Smart Practic

Business and industry leaders discuss how they maximize their companies' financial performance using cutting edge practices. These videos can help show students why corporate finance is a vital topic, regardless of their chosen functional areas. Presidents and CFOs of major corporations, such as Andy Bryant, CFO of Intel Corp., as well as corporate recruiters, are featured in interviews. **SMART PRACTICES VIDEO** icons in the text direct students to **http://smartfinance.swlearning.com**.

SMART PRACTICES VIDEO

Todd Richter, Managing Director, Head of Equity Healthcare Research, Bank of America Securities

"The concepts of value, the things that drive value, don't change."

See the entire interview at **SMARTFinance**

SMART ETHICS VIDEO

Andy Bryant, Executive Vice President of Finance and Enterprise Systems, Chief Financial Officer, Intel Corp.

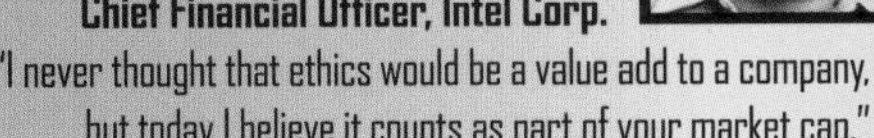

"I never thought that ethics would be a value add to a company, but today I believe it counts as part of your market cap."

See the entire interview at **SMARTFinance**

Smart Ethics Video

These videos show how both academics and business executives view ethics and the impact that ethical or unethical behavior can have on the company's bottom line. **SMART ETHICS VIDEO** icons in the text direct students to **http://smartfinance.swlearning.com** to view these clips.

Smart Ideas Video

Watch the leading academic researchers behind the theory or concepts discussed in class and in the text with Smart Ideas Videos. Each clip runs approximately 2-3 minutes. Video clips feature John Graham (Duke University), Robert Schiller (Yale), Elroy Dimson (London School of Business), Andrew Karolyi (The Ohio State University), Kenneth French (Dartmouth College) and many, many more. **SMART IDEAS VIDEO** icons in the text direct students to **http://smartfinance.swlearning.com** to view these short video clips.

SMART IDEAS VIDEO

Robert Shiller, Yale University

"When the P/E ratio is high it's typically justified by an argument that earnings will go up in the future."

See the entire interview at **SMARTFinance**

Smart Quizzing

The Smart Finance Web site provides quizzes for each chapter to test knowledge.

THOMSON ONE
Business School Edition

If you assign research projects or the Thomson ONE – BSE problems at the end of the chapter, students will use an Internet database of financial data called T ONE – Business School Edition to complete the research the problems. Analysts and financial professionals u database every day to conduct their research. Access to T ONE – BSE is provided with each new textbook and can b at **http://tobsefin.swlearning.com**.

LETTER TO THE STUDENT

As instructors (and former students), we realize that finance can be an intimidating class, especially for students who struggle with quantitative material. In writing this book, we wanted to change that—to lower the intimidation factor in our field and to communicate the excitement and relevance that finance holds for each of us.

Our major goal in writing this book has been to show you how the concepts you've learned from your prerequisite courses— like economics, statistics, and accounting— directly connect to finance concepts. We hope that you'll quickly realize that you already know more than you think you do about finance! If you've learned to measure the costs and the benefits involved in business decisions, you've already learned a primary lesson in finance. You'll see this familiar framework throughout our text.

We realize that while some of you are finance majors, many of you are not. A crucial issue for all finance students is to understand the practical importance of finance. The skills you learn in this class will assist you in your career, regardless of whether you become a Chief Financial Officer, a Marketing Manager, or a Sales Associate. To illustrate how your mastery of this subject will assist you in your career, we've drawn upon experiences of a broad range of professionals who use finance every day. We've filled the book with relevant and timely examples of how financial issues arise in the business world: How has the introduction of the iPod affected Apple Computer and the music industry? Can Governor Arnold Schwarzenegger handle California's growing financial crisis? How can a struggling airline conserve cash after the September 11, 2001 terrorist attacks? All these questions require an understanding of finance to answer; we explore all of these in depth in our text.

Every student needs some extra explanation or support at different points in this course. Consequently, a truly outstanding technology package accompanies this book—a package that will allow you to learn and absorb material at your own pace. Computer animations review important concepts and techniques to help you re-examine complex material until you can grasp the ideas with confidence. You can view each animation as many times as you need to until you understand the concept or technique

Our own students tell us that these animations, found at the Smart Finance Web site, **http://smartfinance.swlearning.com**, are more helpful than any other single feature in the book. You can also visit the Smart Finance Web site to see your choice of nearly one-hundred video clips of finance professionals and scholars, each of whom contributes to the picture of just how often financial issues affect today's world.

We hope your experience with our book is a positive one. If you have any ideas for enhancing this product, please feel free to share them with us. Meanwhile, we wish you the best as you begin your study of finance.

William Megginson
Professor & Rainbolt Chair in Finance
Michael F. Price College of Business
University of Oklahoma
wmegginson@ou.edu

Scott Smart
DaimlerChrysler Faculty Fellow
Department of Finance
Kelley School of Business
Indiana University
ssmart@indiana.edu

Introduction to Corporate Finance

William L. Megginson
University of Oklahoma

Scott B. Smart
Indiana University

Australia · Canada · Mexico · Singapore · Spain · United Kingdom · United States

THOMSON
SOUTH-WESTERN

Introduction to Corporate Finance
William L. Megginson and Scott B. Smart

VP/Editorial Director:
Jack W. Calhoun

VP/Editor-in-Chief:
Dave Shaut

Executive Editors:
Scott Person and Michael R. Reynolds

Sr. Developmental Editor:
Trish Taylor

Marketing Manager:
Heather MacMaster

Production Editors:
Daniel C. Plofchan
Starratt E. Alexander

Manager of Technology, Editorial:
Vicky True

Technology Project Editor:
John Barans

Web Coordinator:
Karen L. Schaffer

Senior First Print Buyer:
Sandee Milewski

Production House:
GEX Publishing Services

Art Director:
Michelle Kunkler

Cover & Internal Designer:
Craig Ramsdell/Ramsdell Design

Cover Images:
© Getty Images

Printer:
R.R. Donnelley, Inc.
Willard, Ohio

Printed in the United States of America
2 3 4 5 08 07 06 05

Student Edition ISBN: 0-324-37986-2

Student Edition
Book Only ISBN: 0-324-37985-4

Instructor's Edition ISBN: 0-324-31744-1

Instructor's Edition
Book Only ISBN: 0-324-31745-X

Library of Congress Control Number:
2004111548

For more information about our products, contact us at:

Thomson Learning Academic Resource Center

1-800-423-0563

Thomson Higher Education
5191 Natorp Boulevard
Mason, OH 45040
USA

Asia (including India)
Thomson Learning
5 Shenton Way
#01-01 UIC Building
Singapore 068808

Australia/New Zealand
Thomson Learning Australia
102 Dodds Street
Southbank, Victoria 3006
Australia

Canada
Thomson Nelson
1120 Birchmount Road
Toronto, Ontario
M1K 5G4
Canada

Latin America
Thomson Learning
Seneca, 53
Colonia Polanco
11560 Mexico
D.F.Mexico

UK/Europe/Middle East/Africa
Thomson Learning
High Holborn House
50/51 Bedford Row
London WC1R 4LR
United Kingdom

Spain (including Portugal)
Thomson Paraninfo
Calle Magallanes, 25
28015 Madrid, Spain

ABOUT THE AUTHORS

William L. Megginson

Bill Megginson is Professor and Rainbolt Chair in Finance at the University of Oklahoma. Dr. Megginson is co-author of the Thomson/South-Western MBA level text ***Corporate Finance,*** first published in 2004. He has published twenty refereed articles in several top academic journals, including the *Journal of Finance,* the *Journal of Financial Economics,* the *Journal of Economic Literature,* the *Journal of Financial and Quantitative Analysis,* the *Journal of Money, Credit, and Banking,* the *Journal of Applied Corporate Finance,* and *Financial Management.* He co-authored a study documenting significant performance improvements in recently privatized companies. This study received one of two Smith Breeden Distinguished Paper Awards for outstanding research published in the *Journal of Finance.* In addition, Dr. Megginson has presented academic papers at over thirty conferences, as well as at the National Bureau of Economic Research, the Federal Reserve Banks of New York and Dallas, the OECD, the World Federation of Exchanges, the United Nations and the World Bank. He is also a voting member of the Italian Ministry of Economics and Finance's Global Advisory Committee on Privatization. Dr. Megginson has a Ph.D. in finance from Florida State University. He has visited 57 countries and has served as a consultant for the New York Stock Exchange, the OECD, the IMF, the World Federation of Exchanges, and the World Bank.

Scott B. Smart

Scott Smart has been a member of the finance faculty at Indiana University since 1990. He is co-author of ***Corporate Finance,*** an MBA level published by Thomson/South-Western. Dr. Smart has been recognized as a 'Master Teacher' by Business Week continuously over the last 10 years, and has won more than a dozen teaching awards. He has published articles in scholarly journals such as the *Journal of Finance,* the *Journal of Financial Economics,* and the *Review of Economics and Statistics.* His research has been cited by the *Wall Street Journal, New York Post, Business Week, Fortune,* and other major newspapers and periodicals. His consulting clients include Intel, Synopsys and Unext. Dr. Smart has served on local boards of directors for Habitat for Humanity and other non-profit groups. Dr. Smart did his undergraduate work at Baylor University and received his PhD. from Stanford University.

TAKING YOUR STUDENTS FURTHER

HOW THIS TEXT INCREASES STUDENT ACCESS

As we sought to make this the most student-friendly introductory finance textbook in the market today, we followed a set of core principles when writing the text and designing the overall support package that accompanies the book.

1. PIQUE INTEREST AND CREATE RELEVANCE FOR STUDENTS WITH REAL-WORLD EXAMPLES THAT MAKE CUTTING-EDGE THEORIES APPEALING, ACCESSIBLE AND PRACTICAL. We feel it's important to grab students' interest and attention from the beginning of the chapter with an interesting, relevant situation such as the budget crisis in California and how Governor Schwarzenegger has chosen to deal with it by issuing bonds under Proposition 57 (Chapter 4). Every chapter of this book begins with a story pulled from recent headlines that illustrates a key chapter concept in an applied setting.

We also strive to provide students with a smooth bridge between theory and practice by highlighting examples in a feature that we call "Applying the Model." These illustrations, many of which use real data from well known companies (such as Wendy's) take concepts and make them easy to understand within an interesting and relevant context.

2. MAXIMIZE THE PEDAGOGICAL AND MOTIVATIONAL VALUE OF TECHNOLOGY. We have often experimented with technology packaged with textbooks, only to find that the included products somehow impede learning and classroom delivery rather than facilitate student interest and understanding. Some technology add-ons, created by subcontractors rather than the text's primary authors, seem to bear almost no relationship to the text they are meant to support. And of course, all too often a technology that we want to use inside or outside of the classroom simply doesn't work.

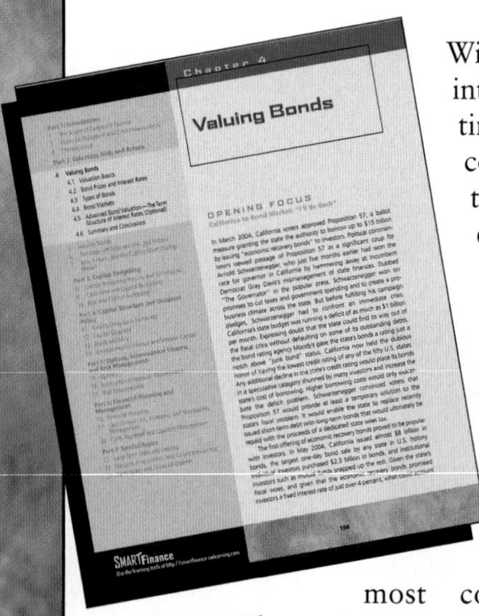
Chapter 4

Valuing Bonds

OPENING FOCUS

SMARTFinance

With such experiences behind us, we wanted to develop an integrated technology package that engaged, motivated, and at times entertained students, while helping them master financial concepts on their own time and at their own pace. We wanted to use technology to allow students to hear firsthand about exciting developments in financial research. We wanted students to hear from business professionals why the material contained in the text is relevant after the final exam is over. *Most of all, as authors of the text, we wanted to take primary responsibility for creating the technology package to ensure that we seamlessly integrated technology with the text's most important concepts and techniques.*

Tests with in-residence and online students have generated almost unanimous praise for these features. In fact, the most common complaint we have heard from students is, "*Why can't we see more of this?*" Visit **http://smartfinance.swlearning.com** to see a sample of the rich content that students can access on the Smart Finance Web site. Access to the Smart Finance Website is free with each new text.

Some examples of the fully integrated technology include (see page viii for more in-depth information):

- **ANIMATED REVIEW TUTORIALS** that explain key concepts;
- **PROBLEM SOLVING ANIMATIONS** that illustrate numerical solution methods as well as develop students' problem-solving intuition;
- **VIDEO CLIPS** of well-known American and international academics and finance practitioners that illustrate the conceptual bases of theory, theory in practice, and ethical issues that financial professionals routinely face, and
- **EXCEL ANIMATIONS** that walk students through problems or through particularly challenging aspects of problems that Excel helps to solve more easily.

In order to describe how to use these technologies in or out of class, and to provide syllabus integration suggestions, an informative ***Resource Integration Guide*** is available to Instructors (ISBN: 0-324-32326-3).

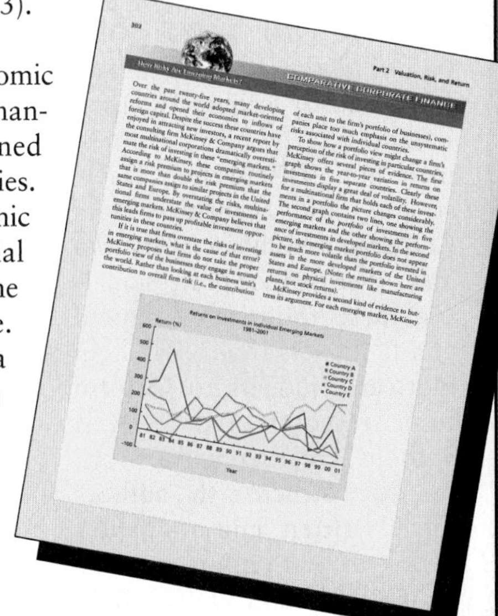
302

How Risky Are Emerging Markets?

Part 2 Valuation, Risk, and Return

COMPARATIVE CORPORATE FINANCE

Over the past twenty-five years, many developing countries around the world adopted market-oriented reforms and opened their economies to inflows of foreign capital. Despite the success these countries have enjoyed in attracting new investors, a recent report by the consulting firm McKinsey & Company argues that most multinational corporations dramatically overestimate the risk of investing in these "emerging markets." According to McKinsey, these companies routinely assign a risk premium to projects in emerging markets that is more than double the risk premium that the same companies assign to similar projects in the United States and Europe. By overstating the risks, multinational firms understate the value of investments in emerging markets. McKinsey & Company believes that this leads firms to pass up profitable investment opportunities in these countries.

If it is true that firms overstate the risks of investing in emerging markets, what is the cause of that error? McKinsey proposes that firms do not take the proper portfolio view of the businesses they engage in around the world. Rather than looking at each business unit's contribution to overall firm risk (i.e., the contribution of each unit to the firm's portfolio of businesses), companies place too much emphasis on the unsystematic risks associated with individual countries.

To show how a portfolio view might change a firm's perception of the risk of investing in particular countries, McKinsey offers several pieces of evidence. The first graph shows the year-to-year variation in returns on investments in five separate countries. Clearly these investments display a great deal of volatility. However, for a multinational firm that holds each of these investments in a portfolio the picture changes considerably. The second graph contains two lines, one showing the performance of the *portfolio* of investments in five emerging markets and the other showing the performance of investments in developed markets. In the second picture, the emerging market portfolio does not appear to be much more volatile than the portfolio invested in assets in the more developed markets of the United States and Europe. (Note: the returns shown here are returns on physical investments like manufacturing plants, not stock returns).

McKinsey provides a second kind of evidence to buttress its argument. For each emerging market, McKinsey

3. PROVIDE A TRULY GLOBAL PERSPECTIVE. The economic world is shrinking—particularly with regard to financial transactions. Formerly centrally-planned economies are moving towards market economies. Many developing nations are making rapid economic progress using markets-based methods. Financial markets play an increasingly important role in the ongoing globalization of business and finance. Rather than grouping international issues into a chapter or two, we integrate a global perspective throughout the text. Every chapter has a unique feature that we call "Comparative Corporate Finance (CCF)" designed to highlight similarities and differences among corporate finance practices around the world.

4. CONSIDER STUDENTS' PREREQUISITES AND CONNECT THE COURSES THEY HAVE TAKEN TO FINANCE. Experienced financial managers consistently tell us that they need people who can see the big picture and who can recognize connections across functional areas. To help students develop a larger sense of what finance is about, why it is relevant to their business studies, and to ease their transition into their own chosen fields, we highlight concepts that most students learn in their introductory economics, statistics, and accounting courses. We then connect these concepts to finance.

Our goal is to create a familiar starting point for students taking finance for the first time—for example, the marginal cost/marginal benefit framework they experienced in prerequisite economics courses. The marginal benefit versus marginal cost decision framework is classic microeconomics, recognizable to anyone who teaches finance. Most current finance textbooks fail to draw this vital connection for students: *Choose to fund only those projects for which the marginal benefits (MB) outweigh the marginal costs (MC)*. Finance is perhaps the discipline best suited to quantify and compare marginal costs (risk) against marginal benefits (returns on investment alternatives).

Several video clips early in the book also emphasize connections between finance and other disciplines. Beginning with what students know and building on that foundation allows us to use an approach that we have used successfully in our own teaching for many years. We wanted our book to reflect that teaching philosophy.

OTHER KEY FEATURES

THAT WILL HELP TAKE YOUR STUDENTS FURTHER...

Excel Appendices appear for 13 relevant chapters (chapters 2-10, 15, 16, 18, and 19). These appendices explicitly show students how to build *Excel* spreadsheets to solve finance problems more easily using modern tools rather than tables or even calculators. *Excel* is clearly the tool of choice for finance courses and for finance professionals today.

Thomson ONE - Business School Edition Problems:

Thomson ONE – BSE is an online database that draws from industry-leading Thomson Financial's data sources, including Disclosure, Datastream, and Securities Data Corporation databases. Analysts and other finance professionals use these tools every day to conduct research. To help motivate students to perform basic research and analysis without creating extra work for the instructor, the authors have written end-of-chapter problems that require students to use Thomson ONE – BSE. See page vii for more in-depth information about using Thomson ONE – BSE.

THOMSON ONE Business School Edition

For instructions on using Thomson ONE, refer to the instructions provided with the Thomson ONE problems at the end of Chapters 1–6 or to "A Guide for Using Thomson ONE."

P7-26. Determine the beta of a portfolio consisting of Priceline.com Inc. (ticker: PCLN), Johnson & Johnson (U:JNJ), Home Depot (U:HD), and Goodyear Tire & Rubber Company (GT). You invest equal amounts of capital in each stock. How does the beta of this portfolio compare with the individual betas? Explain. Instead of investing equal amounts of capital in each stock, you decide to short shares worth $1,000 in each of the two least risky stocks (of the above four stocks) and invest $2,000 each in the two most risky stocks. How do you think the beta of this new portfolio will compare with the individual stock betas? Calculate the beta of this new portfolio and check if it matches your expectations. Consider another alternate portfolio. Now you short shares worth $1,000 in each of the two most risky stocks and invest $2,000 each in the two least risky stocks. How do you think the beta of this new portfolio will compare with the individual stock betas? Calculate the beta of this new portfolio and check if it matches your expectations. Do you think this portfolio will ever be profitable? If so, when?

Learning Objectives highlight the key ideas of each chapter; they appear at the beginning of each chapter.

Concept Review Questions conclude each section within chapters and test students' retention of material. These Concept Review Questions tie directly to the learning objectives that open the chapters. Students can find the answers to the Concept Review Questions on the book Web site at http://megginson.swlearning.com. Click on the book cover and look under "student resources" on the right hand side of the screen. The answers will appear in the same order as they do in the book.

Answers to Self-Test Problems appear in Appendix D at the back of the book.

THOMSON ONE
Business School Edition

Want to bring concepts to life with real data? Do you assign research projects? Would you like your students to conduct research on the Internet? Thomson ONE – Business School Edition meets all of these needs! This tool gives students the opportunity to use a business school version of an Internet-based database that financial analysts and professionals use around the world every day. Relevant chapters include problems specifically for use with Thomson ONE – BSE so that your students find answers in real time. Thomson ONE – BSE includes access to 10-year financial statements downloadable to Excel; one click Peer Set analysis; indices that students can manipulate or compare; and data for international, as well as domestic, companies. This resource is included FREE with each new text.

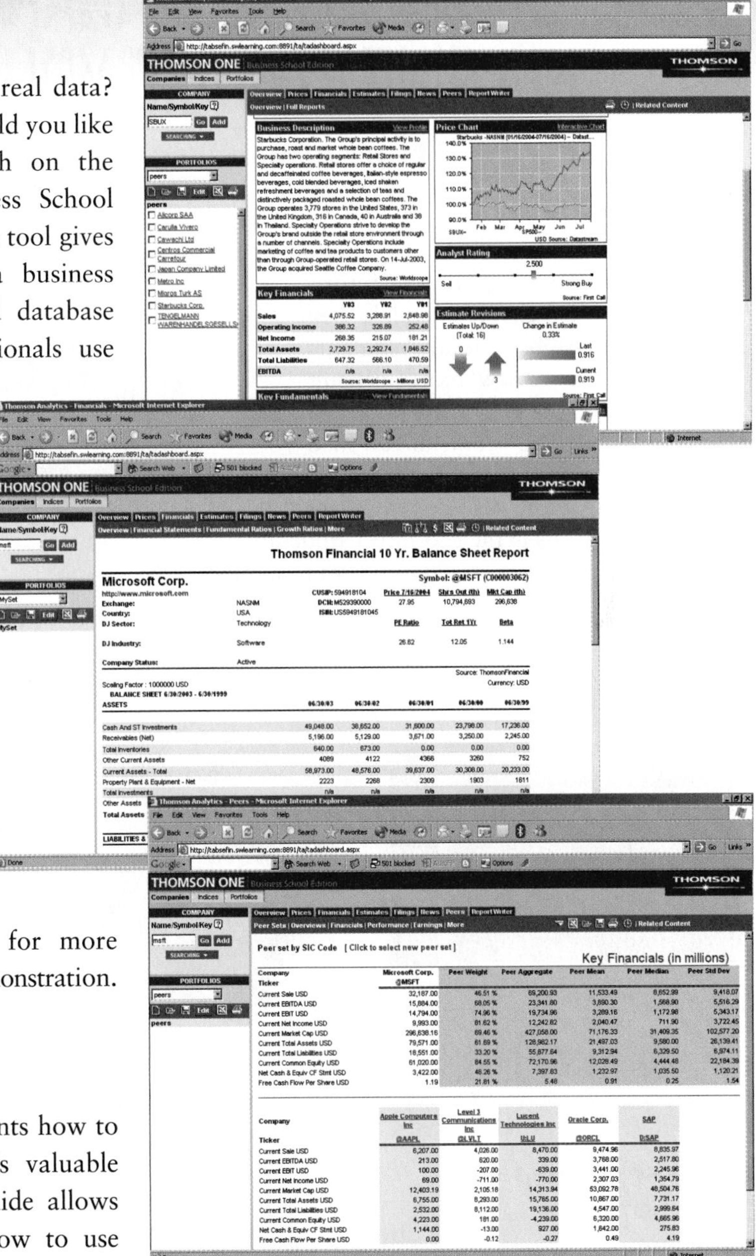

See http://tobsefin.swlearning.com for more information including an animated demonstration.

Guide to Thomson ONE - BSE

This helpful guide shows your students how to use the educational version of this valuable research and analysis tool. This guide allows students to learn for themselves how to use Thomson ONE – BSE at their own pace, saving professors precious class and office hour time. (ISBN: 0-324-31930-4).

Textbook Web site

Find electronic instructor resources: Test Bank, Instructor's Manual, PowerPoint® Lecture Presentations at http://megginson.swlearning.com.

SMART FINANCE HELPING TO TAKE YOU FURTHER...

http://smartfinance.swlearning.com

Smart Concepts

These animated concept review tutorials, organized by chapter, explain key topics step-by-step, offering students opportunities to review more difficult chapter material at their own pace and at convenient times. Students can also decide how much or what parts of the review they want to cover. **SMART CONCEPTS** icons in the text direct students to http://smartfinance.swlearning.com to explore.

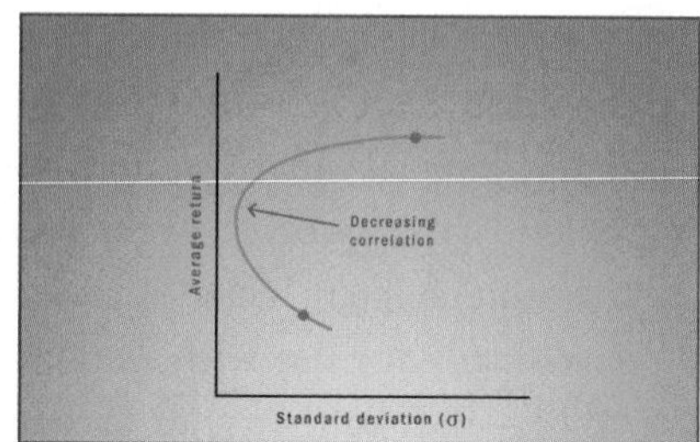

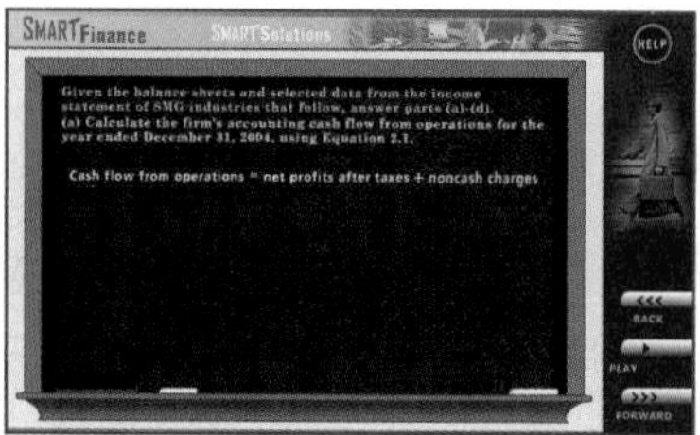

Smart Solutions

The Smart Solutions feature helps improve student's problem-solving skills by demonstrating animated solution steps and offering coaching about how to identify the right technique to apply to particular problems. **SMART SOLUTIONS** icons in the text direct students to http://smartfinance.swlearning.com to explore Smart Solutions.

Smart Excel Animations

Excel animations walk students through problems or through particularly challenging aspects of problems that Excel helps to solve more easily. Additionally, printed appendices for 13 chapters help show how to use Excel to solve chapter problems. **SMART EXCEL** icons in the text direct students to http://smartfinance.swlearning.com to view these resources.

Smart Practices Video

Business and industry leaders discuss how they maximize their companies' financial performance using cutting edge practices. These videos can help show students why corporate finance is a vital topic, regardless of their chosen functional areas. Presidents and CFOs of major corporations, such as Andy Bryant, CFO of Intel Corp., as well as corporate recruiters, are featured in interviews. **SMART PRACTICES VIDEO** icons in the text direct students to **http://smartfinance.swlearning.com**.

SMART PRACTICES VIDEO

Todd Richter, Managing Director, Head of Equity Healthcare Research, Bank of America Securities

"The concepts of value, the things that drive value, don't change."

See the entire interview at **SMARTFinance**

SMART ETHICS VIDEO

Andy Bryant, Executive Vice President of Finance and Enterprise Systems, Chief Financial Officer, Intel Corp.

"I never thought that ethics would be a value add to a company, but today I believe it counts as part of your market cap."

See the entire interview at **SMARTFinance**

Smart Ethics Video

These videos show how both academics and business executives view ethics and the impact that ethical or unethical behavior can have on the company's bottom line. **SMART ETHICS VIDEO** icons in the text direct students to **http://smartfinance.swlearning.com** to view these clips.

Smart Ideas Video

Watch the leading academic researchers behind the theory or concepts discussed in class and in the text with Smart Ideas Videos. Each clip runs approximately 2-3 minutes. Video clips feature John Graham (Duke University), Robert Schiller (Yale), Elroy Dimson (London School of Business), Andrew Karolyi (The Ohio State University), Kenneth French (Dartmouth College) and many, many more. **SMART IDEAS VIDEO** icons in the text direct students to **http://smartfinance.swlearning.com** to view these short video clips.

SMART IDEAS VIDEO

Robert Shiller, Yale University

"When the P/E ratio is high it's typically justified by an argument that earnings will go up in the future."

See the entire interview at **SMARTFinance**

Smart Quizzing

The Smart Finance Web site provides quizzes for each chapter to test knowledge.

THOMSON ONE
Business School Edition

If you assign research projects or the Thomson ONE – BSE problems at the end of the chapter, students will use an Internet database of financial data called Thomson ONE – Business School Edition to complete the research or solve the problems. Analysts and financial professionals use this database every day to conduct their research. Access to Thomson ONE – BSE is provided with each new textbook and can be found at **http://tobsefin.swlearning.com**.

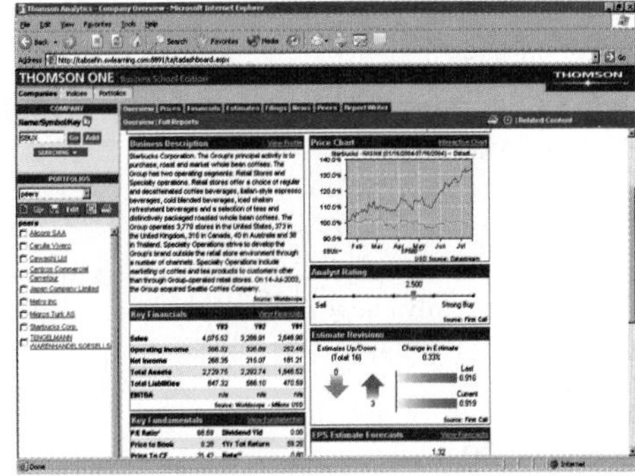

ACKNOWLEDGMENTS

Most people realize that creating a textbook is a collaborative venture. What only authors can truly appreciate is just how many people are involved in planning, writing, editing, producing, and launching a new book. In the paragraphs that follow, we thank the many people who made significant contributions to this book. Although only two people are listed as authors on the title page, we wish to acknowledge the debt we owe to those who have worked so closely with us. We are particularly appreciative of Larry Gitman's willingness to allow us to repurpose materials from our co-authored text, Corporate Finance, for inclusion in this text.

We thank the people at Thomson who pushed us to deliver a top-quality product. This list includes Team Leader Mike Roche and then Vice-President and Editor-in-Chief Dave Shaut. Executive Editor Mike Reynolds lent his considerable expertise and extensive market knowledge to help us get a good start and Executive Editor Scott Person lent his enthusiasm and aggressive marketing tactics to help us launch our product;. Our appreciation extends to freelance developmental editor Joanne Butler, who helped in gathering reviews, analyzing their contents, and summarizing their key points for us. Dan Plofchan, Starratt Alexander, and Cliff Kallemeyn exhibited patience and professionalism as production editors and Kelly Murphy from our production house, GEX Publishing Services went out of her way to create the book that we wanted. Heather MacMaster deserves special thanks for her marketing efforts. We would especially like to thank our devoted Senior Developmental Editor Trish Taylor, with whom we had daily contact to create the best book and supplements possible. Trish has acted as an advocate for our series of books whenever and wherever possible, and we thank her for her constant support.

Several people made written contributions to the book and its supplements. We are grateful to Susan White from the University of Maryland for writing the Instructor's Manual; John Hall from the University of Arkansas at Little Rock, Wendell Licon from Arizona State University, Andreas Rauterkus from Siena University, Chris Pope from the University of Georgia, and especially Bill Chittenden from Texas State University for contributing to our Test Bank; Lance Nail from the University of Alabama at Birmingham for the Resource Integration Guide; Dan Balan for the PowerPoint slides; Michael Sullivan of the University of Nevada, Las Vegas for writing case questions for each chapter; and Ramabhadran Thirumalai for writing problems using the Thomson One-BSE resource. Professor Amy Burnett of St. Edwards University, Austin has written a superb and helpful Study Guide to accompany this text. We particularly appreciate Bridget Lyons for her work in writing the Excel appendices scattered throughout this book. Finally, Bill Megginson wishes to extend special thanks to the students in the classes at the University of Oklahoma where he used early drafts of this book. Even though students received the text free of charge, they paid a price to help us remove errors from earlier drafts.

Technology is an extremely important part of this book, and we wish to express our deep appreciation to South-Western Publishing Company and Thomson Learning for their financial and professional support. In particular, we have been honored to work with technical professionals as competent and supportive as Thomson Learning's Vicky True and John Barans. Many other people have also contributed to creating what we believe to be an outstanding technology package. This list begins with Jack Koning, who made truly amazing contributions in developing the flash animations, and Don Mitchell, whose audio work made the animations come to life. Deryl Dale, Candace Decker, Rebecca Loftin, Neil Charles, Murray McGibbon, Andrew Ellul, Anne Kibler, Doug Hoffman, and Richard Fish all contributed their voices to the animations, and Rebecca Barrett and Joy Hudyma helped create the text's graphics.

Though it would be nice to pretend that our skills as authors are so advanced that we did not have to make repeated passes at writing the chapters you see today, in fact this book has benefited immeasurably from the feedback we have received from reviewers. We would like to thank the following people for their insightful comments and constructive criticism of the text:

BATES, THOMAS
University of Delaware
BERTUS, MARK
Auburn University
BOOTH, ELIZABETH
Michigan State University
CHITTENDEN, WILLIAM
Texas State University
GRAY, GARY
Penn State University
HUESON, ANDREA
University of Miami, FL
KIM, KENNETH
SUNY at Buffalo
LEE, CHUN
Loyola-Marymount
LICON, WENDELL
Arizona State University
NIXON, TERRY
Miami U, Ohio
POPE, CHRISTOPHER
University of Georgia
PUELZ, BOB
Southern Methodist U.
RAUTERKUS, ANDREAS
Siena College
ROBERSON, TODD
Indiana University, Indianapolis
STANSFIELD, JOHN
University of Missouri
STOREY, STANFORD
University of California, Irvine
SULLIVAN, MICHAEL J.
University of Nevada, Las Vegas
YU, JEAN
Oakland University

Last but certainly not least, the authors wish to thank their families and friends who provided invaluable support and assistance. Finally, Peggy Megginson and Susan Smart deserve special thanks for their love and support throughout the long process of creating this book.

WLM, SBS
November 30, 2004

Brief Contents

Contents

Note: Solutions available in a booklet called *Solutions to Concept Review Questions and Self-Test Problems.*

Introduction to Corporate Finance

PART 1

Introduction

Welcome to the study of corporate finance: a field with unmatched career opportunities that are as intellectually challenging as they are financially rewarding. In this book, we explain how financial managers apply a few key principles as they weigh the marginal costs and marginal benefits of important business decisions. When managers take actions that have higher benefits than costs, they create value for shareholders. Our goals in introducing you to these principles are not only to impart useful knowledge, but also to convey our enthusiasm for our chosen field, as well as help you explore whether a career in corporate finance is right for you.

Chapter 1 describes the roles that corporate finance experts play in a variety of businesses and industries. Most of what corporate finance professionals do on a day-to-day basis falls within one of the five basic functions described in the chapter. We recommend that readers revisit the list of five key functions as they work through this book. Most of the chapters place a heavy emphasis on just one or two of these functions, and it is a useful exercise to map the key concepts from each chapter back to the five functions outlined in Chapter 1.

It has been said that accounting is the language of business, and certainly it is true that financial managers need to master accounting concepts and principles to do their jobs well. Chapter 2 offers a broad overview of the most important sources of accounting information: firms' financial statements. Our focus in this chapter is not on how accountants construct these statements (we leave that to your accounting professors). Instead, our goal is to illustrate why these statements are important to financial managers and why finance places so much emphasis on cash flow rather than on measures of earnings, such as net income or earnings per share. We also demonstrate how companies can use the information from financial statements to track their performance over time or to benchmark their results against those achieved by other firms.

Chapter 3 introduces one of the most fundamental concepts in finance called the time value of money. Simply put, the time value of money says that a dollar today is worth more than a dollar in the future. The reasoning behind this statement is straightforward. If you have a dollar in hand today, you can invest it and earn interest, so receiving the dollar now is better than having to wait for it. Because most business decisions involve costs and benefits that are spread out over many months or years, managers need a way to evaluate cash flows that the firm pays or receives at different times. For example, a firm spends $1 million today to purchase an asset that will generate a stream of cash receipts of $225,000 over the next several years. Do the costs of this investment outweigh its benefits, or are the benefits high enough to justify the costs? Chapter 3 explains how managers can make valid cost/benefit comparisons when cash flows occur at different times and using different rates of interest.

Note: Solutions available in a booklet called *Solutions to Concept Review Questions and Self-Test Problems.*

The Scope of Corporate Finance

OPENING FOCUS

Apple Succeeds with iTunes Where Others Had Failed

Ever since global sales of recorded music peaked in 1999, leading music companies have struggled to solve the difficult problem of how to set prices for their products that can compete with the same products for *free*! In 1999, the start-up company Napster pioneered file-sharing programs that allow music lovers to download song tracks over the Internet for free. By 2004, some 900 million music files were available for sharing worldwide. Music companies' sales had been sliced by more than 20 percent from their peak five years before. The challenge for music companies was this: to provide music on demand, at a price customers were willing to pay, while continuing to earn a profit. The recording industry may never discover how to make money selling music electronically—but Apple Computer did.

In April 2003, Apple launched a service called Apple iTunes Music Store from which customers can choose among 500,000 music tracks provided by five major record labels. Steve Jobs, Apple's founder and chief executive officer (CEO), persuaded music companies to allow Apple to sell current and classic songs for 99 cents per track. The service was an immediate hit, selling 1 million songs during its first week alone and more than 70 million during its first twelve months. One customer reportedly spent more than $300,000! The service requires users to download songs using Apple's own software, directly promoting sales of Apple's stylish iPod MP3 player. This device retails for about $300, holds up to 7,500 tracks, and has been widely applauded for its compact design and ease of use. Today, Apple sells more iPods than computers, and the company expects iPod sales to exceed $900 million during 2004.

Perhaps surprisingly, the iTunes Music Store itself has thus far proven only marginally profitable for Apple. The company pays each record label between 60 and 65 cents per track. It spends an additional 25 cents in credit card fees and distribution costs, so the service yields a gross profit margin of only about 10 cents per song. On the other hand, iTunes clearly spurs iPod sales, which are very profitable.

And by keeping download prices so low, Apple both encourages the continued rapid growth of the music download market and discourages competitors from entering the market. In any case, the music companies don't seem to mind. They are at least receiving *some* revenue from songs downloaded over the Internet.

Stories in the popular press tend to focus on the success of iTunes and iPod themselves. However, financial managers behind the scenes at Apple played a number of crucial roles in driving the success of the business. In this chapter, we explain how financial specialists interact with experts in fields as diverse as engineering, marketing, communications, and law to help companies create wealth for their shareholders. We describe the types of activities that occupy financial managers day to day, and highlight some of the most promising career opportunities for students who major in finance. The work that financial analysts do is intellectually challenging, as well as economically rewarding. We hope our overview of the field piques your interest and inspires you to learn more.

Sources: Multiple *Financial Times* articles from April 2003 through June 2004, downloaded from that company's paid Internet service, FT.com (http://www.ft.com). ■

LEARNING OBJECTIVES

After studying this chapter you should be able to:

- Appreciate how finance interacts with other functional areas of any business and see the diverse career opportunities available to finance majors;
- Describe how modern companies obtain funding from financial intermediaries and markets, and discuss the five basic functions that modern financial managers must perform;
- Assess the costs and benefits of the three principal forms of business organization and explain why limited liability companies, with publicly traded shares, dominate economic life in most countries; and
- Define agency costs and explain how shareholders monitor and encourage corporate managers to maximize shareholder wealth by choosing business opportunities for which the marginal benefits (MB) outweigh the marginal cost (MC).

1.1 THE ROLE OF CORPORATE FINANCE IN MODERN BUSINESS

The example in the Opening Focus illustrates not only how managers conduct business in a modern, knowledge-based economy, but also shows the vital role that financial managers play in creating wealth. This story provides important insights into the theory and practice of corporate finance. Modern business involves people with many different skills and backgrounds working together toward common goals. Financial experts play a major role in achieving these goals. The importance (and status) of the finance function and the financial manager within business organizations has risen steadily over the past two decades. Business professionals in many different functional areas now recognize that competent financial professionals can do more than just keep the books and manage the firm's cash. Financial managers can create value in their own right.

This book focuses on the practicing financial manager who is an integral part of the management team in a modern corporation. On the job, a manager must constantly apply financial tools to solve real business problems. Throughout this text, we highlight the one simple question that managers should ask when contemplating all business decisions: Do the marginal benefits (MB) of taking a certain action outweigh the marginal costs (MC) of this action? For instance, at Apple Computer, the finance organization had to estimate the marginal benefits and costs of launching iTunes. *By taking actions that generate benefits in excess of costs, firms generate wealth for their investors.* Managers should take only those actions where the MB is *at least equal* to the MC.

As an introduction to what a financial manager's job entails, the next section discusses how various functional disciplines interact with financial managers. It describes the kinds of jobs that people with financial training generally take. Throughout this book, we assume that the managers we describe work for large, publicly traded corporations, but we maintain this assumption for convenience only. The skills and knowledge needed to contribute effectively toward achieving corporate business objectives are the same as those needed to be a successful entrepreneur, to manage family businesses, or to run a nonprofit organization. Successful financial managers must be able to creatively manage both people and money.

SMART PRACTICES VIDEO

Tom Cole, Deutsche Bank, Leveraged Finance Group

"To be good at finance you have to understand how businesses work."

See the entire interview at **SMARTFinance**

How Finance Interacts with Other Functional Business Areas

Financial professionals interact with experts in a wide range of disciplines to drive successful businesses. Working with Apple's computer scientists, financial managers analyzed the business potential of the iTunes service, as well as the sales potential of the iPod player. Financial managers:

- studied the economics of downloading music over the Internet;
- developed a strategy for providing a fee-based service that would attract customers;
- negotiated licensing agreements with entertainment moguls from the recording industry; and
- worked with technical authorities to ensure that customers could seamlessly download songs.

Apple's financial managers also advised public relations professionals, who were asked to present the new service to a skeptical press and to answer journalists' questions about the service's financial aspects. Additionally, the company's financial managers worked with accounting and information systems staff. Together, they developed payment systems that allow the company to collect large numbers of small-denomination purchases by customers who use credit cards. As the iTunes service grows, financial managers must ensure that Apple will have the cash it needs to continue expanding the business, plus any follow-on services that might develop later.

In sum, although Apple's iPod was primarily a marketing and technology-driven project, the firm's financial organization played pivotal roles in every stage of the deal—from the initial assessment and funding of research, through the actual rollout of iTunes, to managing the cash flows generated by the service, and then to accumulating the capital needed to fund follow-on projects. In more ways than most people imagine, modern finance helps make high technology possible.

Career Opportunities in Finance

This section briefly surveys career opportunities in finance. Though different jobs require different specialized skills, the basic tools of corporate finance are vitally important for all business professionals, whether they work in industrial corporations, on Wall Street, or in the offices of a commercial bank or life insurance company. Three other skills that virtually all finance jobs require are:

- good written and verbal communication skills,
- teamwork, and
- proficiency with computers and the Internet.

For an increasing number of finance jobs, an in-depth knowledge of international business has also become a prerequisite for career success.

We classify finance career opportunities as follows:

- corporate finance,
- commercial banking,
- investment banking,
- money management, and
- consulting.[1]

SMART PRACTICES VIDEO

Joshua Haines, Senior Credit Analyst, The Private Bank

"Most of the basic finance concepts that I learned in my first finance class I still use today."

See the entire interview at **SMARTFinance**

Typical U.S. business graduates who major in finance can expect average starting salaries of $30,000 to $50,000 per year (or more), depending upon their academic credentials and the industry in which they begin their careers.[2] The exact salary you can attain will depend not only on the economic environment, but also your personal negotiating skills and how well you master the knowledge we present in this text.

Corporate Finance. Corporate, or managerial, finance is concerned with the duties of the financial manager in a business. These professionals handle the financial affairs of many types of businesses—financial and nonfinancial, private and public, large and small, profit seeking and not-for-profit. They perform such varied tasks as budgeting, financial forecasting, cash management, credit administration, investment analysis, and funds procurement. In recent years, changing economic and regulatory environments have increased the importance and complexity of the financial manager's duties. The globalization of business has also increased demand for people able to assess and manage the risks associated with volatile exchange rates and rapidly changing political environments. Table 1.1 summarizes key facts relating to various entry- and senior-level corporate finance positions.

---

1. The basic job descriptions and duties are generally taken from the online resources *Careers in Business* (http://www.careers-in-business.com), *Careers in Finance* (http://www.careers-in-finance.com), and other career Web sites such as Monster.com (http://www.monster.com) that highlight the finance profession. Students seeking more detailed descriptions of the varying careers open to finance graduates, as well as in-depth analyses of the specific jobs and responsibilities of different positions, should join the Financial Management Association and obtain a copy of the paperback book titled *Careers in Finance* (Financial Management Association International: Tampa, Florida, 2003).

2. Detailed starting salary information for graduates with a bachelor's degree in business administration (BBA) is available at various Web sites, including *U.S. News & World Report* (http://www.usnews.com/usnews/nycu/work/wohome.htm), Careers.com (http://www.careers.com), the *Wall Street Journal* (http://careers.wsj.com), BenefitsLink (http://www.benefitslink.com), and the "FTCareerPoint" section of the *Financial Times* site (http://ftcareerpoint.ft.com/ftcareerpoint).

Table 1.1
Career Opportunities in Corporate Finance

Position	Description
Financial analyst	Primarily responsible for preparing and analyzing the firm's financial plans and budgets. Other duties include financial forecasting, performing financial ratio analysis, and working closely with accounting.
Capital budgeting manager	Responsible for evaluating and recommending proposed asset investments. May be involved in the financial aspects of implementating approved investments.
Cash manager	Responsible for maintaining and controlling the firm's daily cash balances. Frequently manages the firm's cash collection, short-term borrowing, and banking relationships.
Project finance manager	In large firms, arranges financing for approved asset investments. Coordinates consultants, investment bankers, and legal counsel.
Credit analyst/manager	Administers the firm's credit policy by analyzing or managing the evaluation of credit applications, extending credit, and monitoring and collecting accounts receivable.
Assistant treasurer	Mid-level position in large firms, responsible for overseeing cash management (including banking relationships) and risk management/insurance needs.
Controller	Upper-mid-level position responsible for formulating and implementing integrated financial plans for companies or divisions. This includes supervising the firm's (or division's) accounting and treasury operations and providing foreign-exchange exposure management.
Chief Financial Officer	Top management position charged with developing financial strategies for creating shareholder wealth. Responsible for developing policies covering all aspects of financial management, including dividends, capital structure, securities issuance, mergers and acquisitions, and international expansion. Often a member of firm's board of directors.

Commercial Banking. Commercial banking in the United States has consolidated rapidly in recent years, with the total number of banks shrinking from 14,432 in 1980 to just 7,656 in early 2004. Nonetheless, banks continue to hire large numbers of new business and finance graduates each year, and banking remains a fertile training ground for managers who later migrate to other fields. The key aptitudes required in most entry-level banking jobs are the same as in other areas. In addition to people, computer, and international skills, apprentice bankers must master cash flow valuation, and financial and credit analysis.

Most commercial banks offer at least two basic career tracks: consumer and commercial banking. Consumer banking serves financial needs of a bank's individual customers in its branch network, increasingly via electronic media such as the Internet. Commercial banking, on the other hand, involves extending credit and other banking services to corporate clients, ranging from small, family-owned businesses to *Fortune 500* behemoths. In addition, a great many technologically intensive support positions in banking require excellent finance skills and intimate knowledge of telecommunications and computer technology. Table 1.2 describes career opportunities in commercial banking.

Table 1.2
Career Opportunities in Commercial Banking

Position	Description
Credit analyst	Entry-level position entails analysis of the creditworthiness of a corporate or individual loan applicant. Involves financial and ratio analysis of financial statements, making projections of future cash flows, and often visiting applicants' businesses (corporate loan applicants). Generally a job for BBAs, but MBAs sometimes hired.
Corporate loan officer	Responsible for developing new loan business for the bank and for servicing existing accounts. Often called upon to help develop long-term financing plan for customers and to work with borrowers encountering financial distress. Also expected to market other bank services (cash management, leasing, trust services) to clients.
Branch manager	For BBA employees who select the retail side of commercial banking, this is an early position of real responsibility. Must manage personnel and customers of a bank branch and spearhead searches for new depositors and borrowers.

Table 1.2 (cont.) Career Opportunities in Commercial Banking

Position	Description
Trust officer	Responsible for providing financial advice and products to bank customers—often wealthy ones. Can involve estate planning and/or managing investment assets. Must have (or develop) knowledge of probate law, estate planning, investment planning, and personal taxes.
Mortgage banker	Involves making and servicing mortgage loans to home buyers and businesses. More senior positions involve arranging mortgages for larger real estate developments and commercial properties, as well as securitizing and selling mortgages to syndicators of mortgage-backed securities.
Leasing manager	One of many specialist positions responsible for managing banks' equipment-leasing operations and developing new products and services. Other areas include buying accounts receivable, and data processing services.
Operations officer	Generic classification for many specialist positions requiring knowledge of both banking and information-processing technology. For example, an electronic banking manager would develop the banks' Internet presence and business strategy. Other positions are responsible for internal data processing; coordinating the bank's computer links to ATMs, other banks, and the Federal Reserve Board; and ensuring security of the bank's electronic transactions.

Investment Banking. Along with consulting, investment banking is the career of choice for many highly qualified finance students because of its high income potential and the interesting nature of the work itself. Investment banking involves three main types of activities:

- Helping corporate customers obtain funding by selling securities such as stocks and bonds to investors;
- Providing advice to corporate clients on strategic transactions such as mergers and acquisitions; and
- Trading debt and equity securities for customers or for the firm's own account.

Investment banking was extraordinarily profitable throughout the 1990s, and the top U.S. firms (J. P. Morgan Chase, Merrill Lynch, Morgan Stanley, Goldman Sachs, Citigroup, and a few others) have come to dominate the industry worldwide. But it remains a highly volatile industry. Investment banking is also notorious for being extremely competitive and for demanding long working hours from its professionals (especially the junior ones).

On the other hand, investment banking offers lucrative rewards for those who master the game. Most undergraduates hired by investment banks are assigned duties as financial analysts. Starting salaries for entry-level analyst positions range from $50,000 to more than $70,000, plus bonuses that might average half of their starting salaries. Employees who advance in the investment banking business find that their incomes often rise rapidly—sometimes exponentially. In many ways, investment banking is a star system like professional sports where a handful of top producers receive seven-figure compensation packages, while regular employees earn merely comfortable incomes. Success in this industry demands good analytical and communication skills. Much of the growth in investment banking over the foreseeable future is likely to come from two sources: ongoing development of new financial products and services, and the continued internationalization of corporate finance.

SMART PRACTICES VIDEO

Bill Eckmann, Investment Banker

"Besides finance, there are three subject areas that have really helped me at the beginning of my career in investment banking."

See the entire interview at **SMARTFinance**

Money Management. The past twenty-five years have been very good for stock market investors and finance professionals employed in the money management industry. This industry includes investment advisory firms, mutual fund companies, pension fund managers, trust departments of commercial banks, and the investment arms of insurance companies. In fact, the money management industry encompasses any person or institution that acts as a **fiduciary**—someone who invests and manages money on someone else's behalf. Two powerful economic and demographic trends have created a rapidly growing demand for money management services in the United States and other industrialized countries over the past decade. First, the "baby boomers" (those born between 1946 and 1964) are entering their peak earning years and are beginning to invest large sums to prepare for retirement. Many baby boomers lack the financial expertise to handle their own finances, so the demand for professional money managers has surged.

fiduciary
Someone who invests and manages money on someone else's behalf.

The second major force fueling the growth of the money management industry has been the *institutionalization of investment.* Whereas in the past, individuals owned most financial assets (especially common stocks), today institutional investors dominate the markets. For example, institutional investors own more than 50 percent of outstanding stocks in the United States. Of course, these money managers are not the final owners of the securities they invest in, but they do make almost all the key investment decisions for their clients. The total pool of money managed by institutions is approaching $10 trillion in the United States. This trend toward professional management of institutionally owned financial assets has created employment opportunities in the money management industry and this trend is likely to continue. Table 1.3 lists career opportunities in money management.

Table 1.3
Career Opportunities in Money Management

Position	Description
Securities analyst	Prepares company-specific and industrywide analyses for various classes of publicly traded securities (especially common stock and bonds). Also involves written and verbal presentations of research and recommendations.
Portfolio management, sales	Markets mutual fund shares to individual and/or institutional investors. Also supports pension fund's sales pitch to corporations, as needed. Stockbrokers develop their own client bases.
Portfolio manager	Selects and manages financial assets for inclusion in portfolios designed to meet specific investment preferences (growth, income, international, emerging market bonds). Relative performance of managers is continuously monitored and publicized.
Pension fund manager	Prudently manages assets held by employees' pension fund, controls appropriate administration expenses (trustee and consultant fees, brokerage commissions, etc.), allocates assets among investment managers, and diversifies assets by type of security.
Financial planner	Provides budgeting, insurance, investment, retirement planning, estate planning, and tax advice to individuals. Many practitioners choose to obtain the Certified Financial Planner (CFP®) designation.
Investment adviser	Works for one of the many firms that specialize in providing investment advice, performance evaluation, and quantitative analysis to the money management industry. Requires strong quantitative skills.

Consulting. Management consulting jobs are most coveted by business school graduates. As the name implies, consultants are hired by companies to analyze firms' business processes and strategies and then recommend how practices should change to make firms more competitive. Firms also hire consultants to implement recommendations. Consulting positions offer a unique opportunity early in your career to work with a broad range of businesses. In return, consultants can expect to spend up to 200 days (or even more) yearly on the road.

The above summaries certainly do not represent an exhaustive survey of financial career opportunities. Instead, they illustrate how you can establish a rewarding and satisfying career using the principles of corporate finance covered in this text. We now answer the perplexing question; What exactly should financial managers manage?

CONCEPT REVIEW QUESTIONS

1. What is the "marginal benefits greater than or equal to marginal costs" decision rule, and why should financial managers constantly seek to apply it to business decisions?

2. Think of another company or product besides Apple's iPod and note the connections between other functional areas and finance.

3. List and briefly describe five main career paths open to finance graduates.

1.2 CORPORATE FINANCE ESSENTIALS

Every business requires money to operate, and corporate finance seeks to acquire and manage this money. This section presents several basic concepts involved with the financial management of corporations, beginning with a description of debt and equity capital, the two principal types of long-term funding for all businesses.

Debt and Equity: The Two Flavors of Capital

If you study the financial section of a newspaper or watch the business news on television, you might conclude that businesses have access to many different types of long-term funding, or *capital*. In fact, only two broad types of capital exist: debt and equity. **Debt capital** includes all of a company's long-term borrowing from creditors. The borrower is obliged to pay interest, at a specified annual rate, on the full amount borrowed (called the loan's *principal*), as well as to repay the principal amount at the debt's maturity. All of these payments must be made according to a fixed schedule, and creditors have a legally enforceable claim against the firm. If the company defaults on any of its debt payments, creditors can take legal action to force repayment. In some cases, this means that the creditors can force the borrowing firm into bankruptcy. Companies are forced out of business, and their assets are sold (liquidated) to raise cash, and the cash is then used to repay creditor claims.

debt capital
Borrowed money.

Business owners contribute **equity capital**, which is expected to remain permanently invested in the company. The two basic sources of equity capital are common stock and preferred stock. As discussed in greater depth in Section 1.3 and in Chapter 5, *common stockholders* bear most of the firm's business and financial risk, because they receive returns on their investments only after creditors and preferred stockholders are paid in full. Similar to creditors, *preferred stockholders* are promised a fixed annual payment on their invested capital. Unlike debt, preferred stockholders' claims are not legally enforceable, so these investors cannot force a company into bankruptcy if a preferred stock dividend is missed. If a company falls into bankruptcy and has to be liquidated, preferred stockholders' claims are paid off before any money is paid back to common stockholders.

equity capital
An ownership interest usually in the form of common or preferred stock.

Financial Intermediation and Modern Finance

In the United States, companies can obtain debt capital by selling securities either directly to investors or through financial intermediaries. A **financial intermediary** is an institution that raises capital by issuing liabilities against itself, and then using the funds raised in this way to make loans to corporations and individuals. Borrowers, in turn, repay intermediaries, meaning that debtors have no direct contact with the savers who actually funded the loans. The best-known American financial intermediaries are commercial banks, which issue

financial intermediary
An institution that raises capital by issuing liabilities against itself, and then lends that capital to corporate and individual borrowers.

liabilities such as demand deposits (checking accounts) to companies and individuals and then loan funds to corporations, governments, and households. Banks in the United States are prohibited from making equity investments; banks in other countries are allowed to purchase the common stock of corporate customers. Other significant financial intermediaries include insurance companies, savings and loan institutions, and credit unions.

In addition to making corporate loans, modern financial intermediaries provide a variety of financial services to businesses. By allowing companies and individuals to place their money in demand deposits, banks eliminate the need for everyone to hold large amounts of cash to purchase goods and services. Banks also act as the backbone of a nation's payments system by:

- Collecting payment on checks sent to their corporate customers;
- Making payment on the checks written by their customers to other parties;
- Providing information-processing services to small- and medium-sized businesses; and
- Handling large-volume transactions such as payroll disbursements.

The Growing Importance of Financial Markets. Although modern financial intermediaries are marvels of efficiency, the role of traditional intermediaries such as banks as providers of debt capital to corporations has declined for decades. Instead, nonfinancial corporations have increasingly turned to capital markets for external financing, principally because the rapidly declining cost of information processing makes it much easier for large numbers of investors to obtain and evaluate financial data for thousands of potential corporate borrowers and issuers of common and preferred stock equity. Interestingly, new types of financial intermediaries—especially pension funds and mutual funds—have surged to prominence as corporate finance has shifted towards greater reliance on market-based external funding. These intermediaries are major purchasers of the securities non-financial corporations issue.

primary-market transactions Sales of securities to investors by a corporation to raise capital for the firm.

secondary-market transactions Trades between investors that generate no new cash flow for the firm.

When corporations sell securities to investors in exchange for cash, they raise capital in **primary-market transactions**. In such transactions, firms actually receive the proceeds from issuing securities, so these are a true capital-raising events. Once firms issue securities, investors can sell them to other investors. Trades between investors (called **secondary-market transactions**) generate no new cash flow for the firm, so these are not true capital-raising events. Most stock market transactions are secondary-market trades, whereas a much larger fraction of all bond market transactions involves capital-raising primary offerings. Figure 1.1 details the dramatic growth in the total value of primary stock and bond offerings sold by corporations and other entities over the 1990–2003 period.

Figure 1.1 also points out the enduring importance of U.S. capital markets in global finance. Throughout the 1990–2003 period, U.S. issuers accounted for a remarkably steady two thirds share of the total value of securities issued by corporations around the world each year. To put these "market share" numbers in perspective, the United States represents only about 30 percent of world gross domestic product (GDP) and only about one-eighth of the total value of world trade (exports plus imports). The mix of security issues changed dramatically from year to year, however. In 2003, for example, debt offerings accounted for an unusually high 94.5 percent of the $3.40 trillion total value of securities sold by U.S. corporate issuers.

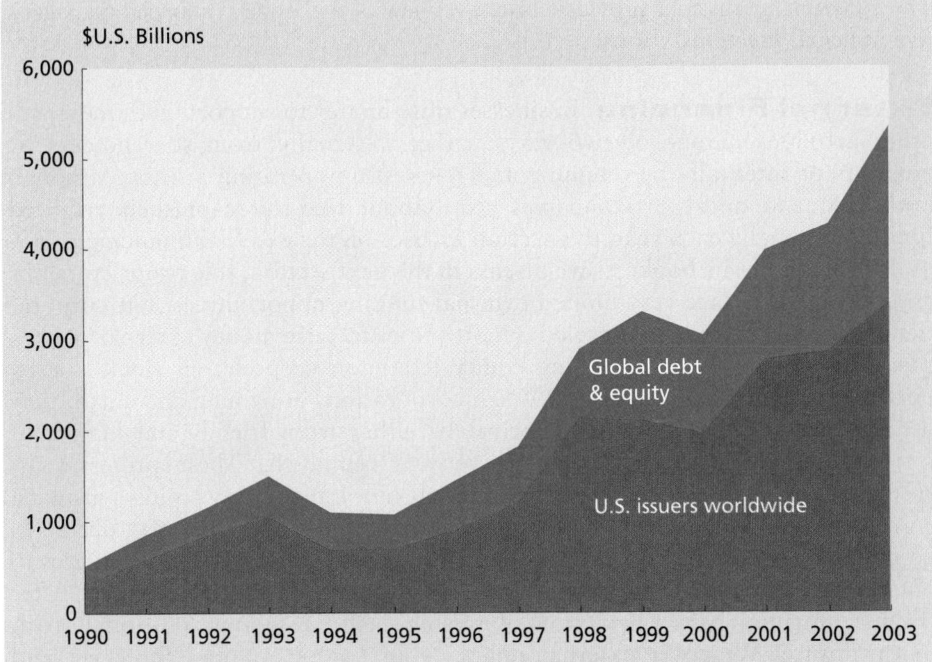

Figure 1.1
The Total Value of Primary (Capital-Raising) Corporate Security Issues, 1990–2003

This figure describes the growth in the volume of security offerings sold directly to investors through capital market issues around the world since 1990. As can be seen, offerings by U.S. issuers typically account for two thirds or more of the global total. These data are from the annual league tables (rankings of investment banks) published by Investment Dealers' Digest *in early January, and include issues by corporations, housing finance authorities and other nonsovereign issuers, but exclude government bond offerings, privatizations, and syndicated bank loans. The $5.33 trillion total for 2003 was a record.*

Source: Investment Dealers' Digest. *Jan. 2004.*

The Five Basic Corporate Finance Functions

Although **corporate finance** is defined generally as the activities involved in managing cash flows (money) in a business environment, a more complete definition would emphasize that the practice of corporate finance involves five basic functions:

- Raising capital to support companies' operations and investment programs (the **external financing function**);
- Selecting the best projects in which to invest firms' resources, based on each project's perceived risk and expected return (the **capital budgeting function**);
- Managing firms' internal cash flows, its working capital, and its mix of debt and equity financing, both to maximize the value of firms' debt and equity claims and to ensure that companies can pay off its obligations when due (the **financial management function**);
- Developing company-wide ownership and corporate governance structures that force managers to behave ethically and make decisions that benefit shareholders (the **corporate governance function**); and
- Managing firms' exposures to all types of risk, both insurable and uninsurable, to maintain an optimal risk-return trade-off and therefore maximize shareholder value (the **risk-management function**).

corporate finance
The activities involved in managing money in a business environment.

external financing function
Raising capital to support companies' operations and investment programs.

capital budgeting function
Selecting the best projects in which to invest the resources of the firm, based on each project's perceived risk and expected return.

financial management function
Managing firms' internal cash flows and its mix of debt and equity financing, both to maximize the value of the debt and equity claims on firms' and to ensure that companies can pay off their obligations when they come due.

corporate governance function
Developing ownership and corporate governance structures for companies that ensure that managers behave ethically and make decisions that benefit shareholders.

risk-management function
Managing firms' exposures to all types of risk, both insurable and uninsurable, in order to maintain optimum risk-return trade-offs and thereby maximize shareholder value.

The following discussions provide a brief overview of the modern financial manager's five principal functions.

External Financing. Businesses raise money to support investment and other activities in one of two ways: either externally from shareholders or creditors or internally by retaining and reinvesting operating profits. Although both U.S. and non-U.S. companies raise about two-thirds of their required funding internally each year, this section focuses on the external financing role—as does much of this book. As we discuss in the next section, sole proprietorships and partnerships face very limited external funding opportunities, but corporations enjoy richer and more varied opportunities to raise money externally. They can raise capital either by selling equity (common or preferred stock), or by borrowing money from creditors. When corporations are young and small, they usually must raise equity capital privately, either from friends and family, or from professional investors such as **venture capitalists**. These professionals specialize in making high-risk/high-return investments in rapidly growing entrepreneurial businesses. Once firms reach a certain size, they may decide to go public by conducting an **initial public offering (IPO)** of stock—selling shares to outside investors and listing the shares for trading on a stock exchange. After IPOs, companies have the option of raising cash by selling additional stock in the future. We cover external financing in Part 4, Capital Structure and Dividend Policy.

venture capitalists
Professional investors who specialize in high-risk/high-return investments in rapidly growing entrepreneurial businesses.

initial public offering (IPO)
Corporations offer shares for sale to the public for the first time; the first public sale of company stock to outside investors.

Capital Budgeting. The capital budgeting function represents firms' financial managers' single most important activity, for two reasons. First, managers evaluate very large investments in the capital budgeting process. Second, companies can prosper in a competitive economy only by seeking out the most promising new products, processes, and services to deliver to customers. Companies such as Intel, General Electric, Shell, Samsung, and Toyota regularly make huge capital outlays. The payoffs from these investments drive the value of their firms and the wealth of their shareholders. For these and other companies, the annual capital investment budget may run to several billion dollars, so the consequences of flawed capital budgeting processes are serious indeed.

The capital budgeting process breaks down into three steps:

1. identifying potential investments;
2. analyzing the set of investment opportunities and identifying those that create shareholder value; and
3. implementing and monitoring the investments selected in Step 2.

The long-term success of almost any firm depends on mastering all three steps. Not surprisingly, capital budgeting is also the area where managers most frequently and explicitly apply the marginal benefit versus marginal cost ($MB \geq MC$) decision rule. Step 2 essentially describes precisely this kind of cost/benefit analysis. We cover capital budgeting in Part 3 of this text.

Financial Management. Financial management involves managing firms' operating cash flows as efficiently and profitably as possible. A key element of this process, known as the *capital structure decision,* is finding the right mix of debt and equity securities to issue that maximizes the firm's overall market value. A second part of the financial management function is ensuring that firms have enough working capital on hand for day-to-day operations. Managing working capital involves obtaining seasonal financing, building up enough inventories to meet customer needs, paying suppliers, collecting from customers, and investing surplus cash, all while maintaining adequate cash balances. Managing working capital effectively requires not only technical and analytical skills, but also people skills. Almost every component of working capital management involves building and maintaining relationships with customers, suppliers, lenders, and others. We cover financial planning and management in Part 6 of this text.

Corporate Governance. Recent corporate scandals—such as financial collapses at Enron, Arthur Andersen, WorldCom, and Parmalat—clearly show that establishing good corporate governance systems is paramount. Governance systems determine who benefits most from company activities; then they establish procedures to maximize firm value and to ensure that employees act ethically and responsibly. Good management does not develop in a vacuum. It results from corporate governance systems that hire and promote qualified, honest people, and that motivate employees to achieve company goals through salary and other incentives.

Developing corporate governance systems present quite a challenge in practice because conflicts inevitably arise among stockholders, managers, and other stakeholders'. A firm's stockholders want managers to work hard and to protect shareholders' interests. But rarely is it in the interest of any *individual* stockholder to spend the time and money needed to ensure that managers act appropriately. If individual stockholders conducted this type of oversight, they would personally bear all the costs of monitoring management, but would share the benefits with all other shareholders. This is a classic example of the **collective action problem** that arises in most relationships between stockholders and managers. Likewise, though managers may wish to maximize shareholder wealth, they do not want to work harder than necessary, especially if others are going to reap most of the benefits. Finally, managers and shareholders may decide together to run a company to benefit themselves at the expense of creditors or other stakeholders who do not generally have a voice in corporate governance.

collective action problem
When individual stockholders expend time and resources monitoring managers, bearing the costs of monitoring management while the benefit of their activities accrues to all shareholders.

As you might expect, a variety of governance mechanisms designed to mitigate conflicts of interest have evolved over time. Strong boards of directors play a vital role in any well-functioning governance system, because boards must hire, fire, pay, and promote senior managers. Boards must also develop *fixed* (salary) and *contingent* (bonus and stock-based) compensation packages that align managers' incentives with those of shareholders. In addition, a firm's auditors play a governance role by certifying the accuracy of financial statements. In the United States, accounting scandals and concerns about auditors' conflicts of interest prompted Congress to pass the **Sarbanes-Oxley Act of 2002 (SOX),** which we discuss in more depth in Section 1.4.

Sarbanes-Oxley Act of 2002 (SOX)
Act of Congress that established new corporate governance standards for U.S. public companies, and that established the Public Company Accounting Oversight Board (PCAOB).

Just as all companies struggle to develop effective corporate governance systems, so do countries. Governments everywhere strive to establish legal frameworks for corporate finance that both encourage competitive businesses to develop and efficient financial markets to run properly. For example, a nation's legal system should allow mergers and acquisitions that increase economic efficiency, but block takeovers that significantly reduce competition. Commercial laws should provide protection for creditors and minority shareholders and limit opportunities for managers or majority shareholders to transfer corporate wealth from investors to themselves. We further discuss the ramifications of corporate governance in Chapters 22 and 23.

SMART CONCEPTS

See the concept explained step-by-step at SMARTFinance

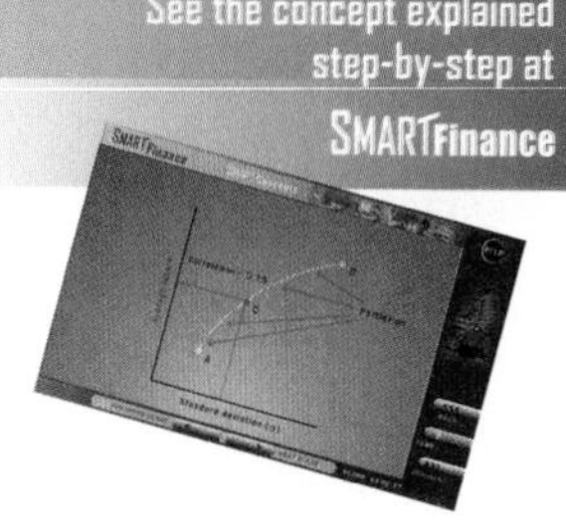

Risk Management. Historically, risk management has identified the unpredictable "acts of nature" risks (fire, flood, collision, and other property damage) to which firms were exposed and has used insurance products or self-insurance to manage those exposures. Today's risk-management function identifies, measures, and manages many more types of risk exposures, including predictable business risks. These exposures include losses that could result from adverse interest rate movements, commodity price changes, and currency value fluctuations. The techniques for managing such risks are among the most sophisticated of all corporate finance practices. The risk-management task attempts to quantify the sources and magnitudes of firms' risk exposure and to decide whether to simply accept these risks or to manage them.

Some risks are easily insurable, such as the risk of loss caused by fire or flood, employee theft, or injury to customers by the company's products. Other corporate risks can be reduced through diversification. For example, rather than use a sole supplier for a key production input, a company may choose to contract with several suppliers, even if it means purchasing the input at slightly more than the lowest possible price. However, the focus of modern risk management is on the market-driven risks mentioned earlier, relating to interest rates, commodity prices, and currency values. Many financial instruments—called *derivatives* because they derive their value from other, underlying assets—have been developed over the past two decades for use in **hedging** (i.e., offsetting) many of the more threatening market risks. These financial instruments are described in depth in Part 5—Chapters 15–17 of this book.

hedging
Procedures used by firms to offset many of the more threatening market risks.

We discuss each of the five major finance functions at length in this textbook, and we hope you come to share our excitement about the career opportunities that corporate finance provides. Never before has finance been as fast-paced, as technological, as international, as ethically challenging, or as rigorous as it is today. These trends have helped make it one of the most popular majors for undergraduate students in U.S. and international business schools. However, all finance careers require an understanding of how effectively applying corporate finance functions can create value for firms.

CONCEPT REVIEW QUESTIONS

4. What is a *financial intermediary*? Why do you think these institutions have steadily been losing "market share" to capital markets as the principal source of external financing for corporations?

5. List the five basic corporate finance functions. What is the general relationship among them?

6. Which of the five basic corporate finance functions might be considered "nontraditional"? Why do you think these functions have become so important in recent years?

1.3 LEGAL FORMS OF BUSINESS ORGANIZATION

Companies exist so that people can organize to pursue profit-making ventures in a formal, legally secure manner. Although companies are organized in numerous ways, only a handful of forms have generally succeeded, and variations of these forms appear throughout the world. This section briefly examines how companies organize themselves legally and discusses the costs and benefits that accrue to each major form. We begin with the organizational forms available to businesses in the United States. After that, we look at the most important organizational forms that non-U.S. businesses use.

Business Organizational Forms in the United States

Historically, three key legal forms of business organization in the United States have worked well: sole proprietorships, partnerships, and corporations. These have recently been joined by a fourth type, limited liability companies, or LLCs. Sole proprietorships are the most common form of organization. However, corporations are by far the dominant form in terms of sales, assets, and total profits. In addition to these classic forms, two very important "hybrid" organizational forms—the limited partnership and the S corporation—have recently emerged.

Sole Proprietorships. As the name implies, a sole proprietorship is a business with a single owner. In fact, in a proprietorship no legal distinction arises between the business and the owner. The business is the owner's personal property, it exists only as long as the owner lives and chooses to operate it, and all business assets belong to the owner personally. Furthermore, the owner/entrepreneur bears personal liability for all debts of the company and pays income taxes on the business's earnings. Sole proprietorships are by far the most common type of business in the United States, accounting for more than 71 percent of the 28.6 million business tax returns filed during 2003. However, proprietorships receive less than 6 percent of business income and employ less than 10 percent of the work force.

Simplicity and ease of operation constitute the proprietorship's principal benefits. However, this organizational form suffers from severe weaknesses that usually limit the firm's long-term growth potential. These include the following:

- *Limited life.* By definition, a proprietorship ceases to exist when the founder dies or retires. Although entrepreneurs can pass the business assets on to their children (or sell them to someone else of their choice), the value of their business—such as business contracts and relationships—tie personally to the entrepreneurs.
- *Limited access to capital.* Proprietorships can obtain operating capital from only two sources: reinvested profits and owners' personal borrowing. In practice, both of these sources are easily exhausted.
- *Unlimited personal liability.* A sole proprietor is personally liable for all debts of the business, including any judgments awarded to plaintiffs in successful lawsuits. The United States is the most litigious society in history (some 20 *million* lawsuits are filed yearly in state courts alone), and a single jury verdict can impoverish even the most successful business family.

joint and several liability
A legal concept that makes each partner in a partnership legally liable for all the debts of the partnership.

Partnerships. A (general) partnership is essentially a proprietorship with two or more owners who have joined their skills and personal wealth. As with sole proprietorships, no legal distinction exists between the business and its owners, each of whom can execute contracts binding on all the others, and each of whom is personally liable for all partnership debts. This is known as **joint and several liability.** Though the owners are not required to formalize the terms of their partnerships in written partnership agreements, most do create such documents. In the absence of partnership agreements, businesses dissolve whenever one of the partners dies or retires. Furthermore, unless a partnership agreement specifies otherwise, each partner shares equally in business income and each has equal management authority. As with proprietorships, partnership income is taxed only once, at the personal level—a definite benefit in favor of these simple forms.

In addition to the tax benefits and ease of formation that partnerships share with proprietorships, partnerships allow a large number of people to pool their capital and expertise to form much larger enterprises. Partnerships enjoy more flexibility than proprietorships. For example, businesses do not automatically terminate after the death or retirement of one partner. Industries in which partnerships are a very important form of organization include accounting, consulting, engineering, law, and medicine.

The drawbacks of partnerships resemble those of sole proprietorships and include the following:

- *Limited life.* Firms' lives can be limited, particularly if only a few partners are involved. Because partnerships are long-term, multi-person business associations, they are also plagued with instability problems as partners leave and others join the business.
- *Limited access to capital.* Firms are still limited to retained profits and personal borrowings if the partnership wants to expand or make capital investments.
- *Unlimited personal liability.* This disadvantage is even worse because the partners are subject to joint and several liability. If one partner makes an unwise or illegal decision, *all* the partners have to pay.

As firms grow larger, the competitive disadvantages of the proprietorship and partnership forms become increasingly severe. Almost all successful companies eventually become corporations. The recent history of the security brokerage industry in the United States shows this very clearly. All the major Wall Street brokerage firms were organized as partnerships before 1970, but during that year Merrill Lynch became a corporation and listed its own shares on the New York Stock Exchange. Over the next three decades, all of the large brokerage houses except Goldman Sachs either switched from partnership to corporate status or were acquired by other financial companies. The last major holdout, Goldman Sachs, finally adopted the corporate form and executed a very successful IPO in May 1999.

Limited partnerships. In many ways, limited partnerships combine the best features of the (general) partnership and the corporate organizational forms. Most of the participants in the partnership (the limited partners) have the limited liability of corporate shareholders, but their share of the profits from the business is taxed as partnership income. In any limited partnership (LP), one or more general partners, each of whom has unlimited personal liability, must oversee the firm's activities. Because the general partners operate the business and they alone are legally exposed to the risk of ruin, they usually receive a greater share of partnership income than their capital contribution alone would merit. The **limited partners** must be totally passive. They contribute capital to the partnership, but they cannot have their names associated with the business, and they cannot take any active role in its operation, even as employees. In return for this passivity, limited partners do not face personal liability for the business's debts. This means limited partners can lose their equity investment in the business, but successful plaintiffs (or tax authorities) cannot look to the limited partners personally for payment of their claims above and beyond the limited partners' initial investments. Best of all, limited partners share in partnership income, which is taxed only once, as ordinary personal income for the partners.

limited partners
One or more totally passive participants in a limited partnership, who do not take any active role in the operation of the business and who do not face personal liability for the debts of the business.

Limited partnerships can provide tax benefits to the limited partners during early years of the business. Disadvantages of LPs include lack of liquidity (that is, limited partnership interests may be difficult to sell) and problems with monitoring and disciplining the general partner(s). In some cases, registering an LP with the Securities and Exchange Commission allows secondary-market trading of partnership interests, which reduces or eliminates the problem of low liquidity.

Corporations. By U.S. law, a corporation is a separate legal entity with many of the same economic rights and responsibilities as those enjoyed by individuals. Corporations can sue and be sued; they can own property and execute contracts in their own names; they can be tried and convicted for crimes committed by their employees. This organizational form has several key competitive advantages over other forms, including the following:

- *Unlimited life.* Once created, corporations have a perpetual life unless they are explicitly terminated.
- *Limited liability.* Firms' shareholders cannot be held personally liable for the firms' debts, although CEOs and chief financial officers (CFOs) can be held personally liable under the Sarbanes-Oxley Act if the debts result from improper accounting practices or fraudulent acts.
- *Individual contracting.* Corporations can contract individually with managers, suppliers, customers, and ordinary employees, and each individual contract can be renegotiated, modified, or terminated without affecting other stakeholders.
- *Unlimited access to capital.* The company itself, rather than its owners, can borrow money from creditors. It can also issue various classes of preferred and common stock to equity investors. Furthermore, the ownership claims (shares of preferred and common stock) of a public company can be freely traded among investors without obtaining permission from other investors. A **public company** has its shares listed for trading on a public security market.

public company
A corporation, the shares of which can be freely traded among investors without obtaining the permission of other investors and whose shares are listed for trading in a public security market.

A **corporation** is a legal entity owned by the shareholders who hold its common stock. Shares of stock carry voting rights, and shareholders vote at annual meetings to elect **boards of directors.** These boards are then responsible for hiring and firing managers and setting overall corporate policies. The rules dictating voting procedures and other aspects of corporate governance appear in the firm's **corporate charter**, the legal document created at the corporation's inception to govern the firm's operations. The charter can be changed only by a shareholder's vote. Also, in contrast to the practice in almost all other countries, incorporation in the United States is executed at the state (rather than the national) level and is governed primarily by state (rather than federal) law. Nonetheless, all fifty states have broadly similar rules for incorporation

corporation
In U.S. law, a separate legal entity with many of the same economic rights and responsibilities as those enjoyed by individuals.

boards of directors
Elected by shareholders to be responsible for hiring and firing managers and setting overall corporate policies.

corporate charter
The legal document created at the corporation's inception to govern its operations.

Figure 1.2
The Finance Function in the Organizational Structure of a Typical Large Corporation

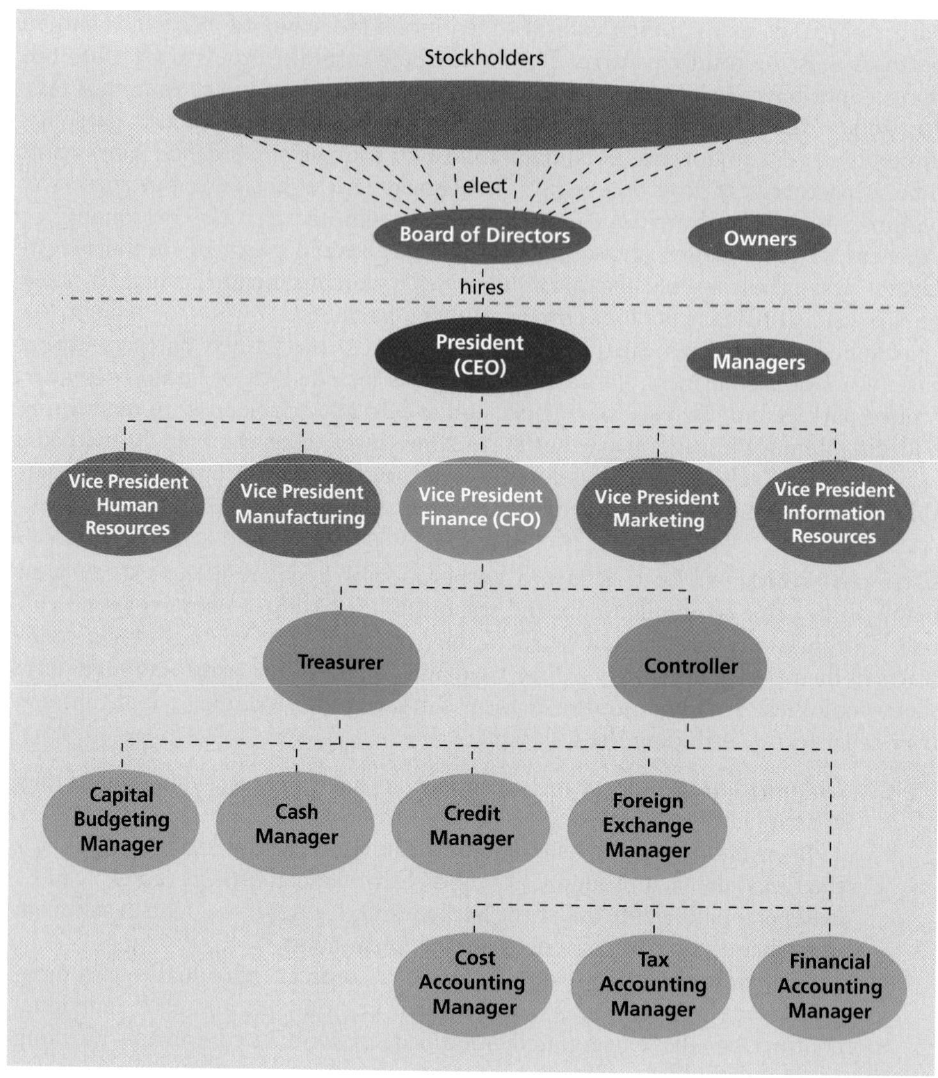

and corporate governance. The top part of Figure 1.2 depicts the relationships among the important parties in a corporation.

shareholders
Owners of common and preferred stock of a corporation.

equity claimants
Owners of a corporation's equity securities.

As Chapter 5 explains, those who hold common and preferred stock own the firm's equity securities. These investors are called **shareholders** or stockholders (the terms are interchangeable). Often they are called **equity claimants** because they hold ownership claims. Generally, preferred stockholders bear less risk than common stockholders, because preferred stock pays a fixed dividend yearly, and preferred stockholders have a more senior claim on the firm's assets in the event of bankruptcy. Therefore, we refer to common stockholders as the firm's ultimate owners. Common stockholders vote periodically to elect members of boards of directors and to amend firms' corporate charter when necessary. Directors typically include the company's top managers as well as outsiders, who are usually successful entrepreneurs or executives of other major corporations. The **president** or **chief executive officer (CEO)** is responsible for managing day-to-day operations and carrying out policies established by the board. The board expects regular reports from the CEO about the firm's current status and future direction. Note the division between owners and managers in a large corporation, as shown by the dashed horizontal line in Figure 1.2. This separation leads to **agency costs**, which arise because of conflicts of interest between shareholders (owners) and managers. Agency costs are discussed in greater depth later in this chapter.

president or chief executive officer (CEO)
The top company manager with overall responsibility and authority for managing daily company affairs and carrying out policies established by the board.

agency costs
Costs that arise due to conflicts of interest between shareholders and managers.

Although corporations dominate economic life around the world, this form has some competitive disadvantages. Many governments tax corporate income at both company and personal levels. In the United States, this treatment, commonly called the **double taxation problem**, has traditionally been the single greatest disadvantage of the corporate form. The **Jobs and Growth Tax Relief Reconciliation Act of 2003** (hereafter, the Tax Relief Act of 2003) dramatically reduced the double taxation problem. To demonstrate the importance of double taxation, we show how this affected the income that shareholders received before and after passage of the Tax Relief Act of 2003. Table 1.4 compares how \$100,000 of operating income would have been taxed for a corporation and for an equivalent company organized as a partnership before 2003. Table 1.5 shows how income is taxed today. Assume that the corporate income tax rate is 35 percent ($T_c = 0.35$), both before and after 2003.

double taxation problem
Taxation of corporate income at both the company and the personal levels—the single greatest disadvantage of the corporate form.

Jobs and Growth Tax Relief Reconciliation Act of 2003
Act of Congress that reduced the rate of personal taxation of dividend income, reducing the double taxation problem.

Before passage of the Tax Relief Act of 2003, both partnership profits and dividend income from corporations were taxed the same way at the personal level in the United States. For ease of exposition, we assume that the personal tax rate on partnership income and corporate dividends was 38 percent ($T_p = 0.38$), and that each type of firm generated \$100,000 in income for the year. The \$100,000 in partnership income was taxed once, at the personal level. The partners then had \$100,000 × (1 – 0.38) = \$62,000 in after-tax disposable income. In contrast, the corporation's operating income was first taxed at the corporate level, where federal taxes took \$100,000 × 0.35 = \$35,000, and then again when the remaining \$65,000 was distributed to shareholders as cash dividends. These were taxed at the personal rate of 38 percent, leaving only \$65,000 × (1 – 0.38) = \$40,300 in after-tax disposable income. (We ignore state taxes in our example, but adding in state tax liabilities would simply make the comparison worse for corporations.)

Table 1.4
Taxation of Business Income for Corporations and Partnerships *Before* Passage of the Jobs and Growth Tax Relief Reconciliation Act of 2003

	Partnership	Corporation
Operating income	\$100,000	\$100,000
Less: Corporate profits tax ($T_c = 0.35$)	0	35,000
Net income	\$100,000	\$ 65,000
Cash dividends or partnership distributions	\$100,000	\$ 65,000
Less: Personal tax on owner income ($T_p = 0.38$)	38,000	24,700
After-tax disposable income	\$ 62,000	\$ 40,300

Table 1.5
Taxation of Business Income for Corporations and Partnerships *After* Passage of the Jobs and Growth Tax Relief Reconciliation Act of 2003

	Partnership	Corporation
Operating income	$100,000	$100,000
Less: Corporate profits tax ($T_c = 0.35$)	0	35,000
Net income	$100,000	$ 65,000
Cash dividends or partnership distributions	$100,000	$ 65,000
Less: Personal tax on dividends ($T_{cg} = 0.15$)		9,750
Less: Personal tax on partnership income ($T_p = 0.35$)	35,000	
After-tax disposable income	$ 65,000	$ 55,250

Table 1.4 shows that business activity conducted through a partnership rather than through a corporation before 2003 could have saved the firm's owners 21.7 cents [($62,000 – $40,300) ÷ $100,000] in taxes on every dollar earned. Even given the massive nontax benefits of the corporate form for most business activities that we noted earlier, this tax "wedge" was a very heavy burden for U.S. companies to shoulder. To lighten this burden, the Bush administration proposed scrapping separate personal taxation of dividends entirely in early 2003. Although dividend taxation was not eliminated, the Jobs and Growth Tax Relief Reconciliation Act of 2003 changed the rate at which dividends were taxed at the personal level. Dividends are now treated as capital gains and taxed at the investor's capital gains tax rate of either 5 or 15 percent. The Jobs and Growth Tax Relief Reconciliation Act of 2003 also reduced the top marginal (federal) tax rate on personal income from 38.6 to 35 percent and reduced the top capital gains tax rate from 20 to 15 percent.

Table 1.5 shows how the new legislation reduces the problem of double taxation on dividends. As before, we assume that the corporation in our example is taxed at the top corporate income tax rate of 35 percent ($T_c = 0.35$) and that the partnership's investors face the top personal income tax rate, which is now 35 percent ($T_p = 0.35$). However, the corporation's shareholders now treat dividends received as capital gains, and we assume that they face the top personal capital gains tax rate of 15 percent ($T_{cg} = 0.15$). Now partners would receive after-tax disposable income of $65,000 [$100,000 × (1 – 0.35)], and shareholders would receive net disposable income of $55,250 [$100,000 × (1 – 0.35) (1 – 0.15)]. As this example shows, the Tax Relief Act of 2003 has reduced the proprietorship's or partnership's tax benefit from a maximum of 21.7 cents on the dollar to only 9.75 cents before state taxes.[3] This differential may be more than offset by the many advantages of the corporate form of business organization noted earlier.

S corporation
An ordinary corporation in which the stockholders have elected to allow shareholders to be taxed as partners while still retaining their limited-liability status as corporate stockholders.

S Corporations. In contrast to regular corporations, **S corporations** (previously called *Subchapter S corporations*) allow shareholders to be taxed as partners while retaining their limited liability status. To be eligible for S status, a firm must meet the following criteria:

[3] A short article describing the key provisions of the Jobs and Growth Tax Relief Reconciliation Act of 2003 can be obtained from the accounting firm Grant Thornton (http://www.gt.com). The Internal Revenue Service's Web site (http://www.irs.gov) also presents a summary of the act's provisions.

- S corporations must have 75 or fewer shareholders.
- The shareholders must be individuals or certain types of trusts (not corporations).
- S corporations cannot issue more than one class of equity security, and cannot be a holding companies. This means they cannot hold a controlling fraction of the stock in another company.

If a corporation can meet these requirements, then election of S corporation status allows the company's operating income to escape taxation at the corporate level.[4] Instead, shareholders claim proportionate fractions of total company profits as personal income and pay tax on this profit at their individual marginal tax rates. As with limited partnerships, S corporation status yields the limited liability benefit of the corporate form, along with the favorable taxation of the partnership form. In addition, S corporations can easily switch back to being regular C corporations whenever companies outgrow the shareholder ceiling (75) or need to issue multiple classes of equity securities. Given the flexibility of this type of organization, many successful companies begin life as S corporations and retain S status until they decide to go public, which forces them to become regular corporations.

Limited Liability Companies. Limited liability companies (LLCs) combine partnerships' pass-through taxation with S corporations' limited liability. All 50 U.S. states allow LLCs, which are easy to set up. The IRS allows LLC owners to elect taxation as either a partnership or as a corporation. Many states allow one-person LLCs, as well as a choice of a finite or infinite life. Even though LLCs are taxed as partnerships, their owners face no personal liability for other partners' malpractice, making this type of company especially attractive for professional service firms. Given the limited liability feature and the flexibility of LLCs, we expect them to continue gaining significant "organizational market share" in coming years.[5]

Forms of Business Organization Used by Non-U.S. Companies

Although any comprehensive survey of international forms of business organization is beyond the scope of this introductory chapter, we briefly survey the most important organizational patterns observed in many industrialized economies. Even a quick glance at non-U.S. systems shows many common patterns. In almost all capitalist economies, some form of limited liability business structure exists, with ownership shares that can be traded freely on national stock markets. Also, as in the United States, these companies dominate economic life almost everywhere.

Limited Liability Companies in Other Industrialized Countries. Although limited liability companies exist around the world, they have different names in different countries. In Britain, they are called public limited companies (plc); in Germany, *Aktiengesellschaft* (AG); in France, *Société Générale;* and in Spain, Mexico, and elsewhere in Latin America, *Sociedad Anónima* (SA). Details vary, but all of these structures are similar to publicly traded corporations in the United States. Key differences between international and U.S. companies revolve around tax treatment of business income and the amount of information that publicly traded companies must

4. According to the February 2004 issue of the Internal Revenue Service *Statistics of Income* summary (http://www.irs.gov/taxstats/index.html), more than 57 percent (3.34 million of 5.85 million) of all corporations that filed tax returns during 2003 were S corporations, which indicates both the popularity of this organizational form and the relatively small average size of U.S. businesses.

5. See http://www.mycorporation.com/incllcbusiness.htm for a comparison of the LLC and corporate forms.

COMPARATIVE CORPORATE FINANCE

The Growth of Stock Market Capitalization

The world's stock markets have increased phenomenally in value and importance during the past twenty years. The figure below traces the rise in the total value of the world's stock markets from 1983 to 2003. This twenty-year period saw a total worldwide market capitalization increase from less than $3.4 trillion to about $35 trillion at its peak in March 2000, before falling and then rebounding to about $29 trillion by the end of December 2003. As the figure shows, the market value of American stocks increased six-fold over these two decades, but non-U.S. markets experienced even faster growth. At its peak in early 2000, the total worldwide stock market capitalization of $35 trillion was roughly equal to the world gross domestic product. The value of stocks traded has actually increased even more than market capitalization over this period, increasing (twenty-seven-fold) from $1.23 trillion in 1983 to $33.32 trillion in 2003.

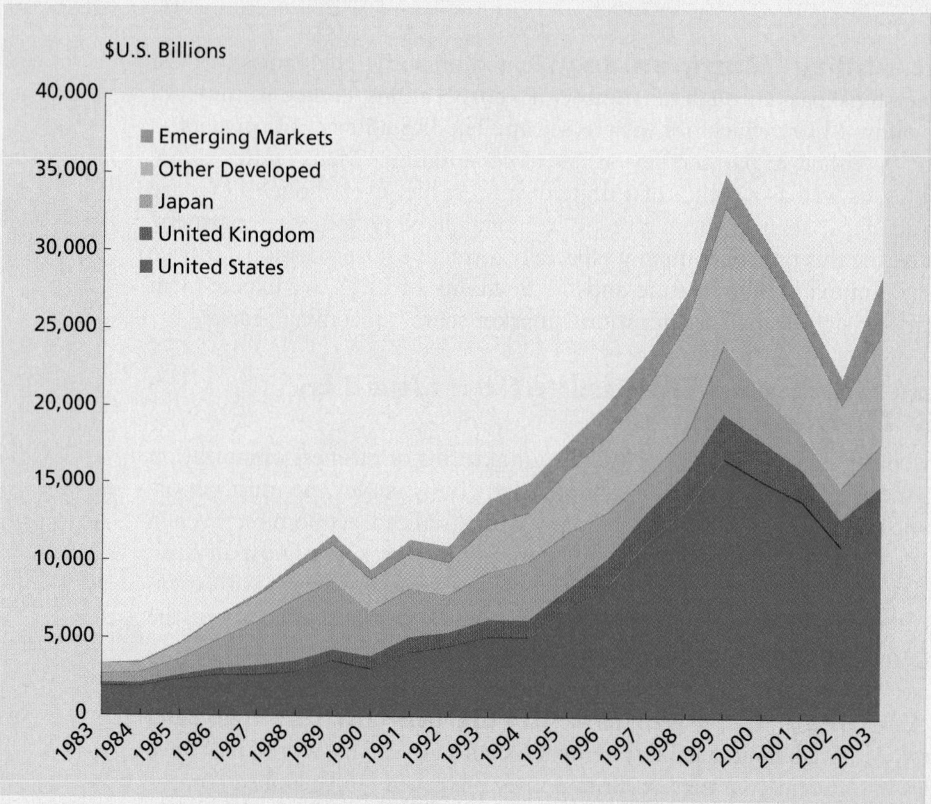

Sources: World Bank (http://www.worldbank.org) and International Federation of Stock Exchanges (http://www.fibv.com)

disclose. Tax rules are typically, though not always, harsher in the United States than elsewhere, and disclosure requirements are invariably greater for U.S. than for non-U.S. companies. The Comparative Corporate Finance insert above shows how these firms' values have surged in markets around the world.

Many countries also distinguish between limited liability companies that can be traded publicly and those that are privately held. In Germany, *Gesellschaft mit beschränkten Haftung* (GmbH) are privately owned, unlisted limited-liability stock companies. In France, these are called *Société à Responsibilité Limitée* (SARL). Private (unlisted) companies, particularly family-owned firms, play important roles in all market economies. For example, the German postwar "economic miracle" was not propelled by giant companies, but rather by midsized, export-oriented companies that pursued niche marketing strategies at home and abroad. These *Mittelstand* (middle market) firms still account for some three quarters of all German economic activity. A similar set of relatively small, entrepreneurial companies has helped propel Taiwan, Singapore, and other Asian nations to growth rates consistently higher than those achieved in the industrialized West.

CONCEPT REVIEW QUESTIONS

7. What are the costs and benefits of each of the three major organizational forms in the United States? Why do you think the various "hybrid" forms of business organization have proven so successful?

8. Comment on the following statement: "Sooner or later, all successful private companies that are organized as proprietorships or partnerships must become corporations."

1.4 THE CORPORATE FINANCIAL MANAGER'S GOALS

In large, publicly traded corporations, owners are typically distinct from managers. Traditionally, finance teaches that managers should act according to the interests of the firm's owners—its stockholders. In the sections that follow, we discuss varying ideas about what a corporate manager's goals *should* be. We first evaluate profit maximization and then describe shareholder wealth maximization. Next, we discuss the *agency costs* arising from potential conflicts between the stockholders' goals and the managers' actions. Finally, we consider the role of ethics in corporate finance and briefly discuss how the Sarbanes-Oxley Act is likely to affect financial management.

What Should a Financial Manager Try to Maximize?

Maximize Profit? Some people believe that the manager's objective always should be to try to maximize profits. To maximize profits, financial managers should take only those actions that are expected to increase the firm's revenues more than its costs. From a practical standpoint, this objective translates into maximizing earnings per share (EPS), defined as earnings available for common stockholders divided by the number of shares of common stock outstanding.

Although it seems a reasonable objective for corporate managers, profit maximization as a goal suffers from several flaws.

- Figures for earnings per share are always historical, reflecting past performance rather than what is happening now or what will happen in the future.

- If managers seek only to maximize profits over a period of time, they may ignore the timing of those profits. Large profits that pay off many years in the future may be less valuable than smaller profits received next year.
- When firms compute profits, they follow certain accounting principles which focus on accrued revenues and costs. A firm that is profitable according to accounting principles may spend more cash than it receives, and an unprofitable firm may have larger cash inflows than outflows. In finance, we place more emphasis on cash than on profits or earnings. As the old saying goes, "You cannot pay your bills with earnings, only with cash."
- Finally, focusing only on earnings ignores variability, or risk. When comparing two investment opportunities, managers must consider both the risks and the expected return of the investments. Corporate finance presumes a trade-off between risk and expected return, and that *risk and expected return are the key determinants of share prices.* However, they affect share prices differently. Higher cash flow generally leads to higher share prices, while higher risk results in lower share prices.

Maximize Shareholder Wealth? Current theory asserts that the firms' proper goal is to maximize shareholders' wealth, as measured by the market price of the firm's stock. A firm's stock price reflects the timing, magnitude, and risk of the *cash flows* that investors expect a firm to generate over time. When considering alternative strategies, financial managers should undertake only those actions that they expect will increase the firm's share price—in other words, actions that will increase the value of the firm's future cash flows. This objective really brings us back to our basic premise for the book: Financial managers should choose actions that generate benefits in excess of costs (MB≥MC).

SMART PRACTICES VIDEO

David Nickel, Controller for Intel Communications Group, Intel Corp.

"Finance's primary role is to try to drive the right business decisions to increase shareholder value."

See the entire interview at **SMARTFinance**

Why does finance regard share value maximization as the primary corporate objective? Why not focus instead on satisfying the desires of customers, employees, suppliers, creditors, or any other stakeholders? Theoretical and empirical arguments support the assertion that managers should focus on maximizing shareholder wealth. A firm's shareholders are sometimes called *residual* claimants, meaning that they have claims only on any of the firm's cash flows that remain after employees, suppliers, creditors, governments, and other stakeholders are paid in full. It may help to visualize all the firm's stakeholders standing in line to receive their share of the firm's cash flows. Shareholders stand at the very end of this line. If the firm cannot pay its employees, suppliers, creditors, and tax authorities first, shareholders receive nothing. Furthermore, by accepting their position as residual claimants, shareholders agree to bear most of the risk of running the firm. If firms did not operate to maximize shareholder wealth, investors would have little incentive to accept the risks necessary to buy stock and provide the funds necessary for a business to thrive.

To understand this point, consider how a firm would operate if it were run in the interests of its creditors. Would such a firm ever make risky investments, no matter how profitable, given that its creditors receive only a fixed return if these investments pay off? Only shareholders have the proper incentives to make risky, value-increasing investments that maximize overall firm value. Thus, only shareholders can force the firm to take on risky, but potentially profitable, ventures.

Focus on Stakeholders? Although the primary goal of managers should be maximizing shareholder wealth, many firms have broadened their focus in recent years to include the interests of other stakeholders—such as employees, customers, tax authorities, and the communities where firms operate. A firm with a stakeholder focus consciously avoids actions that would prove detrimental to stakeholders by transferring other constituents' wealth to shareholders. The goal is not so much to maximize others' interests as it is to preserve those interests.

Considering other constituents' interests is part of the firm's "social responsibility," and keeping other affected groups happy provides long-term benefit to shareholders. Such relationships minimize employee turnover, conflicts, and litigation. In most cases, taking care of stakeholders translates into maximizing shareholder wealth. But conflict between these two objectives inevitably arises. In that case, the firm should ultimately be run to benefit equity holders. Interestingly, even though American corporations are generally expected to act in a socially responsible way, they are rarely *required* by law to do so. The situation is much different in many Western European countries, where corporations are expected to contribute to social welfare almost as much as they are expected to create private wealth.

How Can Agency Costs Be Controlled in Corporate Finance?

Control of modern corporations usually rests in the hands of professional, nonowner managers. We have seen that financial managers' goal should be to maximize shareholder wealth; thus, managers act as agents of the owners, who have hired them to make decisions and to manage the firm for the owners' benefit. Technically, any manager who owns less than 100 percent of the firm's stock is, to some degree, an *agent* of other owners.

In practice, managers also consider their own personal wealth, job security, lifestyle, and prestige, and seek to receive perquisites, such as country club memberships, limousines, and posh offices (provided at company expense, of course). Such concerns often motivate managers to pursue objectives other than shareholder wealth maximization. Voting shareholders, especially large institutional investors, recognize the potential for managers' self-interested behavior, and use a variety of tools to limit such conflicts of interest. Financial economists recognize the *agency costs* that arise when the shareholders' interests and managers' interests conflict.

Types of Agency Costs. Conflict between the goals of a firm's owners and managers gives rise to managerial **agency problems**: costs arising from the likelihood that managers may place personal goals ahead of corporate goals. Shareholders can attempt to overcome these agency problems by:

agency problems
The conflict between the goals of a firm's owners and its managers.

- relying on market forces to exert managerial discipline;
- incurring monitoring and bonding costs necessary to supervise managers; and
- structuring executive compensation packages to align managers' interests with stockholders' interests.

Several market forces constrain a manager's opportunistic behavior. In recent years, large investors have become more active in management. This is particularly true for institutional investors such as mutual funds, life insurance companies, and pension funds, which often hold large blocks of a firm's stock and thus have many votes to wield if issues arise. Institutional investor activists use their influence to pressure underperforming management teams, occasionally applying enough pressure to replace existing CEOs with new ones.

hostile takeover
The acquisition of one firm by another through an open-market bid for a majority of the target's shares if the target firm's senior managers do no support (or, more likely, actively resist) the acquisition.

An even more powerful form of market discipline is the **hostile takeover**. A hostile takeover involves the acquisition of one firm (the *target*) by another (the *bidder*) through an open-market bid, or *tender offer*, for a majority of the target's shares. By definition, a takeover attempt is hostile if the target firm's senior managers do not support (or, more likely, actively resist) the acquisition. The forces that drive hostile takeovers vary over time and from one acquisition to another, but poor financial performance is a common problem among targets of hostile bids. Bidders in hostile deals may believe they can improve the value of the target company, and thereby profit from their investment, by replacing incumbent management. Managers naturally see this as a threat and erect a variety of barriers to thwart potential acquirers. Nevertheless, the constant threat of a takeover provides additional motivation for managers to act in the firm owners' best interests. We discuss mergers and acquisitions in Chapter 22.

In addition to market forces, other devices can encourage managers to behave in shareholders' interests or limit the consequences when managers misbehave. *Bonding expenditures* insure firms against the potential consequences of dishonest acts by managers. For example, managers could be required to accept a portion of their total pay in the form of delayed compensation that must be forfeited in the event of poor performance. *Monitoring expenditures* pay for audits and control procedures that alert shareholders if managers pursue their own interests too aggressively. But, you may ask, "Who monitors the monitors?" In the wake of Enron's bankruptcy, Enron's auditor, Arthur Andersen, experienced the consequences of failing to alert shareholders to the company's problems. Arthur Andersen's audit clients abandoned the firm in droves, and many of the firm's partners quit. The company was later convicted of criminal misconduct in federal court, which forced Arthur Andersen into bankruptcy.

Use of Compensation Contracts to Control Agency Costs. One of the most popular, powerful, and expensive methods of overcoming agency costs and aligning managerial and stockholder interests is through the design of executive compensation contracts. American companies have long used sophisticated (and potentially lucrative) executive compensation contracts, and the practice is spreading to other industrialized countries—though few European or Asian companies offer their managers pay levels that even approach what U.S. managers receive. Compensation contracts give managers incentives to act in the owners' best interests and allow firms to compete for, hire, and retain the best managers available. For this reason, such pay packages are often called "golden handcuffs," because they tie good managers to the firm.

Incentive compensation plans attempt to tie managerial wealth directly to the firm's share price. This primarily involves making outright grants of stock to top managers or, more commonly, giving them *stock options,* which we discuss further in Chapter 15. Options give managers the right to purchase stock at fixed *exercise prices,* usually the market price of the stock at the time the manager receives the options. The idea is that managers who have incentives to take actions to maximize the stock price above the exercise price will increase their own wealth along with other shareholders' equity.

Although experts agree that tying pay to performance can effectively motivate management, the actual workings of many compensation plans have been harshly criticized in recent years. Individual and institutional investors, as well as the SEC, have publicly questioned the wisdom of awarding multimillion-dollar compensation packages (which typically include salary, bonus, and long-term compensation) to executives of poorly performing corporations. For example, the highest-paid U.S. executives in 2003 were Nigel Morris of Capital One Financial (total pay of $147.3 million) and Reuben Mark, CEO of Colgate-Palmolive ($141.1 million). Even the twenty-fifth highest-paid executive received $32.1 million in total pay.[6] According to *Business Week*'s annual survey of executive pay, the average total compensation for CEOs of large U.S. companies increased by 9 percent in 2003 (after three straight years of declines) to $8.1 million. Average levels of CEO compensation in other developed countries tend to be much lower—a fact that critics of CEO pay in the United States do not miss.

Why Are Ethics Important in Corporate Finance?

In recent years, certain businesses' actions have received major media attention. U.S. examples include the following:

- A string of fines totaling more than $1.2 billion paid between 2002 and 2004 by major brokerage firms to investors (and the state of New York) for intentionally misleading investors with regard to buy-and-sell recommendations offered by brokerage firm analysts;
- The June, 2002 insider-trading arrest of Samuel Waksal, founder and CEO of the biotech firm ImClone Systems, who leaked information to family and friends on the failure of the Food and Drug Administration to approve ImClone's marketing application for the cancer drug Erbitux before that information was released to the public;
- The sensational 2004 trials of Dennis Koslowski (Tyco International Ltd) and Martha Stewart (Martha Stewart Living Omnimedia Inc.) on charges of misappropriation of company assets and conspiracy to obstruct justice, respectively.

Europe and Japan have also seen a disturbing number of corporate scandals recently. In January 2004, the Italian government discovered that the Italian milk distribution company Parmalat had used forged documents to obtain loans and to issue bonds. These actions not only landed the company's top executives in jail but also triggered what may become the largest bankruptcy in financial history. Clearly, these and other similar actions, such as those involving Enron, Global Crossing, WorldCom, and Adelphia, have focused attention on the question of ethics, or standards of conduct in business dealings. Today, society in general and the financial community in particular are developing and enforcing higher ethical standards. The U.S. Congress passed the Sarbanes-Oxley Act in 2002 to enforce higher ethical standards and increase penalties for violators, as we discuss in the next section. The goal of these standards is to motivate businesspeople and investors alike to adhere to both the letter and the spirit of laws and regulations concerned with all aspects of business and professional practice.

SMART ETHICS VIDEO

Andy Bryant, Executive Vice President of Finance and Enterprise Systems, Chief Financial Officer, Intel Corp.

"I never thought that ethics would be a value add to a company, but today I believe it counts as part of your market cap."

See the entire interview at **SMARTFinance**

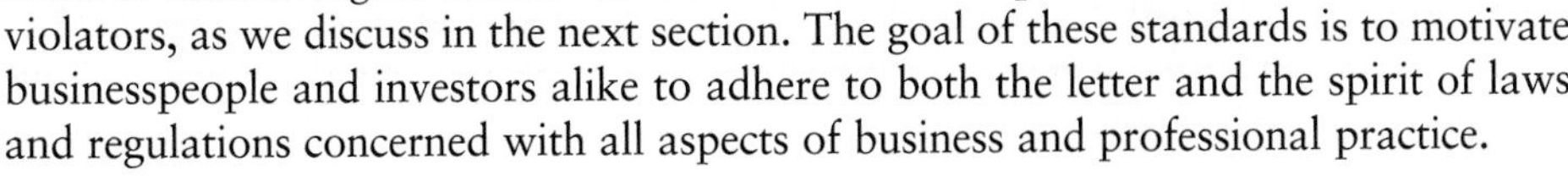

[6] These figures are from a special report on executive pay published each April in *Business Week* magazine. This annual report is viewed with interest by shareholders—and often with dread by the managers fingered as overpaid. The April 19, 2004, report, covering pay for the year 2003, had its share of surprising revelations, but none matched the 2001 report of one of the most attractive noncash bonuses ever paid to an executive. During 2000, the board of Apple Computer purchased a $90 million Gulfstream V business jet for Steve Jobs in recognition of his contribution to the company's turnaround—and as thanks to him for working three years without a salary.

More and more firms are directly addressing ethical issues by establishing corporate ethics policies and guidelines, and by requiring employee compliance with them. Frequently, employees must sign formal pledges to uphold firms' ethics policies. Such policies typically apply to employee actions in dealing with all corporate stakeholders, including the public at large.[7] *Ethical behavior is therefore viewed as necessary for the achievement of firms' goal of maximizing owner wealth.*

How the Sarbanes-Oxley Act Is Changing How Corporate America Conducts Business

As we noted earlier, accounting scandals and concerns about auditors' conflicts of interest prompted the U.S. Congress to pass the Sarbanes-Oxley Act of 2002. This act established a new Public Company Accounting Oversight Board (PCAOB), with the power to license auditing firms and regulate accounting and auditing standards. This act also gave the Securities and Exchange Commission (SEC)—the agency responsible for supervising American capital markets and regulating corporate security issues—greater powers to supervise corporate governance practices in public companies, firms that have shares listed for trading on public stock exchanges. Among many other changes, this act requires both CEOs and CFOs of all large companies to *personally* certify their firms' financial statements.[8] Thus, the CEOs and CFOs can be held personally liable for any questionable or misleading numbers reported to public investors. This act also prevents auditing firms from providing other services—such as consulting, valuation, and tax advisory work—to the companies they are auditing, and mandates that lead auditing partners must rotate off the audit every five years. Perhaps the most crucial internal change the act mandates is to give the firm's audit committee much greater power, responsibility, and independence. The act requires that:

SMART PRACTICES VIDEO

Vince LoForti, Chief Financial Officer, Overland Storage Inc.

"Sarbanes-Oxley has certainly impacted our company in many ways from operations all the way to the board."

See the entire interview at **SMARTFinance**

- each member of the audit committee also be a member of the board of directors;
- each be otherwise independent (not an officer or employee); and
- that at least one of the committee members be a "financial expert."

CONCEPT REVIEW QUESTIONS

9. What are *agency costs?* Why do these tend to increase in severity as a corporation grows larger?

10. What are the relative advantages and disadvantages of using sophisticated management compensation packages to align the interests of managers and shareholders?

11. Why are *ethics* important in corporate finance? What is the likely consequence of unethical behavior by a corporation and its managers?

12. Why did Congress pass the *Sarbanes-Oxley Act of 2002*, and what are its key provisions?

[7] Unfortunately, these steps are hardly enough. Enron had a detailed conflict-of-interest policy in place, but then waived it so that its executives could set up the special-purpose entities that subsequently caused Enron's failure. The result of a lack of effective ethics policies at Enron and numerous other firms has been an increased level of government oversight and regulation.

[8] A summary of the key provisions of the Sarbanes-Oxley Act is presented on the Web site of the American Institute of Certified Public Accountants (AICPA), at http://www.aicpa.org/info/sarbanes_oxley_summary.htm.

1.5 SUMMARY AND CONCLUSIONS

- When making financial decisions, managers should always ask whether the marginal benefits of the decision outweigh the marginal costs. Managers should take actions and accept projects only where the marginal benefits exceed or are equal to marginal costs.
- Finance graduates must interact with professionals trained in all other business disciplines. The five most important career paths for finance professionals are in corporate finance, commercial banking, investment banking, money management, or consulting.
- Corporations can obtain external funding either from financial intermediaries, such as commercial banks, or by issuing securities directly to investors through capital markets. Intermediaries have been steadily losing financial market share to capital markets for several decades.
- The practice of corporate finance involves five basic, related sets of activities: external financing, capital budgeting, financial management, corporate governance, and risk management.
- The three key legal forms of business organization in the United States are sole proprietorships, partnerships, and corporations. Sole proprietorships are most common, but corporations dominate economically. Limited partnerships and S corporations are hybrid forms, combining the limited liability of corporations with the favorable tax treatment of partnerships. A new, fourth form, the limited liability company, has recently become popular because of its flexibility and favorable tax treatment.
- Limited liability companies exist in virtually every country, and those in developed countries share many of the same basic traits.
- The goal of firm managers should be to maximize shareholder wealth rather than maximize profits, because the latter focuses on the past, ignores the timing of profits, relies on accounting values rather than future cash flows, and ignores risk. Shareholder wealth maximization is socially optimal because shareholders are residual claimants who profit only after all other claims are paid in full.
- Agency costs that result from the separation of ownership and control must be addressed satisfactorily for companies to prosper. These costs can be overcome, or at least reduced, by relying on market incentives or threats for corporate control, by incurring monitoring and bonding costs, and by using executive compensation contracts that align the interests of shareholders and managers.
- Ethics, the standards of conduct in business dealings, are important in corporate finance. Ethical behavior is viewed as necessary for the achievement of firms' goal of maximizing owner wealth. The Sarbanes-Oxley Act of 2002 established rules and procedures aimed at eliminating the potential for unethical acts and conflicts of interest in public corporations.

INTERNET RESOURCES

Note: *This textbook includes numerous Internet links throughout the text, both within the discussions and at the end of each chapter. Because some links will likely change or be eliminated during the life of this edition, please go to this book's Web site (*http://megginson.swlearning.com*) to obtain updated links in the event that you encounter a dead link.*

http://money.cnn.com (CNN Money); http://www.yahoo.com (Yahoo!)—Among the best Web sites for general U.S. business information

http://www.ft.com (*Financial Times*)—One of the best Web sites for international business and economic information

http://www.careers.com (CareerBuilder); http://www.monster.com (Monster.com); http://www.usnews.com (*U.S. News & World Report*); http://www.careers.wsj.com (*WSJ Career Journal*)—Web sites for career-related facts and figures

http://www.ameritrade.com (Ameritrade); http://www.schwab.com (Charles Schwab); http://www.etrade.com (E*Trade); http://www.bankone.com (Bank One)—Excellent Web sites maintained by brokerage houses and Internet banking firms

http://www.irs.gov/taxstats/index.html (U.S. Internal Revenue Service's "Statistics of Income" site)—The ideal place to find up-to-date information about the number of businesses filing tax returns and about the distribution of assets and revenues among different organizational forms of business

http://www.sec.gov/edgar.shtml (U.S. Securities and Exchange Commission's EDGAR Web site) Provides online access to all security registrations and financial documents filed by public companies with the SEC since 1994.

KEY TERMS

agency costs
agency problems
boards of directors
capital budgeting function
collective action problem
corporate charter
corporate finance
corporate governance function
corporation
debt capital
double taxation problem
equity capital
equity claimants
external financing function
fiduciary
financial intermediary
financial management function
hedging
hostile takeover
initial public offering (IPO)
Jobs and Growth Tax Relief Reconciliation Act of 2003
joint and several liability
limited partners
president or chief executive officer (CEO)
primary-market transactions
public company
risk-management function
S corporations
Sarbanes-Oxley Act of 2002
secondary-market transactions
shareholders
venture capitalists

QUESTIONS AND PROBLEMS

Q1-1. Why must a financial manager have an integrated understanding of the five basic finance functions? Why is the corporate governance function considered a finance function? Why has the risk-management function become more important in recent years?

Q1-2. Enter the home page of the Careers in Business Web site (http://www.careers-in-business.com), and page through the finance positions listed and their corresponding salaries. What skill sets or job characteristics lead to the variation in salaries? Which of these positions generally require previous work experience?

Q1-3. What are the advantages and disadvantages of different legal forms of business organization? Could the limited liability advantage of a corporation also lead to an *agency problem*? Why? What legal form would an upstart entrepreneur likely prefer?

Q1-4. Can there be a difference between *profit maximization* and *shareholder wealth maximization*? If so, what could cause this difference? Which of the two should be the goal of the firm and its management? Why?

Q1-5. Define a corporate *stakeholder*. Which groups are considered stakeholders? Would stockholders also be considered stakeholders? Compare the shareholder wealth maximization principle with the stakeholder wealth preservation principle in terms of economic systems.

Q1-6. What is meant by an "agency cost" or "agency problem"? Do these interfere with shareholder wealth maximization? Why? What mechanisms minimize these costs/problems?

Q1-7. Are *ethics* critical to the financial manager's goal of shareholder wealth maximization? How are the two related? Is the establishment of corporate ethics policies and guidelines, requiring employee compliance, enough to ensure ethical behavior by employees?

PROBLEMS

Legal Forms of Business Organization

P1-1. Calculate the tax disadvantage to organizing a U.S. business today, after passage of the *Jobs and Growth Tax Relief Reconciliation Act of 2003,* as a corporation versus a partnership under the following conditions. Assume that all earnings will be paid out as cash dividends. Operating income (operating profit before taxes) will be $500,000 per year under either organizational form; the effective corporate profits tax rate is 35 percent ($T_c = 0.35$); the average personal tax rate for the partners of the business is also 35 percent ($T_p = 0.35$); and the capital gains tax rate on dividend income is 15 percent ($T_{cg} = 0.15$). Then, recalculate the tax disadvantage using the same income but with the maximum tax rates that existed before 2003. These rates were 35 percent ($T_c = 0.35$) on corporate profits and 38.6 percent ($T_p = 0.386$) on personal investment income.

P1-2. Calculate the tax disadvantage to organizing a U.S. business as a corporation versus a partnership under the following conditions. Assume that all earnings will be paid out as cash dividends. Operating income (operating profit before taxes) will be $3,000,000 per year under either organizational form; the effective corporate profits tax rate is 30 percent ($T_c = 0.30$); the average personal tax rate for the partners of the business is 35 percent ($T_p = 0.35$); and the capital gains tax rate on dividend income is 15 percent ($T_{cg} = 0.15$). Then, recalculate the tax disadvantage using the same income but with the maximum tax rates that existed before 2003. These rates were 35 percent ($T_c = 0.35$) on corporate profits and 38.6 percent ($T_p = 0.386$) on personal investment income.

The Corporate Financial Manager's Goals

P1-3. Consider the following simple corporate example with one stockholder and one manager. There are two mutually exclusive projects in which the manager may invest and two possible manager compensation contracts that the stockholder may choose to employ. The manager may be paid a flat \$300,000 or receive 10 percent of corporate profits. The stockholder receives all profits net of manager compensation. The probabilities and associated gross profits associated with each project are given below:

Project #1		Project #2	
Probability	Gross Profit	Probability	Gross Profit
33.33%	\$0	50.0%	\$600,000
33.33%	\$3,000,000	50.0%	\$900,000
33.33%	\$9,000,000		

a. Which project maximizes shareholder wealth? Which compensation contract does the manager prefer if this project is chosen?
b. Which project will the manager choose under a flat compensation arrangement?
c. Which compensation contract aligns the interests of the stockholder and the manager so that the manager will act in the best interest of the stockholder?
d. What does this tell you about the structure of management pay contracts?

THOMSON ONE Business School Edition

Access financial information from the Thomson ONE – Business School Edition Web site for the following problem(s). Go to http://tobsefin.swlearning.com/. If you have already registered your access serial number and have a username and password, click **Enter.** Otherwise, click **Register** and follow the instructions to create a username and password. Register your access serial number and then click **Enter** on the aforementioned Web site. When you click Enter, you will be prompted for your username and password (please remember that the password is case sensitive). Enter them in the respective boxes and then click **OK** (or hit **Enter**). From the ensuing page, click **Click Here to Access Thomson ONE – Business School Edition Now!** This opens up a new window that gives you access to the Thomson ONE – Business School Edition database. You can retrieve a company's financial information by entering its ticker symbol (provided for each company in the problem(s)) in the box below "Name/Symbol/Key." For further instructions on using the Thomson ONE – Business School Edition database, please refer to "A Guide for Using Thomson ONE – Business School Edition."

P1-4. What are the total assets and net income available to common shareholders for McDonald's Corp. (ticker: U:MCD) at the end of each of the last five fiscal years? Read this information from the annual financial statements for the same time period.

P1-5. How many shares outstanding does AT&T Corp. (ticker: U:T) have, and what is its current market capitalization? What are its closing, high, and low stock prices over each of the last three fiscal years? What are its earnings per share and dividends per share over the same time period?

Since these exercises depend upon real-time data, your answers will change continuously depending upon when you access the Internet to download your data.

MINICASE

The Scope of Corporate Finance

The potential career paths for someone with expertise in finance are varied and exciting. Career possibilities include the areas of corporate finance, commercial banking, investment banking, asset management, mutual funds and brokerage, insurance, real estate, and venture capital.

ASSIGNMENT

Find descriptions for these and other finance-related careers on the following Web site: http://www.wetfeet.com/asp/careerlist.asp

Think of the ways that our core financial decision can be applied to each of these careers. Remember, our core financial decision takes the approach that: **All financial decisions can be made by asking whether the marginal benefits (MBs) of taking a certain action are greater than or equal to the marginal costs (MCs) of this action.**

CHAPTER 2

Financial Statement and Cash Flow Analysis

OPENING FOCUS

How Do CFOs Feel About the Numbers?

It's been a few long years since the spectacular collapses of Enron, WorldCom, Adelphia, and many other "successful" firms, attributable to accounting fraud. Congress's passage of a big, expensive law, the Sarbanes-Oxley Act of 2002 (SOX), aims to keep it from happening again. Today, prospects are improving, corporate profits are increasing, and chief financial officers (CFOs) are more optimistic about the economy than they have been in years. Many of the perpetrators of the accounting scandals of 2000 have been prosecuted, convicted, and imprisoned.

Has life eased for beleaguered finance professionals? The short answer would be no, but there is cause for optimism, according to a survey of 179 finance executives that *CFO* magazine conducted in March 2004.

Consider the signs of trouble. First, it is alarmingly common for executives to lean on finance employees to "make the numbers work." Nearly half, or 47 percent, report they still feel pressure from their superiors to use aggressive accounting to make results look better. This helps explain how finance executives think about the scandals. Respondents identified personal greed, weak boards of directors, and overbearing CEOs as top causes. It is troubling that the pressure to make the numbers work hasn't lessened. Of those who have felt pressure in the past, only 38 percent think there is less pressure today than three years ago, and 20 percent say there is more.

A second, related concern is that few finance executives have much confidence in the numbers their colleagues are reporting. Only 27 percent say that if they were investing their own money, they would feel "very confident" about the quality and completeness of information available about public companies. (The rest were either "somewhat confident" or "not confident.") CFOs know better than anyone how companies assemble their numbers. Such a lukewarm endorsement should make investors uneasy.

Then, there is the toll exacted by the Sarbanes-Oxley Act of 2002, along with heightened regulatory scrutiny. Three quarters of the respondents report that the scandals have made their jobs harder. In response to a question asking what CFOs would like to say to some of the well-known perpetrators of accounting fraud, one wrote: "Your missteps have tarnished the image of all CFOs and have burdened corporations with unnecessary costs related to Sarbanes-Oxley."

But every cloud has a silver lining. The upheaval of the past few years may have created more work for the CFO, but it has also brought new prominence. Ninety-eight percent of respondents say the scandals have elevated the profile of corporate finance among CEOs and corporate boards, causing them to think about corporate finance more than before.

Most concede that, although costly, the much-loathed SOX is doing some good. Seventy-seven percent said the law makes it easier to resist pressure from a superior to misrepresent results. That is positive news. If it's true that the scandals originated with some overbearing CEOs, then it's up to ethical finance employees to challenge them. Greed will not go away, nor will scandals. But in the future, maybe fewer CFOs will feel the need to ask the question that many respondents did on this survey: "What were they thinking?"

Source: Don Durfee, "It's Better (and Worse) Than You Think," *CFO*, May 3, 2004, from CFO.com Web site: http://www.cfo.com/article/1,5309,13546||C|1,00.html. ■

LEARNING OBJECTIVES

After studying this chapter you should be able to:

- Understand the key financial statements that firms are required to provide to their shareholders;
- Evaluate the firm's cash flows using its financial statements, including the statement of cash flows;
- Calculate and interpret liquidity, activity, and debt ratios;
- Review the popular profitability ratios and the role of the DuPont system in analyzing the firm's returns;
- Compute and interpret the price/earnings and market/book ratios;
- Discuss the basics of corporate taxation of both ordinary income and capital gains.

A major challenge for the financial manager is *measuring* the relevant benefits and costs associated with both existing and proposed operations. The accounting profession provides a variety of "standardized" company data, particularly financial statements, that frequently serve as a starting point for measuring relevant benefits and costs.

SMART PRACTICES VIDEO

Jon Olson, Vice President of Finance, Intel Corp.

"At Intel, accounting is a fundamental requirement of a financial analyst."

See the entire interview at **SMARTFinance**

It is often said that accounting is the language of business. Corporate finance relies heavily on accounting concepts and language, but the primary focus of finance professionals and accountants differs significantly. Accountants apply *generally accepted accounting principles (GAAP)* to construct financial statements that attempt to portray fairly how a company has performed in the past. Accountants generally construct these statements using an **accrual-based approach**, which means that accountants record revenues at the point of sale and costs when they are incurred, not necessarily when a firm receives or pays out cash. These widely accepted accounting principles and practices allow corporate financial managers and others, barring fraud, to feel confident with the financial representation contained in audited financial statements.

accrual-based approach
Revenues are recorded at the point of sale and costs when they are incurred, not necessarily when a firm receives or pays out cash.

cash flow approach
Used by financial professionals to focus attention on current and prospective inflows and outflows of cash.

In contrast to accountants, financial professionals use a **cash flow approach** that focuses more attention on current and prospective inflows (benefits) and outflows (costs) of cash. The financial manager must convert relevant accounting and tax information into cash outflows and cash inflows, which after adjustment for timing differences and risk factors, represents the relevant marginal costs and marginal benefits needed for decision making.

This chapter describes how financial professionals use accounting information and terminology to analyze the firm's cash flows and financial performance. We begin with a brief review of the four major financial statements, then use them to demonstrate some of the key concepts involved in cash flow analysis. We give special emphasis to the firm's cash flows, free cash flows, the classification of inflows and outflows of cash, and the development and interpretation of statements of cash flows. Then, we discuss some popular financial ratios used to analyze the firm's financial performance. Finally, we review the basics of corporate taxation.

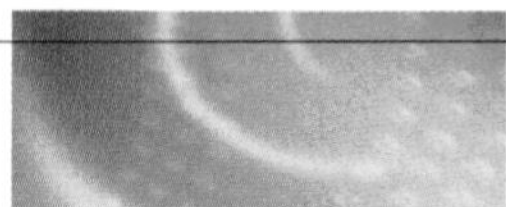

2.1 FINANCIAL STATEMENTS

As noted in Chapter 1, financial managers focus primarily on cash flows rather than on accrual-based accounting data. In spite of this focus, it is important for financial managers to understand financial statements, which serve as a window through which outsiders—investors, lenders, and others—view the firm's financial performance and position.

Although our discussion in this chapter is based on U.S. accounting, the principles covered are quite general. Many national governments require public companies to generate financial statements based on widely accepted accounting rules. In the United States, these generally accepted accounting principles were developed by the Financial Accounting Standards Board (FASB). The FASB is a nongovernmental, professional standards body that examines controversial accounting topics and then issues "rulings" that almost have the force of law, at least in terms of their effect on accounting practices.

The Securities and Exchange Commission (SEC) is responsible for regulating publicly traded U.S. companies, as well as the nation's stock and bond markets. Every other industrialized country has an agency similar to the SEC, and most developed countries mandate that companies generate financial statements that follow international accounting standards (IAS). These are broadly similar to GAAP, although GAAP rules place greater emphasis on public information disclosure than IAS rules do. The SEC adamantly insists that all non-U.S. companies report results based on GAAP to sell their securities directly to U.S. investors. However, the corporate accounting scandals of 2001 and 2002 tarnished the reputation of GAAP and enhanced that of IAS. In response to these scandals, the Sarbanes-Oxley Act of 2002 (SOX) established the Public Company Accounting Oversight Board (PCAOB), which effectively gives the SEC authority to oversee the accounting profession's activities.

The four key financial statements required by the SEC are (1) the balance sheet, (2) the income statement, (3) the statement of retained earnings, and (4) the statement of cash flows.[1] Our chief concern in this section is to review the information presented in these statements. Given the importance of cash flow in financial analysis, we provide in-depth coverage of the statement of cash flows in Section 2.2. Next, we present the financial statements from the 2006 stockholders' report of the Global Petroleum Corporation (GPC). Though fictional, the values constructed for GPC mirror those of a globally active oil company.

Balance Sheet

A firm's balance sheet presents a "snapshot" view of the company's financial position at a specific point in time. By definition, a firm's assets must equal the combined value of its liabilities and stockholders' equity. Phrased differently, either creditors (lenders) or equity investors (owners) finance all of a firm's assets. A balance sheet shows assets on the left-hand side and the claims of creditors and shareholders on the right-hand side. Both assets and liabilities appear in descending order of liquidity, or the length of time it takes for accounts to be converted into cash in the normal course of business. The most liquid asset, *cash*, appears first, and the least liquid, *fixed assets*, comes last. Similarly, *accounts payable* represents the obligations the firm must pay with cash within the next year, whereas the last entry on the right-hand side of the balance sheet, *stockholders' equity*, quite literally never matures.

Table 2.1 presents Global Petroleum Corporation's balance sheet as of December 31, 2006. As is standard practice in annual reports, the table also shows the previous year's (2005) accounts for comparison. *Cash and cash equivalents* are assets such as checking account balances at commercial banks that can be used directly as a means of payment. *Marketable securities* represent very liquid, short-term investments, which financial analysts view as a form of "near cash." *Accounts receivable* represent the amount customers owe the firm from sales made on credit. *Inventories* include raw materials, work in process (partially finished goods), and finished goods held by the firm. The entry for *gross property, plant, and equipment* is the original cost of all real property, structures, and long-lived equipment owned by the firm. *Net property, plant, and equipment* represents the difference between this original value and *accumulated depreciation*—the cumulative expense recorded for the depreciation of fixed assets since their purchase. Governments allow companies to depreciate, or charge against taxable earnings, a fraction of a fixed asset's cost each year to reflect a decline in the asset's economic value over time. The one fixed asset that is not depreciated is land, because it generally does not decline in value over time. Finally, *intangible assets* include valuable items such as patents, trademarks, copyrights, or—in the case of petroleum companies—mineral rights entitling the company to extract oil and gas on specific properties. Although intangible assets are usually nothing more than legal rights, they are often extremely valuable, as the discussion of the market value of global brands in this chapter's Comparative Corporate Finance insert on page 44 vividly demonstrates.

[1] The SEC requires *publicly held corporations*—those whose stock is traded on either an organized securities exchange or over-the-counter exchange and/or those with more than $5 million in assets and 500 or more stockholders—to provide their stockholders with an annual stockholders' report that includes these statements. Although these statement titles are consistently used throughout the text, it is important to recognize that in practice, companies frequently use different statement titles.

Table 2.1
Balance Sheet for Global Petroleum Corporation

Global Petroleum Corporation Balance Sheets at December 31, 2005 and 2006 ($ in millions)

Assets	2006	2005
Current assets		
Cash and cash equivalents	$ 440	$ 213
Marketable securities	35	28
Accounts receivable	1,619	1,203
Inventories	615	530
Other (mostly prepaid expenses)	170	176
Total current assets	$2,879	$2,150
Fixed assets		
Gross property, plant, and equipment	$9,920	$9,024
Less: Accumulated depreciation	3,968	3,335
Net property, plant, and equipment	$5,952	$5,689
Intangible assets and others	758	471
Net fixed assets	$6,710	$6,160
Total assets	**$9,589**	**$8,310**

Liabilities and Stockholders' Equity	2006	2005
Current liabilities		
Accounts payable	$1,697	$1,304
Notes payable	477	587
Accrued expenses	440	379
Total current liabilities	$2,614	$2,270
Long-term liabilities		
Deferred taxes	$ 907	$ 793
Long-term debt	1,760	1,474
Total long-term liabilities	$ 2,667	$2,267
Total liabilities	$ 5,281	$4,537
Stockholders' equity		
Preferred stock	$ 30	$ 30
Common stock ($1 par value)	373	342
Paid-in capital in excess of par	248	229
Retained earnings	4,271	3,670
Less: Treasury stock	614	498
Total stockholders' equity	$ 4,308	$3,773
Total liabilities and stockholders' equity	**$ 9,589**	**$8,310**

Now turn your attention to the right-hand side of the balance sheet. Current liabilities include *accounts payable,* amounts owed for credit purchases by the firm; *notes payable,* outstanding short-term loans, typically from commercial banks; and *accrued expenses,* costs incurred by the firm that have not yet been paid. Examples of accruals include taxes owed to the government and wages due employees. Accounts payable and accruals are often called "spontaneous liabilities" because they tend to change directly with changes in sales.

In the United States and many other countries, laws permit firms to construct two sets of financial statements, one for tax purposes and one for reporting to the public. For example, when a firm purchases a long-lived asset, it can choose to depreciate this asset rapidly for tax purposes, resulting in large, immediate tax write-offs and smaller tax deductions later. When the firm constructs financial statements for release to the public, however, it may choose a different depreciation method, perhaps one that results in higher reported earnings in the early years of the asset's life and lower earnings later. The **deferred taxes** entry on the balance sheet is a long-term liability that reflects the discrepancy between the taxes that firms actually pay and the tax liabilities they report on their public financial statements. **Long-term debt** represents debt that matures more than one year in the future.

The stockholders' equity section provides information about the claims of investors who own preferred and common shares. The **preferred stock** entry shows the historic proceeds from the sale of preferred stock ($30 million for GPC), which is a form of ownership that has preference over common stock with regard to the distribution of income and assets. Next, the amount paid in by the original purchasers of **common stock**, the most basic form of corporate ownership, is shown by two entries—common stock and paid-in capital in excess of par. The common stock entry equals the number of outstanding common shares multiplied by the **par value** per share. The par value of a share of stock is an arbitrary value with little or no economic significance. The entry, **paid-in capital** in excess of par, equals the number of shares outstanding multiplied by the original selling price of the shares, net of the par value. Therefore, the combined value of common stock and paid-in capital equals the proceeds the firm received when it originally sold shares to investors. **Retained earnings** are the cumulative total of the earnings that the firm has reinvested since its inception. It is important to recognize that retained earnings do not represent a reservoir of unspent cash. The retained earnings "vault" is empty because the firm has already reinvested the earnings in new assets.

Finally, the **treasury stock** entry records the value of common shares that the firm currently holds in reserve. Usually, treasury stock appears on the balance sheet because the firm has reacquired previously issued stock through a share repurchase program.

GPC's balance sheet in Table 2.1 shows that the firm's total assets increased by $1,279 million, from $8,310 million in 2005 to $9,589 million in 2006. As expected, the total liabilities and shareholders' equity exactly match these totals in 2005 and 2006.

Income Statement

Table 2.2 on page 46 presents Global Petroleum Corporation's income statement for the year ended December 31, 2006. As with the balance sheet, GPC's income statement also includes data from 2005 for comparison.[2] In the vocabulary of accounting, income (also called *profit, earnings,* or *margin*) equals revenue minus expenses. GPC's income statement, however, has several measures of "income" appearing at different points. The first income measure is *gross profit,* the amount by which *sales revenue* exceeds the *cost of goods sold* (the direct cost of producing or purchasing the goods sold). Next, various operating expenses, including selling expense, general and administrative expense, and depreciation expense, are deducted from gross profits.[3] The resulting *operating profit* of $1,531 million represents the profits earned from the sale of products, although this amount does not include financial and tax costs. *Other income,* earned on

[2] When reporting to shareholders, firms typically also include a **common-size income statement** that expresses all income-statement entries as a percentage of sales.

[3] Depreciation expense can be, and frequently is, included in manufacturing costs—cost of goods sold—to calculate gross profits. Depreciation is shown as an expense in this text to isolate its effect on cash flows.

deferred taxes
Reflect the discrepancy between the taxes that firms actually pay and the tax liabilities they report on their public financial statements.

long-term debt
Debt that matures more than one year in the future.

preferred stock
A form of ownership that has preference over common stock with regard to income and assets.

common stock
The most basic form of corporate ownership.

par value (common stock)
An arbitrary value assigned to common stock on a firm's balance sheet.

paid-in capital
The number of shares of common stock outstanding times the original selling price of the shares, net of the par value.

retained earnings
The cumulative total of the earnings that a firm has reinvested since its inception.

treasury stock
Common shares that were issued and later reacquired by the firm through share repurchase programs and are therefore being held in reserve by the firm.

common-size income statement
An income statement in which all entries are expressed as a percentage of sales.

COMPARATIVE CORPORATE FINANCE

Assessing the Market Values of Global Brands

How much is a global brand name worth? Interbrand Corporation, a New York-based consulting firm, has been trying to answer this question for several years, and *Business Week* has been publishing the rankings annually since 2001. The table details what this firm considers the 25 most valuable brands of 2004. The table also lists the value of these brands in 2003. The total brand values are large and are dominated by brands of U.S.-based companies. Additionally, the rankings are remarkably stable from year to year; the 2003 rankings listed the same top 5, in order, and only one new brand entered the top 25 during 2004. In fact, 23 of the companies in the table below were also among the 25 most valuable brands of 2000, presented in the original *Business Week* ranking.

Although American companies are not required to disclose estimated brand values in their financial statements, large publicly traded British and Australian firms must do so. Brand values do, however, have a significant effect on U.S. accounting rules in one important area—accounting for the "goodwill" created when a firm is acquired by another company for more than the acquired firm's book value. This premium over book value represents the higher market (versus book) value of intangible assets such as patents, copyrights, and trademarks, as well as brand names and business relationships that are not accounted for at all. Until 2001, goodwill was treated as an expense to be charged against the acquiring firms' earnings over a period of years. Now, however, the Financial Accounting Standards Board requires acquirers to periodically assess the fair value of assets that they purchase through acquisitions. If the fair value of those assets declines significantly over time, firms must recognize "goodwill impairment," meaning that some of the value of their intangible assets has vanished. Charges arising from goodwill impairment can have a dramatic effect on reported earnings.

Source: Interbrand Corporation, as reported in Diane Brady, Robert D. Hof, Andy Reinhardt, Moon Ihlwan, Stanley Holmes, and Kerry Capell; "Cult Brands," *Business Week* (August 2, 2004), pp 64–71.

Rank 2004	Rank 2003	Brand	2004 Brand Value ($ in Billions)	2003 Brand Value ($ in Billions)	Percent Change	Country of Ownership
1	1	COCA-COLA	67.39	70.45	–4%	U.S.
2	2	MICROSOFT	61.37	65.17	–6	U.S.
3	3	IBM	53.79	51.77	+4	U.S.
4	4	GE	44.11	42.34	+4	U.S.
5	5	INTEL	33.50	31.11	+8	U.S.
6	7	DISNEY	27.11	28.04	–3	U.S.
7	8	McDONALD'S	25.00	24.70	+1	U.S.
8	6	NOKIA	24.04	27.44	–18	Finland
9	11	TOYOTA	22.67	20.78	+9	Japan
10	9	MARLBORO	22.12	22.18	0	U.S.
11	10	MERCEDES	21.33	21.37	0	Germany
12	12	HEWLETT-PACKARD	20.98	19.86	+6	U.S.
13	13	CITIBANK	19.97	18.57	+8	U.S.
14	15	AMERICAN EXPRESS	17.68	16.83	+5	U.S.
15	16	GILLETTE	16.72	15.98	+5	U.S.

Rank 2004	Rank 2003	Brand	2004 Brand Value ($ in Billions)	2003 Brand Value ($ in Billions)	Percent Change	Country of Ownership
16	17	CISCO SYSTEMS	15.95	15.79	+1	U.S.
17	19	BMW	15.89	15.11	+5	Germany
18	18	HONDA	14.87	15.63	–5	Japan
19	14	FORD	14.46	17.07	–15	U.S.
20	20	SONY	12.76	13.15	-3	Japan
21	25	SAMSUNG	12.56	10.85	+16	South Korea
22	23	PEPSI	12.07	11.78	+2	U.S.
23	21	NESCAFE	11.89	12.34	–4	Switzerland
24	22	BUDWEISER	11.85	11.89	0	U.S.
25	29	DELL	11.50	10.37	+11	U.S.

transactions not directly related to producing and/or selling the firm's products, is added to operating income to yield *earnings before interest and taxes* (*EBIT*) of $1,671 million. When a firm has no "other income," its operating profit and *EBIT* are equal. Next, $123 million of *interest expense*—representing the cost of debt financing—is subtracted from *EBIT* to find *pretax income* of $1,548 million.

The final step is to subtract taxes from pretax income to arrive at *net income,* or *net profit after taxes,* of $949 million. Note that GPC incurred a total tax liability of $599 million during 2006, but only the $367 million *current* portion must be paid immediately. Although the remaining $232 million in deferred taxes must be paid eventually, these are noncash expenses for year 2006. Net income is the proverbial "bottom line" and the single most important accounting number for both corporate managers and external financial analysts. From its net income, the firm paid $3 million in dividends on its $30 million of preferred stock outstanding during both 2005 and 2006. Dividing **earnings available for common stockholders** (net income net of preferred stock dividends) by the number of shares of common stock outstanding results in **earnings per share (*EPS*)**. *EPS* represents the amount earned during the period on each outstanding share of common stock. Because there are 178,719,400 shares of GPC stock outstanding on December 31, 2006, its *EPS* for 2006 is $5.29, which represents a significant increase from the *EPS* of $2.52 GPC managed during 2005. The cash **dividend per share (*DPS*)** paid to GPC's common stockholders during 2006 is $1.93, up slightly from the dividend of $1.76 per share paid in 2005.

earnings available for common stockholders
Net income net of preferred stock dividends.

earnings per share (*EPS*)
Earnings available for common stockholders divided by the number of shares of common stock outstanding.

dividend per share (*DPS*)
The portion of the earnings per share paid to stockholders.

Statement of Retained Earnings

The statement of retained earnings reconciles the net income earned during a given year, and any cash dividends paid, with the change in retained earnings between the start and end of that year. Table 2.3 on page 47 presents this statement for Global Petroleum Corporation for the year ended December 31, 2006. A review of the

Table 2.2
Income Statement for Global Petroleum Corporation

Global Petroleum Corporation Income Statements for the Years Ended December 31, 2005 and 2006 ($ in millions)

	2006	2005
Sales revenue	$ 12,843	$ 9,110
Less: Cost of goods sold[a]	8,519	5,633
Gross profit	$ 4,324	$ 3,477
Less: Operating and other expenses	1,544	1,521
Less: Selling, general and administrative expenses	616	584
Less: Depreciation expense	633	608
Operating profit	$ 1,531	$ 764
Plus: Other income	140	82
Earnings before interest and taxes (*EBIT*)	$ 1,671	$ 846
Less: Interest expense	123	112
Pretax income	$ 1,548	$ 734
Less: Taxes		
Current	367	158
Deferred	232	105
Total taxes	599	263
Net income (net profits after taxes)	$ 949	$ 471
Less: Preferred stock dividends	3	3
Earnings available for common stockholders	$ 946	$ 468
Less: Dividends	345	326
To retained earnings	$ 601	$ 142
Per share data[b]		
Earnings per share (*EPS*)	$ 5.29	$ 2.52
Dividends per share (*DPS*)	$ 1.93	$ 1.76
Price per share	$ 76.25	$71.50

[a] Annual purchases have historically represented about 80 percent of cost of goods sold. Using this relationship, its credit purchases in 2006 were $6,815 and in 2005, they were $4,506.
[b] Based on 178,719,400 and 185,433,100 shares outstanding as of December 31, 2006 and 2005, respectively.

statement shows that the company began the year with $3,670 million in retained earnings and during the year generated net profits after taxes of $949 million. From these profits, it paid a total of $348 million in preferred and common stock dividends, resulting in year-end retained earnings of $4,271 million. Thus, the net increase for GPC is $601 million ($949 million net income minus $348 million in dividends) during 2006.

Statement of Cash Flows

The statement of cash flows provides a summary of a firm's cash flows over the year. This is accomplished by isolating the firm's operating, investment, and financing cash flows and reconciling them with changes in its cash and marketable securities during the year. GPC's statement of cash flows for the year ended December 31, 2006, is presented in Table 2.5 on page 53. (This statement is discussed in greater depth in

Table 2.3
Statement of Retained Earnings for Global Petroleum Corporation

Global Petroleum Corporation Statement of Retained Earnings for the Year Ended December 31, 2006 ($ in millions)		
Retained earnings balance (January 1, 2006)		$3,670
Plus: Net income (for 2006)		949
Less: Cash dividends (paid during 2006)		
Preferred stock	$ 3	
Common stock	345	
Total dividends paid		348
Retained earnings balance (December 31, 2006)		**$4,271**

Section 2.2 on cash flow analysis.) We should also stress that other information presented in financial statements can be very useful to financial managers and analysts. This is especially true about the "notes" to financial statements.

Notes to Financial Statements

A public company's financial statements include detailed explanatory notes keyed to the relevant accounts in the statements. These notes provide detailed information on the accounting policies, calculations, and transactions underlying entries in the financial statements. For example, the notes to General Motors' 2003 financial statements cover 28 of the 95 pages in its annual report. Notes typically provide additional information about a firm's revenue recognition practices, income taxes, fixed assets, leases, and employee compensation plans. This information is particularly useful to professional security analysts who look for clues that shed more light on the firm's past and future performance.

CONCEPT REVIEW QUESTIONS

1. What role do the FASB and SEC play with regard to GAAP?

2. Are balance sheets and income statements prepared with the same purpose in mind? How are these two statements different, and how are they related?

3. Which statements are of greatest interest to creditors, and which would be of greatest interest to stockholders?

2.2 CASH FLOW ANALYSIS

Although financial managers are interested in the information contained in the firm's accrual-based financial statements, their primary focus is on cash flows. Without adequate cash to pay obligations on time, to fund operations and growth, and to compensate owners, the firm will fail. The financial manager and other interested parties can gain insight into the firm's cash flows over a given period of time by both using some popular measures of cash flow and analyzing the firm's statement of cash flows.

The Firm's Cash Flows

Figure 2.1 illustrates the firm's cash flows. Note that the figure treats cash and marketable securities as perfect substitutes. Both cash and marketable securities represent a reservoir of liquidity that increases with *cash inflows* and decreases with *cash outflows*. Also note that the figure divides the firm's cash flows into (1) operating flows, (2) investment flows, and (3) financing flows. The **operating flows** are cash inflows and outflows directly related to the production and sale of the firm's products or services. **Investment flows** are cash flows associated with the purchase or sale of both fixed assets and business equity. Clearly, purchases result in cash outflows, whereas sales generate cash inflows. The **financing flows** result from debt and equity financing transactions. Taking on new debt (short term or long term) results in a cash inflow, whereas repaying existing debt represents a cash outflow. Similarly, the sale of stock results in a cash inflow, whereas the repurchase of stock or payment of cash dividends generates a cash outflow. In combination, the firm's operating, investment, and financing cash flows during a given period will affect the firm's cash and marketable securities balances.

operating flows
Cash inflows and outflows directly related to the production and sale of a firm's products or services.

investment flows
Cash flows associated with the purchase or sale of both fixed assets and business equity.

financing flows
Result from debt and equity financing transactions.

Monitoring cash flow is important for financial managers employed by the firm and for outside analysts trying to estimate how much the firm is worth. There are a variety of cash flow measures that managers and analysts track, but one of the most important is *free cash flow*.

free cash flow (*FCF*)
The net amount of cash flow remaining after the firm has met all operating needs and paid for investments, both long-term (fixed) and short-term (current). Represents the cash amount that a firm could distribute to investors after meeting all its other obligations.

Free Cash Flow.

Free cash flow (*FCF*) is the amount of cash flow available to investors—the providers of debt and equity capital. It represents the net amount of cash flow remaining after the firm has met all operating needs and paid for investments—both long term (fixed) and short term (current). Free cash flow for a given period can be calculated in two steps.

First, we find the firm's **operating cash flow (*OCF*)**, which is the amount of cash flow generated by the firm from its operations. It can be calculated using the following equation:

operating cash flow (*OCF*)
The amount of cash flow generated by a firm from its operations. Mathematically, earnings before interest and taxes (*EBIT*) minus taxes plus depreciation.

$$OCF = EBIT - taxes + depreciation \qquad \text{(Eq. 2.1)}$$

Note that because depreciation is a noncash charge, it is *added back* to determine *OCF*. **Noncash charges**, such as depreciation, amortization, and depletion allowances, are expenses that appear on the income statement but do not involve an actual outlay of cash. Almost all firms list depreciation expense on their income statements, so we focus on depreciation rather than amortization or depletion allowances, but they are treated in a similar fashion. Substituting the values from GPC's 2006 income statement (from Table 2.2) into Equation 2.1, we get GPC's operating cash flow:

noncash charges
Expenses, such as depreciation, amortization, and depletion allowances, that appear on the income statement but do not involve an actual outlay of cash.

$$OCF = \$1{,}671 - \$599 + \$633 = \$1{,}705$$

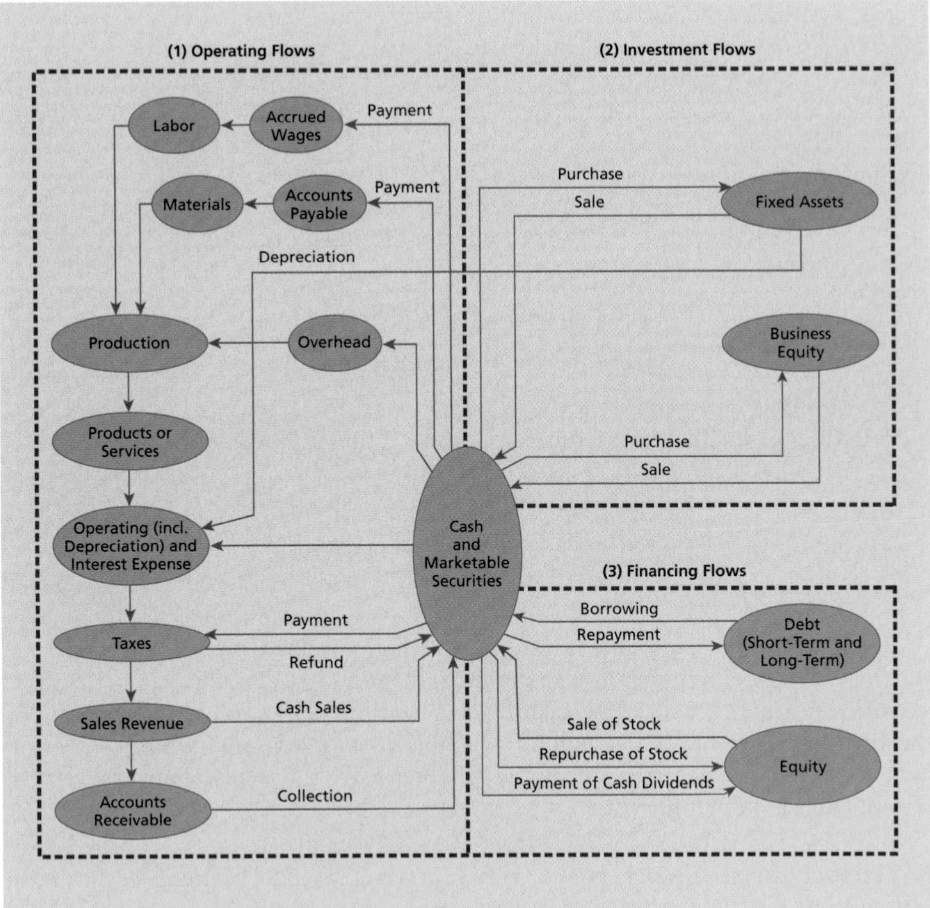

Figure 2.1
The Pattern of Cash Flows Through a Firm

The firm's reservoir of liquidity, containing both cash and marketable securities, is impacted by changes in (1) operating flows, (2) investment flows, and (3) financing flows.

GPC's *OCF* is $1,705 million. Next, we convert this operating cash flow to free cash flow (*FCF*) by deducting the firm's net investments (denoted by the "change" symbol Δ) in fixed and current assets from operating cash flow, as shown in the following equation:

$$FCF = OCF - \Delta FA - (\Delta CA - \Delta A/P - \Delta accruals) \quad \text{(Eq. 2.2)}$$

where

$$\begin{aligned} \Delta FA &= \text{change in gross fixed assets,} \\ \Delta CA &= \text{change in current assets,} \\ \Delta A/P &= \text{change in accounts payable, and} \\ \Delta\text{accruals} &= \text{change in accrued liabilities.} \end{aligned}$$

Note that because they occur automatically with changes in sales, only *spontaneous current liability changes* are deducted from current assets to find the net change in short-term investment. From the preceding calculation, we know that GPC's *OCF* in 2006 was \$1,705 million. Using GPC's 2005 and 2006 balance sheets (Table 2.1), we can calculate the changes in gross fixed assets, current assets, accounts payable, and accruals between 2005 and 2006:

$$\begin{aligned} \Delta FA &= \$9{,}920 - \$9{,}024 = \$896 \\ \Delta CA &= \$2{,}879 - \$2{,}150 = \$729 \\ \Delta A/P &= \$1{,}697 - \$1{,}304 = \$393 \\ \Delta \text{accruals} &= \$440 - \$379 = \$61 \end{aligned}$$

Substituting these values into Equation 2.2, we get the following:

$$\begin{aligned} FCF &= \$1{,}705 - \$896 - (\$729 - \$393 - \$61) \\ &= \$1{,}705 - \$896 - \$275 \\ &= \$534 \end{aligned}$$

Reviewing the second line of the *FCF* calculation above, we see that after subtracting \$896 million in net fixed asset investment and \$275 million in net current asset investment, GPC has free cash flow in 2006 of \$534 million. During 2006, the firm therefore had \$534 million available to pay investors who provide the firm with debt and equity financing. In Chapter 5 we show how analysts use *FCF* to estimate the value of a firm.

Inflows and Outflows of Cash. Table 2.4 classifies the basic inflows and outflows of cash for corporations (assuming other things are held constant). For example, if a firm's accounts payable increases by \$1,000 during the year, this change would be an *inflow of cash*. If the firm's inventory increases by \$2,500, the change would be an *outflow of cash*.

A few additional points can be made about the classification scheme in Table 2.4.

Table 2.4
The Inflows and Outflows of Corporate Cash

Inflows	Outflows
Decrease in any asset	Increase in any asset
Increase in any liability	Decrease in any liability
Net income (profit after tax)	Net loss
Depreciation and other noncash charges	Dividends paid
Sale of common or preferred stock	Repurchase or retirement of stock

1. A *decrease* in an asset, such as the firm's inventory balance, is an *inflow of cash* because cash that has been tied up in the asset is released. Managers can use it for some other purpose, such as repaying a loan. In contrast, an *increase* in the firm's inventory balance (or any other asset) is an *outflow of cash* because additional inventory ties up more of the firm's cash. Similar logic explains why an increase in any liability is an inflow of cash, and a decrease in any liability is an outflow of cash.
2. Our earlier discussion noted why depreciation and other noncash charges are considered cash inflows. Logic suggests that if net income is a cash inflow, then a *net loss* (negative net profits after taxes) is an outflow of cash. The firm must balance its losses with an inflow of cash, such as selling off some of its fixed assets (reducing an asset) or increasing external borrowing (increasing a liability). Note (from Equation 2.1) that a firm can have a *net loss* (*EBIT - taxes*) and still have positive cash flow when depreciation and other noncash charges during the period are greater than the net loss. Therefore, the statement of cash flows treats net income (or net losses) and noncash charges as separate entries.

APPLYING THE MODEL

On March 31, 2004, and on December 31, 2003, Procter & Gamble Co. (P&G) (ticker symbol, PG) reported the following balances in certain current asset and current liability accounts ($ in millions).

Account	March 31, 2004	December 31, 2003
Cash	$5,365	$4,943
Marketable securities	385	351
Accounts receivable	4,093	4,447
Inventory	4,621	4,621
Accounts payable	3,048	2,822
Short-term debt	5,065	5,885

In terms of current assets, accounts receivable declined during the first quarter of 2004, providing an inflow of cash for P&G. Cash increased during the quarter, representing a cash outflow. It may seem strange to think of an increase in cash balances as a use of cash, but that simply means that P&G used some of its cash flow to "invest in liquidity" rather than use the cash for another purpose. Similarly, marketable securities increased during the quarter and represented a cash outflow, whereas inventory remained unchanged and therefore had no effect on cash flow. On the liabilities side, accounts payable increased, representing a cash inflow for P&G, while short-term debt declined, representing an outflow of cash for P&G.

Developing and Interpreting the Statement of Cash Flows

The statement of cash flows summarizes the inflows and outflows of cash during a given period. Accountants construct the statement of cash flows by using the income statement for the year, along with the beginning- and end-of-year balance sheets. The procedure involves classifying balance sheet changes as inflows or outflows of cash; obtaining income statement data; classifying the relevant values into operating, investment, and financing cash flows; and presenting them in the proper format.[4] The statement of cash flows for Global Petroleum Corporation for the year ended December 31, 2006, appears in Table 2.5. Note that the statement assigns positive values to all cash inflows and negative values to all cash outflows. Notice under the investment activities section that the statement records the increase in *gross* fixed assets, rather than *net* fixed assets, as a cash outflow. Depreciation accounts for the difference between changes in gross and net fixed assets, but depreciation expense appears in the operating activities section of the statement. Thus, the focus on changes in gross fixed assets avoids double-counting depreciation in the statement. For a similar reason, the statement does not show a specific entry for the change in retained earnings as an inflow (or outflow) of cash. Instead, the factors that determine the change in retained earnings—profits or losses and dividends—appear as separate individual entries in the statement.

By adding up the items in each category—operating, investment, and financing activities—we obtain the net increase (decrease) in cash and marketable securities for the year. As a check, this value should reconcile with the actual yearly change in cash and marketable securities, obtained from the beginning- and end-of-year balance sheets.

By applying this procedure to GPC's 2006 income statement, and 2005 and 2006 balance sheets, we obtain the firm's 2006 statement of cash flows (see Table 2.5). This statement shows that GPC experienced a $234 million increase in cash and marketable securities during 2006. Looking at GPC's 2005 and 2006 balance sheets in Table 2.1, we see that the firm's cash increased by $227 million, and its marketable securities increased by $7 million between December 31, 2005, and December 31, 2006. The $234 million net increase in cash and marketable securities from the statement of cash flows reconciles with the total change of $234 million in these accounts during 2006. GPC's statement of cash flows therefore reconciles with the balance sheet changes.

The statement of cash flows allows the financial manager and other interested parties to analyze the firm's cash flow over a period of time. Unusual changes in either the major categories of cash flow or in specific items offer clues to problems that a firm may be experiencing. For example, an unusually large increase in accounts receivable or inventories resulting in major cash outflows may signal credit or inventory problems, respectively. Financial managers and analysts can also prepare a statement of cash flows developed from projected, or pro forma, financial statements. They use this approach to determine whether the firm will require additional external financing or will generate excess cash that can be reinvested or distributed to shareholders. After you learn the concepts, principles, and practices of corporate finance presented in the text, you will be able to glean a good amount of useful information from the statement of cash flows.

---

4. For a description and demonstration of the detailed procedures for developing the statement of cash flows, see any recently published financial accounting text, such as Chapter 14 of *Corporate Financial Accounting, 8th ed.*, by Warren, Reeve, and Fess (2005), South-Western Publishing, Mason: Ohio.

Table 2.5
Statement of Cash Flows for Global Petroleum Corporation

This statement is constructed using the firm's income statements and two most recent balance sheets. It groups cash flow into (1) cash flow from operations, (2) cash flow from investments, and (3) cash flow from financing. The net change at the bottom of the statement should match the net change in the cash and marketable securities balance shown between the firm's most recent two balance sheets.

Global Petroleum Corporation Statement of Cash Flows for Year Ended December 31, 2006 ($ in millions)		
Cash flow from operating activities		
Net income (net profit after tax)	$ 949	
Depreciation	633	
Increase in accounts receivable	(416)	
Increase in inventories	(85)	
Decrease in other assets	6	
Increase in accounts payable	393	
Increase in accrued expenses	61	
Cash provided by operating activities		$1,541
Cash flow from investment activities		
Increase in gross fixed assets	($896)	
Increase in intangible and other assets	(287)	
Cash provided (consumed) by investment activities		($1,183)
Cash flow from financing activities		
Decrease in notes payable	($110)	
Increase in deferred taxes	114	
Increase in long-term debt	286	
Changes in stockholders' equity	(66)	
Dividends paid	(348)	
Cash provided (consumed) by financing activities		($ 124)
Net increase in cash and marketable securities		$ 234

CONCEPT REVIEW QUESTIONS

4. How do depreciation and other noncash charges act as sources of cash inflow to the firm? Why does a depreciation allowance exist in the tax laws? For a profitable firm, is it better to depreciate an asset quickly or slowly for tax purposes? Explain.

5. What is *operating cash flow (OCF)?* What is *free cash flow (FCF),* and how is it related to OCF?

6. Why is the financial manager likely to have great interest in the firm's *statement of cash flows*? What type of information can be obtained from this statement?

2.3 ANALYZING FINANCIAL PERFORMANCE USING RATIO ANALYSIS

Analysis of a firm's financial statements is of interest to shareholders, creditors, and the firm's own management. In many cases, the constituents of a firm want to compare its financial condition to that of similar firms, but doing so can be very tricky. For example, suppose you are introduced to a new acquaintance named Bill who tells you that he runs a company that earned a profit of $10 million last year. Would you be impressed? What if you knew that Bill's last name was Gates? Most people would agree that a profit of $10 million would be a great disappointment for Microsoft, the firm run by Bill Gates.

The point here is that the sales, profits, and other items that appear on a firm's financial statements are difficult to interpret unless we have some way to put the numbers in perspective. To analyze financial statements, we need relative measures that normalize size differences. Effective analysis of financial statements is thus based on the knowledge and use of *ratios* or *relative values*. **Ratio analysis** involves calculating and interpreting financial ratios to assess the firm's performance and status.

ratio analysis
Calculating and interpreting financial ratios to assess a firm's performance and status.

Using Financial Ratios

Different constituents will focus on different types of financial ratios. The firm's creditors are primarily interested in ratios that measure the short-term liquidity of the company and its ability to make interest and principal payments. A secondary concern of creditors is the firm's profitability; they want assurance that the business is healthy and will continue to be successful. Both current and prospective shareholders are interested in ratios that measure the firm's current and future levels of risk and return, because these two dimensions directly affect the firm's share price. The firm's managers must be concerned with all aspects of the firm's financial situation, so they use ratios to generate an overall picture of the company's financial health and to monitor the firm's performance from period to period. The managers carefully examine unexpected changes to isolate developing problems.

An additional complication of ratio analysis is that for any given ratio, what is normal in one industry may be highly unusual in another. For example, by dividing a firm's earnings available for common stockholders, by its sales, we obtain the net profit margin ratio. Net profit margins vary dramatically across industries. An outstanding net profit margin in the retail grocery industry could look paltry in the software business. Therefore, when making subjective judgments about the health of a given company, analysts usually compare the firm's ratios to two benchmarks. First, analysts compare the financial ratios in the current year with previous years' ratios. Analysts hope to identify trends that help them evaluate the firm's prospects. Second, analysts compare the ratios of one company with those of other "benchmark" firms in the same industry (or to an industry average obtained from a trade association or third-party provider).

We will use the 2006 and 2005 balance sheets and income statements for Global Petroleum Corporation, presented earlier in Tables 2.1 and 2.2, to demonstrate ratio calculations. We will delete the *millions* after GPC's values. Note that the ratios presented in the remainder of this chapter can be applied to nearly any company. Of course, many companies in different industries use ratios that focus on aspects peculiar to their industry.[5] We will cover the most common financial ratios and group them into five categories: *liquidity, activity, debt, profitability,* and *market* ratios.

liquidity ratios
Measure a firm's ability to satisfy its short-term obligations *as they come due.*

Liquidity Ratios

Liquidity ratios measure a firm's ability to satisfy its short-term obligations *as they come due.* Because a common precursor to financial distress and bankruptcy is low or declining liquidity, liquidity ratios are good leading indicators of cash flow

[5] For example, airlines pay close attention to the ratio of revenues to passenger miles flown. Retailers diligently track the growth in same-store sales from one year to the next.

problems. The two basic measures of liquidity are the *current ratio* and the *quick (acid-test) ratio*.

The **current ratio**, one of the most commonly cited financial ratios, measures the firm's ability to meet its short-term obligations. It is defined as current assets *divided* by current liabilities, and thus presents in ratio form what **net working capital** measures by *subtracting* current liabilities from current assets. The current ratio for GPC on December 31, 2006, is computed as follows:

current ratio
A measure of a firm's ability to meet its short-term obligations, defined as current assets *divided* by current liabilities.

net working capital
A measure of a firm's liquidity calculated by *subtracting* current liabilities from current assets.

$$\text{Current ratio} = \frac{\text{current assets}}{\text{current liabilities}} = \frac{\$2{,}879}{\$2{,}614} = 1.10$$

How high should the current ratio be? The answer depends on the type of business under consideration and on the costs and benefits of having too much versus too little liquidity. For example, a current ratio of 1.0 is considered acceptable for a utility but may be unacceptable for a manufacturing firm. The more predictable a firm's cash flows, the lower the acceptable current ratio. Because GPC is in a business (oil exploration and development) with notoriously unpredictable annual cash flows, its current ratio of 1.10 indicates that GPC takes a fairly aggressive approach to managing its liquidity.

The **quick (acid-test) ratio** is similar to the current ratio except that it excludes inventory, which is usually the least-liquid current asset. The generally low liquidity of inventory results from two factors: (1) many types of inventory cannot be easily sold because they are partially completed items, special-purpose items, and the like; and (2) inventory is typically sold on credit, which means that it becomes an account receivable before being converted into cash. The quick ratio is calculated as follows:

quick (acid-test) ratio
A measure of a firm's liquidity that is similar to the current ratio except that it excludes inventory, which is usually the least-liquid current asset.

$$\text{Quick ratio} = \frac{\text{current assets} - \text{inventory}}{\text{current liabilities}} = \frac{\$2{,}879 - \$615}{\$2{,}614} = 0.866$$

The quick ratio for GPC in 2006 is 0.866. The quick ratio provides a better measure of overall liquidity only when a firm's inventory cannot be easily converted into cash. If inventory is liquid, the current ratio is a preferred measure of overall liquidity. Because GPC's inventory is mostly petroleum and refined products that can be readily converted into cash, the firm's managers probably focus on the current ratio rather than the quick ratio.

Activity Ratios

Activity ratios measure the speed with which the firm converts various accounts into sales or cash. Managers and outsiders use activity ratios as guides to assess how efficiently the firm manages assets such as inventory, receivables, and fixed assets, as well as the current liability, accounts payable.

activity ratios
A measure of the speed with which a firm converts various accounts into sales or cash.

Inventory turnover provides a measure of how quickly a firm sells its goods. GPC's 2006 inventory turnover ratio appears below:

inventory turnover
A measure of how quickly a firm sells its goods.

$$\text{Inventory turnover} = \frac{\text{cost of goods sold}}{\text{inventory}} = \frac{\$8{,}519}{\$615} = 13.85$$

Notice that we used cost of goods sold rather than sales in the numerator because inventory is valued at its cost on the firm's balance sheet. Also note that in the denominator, we use the ending inventory balance of $615 to calculate this ratio. If inventories grow over time or exhibit seasonal patterns, analysts sometimes use the average level of inventory throughout the year rather than the ending balance to calculate this ratio. The resulting turnover of 13.85 indicates that the firm basically sells outs its inventory 13.85 times each year, or slightly more often than once per month. This value is most meaningful when it is compared with that of other firms in the same industry or with the firm's past inventory turnover. An inventory turnover of 20.0 is not unusual for a grocery store, whereas a common inventory turnover for an aircraft manufacturer is 4.0. The value for GPC is in line with that for other oil and gas companies and slightly above the firm's own historic norms.

average age of inventory A measure of inventory turnover, calculated by dividing the turnover figure into 365, the number of days in a year.

Inventory turnover is easily converted into an **average age of inventory** by dividing the turnover figure into 365—the number of days in a year. For GPC, the average age of inventory would be 26.4 days (365 ÷ 13.85). This result means that GPC's inventory balance turns over about every 26 days.

APPLYING THE MODEL

Inventory ratios, like most other financial ratios, vary a great deal from one industry to another. For example, for the four quarters ending March 30, 2004, Intel Corp. reported inventory of $2.80 billion and cost of goods sold for the four quarters ended March 30, 2004, of $13.03 billion. This implies an inventory turnover ratio for Intel of about 4.65, or an average age of inventory of about 78.5 days. With the rapid pace of technological change in the semiconductor industry, Intel cannot afford to hold inventory too long. In contrast, for the four quarters ending March 30, 2004, Robert Mondavi Corp., one of the few publicly traded wineries in the United States, reported cost of goods sold of $288.7 million and inventory of $406.7 million. This yields an inventory turnover ratio for Mondavi of just 0.71, or an average age of inventory of about 514 days. Clearly, the differences in these inventory ratios reflect differences in the economic circumstances of the industries. Whereas the value of semiconductors declines as they age, just the opposite occurs in the wine business, at least up to a point.

average collection period The average amount of time that elapses from a sale on credit until the payment becomes usable funds for a firm. Calculated by dividing accounts receivable by average sales per day. Also called the *average age of accounts receivable.*

The **average collection period**, or *average age of accounts receivable,* is useful in evaluating credit and collection policies.[6] It measures the average amount of time that elapses from a sale on credit until the payment becomes useable funds for a firm. It is computed for GPC by dividing the firm's average sales per day into the accounts receivable balance. On average, in 2006, it took the firm 46.0 days to receive payment from a credit sale.

$$\text{Average sales per day} = \frac{\text{annual sales}}{365} = \frac{\$12{,}843}{365} = \$35.19$$

$$\text{Average collection period} = \frac{\text{accounts receivable}}{\text{average sales per day}} = \frac{\$1{,}619}{\$35.19} = 46.0 \text{ days}$$

[6] The average collection period is sometimes called the *days' sales outstanding (DSO)*. As with the inventory turnover ratio, the average collection period can be calculated using end-of-year accounts receivable or the average receivables balance for the year. The evaluation and establishment of credit and collection policies are discussed in Chapter 19.

The average collection period is meaningful only in relation to the firm's credit terms. If GPC extends 30-day credit terms to customers, an average collection period of 46.0 days may indicate a poorly managed credit or collection department, or both. The lengthened collection period could also be the result of an intentional relaxation of credit-term enforcement in response to competitive pressures. If the firm had extended 45-day credit terms, the 46.0-day average collection period would be quite acceptable. Clearly, additional information is required to evaluate the effectiveness of the firm's credit and collection policies.

Firms use the **average payment period** to evaluate their performance in repaying suppliers. It measures the average length of time it takes the firm to pay its suppliers. It equals the firm's average daily purchases divided into the accounts payable balance. To calculate average daily purchases, an analyst may have to estimate the firm's annual purchases, often by taking a specified percentage of cost of goods sold. This estimate is necessary because annual purchases are not reported on a firm's published financial statements. Instead they are embodied in its cost of goods sold. In the case of GPC, its annual purchases in 2006 were estimated at 80 percent of cost of goods sold, as shown in footnote (a) to its income statement in Table 2.2. Using the annual purchase estimate of \$6,815, GPC's average payment period for 2006 indicates that the firm usually takes 90.9 days to pay its bills.

average payment period
The average length of time it takes a firm to pay its suppliers. Calculated by dividing the firm's accounts payable balance by its average daily purchases.

$$\text{Average purchases per day} = \frac{\text{annual purchases}}{365} = \frac{\$6{,}815}{365} = \$18.67$$

$$\text{Average payment period} = \frac{\text{accounts payable}}{\text{average purchases per day}} = \frac{\$1{,}697}{\$18.67} = 90.9 \text{ days}$$

In a fashion similar to the average collection period, the average payment period is meaningful only when viewed in light of the actual credit terms extended to the firm by its suppliers. If GPC's suppliers, on average, extend 60-day credit terms, the firm's average payment period of 90.9 days indicates that the firm is generally slow in paying its bills. The fact that it takes GPC thirty days longer to pay its suppliers than the 60 days of credit they extended could damage the firm's ability to obtain additional credit and raise the cost of any credit that it may obtain. On the other hand, if the average credit terms granted GPC by its suppliers were 90 days, its 90.9-day average payment period would be very good. It should be clear that an analyst would need further information to draw definitive conclusions from the average payment period with regard to the firm's overall payment policies.

The **fixed asset turnover** measures the efficiency with which a firm uses its fixed assets. The ratio tells analysts how many dollars of sales the firm generates per dollar of fixed asset investment. The ratio equals sales divided by net fixed assets:

fixed asset turnover
A measure of the efficiency with which a firm uses its fixed assets, calculated by dividing sales by the number of dollars of net fixed asset investment.

$$\text{Fixed asset turnover} = \frac{\text{sales}}{\text{net fixed assets}} = \frac{\$12{,}843}{\$6{,}710} = 1.91$$

The fixed asset turnover for GPC in 2006 is 1.91. This means that the company turns over its net fixed assets 1.91 times a year. Said another way, GPC generates almost \$2 in sales for every dollar of fixed assets. As with other ratios, the "normal" level of fixed asset turnover varies widely from one industry to another.

An analyst must be aware that (when using this ratio and the total asset turnover ratio described next) the calculations use the *historical costs* of fixed assets. Because some firms have significantly newer or older assets than others do, comparing fixed asset turnovers of those firms can be misleading. Firms with newer assets tend to have lower turnovers than those with older assets, which have lower book (accounting) values. A naive comparison of fixed asset turnover ratios for different firms may lead an analyst to conclude that one firm operates more efficiently than another, when, in fact, the firm that appears to be more efficient simply has older (i.e., more fully depreciated) assets on its books.

total asset turnover
A measure of the efficiency with which a firm uses all its assets to generate sales; calculated by dividing the dollars of sales a firm generates by the dollars of asset investment.

The **total asset turnover** ratio indicates the efficiency with which a firm uses *all* its assets to generate sales. Like the fixed asset turnover ratio, total asset turnover indicates how many dollars of sales a firm generates per dollar of asset investment. All other factors being equal, analysts favor a high turnover ratio because it indicates that a firm generates more sales (and ideally more cash flow for investors) from a given investment in assets. GPC's total asset turnover in 2006 equals 1.34, calculated as follows:

$$\text{Total asset turnover} = \frac{\text{sales}}{\text{total assets}} = \frac{\$12,843}{\$9,589} = 1.34$$

Debt Ratios

Firms finance their assets from two broad sources, equity and debt. Equity comes from shareholders, whereas debt comes in many forms and from many different lenders. Firms borrow from suppliers, from banks, and from widely scattered investors who buy publicly traded bonds. *Debt ratios* measure the extent to which a firm uses money from creditors rather than shareholders to finance its operations. Because creditors' claims must be satisfied before firms can distribute earnings to shareholders, current and prospective investors pay close attention to the debts on a firm's balance sheet. Lenders share these concerns because the more indebted the firm, the higher the probability that the firm will be unable to satisfy the claims of all its creditors.

financial leverage
Using fixed-cost sources of financing, such as debt and preferred stock, to magnify both the risk and expected return on a firm's investments.

In general, the more debt a firm uses in relation to its total assets, the greater its financial leverage. Fixed-cost sources of financing, such as debt and preferred stock, create **financial leverage** that magnifies both the risk and the expected return on the firm's securities.[7] The more a firm borrows, the riskier its outstanding stock and bonds, and the higher the return that investors require on those securities. A detailed discussion of the effect of debt on the firm's risk, return, and value is in Chapter 12. Here, we emphasize the use of debt ratios to assess a firm's indebtedness and its ability to meet the fixed payments associated with debt.

coverage ratio
A debt ratio that focuses more on income statement measures of a firm's ability to generate sufficient cash flow to make scheduled interest and principal payments.

Broadly speaking, there are two types of debt ratios. One type focuses on balance sheet measures of outstanding debt relative to other sources of financing. The other type, known as the **coverage ratio**, focuses more on income statement measures of the firm's ability to generate sufficient cash flow to make scheduled interest and principal payments. Investors and credit-rating agencies use both types of ratios to assess a firm's creditworthiness.

7. By *fixed cost* we mean that the cost of this financing source does not vary over time in response to changes in the firm's revenue and cash flow. For example, when a firm borrows money at a variable rate, the interest cost of that loan is *not* fixed through time, but the firm's obligation to make interest payments is "fixed" regardless of the level of the firm's revenue and cash flow.

The **debt ratio** measures the proportion of total assets financed by the firm's creditors. The higher this ratio, the greater the firm's reliance on borrowed money to finance its activities. The ratio equals total liabilities divided by total assets, and GPC's debt ratio in 2006 is 0.551, or 55.1 percent:

debt ratio
A measure of the proportion of total assets financed by a firm's creditors.

$$\text{Debt ratio} = \frac{\text{total liabilities}}{\text{total assets}} = \frac{\$5{,}281}{\$9{,}589} = 0.551 = 55.1\%$$

This figure indicates that the company has financed more than half of its assets with debt.

A close cousin of the debt ratio is the **assets-to-equity (A/E) ratio,** sometimes called the **equity multiplier:**

assets-to-equity (A/E) ratio
A measure of the proportion of total assets financed by a firm's equity. Also called the *equity multiplier*.

$$\text{Assets-to-equity} = \frac{\text{total assets}}{\text{common stock equity}} = \frac{\$9{,}589}{\$4{,}278} = 2.24$$

Note that only common stock equity of $4,278 ($4,308 of total equity –$30 of preferred stock equity) is used in the denominator of this ratio. The resulting value indicates that GPC's assets in 2006 are 2.24 times greater than its equity. This value is reasonable given that the debt ratio shows that slightly more than half (55.1 percent) of GPC's assets in 2006 are financed with debt.

equity multiplier
A measure of the proportion of total assets financed by a firm's equity. Also called the *assets-to-equity (A/E) ratio*.

An alternative measure of the firm's leverage that focuses solely on the firm's long-term debt is the **debt-to-equity ratio,** calculated by dividing long-term debt by stockholders' equity. The 2006 value of this ratio for GPC is calculated as follows:

debt-to-equity ratio
A measure of the firm's financial leverage, calculated by divided long-term debt by stockholders' equity.

$$\text{Debt-to-equity ratio} = \frac{\text{long-term debt}}{\text{stockholders' equity}} = \frac{\$1{,}760}{\$4{,}308} = 0.409 = 40.9\%$$

GPC's long-term debts are therefore only 40.9 percent as large as its stockholders' equity. Note, however, that both the debt ratio and the debt-to-equity ratio use book values of debt, equity, and assets. Analysts should be aware that the market values of these variables may differ substantially from book values.

The **times interest earned ratio,** which equals earnings before interest and taxes divided by interest expense, measures the firm's ability to make contractual interest payments. A higher ratio indicates a greater capacity to meet scheduled payments. The times interest earned ratio for GPC in 2006 equals 13.59, indicating that the firm could experience a substantial decline in earnings and still meet its interest obligations:

times interest earned ratio
A measure of the firm's ability to make contractual interest payments, calculated by dividing earnings before interest and taxes by interest expense.

$$\text{Times interest earned} = \frac{\text{earnings before interest and taxes}}{\text{interest expense}} = \frac{\$1{,}671}{\$123} = 13.59$$

Profitability Ratios

Several measures of profitability relate a firm's earnings to its sales, assets, or equity. *Profitability ratios* are among the most closely watched and widely quoted financial ratios. Many firms link employee bonuses to profitability ratios, and stock prices react sharply to unexpected changes in these measures.

gross profit margin A measure of profitability that represents the percentage of each sales dollar remaining after a firm has paid for its goods.

The **gross profit margin** measures the percentage of each sales dollar remaining after the firm has paid for its goods. The higher the gross profit margin, the better. GPC's gross profit margin in 2006 is 33.7 percent:

$$\text{Gross profit margin} = \frac{\text{gross profit}}{\text{sales}} = \frac{\$4,324}{\$12,843} = 0.337 = 33.7\%$$

operating profit margin A measure of profitability that represents the percentage of each sales dollar remaining after deducting all costs and expenses other than interest and taxes.

The **operating profit margin** measures the percentage of each sales dollar remaining after deducting all costs and expenses *other than* interest and taxes. As with the gross profit margin, the higher the operating profit margin, the better. This ratio is of interest because it tells analysts what a firm's bottom line looks like before deductions for payments to creditors and tax authorities. GPC's operating profit margin in 2006 is 11.9 percent:

$$\text{Operating profit margin} = \frac{\text{operating profit}}{\text{sales}} = \frac{\$1,531}{\$12,843} = 0.119 = 11.9\%$$

net profit margin A measure of profitability that represents the percentage of each sales dollar remaining after all costs and expenses, *including* interest, taxes, and preferred stock dividends, have been deducted.

The **net profit margin** measures the percentage of each sales dollar remaining after all costs and expenses, *including* interest, taxes, and preferred stock dividends, have been deducted. Net profit margins vary widely across industries. For example, consider two very profitable U.S. companies, Microsoft and Wal-Mart. For the quarter ending in March, 2004, Microsoft reported a net profit margin of 14.3 percent, more than four times larger than the 3.3 percent net profit margin reported by Wal-Mart one month later. GPC's net profit margin in 2006 of 7.4 percent is calculated as follows:

$$\text{Net profit margin} = \frac{\text{earnings available for common stockholders}}{\text{sales}}$$

$$= \frac{\$946}{\$12,843} = 0.074 = 7.4\%$$

SMART ETHICS VIDEO

Frank Popoff, Chairman of the Board (retired), Dow Chemical

"Overstating or understating the performance of the enterprise is anathema . . . it's just not on."

See the entire interview at **SMARTFinance**

Probably the most closely watched financial ratio of them all is *earnings per share (EPS)*. The earnings per share represent the number of dollars earned on behalf of each outstanding share of common stock. The investing public closely watches *EPS* figures and considers them an important indicator of corporate success. Many firms tie management bonuses to meeting specific *EPS* targets. Earnings per share are calculated as follows:

$$\text{Earnings per share} = \frac{\text{earnings available for common stockholders}}{\text{number of shares of common stock outstanding}}$$

$$= \frac{\$946}{178.7} = \$5.29$$

The value of GPC's earnings per share on common stock outstanding in 2006 is $5.29.[8] This figure represents the dollar amount *earned* on behalf of each share outstanding. The amount of earnings actually *distributed* to each shareholder is the *dividend per share,* which, as noted in GPC's income statement (Table 2.2), rose to $1.93 in 2006 from $1.76 in 2005.

SMART IDEAS VIDEO

John Graham, Duke University

"We asked companies, 'Do you manage your earnings?'"

See the entire interview at **SMARTFinance**

The **return on total assets (*ROA*)**, often called the *return on investment (ROI),* measures the overall effectiveness of management in using its assets to generate returns.[9] The return on total assets for GPC in 2006 equals 9.9 percent:

$$\text{Return on total assets} = \frac{\text{earnings available for common stockholders}}{\text{total assets}}$$

$$= \frac{\$946}{\$9,589} = 0.099 = 9.9\%$$

A closely related measure of profitability is the **return on common equity (*ROE*)**, which captures the return earned on the common stockholders' (owners') investment in the firm. For a firm that uses only common stock to finance its operations, the *ROE* and *ROA* figures are identical. With debt or preferred stock on the balance sheet, these ratios usually differ. When the firm earns a profit, even after making interest payments to creditors and paying dividends to preferred stockholders, the firm's use of leverage magnifies the return earned by common stockholders, and *ROE* exceeds *ROA*. Conversely, if the firm's earnings fall short of the amount it must pay to lenders and preferred stockholders, leverage causes *ROE* to be less than *ROA*. For GPC, the return on common equity for 2006 is 22.1 percent, substantially above GPC's return on total assets:

return on total assets (*ROA*)
A measure of the overall effectiveness of management in generating returns to common stockholders with its available assets.

return on common equity (*ROE*)
A measure that captures the return earned on the common stockholders' (owners') investment in a firm.

$$\text{Return on common equity} = \frac{\text{earnings available for common stockholders}}{\text{common stock equity}}$$

$$= \frac{\$946}{\$4,278} = 0.221 = 22.1\%$$

DuPont System of Analysis. Financial analysts sometimes conduct a deeper analysis of the *ROA* and *ROE* ratios using the **DuPont system**, which uses both income and balance sheet information to break the *ROA* and *ROE* ratios into component pieces. This approach highlights the influence of the net profit margin, total asset turnover, and financial leverage on a firm's profitability. In the DuPont system, the return on total assets equals the product of the net profit margin and total asset turnover:

DuPont system
An analysis that uses both income and balance sheet information to break the ROA and ROE ratios into component pieces.

$$ROA = \text{net profit margin} \times \text{total asset turnover}$$

[8] All per-share values are stated strictly in dollars and cents; they are not stated in millions as are the dollar values used to calculate these and other ratios.

[9] Naturally, all other things being equal, firms prefer a high *ROA*. However, as we will see later, analysts must be cautious when interpreting financial ratios. We recall an old Dilbert comic strip in which Wally suggests boosting his firm's *ROA* by firing the security staff. The reduction in expenses would boost the numerator while the reduction in security would lower the denominator.

By definition, the net profit margin equals earnings available for common stockholders divided by sales, and total asset turnover equals sales divided by total assets. When we multiply these two ratios together, the sales figure cancels, resulting in the familiar *ROA* measure:

$$ROA = \frac{\text{earnings available for common stockholders}}{\text{sales}} \times \frac{\text{sales}}{\text{total assets}}$$
$$= \frac{\$946}{\$12{,}843} \times \frac{\$12{,}843}{\$9{,}589} = 0.074 \times 1.34 = 0.099 = 9.9\%$$
$$ROA = \frac{\text{earnings available for common stockholders}}{\text{total assets}} = \frac{\$946}{\$9{,}589} = 0.099 = 9.9\%$$

Naturally, the *ROA* value for GPC in 2006 obtained using the DuPont system is the same value we calculated before, but now we can think of the *ROA* as a product of how much profit the firm earns on each dollar of sales and of the efficiency with which the firm uses its assets to generate sales. Holding the net profit margin constant, an increase in total asset turnover increases the firm's *ROA*. Similarly, holding total asset turnover constant, an increase in the net profit margin increases *ROA*.

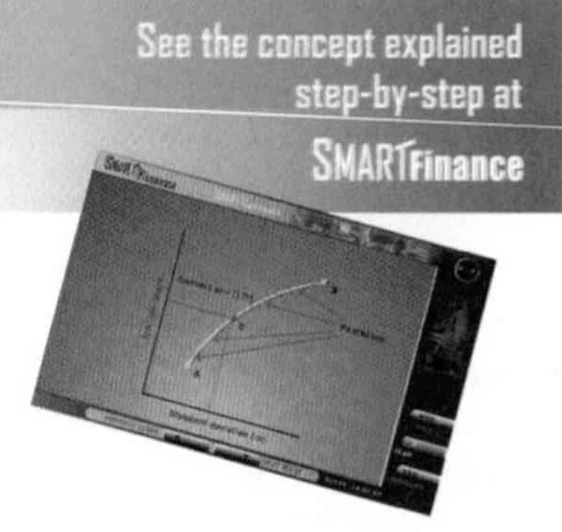

We can push the DuPont system one step further by multiplying the *ROA* times the ratio of *assets-to-equity* (*A/E*), or the *equity multiplier*. The product of these two ratios equals the return on common equity. Notice that for a firm that uses no debt and has no preferred stock, the ratio of assets-to-equity equals 1.0, so the *ROA* equals the *ROE*. For all other firms, the ratio of assets-to-equity exceeds 1. It is in this sense that the ratio of assets-to-equity represents a leverage multiplier.

$$ROE = ROA \times A/E$$

We can apply this version of the DuPont system to GPC in 2006 to recalculate its return on common equity:

$$ROE = \frac{\text{earnings available for common stockholders}}{\text{total assets}} \times \frac{\text{total assets}}{\text{common stock equity}}$$
$$= \frac{\$946}{\$9{,}589} \times \frac{\$9{,}589}{\$4{,}278} = 0.099 \times 2.24 = 0.221 = 22.1\%$$
$$ROE = \frac{\text{earnings available for common stockholders}}{\text{common stock equity}} = \frac{\$946}{\$4{,}278} = 0.221 = 22.1\%$$

Notice that for GPC, the ratio of assets-to-equity is 2.24, which means that GPC's return on common equity is more than twice as large as its return on total assets. Of course, using financial leverage has its risks. Notice what would happen if GPC's return on total assets were a negative number rather than a positive one. The financial leverage multiplier would cause GPC's return on common equity to be even more negative than its ROA.

The advantage of the DuPont system is that it allows the firm to break its return on common equity into a profit-on-sales component (net profit margin) that ties directly to the income statement, an efficiency-of-asset-use component (total asset turnover) that ties directly to the balance sheet, and a financial-leverage-use component (assets-to-equity ratio) that also ties directly to the balance sheet. Analysts can then study the effect of each of these factors on the overall return to common stockholders as is demonstrated in the following Applying the Model example.[10]

APPLYING THE MODEL

The 2006 ratio values for the *ROE*, *ROA*, assets-to-equity ratio, total asset turnover, and net profit margin calculated earlier for GPC are shown below, along with the 2006 industry averages for globally active oil companies.

Ratio	GPC	Industry Average
Return on common equity (*ROE*)	22.1%	19.7%
Return on total assets (*ROA*)	9.9%	12.1%
Assets-to-equity (A/E) ratio	2.24	1.63
Totals asset turnover	1.34	1.42
Net profit margin	7.4%	8.5%

We begin the analysis of GPC's performance during 2006 with its return on common equity of 22.1 percent, which is noticeably above the industry average of 19.7 percent. To learn why GPC's *ROE* outperformed the industry, we look at two components of *ROE*: *ROA* and the assets-to-equity (A/E) ratio. Comparing these ratios for GPC with the industry averages, we see that GPC's *ROA of 9.9 percent was well below the industry average of 12.1 percent*, but because of GPC's *greater use of leverage*—an A/E ratio of 2.24 for GPC versus 1.63 for the industry—GPC was able to generate a higher *ROE* than the average firm. Looking further at the two components of *ROA* (the net profit margin and the total asset turnover), we see that although GPC's total asset turnover of 1.34 is very close to the industry average of 1.42, *its net profit margin of 7.4 percent is below the industry average of 8.5 percent.* It therefore caused GPC's *ROA* to be below the industry average.

Summarizing, it appears that in spite of its inability to manage its costs and generate profit on sales comparable to its competitors, GPC compensated for its below-average *ROA* by using significantly more leverage than its competitors. Clearly GPC took greater risk to compensate for low profits on sales. The firm should focus on its income statement to improve its profitability and may want to reduce its leverage to moderate its risk. It appears that GPC has problems in both its income statement (net profit margin) and its balance sheet (asset-to-equity ratio).

10. Keep in mind that the ratios in the DuPont system are interdependent and that the equation is just a mathematical identity. It is easy to draw questionable conclusions about lines of causality using the DuPont system. For example, consider this farcical version of the formula:

$$ROA = \frac{\text{earnings available for common stockholders}}{\text{sales}} \times \frac{\text{sales}}{\text{assets}} \times \frac{\text{assets}}{\text{CEO age}} \times \frac{\text{CEO age}}{\text{common stock equity}}$$

In this equation, we might interpret the third term on the right as the efficiency with which a CEO of a given age manages the firm's assets. If a younger CEO manages the same quantity of assets, this ratio would increase, and holding all other factors constant, we could say that the firm's *ROE* would increase. This is clearly silly, but mathematically this expression ultimately gives you the firm's *ROE*.

Market Ratios

Market ratios relate the firm's market value, as measured by its current share price, to certain accounting values. These ratios provide analysts with insight into how investors think the firm is performing. Because the ratios include market values, they tend to reflect on a relative basis the common stockholders' assessment of all aspects of the firm's past and expected future performance. Here we consider two popular market ratios, one that focuses on earnings and the other that considers book value.

price/earnings (P/E) ratio
A measure of a firm's long-term growth prospects that represents the amount investors are willing to pay for each dollar of a firm's earnings.

The most widely quoted market ratio, the **price/earnings (P/E) ratio**, is often used as a barometer of a firm's long-term growth prospects. The P/E ratio measures the amount investors are willing to pay for each dollar of the firm's earnings. The price/earnings ratio may indicate the degree of confidence that investors have in the firm's future performance. A high P/E ratio indicates that investors believe a firm will achieve rapid earnings growth in the future; hence, companies with high P/E ratios are referred to as *growth stocks.* Simply stated, investors who believe that future earnings are going to be higher than current earnings are willing to pay a lot for today's earnings, and vice versa.

Using the per-share price of $76.25 for Global Petroleum Corporation on December 31, 2006, and its 2006 *EPS* of $5.29, the P/E ratio at year-end 2006 is computed as follows:

$$\text{Price/earnings (P/E) ratio} = \frac{\text{market price per share of common stock}}{\text{earnings per share}}$$

$$= \frac{\$76.25}{\$5.29} = 14.41$$

This figure indicates that investors were paying $14.41 for each $1.00 of GPC's earnings. It is interesting to note that GPC's price/earnings ratio one year before (on December 31, 2005) had been almost twice as high at 28.37 ($71.50 per share stock price ÷ $2.52 earnings per share).

market/book (M/B) ratio
A measure used to assess a firm's future performance by relating its market value per share to its book value per share.

The **market/book (M/B) ratio** provides another assessment of how investors view the firm's past and, particularly, its expected future performance. It relates the market value of the firm's shares to their book value. The stocks of firms that are expected to perform well—improving profits, growing market share, launching successful products, and so forth—typically sell at higher M/B ratios than those firms with less attractive prospects. Simply stated, firms that investors expect to earn high returns relative to their risk typically sell at higher M/B multiples than those expected to earn low returns relative to risk.

To calculate the M/B ratio for GPC in 2006, we first need to find *book value per share* of common stock:

$$\text{Book value per share} = \frac{\text{common stock equity}}{\text{number of shares of common stock outstanding}}$$

$$= \frac{\$4{,}278}{178.7} = \$23.94$$

Market to book value is then computed by dividing this book value into the current price of the firm's stock:

$$\text{Market/book (M/B) ratio} = \frac{\text{market value per share of common stock}}{\text{book value per share of common stock}}$$

$$= \frac{\$76.25}{\$23.94} = 3.19$$

Investors are currently paying $3.19 for each $1.00 of book value of GPC's stock. Clearly, investors expect GPC to continue to grow in the future, because they are willing to pay more than book value for the firm's shares.

CONCEPT REVIEW QUESTIONS

7. Which of the categories and individual ratios described in this chapter would be of greatest interest to each of the following parties?

- **a.** Existing and prospective creditors (lenders)
- **b.** Existing and prospective shareholders
- **c.** The firm's management

8. How could the availability of cash inflow and cash outflow data be used to improve on the accuracy of the liquidity and debt coverage ratios presented previously? What specific ratio measures would you calculate to assess the firm's liquidity and debt coverage, using cash flow rather than financial statement data?

9. Assume that a firm's total assets and sales remain constant. Would an increase in each of the ratios below be associated with a cash inflow a cash outflow, or would there be no effect on cash?

- **a.** Current ratio
- **b.** Inventory turnover
- **c.** Average collection period
- **d.** Average payment period
- **e.** Debt ratio
- **f.** Net profit margin

10. Use the *DuPont system* to explain why a slower-than-average inventory turnover could cause a firm with an above-average net profit margin and an average degree of financial leverage to have a below-average return on common equity.

11. How can you reconcile investor expectations for a firm with an above-average M/B ratio and a below-average P/E ratio? Could the age of the firm have any effect on this ratio comparison?

2.4 CORPORATE TAXES

Taxation is one of the key measurement challenges facing financial decision makers. Looking at GPC's income statement in Table 2.2, we can see that its taxes for 2006 totaled $599 million on pretax income of $1,548 million; clearly their taxes represent a significant cash outflow. Taxes affect both the benefits and the costs of a proposed action or transaction.

The financial manager needs to estimate the after-tax benefits and costs required by proposed actions to assess their economic viability. Does the financial

Table 2.6
Corporate Income Tax Rates

Taxable income over	Not over	Tax Rate
$ 0	$ 50,000	15%
50,000	75,000	25%
75,000	100,000	34%
100,000	335,000	39%
335,000	10,000,000	34%
10,000,000	15,000,000	35%
15,000,000	18,333,333	38%
18,333,333	....	35%

analyst/decision maker have to be a tax expert? No. But an understanding of the basics of corporate taxation is essential for an effective consultation with tax experts, such as corporate tax counsel or a tax consultant. Asking the right questions and learning the best way to structure and make transactions results in net benefits that create value for owners.

Here we briefly review the most basic corporate tax concepts—the taxation of ordinary income and capital gains. Later in the text, we will apply taxes to various transactions. Keep in mind that (1) the tax code is frequently revised and (2) corporations are subject to tax rates that differ from the personal tax rates applicable to noncorporate businesses such as sole proprietorships and partnerships.

Ordinary Corporate Income

ordinary corporate income Income resulting from the sale of the firm's goods and services.

Ordinary corporate income is income resulting from the sale of the firm's goods and services. Under current tax laws the applicable tax rates are subject to the somewhat progressive tax rate schedule shown in Table 2.6. The purpose of the progressive rates (lower rates on lower taxable amounts) at the bottom of the schedule is to give small corporations a better chance to grow. The following Applying the Model illustrates application of the corporate tax rates.

APPLYING THE MODEL

First Vehicle Corporation (FVC) during 2006 earned pretax income of $2,800,000. What is FVC's tax liability for the year? Using the corporate tax rate schedule, FVC's tax liability is calculated as follows:

$ 50,000 × 0.15 =	$	7,500
($ 75,000 − 50,000) × 0.25 =		6,250
(100,000 − 75,000) × 0.34 =		8,500
(335,000 − 100,000) × 0.39 =		91,650
(2,800,000 − 335,000) × 0.34 =		838,100
Tax liability		$952,000

FVC's tax liability for 2006 on its pretax income of $2,800,000 is therefore $952,000.

average tax rate A firm's tax liability divided by its pretax income.

Average Tax Rate. A useful measure is the firm's **average tax rate**, which is calculated by dividing its tax liability by its pretax income. For example, the average tax rate for FVC in the preceding Applying the Model illustration would be exactly 34 percent ($952,000 ÷ $2,800,000). During 2006, FVC paid an average of 34 cents on each dollar of pretax income earned.

Marginal Tax Rate. More relevant in financial decision making is the **marginal tax rate**, which is the tax rate applicable to the firm's next dollar of earnings. This rate is important because all decisions consider marginal benefits and marginal costs, and therefore, the tax rate used in the analysis should likewise be an incremental, rather than an average rate. Again, referring to the FVC discussions above, we can see that the firm's 2,800,001st dollar of pretax income would be taxed at a 34-percent rate. Therefore, 34 percent is FVC's marginal tax rate at its current level of operations. *Note that because this book focuses on incremental decision making, the tax rates given are always marginal tax rates.*

marginal tax rate
The tax rate applicable to a firm's next dollar of earnings.

Corporate Capital Gains

Corporations experience **capital gains** when they sell capital assets, such as equipment or stock held as an investment, for more than their original purchase price. The amount of the capital gain is equal to the difference between the sale price and initial purchase price. If the sale price is less than the asset's book, or accounting, value, the difference is called a **capital loss**. Under current tax law, corporate capital gains are merely added to operating income and taxed at the ordinary corporate tax rates. The tax treatment of capital losses on depreciable business assets involves a deduction from pretax ordinary income, whereas any other capital losses must be used to offset capital gains. The following Applying the Model demonstrates the tax treatment of a capital gain.

capital gains
The difference between the sale price and the original purchase price resulting from the sale of a capital asset, such as equipment or stock held as an investment.

capital loss
The loss resulting from the sale of a capital asset, such as equipment or stock held as an investment, at a price below its book, or accounting, value.

APPLYING THE MODEL

Assume that First Vehicle Corporation (FVC), introduced previously, decided to sell an entire production line for $850,000. If the firm had originally purchased the line two years earlier for $700,000, how much in capital gain taxes would FVC owe on this transaction if it was in the 34-percent marginal tax bracket on ordinary corporate income? The firm would have realized a $150,000 ($850,000 – $700,000) capital gain on this transaction, which would result in $51,000 ($150,000 × 0.34) of taxes.

CONCEPT REVIEW QUESTIONS

12. How are corporations taxed on ordinary income? What is the difference between the *average tax rate* and the *marginal tax rate* on ordinary corporate income?

13. What are corporate *capital gains* and *capital losses*? How are they treated for tax purposes?

2.5 SUMMARY AND CONCLUSIONS

- The four key financial statements are (1) the balance sheet, (2) the income statement, (3) the statement of retained earnings, and (4) the statement of cash flows. Notes describing the technical aspects of the financial statements are normally included with them.
- Depreciation is the most common noncash charge on income statements; others are amortization and depletion allowances. Depreciation is added back to *EBIT* after taxes to find a firm's operating cash flow. A measure of cash flow that is important to financial analysts is free cash flow, the cash flow available to

investors. Free cash flow equals operating cash flow less the firm's net investment in fixed and current assets.

- The statement of cash flows, in effect, summarizes the firm's cash flows over a specified period of time, typically one year. It presents cash flows divided into operating, investment, and financing flows. When interpreting the statement, an analyst typically looks for unusual changes in either the major categories of cash flow or in specific items to find clues to problems that the firm may be experiencing.
- Financial ratios are a convenient tool for analyzing the firm's financial statements to assess its performance over the given period. A variety of financial ratios are available for assessing various aspects of a firm's liquidity, activity, debt, profitability, and market value. The DuPont system is often used to assess various aspects of a firm's profitability, particularly the returns earned on both the total asset investment and the owners' common stock equity in the firm.
- Financial decision makers must be conversant with basic corporate tax concepts, because taxes are a major measurement challenge that affect both benefits and costs. Taxes are a major outflow of cash to the profitable firm; they are levied on both ordinary income and capital gains. The marginal tax rate is more relevant than the average tax rate in financial decision making.

SELF-TEST PROBLEMS

Answers to Self-Test Problems appear in Appendix D at back of book. Answers to the Concept Review Questions throughout the chapter appear at *http://megginson.swlearning.com*.

ST2-1. Use the financial statements below to answer the questions about S&M Manufacturing's financial position at the end of the calendar year 2006.

a. How much cash and near cash does S&M have at year-end 2006?

S&M Manufacturing, Inc.
Balance Sheet at December 31, 2006 ($000)

Assets		**Liabilities and Equity**	
Current assets		Current liabilities	
Cash	$ 140,000	Accounts payable	$ 480,000
Marketable securities	260,000	Notes payable	500,000
Accounts receivable	650,000	Accruals	80,000
Inventories	800,000	Total current liabilities	$1,060,000
Total current assets	$1,850,000	Long-term debt	
Fixed assets		Bonds outstanding	$1,300,000
Gross fixed assets	$3,780,000	Bank debt (long-term)	260,000
Less: Accumulated depreciation	1,220,000	Total long-term debt	$1,560,000
Net fixed assets	$2,560,000	Stockholders' equity	
Total assets	**$4,410,000**	Preferred stock	$ 180,000
		Common stock (at par)	200,000
		Paid-in capital in excess of par	810,000
		Retained earnings	600,000
		Total stockholders' equity	$1,790,000
		Total liabilities and equity	$4,410,000

S&M Manufacturing, Inc.

Income Statement for Year Ended December 31, 2006 ($000)

Sales revenue		$6,900,000
Less: Cost of goods sold		4,200,000
Gross profits		$2,700,000
Less: Operating expenses		
Sales expense	$ 750,000	
General and administrative expense	1,150,000	
Leasing expense	210,000	
Depreciation expense	235,000	
Total operation expenses		2,345,000
Earnings before interest and taxes		$ 355,000
Less: Interest expense		85,000
Net profit before taxes		$ 270,000
Less: Taxes		81,000
Net profits after taxes		$ 189,000
Less: Preferred stock dividends		10,800
Earnings available for common stockholders		$ 178,200
Less: Dividends		75,000
To retained earnings		$ 103,200
Per share data		
Earnings per share (EPS)	$ 1.43	
Dividends per share (DPS)	$ 0.60	
Price per share	$ 15.85	

a. How much cash and near cash does S&M have at year-end 2006?
b. What was the original cost of all of the firm's real property that is currently owned?
c. How much in total liabilities did the firms have at year-end 2006?
d. How much did S&M owe for credit purchases at year-end 2006?
e. How much did the firm sell during 2006?
f. How much equity did the common stockholders have in the firm at year-end 2006?
g. What is the cumulative total of earnings reinvested in the firm from its inception through the end of 2006?
h. How much operating profit did the firm earn during 2006?
i. What is the total amount of dividends paid out by the firm during the year 2006?
j. How many shares of common stock did S&M have outstanding at year-end 2006?

ST2-2. The partially complete 2006 balance sheet and income statement for Challenge Industries are given on the following page, followed by selected ratio values for the firm based on its completed 2006 financial statements. Use the ratios along with the partial statements to complete the financial statements. *Hint:* Use the ratios in the order listed to calculate the missing statement values that need to be installed in the partial statements.

Challenge Industries, Inc.
Balance Sheet at December 31, 2006 (in $ thousands)

Assets		Liabilities and Equity	
Current assets		Current liabilities	
Cash	$ 52,000	Accounts payable	$150,000
Marketable securities	60,000	Notes payable	?
Accounts receivable	200,000	Accruals	80,000
Inventories	?	Total current liabilities	?
Total current assets	?	Long-term debt	$425,000
Fixed assets (gross)	?	Total liabilities	?
Less: Accumulated depreciation	240,000	Stockholders' equity	
Net fixed assets	?	Preferred stock	?
Total assets	?	Common stock (at par)	150,000
		Paid-in capital in excess of par	?
		Retained earnings	390,000
		Total stockholders' equity	?
		Total liabilities and stockholders' equity	?

Challenge Industries, Inc.
Income Statement for the Year Ended December 31, 2006
(in $ thousands)

Sales revenue		$4,800,000
Less: Cost of goods sold		?
Gross profits		?
Less: Operating expenses		
Sales expense	$690,000	
General and administrative expense	750,000	
Depreciation expense	120,000	
Total operating expenses		1,560,000
Earnings before interest and taxes		?
Less: Interest expense		35,000
Earnings before taxes		?
Less: Taxes		?
Net income (Net profits after taxes)		?
Less: Preferred dividends		15,000
Earnings available for common stockholders		?
Less: Dividends		60,000
To retained earnings		?

Challenge Industries, Inc.
Ratios for the Year Ended December 31, 2006

Ratio	Value
Total asset turnover	2.00
Gross profit margin	40%
Inventory turnover	10
Current ratio	1.60
Net profit margin	3.75%
Return on common equity	12.5%

ST2-3. Use the corporate income tax rate schedule in Table 2.6 to calculate the tax liability for each of the following firms, with the amounts of 2006 pretax income noted.

Firm	2006 Pretax Income	Tax Liability
A	$12,500,000	?
B	200,000	?
C	80,000	?

a. What tax rate—average or marginal—is relevant to financial decisions for these firms?
b. Calculate, compare, and discuss the *average tax rates* for each of the firms during 2006.
c. Find the *marginal tax rates* for each of the firms at the end of 2006.
d. What relationship exists between the average and marginal tax rates for each firm?

INTERNET RESOURCES

Note: *Throughout this textbook you will find numerous Internet links, both within the discussions and at the end of each chapter. Because some links will likely change or be eliminated during the life of this edition, please go to this book's Web site (*http://megginson.swlearning.com*) to obtain updated links in the event you encounter a dead link.*

http://www.sec.gov—SEC site containing the document search and retrieval engine EDGAR; useful for obtaining up-to-date financial statements for publicly traded U.S. firms

http://www.quicken.com—Can retrieve a fairly extensive ratio analysis of a given company by typing in a ticker symbol

http://www.rmahq.org/Ann_Studies/asstudies.html—Can see a sample of a Risk Management Association industry analysis and the material that explains the ratios, quartiles, and other information that is available from RMA

http://www.yahoo.com—Contains a link to Yahoo! Finance for retrieval of recent financial statements and a wide variety of other financial information for any listed U.S. firm and many foreign firms

KEY TERMS

accrual-based approach
activity ratios
assets-to-equity (A/E) ratio
average age of inventory
average collection period
average payment period
average tax rate
capital gains
capital loss
cash flow approach
common stock
common-size income statement
coverage ratio
current ratio
debt ratio
debt-to-equity ratio
deferred taxes
dividend per share (*DPS*)
DuPont system
earnings available for common stockholders
earnings per share (*EPS*)
equity multiplier
financial leverage
financing flows
fixed asset turnover
free cash flow (*FCF*)
gross profit margin
inventory turnover
investment flows
liquidity ratios
long-term debt
marginal tax rate
market/book (M/B) ratio
net profit margin

net working capital
noncash charges
operating cash flow (*OCF*)
operating flows
operating profit margin
ordinary corporate income
paid-in capital
par value (common stock)
preferred stock
price/earnings (P/E) ratio
quick (acid-test) ratio
ratio analysis
retained earnings
return on common equity (*ROE*)
return on total assets (*ROA*)
times interest earned ratio
total asset turnover
treasury stock

QUESTIONS AND PROBLEMS

Q2-1. What information (explicit and implicit) can be derived from financial statement analysis? Does the standardization required by GAAP add greater validity to comparisons of financial data between companies and industries? Are there possible shortcomings to relying solely on financial statement analysis to value companies?

Q2-2. Distinguish between the types of financial information contained in the various financial statements. Which statements provide information on a company's performance over a reporting period, and which present data on a company's current position? What sorts of valuable information may be found in the notes to financial statements? Describe a situation in which the information in the notes would be essential to making an informed decision about the value of a corporation.

Q2-3. If you were a commercial credit analyst charged with the responsibility of making an accept/reject decision on a company's loan request, with which financial statement would you be most concerned? Which financial statement is most likely to provide pertinent information about a company's ability to repay its debt?

Q2-4. What is *operating cash flow (OCF)*? How is it calculated? What is *free cash flow (FCF)*? How is it calculated from *OCF*? Why do financial managers focus attention on the value of *FCF*?

Q2-5. Describe the common definitions of "inflows of cash" and "outflows of cash" used by analysts to classify certain balance sheet changes and income statement values. What three categories of cash flow are used in the statement of cash flows? To what value should the net value in the statement of cash flows reconcile?

Q2-6. What precautions must one take when using ratio analysis to make financial decisions? Which ratios would be most useful for a financial manager's internal financial analysis? For an analyst trying to decide which stocks are most attractive within an industry?

Q2-7. How do analysts use ratios to analyze a firm's *financial leverage?* Which ratios convey more important information to a credit analyst—those revolving around the levels of indebtedness or those measuring the ability to meet the contractual payments associated with debt? What is the relationship between a firm's levels of indebtedness and risk? What must happen for an increase in financial leverage to be successful?

Q2-8. How is the *DuPont system* useful in analyzing a firm's *ROA* and *ROE?* What information can be inferred from the decomposition of *ROE* into contributing ratios? What is the mathematical relationship between each of the individual components (net profit margin, total asset turnover, and assets-to-equity ratio) and *ROE?* Can *ROE* be raised without affecting *ROA?* How?

Q2-9. Provide a general description of the tax rates applicable to U.S. corporations. What is the difference between the *average tax rate* and the *marginal tax rate?* Which is relevant to financial decision making? Why? How do *capital gains* differ from *ordinary corporate income?*

PROBLEMS

Financial Statements

P2-1. Obtain financial statements for Microsoft for the last five years either from its Web site (http://www.microsoft.com) or from the SEC's online EDGAR site (http://www.sec.gov/edgar/searchedgar/webusers.htm). First, look at the statements without reading the notes. Then, read the notes carefully, concentrating on those about executive stock options. Do you have a different perspective after analyzing these notes?

SMART SOLUTIONS

See the problem and solution explained step-by-step at SMARTFinance

Cash Flow Analysis

P2-2. Given the balance sheets and selected data from the income statement of SMG Industries that follow, answer parts (a) – (c).

a. Calculate the firm's *operating cash flow (OCF)* for the year ended December 31, 2006, using Equation 2.1.

b. Calculate the firm's *free cash flow (FCF)* for the year ended December 31, 2006, using Equation 2.2.

c. Interpret, compare, and contrast your cash flow estimates in parts (a) and (b).

SMG Industries Balance Sheets ($ in millions)

Assets	December 31, 2006	December 31, 2005	Liabilities and Stockholders' Equity	December 31, 2006	December 31, 2005
Cash	$ 3,500	$ 3,000	Accounts payable	$ 3,600	$ 3,500
Marketable securities	3,800	3,200	Notes payable	4,800	4,200
			Accruals	1,200	1,300
Accounts receivable	4,000	3,800	Total current liabilities	$ 9,600	$ 9,000
			Long-term debt	$ 6,000	$ 6,000
Inventories	4,900	4,800	Common stock	$11,000	$11,000
Total current assets	$16,200	$14,800	Retained earnings	6,400	5,800
			Total stockholders' equity	$17,400	$16,800
Gross fixed assets	$31,500	$30,100			
			Total liabilities and stockholders' equity	$33,000	$31,800
Less: Accumulated depreciation	14,700	13,100			
Net fixed assets	$16,800	$17,000			
Total assets	$33,000	$31,800			

Income Statement Data (2006, $ in millions)

Depreciation expense	$1,600
Earnings before interest and taxes (*EBIT*)	4,500
Taxes	1,300
Net profits after taxes	2,400

P2-3. Classify each of the following items as an inflow (I) or an outflow (O) of cash, or as neither (N).

Item	Change ($)	Item	Change ($)
Cash	+600	Accounts receivable	–900
Accounts payable	–1,200	Net profits	+700
Notes payable	+800	Depreciation	+200
Long-term debt	–2,500	Repurchase of stock	+500
Inventory	+400	Cash dividends	+300
Fixed assets	+600	Sale of stock	+1,300

Analyzing Financial Performance Using Ratio Analysis

P2-4. Manufacturers Bank is evaluating Aluminum Industries, Inc., which has requested a $3 million loan, to assess the firm's financial leverage and risk. On the basis of the debt ratios for Aluminum, along with the industry averages and Aluminum's recent financial statements (which follow), evaluate and recommend appropriate action on the loan request.

Aluminum Industries, Inc. Income Statement for the Year Ended December 31, 2006

Sales revenue		$30,000,000
Less: Cost of goods sold		21,000,000
Gross profit		$ 9,000,000
Less: Operating expenses		
Selling expense	$3,000,000	
General and administrative expenses	1,800,000	
Lease expense	200,000	
Depreciation expense	1,000,000	
Total operating expense		6,000,000
Operating profit		$ 3,000,000
Less: Interest expense		1,000,000
Net profit before taxes		$ 2,000,000
Less: Taxes (rate = 40%)		800,000
Net profits after taxes		$ 1,200,000

Aluminum Industries, Inc. Balance Sheet as of December 31, 2006

Assets		Liabilities and Stockholders' Equity	
Current assets		Current liabilities	
Cash	$ 1,000,000	Accounts payable	$ 8,000,000
Marketable securities	3,000,000	Notes payable	8,000,000
Accounts receivable	12,000,000	Accruals	500,000
Inventories	7,500,000	Total current liabilities	$16,500,000
Total current assets	$23,500,000	Long-term debt (including financial leases)	$20,000,000
Gross fixed assets (at cost)			
Land and buildings	$11,000,000	Stockholders' equity	
Machinery and equipment	20,500,000	Preferred stock (25,000 shares, $4 dividend)	$ 2,500,000
Furniture and fixtures	8,000,000		
Gross fixed assets	$39,500,000	Common stock (1 million shares, $5 par)	5,000,000
Less: Accumulated depreciation	13,000,000		
Net fixed assets	$26,500,000	Paid-in capital in excess of par	4,000,000
Total assets	$50,000,000		
		Retained earnings	2,000,000
		Total stockholders' equity	$13,500,000
		Total liabilities and stockholders' equity	$50,000,000

Industry Averages

Debt ratio	0.51
Debt-equity ratio	1.07
Times interest earned ratio	7.30

P2-5. Use the information below to answer the questions that follow.

Income Statements for the Year Ended December 31, 2006

	Heavy Metal Manufacturing (HMM)	Metallic Stamping Inc. (MS)	High-Tech Software Co. (HTS)
Sales	$75,000,000	$50,000,000	$100,000,000
-Operating expenses	65,000,000	40,000,000	60,000,000
Operating profit	$10,000,000	$10,000,000	$ 40,000,000
-Interest expenses	3,000,000	3,000,000	0
Earnings before taxes	$ 7,000,000	$ 7,000,000	$ 40,000,000
-Taxes	2,800,000	2,800,000	16,000,000
Net income	$ 4,200,000	$ 4,200,000	$ 24,000,000

Balance Sheets as of December 31, 2006

	Heavy Metal Manufacturing (HMM)	Metallic Stamping Inc. (MS)	High-Tech Software Co. (HTS)
Current assets	$ 10,000,000	$ 5,000,000	$ 20,000,000
Net fixed assets	90,000,000	75,000,000	80,000,000
Total assets	$100,000,000	$80,000,000	$100,000,000
Current liabilities	$ 20,000,000	$10,000,000	$ 10,000,000
Long-term debt	40,000,000	40,000,000	0
Total liabilities	$ 60,000,000	$50,000,000	$ 10,000,000
Common stock	$ 15,000,000	$10,000,000	$ 25,000,000
Retained earnings	25,000,000	20,000,000	65,000,000
Total common equity	$ 40,000,000	$30,000,000	$ 90,000,000
Total liabilities and common equity	$100,000,000	$80,000,000	$100,000,000

a. Use the *DuPont system* to compare the two heavy metal companies shown above (HHM and MS) during 2006. Which of the two has a higher return on common equity? What is the cause of the difference between the two?

b. Calculate the return on common equity of the software company, HTS. Why is this value so different from those of the heavy metal companies calculated in part (a)?

c. Compare the leverage levels between the industries. Which industry receives a greater contribution from return on total assets? Which industry receives a greater contribution from the financial leverage as measured by the assets-to-equity (A/E) ratio?

d. Can you make a meaningful DuPont comparison across industries? Why or why not?

P2-6. Refer to Problem 2-5, and perform the same analysis with real data. Download last year's financial data from Ford Motor Company (http://www2.ford.com), General Motors (http://www.gm.com), and Microsoft (http://www.microsoft.com). Which ratios demonstrate the greatest difference between Ford and General Motors? Which of the two is more profitable? Which ratios drive the greater profitability?

P2-7. A *common-size income statement* for Aluminum Industries' 2005 operations follows. Using the firm's 2006 income statement presented in Problem 2-4, develop the 2006 common-size income statement (see footnote 2) and compare it with the 2005 statement. Which areas require further analysis and investigation?

Aluminum Industries, Inc. Common-Size Income Statement for the Year Ended December 31, 2005

Sales revenue ($35,000,000)		100%
Less: Cost of goods sold		65.9
Gross profit		34.1%
Less: Operating expenses		
Selling expense	12.7%	
General and administrative expenses	6.3	
Lease expense	0.6	
Depreciation expense	3.6	
Total operating expense		23.2
Operating profit		10.9%
Less: Interest expense		1.5
Net profit before taxes		9.4%
Less: Taxes (rate = 40%)		3.8
Net profits after taxes		5.6%

P2-8. Use the following financial data for Greta's Gadgets, Inc. to determine the effect of using additional debt financing to purchase additional assets. Assume that an additional $1 million of assets is purchased with 100 percent debt financing with a 10 percent annual interest rate.

Greta's Gadgets, Inc.

Income Statement for the Year Ended December 31, 2006

Sales	$4,000,000
-Costs and expenses @ 90%	3,600,000
Earnings before interest & taxes	$ 400,000
-Interest (0.10×$1,000,000)	100,000
Earnings before taxes	$ 300,000
-Taxes @ 40%	120,000
Net income	$ 180,000

Greta's Gadgets, Inc.

Balance Sheet as of December 31, 2006

Assets		Liabilities and stockholders' equity	
Current assets	$ 0	Current liabilities	$ 0
Fixed assets	2,000,000	Long-term debt @ 10%	1,000,000
Total assets	$2,000,000	Total liabilities	$1,000,000
		Common stock equity	$1,000,000
		Total liabilities and stockholders' equity	$2,000,000

a. Calculate the current (2006) net profit margin, total asset turnover, assets-to-equity ratio, return on total assets, and return on common equity for Greta's.

b. Now, assuming no other changes, determine the effect of purchasing the $1 million in assets using 100 percent debt financing with a 10 percent annual interest rate. Further, assume that the newly purchased assets generate an additional $2 million in sales and that the costs and expenses remain at 90 percent of sales. For purposes of this problem, further assume a tax rate of 40 percent. What is the effect on the ratios calculated in part (a)? Is the purchase of these assets justified on the basis of the return on common equity?

c. Assume that the newly purchased assets in part (b) generate only an extra $500,000 in sales. Is the purchase justified in this case?

d. Which component ratio(s) of the *DuPont system* is (are) not affected by the change in sales? What does this imply about the use of financial leverage?

P2-9. Tracey White, owner of the Buzz Coffee Shop chain, has decided to expand her operations. Her 2006 financial statements follow. Tracey can buy two additional coffeehouses for $3 million, and she has the choice of completely financing these new coffeehouses with either a 10 percent (annual interest) loan or the issuance of new common stock. She also expects these new shops to generate an additional $1 million in sales. Assuming a 40 percent tax rate and no other changes, should Tracey buy the two coffeehouses? Why or why not? Which financing option results in the better *ROE*?

Buzz Coffee Shops, Inc. 2006 Financial Statements

Balance Sheet		**Income Statement**	
Current assets	$ 250,000	Sales	$500,000
Fixed assets	750,000	-Costs and expenses @ 40%	200,000
Total assets	$1,000,000		
		Earnings before interest and taxes (*EBIT*)	$300,000
Current liabilities	$ 300,000		
Long-term debt	0	-Interest expense	0
Total liabilities	$ 300,000	Net profit before taxes	$300,000
Common equity	$ 700,000	-Taxes @ 40%	120,000
Total liabilities and stockholders' equity	$1,000,000	Net income	$180,000

P2-10. The financial statements of Access Corporation for the year ended December 31, 2006, follow.

Access Corporation Income Statement for the Year Ended December 31, 2006

Sales revenue		$160,000
Less: Cost of goods sold[a]		106,000
Gross profit		$ 54,000
Less: Operating expenses		
Sales expense	$16,000	
General and administrative expense	10,000	
Lease expense	1,000	
Depreciation expense	10,000	
Total operating expense		37,000
Operating profit		$ 17,000
Less: Interest expense		6,100
Net profit before taxes		$ 10,900
Less: Taxes @ 40%		4,360
Net profits after taxes		$ 6,540

[a]Access Corporation's annual purchases are estimated to equal 75 percent of cost of goods sold.

Access Corporation Balance Sheet as of December 31, 2006

Assets		**Liabilities and Stockholders' Equity**	
Cash	$ 500	Accounts payable	$ 22,000
Marketable securities	1,000	Notes payable	47,000
		Total current liabilities	$ 69,000
Accounts receivable	25,000	Long-term debt	$ 22,950
		Total liabilities	$ 91,950
Inventories	45,500	Common stock[a]	$ 31,500
Total current assets	$ 72,000	Retained earnings	26,550
		Total liabilities and stockholders' equity	$150,000
Land	$ 26,000		
Buildings and equipment	90,000		
Less: Accumulated depreciation	38,000		
Net fixed assets	$ 78,000		
Total assets	$150,000		

[a]The firm's 3,000 outstanding shares of common stock closed 2006 at a price of $25 per share.

a. Use the preceding financial statements to complete the following table. Assume that the industry averages given in the table are applicable for both 2005 and 2006.

b. Analyze Access Corporation's financial condition as it relates to (1) liquidity, (2) activity, (3) debt, (4) profitability, and (5) market value. Summarize the company's overall financial condition.

Access Corporation's Financial Ratios

	Industry Average	Actual Ratio 2005	Actual Ratio 2006
Current ratio	1.80	1.84	______
Quick (acid-test) ratio	0.70	0.78	______
Inventory turnover	2.50	2.59	______
Average collection period[a]	37 days	36 days	______
Average payment period[a]	72 days	78 days	______
Debt-to-equity ratio	50%	51%	______
Times interest earned ratio	3.8	4.0	______
Gross profit margin	38%	40%	______
Net profit margin	3.5%	3.6%	______
Return on total assets (*ROA*)	4.0%	4.0%	______
Return on common equity (*ROE*)	9.5%	8.0%	______
Market/book (M/B) ratio	1.1	1.2	______

[a] Based on a 365-day year and on end-of-year figures.

P2-11. Given the following financial statements, historical ratios, and industry averages, calculate the UG Company's financial ratios for 2006. Analyze its overall financial situation both in comparison with industry averages and over the period 2004–2006. Break your analysis into an evaluation of the firm's liquidity, activity, debt, profitability, and market value.

UG Company Income Statement for the Year Ended December 31, 2006

Sales revenue		$10,000,000
Less: Cost of goods sold[a]		7,500,000
Gross profit		$ 2,500,000
Less: Operating expenses		
Selling expense	$300,000	
General and administrative expense	650,000	
Lease expense	50,000	
Depreciation expense	200,000	
Total operating expense		1,200,000
Operating profit (*EBIT*)		$ 1,300,000
Less: Interest expense		200,000
Net profits before taxes		$ 1,100,000
Less: Taxes (rate = 40%)		440,000
Net profits after taxes		$ 660,000
Less: Preferred stock dividends		50,000
Earnings available for common stockholders		$ 610,000
Earnings per share (*EPS*)		$ 3.05

[a] Annual credit purchases of $6.2 million were made during the year.

UG Company Balance Sheet as of December 31, 2006

Assets		Liabilities and Stockholders' Equity	
Current assets		Current liabilities	
Cash	$ 200,000	Accounts payable	$ 900,000
Marketable securities	50,000	Notes payable	200,000
Accounts receivable	800,000	Accruals	100,000
Inventories	950,000	Total current liabilities	$ 1,200,000
Total current assets	$ 2,000,000	Long-term debt (including financial leases)	$ 3,000,000
Gross fixed assets	$12,000,000	Stockholders' equity	
Less: Accumulated depreciation	3,000,000	Preferred stock (25,000 shares, $2 dividend)	$ 1,000,000
Net fixed assets	$ 9,000,000	Common stock (200,000 shares, $3 par)[a]	600,000
Other assets	$ 1,000,000	Paid-in capital in excess of par	5,200,000
Total assets	$12,000,000	Retained earnings	1,000,000
		Total stockholders' equity	$ 7,800,000
		Total liabilities and stockholders' equity	$12,000,000

[a] On December 31, 2006, [a] the firm's common stock closed at $27.50.

Historical and Industry Average Ratios for UG Company

Ratio	Actual 2004	Actual 2005	Industry Average 2006
Current ratio	1.40	1.55	1.85
Quick (acid-test) ratio	1.00	0.92	1.05
Inventory turnover	9.52	9.21	8.60
Average collection period[a]	45.0 days	36.4 days	35.0 days
Average payment period[a]	58.5 days	60.8 days	45.8 days
Fixed asset turnover	1.08	1.05	1.07
Total asset turnover	0.74	0.80	0.74
Debt ratio	0.20	0.20	0.30
Debt-to-equity ratio	0.25	0.27	0.39
Times interest earned ratio	8.2	7.3	8.0
Gross profit margin	0.30	0.27	0.25
Operating profit margin	0.12	0.12	0.10
Net profit margin	0.067	0.067	0.058
Return on total assets (*ROA*)	0.049	0.054	0.043
Return on common equity (*ROE*)	0.066	0.073	0.072
Earnings per share (*EPS*)	$ 1.75	$ 2.20	$ 1.50
Price/earnings (P/E) ratio	12.0	10.5	11.2
Market/book (M/B) ratio	1.20	1.05	1.10

[a] Based on a 365-day year and on end-of-year figures.

P2-12. Choose a company that you would like to analyze and obtain its financial statements. Now, select another firm from the same industry and obtain its financial data from the Internet. Perform a complete ratio analysis on each firm. How well does your selected company compare with its industry peer? Which components of your firm's *ROE* are superior, and which are inferior?

SMART SOLUTIONS

See the problem and solution explained step-by-step at SMARTFinance

Corporate Taxes

P2-13. Thomsonetics, Inc., a rapidly growing early-stage technology company, had the pretax income noted below, for calendar years 2004–2006. The firm was subject to corporate taxes consistent with the rates shown in Table 2.6.

Year	Pretax Income
2004	$ 87,000
2005	$312,000
2006	$760,000

a. Calculate Thomsonetics' tax liability for each year 2004, 2005, and 2006.
b. What was the firm's *average tax rate* in each year?
c. What was the firm's *marginal tax rate* in each year?
d. If in addition to its ordinary pretax income, Thomsonetics realized a capital gain of $80,000 during calendar year 2005, what effect would this have on its tax liability, average tax rate, and marginal tax rate in 2005?
e. Which tax rate—average or marginal—should Thomsonetics use in decision making? Why?

P2-14. Trish Foods, Inc. had pretax ordinary corporate income during 2006 of $2.7 million. In addition, during the year Trish sold a group of nondepreciable business assets that it had purchased for $980,000 three years earlier. Because the assets were not depreciable, their book value at the time of sale was also $980,000. The firm pays corporate income taxes at the rates shown in Table 2.6.

a. Calculate Trish's 2006 tax liability, average tax rate, and marginal tax rate, assuming the group of assets was sold for $1,150,000.
b. Calculate Trish's 2006 tax liability, average tax rate, and marginal tax rate, assuming the group of assets was sold for $890,000.
c. Compare, contrast, and discuss your findings in parts (a) and (b).

THOMSON ONE | Business School Edition

Access financial information from the Thomson ONE – Business School Edition Web site for the following problem(s). Go to http://tobsefin.swlearning.com/. If you have already registered your access serial number and have a username and password, click **Enter**. Otherwise, click **Register** and follow the instructions to create a username and password. Register your access serial number and then click **Enter** on the aforementioned Web site. When you click Enter, you will be prompted for your username and password (please remember that the password is case sensitive). Enter them in the respective boxes and then click **OK** (or hit **Enter**). From the ensuing page, click **Click Here to Access Thomson ONE – Business School Edition Now!** This opens up a new window that gives you access to the Thomson ONE – Business School Edition database. You can retrieve a company's financial information by entering its ticker symbol (provided for each company in the problem(s)) in the box below "Name/Symbol/Key." For further instructions on using the Thomson ONE – Business School Edition database, please refer to "A Guide for Using Thomson ONE – Business School Edition."

P2-15. Compare the profitability of Delta Airlines (ticker: U:DAL) and Continental Airlines (U:CAL) for the latest year. Using the *return on common equity (ROE)*, determine which firm is more profitable. Use the *DuPont system* to determine what drives the difference in the profitability of the two.

P2-16. Analyze the financial condition of Oshkosh B'Gosh (ticker: GOSHA) over the last five years. Use financial ratios that relate to its liquidity, activity, debt, profitability, and market value. In which areas has the company improved, and in which areas has the company's financial position worsened?

Since these exercises depend upon real-time data, your answers will change continuously depending upon when you access the Internet to download your data.

MINICASE

Financial Statement and Cash Flow Analysis

You have been hired by First Citizens Bank as a financial analyst. One of your first job assignments is to analyze the present financial condition of Bradley Stores, Incorporated. You are provided with the following 2006 balance sheet and income statement information for Bradley Stores. In addition, you are told that Bradley Stores has 10,000,000 shares of common stock outstanding, currently trading at $9 per share, and has made annual purchases of $210,000,000.

Your assignment calls for you to calculate certain financial ratios and to compare these calculated ratios with the industry average ratios that are provided. You are also told to base your analysis on five categories of ratios: (a) liquidity ratios, (b) activity ratios, (c) debt ratios, (d) profitability ratios, and (e) market ratios.

Balance Sheet (in 000s)

Cash	$ 5,000	Accounts Payable	$ 15,000
Accounts Receivable	20,000	Notes Payable	20,000
Inventory	40,000	Total Current Liabilities	$ 35,000
Total Current Assets	$ 65,000	Long-Term Debt	$100,000
Net Fixed Assets	135,000	Stockholder Equity	$ 65,000
Total Assets	$200,000	Total Liabilities and Equity	$200,000

Income Statement (in 000s)

Net Sales (all credit)	$300,000
Less: Cost of Goods Sold	250,000
Earnings Before Interest and Taxes	$ 50,000
Less: Interest	40,000
Earnings Before Taxes	$ 10,000
Less: Taxes (40%)	4,000
Net Income	$ 6,000

Industry Averages for Key Ratios

Net Profit Margin	6.4%
Average Collection Period (365 days)	30 days
Debt Ratio	50%
P/E Ratio	23
Inventory Turnover Ratio	12.0
ROE	18%
Average Payment Period (365 days)	20 days
Times Interest Earned Ratio	8.5
Total Asset Turnover	1.4
Current Ratio	1.5
Assets-to-Equity Ratio	2.0
ROA	9%
Quick Ratio	1.25
Fixed Asset Turnover Ratio	1.8

ASSIGNMENT

Use the following guidelines to complete this job assignment. First, identify which ratios you need to use to evaluate Bradley Stores in terms of its (a) liquidity position, (b) business activity, (c) debt position, (d) profitability, and (e) market comparability. Next, calculate these ratios. Finally, compare these ratios to the industry average ratios provided in the problem and answer the following questions.

1. Based on the provided industry average information, discuss Bradley Stores, Inc.'s liquidity position. Discuss specific areas in which Bradley compares positively and negatively with the overall industry.
2. Based on the provided industry average information, what do Bradley Stores, Inc.'s activity ratios tell you? Discuss specific areas in which Bradley compares positively and negatively with the overall industry.
3. Based on the provided industry average information, discuss Bradley Stores, Inc.'s debt position. Discuss specific areas in which Bradley compares positively and negatively with the overall industry.
4. Based on the provided industry average information, discuss Bradley Stores, Inc.'s profitability position. As part of this investigation of firm profitability, include a DuPont analysis. Discuss specific areas in which Bradley compares positively and negatively with the overall industry.

MINICASE

Financial Statement and Cash Flow Analysis (continued)

5. Based on the provided industry average information, how is Bradley Stores, Inc. viewed in the marketplace? Discuss specific areas in which Bradley compares positively and negatively with the overall industry.

6. Overall, what are Bradley's strong and weak points? Knowing that your boss will approve new loans only to companies in a better-than-average financial position, what is your final recommendation (approval or denial of loan)?

Smart *Excel* Appendix

Use the Smart *Excel* spreadsheets and animated tutorials at http://smartfinance.swlearning.com.

Appendix Contents

EXCEL PREREQUISITES

You need to be familiar with the following *Excel* features to use this appendix:

- Creating formulas in *Excel*
- Mathematical operators
- Order of mathematical operations
- Cell formats
- Relative, absolute, and mixed cell references

If this is new to you, be sure to complete the ***Excel Prereqs*** tab of the Chapter 2 *Excel* file before proceeding.

BUILDING FINANCIAL STATEMENTS IN *EXCEL*

Problem: You must perform a financial analysis of Global Petroleum Corporation. Your first step is to build the balance sheet, income statement, statement of retained earnings, and statement of cash flows for Global Petroleum Corporation, in *Excel*. Use the firm information provided in the text tables 2.1, 2.2, 2.3, and 2.5.

To build historical financial statements in *Excel*, follow these steps:

1. Gather the historical financial statements.
2. In a blank *Excel* file, enter (or import) account labels.
3. Enter (or import) account values but not subtotals and totals.
4. Format the cells, as desired, to display appropriate format (dollars, percent, etc.). See ***Excel Prereqs*** tab for instructions.
5. Build a formula for each subtotal and total. Why? To ensure that there are no errors in your account values. Then, check your totals against the historical information.
6. Apply final formatting (lines under subtotals and totals, dollar signs, etc.), as desired.

Approach: Create historic financial statements in *Excel*, using formulas for all subtotals and totals.

Open the Chapter 2 *Excel* file located at the Smart Finance Web site. Open the ***Build finstats*** tab.

Apply the above steps to Global Petroleum to create the balance sheet.

1. Available in the text tables 2.1, 2.2, 2.3, 2.5
2. Account labels have already been entered.
3. Begin with the balance sheet. Enter all account values for current assets. DO NOT enter the current asset subtotal values.
4. If necessary, format the cells. *Save time*: select a group of cells that should have similar formatting and format them all at once.
5. Build a formula to subtotal the current asset values in 2006. Your formula should be:

   =sum(D15:D19)

   Copy the formula across to 2005. Check your results against the historical information in Table 2.1.
6. Apply formatting, as desired (lines under subtotals and totals, dollar signs, etc.).

Repeat these steps for the rest of the balance sheet. Make sure you match the historical balances from Table 2.1.

Apply the steps to complete the income statement. *Careful: Because values are entered in millions of dollars, enter the number of shares in millions.*

Apply the steps to complete the statement of retained earnings. Complete 2006 only. Your ending balance of retained earnings must match the balance sheet value.

Apply the steps to complete the statement of cash flows for 2006. The net increase in cash and marketable securities must equal the change in the account value over the year.

Check your results against the solution provided in the *Excel* file. You can also create the cash flow statement directly from the balance sheet and income statement by creating formulas to pull through values (like net income and depreciation from the income statement) and to pick up changes in account values (like accounts receivable, inventory, fixed assets, accounts payable, and long-term debt) from the balance sheet.

Once you have built the financial statements in Excel, *financial analysis is straightforward and efficient.*

COMMON SIZE THE BALANCE SHEET AND INCOME STATEMENT

Problem: Continue your financial analysis of Global Petroleum Corporation by common sizing the balance sheet and income statement you created.

Use common-size financial statements to evaluate a firm's performance over time and to compare with firms of different sizes. A common-size balance sheet restates the balance sheet to show each account as a percent of total assets rather than as a dollar value. A common-size income statement restates the income statement to show each account as a percent of revenues rather than as a dollar value.

Approach: Common size the balance sheet and income statement created above.

Open the Chapter 2 *Excel* file located at the Smart Finance Web site. Open the *CommonSize* tab.

Start by common sizing the balance sheet. Begin with Cash and cash equivalents in 2006, cell G15. You must create a formula to divide cash by total assets.

Tip: If you set up your formula carefully, you can create a single formula that can be copied across to 2005 and down through the entire balance sheet. You will need to use a mixed reference.

The formula in cell G15 should be
=D15/D$28

This formula locks row 28 so that as you copy your formula down, each account is still divided by total assets. By leaving the column "unlocked," you can copy accurately across to 2005.

Check: If you are correct you will get 100 percent in 2006 and 2005 for total assets and total liabilities and stockholders' equity.

Clean up: The formula above allows you to common size quickly, but you are left with zeroes in rows that were blank. Now delete the zeros, resulting in blank rows such as rows 21 and 22.

After deleting the zeroes in the blank rows, this is part of the solution:

	Solution	
Assets	*2006*	*2005*
Current assets		
Cash and cash equivalents	5%	3%
Marketable securities	0	0
Accounts receivable	17	14
Inventories	6	6
Other (mostly prepaid expenses)	2	2
Total current assets	30	25

Assets	Solution 2006	2005
Fixed assets		
Gross property, plant, and equipment	103%	109%
Less: Accumulated depreciation	–41	–40
Net property, plant, and equipment	62%	69%
Intangible assets and others	8	6
Net fixed assets	70%	75%
Total assets	100%	100%

Apply it

What does the common-size balance sheet tell you? Accounts receivable is a greater percent of total assets in 2006 than in 2005, whereas net property, plant, and equipment is a lower percent of total assets.

Next, common size the income statement. Start with 2006 Revenues and create a single formula that allows you to copy across to 2005 and down throughout the income statement.

The formula in cell G58 should be

=D58/D$58

Copy across for 2005 and down throughout the income statement.

Apply it

What does the common-size income statement sheet tell you? Cost of goods sold rose from 62 percent of sales in 2005 to 66 percent of sales in 2006. Operating expenses fell from 17 percent of sales in 2005 to 12 percent of sales in 2006. While the gross profit margin deteriorated, the operating and net profit margins improved.

CALCULATE FINANCIAL RATIOS

Problem: Complete your financial analysis of Global Petroleum Corporation by calculating the key financial ratios introduced in the chapter.

Approach: Use the balance sheet and income statement created above to calculate financial ratios.

Open the Chapter 2 *Excel* file located at the Smart Finance Web site. Open the Ratios tab.

This tab includes the completed balance sheet and income statements to facilitate ratio calculation. The ratio labels are already entered.

Begin with the liquidity ratios. Create a formula to calculate the current ratio in 2006. It is

=G20/G35

Your result should be 1.10.

Tip: You may have to reformat cells so that ratios appear properly.

Tip: To save time, DO NOT copy the current ratio across for 2005 now. Complete all the 2006 ratios and then, select and copy all the ratios across for 2005 at once.

Solutions to sample ratios appear below. Complete solutions are provided in the file.

Profitability ratios	2006	2005
Gross profit margin	33.7%	38.2%
Operating profit margin	11.9%	8.4%
Net profit margin	7.4%	5.1%
Earnings per share	$5.29	$2.52
Return on total assets	9.9%	5.6%
Return on common equity	22.1%	12.5%

Apply it

What do the financial ratios tell you? While the gross profit margin deteriorated, the operating and net profit margins improved. Return on total assets and return on common equity improved very significantly, and the earnings per share rose dramatically.

Present Value

OPENING FOCUS

Why Is a Lottery's "$315 Million Jackpot" Really Worth Only $170 Million?

The Powerball lottery is a game of chance in which participants pay one dollar for a lottery ticket, select six numbers, and then hope that the numbers selected will be picked in a random, televised drawing. The lottery is operated in the interests of twenty-three participating U.S. state governments, and more than half of the total proceeds from ticket sales flow into the states' operating budgets. Remaining proceeds cover expenses and pay off lucky winners.

Even though the odds against winning these state-sponsored lotteries are astronomically high (so high, in fact, that cynics call the lottery "a tax on the stupid"), the lotteries are very popular. The demand for lottery tickets rises to a near frenzy if several weeks pass without a winner. The jackpot continues to grow until someone finally selects all six winning numbers. The last full week of December 2002 was such a period; after a week of near-record sales, the Powerball jackpot hit dizzying heights. Despite odds of more than 120,000,000:1 against winning, people dreamed of hitting the Christmas-day jackpot, which would pay them thirty annual checks of $10.5 million each. Based on this stream of payouts, Powerball officials touted their jackpot's value at $315 million (30 payments × $10.5 million = $315 million).

What few people noticed about this jackpot was the winner's option to exchange this stream of annual cash flows—which we define in this chapter as a thirty-year annuity due—for a single lump-sum payment of $170 million immediately. Why would anyone want to exchange a $315 million jackpot for a mere $170 million payment? Because the winner receives $170 million right away rather than waiting thirty years for lottery officials to dribble out the entire jackpot. With $170 million in hand, the winner can invest the money and earn interest on it. Having $170 million today is more valuable than having it at some point in the future, but how much more valuable? Does the opportunity to earn interest mean that $170 million today is worth more than $315 million spread over thirty years?

The answer depends on the interest rate. To compare the $170 million lump sum payment with the $315 million stream of payments, we must calculate the "present value" of the stream. For example, suppose an investor could earn 5 percent interest on a relatively safe investment such as U.S. government bonds. If that person invested $10 million today at 5 percent interest, he would have $10.5 million one year later. Thus, we can say that $10 million is the present value of a $10.5 million payment that arrives one year in the future. Similarly, by investing $8.23 million at 5 percent today, an investor would have $10.5 million after five years. Thus, $8.23 million is the present value of a $10.5 million payment arriving in five years.

Applying this process to the entire cash flow stream, we can determine that, if the interest rate on an alternative investment is 5 percent, the present value of thirty annual $10.5 million payments (with the first payment arriving immediately) equals $169.5 million. Phrased differently, any investor who can earn 5 percent on low-risk investments should be almost indifferent to the difference between the $170 million lump sum and the $315 million jackpot. At interest rates above 5 percent, the lump sum becomes more attractive, whereas at interest rates below 5 percent, the stream of annual payments is more appealing. ■

LEARNING OBJECTIVES

After studying this chapter you should be able to:

- Understand how to find the future value of a lump sum invested today;
- Calculate the present value of a lump sum to be received in the future;
- Find the future value of cash flow streams, both mixed streams and annuities;
- Determine the present value of future cash flow streams, including mixed streams, annuities, and perpetuities;
- Apply time-value techniques to compounding more frequently than annually, stated versus effective annual interest rates, and deposits needed to accumulate a future sum;
- Use time-value techniques to find implied interest or growth rates for lump sums, annuities, and mixed streams, and an unknown number of periods for both lump sums and annuities.

Finance is primarily concerned with the *voluntary transfer of wealth* between individuals and across time. The transfer of wealth *between individuals*, which occurs in financial markets, can involve creditors lending money to borrowers in exchange for a promise of repayment with interest, or investors purchasing an ownership interest in a new business venture in exchange for a share in the venture's profits. Likewise, transferring wealth *across time* can take two forms. The first involves determining what the value of an investment made today will be worth at a specific future date, and the second determines the value today of a cash flow to be received at a specific date in the future. We refer to the first such computation as determining the *future value* and the second as determining the *present value*.

Because these wealth transfers are voluntary "trades" of cash today for contractual promises of greater payments in the future, the ability to execute these trades makes all parties better off. The opportunity to borrow and lend using financial markets helps both savers and borrowers. By lending or investing money at a given interest rate, a saver can increase consumption in the future by foregoing some consumption today. The opportunity to receive cash today in exchange for a promise to repay that cash, plus interest, in the future also makes borrowers better off. These borrowers might be individuals, such as new college graduates, who want to obtain financing for new cars and are willing to commit a portion of their future incomes to paying off these loans. Alternatively, "borrowers" might be entrepreneurs with great business plans and managerial talents, who need equity financing to turn their dreams into solid businesses. Perhaps the most relevant example of how borrowing can improve personal welfare is to consider the bargain students make with lenders. Students borrow (often sizable) sums of money to finance their educations, and the knowledge they gain increases their lifetime earnings potential by more than enough to repay the debt. In sum, financial markets improve the welfare of savers, entrepreneurs, and ordinary citizens by allowing borrowing, lending, and investing to occur efficiently.

Transfers of wealth occur between firms and investors just as they do between individuals. Because most decisions that financial managers face involve trading off costs and benefits that are spread out over time, managers need a framework for evaluating cash inflows and outflows that occur at different times. Adjusting for differences in the timing of benefits and costs is a major *measurement challenge*. This challenge is addressed using the **time value of money** techniques, which explicitly recognize that a dollar received today is more valuable than a dollar received in the future, presented in this chapter. Time value is one of the most important concepts in finance.

time value of money
The financial concept that recognizes the fact that a dollar received today is more valuable than a dollar received in the future.

Here we consider several objectives regarding the time value of money. The first is to show how to compute future values, beginning with the simple process of computing the future value of a lump sum and then examining increasingly complex cash flow streams. Second, we demonstrate how to compute the present values of future cash flows, again beginning with a lump sum and then examining streams of future cash flows. Third, we present some special applications of time-value techniques that financial managers commonly employ. The chapter concludes with several additional applications of time-value techniques.

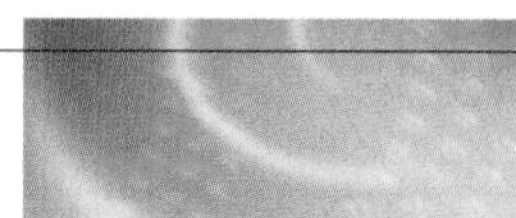

3.1 FUTURE VALUE OF A LUMP SUM

The Concept of Future Value

By consuming less than 100 percent of their present incomes, investors can earn interest on their savings and thereby enjoy higher future consumption. A person who invests $100 today at 5 percent interest expects to receive $105 in one year, representing $5 interest plus the return of the $100 originally invested. In this example, we say that $105 is the **future value** of $100 invested at 5 percent for one year.

future value
The value of an investment made today measured at a specific future date using *compound interest*.

We can calculate the future value of an investment made today by applying compound interest over a specified period of time. **Compound interest** is interest earned both on the principal amount and on the interest earned in previous periods. **Principal** refers to the amount of money on which the interest is paid. To demonstrate these concepts, assume that you have the opportunity to deposit $100 into a risk-free account paying 5 percent annual interest. For simplicity, we assume that interest compounds annually, though in later sections, we show how to compute future values, using semiannual, quarterly, and even continuous compounding periods.

compound interest
Interest earned both on the principal amount and on the interest earned in previous periods.

principal
The amount of money on which interest is paid.

At the end of one year, your account will have a balance of \$105. This sum represents the initial principal of \$100 plus 5 percent (\$5) in interest. This future value is calculated as follows:

$$\text{Future value at end of year } 1 = \$100 \times (1 + 0.05) = \$105$$

If you leave this money in the account for another year, the investment will pay interest at the rate of 5 percent on the new principal of \$105. In other words, you will receive 5 percent interest both on the original principal of \$100 and on the first year's interest of \$5. At the end of this second year, there will be \$110.25 in your account, representing the principal at the beginning of year 2 (\$105) plus 5 percent of the \$105, or \$5.25, in interest. The future value at the end of the second year is computed as follows:

$$\text{Future value at end of year } 2 = \$105 \times (1 + 0.05) = \$110.25$$

Substituting the first equation into the second one yields the following:

$$\begin{aligned}\text{Future value at end of year } 2 &= \$100 \times (1 + 0.05) \times (1 + 0.05)\\ &= \$100 \times (1 + 0.05)^2\\ &= \$110.25\end{aligned}$$

Therefore, \$100 deposited at 5 percent compound annual interest will be worth \$110.25 at the end of two years. This represents two years' interest of 5 percent paid on the original \$100 principal, plus 5 percent paid on the first year's \$5 interest payment, or \$0.25. It is important to recognize the difference in future values that results from compound versus simple interest. **Simple interest** is interest paid only on the initial principal of an investment, not on the interest that accrues in earlier periods. If the investment in our previous example pays 5 percent simple interest, then the future value in any year equals \$100 plus the product of the annual interest payment and the number of years. In this case, its value will be only \$110 at the end of year 2 [\$100 + (2 × \$5)], \$115 at the end of year 3 [\$100 + (3 × \$5)], \$120 at the end of year 4 [\$100 + (4 × \$5)], and so on. Although the difference between a \$110 account balance after two years at simple interest and \$110.25 at compound interest seems rather trivial, the difference grows exponentially over time. For example, with simple interest this account would have a balance of \$250 after thirty years [\$100 + (30 × \$5)], but with compound interest the account balance would be \$432.19 in thirty years [$\$100 \times (1 + 0.05)^{30}$].

simple interest
Interest paid only on the initial principal of an investment, not on the interest that accrues in earlier periods.

The Equation for Future Value

Financial analysts routinely use compound interest. Throughout this book, we generally use compound rather than simple interest. Equation 3.1 gives the general formula for calculating the future value, at the end of *n* years, of a lump sum invested today at an annual interest rate of *r* percent:

$$FV = PV \times (1 + r)^n \qquad \text{(Eq. 3.1)}$$

where FV = future value of an investment,
PV = present value of an investment,
r = annual rate of interest paid,
n = number of years the present value is left on deposit.

time line
A graphical presentation of cash flows over a given period of time.

The following Applying the Model illustrates an application of this equation by showing how you can use the concept of future value to evaluate an investment in a bank certificate of deposit (CD).

APPLYING THE MODEL

In addition to having the opportunity to invest $100 in an open-ended savings account paying 5 percent annual interest, you also have the chance to invest $100 in a CD paying 6 percent annual interest. The difference is that you must leave your money in the CD for five years to earn the full 6 percent interest. If you withdraw the money early, you will face a substantial penalty. You would like to know how much your $100 CD investment will be worth at the end of five years. Substituting $PV = \$100$, $r = 0.06$, and $n = 5$ into Equation 3.1 gives the future value at the end of year 5, expressed as FV:

$$FV = \$100 \times (1+0.06)^5 = \$100 \times (1.3382) = \$133.82$$

Your CD will have an account balance of $133.82 at the end of the fifth year. This is shown on a **time line**, which is a graphical presentation of cash flows over a given period of time, at the top of Figure 3.1.

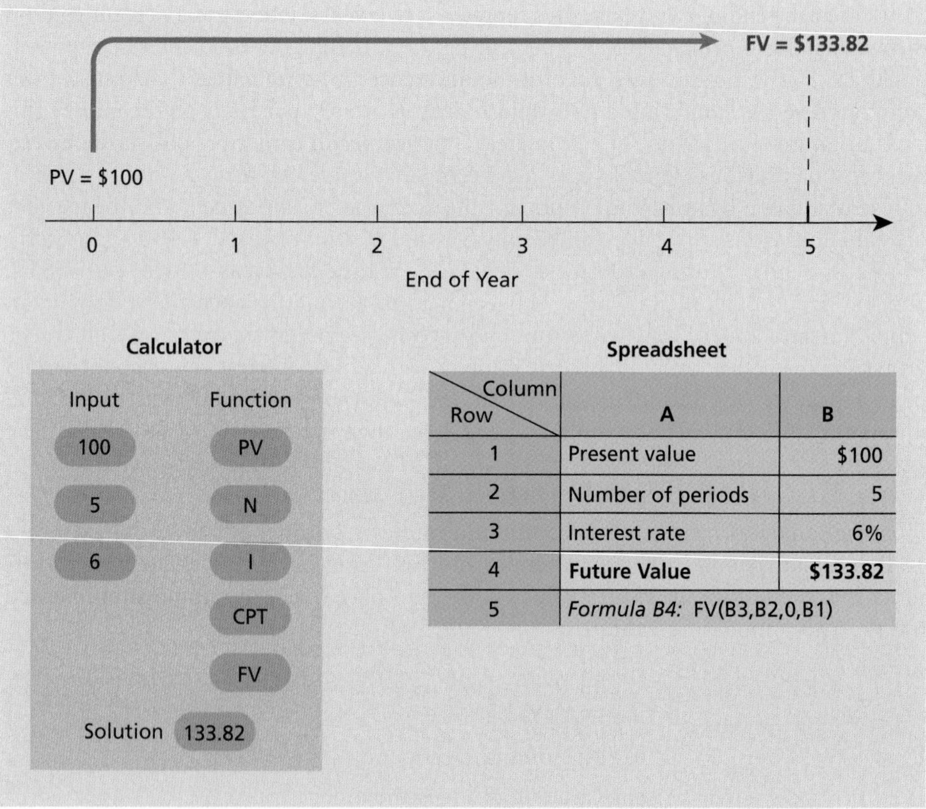

Row \ Column	A	B
1	Present value	$100
2	Number of periods	5
3	Interest rate	6%
4	**Future Value**	**$133.82**
5	*Formula B4:* FV(B3,B2,0,B1)	

Figure 3.1
Time Line for $100 Invested for Five Years at 6% Annual Interest

This figure illustrates how $100 grows to $133.82 over five years if the annual interest rate is 6%. The time line at the top shows the initial deposit as well as the accumulated value after 5 years. The lower left portion of the figure shows how to calculate the future value using a TI BAII PLUS calculator. Keystrokes will vary from one calculator model to another. The lower right portion of the figure shows how to calculate the future value using Excel. *See this chapter's appendix for more instructions on using* Excel *to solve time value of money problems.*

There are three popular methods for simplifying future-value calculations. One method is to use a future-value factor (*FVF*) table, such as Table A1 in Appendix A. Such a table provides future-value factors ($FVF_{r\%,n}$) for various interest rates (r) and holding periods (n). Table 3.1 reproduces a portion of Table A1 from the appendix[1]. To find the future-value factor for 6 percent interest and a five-year holding period ($FVF_{6\%,5}$), we simply move across the interest rates on the horizontal axis of the table until we reach the column labeled "6%," and then move vertically down this column until we find the row labeled "Period 5." We find that $FVF_{6\%,5}$ is equal to 1.338, and this is the number we would multiply by $100 to compute FV_5. Not surprisingly, this matches the previous FV_5 = $133.80, except for a small rounding difference.

A second method is to use a financial calculator.[2] To compute *FV* in the example, you would simply input the number of years (5), the interest rate (6%), and the amount of the initial deposit ($100), and then calculate the future value of $133.82. A simplified financial calculator keypad, showing the keystrokes and the final value for this calculation for the TI BAII PLUS calculator, is shown below the

Table 3.1
Format of a Future-Value Factor (*FVF*) Table

	Interest Rate (r)					
Period	1%	2%	3%	4%	5%	6%
1	1.010	1.020	1.030	1.040	1.050	1.060
2	1.020	1.040	1.061	1.082	1.102	1.124
3	1.030	1.061	1.093	1.125	1.158	1.191
4	1.041	1.082	1.126	1.170	1.216	1.262
5	1.051	1.104	1.159	1.217	1.276	1.338
6	1.062	1.126	1.194	1.265	1.340	1.419
7	1.072	1.149	1.230	1.316	1.407	1.504

1. A complete table of future-value factors is included in Appendix A of this text. Similarly, complete tables of other factors excerpted in this chapter are included in Appendix A.

2. Before using your calculator to make time value of money calculations, make sure it is properly set up. Check the manual that accompanies your calculator to reset it as prescribed here. The following three settings are important:
Setting 1: Most calculators are preset to recognize *monthly* payments, i.e., twelve payments per year. Because in corporate finance we most often work with *annual* payments, *your calculator needs to be set to one payment per year.*
Setting 2: Most calculators are preset to the *END mode,* which means that it recognizes cash flows as occurring at the end of the period, typically a year. *Make sure your calculator is correctly set to END mode.*
Setting 3: Most calculators are preset to show two decimal places to the right of the decimal point. To improve precision, it is recommended that you *reformat your calculator to show four decimal places to the right of the decimal point.*
Three additional points about your calculator should be noted:
Point 1: *Always clear all registers in your calculator before beginning a new set of computations.* This will avoid the inclusion of old data in a new calculation.
Point 2: *The order in which you input values into your calculator doesn't matter for basic present and future value calculations.* The order shown in the most basic calculator demonstrations in this text was chosen for convenience and personal preference. Note that order does matter in some of the more sophisticated calculations demonstrated later in this chapter.
Point 3: *Ignore the minus sign that will frequently precede your solution.* Technically, your calculator differentiates inflows (positive values) and outflows (negative values) by preceding outflows with a minus sign. This means that the present value and future value will have opposite signs. If you input one of these values as a positive number and solve for the other value, it will be preceded by a negative sign, which you can ignore. Sign specification matters only when both the present and future values are inputs, which is explained later in this chapter.

time line in Figure 3.1.[3] The third method of simplifying time-value calculations involves using a financial spreadsheet such as *Excel.* The bottom of Figure 3.1 shows a simplified spreadsheet illustrating the key inputs, the cell formula for the output, and the future value of $133.82.[4]

A Graphic View of Future Value

Remember that we measure future value at the *end* of the given period. Figure 3.2 shows how quickly a $1.00 investment grows over time at various annual interest rates. The figure shows that (1) the higher the interest rate, the higher the future value, and (2) the longer the period of time, the higher the future value. Note that for an interest rate of 0 percent, the future value always equals the present value ($1), but for any interest rate greater than zero, the future value is greater than $1.

CONCEPT REVIEW QUESTIONS

1. Will a deposit made into an account paying *compound interest* (assuming compounding occurs once per year) yield a higher future value after one period than an equal-sized deposit in an account paying *simple interest*? What about future values for investments held longer than one period?

2. How would (a) a *decrease* in the interest rate or (b) an *increase* in the holding period of a deposit affect its future value? Why?

Figure 3.2
The Power of Compound Interest: Future Value of $1 Invested at Different Annual Interest Rates

The figure shows that the future value of $100 increases over time as long as the interest rate is greater than 0%. Notice that each line gets steeper the longer the money remains invested. This is the power of compound interest. For the same reason, the future value grows faster at higher interest rates. Observe how the lines get steeper as the interest rates increase.

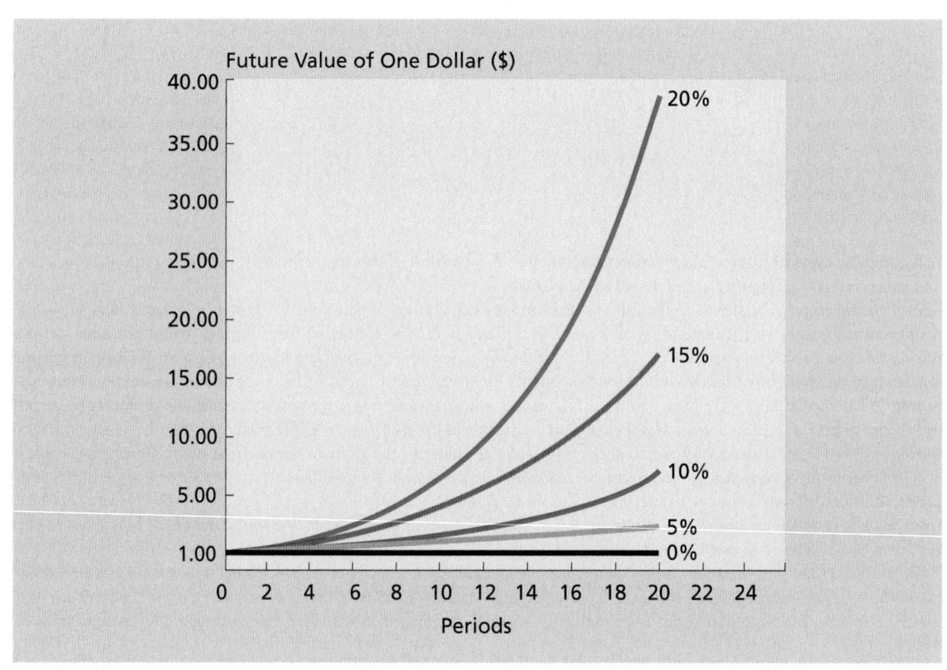

[3] Calculator keystrokes using the same keypad are included with all time lines in this chapter.

[4] The format of *Excel's* future-value formula is "=*FV(rate,nper,pmt,pv,type)*", where: *rate* = interest rate per period; *nper* = number of periods; *pmt* = the size of payments made each year in an annuity (in this case, set to 0 because we are calculating the future value of a lump sum rather than of an annuity); *pv* = the present-value or lump-sum amount; *type* = a 0/1 variable (omitted in our example) that indicates whether payments occur at the beginning or at the end of each period.

If you enter this formula in *Excel,* it will generate the answer, –133.82. You can force Excel to produce a positive future value simply by inserting a minus sign in front of the *FV* equation. (*Note*: The appendix to this chapter provides instructions for solving time value of money problems in *Excel.*)

COMPARATIVE CORPORATE FINANCE

Save Money? Not Me; I'm an American

This chapter shows how money grows over time as it earns interest. But before people can earn interest on their money, they have to save some money to invest. But just how different are the savings patterns of citizens in the major industrialized countries? As the chart below makes clear, personal savings rates are strikingly different both between countries and within the same country at different points in time. Italy has the highest national savings rate (16%) among rich countries in 2002, followed by Belgium, France, and the Czech Republic. The ranking was somewhat different in 1992; while Italy was also the thriftiest rich country then, with a savings rate exceeding 25%, South Korean citizens had the second highest savings rate of 23 percent. Although economists are divided about the determinants of varying national savings rates, systematic and enduring patterns can be observed and it seems clear that economic, demographic, and cultural factors all play important roles in explaining the international differences.

The chart below also shows that savings rates have declined between 1992 and 2002 for fifteen of the twenty countries surveyed. For no country is this more true than the United States. The U.S. savings rate was 8.7 percent in 1992; by 2002 the savings rate of American households had declined to 3.7 percent (and was actually *negative* during 2001). What is going on here? Why did people stop saving during a decade that encompassed the longest economic expansion in U.S. history and that saw the stock market more than triple in value? An even more perplexing question is: how did American corporations finance the $8.5 trillion or so of capital investments they made between 1992 and 2002? There are several partial explanations for this strange mix of generally robust economic health and the seeming extravagance of U.S. citizens. In part, the prosperity of the 1990s reduced the need for people to save as much out of their income, since the rising values of their homes and stock portfolios made it possible to finance a given standard of living in retirement with less foregone consumption today. Record inflows of foreign capital also supported the investment programs of U.S. corporations, as did the U.S government's switch from budget deficit to surplus during the late 1990s (since reversed back to large deficits). These are all only partial answers, however. In truth, economists really do not understand why the U.S. savings rate has fallen so low or why the consequences of this decline have thus far been so muted.

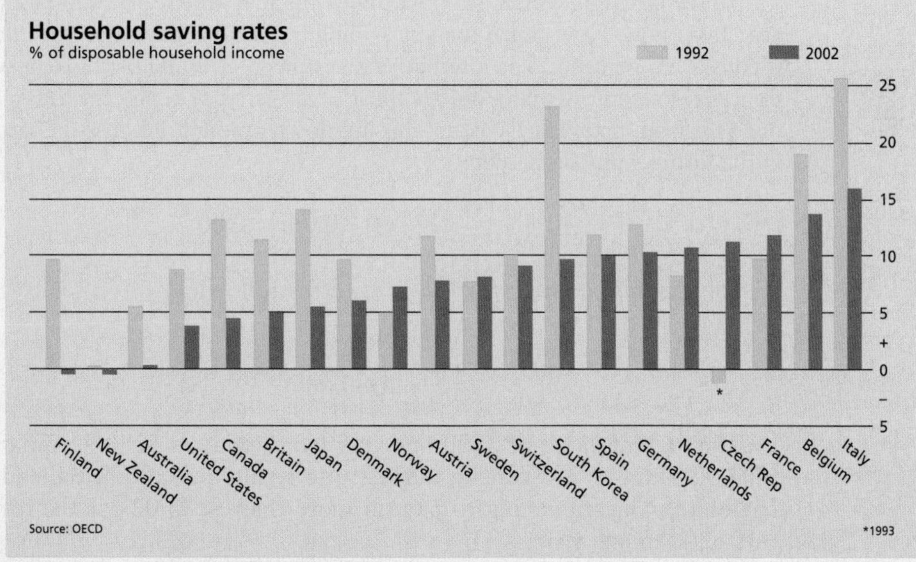

Source: "Household Savings Rates," The Economist (July 2003), downloaded from http://www.economist.com.

3.2 PRESENT VALUE OF A LUMP SUM

present value
The value today of a cash flow to be received at a specific date in the future, assuming an opportunity to earn interest at a specified rate.

We have examined how to project the amount of cash that builds over time as an initial investment earns interest. Now we want to reverse that focus and ask what an investor is willing to pay today to receive a given cash flow at some point in the future. In other words, we want to know the **present value** of the future cash flow. In the Opening Focus, we determined the present value of the lottery's thirty-year *stream* of $10.5 million annual payments, assuming that a lottery winner could invest cash at an interest rate of 5 percent. In this section, we focus on the simpler problem of calculating the present value of a single future cash payment. In the previous section, we saw that the future value of a lump sum depended on the interest rate and on the amount of time that the money would earn that interest rate. Similarly, the present value depends largely on the investment opportunities of the recipient and the timing of the future cash flow.

The Concept of Present Value

discounting
Describes the process of calculating present values.

In everyday language, we say that something is discounted to indicate that it is priced at less than full value. In finance, **discounting** describes the process we use to calculate the present value of future cash flows. To calculate the present value of future cash flows, we must discount the value of the cash flow because we lose the opportunity to earn interest on the money until we receive it. That is, it is better to receive $100 today than to receive it in one year. If we have $100 now, we can earn interest. Therefore, the value right now of a $100 cash flow that will come at some future date is less than $100—to determine how much less, we have to discount the future payment. This process is actually the inverse of compounding interest. Instead of finding the future value of present dollars invested at a given rate, discounting determines the present value of a future amount, assuming an opportunity to earn a given return (r) on the money.[5]

To see how this works, suppose that some investment offers to pay you $300 one year from now. How much are you willing to spend today to acquire this investment if you earn 6 percent on an alternative investment (of equal risk)? To answer this question, determine how many dollars must be invested at 6 percent today to have $300 one year from now. Let PV equal this unknown amount, and use the same notation as in the future-value discussion:

$$PV \times (1+0.06) = \$300$$

Solving this equation for PV gives us the following:

$$PV = \frac{\$300}{(1+0.06)} = \$283.02$$

The present value of $300 one year from today is $283.02. That is, investing $283.02 today at a 6 percent interest rate results in $300 at the end of one year. Therefore, you are willing to pay no more than $283.02 for the investment that pays $300 in one year.

The Equation for Present Value

We can find the present value of a lump sum mathematically by solving Equation 3.1 for PV. In other words, the present value (PV) of some future amount

[5] This interest rate is variously referred to as the *discount rate, required return, cost of capital, hurdle rate,* or *opportunity cost.*

(FV) to be received n periods from now, assuming an opportunity cost of r, is given by Equation 3.2:

$$PV = \frac{FV}{(1+r)^n} = FV \times \left[\frac{1}{(1+r)^n}\right] \quad \text{(Eq. 3.2)}$$

The following Applying the Model illustrates the application of Equation 3.2, using a corporate investment opportunity as an example.

APPLYING THE MODEL

Pam Verity, the financial manager of the Wildcatter Oil Drilling Company, was offered the chance to purchase the right to receive a $1,700 royalty payment eight years from now. The offer came from Sam Long, the owner of the Petroleum Land Management Company. Pam believes that if she had the $1,700 in hand now, she could invest it and earn 8 percent. How much is she willing to pay for the right to receive this royalty payment? Substituting FV = $1,700, $n = 8$, and $r = 0.08$ into Equation 3.2 yields the following:

$$PV = \frac{\$1{,}700}{(1+0.08)^8} = \frac{\$1{,}700}{(1.85093)} = \$918.46$$

Pam finds that the present value of this $1,700 royalty payment is $918.46. If Sam offers to sell Pam the royalty payment for $900 (or any amount less than $918.46), Pam should accept the offer. In this case, the *marginal cost* of the investment ($900) is less than its *marginal benefit* ($918.46). At the top of Figure 3.3 on page 98 is a time line graphically describing this process.

There are three popular methods for simplifying present-value calculations. One method is to use a present-value factor (PVF) table, such as Table A2 in Appendix A. A portion of Table A2 appears below as Table 3.2. Present-value factors for specific discount rates and compounding periods ($PVF_{r\%,n}$) are determined just as they were for future values. To find the relevant factor for the current example, $PVF_{8\%,8}$, move across the top of the table until you reach the 8 percent column, then move down until you reach the row for 8 years. The table indicates that the present value of $1 discounted for 8 years at 8 percent equals $0.540. Multiply that figure by $1,700 to find the present value of the royalty payment, $918 (rounding to the nearest dollar). Using

	Discount Rate (r)							
Period	1%	2%	3%	4%	5%	6%	7%	8%
1	0.990	0.980	0.971	0.962	0.952	0.943	0.935	0.926
2	0.980	0.961	0.943	0.925	0.907	0.890	0.873	0.857
3	0.971	0.942	0.915	0.889	0.864	0.840	0.816	0.794
4	0.961	0.924	0.888	0.855	0.823	0.792	0.763	0.735
5	0.951	0.906	0.863	0.822	0.784	0.747	0.713	0.681
6	0.942	0.888	0.837	0.790	0.746	0.705	0.666	0.630
7	0.933	0.871	0.813	0.760	0.711	0.665	0.623	0.583
8	0.923	0.853	0.789	0.731	0.677	0.627	0.582	0.540

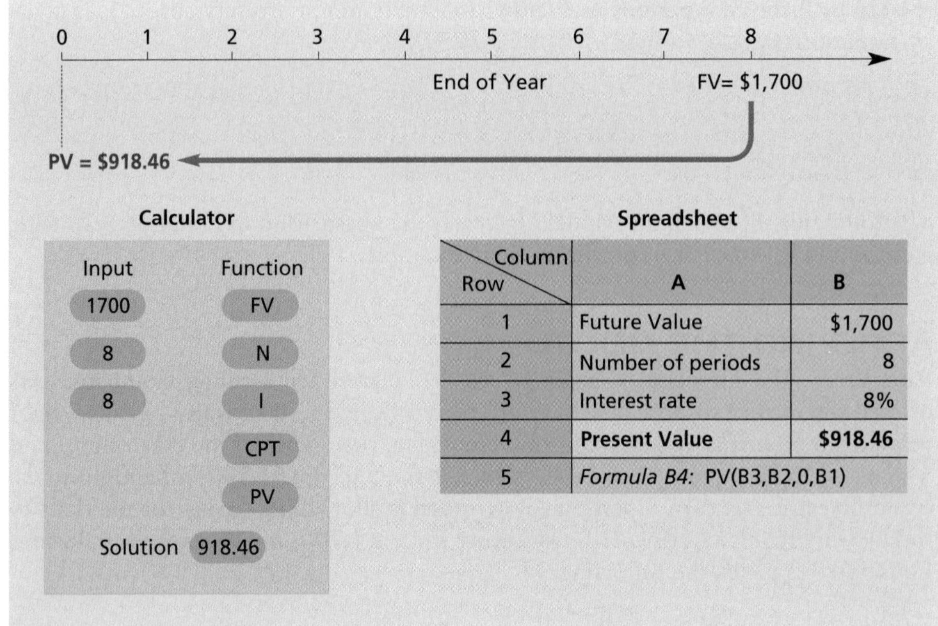

Row \ Column	A	B
1	Future Value	$1,700
2	Number of periods	8
3	Interest rate	8%
4	**Present Value**	**$918.46**
5	*Formula B4:* PV(B3,B2,0,B1)	

Figure 3.3
Present Value of $1,700 To Be Received in 8 Years at an 8% Discount Rate

To calculate the present value of $1,700, we must discount it to reflect the lost opportunity to earn 8% interest on the money for 8 years. In this example, the discounted value of $1,700 equals just $918.46.

financial calculators or spreadsheets, as shown in the lower portion of Figure 3.3, are two other popular methods for simplifying present-value calculations for a lump sum.[6]

A Graphic View of Present Value

For investors who expect to receive cash in the future, Figure 3.4 contains two important messages. First, the present value of a future cash payment declines the longer investors must wait to receive it. Second, the present value declines as the discount rate rises. Note that for a discount rate of 0 percent, the present value always equals the future value ($1). However, for any discount rate greater than zero, the present value falls below the future value.

CONCEPT REVIEW QUESTIONS

3. How are the present value and the future value of a lump sum related—in definition and in terms of mathematics? Notice that for a given interest rate (r) and a given investment time horizon (n), $PVF_{r,n}$ and $FVF_{r,n}$ are inverses of each other. Why?

4. How would (a) an *increase* in the discount rate or (b) a *decrease* in the time period until the cash flow is received affect the present value? Why?

3.3 FUTURE VALUE OF CASH FLOW STREAMS

Financial managers frequently need to evaluate *streams* of cash flows that occur in future periods. Although this is mechanically more complicated than computing the future or present value of a single cash flow, the same basic techniques apply. Two types

[6] The format of the *Excel* function for present value is "=*PV*(*rate,nper,pmt,fv,type*)". The terms in parentheses have similar interpretations to those in *Excel*'s future value function. Note that in the present value function, *Excel* produces an answer with the opposite sign to that of the value entered for the variable "*fv*." In other words, if a lump sum has a positive future value, *Excel* produces a negative estimate for the present value. You can change the sign of *Excel*'s answer simply by putting a minus sign in front of the *PV* equation.

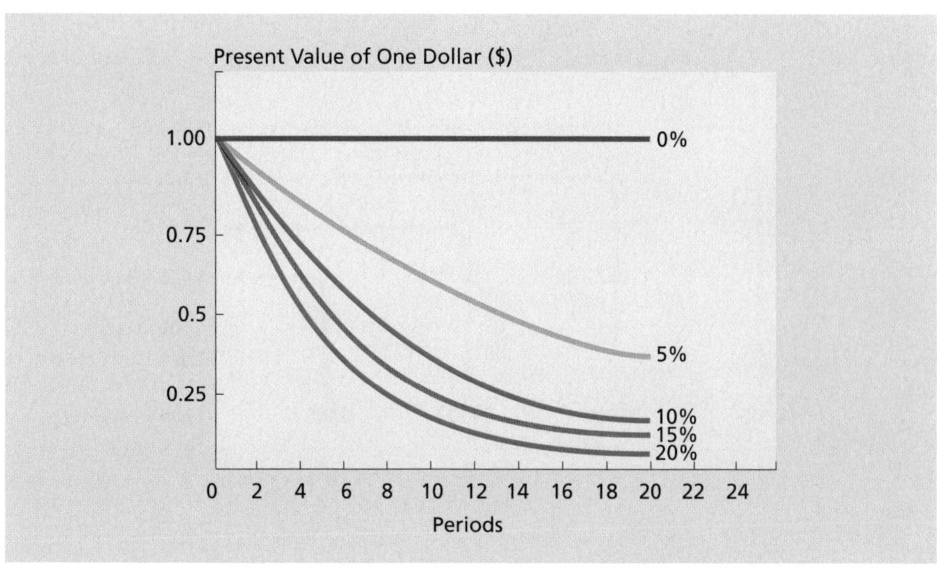

Figure 3.4
The Power of Discounting: Present Value of $1 Discounted at Different Interest Rates

The present value of $1.00 falls as the interest rate rises. Similarly, the longer one must wait to receive a $1.00 payment, the lower the present value of that payment.

of cash flow streams are possible: the mixed stream and the annuity. A **mixed stream** is a series of unequal cash flows reflecting no particular pattern, whereas an **annuity** is a stream of equal periodic cash flows. Either of these cash flow patterns can represent *inflows* earned on investments or *outflows* invested to earn future returns. Because certain shortcuts are possible when evaluating an annuity, we discuss mixed streams and annuities separately.

mixed stream
A series of unequal cash flows reflecting no particular pattern.

annuity
A stream of equal periodic cash flows.

Finding the Future Value of a Mixed Stream

The future value of any stream of cash flows measured at the end of a specified year is merely the sum of the future values of the individual cash flows at that year's end. This future value is sometimes called the *terminal value*. Because each cash flow earns interest, the future value of any stream of cash flows is greater than a simple sum of the cash flows.

APPLYING THE MODEL

We wish to determine the balance at the end of 5 years in an investment account earning 9 percent annual interest, given the following five end-of-year deposits: $400 in year 1, $800 in year 2, $500 in year 3, $400 in year 4, and $300 in year 5. These cash flows appear on the time line at the top of Figure 3.5 on page 100, which also depicts the future-value calculation for this mixed stream of cash flows, followed by the financial calculator and spreadsheet solutions.

The future value of the mixed stream is $2,930.70.[7] Note that the first cash flow, which occurs at the end of year 1, earns interest for four years (end of year 1 to end of year 5); the second cash flow, which occurs at the end of year 2, earns interest for three years (end of year 2 to end of year 5); and so on. As a result of the 9 percent interest earnings, the five deposits, which total $2,400 before interest, grow to more than $2,900 at the end of five years.

[7] There is a $0.01 rounding difference between the future value given on the time line compared with the future-value calculation using a calculator or spreadsheet. As before, *Excel* reports the value $2,930.71 as a negative number because the *FV* function always reverses the signs of the cash flows and the final answer. Notice that to calculate the stream's present value (a necessary input in the *FV* formula), we use the *NPV* function rather than the *PV* function because the latter does not accommodate mixed cash flow streams.

Figure 3.5
Future Value at the End of Five Years of a Mixed Cash Flow Stream Invested at 9%

The future value of a mixed stream of cash flows is merely the sum of the future values of the individual cash flows. For the cash flows shown on the timeline, the individual future values compounded at 9% interest at the end of year 5 are shown at the end of the arrows. Their total of $2,930.70 represents the future value of the mixed stream.

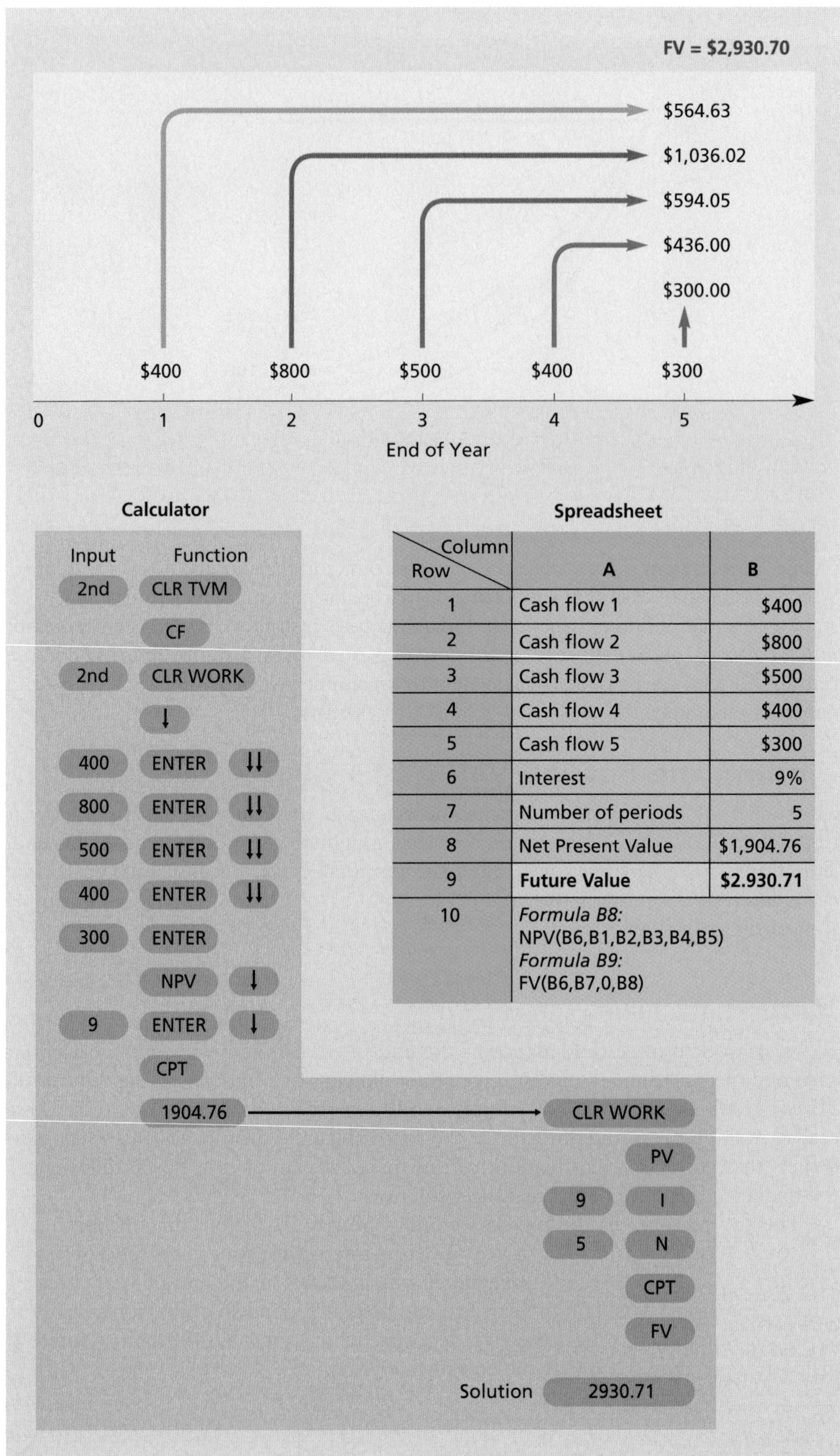

Row \ Column	A	B
1	Cash flow 1	$400
2	Cash flow 2	$800
3	Cash flow 3	$500
4	Cash flow 4	$400
5	Cash flow 5	$300
6	Interest	9%
7	Number of periods	5
8	Net Present Value	$1,904.76
9	**Future Value**	**$2.930.71**
10	*Formula B8:* NPV(B6,B1,B2,B3,B4,B5) *Formula B9:* FV(B6,B7,0,B8)	

Letting CF_t represent the cash flow at the end of year t, the future value of an n-year mixed stream of cash flows (FV) is shown in Equation 3.3:

$$FV = CF_1 \times (1+r)^{n-1} + CF_2 \times (1+r)^{n-2} + \cdots + CF_n \times (1+r)^{n-n} \quad \text{(Eq. 3.3)}$$

Substitute the cash flows shown on the time line and the 9 percent interest rate into Equation 3.3. The values shown to the right of the time line result. They total \$2,930.70.

Simplify the notation for Equation 3.3, as shown in Equation 3.3a, by using the Greek summation symbol, Σ, as a shorthand way of saying that the future value of this n-year mixed stream is equal to the sum of the future values of individual cash flows from periods 1, 2, 3, . . . , n:

$$FV = \sum_{t=1}^{n} CF_t \times (1+r)^{n-t} \quad \text{(Eq. 3.3a)}$$

Although summations economize on the notation needed to express most of the equations presented in this chapter, we present equations in their "noncondensed" format for clarity wherever possible, and we use the summation notation sparingly. Mathematical purists can use their imaginations to construct the more succinct formulations.

Types of Annuities

Before looking at future-value computations for annuities, we distinguish between the two basic types of annuities: the ordinary annuity and the annuity due. An **ordinary annuity** is an annuity for which the payments occur *at the end of each period,* whereas an **annuity due** is one for which the payments occur *at the beginning of each period.* To demonstrate these differences, assume that you choose the better of two annuities as a personal investment opportunity. Both are five-year, \$1,000 annuities. Annuity A is an ordinary annuity and annuity B is an annuity due. Although the amount of each annuity totals \$5,000, the timing of the cash flows differs; each cash flow arrives one year sooner with the annuity due than with the ordinary annuity. In fact, for any positive interest rate, *the future value of an annuity due is always greater than the future value of an otherwise identical ordinary annuity.*[8]

ordinary annuity
An annuity for which the payments occur *at the end of each period.*

annuity due
An annuity for which the payments occur *at the beginning of each period.*

Finding the Future Value of an Ordinary Annuity

The future value of an ordinary annuity can be calculated using the same method demonstrated earlier for a mixed stream.

APPLYING THE MODEL

You wish to save money on a regular basis to finance an exotic vacation in five years. You are confident that, with sacrifice and discipline, you can force yourself to deposit \$1,000 annually, at the *end of each* of the next five years, into a savings

8. Because ordinary annuities arise frequently in finance, we use the term "annuity" throughout this book to refer to ordinary annuities, unless otherwise specified.

account paying 7 percent annual interest. This situation is depicted graphically at the top of Figure 3.6.

Compute the future value (*FV*) of this annuity, using Equation 3.3. Use the assumed interest rate (*r*) of 7 percent and plug in the known values of each of the five yearly ($n = 5$) cash flows (CF_1 to CF_5), as follows:

$$FV = CF_1 \times (1+r)^{n-1} + CF_2 \times (1+r)^{n-2} + \ldots + CF_n \times (1+r)^{n-n}$$

$$\begin{aligned} FV &= CF_1 \times (1+r)^{5-1} + CF_2 \times (1+r)^{5-2} + \ldots + CF_n \times (1+r)^{5-5} \\ &= \$1,000(1.07)^4 + \$1,000(1.07)^3 + \$1,000(1.07)^2 + \$1,000(1.07)^1 \\ &\quad + \$1,000 \\ &= \$1,310.80 + \$1,225.04 + \$1,144.90 + \$1,070 + \$1,000 = \$5,750.74 \end{aligned}$$

The future value of the ordinary annuity is $5,750.74. This is the amount of the money available to you to pay for your vacation. The year-1 cash flow of $1,000 earns 7 percent interest for four years, the year-2 cash flow earns 7 percent interest for three years, and so on.

Fortunately, a shortcut formula exists that simplifies the future-value calculation of an ordinary annuity. Using the symbol *PMT* to represent the annuity's annual payment, Equation 3.4 gives the future value of an annuity that lasts for *n* years (*FV*), assuming an interest rate of *r* percent:

$$FV = PMT \times \left\{ \frac{\left[(1+r)^n - 1 \right]}{r} \right\} \quad \text{(Eq. 3.4)}$$

APPLYING THE MODEL

Demonstrate that Equation 3.4 yields the same answer obtained in the previous model by plugging in the values $PMT = \$1,000$, $n = 5$, and $r = 0.07$:

$$\begin{aligned} FV &= \$1,000 \times \left\{ \frac{\left[(1.07)^5 - 1 \right]}{0.07} \right\} = \$1,000 \times \left[\frac{1.4026 - 1}{0.07} \right] \\ &= \$1,000 \times 5.7507 = \$5,750.74 \end{aligned}$$

Once again, we find the future value of this ordinary annuity to be $5,750.74.

In addition to using algebra, we can use a table such as Table A3 in Appendix A that details future-value factors for ordinary annuities at various interest rates for different holding periods. These are generically labeled $FVFA_{r\%,n}$; the factor corresponding to $r = 7\%$ and $n = 5$ equals $FVFA_{7\%,5}$, which equals 5.751. We can multiply this factor by $1,000 to compute *FV*, which is $5,751. Using financial calculators or spreadsheets, as shown below the time line in Figure 3.6,[9] are two other popular methods for simplifying future-value calculations for annuities.

[9] Notice that when calculating the future value of an ordinary annuity, *Excel* requires only three arguments in the *FV* formula: (1) the interest rate, (2) the number of periods or payments, and (3) the amount of each payment.

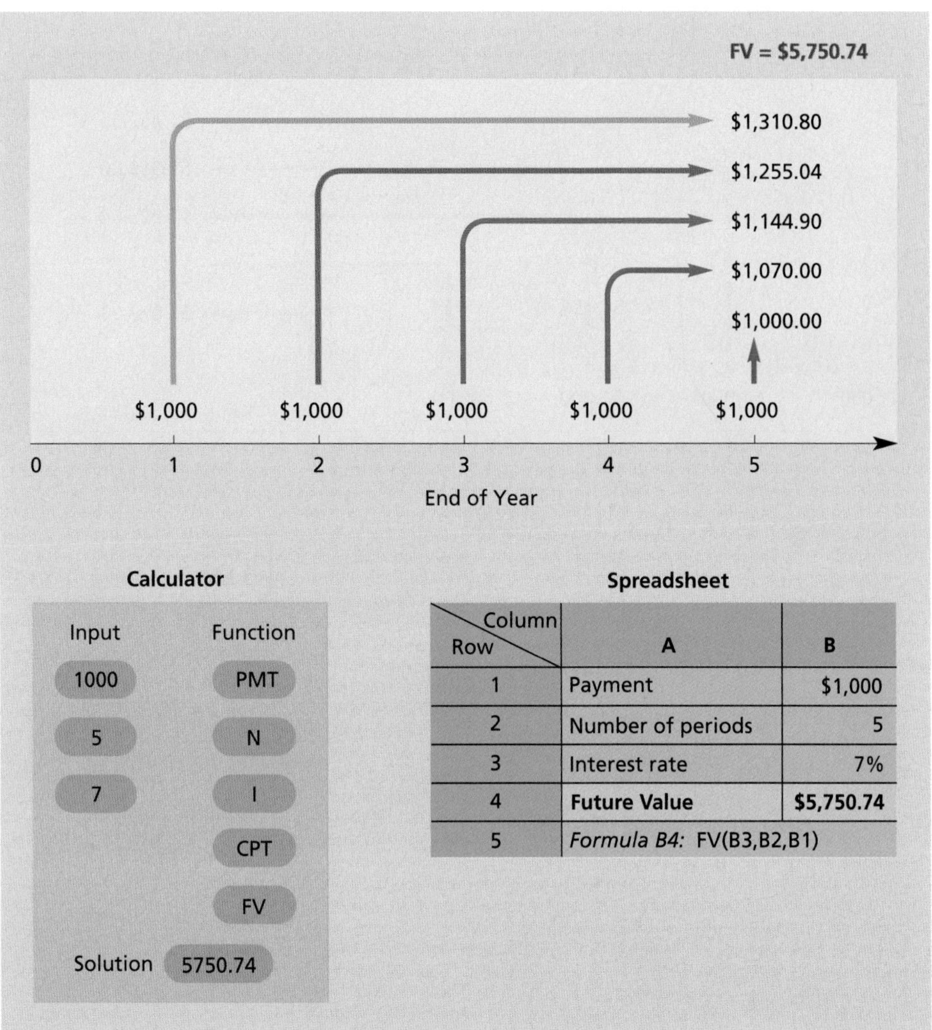

Row \ Column	A	B
1	Payment	$1,000
2	Number of periods	5
3	Interest rate	7%
4	**Future Value**	**$5,750.74**
5	*Formula B4:* FV(B3,B2,B1)	

Figure 3.6
Future Value at the End of Five Years of an Ordinary Annuity of $1,000 Per Year Invested at 7%

The future value of the 5-year $1,000 ordinary annuity at 7% interest at the end of year 5 is $5,750.74, which is well above the $5,000 sum of the annual deposits.

Finding the Future Value of an Annuity Due

The calculations required to find the future value of an annuity due involve only a slight change to those already demonstrated for an ordinary annuity. How much money will you have at the end of five years if you deposit $1,000 annually at the *beginning of each* of the next five years into a savings account paying 7 percent annual interest? This scenario is graphically depicted at the top of Figure 3.7 on page 104. Note that the ends of years 0 through 4 are respectively equivalent to the beginnings of years 1 through 5. The $6,153.29 future value of the annuity due is, as expected, greater than the $5,750.74 future value of the comparable ordinary annuity discussed in the preceding section. Because the cash flows of the annuity due occur at the beginning of the year, the cash flow of $1,000 at the beginning of year 1 earns 7 percent interest for five years, the cash flow of $1,000 at the beginning of year 2 earns 7 percent interest for four years, and so on. Comparing this to the ordinary annuity, it is clear that each $1,000 cash flow of the annuity due earns interest for one more year than the comparable ordinary annuity cash flow. As a result, the future value of the annuity due is greater than the future value of the comparable ordinary annuity.

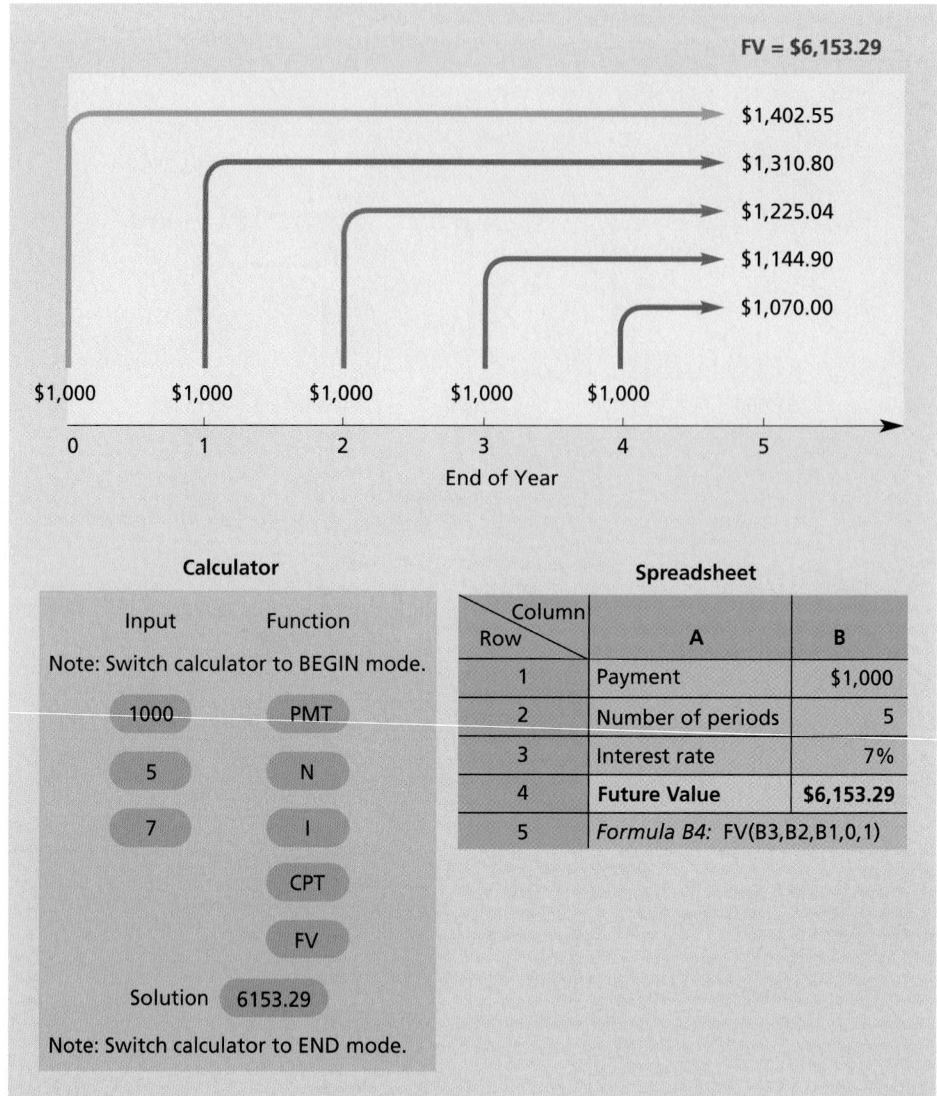

Row \ Column	A	B
1	Payment	$1,000
2	Number of periods	5
3	Interest rate	7%
4	**Future Value**	**$6,153.29**
5	*Formula B4:* FV(B3,B2,B1,0,1)	

Figure 3.7
Future Value at the End of Five Years of an Annuity Due of $1,000 Per Year Invested at 7%

The future value at the end of five years of a $1,000 5-year annuity due that earns 7% annual interest is $6,153.29, which exceeds the $5,750.74 future value of the otherwise identical ordinary annuity (see Figure 3.6). Each deposit in the annuity due earns one more year of interest than the comparable deposit into the ordinary annuity.

Because each cash flow of an annuity due earns one additional year of interest, the equation for the future value of an ordinary annuity, Equation 3.4, can be converted into an expression for the future value of an annuity due, *FV* (annuity due), simply by multiplying it by (1 + *r*), as shown in Equation 3.5:

$$FV(\text{annuity due}) = PMT \times \left\{ \frac{\left[(1+r)^n - 1\right]}{r} \right\} \times (1+r) \qquad \textbf{(Eq. 3.5)}$$

Equation 3.5 demonstrates that the future value of an annuity due always exceeds the future value of a similar ordinary annuity for any positive interest rate. The future value of an annuity due exceeds that of an identical ordinary annuity by a factor of 1 plus the interest rate. We can check this by comparing the results from the two different five-year vacation savings plans presented previously. We determined that the future values of your ordinary annuity and annuity due at the end of year 5, given a 7 percent interest rate, were \$5,750.74 and \$6,153.29, respectively. Multiplying the future value of the ordinary annuity by 1 plus the interest rate yields the future value of the annuity due:

$$FV(\text{annuity due}) = \$5{,}750.74 \times (1.07) = \$6{,}153.29$$

Because the cash flow of the annuity due occurs at the beginning of the period rather than at the end, its future value is greater. In our illustration, you earn about \$400 more with the annuity due and can enjoy a somewhat more luxurious vacation.

CONCEPT REVIEW QUESTIONS

5. How would *the future value of a mixed stream of cash flows* be calculated, given the cash flows and applicable interest rate?

6. Differentiate between an *ordinary annuity* and an *annuity due.* How is the future value of an ordinary annuity calculated, and how (for the same cash flows) can it be converted into the future value of an annuity due?

3.4 PRESENT VALUE OF CASH FLOW STREAMS

Many decisions in corporate finance require financial managers to calculate the present values of cash flow streams that occur over several years. In this section, we show how to calculate the present values of mixed cash flow streams and annuities. We also demonstrate the present-value calculation for a very important cash flow stream, known as a **perpetuity**. A perpetuity is a level (or growing) cash flow stream that continues forever. Perpetuities arise in many applications such as valuing a business as a going concern, or valuing a share of stock with no definite maturity date.

perpetuity
A level or growing cash flow stream that continues forever.

Finding the Present Value of a Mixed Stream

The present value of any cash flow stream is merely the sum of the present values of the individual cash flows. In other words, we apply the same techniques we used to calculate present values of lump sums to calculate the present values of all kinds of cash flow streams.

APPLYING THE MODEL

Shortly after graduation, you receive an inheritance that you use to purchase a small bed-and-breakfast inn as an investment (and a weekend escape). Your plan is to sell the inn after five years. The inn is an old mansion, so you know that appliances, furniture, and other equipment will wear out and need to be replaced or repaired on a regular basis. You estimate that these expenses will total \$4,000 during year 1, \$8,000 during year 2, \$5,000 during year 3, \$4,000 during year 4, and \$3,000 during year 5, the final year of your ownership. For simplicity, assume that the expense payments will be made at the end of each year. Because you have some of your inheritance left over after purchasing the inn (the deceased was indeed generous), you want to set aside a lump sum today from which you can make annual withdrawals to meet these expenses when they come due, as shown in Figure 3.8. Suppose you invest the lump sum in a bank account that pays 9 percent interest. To determine the amount of money you need to put in the account, you must calculate the present value of the stream of future expenses, using 9 percent as the discount rate.

The present value of the mixed stream is $19,047.58. The present-value factors corresponding to each annual cash flow are determined using present-value factor tables such as Table A2, using a financial calculator, or using an *Excel* spreadsheet. The more precise financial calculator and spreadsheet calculations are shown below the time line in Figure 3.8.

There is a general formula for computing the present value of a stream of future cash flows. Continuing to let CF_t represent the cash flow at the end of year t, the present value of an n-year mixed stream of cash flows (PV) is expressed as Equation 3.6:

$$PV = \left[CF_1 \times \frac{1}{(1+r)^1}\right] + \left[CF_2 \times \frac{1}{(1+r)^2}\right] + \ldots + \left[CF_n \times \frac{1}{(1+r)^n}\right] = \sum_{t=1}^{n} CF_t \times \frac{1}{(1+r)^t} \qquad \text{(Eq. 3.6)}$$

Substitute the cash flows shown on the time line in Figure 3.8 and the 9 percent discount rate into Equation 3.6 to obtain the present-value figure, $19,047.58.

Finding the Present Value of an Ordinary Annuity

The present value of an ordinary annuity is found in a manner similar to that used for a mixed stream. Discount each payment and then add up each term to find the annuity's present value.

APPLYING THE MODEL

Braden Company, a producer of plastic toys, was approached by its principal equipment supplier with an intriguing offer for a service contract. The supplier, the Extruding Machines Corporation (EMC), offered to take over all of Braden's equipment repair and servicing for five years in exchange for a onetime payment today. Braden's managers know their company spends $7,000 at the end of every year on maintenance, so EMC's service contract would reduce Braden's cash outflows by this $7,000 annually for five years. Because these are equal annual cash benefits, Braden determines what it is willing to pay for the service contract by valuing it as a five-year ordinary annuity with a $7,000 annual cash flow. If Braden requires a minimum return of 8 percent on all its investments, how much is it willing to pay for EMC's service contract? The calculation of the present value of this annuity is depicted on the time line presented at the top of Figure 3.9 on page 108, followed by the more precise financial calculator and spreadsheet solutions.

Figure 3.8
Present Value of a 5-Year Mixed Stream Discounted at 9%

The present value of the mixed stream is the sum of the present values of the individual cash flows discounted at the 9% rate. The present values of the individual cash flows shown at the end of the arrows are summed to find the $19,047.58 present value of the stream of cash flows.

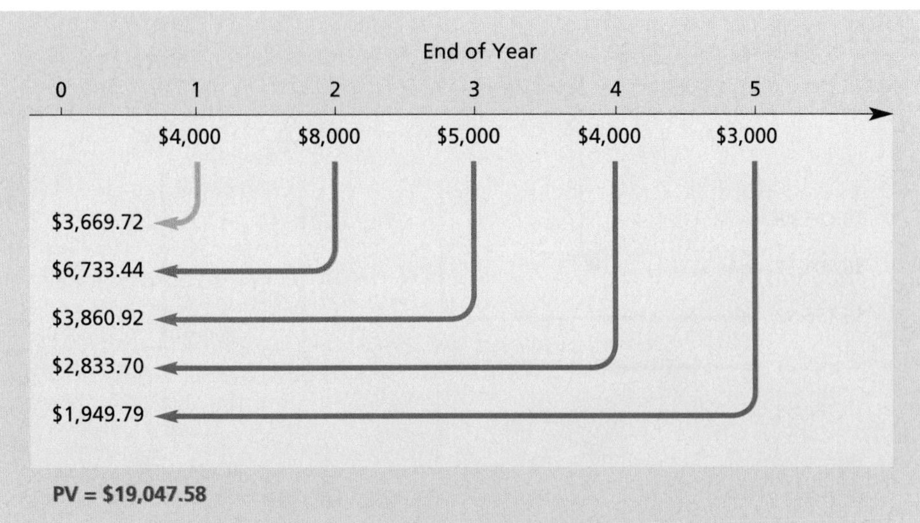

Spreadsheet

Row \ Column	A	B
1	Cash flow 1	4,000
2	Cash flow 2	8,000
3	Cash flow 3	5,000
4	Cash flow 4	4,000
5	Cash flow 5	3,000
6	Interest	9%
7	Number of periods	5
8	**Net Present Value**	**$19,047.58**
9	*Formula B8:* NPV(B6,B1,B2,B3,B4,B5)	

Calculator

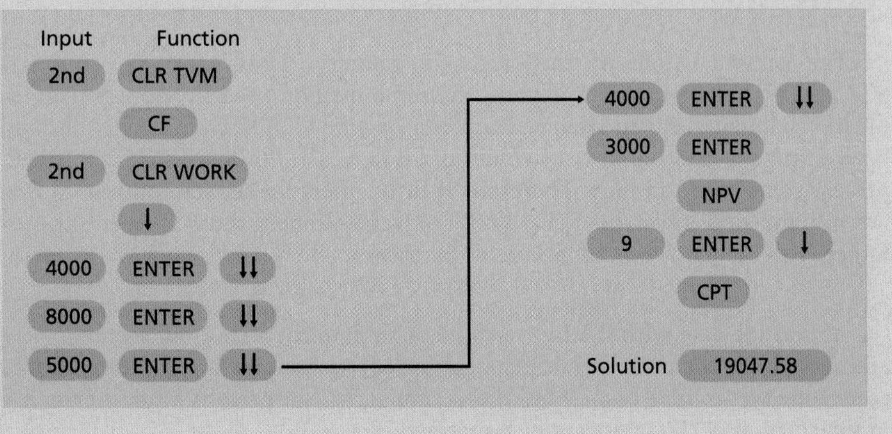

Figure 3.9
Present Value of a 5-Year Ordinary Annuity Discounted at 8%

The present value of the 5-year $7,000 ordinary annuity discounted at 8% is $27,948.97, which is merely the sum of the present values of the individual cash flows shown at the end of the arrows.

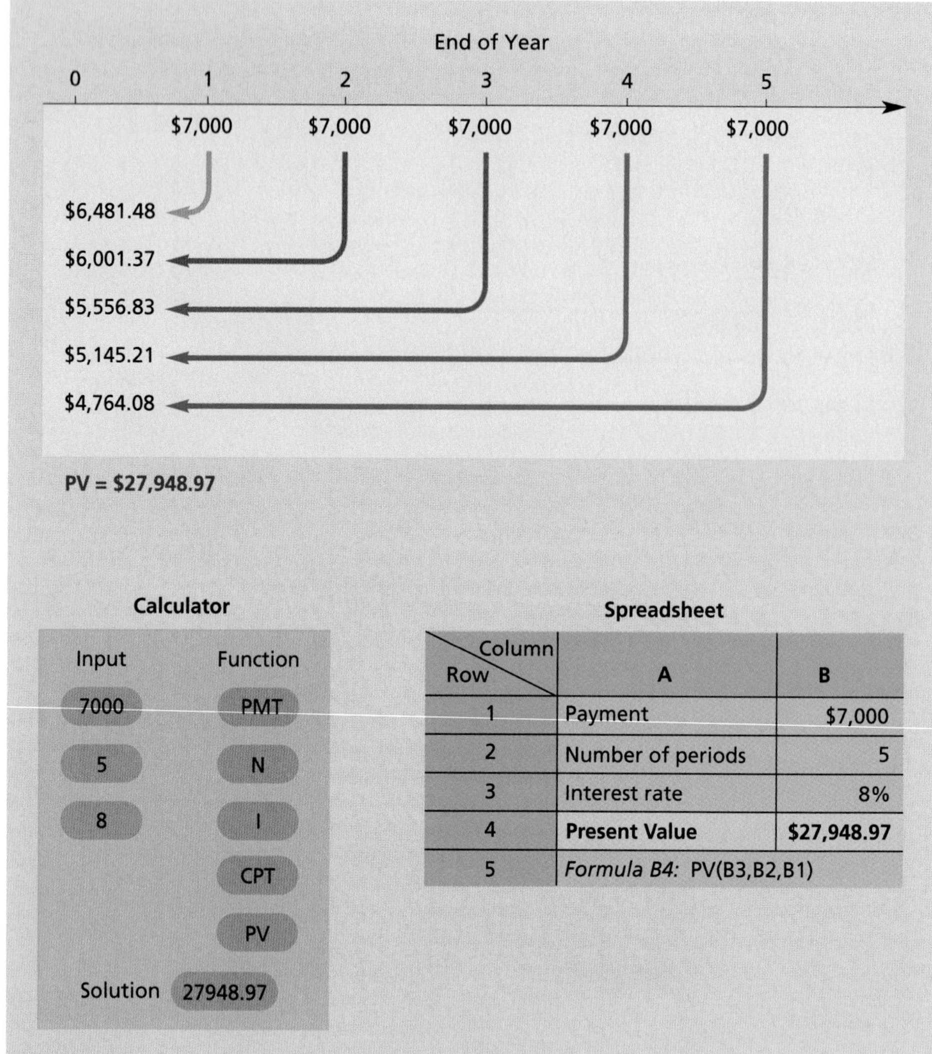

Row \ Column	A	B
1	Payment	$7,000
2	Number of periods	5
3	Interest rate	8%
4	**Present Value**	**$27,948.97**
5	*Formula B4:* PV(B3,B2,B1)	

The present value of this ordinary annuity (EMC's service contract) is $27,948.97, calculated by applying the same method used previously to find the present value of a mixed stream. Each end-of-year $7,000 cash flow is discounted back to time 0, and the present values of all five cash flows are summed to get the present value of the annuity. Therefore, if EMC offers the service contract to Braden for a lump-sum price of $27,948.97 or less, Braden should accept the offer. Otherwise, Braden should continue to perform its own maintenance.

As was the case with the future value of an annuity, a shortcut formula is available to simplify the present-value calculation for an annuity. Using the symbol PMT to denote the annual cash flow, the formula for the present value of an n-year ordinary annuity (PV) appears in Equation 3.7:

$$PV = \frac{PMT}{r} \times \left[1 - \frac{1}{(1+r)^n}\right] \qquad \text{(Eq. 3.7)}$$

APPLYING THE MODEL

Use Equation 3.7 to calculate the present value of the service contract EMC has offered to the Braden Company. Substituting in n = 5 years, r = 0.08, and PMT = $7,000, find the present value (PV) of this ordinary annuity to be $27,948.97, as shown below:

$$PV = \frac{\$7,000}{0.08} \times \left[1 - \frac{1}{(1.08)^5}\right] = \frac{\$7,000}{0.08} \times [1 - 0.6806] = \$27,948.97$$

By now, you know these computations can be simplified using a table such as Table A4 in Appendix A that gives present-value factors for ordinary annuities at various discount rates for different holding periods. Many students find it easier to understand Equation 3.7 when the right-hand side of the equation is expressed simply as the annual cash flow (PMT) times the present-value factor for an annuity paying r percent for n years, or $PVFA_{r\%,n}$. From Table A4, we get $PVFA_{8\%,5}$ = 3.993.When multiplied by the $7,000 annual cash flow, this results in a present value of $27,951, approximately equal to the present value obtained using more precise computations demonstrated beneath the time line in Figure 3.9.

Finding the Present Value of an Annuity Due

The present value of an annuity due is calculated in a fashion similar to that used for an ordinary annuity. Because each cash flow for an annuity due occurs one period earlier—at the beginning rather than at the end of the year—than for an ordinary annuity, an annuity due has a larger present value than an ordinary annuity with the same cash flows, discount rate, and life. The expression for the present value of an annuity due, shown in Equation 3.8, is similar to the equation for the present value of an ordinary annuity (PV) given in Equation 3.7.

$$PV(\text{annuity due}) = \frac{PMT}{r} \times \left[1 - \frac{1}{(1+r)^n}\right] \times (1+r) \qquad \text{(Eq. 3.8)}$$

It is clear from a comparison of Equations 3.7 and 3.8 that the present value of an annuity due is merely the present value of a similar ordinary annuity multiplied by (1 + r). To demonstrate, assume that the Braden Company in the previous illustration wishes to determine the present value of the five-year, $7,000 service contract at an 8 percent discount rate, and that each of the cash flows occurs *at the beginning of the year.* To convert the service contract EMC offered the Braden Company into an annuity due, we assume that EMC would have to pay its annual maintenance cost of $7,000 at the beginning of each of the next five years. Braden is still evaluating what amounts to a five-year annuity; the company will just pay out each annual cash flow a year earlier. The present value of this annuity due is simply (1 + r) times the value of the ordinary annuity: PV(annuity due) = $27,948.97 × (1.08) = $30,184.89. If Braden pays its maintenance costs at the start of each year, the most it is willing to pay EMC for the service contract increases by more than $2,000 to $30,184.89.

Finding the Present Value of a Perpetuity

As noted earlier, a *perpetuity* is a level or growing cash flow stream that continues forever; here we focus on those with level streams, which can be viewed as annuities with infinite lives. One of the first, and certainly the most famous, perpetuities in modern history was the massive "consol" bond issue sold by the British government after the Napoleonic Wars ended in 1815. This bond issue got its name because it consolidated all the existing British war debts into a single issue that paid a constant annual amount of interest into perpetuity. The issue itself never matured, meaning that the principal was never to be repaid.

Currently, not many corporations or governments issue perpetual bonds.[10] Perhaps the simplest modern example of a perpetuity is preferred stock issued by corporations. Preferred shares promise investors a constant annual (or quarterly) dividend payment forever. Though "forever" is a difficult time period to measure, we simply express the lifetime (n) of this security as infinity (∞), and modify our basic valuation formulation for an annuity accordingly. For example, we wish to determine the present value of an annuity (PV) that pays a constant annual dividend amount (PMT) for a perpetual number of years ($n = \infty$) discounted at a rate r. Here, the Greek summation notation is helpful in expressing the formula in Equation 3.9:

$$PV = PMT \times \sum_{t=1}^{\infty} \frac{1}{(1+r)^t} \qquad \text{(Eq. 3.9)}$$

Fortunately, Equation 3.9 also comes in a simplified version, which says that the present value of a perpetuity equals the annual, end-of-year payment divided by the discount rate. Equation 3.10 gives this straightforward expression for the present value of a perpetuity (PV):

$$PV = PMT \times \frac{1}{r} = \frac{PMT}{r} \qquad \text{(Eq. 3.10)}$$

APPLYING THE MODEL

Find the present value of the dividend stream associated with a preferred stock issued by the Alpha and Omega Service Company. A&O, as the company is commonly known, promises to pay $10 per year (at the end of each year) on its preferred shares, and security analysts believe that the firm's business and financial risk merits a required return of 12.5 percent. Substituting the values $PMT = \$10$ per year and $r = 0.125$ into Equation 3.10, we find the following:

$$PV = \frac{\$10}{0.125} = \$80$$

10. Some examples come close to being perpetuities. In July 1993, the Walt Disney Company sold $300 million of bonds that matured in the year 2093, 100 years after they were issued. The market dubbed these "Sleeping Beauty bonds" because their maturity matched the amount of time that Sleeping Beauty slept before being kissed by Prince Charming in the classic story.

The present value of A&O's preferred stock dividends, valued as an annuity with a perpetual life, is $80 per share. In other words, the right to receive $10 at the end of every year for an indefinite period is worth only $80 today if a person can earn 12.5 percent on investments of similar risk. If the person had $80 today and earned 12.5 percent interest on it each year, $10 a year (0.125 × $80) could be withdrawn indefinitely without ever touching the initial $80.

Finding the Present Value of a Growing Perpetuity

As we have seen, perpetuities forever pay a constant periodic amount. However, few aspects of modern life are constant, and most of the cash flows we care about have a tendency to grow over time. This is true for items of income such as wages and salaries, dividend payments from corporations, and Social Security payments from governments.[11] Inflation is one, but only one, factor driving the increase in cash flows over time. We must therefore examine how to adjust the present value of a perpetuity formula to account for expected growth in future cash flows. Suppose we want to calculate the present value (PV) of a stream of cash flows growing forever ($n = \infty$) at the rate g. Given an opportunity cost of r, the present value of the **growing perpetuity** is given by Equation 3.11, which is sometimes called the **Gordon growth model**:[12]

growing perpetuity An annuity promising to pay a growing amount at the end of each year forever.

Gordon growth model The valuation model, named after Myron Gordon, that views cash flows as a *growing perpetuity*.

$$PV = \frac{CF_1}{r-g} \quad r > g \qquad \text{(Eq. 3.11)}$$

Note that the numerator in Equation 3.11 is CF_1, the first year's cash flow. This cash flow is expected to grow at a constant annual rate (g) from now to the end of time. The cash flow for any specific future year(t) can be determined by applying the growth rate (g) as follows:

SMART CONCEPTS

See the concept explained step-by-step at SMARTFinance

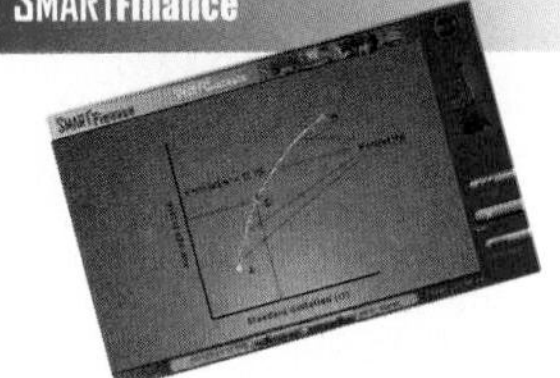

$$CF_t = CF_1 \times (1+g)^{t-1}$$

APPLYING THE MODEL

Gil Bates is a philanthropist who wants to endow a medical foundation with sufficient money to fund ongoing research. Gil is particularly impressed with the research proposal submitted by the Smith Cancer Institute (SCI). The institute requests an endowment sufficient to cover its expenses for medical equipment. Next year, these expenses will total $10 million, and they will grow by 3 percent per year in perpetuity afterward. The institute can earn an 11 percent return on Gil's contribution. How large must the contribution be to finance the institute's medical equipment expenditures in perpetuity? Equation 3.11 tells us that the present value of these expenses equals $125 million, computed as follows:

$$PV = \frac{\$10{,}000{,}000}{0.11-0.03} = \frac{\$10{,}000{,}000}{0.08} = \$125{,}000{,}000$$

[11] Unfortunately, this is also true for expense items such as rent and utility expenses, car prices, and tuition payments.

[12] For this formula to work, the discount rate must be greater than the growth rate. When cash flows grow at a rate equal to or greater than the discount rate, the present value of the stream is infinite.

Note that Gil Bates would have to make an investment of only $90,909,090 ($10,000,000 ÷ 0.11, using Equation 3.10) to fund a nongrowing perpetuity of $10 million per year. The additional investment of about $34 million is required to support the 3 percent annual growth in the payout to SCI.

CONCEPT REVIEW QUESTIONS

7. How would the *present value of a mixed stream of cash flows* be calculated, given the cash flows and an applicable required return?

8. Given the present value of an *ordinary annuity* and the applicable required return, how can this value be easily converted into the present value of an otherwise identical *annuity due?* What is the fundamental difference between the cash flow streams of these two annuities?

9. What is a *perpetuity,* and how is its present value conveniently calculated? How do you find the present value of a *growing perpetuity*?

3.5 SPECIAL APPLICATIONS OF TIME VALUE

Financial managers frequently apply future-value and present-value techniques to determine the values of other variables. In these cases, the future or present values are known, and the equations presented earlier are solved for variables such as the cash flow (*CF* or *PMT*), interest or discount rate (r), or number of time periods (n). Here we consider four of the more common applications and refinements: (1) compounding more frequently than annually, (2) stated versus effective annual interest rates, (3) the calculation of deposits needed to accumulate a future sum, and (4) loan amortization. Then in the final section of this chapter we describe how time-value formulas and concepts can be used to determine interest or growth rates and an unknown number of time periods.

Compounding More Frequently Than Annually

In many applications, interest compounds more frequently than once a year. Financial institutions compound interest semiannually, quarterly, monthly, weekly, daily, or even continuously. This section explores how the present-value and future-value techniques change if interest compounds more than once a year.

semiannual compounding
Interest compounds twice a year.

Semiannual Compounding. **Semiannual compounding** means that interest compounds twice a year. Instead of the stated interest rate being paid once per year, half of the rate is paid twice a year. To demonstrate, consider an opportunity to deposit $100 in a savings account paying 8 percent interest with semiannual compounding. After the first six months, your account grows by 4 percent to $104. Six months later, the account again grows by 4 percent to $108.16. Notice that after one year, the total increase in the account value is $8.16, or 8.16 percent ($8.16 ÷ $100.00). The return on this investment slightly exceeds the stated rate of 8 percent because semiannual compounding allows you to earn interest on interest during the year, increasing the overall rate of return. Table 3.3 shows how the account value grows every six months for the first two years. At the end of two years, the account value reaches $116.99.

Table 3.3
The Future Value from Investing $100 at 8 Percent Interest Compounded Semiannually Over Two Years

Period	Beginning Principal (1)	Future value factor (2)	Future value at end of period [(1) × (2)] (3)
6 months	$100.00	1.04	$104.00
12 months	104.00	1.04	108.16
18 months	108.16	1.04	112.49
24 months	112.49	1.04	116.99

Quarterly Compounding. As the name implies, **quarterly compounding** describes a situation in which interest compounds four times per year. An investment with quarterly compounding pays one-fourth of the stated interest rate every three months. Assume that after further investigation of your savings opportunities, you find an institution that pays 8 percent interest compounded quarterly. After three months, your $100 deposit grows by 2 percent to $102. Three months later, the balance again increases 2 percent to $104.04. By the end of the year, the balance reaches $108.24. Compare that figure with the $108.16 you earn with semiannual compounding. Table 3.4 tracks the growth in the account every three months for two years. At the end of two years, the account is worth $117.17.

quarterly compounding Interest compounds four times per year.

Table 3.5 on page 114 compares values for your $100 deposit at the end of years 1 and 2, given annual, semiannual, and quarterly compounding at the 8 percent rate. As you should expect by now, *the more frequently interest compounds, the greater the amount of money that accumulates.*

A General Equation. We can generalize the preceding examples in a simple equation. Suppose that a lump sum, denoted by PV, is invested at r percent for n years. If m equals the number of times per year that interest compounds, the future value grows as shown in the following equation:

$$FV = PV \times \left(1 + \frac{r}{m}\right)^{m \times n} \quad \text{(Eq. 3.12)}$$

Notice that if $m = 1$, Equation 3.12 reduces to Equation 3.1. The next several examples verify that this equation yields the same ending account values after two years, as shown in Tables 3.3 and 3.4.

Table 3.4
The Future Value from Investing $100 at 8 Percent Interest Compounded Quarterly Over Two Years

Period	Beginning Principal (1)	Future value factor (2)	Future value at end of period [(1) × (2)] (3)
3 months	$100.00	1.02	$102.00
6 months	102.00	1.02	104.04
9 months	104.04	1.02	106.12
12 months	106.12	1.02	108.24
15 months	108.24	1.02	110.41
18 months	110.41	1.02	112.62
21 months	112.62	1.02	114.87
24 months	114.87	1.02	117.17

Table 3.5
The Future Value from Investing $100 at 8 Percent for Years 1 and 2 Given Various Compounding Periods

End of year	Compounding period		
	Annual	Semiannual	Quarterly
1	$108.00	$108.16	$108.24
2	116.64	116.99	117.17

APPLYING THE MODEL

In previous discussions, we calculated the amount that you would have at the end of two years if you deposited $100 at 8 percent interest compounded semiannually and quarterly. For semiannual compounding, $m = 2$ in Equation 3.12; for quarterly compounding, $m = 4$. Substituting the appropriate values for semiannual and quarterly compounding into Equation 3.12 yields the following results:

For semiannual compounding:

$$FV = \$100 \times \left(1 + \frac{0.08}{2}\right)^{2\times 2} = \$100 \times (1 + 0.04)^4 = \$116.99$$

For quarterly compounding:

$$FV = \$100 \times \left(1 + \frac{0.08}{4}\right)^{4\times 2} = \$100 \times (1 + 0.02)^8 = \$117.17$$

These results agree with the values for FV_2 in Tables 3.3 and 3.4. If interest is compounded monthly, weekly, or daily, m would equal 12, 52, or 365, respectively.

continuous compounding
Interest compounds at literally every moment as time passes.

Continuous Compounding. As we switch from annual, to semiannual, to quarterly compounding, the interval during which interest compounds gets shorter, while the number of compounding periods per year gets larger. In principle, there is almost no limit to this process—interest could be compounded daily, hourly, or second by second. **Continuous compounding**, the most extreme case, occurs when interest compounds literally at every moment as time passes. In this case, m in Equation 3.12 would approach infinity, and Equation 3.12 converges to this expression:

$$FV \text{ (continuous compounding)} = PV \times (e^{r\times n}) \qquad \text{(Eq. 3.13)}$$

The number e is an irrational number, like the number π from geometry, which is useful in mathematical applications involving quantities that grow continuously over time. The value of e is approximately 2.7183.[13] As before, increasing the frequency of compounding, in this case by compounding as frequently as possible, increases the future value of an investment.

[13] In one of the more esoteric uses of the Internet, the first 2 million digits of the number e appear at the URL http://antwrp.gsfc.nasa.gov/htmltest/rjn_dig.html. Only the first million will be covered on the exam.

APPLYING THE MODEL

To find the value at the end of two years of your \$100 deposit in an account paying 8 percent annual interest compounded continuously, substitute $n = 2$, $PV =$ \$100, and $r = 0.08$ into Equation 3.13:

$$FV \text{ (continuous compounding)} = \$100 \times (e^{0.08\times2}) = \$100 \times 2.7183^{0.16}$$
$$= \$100 \times 1.1735 = \$117.35$$

The future value with continuous compounding therefore equals \$117.35, which, as expected, is larger than the future value of interest compounded semi-annually (\$116.99) or quarterly (\$117.17).[14]

Stated Versus Effective Annual Interest Rates

Both consumers and businesses need to make objective comparisons of loan costs or investment returns over different compounding periods. To put interest rates on a common basis for comparison, we must distinguish between *stated* and *effective annual interest rates.* The **stated annual rate** is the contractual annual rate charged by a lender or promised by a borrower. The **effective annual rate (*EAR*)**, also known as the *true annual return,* is the annual rate of interest actually paid or earned. The effective annual rate reflects the effect of compounding frequency, whereas the stated annual rate does not. We can best illustrate the differences between stated and effective rates with numerical examples.

stated annual rate
The contractual annual rate of interest charged by a lender or promised by a borrower.

effective annual rate (*EAR*)
The annual rate of interest actually paid or earned, reflecting the impact of compounding frequency. Also called the *true annual return.*

Using the notation introduced earlier, we can calculate the effective annual rate by substituting values for the stated annual rate (r) and the compounding frequency (m) into Equation 3.14:

$$EAR = \left(1 + \frac{r}{m}\right)^m - 1 \qquad \text{(Eq. 3.14)}$$

We can apply this equation using data from preceding examples.

APPLYING THE MODEL

Find the effective annual rate associated with an 8 percent stated annual rate ($r = 0.08$) when interest is compounded annually ($m = 1$), semiannually ($m = 2$), and quarterly ($m = 4$). Substituting these values into Equation 3.14 obtains the following results:

For annual compounding:

$$EAR = \left(1 + \frac{0.08}{1}\right)^1 - 1 = (1 + 0.08)^1 - 1 = 1.08 - 1 = 0.08 = 8.0\%$$

For semiannual compounding:

$$EAR = \left(1 + \frac{0.08}{2}\right)^2 - 1 = (1 + 0.04)^2 - 1 = 1.0816 - 1 = 0.0816 = 8.16\%$$

14. The *Excel* function for continuous compounding is "=exp(argument)". For example, suppose you want to calculate the future value of \$100 compounded continuously for five years at 8 percent. To find this value in *Excel*, first calculate the value of $e^{(0.08\times5)}$, using "=exp(0.08*5)", and then multiply the result by \$100.

For quarterly compounding:

$$EAR=\left(1+\frac{0.08}{4}\right)^4-1=(1+0.02)^4-1=1.0824\ -1=0.0824=8.24\%$$

The results mean that 8 percent compounded quarterly is equivalent to 8.24 percent compounded annually. These values demonstrate two important points: (1) the stated and effective rates are equivalent for annual compounding, and (2) the effective annual rate increases with increasing compounding frequency.

Not surprisingly, the maximum effective annual rate for a given stated annual rate occurs when interest compounds continuously. The effective annual rate for this extreme case can be found by using the following equation:

$$EAR\text{ (continuous compounding)} = e^r - 1 \qquad \text{(Eq. 3.14a)}$$

For the 8 percent stated annual rate (r = 0.08), substitution into Equation 3.14a results in an effective annual rate of 8.33 percent, as follows:

$$e^{0.08}-1=1.0833-1=0.0833=8.33\%$$

annual percentage rate (*APR*)
The stated annual rate calculated by multiplying the periodic rate by the number of periods in one year.

annual percentage yield (*APY*)
The annual rate of interest actually earned reflecting the impact of compounding frequency. The same as the *effective annual rate*.

At the consumer level in the United States, "truth-in-lending laws" *require disclosure* on credit cards and loans of the **annual percentage rate (*APR*)**. The *APR* is the *stated annual rate* found by multiplying the periodic rate by the number of periods in one year. For example, a bank credit card that charges 1.5 percent per month has an *APR* of 18 percent (1.5% per month × 12 months per year). However, the actual cost of this credit card account is determined by calculating the **annual percentage yield (*APY*)**, which is the same as the *effective annual rate*.[15] For the credit card example, 1.5 percent per month interest has an effective annual rate of $[(1.015)^{12} - 1]$ = 0.1956, or 19.56 percent. If the stated rate is 1.75 percent per month, as is the case with many U.S. credit card accounts, the *APY* is a whopping 23.14 percent. In other words, if you are carrying a positive credit card balance with an interest rate like this, pay it off as soon as possible!

Deposits Needed to Accumulate a Future Sum

Suppose that someone wishes to determine the annual deposit necessary to accumulate a certain amount of money at some point in the future. Assume that you want to buy a house five years from now and estimate that an initial down payment of $20,000 will be required. You want to make equal end-of-year deposits into an account paying annual interest of 6 percent, so you must determine what size annuity results in a lump sum equal to $20,000 at the end of year 5. The solution can be derived from the equation for finding the future value of an ordinary annuity.

15. Note that the U.S. truth-in-savings laws *require disclosure* of the *APY* on savings deposits. Clearly, under current law, interest rates on savings are quoted in a more financially accurate way (*APY*) than are the rates charged on credit cards and loans (*APR*).

Earlier in this chapter, we found the future value of an n-year ordinary annuity (FV) by applying Equation 3.4. Solving that equation for PMT, in this case the annual deposit, we get Equation 3.15:

$$PMT = \frac{FV}{\left\{\frac{\left[(1+r)^n - 1\right]}{r}\right\}} \quad \text{(Eq. 3.15)}$$

Once this is done, we substitute the known values of FV, r, and n into the right-hand side of the equation to find the annual deposit required.

APPLYING THE MODEL

Demonstrate the calculation using the situation in which you want to determine the equal annual end-of-year deposits required to accumulate \$20,000 (FV) at the end of five years ($n = 5$), given an interest rate of 6 percent ($r = 6\%$), as follows:

$$PMT = \frac{\$20{,}000}{\left\{\frac{\left[(1.06)^5 - 1\right]}{0.06}\right\}} = \$3{,}547.93$$

You can also use the future-value annuity factor to calculate the required deposit. Note that the denominator of Equation 3.15 is equivalent to the future-value factor for a 6 percent, five-year annuity, which Table A3 shows as $FVFA_{6\%,5} = 5.637$. Dividing the future amount needed (FV = \$20,000) by this factor again gives (except for rounding) an annual cash flow of \$3,547.99. The amount of the annual deposit can alternatively be found, using either a financial calculator or spreadsheet, as shown below.

Deposits (Annuity) Needed to Accumulate a Future Sum

Calculator

Input	Function
20000	FV
5	N
6	I
	CPT
	PMT
Solution	3547.93

Spreadsheet

Row \ Column	A	B
1	Future value	\$20,000
2	Number of periods	5
3	Interest rate	6%
4	**Payment**	**\$3,547.93**
5	*Formula B4:* Pmt(B3,B2,0,B1)	

Loan Amortization

loan amortization
A borrower makes equal periodic payments over time to fully repay a loan.

loan amortization schedule
Used to determine loan amortization payments and the allocation of each payment to interest and principal.

Loan amortization refers to a situation in which a borrower makes equal periodic payments over time to fully repay a loan. For instance, with a conventional, thirty-year home mortgage, the borrower makes the same payment each month for thirty years until the mortgage is completely repaid. To amortize a loan (i.e., to calculate the periodic payment that pays off the loan), you must know the total amount of the loan (the amount borrowed), the term of the loan, the frequency of periodic payments, and the interest rate. To be more specific, the loan amortization process involves finding a level stream of payments (over the term of the loan) with a present value calculated at the loan interest rate equal to the amount borrowed. Lenders use a **loan amortization schedule** to determine these payments and the allocation of each payment to interest and principal.

For example, suppose that you borrow $25,000 at 8 percent annual interest for five years to purchase a new car. To demonstrate the basic approach, we first amortize this loan assuming that you make payments at the end of years 1 through 5. We then modify the annual formula to compute the more typical monthly auto loan payments. To find the size of the annual payments, the lender determines the amount of a five-year annuity discounted at 8 percent that has a present value of $25,000. This process is actually the inverse of finding the present value of an annuity.

Earlier, we found the present value (PV) of an n-year ordinary annuity, using Equation 3.7. Solving that equation for PMT, the annual loan payment, we get Equation 3.16:

$$PMT = \frac{PV}{\left\{\frac{1}{r} \times \left[1 - \frac{1}{(1+r)^n}\right]\right\}} \qquad \text{(Eq. 3.16)}$$

APPLYING THE MODEL

To find the annual payment required on the five-year, $25,000 loan with an 8 percent annual rate, we substitute the known values of PV = $25,000, r = 0.08, and n = 5 into the right-hand side of the equation:

$$PMT = \frac{\$25{,}000}{\left\{\frac{1}{0.08} \times \left[1 - \frac{1}{(1.08)^5}\right]\right\}} = \$6{,}261.41$$

Five annual payments of $6,261.41 are needed to fully amortize this $25,000 loan.

As before, calculate the annual cash flow (PMT) by recognizing that the denominator of Equation 3.16 is equal to the present-value factor of an r percent, n-year annuity ($PVFA_{r\%,n}$). Because Table A4 shows $PVFA_{8\%,5}$ = 3.993, again determine that the payment required to fully amortize this loan is $6,260.96 (slight rounding difference) per year (PMT = $25,000 ÷ 3.993). The amount of the annual loan payment can alternatively be found, using either a financial calculator or spreadsheet, as shown below.

Calculating Loan Amortization Payments

Calculator

Input	Function
25000	PV
5	N
8	I
	CPT
	PMT
Solution	6261.41

Spreadsheet

Row \ Column	A	B
1	Present value	$25,000
2	Number of periods	5
3	Interest rate	8%
4	**Payment**	**$6,261.41**
5	*Formula B4:* Pmt(B3,B2,B1)	

The allocation of each loan payment of $6,261.41 to interest and principal appears in columns 3 and 4 of the *loan amortization schedule* in Table 3.6 on page 120. The portion of each payment representing interest (column 3) declines over the repayment period, and the portion going to principal repayment (column 4) increases. This pattern is typical of amortized loans; with level payments, the interest component declines as the principal falls, leaving a larger portion of each subsequent payment to repay principal.

Though computing amortized loan payments may seem a rather esoteric exercise, it is in fact the present-value formulation that people use most frequently in their personal lives. In addition to calculating auto loan payments, it is used to compute mortgage payments on a home purchase. These consumer loans typically require *monthly payments*. We now demonstrate how to do the amortization calculations using monthly rather than annual payments. First, Equation 3.16a is simply a modified version of Equation 3.16:

$$PMT = \frac{r}{\left[(1+r)^n - 1\right]} \times (1+r)^n \times PV \qquad \textbf{(Eq. 3.16a)}$$

Second, we generalize this formula to more frequent compounding periods by dividing the interest rate by m and multiplying the number of compounding periods by m. This changes the equation as follows:

$$PMT = \frac{\frac{r}{m}}{\left[\left(1+\frac{r}{m}\right)^{m\times n} - 1\right]} \times \left(1+\frac{r}{m}\right)^{m\times n} \times PV \qquad \textbf{(Eq. 3.16b)}$$

APPLYING THE MODEL

Use Equation 3.16b to calculate what a *monthly* car payment will be if you borrow $25,000 for five years at 8 percent annual interest. *PV* will again be the $25,000

Table 3.6
Loan Amortization Schedule $25,000 Principal, for 8 Percent Interest, 5-Year Repayment Period

End of Year	Loan Payment (1)	Beginning of Year Principal (2)	Payments: Interest [0.08 x (2)] (3)	Payments: Principal [(1) – (3)] (4)	End-of-Year Principal [(2) – (4)] (5)
1	$6,261.41	$25,000.00	$2,000.00	$4,261.41	$20,738.59
2	6,261.41	20,738.59	1,659.09	4,602.32	16,136.27
3	6,261.41	16,136.27	1,290.90	4,970.51	11,165.76
4	6,261.41	11,165.76	893.26	5,368.15	5,797.61
5	6,261.41	5,797.61	463.80	5,797.61	0

amount borrowed, but the periodic interest rate ($r \div m$) will be 0.00667, or 0.667 percent per month (0.08 per year ÷ 12 months per year). There will be $m \times n = 60$ compounding periods (12 months/year × 5 years = 60 months). Substituting these values into Equation 3.16b yields a monthly auto loan payment of $506.91:

$$PMT = \frac{\frac{0.08}{12}}{\left[\left(1+\frac{0.08}{12}\right)^{12\times 5} - 1\right]} \times \left(1+\frac{0.08}{12}\right)^{12\times 5} \times \$25,000$$

$$= \frac{0.00667}{\left[(1.00667)^{60} - 1\right]} \times (1.00667)^{60} \times \$25,000$$

$$= \$506.91$$

As a test of your command of the monthly payment formula, see if you can compute the monthly mortgage payment for a home purchased using a thirty-year, $100,000 loan with a fixed 7.5 percent annual interest rate. Note that there are 360 compounding periods (12 months/year × 30 years).[16]

CONCEPT REVIEW QUESTIONS

10. What effect does increasing compounding frequency have on the (a) future value of a given deposit and (b) its *effective annual rate (EAR)?*

11. Under what condition would the stated annual rate equal the effective annual rate (*EAR*) for a given deposit? How do these rates relate to the *annual percentage rate (APR)* and *annual percentage yield (APY)?*

12. How would you determine the size of the annual end-of-year deposits needed to accumulate a given future sum, at the end of a specified future period? What effect does the magnitude of the interest rate have on the size of the deposits needed?

13. What relationship exists between the calculation of the present value of an annuity and amortization of a loan? How can you find the amount of interest paid each year under an amortized loan?

16. The amount of the mortgage payment is $699.21. To find this solution, just enter the formula "=pmt(0.00625,360,100000)" in *Excel.* The first argument in this function is the monthly interest rate, 7.5 percent divided by 12.

3.6 ADDITIONAL APPLICATIONS OF TIME-VALUE TECHNIQUES

As you have probably already guessed, there are a vast number of applications of time-value techniques in modern finance. All are variations of the basic future-value and present-value formulas described earlier in this chapter. Here we expand our repertoire of computational methods to discuss two of the most important specialized uses of time-value techniques: determining (1) implied interest or growth rates and (2) the number of compounding periods.

Implied Interest or Growth Rates

Analysts often need to calculate the compound annual interest or *growth rate* (annual rate of change in values) of a series of cash flows. Because the calculations required for finding interest rates and growth rates, given known cash flow streams, are the same, this section refers to the calculations as those required to find interest or growth rates. We examine each of three possible cash flow patterns: lump sums, annuities, and mixed streams.

Lump Sums. The simplest situation is one in which a person wants to find the interest or growth rate of a single cash flow over time. As an example, assume that you invested $1,000 in a stock mutual fund in December 2001 and that this investment now, in December 2006, is worth $2,150. What was your compound annual rate of return over this five-year period? This is easy to determine, because we are unconcerned about the investment's value during any of the intervening years. We simply want to determine what compound rate of return (r) converted a $1,000 investment ($PV$) into a future amount ($FV$) worth $2,150 in five years ($n$). Note that the number of years of growth (or interest) is the difference between the latest and earliest year number. In this case, $n = 2006 - 2001 = 5$ years. Although the period 2001 through 2006 includes six years, there are only five years of growth because the earliest year (2001) serves as the base year (i.e., time 0) and is then followed by five years of change: 2001 to 2002, 2002 to 2003, 2003 to 2004, 2004 to 2005, and 2005 to 2006. Finding r involves manipulating Equation 3.1 so that we have the value to be determined, in this case $(1 + r)^n$, on the left-hand side of the equation and the two known values, PV and FV, on the right-hand side of the equation, as shown in Equation 3.17:

$$(1+r)^n = \frac{FV}{PV} \qquad \text{(Eq. 3.17)}$$

Substituting in the known values, we obtain the following:

$$(1+r)^5 = \frac{\$2{,}150}{\$1{,}000} = 2.150$$

This says that 1 plus the rate of return $(1 + r)$, compounded for five years ($n = 5$), equals 2.150. Our final step is to calculate the fifth root of 2.150, which is done

Calculating an Interest Rate for a Lump Sum

Calculator

Input	Function
1000	PV
-2150	FV
5	N
	CPT
	I
Solution	16.54

Spreadsheet

Row \ Column	A	B
1	Present value	\$1,000
2	Future value	-\$2,150
3	Number of years	5
4	**Interest rate**	**16.54%**
5	*Formula B4:* RATE(B3,0,B1,B2)	

simply by raising 2.150 to the one-fifth power using the y^x key on a financial calculator, and then subtract 1:

$$r = (2.150)^{0.20} - 1 = 1.1654 - 1 = 0.1654 = 16.54\% \text{ per year}$$

We can use a financial calculator or spreadsheet to more directly solve for a growth or interest rate of a lump sum, as demonstrated in the example above. (Note: The *PV* and *FV* values must be input with opposite signs.)

Annuities. Sometimes you may need to find the interest rate associated with an annuity, which represents the equal annual end-of-year payments on a loan. To demonstrate, assume that your friend John Jacobs can borrow \$2,000 to be repaid in equal annual end-of-year amounts of \$514.18 for the next five years. He wants to find the interest rate on the loan and asks you for assistance. You realize that he is really asking you an annuity valuation question, so you use a variant of the present value of an annuity formula shown in Equation 3.7:

$$PV = PMT \times \left\{ \frac{1}{r} \times \left[1 - \frac{1}{(1+r)^n} \right] \right\}$$

You try to determine the interest rate (r) that will equate the present value of a five-year annuity (PV = \$2,000) to a stream of five equal annual payments (PMT = \$514.18 per year). Because you know PV and PMT, you can rearrange Equation 3.7, putting the unknown value on the left-hand side and the known values on the right:

$$\left\{ \left[\frac{1}{r} \right] \times \left[1 - \frac{1}{(1+r)^n} \right] \right\} = \frac{PV}{PMT} = \frac{\$2{,}000}{\$514.18} = 3.8897$$

Unfortunately, the term on the left-hand side is very difficult to solve directly, but there is an easy shortcut to obtaining the solution. Equation 3.7 can also be expressed using present-value factors as the annual cash flow (*PMT*) times the present-value factor

Calculating an Interest Rate for an Annuity

Calculator

Input	Function
2000	PV
-514.18	PMT
5	N
	CPT
	I
Solution	9.00

Spreadsheet

Row \ Column	A	B
1	Present value	$2,000
2	Payment	-$514.18
3	Number of periods	5
4	**Interest rate**	**9.00**
5	*Formula B4:* Rate(B3,B2,B1)	

for an annuity paying *r* percent for *n* years, or $PVFA_{r\%,n}$, which is the unknown value on the left-hand side of the preceding equation. Substituting, we get the following:

$$PVFA_{r\%,5} = \frac{PV}{PMT} = \frac{\$2,000}{\$514.18} = 3.8897$$

We can then solve this equation by determining the appropriate five-year *PVFA* having a value of 3.8897. Table A4 in Appendix A shows that $PVFA_{9\%,5} = 3.890$, so we can tell John Jacobs that he is being charged about 9 percent on his loan.

We can use a financial calculator or spreadsheet to more directly solve for a growth or interest rate of an annuity, as demonstrated in the example above. (Note: The *PV* and *PMT* values must be input with opposite signs.)

Mixed Streams. As in the previous discussion, finding the unknown interest or growth rate for a lump sum or an annuity is relatively simple, using the formulas presented here, the present-value tables, or a financial calculator or spreadsheet. Finding the unknown interest or growth rate for a mixed stream is very difficult to do using formulas or present-value tables. It can be accomplished by using an iterative trial-and-error approach to find the interest rate that could cause the present value of the stream's inflows to just equal the present value of its outflows. This calculation is often referred to as finding the *yield-to-maturity* or *internal rate of return (IRR)*. A more efficient way to make this type of calculation is to use a financial calculator or spreadsheet that has the IRR function built into it. With this approach, an analyst can input (with all outflows input as negative numbers) all the cash flows—both outflows and inflows—and then use the IRR function to calculate the unknown interest rate. Because this approach is discussed and demonstrated in Chapter 4 with regard to bonds and in Chapter 8 with regard to its use in capital budgeting, a detailed description of its application is not included here.

Number of Compounding Periods

Occasionally, for either a lump sum or an annuity, the financial analyst wants to calculate the unknown number of time periods necessary to achieve a given cash flow goal. We briefly consider this calculation here for both lump sums and annuities.

Lump Sums. If the present (*PV*) and future (*FV*) amounts are known, along with the interest rate (*r*), we can calculate the number of periods (*n*) necessary for the present amount to grow to equal the future amount. For example, assume that you plan to deposit $1,000 in an investment that is expected to earn an 8 percent annual rate of interest. Determine how long it will take to triple your money (to accumulate $3,000). Stated differently, at an 8 percent annual interest rate, how many years (*n*) will it take for $1,000 (*PV*) to grow to $3,000 (*FV*)? This can be expressed by simply rearranging the basic future-value formula, Equation 3.1, to express the unknown value, *n*, on the left-hand side and then plugging in the known values, *FV*, *PV*, and *r*:

$$FV = PV \times (1+r)^n$$

$$(1+0.08)^n = \frac{FV}{PV} = \frac{\$3,000}{\$1,000} = 3.000$$

$$(1.08)^n = 3.000$$

Now what? How do you find the exponent value (*n*) that turns 1.08 into 3.000? Take natural logarithms of both sides of this formula and then express the unknown number of years (*n*) as a ratio of two log values, as follows:

$$n = \frac{\ln(3.000)}{\ln(1.08)} = \frac{1.0986}{0.0770} = 14.275$$

You thus find the number of years to be 14.275, which means that at an 8 percent annual rate of interest, it will take about 14.3 years for your $1,000 deposit to triple in value to $3,000. Use a financial calculator or spreadsheet to more directly solve for the unknown number of periods for a lump sum, as demonstrated below:

Calculating an Unknown Number of Years for a Lump Sum

Calculator

Input	Function
1000	PV
8	I
-3,000	FV
	CPT
	N
Solution	14.275

Spreadsheet

Row \ Column	A	B
1	Present value	$1,000
2	Interest rate	8%
3	Future value	-$3,000
4	**Number of years**	**14.275**
5	*Formula B4:* Nper(B2,0,B1,B3)	

Annuities. Occasionally, we want to determine the unknown life (n) of an annuity that is intended to achieve a specified objective, such as to repay a loan of a given amount (PV) with a stated interest rate (r) and equal annual end-of-year payments (PMT). To illustrate, assume that you can borrow \$20,000 at a 12 percent annual interest rate with annual end-of-year payments of \$3,000. You want to determine how long it will take to fully repay the loan's interest and principal. In other words, how many years (n) will it take to repay a \$20,000 (PV), 12 percent (r) loan if the payments of \$3,000 (PMT) are made at the end of each year? This is similar to the problem of determining the unknown interest rate in an annuity we addressed earlier, except we now know that $r = 12$ percent, and that we are trying to determine the number of years (n). Once again, rearrange the equation that expresses the present value of an annuity (PV) as the product of its payment (PMT) and the present-value factor for an annuity paying r percent for n years ($PVFA_{r\%,n}$):

$$PVFA_{12\%,n} = \frac{PV}{PMT} = \frac{\$20{,}000}{\$3{,}000} = 6.6667$$

We can solve this by finding the 12 percent $PVFA$ value in Table A4 that most closely corresponds to 6.667, which is between 14 years ($PVFA_{12\%,14} = 6.628$) and 15 years ($PVFA_{12\%,15} = 6.811$). Using a financial calculator or spreadsheet, as shown below, we find the number of years to be 14.20, which means that you have to repay \$3,000 at the end of each year for 14 years and about \$600 ($0.20 \times \$3{,}000$) at the end of 14.20 years to fully repay the \$20,000 loan at 12 percent.

Calculating an Unknown Number of Years for an Annuity

Calculator

Input	Function
20000	PV
12	I
-3,000	PMT
	CPT
	N
Solution	14.20

Spreadsheet

Row \ Column	A	B
1	Present value	\$20,000
2	Interest rate	12%
3	Future value	-\$3,000
4	**Number of years**	**14.20**
5	*Formula B4:* Nper(B2,B3,B1)	

CONCEPT REVIEW QUESTIONS

14. How can you find the interest or growth rate for (a) a lump sum amount, (b) an annuity, and (c) a mixed stream?

15. How can you find the number of time periods needed to repay (a) a single-payment loan and (b) an installment loan requiring equal annual end-of-year payments?

3.7 SUMMARY AND CONCLUSIONS

- Financial managers can use future-value and present-value techniques to equate cash flows occurring at different times to compare decision alternatives. Managers rely primarily on present-value techniques and commonly use financial calculators or spreadsheet programs to streamline their computations.
- The future value of a lump sum is found by applying compound interest to the present value (the initial investment) over the period of concern. The higher the interest rate and the further in the future the cash flow's value is measured, the higher its future value.
- The present value of a lump sum is found by discounting the future value at the given interest rate. It is the amount of money today that is equivalent to the given future amount, considering the rate of return that can be earned on the present value. The higher the interest rate and the further in the future the cash flow occurs, the lower its present value.
- The future value of any cash flow stream—mixed stream, ordinary annuity, or annuity due—is the sum of the future values of the individual cash flows. Future values of mixed streams are most difficult to find, whereas future values of annuities are easier to calculate because they have the same cash flow each period. The future value of an ordinary annuity (end-of-period cash flows) can be converted into the future value of an annuity due (beginning-of-period cash flows) merely by multiplying it by 1 plus the interest rate.
- The present value of a cash flow stream is the sum of the present values of the individual cash flows. The present value of a mixed stream is the most difficult to find, whereas present values of annuities are easier to calculate because they have the same cash flow each period. The present value of an ordinary annuity can be converted to the present value of an annuity due merely by multiplying it by 1 plus the interest rate. The present value of an ordinary perpetuity—a level stream that continues forever—is found by dividing the amount of the annuity by the interest rate.
- Some special applications of time value include compounding interest more frequently than annually, stated and effective annual rates of interest, deposits needed to accumulate a future sum, and loan amortization. The more frequently interest is compounded at a stated annual rate, the larger the future amount that will be accumulated and the higher the effective annual rate.
- The annual deposit needed to accumulate a given future sum is found by manipulating the future value of an annuity equation. Loan amortization—determination of the equal periodic payments necessary to fully repay loan principal and interest over a given time at a given interest rate—is performed by manipulating the present value of an annuity equation. An amortization schedule can be prepared to allocate each payment to principal and interest.

- Implied interest or growth rates can be found using the basic future-value equations for lump sums and annuities and require an iterative trial-and-error approach for mixed streams. Using a financial calculator or spreadsheet can greatly simplify these calculations.
- Given present and future cash flows and the applicable interest rate, the unknown number of periods can be found using the basic equations for future values of lump sums and annuities. Using a financial calculator or spreadsheet greatly simplifies these calculations.

SELF-TEST PROBLEMS

Answers to Self-Test Problems appear in Appendix D at back of book. Answers to the Concept Review Questions throughout the chapter appear at http://www.megginson.swlearning.com.

ST3-1. Starratt Alexander is considering investing specified amounts in each of four investment opportunities described below. For each opportunity, determine the amount of money Starratt will have at the end of the given investment horizon.

Investment A: Invest a lump sum of $2,750 today in an account that pays 6 percent annual interest and leave the funds on deposit for exactly fifteen years.

Investment B: Invest the following amounts at the beginning of each of the next five years in a venture that will earn 9 percent annually and measure the accumulated value at the end of exactly five years:

Beginning of Year	Amount
1	$ 900
2	1,000
3	1,200
4	1,500
5	1,800

Investment C: Invest $1,200 at the *end of each year* for the next ten years in an account that pays 10 percent annual interest and determine the account balance at the end of year 10.

Investment D: Make the same investment as in investment C but place the $1,200 in the account at the *beginning of each year.*

ST3-2. Gregg Snead has been offered four investment opportunities, all equally priced at $45,000. Because the opportunities differ in risk, Gregg's required returns (i.e., applicable discount rates) are not the same for each opportunity. The cash flows and required returns for each opportunity are summarized below.

Opportunity	Cash Flows		Required Return
A	$7,500 at the end of 5 years		12%
B	**Year**	**Amount**	15%
	1	$10,000	
	2	12,000	
	3	18,000	
	4	10,000	
	5	13,000	
	6	9,000	
C	$5,000 at the *end of each year* for the next 30 years.		10%
D	$7,000 at the *beginning of each year* for the next 20 years.		18%

a. Find the present value of each of the four investment opportunities.
b. Which, if any, opportunities are acceptable?
c. Which opportunity should Gregg take?

ST3-3. Assume you wish to establish a college scholarship of $2,000 paid at the end of each year for a deserving student at the high school you attended. You would like to make a lump-sum gift to the high school to fund the scholarship into perpetuity. The school's treasurer assures you that they will earn 7.5 percent annually forever.

a. How much must you give the high school today to fund the proposed scholarship program?
b. If you wanted to allow the amount of the scholarship to increase annually after the first award (end of year 1) by 3 percent per year, how much must you give the school today to fund the scholarship program?
c. Compare, contrast, and discuss the difference in your response to parts (a) and (b).

ST3-4. Assume that you deposit $10,000 today into an account paying 6 percent annual interest and leave it on deposit for exactly eight years.

a. How much will be in the account at the end of eight years if interest is compounded
1. annually?
2. semiannually?
3. monthly?
4. continuously?
b. Calculate the *effective annual rate* (*EAR*) for (1) through (4) above.
c. Based on your findings in parts (a) and (b), what is the general relationship between the frequency of compounding and *EAR?*

ST3-5. Imagine that you are a professional personal financial planner. One of your clients asks you the following two questions. Use the time value of money techniques to develop appropriate responses to each question.

a. I borrowed $75,000, am required to repay it in six equal (annual) end-of-year installments of $3,344, and want to know what interest rate I am paying.
b. I need to save $37,000 over the next fifteen years to fund my three-year-old daughter's college education. If I make equal annual end-of-year deposits into an account that earns 7 percent annual interest, how large must this deposit be?

INTERNET RESOURCES

Note: *For updates to links, please go to the book's Web site at* http://megginson.swlearning.com.

http://www.bankrate.com—Offers a variety of automated present and future value calculations, such as a loan amortization calculator and a tool that compares rebates and low-rate financing deals on automobiles

http://www.tcalc.com—Contains numerous financial calculators that can be purchased and added to a Web site

http://www.moneychimp.com—Can try the "How Finance Works" link to learn about many applications of present and future value mathematics; has a number of useful interactive graphs

http://www.financialplayerscenter.com—Provides helpful tutorials on time value concepts

Use the learning tools at http://smartfinance.swcollege.com.

KEY TERMS

annual percentage rate (*APR*)
annual percentage yield (*APY*)
annuity
annuity due
compound interest
continuous compounding
discounting
effective annual rate (*EAR*)
future value
Gordon growth model
growing perpetuity
loan amortization
loan amortization schedule
mixed stream
ordinary annuity
perpetuity
present value
principal
quarterly compounding
semiannual compounding
simple interest
stated annual rate
time line
time value of money

QUESTIONS AND PROBLEMS

Q3-1. What is the importance for an individual of understanding *time value of money* concepts? For a corporate manager? Under what circumstance would the time value of money be irrelevant?

Q3-2. From a time value of money perspective, explain why the maximization of shareholder wealth and the maximization of profits may not offer the same result or course of action.

Q3-3. If a firm's required return were 0 percent, would time value of money matter? As these returns rise above 0 percent, what effect would the increasing return have on future value? Present value?

Q3-4. What would happen to the future value of an annuity if interest rates fell in the late periods? Could the future value of an annuity factor formula still be used to determine the future value?

Q3-5. What happens to the present value of a cash flow stream when the discount rate increases? Place this in the context of an investment. If the required return on an investment goes up, but the expected cash flows do not change, are you willing to pay the same price for the investment, or to pay more or less for this investment than before interest rates changed?

Q3-6. Look at the formula for the present value of an annuity. What happens to its value as the number of periods increases? What distinguishes an annuity from a *perpetuity?* Why is there no future value of a perpetuity?

Q3-7. What is the relationship between the variables in a *loan amortization* calculation and the total interest cost? Consider the variables of interest rates, amount borrowed, down payment, prepayment, and term of loan in answering this question.

Q3-8. Why is it so difficult to find unknown interest or growth rates and numbers of periods when all other variables are known? When must you use trial-and-error techniques?

PROBLEMS

Future Value of a Lump Sum

P3-1. You have $1,500 to invest today at 7 percent interest compounded annually.

a. How much will you have accumulated in the account at the end of the following number of years?
   1. three years
   2. six years
   3. nine years

b. Use your findings in part (a) to calculate the amount of interest earned in
   1. the first three years (years 1 to 3)
   2. the second three years (years 3 to 6)
   3. the third three years (years 6 to 9)

c. Compare and contrast your findings in part (b). Explain why the amount of interest earned increases in each succeeding three-year period.

Present Value of a Lump Sum

P3-2. An Indiana state savings bond can be converted to $100 at maturity six years from purchase. If the state bonds are to be competitive with U.S. savings bonds, which pay 8 percent annual interest (compounded annually), at what price must the state sell its bonds? Assume no cash payments on savings bonds before redemption.

P3-3. You just won a lottery that promises to pay you $1 million exactly ten years from today. Because the $1 million payment is guaranteed by the state in which you live, opportunities exist to sell the claim today for an immediate lump-sum cash payment.

a. What is the least you will sell your claim for if you could earn the following rates of return on similar risk investments during the ten-year period?
   1. 6 percent
   2. 9 percent
   3. 12 percent

b. Rework part (a) under the assumption that the $1 million payment will be received in fifteen rather than ten years.

c. Based on your findings in parts (a) and (b), discuss the effect of both the size of the rate of return and the time until receipt of payment on the present value of a future sum.

Future Value of Cash Flow Streams

P3-4. Dixon Shuttleworth is offered the choice of three retirement-planning investments. The first investment offers a 5 percent return for the first five years, a 10 percent return for the next five years, and a 20 percent return thereafter. The second investment offers 10 percent for the first ten years and 15 percent thereafter. The third investment offers a constant 12 percent rate of return. Determine, for each of the given number of years, which of these investments is the best for Dixon if he plans to make one payment today into one of these funds and to retire in the following number of years.

a. fifteen years
b. twenty years
c. thirty years

P3-5. Robert Blanding's employer offers its workers a two-month paid sabbatical every seven years. Robert, who just started working for the firm, plans to spend his sabbatical touring Europe at an estimated cost of $25,000. To finance his trip, Robert plans to make six annual end-of-year deposits of $2,500 each, starting this year, into an investment account earning 8 percent interest.

a. Will Robert's account balance at the end of seven years be enough to pay for his trip?
b. Suppose Robert increases his annual contribution to $3,150. How large will his account balance be at the end of seven years?

P3-6. Robert Williams is considering an offer to sell his medical practice, allowing him to retire five years early. He has been offered $500,000 for his practice and can invest this amount in an account earning 10 percent per year, compounded annually. If the practice is expected to generate the following cash flows, should Robert accept this offer and retire now?

End of Year	Cash Flow
1	$150,000
2	150,000
3	125,000
4	125,000
5	100,000

P3-7. Gina Coulson has just contracted to sell a small parcel of land that she inherited a few years ago. The buyer is willing to pay $24,000 at the closing of the transaction or will pay the amounts, shown in the following table, at the *beginning* of each of the next five years. Because Gina doesn't really need the money today, she plans to let it accumulate in an account that earns 7 percent annual interest. Given her desire to buy a house at the end of five years after closing on the sale of the lot, she decides to choose the payment alternative—$24,000 lump sum or the mixed stream of payments in the following table—that provides the highest future value at the end of five years.

Mixed Stream	
Beginning of Year (t)	Cash Flow (CF_t)
1	$ 2,000
2	4,000
3	6,000
4	8,000
5	10,000

a. What is the future value of the lump sum at the end of year 5?
b. What is the future value of the mixed stream at the end of year 5?
c. Based on your findings in parts (a) and (b), which alternative should Gina take?
d. If Gina could earn 10 percent rather than 7 percent on the funds, would your recommendation in part (c) change? Explain.

P3-8. For the following questions, assume an ordinary annuity of $1,000 and a required return of 12 percent.

a. What is the future value of a ten-year *ordinary annuity*?
b. If you earned an additional year's worth of interest on this annuity, what would be the future value?
c. What is the future value of a ten-year *annuity due*?
d. What is the relationship between your answers in parts (b) and (c)? Explain.

P3-9. Kim Edwards and Chris Phillips are both newly minted thirty-year-old MBAs. Kim plans to invest $1,000 per month into her 401(k) beginning next month. Chris intends to invest $2,000 per month, but he does not plan to begin investing until ten years after Kim begins investing. Both Kim and Chris will retire at age sixty-seven, and the 401(k) plan averages a 12 percent annual return, compounded monthly. Who will have more 401(k) money at retirement?

Present Value of Cash Flow Streams

P3-10. Given the mixed streams of cash flows shown in the following table, answer parts (a) and (b):

	Cash Flow Stream	
Year	A	B
1	$ 50,000	$ 10,000
2	40,000	20,000
3	30,000	30,000
4	20,000	40,000
5	10,000	50,000
Totals	$150,000	$150,000

a. Find the present value of each stream, using a 15 percent discount rate.
b. Compare the calculated present values, and discuss them in light of the fact that the undiscounted total cash flows amount to $150,000 in each case.

P3-11. As part of your personal budgeting process, you have determined that in each of the next five years you will have budget shortfalls. In other words, you need the amounts shown in the following table at the end of the given year to balance your budget, that is, to make inflows equal outflows. You expect to be able to earn 8 percent on your investments during the next five years and want to fund the budget shortfalls over these years with a single initial deposit.

End of Year	Budget Shortfall
1	$ 5,000
2	4,000
3	6,000
4	10,000
5	3,000

a. How large must the lump-sum deposit into an account paying 8 percent annual interest be today to provide for full coverage of the anticipated budget shortfalls?
b. What effect does an increase in your earnings rate have on the amount calculated in part (a)? Explain.

P3-12. Ruth Nail receives two offers for her seaside home. The first offer is for $1 million today. The second offer is for an owner-financed sale with a payment schedule as follows:

End of Year	Payment
0 (Today)	$200,000
1	200,000
2	200,000
3	200,000
4	200,000
5	300,000

Assuming no differential tax treatment between the two options and that Ruth earns a rate of 8 percent on her investments, which offer should she take?

P3-13. Melissa Gould wants to invest today to assure adequate funds for her son's college education. She estimates that her son will need $20,000 at the end of eighteen years, $25,000 at the end of nineteen years, $30,000 at the end of twenty years, and $40,000 at the end of twenty-one years. How much does Melissa have to invest in a fund today if the fund earns the following interest rate?

a. 6 percent per year with annual compounding
b. 6 percent per year with quarterly compounding
c. 6 percent per year with monthly compounding

P3-14. Assume that you just won the state lottery. Your prize can be taken either in the form of $40,000 at the end of each of the next twenty-five years (i.e., $1 million over twenty-five years) or as a lump sum of $500,000 paid immediately.

a. If you expect to be able to earn 5 percent annually on your investments over the next twenty-five years, ignoring taxes and other considerations, which alternative should you take? Why?

b. Would your decision in part (a) be altered if you could earn 7 percent rather than 5 percent on your investments over the next twenty-five years? Why?

c. On a strict economic basis, at approximately what earnings rate would you be indifferent when choosing between the two plans?

P3-15. For the following questions, assume an end-of-year cash flow of $250 and a 10 percent discount rate.

a. What is the present value of a single cash flow?

b. What is the present value of a 5-year annuity?

c. What is the present value of a 10-year annuity?

d. What is the present value of a 100-year annuity?

e. What is the present value of a $250 perpetuity?

f. Do you detect a relationship between the number of periods of an annuity and its resemblance to a perpetuity? Explain it.

P3-16. Use the following table of cash flows to answer parts (a)–(c). Assume an 8 percent discount rate.

End of Year	Cash Flow
1	$10,000
2	10,000
3	10,000
4	12,000
5	12,000
6	12,000
7	12,000
8	15,000
9	15,000
10	15,000

a. Solve for the present value of the cash flow stream by summing the present value of each individual cash flow.

b. Solve for the present value by summing the present value of the three separate annuities (one current and two deferred).

c. Which method is better for a long series of cash flows with embedded annuities?

P3-17. Joan Wallace, corporate finance specialist for Big Blazer Bumpers, is responsible for funding an account to cover anticipated future warranty costs. Warranty costs are expected to be $5 million per year for three years, with the first costs expected to occur four years from today. How much does Joan have to place into an account today earning 10 percent per year to cover these expenses?

P3-18. Landon Lowman, star quarterback of the university football team, is approached about foregoing his last two years of eligibility and making himself available for the professional football draft. Talent scouts estimate that Landon could receive a signing bonus of $1 million today, along with a five-year contract for $3 million per year (payable at the end of the year). They further estimate that he could negotiate a contract for $5 million per year for the remaining seven years of his career. The scouts believe, however, that Landon will be a much higher draft pick if he improves by playing out his eligibility. If he stays at the university, he is expected to receive a $2 million signing bonus in two years, along with a five-year contract for $5 million per year. After that, the scouts expect Landon to obtain a five-year contract for $6 million per year to take him into retirement. Assume that Landon can earn a 10 percent return over this time. Should Landon stay or go?

P3-19. Matt Sedgwick, facilities and operations manager for the Birmingham Buffalo professional football team, has come up with an idea for generating income. Matt wants to expand the stadium by building skyboxes sold with lifetime (perpetual) season tickets. Each skybox is guaranteed ten season tickets at a cost of $200 per ticket per year for life. If each skybox costs $100,000 to build, what is the minimum selling price that Matt will need to charge for the skyboxes to break even, if the required return is 10 percent?

P3-20. Log on to Hugh Chou's financial calculator Web page (http://www.interest.com/hugh/calc/simple.org) and look over the various calculator links available. Refer to some of the earlier time-value problems and rework them with these calculators. Run through several numerical scenarios to determine the effect of changing variables on your results.

Special Applications of Time Value

P3-21. You plan to invest $2,000 in an individual retirement arrangement (IRA) today at a *stated interest rate* of 8 percent, which is expected to apply to all future years.

a. How much will you have in the account at the end of ten years if interest is compounded as follows?
   1. annually
   2. semiannually
   3. daily (assume a 365-day year)
   4. continuously

b. What is the *effective annual rate (EAR)* for each compounding period in part (a)?

c. How much greater will your IRA account balance be at the end of ten years if interest is compounded continuously rather than annually?

d. How does the compounding frequency affect the future value and effective annual rate for a given deposit? Explain in terms of your findings in parts (a)–(c).

P3-22. Jason Spector has shopped around for the best interest rates for his investment of $10,000 over the next year. He has found the following:

Stated Rate	Compounding
6.10%	annual
5.90%	semiannual
5.85%	monthly

a. Which investment offers Jason the highest *effective annual rate* of return?

b. Assume that Jason wants to invest his money for only six months, and the annual compounded rate of 6.10 percent is not available. Which of the remaining investments should Jason choose?

P3-23. Answer parts (a)–(c) for each of the following cases.

Case	Amount of Initial Deposit ($)	Stated Annual Rate, r (%)	Compounding Frequency, m (times/year)	Deposit Period (years)
A	2,500	6	2	5
B	50,000	12	6	3
C	1,000	5	1	10
D	20,000	16	4	6

a. Calculate the future value at the end of the specified deposit period.

b. Determine the *effective annual rate* (*EAR*).

c. Compare the stated annual rate (r) to the *effective annual rate* (*EAR*). What relationship exists between compounding frequency and the stated and effective annual rates?

P3-24. Tara Cutler is newly married and preparing a surprise gift of a trip to Europe for her husband on their tenth anniversary. Tara plans to invest $5,000 per year until that anniversary and to make her first $5,000 investment on their first anniversary. If she earns an 8 percent rate on her investments, how much will she have saved for their trip if the interest is compounded in each of the following ways?

a. annually
b. quarterly
c. monthly

P3-25. John Tye was hired as the new corporate finance analyst at I-Ell Enterprises and received his first assignment. John is to take the $25 million in cash received from a recent divestiture, use part of these proceeds to retire an outstanding $10 million bond issue, and use the remainder to repurchase common stock. However, the bond issue cannot be retired for another two years. If John can place the funds necessary to retire this $10 million debt into an account earning a 6 percent annual return compounded *monthly,* how much of the $25 million remains to repurchase stock?

P3-26. Find the present value of a three-year, $20,000 ordinary annuity deposited into an account that pays 12 percent annual interest, compounded *monthly*. Solve for the present value of the annuity in the following ways:

a. as three single cash flows discounted at the stated annual rate of interest
b. as three single cash flows discounted at the appropriate effective annual rate of interest
c. as a three-year annuity discounted at the effective annual rate of interest

P3-27. To supplement your planned retirement in exactly forty-two years, you estimate that you need to accumulate $220,000 by the end of forty-two years from today. You plan to make equal annual end-of-year deposits into an account paying 8 percent annual interest.

a. How large must the annual deposits be to create the $220,000 fund by the end of forty-two years?
b. If you can afford to deposit only $600 per year into the account, how much will you have accumulated by the end of the forty-second year?

SMART SOLUTIONS

See the problem and solution explained step-by-step at SMARTFinance

P3-28. Determine the annual deposit required to fund a future annual annuity of $12,000 per year. You will fund this future liability over the next five years, with the first deposit to occur one year from today. The future $12,000 liability will last for four years, with the first payment to occur seven years from today. If you can earn 8 percent on this account, how much will you have to deposit each year over the next five years to fund the future liability?

P3-29. Mary Sullivan, capital outlay manager for PDA Manufacturing, knows that her company is facing a series of monthly expenses associated with installation and calibration of new production equipment. The company has $1 million in a bank account right now that it can draw on to meet these expenses. Funds in this account earn 6 percent interest annually, with monthly compounding. Ms. Sullivan is preparing a budget that will require the firm to make equal monthly desposits into their bank account, starting next month, to ensure that they can pay the expenses they anticipate over the next 24 months (shown below). How much should the monthly bank deposit be?

Months	Repair Costs per Month
1–4	$100,000
5–12	200,000
13–24	500,000

P3-30. Craig and LaDonna Allen are trying to establish a college fund for their son Spencer, who just turned three today. They plan for Spencer to withdraw $10,000 on his eighteenth birthday and $11,000, $12,000, and $15,000 on his subsequent birthdays. They plan to fund these withdrawals with a ten-year annuity, with the first payment to occur one year from today, and expect to earn an average annual return of 8 percent.

a. How much will the Allens have to contribute each year to achieve their goal?
b. Create a schedule showing the cash inflows (including interest) and outflows of this fund. How much remains on Spencer's twenty-first birthday?

P3-31. Joan Messineo borrowed $15,000 at a 14 percent annual interest rate to be repaid over three years. The loan is amortized into three equal annual end-of-year payments.

a. Calculate the annual end-of-year loan payment.
b. Prepare a loan amortization schedule showing the interest and principal breakdown of each of the three loan payments.
c. Explain why the interest portion of each payment declines with the passage of time.

P3-32. You are planning to purchase a building for $40,000, and you have $10,000 to apply as a down payment. You may borrow the remainder under the following terms: a ten-year loan with semiannual repayments and a stated interest rate of 6 percent. You intend to make $6,000 payments, applying the excess over your required payment to the reduction of the principal balance.

a. Given these terms, how long (in years) will it take you to fully repay your loan?
b. What will be your total interest cost?
c. What would be your interest cost if you made no prepayments and repaid your loan by strictly adhering to the terms of the loan?

P3-33. Use a spreadsheet to create amortization schedules for the following five scenarios. What happens to the total interest paid under each scenario?

a. Scenario 1:
Loan amount: $1 million
Annual rate: 5 percent
Term: 360 months
Prepayment: $0
b. Scenario 2: Same as 1, except annual rate is 7 percent
c. Scenario 3: Same as 1, except term is 180 months
d. Scenario 4: Same as 1, except prepayment is $250 per month
e. Scenario 5: Same as 1, except loan amount is $125,000

P3-34. Go to the home page of the Bankrate.com (http://www.bankrate.com) and obtain current average mortgage rates. With this information, go to Hugh Chou's mortgage calculator (http://www.interest.com/hugh/calc/simple.org). Provide the requested variables to create an amortization schedule. Re-create the schedule with different prepayment amounts. What effect does the prepayment have on total interest and the term of the loan?

P3-35. To analyze various retirement-planning options, check out the financial calculator at Bloomberg (http://www.bloomberg.com). Determine the effect of waiting versus immediate planning for retirement. What is the effect of changing interest-rate assumptions on your retirement "nest egg"?

P3-36. For excellent qualitative discussions of the value of compounded interest on saving for future (retirement) obligations, see the following Web sites:

http://www.prudential.com/retirement (Prudential Financial)

http://www.vanguard.com (The Vanguard Group)

http://www.fid-inv.com (Fidelity Investments)

http://www.bloomberg.com (Bloomberg)

What can you conclude about the timing of cash flows and future values available for retirement, considering the information provided on these Web sites?

Additional Applications of Time-Value Techniques

P3-37. Find the rates of return required to do the following:

a. Double an investment in four years
b. Double an investment in ten years
c. Triple an investment in four years
d. Triple an investment in ten years

P3-38. You are given the series of cash flows shown in the following table:

	Cash Flows		
Year	A	B	C
1	$500	$1,500	$2,500
2	560	1,550	2,600
3	640	1,610	2,650
4	720	1,680	2,650
5	800	1,760	2,800
6		1,850	2,850
7		1,950	2,900
8			2,060
9			2,170
10			2,280

a. Calculate the compound annual growth rate associated with each cash flow stream.
b. If year 1 values represent initial deposits in a savings account paying annual interest, what is the annual rate of interest earned on each account?
c. Compare and discuss the growth rate and interest rate found in parts (a) and (b), respectively.

P3-39. Determine the length of time required to double the value of an investment, given the following rates of return.

a. 4 percent
b. 10 percent
c. 30 percent
d. 100 percent

P3-40. You are the pension fund manager for Tanju's Toffees. Your CFO wants to know the minimum annual return required on the pension fund in order to make all required payments over the next five years and not diminish the current asset base. The fund currently has assets of $500 million.

a. Determine the required return if outflows are expected to exceed inflows by $50 million per year.
b. Determine the required return with the following fund cash flows.

End of Year	Inflows	Outflows
1	$55,000,000	$100,000,000
2	60,000,000	110,000,000
3	60,000,000	120,000,000
4	60,000,000	135,000,000
5	64,000,000	145,000,000

c. Consider the cash flows in part (b). What will happen to your asset base if you earn 10 percent? 20 percent?

P3-41. Jill Chew wants to choose the best of four immediate retirement annuities available to her. In each case, in exchange for paying a single premium today, she will receive equal annual end-of-year cash benefits for a specified number of years. She considers the annuities to be equally risky and is not concerned about their differing lives. Her decision will be based solely on the rate of return she will earn on each annuity. The key terms of each of the four annuities are shown in the following table:

Annuity	Premium Paid Today	Annual Benefit	Life (years)
A	$30,000	$3,100	20
B	25,000	3,900	10
C	40,000	4,200	15
D	35,000	4,000	12

a. Calculate to the nearest 1 percent the rate of return on each of the four annuities Jill is considering.
b. Given Jill's stated decision criterion, which annuity would you recommend?

P3-42. Determine which of the following three investments offers you the highest rate of return on your $1,000 investment over the next five years.

Investment 1: $2,000 lump sum to be received in five years

Investment 2: $300 at the end of each of the next five years

Investment 3: $250 at the beginning of each of the next five years

a. Which investment offers the highest return?
b. Which offers the highest return if the payouts are doubled (i.e., $4,000, $600, and $500)?
c. What causes the big change in the returns on the annuities?

P3-43. Consider the following three investments of equal risk. Which offers the greatest rate of return?

	Investment		
End of Year	A	B	C
0	–$10,000	–$20,000	–$25,000
1	0	9,500	20,000
2	0	9,500	30,000
3	24,600	9,500	–12,600

P3-44. You plan to start saving for your son's college education. He will begin college when he turns eighteen and will need $4,000 then and in each of the following three years. You will make a deposit at the end of this year in an account that pays 6 percent compounded annually and an identical deposit at the end of each year, with the last deposit occurring when he turns eighteen. If an annual deposit of $1,484 will allow you to reach your goal, how old is your son now?

P3-45. Log on to MSN Money (http://www.investor.msn.com) and select five stocks to analyze. Use their returns over the last five years to determine the value of $1,000 invested in each stock five years ago. What is the compound annual rate of return for each of the five stocks over the five-year period?

P3-46. The viatical industry offers a rather grim example of present-value concepts. A firm in this business, called a viator, purchases the rights to the benefits from a life insurance contract from a terminally ill client. The viator may then sell claims on the insurance payout to other investors. The industry began in the early 1990s as a way to help AIDS patients capture some of the proceeds from their life insurance policies for living expenses.

Suppose a patient has a life expectancy of eighteen months and a life insurance policy with a death benefit of $100,000. A viator pays $80,000 for the right to the benefit and then sells that claim to another investor for $80,500.

a. From the point of view of the patient, this contract is like taking out a loan. What is the compound annual interest rate on the loan if the patient lives exactly eighteen months? What if the patient lives thirty-six months?

b. From the point of view of the investor, this transaction is like lending money. What is the compound annual interest rate earned on the loan if the patient lives eighteen months? What if the patient lives just twelve months?

SMART SOLUTIONS

See the problem and solution explained step-by-step at

SMARTFinance

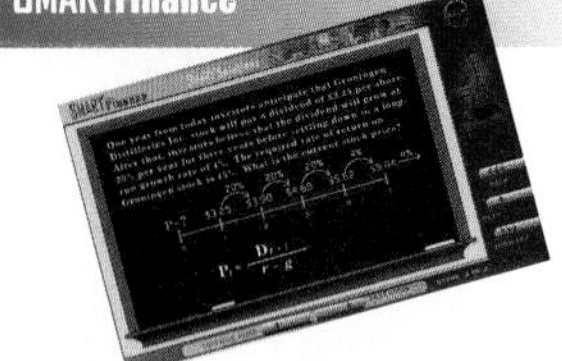

THOMSON ONE Business School Edition

Access financial information from the Thomson ONE – Business School Edition Web site for the following problem(s). Go to http://tobsefin.swlearning.com/. If you have already registered your access serial number and have a username and password, click **Enter.** Otherwise, click **Register** and follow the instructions to create a username and password. Register your access serial number and then click **Enter** on the aforementioned Web site. When you click Enter, you will be prompted for your username and password (please remember that the password is case sensitive). Enter them in the respective boxes and then click **OK** (or hit **Enter**). From the ensuing page, click **Click Here to Access Thomson ONE – Business School Edition Now!** This opens up a new window that gives you access to the Thomson ONE – Business School Edition database. You can retrieve a company's financial information by entering its ticker symbol (provided for each company in the problem(s)) in the box below "Name/Symbol/Key." For further instructions on using the Thomson ONE – Business School Edition database, please refer to "A Guide for Using Thomson ONE – Business School Edition."

P3-47. Compare the performance of Reebok International Limited (ticker: RBK) and Nike Inc. (NKE). Calculate the five-year growth in sales and net income and determine the compound annual growth rate for each company. Does one company dominate the other in growth in both categories?

P3-48. Compare the market performance of Kimberly Clark (ticker: U:KMB) and Procter & Gamble Company (U:PG). Calculate the three-year growth in stock price and the compound annual growth rate in stock price for each company. If you had invested $10,000 in each stock three years ago, what is the current value of each investment?

Since these exercises depend upon real-time data, your answers will change continuously depending upon when you access the Internet to download your data.

MINICASE

Present Value

Casino.com Corporation is building a $25 million office building in Las Vegas and is financing the construction at an 80 percent loan-to-value ratio, where the loan is in the amount of $20,000,000. This loan has a ten-year maturity, calls for monthly payments, and is contracted at an interest rate of 8 percent.

ASSIGNMENT

Using the above information, answer the following questions.

1. What is the monthly payment?
2. How much of the first payment is interest?
3. How much of the first payment is principal?
4. How much will Casino.com Corporation owe on this loan after making monthly payments for three years? (the amount owed immediately after the thirty-sixth payment)
5. Should this loan be refinanced after three years with a new seven-year 7 percent loan, if the cost to refinance is $250,000? To make this decision, calculate the new loan payments and then the present value of the difference in the loan payments.
6. Returning to the original ten-year 8 percent loan, how much is the loan payment if these payments are scheduled for quarterly rather than monthly payments?
7. For this loan with quarterly payments, how much will Casino.com Corporation owe on this loan after making quarterly payments for three years? (the amount owed immediately after the twelfth payment)
8. What is the annual percentage rate on the original ten-year 8 percent loan?
9. What is the *effective annual rate (EAR)* on the original ten-year 8 percent loan?

Smart *Excel* Appendix

Use the Smart *Excel* spreadsheets and animated tutorials at http://smartfinance.swlearning.com.

EXCEL PREREQUISITES

You need to be familiar with the following *Excel* features to use this appendix:

- Creating formulas in *Excel*
- Mathematical operators
- Order of mathematical operations
- Financial functions

If this is new to you, be sure to complete the ***Excel Prereqs*** tab of the Chapter 3 *Excel* file before proceeding.

SOLVING TIME VALUE OF MONEY PROBLEMS IN *EXCEL*

Solving even complex future value, present value, and other time value of money problems is straightforward using *Excel*.

In this appendix, we review three different approaches to solving time value of money problems using *Excel*.

Approach 1. Use the mathematical formula.
Approach 2. Use the financial functions in *Excel*.
Approach 3. Create a basic model and solve using either of the above two approaches.

But first, let's review the *Excel* basics you'll need to solve time value of money problems in *Excel*. If you are new to *Excel*, be sure to review the *Excel* prerequisites for the chapter on the first tab of the Chapter 3 *Excel* file.

4 *EXCEL* BASICS

1. Learn the notation.

As you've seen in the chapter, there are five key variables listed in the table below. The variables are called function arguments in *Excel*. The notation in the text is slightly different than the notation in *Excel*.

Appendix Contents

5 Key Variables	Text notation	*Excel* notation
Present value	*PV*	P_v
Future value	*FV*	F_v
Payment	*PMT*	Pmt
Rate	*R*	Rate
Time or # periods	*N*	nper

If you know four of these variables, you can solve for the fifth.

In the chapter, we normally assume any cash flows occur at the end of the year (ordinary annuity). *Excel* allows for the option of any payment to be at the beginning of the year or at the end of the year. This option is provided for in *Excel* with a sixth variable called type (more on this later).

2. Know the mathematical operator signs in *Excel*.

Remember, all formulas must start with "=".

Mathematical operation	In *Excel* use
Addition	+
Subtraction	-
Multiplication	*
Division	/
Exponent	^

3. Note that cash flow signs matter in *Excel*.

Excel's financial functions have been designed so that the ***cash flow sign matters.*** Cash inflows and outflows MUST have different signs in *Excel*. Cash inflows should have a positive sign and cash outflows a negative sign. This means that if you are looking for a future value of a sum invested, the original funds invested are a cash outflow and have a negative cash flow sign—because the investment is money flowing away. The future value is a cash inflow and has a positive sign. Keep this in mind as you work through the example below.

4. Use *Excel* Smartly!

You can always use *Excel* like a calculator. But *Excel*'s real value in financial analysis is the model you build to change key inputs or assumptions that examine the effect on output. Approach 3 shows you how to build smart financial models in *Excel* to solve time value of money problems, using either the mathematical or the *Excel* function approach.

FUTURE VALUE IN *EXCEL*

Future Value of a Lump Sum

Open the Chapter 3 *Excel* file at the Smart Finance Web site. If you are new to *Excel*, be sure to review the *Excel* prerequisites for the chapter on the first tab of the Chapter 3 *Excel* file. Otherwise, proceed to the worksheet tab labeled ***FV lump sum***. We will solve the following problem, using the three approaches outlined above.

Problem: Find the future value of $1,000 invested for five years at 8%.

Consider the five key variables here:

Present value	$1,000
Future value	You are solving for future value.
Payment	There is no annual payment.
Rate	The rate is 8%.
Number of periods	five years

Approach 1: Use the mathematical formula.

Equation 3.1 on page 91 shows the formula for a future value as

$$FV = PV \times (1+r)^n$$

In a cell in *Excel* type in the formula as

```
=1000*(1.08)^5
```

Formula result: $1,469.33

Note: All solutions are provided in the* Excel *file, so if you have any trouble, check your result against the solution.

Approach 2: Use the future-value function in *Excel*.

A future-value function is built into *Excel*'s financial functions.

As with all *Excel* functions, begin with an equals sign followed by the function symbol, here fv, and the function arguments.

You can use the future-value function directly in a cell by using the following format:

```
=fv(rate,nper,pmt,pv,type)
```

Note: You must start with an "=".

Enter pv as a negative number because the funds are invested—cash outflow.

Type can be left blank (inserting a 1 here changes the payment to the beginning of the year).

Leave no spaces between variables.

Commas are required between variables.

In this example, type in a cell

=fv(8%,5,0,-1000)

Formula result: $1,469.33

You should get the same result as in the first approach.

Approach 3: Create a basic model and solve using either of the above approaches.

The first two approaches help you get a solution quickly and easily, but what if you want to change your initial assumptions? You can redo your calculation or go back in and edit your formula, but another option is to create a basic model.

Financial models built in *Excel* provide the same output but allow you to change your initial assumptions easily. Models are handy for examining the results under different input assumptions. In this example, suppose you want to determine the future value if the rate was changed to 5% or 11%, and to also look at the effect of longer or shorter time horizons.

Our financial models will have three key components:

1. **inputs**
2. **calculation**
3. **output**

The output is the "answer" you want to find. The inputs are the variables used in calculating the output.

In this model, the **output** desired is future value. The **input** assumptions are rate, time, payment, and present value. The **calculation** is straightforward and can be performed using either of the approaches above.

The key to creating a good model is building a formula that makes it easy to change inputs. Why? Because then you won't have to redo your calculations every time you want to change an input assumption. We demonstrate below, using the future-value function in Approach 2.

4 steps in a basic financial model

Step 1: Determine the desired output and select an approach to calculate it (mathematical formula or *Excel* function).

Step 2: Set up an area for input assumptions (done for you in this *Excel* file).

Step 3: Build a formula to calculate output by **USING CELL REFERENCES,** not by typing in the actual numbers (in our solution we use Approach 2).

Step 4: Change the input assumptions, as desired, and analyze the effect on output.

Look at the file provided. Note the section for inputs. Type your input assumptions in here.

Your worksheet should look like this:

Rate	8%
# periods	5
Pmt	0
Present value	(1,000)
Type	

Note that present value is entered as a negative number because the $1,000 is invested (cash outflow). Type can be left blank if payments are zero or occur at the end of the year.

Create a formula for future value by using cell references to the inputs. We use the built-in FV function rather than the mathematical formula, but either approach will work.

Your formula should read

=fv(C31,C32,C33,C34,C35)

Again, the result is $1,469.33.

Apply it

Change the input assumptions and analyze the effect.
If you change the rate input to 5%, the future value is $1,338.23. At 11%, it is $1,685.06.

Return to a rate of 8% but invest for ten years, and the future value is $2,158.92.

Models make financial analysis in *Excel* valuable. Throughout most of this book, we create financial models to solve problems so that it is straightforward to change inputs and analyze the effect on output.

Future Value of an Annuity

In the Chapter 3 *Excel* file, go to the ***FV annuity*** tab and solve the following problem, using the three approaches outlined above.

Problem: Assume that after landing your first job at age twenty-one, you begin saving for retirement. You invest $1,200 at the end of each year for the next forty years and earn 9%. What is the value of your investment at the end of forty years?

Careful: In this problem, there is ***no*** present value because there is no money invested immediately. But there ***is*** an annual payment.

Did you get $405,458.93?
Solutions for each approach are provided to the right of the file.

Apply it

Change the input assumptions and analyze the effect.

- *Suppose you earn 11% instead of 9%?*
  The future value is $698,191.28.
- *Suppose you earn 9%, but you begin saving late and invest for only twenty years?*
  The future value is only $61,392.14.
- *Go back to the original problem but assume the payment is made at the beginning of the year instead of at the end of the year.*
  The type argument allows for any payment to be made at the beginning or at end of the year. Leaving type blank or setting it to zero represents payment at the end of the year (ordinary annuity). Setting at 1 represents payment at the beginning of the year (annuity due).

  The future value is $441,950.24.

  Analysis is much easier with the financial model designed in Approach 3.

  Future Value Challenge:

Problem: Assume that after landing your first job at age twenty-one, you begin saving for retirement. You invest $1,500 immediately. You then invest $1,200 at the end of each year, and your employer matches 100% of your investment. If this occurs for forty years and earns 9% each year, what is the value of your investment at the end of forty years?

Solve using the approach of your choice. The solutions are provided on the ***FV Challenge*** *tab of the* Excel *file.*

PRESENT VALUE IN *EXCEL*

Present Value of a Lump Sum

Open the Chapter 3 *Excel* file at the Smart Finance Web site. Go to the worksheet tab labeled ***PV lump sum***. We will solve the following problem, using the three approaches outlined above.

Problem: Find the present value of $1,000 to be received at the end of five years if the opportunity cost of funds is 8%.

Consider the five key variables here:

Present Value	You are solving for present value.
Future Value	$1,000
Payment	There is no annual payment.

Rate	The rate is 8%.
Number of periods	five years

Approach 1: Use the mathematical formula.

Equation 3.2 on page 97 shows the formula for a present value as

$PV = FV / (1+r)^n$

In a cell in *Excel*, type in the formula as

```
=1000/(1.08)^5
```

Formula result: $680.58

Note: All solutions are provided in the* Excel *file, so if you have any trouble, check your result against the solution.

Approach 2: Use the PV function in *Excel.*

A present-value function is built into *Excel*'s financial functions.

As with all *Excel* functions, begin with an equals sign followed by the function symbol, here pv.

You can use the present-value function directly in a cell by using the following format:

```
=pv(rate,nper,pmt,fv,type)
```

Note: You must start with an "=".

Type is an optional argument and can be left blank (inserting a 1 here changes the payment to the beginning of the year).

Leave no spaces between variables.

Commas are required between variables.

In this example, type in a cell

```
=pv(8%,5,0,1000)
```

Formula result: –$680.58

The present value should appear as a NEGATIVE number, because* Excel *solves for the amount INVESTED today that leads to a future value of $1,000. The intuition is that investing $680.58 today at a rate of 8% is equivalent to $1,000 in five years.

Approach 3: Create a basic model and solve using either of the above approaches.

Try it. *The model is set up for you in the* Excel *file. Enter the inputs and use either the mathematical approach or the built-in present-value function. If you use Approach 2, the present value will appear as a negative number.*

Your worksheet should look like this:

Rate	8%
# periods	5
Pmt	0
Present value	1,000
Type	

If you use the built-in *Excel* present-value function, your formula should read

=pv(C32,C33,C34,C35,C36)

Again, the result is **–$680.58.**

Present Value of an Annuity

In the Chapter 3 *Excel* file, go to the ***PV annuity*** tab and solve the following problem, using the three approaches outline above.

Problem: Find the present value of five annual end-of-year payments of $1,000 if the appropriate rate is 8%.

Your result should be $3,992.71.

OTHER TIME VALUE OF MONEY APPLICATIONS IN *EXCEL*

Excel also includes built-in financial functions to solve for payment, rate, and time. An example of each is provided below and in the *Excel* file.

Payment

Open the Chapter 3 *Excel* file at the Smart Finance Web site. Go to the worksheet tab labeled *Payment.*

Problem: You want to accumulate $1 million by retirement in thirty-five years. Unfortunately, you have not saved anything yet. If you can earn 9% each year, how much do you need to invest annually at the end of the year to reach your goal?

The format for the payment function in *Excel* is

=pmt(rate,nper,pv,fv,type)

here,

=pmt(9%,35,0,1000000)

Type is optional and not included here. DO NOT type in commas in the numbers.

The result is $4,635.84. This appears as a negative number if the *Excel* functions are used because the funds are invested (cash outflows).

Apply it

Change the input assumptions and analyze the effect.

- *Suppose you earn 8% instead of 9%?*
  Your annual payment would increase to $5,803.26.
- *Suppose you earn 9%, but you begin saving late and invest for only twenty-five years?*
  Your annual payment would increase to $11,806.25.

Rate

Open the Chapter 3 *Excel* file at the Smart Finance Web site. Go to the worksheet tab labeled *Rate*.

Problem: You want to accumulate $1 million by retirement in thirty-five years. You have $5,000 to invest immediately. If you invest $1,000 at the end of each year, what rate do you need to earn to reach your goal?

The format for the rate function in *Excel* is

```
=rate(pmt,nper,pv,fv,type)
```

here,

```
=rate(–1000,35,–5000,1000000)
```

The result is 13.37%.

Apply it

Change the input assumptions and analyze the effect.

- *Suppose you invest for forty years instead of 35?*
  The rate you need to earn drops from 13.37% to 11.32%.
- *Suppose you invest $1,500 in each of the thirty-five years?*
  The rate you need to earn drops from 13.37% to 12.36%.
- *Suppose you did not invest $5,000 initially?*
  You need to earn 15.53% to reach $1 million.

***Hint:** If you try this in a blank worksheet, you may get a result of 0. If this occurs, make sure you have formatted the cell as a %.*

Time

Open the Chapter 3 Excel file at the Smart Finance Web site. Go to the worksheet tab labeled *Time*.

Problem: You want to accumulate $1 million by retirement. You have $10,000 to investimmediately. If you invest $1,800 at the end of each year and earn 9.5%, how many years do youneed to save to reach your goal?

The format for the time function in *Excel* is nper, or number of periods.

=nper(rate,pmt,pv,fv,type)

here,

=nper(9.5%,–1800,35,–10000,1000000)

The result is 39.24 years.

Apply it

Change the input assumptions and analyze the effect.

Suppose you did not invest the $10,000 initially?
You need to invest for almost forty-four years to reach $1 million.

EXCEL EXTRAS: DATA TABLES AND GRAPHS

Data tables and graphs are tools that enable you to display the effect of changing inputs on output values. We will show how each can be applied to the first problem we examined—the future value of a lump sum.

DATA TABLES

Open the Chapter 3 Excel file at the Smart Finance Web site. Go to the worksheet tab labeled ***Data table.***

Problem: Create a data table to show the future value of $1,000 invested for different time horizons and different interest rates.

A data table allows you to view the results of a single formula as one or more input variables are changed.

Assume you want to look at $1,000 invested for the following number of years and interest rates:

years: 0, 3, 5, 7, 10, 25

rates: 0%, 2%, 4%, 6%, 8%, 10%, 12%, 14%, 16%, 18%, 20%

Steps to create a data table:

Step 1: Begin with a simple model to calculate future value. You can use the results from the *FV* lump-sum problem.

Approach 3: Create a basic model.

Inputs	
Rate	8%
# periods	5
Pmt	0
Present value	(1,000)
Type	
Output	
Future value	**$1,469.33**

Step 2: Because we are creating a table for various future values, we need to set up the table based on the future-value formula. Select a cell to control the data table. This cell is in the top left corner of the table. Then, use a cell reference to refer to the formula that is the basis of the data table—here Future Value. In the *Excel* file, the cell is color-coded for easy identification.

Step 3: Enter the values for the various inputs—to the right and directly below the control cell. Look at the file; it is set up for you. Note that the rates are entered vertically and the time horizontally. Enter labels.

Step 4: Use the shift and arrow keys to select the entire table areas, INCLUDING the control cell, and row and column variables. DO NOT include the labels.

1,469	0	3	5	7	10	25
0%						
2%						
4%						
6%						
8%						
10%						
12%						
14%						
16%						
18%						
20%						

Step 5: On the toolbar, select **data**, then **table**. The table dialog box will appear.

Step 6: Input the row and column information for the table. You must enter the cell reference from your original model that contains the information needed for the table.

Row input cell: Input the cell reference where the number of periods is entered because the variable in the row is time.

Column input cell: Input the cell reference for rate because the rate is entered in the column.

Step 7: Click OK. The table is completed, and the result is an array formula based on the Table function with two arguments. The result follows:

				Years Invested			
	1,469	**0**	**3**	**5**	**7**	**10**	**25**
	0%	1,000	1,000	1,000	1,000	1,000	1,000
	2%	1,000	1,061	1,104	1,149	1,219	1,641
	4%	1,000	1,125	1,217	1,316	1,480	2,666
	6%	1,000	1,191	1,338	1,504	1,791	4,292
Rates	**8%**	1,000	1,260	1,469	1,714	2,159	6,848
	10%	1,000	1,331	1,611	1,949	2,594	10,835
	12%	1,000	1,405	1,762	2,211	3,106	17,000
	14%	1,000	1,482	1,925	2,502	3,707	26,462
	16%	1,000	1,561	2,100	2,826	4,411	40,874
	18%	1,000	1,643	2,288	3,185	5,234	62,669

This table shows the future value of $1,000 invested at various rates and time horizons.

GRAPHS

Open the Chapter 3 *Excel* file at the Smart Finance Web site. Go to the worksheet tab labeled *Graph.*

Problem: Create a graph to show the future value of $1,000 invested for five years at different interest rates.

Assume you want to look at $1,000 invested five years at the following interest rates:

rates: 0%, 2%, 4%, 6%, 8%, 10%, 12%, 14%, 16%, 18%, 20%

Excel offers a large number of graphing options. In this appendix, we provide a simple illustration of a basic line graph embedded in the file.

Steps to create a graph:

Step 1: Create a table with the information you want to graph. This is done for you here using information from the previous tab on future values and rates.

Step 2: Place your cursor anywhere within the table. On the toolbar, select "insert", then "chart" (or use the chart wizard icon). Choose a line graph.

Step 3: Follow the prompts from the chart wizard. The chart will appear in the worksheet. Drag it to a new location and resize it, as desired.

Notice that the relationship between the future value and the interest rate is not a straight line. The future value increases at an increasing rate as the interest rate rises.

Working with graphs, especially formatting graphs, takes a little practice. Also, there are many options available to reformat axes, add titles and labels, and so on. Experiment and use the *Excel* help function or a basic *Excel* text for more information on graphing.

PART 2

Valuation, Risk, and Return

A bit of wisdom attributed to the English poet Chaucer says, "nothing ventured, nothing gained." Financial markets give us ample evidence that Chaucer knew what he was talking about. Over time, high-risk investments tend to earn higher returns than low-risk investments do. When managers invest corporate funds, or when individuals decide how to allocate their money between different types of investments, they must weigh the potential benefit of higher returns against the cost of taking higher risk. The purpose of the next few chapters is to explore in-depth the relationship between risk and return. We begin in Chapters 4 and 5 by describing two of the most common types of investments available in the market—bonds and stocks.

The bond market is vast, and it plays an extremely important role in the economy. Federal, state, and local governments issue bonds to finance all kinds of public works projects and to cover budget deficits. Corporations sell bonds to meet daily operating needs and to pay for major investments. Chapter 4 describes the basic bond features and explains how investors value bonds.

Chapter 5 examines the stock market. Valuing stocks is more complex than valuing bonds because stocks do not promise fixed payment streams as bonds do. Therefore, Chapter 5 discusses methods that investors and analysts use to estimate the stock values. The chapter also provides a brief explanation of how firms work alongside investment bankers to sell stock to the public and how investors can trade shares of stock with each other.

With the essential features of bonds and stocks in hand, Chapter 6 explores the historical returns earned by different classes of investments. The data illustrate that a fundamental trade-off between risk and return confronts investors. Chaucer was right. Investors who want to get rich have to accept risk as part of the deal.

Chapter 7 quantifies exactly what we mean by the term, "risk." The chapter also introduces one of the most important theories in finance called the Capital Asset Pricing Model, or CAPM. The CAPM estimates the incremental return that investors or corporate managers can expect if they invest in an asset that is risky rather than one that is safe. That is, the CAPM is a tool that lets us evaluate the marginal benefits (higher returns) and marginal costs (higher risk) of alternative investments. It can be useful to individual investors who are trying to decide whether to save for retirement by investing in bonds, in stocks, or in a portfolio that contains both stocks and bonds. But the CAPM also helps corporate managers decide whether it is better to invest a firm's money in a high-risk venture, like building a manufacturing plant in a foreign country, or in a low-risk undertaking, such as upgrading old equipment.

Valuing Bonds

OPENING FOCUS

California to Bond Market: "I'll Be Back"

In March 2004, California voters approved Proposition 57, a ballot measure granting the state the authority to borrow up to $15 billion by issuing "economic recovery bonds" to investors. Political commentators viewed passage of Proposition 57 as a significant coup for Arnold Schwarzenegger, who just five months earlier had won the race for governor in California by hammering away at incumbent Democrat Gray Davis's mismanagement of state finances. Dubbed "The Governator" in the popular press, Schwarzenegger won on promises to cut taxes and government spending and to create a pro-business climate across the state. But before fulfilling his campaign pledges, Schwarzenegger had to confront an immediate crisis. California's state budget was running a deficit of as much as $1 billion per month. Expressing doubt that the state could find its way out of the fiscal crisis without defaulting on some of its outstanding debts, the bond rating agency Moody's gave the state's bonds a rating just a notch above "junk bond" status. California now held the dubious honor of having the lowest credit rating of any of the fifty U.S. states. Any additional decline in the state's credit rating would place its bonds in a speculative category shunned by many investors and increase the state's cost of borrowing. Higher borrowing costs would only exacerbate the deficit problem. Schwarzenegger convinced voters that Proposition 57 would provide at least a temporary solution to the state's fiscal problem. It would enable the state to replace recently issued short-term debt with long-term bonds that would ultimately be repaid with the proceeds of a dedicated state sales tax.

The first offering of economic recovery bonds proved to be popular with investors. In May 2004, California issued almost $8 billion in bonds, the largest one-day bond sale by any state in U.S. history. Individual investors purchased $2.3 billion in bonds, and institutional investors such as mutual funds snapped up the rest. Given the state's fiscal woes, and given that the economic recovery bonds promised investors a fixed interest rate of just over 4 percent, what could account for the issue's high demand? One contributing factor was the U.S. tax code. The interest payments made by any municipal bond (i.e., a bond issued by a state or local government entity) are exempt from federal income tax. The interest on "muni" bonds is also exempt from state income tax for investors who live in the state that issues the bonds. That tax exemption was extremely attractive to high-tax-bracket investors from California, who faced a combined state and federal income tax rate in excess of 40 percent.

Citing the success of the bond issue and an improving California economy, Moody's raised the state's credit rating one level. California announced plans to sell another round of economic recovery bonds in June 2004, but this second offering came with a new twist. The interest rate paid on the second round of bonds would vary with market interest rates rather than remain fixed. In announcing its plans to sell the variable-rate bonds, California was presumably trying to appeal to investors who expected interest rates to rise in the future. Investors who held that view may have passed up the opportunity to invest in the state's initial offering of fixed-rate bonds. By promising investors to increase interest payments if market rates increased, California may be able to issue the variable-rate bonds at an even lower interest rate than the 4 percent paid on the first bond issue. However, making that promise is risky, because an increase in interest rates raises the cost of financing the state's deficits in the future.

Sources: "Wall Street Firm Improves California's Credit Rating," by Rick Jurgens, *Contra Costa Times*, May 22, 2004.
"Economic Recovery Certificates Should Help Put California's Finances Back in Balance," by Jabulani Leffall, *The Daily News of Los Angeles*, May 23, 2004.
"Investors Snatch up $7.9 Billion in California Deficit Bonds," by James B. Kelleher, *The Orange County Register*, May 6, 2004. ■

LEARNING OBJECTIVES

After completing this chapter you should be able to:

- Recall the fundamental concepts that determine how we value assets;
- Understand the vocabulary that describes bonds and the markets in which they trade;
- Interpret the relationship been bond prices and interest rates; and
- Explain the meaning of the "term structure of interest rates."

In the popular imagination, finance is closely associated with stock, bond, and other security markets. References to the closing level of the Dow Jones Industrial Average, the Nikkei 225, the Financial Times Stock Exchange 100, and other market indexes form part of the daily barrage of information that citizens of the world's largest economies absorb. Billions of people understand that these numbers can have a profound influence on their personal and professional lives as more and more countries adopt market-oriented economic policies. However, relatively few people understand the fundamental forces that determine security prices. Though we do not want to understate the complexities of security valuation, a relatively straightforward framework exists that investors can use to value many types of financial assets, including bonds and stocks. This framework says that *the value of any asset equals the present value of future benefits accruing to the asset's owner.*

Notice the importance of the term "present value" in the previous sentence. In Chapter 3, we learned the mechanics of converting a sequence of future cash flows into a single present value. In this chapter and in Chapter 5, we see that calculating present values is fundamental to the process of valuing financial assets. Chapters 8–10 illustrate the use of present-value calculations in valuing physical assets such as a new manufacturing plant or state-of-the-art computer equipment. Time and effort spent mastering present-value concepts earns its return over these chapters.

Our primary objective in this chapter is to describe models used to value debt securities, often called bonds. In the next chapter, we learn about pricing stocks. Why do corporate managers need to understand how to price bonds and stocks? First, firms must occasionally approach bond and stock markets to raise capital for new investments. Understanding how investors in these markets value the firm's securities helps managers determine how to finance new projects. Second, firms periodically make investments by acquiring privately held companies, just as they unload past investments by selling divisions. In either case, knowing how the market values an enterprise guides a manager's expectations regarding the appropriate price for an acquisition or divestiture. Third, a company's stock price provides an external, independent performance assessment of top management, one that a diligent board of directors watches closely. Surely managers who will be judged (and compensated) based on the value of their firm's stock price need to understand the determinants of that price. Fourth, finance theory suggests that the objective of corporate management is to maximize the stock price by correctly weighing the marginal benefits and costs of alternative actions. How can managers take actions to maximize stock prices if they don't know what causes stock prices to rise or fall?

This chapter presents an introduction to bonds and bond valuation. We begin by laying out the principles of valuation—principles that can be applied to a wide variety of valuation problems. After that, we describe the essential features of bonds, and we show how to apply the principles of valuation to calculate bond prices.

4.1 VALUATION BASICS

In a market economy, ownership of an asset confers the rights to the stream of benefits generated by the asset. These benefits may be tangible, such as the interest payments on California's economic recovery bonds mentioned in the Opening Focus, or intangible, such as the pleasure one experiences when viewing a beautiful painting. Either way, *the value of any asset equals the present value of all its future benefits.* Finance theory focuses primarily on tangible benefits, typically the cash flows that an asset pays over time. For instance, a landlord who owns an apartment complex receives a stream of rental payments from tenants. The landlord is also responsible for maintaining the complex, paying taxes, and covering other expenses. If the landlord wants to sell the apartment complex, what price should he expect to receive? According to our fundamental valuation principle above, the price should equal the present value of all future net cash flows. Investors value financial assets such as bonds and stocks in much the same way. First, they estimate how much cash a particular investment distributes over time. Second, investors discount the expected cash payments using the time value of money mathematics covered in Chapter 3. The investment's value, or its current market price, equals the present value of its future cash flows.

This implies that pricing an asset requires knowledge of both its future benefits and the appropriate discount rate that converts future benefits into a present value. For some assets, investors know with a high degree of certainty what the future benefit stream will be. For other investments, the future benefit stream is much harder to predict. Generally, *the greater the uncertainty about an asset's future benefits, the higher the discount rate investors will apply when discounting those benefits to the present.*

Consequently, the valuation process links an asset's future benefits and the uncertainty surrounding those benefits to determine its price. Holding future benefits (cash flows) constant, an inverse relationship exists between risk and value. If two investments promise identical cash flows in the future, investors will pay a higher price for the one with the more credible promise. Or, to state that relationship another way, if a risky asset and a safe asset trade at the same price, the risky asset must offer investors higher future cash flows. This is why, as discussed in the Opening Focus, the state's credit rating was so important to Governor Schwarzenegger and all other California taxpayers. A lower credit rating from Moody's would have made investors more skeptical of California's ability to deliver on its promise to repay investors who purchased the state's bonds. If the credit rating were again to fall, California bonds would have to offer even higher future cash flows (higher interest payments) to attract investors. Luckily, that process works in reverse, so when Moody's increased the state's credit rating, it reassured investors and allowed the state to borrow additional funds at a lower rate.

The Fundamental Valuation Model

Chapters 6 and 7 present an in-depth analysis of the relationship between risk and return. For now, take as given the market's **required rate of return** on a specific investment. The term "required rate of return," is the rate of return that investors expect or require an asset to earn given its risk. The riskier the asset is, the higher will be the return required by investors in the marketplace. We can also say that the required rate of return on an asset is the return available in the market on another equally risky investment. When someone purchases a specific investment, they lose the opportunity to invest their money in another asset. The return on the alternative investment represents an *opportunity cost.*

required rate of return The rate of return that investors require from an investment given the risk of the investment.

How do investors use this required rate of return to determine the prices of different types of securities? Equation 4.1 expresses the fundamental valuation model mathematically, as follows:

$$P_0 = \frac{CF_1}{(1+r)^1} + \frac{CF_2}{(1+r)^2} + \ldots + \frac{CF_n}{(1+r)^n} \quad \text{(Eq. 4.1)}$$

In this equation, P_0 represents the asset's price today (at time 0), CF_t represents the asset's expected cash flow at time t, and r is the required return—the discount rate that reflects the asset's risk. The marginal benefit of owning this asset is the right to receive the cash flows that it pays, and the marginal cost is the opportunity cost of committing funds to this asset rather than to an equally risky alternative. Therefore, Equation 4.1 establishes a price that balances the asset's marginal benefits and costs. The letter n stands for the asset's life, the period over which it distributes cash flows to investors, usually measured in years. As you will see, n may be a finite number, as in the case of a bond that matures in a certain number of years, or it may be infinite, as in the case of a common stock with an indefinite life span. In either case, this equation provides us with a vehicle for valuing almost any type of asset.

SMART PRACTICES VIDEO

Todd Richter, Managing Director, Head of Equity Healthcare Research, Bank of America Securities

"The concepts of value, the things that drive value, don't change."

See the entire interview at **SMARTFinance**

APPLYING THE MODEL

In the wake of the 1998 Master Settlement Agreement between state attorneys general and the tobacco industry, seven tobacco makers agreed to pay roughly $206 billion to the states over the next twenty-five years. States began to receive payments in 1999, but as the softening U.S. economy resulted in reduced state tax collections, many states looked for ways to cash in early on the tobacco lawsuit. "Tobacco bonds" were the solution. By selling the rights to the cash flows from their future tobacco settlement to investors who purchased tobacco bonds, states could capture the present value of future settlement proceeds immediately. Wisconsin closed its 2002–2003 budget shortfall by raising $1.6 billion in one such deal. How did the market determine the value of tobacco bonds in Wisconsin and other states? Suppose that the settlement decreed that a particular state would receive $250 million per year for twenty years, and suppose that the market's required return on investments with this level of risk was 6.5 percent. The present value of this state's settlement proceeds was determined using the shortcut formula for an annuity's present value from Chapter 3 as follows:

$$P_0 = \frac{\$250{,}000{,}000}{(1+0.065)^1} + \frac{\$250{,}000{,}000}{(1+0.065)^2} + \frac{\$250{,}000{,}000}{(1+0.065)^3} + \dots + \frac{\$250{,}000{,}000}{(1+0.065)^{20}}$$

$$P_0 = \$250{,}000{,}000\left(\frac{1-\frac{1}{1.065^{20}}}{0.065}\right) = \$2{,}754{,}626{,}812$$

The state could sell bonds today worth $2.75 billion, using the settlement proceeds to repay bondholders over the next twenty years. To meet its needs for more immediate cash inflow, the state has effectively paid 6.5 percent annual interest to exchange its twenty-year, $250-million annuity for an immediate $2.75 billion.

With this simple framework in hand, we turn to the problem of pricing bonds. Though bond-pricing techniques can get very complex, we focus on "plain-vanilla" bonds: those that promise a fixed stream of cash payments over a finite time period. Among the largest issuers of such "fixed income" securities are national, state, and local governments and multinational corporations.

CONCEPT REVIEW QUESTIONS

1. Why is it important for corporate managers to understand how bonds and stocks are priced?

2. Holding constant an asset's future benefit stream, what happens to the asset's price if its risk increases?

3. Holding constant an asset's risk, what happens to the asset's price if its future benefit stream increases?

4. Keeping in mind Equation 4.1, discuss how you determine the price per acre of farmland in a particular region.

4.2 BOND PRICES AND INTEREST RATES

Bond Vocabulary

Fundamentally, a bond is just a loan. Unlike car loans and home mortgages, which require borrowers to make regular payments, including both an interest component and some repayment of the original loan amount or **principal**, bonds make interest-only payments until they mature. On the **maturity date**, a bond's life formally ends, and both the final interest payment and the original principal amount are due. The principal amount of a bond, also known as the bond's **par value** or *face value*, is typically $1,000 for corporate bonds.

principal
The amount of money on which interest is paid.

maturity date
The date when a bond's life ends and the borrower must make the final interest payment and repay the principal.

par value (bonds)
The face value of a bond, which the borrower repays at maturity.

coupon
A fixed amount of interest that a bond promises to pay investors.

indenture
A legal document stating the conditions under which a bond has been issued.

coupon rate
The rate derived by dividing the bond's annual coupon payment by its par value.

coupon yield
The amount obtained by dividing the bond's coupon by its current market price (which does not always equal its par value).

Though bonds come in many varieties, most bonds share certain basic characteristics. First, many bonds promise to pay investors a fixed amount of interest, called the bond's **coupon.**[1] Most bonds make coupon payments every six months, or semiannually. Because a bond's cash flows are contractually fixed, traders often refer to bonds as *fixed-income securities*. The legal contract between the borrower who issues bonds and the investors who buy them, called the bond **indenture**, specifies the dollar amount of the coupon and when the borrower must make coupon payments. Second, a bond's **coupon rate** equals its annual coupon payment divided by its par value. Third, a bond's **coupon yield** equals the coupon divided by the bond's current market price (which does not always equal its par value).

To illustrate, suppose that a government entity or a firm issues a bond with a $1,000 par value and promises to pay investors $35 every six months until maturity. The bond's *coupon* is $70 per year, and its *coupon rate* is 7 percent ($70 ÷ $1,000). If the current market value of this bond is $980, then its *coupon yield* is 7.14 percent ($70 ÷ $980).

Understanding how to price bonds is important in part because the bond market forms such a large part of the U.S. financial system. Including bonds issued by federal, state, and local government entities, as well as those issued by corporations, there were more than $18.8 trillion in bonds outstanding in the United States at the end of 2003. Compare that figure to the $15.5 trillion total market value of equities (i.e., stocks) outstanding in 2003. Institutional investors such as insurance companies, pension funds, and mutual funds are the largest purchasers of bonds, and individual investors hold about 13 percent of all outstanding bonds.[2] Let's turn now to a basic framework for pricing these instruments.

A Bond Pricing Equation (Assuming Annual Interest)

We can value ordinary bonds by developing a simplified version of Equation 4.1. Remember that a bond makes a fixed coupon payment each year. Assume that the bond makes annual coupon payments of $\$C$ for n years, and at maturity the bond makes its final coupon payment and returns the face value, $\$F$, to investors. (We will

---

1. Historically, bond certificates were printed with coupons attached that the bondholder would literally clip (like coupons in a newspaper) and mail in to receive an interest payment. That is the origin of the term "coupon." In modern times, bonds are registered, meaning that the issuer keeps a record of who owns a given bond. Interest payments are mailed directly to registered owners with no coupon clipping required. Many investors hold their bonds in *street name*, meaning that a brokerage firm registers the bonds in its own name. Because brokerage firms have developed a comparative advantage in processing financial market transactions, holding securities in street name speeds the flow of money between bond issuers and buyers.

2. The source for all these figures is *Flow of Funds Accounts of the United States*, 4th Quarter 2003, published by the Board of Governors of the Federal Reserve System.

deal with the more common occurrence of semiannual coupon payments shortly.) Using these assumptions, we can replace Equation 4.1 with the following:

$$P_0 = \frac{C}{(1+r)^1} + \frac{C}{(1+r)^2} + \dots + \frac{C}{(1+r)^n} + \frac{F}{(1+r)^n} \quad \text{(Eq. 4.2)}$$

Equation 4.2 says that the bond's price equals the present value of an n-year ordinary annuity plus the present value of the lump-sum principal payment. Referring to our equation for the present value of an annuity in Chapter 3, we write the bond-pricing equation as follows:

$$\text{Price} = PV \text{ of coupons} + PV \text{ of principal}$$

$$P_0 = C\left[\frac{1-\frac{1}{(1+r)^n}}{r}\right] + \frac{F}{(1+r)^n}$$

APPLYING THE MODEL

On January 1, 2006, Worldwide United had outstanding a bond with a coupon rate of 9.125 percent and a face value of $1,000. At the end of each year this bond pays investors $91.25 in interest (0.09125 × $1,000). The bond matures at the end of 2016, eleven years from now. Figure 4.1 illustrates the sequence of cash flows that the bond promises investors over time. Notice that we break up the bond's cash payments into two separate components. The first component is an eleven-year annuity of $91.25 annual payments. The second component is a lump-sum payment of $1,000 at maturity.

To calculate the price of this bond, we need to know what rate of return investors demand on bonds that are as risky as Worldwide's bonds. Assume that the market currently requires an 8 percent return on these bonds. At that discount rate, the present value of eleven coupon payments of $91.25 plus the principal repayment equals

$$PV \text{ of coupons} = \$91.25 \times \left[1-(1 \div 1.08)^{11}\right]/0.08 = \$651.43$$

$$PV \text{ of principal} = \$1{,}000 \div 1.08^{11} = \$428.88$$

$$\text{Price of bond} = \$651.43 + \$428.88 = \$1{,}080.31$$

Figure 4.1 also shows how to calculate this bond's price, using a financial calculator or *Excel*. We calculate the price of this bond directly from our fundamental valuation Equation 4.1 as follows:

$$\$1{,}080.31 = \frac{\$91.25}{(1.08)^1} + \frac{\$91.25}{(1.08)^2} + \frac{\$91.25}{(1.08)^3} + \dots + \frac{\$1{,}091.25}{(1.08)^{11}}$$

Notice that this bond sells *above* par value. When a bond sells for more than its par value, we say that the bond trades at a **premium**. Why are Worldwide's bonds trading at a premium? By assumption, the market's required return on an investment like this is just 8 percent, but Worldwide's bonds offer a coupon rate of 9.125 percent. Therefore, if Worldwide's bonds sold at par value, they would offer investors a particularly attractive return, and investors would rush to buy them. As more and more investors purchase Worldwide bonds, the market price of those bonds rises.

premium
A bond that sells for more than its par value.

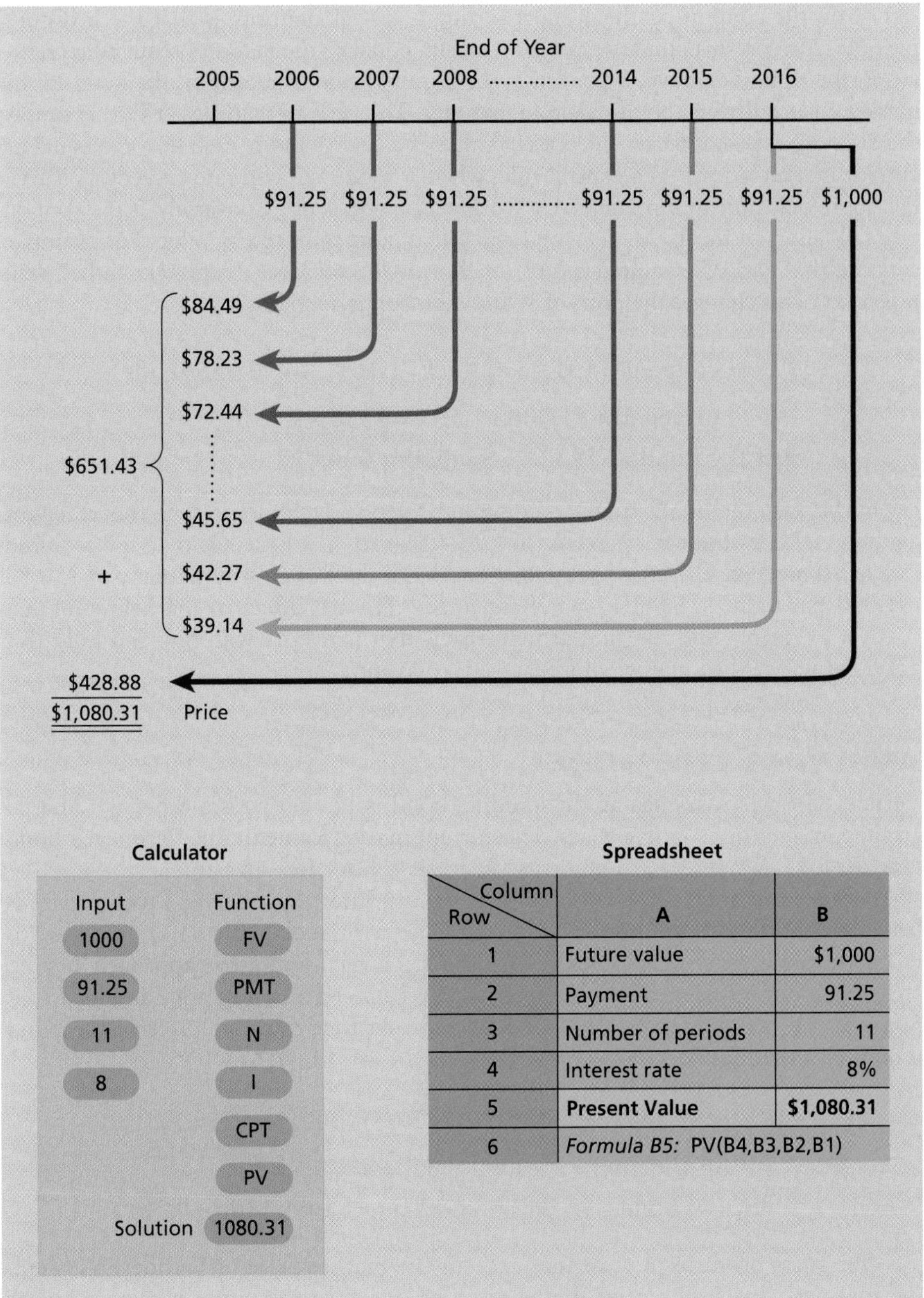

Row \ Column	A	B
1	Future value	$1,000
2	Payment	91.25
3	Number of periods	11
4	Interest rate	8%
5	**Present Value**	**$1,080.31**
6	*Formula B5:* PV(B4,B3,B2,B1)	

Figure 4.1
Time Line for Bond Valuation (Assuming Annual Interest Payments)

Worldwide United 9-1/8% Coupon, $1,000 Par Value Bond, Maturing at End of 2016; Required Return Assumed To Be 8%

Think about the return that an investor earns if she purchases Worldwide bonds today for $1,080.31 and holds them to maturity. Every year, the investor receives a $91.25 cash payment. At the current market price, this represents a coupon yield of about 8.4 percent ($91.25 ÷ $1,080.31), noticeably above the 8 percent required return in the market. However, when the bonds mature, the investor receives a final interest payment plus the $1,000 par value. In a sense, this bond has a built-in loss of $80.31 ($1,000 par value – $1,080.31 purchase price) at maturity because the bond's principal is less than the current price of the bond. The net effect of receiving an above-market return on the coupon payment and realizing a loss at maturity is that the investor's overall return on this bond is exactly 8 percent, equal to the market's required return.

In the example above, 8 percent is the required rate of return on the bond in the market, also called the bond's **yield to maturity**. The yield to maturity (YTM) is simply the discount rate that forces the present value of a bond's future cash flows to equal its current market price.[3] As a general rule, when a bond's coupon rate exceeds its YTM, the bond will trade at a premium as Worldwide's bonds do. Conversely, if the coupon rate falls short of the YTM, the bond will sell at a **discount** to par value. For example, suppose the market's required return on Worldwide bonds is 10 percent rather than 8 percent. This changes the price of Worldwide bonds as follows:

yield to maturity
The discount rate that equates the present value of the bond's cash flows to its market price.

discount
A bond sells at a discount when its market price is less than its part value.

$$PV \text{ of coupons} = \$91.25 \times \left[1 - (1 \div 1.10)^{11}\right] / 0.10 = \$592.68$$

$$PV \text{ of principal} = \$1{,}000 \div 1.10^{11} = \$350.49$$

$$\text{Price of bond} = \$592.68 + \$350.49 = \$943.17$$

In this case the bonds trade at a discount because each month investors receive a coupon yield of about 9.7 percent ($91.25 ÷ $943.17), a little less than the required rate of 10 percent. Offsetting that, the bond has a built-in gain at maturity of $56.83 ($1,000 par value – $943.17 purchase price). The net effect of the below-market coupon payments and the gain at maturity is that investors who buy and hold this bond earn a yield to maturity of exactly 10 percent.

APPLYING THE MODEL

Verhoeven Enterprises has an outstanding bond issue that pays a 6 percent annual coupon and matures in five years. The current market value of one Verhoeven bond is $1,021.35. What yield to maturity do these bonds offer investors?

Because the bond sells at a premium, we can infer that the yield to maturity is less than the bond's coupon rate. We can use a financial calculator or *Excel* to calculate the answer very quickly, but let's try a trial-and-error approach first to strengthen our intuition about the relationship between a bond's price and its YTM. Suppose the bond offers a YTM of 5 percent. At that rate, the price of the bond would be the following:

$$PV \text{ of coupons} = \$60 \times \left[1 - (1 \div 1.05)^{5}\right] / 0.05 = \$259.77$$

$$PV \text{ of principal} = \$1{,}000 \div 1.05^{5} = \$783.53$$

$$\text{Price of bond} = \$259.77 + \$783.53 = \$1{,}043.30$$

Our guess produces a price that exceeds the market price of Verhoeven's bond. Because we calculated a price that is too high, we need to try again using a higher YTM. Discounting the bond's cash flows at a higher YTM results in a lower price. Suppose the YTM equals 5.5 percent. Now we have

$$PV \text{ of coupons} = \$60 \times \left[1 - (1 \div 1.055)^{5}\right] / 0.055 = \$256.22$$

$$PV \text{ of principal} = \$1{,}000 \div 1.055^{5} = \$765.13$$

$$\text{Price of bond} = \$256.22 + \$765.13 = \$1{,}021.35$$

3. You can use a financial calculator to calculate a bond's YTM given its current market price and its coupon payments. *Excel* has a built-in function for finding a bond's YTM. See the appendix to this chapter for details.

The YTM equals 5.5 percent because that is the discount rate that equates the present value of the bond's cash flows with its current market price.

Semiannual Compounding

Most bonds issued in the United States make two interest payments per year rather than one. Adjusting our bond-pricing framework to handle semiannual interest payments is easy. If the bond matures in n years and the annual coupon equals $\$C$, then the bond now makes $2n$ payments equal to $\$C \div 2$. Similarly, if the bond's annual yield to maturity equals r, we replace that with a semiannual yield of $r \div 2$. This produces a modified version of Equation 4.2[4]:

$$P_0 = \frac{C/2}{(1+\frac{r}{2})^1} + \frac{C/2}{(1+\frac{r}{2})^2} + \ldots + \frac{C/2}{(1+\frac{r}{2})^{2n}} + \frac{F}{(1+\frac{r}{2})^{2n}} \quad \text{(Eq. 4.3)}$$

Expressing this equation as a sum of the present value of an ordinary annuity and the present value of a lump sum, we have the following:

$$P_0 = C/2 \left[\frac{1 - \frac{1}{(1+\frac{r}{2})^{2n}}}{\frac{r}{2}} \right] + \frac{F}{(1+\frac{r}{2})^{2n}}$$

For example, the Peterson Fishing Co. issues a three-year bond that offers a 6 percent coupon rate paid semiannually. This means that the annual coupon equals \$60, and there are two \$30 payments each year. Suppose that 6 percent per year is also the market's required return on Peterson bonds. The market price of the bonds equals

$$PV \text{ of coupons} = \$30\left[1-(1 \div 1.03)^6\right]/0.03 = \$162.52$$

$$PV \text{ of principal} = \$1{,}000/(1.03)^6 = \$837.48$$

$$\text{Price of bond} = \$162.52 + \$837.48 = \$1{,}000$$

Because this bond offers investors a return exactly equal to the required rate in the market, the bond sells at par value. Notice, too, that the effective annual yield on this bond is slightly higher than 6 percent. If the semiannual yield is 3 percent, the effective annual yield equals 6.09 percent ($1.03^2 - 1$).

Again, we emphasize the fundamental lesson: *the price of a bond equals the present value of its future cash flows*. We now turn to a more in-depth development of the concepts underlying bond valuation, starting with a discussion of interest rate risk.

4. The yield to maturity on a bond is typically quoted like an APR. That is, the bond's annual YTM equals the semiannual yield times 2. This implies that the effective annual YTM is slightly above the quoted YTM.

Bond Prices and Interest Rates

A bond's market price changes frequently as time passes. Whether a bond sells at a discount or a premium, its price will converge to par value (plus the final interest payment) as the maturity date draws near. Imagine a bond that matures one day from now. The bond's final cash flow consists of its par value plus the last coupon payment. If this payment arrives just one day in the future, you determine the bond's price by discounting this payment for one day. Therefore, the price and the final payment are virtually identical.

SMART CONCEPTS

Economic Forces Affecting Bond Prices. A variety of economic forces can change bond prices, but the most important factor is the prevailing market interest rate. When the market's required return on a bond changes, the bond's price changes in the opposite direction. The higher the bond's required return, the lower its price, and vice versa. How much a bond's price responds to changes in required returns depends on several factors, especially the bond's maturity.

Figure 4.2 shows how the prices of two bonds change as their required returns change. Both bonds pay a 6 percent coupon, but one matures in two years, whereas the other matures in ten years. As the figure shows, when the required return equals the coupon rate, 6 percent, both bonds trade at par. However, as the required return increases, the bonds' prices fall. The decline in the ten-year bond's price exceeds that of the two-year bond. Likewise, as the required return decreases, the prices of both bonds increase. But the ten-year bond's price increases faster than does that of the two-year bond. The general lessons are *(1) bond prices and interest rates move in opposite directions, and (2) the prices of long-term bonds display greater sensitivity to changes in interest rates than do the prices of short-term bonds.*

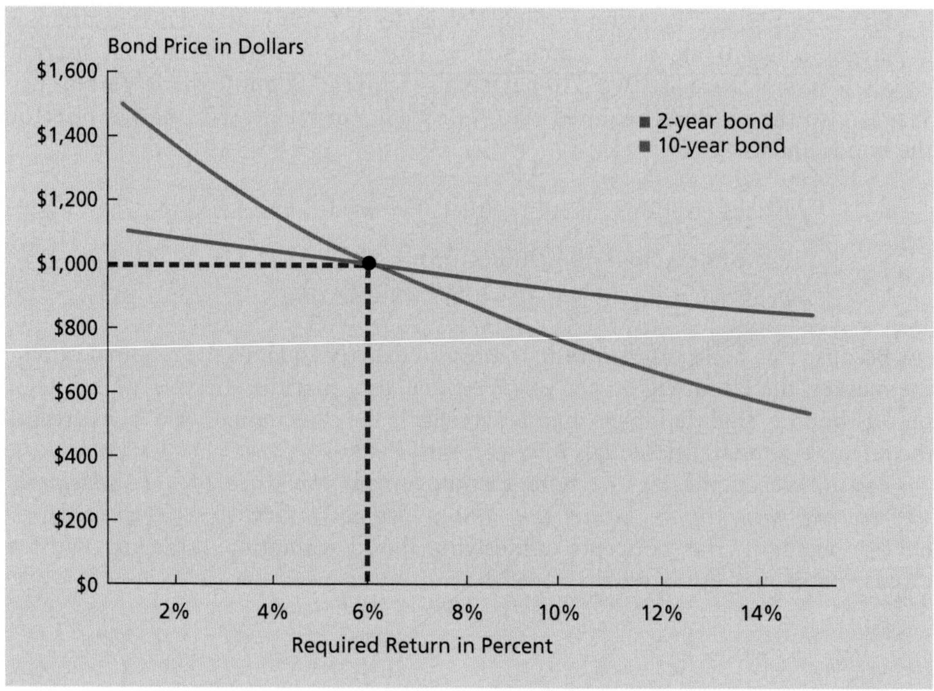

Figure 4.2
The Relationship Between Bond Prices and Required Returns for Bonds with Differing Times to Maturity but the Same 6% Coupon Rate

Bond prices move in the opposite direction of market interest rates. This figure shows that the prices of two-year and ten-year bonds fall as the required return rises (and vice versa), but the magnitude of this effect is much greater for the ten-year bond. Typically, long-term bond prices are much more sensitive to rate changes than short-term bond prices are.

Interest Rate Risk. Figure 4.2 illustrates the importance of **interest rate risk**—that changes in market interest rates will move bond prices. Figure 4.3 shows just how volatile interest rates have been in the United States. The blue line plots the historical YTM on ten-year U.S. government bonds.[5] The yields offered by these bonds peaked in 1981 at almost 14 percent, but recently Treasury bond yields have been much lower. The point of the graph is simple—because interest rates fluctuate widely, investors must be cognizant of the interest rate risk inherent in these instruments.

interest rate risk
The risk that changes in market interest rates will cause fluctuations in a bond's price. Also, the risk of suffering losses as a result of unanticipated changes in market interest rates.

One of the main factors causing interest rate movements is inflation. When investors buy financial assets, they expect these investments to provide a return that exceeds the inflation rate. This is important to people because they want to achieve a better standard of living by saving and investing their money. If asset returns do no more than keep up with inflation, then investors are not really better off having invested their funds. For example, suppose you want to expand your CD collection. You have \$150 to spend, and each CD costs \$15, so you can purchase ten new CDs. Alternatively, suppose you save your money and invest it in an asset earning a 10 percent return. You reason that after one year, you will have \$165 (\$150 × 1.10), and with that you can buy eleven CDs rather than ten. However, imagine that while your money is invested, the price of CDs increases by 10 percent from \$15 to \$16.50. This means that at the end of the year, your \$165 enables you to purchase just ten CDs, exactly what you could have purchased a year earlier. In real terms, you are no better off at the end of the year than you were at the start.

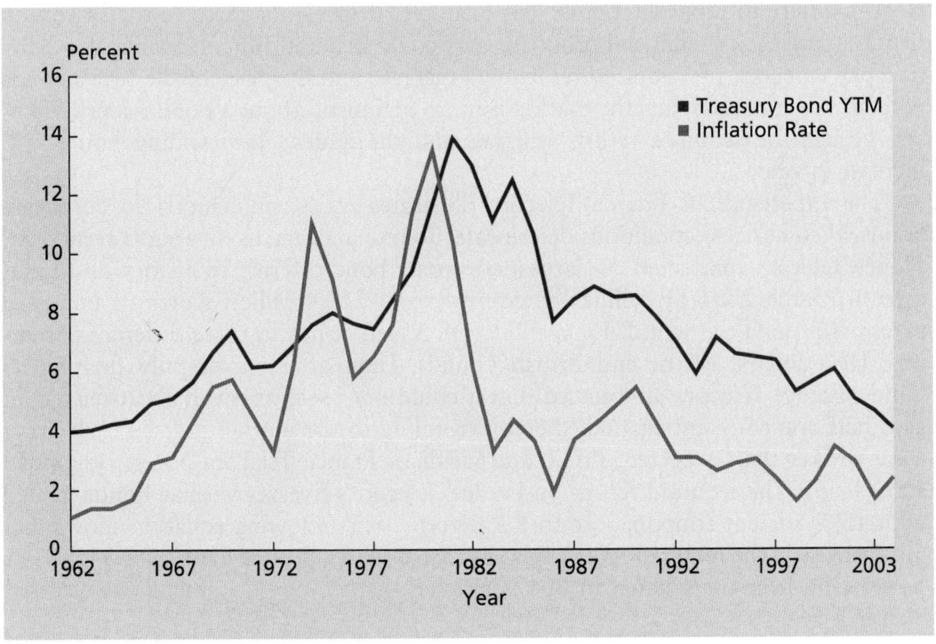

Figure 4.3
Treasury Bond Yields and Inflation Rates 1962–2003

This figure shows how volatile interest rates have been over time and how inflation is one underlying cause of the volatility. The blue line shows the yield to maturity on a ten-year Treasury bond, and the red line shows the rate of inflation each year. Bond yields are generally a little higher than inflation because investors want to earn a positive real rate of return. Because changes in interest rates cause bond prices to fluctuate, bond investors must be aware of interest rate risk.

Source: *http://www.federalreserve.gov* and *http://www.bls.gov/cpi/home.htm*

[5] We discuss the specific features of Treasury securities later in this chapter. The line in Figure 4.3 shows what the yield to maturity was on a newly issued ten-year Treasury bond, in each year from 1962 to 2003. In other words, at each point on the graph, you are looking at the yield on a bond with a constant maturity of ten years.

real return
Approximately, the difference between an investment's stated or nominal return and the inflation rate.

nominal return
The stated return offered by an investment unadjusted for the effects of inflation.

The lesson here is that the bond yields must offer investors a positive **real return.** The real return on an investment *approximately* equals the difference between its stated or **nominal return** and the inflation rate. In the previous example, the nominal return on your investment is 10 percent, but so is the inflation rate, so the investment's real return is zero. Mathematically, if r equals the nominal return, i equals the inflation rate, and r_{real} equals the real rate, then we can write the following:

$$(1+r)=(1+i)(1+r_{real})$$

$$\frac{(1+r)}{(1+i)}-1=r_{real}$$

$$\frac{(1+0.10)}{(1+0.10)}-1=0=r_{real}$$

Look once more at Figure 4.3. The red line plots the annual rate of inflation. The graph shows that interest rates were high in 1980 because inflation was high at the same time. Over the past two decades, as the inflation rate gradually fell, so did interest rates. Because bonds are generally priced to offer a positive real return, nominal interest rates are higher when inflation is high, as was the case around 1980, and rates are lower when inflation is low, as is the case now.[6]

Changes in Issuer Risk. When macroeconomic factors change, yields may change simultaneously on a wide range of bonds. But the market's required return *on a particular bond* can also change because the market reassesses the borrower's ability to repay investors. For example, if investors perceive that a certain firm is experiencing financial problems that could make it difficult for the company to repay its debts, the required return will increase and the price of the firm's bonds will fall. Conversely, when the market is more optimistic about a bond issuer's financial health, the required return will fall and the issuer's outstanding bonds will increase in value.

The experience of France Telecom illustrates what can happen to corporate bonds when business conditions deteriorate. To refinance its massive short-term debt, France Telecom conducted the largest corporate bond offering in history up to that time in March 2001 by selling the equivalent of $16.4 billion worth of bonds to investors around the world. France Telecom issued bonds in three different currencies: U.S. dollars, euros, and British pounds. Days after successfully floating its bonds, France Telecom announced that it could not retire as much short-term debt as it had originally anticipated, thereby signaling to the market that its cash flows were weaker than expected. Prices and yields of France Telecom bonds responded accordingly. The required return on France Telecom's five-year dollar bonds, issued with a 7.2 percent coupon, rose to 8.5 percent. The following equation shows that this increase in the required return was associated with a decline in price of $52.07, or 5.2 percent, from the original $1,000 par value:

[6] In Figure 4.3, it appears that real interest rates were negative in 1974–75 and again in 1980–81. Keep in mind that if an investor buys a ten-year bond and holds it to maturity, the real return depends on the inflation that occurs over the bond's life. The figure simply plots the yields on ten-year bonds when they are issued against the inflation rate in that year.

$$P_0 = \$72/2\left[\frac{1-\frac{1}{(1+\frac{0.085}{2})^{10}}}{\frac{0.085}{2}}\right]+\frac{\$1{,}000}{(1+\frac{0.085}{2})^{10}} = \$947.93$$

Fortunately, the same effect can occur in reverse. Consider what might have happened if France Telecom's business had improved suddenly after the bond issue. Suppose that the bond market became convinced that France Telecom's brighter cash flow outlook lowered the risk of the five-year bonds. If investors lowered their required return on these bonds to 6.5 percent, the price of the five-year bonds would have risen to $1,029.48.

You might argue that this entire discussion is irrelevant if an investor holds a bond to maturity. If a bond is held to maturity, there is a good chance that the investor will receive all interest and principal payments as promised, so any price decrease (or increase) that occurs between the purchase date and the maturity date is just a "paper loss." Though the tax code may ignore investment gains and losses until investors realize them, financial economists argue that losses matter, whether investors realize them by selling assets or whether the losses exist only on paper. For example, when the France Telecom bond's value falls from $1,000 to $947.93, an investor holding the bond experiences an opportunity loss. Because the bond's price has fallen, the investor no longer has the opportunity to invest $1,000 elsewhere.

CONCEPT REVIEW QUESTIONS

5. How is a bond's *coupon rate* different from its *coupon yield*?

6. In general, when will a bond sell at a *discount*?

7. Explain the meaning of the term "interest rate risk."

8. Why do bond prices and bond yields move in opposite directions?

4.3 TYPES OF BONDS

The variety of bonds trading in modern financial markets is truly remarkable. In this section, we offer a brief description of the most common types of bonds available today. Many investors see bonds as a rather unexciting investment that provides a steady, predictable stream of income. That description fits some bonds reasonably well, but many bonds are designed with exotic features that make their returns as volatile and unpredictable as shares of common stock.

Bond trading occurs in either the primary or secondary market. *Primary market* trading refers to the initial sale of bonds by firms or government entities. Primary market trading varies depending on the type of bond being considered. For example, the U.S. Treasury sells bonds through an auction process. Most bonds sold at Treasury auctions go to a relatively small group of authorized government bond dealers, though individual investors can participate in Treasury auctions, too. When corporations and state and local government bodies issue bonds in the primary market, they do so with the help of *investment bankers*. Investment bankers assist bond issuers with the design, marketing, and distribution of new bond issues.

Once bonds are issued in the primary market, investors trade them with each other in the *secondary market*. However, many bonds issued in the primary market are purchased by institutional investors who hold the bonds for a long time. As a result, secondary market trading in bonds can be somewhat limited. For instance, if General Motors raises money by conducting a new bond offering, it is likely that their bonds will not trade as actively as General Motors common stock does. Although some specific bond issues do not trade a great deal once they are issued, the sheer size of the bond market means that investors interested in adding bonds to their portfolio have a wide range of choices. We now turn to an overview of the choices available to bond investors. There are several ways to structure an overview of the bond market, beginning with the types of bond issuers.

By Issuer

Bonds come in many varieties and are classified in different ways. Perhaps the simplest classification scheme puts bonds into categories based upon the identity of the issuer. Large companies who need money to finance new investments and to fulfill other needs issue **corporate bonds.** Corporations issue bonds with maturities ranging from 1 to 100 years. When a company issues a debt instrument with a maturity of one to ten years, that instrument is usually called a *note* rather than a bond, but notes and bonds are essentially identical instruments. Most corporate bonds have a par value of $1,000 and pay interest semiannually.

corporate bonds
Bonds issued by corporations.

In the chapter's Opening Focus, we introduced another category known as **municipal bonds,** bonds issued by local and state government entities. In the United States, federal law gives local and state governments a significant break by exempting interest received on municipal bonds from the bondholder's federal income tax. Obviously, this makes municipal bonds especially attractive to investors who face high marginal tax rates. For instance, suppose a corporate bond selling at par offers an investor a coupon rate of 6 percent. If the investor's tax rate on interest income is 33 percent, then the after-tax return on this bond would be 4 percent [6% × (1 – 33%)]. Now suppose there is a municipal bond that is no more or less risky than the corporate bond, and it offers a return of 4 percent. Because this return is tax-free, the municipal bond's return is competitive with the return offered by the corporate bond on an after-tax basis. To put this another way, the tax exemption on municipal bond interest allows state and local governments to raise money at lower interest rates than they would otherwise be able to do.

municipal bonds
Issued by U.S. state and local governments. Interest received on these bonds is exempt from federal income tax.

The largest single issuer of bonds is the U.S. government. The debt instruments issued by the government range in maturity from a few weeks to twenty years. **Treasury bills** are debt instruments that mature in less than a year. The maturities of **Treasury notes** range from one to ten years. Before 2001, the government also issued **Treasury bonds** with maturities of up to thirty years, but the Treasury has not issued thirty-year bonds in recent years. Of course, there are many Treasury bonds originally issued with thirty-year maturities still outstanding in the market. The federal government issues these instruments to raise money to cover budget deficits, and these securities are backed by the "full faith and credit" of the United States. That pledge means that investors generally regard Treasury bills, notes, and bonds as very safe investments. As with all bonds, Treasury bond prices can fluctuate as market interest rates change, but it is generally accepted that Treasury bonds will make all promised cash payments on time and in full. Interest from Treasury securities is subject to federal income tax but not state income tax.

Treasury bills
Debt instruments issued by the federal government that mature in less than one year.

Treasury notes
Debt instruments issued by the federal government with maturities ranging from 1 to 10 years.

Treasury bonds
Debt instruments issued by the federal government with maturities longer than 10 years.

Some federal government agencies issue their own bonds, called **agency bonds**, to finance operations. The government charters these agencies with the task of providing credit for certain sectors of the economy such as farming, real estate, and education. The Federal Home Loan Bank (FHLB), the Federal National Mortgage Association (FNMA or "Fannie Mae"), the Government National Mortgage Association (GNMA or "Ginnie Mae"), and the Federal Home Loan Mortgage Corporation (FHLMC or "Freddie Mac") are the major mortgage-related agencies that issue bonds. At the end of 2003, these agencies had more than $6 trillion in outstanding debt instruments. Some of these agencies are federally owned, and others are federally sponsored. What this implies is that agency debt is not necessarily backed by the full faith and credit of the Treasury, so investors recognize that agency debt carries a small amount of additional risk relative to Treasury securities.

agency bonds
Bonds issued by federal government agencies. Agency bonds are not explicitly backed by the full faith and credit of the U.S. government. Agencies issue bonds to promote the formation of credit in certain sectors of the economy such as real estate, education, and farming.

Figure 4.4 shows the quantity of Treasury, agency, municipal, and corporate bonds *issued* in the primary market during the first quarter of 2004.[7] Clearly federal, state, and local government bodies are very active in the bond market, raising $637 billion in just one quarter. Corporate borrowers barely accounted for one-fourth of the total amount issued. Figure 4.5 on page 172 provides a breakdown of the total amount *outstanding* at the end of that quarter. Again, government institutions raise much more money by issuing bonds than do corporations. Finally, Figure 4.6 provides some information on *secondary market trading* in these bonds. Notice that Treasury securities account for a disproportionate share of volume. Roughly 13 percent of all outstanding Treasury bonds trade on an average day ($480 billion traded divided by $3.7 trillion outstanding).

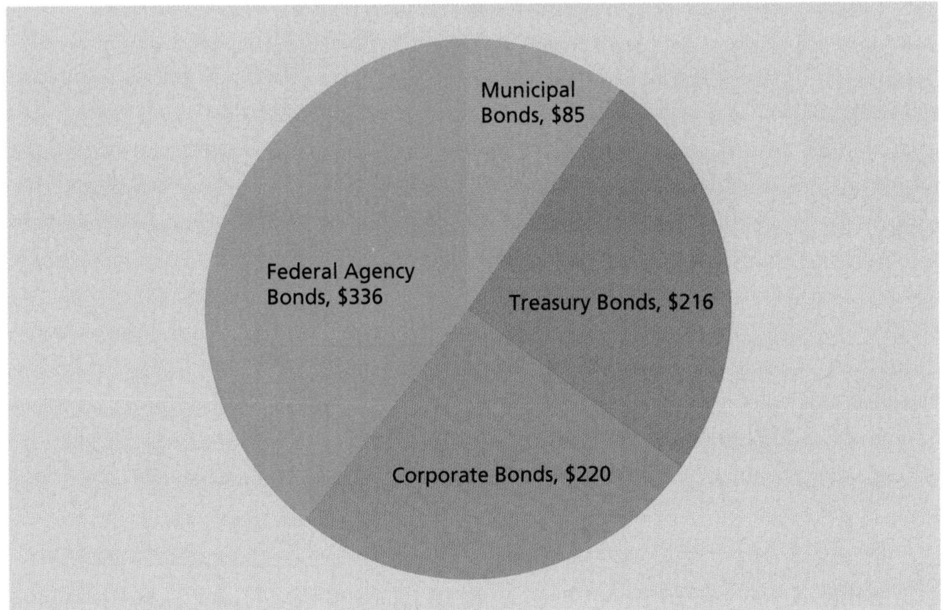

Figure 4.4
New Bonds Sold by Type of Issuer 1st Quarter 2004 ($ billions)

Source: *http://www.investinginbonds.com*

7. The figures for Treasury bonds combine Treasury bills, notes, and bonds.

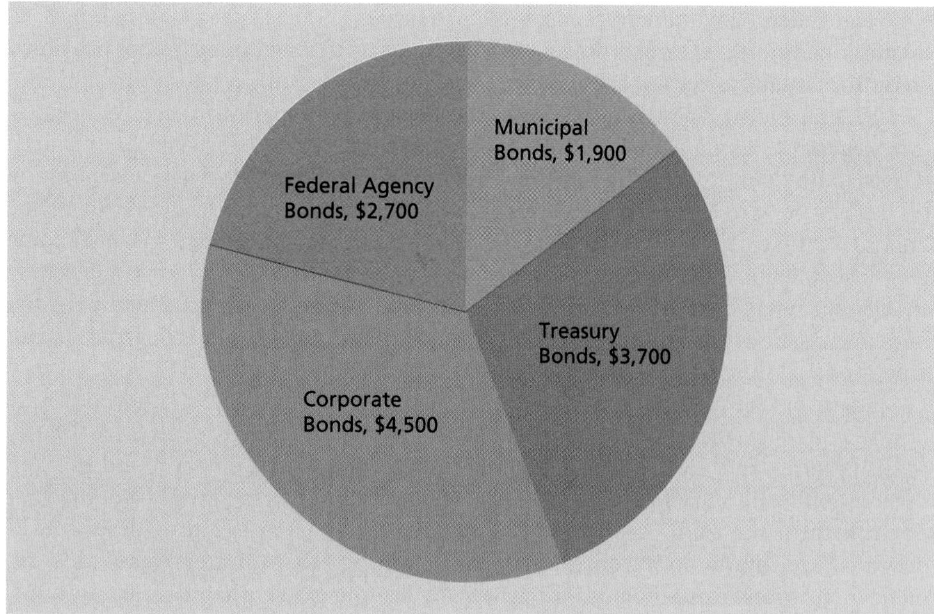

Figure 4.5
Total Outstanding Treasury, Agency, Municipal, and Corporate Bonds 1st Quarter 2004 ($ billions)

Source: http://www.investinginbonds.com

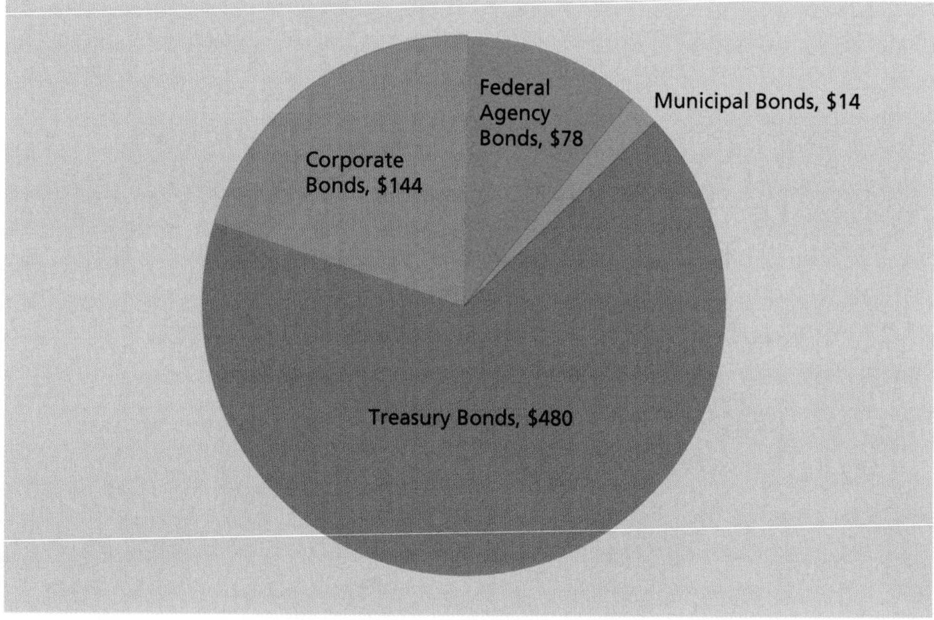

Figure 4.6
Daily Trading Volume in Treasury, Agency, Municipal, and Corporate Bonds 1st Quarter 2004 ($ billions)

Source: http://www.investinginbonds.com

In this section, our focus has been on bond issues. Why do firms and government entities sell bonds? The simple answer is that bond issuers need money—money to finance a deficit, to build public infrastructure, or to pay for expanded manufacturing facilities. An important characteristic that distinguishes corporations from government entities is that when the latter group needs to issue a security to raise funds, they are essentially limited to issuing a bond or other debt instrument. Corporations, on the other hand, can issue either debt (bonds) or equity (stock).

Debt securities offer a series of cash payments that are, for the most part, contractually fixed. The cash payout that bond investors expect from a firm generally does not fluctuate each quarter as the firm's earnings do, and if a firm fails to live up to its promise to make interest and principal payments, bondholders can take legal action against the company and force it into bankruptcy court.

In contrast, common stock, which we cover in the next chapter, represents an ownership or equity claim on the firm's cash flows. Unlike bondholders, stockholders generally have the right to vote on corporate matters ranging from electing a board of directors to approving mergers and acquisitions. However, stockholders have no specific legal entitlement to receive periodic cash payments. Whether stockholders receive any cash payments at all depends on the firm's profitability and on the board of directors' decision to distribute cash to investors.

As we will see, some bonds have features that put them into a gray area between pure debt and equity. In the rest of this section, we discuss a wide range of bond features commonly observed in the corporate bond market.

floating-rate bonds Bonds that make coupon payments that vary through time. The coupon payments are usually tied to a benchmark market interest rate. Also called variable-rate bonds.

prime rate The rate of interest charged by U.S. banks on loans to business borrowers with excellent credit records.

London Interbank Offered Rate (LIBOR) The interest rate that banks in London charge each other for overnight loans. Widely used as a benchmark interest rate for short-term floating-rate debt.

federal funds rate The interest rate that U.S. banks charge each other for overnight loans.

spread The difference between the rate that a lender charges for a loan and the underlying benchmark interest rate. Lenders charge higher spreads to less creditworthy borrowers.

By Features

Fixed versus floating rates. As we have already discussed, most bonds require the borrower to make periodic coupon payments and to repay the bond's face value at maturity. The coupon payments themselves may be fixed in dollar terms over the bond's life, or the coupons may adjust occasionally, if market interest rates change while the bond is outstanding. **Floating-rate bonds** provide some protection against interest rate risk for investors. If market interest rates increase, then eventually, so do the bond's coupon payments. Of course this makes the borrowers' future cash obligations somewhat unpredictable, because the *interest rate risk* of floating-rate bonds is effectively transferred from the buyer to the issuer.

The interest rate on floating-rate bonds is typically tied to a widely quoted market interest rate. Several benchmark interest rates that are often used to determine how a floating-rate bond's interest rate changes over time are the one-year Treasury rate, the prime rate, and the London Interbank Offered Rate. The **prime rate** is the interest rate charged by large banks to "prime" customers, usually businesses that have an excellent record of repaying their debts on time. The **London Interbank Offered Rate (LIBOR)** is a rate at which large banks can borrow from one another, and it is perhaps the most common benchmark interest rate for short-term debt. The equivalent of LIBOR in the United States is the **federal funds rate**, the rate for overnight lending between banks.

The interest rate on floating-rate bonds is typically specified by starting with one of the benchmark rates above and then adding a **spread**. The spread, also called the *credit spread*, is added to the benchmark interest rate, according to the risk of the borrower. Lenders charge higher spreads for less creditworthy borrowers.

APPLYING THE MODEL

On February 14, 2004, Chattem, producer and marketer of such products as Gold Bond skin powder, Aspercreme, and other over-the-counter health-care products, announced that it had issued $200 million in floating-rate notes tied to LIBOR. At the time of the announcement, LIBOR stood at approximately 1.5 percent. With a 3 percent spread, Chattem would pay an interest rate of 4.5 percent on its notes, but that interest rate would adjust every quarter. Thus, Chattem's interest expenses might rise or fall, depending on how LIBOR evolved over time.

Treasury Inflation-Protected Securities (TIPS)
Notes and bonds issued by the federal government that make coupon payments that vary with the inflation rate.

In addition to the fixed-rate notes and bonds that it issues, the U.S. Treasury also offers a floating-rate debt instrument called **Treasury Inflation-Protected Securities (TIPS).** The Treasury sells TIPS with maturities up to 20 years. Rather than making coupon payments that are tied to a specific market interest rate such as LIBOR, TIPS pay a variable coupon that depends on the U.S. inflation rate. Some investors find these securities attractive because, as their name implies, TIPS offer a return that is protected against unexpected increases in inflation. For example, suppose an investor buys a ten-year inflation-indexed note with a par value of $1,000 and a coupon rate of 2 percent. If there is no inflation, the investor will receive a coupon payment of $10 (2% × $1,000 × ½) every six months. However, suppose that in the first six months after the investor bought this note, the United States experienced a 10 percent increase in prices (i.e., a 10 percent inflation rate). When the first coupon payment is due, the U.S. Treasury increases the note's par value by the inflation rate, from $1,000 to $1,100. The 2 percent coupon rate then applies to the new principal value. The first coupon payment will be $11 (2% × $1,100 × ½). Notice that the coupon payment increases at the rate of inflation (from $10 to $11, a 10 percent increase). This means that TIPS offer investors a constant *real* coupon rather than the constant *nominal* coupon guaranteed by ordinary Treasury securities.[8]

Secured versus unsecured. What assurances do lenders have that borrowers will fulfill their obligations to make interest and principal payments on time? In the case of *unsecured debt*, the only assurance is the borrower's promise to repay, combined with the recourse offered by the legal system if the borrower does not make all promised payments. An unsecured corporate bond is usually called a **debenture.** If a corporation has conducted more than one offering of debentures, some issues may have a lower priority claim than others. The term **subordinated debentures** refers to unsecured bonds that have legal claims inferior to, or subordinate to, other outstanding bonds. The terms *senior* and *junior* describe the relative standing of different bond issues, with senior bonds having a higher priority claim than junior bonds.

debentures
Unsecured bonds backed only by the general faith and credit of the borrowing company.

subordinated debentures
An unsecured bond that has a legal claim inferior to other outstanding bonds.

In some cases, however, firms pledge **collateral** when they issue bonds. Collateral refers to assets the bondholders can legally claim if a borrower defaults on a loan. When a bond is backed by collateral, we say that the bond is *secured.* Examples of secured bonds are **mortgage bonds**, which are bonds secured by real estate or buildings; **collateral trust bonds**, which are bonds secured by financial assets held by a trustee; and **equipment trust certificates**, which are bonds secured by various types of physical equipment and are typically related to transportation.

collateral
The specific assets pledged to secure a loan.

mortgage bonds
A bond secured by real estate or buildings.

collateral trust bonds
A bond secured by financial assets held by a trustee.

equipment trust certificates
A secured bond often used to finance transporation equipment.

Zero-coupon bonds. Most bonds make periodic interest payments called coupons, but a few bonds, called zero-coupon bonds, pay no interest at all. Why would anyone purchase a bond that pays no interest? The incentive to purchase zero-coupon bonds is that they sell below face value. For that reason, zero-coupon bonds are also called discount bonds or **pure discount bonds.**[9] An investor who purchases a discount bond receives a capital gain when the bond matures and pays its face value.

pure discount bonds
Bonds that pay no interest and sell below par value. Also called *zero-coupon bonds.*

The best-known example of a pure discount bond is a U.S. *Treasury bill*, or *T-bill.* T-bills are issued by the U.S. government, like Treasury notes and bonds discussed earlier, but they mature in one year or less, have a par value of $10,000, and distribute cash only at maturity. There are no intermediate coupon payments such as those paid

8. TIPS have proven to be so popular with investors that some corporations have recently offered their own inflation-indexed bonds to investors.

9. Be sure you understand the difference between a pure discount bond—a bond that makes no coupon payments at all—and an ordinary bond that sells at a discount. An ordinary bond sells at a discount when its coupon rate is below the rate of return that investors require to hold the bond.

by notes and bonds. For example, the Treasury recently sold a $10,000 face value bill that matures in six months. The selling price of this T-bill was $9,950.70. An investor who purchases the bill and holds it to maturity earns a return of 0.5 percent over the next six months.

$$\frac{\$10,000 - \$9,950.70}{\$9,950.70} = 0.005 = 0.5\%$$

We can convert that return to an annual rate by multiplying it by 2, so the annual (simple interest) return on the T-bill equals about 1 percent.

Another example of a zero-coupon bond is a **Treasury STRIP**. The Treasury creates STRIP securities by issuing an ordinary coupon-paying note or bond, then stripping off the individual coupon and principal payments the security makes, and selling them as separate securities. For example, suppose a five-year, $1,000 par Treasury note offers a coupon rate of 5 percent. This means that the note will make ten coupon payments of $25 each at six-month intervals (5% × $1,000 × ½) and one $1,000 payment at maturity. The Treasury can create eleven distinct STRIP securities by selling each of these payments separately. Suppose an investor pays $765.13 for the right to receive the $1,000 principal payment in five years. Calculate the investor's return on this instrument by solving for its yield to maturity:

Treasury STRIP
A zero-coupon bond representing one coupon payment or the final principal payment made by an existing Treasury note or bond.

$$\$765.13 = \frac{\$1,000}{(1+r)^5} \qquad r = 0.055 \text{ or } 5.5\%$$

Special tax rules apply to zero-coupon bonds. In the United States, the Internal Revenue Service recognizes that capital gains, which accrue to owners of zero-coupon bonds, are a kind of implicit interest payment. Therefore, as the bond's price slowly appreciates as the maturity date draws near, each year's capital gain is taxable, whether the investor sells the bond and realizes a gain or not. Table 4.1 shows how the price of a zero-coupon bond rises as time passes and illustrates the investor's tax liability each year.

Convertible and exchangeable bonds. Some bonds issued by corporations combine the features of debt and equity. Like ordinary bonds, **convertible bonds** pay investors a relatively safe stream of fixed coupon payments. But convertible bonds also give investors the right to convert their bonds into the common stock of the firm that issued the bonds. This means that if the stock prices increased, bondholders can share in that gain. An example illustrates.

convertible bond
A bond that gives investors the option to redeem their bonds for shares of the issuer's stock rather than cash.

Years to Maturity	Yield to Maturity	Bond Price	Taxable Capital Gain
5	0.055	$ 765.13	
4	0.055	$ 807.22	$42.08
3	0.055	$ 851.61	$44.40
2	0.055	$ 898.45	$46.84
1	0.055	$ 947.87	$49.41
0	0.055	$1,000.00	$52.13

Table 4.1
Zero-Coupon Bond Prices and Taxable Income

Zero-coupon bonds pay no interest, so investors earn their return by purchasing them at a discount and letting them appreciate over time. This table illustrates how the discount bond's price rises as maturity approaches. The last column shows the investor's taxable gain each year.

APPLYING THE MODEL

On February 10, 2004, the parent company of American Airlines, AMR Corp. (ticker, AMR), announced a $300-million offering of convertible bonds maturing in 2024. The bonds offered investors a coupon rate of 4.5 percent, paid semiannually, and bondholders also received the right to exchange each $1,000 par value bond for 45.3515 AMR common shares. At what stock price does it make sense for bondholders to exercise the right to convert their bonds into shares? Consider that each bond is worth either $1,000 or 45.3515 times AMR's stock price. The break-even point occurs when AMR's stock price equals $22.05 ($1,000 ÷ 45.3515). At any lower price, bondholders are better off taking $1,000 in cash, but at any higher price, the shares are worth more than the bonds' face value. Moreover, there is no upper limit to the return that AMR convertible bondholders can earn. Once the price of AMR stock exceeds $22.05, each additional $1 increase in the stock price is worth an additional $45.3515 to bondholders.

exchangeable bonds
Bonds issued by corporations which may be converted into shares of a company other than the company that issued the bonds.

Exchangeable bonds work in much the same way that convertible bonds do, except that exchangeable bonds are convertible into common shares of a company other than the company that issued the bonds. Exchangeable bonds' are often used when one company owns a large block of stock in another firm that it wants to divest. Although the option to convert bonds into shares generally resides with the investor who holds a convertible bond, exchangeable bonds' conversion rights can vary. Sometimes the bond indenture requires that, at maturity, bondholders accept common stock in the underlying firm. In that case, the securities are called *mandatory exchangeable bonds*.

callable
Bonds that the issuer can repurchase from investors at a predetermined price known as the *call price*.

call price
The price at which a bond issuer may call or repurchase an outstanding bond from investors.

Callable and putable bonds. Most corporate bonds and some government bonds are **callable**. This means that the bond issuer retains the right to repurchase the bonds in the future at a predetermined price known as the **call price**. That right is valuable when market interest rates fall. Recall that bond prices generally rise as market interest rates fall. A firm that issued noncallable bonds when rates were high may want to retire those bonds and reissue new ones after a decline in interest rates. However, retiring the outstanding bonds requires paying a significant premium over par value. With callable bonds, the call price establishes an upper limit on how much the firm must pay to redeem previously issued bonds. Investors recognize that the call feature works to the advantage of the bond issuer, so callable bonds must generally offer higher coupon rates than otherwise similar noncallable bonds.

putable bonds
Bonds that investors can sell back to the issuer at a predetermined price under certain conditions.

Putable bonds work in just the opposite way. **Putable bonds** allow investors to sell their bonds back to the issuing firm. This option is valuable to bondholders because it protects them against a decline in the value of their bonds. Therefore, putable bonds can offer lower coupon rates than otherwise similar nonputable bonds.

default risk
The risk that the corporation issuing a bond may not make all scheduled payments.

Protection from default risk. Besides interest rate risk, bond investors also have to worry about default risk. **Default risk** refers to the possibility that a bond issuer may not be able to make all scheduled interest and principal payments on time and in full. The *bond indenture,* the contract between a bond issuer and its creditors, usually contains a number of provisions designed to protect investors from default risk.

We have already discussed some of these features, including a bond issue's seniority and whether it is secured or unsecured. Additional examples of these provisions include sinking funds and protective covenants. A **sinking fund** provision requires the borrower to make regular payments to a third-party trustee. The trustee then uses those funds to repurchase outstanding bonds. Usually sinking fund provisions require the trustee to retire bonds gradually, so that by the time a bond issue's maturity date arrives, only a fraction of the original issue remains outstanding. The trustee may purchase previously issued bonds on the open market, or the trustee may repurchase bonds by exercising a call provision, as described above.

sinking fund
A provision in a bond indenture that requires the borrower to make regular payments to a third-party trustee for use in retiring the bond

Protective covenants
Provisions of the bond indenture that stipulate actions that the borrower must do (positive covenants) or actions that the borrower must not do (negative covenants).

Protective covenants, part of the bond indenture, specify requirements that the borrower must meet as long as bonds remain outstanding. *Positive covenants* specify things that the borrower must do. For example, positive covenants may require a borrower to file quarterly audited financial statements, to maintain a minimum amount of working capital, or to maintain a certain level of debt coverage ratios. *Negative covenants* specify things that the borrower must not do, such as pay unusually high dividends, sell off assets, or issue additional senior debt.

Clearly investors have a lot of choices when they consider buying bonds. The number and variety of fixed-income investments available in the market is truly astounding and far exceeds the number of common stocks available for trading. Let us turn now to the bond markets to see how bonds are traded, how bond prices are quoted, and what external information is available to bond traders to help them make investment decisions.

SMART IDEAS VIDEO
Annette Poulsen, University of Georgia
"There is a tradeoff between flexibility for the corporation and protection for the bondholder."
See the entire interview at **SMARTFinance**

CONCEPT REVIEW QUESTIONS

9. What are the main types of issuers of bonds in the United States?

10. What is the difference between a *pure discount bond* and an ordinary bond that sells at a discount?

11. Explain who benefits from the option to *call* a bond, and who benefits from the option to *convert* a bond into shares of common stock.

4.4 BOND MARKETS

In terms of the dollar volume of securities traded each day, the bond market is much larger than the stock market. Though some bonds are listed on stock exchanges, most bonds trade in an electronic over-the-counter (OTC) market. The OTC market is not a single physical location where bonds are traded. It is a collection of dealers around the country and around the world who stand ready to buy and sell bonds. Dealers communicate with one another and with investors via an electronic network. Because trades are decentralized and negotiated privately, it is usually difficult to obtain accurate, up-to-date price information on most bonds. Nevertheless, it is useful to see how bond prices are quoted in different segments of the market.

Figure 4.7
Price Quotes for Treasury Securities

The figure shows bid and ask prices for Treasury securities maturing between November 2008 and February 2010. The first column lists the coupon rate offered by each security, and the final column shows each security's yield to maturity based on the ask price.

Source: The Wall Street Journal, June 4, 2004. Reprinted with permission.

Treasury Bonds, Notes and Bills

RATE	MATURITY MO/YR	BID	ASKED	CHG	ASK YLD
Government Bonds & Notes					
4.750	Nov 08n	104:07	104:08	2	3.70
3.375	Dec 08n	98:12	98:13	3	3.76
3.250	Jan 09n	97:22	97:23	4	3.79
3.875	Jan 09i	111:30	111:31	-5	1.20
3.000	Feb 09n	96:16	96:17	4	3.81
2.625	Mar 09n	94:24	94:25	3	3.83
3.125	Apr 09n	96:26	96:27	3	3.84
3.875	**May 09n**	**100:00**	**100:01**	**3**	**3.87**
5.500	May 09n	107:13	107:14	3	3.83
6.000	Aug 09n	109:20	109:21	4	3.93
10.375	Nov 09	103:30	103:31	-1	1.37
4.250	Jan 10i	114:28	114:29	-5	1.47
6.500	Feb 10n	112:10	112:11	4	4.05
11.750	Feb 10	106:29	106:30	-3	1.68

Bond Price Quotations

ask
The price that an investor pays to a dealer to purchase a security. Also, the price at which a dealer stands ready to sell securities to investors.

bid
The price that an investor receives when they sell a security to a dealer. Also, the price at which a dealer stands ready to buy securities from investors.

bid-ask spread
The difference between the price at which a dealer is willing to buy and the price at which the dealer will sell. By selling at the ask, which is higher than the bid, the dealer makes a profit on each trade.

Figure 4.7 shows representative price quotes for U.S. Treasury securities taken from *The Wall Street Journal* on Friday, June 4, 2004. The first column lists the coupon rate of each security. The second column lists the month and year that each security matures. Where the letter "n" appears, it denotes that the particular instrument being described is a Treasury note. For example, look at the rows in Figure 4.7 that are highlighted. The first highlighted row indicates that a Treasury note maturing in February 2009 offers a coupon rate of 3.000 percent. Given that the note's par value equals $1,000, this coupon rate implies that the bond will make two coupon payments of $15 each year. The columns labeled "bid" and "ask" show the market price of each note. The **ask** price is the price that a trader pays to a dealer to buy a note, and the **bid** price is the price a trader receives if he sells a note to a dealer. Notice that the ask price is always higher than the bid. This **bid-ask spread** represents income to the bond dealer.

By convention, Treasury note and bond prices are quoted as a percentage of par value and in increments of 32nds of a dollar. For example, look at the note that matures in August 2009. The bid price of 109:20 means that an investor who owned this note could sell it for 109 and 20/32nds percent of par value. The fraction 20/32 equals 0.625, so this bond's dollar bid price equals $1,096.25 ($1,000 × 1.09625). The next-to-last column shows how much the note's price changed on the previous trading day, and the final column calculates the note's yield to maturity based on the ask price. To calculate the ask yield, use Equation 4.3.

APPLYING THE MODEL

Figure 4.7 shows that a note offering a coupon rate of 5.500 and maturing on May 2009 has an ask price of 107:14. The figure lists the ask yield on this bond at 3.83 percent. To derive this yield, let us make a simplifying assumption. Figure 4.7 was taken from *The Wall Street Journal* on June 5, 2004. The note we are interested in makes coupon payments each May and November, so assume that the most recent coupon payment was just made. This means that the next coupon payment will arrive in six months.[10] Each semiannual coupon payment equals \$27.50. The Treasury pays the next coupon in November 2004 and the final one in May 2009, so ten payments remain. The ask price in dollar terms equals 107 and 14/32nds percent of par value. Because 14/32 equals 0.4375, the ask price is

$$\$1,000 \times 1.074375 = \$1,074.375$$

Now apply Equation 4.3 and use *Excel* or a financial calculator to find the note's ask yield to maturity:

$$\$1,074.375 = \frac{\$27.50}{(1+\frac{r}{2})^1} + \frac{\$27.50}{(1+\frac{r}{2})^2} + \ldots.. + \frac{\$1,027.50}{(1+\frac{r}{2})^{10}}$$

$$r = 0.0385 = 3.85\%$$

Our solution is within 0.02 percentage points (or 2 *basis points*) of the yield quoted in Figure 4.7. The slight difference occurs because of our simplifying assumption that the next coupon will arrive in exactly six months.

If you look closely at the highlighted rows, you will notice an interesting pattern. The coupon rates offered on these notes vary from 2.625% on the note maturing in March to 6.000% on the note maturing in August. However, the yields on the notes do not vary as much, ranging from 3.81 to 3.93 percent. The variation in coupon rates suggests that, although these instruments mature within seven months of each other, they may have been issued originally at different times in different market conditions. The difference in coupons offered by the notes maturing in February (3.000 percent) and August (6.000 percent) indicate that the August 2009 note was originally issued at a time when interest rates were much higher than when the February 2009 bond was first issued. Even though the coupons on these notes vary a great deal, the yields do not. This means that the market's current required return is a little less than 4 percent and that the prices of previously issued notes and bonds adjust until they offer competitive yields.

Also notice that three of the securities we've highlighted sell at a discount, one sells close to par value, and two sell at a premium. This reflects the difference between the market's required rate of return (again, just under 4 percent) and the coupon each note offers. Those notes with coupon rates below the required rate trade at a discount, and those notes with coupon rates above the required rate trade at a premium. The note trading near par offers a coupon of 3.875 percent. Because its coupon is so close to the required rate in the market, it sells very close to par.

---

10. In fact, the May coupon payment was made a few weeks before June 5, so the next coupon payment would come in a little less than six months. By making an assumption about the timing of this note's cash flows that is incorrect by a couple of weeks, we derive a yield that is slightly different from that reported in the figure. However, we stick with our assumption because it allows us to keep the discounting simple, with cash flows arriving exactly every six months.

Table 4.2 shows market data for some heavily traded corporate bonds. The first column lists the name and ticker symbol of the bond issuer. The second column shows the annual coupon rate, and the third column reports the maturity date. Corporate bond prices are quoted as a percent of par value, but without the convention of quoting in 32nds of a dollar. For example, the first row of the table indicates that the AT&T Wireless Services bond paying a coupon rate of 8.75 percent and maturing on March 1, 2031, recently sold for $1,298.06 (or 129.806 percent of par value). Given the price, coupon, and maturity date, the next column calculates the AT&T bond's yield to maturity, which equals 6.414 percent.

yield spread
The difference in yield to maturity between two bonds or two classes of bonds with similar maturities.

Traders often refer to the **yield spread** on a particular bond. The yield spread equals the difference in yield to maturities between a corporate bond and a Treasury bond at roughly the same maturity. By convention, yield spreads are quoted in terms of basis points, where one basis point equals 1/100 of 1 percent. Because corporate bonds are riskier than Treasury bonds, they offer higher yields, so the yield spread is always a positive number. The fifth and sixth columns of Table 4.2 report data on yield spreads. The fifth column gives the yield spread between the corporate bond in question and a similar maturity Treasury bond. The sixth column specifies what we mean by a "similar" bond. The column heading, UST, stands for U.S. Treasury, and the numbers in the column refer to the maturity of the Treasury security to which each corporate bond is compared to calculate the yield spread. Looking at those two columns, we see that the AT&T Wireless bond offers a yield that is 150 basis points (or 1.5 percentage points) above the yield on a Treasury bond maturing in thirty years. The thirty-year Treasury bond is a relevant comparison because the AT&T bond's maturity is so far off in the future at 2031. Notice that the yield spread on Vodafone bonds, which mature in 2010, is reported relative to a five-year Treasury note.

As you might expect, bond spreads reflect a direct relationship with default risk. The greater the risk that the borrower may default on its debts, the higher the spread that bonds issued by the borrower must offer investors to compensate them for the risk that they take. For investors, estimating the default risk of a particular bond issue is a crucial element in determining what the required return on the bond should be. Fortunately, bond investors have several resources at their disposal to help them make this evaluation.

Table 4.2
Market Data for Actively Traded Corporate Bonds

Company (Ticker)	Coupon	Maturity	Last Price	Last Yield	Estimated Spread	UST	Est $ Vol (000s)
AT&T Wireless Services (AWE)	8.750	March 1, 2031	129.806	6.414	150	30	211,915
Goldman Sachs Group (GS)	6.345	February 15, 2034	101.131	6.261	135	30	98,407
SBC Communications (SBC)	5.875	August 15, 2012	107.161	4.836	80	10	73,867
Vodafone Group PLC (VOD)	7.750	February 15, 2010	119.546	4.041	104	5	58,125

Rating Description	Moody's	S&P and Fitch	
Highest quality	Aaa	AAA	Investment-
High quality	Aa1, Aa2, Aa3	AA+, AA, AA-	grade
Upper medium	A1, A2, A3	A+, A, A-	bonds
Medium	Baa1, Baa2, Baa3	BBB+, BBB, BBB-	
Non-investment grade	Ba1 BB+		
Speculative	Ba2, Ba3	BB, BB-	Junk
Highly speculative	B1, B2, B3	B+, B, B-	bonds
Very risky, default	Caa1 or lower	CCC+ or lower	

Table 4.3
Bond Ratings

Bond rating agencies such as Moody's, Standard and Poors, and Fitch assign bond ratings based on their assessment of the borrower's ability to repay. Bonds in the top four ratings categories are investment grade bonds, while those rated lower are junk bonds.

Bond Ratings

For information on the likelihood that a particular bond issue may default, investors turn to bond rating agencies such as Standard & Poor's, Moody's, and Fitch. These organizations provide an independent assessment of the risk of most publicly traded bond issues, and they assign a letter **bond rating** to each issue to indicate its degree of risk. Table 4.3 lists the major bond-rating categories provided by each of the agencies and the interpretation associated with each rating class. Bonds rated BBB- or higher by S&P and Fitch, and Baa3 or higher by Moody's fall into the investment-grade category. Bonds rated lower than that are called non-investment grade or **junk bonds**. Recall from the Opening Focus that in early 2004, the state budget crisis in California was so bad that the state's outstanding bonds were rated just one level above the junk bond-category. The term "junk bonds" has a pejorative connotation but simply means that these bonds are riskier than investment-grade bonds are. For example, for bonds in the investment grade category, the probability of default is extremely low, perhaps as low as 1 percent. A recent study put the probability of a B-rated bond defaulting in its first year at almost 8 percent.[11]

bond ratings
Grades assigned to bonds by specialized agencies that evaluate the capacity of bond issuers to repay their debts. Lower grades signify higher default risk.

junk bonds
Bonds rated below investment grade (also known as high yield bonds).

Table 4.4 shows the relationship between bond ratings and yield spreads for corporate bonds at different maturities.[12] As before, the yield spreads are quoted in basis points. The first entry in the top left corner of the table shows a corporate bond with the highest possible Aaa/AAA rating and a maturity of one year. It offered investors a yield to maturity that was just ten basis points higher than a one-year Treasury bill on February 20, 2004. Moving across the row, we see that yield spreads increase with time to maturity. As expected, yield spreads increase as you move down the rows. The bottom row shows that the lowest-rated bonds, those that are at or

11. "Default Curves and the Dynamics of Credit Spreads," by Wesley Phoa, in *Professional Perspectives on Fixed Income Portfolio Management*, Frank J. Fabozzi, ed., John Wiley & Sons, 2002.

12. We focus exclusively on corporate bonds in Table 4.4 because the yields on corporate and municipal bonds with the same rating will be quite different. As noted earlier, interest payments from municipal bonds are not subject to federal income tax. This means that investors will accept a lower yield on a municipal bond than they will accept on a corporate bond having the same rating.

Table 4.4
The Relationship Between Bond Ratings and Spreads at Different Maturities

The table shows the difference in yields, as of February 2004, between bonds in different ratings categories and Treasury securities having the same maturity. For instance, 5-year bonds with a AAA rating offered a yield that was 29 basis points higher than the 5-year Treasury note in February 2004. Note that yield spreads rise with maturity just as they rise as the bond rating falls.

Source: http://www.bondsonline.com, February 20, 2004

Rating	1 yr	2 yr	3 yr	5 yr	7 yr	10 yr	30 yr
Aaa/AAA	10	12	23	29	46	58	78
Aa1/AA+	19	27	28	40	56	69	90
Aa2/AA	21	33	35	44	59	71	93
Aa3/AA-	22	36	37	49	63	75	101
A1/A+	44	49	53	61	76	90	113
A2/A	47	52	55	63	78	92	117
A3/A-	51	55	58	67	81	95	118
Baa1/BBB+	59	69	77	87	117	139	165
Baa2/BBB	62	77	5	92	124	147	172
Baa3/BBB-	69	82	87	97	129	154	177
Ba1/BB+	330	340	350	360	380	400	420
Ba2/BB	340	350	360	370	390	410	430
Ba3/BB-	350	360	370	380	400	420	440
B1/B+	470	480	490	520	560	600	650
B2/B	480	490	500	530	570	610	660
B3/B-	490	500	510	540	580	620	670
Caa/CCC	890	900	910	935	945	955	985

near the point of default, offer yields that are 9 to 10 percent higher than comparable maturity Treasury securities. To illustrate an extreme case, suppose that the yield to maturity on a ten-year Treasury bond equals 3 percent. The next-to-last entry in Table 4.4 shows that a ten-year corporate bond rated Caa/CCC must offer a yield that is 9.55 percent higher than the Treasury bond, or 12.55 percent. If that seems like an attractive return, remember the risk dimension. An investor who buys a large number of bonds rated Caa/CCC will almost certainly not earn an average yield of 12.55 percent, because some of these bonds will default. When default occurs, bondholders usually do not receive all the payments they were originally promised, so the yield they realize on their bonds falls short of the promised yield to maturity.[13]

Thus far, we have maintained a simplifying assumption in our valuation models. You can see that assumption embedded in Equations 4.1 and 4.2. Both equations assume that we can apply a single discount rate, r, to determine the present value of cash payments made at any and all future dates. In other words, the models assume that investors require the same rate of return on an investment that pays cash one year from now and on one that pays cash ten years from now. In reality, required rates of return depend on the exact timing of cash payments, as the next section illustrates.

CONCEPT REVIEW QUESTIONS

12. Calculate a bond's yield to maturity using the *ask* price, then repeat the calculation using the bond's *bid* price. Which yield to maturity is higher?

13. The price of a certain Treasury note is quoted as 98:10. What is the dollar price of this note if its par value is $1,000?

14. Explain why the *yield spread* on corporate bonds versus Treasury bonds must always be positive. Is the same true for the yield spread on municipal bonds?

[13] According to The Salomon Center for the Study of Financial Institutions, the default rate among junk bonds reached a record 12.8% in 2002. In a very rough sense, this means that one of eight junk bond issues in the market defaulted that year. The Center estimates that investors who held defaulted bonds recovered only 25% of par value. With the improving economy in 2003, the default rate fell to 4.6% and the recovery rate increased to 45%.

4.5 ADVANCED BOND VALUATION—THE TERM STRUCTURE OF INTEREST RATES (OPTIONAL)

The Yield Curve

A quick glance at Table 4.4 reveals an important fact: bond yields vary with maturity. The difference in the yield spread between a one-year and a thirty-year bond varies from 68 (78 – 10) basis points for Aaa/AAA bonds to 100 basis points, or more, for junk bonds. Though Table 4.4 reports yield spreads rather than yields, the data suggest that a positive relationship exists between time to maturity and yield to maturity for bonds in any risk category.

Financial experts refer to the relationship between time to maturity and yield to maturity for bonds of equal risk as the **term structure of interest rates.** The term structure of interest rates indicates whether yields rise, fall, or remain constant across bonds with different maturities. The simplest way to communicate information about the term structure is to draw a graph that plots yield to maturity on the *y*-axis and time to maturity on the *x*-axis. Each day, *The Wall Street Journal* and many other financial publications print this graph, usually for a sample of Treasury securities. A graph showing the term structure of interest rates is called the **yield curve.**

term structure of interest rates
The relationship between yield to maturity and time to maturity among bonds having similar risk.

yield curve
A graph that plots the relationship between yield to maturity and maturity for a group of similar bonds.

Figure 4.8 shows how the yield curve for U.S. government bonds looked at four different dates. Usually, long-term bonds offer higher yields than short-term bonds do, and the yield curve slopes up. That was the case in January 1983 and in July 1993. However, the level of the yield curve was much higher in 1983 than in 1993. Differences in expected inflation rates in those two years largely explain why the yield curve was so much higher in 1983. In the 24 months before January 1983, the annual rate of U.S. inflation had averaged about 6 percent. Assume that investors expected inflation to remain roughly at that level in the near term. Investors who purchased short-term Treasury bills in January 1983 earned a return of about 7.5 percent, slightly higher than the expected inflation rate. In contrast, in the 24 months before July 1993, the annual inflation rate averaged just under 3 percent. In July 1993, T-bills offered a return of roughly 3.75 percent, again just slightly above the level of expected inflation at that time. In other words, because investors required a positive *real return* on bonds, the nominal bond returns had to be higher in 1983 compared with 1993 because inflation was higher in the earlier period.[14]

The other two graphs in Figure 4.8 illustrate that the shape of the yield curve can change over time. In February 1998, the yield curve was nearly flat, with yields on short-term and long-term bonds hovering around 5 percent. But by November 2000, the yield curve had inverted, with short-term yields lying slightly above long-term yields. Why the yield curve sometimes slopes up and at other times slopes down is a complex problem. However, there is an interesting link between the slope of the yield curve and overall macroeconomic growth.

---

14. The nominal rate of return offered by a bond or any other financial asset should include an estimate of the expected inflation rate in the future rather than merely reflect the inflation rate of the recent past. We discuss the relationship between expected inflation and returns in more depth in the next two chapters. Go to http://www.smartmoney.com/bonds/ to see how the yield curve has behaved in the United States since 1977. Click the link for the Living Yield Curve.

Figure 4.8
The Term Structure of Interest Rates

The figure shows how the yield curve looked on four different dates. Most of the time, the yield curve slopes up because long-term bond yields exceeds short-term bond yields. However, before recessions the yield curve often inverts as it did in November 2000.

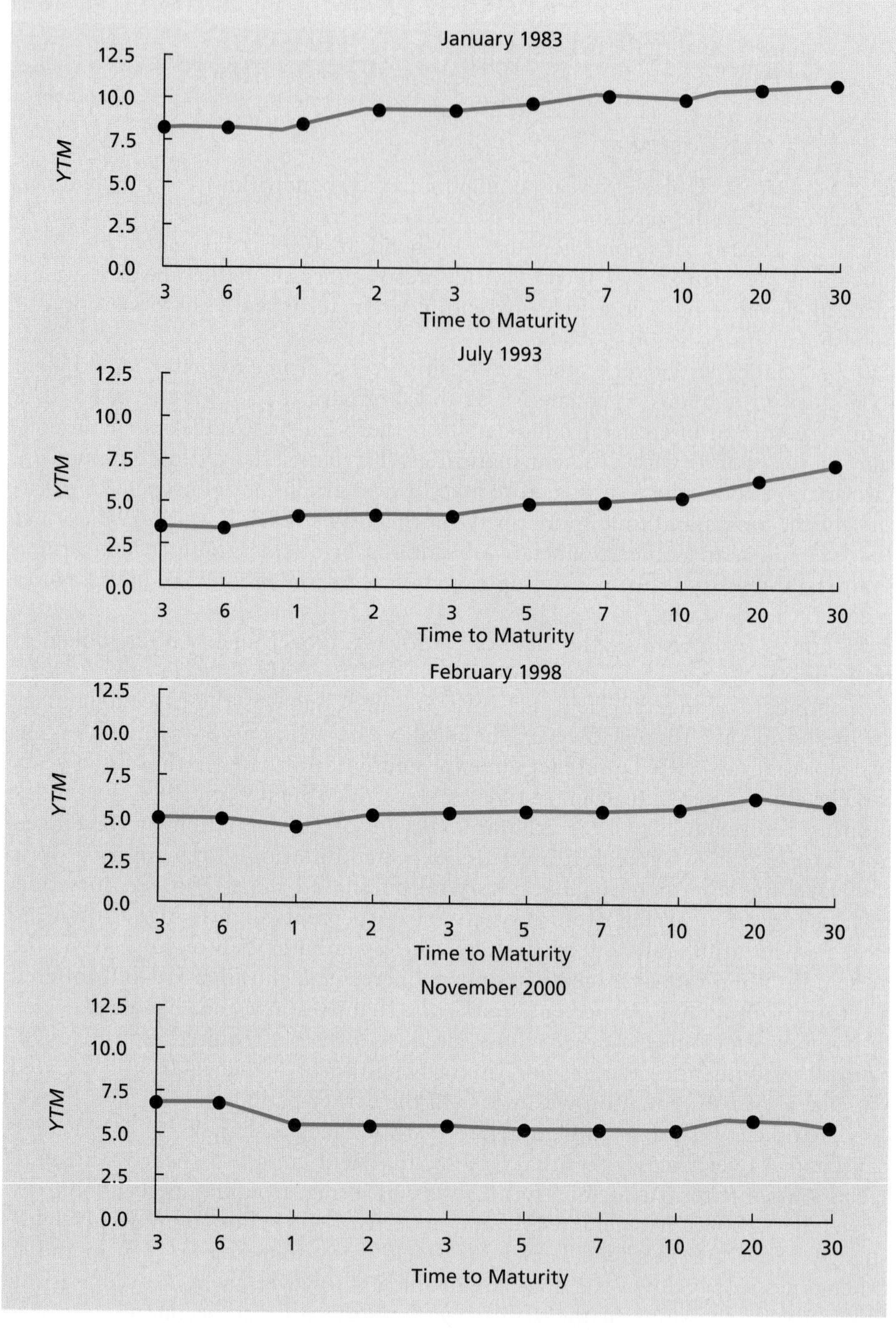

Historically, when the yield curve inverts (i.e., switches from an upward slope to a downward slope), a recession usually follows. In fact, several research studies show that economic forecasts based on the yield curve's slope more accurately predict recessions than many forecasts produced using complex statistical models.

One reason for this pattern is as follows. Suppose a firm receives new information from its sales force indicating that orders for the firm's products are likely to fall in the near term. This prompts the firm to cut back on planned investment. That means the firm's need for long-term borrowing to finance new investment is diminished. If this happens to just a few firms, it is not likely to have a noticeable effect on financial markets. But if it happens to many firms simultaneously (because demand is falling for many products at once, as happens during a recession), the aggregate demand for new financing to pay for investment will fall. Firms will not need to issue long-term bonds to borrow money for new factories or new equipment. A reduction in the demand for long-term borrowing can cause long-term interest rates to fall relative to short-term rates, and the yield curve may invert. The yield curve may also invert because short-term rates rise above long-term rates. This may occur when the Federal Reserve increases short-term rates to fight inflation. As this chapter's Comparative Corporate Finance insert explains, research in this area shows that the yield curve works well as a predictor of economic activity, not only in the United States, but also in Canada, Germany, and other large industrialized economies.

The Expectations Theory

Economists have studied the yield curve intensely for several decades, trying to understand how it behaves and what it portends for the future. As a result of that research, we know that economic growth forecasts that include the slope of the yield curve perform well relative to forecasts that ignore the yield curve. Can the yield curve also tell us something about the direction in which interest rates are headed? The answer is a highly qualified yes. To understand the logic underlying the hypothesis that the slope of the yield curve may predict interest rate movements, consider the following example.

Russell wants to invest $1,000 for two years. He does not want to take much risk, so he plans to invest the money in U.S. Treasury securities. Consulting the Treasury Web site, Russell learns that 1-year Treasury bonds currently offer a 5 percent YTM, and 2-year bonds offer a 5.5 percent YTM. At first, Russell thinks his decision about which investment to purchase is easy. He wants to invest for two years, and the 2-year bond pays a higher yield, so why not just buy that one? Thinking further, Russell realizes that he could invest his money in a 1-year bond and reinvest the proceeds in another 1-year bond when the first bond matures. Whether that strategy will ultimately earn a higher return than that of simply buying the 2-year bond depends on what the yield on a 1-year bond will be one year from now. For example, if the 1-year bond rate rises to 7 percent, Russell will earn 5 percent in the first year and 7 percent in the second year, for a grand total of 12 percent (12.35 percent after compounding). Over the same period, the 2-year bond offers just 5.5 percent per year or 11 percent total (11.30 percent after compounding). In this scenario, Russell earns more by investing in two 1-year bonds than in one 2-year bond. But what if the yield on a 1-year bond is just 5 percent next year? In that case, Russell earns 10 percent over two years (or 10.25 percent after compounding), and he is better off buying the 2-year bond. If next year's yield on the 1-year bond is about 6 percent, then Russell will earn approximately the same return over the two years no matter which investment strategy he chooses.

COMPARATIVE CORPORATE FINANCE

Is the Yield Curve a Good Economic Predictor?

Economists have known for many years that the slope of the yield curve—that is, the difference between yields on short-term and long-term Treasury securities—helps predict future economic growth in the United States. The same is true in many other countries, although the reliability of growth forecasts based on the yield curve varies internationally. The chart below measures the reliability of forecasts based on the yield curve in eleven different countries.

For each country, the chart shows the ability of the yield curve to predict, one year in advance, changes in three different measures of economic activity: the percentage change in real gross domestic product (GDP), the percentage change in industrial production, and the change in the unemployment rate. The vertical height of the bars measures forecast reliability. A forecast which perfectly predicted future economic activity plots at 100 percent, whereas an utterly useless forecast plots at 0 percent.

The chart indicates that the yield curve is most useful in predicting future economic activity in the United States and Canada. The yield curve's predictive power is weaker, but still significant, in most European countries. Curiously, the yield curve's performance is worst in the East, showing almost no ability to predict changes in economic variables in Japan and Australia.

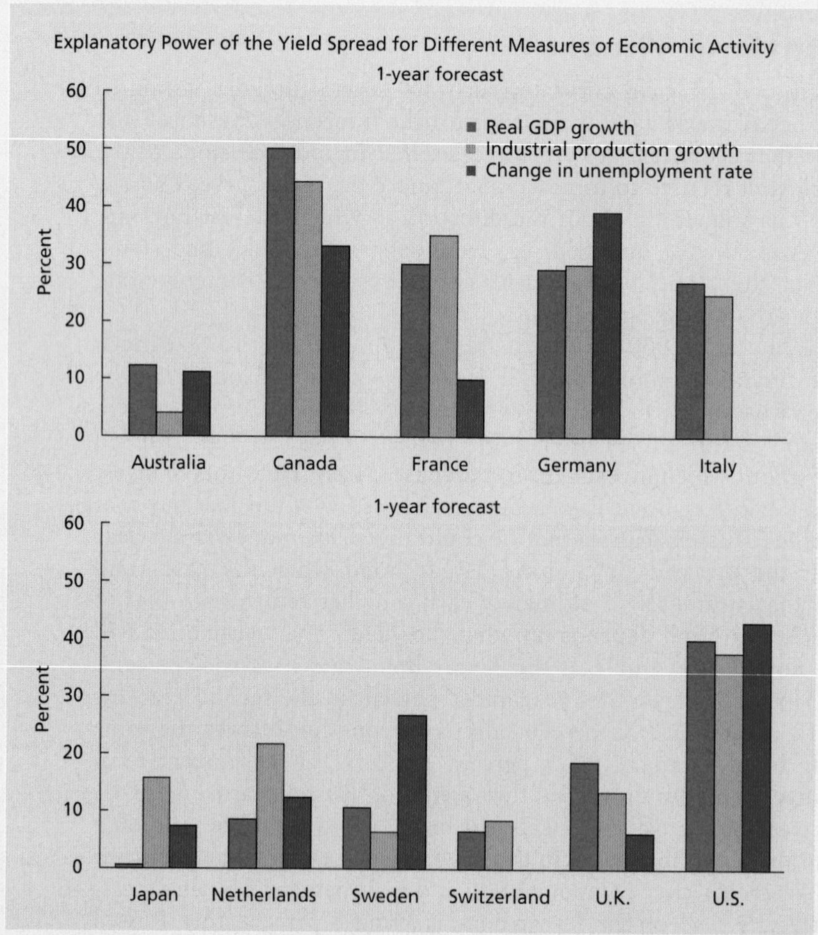

Source: Catherine Bonser-Neal and Timothy R. Morley, "Does the Yield Spread Predict Real Economic Activity? A Multicountry Analysis," Federal Reserve Bank of St. Louis, *Economic Review*, (1997), vol. 82, no. 3, pp. 37–53.

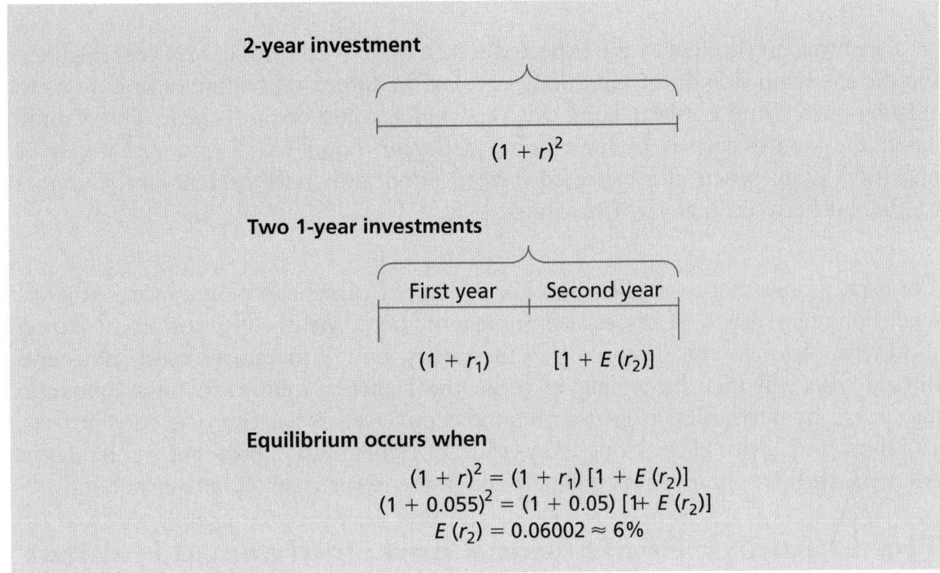

Figure 4.9
The Expectations Hypothesis

The expectations hypothesis says that investors should earn the same expected return by purchasing one 2-year bond or two 1-year bonds. In this example, equilibrium occurs when the expected return on a 1-year bond next year, $E(r_2)$, is 6%. Only then do the two investments strategies provide the same expected return.

This example illustrates the **expectations theory** of the term structure: in equilibrium, investors should expect to earn the same return whether they invest in long-term Treasury bonds or a series of short-term Treasury bonds. If the yield on 2-year bonds is 5.5 percent when the yield on 1-year bonds is 5 percent, then investors must expect next year's yield on a 1-year bond to be 6 percent. Suppose not. If they expect a higher yield than 6 percent, investors are better off purchasing a series of 1-year bonds than from buying the 2-year bond. Conversely, if investors expect next year's bond rate to be less than 6 percent, they will flock to the 2-year bond. Equilibrium occurs when investors' expectations are such that the expected return on a 2-year bond equals the expected return on two 1-year bonds. In this example, equilibrium occurs when investors believe that next year's interest rate will be 6 percent.

expectations theory
In equilibrium, investors should expect to earn the same return whether they invest in long-term Treasury bonds or a series of short-term Treasury bonds.

Figure 4.9 illustrates this idea. The first part of the figure shows that the value of \$1 invested in one 2-year bond will grow to $(1 + r)^2$. In this expression, r represents the current interest rate on a 2-year bond. Next, the figure shows that investors expect \$1 invested in a sequence of two 1-year bonds to grow to $(1 + r_1)[1 + E(r_2)]$. Here, r_1 represents the current 1-year bond rate, and $E(r_2)$ represents the expected 1-year bond rate in the second year. Equilibrium occurs when the two strategies have identical expected returns, or when the expected 1-year interest rate is about 6 percent.

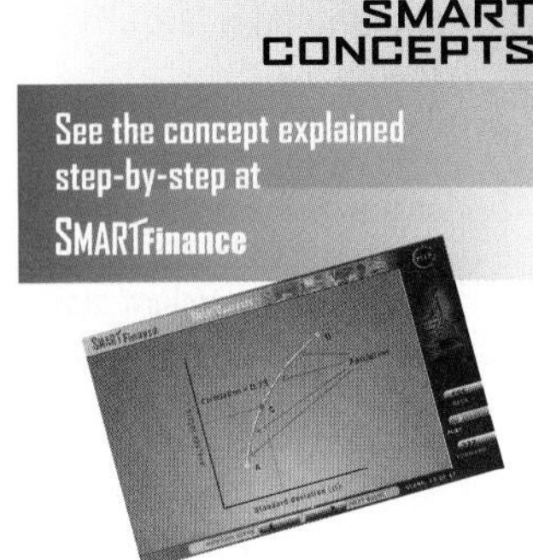

APPLYING THE MODEL

Suppose a 1-year bond currently offers a yield of 5 percent, and a 2-year bond offers a 4.5 percent yield. Under the expectations hypothesis, what interest rate do investors expect on a 1-year bond next year? Remember that the expectations hypothesis says that investors should earn the same expected return by investing in either two 1-year bonds or one 2-year bond. Therefore, the break-even calculation is

$$(1+0.05)(1+E(r_2))=(1+0.045)^2$$
$$(1+E(r_2))=(1.045)^2 \div (1.05)$$
$$E(r_2)=0.04 \text{ or } 4\%$$

The term $E(r_2)$ refers to the expected return on a 1-year bond next year (year 2). On the left-hand side of the equation, we have the return that an investor expects to earn by purchasing a 1-year bond this year and another one next year. That should equal the return earned by purchasing a 2-year bond today and holding it to maturity. Only when the expected 1-year bond rate is 4 percent are investors indifferent between these two strategies.

The expectations theory implies that when the yield curve is sloping upward—that is, when long-term bond yields exceed short-term bond yields—investors must expect short-term yields to rise. According to the theory, only if investors expect short-term rates to rise will they be willing to forgo the higher current yield on a long-term instrument by purchasing a short-term bond. Conversely, when the yield curve inverts, and short-term yields exceed long-term yields, investors must expect short-term rates to fall. Only then would investors willingly accept the lower yield on long-term bonds.

The Liquidity Preference and Preferred Habitat Theories

Unfortunately, the slope of the yield curve does not always provide a reliable signal of future interest rate movements, perhaps because the expectations theory ignores several factors that are important to investors and that influence the shape of the yield curve. The first factor is that investors may have a preference for investing in short-term securities. As we have seen, when market interest rates change, the prices of long-term bonds fluctuate more than the prices of short-term bonds. This added risk might deter some investors from investing in long-term bonds. To attract investors, perhaps long-term bonds must offer a return that exceeds the expected return on a series of short-term bonds. Therefore, when the yield curve slopes up, we cannot be sure whether this is the result of investors expecting interest rates to rise in the future, or simply a reflection of compensation for risk. The **liquidity preference theory** of the term structure recognizes this problem. It says that the slope of the yield curve is influenced not only by expected interest rate changes but also by the liquidity premium that investors require on long-term bonds.

liquidity preference theory
States that the slope of the yield curve is influenced not only by expected interest rate changes, but also by the liquidity premium that investors require on long-term bonds.

A second factor clouds the interpretation of the slope of the yield curve as a signal of interest rate movements if certain investors always purchase bonds with a particular maturity. For instance, pension funds that promise retirement income to investors and life insurance companies that provide death benefits to policyholders have very long-term liabilities. These companies may have a strong desire to invest in long-term bonds (the longest available in the market) to match their liabilities, even if long-term bonds offer low expected returns relative to a series of short-term bonds. Economists use the **preferred habitat theory** (or the *market segmentation theory*) to describe the effect of this behavior on the yield curve. If short-term bond rates exceed long-term rates, the cause may be that the demand for long-term bonds is very high relative to their supply. This demand drives up long-term bond prices and drives down their yields. If the investors purchasing long-term bonds have a strong preference for investing in those securities, despite their low yields, then a yield curve that slopes down does not necessarily imply that investors expect interest rates to fall.[15]

preferred habitat theory
A theory that recognizes that the shape of the yield curve may be influenced by investors who prefer to purchase bonds having a particular maturity regardless of the returns those bonds offer compared to returns available at other maturities.

15. Do you have a favorite place to go to enjoy a beer with your peers? Is the price of beer there the lowest price in town? If not, you are behaving according to the preferred habitat theory. You prefer to go to a particular establishment to socialize, even though you could buy the same beer at another location for less money. In the same way, some investors prefer to invest in long-term bonds even though a series of sort-term bonds might offer a higher expected return.

Conclusion

Valuing assets, both financial assets and real assets, is what finance is all about. In this chapter, we have learned some simple approaches for pricing bonds, which are among the most common and most important financial instruments in the market. A bond's price depends on how much cash flow it promises investors, how that cash flow is taxed, how likely it is that the issuers fulfill its promises (i.e., default risk), whether investors expect high or low inflation, and whether interest rates rise or fall over time. In the next chapter, we apply many of these same ideas to the pricing of common and preferred stock.

15. Explain why the height of the yield curve depends on inflation.

16. Suppose the Treasury issues two 5-year bonds. One is an ordinary bond that offers a fixed nominal coupon rate of 4 percent. The other bond is an inflation-indexed bond (or TIPS). When the TIPS bond is issued, will it have a coupon rate of 4 percent, more than 4 percent, or less than 4 percent?

CONCEPT REVIEW QUESTIONS

4.6 SUMMARY AND CONCLUSIONS

- Valuation is a process that links an asset's return with its risk. To value most types of assets, one must first estimate the asset's future cash flows and then discount them at an appropriate discount rate.
- Pricing bonds is an application of the general valuation framework. A bond's price equals the present value of its future cash flows, which consist of coupon and principal payments.
- The yield to maturity is a measure of the return that investors require on a bond. The YTM is the discount rate that equates the present value of a bond's cash flows to its current market price.
- Bond prices and interest rates are inversely related. When interest rates rise (fall), bond prices fall (rise), and the prices of long-term bonds are more responsive in general to changes in interest rates than short-term bond prices are.
- Bonds are categorized based on who issues them or on any number of features such as convertibility, callability, maturity, and so on.
- Bond rating agencies help investors evaluate the risk of bonds. Bonds with lower ratings must offer investors higher yields.
- The return that is most important to investors is the real, or inflation-adjusted, return. The real return is roughly equal to the nominal return minus the inflation rate.
- The "term structure of interest rates" describes the relationship between time to maturity and yield to maturity on bonds of equivalent risk. A graph of the term structure is called the yield curve. The slope of the yield curve is highly correlated with future economic growth.

SELF-TEST PROBLEMS

Answers to Self-Test Problems appear in Appendix D at back of book. Answers to the Concept Review Questions throughout the chapter appear at http://megginson.swlearning.com.

ST4-1. A five-year bond pays interest annually. The par value is $1,000 and the coupon rate equals 7 percent. If the market's required return on the bond is 8 percent, what is the bond's market price?

ST4-2. A bond that matures in two years makes semiannual interest payments. The par value is $1,000, the coupon rate equals 4 percent, and the bond's market price is $1,019.27. What is the bond's yield to maturity?

ST4-3. Two bonds offer a 5 percent coupon rate, paid annually, and sell at par ($1,000). One bond matures in two years and the other matures in ten years.

a. What are the YTMs on each bond?
b. If the YTM changes to 4 percent, what happens to the price of each bond?
c. What happens if the YTM changes to 6 percent?

INTERNET RESOURCES

http://www.investinginbonds.com—Contains a wealth of information about markets for Treasury, corporate, and municipal bonds, including easy-to-read tutorials on bond basics, reading bond price quotations, and many other topics

http://www.bondmarkets.com—An extremely comprehensive site with extensive coverage of current events, policy issues, and research related to the bond markets; has an extensive list of links to other bond sites on the Web

http://www.financenter.com—A consumer-oriented site offering various online financial calculators that allow you to calculate a bond's after-tax yield to maturity, the effect of interest rate movements on a bond's price, and many other figures

http://www.stockcharts.com/charts/YieldCurve.html—Offers a Java-animated yield curve juxtaposed to a plot of the S&P 500, a stock index that includes 500 of the biggest and most important firms in the market; allows you to watch historical movements in stock and bond markets simultaneously

http://www.bondsonline.com—Provides an enormous amount of information on the bond markets

KEY TERMS

agency bonds
ask
bid
bid-ask spread
bond rating
call price
callable
collateral
collateral trust bonds
convertible bonds
corporate bonds
coupon
coupon rate
coupon yield
debenture
default risk
discount
equipment trust certificates
exchangeable bonds
expectations theory
federal funds rate
floating-rate bonds

indenture
interest rate risk
junk bonds
liquidity preference theory
London Interbank Offered Rate
maturity date
mortgage bonds
municipal bonds
nominal return
par value
preferred habitat theory
premium
prime rate
principal
protective covenants
pure discount bonds
putable bonds
real return
required rate of return
sinking fund
spread
subordinated debentures
term structure of interest rates
Treasury bills
Treasury bonds
Treasury Inflation-Protected Securities
Treasury notes
Treasury STRIP
yield curve
yield spread
yield to maturity

QUESTIONS AND PROBLEMS

Q4-1. What is the relationship between the price of a financial asset and the return that investors require on that asset, holding other factors constant?

Q4-2. Define the following terms commonly used in bond valuation: (a) *par value,* (b) *maturity date,* (c) *coupon,* (d) *coupon rate,* (e) *coupon yield,* (f) *yield to maturity (YTM),* and (g) *yield curve.*

Q4-3. Under what circumstances will a bond's *coupon rate* exceed its *coupon yield*? Explain in economic terms why this occurs.

Q4-4. What is the difference between a *pure discount bond* and a bond that trades at a discount? If issuers successfully sell pure discount bonds in the market, investors must want them. Can you explain why any bond purchaser might prefer to purchase a pure discount bond rather than a bond that pays interest?

Q4-5. A firm issues a bond at *par value*. Shortly thereafter, interest rates fall. If you calculate the *coupon rate*, *coupon yield*, and *yield to maturity* for this bond after the decline in interest rates, which of the three values is highest and which is lowest? Explain.

Q4-6. Twenty-five years ago, the U.S. government issued thirty-year bonds with a *coupon rate* of about 8 percent. Five years ago, the U.S. government sold ten-year bonds with a *coupon rate* of about 5 percent. Suppose that the current *coupon rate* on newly issued five-year Treasury bonds is 2.5 percent. For an investor seeking a low-risk investment maturing in five years, do the bonds issued twenty-five years ago with a much higher *coupon rate* provide a more attractive return than the new five-year bonds? What about the ten-year bonds issued five years ago?

Q4-7. Describe how and why a bond's *interest rate risk* is related to its maturity.

Q4-8. Explain why *municipal bonds* can offer lower interest rates than equally risky corporate bonds.

Q4-9. Explain why the *yield to maturity* on a *junk bond* is not a particularly good measure of the return you can expect if you buy it and hold it until maturity.

Q4-10. Under the *expectations theory*, what does the slope of the *yield curve* reveal about the future path of interest rates?

Q4-11. If the yield curve typically slopes upward, what does this imply about the long-term path of interest rates if the expectations theory is true?

Q4-12. Go to http://www.stockcharts.com/charts/YieldCurve.html and click on the animated yield-curve graph (be sure JAVA is enabled on your browser). Answer the following questions:

a. Is the yield curve typically upward sloping, downward sloping, or flat?

b. Notice the behavior of the yield curve and the S&P 500 between July 28, 1998, and October 19, 1998. In August 1998, Russia defaulted on billions of dollars of foreign debt. Then, in late September came the news that at the behest of the Federal Reserve, fifteen financial institutions would infuse $3.5 billion in new capital into hedge fund Long-Term Capital Management, which had lost nearly $2 billion in the previous month. Comment on these events as they relate to movements in the yield curve and the S&P 500 that you see in the animation.

Q4-13. At http://www.nber.org/cycles.html, you can find the official beginning and ending dates for U.S. business cycles, according to the National Bureau of Economic Research (NBER). For example, the NBER indicates that the U.S. economy was in recession from January 1980 to July 1980, from July 1981 to November 1982, and from July 1990 to March 1991. Next, go to http://www.smartmoney.com/onebond/index.cfm?story=yieldcurve and click on the animation of the Living Yield Curve. Pause the animation at November 1978. Then, click one frame at a time until May 1980. Pause again at November 1981, and click one frame at a time until August 1982. Let the animation play again until you reach March 1989. What association do you notice between the shape of the yield curve and the NBER's dates for recessions?

Q4-14. Look again at the yield-curve animation found at the SmartMoney Web site, http://www.smartmoney.com/onebond/index.cfm?story=yieldcurve. Make a note of the overall level of the yield curve from about mid-1979 to mid-1982. Compare that with the level of the curve for most of the 1990s. What accounts for the differences in yield-curve levels in these two periods?

PROBLEMS

Valuation Fundamentals

P4-1. A best-selling author decides to cash in on her latest novel by selling the rights to the book's royalties for the next four years to an investor. Royalty payments arrive once per year, starting one year from now. In the first year, the author expects $400,000 in royalties, followed by $300,000, then $100,000, then $10,000 in the three subsequent years. If the investor purchasing the rights to royalties requires a return of 7 percent per year, what should the investor pay?

P4-2. An oil well produces 20,000 barrels of oil per year. Suppose the price of oil is $20 per barrel. You want to purchase the right to the oil produced by this well for the next five years. At a discount rate of 10 percent, what is the value of the oil rights? (You can assume that the cash flows from selling oil arrive at annual intervals.)

Bond Prices and Interest Rates

P4-3. A $1,000 par value bond makes two interest payments each year of $45 each. What is the bond's *coupon rate*?

P4-4. A $1,000 par value bond has a *coupon rate* of 8 percent and a *coupon yield* of 9 percent. What is the bond's market price?

P4-5. A bond sells for $900 and offers a *coupon yield* of 7.2 percent. What is the bond's annual coupon payment?

P4-6. A bond offers a *coupon rate* of 5 percent. If the par value is $1,000 and the bond sells for $1,250, what is the *coupon yield*?

P4-7. A bond makes two $45 interest payments each year. Given that the bond's par value is $1,000 and its price is $1,050, calculate the bond's *coupon rate* and *coupon yield*.

P4-8. Calculate the price of a five-year, $1,000 par value bond that makes semiannual payments, has a *coupon rate* of 8 percent, and offers a *yield to maturity* of 7 percent. Recalculate the price assuming a 9 percent YTM. What is the general relationship that this problem illustrates?

SMART SOLUTIONS

See the problem and solution explained step-by-step at SMARTFinance

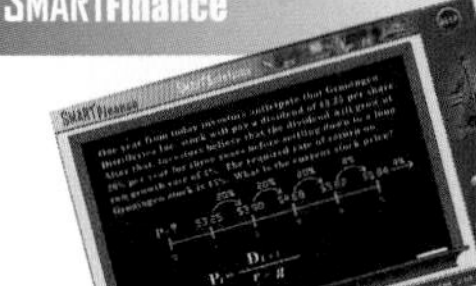

P4-9. A $1,000 par value bond makes annual interest payment of $75. If it offers a *yield to maturity* of 7.5 percent, what is the price of the bond?

P4-10. A $1,000 par value bond pays a *coupon rate* of 8.2 percent. The bond makes semiannual payments, and it matures in four years. If investors require a 10 percent return on this investment, what is the bond's price?

P4-11. Griswold Travel Inc. has issued six-year bonds that pay $30 in interest twice each year. The par value of these bonds is $1,000, and they offer a *yield to maturity* of 5.5 percent. How much are the bonds worth?

P4-12. Bennifer Jewelers recently issued ten-year bonds that make annual interest payments of $50. Suppose you purchased one of these bonds at par value when it was issued. Right away, market interest rates jumped, and the YTM on your bond rose to 6 percent. What happened to the price of your bond?

P4-13. You are evaluating two similar bonds. Both mature in four years, both have a $1,000 *par value*, and both pay a *coupon rate* of 10 percent. However, one bond pays that coupon in annual installments, whereas the other makes semiannual payments. Suppose you require a 10 percent return on either bond. Should these bonds sell at identical prices or should one be worth more than the other? Use Equations 4.2 and 4.3, and let $r = 10\%$. What prices do you obtain for these bonds? Can you explain the apparent paradox?

P4-14. A bond makes annual interest payments of $75. The bond matures in four years, has a *par value* of $1,000, and sells for $975.30. What is the bond's *yield to maturity (YTM)*?

P4-15. Johanson VI Advisors issued $1,000 par value bonds a few years ago with a coupon rate of 7 percent, paid semiannually. After the bonds were issued, interest rates fell. Now with three years remaining before they mature, the bonds sell for $1,055.08. What YTM do these bonds offer?

P4-16. A bond offers a 6 percent coupon rate and sells at par. What is the bond's *yield to maturity*?

Types of Bonds

P4-17. The *nominal interest rate* is 9 percent and the inflation rate is 7 percent. What is the *real interest rate*?

P4-18. The rate of inflation is 5 percent and the *real interest rate* is 3 percent. What is the *nominal interest rate*?

SMART SOLUTIONS

See the problem and solution explained step-by-step at SMARTFinance

P4-19. Suppose investors face a tax rate of 40 percent on interest paid by corporate bonds. Suppose AAA-rated corporate bonds currently offer yields of about 7 percent. Approximately what yield would AAA-rated municipal bonds need to offer to be competitive?

P4-20. Investors face a tax rate of 33 percent on interest paid by corporate bonds. If municipal bonds currently offer yields of 6 percent, what yield would equally risky corporate bonds need to offer to be competitive?

P4-21. You purchase a U.S. Treasury inflation-indexed bond at par value of $1,000. The bond offers a coupon rate of 6 percent paid semiannually. During the first six months that you hold the bond, prices in the United States rise by 2 percent. What is the new par value of the bond, and what is the amount of your first coupon payment?

P4-22. What is the price of a zero-coupon bond that has a par value of $1,000? The bond matures in thirty years and offers a *yield to maturity* of 4.5 percent. Calculate the price one year later, when the bond has twenty-nine years left before it matures (assume the yield remains at 4.5 percent). What is the return that an investor earns if they buy the bond with thirty years remaining and sell it one year later?

Bond Markets

P4-23. A Treasury bond's price is quoted as 98:11. What is the price of the bond if its par value is $1,000?

P4-24. A corporate bond's price is quoted as 102.312. If the bond's par value is $1,000, what is its market price?

Advanced Bond Valuation

P4-25. A one-year Treasury security offers a 4 percent *yield to maturity* (YTM). A two-year Treasury security offers a 4.25 percent YTM. According to the *expectations hypothesis*, what is the expected interest rate on a one-year security next year?

P4-26. A one-year Treasury bill offers a 6 percent *yield to maturity*. The market's consensus forecast is that one-year T-bills will offer 6.25 percent next year. What is the current yield on a 2-year T-bill if the *expectations hypothesis* holds?

THOMSON ONE Business School Edition

Access financial information from the Thomson ONE – Business School Edition Web site for the following problem(s). Go to http://tobsefin.swlearning.com/. If you have already registered your access serial number and have a username and password, click **Enter**. Otherwise, click **Register** and follow the instructions to create a username and password. Register your access serial number and then click **Enter** on the aforementioned Web site. When you click Enter, you will be prompted for your username and password (please remember that the password is case sensitive). Enter them in the respective boxes and then click **OK** (or hit **Enter**). From the ensuing page, click **Click Here to Access Thomson ONE – Business School Edition Now!** This opens up a new window that gives you access to the Thomson ONE – Business School Edition database. You can retrieve a company's financial information by entering its ticker symbol (provided for each company in the problem(s)) in the box below "Name/Symbol/Key." For further instructions on using the Thomson ONE – Business School Edition database, please refer to "A Guide for Using Thomson ONE – Business School Edition."

P4-27. Which of the following two companies will have a higher bond rating: Abbott Laboratories Inc (ticker: U:ABT) or Bristol Myers Squibb Company (U:BMY)? Bond rating agencies, such as Standard and Poor's, Moody's, and Fitch, investigate, among other things, a company's debt and profitability ratios (see Chapter 2 for these ratios) to rate its bonds. Examine these ratios for the two companies and explain which company's bonds are likely to have a higher rating and why.

Since these exercises depend upon real-time data, your answers will change continuously depending upon when you access the Internet to download your data.

MINICASE

Valuing Bonds

You open your *Wall Street Journal* (WSJ) on the morning of February 16, 2005, and see the following bond quote for General Mills, Incorporated. Based on this WSJ information, answer the following questions.

Company (ticker)	Coupon	Maturity	Last Price	Last Yield	Est Spread	UST	Est $ Vol (000's)
General Mills (GIS)	6.000	Feb. 15, 2012	109.305	???	60	10	45,040

ASSIGNMENT

1. What is the YTM for this General Mills Corporate Bond?
2. What is the coupon yield of this bond over the next year?
3. If your required rate of return for a bond of this risk-class is 4.7 percent, what value do you place on this General Mills, Inc. bond?
4. At this required rate of return of 4.7 percent are you interested in purchasing this bond?
5. If you purchased this General Mills, Inc. bond for 1,093.05 yesterday and the market rate of interest for this bond increased to 4.5 percent today, do you have a gain or loss? How much is that gain or loss in dollars?

Smart *Excel* Appendix

Appendix Contents

Use the Smart *Excel* spreadsheets and animated tutorials at http://smartfinance.swlearning.com.

EXCEL PREREQUISITES

You need to be familiar with the following *Excel* features to use this appendix:

- The use of cell references in a formula
- Relative cell references
- Absolute and mixed cell references

If this is new to you, be sure to complete the ***Excel Prereqs*** tab of the Chapter 4 *Excel* file before proceeding.

BASIC BOND VALUATION IN *EXCEL*

Annual Interest Payments

Open the Chapter 4 Excel file at the Smart Finance Web site.

Problem: Find the value of a $1,000 par value bond with a coupon rate of 9%, interest paid annually, and 10 years to maturity if the current yield to maturity is 8.25%.

To determine a bond's price you must design a model to forecast the bond's cash flows and calculate the present value of these cash flows. Remember the components of a basic model: inputs, calculations, and output. The output is the bond's price. The inputs are the assumptions regarding coupon rate, par value, time to maturity, and current yield to maturity. Use the inputs to calculate the bond's cash flows and determine the present value of the cash flows.

We will create models to solve the problem, using two different approaches: the present-value function built into *Excel* and the mathematical formula approach.

Recall from the Chapter 3 appendix the four steps in building a basic financial model.

Step 1: Determine the desired output and select an approach to calculate it (mathematical formula or *Excel* function).
Step 2: Set up an area for input assumptions (done for you in this *Excel* file).
Step 3: Build a formula to calculate output by **USING CELL REFERENCES**, not by typing in the actual numbers.
Step 4: Change the input assumptions, as desired, and analyze the effect on output.

Consider the five key variables here:

Present value	You are solving for the present value or bond price.
Future value	the bond's par value of $1,000
Payment	the annual interest payment
Rate	the current yield to maturity of 8.25%
Number of periods	10 years

Approach 1: Use the present-value function in *Excel*.

Valuing bonds using the present-value function in *Excel* is straightforward. The function has the following format:

=pv(rate,nper,pmt,fv,type)

Type allows for payment at the beginning (if type = 1) or at the end (if type = 0) of the year. If type is omitted, the default is year-end cash flows.

1. On the ***Bond basics*** tab of the Chapter 4 *Excel* file, fill in the input assumptions.
2. Under Calculations, create a formula for the coupon payment by multiplying the par value times the coupon rate.
3. Under Output, use the present-value function to find the bond price.

Solutions are provided in the file. The formula result is –$1,049.76.

The sign is negative because the bond's price represents cash outflow for an investor who buys the bond and receives the interest and principal payments over the next 10 years.

Apply it

Change the input assumptions and analyze the effect.

- *Suppose the yield to maturity is 9.5% instead of 8.25%.*
  As rates rise, bond values fall. At 9.5%, the bond value is $968.61.
- *Suppose the time to maturity is 25 years instead of 10 years (leave YTM at 8.25%).*
  The bond price is $1,078.38.

Approach 2: Use the mathematical formula.

Equation 4.2 in the chapter shows the formula for a bond's price as the present value of the future cash flows from interest payments and par value.

1. On the ***Bond basics*** tab of the Chapter 4 *Excel* file, fill in the input assumptions.

   Your input section should look like this:

   Inputs

Enter the inputs	
Par value	$1,000.00
Coupon rate	9%
# periods	10
Yield to maturity	8.25%

2. Next, begin the calculations section by inserting the years, beginning with Year 0. Simply type in the number; do not type the word, Year.
3. In the Year 1 column, create a formula for the annual coupon interest payment, using cell references. Remember to use absolute cell references, as needed (see the prerequisites tab if you are not familiar with absolute cell references). Copy this formula across for the life of the bond.

   The formula is =par value * coupon rate
   =$C$44*$C$45

4. In the final year, use a cell reference for the par value.
5. Create a formula using cell references to sum the cash flows in Year 1 and copy across for the life of the bond.
6. Create a formula to find the present value of each year's cash flows. Again, use absolute cell references, as needed.

   The formula in Year 1 is =total cash flow / (1 + YTM) ^ Year #
   =D53/(1+$C$47)^D50

   When complete, your calculations section should look like this:

Calculations

Year	0	1	2	3	4	5	6	7	8	9	10
Coupon payment		$90.00	$90.00	$90.00	$90.00	$90.00	$90.00	$90.00	$90.00	$90.00	$90.00
Principal payment											$1,000.00
Total cash flow		$90.00	$90.00	$90.00	$90.00	$90.00	$90.00	$90.00	$90.00	$90.00	$1.090.00
PV of cash flow		$83.14	$76.80	$70.95	$65.54	$60.55	$55.93	$51.67	$47.73	$44.10	$493.34

The last row shows the present value of each year's cash flows. The sum of these values is the bond price.

7. In the output section, create a formula to find the bond's price by summing the present values.

All solutions are provided in the Excel *file so you can check your result against the solution. The bond's price is $1,049.76.*

You should get the same result as in the first approach.

Now try changing the input assumptions as you did with Approach 1.

Data Tables and Graphs

In the Chapter 3 appendix, we illustrate how to create data tables and graphs. Applications to bond valuation are provided in the Chapter 4 file on the Data table and Graph tabs.

BOND VALUATION WITH SEMIANNUAL INTEREST PAYMENTS

Now consider a bond that pays interest semiannually. Again, solve the following problem using the two different approaches: the present-value function built into *Excel* and the mathematical formula.

Problem: Find the value of a $1,000 par value bond with an annual coupon rate of 7% and four years to maturity if the current yield to maturity is 7.75%. What if interest is paid semiannually instead of annually?

Approach 1: Use the present-value function in *Excel*.

Again, use the present-value function but adapt it to handle semiannual payments.

=pv(rate,nper,pmt,fv,type)

To use the present-value function with semiannual interest payments, adjust the rate, the number of periods, and the payment to semiannual numbers. We do this in the calculation section.

For bonds paying interest semiannually:

Rate:	The six-month rate is one half of the YTM.
Nper:	The number of six-month periods is two times the number of years.
Pmt:	The semiannual interest payment is one half the annual interest payment.
FV:	Par value is not affected.

This problem is set up on the ***Semibond*** tab of the Chapter 4 *Excel* file.

Formula result: $974.62

Approach 2: Use the mathematical formula.

1. On the ***Semibond*** tab of the Chapter 4 *Excel* file, fill in the input assumptions.
2. Next, insert the number of periods rather than years under calculations, beginning with Period 0. There will be eight periods on a 4-year bond with semiannual interest.
3. In the Year 1 column, create a formula for the semiannual coupon interest payment, using cell references. Remember to use absolute cell references, as needed (see the prerequisites tab if you are not familiar with absolute cell references). Copy this formula across for the life of the bond.
4. In the final period, use a cell reference for the par value.
5. Create a single formula to sum the cash flows in each period and copy across for the life of the bond.
6. Create a formula to find the present value of each period's cash flows. Again, use absolute cell references, as needed. The key difference here is to use the yield to maturity divided by 2 to discount.

   The formula to find present value in Year 1 in cell D55 is

   =total cash flow / (1 + YTM) ^ Year #
   =D54/(1+$C$48/2)^D51

   When complete, your calculations section should look like this:

Calculations

6-month period	0	1	2	3	4	5	6	7	8
Coupon payment		$35.00	$35.00	$35.00	$35.00	$35.00	$35.00	$35.00	$35.00
Principal payment									$1,000.00
Total cash flow		$35.00	$35.00	$35.00	$35.00	$35.00	$35.00	$35.00	$1,035.00
PV of cash flow		$36.69	$32.44	$31.23	$30.06	$28.94	$27.86	$26.82	$763.58

7. In the output section, create a formula to find the bond's price by summing the present values.

   Again, you should find that the bond's price is $974.62.

YIELD TO MATURITY

It is simple to find yield to maturity on a bond, using *Excel*'s rate function.

Problem: Find the yield to maturity of a 5-year $1,000 par value bond with a coupon rate of 9.5% and a current price of $1,145. Solve for both annual and semi-annual payments of interest. Does the yield differ with the timing of interest payments?

Approach 3: Use the rate function in *Excel*.

The rate function can be used to solve for the yield to maturity on a bond. The format of the function is

=rate(nper,pmt,pv,fv)

For the bond paying interest annually, the solution is straightforward. Remember, the present value must be entered as a negative number.

The yield to maturity is 6.05%.

For the bond paying interest semiannually, you must adapt to handle semiannual payments and periods. Again use the rate function, but nper is the number of six-month periods, and pmt is the semiannual interest payment.

The resulting yield to maturity will be a six-month rate, so it MUST BE DOUBLED to find the actual yield to maturity.

In the model, we handle this by using the following equation:

=rate(nper,pmt,pv,fv)*2

This problem is set up on the **YTM** of the Chapter 4 *Excel* file. **The formula result is 6.09%.**

SMART EXCEL

See this problem explained in Excel at SMARTFinance

Apply it

Why is the semiannual YTM higher than the annual YTM?

Intuitively, if two bonds have the same discount rate and pay the same cash flow, but one bond pays sooner than the other, then the bond paying sooner should have a higher price. But in this example, we created the problem with the assumption that both bonds had the same price—$1,145. The two bonds have the same cash flow, but because the semiannual bond pays sooner, it has a higher resulting yield.

Valuing Stocks

OPENING FOCUS

The Year of the Dividend

Call it the year of the dividend. In August 2003, Thomson Financial released a forecast predicting that the companies that made up the much-watched Standard & Poor's 500 Stock Index would increase their aggregate dividend payout by 8.2 percent, more than double the growth rate in aggregate S&P 500 dividends over the previous twelve years. Analysts offered many possible explanations for the dividend surge. In 2003, the U.S. economy continued its recovery from recession. Firms, seeing profitable times ahead, were willing to put more of their cash in investors' hands. In addition, the U.S. Congress passed a tax law that cut personal taxes on dividends. Finally, corporate scandals at Enron, Tyco, and WorldCom, coupled with steep declines in technology stocks during 2001–2002, prompted many investors to seek out more established companies with long histories of paying dividends.

Whatever the explanation, many firms touted their dividend achievements. The manufacturing concern Leggett & Platt (ticker symbol LEG) announced its thirty-third consecutive year of dividend increases. During that span, Leggett & Platt managed to increase dividends per share at a compound annual growth rate of roughly 15 percent. Diversified conglomerate General Electric (ticker symbol GE) increased its dividend for the twenty-eighth consecutive year, continuing a string of uninterrupted quarterly dividends that spanned more than a century.

The purpose of this chapter is to introduce you to simple models for valuing both common and preferred stock. The first section describes the contractual features of common and preferred stock. Understanding these features is the first step in valuing stock. The second section describes how firms work with investment bankers to issue new securities. Investment banking is one of the most exciting, demanding, and lucrative career opportunities in finance, so this part of the chapter may help you decide whether that career path appeals to you. The third section explains how investors trade securities in the secondary market, and it gives an overview of the major trading venues in the United States.

The technical part of valuing stocks begins in the fourth section. We continue the theme from Chapter 4: that the price of any financial asset equals the present value of future cash flow distributed to owners of that asset. In the case of both common and preferred stock, the most obvious source of cash flow is dividends. Therefore, this chapter offers a discussion of several models that calculate the price of a share of stock by estimating and discounting the dividends that the stock pays over a very long horizon. Before we delve into the technical aspects of valuing stocks, we begin with a description of the features that distinguish debt from equity, and preferred stock from common stock. Next, we discuss how firms, with the help of their investment bankers, sell new securities to the public and how investors trade those securities with each other. Following our discussion of valuation models that calculate stock prices based on discounted dividends, the final two sections examine alternative valuation models that do not focus exclusively on dividend payments.

LEARNING OBJECTIVES

After studying this chapter you should be able to:

- Describe the differences between preferred and common stock;
- Understand how investment bankers help firms issue equity securities in the primary market;
- List the major U.S. secondary markets in which investors trade stocks;
- Calculate the estimated value of preferred and common stock using zero, constant, and variable growth models;
- Value an entire company using the free cash flow approach; and
- List alternative approaches for pricing stocks that do not rely on discounted cash flow analysis.

This chapter focuses on valuing preferred and common stocks. We begin by describing the essential features of these instruments, comparing and contrasting them with the features of bonds that we covered in the previous chapter. Then, we explain how firms, with the assistance of investment bankers, issue these securities to investors and how trades between investors occur on an ongoing basis once the securities have been issued. Next, we apply the information from this chapter's first two sections to the basic discounted cash flow valuation framework from Chapter 4 to develop a method for pricing preferred and common stock. We introduce three simple approaches—the zero, constant, and variable growth models—for valuing stocks based on the dividend streams they pay over time. We also present the free cash flow approach for valuing the entire enterprise. Finally, we review some other popular stock valuation measures, including book value, liquidation value, and price/earnings multiples.

5.1 THE ESSENTIAL FEATURES OF PREFERRED AND COMMON STOCK

Debt Versus Equity

Periodically, firms issue new securities to investors to raise capital by selling either of two broad types of securities to investors: debt or equity. Debt securities, such as bonds, generally offer investors a legally enforceable claim with cash flows that are either fixed or vary according to a predetermined formula. Debt holders typically have little say in how a firm conducts its business. Instead, the investors who purchase a firm's debt securities can force the firm into bankruptcy court if it does not make scheduled interest and principal payments on time.

Equity securities, such as common stock, are quite different. Firms issuing common stock make no specific promises to investors about how much cash they will receive or when. Loosely speaking, a firm distributes cash to common stockholders if it is generating enough cash from its operations to pay expenses and to undertake new profitable investment opportunities. In other words, whether investors in common stock receive any cash at all depends on how well the firm performs. Lacking a solid commitment from the firm to distribute cash, holders of common stock cannot push a firm into bankruptcy simply because they are unhappy with the outcome of their investment. However, unlike bondholders, common stockholders collectively own the company. Their shares entitle them to vote on important matters ranging from electing a board of directors that monitors senior management to restructuring the firm through mergers and acquisitions. When equity investors become dissatisfied with the returns they have earned on their shares, they may exercise their voting rights to oust incumbent management, or they may seek to influence how executives manage the firm in other ways.

The preceding two paragraphs should give you a sense that debt and equity are associated with very different marginal benefits and costs for investors. They differ in terms of both the risks they require investors to take and the potential rewards for taking those risks. Comparatively, debt securities offer investors a relatively safe and predictable return. But safety comes at a price. Bond returns are rarely high enough to generate a lot of wealth quickly, and bondholders exercise almost no direct influence on corporate decisions. Common stockholders accept more risk than bondholders do. For example, an investor who purchased $10,000 worth of Microsoft stock when it debuted in 1986 has seen that investment grow to more than $2.6 million by June 2004. At the other end of the spectrum, someone who spent $10,000 on just about any of the notorious "dot-com" Internet stocks issued in the late 1990s has almost nothing left from that investment today.[1] Because common stockholders are asked to take large risks, they have the opportunity to exercise some control over corporate decisions through their voting rights, and they tend to earn higher returns (at least on average) than bond investors do.

Whereas the last chapter focused on debt, in this chapter we turn our attention to equity. As a starting point, we look at a security that is a bit of a hybrid, having some resemblance to bonds and some to common stock. That security is preferred stock.

Preferred Stock

dividend
A periodic cash payment that firms make to investors who hold the firms' preferred or common stock.

Some features of preferred stock resemble the features of debt. When a firm issues preferred stock, it promises investors a fixed periodic cash payment, called a **dividend**, much like the semiannual interest payments made to bondholders. Firms usually pay preferred dividends on a quarterly basis. Like bondholders, preferred stockholders do not have the right to vote on important corporate decisions, so they exercise almost no direct control over management. Preferred stock is a claim that, in many respects, is *senior to common stock,* meaning that preferred stockholders have a higher priority claim on a firm's cash flows. For instance, most companies that issue preferred

1. Of course, there are notable exceptions such as eBay. However, the vast majority of Internet stocks proved to be disastrous investments. The case of the company called TheGlobe.com is illustrative. Originally offered to investors in mid-1998 at $9 per share, TheGlobe.com's stock quickly rose to $97, but the gains were short-lived. Three years later the company folded, and the final stock price recorded for the firm was just $0.08 per share.

stock are required to pay the promised dividend on preferred shares before they can pay a dividend on their common stock. Similarly, most preferred stock has a feature known as *cumulative dividends*, meaning that if a firm misses any preferred dividend payments, it must catch up and pay preferred shareholders for all the dividends they missed (along with the current dividend) before it can pay dividends on common stock. In all these instances, preferred stock seems more like debt than equity.

In other respects, preferred stock looks more like equity than debt. From a tax perspective, preferred dividends are treated like common stock dividends; neither can be treated as a tax-deductible expense for the firm. Interest payments on debt are tax deductible. Though preferred stock is *senior to common stock* in many ways, preferred shareholders hold a claim that is *junior to bonds,* meaning that preferred shareholders hold a lower priority claim than bondholders do. In particular, preferred shareholders cannot take a firm to court for failure to pay dividends as bondholders can do if a firm misses interest or principal payments. Finally, most preferred shares do not have a specific maturity date and can remain outstanding indefinitely, similar to common stock.

Although some industrial firms issue preferred stock, it is most often issued by public utilities. Historically, public utilities in the United States have been highly regulated, with state agencies exercising some control over the rates that utilities can charge for their services. Though preferred dividends are not tax deductible, utilities can argue with regulators for higher rates by treating preferred dividends as a cost of doing business. Because preferred stock falls under the equity section of the balance sheet, issuing preferred stock increases equity and can also enhance a firm's credit rating and its capacity to issue additional debt.

Other corporations frequently issue preferred stock as part of a merger or acquisition. In these transactions in which one company buys another, special tax advantages arise that create an incentive for firms to issue preferred stock. Another tax incentive favoring preferred stock occurs when one corporation owns the preferred stock of another company, the firm receiving preferred dividends can exclude a large fraction of those dividends from taxable income. As a result, corporations, rather than individuals, own much of the preferred stock that is issued in the United States.

Common Stock

Common Stockholders as Residual Claimants. Because common stockholders own the firm, they generally retain all the important decision rights concerning what the firm does and how it is governed. However, shareholders cannot receive cash distributions from the company unless the firm first pays what it owes to its creditors and preferred shareholders. Because shareholders hold the right to receive only the cash flow that remains after all other claims against the firm have been satisfied, they are sometimes called **residual claimants**. Obviously, holding the most junior claim on a firm's assets and cash flows is very risky. For this reason, common stockholders generally expect to earn a higher, though more variable, return on their investment than do bondholders or preferred shareholders.

residual claimants
Investors who have the right to receive cash flows only after all other claimants have been satisfied. Common stockholders are typically the residual claimants of corporations.

Stockholder Voting Rights. As residual claimants, stockholders receive several important rights. The most important is the right to vote at any shareholders' meeting.[2] Most U.S. corporations have a single class of common

[2] U.S. public corporations must hold a general shareholders' meeting at least once per year. Additionally, special shareholders' meetings may be held to allow stockholders to vote on especially important questions, such as approving corporate mergers, divestitures, or major asset sales.

majority voting system System that allows each shareholder to cast one vote per share for each open position on the board of directors.

stock outstanding, and every shareholder has the same rights and responsibilities. Most U.S. corporations also have a **majority voting system**, which allows each shareholder to cast one vote per share for each open position on the board of directors. It stands to reason that the owners (or owner) of 50.1 percent of the firm's stock can decide every contested issue and can elect the people they want to become directors. In practice, an investor or group of investors can control a corporation even if they own less than a majority of the oustanding stock. All the controlling group needs is a *majority of the votes cast* on a ballot issue, and in most corporate elections, many shareholders do not vote at all.

U.S. companies occasionally have two or more outstanding classes of stock, usually with different voting rights for each class. In these cases, corporate insiders generally concentrate their holdings in the superior voting-share class. Ordinary investors hold relatively more of the inferior voting-share class. This *dual-class* common stock structure is much more common in many other countries than it is in the United States, at least partly because both the New York Stock Exchange (NYSE) and the Securities and Exchange Commission (SEC) have at times discouraged American companies from adopting such structures.[3] The Internet search engine company Google is the most prominent recent example of a U.S. firm choosing the dual-class structure. In its initial public offering, Google sold common stock to outside investors who had one vote per share. Certain Google insiders received a special class of stock entitled to ten votes per share. A dual-class structure allows insiders to raise the capital they need to finance growth, without losing voting control.

proxy statements A document mailed to shareholders that describes the matters to be decided by a shareholder vote in an upcoming annual meeting. Shareholders can sign their proxy statements and grant their voting rights to other parties.

proxy fight A ploy used by outsiders to attempt to gain control of a firm by soliciting a sufficient number of votes to unseat existing directors.

Proxies and Proxy Contests. Because most investors who own a few shares do not attend annual meetings to vote, they may sign **proxy statements** giving their votes to another party. The firm's current managers generally receive most of the stockholders' proxies, partly because managers can solicit them at company expense. Occasionally, when the ownership of the firm is widely dispersed, outsiders may try to gain control by waging a **proxy fight**, an attempt to solicit a sufficient number of votes to unseat existing directors.

A significant fraction of stockholders routinely fail to exercise their right to vote. In some cases, brokers and banks that hold shares in "street name" are allowed to vote on behalf of their clients, and they almost always side with management. Recent studies have found that when managers submit proposals for shareholder votes and believe the votes will be close, they craft the proposal in a way that maximizes the votes cast by brokers and banks. Therefore, managers have a limited ability to manipulate the proxy process to obtain outcomes favorable to their own interests.

Rights to Dividends and Other Distributions. A firm's board of directors decides whether to pay dividends or not. Most U.S. corporations that pay dividends pay them quarterly, whereas the common practice in other developed countries is to pay dividends semiannually or annually. Firms usually pay dividends in cash, but they may also make dividend payments using stock or (on rare occasions) merchandise. Common stockholders have no guarantee that the firm will pay dividends, but shareholders nevertheless come to expect certain payments based on the historical dividend pattern of the firm. The dividend decision and its effect

3. For most of its modern history, the New York Stock Exchange automatically delisted any firm that adopted a dual-class common stock structure and also refused to list any company with such a structure. The exchange was forced to back off this policy, in 1986, when General Motors adopted a two-class structure as part of its acquisitions of Hughes and EDS. Two years later, however, the SEC issued a ruling prohibiting publicly traded companies from adopting dual-class structures, though the ruling did allow firms going public with such structures to retain them.

on firm valuation have perplexed researchers for decades, and we examine it in detail in Chapter 13.

Just as shareholders have no guarantee that they will receive dividends, they have no assurance they will receive any cash settlement in the event that the firm is liquidated. Because of limited liability, however, shareholders cannot lose more than they invest in the firm. Moreover, common stockholders can receive unlimited returns through dividends and through the appreciation in the value of their holdings. In other words, although nothing is guaranteed, the *possible* rewards for providing equity capital can be considerable.

The Equity Section of the Balance Sheet. Table 5.1 details the stockholders' equity accounts of Halogen Actuated Lighting (HAL). As of December 31, 2006, HAL had only common stock outstanding. During 2006, the company paid off the $247 million of preferred stock that it had outstanding at the end of 2005 and did not issue any new preferred stock in replacement. Several terms that appear in the stock accounts require an explanation, beginning with "par value." As discussed in Chapter 2, common stock can be sold with or without **par value**, which, in the United States, is a rather archaic term having little real economic significance. Because many states prohibit firms from selling shares at a price below par value, there is a clear incentive to set this value low. For this reason, HAL follows a standard convention of setting par value quite low, at $0.20 per share, so that such laws are unlikely ever to prove a binding constraint.[4]

par value (stock)
An arbitrary value assigned to common stock on a firm's balance sheet.

shares authorized
The shares of a company's stock that shareholders and the board authorize the firm to sell to the public.

shares issued
The shares of a company's stock that have been issued or sold to the public.

At the end of 2006, HAL had 4,687,500,000 **shares authorized**, meaning that the firm's stockholders had given HAL's board of directors the right to sell up to this number of shares without further stockholder approval.[5] At that time, there were 1,913,513,218 **shares issued** and outstanding (compared with 1,893,940,595 at year-end 2005), with a total par value of $382,702,644 ($0.20/share × 1,913,513,218 shares). The total book value of common stock equals $14,248 million, so we

Table 5.1
Stockholders' Equity Accounts for HAL, December 31, 2006, and 2003 ($ millions)

	2006	2005
Preferred stock, par value $0.01 per share	—	$ 247
Shares authorized: 150,000,000		
Shares issued: (2005) 2,546,011		
Common stock, par value $0.20 per share	$14,248	12,400
Shares authorized: 4,687,500,000		
Shares issued: (2006: 1,913,513,218; 2005: 1,893,940,595)		
Retained earnings	30,142	23,784
Less: Treasury stock, at cost	20,114	13,800
Shares: (2006: 190,319,489; 2005: 131,041,411)		
Less: Employee benefits trust, at cost (shares, 2005: 20,000,000)	—	1,712
Less: Accumulated gains and losses not affecting retained earnings	662	295
Total stockholders' equity	$23,614	$20,624

[4] Outside the United States, par values are often higher because it is common practice for firms to quote dividend payments and other cash distributions as a percentage of par value.

[5] Though we changed the names and dates for this example, the numbers for HAL are real. Following Stanley Kubrick's example in *2001: Space Odyssey*, the data for our mythical company HAL actually came from recent financial reports for International Business Machines Corporation (IBM).

additional paid-in capital The difference between the price the company received when it sold stock in the primary market and the par value of the stock, multiplied by the number of shares sold. This represents the amount of money the firm received from selling stock, above and beyond the stock's par value.

market capitalization The value of the shares of a company's stock that are owned by the stockholders: the total number of shares issued multiplied by the current price per share.

calculate the amount of **additional paid-in capital**, or capital in excess of par value, that HAL received for these shares as $13,865 million ($7.25 per share). This equals the difference between the $14,248 million book value and the $383 million par value. Since HAL's stock price was $126.39 per share at the end of December 2006, we determine that HAL's **market capitalization** on that date was $241.86 billion ($126.39/share × 1,914,000,000 shares outstanding).

In addition to the shares outstanding at the end of 2006, HAL has been aggressively repurchasing its shares in the open market for several years. The company repurchased 59.3 million shares worth $6.3 billion in 2006. The stock repurchased during 2006 was held as **treasury stock**, with a book value of $20,114 million on December 31, 2006. HAL holds these shares as part of its employee stock-purchase plan.

Finally, HAL's accounts show that the firm has retained earnings of $30,142 million at year-end 2006. This represents the cumulative amount of profits that the firm has reinvested over the years. Don't be fooled by the $30.1 billion balance of this account. Retained earnings do not represent a pool of cash that the firm can use should a need for cash arise. Retained earnings simply reflect earnings that HAL reinvested in previous years.

CONCEPT REVIEW QUESTIONS

1. Why are common stockholders viewed as "residual owners"? What rights do they get in exchange for taking more risk than creditors and preferred shareholders take?

2. Most large Japanese corporations hold their annual shareholders' meeting on the same day and require voting in person. Therefore, it is impossible for a shareholder who owns stock in more than one company to go to more than one annual meeting. What does this practice say about the importance and clout of individual shareholders in Japanese corporate governance?

5.2 PRIMARY MARKETS AND ISSUING NEW SECURITIES

treasury stock Common shares that have been issued but are no longer outstanding because the firm repurchased them.

investment banks Financial institutions that assist firms in the process of issuing securities to investors. Investment banks also advise firms engaged in mergers and acquisitions, and they are active in the business of selling and trading securities in secondary markets.

Before we turn to a discussion about how investors trade and price preferred and common stocks, we offer a brief overview of how firms issue equity securities to investors. As previously noted, the *primary market* refers to the market in which firms originally issue new securities. Once the securities have been issued in the primary market, investors can trade them in the *secondary market*. In this section, we examine the primary market and how investment bankers help firms sell new securities. Section 5.3 looks at the secondary market.

Investment banks (IBs) play an important role in helping firms raise long-term debt and equity financing in the world's capital markets. **Investment banks** sell new security issues and assist and advise corporations about major financial transactions, such as mergers and acquisitions, in exchange for fees and commissions. During the past twenty years, and especially since 1990, the global investment banking industry has grown dramatically in scale and in the variety of services it provides to corporations. Furthermore, with the recent repeal of the United States *Glass-Steagall Act*, commercial banks formerly excluded from providing investment banking services can now enter that business. Investment banks headquartered in the United States dominate the top ranks of global IB firms.[6] J. P. Morgan Chase, Morgan Stanley, Goldman Sachs, Citigroup, and Merrill Lynch are the five U.S. banks having the highest market share. Here we briefly review the key services provided by investment banks before, during, and after security offerings.

Key Investment Banking Activities

Investment banks provide a broad range of services to corporations. Table 5.2 breaks out the key sources of revenue for the eight largest U.S.-based investment banks in 2000. The three principal lines of business are

- *corporate finance,*
- *trading,* and
- *asset management.*

Of the three business lines, corporate finance enjoys the highest visibility and includes activities such as new security issues and merger and acquisitions (M&A) advisory work. Corporate finance tends to be the most profitable line of business, especially for more prestigious banks such as Goldman Sachs and Morgan Stanley, which can charge the highest underwriting and advisory fees. However, corporate finance generates less than one fourth of the typical IB's revenues and less than 20 percent for three of the eight banks.

Investment banks earn revenue from trading debt-and-equity securities in two important ways. First, they act as dealers, facilitating trade between unrelated parties and earning fees in return. Second, they hold inventories of securities and may make or lose money as inventory values fluctuate. Table 5.2 reveals that revenues generated from trading activities, on average, account for one quarter of large banks' revenues. Finally, asset management encompasses several different activities, including managing money for individuals with high net worth, operating and advising mutual funds, and managing pension funds. As the table shows, revenues from asset management exceed those from the other primary investment banking services.

SMART PRACTICES VIDEO

David Baum, Co-head of M&A for Goldman Sachs in the Americas

"You sit right at the crossroads of industry and capital markets."

See the entire interview at **SMARTFinance**

The Investment Banker's Role in Equity Issues

We now turn to the services which investment banks provide to companies issuing new securities. The focus is on U.S. practices, although security issues around the world increasingly conform to U.S. standards. As usual, we focus on common stock issues, though the procedures for selling bonds and preferred stocks are substantially similar. Investment banks play several different roles throughout the securities-offering process. For stock offerings, the complexity of the investment banker's job depends on (1) whether a firm is selling equity for the first time, and in the process, converting from private to public ownership, or (2) whether the firm has previously issued stock and is simply going back to the equity market to raise money. The first type of transaction is much more complex and is called an **initial public offering (IPO)**. The second type is known as a **seasoned equity offering (SEO)**, implying that the stock offered for sale has previously been "seasoned" in the market. Below, we describe the investment banker's role in an IPO, though the description would change little for an SEO.

initial public offering (IPO) A corporation offers its shares for sale to the public for the first time; the first public sale of company stock to outside investors.

seasoned equity offering (SEO) An equity issue by a firm that already has common stock outstanding.

---

6. The U.S. preeminence is at least partly a result of the U.S. investment banking industry being deregulated much earlier than Europe's. In particular, the SEC forced U.S. investment banks to end fixed stock trading commissions in May 1975, which prompted both a competitive free-for-all and rapid growth in share trading volume and securities issuance. In contrast, British capital markets were not significantly deregulated until the "Big Bang" reforms were implemented in 1986. Continental European (and Japanese) markets were opened fully only during the 1990s.

Table 5.2
Composition of Investment Banking Revenues of Leading U.S.-Based Investment Banks (IB) in 2000 (% of Revenues)

Source: Roy C. Smith, "Strategic Directions in Investment Banking—A Retrospective Analysis," Journal of Applied Corporate Finance *14 (Spring 2001), pp. 111–123, table 4.*
Note: All numbers are expressed as a % of that firm's net revenues.

	Corporate Finance			Trading				Asset Management			Total IB
Firm	Under-writing	M&A	Total	Fixed Income	Equities	Principal Investing	Total	Fees	Commis-sions & Other	Total	Revenues ($ in millions)
J. P. Morgan Chase	13.8%	7.4%	21.2%	22.0%	8.6%	3.4%	34.0%	44.8%	—	44.8%	$20,597
Morgan Stanley	11.6	9.1	20.7	11.4	20.0	0.8	20.8	31.6	15.5	47.1	23,561
Goldman Sachs	16.8	15.6	32.4	18.1	21.0	0.8	21.8	5.7	22.0	27.7	16,590
Citigroup	16.9	—	16.9	14.9	7.2	18.7	25.9	18.7	23.5	42.2	24,161
Merrill Lynch	10.0	5.2	15.2	8.7	13.6	11.8	25.4	21.2	29.6	50.8	26,787
Bank of America	20.7	5.1	25.8	28.3	20.6	—	20.6	18.2	7.2	25.4	5,853
Lehman Brothers	18.5	10.0	28.8	21.2	27.0	—	27.0	—	23.0	23.0	7,707
Bear Stearns	7.4	11.0	18.7	16.1	14.5	10.5	25.0	—	40.2	40.2	5,476
Average			22.5%				25.1%			37.7%	

Although it is possible for firms to issue securities without the assistance of investment bankers, in practice, almost all firms enlist IBs when they issue equity. Broadly speaking, firms can choose an investment banker in one of two ways. The most common approach is a **negotiated offer**, where, as the name implies, the issuing firm negotiates the terms of the offer directly with one investment bank. In the other approach, a **competitively bid offer**, the firm announces the terms of its intended equity sale, and investment banks bid for the business. The vast majority of equity sales are negotiated offerings rather than competitive offers. Firms issuing securities often enlist the services of more than one investment bank. In these cases, it is typical for one of the banks to be named the **lead underwriter**, and the other participating banks are known as *comanagers*.

Investment bankers sell equity under two types of contracts. In a **best efforts** arrangement, the investment bank makes no guarantee about the ultimate success of the offering. Instead, it promises to give its best effort to sell the firm's securities at the agreed-upon price, but if insufficient demand emerges for the issue, the firm withdraws the issue from the market. Best efforts offerings are most common for very small, high-risk companies. The investment bank receives a commission based on the number of shares sold in a best efforts deal.

By contrast, in a **firm-commitment** offering, the investment bank agrees to **underwrite** the issue, meaning that the bank actually purchases the shares from the firm and resells them to investors. In theory, this arrangement requires the investment bank to bear the risk of inadequate demand for the firm's shares. Bankers mitigate this risk in two ways. First, the lead underwriter forms an **underwriting syndicate** consisting of many investment banks. These banks collectively purchase the firm's shares and market them, thereby spreading the risk exposure across the syndicate. Second, underwriters go to great lengths to determine whether sufficient demand for a new issue exists before it comes to market. They generally set the issue's *offer price* and take possession of the securities no more than a day or two before the issue date. With such research efforts before sale, the risk that the investment bank might not be able to sell the shares that it underwrites is small.

In firm-commitment offerings, investment banks receive compensation for their services via the **underwriting spread**, the difference between the price at which the banks purchase shares from firms (the *net price*) and the price at which they sell the shares to institutional and individual investors (the *offer price*). In some offerings, the underwriters receive additional compensation in the form of warrants that grant underwriters the right to buy shares of the issuing company at a fixed price. Underwriting fees can be quite substantial, especially for firms issuing equity for the first time. The vast majority of U.S. initial public offerings have underwriting spreads of exactly 7 percent, although lower spreads are common in very large IPOs. For example, if a firm conducting an IPO wants to sell shares worth $100 million, it will receive $93 million in proceeds from the offer. The underwriter earns the gross spread of $7 million. At the other extreme, large debt offerings of well-known issuers have underwriting spreads in the 0.5 percent range.

Just what do investment banks do to earn their fees? Investment banks perform a wide variety of services, ranging from carrying out the analytical work required to price a new security offering, to assisting the firm with regulatory compliance, marketing the new issues, and developing an orderly market for the firm's securities once they begin trading. The chronology of a typical equity offering provides a useful framework for describing these services.

negotiated offer
The issuing firm negotiates the terms of the offer directly with one investment bank.

competitively bid offer
The firm announces the terms of its intended equity sale, and investment banks bid for the business.

lead underwriter
The investment bank that takes the primary role in assisting a firm in a public offering of securities.

best efforts
The investment bank promises to give its best effort to sell the firm's securities at the agreed-upon price; but if there is insufficient demand for the issue, then the firm withdraws the issue from the market.

firm-commitment
An offering in which the investment bank underwrites the firm's securities and thereby guarantees that the firm will successfully complete its sale of securities.

underwrite
The investment banker purchases shares from a firm and resells them to investors.

underwriting syndicate
Consists of many investment banks that collectively purchase the firm's shares and market them, thereby spreading the risk exposure across the syndicate.

underwriting spread
The difference between the net price and the offer price.

Services Provided Before the Offering. Early in the process of preparing for an equity offering, an investment bank helps the firm file the necessary documents with regulators, starting with the *registration statement,* which provides a wealth of information about the securities being offered, as well as the firm selling them. Preparing this document may sound like a rather trivial undertaking, but, in fact, it is one of the most time-consuming parts of the capital-raising process, especially for IPOs. When a firm files documents with the Securities and Exchange Commission, it must take great pains to be sure that the information provided is timely and accurate. Firms can spend weeks with their bankers putting this document together. The investment bankers also prepare a **prospectus**, a document containing extensive details about the firm and the security it intends to offer. The investment bank circulates the prospectus among potential investors as a starting point for marketing the new issue. The cover of the prospectus for the May 2004 IPO of Internet diamond seller, Blue Nile, appears as Figure 5.1.

prospectus
A document that describes the securities being offered for sale and the company offering them.

SMART PRACTICES VIDEO

Jay Goodgold, Managing Director, Equities Division, Goldman Sachs

"The goal here on the road show is to see the major institutional clients in Boston, New York, Chicago, Denver, Los Angeles, San Franciso, London, Paris, Frankfurt, and Tokyo."

See the entire interview at **SMARTFinance**

While it is preparing the necessary legal documents, the investment bank must also begin to estimate the value of the securities the firm intends to sell. Generally speaking, this task is simpler for debt than for equity, and of course, it is easier to value the equity of a company that already has shares trading on the market than to value the shares in an IPO. Investment banks use a variety of methods to value IPO shares, including discounted cash flow models and market "comparables," both of which are described later in this chapter. In the latter case, an investment bank compares the firm issuing equity with similar publicly traded firms, often estimating the value of the new stock issue by applying a price/earnings multiple to the issuing firm's current or projected per-share earnings or cash flow.

Several weeks before the scheduled offering, the firm and its bankers take a whirlwind tour of major U.S. and international cities to solicit demand for the offering from investors. Affectionately called the **road show**, this grueling process usually lasts a week or two. It gives managers the opportunity to pitch their business plan to prospective investors. The investment banker's goal in this process is to build a book of orders for stock that is greater (often many times greater) than the amount of stock the firm intends to sell. The expressions of interest by investors during the road show are not legally binding purchase agreements. The investment bank typically does not commit to an offer price at this point. Instead, bankers give investors a range of prices at which they expect to sell the offer, based on their assessment of demand. Given the tentative nature of the demand expressed on the road show, the banker seeks to **oversubscribe** the offering to minimize the bank's underwriting risk. Naturally, one way to create excess demand for an offering is to set the offer price below the market-clearing level. The vast majority of IPOs in the United States and other countries are underpriced, meaning that once IPO shares begin trading, they do so at a price that is above the original offer price set by the firm and its bankers.

road show
A tour of major cities taken by a firm and its bankers several weeks before a scheduled offering.

oversubscribe
When the investment banker builds a book of orders for stock that is greater than the amount of stock the firm intends to sell.

Services Provided During and After the Offering. The lead underwriter conducts the security offering, ensuring that on the issue date, participating investors receive their shares, as well as copies of the final prospectus.

PROSPECTUS

3,740,000 Shares

Common Stock

This is Blue Nile, Inc.'s initial public offering. We are selling 2,000,000 shares and the selling stockholders are selling 1,740,000 shares. We will not receive any proceeds from the sale of shares by the selling stockholders.

The initial public offering price of our common stock is $20.50 per share. Prior to the offering, there has been no public market for the shares. Our common stock has been approved for quotation on the Nasdaq National Market under the symbol "NILE."

Investing in our common stock involves risks that are described in the "Risk Factors" section beginning on page 5 of this prospectus.

	Per Share	Total
Public offering price	$20.50	$76,670,000
Underwriting discount	$1.435	$5,366,900
Proceeds, before expenses, to Blue Nile, Inc.	$19.065	$38,130,000
Proceeds, before expenses, to the selling stockholders	$19.065	$33,173,100

The underwriters may also purchase up to an additional 300,910 shares from us, and up to an additional 260,090 shares from the selling stockholders, at the public offering price, less the underwriting discount, within 30 days from the date of this prospectus to cover overallotments.

Neither the Securities and Exchange Commission nor any state securities commission has approved or disapproved of these securities or determined if this prospectus is truthful or complete. Any representation to the contrary is a criminal offense.

The shares will be ready for delivery on or about May 25, 2004.

Merrill Lynch & Co. **Bear, Stearns & Co. Inc.**

Thomas Weisel Partners LLC

The date of this prospectus is May 19, 2004.

Figure 5.1
Prospectus for Blue Nile, Inc.'s Initial Public Offering

The Blue Nile IPO prospectus provides investors with information that they need to determine whether they want to buy shares in the offering. On the front page, shown here, you can see that Blue Nile plans to sell 3.74 million shares for $20.50 each, and the shares will trade on Nasdaq.

Source: Prospectus cover for Blue Nile. Reprinted with permission.

The lead underwriter exercises some discretion over the distribution of shares among syndicate members and the **selling group**, investment banks that may assist in selling shares but are not formal members of the syndicate. In oversubscribed offerings, the lead underwriter may exercise a **Green Shoe option** (or *overallotment option*), essentially an option to sell as much as 15 percent more shares than originally planned.

selling group
Consists of investment banks that may assist in selling shares but are not formal members of the underwriting syndicate.

Green Shoe option
An option to sell more shares than originally planned.

Table 5.3
Key Steps in the Initial Public Offering Process

Source: Katrina Ellis, Roni Michaely, and Maureen O'Hara, "When the Underwriter is the Market Maker: An Examination of Trading in the IPO Aftermarket," Journal of Finance *55 (June 2000), pp. 1039–1074.*

Major Steps and Main Events	Role of the Underwriter
1. Initial step	
Select book-running manager and co-manager	Book-running manager's role includes forming the syndicate and overseeing the entire process.
Letter of intent	Letter specifies gross spread and Green Shoe (overallotment) option, and protects underwriter from unexpected expenses. Doesn't guarantee price or number of shares to be issued.
2. Registration process	
Registration statement and due diligence	After conducting due diligence, underwriter files necessary registration statement with SEC.
Red herring	Once registration statement is filed with SEC, it is transformed into a preliminary prospectus (red herring).
3. Marketing	
Distribute prospectus; road show	Red herring is sent to salespeople and institutional investors around the country. Concurrently, company and underwriter conduct a road show, and the IB builds a book based on expressed demand—but not legally binding.
4. Pricing and allocation	
Pricing; allocation	Once registration statement has SEC approval, underwriter asks the SEC to accelerate the date on which the issue becomes effective. Firm and underwriter meet the day before the offer to determine price, number of shares, and allocation of shares.
5. Aftermarket activities	
Stabilization; overallotment option	Underwriter supports the stock price by purchasing shares if price declines. If stock price goes up, underwriter uses overallotment option to cover short position. If price goes down, underwriter covers over-allotment by buying stock in open market.
Research coverage	Final stage of IPO process begins 25 calendar days after IPO, when the "quiet period" ends. Only after this can underwriter and other syndicate members comment on the value of the firm and provide earnings estimates.

price stabilization
Purchase of shares by an investment bank when a new issue begins to falter in the market, keeping the market price at or slightly above the offer price.

Once a firm's securities begin trading, the underwriter may engage in **price stabilization**. The reputation of an underwriter suffers if investors buy shares in an offering only to find that, once trading begins, the share price falls below the offer price. Because investment banks repeatedly approach investors with new share issues, it is very costly for them if investors lose confidence in the banks' ability to price new issues. Therefore, if a new issue begins to falter in the market, the investment bank may buy shares on its own account, keeping the market price at or slightly above the offer price for an indefinite period. With limited capital, investment banks do not want to take large positions in the shares they underwrite, so the threat of having to stabilize the market gives underwriters an additional incentive to underprice new issues at the outset.

After a share offering is successfully sold, the lead underwriter often serves as the principal *market maker* for trading in the firm's stock. A market maker maintains an inventory of the firm's stock and continuously quotes bid and ask prices at which it is willing to buy or sell to investors. In this role, the lead underwriter purchases shares from investors wishing to sell, and sells shares to investors wishing to buy, thus "making a market" in the new issue. The lead underwriter also assigns one or more research analysts to cover the issuing firm. The research reports these analysts write (which naturally tend to be flattering) help generate additional interest in trading the firm's securities. In fact, some firms choose their investment bankers largely based on the reputation of the analyst who will cover the stock once it goes public. Table 5.3 summarizes the chronology of an investment bank's activities through the IPO process.

SMART ETHICS VIDEO

Kent Womack, Dartmouth College,
"It's very easy for analysts to have conflict of interest problems."

See the entire interview at **SMARTFinance**

To conclude this section, we want to highlight the conflicts that investment bankers may face. Firms issuing securities, on the one hand, want to obtain the highest possible price for their shares (or bonds). Firms also want favorable coverage from securities analysts employed by their investment bankers. Investors, on the other hand, want to purchase securities at prices low enough to ensure that they will earn a high return on their investments. Investors also value dispassionate, unbiased advice from analysts. Investment bankers must therefore walk a thin line, both ethically and economically, to please their constituents. Firms issuing securities are wise to remember this. Investment bankers deal with investors, especially large institutional investors, on a repeated basis. They must approach this group each time a new offering comes to the market. In contrast, over its entire life, a firm conducts just a single IPO.[7]

SMART ETHICS VIDEO

Jay Ritter, University of Florida,
"Lots of buyers were willing to give things to the underwriters in terms of, for instance, generating extra commissions business."

See the entire interview at **SMARTFinance**

CONCEPT REVIEW QUESTIONS

3. What is the difference between a *primary market* and a *secondary market*?

4. What do firms and their investment bankers hope to learn on the road show?

5. How are underwriters compensated?

[7] A chief executive officer of a company that conducted an IPO during the 1990s told us, "You have two friends in an IPO: your lawyer and your accountant." Notice that the investment banker didn't make the list.

5.3 SECONDARY MARKETS FOR EQUITY SECURITIES

brokers
Agents who facilitate secondary-market trading by bringing buyers and sellers together.

dealers
Also called market makers, dealers faciliate secondary-market trading by standing ready to buy and sell securities with other investors.

The secondary market permits investors to execute transactions among themselves—it's the marketplace where investors can easily sell their holdings to others. Helping investors facilitate these trades are **brokers** and **dealers.** Brokers help bring buyers and sellers together. Dealers maintain an inventory of stock and stand ready to buy and sell shares with investors at any time. Dealers are also called *market makers* because of the important role they play in bringing about a smoothly functioning secondary market. Included among the secondary markets are the various *securities exchanges,* in which orders from buyers and sellers come together in one physical location for the purpose of executing trades.

In addition, there is the *over-the-counter (OTC) market,* made up of a nationwide network of brokers and dealers who execute transactions in securities that are not listed on one of the exchanges. The securities exchanges typically handle securities of larger, better-known companies, and the over-the-counter market handles many of the smaller, lesser-known firms. There are many exceptions to that rule, however. The exchanges are well-structured institutions that bring together the market forces of supply and demand. The OTC market is basically a mass telecommunications network linking buyers and sellers.

listed securities
Securities that trade on major stock exchanges.

Securities Exchanges. The market forces of supply and demand come together in the major stock exchanges. So-called **listed securities** trade on these exchanges and account for about 60 percent of the total dollar volume of all shares traded in the U.S. stock market. Much of the trading in listed securities is carried out in one place (such as the New York Stock Exchange on Wall Street) and under a broad set of rules by people who are *members* of the exchange. Members are said to "own a seat" on the exchange, a privilege obtained by meeting certain financial requirements. Only the securities of companies that have met established listing requirements are traded on the exchange. Those firms must comply with various regulations to ensure that they do not make financial or legal misrepresentations to their stockholders. Trading takes place in an auction format that brings together buyers and sellers and allows them to make transactions at competitive prices. Firms must not only comply with the rules of the specific exchange, but also fulfill certain requirements as established by the SEC.

New York Stock Exchange
The largest and most prestigious stock exchange in the world.

The **New York Stock Exchange** is the largest and most prestigious securities exchange in the world. Known as "the big board," it lists almost 360 billion shares of stock that, at the end of 2003, had a market value of some $17.3 trillion. Average daily trading volume on the NYSE is about 1.4 billion shares worth more than $38 billion. Membership on the NYSE is limited to 1,366 seats. Brokerage firms own most seats, with Merrill Lynch, the largest of these firms, holding more than twenty seats.

The NYSE has the most stringent listing requirements of all the exchanges and requires listed firms to meet certain standards, including the following:

- at least 2,000 stockholders, each owning at least 100 shares
- $10 million in aggregate earnings over the three years before listing
- at least $2 million in earnings in any of the three years before listing
- positive earnings in the year before listing
- at least $100 million total market value of outstanding common stock

COMPARATIVE CORPORATE FINANCE

Pssst ... Want to Buy a Stock (Exchange)?

International investors have long been able to purchase the shares of many different types of companies that are listed on global stock markets. Recently, however, these same investors have been offered the opportunity to purchase shares in many of the stock exchanges themselves. Since the mid-1990s, no fewer than fifteen of the fifty-six exchanges that are members of the World Federation of Exchanges have sold shares to investors and listed these shares for trading, usually on the exchange itself. Five of the eight largest non-U.S. stock exchanges (London Stock Exchange, Euronext, Deutsche Börse, TSX Toronto Stock Exchange, and Hong Kong Exchanges and Clearing) are now listed companies, and several other exchanges are considering a public listing. In the United States, the New York Stock Exchange is considering a listing of shares, and the Chicago Mercantile Exchange (where investors can trade a wide range of financial products, including commodities and foreign currencies) went public during 2003.

Although the idea of buying shares in a stock exchange may seem odd at first, there are strong business reasons for exchanges to become fully private, profit-making companies with their own boards of directors and publicly traded shares. Exchanges have traditionally been either mutual associations, owned by individuals and brokerage firms, or member-owned limited companies. Unfortunately, these structures have proven to be cumbersome in today's rapidly changing global financial markets, where the ability to make rapid decisions and exploit fleeting opportunities is crucial. An additional problem was that exchanges wanting to undertake acquisitions had to pay for their targets with cash. Exchanges did not have publicly traded stock to use for payment. By setting themselves up as full-fledged corporations with listed shares, stock exchanges can make decisions quickly and use their stock as a currency for acquistions. They can also adopt stock-based employee compensation programs.

No company has been a more enthusiastic advocate of public listing than Euronext N.V., Europe's second-largest exchange (as measured by market capitalization). Formed by the merger of the Paris Bourse, the Amsterdam Stock Exchange, and the Brussels Stock Exchange in September 2000, this company executed an initial public offering and listed shares (on Euronext) in July 2001. In early 2002, Euronext acquired the London International Financial Futures and Options Exchange and merged with the Lisbon Stock Exchange, bringing the total number of exchanges in the group to five. As the chart below makes clear, Euronext shareholders also have reason to cheer the group's effortsTheir shares have retained their value far better since July 2001 than have other European stocks—as measured by the return performance French CAC 40 stock index. Euronext shares have also traded at a very respectable 15–18 times earnings throughout this difficult period.

How are the shares of exchange stocks valued? Just like any other company's shares: investors forecast the per-share cash flows that the company will generate in the future, and then use an appropriate risk-adjusted discount rate to determine the present value of those cash flows. Based on the share price performance of Euronext, the Deutsche Börse, and other listed exchanges, we expect to see continued growth in the number of stock exchanges that sell their own service to public investors.

Stock Price Performance of Euronext Versus the CAC 40 Index

July 2001 through February 5, 2004

Sources: Exchange listing information comes from personal correspondence with Thomas Krantz, secretary-general of the World Federation of Exchanges, and Lorenzo Gallai, *Cost and Revenue Survey 2002*, World Federation of Exchanges (Paris, August 2003), downloadable from http://www.world-exchanges.org. Euronext stock price data comes the *Financial Times* Web site (http://www.ft.com), and the charts are created by BigCharts.Com.

The NYSE also requires firms to pay a listing fee that ranges between $150,000 and $250,000, depending on how much stock the firm has outstanding. Firms that fail to continue to meet listing requirements can be *delisted*. More than 3,200 firms from around the world list their shares on the NYSE.

American Stock Exchange
A major stock exchange in the United States though not as large as the NYSE in terms of daily trading volume or the market capitalization of listed companies.

The **American Stock Exchange** (AMEX) is the second-largest U.S. exchange in terms of the number of listed companies; when it comes to the dollar volume of trading, however, the AMEX is actually smaller than the largest regional exchange (the Midwest in Chicago). The AMEX's organization and procedures are similar to those of the NYSE, but its membership costs and listing requirements are not as stringent. There are approximately 850 seats on the AMEX, and it is home to about 800 listed stocks and a handful of listed corporate bonds. The AMEX handles only about 4 percent of the total annual dollar volume of shares traded on security exchanges. In contrast, the NYSE handles about 90 percent of all common shares traded on organized exchanges, so the AMEX is nowhere near the NYSE in terms of size or stature.

In addition to the NYSE and AMEX, there are a handful of so-called regional exchanges. Each of these exchanges typically list the securities of about 100 to 500 firms. As a group they handle around 6 percent of all shares traded on organized exchanges. The best known of these are the Midwest, Pacific, Philadelphia, Boston, and Cincinnati exchanges. These exchanges deal primarily in securities with local and regional appeal. Most are modeled after the NYSE, but their membership and listing requirements are considerably more lenient. To enhance their trading activity, regional exchanges often list securities that are also listed on the NYSE or AMEX.

Of course, stock exchanges are not limited to the United States. A recent study reported that 103 countries around the world had active stock markets by the turn of the century. As the Comparative Corporate Finance feature on the previous page explains, more and more of these exchanges are converting to public ownership and making their shares available for public trading.

The Over-the-Counter (OTC) Market. Unlike an exchange with a centralized location where trading occurs, the OTC market does not have a single, physical location. Instead, it exists as an intangible relationship between buyers and sellers of securities. Securities traded in this market are sometimes called *unlisted securities*. The OTC accounts for about 40 percent of the total dollar volume of domestic shares traded, and today trades close to 35,000 issues. The market is linked by a mass telecommunications network. Unlike transactions in the physical securities exchanges, trade in the OTC market represents direct transactions between investors and securities dealers That is, the investors buy from and sell to the securities dealers, whereas on the listed securities exchanges the broker acts as an intermediary between buyers and sellers. More common stocks trade in the OTC market than on the exchanges. Dealers make markets in certain OTC securities by offering to either buy or sell them at stated prices.

National Association of Securities Dealers Automated Quotation (Nasdaq) System
An electronic system that facilitates trading in OTC stocks.

A part of the OTC market is made up of a select list of stocks that trade on the **National Association of Securities Dealers Automated Quotation (Nasdaq) System,** which provides up-to-the-minute prices on thousands of stocks. About 7,000 issues actively trade in the Nasdaq portion of the OTC market, and about 2,700 of these are part of the *National Market System* (NMS). The NMS is reserved for the biggest and most actively traded stocks—those that generally have a national following. These securities are widely quoted, and the trades are executed here about as quickly and inexpensively as on the floor of the NYSE. A number of large, well-known firms trade on the Nasdaq NMS such as Intel, Oracle, and Microsoft.

NEW YORK STOCK EXCHANGE COMPOSITE TRANSACTIONS

YTD % CHG	52-WEEK HI	52-WEEK LO	STOCK (SYM)	DIV	YLD %	PE	VOL 100s	CLOSE	NET CHG
			D						
-8.8	21.42	14.35	DPL Inc **DPL**	.96f	5.0	17	3210	19.05	0.05
11.1	32	23.37	DRS Tch **DRS**		...	17	1652	30.86	-0.10
14.2	48.63	34.30	DST Sys **DST**		...	16	7675	47.68	0.25
3.1	42.29	34	DTE Engy **DTE**	2.06	5.1	12	4476	40.61	0.25
1.1	49.85	33.67	DmlrChrylr **DCX**	1.82e	3.9	...	12927	46.71	0.17
6.7	23.20	11.14	Dana Cp **DCN**	.48	2.5	12	11597	19.58	-0.50
9.9	50.85	32.66	Danaher **DHR** s	.06f	.1	28	15539	50.40	...
9.1	17.89	13.05	Danone ADS **DA** s	.29e	1.6	...	236	17.72	0.04
-2.9	25.60	18.25	Darden **DRI**	.08	.4	15	9028	20.42	-0.19
45.6	19.59	9.72	♣DaveBusters **DAB**		...	24	632	18.46	0.02
13.3	34.65	17.07	DaVita **DVA** s		...	16	4873	29.46	-0.61
19.1	6.38	3.48	DeRigo ADS **DER**		...	...	118	6.06	0.06
11.6	37.49	26.94	DeanFoods **DF**		...	16	6676	36.67	0.01
3.9	74.93	44.23	Deere **DE** x	1.12	1.7	18	13378	67.58	-1.90
-3.3	11.75	8.24	DelMonte **DLM**		...	13	16306	10.06	0.16
-2.0	57.33	29.57	Delhaize ADS **DEG**	1.22e	2.4	...	147	50.02	0.97
3.0	11.78	7.85	♣Delphi **DPH**	.28	2.7	dd	8460	10.52	-0.19
19.4	44.11	30.30	DelphiFnl **DFG** s	.32	.7	13	1690	43	0.20
-40.5	**15.60**	**4.53**	**DeltaAir DAL**		**...**	**dd**	**70033**	**7.03**	**0.42**
-15.4	26.63	20.67	Delta&Pine **DLP**	.48	2.2	41	2588	21.50	-0.24
23.5	38.25	26.25	DelticTimber **DEL**	.25	.7	51	214	37.55	0.25
3.8	48.10	38.47	DeluxeCp **DLX**	1.48	3.5	12	2651	42.88	-0.24
45.2	**21.73**	**11.23**	**♣DnbryRes DNR**		**...**	**20**	**5239**	**20.20**	**-1.27**
14.7	17.31	12.55	Dept56 **DFS**		...	15	458	15.03	0.03
7.3	10.11	5.09	DescSA ADS **DES**		...	...	8	5.74	-0.09
-3.5	94.99	56.20	DtscheBK **DB**	3.36e	4.2	...	731	79.30	1.43
-2.3	21.34	13.91	♣DtscheTel ADS **DT**		...	...	9475	17.72	0.32
7.2	42.55	27.71	DevDivRlty **DDR**	1.84	5.1	15	3917	36	...
10.6	32.38	21.80	DeVry **DV**		...	36	4774	27.80	0.80
5.4	57.60	40.18	Diageo ADS **DEO**	1.87e	3.4	...	2270	55.70	0.33
-7.5	51.68	34.70	DiagnstPdt **DP**	.24	.6	20	643	42.47	0.45
13.3	26.85	17.06	DmndOffshr **DO**	.25	1.1	dd	6293	23.23	-0.39
40.6	34.42	16.83	DicksSprtgGds **DKS** s		...	31	13504	34.20	0.77
-3.9	57.43	41.78	Diebold **DBD**	.74	1.4	21	1798	51.76	-0.02
39.4	23.51	12.87	Dillards **DDS** x	.16	.7	50	8506	22.94	0.46
-14.8	7.72	5.50	♣Dimon **DMN**	.30	5.2	...	846	5.75	-0.05
2.4	18.81	12.74	DIRECTV **DTV**		...	...	17319	16.95	0.35
8.2	28.41	18.85	Disney **DIS**	.21	.8	26	53583	25.24	0.06
-25.5	22	12.22	Dist&Srv ADS **DYS**	.43e	2.8	...	447	15.40	-0.04

Figure 5.2
Stock Price Quotes

The figure illustrates how stock prices are quoted and reported in financial newspapers. For each stock, the columns report data including the stock's year-to-date performance, the high and low prices over the past year, the dividend, the price to earnings ratio, and the current market price.

Source: The Wall Street Journal, *June 29, 2004 Reprinted with permission.*

Market Reporting. Summary statistics are reported daily on the activity of widely followed stocks. Regardless of the market on which a stock trades, its price quotation typically appears in a standardized format. To see how price quotations work and what they mean, consider the quotes that appear daily in *The Wall Street Journal*. As we'll see, the quotations provide not only current prices, but a great deal of additional information as well. A portion of the NYSE stock quotations from *The Wall Street Journal* appears in Figure 5.2. Let's use the highlighted Disney quotations for purposes of illustration. These quotes were published on June 29, 2004, and are for trades that occurred the day before. A glance at the quotes shows that stocks, like most other securities, are priced in dollars and cents.

Looking at the Disney quotes, the first column (YTD % CHG) gives the stock's year-to-date change in price; note that Disney's stock has gone up 8.2 percent since the first of the year. The two columns labeled "HI" and "LO" show the highest and lowest prices at which the stock sold during the past fifty-two weeks. You can see that Disney has traded between $28.41 and $18.85 during the preceding fifty-two-week period. Listed to the right of the company's name is its stock symbol (Disney goes by the three-letter initialism DIS). These ticker symbols are the abbreviations used on the market tapes seen in brokerage offices and on television, as well as on Internet sites such as Yahoo!, to identify specific securities. The figure listed right after the stock symbol is the annual cash dividend paid on each share of stock. This is followed by the dividend yield. (Note: Because Disney paid a cash dividend of $0.21 per share, its dividend yield is just 0.8 percent, which equals the ratio of the dividend divided by the closing stock price.) The next entry is the

P/E ratio, which is the current market price divided by the per-share earnings for the most recent twelve-month period. Note that Disney was trading at twenty-six times its earnings.

The daily trading volume follows the P/E ratio. Here, the sales numbers are listed in round lots (of 100 shares), so a figure of 53,583 for Disney indicates that 5,358,300 shares of Disney stock traded that day. The next entry, labeled "CLOSE," shows the closing (final) price of $25.24 at which the stock price traded on the day in question. Finally, as the last (NET CHG) column shows, Disney closed up $0.06. This means the stock closed six cents higher than it did the day before.

The same quotation system is used for Nasdaq National Market stocks. However, a slightly different procedure is used with AMEX and OTC securities that are not part of the National Market system. For many AMEX and OTC stocks, only the stock name, symbol, volume, closing price, and change in price are reported.

CONCEPT REVIEW QUESTIONS

6. When you buy a stock in the secondary market, does the firm that issued the stock receive cash?

7. List several differences between the NYSE and the Nasdaq.

5.4 STOCK VALUATION

Pricing common stocks is much more difficult than valuing bonds. Unlike bonds, common stocks generally do not promise a fixed cash flow stream over time. The cash flows that accrue to common stockholders are variable and uncertain. Because common shares have no specific expiration date (as bonds do), estimates of the cash flows accruing to common shareholders must necessarily take a long-term view. Whereas investors can easily calculate a bond's yield to maturity for an estimate of the return that the market requires on that bond, no mechanical calculation can provide an equally accurate picture of the market's required rate of return on a share of stock.

Despite these difficulties, the principles involved in valuing stock mirror those we adopted to determine bond prices in Chapter 4. First, we estimate the cash flows that a stockholder receives over time. Second, we determine a discount rate that reflects the risk of those cash flows. Third, we estimate the stock's price by calculating the present value. In other words, valuing stock is simply another application of Equation 4.1.

Preferred Stock Valuation

In Section 5.1, we noted that preferred stock represents a hybrid security with some features of both debt and equity. Preferred shares typically offer a fixed stream of cash flows with no specific maturity date. For that reason, we treat preferred stock as a security with an infinite life in our valuation formulas.

In Chapter 3, you learned a shortcut for valuing a *perpetuity*—an annuity with an infinite life. For a perpetuity that makes annual cash payments, with the first payment arriving in one year, the present value equals the next payment divided by the discount rate.[8] To find today's value of a preferred stock, PS_0, we use the

[8] Look once more at Equation 3.10 on page 110 for a refresher on this point.

equation for the present value of a perpetuity, dividing the preferred dividend, D_P, by the required rate of return on the preferred stock, r_P:

$$PS_0 = \frac{D_p}{r_p} \quad \text{(Eq. 5.1)}$$

APPLYING THE MODEL

Suppose that a particular preferred stock pays an annual dividend of \$8. If the next dividend payment occurs in one year and the market's required return on this stock is 10 percent, then its price will be \$80 (\$8 ÷ 0.10). If you know the price of a preferred stock, you can easily determine its yield by dividing the dividend by the price.

Equation 5.1 is valid if dividend payments arrive annually and if the next dividend payment comes in one year. However, simple modifications to the equation can handle dividend payments at other frequencies. For instance, for a preferred stock that pays quarterly dividends, simply divide the quarterly payment by a quarterly discount rate to calculate the price per share.

The Basic Common Stock Valuation Equation

Like the value of bonds and preferred stock, the value of a share of common stock equals the present value of all future benefits that investors expect it to provide. Unlike bonds, which have contractual cash flows, common stocks have cash flows that are noncontractual and unspecified. What are the benefits expected from a share of common stock? When you buy a share of stock, you may expect to receive a periodic dividend payment from the firm, and you probably hope to sell the stock at a future date for more than its purchase price. But when you sell the stock, you are simply passing the rights to future benefits to the buyer. The buyer purchases the stock from you in the belief that the future benefits—dividends and capital gains—justify the purchase price. This logic extends to the next investor who buys the stock from the person who bought it from you, and so on, forever. Simply put, the value of common stock equals the present value of all future dividends that investors expect the stock to distribute.[9]

The easiest way to understand this argument is as follows. Suppose that an investor buys a stock today for price P_0, receives a dividend equal to D_1 at the end of one year, and immediately sells the stock for price P_1. The return on this investment is easy to calculate:

$$r = \frac{D_1 + P_1 - P_0}{P_0}$$

[9] Firms can distribute cash directly to shareholders in forms other than dividends. For instance, many firms regularly buy back their own shares. Also, when an acquiring firm buys a target, it may distribute cash to the target's shareholders. In this discussion, we assume for simplicity that cash payments always come in the form of dividends, but the logic of the argument does not change even if we allow for other forms of cash payments.

The numerator of this expression equals the dollar profit or loss. Dividing that by the purchase price converts the return into percentage form. Rearrange this equation to solve for the current stock price:

$$P_0 = \frac{D_1 + P_1}{(1+r)^1} \quad \text{(Eq. 5.2)}$$

This equation indicates that the value of a stock today equals the present value of cash that the investor receives in one year. But what determines P_1, the selling price at the end of the year? Use Equation 5.2 again, changing the time subscripts to reflect that the price next year will equal the present value of the dividend and selling price received two years from now:

$$P_1 = \frac{D_2 + P_2}{(1+r)^1}$$

Now, take this expression for P_1 and substitute it back into Equation 5.2:

$$P_0 = \frac{D_1 + \frac{D_2 + P_2}{(1+r)^1}}{(1+r)^1} = \frac{D_1}{(1+r)^1} + \frac{D_2 + P_2}{(1+r)^2}$$

We have an expression that says that the price of a stock today equals the present value of the dividends it will pay over the next two years, plus the present value of the selling price in two years. Again we could ask, what determines the selling price in two years, P_2? By repeating the last two steps over and over, we can determine the price of a stock today, as shown in Equation 5.3:

$$P_0 = \frac{D_1}{(1+r)^1} + \frac{D_2}{(1+r)^2} + \frac{D_3}{(1+r)^3} + \frac{D_4}{(1+r)^4} + \frac{D_5}{(1+r)^5} + \ldots \quad \text{(Eq. 5.3)}$$

The price today equals the present value of the entire dividend stream that the stock will pay in the future. Now consider the problem that an investor faces if she tries to determine whether a particular stock is over-valued or under-valued. In deciding whether to buy the stock, the investor must weigh the marginal benefits of owning the stock (the future dividend stream) against the marginal cost of acquiring it (the market price). As we will see in Chapter 7, finding stocks or other financial assets with marginal benefits that exceed their marginal costs is very difficult.

To calculate the stock price using Equation 5.3, an analyst must have two inputs: the future dividend amounts and the appropriate discount rate. Neither input is easy to estimate. Here's that measurement challenge again! The discount rate, or the rate of return required by the market on this stock, depends on the stock's risk. We defer a full discussion of how to measure a stock's risk and how to translate that into a required rate of return until Chapters 6 and 7. Here, we focus on the problem of estimating dividends. In most cases, analysts can formulate reasonably accurate estimates of dividends one year into the future. The real trick is to determine how quickly dividends will grow over time. Our discussion of stock valuation centers on three possible scenarios for dividend growth: zero growth, constant growth, and variable growth.

Zero Growth

zero growth model The simplest approach to stock valuation that assumes a constant dividend stream.

The simplest approach to dividend valuation, the **zero growth model**, assumes a constant dividend stream. If dividends do not grow, we can write the following equation:

$$D_1 = D_2 = D_3 = \ldots = D$$

Plugging the constant value D for each dividend payment into Equation 5.3, you can see that the valuation formula simply reduces to the equation for the present value of a perpetuity:

$$P_0 = \frac{D}{r}$$

In this special case, the formula for valuing common stock is essentially identical to that for valuing preferred stock.

APPLYING THE MODEL

One company that might appear to fit the zero growth model is Wendy's International (ticker symbol WEN). Wendy's paid an uninterrupted string of $0.06 per share quarterly dividends from 1985 through 2003. Perhaps after eighteen years of identical dividends, investors believe Wendy's will continue to pay the same dividend, $0.24 per year, forever. What price would they be willing to pay for Wendy's stock?

The answer depends on Wendy's required rate of return. If investors demand a 10 percent return on Wendy's stock, the stock should be worth $0.24 ÷ 0.10 = $2.40.[10] In fact, in late 2003 and early 2004, Wendy's stock traded for just under $40 per share. This implies one of two things: Either investors require a rate of return on Wendy's stock that is much less than 10 percent, or they expect to receive higher cash distributions in the future than they have received in the past. We lean toward the latter interpretation. As it turns out, investors who held Wendy's stock at the end of 2003 didn't have to wait long to receive higher dividends, because the company doubled its payout in February 2004.

10. You can apply the same formula to quarterly dividends as long as you make an appropriate adjustment in the interest rate. For example, if investors expect a 10 percent effective annual rate of return on Wendy's stock, they expect a quarterly return of $(1.10)^{0.25}-1$, or 2.41 percent. Using this figure, you can recalculate the stock price by dividing $0.06, the quarterly dividend, by 0.0241 to obtain $2.49. Why is Wendy's stock more valuable in this calculation? Since Wendy's dividends arrive more often than once a year, the present value of the dividend stream is greater.

Constant Growth

Of all the relatively simple stock valuation models that we consider in this chapter, the *constant growth model* probably sees the most use in practice. The model assumes that dividends will grow at a constant rate, *g*. If dividends grow at a constant rate forever, we calculate the value of that cash flow stream by using the formula for a growing perpetuity, given in Chapter 3. Denoting next year's dividend as D_1, we determine the value today of a stock that pays a dividend growing at a constant rate:[11]

$$P_0 = \frac{D_1}{r-g} \quad \text{(Eq. 5.4)}$$

Gordon growth model Values a share of stock under the assumption that dividends grow at a constant rate forever.

The constant growth model in Equation 5.4 is commonly called the **Gordon growth model**, after Myron Gordon, who popularized this formula during the 1960s and 1970s.

APPLYING THE MODEL

Few public companies have achieved a longer streak of uninterrupted dividend increases than People's Energy Corp. (ticker symbol, PGL). A holding company that owns several public utilities in the Midwest, People's Energy increased its dividend each year from 1983 through 2003. Over this period, the company increased its dividend at an average annual rate of about 3.8 percent per year. Suppose that investors expect People's Energy to pay a dividend next year of $2.15 per share, and they expect that dividend to continue growing at 3.8 percent per year indefinitely. What would they pay for PGL stock?

Assume that the required rate of return on utility stocks is about 9 percent. Substituting into the constant growth model, Equation 5.4, the result suggests that PGL's stock price should be the following:

$$P = \frac{\$2.15}{0.09 - 0.038} = \$41.35$$

In fact, in late 2003 and early 2004, PGL stock traded in the range of $40–$45, so the growth model appears to do a fairly good job of predicting PGL's price.

We do not want to overstate the accuracy of the constant growth model. We based our calculations on a reasonable set of assumptions, using the long-run growth rate in dividends for *g* and an estimate of the required rate of return on utility stocks for *r*. By making small adjustments to the dividend, the required rate of return, or the growth rate, we could easily obtain an estimate for People's Energy stock that matches the current market price in early 2004. But we could also obtain a very different price with an equally reasonable set of assumptions. For instance, increasing the required rate of return from 9 percent to 9.5 percent and decreasing the dividend growth rate from 3.8 percent to 3.3 percent decreases the price to $34.68. Obviously, analysts want to estimate the inputs for Equation 5.4 as precisely as possible, but the amount of uncertainty inherent in estimating required rates of return and growth rates makes obtaining precise valuations very difficult.

[11] To apply this equation, one must assume that $r>g$ and that *g* itself is constant. Of course, some firms may grow very rapidly for a time, so that $g>r$ temporarily.

Nevertheless, the constant growth model provides a useful way to frame stock-valuation problems, highlighting the important inputs and, in some cases, providing price estimates that seem fairly reasonable. But the model should not be applied blindly to all types of firms, especially not to those enjoying rapid, albeit temporary, growth.

Variable Growth

The zero and constant growth common stock valuation models just presented do not allow for any shift in expected growth rates. Many firms go through periods of relatively fast growth, followed by a period of more stable growth. Valuing the stock of such a firm requires a **variable growth model**, one in which the dividend growth rate can vary. Using our earlier notation, let D_0 equal the last or most recent per-share dividend paid, g_1 equal the initial (fast) growth rate of dividends, g_2 equal the subsequent (stable) growth rate of dividends, and N equal the number of years in the initial growth period. We can write the general equation for the variable growth model as follows:

variable growth model Assumes that the growth rate dividend will vary during different periods of time, when calculating the value of a firm's stock.

$$P_0 = \underbrace{\frac{D_0(1+g_1)^1}{(1+r)^1} + \frac{D_0(1+g_1)^2}{(1+r)^2} + \ldots \frac{D_0(1+g_1)^N}{(1+r)^N}}_{PV \text{ of dividends during initial growth phase}} + \underbrace{\left[\frac{1}{(1+r)^N} \times \frac{D_{N+1}}{r-g_2}\right]}_{\substack{PV \text{ of stock price} \\ \text{at the end of the} \\ \text{initial growth phase}}} \quad \text{(Eq. 5.5)}$$

SMART CONCEPTS

See the concept explained step-by-step at SMARTFinance

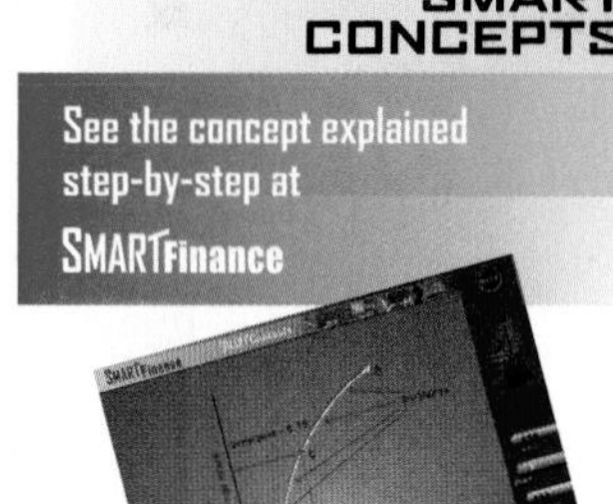

As noted by the labels, the first part of the equation calculates the present value of the dividends expected during the initial fast-growth period. The last term, $D_{N+1} \div (r - g_2)$, equals the value, *as of the end of the fast-growth stage*, of all dividends that arrive after year N. To calculate the *present value* of this growing perpetuity, we must multiply the last term by $1 \div (1 + r)^N$.

APPLYING THE MODEL

Imagine that a food company develops a new carbohydrate-free ice cream. As the popularity of this product increases, the firm (unlike its customers) grows quite rapidly, perhaps 20 percent per year. Over time, as the market share of this new food increases, the firm's growth rate will reach a steady state. At that point, the firm may grow at the same rate as the overall economy, perhaps 5 percent per year. Assume that the market's required rate of return on this stock is 14 percent.

To value this firm's stock, you need to break the future stream of cash flows into two parts. The first consists of the period of rapid growth, and the second is the constant-growth phase. Suppose that the firm's most recent (Year 0) dividend was \$2 per share. You anticipate that the firm will increase the dividend by 20 percent per year for the next three years. After that period the dividend will grow at 5 percent per year indefinitely. The expected dividend stream over the next 7 years looks like this:

Fast Growth Phase (g_1 = 20%)		Stable Growth Phase (g_2 = 5%)	
Year 0	\$2.00	Year 4	\$3.63
Year 1	2.40	Year 5	3.81
Year 2	2.88	Year 6	4.00
Year 3	3.46	Year 7	4.20

The value of the dividends during the fast growth phase is calculated as follows:

$$PV \text{ of dividends (initial phase)} = \frac{\$2.40}{(1.14)^1} + \frac{\$2.88}{(1.14)^2} + \frac{\$3.46}{(1.14)^3}$$
$$= \$2.10 + \$2.22 + \$2.34 = \$6.66$$

The stable growth phase begins with the dividend paid four years from now. The final term of Equation 5.5 is similar to Equation 5.4, which indicates that the value of a constant-growth stock at time t equals the dividend a year later, at time $t + 1$, divided by the difference between the required rate of return and the growth rate. Applying that formula here means valuing the stock at the end of Year 3, just before the constant growth phase begins:

$$P_3 = \frac{D_4}{r - g} = \frac{\$3.63}{0.14 - 0.05} = \$40.33$$

Don't forget that \$40.33 is the estimated price of the stock *three years from now.* Today's present value equals \$40.33 ÷ $(1.14)^3$ = \$27.22. This represents the value today of all dividends that occur in Year 4 and beyond. Putting the two pieces together, we get the following:

$$\text{Total value of stock, } P_0 = \$6.66 + \$27.22 = \$33.88$$

Figure 5.3 depicts a time line for this calculation. The following single algebraic expression shows the same information in a more compact form:

$$P_0 = \frac{\$2.40}{(1.14)^1} + \frac{\$2.88}{(1.14)^2} + \frac{\$3.46 + \$40.33}{(1.14)^3} = \$33.88$$

The numerator of the last term contains both the final dividend payment of the fast-growth phase, \$3.46, and the present value *as of the end of Year 3* of all future dividends, \$40.33. The value of the firm's stock using the variable growth model is \$33.88.

How to Estimate Growth

By now it should be apparent that a central component in many stock-pricing models is the growth rate. Unfortunately, analysts face a tremendous challenge in estimating a firm's growth rate, whether that growth rate refers to dividends, earnings, sales, or almost any other measure of financial performance. A firm's rate of growth depends on several factors. Among the most important, however, are the size of the investments it makes in new and existing projects and the rate of return those investments earn.

A simple, but rather naive method for estimating how fast a firm will grow uses information from financial statements. This approach acknowledges the importance of new investments in driving future growth. First, calculate the magnitude of new investments that the firm can make by determining its *retention rate, rr*, the fraction of the firm's earnings that it retains. Second, calculate the firm's return on common equity, *ROE* (see Chapter 2), to estimate the rate of return that new investments will generate. The product of those two values is the firm's growth rate, g.

$$g = rr \times ROE \qquad \text{(Eq. 5.6)}$$

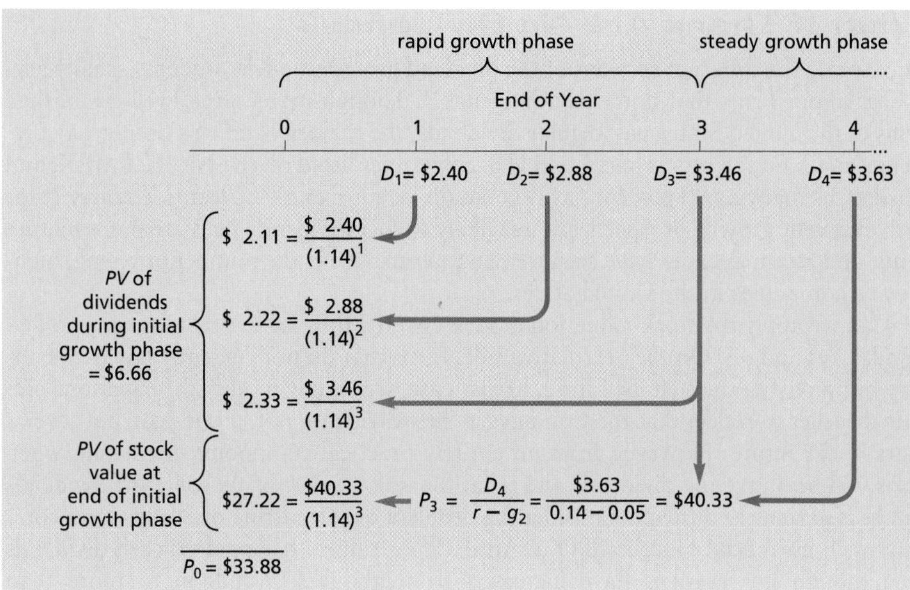

Figure 5.3
Valuing a Stock Using the Variable Growth Model

The stock's value consists of (1) the present value of dividends during the three-year rapid-growth phase and (2) the present value of the constant-growth perpetuity which begins in four years.

APPLYING THE MODEL

Simon Manufacturing traditionally retains 75 percent of its earnings to finance new investments and pays out 25 percent as dividends. Last year, Simon's earnings available for common stockholders were $44.6 million. The book value of its common stock equity was $297.33 million, resulting in a return on common equity of 15 percent. Substituting into Equation 5.6 and multiplying the retention rate by the return on common equity, we estimate Simon's growth rate:

$$g = 0.75 \times 0.15 = 0.1125$$

The resulting estimate of Simon Manufacturing's growth rate is 11.25 percent.

An alternative approach to estimating growth rates makes use of historical data. Analysts track a firm's sales, earnings, and dividends over several years in an attempt to identify growth trends. But how well do growth rates from the past predict growth rates in the future? Unfortunately, the relationship between past and future growth rates for most firms is surprisingly weak. The fact that growth rates are largely unpredictable should not come as a great surprise. One of the most fundamental ideas in economics is that competition limits the ability of a firm to generate abnormally high profits for a sustained period. When one firm identifies a profitable business opportunity, people notice, and entrepreneurs (or other companies) attempt to enter the same business. As more and more firms enter, profits (or the growth rate in profits) fall. At some point, if the industry becomes sufficiently competitive, profits fall to such a low level that some firms exit. As firms exit, profits for the remaining firms rise again. The constant pressure created by these competitive forces means that it is rare to observe a firm with a consistent, long-term growth trend. Perhaps one reason that companies such as Microsoft and Intel are so well known is that their histories of exceptional long-run growth are so uncommon.

SMART IDEAS VIDEO
Kenneth French, Dartmouth College,
"Competition is one of the most pervasive forces out there in the economy."

See the entire interview at **SMARTFinance**

What If There Are No Dividends?

After seeing the different versions of the dividend growth models, students usually ask, "What about firms that don't pay dividends?" Though many large, well-established firms in the United States pay regular dividends, the majority of firms do not pay dividends at all. Of the more than 5,000 U.S. companies listed on the NYSE, AMEX, and Nasdaq, as many as 80 percent pay no cash dividends in a given year.[12] Younger firms with excellent growth prospects are less likely to pay dividends than are more mature firms, and recent decades have seen tremendous growth in the number of young, high-growth companies in the United States.

Can we apply the stock-valuation models covered thus far to firms that pay no dividends? Yes and no. On the affirmative side, firms that do not currently pay dividends may begin paying them in the future. In that case, we simply modify the equations presented earlier to reflect that the firm pays its first dividend, not in one year, but several years in the future. However, from an entirely practical standpoint, predicting when firms will begin paying dividends and what the dollar value of those far-off dividends will be is extremely difficult. Consider the problem of forecasting dividends for a company such as Yahoo! Since its IPO in April 1996, Yahoo! has paid no cash dividends even though its revenues have increased from about $19 million to more than $950 million. Although the company reported a net loss in 2001, it was profitable in the three previous years and in 2002–2003. Is Yahoo! ready to start paying dividends, will it continue to reinvest income to finance growth, or will it be acquired by another firm? In all likelihood, investors will have to wait several years to receive Yahoo!'s first dividend, and there is no way to determine with any degree of precision when that dividend will arrive. Consequently, when analysts attempt to estimate the value of Yahoo!, they generally use methods other than the dividend growth model.

What happens if a company never plans to pay a dividend or otherwise to distribute cash to investors? Our answer to this question is that for a stock to have value, there must be an expectation that the firm will distribute cash in some form to investors at some point in the future. That cash could come in the form of dividends or share repurchases. If the firm is acquired by another company for cash, the cash payment comes when the acquiring firm purchases the shares of the target. Investors must believe that they will receive cash at some point in the future. If you have a hard time believing this, we invite you to buy shares in the Megginson and Smart Corporation, a firm expected to generate an attractive revenue stream from selling its products and services. This firm promises never to distribute cash to shareholders in any form. If you buy shares, you will have to sell them to another investor later to realize any return on your investment. How much are you willing to pay for these shares?

CONCEPT REVIEW QUESTIONS

8. Why is it appropriate to use the perpetuity formula from Chapter 3 to estimate the value of preferred stock?

9. When a shareholder sells common stock, what is being sold? What gives a share of common stock value?

10. Using a dividend forecast of $2.15, a required return of 9 percent, and a growth rate of 3.8 percent, we obtained a price for People's Energy Corp. of $41.35. What would happen to this price if the market's required return on People's Energy stock increased?

---

[12] We expect this percentage to drop during the next few years as a result of the more favorable personal tax treatment afforded dividends in the 2003 Tax Act.

5.5 VALUING THE ENTERPRISE—THE FREE CASH FLOW APPROACH

One way to deal with the valuation challenges presented by a firm that does not pay dividends is to value the firm's ability to generate cash rather than try to value only the firm's shares. The advantage of this procedure is that it requires no assumptions about when the firm distributes cash dividends to stockholders. Instead, when using the free cash flow approach, we begin by asking, what is the total operating cash flow generated by a firm? Next, we subtract from the firm's operating cash flow the amount needed to fund new investments in both fixed assets and current assets. The difference is total **free cash flow (*FCF*)**. Free cash flow, as noted in Chapter 2, represents the cash amount that a firm could distribute to investors after meeting all its other obligations. Note that we used the word *investors* in the previous sentence. Total free cash flow is the amount that the firm could distribute to *all types of investors,* including bondholders, preferred shareholders, and common stockholders. Once we have estimates of the *FCF*s that a firm will generate over time, we can discount them at an appropriate rate to obtain an estimate of the total enterprise value.

free cash flow (*FCF*)
The net amount of cash flow remaining after the firm has met all operating needs and paid for investments, both long-term (fixed) and short-term (current). Represents the cash amount that a firm could distribute to investors after meeting all its other obligations.

But what do we mean by "an appropriate discount rate"? This is a subtle issue that we discuss in much greater detail in Chapter 10. To understand the main idea, recall that *FCF* represents the total cash available for all investors. We suspect that debt is not as risky as preferred stock, and that preferred stock is not as risky as common stock. This means that bondholders, preferred shareholders, and common stockholders each have a different required return in mind when they buy a firm's securities. Somehow we have to capture these varying required rates of return to come up with a single discount rate to apply to free cash flow, the aggregate amount available for all three types of investors. The solution to this problem is known as the **weighted average cost of capital (*WACC*)**.[13] The *WACC* is the after-tax, weighted average required return on all types of securities issued by the firm, where the weights equal the percentage of each type of financing in the firm's overall capital structure. For example, suppose that a firm finances its operation with 50 percent debt and 50 percent equity. Suppose that a firm pays an after-tax return of 8 percent on its outstanding debt and that investors require a 16 percent return on the firm's shares. The *WACC* for this firm would be calculated as follows:

weighted average cost of capital (*WACC*)
The after-tax, weighted average required return on all types of securities issued by a firm, in which the weights equal the percentage of each type of financing in a firm's overall capital structure.

$$WACC = (0.50 \times 8\%) + (0.50 \times 16\%) = 12\%$$

If we obtain forecasts of the *FCF*s, and if we discount those cash flows at a 12 percent rate, the resulting present value is an estimate of the total value of the firm, which we denote V_F.

When analysts value free cash flows, they use some of the same types of models that we have used to value other kinds of income. We could assume that a firm's free cash flows will experience zero, constant, or variable growth. In each instance the procedures and equations would be the same as those introduced earlier for dividends, except we would now substitute *FCF* for dividends.

Remember, our goal in using the free cash flow approach is to develop a method for valuing a firm's shares without making assumptions about its dividends. The free cash flow approach begins by estimating the total value of the firm. To find out

13. We provide only a brief sketch of the *WACC* concept at this point, deferring a deeper analysis until Chapter 10.

what the firm's shares are worth, V_S, we subtract from the total enterprise value, V_F, the value of the firm's debt, V_D, and the value of the firm's preferred stock, V_P. Equation 5.7 depicts this relationship:

$$V_S = V_F - V_D - V_P \quad \text{(Eq. 5.7)}$$

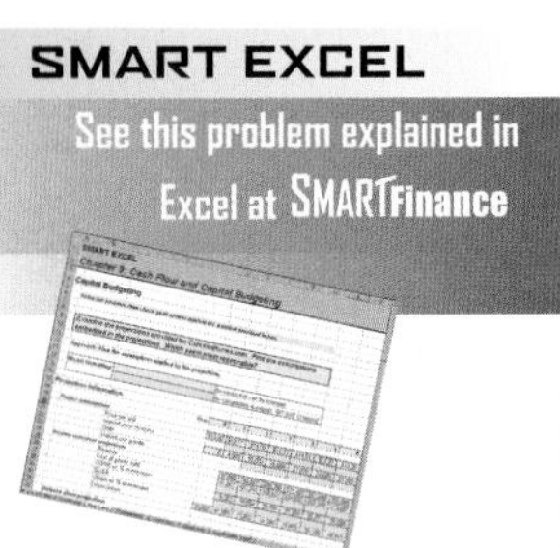

SMART EXCEL
See this problem explained in Excel at SMARTFinance

We already know how to value bonds and preferred shares, so this step is relatively straightforward. Once we subtract the value of debt and preferred stock from the total enterprise value, the remainder equals the total value of the firm's shares. Simply divide this total by the number of shares outstanding to calculate the value per share, P_0.

APPLYING THE MODEL

Had a good steak lately? One of the better-known purveyors of high-quality steak is Mortons of Chicago, operated by Mortons Restaurant Group (MRG). Its stock traded in the $20–$25 range in the first quarter of 2001. At the end of 2000, Mortons had debt with a market value, V_D, of about $66 million, no preferred stock (V_P = 0) and 4,148,002 shares of common stock outstanding. Its year-2000 free cash flow, calculated using the techniques presented in Chapter 2, was about $4.8 million. Its revenues and operating profits both grew at compound annual rates of about 14 percent between 1998 and 2000. Indeed, many consumers were returning to beef during that period. At the same time the steak-house market was growing, competition was beginning to heat up. We assume that Mortons will experience about 14 percent annual growth in *FCF* from 2000 to 2004, followed by 7 percent annual growth thereafter, because of increasing competition as well as changing consumer tastes and preferences. A rough estimate of Mortons' *WACC* of 11 percent is deemed applicable in this valuation.

Mortons' forecast free cash flow for the fast growth period, 2000 to 2004, and for the year 2005, which begins the infinite-lived period of stable growth, are calculated in the following table:

End of Year	Growth Status	Growth Rate (%)	*FCF* Calculation	*FCF*
2000	Historic	Given	$4,800,000	
2001	Fast	14	$4,800,000 × (1.14)^1 =	$5,472,000
2002	Fast	14	$4,800,000 × (1.14)^2 =	$6,238,080
2003	Fast	14	$4,800,000 × (1.14)^3 =	$7,111,411
2004	Fast	14	$4,800,000 × (1.14)^4 =	$8,107,009
2005	Stable	7	$8,107,009 × (1.07)^1 =	$8,674,499

Replacing dividends with free cash flow in Equation 5.5, and substituting $N = 4$, $r = 0.11$, and $g_2 = 0.07$, we can now estimate Mortons' enterprise value at the beginning of 2001, V_F:

$$V_F = \frac{\$5{,}472{,}000}{(1.11)^1} + \frac{\$6{,}238{,}080}{(1.11)^2} + \frac{\$7{,}111{,}411}{(1.11)^3} + \frac{\$8{,}107{,}009}{(1.11)^4} + \left[\frac{1}{(1.11)^4} \times \frac{\$8{,}674{,}499}{(0.11-0.07)}\right]$$
$$= \$4{,}929{,}730 + \$5{,}062{,}966 + \$5{,}199{,}802 + \$5{,}340{,}338 + \$142{,}854{,}029$$
$$= \$163{,}386{,}865$$

Substituting Mortons' enterprise value of \$163,386,865, its debt value, V_D, of \$66 million, and its preferred stock value, V_P, of \$0 into Equation 5.7, we get its total share value, V_S:

$$V_S = \$163{,}386{,}865 - \$66{,}000{,}000 - \$0 = \$97{,}386{,}865$$

Dividing the total share value by the 4,148,002 shares outstanding at the beginning of 2001, we get the per-share value of Mortons' stock, P_{2001}.

$$P_{2001} = \frac{\$97{,}386{,}865}{4{,}148{,}002} = \$23.48$$

Our estimate of Mortons' total share value at the beginning of 2001 of \$97,386,865, or \$23.48 per share, is within its actual trading range of \$20–\$25 per share during the first quarter of 2001.[14]

The free cash flow approach offers an alternative to the dividend discount model that is especially useful when valuing shares that pay no dividends. Security analysts also estimate share values using several models that do not rely on the discounted cash flow methods we have studied so far. We next take a look at some of those alternatives.

11. How can the *free cash flow approach* to valuing an enterprise be used to resolve the valuation challenge presented by firms that do not pay dividends? Compare and contrast this model with the dividend valuation model.

CONCEPT REVIEW QUESTIONS

[14] Here's an interesting postscript for this example. As it was for many businesses, 2001 was a tough year for Mortons. The company experienced significant declines in revenues, earnings, and cash flows, highlighting the difficulties we mentioned earlier in predicting how fast a firm will grow over time. By the first quarter of 2002, Mortons stock had fallen by roughly 75 percent, trading at times for less than \$10 per share. However, some rather important investors thought Mortons was a bargain at that price. The company received a number of acquisition bids from private investors. Mortons' board accepted an offer of \$17 per share from the private equity group Castle Harlan, Inc. The board had rejected an earlier \$17 per share offer from Carl Icahn after Castle responded by increasing its offer from \$16 to \$17. In fact, Castle raised its bid four times in response to bids from Icahn. The total offer was \$71.2 million for sixty-six restaurants that generated revenues of \$233 million in 2001.

5.6 OTHER APPROACHES TO COMMON STOCK VALUATION

Practitioners employ many different approaches to value common stock. The more popular approaches include the use of book value, liquidation value, and some type of a price/earnings multiple.

book value
The value of a firm's equity as recorded on the firm's balance sheet.

Book Value. **Book value** refers to the value of a firm's equity shown on its balance sheet. Calculated using generally accepted accounting principles (GAAP), the book value of equity reflects the historical cost of the firm's assets, adjusted for depreciation, net of the firm's liabilities. Because of its backward-looking emphasis on historical cost figures, book value usually provides a conservative estimate of true market value. Book value is usually less than market value in part because book value does not incorporate information about a firm's potential to generate cash flows in the future. An exception to this general rule occurs when firms experience financial distress. In some cases, such as when a firm's earnings prospects are very poor, the book value of equity may actually exceed its market value.

Liquidation Value. To calculate liquidation value, analysts estimate the amount of cash that remains if the firm's assets are sold and all liabilities paid. Liquidation value may be more or less than book value, depending on the marketability of the firm's assets and the depreciation charges that have been assessed against fixed assets. For example, an important asset on many corporate balance sheets is real estate. The value of raw land appears on the balance sheet at historical cost, but, in many cases, its market value is much higher. In that instance, liquidation value exceeds book value. In contrast, suppose that the largest assets on a firm's balance sheet are highly customized machine tools, purchased two years ago. If the firm depreciates these tools on a straight-line basis over five years, the value shown on the books would equal 60 percent of the purchase price. However, there may be no secondary market for tools that have been customized for the firm's manufacturing processes. If the firm goes bankrupt, and the machine tools have to be liquidated, they may sell for much less than book value.

SMART PRACTICES VIDEO
Bill Eckmann, Investment Banker
"Besides the DCF analysis, everyday I also use the comparable company analysis."

See the entire interview at **SMARTFinance**

Price/Earnings Multiples. As noted in Chapter 2, *the price/earnings (P/E) ratio* reflects the amount investors are willing to pay for each dollar of earnings. The P/E simply equals the current stock price divided by annual earnings per share (*EPS*). The *EPS* used in the denominator of the P/E ratio may reflect either the earnings that analysts expect a firm to generate over the next year or earnings from the previous year.[15] An analyst using this method to value a stock might proceed as follows: First, the analyst forecasts what the firm's *EPS* will be in the next quarter or year. Second, the analyst calculates the average P/E ratio for a group of "comparable firms" in the same industry. Third, the analyst obtains an estimate of the stock price by multiplying the earnings forecast times the average or median P/E ratio for comparable firms.

[15] Analysts refer to "leading" or "trailing" P/E ratios, depending on whether the earnings number in the denominator is a forecast or a historical value.

Though P/E ratios are widely quoted in the financial press, interpreting them can be difficult. Stock analysts frequently tie a firm's P/E ratio to its growth prospects, using logic similar to the following: Suppose one firm has a P/E ratio of 50, and another has a P/E of 20. Why would investors willingly pay $50 per dollar of earnings for the first company and only $20 per dollar of earnings for the second? One possibility is that investors expect the first firm's earnings to grow more rapidly than those of the second firm.

To see this relationship more clearly, look again at Equation 5.4, which indicates that the price of a stock depends on three variables: the dividend next period, the dividend growth rate, and the required rate of return on the stock. We can modify this formula by assuming that a firm pays out a constant percentage of its earnings as dividends. If we denote this payout percentage as *d* and next year's earnings per share as E_1, we can rewrite Equation 5.4 as follows:

$$P_0 = \frac{dE_1}{r-g}$$

where we replace the dividend next year in the numerator with the payout ratio times earnings next year. Now, divide both sides of this equation by E_1 to obtain the following:

$$\frac{P_0}{E_1} = \frac{d}{r-g}$$

On the left-hand side is the P/E ratio using next period's earnings. Notice that if the value of *g* increases, so does the P/E ratio. That provides some justification for the common notion that stocks with high P/E ratios have high growth potential. However, the equation illustrates that either an increase in the dividend payout or a decrease in the required rate of return also increases the P/E ratio. Therefore, when comparing P/E ratios of different firms, we cannot conclude that the firm with the higher P/E ratio necessarily has better growth prospects. In addition, interpreting a P/E ratio is virtually impossible when the firm's earnings are negative or close to zero.

For example, on July 28, 2004, *The Wall Street Journal* reported a price/earnings ratios of 88 for Unova, a company that develops computer and manufacturing systems designed to help customers improve manufacturing efficiency. Did the high P/E ratio signal bright growth prospects for Unova? Not exactly. The P/E ratio was high because Unova barely earned a small profit over the preceding 12 months. Dividing the stock price by earnings per share (which were just a few pennies) resulted in the unusually high P/E ratio.

SMART IDEAS VIDEO

Robert Shiller, Yale University,

"When the P/E ratio is high it's typically justified by an argument that earnings will go up in the future."

See the entire interview at **SMARTFinance**

Despite the difficulties associated with P/E ratios, analysts frequently use them to make rough value assessments. For instance, an analyst might calculate the average P/E ratio in a particular industry and then compare that average with the P/E ratio for a specific firm. If a particular stock's P/E ratio falls substantially above (below) the industry average, the analyst might suspect that the stock is overvalued (undervalued). In the same way, analysts sometimes look at the aggregate P/E ratio for the entire stock market to make judgments about whether stocks generally are over- or undervalued.

CONCEPT REVIEW QUESTIONS

12. Why might the terms *book value* and *liquidation value,* used to determine the value of a firm, be characterized as viewing the firm as "dead rather than alive"? Explain why those views are inconsistent with the discounted cash flow valuation models.

13. Why is it dangerous to conclude that a firm with a high P/E ratio will probably grow faster than a firm with a lower P/E ratio?

5.7 SUMMARY AND CONCLUSIONS

- Preferred stock has both debt-and-equity-like features and does not convey an ownership position in the firm.
- Common stock represents a residual claim on a firm's cash flows, and common stockholders have the right to vote on corporate matters.
- Stock markets can be classified as either primary or secondary. Stocks are sold for the first time in the primary market, but after that, trading occurs in the secondary market.
- Investment bankers play an important role in helping firms issue new securities.
- Stocks trade both on organized exchanges and in an electronic over-the-counter market.
- The same principles apply to the valuation of preferred and common stock. The value of a share depends on the cash flow that the share pays to its owner over time.
- Because preferred stock pays a constant dividend with no specific expiration date, it can be valued using the perpetuity formula from Chapter 3.
- The approach used to value common stock depends on investors' expectations of dividend growth. Zero dividend growth, constant dividend growth, and variable dividend growth can all be incorporated into the basic valuation approach.
- Estimating dividend growth is very difficult. A starting point is to multiply the retention rate times the return on equity.
- Analysts use the free cash flow approach to value the entire enterprise. From that they derive a price per share.
- Other approaches to valuation rely on book value, liquidation value, or price/earnings multiples.

SELF-TEST PROBLEMS

Answers to Self-Test Problems appear in Appendix D at back of book. Answers to the Concept Review Questions throughout the chapter appear at http://megginson.swlearning.com.

ST5-1. Omega Healthcare Investors (ticker symbol, OHI) pays a dividend on its Series B preferred stock of $0.539 per quarter. If the price of Series B preferred stock is $25 per share, what quarterly rate of return does the market require on this stock, and what is the effective annual required return?

ST5-2. The restaurant chain Applebee's International, Inc. (ticker symbol, APPB) announced an increase of their quarterly dividend from $0.06 to $0.07 per share in

December 2003. This continued a long string of dividend increases. Applebee's was one of few companies that had managed to increase its dividend at a double-digit clip for more than a decade. Suppose you want to use the dividend growth model to value Applebee's stock. You believe that dividends will keep growing at 10 percent per year indefinitely, and you think the market's required return on this stock is 11 percent. Let's assume that Applebee's pays dividends annually and that the next dividend is expected to be $0.31 per share. The dividend will arrive in exactly one year. What would you pay for Applebee's stock right now? Suppose you buy the stock today, hold it just long enough to receive the next dividend, and then sell it. What rate of return will you earn on that investment?

INTERNET RESOURCES

http://www.nyse.com—At the New York Stock Exchange site you can learn about listing requirements, gather statistics on listed stocks and trading volume, and stay abreast of current market events.

http://www.nasdaq.com—Learn about the Nasdaq and conduct research on stocks traded there.

http://www.mergent.com/Dividend_Achievers.asp—Mergent's site collects data on "dividend achievers," firms that have increased their dividend payments for ten or more consecutive years.

http://www.dividenddiscountmodel.com—Here is a Web site devoted to the dividend discount model for valuing stocks.

KEY TERMS

additional paid-in capital
American Stock Exchange
best efforts
book value
brokers
competitively bid offer
dealers
dividend
firm-commitment
free cash flow (*FCF*)
Gordon growth model
Green Shoe option
initial public offering (IPO)
investment banks
lead underwriter
listed securities
majority voting system
market capitalization
negotiated offer
New York Stock Exchange
National Association of Securities Dealers Automated Quotation (Nasdaq) System
oversubscribe
par value (stock)
price stabilization
prospectus
proxy fight
proxy statements
residual claimants
road show
seasoned equity offering (SEO)
selling group
shares authorized
shares issued
treasury stock
underwrite
underwriting spread
underwriting syndicate
variable growth model
weighted average cost of capital (*WACC*)
zero growth model

QUESTIONS AND PROBLEMS

Q5-1. How is preferred stock different from common stock?

Q5-2. What is a *prospectus?*

Q5-3. Describe the role of the *underwriting syndicate* in a *firm-commitment offering.*

Q5-4. Why is the relationship between an investment banker and a firm selling securities somewhat adversarial?

Q5-5. Does secondary market trading generate capital for the company whose stock is trading?

Q5-6. How do you estimate the required rate of return on a share of preferred stock if you know its market price and its dividend.

Q5-7. The value of common stocks cannot be tied to the present value of future dividends because most firms don't pay dividends. Comment on the validity, or lack thereof, of this statement.

Q5-8. A common fallacy in stock market investing is assuming that a good company makes a good investment. Suppose we define a good company as one that has experienced rapid growth (in sales, earnings, or dividends) in the recent past. Explain the reasons why shares of good companies may or may not turn out to be good investments.

Q5-9. Why is it not surprising to learn that growth rates rarely show predictable trends?

Q5-10. The *book value* of a firm's common equity is usually lower than the market value of the common stock. Why? Can you describe a situation in which the *liquidation value* of a firm's equity could exceed its market value?

PROBLEMS

The Essential Features of Preferred and Common Stock

P5-1. The equity section of the balance sheet for Hilton Web-Cams looks like this:

Common stock, $0.25 par	$ 400,000
Paid-in capital surplus	$4,500,000
Retained earnings	$1,100,000

a. How many shares has the company issued?
b. What is the book value per share?
c. Suppose that Hilton Web-Cams has made only one offering of common stock. At what price did it sell shares to the market?

P5-2. The equity section of the balance sheet for Jackson Halftime Entertainment, Inc. appears below:

Common stock, $0.60 par value	$________
Paid-in capital surplus	$10,000,000
Retained earnings	$22,000,000

If the company originally raised $11,000,000 in its stock issue, how many shares did it sell and at what price?

Primary Markets and Issuing New Securities

P5-3. Owners of the Internet bargain site FROOGLE.com have decided to take their company public by conducting an initial public offering of common stock. They have agreed with their investment banker to sell 3.3 million shares to investors at an offer price of $14 per share. The underwriting spread is 7 percent.

a. What is the net price that FROOGLE.com will receive for its shares?
b. How much money will FROOGLE.com raise in the offering?
c. What do FROOGLE.com's investment bankers make on this transaction?

Secondary Markets for Equity Securities

P5-4. The following stock quotes were taken from a recent issue of *The Wall Street Journal*:

YTD % Chg	52-Week HI	52-Week LO	Stock (SYM)	DIV	Yld (%)	PE	Vol 100s	Close	Net Chg
12.7	46.8	33.0	Smucker SJM	0.92	2.1	20	1349	44.86	0.05
−11.8	44.3	31.1	Verizon VZ	1.54	4.5	15	61517	34.17	0.04

a. Which company had higher earnings per share over the last year?
b. What was the closing price of Verizon as reported in the paper yesterday?
c. Which company's stock earned a higher percentage return on the day as reported here?

P5-5. Fill in the missing figures in the table.

YTD % Chg	52-Week HI	52-Week LO	Stock (SYM)	DIV	Yld (%)	PE	Vol 100s	Close	Net Chg
19.7	94.5	73.17	IBM IBM	0.64		28	35964	92.79	−0.60
−16.4	60.1	40.57	Merck MRK		3.3	14	66805	44.77	0.56

Stock Valuation

P5-6. Argaiv Towers has outstanding an issue of preferred stock with a par value of $100. It pays an annual dividend equal to 8 percent of par value. If the required return on Argaiv preferred stock is 6 percent, and if Argaiv pays its next dividend in one year, what is the market price of the preferred stock today?

P5-7. Artivel Mining Corp.'s preferred stock pays a dividend of $5 each year. If the stock sells for $40 and the next dividend will be paid in one year, what return do investors require on Artivel preferred stock?

P5-8. Silaic Tools has issued preferred stock that offers investors a 10 percent annual return. The stock current sells for $80, and the next dividend will be paid in one year. How much is the dividend?

P5-9. Suppose a preferred stock pays a quarterly dividend of $2 per share. The next dividend comes in exactly one-fourth of a year. If the price of the stock is $80, what is the effective annual rate of return that the stock offers investors?

P5-10. A particular preferred stock pays a $1 quarterly dividend and offers investors an effective annual rate of return of 12.55 percent. What is the price per share?

P5-11. The C. Alice Stone Company's common stock has paid a $3 dividend for so long that investors are now convinced that the stock will continue to pay that annual dividend forever. If the next dividend is due in one year and investors require an 8 percent return on the stock, what is its current market price? What will the price be immediately after the next dividend payment?

SMART SOLUTIONS

See the problem and solution explained step-by-step at SMARTFinance

P5-12. Propulsion Sciences' (PS) stock dividend has grown at 10 percent per year for many years. Investors believe that a year from now the company will pay a dividend of \$3 and that dividends will continue their 10 percent growth indefinitely. If the market's required return on PS stock is 12 percent, what does the stock sell for today? How much will it sell for a year from today after the stockholders receive their dividend?

P5-13. Investors believe that a certain stock will pay a \$4 dividend next year. The market price of the stock is \$66.67, and investors expect a 12 percent return on the stock. What long-run growth rate in dividends is consistent with the current price of the stock?

P5-14. Gail Dribble is analyzing the shares of Petscan Radiology. Petscan's stock pays a dividend once each year, and it just distributed this year's \$0.85 dividend. The market price of the stock is \$12.14. Gail estimates that Petscan will increase its dividends by 7 percent per year forever. After contemplating the risk of Petscan stock, Gail is willing to hold the stock only if it provides an annual expected return of at least 13 percent. Should she buy Petscan shares or not?

P5-15. Carbohydrates Anonymous (CA) operates a chain of weight-loss centers for carb lovers. Its services have been in great demand in recent years, and its profits have soared. CA recently paid an annual dividend of \$1.35 per share. Investors expect that the company will increase the dividend by 20 percent in each of the next three years, and after that they anticipate that dividends will grow by about 5 percent per year. If the market requires an 11 percent return on CA stock, what should the stock sell for today?

P5-16. Hill Propane Distributors sells propane gas throughout the eastern half of Texas. Because of population growth and a construction boom in recent years, the company has prospered and expects to continue to do well in the near term. The company will pay a \$0.75 per-share dividend to investors one year from now. Investors believe that Hill Propane will increase that dividend at 15 percent per year for the subsequent five years, before settling down to a long-run dividend growth rate of 3 percent. Investors expect an 8 percent return on Hill Propane common shares. What is the current selling price of the stock?

P5-17. Yesterday, September 22, 2006, Wireless Logic Corp. (WLC) paid its annual dividend of \$1.25 per share. Because WLC's financial prospects are particularly bright, investors believe the company will increase its dividend by 20 percent per year for the next four years. After that, investors believe WLC will increase the dividend at a modest annual rate of 4 percent. Investors require a 16 percent return on WLC stock, and WLC always makes its dividend payment on September 22 of each year.

a. What is the price of WLC stock on September 23, 2006?
b. What is the price of WLC stock on September 23, 2007?
c. Calculate the percentage change in price of WLC stock from September 23, 2006, to September 23, 2007.
d. For an investor who purchased WLC stock on September 23, 2006, received a dividend on September 22, 2007, and sold the stock on September 23, 2007, what was the total rate of return on the investment? How much of this return came from the dividend, and how much came from the capital gain?
e. What is the price of WLC stock on September 23, 2010?
f. What is the price of WLC stock on September 23, 2011?
g. For an investor who purchased WLC stock on September 23, 2010, received a dividend on September 22, 2011, and sold the stock on September 23, 2011, what was the total rate of return on the investment? How much of this return came from the dividend, and how much came from the capital gain? Comment on the differences between your answers to this question and your answers to part (d).

P5-18. Today's date is March 30, 2006. E-Pay, Inc. stock pays a dividend every year on March 29. The most recent dividend was $1.50 per share. You expect the company's dividends to increase at a rate of 25 percent per year through March 29, 2009. After that, you expect that dividends will increase at 5 percent a year. Investors require a 14 percent return on E-Pay stock. Calculate the price of the stock on the following dates: March 30, 2006; March 30, 2010; and September 30, 2007.

P5-19. One year from today, investors anticipate that Groningen Distilleries Inc. stock will pay a dividend of $3.25 per share. After that, investors believe that the dividend will grow at 20% per year for three years before settling down to a long-run growth rate of 4%. The required rate of return on Groningen stock is 15%. What is the current stock price?

SMART SOLUTIONS

See the problem and solution explained step-by-step at

SMARTFinance

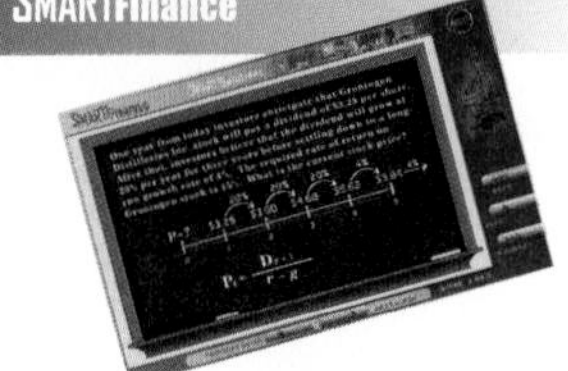

P5-20. Investors expect the following series of dividends from a particular common stock:

Year One	$1.10
2nd year	$1.25
3rd year	$1.45
4th year	$1.60
5th year	$1.75

After the fifth year, dividends will grow at a constant rate. If the required rate of return on this stock is 9 percent and the current market price is $45.64, what is the long-term rate of dividend growth expected by the market?

P5-21. In the constant-growth model we can apply the equation $P = D/(r\text{-}g)$, only under the assumption that $r>g$. Suppose someone tries to argue with you that for a certain stock, $r<g$, forever, not just during a temporary growth spurt. Why can't this be the case? What would happen to the stock price if this were true? If you try to answer simply by looking at the formula, you will almost certainly get the wrong answer. Think it through.

P5-22. Stephenson Technologies (ST) produces the world's greatest single-lens-reflex (SLR) camera. The camera has been a favorite of professional photographers and serious amateurs for several years. Unfortunately, the camera uses old film technology and does not take digital pictures. Ron Stephenson, owner and chief executive officer of the company, decided to let the business continue for as long as it can without making any new research-and-development investments to develop digital cameras. Accordingly, investors expect ST common stock to pay a $4 dividend next year and shrink by 10 percent per year indefinitely. What is the market price of ST stock if investors require a 12 percent return?

Valuing the Enterprise—The Free Cash Flow Approach

P5-23. Roban Corporation is considering going public but is unsure of a fair offering price for the company. Before hiring an investment banker to assist in making the public offering, managers at Roban decide to make their own estimate of the firm's common stock value. The firm's chief financial officer gathers data for performing the valuation using the free cash flow valuation model.

The firm's weighted average cost of capital is 12 percent. It has $1,400,000 of debt at market value and $500,000 of preferred stock at its assumed market value. The estimated free cash flows over the next five years, 2007 through 2011, are given below. Beyond 2011 to infinity, the firm expects its free cash flow to grow by 4 percent annually.

Year	Free cash flow
2007	$250,000
2008	290,000
2009	320,000
2010	360,000
2011	400,000

a. Estimate the value of Roban Corporation's entire company by using the *free cash flow approach.*

b. Use your finding in part (a), along with the data provided above, to find Roban Corporation's common stock value.

c. If the firm plans to issue 220,000 shares of common stock, what is its estimated value per share?

P5-24. Dean and Edwards, Inc. (D&E) is a firm that provides temporary employees to businesses. D&E's client base has grown rapidly in recent years, and the firm has been quite profitable. The firm's cofounders, Mr. Dean and Mr. Edwards, believe in a conservative approach to financial management and therefore have not borrowed any money to finance their business. A larger company in the industry has approached D&E about buying them out. In the most recent year, 2006, D&E generated free cash flow of $1.4 million. Suppose that D&E projects that these cash flows will grow at 15 percent per year for the next four years, and then will settle down to a long-run growth rate of 7 percent per year. The cofounders want a 14 percent return on their investment. What should be their minimum asking price from the potential acquirer?

Other Approaches to Common Stock Valuation

P5-25. Dauterive Barber Shops (DBS) specializes in providing quick and inexpensive haircuts for middle-aged men. The company retains about half of its earnings each year and pays the rest out as a dividend. Recently, the company paid a $3.25 dividend. Investors expect the company's dividends to grow modestly in the future, about 4 percent per year, and they require a 9 percent return on DBS shares. Based on next year's earnings forecast, what is DBS's price/earnings ratio? How would the price/earnings ratio change if investors believed that DBS's long-term growth rate was 6 percent rather than 4 percent? Retaining the original assumption of 4 percent growth, how would the price/earnings ratio change if investors became convinced that DBS was not very risky and were willing to accept a 7 percent return on their shares going forward?

THOMSON ONE Business School Edition

Access financial information from the Thomson ONE – Business School Edition Web site for the following problem(s). Go to http://tobsefin.swlearning.com/. If you have already registered your access serial number and have a username and password, click **Enter.** Otherwise, click **Register** and follow the instructions to create a username and password. Register your access serial number and then click **Enter** on the aforementioned Web site. When you click Enter, you will be prompted for your username and password (please remember that the password is case sensitive). Enter them in the respective boxes and then click **OK** (or hit **Enter**). From the ensuing page, click **Click Here to Access Thomson ONE – Business School Edition Now!** This opens up a new window that gives you access to the Thomson ONE – Business School Edition database. You can retrieve a company's financial information by entering its ticker symbol (provided for each company in the problem(s)) in the box below "Name/Symbol/Key." For further instructions on using the Thomson ONE – Business School Edition database, please refer to "A Guide for Using Thomson ONE – Business School Edition."

P5-26. What rate of return do investors require on General Electric (ticker: U:GE) common stock? Use the annual dividends per share reported for the last five years to determine the compound annual growth rate in dividends. Assume that General Electric maintains this growth rate forever and has just paid a dividend. Use the latest available closing price as the current stock price. How does this required rate of return compare with the compound annual stock return over the last five years? Have investors been compensated sufficiently?

P5-27. Are shares of Eli Lilly & Company (ticker: U:LLY) currently under- or overpriced? Calculate the average P/E ratio over the last five fiscal years. Assuming that Eli Lilly maintains this average P/E into the future, determine the price per share using the average EPS estimate for the next fiscal year end. Is this estimate higher or lower than the latest closing price for Eli Lilly?

Since these exercises depend upon real-time data, your answers will change continuously depending upon when you access the Internet to download your data.

MINICASE

Valuing Stocks

Your investment adviser has sent you three analyst reports for a young, growing company named Vegas Chips, Incorporated. These reports depict the company as speculative, but each one poses different projections of the company's future growth rate in earnings and dividends. All three reports show that Vegas Chips earned $1.20 per share in the year ended previously. There is consensus that a fair rate of return to investors for this common stock is 14 percent, and that management expects to consistently earn a 15 percent return on the book value of equity (ROE = 15 percent).

ASSIGNMENT

1. The analyst who produced report A makes the assumption that Vegas Chips will remain a small, regional company that, although profitable, is not expected to grow. In this case, Vegas Chips' management is expected to elect to pay out 100 percent of earnings as dividends. Based on this report, what model can you use to value a share of common stock in Vegas Chips? Using this model, what is the value?
2. The analyst who produced report B makes the assumption that Vegas Chips will enter the national market and grow at a steady, constant rate. In this case, Vegas Chips' management is expected to elect to pay out 40 percent of earnings as dividends. This analyst discloses news that this dividend has just been committed to current stockholders. Based on this report, what model can you use to value a share of common stock in Vegas Chips? Using this model, what is the value?
3. The analyst who produced report C also makes the assumption that Vegas Chips will enter the national market but expects a high level of initial excitement for the product that is then followed by growth at a constant rate. Earnings and dividends are expected to grow at a rate of 50 percent over the next year, 20 percent for the following two years, and then revert back to a constant growth rate of 9 percent thereafter. This analyst also discloses that Vegas Chips' management has just announced the pay out of 40 percent of the recently reported earnings to current stockholders. Based on this report, what model can you use to value a share of common stock in Vegas Chips? Using this model, what is the value?
4. Discuss the feature(s) that drives the differing valuation of Vegas Chip', Incorporated. What additional information do you need to garner confidence in the projections of each analyst report?

Smart *Excel* Appendix

Use the Smart *Excel* spreadsheets and animated tutorials at http://smartfinance.swlearning.com.

EXCEL PREREQUISITES

You need to be familiar with the following *Excel* features to use this appendix:

- The use of the fill-series feature on the edit menu
- Creating a cumulative formula

If this is new to you, be sure to complete the ***Excel Prereqs*** tab of the Chapter 5 *Excel* file before proceeding.

CALCULATING DOLLAR AND PERCENT RETURNS

In the text, the return on an investment in equity is shown as

$$r = (D_1 + P_1 - P_0) / P_0$$

The numerator provides the dollar return, and dividing that by the purchase price converts the return into percentage form.

Problem: You just bought shares in FastFood, Inc. at $42 per share. You expect the dividend per share for the stock to total $1.20 over the next year and believe the price will rise to $46.50. Under these assumptions, find the dollar and percent return on an investment in one share. Now suppose the stock price falls to $38.50. What is the return?

Approach: Create a simple model that allows you to find the dollar and percent return on an equity investment.

Try it yourself in a blank *Excel* file. Think about what to include in inputs and how to set up your calculations and output. Alternatively, you can use the setup file provided on the Return tab of the Chapter 5 *Excel* file at the Smart Finance Web site.

If the ending price is $46.50, the capital gain is $4.50. With the dividend, the dollar return is $5.70 and the percent return is 13.6%. Assuming an ending price of

\$38.50, there is a capital loss of \$3.50. With the dividend, the dollar loss is \$2.30 and the percent return is –5.5%.

STOCK VALUATION UNDER CONSTANT GROWTH

Problem: Campus Bookstores' stock dividend has grown at 7% per year for many years. The firm just paid a dividend of \$2.20, and investors believe that dividends will continue to grow at 7% indefinitely. If the market assessment of the required return for Campus Bookstores is 10%, what should the stock sell for today?

To determine a stock price you must design a model to forecast the stock's cash flows and calculate the present value of these cash flows. Remember the components of a basic model: inputs, calculations, and output. The output is the stock price. The inputs are the assumptions about future dividends, growth, and the required return on the stock. In the calculations section, find the dividend expected next year. The stock price is the output derived from the Gordon Constant Growth model.

Approach 1: Gordon model

Try it yourself in a blank *Excel* file. Think about what to include in inputs and how to set up your calculations and output. Alternatively, you can use the setup file provided on the *Stockval const growth* tab of the Chapter 5 *Excel* file.

You should get a price of \$78.47. (If you get a slightly different price, it may be the result of rounding. We did not round the Year 1 dividend).

Apply it

Suppose the growth is 9%, 0%, or −3%.

At a growth rate of 9%, the price is \$239.80.
At a growth rate of 0%, the price is \$22.00.
At a growth rate of −3%, the price is \$16.42.

Approach 2: Valuation Based on Dividends Received Over a Finite Time Period

It is interesting to know how much of the stock's value comes from cash flows (dividends) in early years versus the value derived from later cash flows. Another approach sometimes used in valuation is to look at a predetermined finite horizon (as with bonds). Unlike bonds, stocks do not mature, but this approach enables you to see how much a stock's value depends on dividend payments over different horizons.

Again, solve the Campus Bookstores' problem, but now consider only the value of dividends received over the next fifty years.

Under this approach, you will need to estimate the dividends over some selected time period (here fifty years) and then find the present value of these dividends using the required return as the discount rate. It is quite similar to the bond valuation approach except that the cash flows are dividends.

1. On the ***Stockval const growth*** tab of the Chapter 5 *Excel* file, fill in the input assumptions.

2. In the Calculations section, fill in the Year numbers from 0 through 50. This is simple if you use the fill-series feature described on the ***Prereqs*** tab.
3. In the Calculations section, you need to enter the last dividend paid under Year 0 for use in the formula for future dividends. Enter the last dividend in the Year 0 column by using a cell reference to the input assumption. (In cell C41 type =C35)
4. Next, create a formula for the dividend in Year 1. It is equal to the previous year's dividend (shown in Year 0) multiplied by 1 plus the growth rate. Copy this formula across for all years.

   If you have an error, check that you used an absolute reference for the growth rate and that you used parentheses. The formula is:

   $=D_0*(1+g)$

5. Create a formula to find the present value of the dividend in each year. Copy across. You will get an error if you do not absolute reference the required return. The formula is:

   =Div / (1+ req return)^ year #

6. Now create a cumulative formula (covered on the ***Prereqs*** tab) to find the cumulative present value of dividends throughout each year.

   The formula under Year 1 is:

   =sum($D$42:D42)

   This row will show you what a stock is worth if based on dividends it pays over some finite time horizon. In this example, the total present value of the first ten years of dividends is $18.96.

   The first part of your calculations should look like this:

Calculations

Year	0	1	2	3	4	5	6	7	8	9	10
Dividend	$2.20	$2.35	$2.52	$2.70	$2.88	$3.09	$3.30	$3.53	$3.78	$4.04	$4.33
PV of dividend		$2.14	$2.08	$2.02	$1.97	$1.92	$1.86	$1.81	$1.76	$1.72	$1.67
Cumulative PV of dividends		$2.14	$4.22	$6.25	$8.22	$10.13	$12.00	$13.81	$15.57	$17.29	$18.96

7. Under Output, use a cell reference to the Cumulative *PV* of dividends in Year 50 to show the value based off a fifty-year time horizon.

Solutions are provided in the file. The formula result is $58.78. This is significantly less than the price of $78.47 found using the Gordon model. This suggests that about $20 of the $78.47 stock price found under the Gordon model comes from dividends received after the first fifty years.

Apply it

- *Suppose the growth is 9%, 0%, or −3%.*

  At a growth rate of 9%, the price is $87.91 (compared to $239.80 using the Gordon model).
  At a growth rate of 0%, the price is $21.81 (compared to $22.00 using the Gordon model).
  At a growth rate of −3%, the price is $16.38 (compared to $16.42 using the Gordon model).

  Between the Gordon approach and the finite horizon approach, how is the difference in price related to the growth rate?

With lower growth rates, the dividends received in the earlier years account for a higher fraction of today's stock prices. Thus, when the growth rate is low, the two approaches yield fairly close results. With high dividend growth the results differ dramatically.

STOCK VALUATION UNDER VARIABLE GROWTH

Problem: SnackHappy Foods has created a line of low carbohydrate desserts. Demand for these products has pushed the firm's growth rate from its historical average of 7% to 40% over the last year. Management knows this rate is not sustainable but does expect several years of high growth. It estimates dividend growth over the next two years to be 30%, followed by 15% growth in Years 3–5 before a return to the long-run dividend growth rate of 7%. Use the model developed in the chapter to find the expected stock price of SnackHappy, assuming the firm just paid an annual dividend of $0.85 and the market's required return for SnackHappy is 11.5%.

Approach 1: Gordon model

Recall from the text that under variable growth, you need to break the future stream of cash flows into two parts: the variable growth phase and the stable or constant growth phase.

Your model must calculate the present value of dividends, one dividend at a time, during the high growth phase. The model must also calculate the price of the stock at the end of the high growth phase using the Gordon model.

The stock price is the sum of the present value of the dividends during the variable growth period and the present value of the stock price when growth becomes stable.

The key to using this model is to remember that you forecast the dividend into the first constant growth period to find the stock price when growth stabilizes.

Recall that the formula to find the price of a constant growth stock today is $P_0 = D_1 / (r - g)$.

You must use the NEXT dividend expected. To value today (time 0), use the expected Year 1 dividend.

Likewise, if growth stabilizes beginning in Year 6, you would find the present value of dividends during the first five years. Then, find the price of the stock when growth becomes constant, at the end of the five years. Use the dividend expected in Year 6 in the formula.

The price at the end of Year 5 is:

$$P_5 = D_6 / (r - g)$$

Since this is the value at the end of Year 5, it must be discounted for five years to find the present value.

Open the Chapter 5 *Excel* file and turn to the ***Stockval var growth*** tab.

Enter the input information. **Careful: Start the years row with 0 since we need Year 0.**

Note that the calculations section is in two parts: the first part is used to determine the dividends during the variable growth phase (the first five years). Then, these dividends are stated in present-value form.

The second part is used to find the value of the stock when growth becomes stable. This price is also then stated in present-value form.

Your results should look like this:

Inputs							
Year	0	1	2	3	4	5	6
Last dividend (just paid)	$0.85						
r = required return	11.5%						
g = growth rate expected		30%	30%	15%	15%	15%	7%
Calculations							
Variable growth phase							
Dividends	$0.85	$1.11	$1.44	$1.65	$1.90	$2.18	
Present value of dividends		$0.99	$1.16	$1.19	$1.23	$1.27	
Stable growth phase							
Dividend in first year of stable growth							$2.34
Stock price when growth becomes stable						$51.95	
Present value of price	$27.03						
Output							
Stock price	$32.87						

The output, stock price, is the sum of the present value of dividends paid during the variable growth phase (the *PV* of dividends received in Years 1–5) and the present value of the stock when stable growth is reached. The value of the stock as the firm enters stable growth is $51.95. The present value of $51.95 to be received in five years discounted at 11.5%, is $27.03.

If you find this confusing, recall that the dividend in Year 6 is found only to estimate the price in Year 5, just as, under constant growth, the dividend in Year 1 is used to estimate the price today.

$P_0 = D_1 / (r - g)$ and $P_5 = D_6 / (r - g)$

Apply it

After you complete the model, change the expected growth rates and watch how price reacts.

Approach 2: Valuation Based on Dividends Received Over a Finite Time Period

As with constant growth stocks, you may want to determine the price based on a finite time period.

Again, solve the SnackHappy problem, but now consider only the value of dividends received over the next forty years. The main difference from the solution on the previous tab is that the dividend calculation refers to growth rate estimates in the inputs. Use the fill-series feature to input the years.

With this approach, there is no need to use the two stages because dividends are simply estimated and then put in present-value form for the desired time horizon.

The first part of your model should look like this (Years 11–40 are not displayed here):

Inputs											
Year	0	1	2	3	4	5	6	7	8	9	10
Last dividend	$0.85										
r = required return	11.5%										
g = growth rate expected		30%	30%	15%	15%	15%	7%	7%	7%	7%	7%
Calculations											
Dividend	$0.85	$1.11	$1.44	$1.65	$1.90	$2.18	$2.34	$2.50	$2.68	$2.86	$3.06
PV of dividend		$0.99	$1.16	$1.19	$1.23	$1.27	$1.22	$1.17	$1.12	$1.08	$1.03
Cumulative PV of dividends		$0.99	$2.15	$3.34	$4.57	$5.84	$7.05	$8.22	$9.34	$10.41	$11.45
Output											
Price for 40-year time horizon	$28.85										

Note that the value under a forty-year time horizon is about $4 less than under the infinite horizon price of $32.87.

FREE CASH FLOW VALUATION OF AN ENTERPRISE

Problem: Turn to the Morton's valuation in Section 5.2 of the text. Set up a model to value the enterprise, using the free cash flow approach.

We will value the enterprise, using the two approaches from the previous problem.

Open the setup file on the tab labeled ***EnterValue***. The first approach is similar to the calculations in the text. Complete the model and compare to the solution.

In the second approach, assume you have been asked to value the enterprise based upon fifty years of free cash flows to assess how much of the enterprise value is derived from cash flows in the early years.

Apply it

Change your growth estimates and analyze the effect on enterprise value and stock price.

Small changes in growth rates can have large effects on values. Also, as growth rate estimates increase, the difference in values between the two approaches becomes greater. At higher growth rates a larger fraction of today's price comes from dividends in later years.

The Trade-off Between Risk and Return

OPENING FOCUS

Daedalus or Icarus—Risk Propels Money Manager to Extreme Highs and Lows

In Greek mythology, Daedalus was a craftsman and inventor who built wings made of feathers and wax so that he and his son Icarus could flee the court of King Minos on the island of Crete. Daedalus and Icarus managed to escape, but Icarus, exhilarated by the thrill of flying, ascended too high. The sun's heat melted the wax on Icarus' wings, and he fell to his death.

The ups and down of Icarus' flight are all too familiar for Stephen Coleman, chief investment officer of the money management firm, Daedalus Capital, in St. Louis. Eschewing conventional wisdom that preaches the benefits of diversification to reduce risk, Coleman invests in just 10–12 stocks at any given time. In early 2000, Coleman was a top-ranked money manager, according to the trade magazine, *Pensions & Investments*. However, when the U.S. stock market turned from bullish to bearish, Coleman's returns swooned. In 2001, when the S&P 500 stock index dipped 12 percent, the value of Coleman's portfolio fell by 68 percent. The lackluster performance of Daedalus Capital's products continued in 2002, and investors began to appreciate just how risky Coleman's investment philosophy was. As investors took their funds elsewhere in a search for better returns, the money managed by Coleman declined to $30 million from a peak of $300 million.

In 2003, the U.S. stock market turned upward, and Coleman's returns skyrocketed. In the 12 months ending in September 2003, Daedalus's clients enjoyed a gain of 209 percent. *Pensions & Investments* once more put Coleman back at the top of their money manager rankings. Coleman's returns were more than 100 percentage points higher than those earned by the second-ranked money manager. A close inspection of Coleman's investment choices helps explain why his returns fluctuate so wildly. In most years, Coleman buys stock in high-technology companies, sometimes favoring those firms that appear to be on the brink of bankruptcy. For example, in late 2002, he purchased Nortel Networks at $1.01 per share and watched the stock rise to $4.20 in a few months. Since heading up the fund in 1995, Coleman earned an average annual return of 18 percent, compared to 12 percent for the S&P 500 Index. Investors who stayed with the fund over the past decade were well rewarded, but they must have had a lot of sleepless nights along the way.

Source: (1) "Daedalus' Coleman Outshines Rivals with 209% Return," by David Nicklaus, *St. Louis Post-Dispatch,* November 14, 2003; (2) "Daedalus' Coleman Invents His Own Way," *Investment Management Weekly,* April 26, 2004; (3) Daedalus Web site: http://www.wegrowmoney.com ■

LEARNING OBJECTIVES

After studying this chapter you should be able to:

- Calculate an investment's total return in dollar or percentage terms, identify the components of the total return, and explain why total return is a key metric for assessing an investment's performance;
- Describe the historical performance of asset classes such as Treasury bills, Treasury bonds, and common stocks and articulate the important lessons that history provides;
- Calculate the standard deviation from a series of historical returns; and
- Distinguish between systematic and unsystematic risk, explain why systematic risk is more closely linked to returns than is unsystematic risk, and illustrate how diversification reduces volatility.

Finance teaches that investment returns are related to risk. From a purely theoretical perspective, it seems logical that risk and return should be linked, but the notion that an unavoidable trade-off between the two exists is grounded in fact. In countries around the world, historical capital market data offer compelling evidence of a positive relationship between risk and return. That evidence is a major focus of this chapter.

Naturally, most of us like to earn high returns on the money we save and invest. The returns we earn (and therefore the additional consumption we can undertake later in life) represent the marginal benefit of investing. At the same time, most investors would rather avoid dramatic swings in their wealth. Unfortunately, the higher the return that investors desire, the greater the risk they must bear. Risk represents the marginal cost of investing. Therefore, when individuals decide how to invest their money, they have to weigh the marginal benefit of a higher return against the marginal cost of additional risk. Not everyone will strike this balance in exactly the same way, but the historical data on risk and return that we study in this chapter provides evidence that markets present investors with an unavoidable trade-off between risk and reward.

In Chapters 4 and 5, we argued that corporate bonds are more risky than U.S. Treasury securities and that common stocks are riskier than either corporate or Treasury bonds. Based on that assessment, we should expect a relationship like that shown in Figure 6.1. If we arrange these assets from least to most risky, we expect returns to rise, as we move from left to right in the figure. Soon we will see that this is exactly the pattern revealed by historical data.

What is it worth?—perhaps the most important question in finance. For an investor contemplating a stock purchase or for a corporate manager weighing a

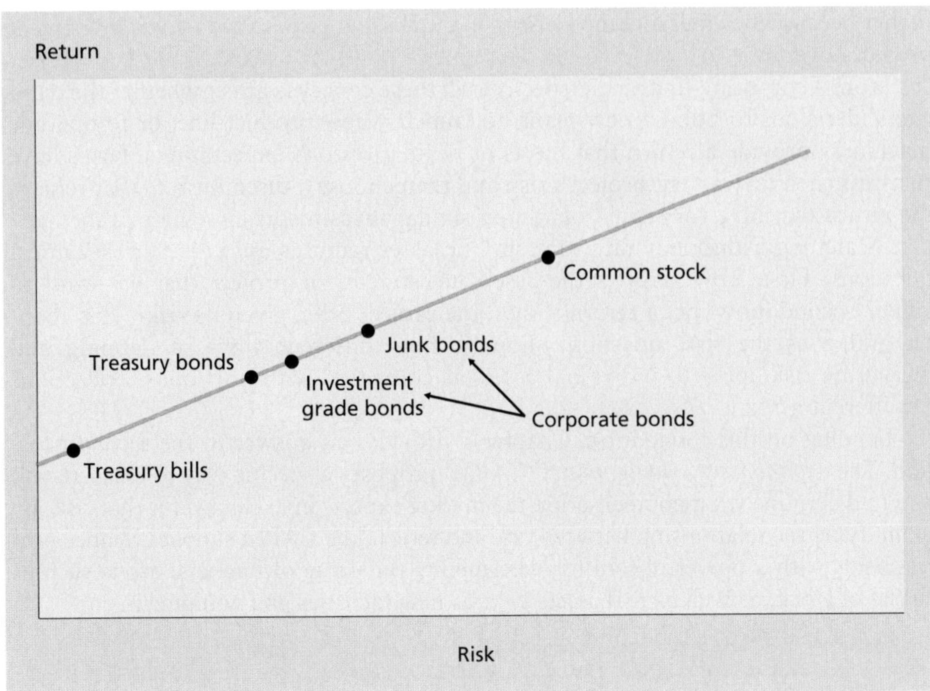

Figure 6.1
The Trade-off Between Risk and Return

Intuitively, we expect that investors seeking higher returns must be willing to accept higher risk. Moving along the line from safe assets such as Treasury bills to much riskier investments such as common stocks, returns should rise.

new plant construction proposal, placing a value on risky assets is fundamental to the decision-making process. The procedure for valuing a risky asset involves three basic steps:

(1) determining the asset's expected cash flows,
(2) choosing a discount rate that reflects the asset's risk, and
(3) calculating the present value.

Finance professionals apply these three steps, known as *discounted cash flow (DCF) analysis,* to value a wide range of real and financial assets. Chapter 3 introduced you to the rather mechanical third step of this process—converting a sequence of future cash flows into a single number reflecting an asset's present value. Chapters 4 and 5 focused more on the first step in the process—projecting future cash flows. In this chapter and in Chapter 7, we will emphasize the second step in DCF valuation—determining an appropriate discount rate.

We begin by establishing a precise measure of an investment's performance called the total return. An asset's total return captures any income that the asset pays as well as any changes in the asset's price. With the definition of total return in hand, we proceed to study the historical performance of broad asset classes such as stocks and bonds in the U.S. and other countries. Our analysis examines both the nominal and real returns that different investments have earned over time. During the last century, prices in the U.S. rose by a factor of 22. That is, the *purchasing power* of $1 in 1900 was roughly equivalent to the purchasing power of $22 today. Because inflation gradually erodes the value of a dollar, we focus on the real returns offered by various asset classes, not just their nominal returns. When people save their money and invest it, they do so in the hope of living more comfortably in the future. Their objective is not just to accumulate a large sum of money but to be able to spend that money to buy the necessities (and the luxuries) of life. Real returns matter because they measure the increase in purchasing power that a given investment provides over time.

From a corporate finance perspective, all these concerns affect whether the managers' decisions to build a new plant, to launch a new product line, or to upgrade machinery provide a return that meets or beats investor's expectations. Firms have to assess each investment project's risk and then choose a discount rate that reflects the return that investors could obtain on similar investments elsewhere in the market. Matching a discount rate to a specific asset requires answers to two critical questions. First, how risky is the asset, investment, or project that we want to value? Second, how much return should the project offer, given its risk? This chapter addresses the first question, showing how different ways of defining and measuring risk apply to individual assets as compared with *portfolios* (collections of different assets).

Building on this foundation, Chapter 7 provides an answer to the second question. The *capital asset pricing model (CAPM)* proposes a specific way to measure risk and to determine what compensation the market expects in exchange for that risk. By quantifying the relationship between risk and return, the CAPM supplies finance professionals with a powerful tool for determining the value of financial assets such as shares of stock, as well as real assets such as new factories and equipment.

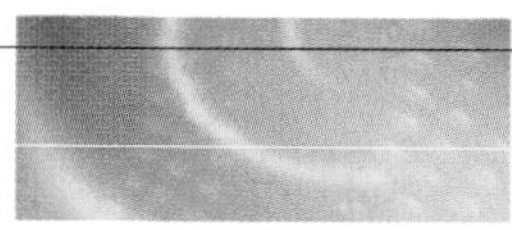

6.1 UNDERSTANDING RETURNS

Probably the first question that enters the mind of investors when they decide whether to undertake an investment is, "How much money will this investment earn?" In finance, we refer to the total gain or loss on an investment as the **total return**. The total return, expressed either in dollar terms or on a percentage basis, measures the increase (or decrease) in wealth that an investor experiences from holding a particular asset such as a share of common stock or a bond.

total return
A measure of the performance of an investment that captures both the income it paid and its capital gain or loss over a stated period of time.

The Components of Total Return

An investment's total return consists of two components. The first part is the income stream the investment produces. For bonds, the income stream comes in the form of interest. For common or preferred stock, dividends provide the income stream. As we learned in Chapters 4 and 5, the financial press regularly provides investment performance measures that primarily focus on an asset's income stream. For example, the *coupon yield,* which equals the coupon payment divided by the bond's market price, describes how much money the bondholder earns in interest as a percentage of the price of the bond. Similarly, the *dividend yield,* equal to a stock's annual dividend payment divided by the stock price, highlights the income component of stock returns.

Measures such as the coupon yield and dividend yield may provide investors with useful information, but any performance measure that focuses entirely on an investment's income stream misses the second, and often the most important, component of total returns. That component is the change in the asset's price, called the **capital gain** or **capital loss.** For some investments, such as zero-coupon bonds and stocks that do not pay dividends, the capital gain or loss is the *only* component of total return because there is no income. For other investments, the price change may be more or less important than the income stream in determining the investment's total return.

capital gain
The increase in the price of an asset that occurs over a period of time.

capital loss
The decrease in the price of an asset that occurs over a period of time.

For example, suppose that an investor spends $1,000 to purchase a newly issued 10-year corporate bond that pays an annual coupon of $60. In this case, the coupon rate and the coupon yield are both 6 percent ($60 ÷ $1,000). Because this bond sells at par value, we know that the market requires a six percent return on the bond. Suppose we want to assess the performance of this investment after one year. To do that, we need to add up both the income paid by the bond and any price change that occurs during the year. At the end of the year, the investor receives a $60 coupon payment, but what is her bond worth? We know from Chapter 4 that the answer to that question depends on what happens to market interest rates during the year. Suppose that the market's required return on this bond has risen from 6 percent to 8 percent. At the end of the first year, the bond has nine years left until maturity. Discounting the remaining cash flows at 8 percent, we find that the bond's market price equals just $875.06:

$$P = \frac{\$60}{1.08^1} + \frac{\$60}{1.08^2} + \frac{\$60}{1.08^3} + \ldots + \frac{\$1{,}060}{1.08^9} = \$875.06$$

The investor's total return is considerably less than the 6 percent coupon yield. In fact, the capital loss caused by rising interest rates results in a negative total return. The investor earns income of $60, but she also experiences a capital loss of $124.94 ($1,000 – $875.06). That loss more than offsets the interest payment, and our investor ends the year with less wealth than when she started.

Note that the investor's total return this year does not depend on whether she sells the bond or continues to hold it. Selling or not selling the bond determines whether the capital loss in this example is *realized* or *unrealized,* but it has no affect on the investor's wealth (at least if we ignore taxes). At the end of the year, the investor has $60 in cash plus a bond worth $875.06. That is equivalent to owning $935.06 in cash, which would be the investor's position if she sells the bond.[1] In any case, this example illustrates that both the income and capital gain or loss components influence an investor's wealth. *The important lesson to remember is that one must focus on the total return when assessing an investment's performance.*

Dollar Returns and Percentage Returns

We can describe an investment's total return either in dollar terms or in percentage terms. Consider again the bond example in the previous two paragraphs. To calculate the *dollar return* on this investment, we simply add the income component to the capital gain or loss:

$$\text{Total dollar return} = \text{income} + \text{capital gain or loss} \quad \text{(Eq. 6.1)}$$

Earlier we defined an investment's total return as the change in wealth that it generates for the investor. In the present example, the investor begins with $1,000.

1. Unrealized losses are sometimes called paper losses. This term simply means that the value of the paper that an investor holds, a bond or stock certificate, has gone down. Some investors believe that paper losses are irrelevant and that losses only matter when they are realized because an investor sells. We hope you will not be trapped by this fallacy. Bill Gates is one of the world's richest people because he owns a large quantity of Microsoft stock. If an antitrust action by the U.S. government causes Microsoft shares to fall by half, then Bill Gates is much less wealthy, even if he doesn't sell his stock. That his loss is only "on paper" does not mean that the loss isn't meaningful.

A year later, she receives \$60 and she owns a bond worth \$875.06. Therefore, end-of-year wealth equals \$935.06. The change in wealth during the year equals –\$64.94 (\$935.06 – \$1,000), which we can verify by plugging the appropriate values into Equation 6.1:

$$\text{Total dollar return} = \$60 + (-\$124.94) = -\$64.94$$

Dollar returns tell us, in an absolute sense, how much wealth an investment generates over time. Other things being equal, investors prefer assets that provide higher dollar returns. However, comparing the dollar returns of two different investments can be treacherous, as the following example illustrates.

APPLYING THE MODEL

Terrell purchases 100 shares of Micro-Orb stock for \$25 per share. A year later, the stock pays a dividend of \$1 per share and sells for \$30. Terrell's total dollar return is:

$$\text{Total dollar return} = (100 \text{ shares}) \times (\text{income} + \text{capital gain})$$

$$\text{Total dollar return} = 100 \times (\$1 + \$5) = \$600$$

Meanwhile, Owen purchases 50 shares of Garcia Transportation Inc. for \$15 per share. Garcia shares pay no dividends, but at the end of the year, the stock sells for \$25. Owen's total dollar return equals:

$$\text{Total dollar return} = 50 \times (\$10) = \$500$$

Based on these figures, it appears that Terrell had a better year than Owen did. But before we reach that conclusion, we ought to recognize that at the beginning of the year, Terrell's investment was much larger than Owen's.

The preceding example illustrates a problem we encounter when comparing dollar returns on different investments. Terrell's dollar return exceeds Owen's by \$100, but that does not necessarily mean that Terrell's stock performed better. Terrell spent \$2,500 to purchase 100 Micro-Orb shares, while Owen devoted just \$750 to his investment in Garcia Transportation. Intuitively, we might expect Terrell to earn a higher dollar return than Owen because he invested so much more than Owen did.

Another way to compare outcomes is to calculate the *percentage return* on each investment. The total percentage return equals the total dollar return divided by the initial investment:

$$\text{Total percentage return} = \text{total dollar return} \div \text{initial investment} \quad \text{(Eq. 6.2)}$$

APPLYING THE MODEL

Given that Terrell initially invested \$2,500, while Owen invested just \$750, we can calculate their total returns on a percentage basis as follows:

$$\text{Terrell's return} = \frac{100 \times (\$1 + \$5)}{\$2,500} = \frac{\$600}{\$2,500} = 0.24 = 24\%$$

$$\text{Owen's return} = \frac{50 \times (\$10)}{\$750} = \frac{\$500}{\$750} = 0.67 = 67\%$$

On a percentage basis, Owen's investment performed better than Terrell's did, but on a dollar return basis the opposite is true. The conflict arises here because the initial amount invested by Terrell is so much larger than Owen's up-front investment. Which investment would you rather have, one that makes you \$600 richer or one that increases your initial stake by 67 percent? Comparing the returns on investments that involve different amounts of money is a fundamental problem to which we will return in Chapter 8. For now, we only say that dollar returns and percentage returns can lead to different relative rankings of investment alternatives.

Just as the total dollar return was the sum of an investment's income and its capital gain or loss, *the total percentage return equals the sum of the investment's yield and its percentage capital gain or loss.* Recall that the dividend yield equals a stock's dividend divided by its market price. Using the beginning-of-year price of Micro-Orb stock to calculate its dividend yield, we have:

$$\text{Micro-Orb dividend yield} = \$1 \div \$25 = 0.04 = 4\%$$

Similarly, the percentage capital gain equals:

$$\text{Micro-Orb capital gain} = \$5 \div \$25 = 0.20 = 20\%$$

Therefore, the total percentage return on Micro-Orb equals the sum of the dividend yield and the percentage capital gain:

$$\text{Micro-Orb total percentage return} = 4\% + 20\% = 24\%$$

To summarize the important points from this section,

- Measuring an investment's performance requires a focus on total return.
- The total return consists of two components, income and capital gain or loss.
- We can express total returns either in dollar terms or in percentage terms.
- When ranking the performance of two or more investments relative to each other, it is important to be careful that the amount of money initially invested in each asset is the same.
- If one asset requires a much larger up-front monetary commitment than the other, then dollar returns and percentage returns may lead to different performance rankings.

CONCEPT REVIEW QUESTIONS

1. In Chapter 4, we defined several bond return measures, including the *coupon*, the *coupon rate*, the *coupon yield*, and the *yield to maturity*. Indicate whether each of these measures (a) focuses on the total return or just one of the components of total return and (b) focuses on dollar returns or percentage returns.

2. You buy a stock for $40. During the next year, it pays a dividend of $2, and its price increases to $44. Calculate the total dollar and total percentage return and show that each of these is the sum of the dividend and capital gain components.

6.2 THE HISTORY OF RETURNS (OR HOW TO GET RICH SLOWLY)

British writer Aldous Huxley once said, "That men do not learn very much from the lessons of history is the most important of all lessons that history has to teach." We are more optimistic. Certainly what we can learn from the history of financial markets benefits investors who study that history. Perhaps the most important lesson is this: an unavoidable trade-off exists between risk and return, so investors seeking higher returns almost always have to accept higher risk.

Nominal and Real Returns on Stocks, Bonds, and Bills

Figure 6.2 shows how a one-dollar investment in each of three different asset classes grew over the last 104 years in the United States.[2] The three types of investments shown in the figure are Treasury bills, long-term Treasury bonds, and common stocks. Recall from Chapter 4 that *Treasury bills* are among the safest investments in the world. They mature in one year or less and thus are not highly sensitive to interest rate movements.[3] They are backed by the full faith and credit of the U.S. government. *Treasury bonds* receive that same backing, but because they are long-term instruments, their prices can fluctuate dramatically as interest rates change. Common stocks are the riskiest of the three investments. As you know by now, the performance of a particular stock depends on the ability of the company to generate cash. Investors have no guarantee when they buy stock that it will perform well.

A quick glance at Figure 6.2 reveals that from 1900–2003, common stocks far outperformed Treasury bonds and bills.[4] One dollar invested in a portfolio of common stocks in 1900 grew to $15,579 by the end of 2003. In contrast, a one-dollar investment in T-bonds or T-bills grew to just $148 or $61, respectively. In comparing the values of these investments in 1900 to their 2003 levels, it is important to remember that the price level in the U.S. was not constant over this period. The fourth line in Figure 6.2 shows how inflation gradually changed the purchasing power of a dollar. The figure shows that the price level increased by a factor of 22 from 1900 to 2003, which means that the purchasing power of $1 in 1900 is roughly equivalent to the purchasing power of $22 in 2003.

2. The term "asset class" simply refers to a distinct type of investment or to a group of assets that share common characteristics.

3. Or, using terms we have learned, they carry negligible interest rate risk and no default risk.

4. The lines in this figure incorporate both the income component and the capital gain component of returns, and they assume that the initial investment and the total dollar return on each asset are reinvested each year.

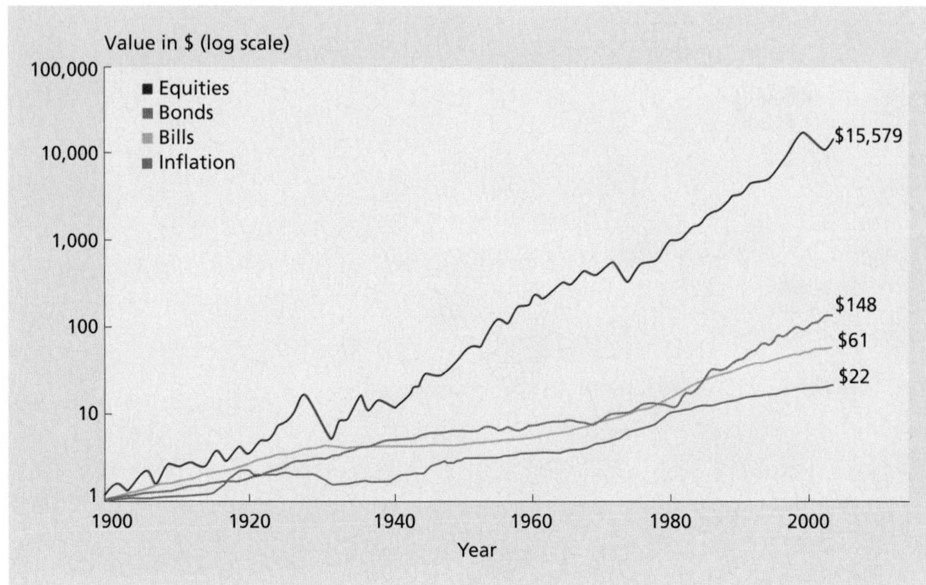

Figure 6.2
The Value of $1 Invested in Equities, Treasury Bonds, and Bills, 1900–2003

The figure shows that $1 invested in common stocks in 1900 would have grown to $15,579 by 2003. In comparison, one dollar invested in Treasury bonds would have grown to $148, while a dollar invested in Treasury bills would have reached just $61 by 2003.

Source: Triumph of the Optimists, 101 Years of Global Investment Returns, *by Elroy Dimson, Paul Marsh, Mike Staunton. Published by Princeton University Press. Additional updates provided by Dimson, et al. Reprinted with permission.*

Figure 6.3 takes inflation out of the picture by plotting the performance of the three types of investments in *real,* inflation-adjusted terms.[5] Even after adjusting for inflation, Figure 6.3 demonstrates that common stocks outperformed other investments, increasing in real terms from $1 to $719 in 104 years. As before, the increase in wealth from investing in Treasury bonds or bills was far less. In fact, a one-dollar investment in Treasury bills grew, in real terms, to just $2.8 over the century. You have to wait a long time to get rich if you are investing in Treasury bills.

The Risk Dimension

In both Figure 6.2 and Figure 6.3 another important difference between the three asset classes emerges. The line plotting the growth of one dollar invested in Treasury bills is relatively smooth. The line for bonds moves up and down a little more, and the line representing common stocks looks very jagged indeed. This implies that although a portfolio invested entirely in common stocks grows more rapidly than a portfolio invested in either bonds or bills, the common stock portfolio displays more dramatic ups and downs from year to year. In the long run, common stock investors

[5] Recall that the relationship between nominal returns, real returns, and inflation is given by the following equation:

$$(1 + \text{nominal}) = (1 + \text{real})(1 + \text{inflation})$$

If the nominal return on a share of stock is 15 percent in a certain year and the inflation rate is 10 percent, then we can solve for the real rate as follows:

$$(1 + 0.15) = (1 + \text{real})(1 + 0.10)$$
$$(1 + \text{real}) = (1 + 0.15) \div (1 + 0.10)$$
$$(1 + \text{real}) = 1.0454$$
$$\text{real} = 0.0454 = 4.54\%$$

Figure 6.3
The Real Value of $1 Invested in Equities, Treasury Bonds, or Bills, 1900–2003

Source: Triumph of the Optimists, 101 Years of Global Investment Returns, *by Elroy Dimson, Paul Marsh, Mike Staunton. Published by Princeton University Press. Additional updates provided by Dimson, et al. Reprinted with permission.*

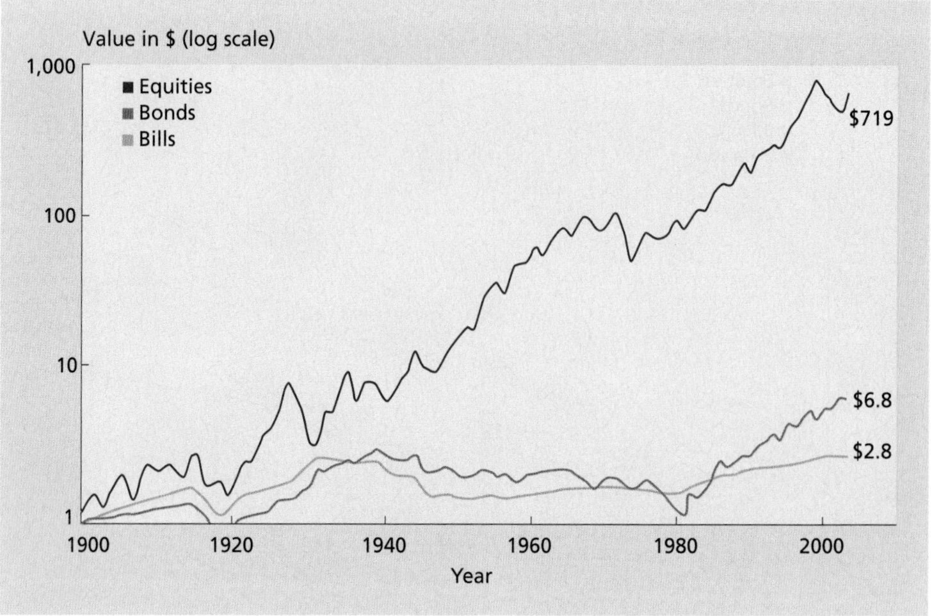

may grow wealthier than bond investors do, but their path to riches is a bumpy one. Some investors may be willing to pass up higher returns on stocks in exchange for the additional security of bonds or bills.

Table 6.1 summarizes the information in Figures 6.2 and 6.3. Both in nominal and in real terms, the average return on equities is far higher than the average return on Treasury bonds or bills.[6] However, notice the difference in returns between the best and worst years for common stocks, and compare that to the differences in the best and worst years for the other asset classes. In 1933, common stocks experienced their highest nominal return of 57.6 percent, but that outstanding performance followed on the heels of the worst year for stocks, 1931, with a nominal return of −43.9 percent. The difference in the best and the worst in returns is more than 100 percent! In contrast, Treasury bills moved within a much narrower band, with a top nominal return of 14.7 percent and a minimum nominal return of 0 percent.

Figure 6.4 shows the nominal return for each of the three asset classes in every year from 1900–2003. The wider range of outcomes on stocks relative to Treasury bonds, and likewise on bonds relative to bills, is readily apparent. But so is the tendency for stocks to earn higher average returns than T-bonds and for T-bonds to outperform T-bills. Figure 6.4 highlights the average return for each investment, the best and worst years, and a few recent years for comparison. Notice that 2003 was a particularly good year for stocks, in sharp contrast to 2002, which was a poor year. Just the opposite was true for Treasury bonds, with above-average returns in 2002 and below-average returns in 2003.

---

[6] The formula for calculating the average return is straightforward. If there are N years of historical data and the return in any particular year t is R_t, then the average return equals the sum of the individual returns divided by N:

$$\text{Average return} = \frac{\sum_{t=1}^{N} R_t}{N}$$

Table 6.1
Percentage Returns on Bills, Bonds, and Stocks, 1900–2003

Stocks earn the highest average returns, but they fluctuate over a wide range. Treasury bill returns move within a fairly narrow range, but T-bills earn low average returns. Treasury bonds fall between stocks and bills along both dimensions.

	Nominal (%)			Real (%)		
Asset Class	Average	Best Year	Worst Year	Average	Best Year	Worst Year
Bills	4.1	14.7	0.0	1.1	19.7	–15.1
Bonds	5.2	40.4	–9.2	2.3	35.1	–19.4
Stocks	11.7	57.6	–43.9	8.5	56.8	–38.0

Source: Triumph of the Optimists, 101 Years of Global Investment Returns, *by Elroy Dimson, Paul Marsh, Mike Staunton. Published by Princeton University Press. Additional updates provided by Dimson, et al. Reprinted with permission.*

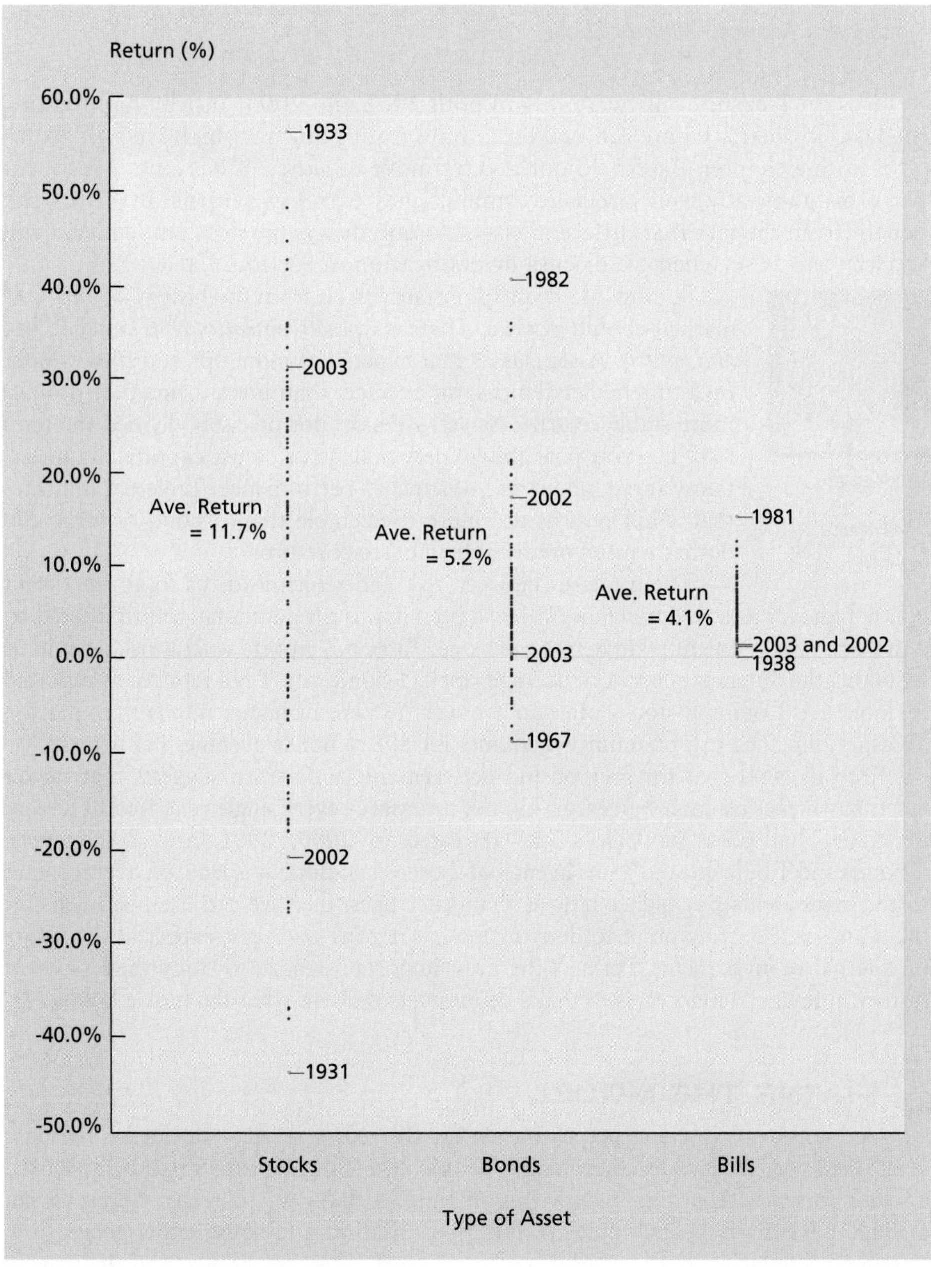

Figure 6.4
Nominal Returns on Stocks, Treasury Bonds, and Bills, 1900–2003

The dots in the figure show the return on each asset class in every year from 1900–2003. Notice that common stock returns cover a wider range than returns on Treasury bonds or bills. But common stocks also earn the highest average returns. Observe how stocks and bonds moved in opposite directions in 2002 and 2003.

Source: Triumph of the Optimists, 101 Years of Global Investment Returns, *by Elroy Dimson, Paul Marsh, Mike Staunton. Published by Princeton University Press. Additional updates provided by Dimson, et al. Reprinted with permission.*

Table 6.2
Risk Premiums for Stocks, Bonds, and Bills, 1900–2003

The risk premium refers to the additional return offered by an investment, relative to an alternative, because it is more risky than the alternative. Stocks offer a risk premium over Treasury bonds and bills, and T-bonds offer a risk premium over T-bills.

Comparison	Risk Premium (%)
Stocks – Bills	11.7 – 4.1 = 7.6
Stocks – Bonds	11.7 – 5.2 = 6.5
Bonds – Bills	5.2 – 4.1 = 1.1

Source: Triumph of the Optimists, 101 Years of Global Investment Returns, *by Elroy Dimson, Paul Marsh, Mike Staunton. Published by Princeton University Press. Additional updates provided by Dimson, et al. Reprinted with permission.*

Returns on Treasury bills were low in both 2002 and 2003. Just by highlighting the last few years, Figure 6.4 makes an important point to which we will return later in this chapter. Assets do not always move together. When one investment performs unusually well, other investments may earn low returns. Investors can benefit from the fact that different assets do not always move in tandem. We will see why this is so when we discuss diversification in Section 6.4.

By now the most important lesson from the history of financial markets should be clear. *There is a positive relationship between risk and return.* Asset classes that experience more ups and downs offer investors higher returns, on average, than investments that provide more stable returns. As yet, we have not precisely defined the term risk, but you probably expect that "risk" must capture the uncertainty surrounding an investment's performance. Table 6.1 indicates that T-bill returns are more predictable than T-bond returns, and both are more predictable than stock returns.

risk premium
The additional return that an investment must offer, relative to some alternative, because it is more risky than the alternative.

The trade-off between risk and return leads us to an important concept known as a **risk premium**. The risk premium is the additional return offered by a more risky investment relative to a safer one. Table 6.2 reports several risk premiums by taking the differences between average stock, T-bond, and T-bill returns, as reported in Table 6.1. Common stocks offer an average 7.6 percent higher return than that on Treasury bills. The risk premium on equities relative to bonds averages 6.5 percent.

Keep in mind that the relationship between risk and return suggests that riskier assets pay higher returns *on average,* but not necessarily every single year. Recent history illustrates that point as U.S. stocks retreated in 2000, 2001, and 2002, while T-bonds and T-bills showed gains in each of those years. But if it is true, on average, that riskier investments pay higher returns than safer ones, then we can use historical risk premiums as a starting point to determine what returns we might expect in the future on alternative investments. Perhaps the most important reason to study the lessons of history in financial markets is to make better guesses about what the future holds.

APPLYING THE MODEL

Suppose you want to construct a forecast for the return on U.S. stocks for the next year. One approach is to use the average historical value, 11.7 percent (from Table 6.1), as your forecast. A problem with this method is that 11.7 percent represents an average over many years, some having high inflation and some experiencing low inflation. Similarly, in some past years, interest rates on bonds and bills were relatively high; in other years, rates were much lower. You can make use of current market information to construct a better forecast than the average historical return.

For example, suppose you look at Treasury bills trading in the market at the time that you want to develop a forecast for equity returns. At that time, you find that Treasury bills offer a yield to maturity of about 2 percent. From Table 6.2, you see that the average risk premium on equities relative to T-bills is 7.6 percent. Add that premium to the current Treasury bill yield to arrive at a forecast for equity returns of 9.6 percent (2% + 7.6%). This should be a superior forecast compared to the simple historical average because the estimate of 9.6 percent reflects current market conditions (such as expected inflation rates and required returns on low-risk investments).

Analysts use data on risk premiums for many different purposes. In Chapter 4, we saw that bonds receiving lower ratings from bond-rating agencies must pay higher yields. Bond traders know this and use data on the risk premium between relatively safe bonds (like Treasury bonds or AAA-rated corporate bonds) and riskier bonds to price complex financial instruments. As we will see in future chapters, corporate executives use the risk premium on equities relative to Treasury securities to estimate the rate of return that their investors expect on major capital expenditures. We will return to the subject of the equity risk premium several times in this book, but next, we need to explore the meaning of the word *risk* in more depth.

CONCEPT REVIEW QUESTIONS

3. Why do investors need to pay attention to *real returns*, as well as *nominal returns*?

4. Look at Figure 6.3. The figure is drawn using a logarithmic vertical scale which means that if an investment offers a constant rate of return over time, the growing value of that investment would plot as a straight line. This implies that the steeper the line is, the higher is the rate of return on the investment. Given this, which investment looks like it performed best in *real terms* from 1920–1930? What about from 1999–2003?

5. In Table 6.1, why are the *average real returns* lower than the *average nominal returns* for each asset class? Is it always true that an asset's nominal return is higher than its real return?

6.3 VOLATILITY AND RISK

The Distribution of Historical Stock Returns

We begin our analysis of risk with one more historical illustration. Figure 6.5 shows a histogram of stock returns since 1900. The shape of this histogram is probably familiar to you because it is somewhat reminiscent of a bell curve, also known as a *normal distribution*. In most years, stocks earned a return not far from the historical average of 11.7 percent. Of the 104 annual returns shown in the figure, more than half (58 to be exact) fall in a range between 0 and 30 percent. Extremely high or low returns occur less frequently. The only two years that showed losses of 30 percent or more were 1931 and 1937, while 1933 and 1954 were the only two years in which stocks rose more than 50 percent. Collectively, these years with very high or very low returns represent about 4 percent of the data from the last century.

Figure 6.5 gives us a sense that stock returns can be quite volatile, and it tells us something about the relative frequencies of different outcomes in the U.S. stock market. We are interested in these frequencies not only for their historical significance but also

< -30	-30 to -20	-20 to -10	-10 to 0	0 to 10	10 to 20	20 to 30	30 to 40	40 to 50	> 50
						1999			
						1998			
						1996			
						1989			
						1983			
				1992		1979			
				1987		1976			
				1984		1967			
				1978		1963			
				1970	1993	1961			
				1960	1988	1955			
				1956	1986	1951	2003		
			1994	1953	1982	1950	1997		
			1990	1948	1972	1949	1995		
		2001	1981	1947	1971	1944	1991		
		2000	1977	1939	1968	1943	1985		
		1973	1966	1934	1965	1938	1980		
		1969	1946	1926	1964	1925	1975		
		1962	1941	1923	1959	1924	1945		
		1957	1940	1916	1952	1919	1936		
	2002	1929	1932	1912	1942	1909	1928		
	1974	1920	1914	1911	1921	1905	1927	1958	
1937	1930	1917	1913	1906	1918	1904	1922	1935	1954
1931	1907	1903	1910	1902	1901	1900	1915	1908	1933

Percent Return in a Given Year

Figure 6.5
Histogram of Nominal Returns on Equities, 1900–2003

The figure illustrates the performance of stocks in the U.S. in every year from 1900–2003. For example, stock returns were between –20% and –30% in 1907, 1930, 1974, and 2002. The figure suggests that the historical distribution of stock returns is at least roughly approximated by a bell curve, or a normal distribution.

Source: Triumph of the Optimists, 101 Years of Global Investment Returns, *by Elroy Dimson, Paul Marsh, Mike Staunton. Published by Princeton University Press. Additional updates provided by Dimson, et al. Reprinted with permission.*

for what they may tell us about future stock market returns. For example, a question that investors may want to ask is, "What is the probability that a portfolio of stocks will lose money in any given year?" Without a crystal ball, no one can answer that question precisely, but a close inspection of Figure 6.5 shows that returns were negative in 28 out of the last 104 years, or about 27 percent of the time. At least as a starting point, we can estimate a 27 percent probability that stocks will lose money in a particular year.

If we could list every possible outcome that might occur in the stock market and attach an exact probability to each outcome, then we would have a *probability distribution*. Some probability distributions are easy to describe. For example, the probability distribution that governs outcomes of a coin toss is given below:

Outcome	Probability
Heads	50%
Tails	50%

Unfortunately, the probability distribution for future stock returns is unknown. We rely on Figure 6.5 to give us clues about the characteristics of this distribution. From the shape of the figure, we may conjecture that the unknown distribution of stock returns is a normal curve with a mean return (or average return) of

11.7 percent. A normal distribution is symmetric, so there is an equal chance of experiencing an above-average and a below-average outcome. Since 1900, the split between above-average and below-average years in the stock market is 55 to 49, very close to even. This suggests that our assumption of an underlying normal distribution may be a good approximation to reality.[7]

The Variability of Stock Returns

variance
A measure of volatility equal to the sum of squared deviations from the mean divided by one less than the number of observations in the sample.

Every normal distribution has two key characteristics: its mean and its variance. As you may recall from statistics, the **variance** measures the dispersion of observations around the mean of the distribution. To be more precise, the variance is the expected value (or the average value) of squared deviations from the mean. In equations, variance is usually noted by the Greek symbol σ^2. Suppose we are estimating the variance of stock returns using N years of historical data. The return in any given year t is R_t, and the average return is $\overline{R}$. We calculate the variance using the equation below:

$$\text{Variance} = \sigma^2 = \frac{\sum_{t=1}^{N}(R_t - \overline{R})^2}{N-1} \qquad \text{(Eq. 6.3)}$$

Table 6.3 illustrates a variance calculation using stock returns in the U.S. from 1994–2003. Over this period, the average annual return equals 12.5 percent, almost a full percentage point more than the 11.7 percent historical average from 1900–2003. In the table's third column, we subtract the average return from the actual return in each year. The fourth column squares that difference. We square deviations from the mean so that both positive and negative deviations contribute to the variance calculation. If we simply added up positive and negative deviations from the mean, then the resulting sum would be zero by virtue of the definition of a mean. To find the variance, add up the numbers in the fourth column and then divide the sum by nine.[8] The calculations show that the variance of stock returns equals 442.2. Interpreting the number 444.2 is a little tricky because it is expressed in units of percent squared. Remember, to calculate the variance we worked with numbers in percent form and then squared them. What exactly does 444.2%^{2} mean?

Fortunately, we don't have to struggle to interpret these odd units. Instead, if we take the square root of the variance, we are back in percentage units, and we have the standard deviation. The **standard deviation** is just another measure of dispersion around the mean, but in the case of investment returns, it is easier to interpret because it is expressed in percentage terms.

standard deviation
A measure of volatility equal to the square root of variance.

7. Extensive research on the distribution of equity return teaches us that the normal distribution is only a rough approximation of the actual returns distribution. For example, equity returns do not appear to be distributed symmetrically around the mean. This makes sense in light of the limited liability feature of the U.S. legal system. A fortunate stockholder might earn a return in excess of 100 percent in any given year, but no investors can experience a loss greater than 100 percent (unless they are buying stocks using borrowed money). When we examine historical stock returns, we do observe outcomes that are far above the mean more frequently than we see outcomes well below the mean.

8. You may wonder why we are dividing by 9 if we have ten years of data. The reason is technical and has to do with a statistical concept, known as degrees of freedom. The technical issue is not terribly important here, and with a very large sample, dividing by either N or N–1 will make little difference in the variance calculation. The careful reader may also wonder whether the first entry in the table's third column is a typo. The third column shows the difference between the yearly return reported in the second column and the average return of 12.5 percent. You might expect the first entry in column three to be –12.6 (–0.1 – 12.5). However, the entry of –12.5 is correct and appears to be off by 0.1 due to rounding.

Table 6.3
Calculating the Variance of Stock Returns from 1994–2003

To calculate the variance, first find the average return. Next, take the difference between the actual return in each year and the average return, then square that difference. Add up the squared differences and divide the sum by one less than the number of years in the sample.

Source: Triumph of the Optimists, 101 Years of Global Investment Returns, *by Elroy Dimson, Paul Marsh, Mike Staunton. Published by Princeton University Press. Additional updates provided by Dimson, et al and based upon Megginson and Smart's calculations. Reprinted with permission.*

Year	Return (%)	Return(%) – 12.5	(Return(%) – 12.5)^2
1994	–0.1	–12.5	157.3
1995	36.4	24.0	574.5
1996	21.2	8.7	76.3
1997	31.3	18.8	353.9
1998	23.4	11.0	119.9
1999	23.6	11.1	122.8
2000	–10.9	–23.4	546.3
2001	–11.0	–23.5	550.0
2002	–20.9	–33.3	1,111.5
2003	31.6	19.2	367.2
Sum	124.8		3,979.7
Average Return	**12.5** (124.8 ÷ 10)		
Variance			**442.2** (3,979.7 ÷ 9)
Standard deviation			**21.0**

$$\text{Standard deviation} = \sqrt{\text{variance}} = \sqrt{442.2} = 21.0\%$$

If we use the complete 104-year history of U.S. returns, rather than just the last decade, we arrive at the following estimates of the mean and standard deviation of historical returns:

$$\text{average return} = 11.7\% \qquad \text{standard deviation} = 20.1\%$$

SMART EXCEL
See this problem explained in Excel at SMARTFinance

These figures indicate that the U.S. experience from 1994–2003 described in Table 6.3, is roughly similar to the entire twentieth century. The mean and the standard deviation were both about 1 percent higher in the last decade compared to the last century.

Let's return to our assumption that the underlying probability distribution governing stock returns is approximately normal. We now have estimates of the mean (11.7%) and the standard deviation (20.1%) of that distribution. Those estimates allow us to make a few other interesting descriptive statements about the behavior of common stocks. First, for any normal distribution, 68 percent of all observations fall between one standard deviation above and one standard deviation below the mean, and 95 percent of the observations should be within two standard deviations of the mean. In the present context, this implies that stock returns should fall between –8.4 percent and 31.8 percent (11.7 plus or minus 20.1) in a little more than two thirds of the years. Returns greater than 51.9 percent or less than –28.5 percent (11.7 plus or minus 40.2) should occur about 5 percent of the time. How does that prediction compare with the historical evidence? From 1900–2003, returns fell within the range of –8.4 to 31.8 percent in 69 years, or 66.3 percent of the time. There was only one year with a return greater than 51.9 percent, and there were three years with returns less than –28.5 percent. So these extreme, "two-sigma" outliers occurred a little less than 4 percent of the time. All in all, the distribution of historical returns seems very close to a bell curve.

Table 6.4 shows the average annual return and the standard deviation of returns for stocks, Treasury bonds and Treasury bills during the last century. We saw the

Table 6.4
Average Returns and Standard Deviation for Equities, Bonds, and Bills, (1900–2003)

	Nominal Returns		Real Returns	
Asset	Average (%)	Std. Dev. (%)	Average(%)	Std. Dev.(%)
Equities	11.7	20.1	8.5	20.4
Bonds	5.2	8.2	2.3	10.0
Bills	4.1	2.8	1.1	4.7

Source: Triumph of the Optimists, 101 Years of Global Investment Returns, *by Elroy Dimson, Paul Marsh, Mike Staunton. Published by Princeton University Press. Additional updates provided by Dimson, et al. Reprinted with permission.*

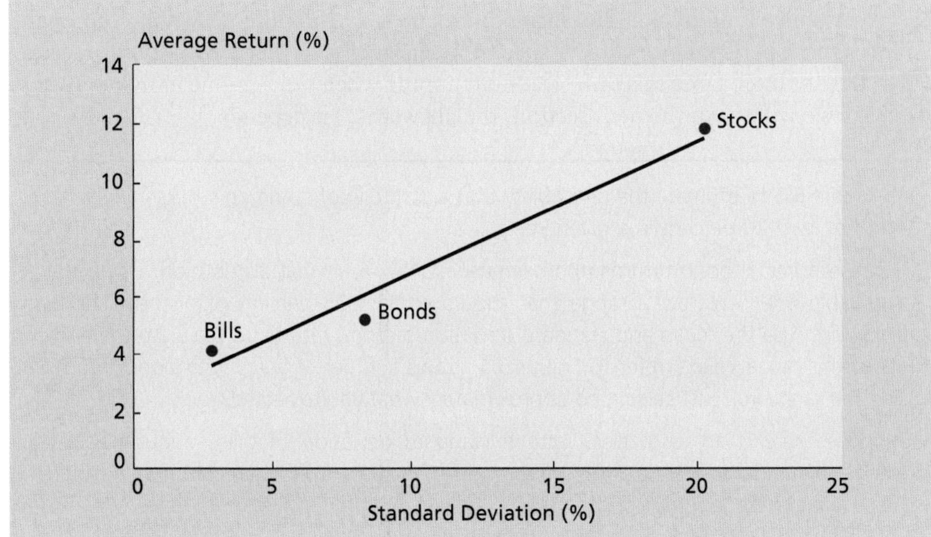

Figure 6.6
The Relationship Between Average (Nominal) Return and Standard Deviation for Stocks, Treasury Bonds, and Bills, 1900–2003

The figure indicates that a positive relationship exists between the average returns offered by an asset class and the standard deviation of returns.

Source: Triumph of the Optimists, 101 Years of Global Investment Returns, *by Elroy Dimson, Paul Marsh, Mike Staunton. Published by Princeton University Press. Additional updates provided by Dimson, et al. Reprinted with permission.*

average returns previously in Table 6.1, but now we have a specific measure of risk to couple with the mean returns. Once again, we see evidence that risk and return are positively linked, at least if we define risk to mean volatility (as captured by standard deviation). The average return on stocks is more than double the average bond return, but stocks are roughly 2.5 times more volatile than bonds. Bonds offer a premium over bills, but the standard deviation of bond returns is nearly three times the standard deviation for bills. Switching from nominal to real returns lowers the average returns, but it does not change the basic story. Asset classes that display greater volatility pay higher returns on average.

Figure 6.6 plots the relationship between average returns and standard deviation for stocks, bonds, and bills. In the figure, we chose to plot nominal returns, but switching to real returns would make very little difference. The figure also includes a trend line through the three data points. Notice that the relationship shown in the figure is almost perfectly linear, meaning that the dots fall very close to the trend line.[9]

[9] The trend line here is estimated using linear regression. We will discuss regression lines again in Chapter 7, but you may recall that a measure of "goodness of fit" for a regression line is the R-square statistic. The R-square value ranges between 0 percent and 100 percent, with a higher number indicating a stronger relationship between the two variables. In Figure 6.6, the R-square value of our line is almost 97, indicating a very tight relationship between standard deviation and returns.

This is not the last time that we will see evidence of a straight-line relationship between risk and return. What are the implications of such a relationship? The most important implications are that (1) investors who want higher returns have to take more risk, and (2) the incremental reward from accepting more risk is constant. In other words, if an investor wants to increase his return from 5 percent to 10 percent, the additional risk that he has to accept is the same as the additional risk that another investor has to accept to increase her returns from 10 percent to 15 percent. In economics, we frequently see evidence of diminishing returns. This evidence shows up in graphs as a curve with a decreasing slope. For example, a factory can produce more output if there are more workers present, but at some point the incremental output produced by an additional worker (i.e., the marginal product) begins to fall as diminishing returns set in. With respect to risk and return, Figure 6.6 shows no similar evidence of diminishing returns to risk taking.

Thus far, we have seen that a trade-off between risk and return exists for major asset classes including stocks, Treasury bonds, and bills. Suppose we want to compare the investment performance of two specific assets such as a share of General Electric and a share of Intel. Does this same trade-off appear when we examine individual securities? As we will see in the next section, the answer is, "it depends."

CONCEPT REVIEW QUESTIONS

6. Use Figure 6.5 to estimate the probability that a portfolio of common stocks will earn a return of at least 20 percent in a given year.

7. Suppose nominal bond returns approximately follow a normal distribution. Using the data in Table 6.4, construct a range that should contain 95 percent of historical bond returns. (*Hint:* Use the mean and standard deviation of bond returns to calculate the endpoints of this range.) Next, refer to Figure 6.4. Is the number of years with bond returns outside the range you just calculated approximately what you expected?

8. Suppose there is an asset class with a standard deviation that lies about halfway between the standard deviations of stocks and bonds. Based on Figure 6.6, what would you expect the average return on this asset class to be?

6.4 THE POWER OF DIVERSIFICATION

Systematic and Unsystematic Risk

In this section, our objective is to take the lessons we've learned about risk and return for major asset classes and apply those lessons to individual securities. As a starting point, examine Table 6.5 which shows the average annual return and the standard deviation of returns during the past decade for several well-known stocks. The average return and the average standard deviation for this group of stocks appear at the bottom of the table. Several observations are in order.

First, the average return for this group of stocks is higher than the average return for all stocks in the last ten years, as shown in Table 6.3. This group's average return is 14.7 percent. Perhaps one reason these firms are so familiar is because they have performed relatively well in the recent past. Second, and more important, most of these individual stocks have a much higher standard deviation than was reported in Table 6.3, where we showed that a *portfolio* of all common stocks had a standard deviation of 21.0 percent from 1994–2003. Table 6.5 illustrates that ten of eleven individual stocks have a standard deviation in excess of 21.0 percent. In

Company	Ave. Return (%)	Std Deviation (%)
Anheuser-Busch	19.2	16.1
Coca-Cola	12.1	22.6
Wendy's International	11.8	23.3
Archer Daniels Midland	7.6	23.5
General Motors	8.3	26.0
General Electric	20.3	32.1
Merck	17.8	32.7
Nordstrom	14.3	38.1
Wal-Mart	22.7	44.7
American Airlines (AMR)	10.0	47.8
Advanced Micro Devices	17.6	56.4
Average for all 11 stocks	**14.7**	**33.0**

Table 6.5
Average Returns and Standard Deviation for 11 Stocks (1994–2003)

Compared to the figures reported for all common stocks in Table 6.3, these stocks earned slightly higher returns, but their standard deviations were much higher.

Source: Megginson and Smart's computations using data from the Center on Research on Security Prices.

fact, the average standard deviation across these eleven securities is 33.0 percent. Is that because we are featuring riskier-than-average stocks in Table 6.5?

In fact, the stocks listed in this table are not unusually volatile. Most of these firms are corporate giants, household names because of their past success. The truth is that these companies are *less volatile* than the average firm with publicly traded stock. From 1994–2003, the standard deviation of the typical stock in the U.S. was about 60 percent per year! That raises an interesting question. *If the average stock's standard deviation is about 60 percent, then how can the standard deviation of the entire stock market be only 21 percent?*

This is a key point. Individual stocks generally display much higher volatility than portfolios of stocks do.[10] **Diversification**, the act of investing in many different assets rather than just one or two, explains why a portfolio usually has a lower standard deviation than the individual stocks that make up that portfolio. We can offer some simple intuition to explain this. In any given year, some stocks in a portfolio will have high returns, while other stocks in the portfolio will earn lower returns. Each year, the ups and downs of individual stocks at least partially cancel each other out, so the standard deviation of the portfolio is less than the standard deviations of the individual stocks. The diversification principle works not only for individual stocks but also for broad classes of investments such as stocks trading in different countries.

diversification
The act of investing in many different assets rather than just a few.

Figure 6.7 on page 268 demonstrates the impact of diversification with just two stocks, Coca-Cola and Wendy's International. In each year from 1994–2003, we plot the return on these two stocks. Recall from Table 6.5 that both Coca-Cola and Wendy's have an average return close to 12 percent, so we have drawn a horizontal line across the bar chart to highlight the average performance for these firms. Notice that in the years 1995, 1997–1999, and 2002–2003, Coca-Cola's returns and Wendy's returns were moving together in the sense that both stocks displayed above-average or below-average performance in the same year. However, in 1994, 1996, 2000, and 2001, one stock had an above-average year, while the other had a below-average year. What would happen if we formed a portfolio by investing some of our money in Coca-Cola and the rest in Wendy's?

10. The same statement could be made for other types of assets (e.g., individual bonds are more volatile than a portfolio of bonds).

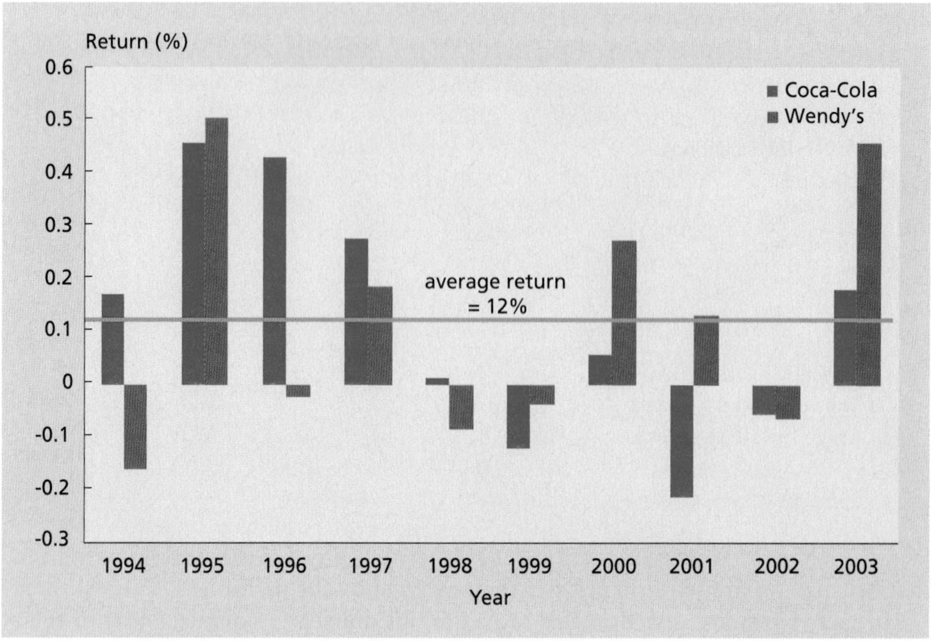

Figure 6.7
Annual Returns on Coca-Cola and Wendy's International

The figure illustrates how diversification reduces volatility. Both Wendy's and Coca-Cola stock earned an average return of about 12% from 1994–2003, but the two stocks did not always move in sync. In some years, one stock had an above-average year while the other stock performed below average. The net effect of this is that a portfolio containing both Wendy's and Coca-Cola would be less volatile than either stock held in isolation.

Source: Megginson and Smart's computations using data from the Center on Research on Security Prices.

In the years in which Coca-Cola and Wendy's move together, our portfolio return would be quite volatile, just as the individual stock returns are volatile. For example, our portfolio return in 1995 would be very high because both stocks did well that year, and in 2002, the portfolio would perform poorly because both stocks did. However, in some other years the excellent performance of one stock will be largely offset by the sub-par performance of the other, and the portfolio's results will be close to the average return of 12 percent. In other words, the portfolio's return does not deviate as far or as often from the average as the individual stock returns do. As a result, the standard deviation for the portfolio will be less than the standard deviation of either Coca-Cola or Wendy's.

Now extend that logic to portfolios containing more than two stocks. Figure 6.8 indicates that the standard deviation of a portfolio falls as the number of stocks in the portfolio rises. The dot in the upper-left corner of the graph represents a portfolio invested entirely in Advanced Micro Devices (AMD). As Table 6.5 indicates, this stock had a standard deviation of 56.4 percent. Next, move down and to the right to the dot which represents a portfolio containing an equal share of AMD and American Airlines (AMR) stock. From 1994–2003, the standard deviation of this portfolio was roughly 45 percent, a figure which is lower than the standard deviation of either AMD or AMR alone. Continuing down and to the right we reach a point which shows the position of a portfolio containing AMD, AMR, and Wal-Mart, in equal proportions. The standard deviation of this three-stock portfolio is 35 percent. Again, the portfolio's standard deviation is lower than any of the stocks it contains. Finally, the last dot on the far right shows what happens when we invest an equal amount in each of the eleven stocks shown in Table 6.5. In this case, the portfolio's standard deviation is 22 percent, just a little above the standard deviation of the overall market (the 21 percent figure for the standard deviation of all stocks comes from Table 6.3).

As you can see, there are diminishing returns to diversification.[11] Adding more stocks to this portfolio would lower the portfolio's volatility. But even if the

11. Refer back to the Opening Focus. One justification that Stephen Coleman has offered for investing in just a handful of stocks at any one time is that it is possible to capture most of the benefits of diversification with a relatively small number of securities. Figure 6.8 suggests that this may be true, but keep in mind that the stocks in this figure come from different industries, whereas the stocks held by Daedalus Capital are drawn mostly from the high-tech sector.

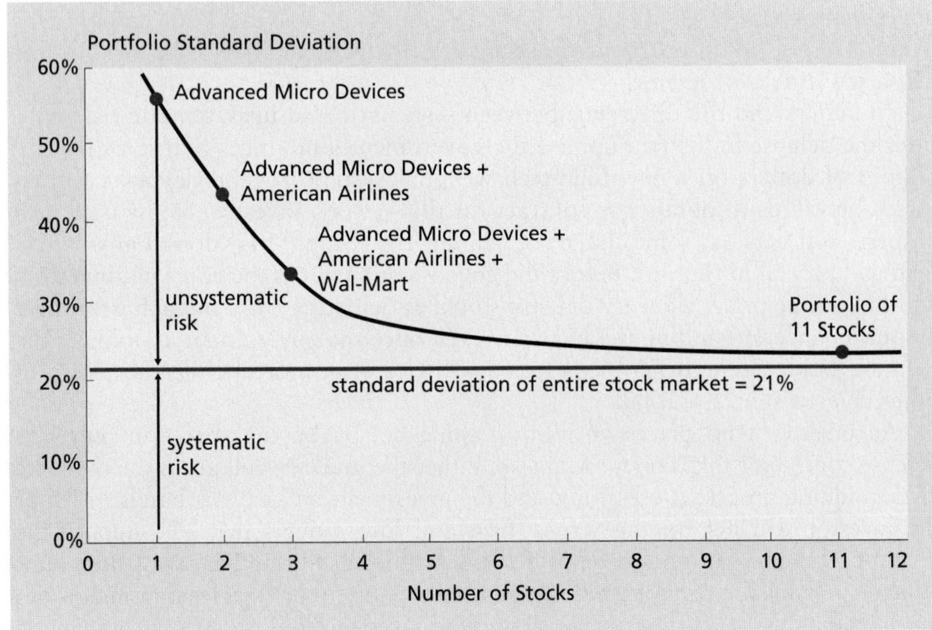

Figure 6.8
The Relationship Between Portfolio Standard Deviation and the Number of Stocks in the Portfolio

The standard deviation of a portfolio tends to decline as more stocks are added to the portfolio. The standard deviations of AMD and American Airlines stocks are 56.4% and 47.8% respectively when they are held in isolation. However, the standard deviation of a portfolio containing equal investments in both stocks is just 45%. The portfolio is less volatile than either stock in the portfolio. The risk that diversification eliminates is called unsystematic risk. The risk that remains, even in a diversified portfolio, is called systematic risk.

Source: Megginson and Smart's computations using data from the Center on Research on Security Prices.

portfolio contains every available stock in the market, the standard deviation will not drop below 21 percent.[12] *Diversification lowers volatility, but only up to a point.* No matter how diversified the portfolio is, there will still be some volatility remaining. In finance, the risk that remains even in a well-diversified portfolio is called **systematic risk.**[13] The term systematic risk refers to a risk that occurs systematically across many different stocks. Examples of systematic risks would include the recession/expansion phases of the macroeconomy, as well as changes in inflation, interest rates, and exchange rates. On September 11, 2001 and in the days that followed, U.S. investors learned that terrorism is a type of systematic risk, as the vast majority of stocks fell in response to the attacks on the World Trade Center and the Pentagon.

systematic risk
Risk that cannot be eliminated through diversification.

Look again at the dot in Figure 6.8 showing the standard deviation of a portfolio containing nothing but AMD shares. The standard deviation here is almost 60 percent, which, as previously noted, roughly equals the standard deviation for the average stock trading in the U.S. market. If AMD's standard deviation equals 60 percent, but the standard deviation of a portfolio containing AMD (and many other assets) is only 21 percent, this suggests that most of AMD's risk disappears once we put AMD inside a portfolio. What is true for AMD is true for most stocks. A substantial fraction of the volatility of an individual stock vanishes when investors hold the stock as part of a diversified portfolio. The risk of an individual stock that disappears when one diversifies is called

SMART ETHICS VIDEO
Utpal Bhattacharya, Indiana University,
"The cost of equity goes up if insider trading laws are not enforced."

See the entire interview at **SMARTFinance**

12. Of course it is possible to construct some portfolio of stocks with a standard deviation below 21 percent. To do this we would have to buy stocks that are less risky than average. Such a portfolio would generate lower returns than one more broadly diversified.

13. Other terms used to describe this type of risk are nondiversifiable risk and market risk. The meaning of nondiversifiable risk is self-evident. Market risk conveys the sense that we are concerned with risks that affect the broad market, not just a few stocks or even a few sectors in the market.

unsystematic risk Risk that can be eliminated through diversification.

unsystematic risk.[14] As the name implies, unsystematic risks are those risks which are not common to many securities. Instead, unsystematic risks affect just a few stocks at a time.

To understand the difference between systematic and unsystematic risk, consider the defense industry. Suppose the government announces that it will spend billions of dollars on a new high-tech weapons system. Several defense contractors submit bids to obtain the contract for this system. Investors know that each of these contracts has some chance of winning the bid, but they don't know which firm will prevail in the end. Before the government awards the contract, investors will bid up the prices of every defense stock, anticipating that for each firm there is some chance of winning the bid. However, once the government announces the winning bidder, that firm's stock price will rise even more, while the prices of other defense stocks will fall.

An investor who places an all-or-nothing bet by buying shares in only one defense contractor takes on a lot of risk. Either the investor will guess the outcome of the bidding process successfully, and the investment will pay off handsomely, or the investor will bet on the wrong firm and lose money. Instead, suppose the investor diversifies and holds a position in each defense firm. That way, no matter which firm wins the contract, the investor will be sure to have at least a small claim on the value of that deal. By diversifying the investor eliminates the unsystematic risk in this situation. However, suppose there is a chance that the defense department will cancel their plans to build the weapons system. When that announcement is made, all defense stocks will fall and diversifying across all of these firms will not help an investor avoid that loss.[15]

Risk and Return Revisited

Remember that our goal in this section is to be able to say something useful about the relationship between risk and return for individual assets. We already know that asset classes that pay higher returns have higher standard deviations. Is the same thing true for securities within a particular asset class? Do individual stocks with higher standard deviations earn higher returns over time?

Figure 6.9 plots the average return and standard deviation for the eleven stocks featured in Table 6.5. Unlike the predictable, almost linear relationship between standard deviation and returns that we observed for asset classes, no obvious pattern leaps out of this figure. If we compare the standard deviations and average returns of Archer Daniels Midland (ADM) to those of Wal-Mart, then the positive relation between these two variables seems to hold. Clearly Wal-Mart stock was more volatile than ADM during this period, and Wal-Mart investors earned much higher returns. However, comparing ADM to Anheuser-Busch, Anheuser-Busch shares were actually less volatile than ADM shares were, but shareholders of the famous brewer earned returns nearly as high as those achieved by Wal-Mart. Similarly, American Airlines (AMR) stock was a little more volatile than Wal-Mart, but AMR shareholders earned very low returns in comparison.

Why does the relationship between risk and return observed for asset classes in Figure 6.6 seem to break down when we focus on specific securities? The horizontal axis in Figure 6.9 offers a clue. Remember that the standard deviation of a single stock

14. Unsystematic risk is sometimes called diversifiable risk, unique risk, firm-specific risk, or idiosyncratic risk. Each of these terms implies that we are talking about risks that apply to a single firm or a few firms, not to many firms simultaneously.

15. A clever reader might argue that if the government spends less on defense, then more is spent on something else. So an investor may be able to diversify this risk away by holding a broad portfolio of stocks rather than just a portfolio of defense stocks. In that case, our illustration is once again about unsystematic rather than systematic risk.

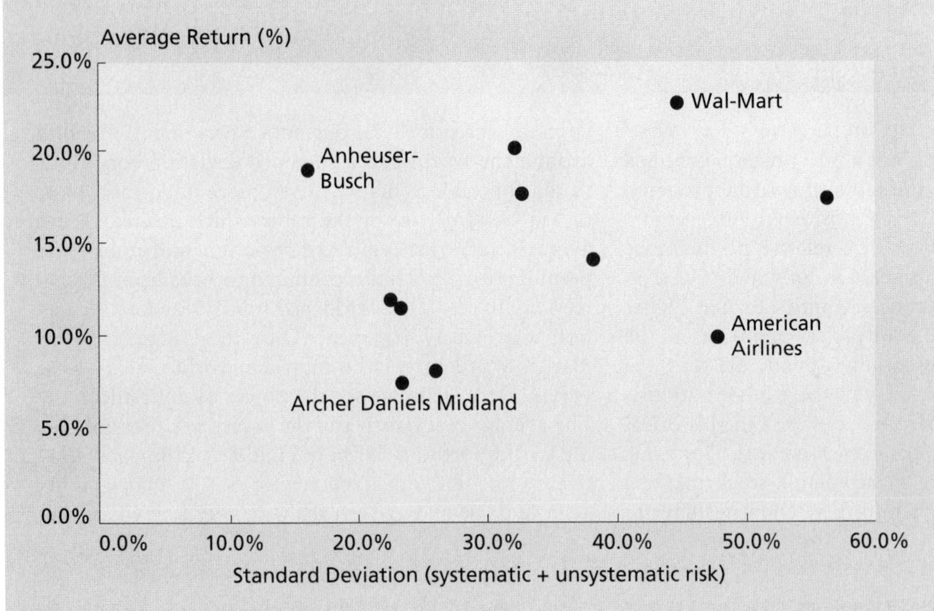

Figure 6.9
Average Return and Standard Deviation for 11 Stocks, 1994–2003

In contrast to the positive relationship between average returns and standard deviations for assest clases shown previously in Figure 6.6, this figure shows no such pattern for individual assets. There is no obvious tendency for the stocks that have earned the highest returns to be the most volatile. This suggests that for an individual stock, standard deviation may not be an appropriate measure of that stock's risk because it is unrelated to the stock's returns.

Source: Megginson and Smart's computations using data from the Center on Research on Security Prices.

contains both systematic and unsystematic components. *If investors are wise enough to diversify, then the unsystematic component of risk is irrelevant because diversification eliminates unsystematic risks.* How difficult is it for investors to remove exposure to unsystematic risk? In fact, it is very easy for them to do so. The mutual fund industry is built on the idea of allowing many investors to pool their money so that even people with relatively little money to invest can buy a stake in a well-diversified portfolio. This Chapter's Comparative Corporate Finance insert shows that it is possible to eliminate some unsystematic risk by diversifying globally.

If diversification is easy, and if it eliminates unsystematic risk, then what reward should investors expect if they choose not to diversify and to bear systematic risk? Just by equating marginal costs and benefits, we can predict that *bearing unsystematic risk offers no incremental reward.* The market rewards investors for bearing systematic risk but not unsystematic risk. Investors can eliminate their exposure to unsystematic risk at almost no cost by diversifying, so the marginal benefit of bearing unsystematic risk equals zero. The market offers higher returns only for investments that have higher systematic risk.

SMART CONCEPTS

See the concept explained step-by-step at SMARTFinance

In Figure 6.6, we observed an almost linear relation between standard deviation and average return for three asset classes: stocks, bonds, and bills. In Figure 6.9, the relationship between standard deviation and return is not as clear. The difference between the figures is that in one case (Figure 6.6), we are looking at portfolios of assets, and in the other case (Figure 6.9), we are looking at individual assets. A well-diversified portfolio contains very little unsystematic risk. This is why the standard deviation of a portfolio of stocks is typically so much lower than the standard deviation of a single stock. For a portfolio, the standard deviation of returns consists almost entirely of systematic risk. For an individual asset, the standard deviation contains both types of risk. Therefore, if the market rewards systematic risk only, then in Figure 6.6, we see a nice linear relationship between portfolio standard deviation (systematic risk) and average returns, but in Figure 6.9, standard deviation (systematic + unsystematic risk) seems almost unrelated to average returns.

To conclude this chapter, let us take a step back and think about our original objective. The fundamental goal of finance is to value things. Usually, valuation

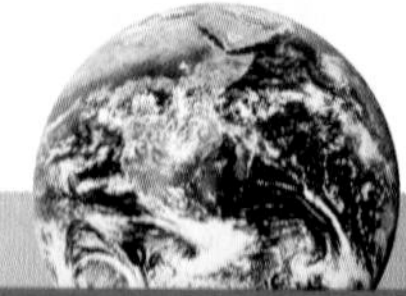

COMPARATIVE CORPORATE FINANCE

Risk Premiums Around the World

The tendency for stocks to outperform safer investments like Treasury bills is not a phenomenon confined to the United States. As the table shows, the premium on equities relative to bills was positive in fifteen other countries from 1900–2003. The relative performance of equities vs. bills was highest in Italy and lowest in Denmark, but in all countries equities earned higher returns than bills. The equity risk premium in the United States was not especially remarkable over the last century when compared with these other nations.

The second column of numbers shows the historical standard deviation of stocks in each country. Germany, Japan, and Italy had the most volatile stock markets over the past century (what do these countries have in common historically?), but notice how many markets around the world had a standard deviation very close to that of the U.S. market. Even more important, look at the bottom row of the table which calculates the average real return, standard deviation, and equity risk premium for a portfolio containing stocks from all sixteen countries. The world portfolio's standard deviation was just 17.4 percent. Only the Canadian stock market was less volatile than the world market as a whole. Here again we see the power of diversification. The average real return and the equity risk premium on the world portfolio fell in the middle of the pack relative to the individual countries, but it managed to achieve those average returns with very low volatility.

Real Equity Returns and Risk Premiums Around the World 1900–2003

Country	Ave. Real Return on Equities	Standard Deviation	Risk Premium vs. Bills
Australia	9.0%	17.7%	8.3%
Belgium	4.1	22.0	4.5
Canada	7.4	16.9	5.7
Denmark	6.5	20.2	4.0
France	5.6	22.7	9.0
Germany	8.3	32.4	9.6
Ireland	6.7	22.2	5.7
Italy	6.3	29.3	10.3
Japan	8.9	30.1	9.5
South Africa	9.0	22.5	7.9
Spain	5.6	22.0	5.1
Sweden	9.7	22.7	7.7
Switzerland	6.0	19.7	5.0
The Netherlands	7.0	21.4	6.4
United Kingdom	7.2	20.1	6.0
United States	8.5	20.4	7.4
World	7.1	17.4	6.0

Source: The Triumph of the Optimists, 101 Years of Global Investment Returns, by Elroy Dimson, Paul Marsh, Mike Staunton. Published by Princeton University Press. Reprinted with permission.

involves projecting an asset's future cash flows, choosing a discount rate that is appropriate, given the asset's risk, and then calculating the present value. In this chapter, we have made some progress in understanding the second step of the valuation process. We know that what really matters is an investment's total return, and we want to know how that return relates to risk. Not all risks are equal, however, so we need to focus on an asset's systematic risk because that is what should drive the asset's return in the market. Diversified portfolios contain very little unsystematic risk; thus a measure like the standard deviation of the portfolio's return provides a good measure of the portfolio's systematic risk. As expected, a portfolio's standard deviation and its return are closely linked.

But complications arise for individual assets because their fluctuations reflect both systematic and unsystematic factors. Therefore, the standard deviation of returns for a single stock does not focus exclusively on the stock's systematic risk. As a result, when we compare standard deviations and average returns across many different stocks, we do not see a reliable pattern between those two variables.

This is an important problem because both managers and investors have to assess the risk of individual investments, not just portfolios. They need a way to measure the systematic risk, and only the systematic risk, of each and every asset. If it is possible to quantify an individual asset's systematic risk, then we should expect that measure of risk to be reliably related to returns. This is precisely our focus in Chapter 7.

CONCEPT REVIEW QUESTIONS

9. Why is the standard deviation of a portfolio usually smaller than the standard deviations of the assets that comprise the portfolio?

10. In Figure 6.8, why does the line decline steeply at first and then flatten out?

11. Explain why the dots in Figure 6.9 appear to be almost randomly scattered.

6.5 SUMMARY AND CONCLUSIONS

- An important measure of an investment's performance is its total return. The total return is the sum of the income that the investment pays, plus any change in the price of the investment.
- Total returns can be expressed either in dollar or percentage terms.
- Historically, stocks have earned higher average returns than bonds, and bonds have earned higher returns than bills. However, higher returns come at the price of higher volatility.
- Real returns measure the change in purchasing power over time, whereas nominal returns measure the change in dollars accumulated. Investors who care about what they can consume with their wealth should focus on real returns.
- Historically, stock returns are approximately normally distributed.
- One measure of risk is standard deviation, which captures deviations from the average outcome. For broad asset classes, the relationship between average returns and standard deviation is nearly linear.
- The volatility (standard deviation) of individual stocks is generally higher than the volatility of a portfolio. This suggests that diversification lowers risk.
- There is a point beyond which additional diversification does not reduce risk. The risk that cannot be eliminated through diversification is called systematic risk, whereas the risk that disappears in a well-diversified portfolio is called unsystematic risk. The variance or standard deviation of any investment equals the sum of the systematic and unsystematic components of risk.

- Because investors can easily eliminate unsystematic risk by diversifying, the market should only reward investors based on the systematic risk that they bear.
- For individual investments, there is no strong linear relationship between average returns and standard deviation. This is the case, because standard deviation includes both systematic and unsystematic risk, and returns should only be linked to systematic risk.

SELF-TEST PROBLEMS

Answers to Self-Test Problems appear in Appendix D at back of book. Answers to the Concept Review Questions throughout the chapter appear at http://megginson.swlearning.com.

ST6-1. Using Table 6.3, calculate the standard deviation of stock returns from 1999–2003. Over the last five years, were stocks more or less volatile than they were over the last ten years?

ST6-2. Table 6.3 shows that the average return on stocks from 1994–2003 was 12.5 percent. Not shown in the table are the average returns on bonds and bills over the same period. The average return on bonds was 8.7 percent, and for bills the average return was 4.2 percent. From these figures, recalculate the risk premiums shown in Table 6.2 and compare recent history to the long-run numbers.

ST6-3. Suppose that Treasury bill returns follow a normal distribution with a mean of 4.1 percent and a standard deviation of 2.8 percent. This implies that, 68 percent of the time, T-bill returns should fall within what range?

INTERNET RESOURCES

http://www.yahoo.com—At Yahoo you can download monthly or daily prices for most stocks that trade in the U.S.

http://www.nyse.com—The New York Stock Exchange Web site provides up-to-the-minute price information and a virtual tour of the exchange floor.

http://www.globalfindata.com—This is an excellent resource for free historical data on stock returns, bond returns, and inflation for the U.S. and other countries.

http://www.morningstar.com—Use this site to obtain historical returns and estimates of volatility such as standard deviation for mutual funds.

KEY TERMS

capital gain
capital loss
diversification
risk premium
standard deviation
systematic risk
total return
unsystematic risk
variance

QUESTIONS AND PROBLEMS

Q6-1. Why is it important to focus on *total returns* when measuring an investment's performance?

Q6-2. Why do *real returns* matter more than *nominal returns*?

Q6-3. Under what conditions will the components of a bond's return have the opposite sign?

Q6-4. Explain why dollar returns and percentage returns can sometimes send conflicting signals when comparing two different investments.

Q6-5. Do the rankings of investment alternatives depend on whether we rank based on *nominal returns* or *real returns*?

Q6-6. Look at Table 6.1. Compare the best and worst years for T-bills in terms of their *nominal returns,* and then compare the best and worst years in terms of *real returns*. Comment on what you find.

Q6-7. Notice in Figure 6.4 that 1981 was the top year for nominal bill returns, and 1982 was the top year for nominal bond returns. Why do you think that these two years saw such high returns on bonds and bills?

Q6-8. Table 6.2 calculates the risk premiums on stocks and bonds relative to T-bills by taking the difference in average nominal total returns on each asset class. Would these risk premiums be much different if we calculated them using real rather than nominal returns?

Q6-9. When measuring the volatility of an investment's returns, why is it easier to focus on standard deviation rather than variance?

Q6-10. Are there diminishing returns to risk taking?

Q6-11. Notice in Table 6.5 that the stocks with the lowest standard deviations are Anheuser-Busch, Coca-Cola, Archer Daniels Midland, and Wendy's. Is this a surprise?

Q6-12. Look at Figure 6.9. The unlabeled dot on the far right of the graph represents the average return and standard deviation of Advanced Micro Devices. Down and to the left from that point is the position of American Airlines. Imagine that you form a portfolio with half your money in AMD and half in AMR. Where do you think that portfolio would plot in Figure 6.9? For a hint, see Figure 6.8.

Q6-13. Classify each of the following events as a source of *systematic* or *unsystematic* risk.

a. Alan Greenspan retires as Chairman of the Federal Reserve and Arnold Schwarzenegger is appointed to take his place.
b. Martha Stewart is convicted of insider trading and is sentenced to prison.
c. An OPEC embargo raises the world market price of oil.
d. A major consumer products firm loses a product liability case.
e. The Supreme Court rules that no employer can layoff an employee without first giving thirty days notice.

PROBLEMS

Understanding Returns

P6-1. You purchase 1,000 shares of Spears Grinders, Inc. stock for $45 per share. A year later, the stock pays a dividend of $1.25 per share, and it sells for $49.

a. Calculate your total dollar return.
b. Calculate your total percentage return.
c. Do the answers to parts (a) and (b) depend on whether you sell the stock after one year or continue to hold it?

P6-2. A financial adviser claims that a particular stock earned a total return of 10 percent last year. During the year the stock price rose from $30 to $32.50. What dividend did the stock pay?

P6-3. D. S. Trucking Company stock pays a $1.50 dividend every year without fail. A year ago, the stock sold for $25 per share, and its total return during the past year was $20%. What does the stock sell for today?

P6-4. Nano-Motors Corp. has stock outstanding which sells for $10 per share. Macro-Motors, Inc. shares cost $50 each. Neither stock pays dividends at present.

a. An investor buys 100 shares of Nano-Motors. A year later, the stock sells for $15. Calculate the total return in dollar terms and in percentage terms.
b. Another investor buys 100 shares of Macro-Motors stock. A year later, the stock has risen to $56. Calculate the total return in dollar terms and in percentage terms.
c. Why is it difficult to say which investor had a better year?

SMART SOLUTIONS

See the problem and solution explained step-by-step at SMARTFinance

P6-5. David Rawlings pays $1,000 to buy a 5-year Treasury bond that pays a 6 percent coupon rate (for simplicity, assume annual coupon payments). One year later, the market's required return on this bond has increased from 6 percent to 7 percent. What is Rawlings total return (in dollar and percentage terms) on the bond?

P6-6. G. Welch purchases a corporate bond that was originally issued for $1,000 several years ago. The bond has four years remaining until it matures, the market price now is $1,054.45, and the *yield to maturity (YTM)* is 4 percent. The bond pays an annual coupon of $55, with the next payment due in one year.

a. What is the bond's *coupon rate*? Its *coupon yield*?
b. Suppose Welch holds this bond for one year and the YTM does not change. What is the total percentage return on the bond? Show that on a percentage basis, the *total return* is the sum of the interest and capital gain/loss components.
c. If the yield to maturity decreases during the first year from 4 percent to 3.5 percent, what is the total percentage return that year?

P6-7. In this advanced problem, let's look at the behavior of ordinary Treasury bonds and inflation-indexed bonds, or TIPS. We will simplify by assuming annual interest payments rather than semiannual. Suppose over the next five years, investors expect 3 percent inflation each year. The Treasury issues a 5-year ordinary bond that pays $55 interest each year. The Treasury issues a 5-year TIPS that pays a coupon rate of 2 percent. With TIPS, the coupon payment is determined by multiplying the coupon rate times the inflation-adjusted principal value. Like ordinary bonds, TIPS begin with a par value or principal value of $1,000. However, that principal increases over time as inflation occurs. Assuming that inflation is in fact equal to 3 percent in each of the next five years, then the cash flows associated with each bond would look like this:

Year	T-bond Pays	TIPS Pays	Inflation-adjusted Principal (TIPS)	Coupon pymt calculation
0 (cost)	−1,000.00	−1,000.00	−1,000.00	NA
1	55.00	20.60	1,030.00	1,000.00(1.03) × 2%
2	55.00	21.22	1,060.90	1,030.00(1.03) × 2%
3	55.00	21.85	1,092.73	1,060.90(1.03) × 2%
4	55.00	22.51	1,125.51	1,092.73(1.03) × 2%
5	1,055.00	1,182.46	1,159.27	1,125.51(1.03) × 2%

In the last row of the table, notice the final TIPS payment includes the return of the inflation-adjusted principal ($1,159.27), plus the final coupon payment.

a. Calculate the *yield to maturity (YTM)* of each bond. Why is one higher than the other? Show that the TIPS YTM equals the product of the real interest rate and the inflation rate.

b. What is the *real return* on the T-bond?

c. Suppose the *real return* on the T-bond stays constant, but investors expect 4 percent inflation rather than 3 percent. What happens to the required return on the T-bond in nominal terms?

d. Imagine that during the first year, the inflation that actually occurred was 3 percent, as expected. However, suppose that by the end of the first year, investors had come to expect 4 percent inflation for the next four years. Fill out the remaining cash flows for each bond in the table below.

Year	T-bond Pays	TIPS Pays	Inflation-adjusted Principal (TIPS)	Coupon pymt calculation
0 (cost)	−1,000.00	−1,000.00	−1,000.00	NA
1	55.00	20.60	1,030.00	1,000.00(1.03) × 2%
2				
3				
4				
5				

e. Now calculate the market price of the Treasury bond as of the end of the first year. Remember to discount the bond's remaining cash flows, using the nominal required return that you calculated in part (c). Given this new market price, what is the total return offered by the T-bond the first year?

f. Next, calculate the market price of the TIPS bond. Remember, at the end of the first year, the YTM on the TIPS will equal the product of one plus the real return (2%) and one plus the inflation rate (4%). What is the total nominal return offered by TIPS the first year?

The History of Returns (or How to Get Rich Slowly)

P6-8. Refer to Figure 6.2. At the end of each line, we show the nominal value in 2003 of a $1 investment stocks, bonds, and bills. Calculate the ratio of the 2003 value of $1 invested in stocks divided by the 2003 value of $1 invested in bonds. Now recalculate this ratio, using the real values in Figure 6.3. What do you find?

P6-9. The U.S. stock market hit an all-time high in October 1929 before crashing dramatically. Following the market crash, the U.S. entered a prolonged economic downturn dubbed "The Great Depression." Using Figure 6.2, estimate how long it took for the stock market to fully rebound from its fall which began in October 1929. How did bond investors fare over this same period? (Note: A precise answer is hard to obtain from the figure, so just make your best guess.)

P6-10. Refer again to Figure 6.2 which tracks the value of $1 invested in various assets starting in 1900. At the stock market peak in 1929, look at the gap that exists between equities and bonds. At the end of 1929, the $1 investment in stocks was worth about five times more than the $1 investment in bonds. About how long did investors in stocks have to wait before they would regain that same performance edge? Again, getting a precise answer from the figure is difficult, so make an estimate.

P6-11. The *nominal return* on a particular investment is 11 percent and the inflation rate is 2 percent. What is the *real return*?

P6-12. A bond offers a *real return* of 5 percent. If investors expect 3 percent inflation, what is the *nominal rate of return* on the bond?

P6-13. If an investment promises a nominal return of 6 percent and the inflation rate is 1 percent, what is the real return?

P6-14. The following data shows the rate of return on stocks and bonds for several recent years. Calculate the *risk premium* on equities vs. bonds each year and then calculate the average risk premium. Do you think, at the beginning of 2000, investors expected the outcomes we observe in this table?

Year	2000	2001	2002	2003
Return on stocks (%)	–10.9	–11.0	–20.9	31.6
Return on bonds (%)	21.5	3.7	17.8	1.4
Risk premium (%)				

P6-15. The table below shows the average return on U.S. stocks and bonds for 25-year periods ending in 1925, 1950, 1975, and 2000. Calculate the *equity risk premium* for each quarter century. What lesson emerges from your calculations?

Ave. Return	1925	1950	1975	2000
Stocks	9.7%	10.2%	11.4%	16.2%
Bonds	3.5%	4.1%	2.4%	10.6%
Risk Premium				

Source: The Triumph of the Optimists, 101 Years of Global Investment Returns, by Elroy Dimson, Paul Marsh, Mike Staunton. Published by Princeton University Press. Reprinted with permission.

P6-16. The current yield to maturity on a 1-year Treasury bill is 2 percent. You believe that the expected risk premium on stocks vs. bills equals 7.6 percent.

a. Estimate the expected return on the stock market next year.

b. Explain why the estimate in part (a) may be better than simply assuming that next year's stock market return will equal the long-term average return.

Volatility and Risk

SMART SOLUTIONS

See the problem and solution explained step-by-step at SMARTFinance

P6-17. Using Figure 6.5, how would you estimate the probability that the return on the stock market will exceed 30 percent in any given year?

P6-18. In this problem, use Figure 6.5 to estimate the expected return on the stock market. To estimate the expected return, create a list of possible returns and assign a probability to each outcome. To find the expected return, multiply each possible return by the probability that it will occur and then add up across outcomes. Notice that Figure 6.5 divides the range of possible returns into intervals of 10 percent (except for very low or very high outcomes). Create a list of potential future stock returns by taking the midpoint of the various ranges as follows:

Possible Stock Returns (%)									
−35	−25	−15	−5	5	15	25	35	45	55
$\frac{2}{104}$	$\frac{4}{104}$							$\frac{3}{104}$	$\frac{2}{104}$

Expected return = $(\frac{2}{104})(-35) + (\frac{4}{104})(-25) + \ldots + (\frac{3}{104})(45) + (\frac{2}{104})(55) = ?$

Figure 6.5 shows that four years out of 104 had returns of between −20% and −30%. Let us capture this fact by assuming that if returns do occur inside that interval that the typical return would be −25% (in the middle of the interval). The probability associated with this outcome is 4/104 or about 3.8%. Fill in the missing values in the table and then fill in the missing parts of the equation to calculate the expected return.

P6-19. Here are the nominal returns on stocks, bonds, and bills for the 1920s and 1930s. For each decade, calculate the standard deviation of returns for each asset class. How do those figures compare with the more recent numbers for stocks presented in Table 6.3 and the long-run figures for all three asset types in Table 6.4?

Nominal Returns (%) on Stocks, Bonds, and Bills

	1920s				1930s		
	Stocks	Bonds	Bills		Stocks	Bonds	Bills
1920	−17.9	5.8	7.6	1930	−28.3	4.7	2.4
1921	11.6	12.7	7.0	1931	−43.9	−5.3	1.1
1922	30.6	3.5	4.7	1932	−9.8	16.8	1.0
1923	3.0	5.7	5.2	1933	57.6	−0.1	0.3
1924	27.0	6.4	4.1	1934	4.4	10.0	0.2
1925	28.3	5.7	4.1	1935	44.0	5.0	0.2
1926	9.5	7.8	3.3	1936	32.3	7.5	0.2
1927	33.1	8.9	3.1	1937	−34.6	0.2	0.3
1928	38.7	0.1	3.6	1938	28.2	5.5	0.0
1929	−14.5	3.4	4.7	1939	2.9	5.5	0.0

Source: The Triumph of the Optimists, 101 Years of Global Investment Returns, by Elroy Dimson, Paul Marsh, Mike Staunton. Published by Princeton University Press. Reprinted with permission.

P6-20. Use the data below to calculate the standard deviation of nominal and real Treasury bill returns from 1972–1982. Do you think that when they purchased T-bills, investors expected to earn negative real returns as often as they did during this period? If not, what happened that took investors by surprise?

Year	Nominal Return (%)	Real Return (%)
1972	3.8	0.4
1973	6.9	−1.7
1974	8.0	−3.7
1975	5.8	−1.1
1976	5.1	0.3
1977	5.1	−1.5
1978	7.2	−1.7
1979	10.4	−2.6
1980	11.2	−1.0
1981	14.7	5.3
1982	10.5	6.4

Source: The Triumph of the Optimists, 101 Years of Global Investment Returns, by Elroy Dimson, Paul Marsh, Mike Staunton. Published by Princeton University Press. Reprinted with permission.

P6-21. Based on Figure 6.6, about what rate of return would a truly risk-free investment (i.e., one with a standard deviation of zero) offer investors?

The Power of Diversification

P6-22. Troy McClain wants to form a portfolio of four different stocks. Summary data on the four stocks appears below. First, calculate the average standard deviation across the four stocks and then answer this question. If Troy forms a portfolio by investing 25% of his money in each of the stocks in the table, it is very likely that the standard deviation of this portfolio's return will be (more than, less than, equal to) 43.5%. Explain your answer.

Stock	Return	Std. Dev.
#1	14%	71%
#2	10%	46%
#3	9%	32%
#4	11%	25%

SMART EXCEL

See this problem explained in Excel at SMARTFinance

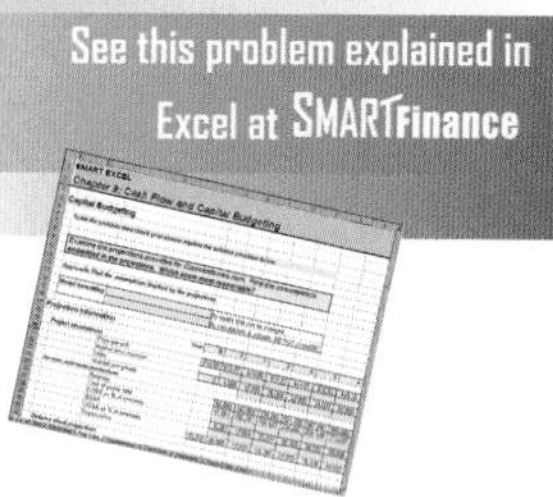

P6-23. The table below shows annual returns on chip maker Advanced Micro Devices and the pharmaceutical producer Merck. The last column of the table shows the annual return that a portfolio invested 50% in AMD and 50% in Merck would have earned each year. The portfolio's return is simply a weighted average of the returns of AMD and Merck. An example portfolio return calculation for 1994 is given at the top of the table.

Year	AMD	Merck	50-50 portfolio
1994	40.1%	14.9%	27.5% (= $\frac{1}{2}$ × 40.1% + $\frac{1}{2}$ × 14.9%)
1995	−33.7%	76.4%	
1996	56.1%	24.0%	
1997	−31.1%	35.5%	
1998	63.4%	41.2%	
1999	−0.2%	−7.4%	
2000	−4.5%	41.7%	
2001	14.8%	−35.9%	
2002	−59.3%	−1.1%	
2003	130.7%	−11.2%	
Std. Dev.			

a. Plot a graph similar to Figure 6.7 showing the returns on AMD and Merck each year.

b. Fill in the blanks in the table above by calculating the 50-50 portfolio's return each year from 1995–2003 and then plot this on the graph you created for part (a). How does the portfolio return compare to the returns of the individual stocks in the portfolio?

c. Calculate the standard deviation of AMD, Merck, and the portfolio and comment on what you find.

P6-24. The table below shows annual returns for Merck and one of its major competitors, Eli Lilly. The final column shows the annual return on a portfolio invested 50% in Lilly and 50% in Merck. The portfolio's return is simply a weighted average of the returns of the stocks in the portfolio, as shown in the example calculation at the top of the table.

Year	Eli Lilly	Merck	50-50 portfolio
1994	15.4%	14.9%	15.1% (= $\frac{1}{2} \times$ 15.4% + $\frac{1}{2} \times$ 14.9%)
1995	77.2%	76.4%	
1996	32.6%	24.0%	
1997	93.6%	35.5%	
1998	29.1%	41.2%	
1999	−24.3%	−7.4%	
2000	41.9%	41.7%	
2001	−14.4%	−35.9%	
2002	−17.6%	−1.1%	
2003	13.1%	−11.2%	
Std. Dev.			

a. Plot a graph similar to Figure 6.7 showing the returns on Lilly and Merck each year.

b. Fill in the blanks in the table above by calculating the 50-50 portfolio's return each year from 1995–2003 and then plot this on the graph you created for part (a). How does the portfolio return compare to the returns of the individual stocks in the portfolio?

c. Calculate the standard deviation of Lilly, Merck, and the portfolio and comment on what you find.

P6-25. In this problem, you will generate a graph similar to Figure 6.8. The table below shows the standard deviation for various portfolios of stocks listed in Table 6.5. Plot the relationship between the number of stocks in the portfolio and the portfolio's standard deviation. Comment on how the resulting graph is similar to and different from Figure 6.8. In answering this question, it may be helpful to examine the order of stocks listed in Table 6.5 and compare that to the order in which stocks were added to portfolios in Figure 6.8 and in the table below.

Stocks in the Portfolio	Std. Deviation (%)
Anheuser-Busch	16.1
AB + Coca-Cola	15.9
AB+Coke+Wendy's	15.1
AB+Coke+Wendy's+Archer	13.6
AB+Coke+Wendy's+Archer+Gen. Motors	13.1
AB+Coke+Wendy's+Archer+GM+GE	14.7

THOMSON ONE Business School Edition

Access financial information from the Thomson ONE – Business School Edition Web site for the following problem(s). Go to http://tobsefin.swlearning.com/. If you have already registered your access serial number and have a username and password, click **Enter.** Otherwise, click **Register** and follow the instructions to create a username and password. Register your access serial number and then click **Enter** on the aforementioned Web site. When you click Enter, you will be prompted for your username and password (please remember that the password is case sensitive). Enter them in the respective boxes and then click **OK** (or hit **Enter**). From the ensuing page, click **Click Here to Access Thomson ONE – Business School Edition Now!** This opens up a new window that gives you access to the Thomson ONE – Business School Edition database. You can retrieve a company's financial information by entering its ticker symbol (provided for each company in the problem(s)) in the box below "Name/Symbol/Key." For further instructions on using the Thomson ONE – Business School Edition database, please refer to "A Guide for Using Thomson ONE – Business School Edition."

P6-26. Compare the average annual returns and standard deviations of annual returns of AOL Timer Warner, Inc. (ticker: U:AOL), FedEx Corp (FDX), and Motorola, Inc. (U:MOT) to those of a portfolio containing the three companies' stocks. Calculate the average and standard deviation of annual returns for each company. Now assume that you form a portfolio by investing equal amounts of money in each stock. Determine the annual returns for this portfolio. To calculate the portfolio's return in each year, simply calculate a weighted-average of the returns of the stocks in the portfolio. The weight given to each stock is one-third. For example, if the returns on AOL, FDX, and MOT are 10%, –3%, and 20% in a certain year, then the portfolio return for that year equals:

$$(\tfrac{1}{3})(10\%) + (\tfrac{1}{3})(-3\%) + (\tfrac{1}{3})(20\%) = 9\%$$

After calculating the portfolio's return in each year, then calculate the average and standard deviation of the portfolio's annual returns.

How do these compare to the average and standard deviation of annual returns of the three firms taken separately? What can you infer about the risk and return of the portfolio compared to those of the individual firms? Does your answer change if you invest 40 percent of your capital in Motorola, 35 percent in AOL Time Warner, and the remaining funds in FedEx?

P6-27. Compare the nominal and real annual returns for Oracle Corp. (ticker: ORCL). Determine the annual nominal rate of return for Oracle over the last ten years. Use the CPI inflation calculator at the Bureau of Labor Statistics Web site (http://data.bls.gov/cgi-bin/cpicalc.pl) to determine annual inflation rates over the last ten years. Calculate the real annual rates of return for Oracle. Is the real rate of return less than the nominal rate of return every year? Why? What do you think will happen to this relationship if the inflation in any given year were negative?

Since these exercises depend upon real-time data, your answers will change continuously depending upon when you access the Internet to download your data.

MINICASE

The Trade-off Between Risk and Return

ASSIGNMENT

Use the following information to compare the recent performance of the S&P 500 Index, the NASDAQ Index, and the Treasury Bill Index. Each of these index numbers is calculated in a way that assumes that investors reinvest any income they receive, so the total return equals the percentage change in the index value each year. The last column shows the level of the Consumer Price Index (CPI) at the end of each year, so the percentage change in the index indicates the rate of inflation for a particular year. Note that because the data start on December 31, 1983, it is not possible to calculate returns or an inflation rate in 1983.

For the S&P500, the Nasdaq, and the T-bill series calculate (a) the cumulative return over twenty years, (b) the average annual return in nominal terms, (c) the average annual return in real terms, and (d) the standard deviation of the nominal return. Based on these calculations, discuss the risk/return relationship between these indexes. Which asset class earned the highest average return? For which asset class were returns most volatile? Plot your results on a graph with the standard deviation of each asset class on the horizontal axis and the average return on the vertical axis.

Date	S&P 500	NASDAQ	T-Bills	CPI
12/31/1983	164.93	278.60	681.44	101.3
12/31/1984	167.24	247.35	748.88	105.3
12/31/1985	211.28	324.39	806.62	109.3
12/31/1986	242.17	348.81	855.73	110.5
12/31/1987	247.08	330.47	906.02	115.4
12/31/1988	277.72	381.38	968.89	120.5
12/31/1989	353.40	454.82	1050.63	126.1
12/31/1990	330.22	373.84	1131.42	133.8
12/31/1991	417.09	586.34	1192.83	137.9
12/31/1992	435.71	676.95	1234.36	141.9
12/31/1993	466.45	776.80	1271.78	145.8
12/31/1994	459.27	751.96	1327.55	149.7
12/31/1995	615.93	1052.13	1401.97	153.5
12/31/1996	740.74	1291.03	1473.98	158.6
12/31/1997	970.43	1570.35	1550.49	161.3
12/31/1998	1229.23	2192.68	1625.77	163.9
12/31/1999	1469.25	4069.31	1703.84	168.3
12/31/2000	1320.28	2470.52	1805.75	174.0
12/31/2001	1148.08	1950.40	1865.85	176.7
12/31/2002	879.82	1335.51	1895.83	180.9
12/31/2003	1111.92	2003.37	1915.29	184.3

Smart *Excel* Appendix

Appendix Contents

Use the Smart *Excel* spreadsheets and animated tutorials at http://smartfinance.swlearning.com.

EXCEL PREREQUISITES

You need to be familiar with the following *Excel* features to use this appendix:

- Exponentiation in *Excel*
- Statistical functions

If this is new to you, be sure to complete the ***Excel Prereqs*** tab of the Chapter 6 *Excel* file **at the Smart Finance Web site** before proceeding.

CALCULATING DOLLAR AND PERCENT RETURNS

Problem: Exactly one year ago, you bought 50 shares of FastFood, Inc. at a price of $32 per share. You received dividends of $1.20 per share. Today, the price of FastFood is $38.75. Your sister bought 75 shares of PriceyCoffee exactly one year ago at a price of $29.75. She received dividends of $0.80 per share. PriceyCoffee is trading today at $34.50. Find the dollar and percent returns of each investment. Who earned a higher return?

In an equity investment, return is derived from two sources: dividend income and capital gains. The dividend income is equal to the dividend per share multiplied by the number of shares purchased. The capital gain (or loss) is equal to the change in price multiplied by the number of shares purchased.

Approach: Create a simple model that allows you to find the dividend income and capital gain as well as the total dollar and percent return on an equity investment.

Try it yourself in a blank *Excel* file. Think about what to include in inputs and how to set up your calculations and output. Alternatively, you can use the setup file provided on the ***Returns*** tab of the Chapter 6 *Excel* file.

SMARTFinance
Use the learning tools at

We set up the model as follows:

Inputs	Beginning stock price	
	Ending stock price	
	Annual dividend	
	# shares purchased	
Calculations	Funds invested	
	Capital gain/loss	
	Total $ dividends	
Output	**Dollar return**	
	Percent return	

Calculate funds invested by multiplying the beginning price by the number of shares purchased. You should find that your dollar returns was $397.50 which translates into a percentage return of 24.8%. Your sister had a higher dollar return, $416.25, but a lower percent return, 18.7%, due to her higher initial investment.

Apply it

What if you change the number of shares purchased?

Suppose you each purchase 100 shares.

The dollar return varies (you earn $795 and she earns $555.), but the percent returns are not affected because the return on investment remains constant.

NOMINAL AND REAL RETURNS

Create a simple model in *Excel* to solve for real or nominal returns.

Problem: You are considering a one-year investment with a nominal return of 11%. You think inflation will be 2.5% this year. If so, what is your expected real rate of return?

To determine the real rate of return, use the text equation:

(1+ nominal return) = (1+ real return) * (1+ inflation rate)

Solving the equation for real return yields:

Real return = (1+ nominal return) / (1+ inflation rate) – 1

Approach: Set up a basic model to solve for the real rate of return.

Try it yourself in a blank *Excel* file. Think about what to include in inputs and how to set up your calculations and output. Alternatively, you can use the setup file provided on the ***Nom & Real Return*** tab of the Chapter 6 *Excel* file. You should get a real rate of return of 8.3%.

Apply it

What if inflation is not what you expected?

Suppose inflation is 4.5%? 1.5%?

Higher levels of inflation lead to lower real returns. At 4.5% inflation, the real rate of return is 6.2%; at 1.5% inflation, the real rate of return is 9.4%.

CALCULATING THE AVERAGE, VARIANCE, AND STANDARD DEVIATION

Problem: Table 6.3 in the text examined stock returns from 1994–2003. Use the text data in that table and calculate the average return, variance of returns, and standard deviation of returns for the 1994–2003 period.

Approach 1: Use the mathematical equations.

Open the Chapter 6 *Excel* file and turn to the ***Stats*** tab.

Enter the year and return data in the input section.

Next, create a formula to calculate average return.

The model also includes calculations to facilitate calculation of variance. Complete these calculations. Find the desired output: average return, variance, and standard deviation.

You should get the following results. Note that these values differ just slightly from those in the text because we did not round here.

Output

Average Return	12.46
Variance	442.36
Std deviation	21.03

Approach 2: Use the statistical functions in *Excel*.

Excel includes a number of built-in statistical functions, including average, variance, and standard deviation. Use of these functions is detailed on the ***Prereqs*** tab of the Chapter 6 *Excel* file.

The **average** function returns the average of a group of numbers. You can use the function by either typing in individual values or using cell references.

The format is:

=average(value1, value2,....) or =average(cell ref:cell ref)

The **variance** function returns the variance of a group of numbers. You can use the function by either typing in individual values or using cell references.

The format is:

=var(value1, value2,....) or =var(cell ref:cell ref)

The **standard deviation** function returns the standard deviation of a group of numbers. You can use the function by either typing in individual values or using cell references.

The format is:

=stdev(value1, value2,....) or =stdev(cell ref:cell ref)

To solve, using Approach 2, again enter the years and returns as inputs. Then use the built-in statistical functions to find the average return, variance of returns, and standard deviation of returns.

You should get the same results as with Approach 1.

Apply it

An advantage of using the built-in functions is that it is easy to look at statistics for sub-periods.

Find the average return, variance of returns, and standard deviation of returns for

- *1995–1999*
- *1996–2000*
- *2000–2003*

You should get the following results.

1995–1999		*1996–2000*		*2000–2003*	
Average return	27.18	Average return	17.72	Average return	(2.80)
Variance	41.21	Variance	270.62	Variance	547.94
Std deviation	6.42	Std deviation	16.45	Std deviation	23.41

Interpret

The period selected for analysis has a tremendous impact on the results.

CALCULATING PORTFOLIO RISK AND RETURN STATISTICS

You may also want to find the average return, variance of returns, and standard deviation of returns for a portfolio.

Problem: Solve Problem 6-23 in which you were asked to compare investments in Merck, AMD, and a portfolio with 50% invested in each.

Approach: Build a basic model and use the statistical functions.

Open the Chapter 6 *Excel* file and turn to the ***Portfolios*** tab.

Enter the year and return data for AMD and Merck in the input section. Then, enter the percent of the portfolio invested in each. The percents must add up to 100% each year. Because there is 50% invested in each firm in each year, type in 50% for the percent in AMD in 1994. Then, copy down for Merck and across all years.

Calculate portfolio return in Year 1 as the weighted average return. Your formula in 1994 should be:

=C15*C17+C16*C18

Copy the formula across for all years.

Then, use the statistical functions to find the average return for AMD, Merck, and the portfolio.

Here are our results:

Output

	AMD	Merck	Portfolio
Average return	0.18	0.18	0.18
Variance	0.32	0.11	0.08
Std deviation	0.56	0.33	0.29

Apply it

What if you vary the percent of the portfolio invested in AMD and Merck?

- *Consider a portfolio with 75% in AMD and 25% in Merck.*
- *Consider a portfolio with 25% in AMD and 75% in Merck.*

Interpret

Interestingly, in this example, varying the percents invested in each stock does not change the average portfolio return.

Is this typical?

No. This occurs only because AMD and Merck have approximately the same average return. The variance and standard deviation of the portfolio are, however, affected. With 75% in AMD and 25% in Merck, the variance is 0.17 and the standard deviation 0.41. With 25% in AMD and 75% in Merck, the variance drops to 0.06 and standard deviation to 0.25.

Risk, Return, and the Capital Asset Pricing Model

OPENING FOCUS

High Beta Sinks IPO

On March 24, 2004, German manufacturer Wacker Siltronic announced that it had postponed its plan to raise money by selling shares to the public in an initial public offering. Siltronic, one of only three firms in the world capable of producing state-of-the-art 300-mm silicon wafers, cancelled its IPO in response to the terrorist attacks in Madrid, Spain, just before the Spanish elections. Their IPO would have been the first in Germany in more than a year, but Siltronic felt that market conditions were not right for their offering. As is common in high-tech industries, Siltronic's share price would be very sensitive to changing market conditions brought about either by economic events or political events such as the terrorist strike that occurred in Madrid on March 11, 2004. Financial analysts call stocks like Siltronic—that move very sharply in response to movements in the broader stock market—high-beta stocks. As European stock markets moved lower in response to the terrorist threat, Siltronic executives perceived that unfolding events would substantially decrease the price they could obtain on a new share offering. Rather than issuing shares at an unfavorable price, Siltronic executives decided to take a wait-and-see approach. Ewald Walraven, an analyst with ING Financial Markets, articulated the company's concerns by saying, "High-beta tech stocks are the natural losers in this climate."

Sources: (1) AFX.com, March 24, 2004, "Siltronic pulls IPO citing market conditions"; (2) Siltronic Web site.

LEARNING OBJECTIVES

After studying this chapter you will be able to:

- Illustrate three different approaches for estimating an asset's expected return;
- Calculate a portfolio's expected return and its beta;
- Explain how the Capital Asset Pricing Model (CAPM) links an asset's beta to its expected return; and
- Describe the concept of market efficiency and its important lessons for investors.

In this chapter, we continue our study of the relationship between risk and return. We will see that a stock's beta, a measure of how much a stock's returns vary in response to variations in overall market returns, *is an important determinant of its expected return*. This is the central insight of the Capital Asset Pricing Model (CAPM), one of the most important ideas in modern finance. The scholars who developed the model earned a Nobel Prize in Economics in 1990 for their research. The CAPM is useful not only for investors in financial markets but also for managers who need to understand what returns stockholders expect on the money they contribute to corporate ventures.

7.1 EXPECTED RETURNS

expected return
A forecast of the return that an asset will earn over some period of time.

Ultimately, people want to know what return they can expect from an investment. Investors and corporate managers decide upon investments based on their best judgments about what the future will hold. In finance, when we use the term **expected return**, we have in mind a "best guess" estimate of how an investment will perform in the future. For example, in Chapter 6, we saw ample evidence that investors should expect higher returns on stocks than on bonds. Intuitively, such an expectation makes sense because stocks are riskier than bonds, and investors should expect a reward for bearing risk. However, the claim that expected returns on stocks exceed expected returns on bonds does not imply that stocks will actually outperform bonds in any given year. Rather, it means that it is more reasonable to expect that stocks will outperform bonds rather than bonds outperforming stocks.

In Chapter 6, we noted that the marginal benefit that an investment provides is its return, but the associated marginal cost is the investment's risk. In this chapter, we develop an explicit link between risk and return, and therefore between marginal costs and benefits of investing. To establish that link, we have to deal with a major challenge. *Expected returns are inherently unobservable.* Analysts have many techniques at their disposal to form estimates of expected returns, but it is important to remember that the numbers produced by these models are just estimates. As a starting point, let's see how analysts might use historical data to make educated guesses about the future.

The Historical Approach

Analysts employ at least three different methods to estimate an asset's expected return. The first method relies on historical data and assumes that the future and the past share much in common. Chapter 6 reported an average risk premium on U.S. stocks relative to Treasury bills of 7.6 percent over the last 104 years. If a Treasury bill currently offers investors a 2 percent yield to maturity, then the sum of the bill yield and the historical equity risk premium (2.0% + 7.6% = 9.6%) provides one measure of the expected return on stocks for the future.

Can we apply that logic to an individual stock to estimate its expected return? Consider the case of General Motors. GM stock has been trading in the U.S. for many years, so we could calculate its long-run average return, just as we did for the U.S. stock market. Suppose that over many decades, GM's return has averaged 17%. Suppose also that over the same time period, the average return on Treasury bills was 4.1%. Thus, GM stockholders have enjoyed a historical risk premium of 12.9% (17.0% – 4.1%). Therefore, we might estimate GM's expected return as follows:

$$\text{GM expected return} = \text{Current Tbill rate} + \text{GM historical risk premium}$$
$$\text{GM expected return} = 2\% + 12.9\% = 14.9\%$$

Although simple and intuitively appealing, this approach suffers from several drawbacks. First, over its long history, GM has experienced many changes, ranging from executive turnover to technological breakthroughs in manufacturing to increased competition from domestic and foreign rivals. Presumably, GM stockholders earned returns year by year and decade by decade that compensated them for the risks associated with holding GM shares, but those risks vary over time. Calculating GM's historical risk premium over the last seventy-five years blends all these changes into a single number, and that number may or may not reflect GM's current status. Thus, the historical approach yields merely a naïve estimate of the expected return in any given year. Investors need to know whether GM's shares today are more risky, less risky, or just as risky as the long-term premium indicates.

A second flaw in applying this approach broadly is that most stocks in the market do not have as long a history as GM does to forecast the expected return. Just since 1999, more than 1,000 new firms listed their stock on U.S. markets. These firms show no long-run track record to learn from—only a few years of rather volatile recent history.

The Probabilistic Approach

Another method for estimating expected returns uses statistical concepts. When statisticians want to estimate the expected value of some unknown quantity, they first list all *possible* values that the variable of interest might take, as well as the probability that each outcome will occur. In principle, analysts can use the same approach to calculate the expected return on stocks and other financial assets. A potential advantage of this approach is that it does not require an analyst to assume that the future will look just like the past. Professional judgment plays a larger role here.

General Motors falls into a category of stocks that traders call "cyclicals," because these stocks' fortunes rise and fall dramatically with the business cycle. To project the expected return on GM stock, an analyst can estimate the probabilities associated with different states of the overall economy. The table below illustrates how this can work. The analyst assumes that the economy will be in one of three possible states next year: boom, expansion, or recession. The current climate presents a 20 percent chance that the economy will experience a recession, and the probabilities of a normal expansion or a boom are 70 percent and 10 percent, respectively. Next, the analyst projects that if the economy slips into recession, GM stockholders will experience a 30 percent loss. If the economy continues to expand normally, then GM's stock return will be 15 percent. If the economy booms, GM stock will do very well, earning a total return of 55 percent.

Outcome	Probability	GM Return
Recession	20%	–30%
Expansion	70%	15%
Boom	10%	55%

To calculate the expected return on GM shares, multiply each possible return times the probability that it will occur and then add up the returns across all three possible outcomes:

$$\text{GM expected return} = 0.20(-30\%) + 0.70(15\%) + 0.10(55\%) = 10\%^{1}$$

With an estimate of the expected return in place, the analyst can use the same basic model to estimate the variance and standard deviation of GM stock. To do so, subtract the 10 percent expected return from the actual return on GM stock in each state of the economy. Then, square that difference and multiply it by the probability of recession, expansion, or boom. The accompanying table illustrates the calculation.

Outcome	Probability	GM Return	Return – 10%	(Return – 10%)^2
Recession	20%	–30%	–40%	1,600%^{2}
Expansion	70%	15%	5%	25%^{2}
Boom	10%	55%	45%	2,025%^{2}

$$\text{Variance} = (0.20)(1{,}600\%^2)+(0.70)(25\%^2)+(0.10)(2{,}025\%^2) = 540\%^2$$

$$\text{Standard Deviation} = \sqrt{540\%^2} = 23.2\%$$

[1] It is easy to generalize this equation. Rather than assuming that there are just three possible outcomes for GM stock, suppose that there are N distinct states., where N can be any number. Each state occurs with a particular probability ($p_1+p_2+...p_N=1.0$) and results in a specific return on GM shares (R_1, R_2, R_3,....). In this case, the expected return equals:

$$E(R) = p_1R_1 + p_2R_2 + p_3R_3 + ... + p_NR_N$$

The analyst can apply the same model to any stock with returns tied to the business cycle. For example, purchases of Coca-Cola do not vary over the business cycle as much as car purchases do, so Coke stock should be less sensitive to economic conditions than GM's stock is. Perhaps when the economy is booming, Coke shareholders earn 36 percent. Under normal economic conditions, Coke stock earns 12 percent, but during an economic slump, the return on Coke shares equals –15 percent. Maintaining the same assumptions about the probabilities of recession, expansion, and boom, estimates of Coke's expected return, variance, and standard deviation can be constructed as follows:

Outcome	Probability	Coke Return	Return – 9%	(Return – 9%)^2
Recession	20%	–15%	–24%	576%^{2}
Expansion	70%	12%	3%	9%^{2}
Boom	10%	36%	27%	729%^{2}

Expected return = (0.20)(–15%) + (0.70)(12%) + (0.10)(36%) = 9%

Variance = (0.20)(576%^{2})+(0.70)(9%^{2})+(0.10)(729%^{2}) = 194.4%^{2}

Standard Deviation = $\sqrt{194.4\%^2}$ = 13.9%

But the probabilistic approach has its own drawbacks. To calculate expected returns for GM and Coca-Cola, we started with a simplifying assumption that only three possible outcomes or scenarios were possible. Clearly, the range of potential outcomes is much broader than this. Similarly, we assumed that we could know the probability of each scenario in advance. Where did those probabilities come from? Analysts can draw from historical experience, for example, by estimating the probability of a recession by studying the frequencies of recessions in the past. If history shows that recessions occur in roughly one year out of every five, then 20 percent might be a reasonable estimate of the probability of a recession in the future; then again, it might be well off the mark. In any case, the probabilistic approach involves a high degree of subjectivity. It requires analysts to specify possible future outcomes for stock returns and to attach a probability to each outcome. Once again, these assumptions about possible states of the economy can be somewhat naïve if the assumptions are based on historical data.

The Risk-Based Approach

A third approach to estimate an asset's expected return is more theoretically sound and is used in practice by most corporate finance professionals. It requires an analyst to first measure the risk of the asset and then to translate that risk measure into an expected return estimate. This approach involves a two-step process. The first step is to define what we mean by risk and to measure it, and the second step is to quantify how much return we should expect on an asset with a given amount of risk.

Measuring the Risk of a Single Asset. Recall that Chapter 6 introduced the notions of systematic and unsystematic risk. Remember these concepts:

- *Systematic risks* simultaneously affect many different securities, whereas unsystematic risks affect just a few securities at a time. Systematic risk refers to events, such as unexpected changes in the overall health of the economy, interest rate movements, or changes in inflation. Events that we classify as examples of *unsystematic risk* include the failure of a firm's new product to gain market share, a scandal involving top management at a particular company, or the loss of a key employee.[2]
- Investors *can eliminate unsystematic risk by diversifying,* but diversification cannot eradicate systematic (or market) risk. Because it is easy for investors to shed one type of risk but not the other, the *market pays investors for bearing systematic risk.* That is, assets with more exposure to systematic risk generally offer investors higher returns than assets with less exposure to systematic risk. We see evidence of that proposition in the historical record, such as the higher long-term average return on stocks compared to T-bonds or T-bills.
- The standard deviation of an asset's returns measures how much returns fluctuate around the average. Standard deviation makes no distinction between a movement in returns caused by systematic factors, such as an increase in the price of oil, and movements associated with unsystematic factors, such as the outcome of a product liability lawsuit filed against one firm. In other words, *the standard deviation measures an asset's total risk, equal to the sum of its systematic and unsystematic components*. Because only the systematic component of risk influences an asset's expected return, an asset's standard deviation is an unreliable guide to its expected return.

If systematic risk means risk that affects the entire market, then for an individual stock, we need to know the extent to which the stock moves when the market moves. We need a measure that captures *only* the systematic component of a stock's volatility, because *only* that component should be related to the asset's expected return. When an event having a positive (or negative) effect on the overall market also has a pronounced positive (or negative) effect on a particular stock, then that stock has a high degree of systematic risk and should also have a high expected return.

For a visual explanation of this idea, examine Figures 7.1A and 7.1B. The figure shows scatter plots of weekly stock returns for two companies, The Sharper Image and ConAgra, versus the weekly return on the Standard and Poors 500 Stock Index (S&P 500).[3] For example, each dot in Figure 7.1A shows the return on The Sharper Image stock and the return on the S&P 500 in a particular week. Through each scatter plot we have drawn a trendline, estimated by using the method of linear regression. This trendline shows the average tendency for each stock to move with the market.

2. Notice that all these examples are negative events, in the sense that we expect them to cause the firm's stock price to fall. Of course, risk means that outcomes can be surprisingly good, just as they can be surprisingly bad.

3. The S&P 500 is a market index consisting of 500 large U.S. stocks. It is one of the most widely watched barometers of the overall U.S. stock market, so we use it here as a proxy for the entire market.

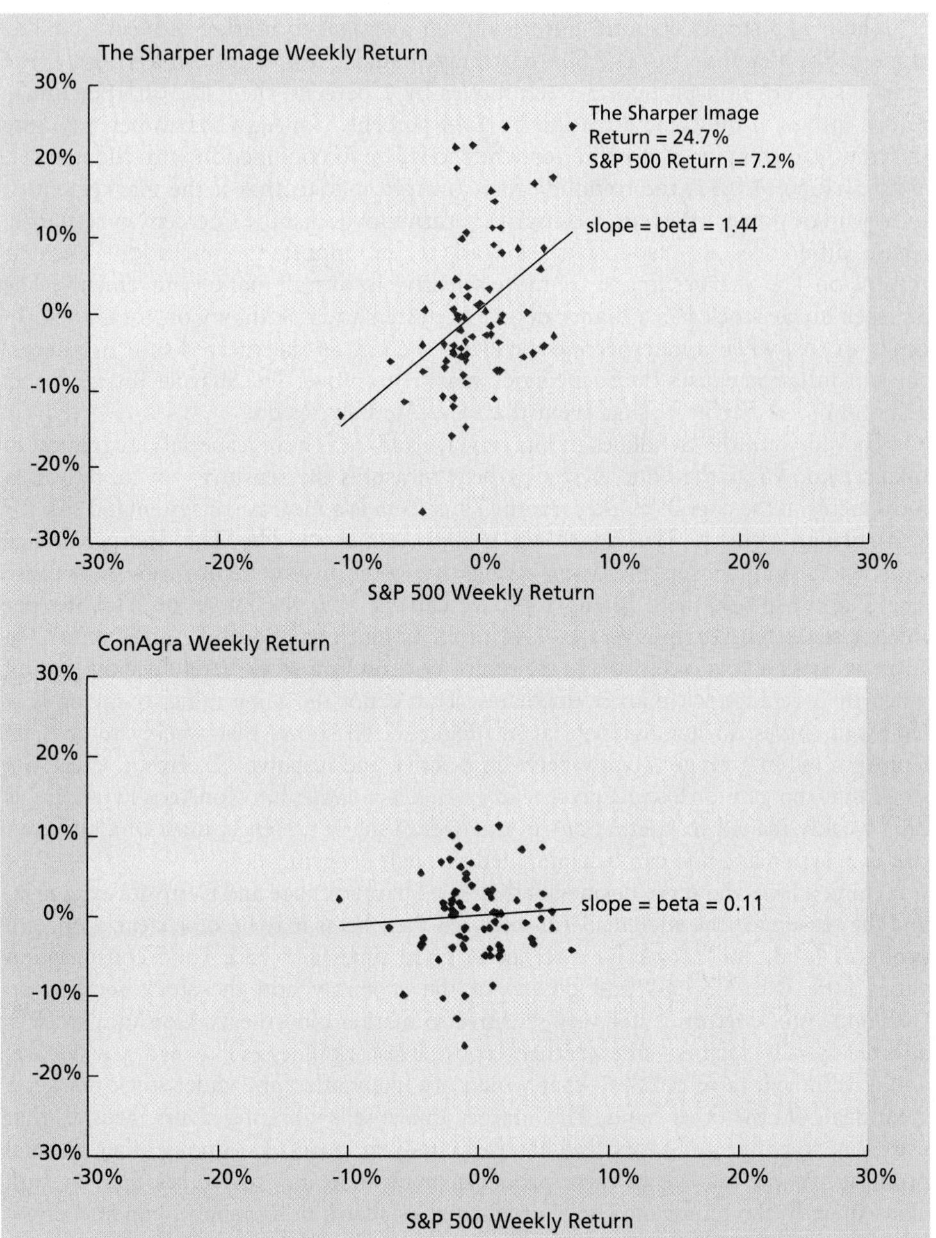

Figure 7.1A
Scatter Plot of Weekly Returns on The Sharper Image vs. The S&P 500 Stock Index

Figure 7.1B
Scatter Plot of Weekly Returns on ConAgra vs. The S&P 500 Stock Index

The figure shows a scatter plot of weekly returns on The Sharper Image stock (Figure 7.1A) and ConAgra stock (Figure 7.1B) versus the weekly return on the S&P 500 stock index. The scatter plots reveal a strong association between movements in the overall market return and movements in The Sharper Image. The link between market movements and ConAgra is much weaker.

These two stocks respond differently, on average, to market movements. The slope of the trendline for The Sharper Image equals 1.44. Thus, on average, if the market's return in a particular week moves by 1 percent, then The Sharper Image return moves in the same direction by 1.44 percent. ConAgra shares behave quite differently, displaying almost no tendency to move in conjunction with the market. With a slope of 0.11, the trendline for ConAgra tells us that if the market return moves up or down 1 percent, ConAgra's return moves just 0.11 percent in response. These differences in responsiveness lead to an important conclusion. Because returns on The Sharper Image are more sensitive to overall market movements, The Sharper Image stock has a higher degree of systematic risk than ConAgra stock. In other words, when a macroeconomic event such as an unexpected shift in interest rates or inflation causes the entire stock market to move, The Sharper Image shares respond more sharply to that event than ConAgra shares do.

beta
A standardized measure of the risk of an individual asset, one that captures only the systematic component of its volatility.

The slopes of the trendlines in Figure 7.1A and 7.1B have a special designation in finance, known as the **beta**. A stock's beta measures the sensitivity of its return to movements in the overall market return. Thus, beta is a measure of systematic risk for a particular security. The return on a high-beta stock like The Sharper Image experiences dramatic up-and-down swings when the market return moves. Because The Sharper Image's beta equals 1.44, we can say that the return on The Sharper Image's shares moves, on average, 1.44 times as much as does the market return. In contrast, with a beta of just 0.11, the return on ConAgra stock barely responds at all when the overall stock market fluctuates. This is not the same thing as saying that ConAgra shares do not fluctuate at all. Figure 7.1B shows that weekly returns on ConAgra fall in a range roughly between positive and negative 12 percent. Clearly, a stock that can gain or lose 12 percent in a week is volatile, but ConAgra's volatility is only weakly related to fluctuations in the overall market. Hence, most of ConAgra's risk is unsystematic and can be eliminated through diversification.

Think a little about the businesses that The Sharper Image and ConAgra engage in, and the reason for the wide disparity between their betas may become clear. ConAgra produces food, and people have to eat in good times and bad. Food consumption varies little with the ups and downs of the economy and the stock market, so ConAgra's stock return is not very sensitive to market movements. ConAgra stock is affected more by factors—like weather (crops), livestock illnesses like mad cow disease, and government farm policies—that would not likely affect the wider stock market a great deal. On the other hand, The Sharper Image sells vibrating chairs, brushes that use ozone to reduce pet odors, and handheld body-fat analyzers, among other unusual products. People indulge in these products much more in good times than in bad. Consequently, the return on The Sharper Image's shares moves sharply up and down in response to changing macroeconomic conditions.

Risk and Expected Returns. The risk-based approach to calculating expected returns involves two steps. The first step is to develop a measure of a particular asset's systematic risk. In *beta* we have such a measure. The second step involves translating the asset's beta into an estimate of expected return. To see how that process works, examine Figure 7.2.

In Figure 7.2, we plot the beta against the expected return for two important assets. First, suppose an asset is available that pays a return equal to 4 percent with certainty. We designate this as the risk-free asset because it pays 4 percent no matter

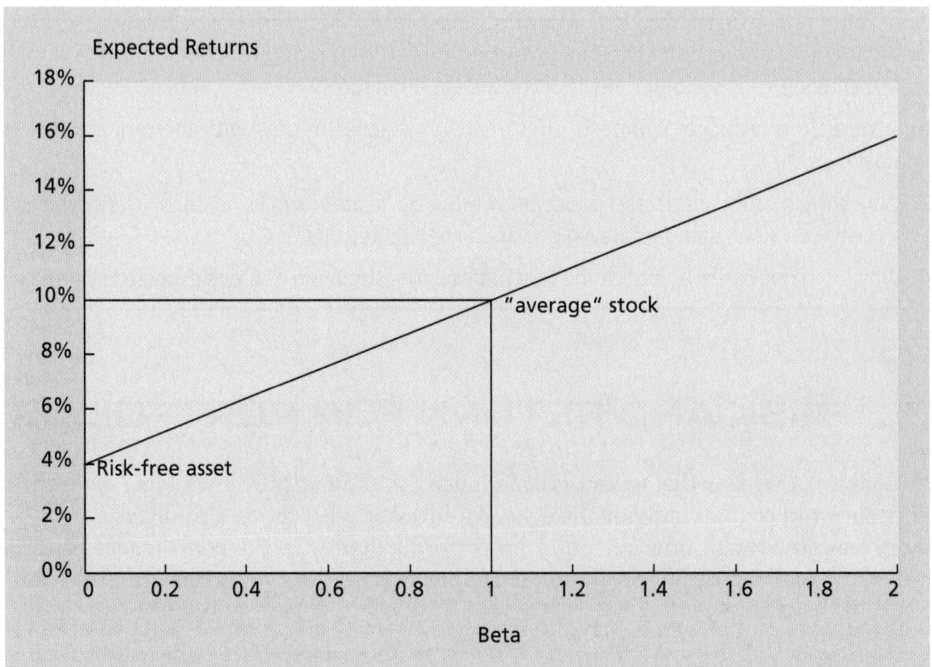

Figure 7.2
Beta and Expected Returns

An investor willing to accept an average level of systematic risk, by holding a stock with a beta of 1.0, expects a return of 10%. By holding only the risk-free asset, an investor can earn 4%, without having to accept any systematic risk at all.

what the market return may be. In reality, no asset can promise a completely risk-free return, but a U.S. Treasury bill comes very close. Therefore, think of a T-bill each time we refer to a risk-free asset. By definition, *a risk-free asset has no systematic risk, and so its beta equals zero*. We also say that 4 percent is the risk-free rate.

The second asset plotted in Figure 7.2 is an average stock. The term "average stock" means that this security's sensitivity to market movements is neither especially high, like The Sharper Image, nor especially low, like ConAgra. By definition, *the beta of the average stock equals 1.0*. On average, its return goes up or down by 1 percent when the market return goes up or down by 1 percent. Assume for a moment that the expected return on this stock equals 10 percent.

By drawing a straight line connecting the two points in Figure 7.2, we gain some insight into the relationship between beta and expected returns. An investor who is unwilling to accept any systematic risk at all can hold the risk-free asset and earn 4 percent. An investor who is willing to bear an average degree of systematic risk, by investing in a stock with a beta equal to 1.0, expects to earn 10 percent. But how about an investor who wants to take an intermediate level of risk, by holding a stock with a beta of 0.5? Or an investor who has a high tolerance for risk and prefers to hold a stock with a beta of 1.5?

As you might guess, we can simply find the desired beta along the horizontal axis and then go up to the line to find that asset's expected return. For example, a stock with a beta of 0.5 has an expected return of 7 percent, while a stock with a beta of 1.5 has an expected return of 13 percent. The line in Figure 7.2 plays a very important role in finance, and we will return to it later in this chapter. For now, the important lesson is that *beta measures an asset's systematic risk and risk that has a direct relationship with expected returns*.

CONCEPT REVIEW QUESTIONS

1. What is the difference between an asset's *expected return* and its actual return? Why are expected returns so important to investors and managers?

2. Contrast the historical approach to estimating expected returns with the probabilistic approach.

3. Why should *stock betas* and expected returns be related, while no such relationship exists between stock standard deviations and expected returns?

4. Why is the risk-based approach the best method for estimating a stock's expected return?

7.2 RISK AND RETURN FOR PORTFOLIOS

In Chapter 6, we saw that investors can reduce risk dramatically by holding diversified portfolios rather than individual stocks. An investor who chooses to diversify will be more concerned with how her portfolio performs than with the performance of each individual security in the portfolio. Therefore, we need a way to measure risk and return for portfolios.

Portfolio Expected Return

Suppose an individual has \$10,000 to invest, and she decides to divide that money between two different assets. Asset 1 has an expected return of 8 percent, and Asset 2 has an expected return of 12 percent. Our investor puts \$4,000 in Asset 1 and \$6,000 in Asset 2. What is the expected return on the portfolio?

portfolio weights
The percentage invested in each of several securities in a portfolio. Portfolio weights must sum to 1.0 (or 100%).

To begin, we must calculate the fraction of the individual's wealth invested in each asset, known as the **portfolio weights**. The fraction invested in Asset 1 equals 0.40 (\$4,000/\$10,000), and the fraction invested in Asset 2 equals 0.60 (\$6,000/\$10,000). Notice that the portfolio weights add up to 1.0.

The portfolio's expected return equals the weighted average of the expected returns of the securities in the portfolio. In this case, the expected return equals:

$$\text{Expected return} = (0.40)(8\%) + (0.60)(12\%) = 10.4\%$$

We can write down a more general expression describing a portfolio's expected return. Suppose a portfolio contains N different securities. The expected returns on these securities are $E(R_1)$, $E(R_2)$, ..., $E(R_N)$. Finally, the portfolio weights are w_1, w_2, ..., w_N. The portfolio expected return $E(R_p)$ is given by the following equation:

$$E(R_p) = w_1 E(R_1) + w_2 E(R_2) + \ldots + w_N E(R_N) \quad \text{(Eq. 7.1)}$$
$$w_1 + w_2 + \ldots + w_N = 1$$

APPLYING THE MODEL

Calculate the expected return on the portfolio described in the following table.

Stock	$E(R)$	$ Invested
IBM	10%	$ 2,500
GE	12%	$ 5,000
Sears	8%	$ 2,500
Pfizer	14%	$10,000

First, calculate the portfolio weights. The total dollar value of the portfolio is $20,000. The weights for the investments in Pfizer and Sears are 0.125 ($2,500/$20,000). The fraction invested in GE is 0.25, and the weight associated with Pfizer is 0.50. Now multiply those weights times the expected return for each stock and add up:

$$E(R_p) = (0.125)(10\%) + (0.25)(12\%) + (0.125)(8\%) + (0.5)(14\%) = 12.25\%$$

SMART CONCEPTS

See the concept explained step-by-step at

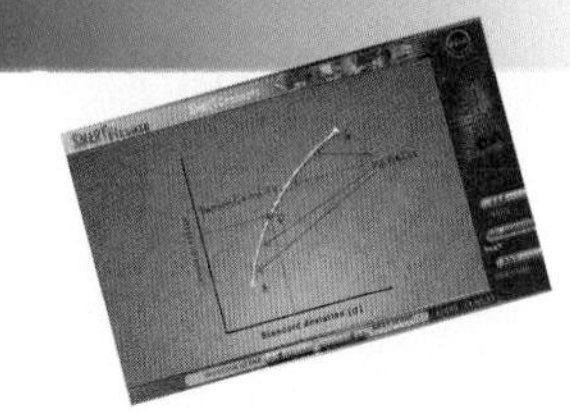

Short Selling (Optional). We noted that the portfolio weights have to add up to one. It is natural to assume that these weights also fall in a range between zero and one, meaning that an investor can invest nothing or everything in any particular asset. However, a more exotic arrangement is possible, one that results in a negative portfolio weight for a particular asset. A negative portfolio weight means that rather than investing in the given asset, an individual is borrowing that asset, selling it, and using the proceeds to invest more in something else. When investors borrow a security and sell it to raise money to invest in something else, they are said to be **selling short**. Here's how that works.

Consider two assets in the market, Rocket.com and BricksNMortar Inc. Both stocks currently sell for $10 and pay no dividends. You are optimistic about Rocket.com's prospects, and you expect its return next year to be 25 percent. In contrast, you believe that BricksNMortar will earn just 5 percent. You have $1,000 to invest, but you'd like to invest more than that in Rocket.com. To do this, you phone a friend who owns 50 shares of BricksNMortar and persuade him to let you borrow the shares, by promising that you'll return them in one year. Once you receive the shares, you sell them in the market, immediately raising $500. Next, you combine those funds with your own money and purchase $1,500 (150 shares) of Rocket.com. Your portfolio expected return looks like this:

$$E(R_p) = (-0.5)(5\%) + (1.5)(25\%) = 35\%$$

selling short
Borrowing a security and selling it for cash at the current market price. An investor who sells short must eventually return the security to the lender by purchasing it at the then-current market price. Therefore, a short seller hopes that either (1) the price of the security sold short will fall, or (2) the return on the security sold short will be lower than the return on the asset in which the proceeds from the short sale were invested.

In this equation, the weight invested in Rocket.com equals 1.5 ($1,500 ÷ $1,000), or 150% of your total wealth. You can invest more than 100 percent of your wealth (i.e., more than $1,000) because you borrowed from someone else. The weight invested in BricksNMortar equals –0.5 because you took out a $500 loan equivalent to half your wealth. If you are right and BricksNMortar shares go up from $10 to $10.50 during the year (an increase of 5 percent), then you will effectively pay your friend 5 percent interest when you repurchase the BricksNMortar shares and return them next year. This loan will be very profitable if Rocket.com stock increases as rapidly as you expect. For example, in one year's time, if BricksNMortar sells for $10.50 and Rocket.com sells for $12.50 (up 25 percent), your position will look like this:

Beginning of Year		
Initial investment	$1,000	
Borrowed funds	$ 500	(50 shares @ $10)
Rocket shares	$1,500	(150 shares @ $10)
End of Year		
Sell Rocket shares	$1,875	(150 shares @ $12.50)
Return borrowed Shares	–$ 525	(50 shares @ $10.50)
Net cash earned	$1,350	
Rate of return = ($1,350 – $1,000) / $1,000 = 0.35 = 35%		

Notice that the expected return on this portfolio exceeds the expected return of either stock in the portfolio. When investors take a short position in one asset to invest more in another asset, they are using *financial leverage*. As noted in Chapter 12, leverage magnifies expected returns, but it also increases risk.

Portfolio Risk

Based on the calculation of a portfolio's expected return, you may expect that a portfolio's risk is equal to a weighted average of the risks of the assets that comprise the portfolio. That statement is partly right and partly wrong. When we shift our focus from expected return to risk, we have to be very careful about the measure of risk that we use in our calculations.

For instance, in Table 6.5 in the previous chapter, we estimated the standard deviation of returns for Advanced Micro Devices to be 56.4 percent. The same table reported a standard deviation for American Airlines (AMR) of 47.8 percent. Suppose we form a portfolio invested equally in AMD and AMR shares. With portfolio weights of 0.50, you might guess that the standard deviation of this portfolio equals:

$$\text{Portfolio standard deviation} = (0.50)(56.4\%) + (0.50)(47.8\%) = 52.1\%$$

As reasonable as that guess seems, it is wrong. In the previous chapter, Figure 6.8 showed that a portfolio invested in equal proportions of AMD and AMR had a standard deviation of just 45 percent! As a general rule, the standard deviation of a portfolio is almost always less than the weighted average of the standard deviations of the stocks in the portfolio. This is diversification at work. Combining securities together eliminates some of their unsystematic risk, so the portfolio is less volatile than the average stock in the portfolio.

SMART IDEAS VIDEO

Andrew Karolyi, The Ohio State University

"Investors who seek to diversify internationally to reduce their global risk can leave money on the table if they ignore the unique industrial compositions of markets."

See the entire interview at **SMARTFinance**

However, diversification does not eliminate systematic risk. Therefore, if we redefine portfolio risk and focus on systematic risk only, not on standard deviation, which includes both systematic and unsystematic risk, then the simple weighted average formula works. For example, suppose AMD stock has a beta of 1.8 and AMR's beta equals 1.4. The beta of a portfolio with equal investments in each stock is:

$$\text{Portfolio Beta} = \beta_{\text{p}} = (0.50)(1.8) + (0.05)(1.4) = 1.6$$

APPLYING THE MODEL

Calculate the beta of the portfolio described in the following table.

Stock	Beta	$ Invested
IBM	1.00	$ 2,500
GE	1.33	$ 5,000
Sears	0.67	$ 2,500
Pfizer	1.67	$10,000

The portfolio weights here are the same as in the previous *Applying the Model,* so the portfolio beta equals:

$$\beta_{\text{p}} = (0.125)(1.00) + (0.25)(1.33) + (0.125)(0.67) + (0.50)(1.67) = 1.38$$

The Comparative Corporate Finance insert illustrates why distinguishing between systematic and unsystematic risk is important, not just for investors who buy stocks and bonds, but also for corporations that build factories, invest in distribution networks, and make other kinds of investments in physical assets.

CONCEPT REVIEW QUESTIONS

5. How can the weight given to a particular stock in a portfolio exceed 100 percent?

6. Why is the standard deviation of a portfolio typically less than the weighted average of the standard deviations of the assets in the portfolio, while a portfolio's beta equals the weighted average of the betas of the stocks in the portfolio?

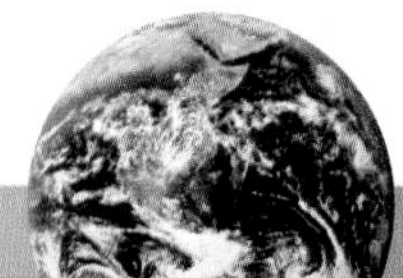

COMPARATIVE CORPORATE FINANCE

How Risky Are Emerging Markets?

Over the past twenty-five years, many developing countries around the world adopted market-oriented reforms and opened their economies to inflows of foreign capital. Despite the success these countries have enjoyed in attracting new investors, a recent report by the consulting firm McKinsey & Company argues that most multinational corporations dramatically overestimate the risk of investing in these "emerging markets." According to McKinsey, these companies routinely assign a risk premium to projects in emerging markets that is more than double the risk premium that the same companies assign to similar projects in the United States and Europe. By overstating the risks, multinational firms understate the value of investments in emerging markets. McKinsey & Company believes that this leads firms to pass up profitable investment opportunities in these countries.

If it is true that firms overstate the risks of investing in emerging markets, what is the cause of that error? McKinsey proposes that firms do not take the proper portfolio view of the businesses they engage in around the world. Rather than looking at each business unit's contribution to overall firm risk (i.e., the contribution of each unit to the firm's portfolio of businesses), companies place too much emphasis on the unsystematic risks associated with individual countries.

To show how a portfolio view might change a firm's perception of the risk of investing in particular countries, McKinsey offers several pieces of evidence. The first graph shows the year-to-year variation in returns on investments in five separate countries. Clearly these investments display a great deal of volatility. However, for a multinational firm that holds each of these investments in a portfolio the picture changes considerably. The second graph contains two lines, one showing the performance of the *portfolio* of investments in five emerging markets and the other showing the performance of investments in developed markets. In the second picture, the emerging market portfolio does not appear to be much more volatile than the portfolio invested in assets in the more developed markets of the United States and Europe. (Note: the returns shown here are returns on physical investments like manufacturing plants, not stock returns).

McKinsey provides a second kind of evidence to buttress its argument. For each emerging market, McKinsey

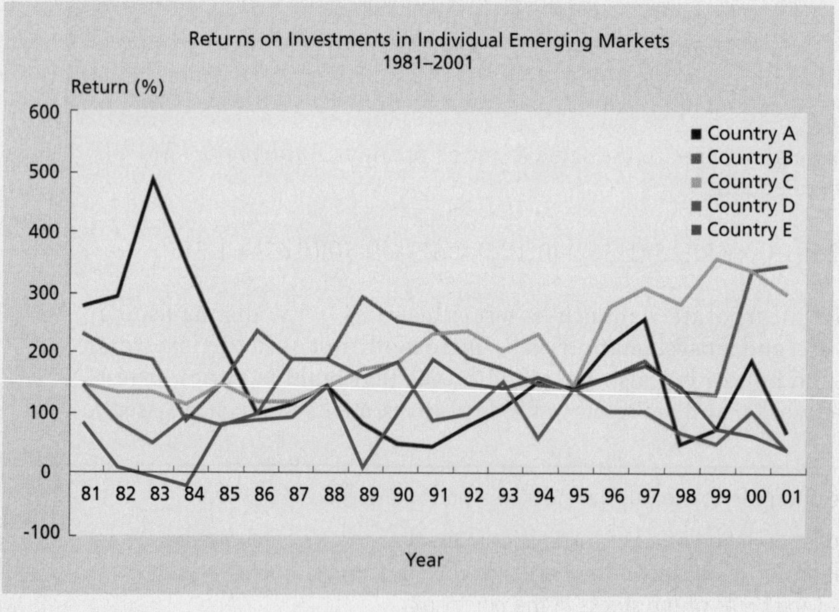

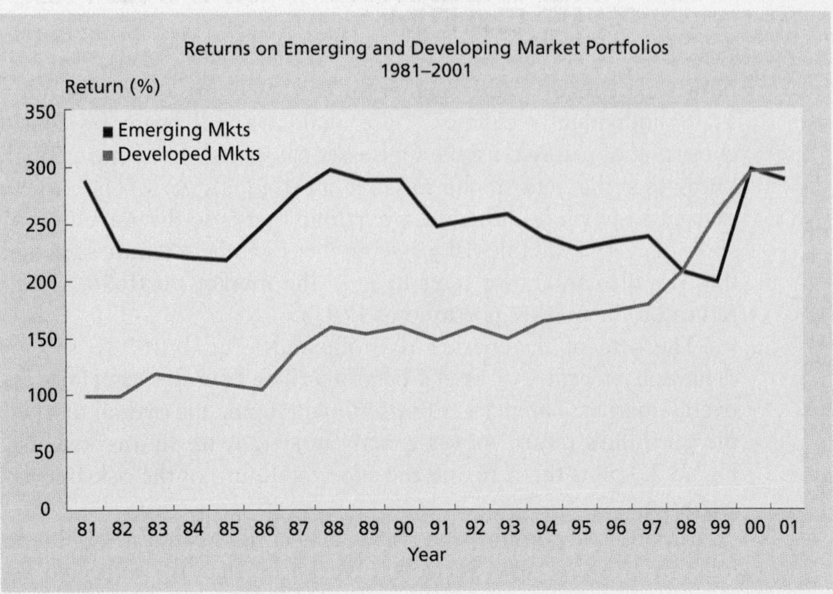

calculates that market's beta relative to a world market index. By definition, the world market's beta equals 1.0. Especially risky countries should have betas much greater than 1.0, while supposedly "safe" countries like the United States should have betas below 1.0. The bar chart shows betas for the United States, Europe, and twenty-two emerging markets. Ten emerging markets have a beta below that of the U.S. market, and in only one country, Russia, does the market beta justify a risk premium double that of the United States. The three charts here tell a common story. Investments that seem to be very risky when considered in isolation look much less risky as part of a portfolio. That's a lesson that applies to individual investors as well as to multinational corporations.

Source: "Are Emerging Markets as Risky as You Think?" by Marc H. Goedhart and Peter Haden, *McKinsey on Finance*, Spring 2003.

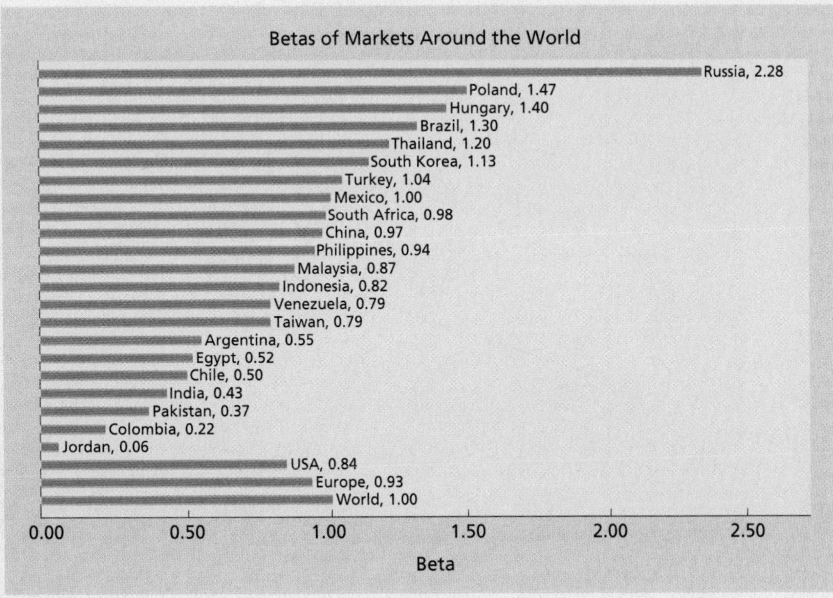

7.3 THE SECURITY MARKET LINE AND THE CAPM

Now we are ready to tie together the concepts of risk and return for portfolios as well as for individual securities. Once again we will begin by considering a portfolio consisting of just two assets. One asset pays a risk-free return equal to R_f. We already know that the beta of the risk-free asset equals zero. The other asset is a broadly diversified portfolio. Imagine a portfolio that is so diversified that it contains at least some of every available risky asset in the economy. Because such a portfolio represents the overall market, we refer to it as the **market portfolio**. Designate the expected return on the market portfolio as $E(R_m)$.

market portfolio
A portfolio that contains some of every asset in the economy.

The beta of the market portfolio must equal 1.0. To see why, reconsider the definition of beta. An asset's beta describes how the asset moves in relation to the overall market. The market portfolio will mimic the overall market perfectly. Because the portfolio's return moves exactly in sync with the market, its beta must be 1.0. Figure 7.3 plots the beta and the expected return of the risk-free asset and the market portfolio.

Suppose we combine the risk-free asset, let's call it a T-bill, and the market portfolio to create a new portfolio. We know that the expected return on this new portfolio must be a weighted average of the expected returns of the assets in the portfolio. Similarly, we know that the beta of the portfolio must be a weighted average of the betas of a T-bill and the market. This implies that the new portfolio we've created must lie along the line connecting the risk-free asset and the market portfolio in Figure 7.3. What are the properties of this line?

With two points identified on the line, the T-bill and the market portfolio, we can calculate the line's slope by taking the rise over the run:

$$\text{Slope} = \frac{E(R_m) - R_f}{1 - 0} = E(R_m) - R_f$$

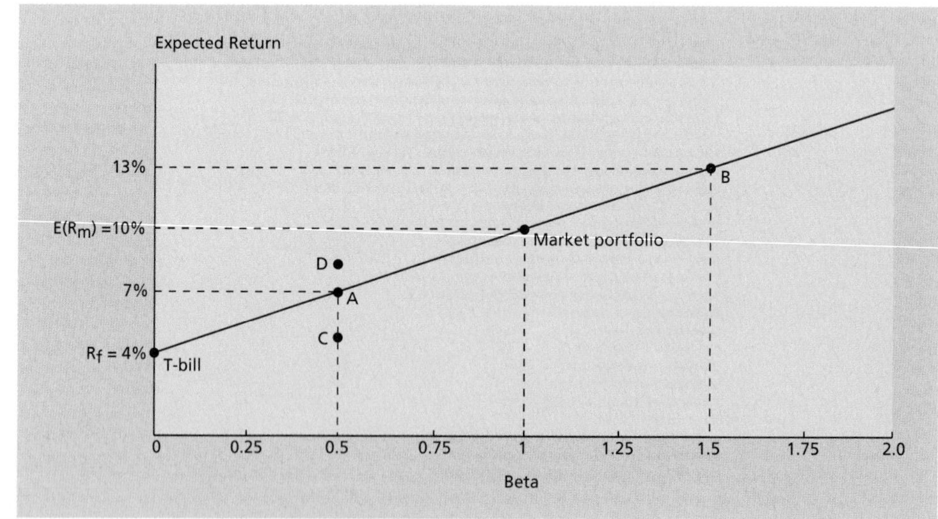

Figure 7.3
The Security Market Line

The Security Market Line plots the relationship between an asset's beta and its expected return. The line shows how an investor can construct a portfolio of T-bills and the market portfolio to achieve the desired level of risk and return. One investor might choose a relatively conservative portfolio, mixing T-bills and the market portfolio in equal proportions. Another investor could construct a very risky portfolio by investing his own money and borrowing more to invest in the market.

This expression should be familiar. The difference in returns between a portfolio of risky securities and a risk-free asset is the **market risk premium**. The market risk premium indicates the reward that investors receive if they hold the market portfolio.

market risk premium The additional return earned (or expected) on the market portfolio over and above the risk-free rate.

The intercept of the line in Figure 7.3 equals R_f. From elementary algebra we know that the equation for a straight line is $y = b + mx$ where b is the intercept and m is the slope. In Figure 7.3, the variable we measure on the y-axis is the expected return on some portfolio of T-bills and the market portfolio. The variable we measure on the x-axis is the beta of this portfolio. Therefore, the equation of the line plotted in this figure is

$$E(R_p) = R_f + B_p\left[E(R_m) - R_f\right]$$

The equation says that the expected return on any portfolio consisting of T-bills and the market portfolio depends on three things: the risk-free rate, the portfolio beta, and the market risk premium. It's easy to verify that this equation works with a numerical illustration.

APPLYING THE MODEL

Suppose the risk-free rate is 4 percent, and the expected return on the market portfolio is 10 percent. This implies that the market risk premium is 6 percent. What is the expected return on a portfolio invested equally in T-bills and stocks? There are actually several ways to get the answer. First, we know that the expected return on the portfolio is simply the weighted average of the expected returns of the assets in the portfolio, so we have:

$$E(R_p) = (0.5)(4\%) + (0.5)(10\%) = 7\%$$

Alternatively, we could begin by calculating the beta of this portfolio. The portfolio beta is a weighted average of the betas of T-bills and the market portfolio, so we obtain:

$$\beta_p = (0.5)(\text{Tbill beta}) + (0.5)(\text{market beta}) = (0.5)(0) + (0.5)(1.0) = 0.5$$

Now, using the equation of the line in Figure 7.3, we calculate the portfolio's expected return as follows:

$$E(R_p) = 4\% + (0.5)\left[10\% - 4\%\right] = 7\%$$

The position of this portfolio appears as point A in Figure 7.3.

What if an investor is willing to hold a position that is even more risky that the market portfolio? One option is to borrow money. When investors buy T-bills, they are essentially loaning money to the government. Suppose investors also borrow money at the risk-free rate. To be more precise, suppose a certain investor has \$10,000 to invest, but he raises an additional \$5,000 by borrowing. The investor then puts all \$15,000 in the market portfolio. The portfolio weight on T-bills becomes –0.50, and the weight invested in the market portfolio increases to 1.50. The investor now holds a portfolio with a beta greater than one and an expected return greater than 10 percent, as confirmed in the following calculations:

$$\beta_p = -(0.5)(0) + (1.5)(1.0) = 1.5$$

$$E(R_p) = 4\% + (1.5)\left[10\% - 4\%\right] = 13\%$$

SMART IDEAS VIDEO

William Sharpe, Stanford University, Co-founder, Financial Engines

"To the extent that there is a premium for bearing risk, it is a premium for bearing the risk of doing badly in bad times."

See the entire interview at SMARTFinance

In Figure 7.3, the investor's portfolio lies up and to the right from the market portfolio at point B.

At this point, we must stop and make a crucial observation. If it is true, as the preceding *Applying the Model* shows, that a portfolio with a beta of 0.5 offers an expected return of 7 percent, then in equilibrium it must also be true that any individual security with a beta of 0.5 offers the same return. To understand this claim, examine point C in Figure 7.3. This point represents a stock with a beta of 0.5 and an expected return of less than 7 percent. Rational investors who own C will sell it, because they can create an equally risky portfolio that offers a higher return, by combining T-bills and the market portfolio. As investors sell asset C, its price will fall. We know that prices and returns of financial assets move in opposite directions, so as the price of C falls, its expected return rises until it reaches 7 percent.

Similarly, consider point D in the figure. Point D represents an asset with a beta of 0.5 but an expected return greater than 7 percent. This asset is a true bargain because it offers investors a higher rate of return than they can earn on a 50-50 portfolio of T-bills and stocks, without requiring them to take on extra risk. Investors will rush to buy stock D, and their buying pressure will drive up the price and push down the return of stock D. As soon as the expected return on D reaches 7 percent, the market once again reaches equilibrium.

Capital Asset Pricing Model (CAPM)
States that the expected return on a specific asset equals the risk-free rate plus a premium that depends on the asset's beta and the expected risk premium on the market portfolio.

Figure 7.3 therefore plots the relationship between betas and expected returns for individual securities as well as for portfolios. This relationship is called The Security Market Line, and the equation of this line is the fundamental risk and return relationship predicted by the **Capital Asset Pricing Model (CAPM)**. The CAPM says that the expected return on any asset i, denoted by $E(R_i)$, depends on the risk-free rate, the security's beta, and the market risk premium:

$$E(R_i) = R_f + \beta_i \left(E(R_m) - R_f\right) \quad \text{(Eq. 7.2)}$$

SMART CONCEPTS

See the concept explained step-by-step at SMARTFinance

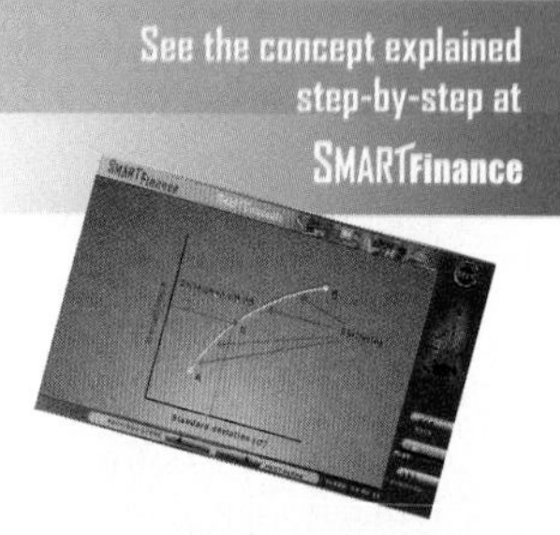

The Capital Asset Pricing Model stands as one of the most important ideas in all of finance. Financial managers in nearly all large corporations know the model's key predictions, and they use the CAPM to establish required rates of return on all types of investment projects. The CAPM helps managers understand what returns the market requires on projects having different risk levels. That knowledge improves the quality of corporate investment decisions. As useful as it is, however, the CAPM is not a crystal ball. It gives us some insights about expected returns, but that is not the same thing as predicting how the future will unfold. In the next section, we explore the extent to which actual stock returns, rather than expected returns, may be predictable.

CONCEPT REVIEW QUESTIONS

7. List the three factors that influence a stock's expected return according to the CAPM.

8. If a particular stock had no systematic risk, only unsystematic risk, what would be its expected return?

7.4 ARE STOCK RETURNS PREDICTABLE?

Microsoft Corp. debuted as a public company with its initial public offering (IPO) on March 13, 1986. On that day, one Microsoft share sold for $21. In the eighteen years that followed, stock splits turned a single share purchased at the IPO into 288 shares, worth an amazing $7,200 by March 2004. That represents a compound annual return of more than 38 percent per year! The purpose of this section is to investigate whether such a spectacular outcome could have been anticipated by smart investors.

Suppose upon graduating from business school you decide to forsake a career in the corporate world and open your own business. The question is, what kind of business should you start? A friend suggests opening a pizza restaurant. Having learned a few valuable lessons in school, you respond that the pizza business is a terrible place to start. Most communities are already saturated with pizza parlors. Most of those offer the similar varieties of pizza with a similar ambience, or lack thereof. You want to find a niche that is less competitive. You reason that getting rich selling pizzas is nearly impossible.

As competitive as the pizza business is, it hardly compares with the competitive environment of modern financial markets. The sheer size and transparency of financial markets make them more competitive than most markets for goods and services. Financial asset prices are set by open auction in arenas that are typically governed by rules designed to make the auction process as fair and open as possible. Each day, thousands of professional financial analysts (to say nothing of the tens of thousands of amateurs) worldwide scrutinize all available information about high-profile stocks such as Microsoft, hoping to find any bit of information overlooked by the crowd that might lead to an advantage in determining the fair value of Microsoft shares. The rapid growth of electronic media during the past two decades, especially the Internet, has caused an explosion in the total volume of financial information available to investors and has accelerated the speed with which that information arrives. All of this means that being a better-than-average stock prognosticator is probably more difficult than building a better pizza.

In finance, the idea that competition in financial markets creates an equilibrium in which it is exceedingly difficult to identify undervalued or overvalued stocks is called the **efficient markets hypothesis (EMH)**. The EMH says that financial asset prices rapidly and fully incorporate new information. An interesting implication of this prediction is that asset prices move almost randomly over time. We have to use the qualifier, "almost" in the previous sentence because there is a kind of baseline predictability to asset returns that is related to risk. For example, over time, we expect stocks to earn higher returns than bonds, because stocks are riskier. Indeed, the historical record confirms this prediction. But in any given year, stocks may do very well or very poorly relative to bonds. The efficient markets hypothesis says that it is nearly impossible to predict exactly when stocks will do well relative to bonds or when the opposite outcome will occur.

efficient markets hypothesis (EMH)
Asserts that financial asset prices fully reflect all available information (as formally presented by Eugene Fama in 1970).

The seemingly random changes in stock prices occur because prices respond only to new information, and new information is almost by definition unpredictable. A few examples will illustrate this point.

Unconvinced that market efficiency makes stock prices nearly unpredictable, you dig through the archives of historical stock returns searching for trading strategies that, with the benefit of hindsight, would have been extraordinarily profitable. Your benchmark for success is the average annual return that an investor who bought stocks and held them every year would have

SMART PRACTICES VIDEO

Todd Richter, Managing Director, Head of Equity Healthcare Research, Bank of America Securities

"I don't necessarily believe that markets are efficient. I believe that markets tend toward efficiency."

See the entire interview at **SMARTFinance**

earned over the past century, 11.7 percent. The first strategy you test is the following:

Strategy 1: Buy stocks after particularly bad years when the market was down 10 percent or more. After a bad year, the market will surely bounce back.

Outcome: From 1900–2003, there were sixteen years in which the stock market fell by more than 10 percent. The average return the next year was 8 percent. The buy-and-hold approach easily beats this strategy.

Undeterred, you decide that perhaps another way to make money is to be out of the market when returns are poor. So you try the opposite approach:

Strategy 2: Sell stocks after particularly good years when the market was up 30 percent or more. After such a good year, stocks will surely display subpar performance the next year.

Outcome: From 1900–2003, there were seventeen years in which the stock market rose by more than 30 percent, excluding 2003. (We don't know how 2004 will turn out yet.) The average return on the market the next year was 10.6 percent. So these seventeen years did have below-average performance, but just barely. In any event, 10.6 percent is a higher return that an investor holding bonds or bills would have earned in these years. Again, the buy-and-hold approach seems superior.

Still searching for a strategy that will help you get rich quick, you decide that basing your trading rules on a single year's stock market performance is too short-sighted. This time you try:

Strategy 3: Buy stocks in any year in which the market has increased for the previous two years.

Outcome: Over the past century, stock prices increased in consecutive years fifty-five times. In the year following two consecutive years of positive stock returns, the average market return was 9 percent. Once again, while these years earned lower-than-average returns, investing in stocks still earned higher average returns than bonds or bills.

Of course, there is no end to the number of trading rules like these that can be tested using the historical data. In the vast majority of cases, these trading strategies do not generate significantly higher returns than a simple buy-and-hold approach. This suggests that stock prices are indeed nearly unpredictable.

The most compelling evidence that markets are efficient is a comparison of **passively managed** versus **actively managed** mutual funds. A mutual fund that adopts a passive management style is called an **index fund.** Index fund managers make no attempt to analyze stocks to determine which ones will perform well and which ones will do poorly. Instead, these managers try to mimic the performance of a market index, such as the S&P 500, by buying the stocks that make up the index. In contrast, fund managers adopting an active management style do extensive analysis to identify mispriced stocks. Active managers trade more frequently than passive managers do and in the process, generate higher expenses for their shareholders. Though there are notable exceptions (such as legendary managers Peter Lynch, Warren Buffet, and Bill Gross), most research indicates that active funds earn lower returns, after expenses, than passive funds do. Buy-and-hold wins again.

If this section concludes with the statement that stock returns are essentially unpredictable, then it is fair to ask why we place so much emphasis on the

passively managed
An approach to running a mutual fund in which the fund manager makes no attempt to identify over valued or under valued stocks, but instead holds a diversified portfolio and attempts to minimize the costs of operating the fund.

actively managed
An approach to running a mutual fund in which the fund manager does research to identify under valued and over valued stocks.

index fund
A passively managed fund that tries to mimic the performance of a market index such as the S&P 500.

SMART CONCEPTS

See the concept explained step-by-step at SMARTFinance

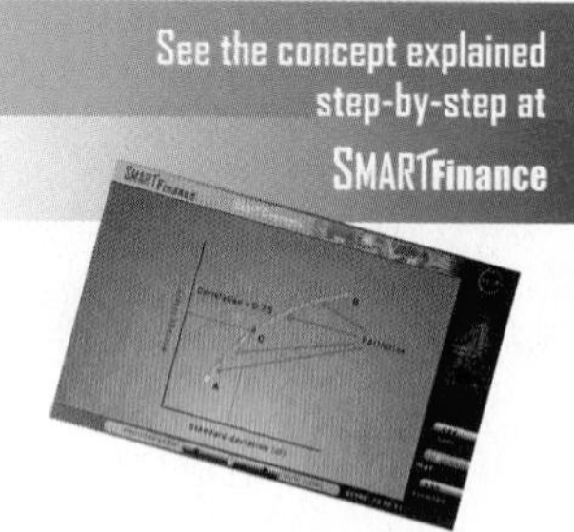

CAPM. After all, the CAPM's purpose is to provide an estimate of how a stock will perform in the future. If stock returns move essentially at random, then does the CAPM have any place in the practice of corporate finance?

It is true that the CAPM provides only an estimate of a stock's expected return and that actual outcomes deviate considerably (and unpredictably) from that estimate in any given year. Even so, the CAPM gives analysts a tool for measuring the systematic risk of any particular asset. Because assets with high systematic risk should, on average, earn higher return than assets with low systematic risk, the CAPM offers a framework for making educated guesses about the risk and return of investment alternatives. Though it is hardly infallible, that framework enjoys widespread use in corporate finance, as we will see in subsequent chapters.

CONCEPT REVIEW QUESTIONS

9. If the stock market is *efficient*, what makes it efficient?

10. If prices move almost at random, then why should we place any value on the CAPM, which makes predictions about expected asset returns?

7.5 SUMMARY AND CONCLUSIONS

- Investors and managers must make decisions based on expected returns.
- Estimates of expected returns may be obtained from historical data, from probabilistic calculations, or from a risk-based approach.
- An asset's beta measures its systematic risk, and it is this risk that should be linked to expected returns.
- The expected return of a portfolio equals a weighted average of the expected returns of the assets in the portfolio. The same can be said of the portfolio's beta.
- The standard deviation of a portfolio usually does not equal the weighted average of the standard deviation of the stocks in the portfolio. This is because some of the unsystematic fluctuations of individual stocks cancel each other out in a portfolio. A fully diversified portfolio contains only systematic risk.
- The CAPM predicts that the expected return on a stock depends on the stock's beta, the risk-free rate, and the market risk premium.
- In an efficient market, competition for information makes asset prices nearly unpredictable.

SELF-TEST PROBLEMS

Answers to Self-Test Problems appear in Appendix D at back of book. Answers to the Concept Review Questions throughout the chapter appear at http://megginson.swlearning.com.

ST7-1. Calculate the mean, variance, and standard deviations for a stock with the probability distribution outlined in the accompanying table:

Outcome	Probability	Stock Return
Recession	10%	−40%
Expansion	60%	20%
Boom	30%	50%

ST7-2. You invest $25,000 in T-bills and $50,000 in the market portfolio. If the risk-free rate equals 2 percent and the expected market risk premium is 6 percent, what is the expected return on your portfolio?

ST7-3. The risk-free rate equals 4 percent, and the expected return on the market is 10 percent. If a stock's expected return is 13 percent, what is the stock's beta?

INTERNET RESOURCES

http://www.yahoo.com—Type in the ticker for a stock or a mutual fund and gain access to historical returns and other information, including the stock's (or fund's) beta.

http://www.money.cnn.com/markets—Useful for obtaining current stock price and interest rate data.

KEY TERMS

actively managed
beta
Capital Asset Pricing Model (CAPM)
efficient markets hypothesis (EMH)
expected return
index fund
market portfolio
market risk premium
passively managed
portfolio weights
selling short

QUESTIONS AND PROBLEMS

Q7-1. Based on the charts below, which stock has more *systematic risk*, and which stock has more *unsystematic risk*?

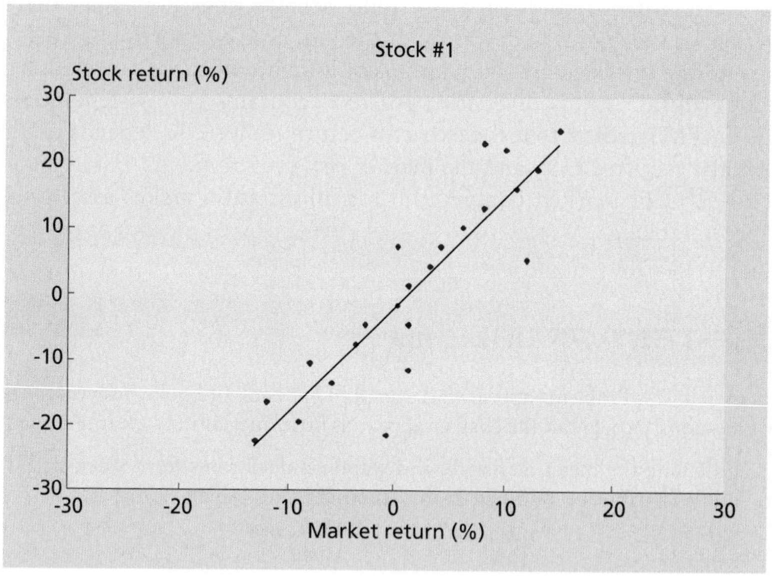

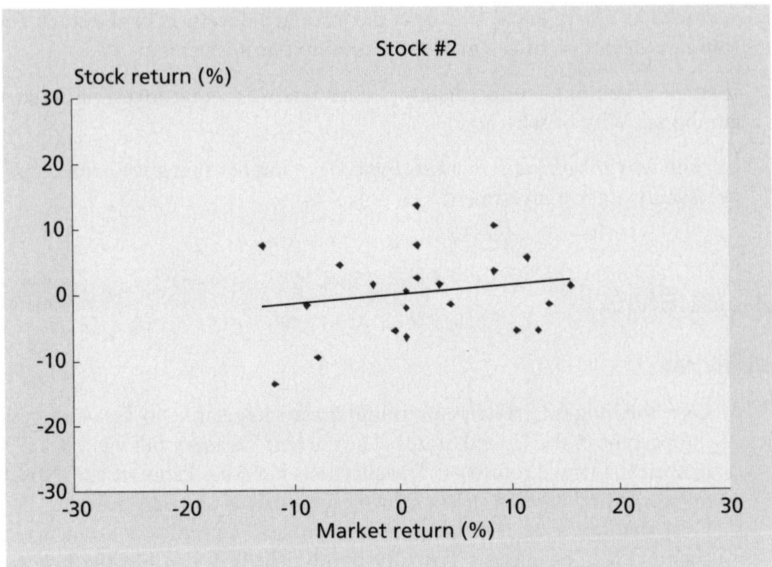

Q7-2. The table below shows the expected return and standard deviation for two stocks. Is the pattern shown in the table possible? Explain your answer.

Stock	Beta	Std. Dev.
#1	1.5	22%
#2	0.9	35%

Q7-3. Which type of company do you think will have a higher beta: fast-food chain or a cruise-ship firm? Why?

Q7-4. Is the data in the following table believable? Explain your answer.

Stock	Std. Dev.
#1	40%
#2	60%
50-50 Portfolio	50%

Q7-5. How can investors hold a portfolio with a weight of more than 100 percent in a particular asset?

Q7-6. According to the *Capital Asset Pricing Model,* is the following data possible? Explain your answer.

Asset	Return	Std. Dev.
#1	4%	0%
#2	2%	20%

Q7-7. Stock A has a beta of 1.5, and Stock B has a beta of 1.0. Determine whether each statement below is true or false.

a. Stock A must have a higher standard deviation than Stock B.
b. Stock A has a higher expected return than Stock B.
c. The expected return on Stock A is 50 percent higher than the expected return on B.

Q7-8. If an asset lies above the security market line, is it overpriced or underpriced? Explain why.

Q7-9. A stock has a beta equal to 1.0. Is the standard deviation of the stock equal to the standard deviation of the market? Explain your answer.

Q7-10. If stock prices move unpredictably, does this mean that investing in stocks is just gambling? Why or why not?

Q7-11. Explain why *the efficient markets hypothesis* implies that a well-run company is not necessarily a good investment?

PROBLEMS

Expected Returns

P7-1. **a.** Over the long run, the risk-premium on stocks relative to Treasury bills has been 7.6 percent in the United States. The current Treasury bill yield is 1.5%, but the historical average return on Treasury bills is 4.1%. Estimate the expected return on stocks and explain how and why you arrived at your answer.

b. Over the long run, the risk-premium on stocks relative to Treasury bonds has been 6.5%. The current Treasury bond yield is 4.5%, but the historical return on T-bonds is 5.2%. Estimate the expected return on stocks and explain how and why you arrived at your answer.

c. Compare your answers above and explain any differences.

P7-2. The table below shows the difference in returns between stocks and Treasury bills and the difference between stocks and Treasury bonds at ten year intervals.

Years	Stocks vs. Bonds	Stocks vs. Bills
1964–73	3.7%	8.3%
1974–83	0.2%	8.6%
1984–93	7.5%	5.4%
1994–2003	4.8%	2.1%

a. At the end of 1973, the yield on Treasury bonds was 6.6% and the yield on T-bills was 7.2%. Using these figures and the historical data above from 1964–1973, construct two estimates of the expected return on equities as of December 1973.

b. At the end of 1983, the yield on Treasury bonds was 6.6% and the yield on T-bills was 7.2%. Using these figures and the historical data above from 1974–1983, construct two estimates of the expected return on equities as of December 1983.

c. At the end of 1993, the yield on Treasury bonds was 6.6% and the yield on T-bills was 2.8%. Using these figures and the historical data above from 1984–1993, construct two estimates of the expected return on equities as of December 1993.

d. At the end of 2003, the yield on Treasury bonds was 5.0% and the yield on T-bills was 1.0%. Using these figures and the historical data above from 1994–2003, construct two estimates of the expected return on equities as of December 2003.

e. What lessons do you learn from this exercise? How much do your estimates of the expected return on equities vary over time, and why do they vary?

P7-3. Use the information below to estimate the expected return on the stock of W. M. Hung Corporation.

Long-run average stock return = 10%
Long-run average T-bill return = 4%
Current T-bill return = 2%

P7-4. Calculate the expected return, variance, and standard deviation for the stocks in the table below.

		Stock Returns in Each Scenario		
Product Demand	Probability	Stock 1	Stock 2	Stock 3
High	20%	30%	20%	15%
Medium	60%	12%	14%	10%
Low	20%	–10%	–5%	–2%

P7-5. Calculate the expected return, variance, and standard deviation for each stock listed below.

		Stock Returns in Each State		
State of the Economy	Probability	Stock A	Stock B	Stock C
Recession	15%	–20%	–10%	–5%
Normal Growth	65%	18%	13%	10%
Boom	20%	40%	28%	20%

P7-6. Refer to Figure 7.2 and answer the following questions.

a. What return would you expect on a stock with a beta of 2.0?

b. What return would you expect on a stock with a beta of 0.66?

c. What determines the slope of the line in Figure 7.2?

Risk and Return for Portfolios

P7-7. Calculate the portfolio weights implied by the dollar investments in each of the asset classes below.

Asset	$ Invested
Stocks	$10,000
Bonds	$10,000
T-bills	$ 5,000

P7-8. Kevin Federline recently inherited $1 million and has decided to invest it. His portfolio consists of the following positions in several stocks. Calculate the portfolio weights to fill in the bottom row of the table.

	Intel	General Motors	Procter & Gamble	Exxon Mobil
Shares	7,280	5,700	5,300	6,000
Price per share	$25	$45	$55	$45
Portfolio weights				

P7-9. Victoria Beckham is a financial advisor who manages money for high-net-worth individuals. For a particular client, Victoria recommends the following portfolio of stocks.

	Global Recording Artists (GRA)	Soccer Intl. (SI)	Liquid Oxygen Corp. (LO)	Viva Mfg. (VM)	Wannabe Travel (WT)
Shares	8,000	9,000	7,000	10,500	4,000
Price per share	$40	$36	$45	$30	$60
Portfolio weights					

a. Calculate the portfolio weights implied by Ms. Beckham's recommendations. What fraction of the portfolio is invested in GRA and SI combined?

b. Suppose that the client purchases the stocks suggested by Ms. Beckham, and a year later the prices of the five stocks are as follows: GRA($60), SI($50), LO($38), VM($20), WT($50). Calculate the portfolio weights at the end of the year. Now what fraction of the portfolio is held in GRA and SI combined?

P7-10. Calculate the expected return, variance, and standard deviation for the stocks in the table below. Next, form an equally weighted portfolio of all three stocks and calculate its mean, variance, and standard deviation.

State of the Economy	Probability	Returns in Each State of the Economy Cycli-Cal Inc.	Home Grown Crop.	Pharma-Cel
Boom	20%	40%	20%	20%
Expansion	50%	10%	10%	40%
Recession	30%	–20%	–10%	–30%

P7-11. You analyze the prospects of several companies and come to the following conclusions about the expected return on each:

Stock	Expected Return
Starbucks	18%
Sears	8%
Microsoft	16%
Limited Brands	12%

You decide to invest \$4,000 in Starbucks, \$6,000 in Sears, \$12,000 in Microsoft, and \$3,000 in Limited Brands. What is the expected return on your portfolio?

P7-12. Calculate the expected return of the portfolio described in the accompanying table.

Stock	\$ Invested	Expected Return
A	\$40,000	10%
B	\$20,000	14%
C	\$25,000	12%

P7-13. Calculate the portfolio weights based on the dollar investments in the table below. Interpret the negative sign on one investment. What is the size of the initial investment on which an investor's rate of return calculation should be based?

Stock	\$ Invested
1	\$10,000
2	–\$ 5,000
3	\$ 5,000

P7-14. Pete Pablo has \$20,000 to invest. He is very optimistic about the prospects of two companies, 919 Brands Inc. and Diaries.com. However, Pete has a very pessimistic view of one firm, a financial institution known as Lloyd Bank. The current market price of each stock and Pete's assessment of the expected return for each stock appear below.

Stock	Price	Expected Return
919 Brands	\$60	10%
Diaries.com	\$80	14%
Lloyd Bank	\$70	–8%

a. Pete decides to purchase 210 shares of 919 Brands and 180 shares of Diaries.com. What is the expected return on this portfolio? Can Pete construct this portfolio with the amount of money he has to invest?

b. If Pete sells short 100 shares of Lloyd Bank, how much additional money will he have to invest in the other two stocks?

c. If Pete buys 210 shares of 919 Brands and 180 shares of Diaries.com, and he simultaneously sells short 100 shares of Lloyd Bank, what are the resulting portfolio weights in each stock? (Hint: the weights must sum to one, but they need not all be positive).

d. What is the expected return on the portfolio described in part (c)?

P7-15. Shares in Springfield Nuclear Power Corp. currently sell for \$25. You believe that the shares will be worth \$30 in one year, and this implies that the return you expect on these shares is 20% (the company pays no dividends).

a. If you invest $10,000 by purchasing 400 shares, what the expected value of your holdings next year?

b. Now suppose that you buy 400 shares of SNP, but you finance this purchase with $5,000 of your own funds and $5,000 that you raise by selling short 100 shares of Nader Insurance Inc. Nader Insurance shares currently sell for $50, but next year you expect them to be worth $52. This implies an expected return of 4%. If both stocks perform as you expect, how much money will you have at the end of the year after you repurchase 100 Nader shares at the market price and return them to your broker? What rate of return on your $5,000 investment does this represent?

c. Suppose you buy 400 shares of SNP and finance them as described in part (b). However, at the end of the year SNP stock is worth $31. What was the percentage increase in SNP stock? What is the rate of return on your portfolio (again, after you repurchase Nader shares and return them to your broker)?

d. Finally, assume that at the end of one year, SNP shares have fallen to $24. What was the rate of return on SNP stock for the year? What is the rate of return on your portfolio?

e. What is the general lesson illustrated here? What is the impact of short selling on the expected return and risk of your portfolio?

P7-16. You are given the following data on several stocks:

State of the Economy	Probability	Returns in Each State of Economy: Gere Mining	Reubenfeld Films	DeLorean Automotive
Boom	25%	40%	24%	–20%
Expansion	50%	12%	10%	12%
Recession	25%	–20%	–12%	40%

a. Calculate the expected return and standard deviation for each stock.

b. Calculate the expected return and standard deviation for a portfolio invested equally in Gere Mining and Reubenfeld Films. How does the standard deviation of this portfolio compare to a simple 50-50 weighted average of the standard deviations of the two stocks?

c. Calculate the expected return and standard deviation for a portfolio invested equally in Gere Mining and DeLorean Automotive. How does the standard deviation of this portfolio compare to a simple 50-50 weighted average of the standard deviations of the two stocks?

d. Explain why your answers regarding the portfolio standard deviations are so different in parts (b) and (c).

P7-17. In an odd twist of fate, the return on the stock market has been exactly 1 percent in each of the last eight months. The return on Simon Entertainment stock in the past eight months has been as follows: 8%, 4%, 16%, –10%, 26%, 22%, 1%, –55%. From this information, estimate the beta of Simon stock.

P7-18. Petro-Chem Inc. stock has a beta equal to 0.9. Digi-Media Corp.'s stock beta is 2.0. What is the beta of a portfolio invested equally in these two stocks?

The Security Market Line and the CAPM

P7-19. The risk-free rate is currently 5%, and the expected risk premium on the market portfolio is 7%. What is the expected return on a stock with a beta of 1.2?

P7-20. The expected return on the market portfolio equals 12%. The current risk-free rate is 6%. What is the expected return on a stock with a beta of 0.66?

P7-21. The expected return on a particular stock is 14%. The stock's beta is 1.5. What is the risk-free rate if the expected return on the market portfolio equals 10%?

P7-22. If the risk-free rate equals 4% and a stock with a beta of 0.75 has an expected return of 10%, what is the expected return on the market portfolio?

P7-23. You believe that a particular stock has an expected return of 15%. The stock's beta is 1.2, the risk-free rate is 3%, and the expected market risk premium is 6%. Based on this, is your view that the stock is overvalued or undervalued?

P7-24. A particular stock sells for $30. The stock's beta is 1.25, the risk-free rate is 4%, and the expected return on the market portfolio is 10%. If you forecast that the stock will be worth $33 next year (assume no dividends), should you buy the stock or not?

P7-25. Currently the risk-free rate equals 5% and the expected return on the market portfolio equals 11%. An investment analyst provides you with the following information:

Stock	Beta	Expected Return
A	1.33	12%
B	0.7	10%
C	1.5	14%
D	0.66	9%

a. Indicate whether each stock is overpriced, underpriced, or correctly priced.
b. For each stock, subtract the risk-free rate from the stock's expected return and divide the result by the stock's beta. For example, for asset A this calculation is (12% – 5%) ÷ 1.33. Provide an interpretation for these ratios. Which stock has the highest ratio and which has the lowest?
c. Show how a smart investor could construct a portfolio of stocks C and D that would outperform stock A.
d. Construct a portfolio consisting of some combination of the market portfolio and the risk-free asset such that the portfolio's expected return equals 9%. What is the beta of this portfolio? What does this say about stock D?
e. Divide the risk premium on stock C by the risk premium on stock D. Next, divide the beta of stock C by the beta of stock D. Comment on what you find.

THOMSON ONE Business School Edition

For instructions on using Thomson ONE, refer to the instructions provided with the Thomson ONE problems at the end of Chapters 1–6 or to "A Guide for Using Thomson ONE."

P7-26. Determine the beta of a portfolio consisting of Priceline.com Inc. (ticker: PCLN), Johnson & Johnson (U:JNJ), Home Depot (U:HD), and Goodyear Tire & Rubber Company (GT). You invest equal amounts of capital in each stock. How does the beta of this portfolio compare with the individual betas? Explain. Instead of investing equal amounts of capital in each stock, you decide to short shares worth $1,000 in each of the two least risky stocks (of the above four stocks) and invest $2,000 each in the two most risky stocks. How do you think the beta of this new portfolio will compare with the individual stock betas? Calculate the beta of this new portfolio and check if it matches your expectations. Consider another alternate portfolio. Now you short shares worth $1,000 in each of the two most risky stocks and invest $2,000 each in the two least risky stocks. How do you think the beta of this new portfolio will compare with the individual stock betas? Calculate the beta of this new portfolio and check if it matches your expectations. Do you think this portfolio will ever be profitable? If so, when?

P7-27. Determine whether the stock of Hershey Foods (ticker: HSY) was mispriced (either underpriced or overpriced) at any time over the last five years. Assume that the beta for Hershey Foods stayed constant over the last five years and use the latest available beta. Further, assume that the S&P 500 Composite Index (DSMnemonic: S&PCOMP) proxies for the market portfolio and calculate the annual returns for the index over the last five years. You can access the three month T-bill yields from Yahoo! Finance (http://finance.yahoo.com).[4] Use the Capital Asset Pricing Model (CAPM) to estimate the expected annual stock returns for Hershey Foods for each year. Compare the expected stock returns to the actual annual returns for each year and determine if the stock was mispriced.

Since these exercises depend upon real-time data, your answers will change continuously depending upon when you access the Internet to download your data.

MINICASE

Risk, Return, and the Capital Asset Pricing Model

As a first day intern at Tri-Star Management Incorporated the CEO asks you to analyze the following information pertaining to two common stock investments, Tech.com Incorporated and Sam's Grocery Corporation. You are told that a one-year Treasury Bill will have a rate of return of 5% over the next year. Also, information from an investment advising service lists the current beta for Tech.com as 1.68 and for Sam's Grocery as 0.52. You are provided a series of questions to guide your analysis.

		Estimated Rate of Return		
Economy	Probability	Tech.com	Sam's Grocery	S&P 500
Recession	30%	–20%	5%	– 4%
Average	20%	15%	6%	11%
Expansion	35%	30%	8%	17%
Boom	15%	50%	10%	27%

ASSIGNMENT

1. Calculate the expected rate of return for Tech.com Incorporated, Sam's Grocery Corporation, and the S&P 500 Index.
2. Calculate the standard deviations in estimated rates of return for Tech.com Incorporated, Sam's Grocery Corporation, and the S&P 500 Index.
3. Which is a better measure of risk for the common stock of Tech.com Incorporated and Sam's Grocery Corporation—the standard deviation you calculated in Question 2 or the beta?
4. Based on the beta provided, what is the expected rate of return for Tech.com Incorporated and Sam's Grocery Corporation for the next year?
5. If you form a two-stock portfolio by investing \$30,000 in Tech.com Incorporated and \$70,000 in Sam's Grocery Corporation, what is the portfolio beta and expected rate of return?
6. If you form a two-stock portfolio by investing \$70,000 in Tech.com Incorporated and \$30,000 in Sam's Grocery Corporation, what is the portfolio beta and expected rate of return?
7. Which of these two-stock portfolios do you prefer? Why?

4. On the left-hand side, under Investing, click on Indices under Today's Markets. Click on the symbol next to 13-Week Bill under Treasury Securities. Click on Historical Prices on the left-hand side menu. This gives you historical three month (or thirteen week) T-bond yields.

Smart *Excel* Appendix

Appendix Contents

Excel prerequisites

- Relative, absolute, and mixed cell references, covered in Chapter 4

Learn to solve for

- Expected stock returns using the historical approach
- Expected stock returns using the probabilistic approach
- Expected stock returns using the CAPM approach
- Expected portfolio return and risk measures

Use the Smart *Excel* spreadsheets and animated tutorials at http://smartfinance.swlearning.com.

EXCEL PREREQUISITES

There are no new *Excel* features used in this appendix, but there is extensive use of absolute and mixed cell references. This material is reviewed and extended on the ***Excel Prereqs*** tab of the Chapter 7 file located at the **Smart Finance Web site.**

EXPECTED RETURN

Problem: You are considering investing in four companies and want to determine the expected return on each investment, if held on its own, over the next year. You are interested in comparing the expected return using three approaches: historical, probabilistic, and CAPM. You also want to find the return on a portfolio invested equally in each of the four investments. Last, you want to assess the risk of the potential investments. Information on the investments and current market conditions is provided here and below. You have return information for the 1964–2003 period. The current Treasury bill rate is 2.2%, and the average Treasury bill return over the period 1964–2003 was 4.1%. The expected return on a market portfolio is 11%. You want to consider returns under three possible economic scenarios over the next year: weak economy, average economy, strong economy. You believe the probability of a weak economy is 20%, the probability of an average economy is 50%, and the probability of a strong economy is 30%.

	Petrochemical	High Pressure Tires	J.R.R. Toykins	Karma-ceuticals
Average Return 1964–2003	0.121	0.098	0.111	0.178
Beta	1.2	0.9	1.0	1.6
Return in a weak economy	–0.25	0.22	–0.15	–0.40
Return in an avg economy	0.13	0.14	0.11	0.38
Return in a strong economy	0.35	–0.05	0.25	0.25

HISTORICAL APPROACH TO CALCULATING EXPECTED RETURN

Use the historical approach to find the expected return on an investment in each of the four companies, as well as the portfolio invested equally in each of the four firms.

Remember, the expected return under the historical approach is found by adding the historical average risk premium for the firm (the premium over the historical average Treasury bill rate) to the current risk-free rate.

The portfolio return is a weighted average of the individual stock returns, as calculated in Chapter 6.

Approach: Create a simple model based on the historical risk premium to find the expected return.

Try it yourself in a blank *Excel* file. Think about what to include in inputs and how to set up your calculations and output. Alternatively, you can use the setup file provided on the ***Historical*** tab of the Chapter 7 *Excel* file at the Smart Finance Web site.

We set up the model as follows:

Approach: Build a simple model to estimate individual stock returns and portfolio returns.

Model formatting		
		For inputs that can be changed
		For calculations & outputs; DO NOT CHANGE

Inputs

Treasury bill data	
Avg return Tbills 1964 to 2003	
Current Tbill rate	

Firm data	Petrochemical	High Pressure Tires	J.R.R. Toykins	Karma-ceuticals
Avg return 1964 to 2003				
Portfolio weights				

Calculations

Avg risk premium 1964 to 2003				

Output

	Petrochemical	High Pressure Tires	J.R.R. Toykins	Karma-ceuticals	*Portfolio*
Expected return					

In this model, we introduce new formatting. Blue background is used to denote inputs that can be changed. Green shading denotes formulas in calculatios and output that should not be changed. Smart *Excel* users employ color, borders, and even alternative fonts to make their spreadsheets easier for others to share and interpret. The formatting in this model signals to a user that anything in blue can be changed, while cells in green should not be altered. We will use this optional format in Chapter 7 to provide an introduction to alternative model designs and formats.

	Petrochemical	High Pressure Tires	J.R.R. Toykins	Karma-ceuticals	Portfolio
Expected return	10.2%	7.9%	9.2%	15.9%	10.8%

You should get the results above. The portfolio return is with weights of 25% in each of the four firms.

Apply it

What if you change the portfolio weights?

- *Suppose you invest 50% in Petrochemical, 50% in Karma-ceuticals, and 0% in the other two stocks.*
  Simply change the weights in cells C26–F26. Now the return is 13.1%.
- *Suppose you invest 25% in High Pressure Tires, 25% in Petrochemical, 50% in J.R.R. Toykins, and 0% in Karma-ceuticals.*
  The return is 9.1%.

PROBABILISTIC APPROACH TO CALCULATING EXPECTED RETURN

The historical approach provides an estimate of expected return based on historical data. What if you believe the future will not look like the past? You may want to develop future scenarios, consider the probability of each scenario, and estimate returns in each scenario. The scenarios could be based on economic conditions, product demand, or competitor responses. This is the probabilistic approach to estimating return. In this example, we look at three possible economic scenarios.

Use the probabilistic approach to find the expected return on an investment in each of the four companies, as well as the equally-weighted portfolio. Also find the variance and standard deviation of returns for the individual stocks and the portfolio.

The expected return under the probabilistic approach is a probability weighted average. The expected return is found by multiplying the return in each scenario by the probability of the scenario and then summing for all scenarios. The probabilities must sum to 100%.

Using the probabilistic approach, the variance and standard deviation cannot be calculated using the formulas in Chapter 6 and cannot be found using the *Excel* functions, because we need to consider the probabilities. You can find information on the calculation of variance and standard deviation with probabilities on page 288 of the chapter.

Approach: Create a basic model to find expected return, variance, and standard deviation using the probabilistic approach.

Open the setup file provided on the ***Probab*** tab of the Chapter 7 *Excel* file.

Enter the input data in the blue-shaded cells of the *Inputs & Portfolio Calculations* section. Note that portfolio calculations are included in this section. In earlier chapters, we placed inputs in a separate section to clearly distinguish the model inputs from calculations and output. In general, we recommend this. In this model, however, the portfolio returns in each economic condition are most easily calculated and most clearly displayed right next to the inputs. Therefore, we decided to include these calculations in the input section but use the green shading to highlight to users that these are not inputs and should not be changed. The portfolio calculations are formulas based on the inputs.

To find the portfolio return in the weak economy, multiply the portfolio weight of each investment by its return in the weak economy and sum the results.

In this example, the equally-weighted portfolio's return in a weak economy is: =25%*–0.25 + 25%*0.22+ 25%*–0.15+25%*–0.40 = –0.145

Apply it

- *Why does High Pressure Tires have such a high return in the weak economy?* Now try to create a formula in the *Excel* file for the portfolio return in each economic scenario.

Tip: If you set up your formula carefully, you can copy across for the other firms and the portfolio.

How? Make sure you absolute reference the probabilities in the formula.
The formula for this, in cell H20, should read:

=$D$23*D20+$E$23*E20+$F$23*F20+$G$23*G20

The result is –0.145.
Copy down for the average and strong scenarios.
Your *Inputs & Portfolio Calculations* section should look like this:

Inputs and Portfolio Calculations **Percent Return**

Economic Conditions	Probability	Petrochem.	H.P. Tires	J.R.R. Toykins	Karma.	Portfolio Calcs
Weak economy	20%	–0.250	0.220	–0.150	–0.400	–0.145
Average economy	50%	0.130	0.140	0.110	0.380	0.190
Strong economy	30%	0.350	–0.050	0.280	0.250	0.208
Portfolio weights		25%	25%	25%	25%	

While few companies really have such countercyclical results, assume this company manufactures replacement tires for automobiles. In weak economic conditions, the firm's sales are relatively high, as people buy fewer new cars and hold on to older cars longer. Older cars are more likely to need replacement tires.

Expected Return

Next, complete the return section of the *Calculations* section. Create a formula for the expected return for Petrochemical.

The formula is:
Expected return = probability of a weak economy *return in the weak economy
+ probability of an average economy *return in the average economy
+ probability of a strong economy *return in the strong economy

You should find the expected return for Petrochemical is 12%; the portfolio return is 12.8%.

Apply it

- ***Can you find another approach to solving for the portfolio return?***
  Once you have found the expected returns for the individual stocks, you can find the portfolio return by taking a portfolio weighted average of the individual stock returns. Your results will be the same—12.8%.

  This illustrates that you can find the portfolio return two different ways.
  1. Use the portfolio return in each scenario and find the probability weighted average.
  2. Use the expected returns of the individual stocks and find the portfolio weighted average.

- ***Can you find portfolio variance as portfolio weighted averages of the individual firm variances?***
  No, diversification often lowers portfolio variance. To find portfolio variance you need information on the portfolio return in each scenario to use in the calculations.

Variance Calculations

Calculating variance under scenarios can be confusing. The calculations are described on page 292 of the chapter. We broke the calculation into three steps in the ***Probab*** tab of the *Excel* file.

Step 1: Set up a formula to find the return minus the expected return. Start with Petrochemical in the weak economy. You'll save time if you set up a formula that you can copy across all firms and the portfolio and that can be copied down through all three scenarios. To accomplish this, you'll need to use mixed cell references. You may want to review the information on mixed cell references at the bottom of the ***Excel Prereqs*** tab.

The formula is: = Petrochemical return in weak economy minus Petrochemical expected return
= –0.25 – 0.12
=D20 – D$26

Use a mixed cell reference for the expected return. **DO** lock the row so that when you copy the formula down for Petrochemical in the other scenarios, the formula refers back to the expected return. **DO NOT** lock the column so that you can copy the formula across for the other firms and the portfolio.

Copy the formula down through the average and strong economic scenarios, and across through the other firms and the portfolio.

Step 2: Take the result from Step 1, square it, and then multiply by the probability of that economic scenario.

Start with Petrochemical in the weak economy.

The formula is = Return minus expected return squared * probability
=–0.37 squared * 20%
=D31^2*$C20

Again, you want to create one formula that can be copied down and across, so be careful with your cell references. **DO NOT** lock the row so that you can copy down for other scenarios. **DO** lock column C since all probabilities are in column C. This enables you to accurately copy across.

Copy the formula down through the average and strong economic scenarios, and across through the other firms and the portfolio.

Step 3: Find the variance by summing the results of Step 2 for all three scenarios.

Your variance calculations should match this:

Variance Calcs

1. Find return minus exp return	Petrochemical	High Pressure Tires	J.R.R. Toykins	Karma-ceuticals	Portfolio Calcs
weak economy	–0.370	0.121	–0.259	–0.585	–0.273
avg economy	0.010	0.041	0.001	0.195	0.062
strong economy	0.230	–0.149	0.171	0.065	0.079
*2. (Ret- exp ret)^2*Prob'y*					
weak economy	0.027	0.003	0.013	0.068	0.015
avg economy	0.000	0.001	0.000	0.019	0.002
strong economy	0.016	0.007	0.009	0.001	0.002
3. Variance	0.043	0.010	0.022	0.089	0.019

Output

Now go to the output section and complete the model. Expected return and variance have already been calculated, so use cell references to pull the information through to this section. Standard deviation is the square root of variance. The final results are:

Output

	Petrochemical	High Pressure Tires	J.R.R. Toykins	Karma-ceuticals	Portfolio
Exp Return	0.120	0.099	0.109	0.185	0.128
Variance	0.043	0.010	0.022	0.089	0.019
Standard deviation	0.208	0.102	0.149	0.298	0.137

Apply it

- ***Is the standard deviation of the portfolio a weighted average of the standard deviations of the individual stocks?***
  No. Since the stocks in the portfolio do not move exactly in sync with each other, the portfolio standard deviation is less than the weighted average. The weighted average of the four standard deviations (assuming 25% in each stock) is 0.189, while the portfolio standard deviation in 0.137.
- ***Change the scenario probabilities and note the effect. Be certain that the probabilities sum to 100%.***
  You will find that if the likelihood of a weak economy is 30%, an average economy is 50%, and a strong economy is 20%, the portfolio return drops to 9.3%.
- ***Change the portfolio weights and note the effect. Weights must also sum to 100%.***
  Changes in portfolio weights can also effect portfolio return significantly.

CAPM APPROACH TO CALCULATING EXPECTED RETURN

Next, use the CAPM approach to find the expected return to on investment in each of the four companies as well as the portfolio invested equally in each of the four firms. Also find the portfolio beta.

Approach: Create a basic model to find expected return and portfolio beta, using the CAPM approach.

Open the setup file provided on the *CAPM* tab of the Chapter 7 *Excel* file. Enter the input data in the blue-shaded cells of the *Inputs & Portfolio Calculations* section. Note that portfolio calculations are again included in this section.

Complete the portfolio beta calculation. The portfolio beta is a weighted average of the firm betas. Your completed section should appear as:

Inputs and Portfolio Calculations

			High Pressure		Karma-	Portfolio
Current Tbill rate	0.022	Petrochemical	Tires	J.R.R. Toykins	ceuticals	Calcs
Expected market return	0.110					
Beta		1.20	0.90	1.00	1.60	1.18
Portfolio weights		25%	25%	25%	25%	

Next, use the input information and portfolio beta to solve for the expected return of the individual stocks and the portfolio. Set up the formula for Petrochemical so that you can copy it across for the other firms and the portfolio. Use absolute cell references, as needed.

Again, we provide an alternative calculation for portfolio return to illustrate that the return using the CAPM, with the portfolio beta, yields the same result as a portfolio weighted average of the individual firm expected returns.

The results are:

	Petrochemical	High Pressure Tires	J.R.R. Toykins	Karma-ceuticals	Portfolio Calcs
Exp return	0.128	0.101	0.110	0.163	0.125
Exp return (alternative portfolio calc.)					0.125
Beta	1.20	0.90	1.00	1.60	1.18

Apply it

- *Suppose the entire portfolio is invested in J.R.R. Toykins.*
  The expected return is 11%, the same return expected on the market index. Why? Because J.R.R. Toykins has a beta of 1.0 and is about as risky as the market.
- *Suppose the current Treasury bill rate increases to 6%, and you invest 25% of your portfolio in each of the firms.*
  You will get expected returns as follows:

Output

	Petrochemical	High Pressure Tires	J.R.R. Toykins	Karma-ceuticals	Portfolio Calcs
Exp return	0.120	0.105	0.110	0.140	0.119
Exp return (alternative portfolio calc.)					0.119
Beta	1.20	0.90	1.00	1.60	1.18

The expected returns are identical for J.R.R. Toykins, higher for High Pressure Tires, and lower for Petrochemical and Karma-ceuticals.

- *Why?*

  The CAPM equation for expected return is:
  $E(R) = R_f + (R_m - R_f) * B$

  This equation can be rewritten as:
  $E(R) = R_f * (1 - B) + B * R_m$

When beta is equal to one, as with J.R.R. Toykins, the term $R_f * (1–B)$ falls out, leaving R_m, so changes in the risk-free rate have no effect on expected return.

When beta exceeds one, as with Petrochemical and Karma-ceuticals, an increase in the risk-free rate leads to a decrease in expected return.

Finally, when beta is less than one, as with High Pressure Tires, an increase in the risk-free rate leads to an increase in expected return.

This assumes the expected market rate remains at 11%.

PART 3

Capital Budgeting

The long-run success or failure of most businesses depends more on the quality of its investment decisions than on any other factor. For many firms, the most important investment decisions are those that involve the acquisition of fixed assets like land or plant and equipment. In finance, we refer to the process of making these investment decisions as *capital budgeting*. This part of the text focuses exclusively on capital budgeting.

Chapter 8 describes some of the methods that firms use to evaluate investment opportunities. Several methods are used widely, but from a purely theoretical perspective, one method dominates the others. The preferred approach is the Net Present Value (or *NPV*) method. In an *NPV* analysis, a financial manager compares the incremental cash outflows and inflows (*marginal costs* and *marginal benefits*, again) associated with a particular investment and discounts those cash flows at a rate that reflects the investment's risk. The investment rule is to invest when the *NPV* is positive, because only then do the investment's marginal benefits exceed its marginal costs.

Chapter 9 goes deeper into *NPV* analysis by showing how analysts derive the cash flow estimates necessary to calculate a project's *NPV*. Experienced analysts know that certain types of cash flows occur in almost any investment project, so Chapter 9 lists several categories of cash flows and explains how to treat them properly in an *NPV* calculation.

Chapter 10 focuses on the second step in calculating *NPVs*—choosing an interest rate at which the investment's cash flows will be discounted. Conceptually, the discount rate that a manager chooses should reflect the risk of the investment being analyzed. Analysts should use higher discount rates when they evaluate riskier investment projects. Furthermore, managers should "look to the market" to decide what rate of return investors expect the firm to achieve. Because every firm's assets are financed by some combination of debt and equity, it is possible for managers to discern the underlying required return on the assets they invest in by calculating the weighted average cost of capital (or *WACC*). The *WACC* establishes an important "hurdle rate" for firms. On average, if the firm purchases assets that generate returns higher than the firm's *WACC*, then the firm makes its investors very happy, and it creates wealth for shareholders.

Note: Solutions available in a booklet called *Solutions to Concept Review Questions and Self-Test Problems.*

CHAPTER 8

Capital Budgeting Process and Techniques

OPENING FOCUS

Tantalized by Tantalum

On January 9, 2002, the *Financial Times* reported a 53 percent increase in the stock price of Tertiary Minerals PLC (London Stock Exchange ticker symbol, TYM). The market was apparently reacting to an independent report that one of Tertiary's major investments could generate an internal rate of return of 33 percent over several years. Specifically, the analysis referred to Tertiary's opportunity to extract tantalum, a metal used in cell phones and other electronic devices, from deposits located on the southwest coast of Finland. One month later, the company's shares jumped another 58 percent on news that it won a five-year license to explore tantalum reserves in Saudi Arabia.

Tantalized by tantalum? A firm's investments in capital assets (whether in the form of physical plant and equipment, or intangible assets such as brands, trademarks, and patents) are largely responsible for creating and maintaining its competitive advantage. Financial markets monitor firms' investment decisions very closely, and share prices reflect investors' beliefs about the likely success or failure of these endeavors.

For example, consider what happened to the stock of BHP Billton, an Australian natural resources firm, when it announced on April 4, 2002, that it planned to open a new iron ore mine in the Pilbara region of Western Australia. An analyst at Credit Suisse First Boston projected that BHP would spend $213 million to open the mine and that the project would increase the firm's value by about $400 million, equivalent to just under A$0.13 (Australian dollars) per BHP common share. Dealers with two Australian financial services firms, Macquarie Equities and JB Were Stockbroking, echoed the view that the investment would create value for BHP shareholders, an opinion that traders on the Australian Stock Exchange apparently shared. BHP stock rose slightly less than 1 percent, or about A$0.08 per share on news of the pending investment.

When managers, analysts, and investors evaluate the major investments that firms undertake, they have several tools at their disposal to help them determine whether the investments benefit or harm shareholders. Two of the most widely used investment evaluation techniques are the net present value and internal rate of return methods. Read on to learn how to apply these techniques to the investment decision process.

Sources: "BHP Billton Higher after New Iron Ore Project Approval," *AFX News Limited* (April 4, 2002); "Europower Boosted by Approach," *Financial Times* (January 9, 2002); "Tertiary Tantalizes Investors," *Investors Chronicle* (February 8, 2002).

LEARNING OBJECTIVES

After studying this chapter you should be able to:

- Understand capital budgeting procedures and the characteristics that management desires in a capital budgeting technique;
- Evaluate the use of the accounting rate of return, the payback period, and the discounted payback to evaluate proposed capital expenditures;
- Discuss the logic, calculation, and pros and cons of using net present value (*NPV*) to evaluate proposed capital expenditures;
- Describe the logic, calculation, advantages, and problems associated with the use of internal rate of return (*IRR*) to evaluate proposed capital expenditures;
- Differentiate between the *NPV* and *IRR* techniques by focusing on the scale and timing problems associated with mutually exclusive capital budgeting projects; and
- Discuss the profitability index and recent findings with regard to the actual use of *NPV* and *IRR* in business practice.

On a daily basis, firms make decisions that have financial consequences. Some decisions, such as extending credit to a customer or ordering inventory, have consequences that are short-lived. Moreover, managers can reverse these short-term actions with relative ease. In contrast, some decisions that managers face have a long-term impact on the firm and can be very difficult to unwind once started. Major investments in plant and equipment fit this description, but so might spending on advertising designed to build brand awareness and loyalty among consumers. The terms **capital investment** and **capital spending** refer to investments in these kinds of long-lived assets, and the term **capital budgeting** refers to the process of identifying which of these investment projects a firm should undertake. The capital budgeting process involves three basic steps:

capital investment
Investments in long-lived assets such as plant, equipment, and advertising.

capital spending
Investments in long-lived assets such as plant, equipment, and advertising.

capital budgeting
The process of identifying which long-lived investment projects a firm should undertake.

1. Identifying potential investments;
2. Analyzing the set of investment opportunities, identifying and perhaps prioritizing those that will create shareholder value; and
3. Implementing and monitoring the investment projects selected in Step 2.

The capital budgeting process begins with an idea and ends with implementation and monitoring. Ideas for investment projects can come from virtually anywhere within the firm. Marketing may propose that the firm spend money to reach a new class of customers. Operations may want to modernize equipment to realize production efficiencies. Engineering may seek resources to engage in research and development designed to improve existing products or create new ones. Information Systems may want to upgrade the firm's computer network to enable more efficient information-sharing across functional areas and physical locations. Each group will undoubtedly have a compelling story to justify spending money on its pet project. The firm will analyze each proposal considering its risk and return and their combined effect on its value; some projects will be approved and others rejected.

Once a project gains approval, the attention of financial managers turns to implementation. They devote a significant fraction of their time to Step 3, implementing and monitoring investments that the firm has decided to make. When firms undertake a capital investment, they almost always do so with a specific budget, outlining the financial objectives and constraints of that investment. Financial managers work to ensure that project managers adhere to budget guidelines, and they help track a project's success over time to determine whether an investment's initial promises were realized.

Without understating the importance of Step 1 (which we discuss in Chapter 9) and Step 3, our focus in this chapter is on the second stage of the process, evaluating the merits of investment proposals. Here we ignore risk and assume that projects are equally risky; in Chapter 10, we relax this assumption and develop techniques that are consistent with Chapters 6 and 7, which recognize differences in project risk. In practice, firms use many different techniques to justify their capital investments, ranging from simple to sophisticated. In this chapter, we describe several of these techniques, highlighting their strengths and weaknesses. In the end, the preferred technique for evaluating most capital investments is the one called "net present value."

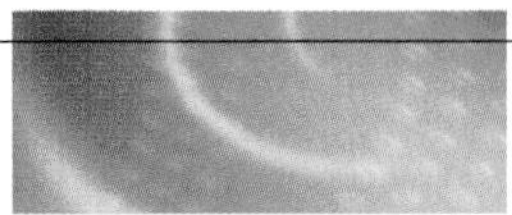

8.1 INTRODUCTION TO CAPITAL BUDGETING

What Do Managers Really Want?

Firms use a variety of techniques to evaluate capital investments. Some techniques involve very simple calculations and are intuitively easy to grasp. Financial managers prefer (1) an easily applied technique that (2) considers cash flow, (3) recognizes the time value of money, (4) fully accounts for expected risk and return, and (5) when applied, leads to higher stock prices. Easy application accounts for the popularity of some simple capital budgeting methods such as *accounting rate of return* and the *payback period* (both defined later).

Unfortunately, when comparing simple capital budgeting methods with more complex ones, other things are decidedly not equal. More complex methods such as *net present value (NPV), internal rate of return (IRR),* or the *profitability index (PI)* generally lead to better decision making because they take into account issues such as cash flow, the time value of money, the expected risk and return, and the effect on share value, factors which are neglected or ignored by simpler methods. Moreover, we will learn that the net present value approach provides a direct estimate of the increase or decrease in shareholder value resulting from a particular investment. Managers who seek to maximize shareholder value must understand not only how to use the more complex techniques but also the logic that explains why some methods are better than others. As challenging as that sounds, there is no reason to worry. We have already seen these tools at work in valuing bonds and stocks, and now we will apply the discounted cash flow apparatus to real assets such as plant and equipment.

A Capital Budgeting Problem

We apply each of the decision-making techniques in this chapter to a single, simplified business problem currently facing Global Wireless Incorporated, a (fictitious) U.S.-based worldwide provider of wireless telephony services. At this time, wireless carriers are scrambling to attract and retain customers in this highly competitive market. According to customer surveys, the number one reason for selecting a given carrier (or for switching to a new one) is the quality of service. Customers who lose

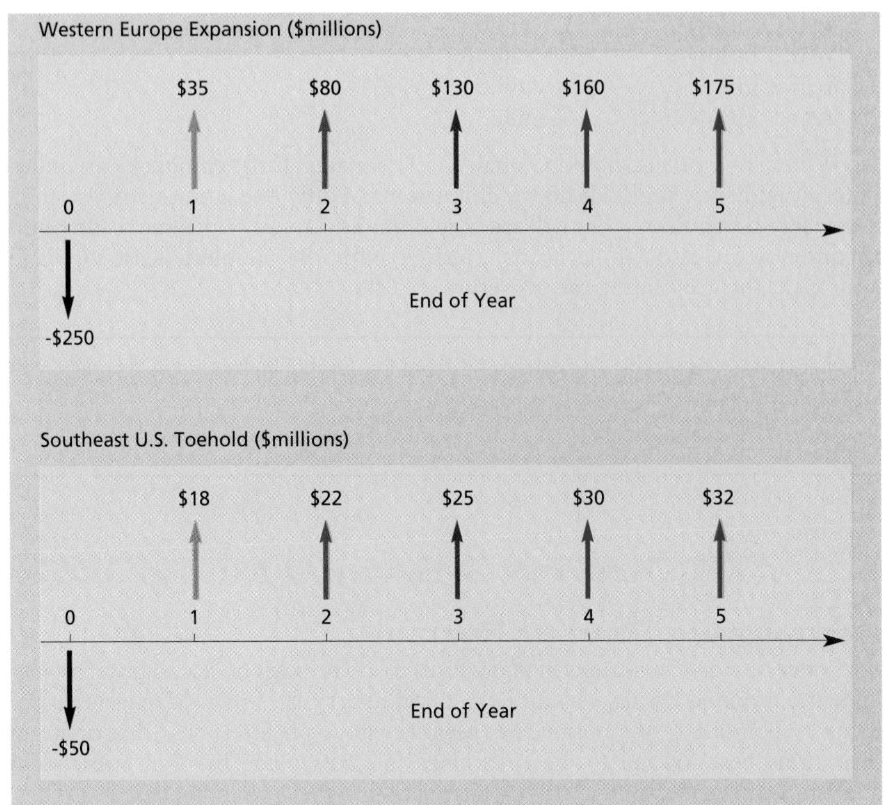

Figure 8.1
Global Wireless Investment Proposals

The figure depicts on time lines the cash flows for Global Wireless's major expansion—the Western Europe expansion, and the Southeast U.S. toehold.

calls as they commute to work or travel from one business location to another are apt to switch if another carrier offers fewer service interruptions.

Against this backdrop, Global Wireless is contemplating a major expansion of its wireless network in two different regions. Figure 8.1 depicts the projected cash inflows and outflows of each project over the next five years. By investing $250 million, Global Wireless could add up to 100 new cell sites to its existing base in Western Europe, giving it the most comprehensive service area in that region. Company analysts project that this investment could generate year-end net after-tax cash inflows that could grow over the next five years, as outlined below:

Initial Outlay	–$250 million
Year 1 inflow	$ 35 million
Year 2 inflow	$ 80 million
Year 3 inflow	$130 million
Year 4 inflow	$160 million
Year 5 inflow	$175 million

Alternatively, Global Wireless could make a much smaller investment to establish a toehold in a new market in the southeast United States. For an initial investment of $50 million, Global Wireless believes it can create a southeast network, with its hub centered in Atlanta, Georgia. The projected end-of-year cash flows associated with this project are as follows:

Initial Outlay	–$50 million
Year 1 inflow	$18 million

Year 2 inflow	\$22 million
Year 3 inflow	\$25 million
Year 4 inflow	\$30 million
Year 5 inflow	\$32 million

Which investment should Global Wireless make? If the company can undertake both investments, should it do so? If it can make only one investment, which one is better for shareholders? We will see how different capital budgeting techniques lead to different investment decisions, starting with the simplest, least-sophisticated approach, the accounting rate of return.

CONCEPT REVIEW QUESTION

1. What characteristics does management desire in a capital budgeting technique? Why?

8.2 ACCOUNTING-BASED METHODS

Accounting Rate of Return

For better or worse, managers in many firms focus as much on how a given project will influence reported earnings as on how it will affect cash flows. Managers justify this focus by pointing to the positive (or negative) stock-price response that occurs when their firms beat (or fail to meet) earnings forecasts made by Wall Street securities analysts. Managers may also pay more attention to the accounting-based earnings of a project than they pay to its cash flows because their compensation is based on meeting accounting-based performance measures such as earnings-per-share or return-on-total-assets targets. Consequently, many firms decide whether to invest in a given project, based on the rate of return the investment will earn on an accounting basis.

Companies have many different ways of defining a *hurdle rate* for their investment in terms of accounting rates of return. Almost all these metrics involve two steps: (1) to identify the net income associated with the project in each year of its life, and (2) to measure the amount of invested capital, as shown on the balance sheet, devoted to the project in each year. Given these two figures, a firm may calculate an **accounting rate of return** by dividing net income by the book value of assets, either on a year-by-year basis or by taking an average over the project's life. Note that this measure is comparable to *return on total assets (ROA),* also called *return on investment (ROI),* introduced in Chapter 2, for measuring a firm's overall effectiveness in generating returns with its available assets. Companies will usually establish some minimum accounting rate of return that projects must earn before they can be funded. When more than one project exceeds the minimum standard, firms prioritize projects, based on their accounting rates of return, and invest in projects with higher returns first.

accounting rate of return Calculation of a hurdle rate by dividing net income by the book value of assets, either on a year-by-year basis or by taking an average over the project's life.

APPLYING THE MODEL

Suppose that the practice at Global Wireless is to calculate a project's accounting rate of return by taking the project's average contribution to net income and dividing by its average book value. Global Wireless ranks projects based on this measure and accepts those that offer an accounting rate of return of at least 25 percent. So far, we have been given the cash flows from each of the two projects that Global Wireless is evaluating. Chapter 9 discusses in more depth the differences between cash flow and net income, but for now, we will assume that we can determine each project's contribution to net income by subtracting depreciation from cash flow each year. We will assume that the company depreciates fixed assets on a straight-line basis over five years. Therefore, the Western Europe project will have an annual depreciation charge of $50 million (one fifth of $250 million), and the southeast U.S. project will have an annual depreciation charge of $10 million (one fifth of $50 million). These assumptions yield the following net income figures for the next five years:

Year	Western Europe Project ($ in millions)	Southeast U.S. Project ($ in millions)
1	−15	8
2	30	12
3	80	15
4	110	20
5	125	22

The Western Europe project begins with a book value of $250 million. After five years of depreciation it has a book value of $0. Therefore, the average book value of that project is $125 million [($250 – $0) ÷ 2]. The project's average net income equals $66 million [(–$15 + $30 + $80 + $110 + $125) ÷ 5], so its average accounting rate of return is an impressive 52.8 percent ($66 ÷ $125). The same steps applied to the southeast U.S. project yield an average book value of $25 million [($50 – $0) ÷ 2], an average net income of $15.4 million [($8 + $12 + $15 + $20 + $22) ÷ 5], and an accounting rate of return of 61.6 percent ($15.4 ÷ $25). On the basis of this analysis, Global Wireless should be willing to invest in either project, but it would rank the southeast U.S. investment above the Western Europe expansion.

Pros and Cons of the Accounting Rate of Return. Because of their convenience, ease of calculation, and ease of interpretation, accounting-based measures are used by many firms to evaluate capital investments. However, these techniques have serious flaws. First, as the preceding *Applying the Model* demonstrates, the decision about what depreciation method to use has a large effect on both the numerator and the denominator of the accounting rate of return formula. Second, this method makes no adjustment for the time value of money or project risk. Third, investors should be more concerned with the market value than the book value of the assets that a firm holds. After five years, the book value of Global Wireless's investment (in either project) is zero, but the market value will almost certainly be positive and may be even greater than the initial amount invested. Fourth, as explained in Chapter 2, finance theory teaches that investors should focus on a company's ability to generate cash rather than on its net income. Fifth, the choice of the 25 percent accounting return hurdle rate is essentially arbitrary. This rate is not based on rates available on similar investments in the market, but reflects a purely subjective judgment on the part of management.

CONCEPT REVIEW QUESTIONS

2. Why do managers focus on the effect that an investment will have on reported earnings rather than on the investment's cash flow consequences?

3. What factors determine whether the annual *accounting rate of return* on a given project will be high or low in the early years of the investment's life? In the latter years?

8.3 PAYBACK METHODS

The Payback Decision Rule

payback period
The amount of time it takes for a given project's cumulative net cash inflows to recoup the initial investment.

The payback method is the simplest of all capital budgeting decision-making tools. It enjoys widespread use, particularly in small firms. Firms using the payback approach typically define a minimum acceptable payback period. The **payback period** is the amount of time it takes for a given project's cumulative net cash inflows to recoup the initial investment. If a firm decides that it wants to avoid any investment that does not "pay for itself" in three years or less, then the payback decision rule is to accept projects with a payback period of three years or less and reject all other investments. If several projects satisfy this condition, then firms may prioritize investments, based on which ones achieve payback more rapidly. The decision to use three years as the cutoff point is somewhat arbitrary, and there are no hard-and-fast guidelines that establish what the "optimal" payback period should be. Nevertheless, suppose that Global Wireless uses 2.75 years as its cutoff when doing payback analysis. What investment decision would it make?

APPLYING THE MODEL

The investment to expand the wireless network in Western Europe requires an initial outlay of $250 million. According to the firm's cash flow projections, this project will bring in just $245 million in its first three years ($35 million in year 1 + $80 million in year 2 + $130 million in year 3) and $405 million after four years ($245 million in the first 3 years + $160 million in year 4). So the firm will fully recover its $250 million initial outlay sometime between years 3 and 4. Because the firm only needs to recover $5 million ($250 million initial outlay – $245 million recovered in the first 3 years) in year 4, assuming cash flow occurs at a constant rate throughout the year, we can estimate the fraction of year 4 as 0.03, by dividing the $5 million that needs to be recovered in year 4 by the $160 million expected to be recovered in that year. *The payback period for Western Europe is therefore 3.03 years, so Global Wireless would reject the investment because this payback period is longer than the firm's maximum 2.75-year payback period.*

The toehold investment in the southeast U.S. project requires just $50 million. In its first two years, this investment generates $40 million in cash flow ($18 million in year 1 + $22 million in year 2). By the end of year 3, it produces a cumulative cash flow of $65 million ($40 million in the first 2 years + $25 million in year 3). Thus, the project earns back the initial $50 million at some point between years 2 and 3. It needs to recover $10 million ($50 million initial outlay – $40 million recovered in the first 2 years) in year 3. We can estimate the fraction of year 3 as 0.40, by dividing the $10 million that needs to be recovered in year 3 by the $25 million expected to be recovered that year. *The payback for the southeast U.S. project is therefore 2.40 years. Global Wireless would undertake the investment because this payback period is shorter than the firm's maximum 2.75-year payback period.*

Pros and Cons of the Payback Method

Simplicity is the main virtue of the payback approach. Once a firm estimates a project's cash flows, it is a simple matter of addition to determine when the cumulative net cash inflows equal the initial outlay. The intuitive appeal of the payback method is strong. It sounds reasonable to expect a good investment to pay for itself in a fairly short period of time. Furthermore, by requiring projects to earn back the initial cash outlay within a few short years, the payback approach recognizes the time value of money, although it fails to explicitly consider it. Some managers say that establishing a short payback period is one way to account for a project's risk exposure. Projects that take longer to pay off are intrinsically riskier than those that recoup the initial investment more quickly. Because of its ability to measure the project's exposure to the risk of not recovering the initial outlay, the payback period is a very popular decision-making technique in highly uncertain situations. It is popular for international investments made in unstable economic/political environments and in risky domestic investments such as oil drilling and new business ventures. In these situations, it is frequently used as the primary decision-making technique.

The payback period is an effective criterion when management has to worry about financing constraints, because it indicates how quickly the firm can recover cash flows for use in debt repayment or for financing other attractive investment opportunities. Career concerns may also lead managers to prefer the payback rule. Particularly in large companies, managers rotate quite often from one job to another. To obtain promotions and to enhance their reputations, managers want to make investments that enable them to point to success stories at each stage of their careers. A manager who expects to stay in a particular position in the firm for just two or three years may prefer to undertake investments that recover costs quickly rather than projects that have payoffs far into the future. In that case, selecting projects based on how quickly they meet the payback requirement offers considerable appeal to someone trying to build a career. (Note: This is viewed as a disadvantage when it results in an *agency problem*—achievement of the managers' career goals is not always in the best interests of shareholders.)

Despite these apparent virtues, the payback method suffers from several serious problems. First, the payback cutoff period is simply a judgemental choice with little or no connection to shareholder value maximization. How can we be sure that accepting projects that pay back within 2.75 years will maximize shareholder wealth rather than accepting projects that pay back within two years or four years? Second, the way that the payback method accounts for the time value of money is crude in the extreme. The payback method assigns a 0 percent discount rate to cash flows that occur before the cutoff point. That is, if the payback period is three years, then cash flows that occur in years 1, 2, and 3 receive equal weight in the payback calculation. Beyond the cutoff point, the payback method implicitly assigns an infinite discount rate to all future cash flows, thereby ignoring them. In other words, cash flows in year 4 and beyond receive zero weight (or have zero present value) in today's decision to invest or not to invest.[1] Third, using the payback period as a way to control for project risk is equally crude. Finance teaches that riskier investments should offer higher returns. If it is true, as managers sometimes argue, that riskier projects have longer payback periods, then the payback rule simply rejects all such investments, whether they offer higher returns in the long run. Managers who naively follow the payback rule tend to underinvest in long-term projects that could offer substantial rewards for shareholders. Fourth, if career concerns lead managers to favor projects with very quick payoffs, then firms should adjust the way that they evaluate employees. Firms could reduce incentives for managers to focus on short-term successes by rewarding them for their efforts in meeting the short-term goals of long-term projects (e.g., staying on budget, meeting revenue forecasts), as well as for long-term results.

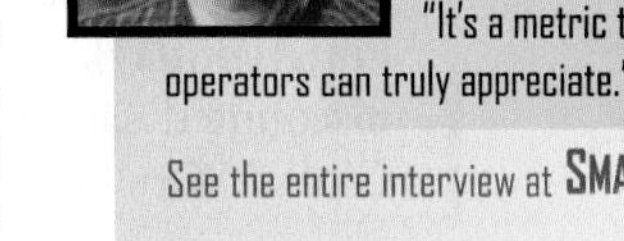

SMART PRACTICES VIDEO

Dan Carter, Executive Vice President, Chief Financial Officer, Charlotte Russe

"It's a metric that frankly most of our operators can truly appreciate."

See the entire interview at **SMARTFinance**

[1] We know that the present value of a future cash flow becomes smaller and smaller as we discount at higher and higher interest rates. Discounting at an infinite interest rate results in a future cash flow having zero present value.

Discounted Payback

discounted payback The amount of time it takes for a project's discounted cash flows to recover the initial investment.

The **discounted payback** rule is essentially the same as the payback rule except that in calculating the payback period, managers discount cash flows first. In other words, the discounted payback method calculates how long it takes for a project's discounted cash flows to recover the initial outlay. This represents a minor improvement over the simple payback method in that it does a better job of accounting for the time value of cash flows that occur within the payback cutoff period. As with the ordinary payback rule, discounted payback totally ignores cash flows that occur beyond the cutoff point.

APPLYING THE MODEL

Suppose that Global Wireless uses the discounted payback method, with a discount rate of 18 percent and a cutoff period of 2.75 years. The following schedules show the present values of each project's cash flows during the first three years.[2] For example, $29.7 million is the present value of the $35 million that the Western Europe investment is expected to earn in its first year, $57.4 million is the present value of the $80 million that the project is expected to earn in its second year, and so on.

Present Value	Western Europe Project ($ in millions)	Southeast U.S. Project ($ in millions)
PV of year 1 inflow	29.7	15.2
PV of year 2 inflow	57.4	15.8
PV of year 3 inflow	79.1	15.2
Cumulative PV years 1–3	166.2	46.2

Recall that the initial outlay for the Western Europe expansion project is $250 million, whereas it is $50 million for the southeast U.S. toehold project. Because, after three years, neither project's cumulative present value of cash flows exceeds its initial outlay (Western Europe: Cumulative PV years 1–3 = $166.2 million < $250 million initial outlay and Southeast U.S.: Cumulative PV years 1–3 = $46.2 million < $50 million initial outlay), it is clear that neither investment satisfies the condition that the discounted cash flows recoup the initial investment in 2.75 years or less. Therefore, Global Wireless would reject both projects.

Pros and Cons of Discounted Payback

The discounted payback rule offers essentially the same set of advantages and disadvantages as ordinary payback analysis does. The primary advantage is its relative simplicity. Discounted payback does correct the payback rule's problem of implicitly applying a 0 percent discount rate to all cash flows that occur before the cutoff point. However, like the ordinary payback rule, the discounted payback approach ignores cash flows beyond the cutoff point, in essence, applying an infinite discount rate to these cash flows. In the final analysis, even though it represents a marginal improvement over the simplest version of the payback rule, discounted payback analysis is likely to lead managers to underinvest in profitable projects with long-run payoffs.

2. We are assuming here that the first year's cash flows occur one year after the initial investment (end of year 1), the second year's cash flows occur two years after the initial investment (end of year 2), and so on.

By now you may have noticed some common themes in our discussion of the pros and cons of different approaches to capital budgeting. None of the methods discussed thus far factor all the cash flows of a project into the decision-making process. Each of these methods fails to properly account for the time value of money, and none of them deal adequately with differences in risk from one investment to another. We now turn our attention to a method that solves all these difficulties and therefore enjoys widespread support from both academics and businesspeople.

CONCEPT REVIEW QUESTIONS

4. What factors account for the popularity of the *payback method*? In what situations is it often used as the primary decision-making technique? Why?

5. What are the major flaws of the *payback period* and *discounted payback* approaches?

8.4 NET PRESENT VALUE

Net Present Value Calculations

The **net present value (*NPV*)** of a project is the sum of the present value of all its cash flows, both inflows and outflows, discounted at a rate consistent with the project's risk. Calculating the *NPV* of an investment project is relatively straightforward. First, write down the net cash flows that the investment will generate over its life. Second, discount these cash flows at an interest rate that reflects the degree of risk inherent in the project. (Note: The development of this rate is discussed in Chapter 10.) The resulting sum of discounted cash flows equals the project's net present value. The *NPV* decision rule says to invest in projects when the net present value is greater than zero:[3]

net present value (*NPV*) The sum of the present value of all of a given project's cash flows, both inflows and outflows, discounted at a rate consistent with the project's risk. Also, a method for valuing capital investments.

$$NPV = CF_0 + \frac{CF_1}{(1+r)^1} + \frac{CF_2}{(1+r)^2} + \frac{CF_3}{(1+r)^3} + \ldots + \frac{CF_N}{(1+r)^N} \quad \text{(Eq. 8.1)}$$

In this expression, CF_t represents net cash flow in year t, r is the discount rate, and N represents the life of the project. The cash flows in each year may be positive or negative, though we usually expect projects to generate cash outflows initially and cash inflows later on. For example, suppose that the initial cash flow, CF_0, is a negative number representing the outlay necessary to get the project started, and suppose that all subsequent cash flows are positive. In this case, the *NPV* can be defined as the *present value of future cash inflows minus the initial outlay*. The *NPV* decision rule says that firms should invest when the sum of the present values of future cash inflows exceeds the initial project outlay. That is, $NPV > \$0$, when the following occurs:

$$-CF_0 < \frac{CF_1}{(1+r)^1} + \frac{CF_2}{(1+r)^2} + \frac{CF_3}{(1+r)^3} + \ldots + \frac{CF_N}{(1+r)^N}$$

[3] What about investments with $NPV = \$0$? A zero *NPV* represents a kind of wealth-creation breakeven point. That is, when an investment's *NPV* is positive, a firm creates wealth for its shareholders. When the *NPV* is negative, the firm destroys wealth by undertaking the project. When the *NPV* is zero, although investing will increase the book value of the firm's assets, it neither creates nor destroys wealth. Therefore, in this case, shareholders are generally indifferent to whether the firm accepts or rejects the project.

Simply stated, the *NPV* decision rules are:

$NPV > \$0$	invest
$NPV < \$0$	do not invest

Why does the *NPV* rule generally lead to good investment decisions? Remember that the firm's goal in choosing investment projects is to maximize shareholder wealth. Conceptually, the discount rate, r, in the *NPV* equation represents an opportunity cost, the highest rate of return that investors can obtain in the marketplace on an investment with risk equal to the risk of the specific project. When the *NPV* of a cash flow stream equals zero, that stream of cash flows provides a rate of return exactly equal to shareholders' required return. Therefore, when a firm finds a project with a positive *NPV*, the project offers a return that exceeds shareholders' expectations. A firm that consistently finds positive *NPV* investments will consistently surpass shareholders' expectations and enjoy a rising stock price. The *NPV*, in effect, represents the amount of additional value created by the investment. Clearly, the acceptance of positive *NPV* projects is consistent with the firm's value-creation goal. Conversely, if the firm makes an investment with a negative *NPV*, the investment will destroy value and disappoint shareholders. A firm that regularly makes negative *NPV* investments will see its stock price lag as it persists in generating lower-than-required returns for stockholders.

We can develop an analogy, drawing on what we already know about valuing bonds, to drive home the point about the relationship between stock prices and the *NPV* rule. Suppose that at a given point in time, investors require a 5 percent return on five-year Treasury bonds. Of course, this means that if the U.S. Treasury issues five-year, \$1,000 par value bonds paying an annual coupon of \$50, the market price of these bonds will be \$1,000, exactly equal to par value.[4]

$$\$1,000 = \frac{\$50}{1.05^1} + \frac{\$50}{1.05^2} + \ldots + \frac{\$1,050}{1.05^5}$$

Now apply *NPV* logic. If an investor purchases one of these bonds for \$1,000, the *NPV* equals zero because the bond's cash flows precisely satisfy the investor's expectation of a 5 percent return.

$$NPV = \$0 = -\$1,000 + \frac{\$50}{1.05^1} + \frac{\$50}{1.05^2} + \ldots + \frac{\$1,050}{1.05^5}$$

Next, imagine that in a fit of election-year largesse, the U.S. Congress decrees that the coupon payments on all government bonds will double, so this bond now pays \$100 in interest per year. If the bond's price remains fixed at \$1,000, this investment's *NPV* will suddenly switch from zero to positive:

$$NPV = \$216.47 = -\$1,000 + \frac{\$100}{1.05^1} + \frac{\$100}{1.05^2} + \ldots + \frac{\$1,100}{1.05^5}$$

Of course, the bond's price will not remain at \$1,000. Investors will quickly recognize that at a price of \$1,000 and with a coupon of \$100, the return offered by these bonds substantially exceeds the required rate of 5 percent. Investors will flock to buy the bonds, rapidly driving up bond values until prices reach the point

4. Though Treasury bonds pay interest semiannually, we assume annual interest payments here to keep the example simple.

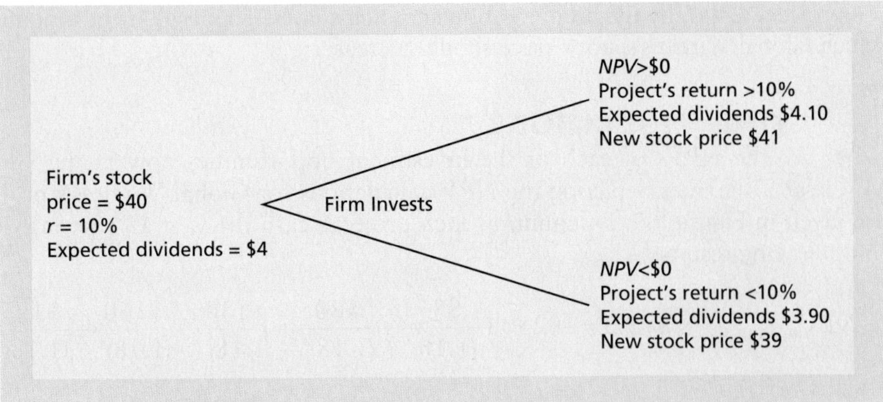

Figure 8.2
The *NPV* Rule and Shareholder Wealth

If a firm invests in a project that earns more than its required return, its expected dividends and stock price are expected to rise. If the project earns less than the required return, the expected dividends and stock price are expected to fall.

at which buying bonds becomes a zero *NPV* investment once again.[5] In the new equilibrium, the bond's price will rise by $216.47, exactly the amount of the *NPV* that was created when Congress doubled the coupon payments:

$$NPV = \$0 = -\$1{,}216.47 + \frac{\$100}{1.05^1} + \frac{\$100}{1.05^2} + \ldots + \frac{\$1{,}100}{1.05^5}$$

SMART PRACTICES VIDEO

Chris Muscarella, Professor of Finance and L.W. 'Roy' and Mary Lois Clark Teaching Fellow

"We look at the impact on stock prices of firms' capital budgeting decisions."

See the entire interview at **SMARTFinance**

The same forces drive up a firm's stock price when it makes a positive *NPV* investment, as shown in Figure 8.2. In the figure, we depict a firm that investors believe will pay an annual dividend of $4 in perpetuity. If investors require a 10 percent return on this firm's stock, the price will be $40.[6] What happens if the firm makes a new investment? If the return on this investment is greater than 10 percent, it will have a positive *NPV*. Investors will recognize that the firm has made an investment that exceeds their expectations, and investors will raise their forecast of future dividends, perhaps to $4.10 per year. At that level, the new stock price will be $41. The same thing happens in reverse if the firm makes an investment that earns a return below 10 percent. At that rate, the project has a negative *NPV*. Shareholders recognize that this investment's cash flows fall below their expectations, so they lower their estimates of future dividends to $3.90 per year. As a consequence, the stock price falls to $39.

Now apply this thought process to Global Wireless. Suppose that its shareholders demand an 18 percent return on their shares. According to the principles we discussed in Chapter 5, the price of Global Wireless stock will reflect the value of all future cash distributions that investors expect from the company, discounted at a rate of 18 percent. But what if Global Wireless discovers that it can make an investment that offers a return substantially above 18 percent? By definition, such an investment has a positive *NPV*, and by undertaking it, Global Wireless will increase the price of its stock as investors come to realize that the company is able to distribute higher-than-anticipated cash flows as a result of the investment opportunity. How far will the stock price rise? Simply divide the project's *NPV* (which represents the amount of wealth

5. Recall that in Chapter 7, we said that an underpriced stock would lie above the security market line. The same thing is happening here. At a price of $1,000, the bond is underpriced if Congress raises the bond's coupon to $100. The price of the bond rises, and its expected return falls.

6. Remember that the price of a stock that pays a constant dividend in perpetuity equals the annual dividend divided by the required rate of return—in this case, $4 ÷ 0.10 = $40.

the project creates) by the number of outstanding shares. The result is the amount by which Global Wireless's stock price should increase.

APPLYING THE MODEL

What are the *NPV*s of each of the investment opportunities now facing Global Wireless? Time lines depicting the *NPV* calculations for Global Wireless's projects are given in Figure 8.3. Discounting each project's cash flows at 18 percent yields the following results:[7]

$$NPV_{WesternEurope} = \$75.3 = -\$250 + \frac{\$35}{(1.18)^1} + \frac{\$80}{(1.18)^2} + \frac{\$130}{(1.18)^3} + \frac{\$160}{(1.18)^4} + \frac{\$175}{(1.18)^5}$$

$$NPV_{SoutheastU.S.} = \$25.7 = -\$50 + \frac{\$18}{(1.18)^1} + \frac{\$22}{(1.18)^2} + \frac{\$25}{(1.18)^3} + \frac{\$30}{(1.18)^4} + \frac{\$32}{(1.18)^5}$$

Both projects increase shareholder wealth, so both are worth undertaking. One could say that "both projects outrun the firm's 18 percent required return and are therefore acceptable." However, if the company can make only one investment, it should choose to expand its presence in Western Europe. That investment increases shareholder wealth by $75.3 million, whereas the southeast U.S. investment increases wealth by only about one third as much. If Global Wireless has 100 million shares of common stock outstanding, then accepting the Western Europe project should increase the stock price by about $0.75 ($75.3 million ÷ 100 million shares). Accepting the southeast U.S. investment would increase the stock price by almost $0.26 ($25.7 million ÷ 100 million shares).

Pros and Cons of *NPV*

The net-present-value method solves all the problems we have identified with the payback and discounted payback rules, as well as the problems associated with decision rules that are based on the accounting rate of return. First, the *NPV* rule focuses on cash flow, not accounting earnings. Second, when properly applied, the net-present-value method makes appropriate adjustments for the time value of money. Third, the decision rule to invest when *NPV*s are positive and to refrain from investing when *NPV*s are negative reflects the firm's need to compete for funds in the marketplace rather than an arbitrary judgment of management. Fourth, the *NPV* approach offers a relatively straightforward way to control for differences in risk among alternative investments. Cash flows on riskier investments should be discounted at higher rates. Fifth, the *NPV* method incorporates all the cash flows that a project generates over its life, not just those that occur in the project's early years. Sixth, the *NPV* gives a direct estimate of the change in shareholder wealth resulting from a given investment.

Although we are enthusiastic supporters of the *NPV* approach, especially when compared with the other decision methods examined thus far, we must acknowledge that the *NPV* rule suffers from a few weaknesses. Relative to alternative capital budgeting tools, the *NPV* rule seems less intuitive to many users. When you hear that Global Wireless's southeast U.S. project has an *NPV* of $25.7 million, does that seem more or less intuitive than learning that the investment pays back its initial cost in 2.4 years or that it earns an accounting rate of return of 61.6 percent?

7. Of course, you can make this calculation using a financial calculator or *Excel*, as shown below the time lines in Figure 8.3.

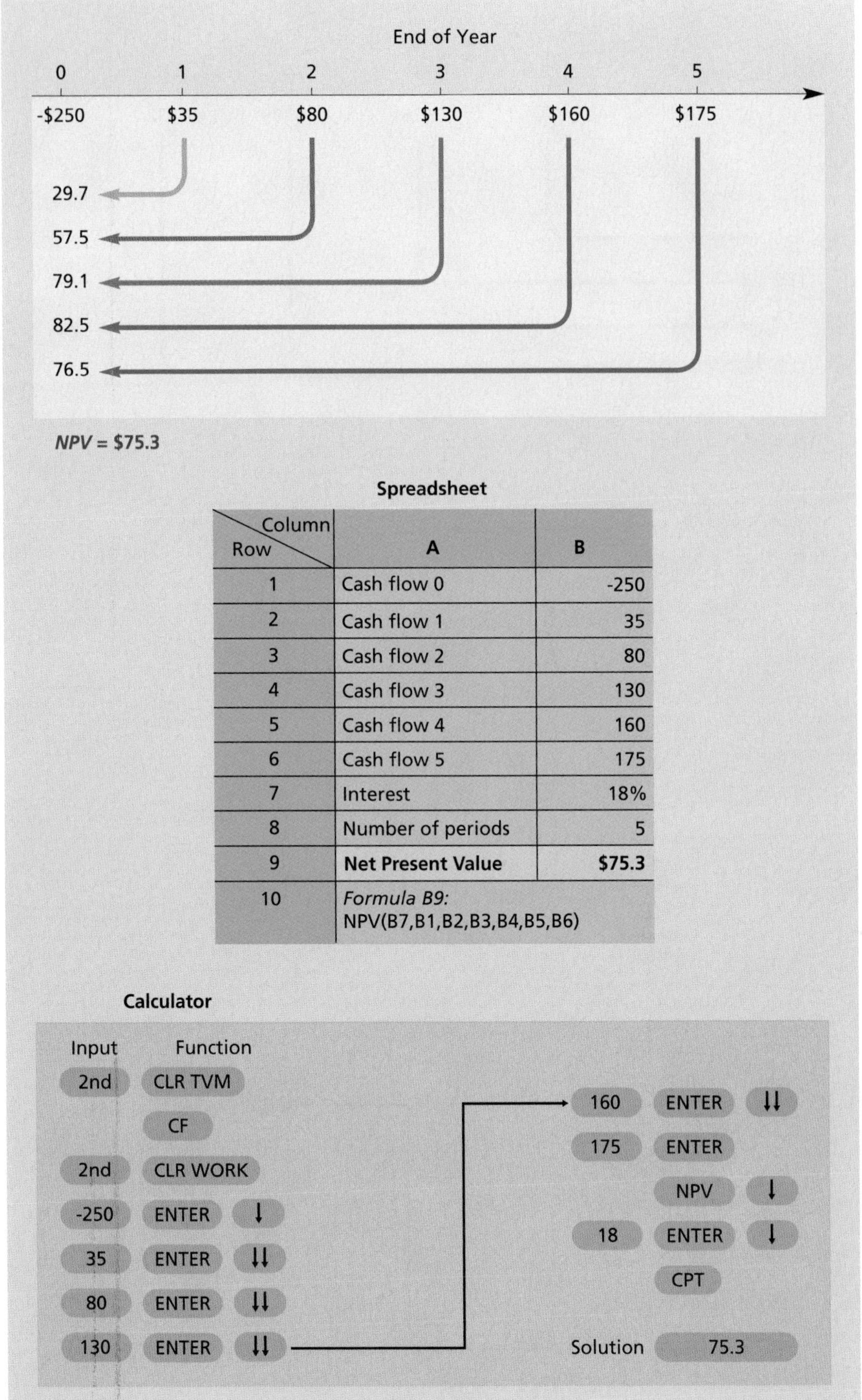

Row \ Column	A	B
1	Cash flow 0	-250
2	Cash flow 1	35
3	Cash flow 2	80
4	Cash flow 3	130
5	Cash flow 4	160
6	Cash flow 5	175
7	Interest	18%
8	Number of periods	5
9	**Net Present Value**	**$75.3**
10	*Formula B9:* NPV(B7,B1,B2,B3,B4,B5,B6)	

Figure 8.3a
NPV of Global Wireless's Projects at 18% ($millions)

Western Europe Project

The net present value (NPV) of Global Wireless's Western Europe Project is $75.3 million, which means that it is acceptable (NPV > $0) and therefore creates wealth for its shareholders. This project would be preferred over the Southeast U.S. Project which has a lower NPV as shown in Figure 8.3b.

Figure 8.3b
NPV of Global Wireless's Projects at 18% ($millions)

Southeast U.S. Project

The net present value (NPV) *of Global Wireless's Southeast U.S. Project is $25.7 million, which means that it is acceptable (*NPV *> $0) and therefore creates value for shareholders. This project is inferior to the Western Europe Project which has a higher* NPV *as shown in Figure 8.3a.*

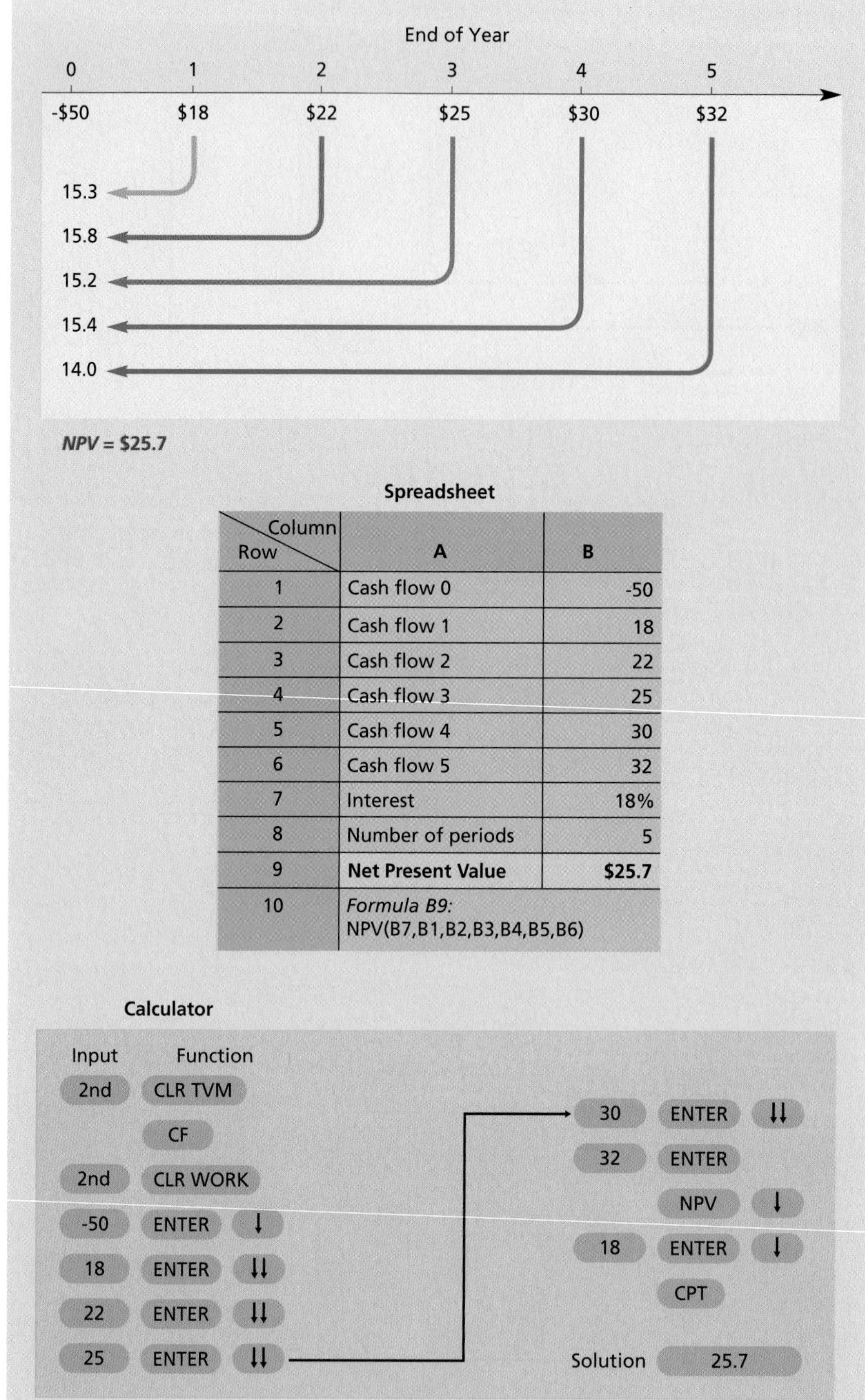

Row \ Column	A	B
1	Cash flow 0	-50
2	Cash flow 1	18
3	Cash flow 2	22
4	Cash flow 3	25
5	Cash flow 4	30
6	Cash flow 5	32
7	Interest	18%
8	Number of periods	5
9	**Net Present Value**	**$25.7**
10	*Formula B9:* NPV(B7,B1,B2,B3,B4,B5,B6)	

Though the mathematics of an *NPV* calculation can hardly be called sophisticated, it is still easier to calculate a project's payback period than its *NPV*.

Whereas most large corporations apply the *NPV* method, perhaps in conjunction with other capital budgeting tools, to make major investment decisions, the *NPV* rule has a close cousin known as the *internal rate of return,* that is even more widely used. The internal rate of return uses essentially the same mathematics as *NPV* does for evaluating a project's merits. The output of internal rate of return analysis is a single, intuitively appealing number representing the return that an investment earns over its life. In most cases, the internal rate of return yields investment recommendations that are in agreement with the *NPV* rule, although important differences between the two approaches arise when ranking alternative projects.

CONCEPT REVIEW QUESTIONS

6. What does it mean if a project has an *NPV* of $1 million?

7. Why might the discount rates used to calculate the *NPVs* of two competing projects differ at a given point in time?

8.5 INTERNAL RATE OF RETURN

Finding a Project's *IRR*

All methods used for evaluating investment projects, accounting rate of return, payback, and discounted payback suffer from common problems—the complete or partial failure to make adjustments for the time value of money and for risk. Alternative methods exist that correct these shortcomings. Perhaps the most popular and most intuitive of these alternatives is known as the **internal rate of return (*IRR*)** method. An investment's internal rate of return is analogous to a bond's *yield-to-maturity (YTM),* a concept we introduced in Chapter 4. Recall that the *YTM* of a bond is the discount rate that equates the present value of the bond's future cash flows to its market price. The *YTM* measures the compound annual return that an investor earns by purchasing a bond and holding it until maturity (provided that all payments are made as promised and that interest payments can be reinvested at the same rate). In a similar vein, the *IRR* of an investment project is the compound annual rate of return on the project, given its up-front costs and subsequent cash flows.

internal rate of return (*IRR*)
The compound annual rate of return on a project, given its up-front costs and subsequent cash flows.

A project's *IRR* is the discount rate that makes the net present value of all project cash flows equal to zero:

$$NPV = \$0 = CF_0 + \frac{CF_1}{(1+r)^1} + \frac{CF_2}{(1+r)^2} + \frac{CF_3}{(1+r)^3} + \ldots + \frac{CF_N}{(1+r)^N} \quad \text{(Eq. 8.2)}$$

To find a project's *IRR*, we must begin by specifying the project's cash flows. Next, using a financial calculator, a spreadsheet, or even trial and error, we find the discount rate that equates the present value of cash flows to zero. Once we have the *IRR* in hand, we compare it with a prespecified hurdle rate established by the firm. The hurdle rate represents the firm's minimum acceptable return for a given project, so *the decision rule is to invest only if the project's* IRR *exceeds the hurdle rate.*

But where does the hurdle rate come from? How do firms decide whether to require projects to exceed a 10 percent hurdle or a 20 percent hurdle? The answer to this question provides insight into another advantage of *IRR* over capital budgeting

Figure 8.4
NPV Profile and Shareholder Wealth

The net present value (NPV) *profile for the "typical" project, which begins with an initial outflow followed by a series of inflows, shows that the* NPV *declines as the discount rate used to calculate the* NPV *increases. The project's* IRR *is the discount rate that causes the* NPV *to equal zero.*

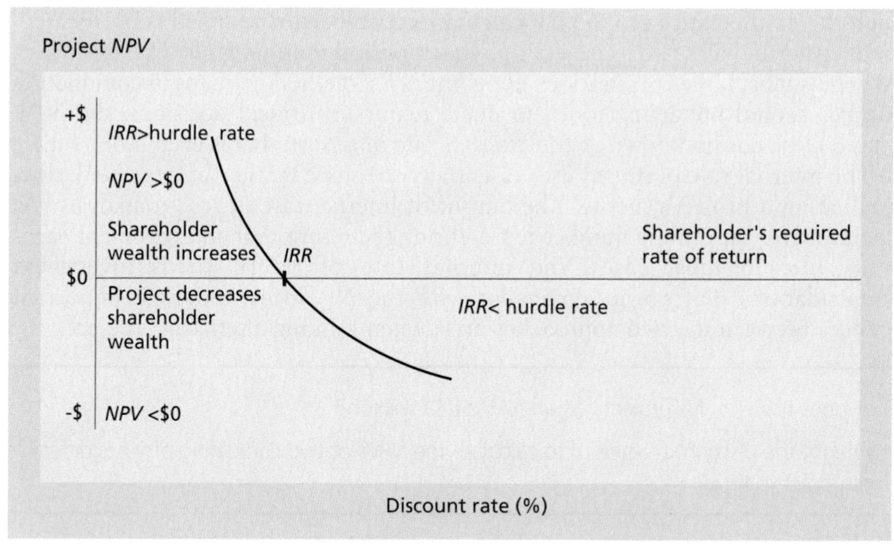

methods that focus on a project's accounting rate of return or payback period. A company should set the hurdle rate at a level that reflects market returns on investments that are just as risky as the project under consideration. For example, if the project at hand involves expanding a chain of fast-food restaurants, then the hurdle rate should reflect the returns that other fast-food businesses offer investors in the marketplace. Therefore, the *IRR* method, like the *NPV* method, establishes a hurdle rate or a decision criterion that is *market-based,* unlike the accounting-based and payback approaches that establish arbitrary thresholds for investment approval. In fact, *for a given project, the hurdle rate used in* IRR *analysis should be the discount rate used in* NPV *analysis.*

net present value (*NPV*) profile
A plot of a project's *NPV* (on the y axis) against various discount rates (on the x axis). It is used to illustrate the relationship between the *NPV* and the *IRR* for the typical project.

Figure 8.4 is a **net present value (*NPV*) profile**, which plots a project's *NPV* (on the *y* axis) against various discount rates (on the *x* axis). The *NPV* profile can be used to illustrate the relationship between the *NPV* and the *IRR* for a typical project. By "typical," we mean a project with cash flows that begin with an initial outflow, followed by a series of inflows. In this case, the *NPV* declines as the discount rate used to calculate the *NPV* increases. Not all projects have this feature, as we will soon see. The line in Figure 8.4 plots the *NPV* of a project at various discount rates. When the discount rate is relatively low, the project has a positive *NPV*. When the discount rate is high, the project has a negative *NPV*. *At some discount rate, the NPV of the project will equal zero, and that rate is the project's IRR.*

APPLYING THE MODEL

Suppose that Global Wireless requires its analysts to calculate the *IRR* of all proposed investments, and the company agrees to undertake only those investments that offer an *IRR* exceeding 18 percent, a rate that Global Wireless believes to be an industry standard. Figure 8.5 presents a time line depicting the *IRR* calculation procedure for Global Wireless's two projects. Calculating the *IRR* for each of Global Wireless's potential investments involves solving these two equations:

$$\$0 = -\$250 + \frac{\$35}{(1+r_{WE})^1} + \frac{\$80}{(1+r_{WE})^2} + \frac{\$130}{(1+r_{WE})^3} + \frac{\$160}{(1+r_{WE})^4} + \frac{\$175}{(1+r_{WE})^5}$$

$$\$0 = -\$50 + \frac{\$18}{(1+r_{SE})^1} + \frac{\$22}{(1+r_{SE})^2} + \frac{\$25}{(1+r_{SE})^3} + \frac{\$30}{(1+r_{SE})^4} + \frac{\$32}{(1+r_{SE})^5}$$

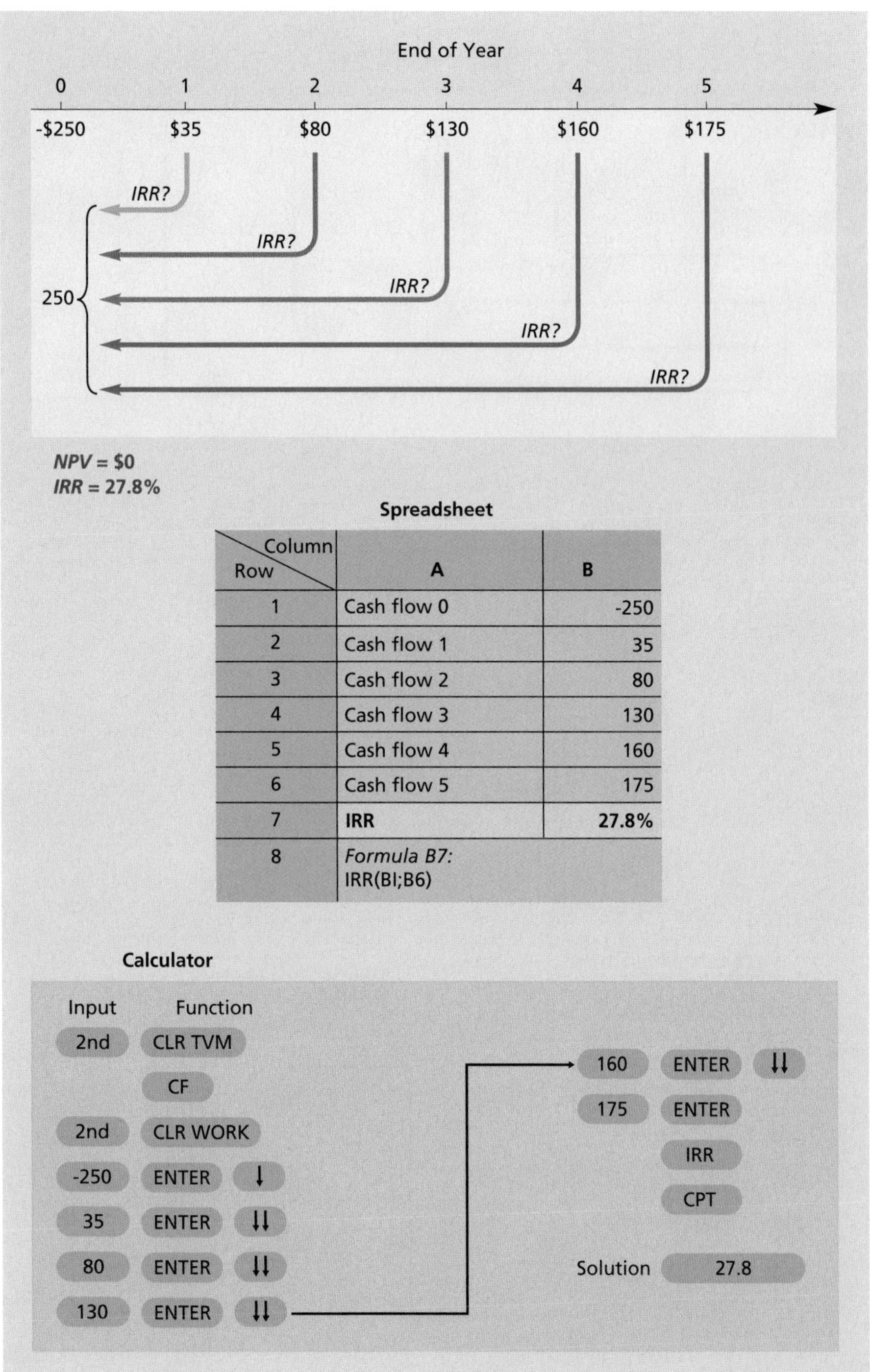

Row \ Column	A	B
1	Cash flow 0	-250
2	Cash flow 1	35
3	Cash flow 2	80
4	Cash flow 3	130
5	Cash flow 4	160
6	Cash flow 5	175
7	**IRR**	**27.8%**
8	*Formula B7:* IRR(BI;B6)	

Figure 8.5a
IRR of Global Wireless's Projects ($millions)

Western Europe Project

The internal rate of return (IRR) *for Global Wireless's Western Europe Project is 27.8%, which is the discount rate that causes the project's cash flows to have an* NPV *of $0. The project is acceptable because its* NPV *is greater than the firm's 18% hurdle rate. Because the* IRR *for the Western Europe Project is less than the 36.7%* IRR *for the Southeast U.S. Project shown in Figure 8.5b, the Southeast U.S. Project is preferred.*

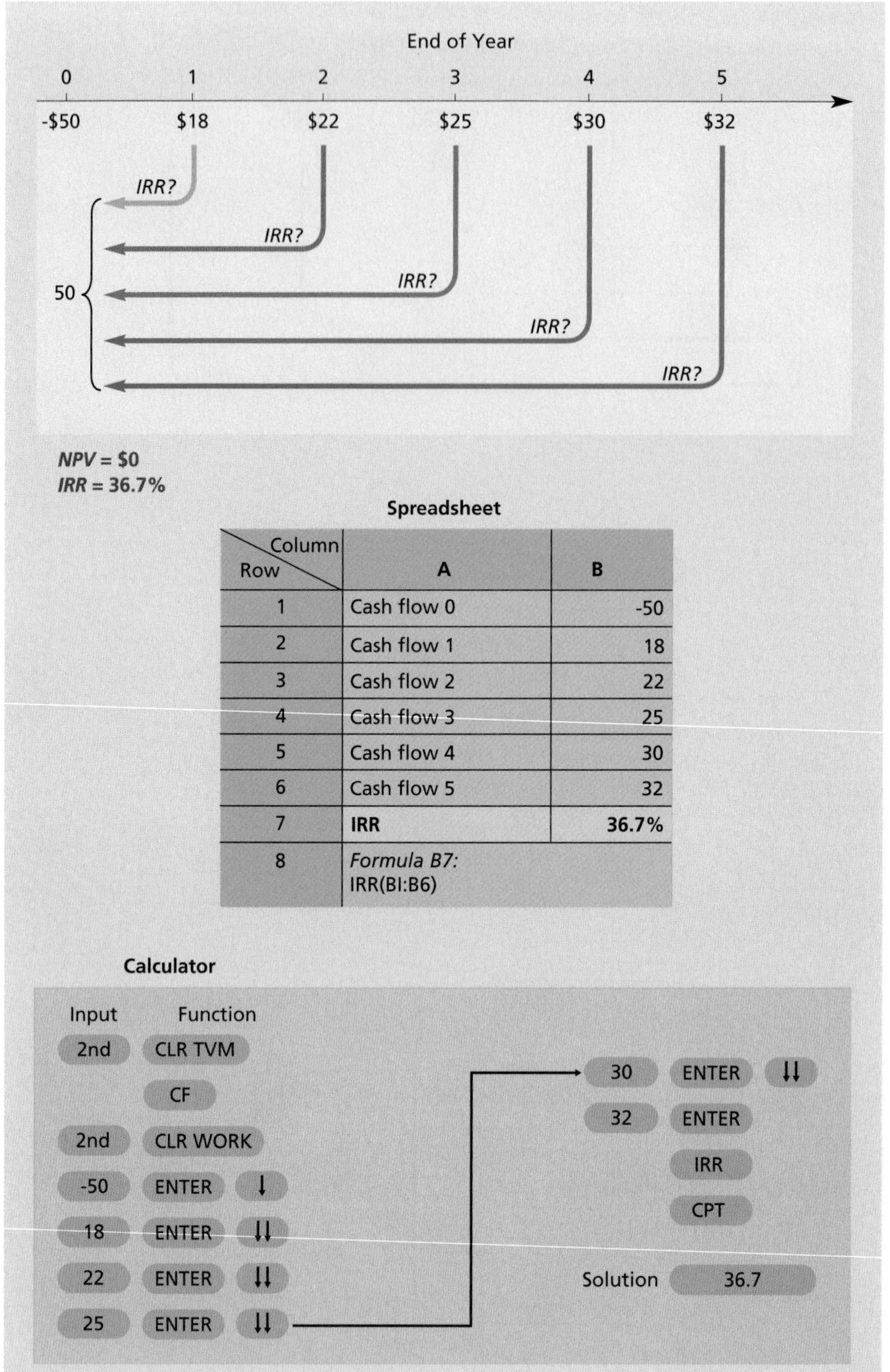

Column / Row	A	B
1	Cash flow 0	-50
2	Cash flow 1	18
3	Cash flow 2	22
4	Cash flow 3	25
5	Cash flow 4	30
6	Cash flow 5	32
7	**IRR**	**36.7%**
8	*Formula B7:* IRR(BI:B6)	

Figure 8.5b
IRR of Global Wireless's Projects ($millions)

Southeast U.S. Project

The internal rate of return (IRR) *for Global Wireless's Southeast U.S. Project is 36.7%, which is the discount rate that causes the project's cash flow to have an* NPV *of $0. Because the* IRR *for this project is above the 27.8%* IRR *for the Western Europe Project, this project is preferred.*

The numerical values in these equations come from each project's cash flow estimates, and the terms r_{WE} and r_{SE} represent the *IRR* for the Western Europe and southeast U.S. investments, respectively. Solving these expressions yields the following:[8]

$r_{WE} = 27.8\%$
$r_{SE} = 36.7\%$

Because both investments exceed the hurdle rate of 18 percent, Global Wireless would like to undertake both projects. But what if it can invest in only one project or the other? Should the company invest in the southeast U.S. project because it offers a higher *IRR* than the alternative?

Advantages of the *IRR* Method

The question of how to rank investments that offer different *IRR*s points to an important weakness of this method. However, before considering the problems associated with *IRR* analysis, let us discuss the advantages that make it one of the most widely used methods for evaluating capital investments.

First, the *IRR* makes an appropriate adjustment for the time value of money. The value of a dollar received in the first year is greater than the value of a dollar received in the second year. Even cash flows that arrive several years in the future receive some weight in the analysis (unlike payback, which totally ignores distant cash flows). Second, the hurdle rate itself can be based on market returns obtainable on similar investments. This takes away some of the subjectivity that creeps into other analytical methods, like the arbitrary threshold decisions that must be made when using accounting rate of return or payback, and it allows managers to make explicit, quantitative adjustments for differences in risk across projects. Third, because the "answer" that comes out of an *IRR* analysis is a rate of return, its meaning is easy for both financial and nonfinancial managers to grasp intuitively. They can easily compare a project's *IRR* with objective as well as subjective hurdle rates to assess its economic viability. As we will see, however, the intuitive appeal of the *IRR* approach has its drawbacks, particularly when ranking investments with different *IRR*s. Fourth, the *IRR* technique focuses on cash flow rather than on accounting measures of income.

Though it represents a substantial improvement over accounting rate of return or payback analysis, the *IRR* technique has some quirks and problems that in certain situations should concern analysts. Some of these problems arise from the mathematics of the *IRR* calculation, but other difficulties come into play only when companies must discriminate between **mutually exclusive projects.** If the *IRR*s of several projects exceed the hurdle rate (or *NPV*s exceed \$0), but only a subset of those projects can be undertaken at the given time, how does the firm choose? It turns out that the intuitive approach, selecting those projects with the highest *IRR*s, can lead to bad decisions in certain cases.

mutually exclusive projects
The situation that occurs when the *IRRs* of several projects exceed the hurdle rate (or the *NPVs* exceed \$0), but only a subset of those projects can be undertaken at the given time.

Problems with the Internal Rate of Return

There are two classes of problems that analysts encounter when evaluating investments using the *IRR* technique. The first class can be described as "mathematical problems," which are difficulties in interpreting the numbers that one obtains from solving an *IRR* equation. For example, consider a simple project with cash flows at three different points in time:

CF_0	CF_1	CF_2
0	1	2

years →

[8] Of course, you can make this calculation using a financial calculator or *Excel*, as shown below the time lines in Figure 8.5.

CF_0 is the immediate cash flow when the project begins, and CF_1 and CF_2 are cash flows that occur at the end of years 1 and 2, respectively. Note that conceptually the values of CF_0, CF_1, and CF_2 could be either positive or negative. Solving for this project's *IRR* means setting the net present value of all these cash flows equal to zero:

$$NPV = \$0 = CF_0 + \frac{CF_1}{(1+r)^1} + \frac{CF_2}{(1+r)^2}$$

Notice that this equation involves terms such as $[1/(1+r)]^1$ and $[1/(1+r)]^2$. In other words, this is a quadratic equation in terms of $[1/(1+r)]$. Remember factoring equations such as $x^2 - 5x + 6 = 0$? That equation factors into $(x-2)(x-3)$ and has two correct values for x, $x = 2$ or 3. This is the same issue we sometimes face when calculating a project's *IRR* where $x = [1/(1+r)]$. Simply stated, solving a quadratic equation can result in a variety of possible outcomes, including (1) a unique solution, (2) multiple solutions, and (3) no real solution. The following examples illustrate the problems with multiple *IRR*s and no real solution.

Multiple *IRR*s. One difficulty with the *IRR* method can occur when a project's cash flows alternate between negative and positive values—that is, when the project generates an alternating series of net cash inflows and outflows. In that case, there may be more than one solution to the *IRR* equation. As an example, consider a project with the following stream of cash flows:

Year	*CF* ($ in millions)
0	+100
1	−460
2	+791
3	−602.6
4	+171.6

Admittedly, this project has a rather strange sequence of alternating net cash inflows and outflows, but it is not hard to think of real-world investments that generate cash flow streams that flip back and forth like this. For example, think about high-technology products. A new product costs money to develop. It generates plenty of cash for a year or two, but it quickly becomes obsolete. Obsolescence necessitates more spending to develop an upgraded version of the product, which then generates cash again. The cycle continues indefinitely.

Figure 8.6 presents the *NPV* profile for a project with the cash flows shown above at various discount rates. Notice that there are several points on the graph at which the project *NPV* equals zero. In other words, there are several *IRR*s for this project, including 0 percent, 10 percent, 20 percent, and 30 percent. How does one apply the *IRR* decision rule in a situation such as this? Suppose that the hurdle rate for this project is 15 percent. Two of the four *IRR*s on this project exceed the hurdle rate, and two fall below the hurdle rate. Should the firm invest or not? The only way to know for sure is to check the *NPV*. On the graph, we see that at a discount rate of 15 percent, the project's *NPV* is positive, so the firm should invest.

The general rule of thumb is that the maximum number of *IRR*s that a project can have equals the number of sign changes in the cash flow stream. Therefore, in the typical project with cash outflows up front and cash inflows later on, there is just one sign change, and there will be at most one *IRR*. In the previous example, there are four sign changes in the cash flow stream and four different *IRR*s. *In the event that you have to evaluate a project with more than one sign change in the cash flows, beware of the*

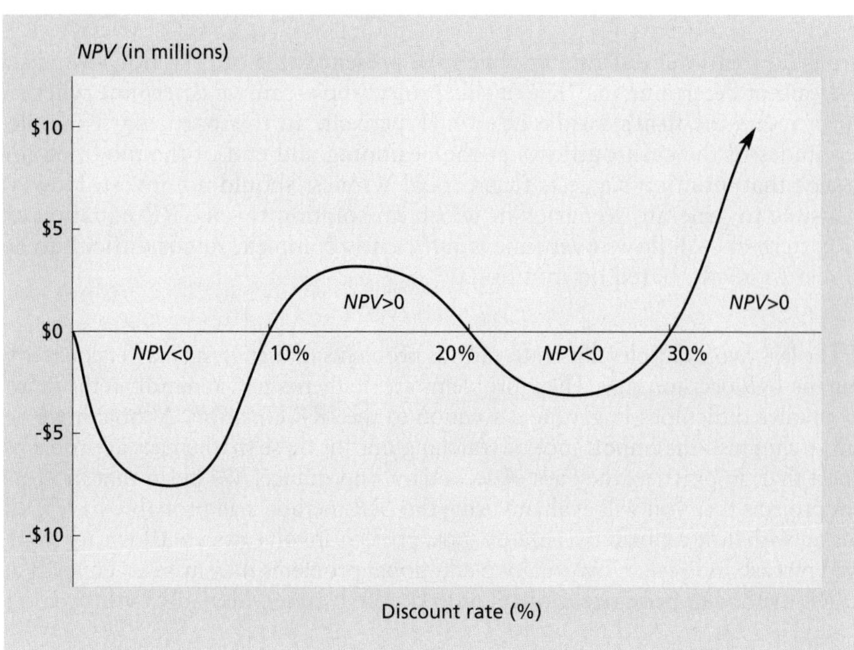

Figure 8.6
NPV Profile for a Project with Multiple *IRRs*

This project with alternating cash inflows and outflows has an NPV *profile that reflects multiple* IRRs*. At each discount rate for which the* NPV *= $0, there is an* IRR*. In this case,* IRRs *occur at 0%, 10%, 20%, and 30%.*

multiple IRR problem. In this situation, the *NPV* profile must be analyzed because use of the *IRR* typically does not result in the correct decision.

No Real Solution. Occasionally, when you enter the cash flows from a particular investment into a calculator or a spreadsheet, you may receive an error message indicating that there is no solution to the problem. For some cash flow patterns, it is possible that there is no real discount rate that equates the project's *NPV* to zero. In these cases, the only solution to the *IRR* equation involves imaginary numbers, hardly something that we can compare with a firm's hurdle rate.

APPLYING THE MODEL

When we first looked at the Global Wireless Western Europe expansion project, we examined cash flows over a five-year project life. Let's modify the example a little. Suppose that the project life is six years rather than five, and in the sixth year, the firm must incur a large negative cash outflow. The modified cash flow projections look like this:

Year	Western Europe Project ($ in millions)
0	–250
1	35
2	80
3	130
4	160
5	175
6	–355

When we attempt to calculate the *IRR* for this stream of cash flows, we find that our financial calculator (or *Excel*) returns an error code. The problem is that for this stream of cash flows, there is no real solution to the *IRR* equation. That is, there is no (real) interest rate at which the present value of cash flows equals zero. If we cannot determine the *IRR* of this project, how can we determine whether the project meets the firm's hurdle rate of 18 percent? In this particular example, the magnitudes of the cash outflows at the beginning and end of the modified project are such that intuition suggests that Global Wireless should not invest. However, it is possible to generate scenarios in which no solution to the *IRR* equation exists. The pattern of cash flows over time is sufficiently complex, so it is difficult to decide whether to invest, based on intuition.

The last two examples illustrate various problems that analysts may encounter when using the *IRR* decision rule. These problems are mathematical in nature in the sense that they involve difficulties in getting a solution to the *IRR* equation. Although we do not want to diminish the importance of watching out for these mathematical problems, we suspect that, in practice, they are of secondary importance. We mean that most investment projects that you will evaluate using the *IRR* method will probably have a unique solution with little ambiguity (because most projects involve cash outflows up front, followed by cash inflows). However, two additional problems may arise when analysts use the *IRR* method to prioritize projects or to choose between mutually exclusive projects.

IRR, *NPV*, and Mutually Exclusive Projects

The Scale Problem. Suppose that a friend promises to pay you $2 tomorrow if you lend him $1 today. If you make the loan and your friend fulfills his end of the bargain, you will have made an investment with a 100 percent *IRR*.[9] Now consider a different case. Your friend asks you to lend him $100 today in exchange for $150 tomorrow. The *IRR* on that investment is 50 percent, exactly half the *IRR* of the first example. Both of these loans offer very high rates of return. Assuming that you trust the friend to repay you in either case, which investment would you choose if you could choose only one? The first investment increases your wealth by $1, and the second increases your wealth by $50. Even though the rate of return is lower on the second investment, most people would prefer to lend the larger amount because of its substantially greater payoff.

The point of these examples is not to tempt you to enter the loan-shark business, but rather to illustrate the *scale problem* inherent in *IRR* analysis. When choosing between mutually exclusive investments, we cannot conclude that the one offering the highest *IRR* necessarily provides the greatest wealth-creation opportunity. When several alternative investments offer *IRR*s that exceed a firm's hurdle rate, choosing the investment that maximizes shareholder wealth involves more than picking the project with the highest *IRR*. For example, take another look at the investment opportunities faced by Global Wireless, opportunities that vary dramatically in scale.

APPLYING THE MODEL

Here again are the *NPV* and *IRR* figures for the two investment alternatives.

Project	*IRR*	*NPV* (@18%)
Western Europe	27.8%	$75.3 million
Southeast U.S.	36.7	25.7 million

9. The *IRR* is 100 percent per day in this example, which is not a bad return if you annualize it.

If we had to choose just one project, and we ranked them based on their *IRR*s, we would choose to invest in the southeast U.S. project. But we have also seen that the Western Europe project generates a much higher *NPV*, meaning that it creates more wealth for Global Wireless shareholders. The *NPV* criterion tells us to expand in Western Europe rather than in the southeast United States. Why the conflict? The scale of the Western Europe expansion is roughly five times that of the southeast U.S. project. Even though the southeast U.S. investment provides a higher rate of return, the opportunity to make the much larger Western Europe investment (an investment that also offers a return well above the firm's hurdle rate) is more attractive.

Fortunately for analysts who prefer to use the *IRR* method, there is a resolution to the scale problem. Discussion of this procedure is beyond the scope of this introductory text. Suffice it to say that the methodology allows one to use the *IRR* technique to find precisely the same solution that would result using *NPV*.[10]

The Timing Problem. Managers of public corporations often receive criticism for neglecting long-term investment opportunities for the sake of meeting short-term financial performance goals. We prefer to remain noncommittal on whether corporate managers, as a rule, put too much emphasis on short-term performance. However, we agree with the proposition that a naive reliance on the *IRR* method can lead to investment decisions that sometimes favor investments with short-term payoffs over those that offer returns over a longer horizon. The *Applying the Model* illustrates the problem we have in mind.

APPLYING THE MODEL

A company wants to evaluate two investment proposals. The first involves a major effort in new product development. The initial cost is $1 billion, and the company expects the project to generate relatively meager cash flows in the first four years, followed by a big payoff in year 5. The second investment is a significant marketing campaign to attract new customers. It too has an initial outlay of $1 billion, but it generates significant cash flows almost immediately and lower levels of cash in the later years. A financial analyst prepares cash flow projections and calculates each project's *IRR* and *NPV* as shown in the following table (the firm uses 10 percent as its hurdle rate):

Cash Flow	Product Development ($ in millions)	Marketing Campaign ($ in millions)
Initial Outlay	–1,000	–1,000
Year 1	0	450
Year 2	50	350
Year 3	100	300
Year 4	200	200
Year 5	1,500	100
Technique		
IRR	14.1%	15.9%
NPV (@10%)	$184.44	$122.44

The analyst observes that the first project generates a higher *NPV*, whereas the second offers a higher *IRR*. Bewildered, he wonders which project to recommend to senior management.

10. See Scott B. Smart, William L. Megginson, and Lawrence J. Gitman, *Corporate Finance* (Mason, OH: South-Western, 2004), p. 245, for a demonstration of this procedure.

Even though both projects require the same initial investment and both last for five years, the marketing campaign generates more cash flow in the early years than the product development proposal. Therefore, in a relative sense, the payoff from product development occurs later than the payoff from marketing. We know from our discussion of interest-rate risk in Chapter 4 that when interest rates change, long-term bond prices move more than short-term bond prices do. The same phenomenon is at work here. Figure 8.7 plots the *NPV* profiles for the two projects on the same set of axes. Notice that one line, the line plotting *NPV*s for the product development idea, is much steeper than the other. In simple terms, this means that the *NPV* of that investment is much more sensitive to the discount rate than is the *NPV* of the marketing campaign.

Each investment's *IRR* appears in Figure 8.7 where the *NPV* lines cross the *x*-axis. Figure 8.7 shows that both *IRR*s exceed the hurdle rate of 10 percent and that the marketing campaign has the higher *IRR*. The two lines intersect at a discount rate of 12.5 percent. At that discount rate, the *NPV*s of the projects are equal. At discount rates below 12.5 percent, product development, which has a longer-term payoff, has the higher *NPV*. At discount rates above 12.5 percent, the investment in the marketing campaign offers a larger *NPV*. Given that the required rate of return on investments for this particular firm is 10 percent, the firm should choose to spend the $1 billion on product development. However, if the firm bases its investment decision solely on achieving the highest *IRR*, it will choose the marketing campaign proposal instead.

SMART CONCEPTS

In summary, we can say that when the timing of cash flows is very different from one project to another, the project with the highest *IRR* may or may not have the highest *NPV*. As in the case of the scale problem, the timing problem can lead firms to reject investments that they should accept. We want to emphasize that this problem (and the scale problem) occurs only when firms must choose between mutually exclusive projects. In the previous example, if the firm could invest in both projects, it should.

When firms must prioritize projects, leaving some acceptable projects on the table, there are two ways they can avoid falling into the timing trap. First, using *NPV* will lead to the correct decision when evaluating projects with very different cash flow patterns over time. Second, analysts can use mathematical techniques that

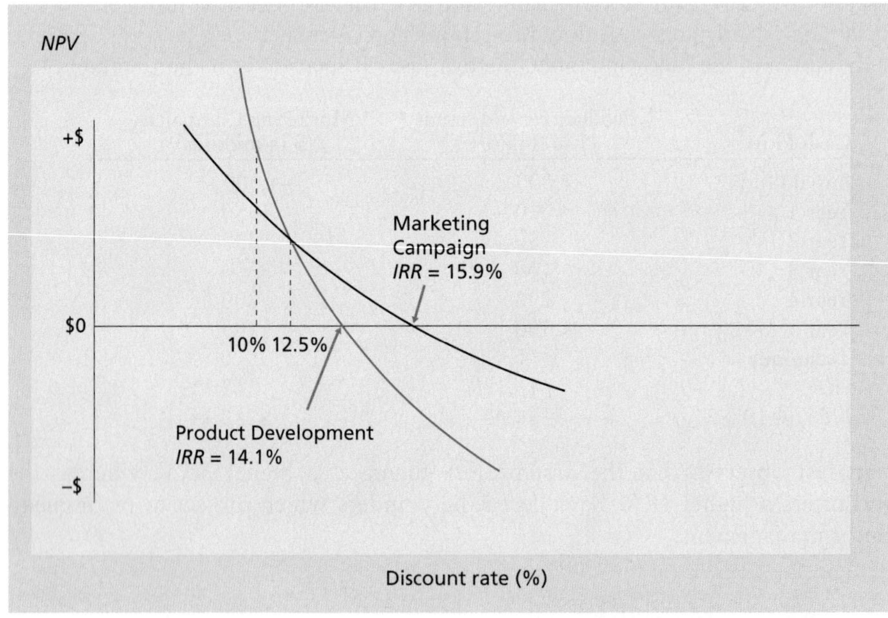

Figure 8.7
NPV Profiles Demonstrating the Timing Problem

Because of the differences in the timing of the two projects' cash flows, the Marketing Campaign has a higher IRR *than the Product Development proposal, and both* IRRs *exceed the 10% hurdle rate. But the* NPV *for the Product Development proposal at 10% exceeds the* NPV *for the Marketing Campaign.*

are beyond the scope of this introductory text to resolve the timing problem. The methodology allows one to use the *IRR* technique to find precisely the same solution that would result using *NPV*.[11] **Clearly, the most straightforward and, theoretically, the best decision technique is net present value (*NPV*).**

CONCEPT REVIEW QUESTIONS

8. Describe how the *IRR* and *NPV* approaches are related.

9. If the *IRR* for a given project exceeds a firm's hurdle rate, does that mean that the project necessarily has a positive *NPV*? Explain.

10. Describe the "scale problem" and the "timing problem" and explain the potential effects of these problems on the choice of mutually exclusive projects, using *IRR* versus *NPV*.

8.6 PROFITABILITY INDEX

A final capital budgeting tool that we discuss is the **profitability index (*PI*)**. Like the *IRR*, the profitability index is a close cousin of the *NPV* approach. Mathematically, for simple projects that have an initial cash outflow (CF_0) followed by a series of inflows (CF_1, CF_2,...,CF_N), the *PI* equals the present value of a project's cash inflows divided by the initial cash outflow.

profitability index (*PI*) A capital budgeting tool, defined as the present value of a project's cash inflows divided by its initial cash outflow.

$$PI = \frac{\frac{CF_1}{(1+r)^1} + \frac{CF_2}{(1+r)^2} + \ldots + \frac{CF_N}{(1+r)^N}}{CF_0} \quad \text{(Eq. 8.3)}$$

The decision rule to follow when evaluating investment projects using the *PI* is to invest when the *PI* is greater than 1.0 (i.e., when the present value of cash inflows exceeds the initial cash outflow) and to refrain from investing when the *PI* is less than 1.0. Notice that if the *PI* is above 1.0, the *NPV* must be greater than zero. That means that the *NPV* and *PI* decision rules will always yield the same investment recommendation when we are simply trying to decide whether to accept or reject a single project.

APPLYING THE MODEL

To calculate the *PI* for each of Global Wireless's investment projects, calculate the present value of its cash inflows from years 1–5 and then divide by the initial cash outflow to obtain the following result:

Project	*PV* of *CF* (1–5) ($ in millions)	Initial Outlay ($ in millions)	*PI*
Western Europe	325.3	250	1.3
Southeast U.S.	75.7	50	1.5

Because both projects have a *PI* greater than 1.0, both are worthwhile. However, notice that if we rank projects based on the *PI*, the southeast U.S. project looks better.

[11] Smart, Megginson, and Gitman, Op. cit., p. 247.

Because the *NPV*, *IRR*, and *PI* methods are so closely related, they share many of the same advantages relative to accounting rate of return or payback analysis, and there is no need to reiterate those advantages here. However, it is worth pointing out that the *PI* and the *IRR* share an important flaw. Both suffer from the *scale problem* described earlier. Recall that our *NPV* calculations suggested that the Western Europe project created more value for shareholders than the southeast U.S. endeavor, whereas the *IRR* and *PI* comparisons suggest just the opposite project ranking. The reason that the *IRR* and *PI* analyses identify the southeast U.S. project as the superior investment is that they do not take into account the differences in scale between the two projects. For the southeast U.S. project, the *PI* indicates that project cash inflows exceed the initial cash outflow by 50 percent on a present-value basis. The present value of cash inflows for the Western Europe investment exceeds the initial cash outflow by just 30 percent. But the Western Europe project is much larger, and as our *NPV* figures reveal, it generates considerably more wealth for Global Wireless stockholders.[12]

CONCEPT REVIEW QUESTIONS

11. How are the *NPV*, *IRR*, and *PI* approaches related?

12. What important flaw do both the *IRR* and *PI* share? Explain.

8.7 WHICH TECHNIQUES DO FIRMS ACTUALLY USE?

In a recent survey of 392 chief financial officers (CFOs), Graham and Harvey (2001) studied the capital budgeting methods that companies use to make real investment decisions. They asked CFOs to indicate how frequently they used several capital budgeting methods by ranking them on a scale ranging from 0 (never) to 4 (always). The techniques CFOs use most often are *NPV* (score = 3.08) and *IRR* (score = 3.09), with roughly 75 percent of CFOs indicating that they always or almost always use these techniques. A thirty-year-old study by Gitman and Forrester (1977) found that only 9.8 percent of large firms used *NPV* as a primary capital budgeting tool, so Graham and Harvey's results clearly illustrate that the popularity of the *NPV* approach has grown over time. Interestingly, the popularity of the *NPV* approach is correlated both with the size of the firm and the educational background of its CFO. Large, publicly traded firms run by CFOs with MBAs are much more likely to rely on the *NPV* method than are small, private firms headed by CFOs without MBAs.

SMART PRACTICES VIDEO

Beth Acton, Vice President and Treasurer of Ford Motor Co. (former)

"We look at capital investments in a very similar fashion whether they're routine or large investments."

See the entire interview at **SMARTFinance**

Third on the list of most frequently used capital budgeting tools is the payback method. Small firms, in particular, use the payback approach almost as often as they use *NPV* and *IRR*. Older CFOs and those without MBA degrees also tend to make decisions based on payback analysis much more frequently than do other CFOs. Most CFOs reported that they rarely used accounting rate of return, discounted payback, or the profitability index when making investment decisions. The Comparative Corporate Finance insert compares Graham and Harvey's results to similar studies conducted in Sweden, South Africa, and the United Kingdom. All these papers point to the preeminence of discounted cash flow analysis in making investment decisions around the world.

12. The use of the profitability index in capital rationing, which occurs when the firm has more acceptable projects than it can fund from its current budget, is discussed in Chapter 9.

COMPARATIVE CORPORATE FINANCE

Capital Budgeting in Sweden, South Africa, and the United Kingdom

We have seen that managers of publicly traded U.S. firms use discounted cash flow techniques in capital budgeting far more today than in the past. But what of managers in other countries? Three recent academic studies present survey evidence of how frequently discounted cash flow techniques are used by managers of Swedish, South African, and British companies. The results are somewhat encouraging. Sandahl and Sjögren (2003) find that 64.8 percent of the 128 responding Swedish companies use either *NPV* (52.3 percent) or *IRR* (22.7 percent), or both, with larger firms more likely to use one of these methods than smaller companies. On the other hand, 78.1 percent of the responding companies use the payback period. This is by far the most commonly employed tool for companies that use only one capital budgeting decision rule, with 58.3 percent using payback versus 12.5 percent for both *NPV* and *IRR*.

In a survey of companies listed on the Industrial Sector of the Johannesburg Stock Exchange, Hall (2000) finds that two thirds of responding South African firms use discounted cash flow techniques to make capital budgeting decisions. Specifically, 32.3 percent of these firms report that they believe that the *IRR* method is the best tool for evaluating capital investments, while 16.9 percent say that *NPV* is their preferred tool, and 16.9 percent rely on discounted payback. Moreover, the importance of these techniques in the investment decision process rises with the size of the firm. Among the smallest South African firms in the survey, just over 14 percent calculate the *NPV* or *IRR* of their investment projects, but 75 percent of the largest firms do. Finally, a study published in Lumby (1991) reports similar patterns among UK firms, with 54 percent using discounted cash flow techniques. The same positive relationship between a firm's size and its tendency to use discounted cash flow analysis that exists in South Africa also emerges in the United Kingdom.

Sources: Gert Sandahl and Stefan Sjögren, "Capital Budgeting Methods Among Sweden's Largest Groups of Companies: The State of the Art and a Comparison with Earlier Studies," *International Journal of Production Economics* 84 (April 2003), pp. 51–69; J. H. Hall, "An Empirical Investigation of the Capital Budgeting Process," (2000), University of Pretoria working paper; and L. Lumby, *Investment Appraisal and Investment Decisions*, 4th ed. London: Chapman & Hall, 1991.

8.8 SUMMARY AND CONCLUSIONS

- The capital budgeting process involves generating, reviewing, analyzing, selecting, and implementing long-term investment proposals that are consistent with the firm's strategic goals.
- Other things being equal, managers would prefer an easily applied capital budgeting technique that considers cash flow, recognizes the time value of money, fully accounts for expected risk and return, and when applied, leads to higher stock prices.
- Though simplicity is a virtue, the simplest approaches to capital budgeting do not always lead firms to make the best investment decisions.
- Capital budgeting techniques include the accounting rate of return, the payback period, and the discounted payback period, which are less-sophisticated techniques because they do not explicitly deal with the time value of money and are not tied to the firm's wealth-maximization goal. More-sophisticated techniques include net present value (*NPV*), internal rate of return (*IRR*), and profitability index (*PI*). These methods often give the same accept-reject decisions but do not necessarily rank projects the same.
- Table 8.1 summarizes the definitions, advantages and disadvantages of each of the capital budgeting techniques presented in this chapter.
- Using the *IRR* approach can lead to poor investment decisions when projects have cash flow streams alternating between net inflows and outflows. The *IRR* technique may provide suboptimal project rankings when different investments have very different scales or when the timing of cash flows varies dramatically from one project to another.

- Although the *NPV* and *IRR* techniques give the same accept or reject decisions, these techniques do not necessarily agree in ranking mutually exclusive projects. Because of its lack of mathematical, scale, and timing problems, the most straightforward and, theoretically, the best decision technique is net present value (*NPV*).
- The profitability index is a close cousin of the *NPV* approach, but it suffers from the same scale problem as the *IRR* approach.

Table 8.1
Analysis of Capital Budgeting Techniques

Technique	Definition	Advantages	Disadvantages
Accounting Rate of Return	Net income divided by the book value of assets, either on a year-to-year basis or averaged over the project's life.	• Convenience • Ease of calculation • Ease of interpretation	• Significantly effected by the depreciation method used by the firm • Makes no adjustment for project's risk or the time value of money • Considers book values, not market values, of firm's assets • Focuses on income rather than cash flow • Relies on an arbitrary hurdle rate
Payback Period	Amount of time for cumulative net cash inflow to recoup initial investment.	• Simple to calculate • Intuitively appealing • Gives some consideration to the time value of money • Accounts for project risk exposure	• Relies on an arbitrary cutoff period • Method of accounting for time value of money is crude in the extreme • Ignores cash flows after the payback period • Crude method of controlling for project risk • Career concerns may cause managers to incorrectly favor projects with short paybacks
Discounted Payback	Same as payback except that cash flows are discounted and then the payback is calculated.	• Same as for the payback period except it explicitly considers time value of money in the cash flows that occur before the payback period	• Same as for the payback period except it does recognize time value for the payback period
Net Present Value (*NPV*)	The sum of the present values of all of a project's cash flows, both inflows and outflows, discounted at a rate consistent with the project's risk.	• Focuses on cash flows not accounting values • Makes appropriate adjustments for the time value of money • Reflects the firm's need to compete for funds in the marketplace rather than arbitrary judgment • Provides a convenient way to control for differences	• *NPV* is less intuitive than payback or a rate of return measure • More difficult to compute than is the payback period

Table 8.1 (continued)
Analysis of Capital Budgeting Techniques

Technique	Definition	Advantages	Disadvantages
		in risk among investment alternatives through discount rate adjustments • Incorporates all cash flows the project will generate over its life, not just those in the early years • Gives a direct estimate of the change in shareholder wealth resulting from a given investment	
Internal Rate of Return (*IRR*)	The compound annual rate of return on a project, given its up-front costs and subsequent cash flows.	• Makes an appropriate adjustment for the time value of money • Hurdle rate can be based on market returns obtainable on similar investments • Because it is a rate of return, it is easy for both financial and nonfinancial managers to grasp it intuitively • Focuses on cash flow rather than accounting measures of income	• Can have multiple *IRR*s when a project's cash flows alternate between inflows and outflows • For some cash flow patterns, there is no real discount rate that equates a project's *NPV* to zero, and therefore, there is no real *IRR* • For mutually exclusive projects, due to the "scale problem" the project with the highest *IRR* may not provide the greatest wealth creation opportunity • For mutually exclusive projects, *IRR* can lead to investment decisions that sometimes favor investments with short-term payoffs over those that offer returns over a longer horizon
Profitability Index (*PI*)	The ratio present value of a project's cash inflows divided by its initial cash outflow	• Same as *NPV*	• Same as *NPV* except suffers from the same "scale problem" as *IRR*, i.e., the project with the highest *PI* may not provide the greatest wealth-creation opportunity

SELF-TEST PROBLEMS

Answers to Self-Test Problems appear in Appendix D at back of book. Answers to the Concept Review Questions throughout the chapter appear at http://megginson.swlearning.com.

ST8-1. Nader International is considering investing in two assets—A and B. The initial outlay, annual cash flows, and annual depreciation for each asset is shown in the table below for the assets' assumed five-year lives. As can be seen, Nader will use straight-line depreciation over each asset's five-year life. The firm requires a 12 percent return on each of those equally risky assets. Nader's maximum payback period is 2.5 years, its maximum discounted payback period is 3.25 years, and its minimum accounting rate of return is 30 percent.

	Asset A		Asset B	
Initial Outlay (CF_0)	$200,000		$180,000	
Year (t)	Cash Flow (CF_t)	Depreciation	Cash Flow (CF_t)	Depreciation
1	$ 70,000	$40,000	$80,000	$36,000
2	80,000	40,000	90,000	36,000
3	90,000	40,000	30,000	36,000
4	90,000	40,000	40,000	36,000
5	100,000	40,000	40,000	36,000

a. Calculate the *accounting rate of return* from each asset, assess its acceptability, and indicate which asset is best, using the accounting rate of return.

b. Calculate the *payback period* for each asset, assess its acceptability, and indicate which asset is best, using the payback period.

c. Calculate the *discounted payback* for each asset, assess its acceptability, and indicate which asset is best, using the discounted payback.

d. Compute and contrast your findings in parts (a), (b), and (c). Which asset would you recommend to Nader, assuming that they are mutually exclusive? Why?

ST8-2. JK Products, Inc. is considering investing in either of two competing projects that will allow the firm to eliminate a production bottleneck and meet the growing demand for its products. The firm's engineering department narrowed the alternatives down to two—Status Quo (SQ) and High Tech (HT). Working with the accounting and finance personnel, the firm's CFO developed the following estimates of the cash flows for SQ and HT over the relevant six-year time horizon. The firm has an 11 percent required return and views these projects as equally risky.

	Project SQ	Project HT
Initial Outflow (CF_0)	$670,000	$940,000
Year (t)	Cash Inflows (CF_t)	
1	$250,000	$170,000
2	200,000	180,000
3	170,000	200,000
4	150,000	250,000
5	130,000	300,000
6	130,000	550,000

a. Calculate the *net present value* (*NPV*) of each project, assess its acceptability, and indicate which project is best, using *NPV*.

b. Calculate the *internal rate of return* (*IRR*) of each project, assess its acceptability, and indicate which project is best, using *IRR*.

c. Calculate the *profitability index* (*PI*) of each project, assess its acceptability, and indicate which project is best, using *PI*.

d. Draw the *NPV profile* for project SQ and HT on the same set of axes and use this diagram to explain why the *NPV* and the *IRR* show different preferences for these two mutually exclusive projects. Discuss this difference in terms of both the "scale problem" and the "timing problem."

e. Which of the two mutually exclusive projects would you recommend that JK Products undertake? Why?

INTERNET RESOURCES

Note: *For updates to links, please go to the book's Web site at* http://megginson.swlearning.com

http://www.teachmefinance.com/—A site that has definitions and examples of many finance concepts, including most of the capital budgeting tools discussed in this chapter.

http://clinton3.nara.gov/pcscb/—Contains a report by the President's Commission to Study Capital Budgeting, a group created in 1997 to evaluate capital budgeting techniques used by other governments and the private sector.

http://www.swlearning.com/finance/finance_news/fin_capital_budgeting.html/—A site maintained by South Western Publishing Company that summarizes news events relating to capital budgeting and investment evaluation techniques.

KEY TERMS

accounting rate of return
capital budgeting
capital spending
capital investment
discounted payback
internal rate of return (*IRR*)
mutually exclusive projects
net present value (*NPV*)
net present value (*NPV*) profile
payback period
profitability index (*PI*)

QUESTIONS AND PROBLEMS

Q8-1. Can you name some industries where the payback period is unavoidably long?

Q8-2. In statistics, you learn about Type I and Type II errors. A Type I error occurs when a statistical test rejects a hypothesis when the hypothesis is actually true. A Type II error occurs when a test fails to reject a hypothesis that is actually false. We can apply this type of thinking to capital budgeting. A Type I error occurs when a firm rejects an investment project that would actually enhance shareholder wealth. A Type II error occurs when a firm accepts a value-decreasing investment, which should have been rejected.

a. Describe the features of the payback rule that could lead to Type I errors.
b. Describe the features of the payback rule that could lead to Type II errors.
c. Which error do you think is more likely to occur when firms use payback analysis? Does your answer depend on the length of the cutoff payback period? You can assume a "typical" project cash flow stream, meaning that most cash outflows occur in the early years of a project.

Q8-3. Holding the cutoff period fixed, which method has a more severe bias against long-lived projects, payback or discounted payback?

Q8-4. For a firm that uses the *NPV* rule to make investment decisions, what consequences result if the firm misestimates shareholders' required returns and consistently applies a discount rate that is "too high"?

Q8-5. "Cash flow projections more than a few years out are not worth the paper they're written on. Therefore, using payback analysis, which ignores long-term cash flows, is more reasonable than making wild guesses as one has to do in the *NPV* approach." Respond to this comment.

Q8-6. "Smart analysts can massage the numbers in *NPV* analysis to make any project's *NPV* look positive. It is better to use a simpler approach like payback or accounting rate of return that gives analysts fewer degrees of freedom to manipulate the numbers." Respond to this comment.

Q8-7. In what way is the *NPV* consistent with the principle of shareholder wealth maximization? What happens to the value of a firm if a positive *NPV* project is accepted? If a negative *NPV* project is accepted?

Q8-8. A particular firm's shareholders demand a 15 percent return on their investment, given the firm's risk. However, this firm has historically generated returns in excess of shareholder expectations, with an average return on its portfolio of investments of 25 percent.

a. Looking back, what kind of stock-price performance would you expect to see for this firm?
b. A new investment opportunity arises, and the firm's financial analysts estimate that the project's return will be 18 percent. The CEO wants to reject the project because it would lower the firm's average return and therefore lower the firm's stock price. How do you respond?

Q8-9. What are the potential faults in using the *IRR* as a capital budgeting technique? Given these faults, why is this technique so popular among corporate managers?

Q8-10. Why is the *NPV* considered to be theoretically superior to all other capital budgeting techniques? Reconcile this result with the prevalence of the use of *IRR* in practice. How would you respond to your CFO if she instructed you to use the *IRR* technique to make capital budgeting decisions on projects with cash flow streams that alternate between inflows and outflows?

Q8-11. Outline the differences between *NPV*, *IRR*, and *PI*. What are the advantages and disadvantages of each technique? Do they agree with regard to simple accept or reject decisions?

Q8-12. Under what circumstances will the *NPV*, *IRR*, and *PI* techniques provide different capital budgeting decisions? What are the underlying causes of the differences often found in the ranking of mutually exclusive projects using *NPV* and *IRR*?

PROBLEMS

Accounting-Based Methods

P8-1. Kenneth Gould is the general manager at a small-town newspaper that is part of a national media chain. He is seeking approval from corporate headquarters (HQ) to spend $20,000 to buy some Macintosh computers and a laser printer to use in designing the layout of his daily paper. This equipment will be depreciated using the straight-line method over four years. These computers will replace outmoded equipment that will be kept on hand for emergency use.

HQ requires Kenneth to estimate the cash flows associated with the purchase of new equipment over a four-year horizon. The impact of the project on net income is derived by subtracting depreciation from cash flow each year. The project's average accounting rate of return equals the average contribution to net income divided by the average book value of the investment. HQ accepts any project that (1) has an average accounting rate of return that exceeds the cost of capital of 15 percent, and (2) returns the initial investment within four years (on a cash flow basis). The following are Kenneth's estimates of cash flows:

	Year 1	Year 2	Year 3	Year 4
Cost Savings	$7,500	$9,100	$9,100	$9,100

a. What is the average contribution to net income across all four years?
b. What is the average book value of the investment?
c. What is the average *accounting rate of return*?
d. What is the *payback period* of this investment?
e. Critique the company's method for evaluating investment proposals.

Payback Methods

P8-2. Suppose that a thirty-year U.S. Treasury bond offers a 4 percent coupon rate, paid semiannually. The market price of the bond is $1,000, equal to its par value.

a. What is the *payback period* for this bond?
b. With such a long payback period, is the bond a bad investment?
c. What is the *discounted payback period* for the bond, assuming its 4 percent coupon rate is the required return? What general principle does this example illustrate regarding a project's life, its discounted payback period, and its *NPV*?

P8-3. The cash flows associated with three different projects are as follows:

Cash Flows	Alpha ($ in millions)	Beta ($ in millions)	Gamma ($ in millions)
Initial Outflow	−1.5	−0.4	−7.5
Year 1	0.3	0.1	2.0
Year 2	0.5	0.2	3.0
Year 3	0.5	0.2	2.0
Year 4	0.4	0.1	1.5
Year 5	0.3	−0.2	5.5

a. Calculate the *payback period* of each investment.
b. Which investments does the firm accept if the cutoff payback period is three years? Four years?
c. If the firm invests by choosing projects with the shortest payback period, which project would it invest in?
d. If the firm uses *discounted payback* with a 15 percent discount rate and a four-year cutoff period, which projects will it accept?
e. One of these almost certainly should be rejected, but may be accepted if the firm uses payback analysis. Which one?
f. One of these projects almost certainly should be accepted (unless the firm's opportunity cost of capital is very high), but may be rejected if the firm uses payback analysis. Which one?

Net Present Value

P8-4. Calculate the *net present value* (*NPV*) for the following twenty-year projects. Comment on the acceptability of each. Assume that the firm has an opportunity cost of 14 percent.

a. Initial cash outlay is $15,000; cash inflows are $13,000 per year.
b. Initial cash outlay is $32,000; cash inflows are $4,000 per year.
c. Initial cash outlay is $50,000; cash inflows are $8,500 per year.

P8-5. Michael's Bakery is evaluating a new electronic oven. The oven requires an initial cash outlay of $19,000 and will generate after-tax cash inflows of $4,000 per year for eight years. For each of the costs of capital listed, (1) calculate the *NPV*, (2) indicate whether to accept or reject the machine, and (3) explain your decision.

a. The cost of capital is 10 percent
b. The cost of capital is 12 percent.
c. The cost of capital is 14 percent.

P8-6. Using a 14 percent cost of capital, calculate the *NPV* for each of the projects shown in the following table and indicate whether or not each is acceptable.

	Project A	Project B	Project C	Project D	Project E
Initial Cash Outflow (CF_0)	$20,000	$600,000	$150,000	$760,000	$100,000
Year (t)			Cash Inflows (CF_t)		
1	$ 3,000	$120,000	$ 18,000	$185,000	$ 0
2	3,000	145,000	17,000	185,000	0
3	3,000	170,000	16,000	185,000	0
4	3,000	190,000	15,000	185,000	25,000
5	3,000	220,000	15,000	185,000	36,000
6	3,000	240,000	14,000	185,000	0
7	3,000		13,000	185,000	60,000
8	3,000		12,000	185,000	72,000
9	3,000		11,000		84,000
10	3,000		10,000		

P8-7. Scotty Manufacturing is considering the replacement of one of its machine tools. Three alternative replacement tools—A, B, and C—are under consideration. The cash flows associated with each are shown in the following table. The firm's cost of capital is 15 percent.

	A	B	C
Initial Cash Outflow (CF_0)	\$95,000	\$50,000	\$150,000
Year (t)		Cash Inflows (CF_t)	
1	\$20,000	\$10,000	\$ 58,000
2	20,000	12,000	35,000
3	20,000	13,000	23,000
4	20,000	15,000	23,000
5	20,000	17,000	23,000
6	20,000	21,000	35,000
7	20,000	-	46,000
8	20,000	-	58,000

a. Calculate the *NPV* of each alternative tool.
b. Using *NPV*, evaluate the acceptability of each tool.
c. Rank the tools from best to worst, using *NPV.*

SMART SOLUTIONS

See the problem and solution explained step-by-step at SMARTFinance

P8-8. Erwin Enterprises has 10 million shares outstanding with a current market price of \$10 per share. There is one investment available to Erwin, and its cash flows are provided below. Erwin has a cost of capital of 10 percent. Given this information, determine the impact on Erwin's stock price and firm value if capital markets fully reflect the value of undertaking the project.

Initial Cash Outflow = \$10,000,000

Year	Cash Inflow
1	\$3,000,000
2	\$4,000,000
3	\$5,000,000
4	\$6,000,000
5	\$9,800,000

Internal Rate of Return

P8-9. For each of the projects shown in the following table, calculate the *internal rate of return* (*IRR*).

	Project A	Project B	Project C	Project D
Initial Cash Outflow (CF_0)	\$72,000	\$440,000	\$18,000	\$215,000
Year (t)			Cash Inflows (CF_t)	
1	\$16,000	\$135,000	\$ 7,000	\$108,000
2	20,000	135,000	7,000	90,000
3	24,000	135,000	7,000	72,000
4	28,000	135,000	7,000	54,000
5	32,000	-	7,000	-

P8-10. William Industries is attempting to choose the better of two mutually exclusive projects for expanding the firm's production capacity. The relevant cash flows for the projects are shown in the following table. The firm's cost of capital is 15 percent.

	Project A	Project B
Initial Cash Outflow (CF_0)	\$550,000	\$358,000
Year (t)	Cash Inflows (CF_t)	
1	\$110,000	\$154,000
2	132,000	132,000
3	165,000	105,000
4	209,000	77,000
5	275,000	55,000

a. Calculate the *IRR* for each of the projects.
b. Assess the acceptability of each project based on the *IRR*s found in part (a).
c. Which project is preferred, based on the *IRR*s found in part (a)?

P8-11. Contract Manufacturing, Inc. is considering two alternative investment proposals. The first proposal calls for a major renovation of the company's manufacturing facility. The second involves replacing just a few obsolete pieces of equipment in the facility. The company will choose one project or the other this year, but it will not do both. The cash flows associated with each project appear below, and the firm discounts project cash flows at 15 percent.

Year	Renovate	Replace
0	–$9,000,000	–$1,000,000
1	3,500,000	600,000
2	3,000,000	500,000
3	3,000,000	400,000
4	2,800,000	300,000
5	2,500,000	200,000

a. Rank these investments based on their *NPV*s.
b. Rank these investments based on their *IRR*s.
c. Why do these rankings yield mixed signals?

P8-12. Consider a project with the following cash flows and a firm with a 15 percent cost of capital.

End of Year	Cash Flow
0	–$20,000
1	50,000
2	– 10,000

a. What are the two *IRR*s associated with this cash flow stream?
b. If the firm's cost of capital falls between the two *IRR* values calculated in part (a), should it accept or reject the project?

P8-13. A certain project has the following stream of cash flows:

Year	Cash Flow
0	$ 17,500
1	– 80,500
2	138,425
3	– 105,455
4	30,030

a. Fill in the following table:

Cost of Capital (%)	Project *NPV*
0	______
5	______
10	______
15	______
20	______
25	______
30	______
35	______
50	______

b. Use the values developed in part (a) to draw an *NPV profile* for the project.
c. What is this project's *IRR?*
d. Describe the conditions under which the firm should accept this project.

Profitability Index

P8-14. Evaluate the following three projects, using the profitability index. Assume a cost of capital of 15 percent.

	Project		
Cash Flows	Liquidate	Recondition	Replace
Initial Cash Outflow	–$100,000	–$500,000	–$1,000,000
Year 1 cash inflow	50,000	100,000	500,000
Year 2 cash inflow	60,000	200,000	500,000
Year 3 cash inflow	75,000	250,000	500,000

a. Rank these projects by their *PI*s.
b. If the projects are independent, which would you accept according to the *PI* criterion?

c. If these projects are mutually exclusive, which would you accept according to the *PI* criterion?
d. Apply the *NPV* criterion to the projects, rank them according to their *NPV*s, and indicate which you would accept if they are independent and mutually exclusive.
e. Compare and contrast your answer from part (c) with your answer to part (d) for the mutually exclusive case. Explain this result.

P8-15. You have a \$10 million capital budget and must make the decision about which investments your firm should accept for the coming year. Use the following information on three mutually exclusive projects to determine which investment your firm should accept. The firm's cost of capital is 12 percent.

Cash Flows	Project 1	Project 2	Project 3
Initial Cash Outflow	–\$4,000,000	–\$5,000,000	–\$10,000,000
Year 1 cash inflow	1,000,000	2,000,000	4,000,000
Year 2 cash inflow	2,000,000	3,000,000	6,000,000
Year 3 cash inflow	3,000,000	3,000,000	5,000,000

a. Which project do you accept on the basis of *NPV*?
b. Which project do you accept on the basis of *PI*?
c. If these are the only investments available, which one do you select?

Which Techniques Do Firms Actually Use?

P8-16. Both Old Line Industries and New Tech, Inc. use the *IRR* to make investment decisions. Both firms are considering investing in a more efficient \$4.5 million mail-order processor. This machine could generate after-tax savings of \$2 million per year over the next three years for both firms. However, due to the risky nature of its business, New Tech has a much higher cost of capital (20 percent) than does Old Line (10 percent). Given this information, answer parts (a)–(c).

a. Should Old Line invest in this processor?
b. Should New Tech invest in this processor?
c. Based on your answers in parts (a) and (b), what can you infer about the acceptability of projects across firms with different costs of capital?

P8-17. Butler Products has prepared the following estimates for an investment it is considering. The initial cash outflow is \$20,000, and the project is expected to yield cash inflows of \$4,400 per year for seven years. The firm has a 10 percent cost of capital.

a. Determine the *NPV* for the project.
b. Determine the *IRR* for the project.
c. Would you recommend that the firm accept or reject the project? Explain your answer.

P8-18. Reynolds Enterprises is attempting to evaluate the feasibility of investing \$85,000, CF_0, in a machine having a five-year life. The firm has estimated the *cash inflows* associated with the proposal as shown below. The firm has a 12 percent cost of capital.

End of Year (t)	Cash Inflows (CF_t)
1	\$18,000
2	22,500
3	27,000
4	31,500
5	36,000

a. Calculate the *payback period* for the proposed investment.
b. Calculate the *NPV* for the proposed investment.
c. Calculate the *IRR* for the proposed investment.
d. Evaluate the acceptability of the proposed investment using *NPV* and *IRR*. What recommendation would you make relative to implementation of the project? Why?

P8-19. Sharpe Manufacturing is attempting to select the best of three mutually exclusive projects. The initial cash outflow and after-tax cash inflows associated with each project are shown in the following table.

Cash Flows	Project X	Project Y	Project Z
Initial Cash Outflow (CF_0)	\$80,000	\$130,000	\$145,000
Cash Inflows (CF_t), Years (t) = 1–5	27,000	41,000	43,000

a. Calculate the *payback period* for each project.
b. Calculate the *NPV* of each project, assuming that the firm has a cost of capital equal to 13 percent.
c. Calculate the *IRR* for each project.
d. Summarize the preferences dictated by each measure and indicate which project you would recommend. Explain why.

P8-20. Wilkes, Inc. must invest in a pollution-control program in order to meet federal regulations to stay in business. There are two programs available to Wilkes: an all-at-once program that will be immediately funded and implemented, and a gradual program that will be phased in over the next three years. The immediate program costs \$5 million, whereas the phase-in program will cost \$1 million today and \$2 million per year for the following three years. If the cost of capital for Wilkes is 15 percent, which pollution-control program should Wilkes select?

P8-21. A consumer product firm finds that its brand of laundry detergent is losing market share, so it decides that it needs to "freshen" the product. One strategy is to maintain the current detergent formula but to repackage the product. The other strategy involves a complete reformulation of the product in a way that will appeal to environmentally conscious consumers. The firm will pursue one strategy or the other but not both. Cash flows from each proposal appear below, and the firm discounts cash flows at 13 percent.

SMART SOLUTIONS

See the problem and solution explained step-by-step at SMARTFinance

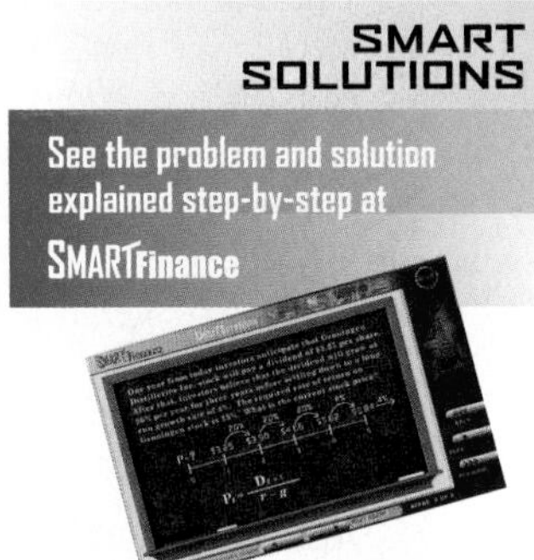

Year	Repackage	Reformulate
0	–\$3,000,000	–\$25,000,000
1	2,000,000	10,000,000
2	1,250,000	9,000,000
3	500,000	7,000,000
4	250,000	4,000,000
5	250,000	3,500,000

a. Rank these investments based on their *NPVs*.
b. Rank these investments based on their *IRRs*.
c. Rank these investments based on their *PIs*.
d. Draw *NPV profiles* for the two projects on the same set of axes and discuss these profiles.
e. Do these investment rankings yield mixed signals?

P8-22. Lundblad Construction Co. recently acquired ten acres of land and is weighing two options for developing the land. The first proposal is to build ten single-family homes on the site. This project would generate a quick cash payoff as the homes are sold over the next two years. Specifically, Lundblad estimates that it would spend \$2.5 million on construction costs immediately, and it would receive \$1.6 million as cash inflows in each of the next two years.

The second proposal is to build a strip shopping mall. This project calls for Lundblad to retain ownership of the property and to lease space for retail businesses that would serve the neighborhood. Construction costs for the strip mall are also about \$2.5 million, and the company expects to receive \$350,000 annually (for each of fifty years, starting one year from now) in net cash inflows from leasing the property. Lundblad's cost of capital is 10 percent.

a. Rank these projects based on their *NPVs*.
b. Rank these projects based on their *IRRs*.
c. Rank these projects based on their *PIs*. Do these rankings agree with those based on *NPV* or *IRR*?
d. Draw *NPV profiles* for these projects on the same set of axes. Use this graph to explain why, in this case, the *NPV* and *IRR* methods yield mixed signals.
e. Which project should Lundblad choose?
f. Which project should Lundblad choose if its cost of capital is 13.5 percent? 16 percent? 20 percent?

MINICASE

Capital Budgeting Process And Techniques

Contact Manufacturing, Inc., is considering two alternative investment proposals. The first proposal calls for a major renovation of the company's manufacturing facility. The second involves replacing just a few obsolete pieces of equipment in the facility. The company will choose one project or the other this year, but it will not do both. The cash flows associated with each project appear below and the firm discounts project cash flows at 15 percent.

Year	Renovate	Replace
0	–\$9,000,000	–\$2,400,000
1	3,000,000	2,000,000
2	3,000,000	800,000
3	3,000,000	200,000
4	3,000,000	200,000
5	3,000,000	200,000

ASSIGNMENT

1. Calculate the *payback period* of each project and based on this criteria for which project would you recommend acceptance?
2. Calculate the *net present value* (*NPV*) of each project and based on this criteria for which project would you recommend acceptance?
3. Calculate the *internal rate of return* (*IRR*) of each project and based on this criteria for which project would you recommend acceptance?
4. Calculate the *profitability index* (*PI*) of each project and based on this criteria for which project would you recommend acceptance?
5. Overall, you should find conflicting recommendations based on the various criteria. Why is this occurring?
6. Chart the *NPV profiles* of these projects. Label the intersection points on the X and Y axis and the crossover point.
7. Based on this *NPV profile* analysis and assuming the *WACC* is 15%, which project is recommended? Why?
8. Based on this *NPV profile* analysis and assuming the *WACC* is 25%, which project is recommended? Why?
9. Discuss the important elements to consider when deciding between these two projects.

Smart *Excel* Appendix

Appendix Contents

Use the Smart *Excel* spreadsheets and animated tutorials at http://smartfinance.swlearning.com.

EXCEL PREREQUISITES

You need to be familiar with the following *Excel* features to use this appendix:

- Creating a cumulative formula
- Use of the average function

This material was covered in Chapters 5 and 6 but is repeated on the ***Excel Prereqs*** tab of the Chapter 8 *Excel* file located at the *Smart Finance Web site.*

CAPITAL BUDGETING TECHNIQUES

Problem: Evaluate the capital budgeting decision faced by Global Wireless Inc. as described in Chapter 8.

Global Wireless is contemplating a major expansion of its wireless network in two different regions. By investing $250 million, it can add up to 100 new cell sites to its existing base in Western Europe. By investing $50 million, it can enter a new market in the Southeast United States. Company analysts project the following year-end net after-tax cash flows. The firm uses an 18 percent discount rate.

	Western Europe Project (in $ millions)	**Southeast U.S. Project** (in $ millions)
Initial outlay	–$250	–$50
Year 1 cash flow	$35	$18
Year 2 cash flow	$80	$22
Year 3 cash flow	$130	$25
Year 4 cash flow	$160	$30
Year 5 cash flow	$175	$32

ACCOUNTING RATE OF RETURN

Approach: Find the project net income and divide by the book value of assets.

To find the accounting rate of return, follow these steps:

1. Fill in the input assumption on project cash flows and the depreciable life of the assets. In this example, both projects are assumed to have a 5-year straight-line depreciation.
2. Find the annual depreciation for each project. Here, this is equal to the initial investment divided by the depreciable life. (Remember to use absolute references, as needed.)
3. Create a formula to calculate the annual project net income. In the Global Wireless example, this is assumed to be project cash flow minus depreciation. Then, use the average function to find average annual income over the project life.
4. Create a formula to find the asset book value. Each year this is the starting value less depreciation. Then, use the average function to find the average asset book value.
5. The accounting rate of return is the average income divided by the average book value.

   Your results should match:

Calculations

Year	0	1	2	3	4	5
Western Europe Project						
Depreciation		(50)	(50)	(50)	(50)	(50)
Net income		(15)	30	80	110	125
Average net income	66					
Asset book value	250	200	150	100	50	0
Average book value	125					
Southeast U.S. Project						
Depreciation		(10)	(10)	(10)	(10)	(10)
Net income		8	12	15	20	22
Average net income	15					
Asset book value	50	40	30	20	10	0
Average book value	25					

Output

Accounting ROR Western Europe Project	52.8%
Accounting ROR Southeast U.S. Project	61.6%

PAYBACK

Approach: Find the cumulative cash flows from the project.

Open the Chapter 8 *Excel* file located at the Smart Finance Web site. Open the *Payback* tab.

Enter the input information. Begin years with 0. Enter the cash flow assumptions for each project.

To find the project payback, follow these steps:

1. Create a formula to calculate the cumulative cash flow in each year. In year 0 (set up), this is the initial investment. In year 1, it is the initial investment plus the cash flows in year 1. Try to set up one formula that can be accurately copied across all years and copied down for the second project's cumulative cash flows. See the ***Excel Prereqs*** tab for help.
2. The year in which the initial investment is recovered is the payback year.

Apply it

- *Which project has a more favorable payback?*
  The Southeast U.S. project has a faster payback.

  Your results should be:

Year	0	1	2	3	4	5
Cumulative cash flow – Western Europe		35	115	245	405	580
Cumulative cash flow – Southeast United States		18	40	65	95	127

Payback occurs when the initial investment is recovered. Because the initial investment for the Western Europe project is $250 million, payback is in the fourth year. The initial investment for the U.S. project is $50 million so payback is in the third year.

DISCOUNTED PAYBACK

Approach: Find the present value of the project cash flows and then find the cumulative cash flows using the discounted cash flows.

To find the discounted project payback, follow these steps:

1. Create a formula to calculate the present value of each year's cash flows. Copy across for all years.
2. Create a single formula to find the cumulative cash flow, based on the discounted cash flows.
3. The year in which the initial investment is recovered is the payback year.

Your results should be:

Year	0	1	2	3	4	5
PV of cash flows – Western Europe		30	57	79	83	76
PV of cash flow – Southeast United States		15	16	15	15	14
Cum disc cash flow – Western Europe		30	87	166	249	325
Cum disc cash flow – Southeast United States		15	31	46	62	76

NET PRESENT VALUE

Approach: Use the *NPV* function.

To find the project net present values, use the npv function in *Excel*. The format is:

=CF0 + npv(rate,CF1,CF2,...CFn) or
=CF0 + npv(rate,CF1:CFn)

where the rate is the discount rate, CF0 is the initial investment, CF1 is the cash flow in year 1, and CFn is the cash flow in the final year.

Important: When using the NPV *function, DO NOT include the year 0 cash flow within the function because it will then get discounted.* The *NPV* function discounts the first cash flow for one year, the second for two years, etc.

The formula to find the net present value of the Western Europe project is:

= initial investment + NPV(rate, CF1:CF5)
=D16+ npv(D18,E16:I16)
=$75.3 million.

The net present value of the Southeast U.S. project is $25.7 million.

Apply it

Sum the present values for the cash flows from year 0 through year 5 for the Western Europe project. What is your result?

The result is $75.3 million, the project net present value. You can find the *NPV* by either using the *NPV* function or discounting the cash flows and summing the present values. This alternative calculation is shown in the file solution.

Analyze the impact of the discount rate on the decision faced by Global Wireless.

- *Suppose the discount rate is 15%?*
- *Suppose the discount rate is 21%?*

The net present values are:

NPV with discount rate of:	15%	21%
Western Europe project	$104.8 million	$49.1 million
Southeast U.S. project	$31.8 million	$20.3 million

At a lower discount rate, both projects look more attractive. At higher discount rates, the present value of the cash inflows falls.

INTERNAL RATE OF RETURN

Approach: Use the *IRR* function.

To find the project net present values, use the irr function in *Excel*. The format is:

=irr(CF0,CF1,CF2,...CFn) or
=irr(CF0:CFn)

where CF0 is the initial investment, CF1 is the cash flow in year 1, and CFn is the cash flow in the final year.

Important: When using the IRR *function, DO include the year 0 cash flow within the function.*

The formula to find the net present value of the Western Europe project is:

= irr(CF0:CF5)
=irr(D16:I16)
=27.8%

The internal rate of return of the Southeast U.S. project is 36.7%.

Apply it

Analyze the impact of the discount rate on the decision faced by Global Wireless.

- *Suppose the discount rate is 15%?*
- *Suppose the discount rate is 21%?*

Changing the discount rate has no effect on the internal rate of return since the discount rate is not part of the internal rate of return calculation. The internal rate of return is the rate that leads to a net present value of zero.

PROFITABILITY INDEX

Approach: Compare the ratio of the present value of the project's cash flows (excluding the initial investment) with the initial investment.

To find the profitability index, sum the cash flows from the project from year 1 on, divide this sum by the initial investment. This ratio will be a negative number if the initial investment is negative. Change the sign to a positive number by beginning the formula with a negative sign.

= – (sum of the present value of cash flows from year 1 through project end)/ initial investment
= – sum(E22:I22)/D22
=1.30

For Southeast U.S., the profitability index equals 1.51.

Apply it

Analyze the impact of the discount rate on the decision faced by Global Wireless.

- *Suppose the discount rate is 15%?*
- *Suppose the discount rate is 21%?*

The profitability index is:

PI with discount rate of:	15%	21%
Western Europe project	1.42	1.20
Southeast U.S. project	1.64	1.41

SOLVE PROBLEM 8-21

Solve Problem 8-21

Find the project net present value, the internal rate of return, and the profitability index. Our solution is provided on the final two tabs in the *Excel* file.

Now follow these steps to create the *NPV* profile.

To create a net present value profile, follow these steps:

1. Begin with the solution.
2. Create a table with the project *NPVs* at different discount rates. To create the table, enter the various discount rates in the first column. Then, in the next column, create a formula for *NPV* that refers to the discount rate. Copy the formula down through the various discount rates and across for other projects. It should be set up like the table below, although in the file we continue through rates of 20 percent:

The discount rates are typed in (to save time, use the fill-series feature on the edit menu). The NPVs *are the result of the formula.*

3. Create a graph by selecting the two columns of *NPVs* and using the graph icon. Select a line graph.

The graph shows the net present-value profile of the two projects. You will have to add titles and reformat slightly to get your graph to look like our solution.

Discount Rate	*NPV* of Repackage	*NPV* of Reformulate
0%	1,250,000	8,500,000
1%	1,168,975	7,691,837
2%	1,090,801	6,916,136
3%	1,015,337	6,171,172
4%	942,453	5,455,327
5%	872,025	4,767,090

Apply it

- *What does the* NPV *profile indicate?*

The *NPV* profile shows the project *NPVs* at different discount rates. Note that at very low discount rates, the *NPV* of the reformulate project is much higher than the *NPV* of the repackage project.

Cash Flow and Capital Budgeting

OPENING FOCUS

Boeing Bets Big on the Dreamliner

Capital budgeting decisions are very important for most firms, but these decisions usually do not involve "betting the company" on a single investment project. The decision that the board of directors of the Boeing Company faced in December 2003, however, was truly that stark, because the directors had to decide whether to commit at least $6 billion (and perhaps as much as $8 billion) to develop and market an entirely new 200-passenger commercial aircraft, the 7E7 "Dreamliner." Not only were the financial stakes enormous but also Boeing had not launched a new aircraft in over a decade. It was saddled with an aging product line that left it reeling from the competitive onslaught represented by its arch-rival Airbus's modern fleet of fuel-efficient aircraft. Whereas Boeing had proposed, then canceled, no less than six new aircraft projects over the previous twelve years, Airbus had successfully launched a string of new planes, most recently the 550-passenger A380. If Boeing did not develop a winning new plane, it faced the real prospect of eventually being swept out of the commercial aircraft-manufacturing business.

This chapter will describe the processes involved in generating estimates of the initial investment required to launch a capital investment project, the net cash flows that this project will generate over its economic life, and the final-period cash flows that result at the project's termination date. Boeing's managers and directors performed precisely this exercise in deciding whether to launch the Dreamliner. Their task was almost unimaginably complex because of the scale of the project and the uncertainty involved in estimating the different cash flows. To generate estimates of the initial investment required, Boeing had to account for three special circumstances that few other manufacturers had to address. First, the Dreamliner would be built using far more carbon-fiber and other new materials than any other commercial aircraft in history, and therefore would employ brand new assembly techniques. Boeing had to account for an unusually high level of technological risk during the plane's development stage. The other two factors complicating their estimation of the initial investment required would actually benefit Boeing by reducing the company's own financial exposure. As with previous aircraft projects, Boeing would be able to count on the suppliers of jet engines and other major subassemblies to incur up to half of the Dreamliner's overall development costs. Additionally, by shrewdly causing several American states to compete with each other to attract the assembly plant for the 7E7, Boeing was able to entice the state of Washington to offer tax and other incentives worth $3.2 billion over twenty years and to raise the state's gasoline tax by 5 cents per gallon to fund a $4.2 billion Seattle-area transportation plan that Boeing had wanted. As we stress repeatedly in this chapter, Boeing's managers were correct to focus on incremental, after-tax cash flows in estimating both the initial investment required to begin producing the Dreamliner and the cash flows that would result from manufacturing and selling the airplane.

As you might expect, generating these long-term, after-tax cash flow estimates for the Dreamliner was also very challenging for Boeing's managers and directors. The company estimates that between 2,000 and 3,000 aircraft in the 7E7's market segment will be purchased by the world's airlines over the next twenty years. The total value of these sales will be about $1.9 trillion. If Boeing could count on dominating this market over the coming two decades as thoroughly as it had traditionally dominated other aircraft markets, the 7E7 project would likely prove extremely profitable. However, the year 2003 marked the first time in history that Airbus sold more planes than Boeing, so even if Boeing's twenty-year sales forecast proved accurate, there was no guarantee that the company would be able to grab a large share of these sales. Therefore, Boeing faced great uncertainty in forecasting the cash inflows that would result from launching the Dreamliner. Finally, in the commercial aircraft industry, the price of success is a never-ending requirement to make ever larger capital investments to stay competitive. To that end, Boeing had to project how the possibility of a successful Dreamliner launch would affect its future capital budgeting plans.

So what did Boeing's board decide to do? On December 17, 2003, the company announced that the board had given the go-ahead to launch the 7E7. The Dreamliner will become a reality. And in April 2004, All Nippon Airways placed the first firm order for 50 Dreamliners (worth $6 billion) with Boeing, thus becoming the planes all-important launch customer.

Sources: "Boeing May Count on New Dreamliner to Regain Lead from Airbus," Bloomberg.com (October 3, 2003); Caroline Daniel, "Boeing to Offer Mid-sized 7E7 Jet Next Year," *Financial Times* (December 17, 2003); and Jack Lyne, "Boeing's $900-Million 7E7 Plant Nearing Touchdown," *Site Selection* magazine (September 2003).

LEARNING OBJECTIVES

After studying this chapter you should be able to:

- Differentiate between cash flow and accounting profit with regard to incremental cash flow, financing costs, taxes, and noncash expenses;
- Discuss depreciation, fixed asset expenditures, working capital expenditures, and terminal value;
- Understand relevant cash flows and the effects of sunk costs, opportunity costs, and cannibalization on them;
- Demonstrate the procedures for determining the relevant cash flows for a capital budgeting problem;
- Understand how to analyze capital rationing decisions, competing replacement projects with unequal lives, and excess capacity utilization projects; and
- Describe how the human element can affect the capital budgeting process and its outcomes.

Chapter 8 described various capital budgeting techniques that analysts use to evaluate and rank investment proposals. Each of the examples in Chapter 8 began with a sequence of cash flows, although we did not discuss the origins of those cash flow figures. This chapter describes procedures for determining a project's relevant cash flows, the inputs for the capital budgeting decision tools from Chapter 8. We begin with an overview of the kinds of cash flows that may appear in almost any type of investment. Then, we consider the relevant cash flows and some challenges in estimating them. Next, an extended capital budgeting example is presented and we discuss special problems and situations that frequently arise in the capital budgeting process. The chapter concludes with a brief discussion of the human element in capital budgeting.

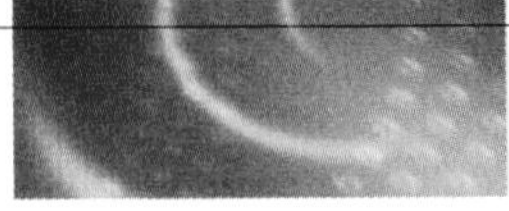

9.1 TYPES OF CASH FLOWS

Cash Flow vs. Accounting Profit

When accountants prepare financial statements for external reporting, they have a very different purpose in mind than financial analysts have when they evaluate the merits of an investment. Accountants want to produce financial statements that fairly and accurately represent the state of a business at any given time, as well as over a period of time. Given this purpose, accountants measure the inflows and outflows of a business's operations on an *accrual basis* rather than on a *cash basis*. For example, accountants typically credit a firm for earning revenue once a sale is made, even though customers may not pay cash for their purchases for several weeks or months. Similarly, accountants typically will not record the full cost of an asset as an expense if they expect the asset to confer benefits to the firm over a long period of time. The best example of this approach is depreciation. If a firm spends $1 billion on an asset that it plans to use over ten years, accountants may count only one tenth of the purchase price, or $100 million, as a current-year depreciation expense.

Simply stated, *financial analysts focus solely on cash flows when evaluating potential investments*. In doing this, they estimate the "relevant cash flows" by focusing on the incremental cash flows, ignoring financing costs, considering taxes, and adjusting for any noncash expenses such as depreciation. Here, we briefly consider the effect of each of these items on cash flow.

Focusing on Incremental Cash Flows. For capital budgeting purposes, financial analysts focus on *incremental* cash inflows and outflows, emphasizing that no matter what earnings a firm may show on an accrual basis, it cannot survive for long unless it generates cash to pay its bills. If a firm purchases an asset for $500 million, with a purchase contract requiring an immediate payment, then the firm must come up with $500 million in cash, even if it plans to deduct only a portion of the purchase price each year as depreciation expense. The importance placed on cash flow in capital budgeting also reflects the *time value of money*. If a firm sells a product for $1,000, the value of that sale is greater if the customer pays immediately, rather than 30 or 90 days in the future. To develop the relevant cash flows, the financial analyst must determine the **incremental cash flows,** which are the cash flows that directly result from the proposed investment. These cash flows effectively represent the *marginal costs* (*MC*) and the *marginal benefits* (*MB*) expected to result from undertaking the proposed investment. Once these *MCs* and *MBs* are estimated, capital budgeting techniques (described in Chapter 8) can be applied to them to account for time value of money and risk. These procedures allow the analyst to choose only those projects that increase shareholder value. The procedures for estimating incremental cash flows are demonstrated later in this chapter.

incremental cash flows
Cash flows that directly result from a proposed investment. They effectively represent the *marginal costs (MC)* and *marginal benefits (MB)* expected to result from undertaking a proposed investment.

Ignoring Financing Costs. Much of this chapter focuses on which cash flows to include in calculating a project's *NPV*. We should also mention an important category of cash flows that should be excluded—financing cash flows. When calculating a project's *NPV*, analysts should ignore the costs of raising the money to finance the project, whether those costs are in the form of interest expense from debt financing or dividend payments to equity investors. It may seem counter-intuitive to ignore an item, such as interest expense, which appears on the income statement, but it is necessary to do so because financing costs are fully captured in the process of discounting a project's future cash flows to the present. In previous chapters, we have seen that the discounted present value of a cash flow is less than its future value. When analysts discount a project's future cash flows, they take into account the opportunity that investors have to invest in other firms. Therefore, if an analyst deducted cash outflows to investors, such as interest and dividend payments, the analyst would, in effect, double-count the financing costs of the investment.

In an operational sense, when using the income statement to develop an investment's relevant cash flows, we ignore financing costs by focusing on *earnings before interest* rather than earnings after deduction of interest expense. Given the structure of an income statement, earnings before interest excludes all dividends paid to preferred and/or common stockholders as well. The deduction of interest expense and dividends would double-charge the firm for its financing costs—once in the cash flows and again in the discount rate used to find present value. As we demonstrate later in this chapter, *both interest and dividends are ignored when developing an investment's relevant cash flows.*

Considering Taxes. Analysts should measure all cash flows of a project on an after-tax basis. Remember, when deciding whether an investment is worth taking, we must determine whether the cash flows of the project are sufficient to meet or exceed shareholders' expectations. *The firm can only distribute after-tax cash flows to investors, and thus, only after-tax cash flows are relevant in the decision process.* The tax consequences associated with a particular investment can be very complex, in part because cash flows from a single investment may fall under several tax jurisdictions (local, state, national, international, etc.) and may be subject to both ordinary and capital gains taxes. It is important to note that because the discount rate (required return) is an after-tax value, we can ignore the tax shield resulting from the pretax deduction of interest, which, as noted above, does not enter into the calculation of an investment's cash flows. Simply stated, *an after-tax point of view is consistent with ignoring financing costs when determining relevant cash flows.*

An examination of all the nuances of the tax code is well beyond the scope of this book, but we offer simplified illustrations of the principles involved in measuring after-tax cash flows. The most important of these principles is that financial managers should measure the after-tax cash flows of a given investment by using the firm's **marginal tax rate**, which, as noted in Chapter 2, equals the tax rate applicable to the next dollar of income. For convenience, throughout this chapter, we assume that the marginal tax rate equals 40 percent.

marginal tax rate
The percentage of taxes owed on the next dollar of income.

noncash expenses
Tax-deductible expenses for which there is no corresponding cash outflow. They include depreciation, amortization, and depletion.

Adjusting for Noncash Expenses. Another tax-related principle relevant to measuring pertinent cash flows is that analysts cannot entirely ignore **noncash expenses** (tax-deductible expenses for which there is no corresponding cash outflow) when projecting cash flows. Noncash expenses include depreciation, amortization, and depletion. We focus solely on depreciation, which is the most common noncash expense involved in making capital investments. Depreciation plays a key role when projecting cash flows. As a noncash expense, it reduces not only taxable income but also the cash outflows associated with tax payments. There are two ways to calculate cash flows that take this effect into account. First, we can add noncash expenses back to *net income before interest and after taxes*. Second, we can ignore noncash expenses when calculating *net income before interest and after taxes*, and then add back the tax savings created by noncash deductions.[1]

APPLYING THE MODEL

Let's examine two ways to treat noncash expenses to obtain cash flow numbers for a simple project. Suppose a firm spends \$30,000 in cash to purchase a fixed asset today that it plans to fully depreciate on a straight-line basis over three years. Acquiring this machine, the firm can now produce 10,000 units of some product each year. The product costs \$1 to make and sells for \$3. The following is a simple income statement (that ignores any financing costs) for a typical year of this project:

Sales	\$30,000
Less: Cost of goods	10,000
Gross profit	\$20,000
Less: Depreciation	10,000
Pretax income	\$10,000
Less: Taxes (40%)	4,000
Net income after taxes	\$ 6,000

How much cash flow does this project generate in a typical year? There are two ways to arrive at the answer. First, take net income after taxes and add back depreciation, for which there was no cash outlay:

Cash flow = net income after taxes + depreciation
= \$6,000 + \$10,000 = \$16,000

Second, calculate net income after taxes, ignoring depreciation expense, and then add back the tax savings generated by the depreciation deduction:

Sales	\$30,000	
Less: Cost of goods	10,000	
Pretax income	\$20,000	
Less: Taxes (40%)	8,000	
After-tax income	\$12,000	
Plus: Depreciation tax savings	4,000	(40% × \$10,000)
Total cash flow	\$16,000	

Depreciation

The largest noncash item for most investment projects is depreciation. Analysts must know the magnitude and timing of depreciation deductions for a given project because these deductions affect the amount of taxes that the firm will pay. Treating depreciation properly is complicated because the law allows firms to use several different depreciation methods. For example, in the United States and the United Kingdom, firms can (and do) keep separate sets of books, one for tax purposes and one for financial reporting purposes, using different depreciation methods for each set. Their goal is to show low

1. Deriving accurate cash flow numbers from real financial statements issued by real companies is considerably more complex than the following simple example may lead you to believe, primarily due to the need to measure cash flows *before interest and after taxes*.

Table 9.1
U.S. tax depreciation allowed for various MACRS asset classes. Figures represent the percentage of an asset's depreciable basis that is depreciable in each year.

TAX DEPRECIATION SCHEDULES BY ASSET CLASS						
YEAR(S)	3-YEAR	5-YEAR	7-YEAR	10-YEAR	15-YEAR	20-YEAR
1	33.33	20.00	14.29	10.00	5.00	3.75
2	44.45	32.00	24.49	18.00	9.50	7.22
3	14.81	19.20	17.49	14.40	8.55	6.68
4	7.41	11.52	12.49	11.52	7.70	6.18
5		11.52	8.93	9.22	6.93	5.71
6		5.76	8.93	7.37	6.23	5.28
7			8.93	6.55	5.90	4.89
8			4.45	6.55	5.90	4.52
9				6.55	5.90	4.46
10				6.55	5.90	4.46
11				3.29	5.90	4.46
12					5.90	4.46
13					5.90	4.46
14					5.90	4.46
15					5.90	4.46
16					2.99	4.46
17–20						4.46
21						2.25

taxable income to the taxing authorities and stable, growing income to investors. As a result, most U.S. and U.K. firms use accelerated depreciation methods for tax purposes and straight-line depreciation for financial reporting. In contrast, in nations such as Japan, Sweden, and Germany, the law requires that the income firms report to the tax authorities be substantially the same as the income they report to investors. Naturally, firms in these countries want to enjoy the tax benefits of accelerated depreciation, so they depreciate assets using methods such as double-declining balance or sum-of-the-years' digits almost exclusively.[2] Because we are interested in the cash flow consequences of investments, and because depreciation only affects cash flow through taxes, *we consider only the depreciation method that a firm uses for tax purposes when determining project cash flows.*

Table 9.1 illustrates the tax depreciation allowed in the United States on various classes of equipment. The Tax Reform Act of 1986 set forth a **modified accelerated cost recovery system (MACRS)**, which defined the allowable annual depreciation deductions for various classes of assets. Automobiles used for business purposes fall under the three-year class, computer equipment is part of the five-year class, and most manufacturing equipment is part of the seven-year class. A quick glance at the table reveals that U.S. tax laws allow firms to take larger depreciation deductions in the early years of an asset's life. The cash flow effect of this system is to accelerate the tax benefits associated with depreciation.[3]

modified accelerated cost recovery system (MACRS)
Set forth in the Tax Reform Act of 1986 to define the allowable annual depreciation deductions for various classes of assets.

2. The International Forum on Accountancy Development (IFAD) maintains a Web site where you can find a brief overview of accounting standards in 62 different countries, all benchmarked against international accounting standards (IAS). See Internet Resources in this chapter.

3. That is, the tax benefits accrue faster than would be the case under straight-line depreciation. An observant reader of Table 9.1 will notice that the law grants four years of depreciation deductions on the three-year asset class, six years of deductions for assets in the five-year class, and so on. There appears to be one "extra year" of depreciation for each asset class because the first year's deduction reflects an assumption that, on average, investments in fixed assets are in service for just one half of the first year. The last half-year of depreciation deductions for an asset falling in the N-year class occurs in year $N + 1$. This is the same as assuming the equipment is put into service on July 1 of the first year. Special rules apply to real estate assets. In general, land is not depreciable. The law does allow depreciation deductions for structures, with the depreciable life of the structure depending on whether it is a commercial or residential property.

Fixed Asset Expenditures

Many capital budgeting decisions involve the acquisition of a fixed asset. The cost of this investment often appears as the initial cash outflow for a project (assuming that the firm pays the full purchase price in one cash payment). Additional factors that influence the cash consequences of fixed asset acquisitions include installation costs and proceeds from sales of any existing fixed assets that are being replaced.

In many cases, the cost of installing new equipment can be a significant part of a project's initial outlay. For tax purposes, firms must combine the asset's purchase price and its installation cost to arrive at the asset's *depreciable basis*. Though depreciation itself is not a cash outflow, we have seen that depreciation deductions affect future cash flows by lowering taxes. Depreciation deductions influence taxes through another channel when firms sell old fixed assets. Specifically, when a firm sells an old piece of equipment, there is a tax consequence if the selling price exceeds or falls below the old equipment's *book value*. If the firm sells an asset for more than its book value, the firm must pay taxes on the difference. If a firm sells an asset for less than its book value, then it can treat the difference as a tax-deductible expense.

APPLYING THE MODEL

Electrocom Manufacturing purchased $100,000 worth of new computers three years ago. Now it is replacing these machines with newer, faster computers. The firm has a 40 percent tax rate. Because computers qualify as five-year equipment under MACRS depreciation rules, the company has depreciated 71.20 percent (20.00% in year 1 + 32.00% in year 2 + 19.20% in year 3) of the old machines' cost, leaving a book value of $28,800. Electrocom sells its old computers to another firm for $10,000. This allows Electrocom to report a loss on the sale of $18,800 ($28,800 book value – $10,000 sale price). Assuming that Electrocom's business is otherwise profitable, it can deduct this loss from other pretax income, resulting in a tax savings of $7,520 (0.40 × $18,800).

Working Capital Expenditures

Consider a retail firm evaluating the opportunity to open a new store. Part of the cash outflow of this investment involves expenditures on fixed assets such as shelving, cash registers, and merchandise displays, but stocking the store with inventory constitutes another important cash outflow. A portion of this cash outflow may be deferred if the firm can purchase inventory from suppliers on credit. By the same token, cash inflows from selling the inventory may be delayed if the firm sells to customers on credit.

Just as a firm must account for cash flows on fixed assets, it must also weigh the cash inflows and outflows associated with *changes* in **net working capital**, which equals the difference between current assets and current liabilities. Frequently, the term **working capital** is used to refer to what is more correctly known as "net working capital." *An increase in net working capital represents a cash outflow.* Notice that, assuming all other current accounts remain unchanged, net working capital increases if current assets rise (e.g., if the firm buys more inventory) or if current liabilities fall (e.g., if the firm pays down accounts payable). As noted in Chapter 2 (see Table 2.5), any increase (decrease) in a current asset account or any decrease (increase) in a current liability account

net working capital
The difference between a firm's current assets and its current liabilities. Often used as a measure of liquidity.

working capital
Refers to what is more correctly known as *net working* capital.

results in a cash outflow (inflow).[4] Net working capital decreases when current assets fall (as when a firm sells inventory) or when current liabilities increase (as when the firm borrows from suppliers). Therefore, *a decrease in net working capital represents a cash inflow.*

APPLYING THE MODEL

Have you ever noticed the cottage industries that temporarily spring up around certain big events? Think about the booths that open in shopping malls near the end of each year and sell nothing but calendars. Suppose you are evaluating the opportunity to operate one of these booths from November to January. You begin by ordering (on credit) $15,000 worth of calendars. Your suppliers require a $5,000 payment on the first day of each month, starting in December. You anticipate that you will sell (entirely on a cash basis) 30 percent of your inventory in November, 60 percent in December, and 10 percent in January. You plan to keep $500 in the cash register until you close the booth on February 1. Your balance sheet at the beginning of each month looks like this:

	Oct. 1	Nov. 1	Dec. 1	Jan. 1	Feb. 1
Cash	$0	$ 500	$ 500	$ 500	$ 0
Inventory	0	15,000	10,500	1,500	0
Accounts payable	0	15,000	10,000	5,000	0
Net working capital	0	500	1,000	–3,000	0
Monthly net working capital *change*	NA	+500	+500	–4,000	+3,000

The cash flows associated with *changes* in net working capital are as follows:

$500 cash outflow from October to November
$500 cash outflow from November to December
$4,000 cash inflow from December to January
$3,000 cash outflow from January to February

Notice that at the start of November, purchases of inventory are entirely on credit, so the increase in inventory is exactly offset by an increase in accounts payable. The only working capital cash outflow occurs because you must raise $500 to put in the cash register. During November, sales reduce your inventory by $4,500 (inflow), but you pay suppliers $5,000 (outflow). You still have the same amount in the cash register as before, $500, so on net you have an outflow of $500, exactly equal to the increase in net working capital from the prior month. During the month of December, sales reduce your inventory by

4. Of course, one important current asset account is cash. It may seem counterintuitive to argue that if the balances in the cash account increase, then that should be treated as a cash outflow. However, consider again the example of a new retail store. If the company opens a new store, a small amount of cash will have to be held in that store for transactions purposes. Holding fixed the amount of cash that the firm maintains in all of its other stores and in its corporate accounts, opening a new store requires a net increase in the firm's cash holdings. If the firm did not open the new store, then it could invest the cash that it would have held in reserve in the new store in a different project. Likewise, consider what happens if the company decides to close one of its stores. The cash kept in reserve at that location can be redeployed for another use, so reducing cash at that store represents a cash inflow to the firm as a whole. As we will see in Chapter 19, cash management tools have become so sophisticated today that few investments require significant changes in cash holdings. Changes in the other working capital items, such as inventory, receivables, and payables, typically have a much greater cash flow impact than changes in cash balances.

$9,000 (inflow), and you pay $5,000 to suppliers (outflow). That leaves you with cash inflow of $4,000, equal to the decrease in net working capital during the month. By February 1, sales reduce your inventory by the remaining $1,500 in calendars (inflow), you empty $500 from the cash register (inflow), and you pay the last $5,000 to suppliers (outflow). The net effect is a $3,000 cash outflow during January.[5]

Terminal Value

Some investments have a well-defined life span. The life span may be determined by the physical life of a piece of equipment, by the length of time until a patent expires, or by the period of time covered by a leasing or licensing agreement. Often, however, investments have an indefinite life. For example, when a company acquires another company as a going concern, as noted in the stock valuation discussion in Chapter 5, it generally expects the acquired company's assets to continue to generate cash flow for a very long period of time.

When managers invest in an asset with a long life span, they typically do not construct cash flow forecasts more than five to ten years into the future. These long-term forecasts are so inaccurate that the fine detail in an item-by-item cash flow projection is not very meaningful. Instead, managers project detailed cash flow estimates for five to ten years, then calculate a project's **terminal value**, the value of a project at a given future date. There are a number of ways to calculate terminal value.

terminal value
The value of a project at a given future date.

Perhaps the most common approach to calculate terminal value is to take the final year of cash flow projections and make an assumption that all future cash flows from the project will grow at a constant rate. For example, in valuing a large acquisition, many acquiring firms project the target company's cash flows for five to ten years in the future. After that, they assume that cash flows will grow at a rate equal to the growth rate in gross domestic product (GDP) for the economy.[6]

APPLYING THE MODEL

Suppose that analysts at JDS, Inc. were analyzing the potential acquisition of SDL, Inc. They projected that the acquisition of SDL, Inc. would generate the following new stream of cash flows:

Year 1	$0.50 billion
Year 2	1.00 billion
Year 3	1.75 billion
Year 4	2.50 billion
Year 5	3.25 billion

In year 6 and beyond, analysts believed that cash flows would continue to grow at 5 percent per year. What is the terminal value of this investment? Recall that in

[5] Notice that we are only looking at the working capital cash flows associated with this project. We have not considered any fixed asset investment up front. We are not considering the profits from selling calendars at a markup, nor the labor costs of operating the booth.

[6] We emphasize that when companies assume that an investment's cash flows will grow at some rate in perpetuity, the rate of growth in GDP, either in the local economy or the world economy, serves as a maximum potential long-run growth rate. Why? If an investment generates cash flows that grow forever at a rate that exceeds the growth of GDP, then mathematically, that one investment eventually becomes the entire economy.

Chapters 3 and 5, we learned that we can determine the present value, at a discount rate r, of a stream of cash flows growing at a perpetual rate, g, by using the following formula:

$$PV_t = \frac{CF_{t+1}}{r-g}$$

We know that the year-6 cash flow is 5 percent more than in year 5, or \$3.41 billion (1.05 × \$3.25 billion). Put that figure in the numerator of the equation. We also know that g = 5 percent. Suppose that JDS, Inc. discounted the cash flows of this investment at 10 percent. Using the formula above, we can determine that the present value, *as of year 5*, of cash flows in years 6 and beyond equals the following:

$$PV_5 = \frac{\$3.41}{0.10-0.05} = \$68.20$$

This means that the terminal value, the value of the project at the end of year 5, equals \$68.20 billion. To determine the entire value of the project, discount this figure along with all the other cash flows at 10 percent to obtain a total value of \$48.67 billion:[7]

$$\frac{\$0.5}{1.10^1}+\frac{\$1}{1.10^2}+\frac{\$1.75}{1.10^3}+\frac{\$2.5}{1.10^4}+\frac{\$3.25}{1.10^5}+\frac{\$68.2}{1.10^5} = \$48.67$$

Given this set of assumptions, the most JDS, Inc. should pay to acquire SDL, Inc. is about \$48.67 billion.

Notice in the preceding example that the terminal value was very large relative to all the other cash flows. If we discount the terminal value for five years at 10 percent, we find that \$42.35 billion of the project's total \$48.67 billion present value comes from the terminal-value assumptions. Those proportions are not uncommon for long-lived investments, illustrating just how important estimates of terminal value can be in assessing an investment's merit. Analysts must think very carefully about the assumptions they make when calculating terminal value. For example, the growth rate used to calculate a project's terminal value does not always equal the long-run growth rate of the economy. A factory with fixed capacity might offer zero growth in cash flows, or growth that just keeps pace with inflation, once the firm hits the capacity constraint.

Several other methods maintain widespread application in terminal-value calculations. One method calculates terminal value by multiplying the final year's cash flow estimate by a market multiple such as a *price-to-cash-flow ratio* for publicly traded firms with characteristics similar to those of the investment. For example, the last specific cash flow estimate for the SDL, Inc. acquisition was \$3.25 billion in year 5. JDS, Inc. may observe that the average price-to-cash-flow ratio for companies in this industry is 20. Multiplying \$3.25 billion by 20 results in a terminal value estimate of \$65 billion, quite close to the estimate obtained from the perpetual growth model. One hazard in using this approach is that market multiples fluctuate through time, which means that when year 5 finally arrives, even if SDL, Inc. generates \$3.25 billion in cash flow as anticipated, the market may place a much lower value on that cash flow than it did when the acquisition originally took place.

7. Notice that this is the gross present value, not the *NPV*, because we are not deducting any up-front costs incurred to acquire SDL, Inc.

Other approaches to this problem use an investment's book value or its expected liquidation value to estimate the terminal-value figure. Using *book value* is most common when the investment involves a physical plant and equipment with a limited useful life. In such a case, firms may plausibly assume that after a number of years of depreciation deductions, the asset's book value will be zero. Depending on whether the asset has fairly standard characteristics that would enable other firms to use it, its *liquidation value* may be positive or it may be zero.[8] Finding liquidation value often involves inclusion of the tax cash flows that result from selling the asset for a price that differs from its book value at the time of sale. Some assets may even have negative terminal values if disposing of them entails substantial costs. Projects that involve the use of substances hazardous to the environment fit this description. When an investment has a fixed life span, part of the terminal value or terminal cash flow may also include recovery of working capital investments. When a retail store closes, for example, the firm realizes a cash inflow from liquidating inventory.

CONCEPT REVIEW QUESTIONS

1. Why is it important for the financial analyst to (a) focus on incremental cash flows, (b) ignore financing costs, (c) consider taxes, and (d) adjust for noncash expenses when estimating a project's relevant cash flows?

2. Why do we consider *changes* in net working capital associated with a project to be cash inflows or outflows rather than consider the absolute level of net working capital?

3. For what kinds of investments does terminal value account for a substantial fraction of the total project *NPV*, and for what kinds of investments is terminal value relatively unimportant?

9.2 THE RELEVANT CASH FLOWS

The **relevant cash flows** for an investment are all the incremental, after-tax, cash flows (initial outlay, operating cash flow, and terminal value) associated with a proposed investment. As noted in Section 9.1, these cash flows ignore financing costs, include working capital outlays and recovery, and reflect adjustments for any noncash expenses, typically depreciation. Here we consider incremental cash flows in greater detail and discuss sunk costs, opportunity costs, and cannibalization—a few challenges to correctly measuring relevant cash flows. An understanding of these challenges allows you to more accurately estimate a proposed investment's relevant cash flows.

relevant cash flows
All of the incremental, after-tax cash flows (initial outlay, operating cash flow, and terminal value) associated with a proposed investment.

Incremental Cash Flow

We have seen that many investment problems have similar types of cash flows that analysts must estimate: initial outlays on fixed assets and working capital, operating cash flow, and terminal value. But in a broader sense, there is only one type of cash flow that matters in capital budgeting analysis—*incremental cash flow*. To rephrase the oath that witnesses take in television courtroom dramas, analysts must focus on "all incremental cash flow and nothing but incremental cash flow." Determining which cash flows are incremental and which are not for a given project can become complicated at times.

8. It has been estimated that firms can expect to recover no more than 20–50 percent of the original purchase cost of a new machine, once it has been installed. This finding is applicable even for assets with reasonably active secondary markets.

Consider, for example, the incremental cash flows associated with the decision of an employed person with a bachelor's degree to leave his job and return to school to pursue an MBA degree. Many of the incremental outflows are fairly obvious, such as tuition and fees, the cost of textbooks, and possibly relocation expenses. What about expenditures on room and board? Whether or not a student decides to pursue an MBA, he or she still has to eat and have a place to sleep at night. Therefore, room and board expenditures are not incremental to the decision to go back to school.[9]

SMART PRACTICES VIDEO

Paul Savastano, Director of Information Technology, Sprint Corp.

"So the challenge becomes, how do you quantify the benefits when a big piece of the investment is going to be for things that people never see?"

See the entire interview at SMARTFinance

The cash inflows associated with an investment in an MBA degree are more difficult to estimate. For most students, obtaining an MBA degree offers the opportunity to earn higher pay after graduation than they earned before returning to school. Furthermore, most students hope that, after obtaining an MBA, their salary will increase at a much faster rate than it otherwise would have. The net cash flow equals the difference in the salary that a student earns with an MBA versus the salary earned without an MBA, after taxes, of course.

APPLYING THE MODEL

Norm Paul earns $60,000 per year working as an engineer for an auto manufacturer, and he pays taxes at a flat rate of 35 percent. He expects salary increases each year of about 5 percent. Lately, Norm has been thinking about going back to school to earn an MBA. A few months ago, he spent $1,000 to enroll in a Graduate Management Admission Test (GMAT) study course. He also spent $2,000 visiting various MBA programs in the United States. From his research on MBA programs, Norm has learned a great deal about the costs and benefits of the degree. At the beginning of each of the next two years, his out-of-pocket costs for tuition, fees, and textbooks will be $35,000. He expects to spend roughly the same amount on room and board in graduate school that he spends now. At the end of two years, he anticipates that he will receive a job offer with a salary of $90,000, and he expects that his pay will increase by 8 percent per year over his career (about the next 30 years). The schedule of incremental cash flows for the next few periods, excluding the salary that Norm gives up if he goes back to school (more on that later), looks like this:

Year 0	–$35,000
Year 1	– 35,000
Year 2	+ 15,503
Year 3	+ 18,032

The cash outflows at time zero and for year 1 are obvious. The cash inflow figures for years 2 and 3 require some explanation. Had Norm stayed at his current job for the next two years, rather than go back to school, his pay would have increased to $66,150 [$\$60,000 \times (1 + 0.05)^2$]. Therefore, the difference between that figure and his $90,000 post-MBA salary represents a net cash inflow of $23,850. Assuming that Norm pays about 35 percent of his earnings in taxes, the after-tax inflow would be $15,503 [$23,850 × (1.00 – 0.35)]. In year 3, Norm expects to earn 8 percent more, or $97,200, compared with what he would have earned at his old job, $69,458 [$66,150 × (1 + 0.05)]. The after-tax cash inflow in year 3 equals $18,032 [($97,200 – $69,458) × (1.00 – 0.35)]. If you carry these steps out for 30 years, you will quickly see that the MBA has a substantial positive *NPV* at almost any reasonable discount rate.

9. Of course, there may be a difference between money spent on housing and food, depending on whether the person is a student or a working professional. The difference in spending would be an incremental cash flow, but it could be an incremental inflow (if these costs are lower in graduate school) or an outflow (if the MBA program is located in a city with a high cost of living).

Sunk Costs

A **sunk cost** is a cost that has already been paid and is therefore not recoverable; thus, it is irrelevant to the investment decision. For instance, in the preceding *Applying the Model* example, Norm's cash outflows did not include the money he had already spent on the GMAT review and on visits to MBA programs. Clearly, these costs are not recoverable as a result of his decision whether to give up his job and return to school. The money has already been spent and therefore has no bearing on his investment decision. Simply stated, *sunk costs are irrelevant and therefore should be ignored when determining an investment's relevant cash flows.*

sunk costs
Costs that have already been paid and are therefore not recoverable.

Opportunity Costs

We made a number of simplifying assumptions in the preceding *Applying the Model* example. For instance, we assumed that Norm received his pay in a lump sum each year and that he faced a flat tax rate. Of course, the incremental salary that Norm earns arrives monthly, and his higher earnings may be taxed at a higher rate. All these effects are easy to account for, although the calculations become a bit more tedious.

However, there is one major error in our analysis of Norm's investment problem. We ignored a significant opportunity cost. Undertaking one investment frequently means passing on an alternative. In capital budgeting, the **opportunity costs** of an investment are the cash flows that the firm (or in this case, the individual) will not receive from other investments (or actions) as a result of undertaking the proposed investment. If Norm did not attend school, he would earn $60,000 [$39,000 after taxes ($60,000 × (1.00 – 0.35))] the first year and $63,000 [$40,950 after taxes ($63,000 × (1.00 – 0.35))] the second year. This is Norm's *opportunity cost* of getting an MBA, and it is just as important in the overall calculation as his out-of-pocket expenses for tuition, fees, and books. Though it is still true, given the assumptions of our example, that the *NPV* of an MBA is positive, the value of the degree falls substantially once we recognize opportunity costs. As every MBA student knows, opportunity costs are real, not just hypothetical numbers from a textbook. Directors of MBA programs all over the world know that MBA applications are countercyclical. That is, the number of students applying to MBA programs rises during economic downturns and falls during booms. The most plausible explanation of this phenomenon is that potential MBA students face higher opportunity costs when the economy is strong.

opportunity costs
Lost cash flows on an alternative investment that the firm or individual decides not to make.

What kinds of opportunity costs do businesses encounter in capital budgeting problems? Assume that JDS, Inc., introduced in an earlier *Applying the Model* example, acquired SDL, Inc. by issuing $41 billion worth of stock to acquire the shares of SDL. (Note that this transaction was made at a price well below the $48.67 billion maximum price we calculated earlier.) Assume that at the time of this acquisition some "experts" indicated that the cash flow consequence of this transaction was nil, because "the firms just traded pieces of paper, and no one paid or received cash." This view ignores JDS, Inc.'s opportunity cost. Though it may be true that JDS, Inc. could not have raised $41 billion in cash had it attempted to sell the same number of shares that it gave to SDL, Inc. shareholders in the acquisition, JDS, Inc. certainly could have raised a substantial amount of cash from a stock sale. The amount of cash that JDS, Inc. gave up by issuing shares to pay for the acquisition, rather than selling them, is the opportunity cost of the acquisition.

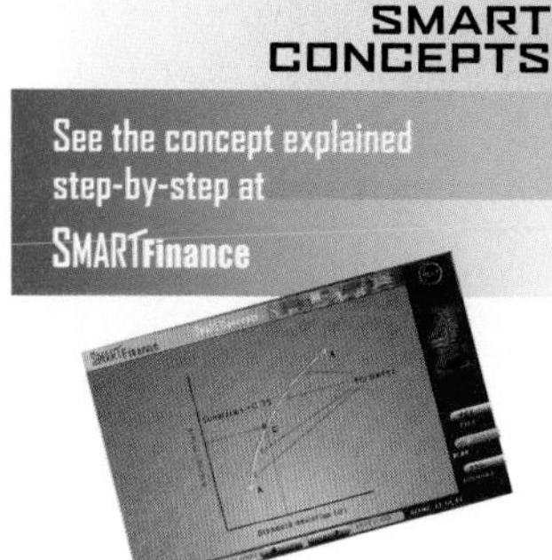

Probably the most common type of opportunity cost encountered in capital budgeting problems involves the alternative use of an asset owned by a firm. Suppose that a company owns raw land that it purchased some years ago in anticipation of an expansion opportunity. Now the firm is ready to expand by building new facilities on the raw land. Even though the firm may have paid for the land many years ago, using the land for expansion entails an incremental opportunity cost. The opportunity cost is the cash that could be raised if the firm sold the land or leased it for another purpose. That cost (the revenue given up) should be factored into the *NPV* calculation for the firm's expansion plans.

Cannibalization

cannibalization
Loss of sales of an existing product when a new product is introduced.

Incremental cash flows show up in surprising forms. One type of incremental cash outflow that firms must be careful to measure when launching a new product is called **cannibalization.** This involves the "substitution effect" that frequently occurs when a firm introduces a new product. Typically, some of the new product's sales come at the expense of the firm's existing products. In the food products industry, sales of a low-fat version of a popular product may reduce sales of the original (presumably, high-fat) version. Some consumers may effectively substitute purchase of the new "improved" product for purchase of the original product. Firms must be careful to consider the incremental cash outflows from existing product sales that are cannibalized by a newer product.[10]

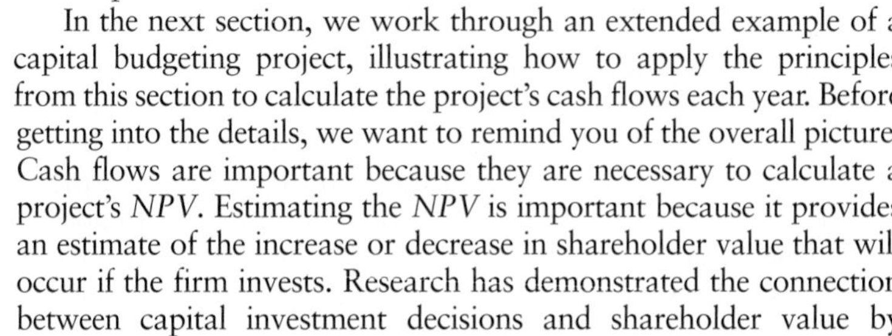

SMART ETHICS VIDEO
Scott Lee, Texas A&M University
"We have found evidence that the market punishes firms that were involved in defense procurement fraud."
See the entire interview at SMARTFinance

In the next section, we work through an extended example of a capital budgeting project, illustrating how to apply the principles from this section to calculate the project's cash flows each year. Before getting into the details, we want to remind you of the overall picture. Cash flows are important because they are necessary to calculate a project's *NPV*. Estimating the *NPV* is important because it provides an estimate of the increase or decrease in shareholder value that will occur if the firm invests. Research has demonstrated the connection between capital investment decisions and shareholder value by showing that stock prices rise on average when firms publicly announce significant new capital investment programs. This suggests that, on average, firms invest in positive *NPV* projects. The Comparative Corporate Finance insert offers evidence supporting the overall picture—what matters is not just the amount of investment that firms undertake but how efficiently they invest.

CONCEPT REVIEW QUESTIONS

4. What is meant by a potential investment's *relevant cash flows?* What are *sunk costs* and *cannibalization*, and do they affect the process of determining a proposed investment's incremental cash flows?

5. A real estate development firm owns a fully leased forty-story office building. A tenant recently moved its offices out of two stories of the building, leaving the space temporarily vacant. If the real estate firm considers moving its own offices into this forty-story office building, what cost should it assign for the space? Is the cost of the vacant space zero because the firm paid for the building long ago, a cost that is *sunk*, or is there an incremental *opportunity cost?*

6. Suppose that an analyst makes a mistake and calculates the *NPV* of an investment project by discounting the project's *contribution to net income* each year rather than by discounting its *relevant cash flows*. Would you expect the *NPV* based on net income to be higher or lower than the *NPV* calculated using the relevant cash flows?

[10] On a capital budgeting exam problem, one of our students mentioned that a firm needed to be wary that its new product should not "cannibalize the existing sales force." Needless to say, that is not the kind of cannibalization that we have in mind, although should it occur, it would certainly represent an incremental cash outflow.

COMPARATIVE CORPORATE FINANCE

Is a High Investment Rate Good for a Nation's Economic Health?

Most people accept as a given that a high investment rate, measured as capital investment spending as a percent of GDP, is strongly correlated with rapid growth in industrial production and overall employment. However, as the table below makes clear, no such strong relationship exists for industrialized countries over the period 1990 to 2002. The industrialized country with the highest investment rate, Japan, saw industrial production fall by 8 percent and total employment decline by 17 percent between 1990 and 2002. Similarly, the large continental European economies of France, Germany, and Italy had above average investment rates *throughout* the period from 1990 to 2002, but industrial production grew more slowly than the average for all industrial countries. All three nations experienced large net employment *declines* over these twelve years. Country-specific factors help explain the exceptional performance of two of the smaller countries in the table, Ireland and Norway. Ireland adopted an explicit open market strategy during the 1980s and attracted large net inflows of foreign direct investment thereafter—with a spectacular payoff in industrial production, plus a more muted, but still significant, increase in employment. Norway benefited from an investment boom resulting from exploration and development of massive North Sea petroleum deposits. However, by far the best performing large economy was the United States. Despite having a below-average investment rate throughout this period, industrial production increased by 43 percent and employment by 19.5 percent between 1990 and 2002. The moral is clear: how efficiently capital is invested is far more important to a nation's economic health than is the absolute level of investment.

Country	Capital Investment Spending (as a % of GDP)		Industrial Production Index (1995 = 100)		Total Employment (1995 = 100)	
	1990	2002[a]	1990	2002[a]	1990	2002[a]
United States	18.0%	18.4%	86.5	123.6	93.4	111.6
Canada	20.7	19.9	88.8	119.8	112.6	117.4
Japan	32.8	25.5	105.3	96.4	101.7	84.3
France	23.4	19.3	100.4	115.9	113.6	97.1
Germany	24.6	23.2	103.2	111.8	100.0[b]	85.9[b]
Ireland	21.0	22.0	62.1	255.3	90.7	112.3
Italy	22.2	19.9	93.5	108.2	107.7	102.3
Spain	25.4	26.0	96.9	118.1	104.5	120.2
Norway	23.3	18.9	86.5	110.3	97.7	102.8
Sweden	21.3	17.2	87.8	124.9	124.7	93.1
Switzerland	28.3	17.2	97.0	121.4	119.4	93.3
United Kingdom	20.2	16.0	94.1	100.0	102.5	109.8
Industrial country average	**22.6%**	**19.9%**	**95.2**	**111.0**	**102.4**	**99.2**

[a] Or most recent year, usually 2001.

[b] Employment index for Germany, 1990 = 100 and data ends 1994.

Source: International Monetary Fund, *International Financial Statistics Yearbook 2003* (Washington, D.C.).

9.3 CASH FLOWS FOR CLASSICALTUNES.COM

Classicaltunes.com is a (fictitious) profitable Internet-based music club selling classical-music CDs to its members.[11] The company is considering a proposal to expand its music selection to include jazz recordings. Management believes that many lovers of classical music also enjoy jazz, and so the company has a built-in clientele for the new music offerings. If the company decides to undertake this project, it will begin selling jazz-music CDs next month when its new fiscal year begins. The company would therefore make the required investment before the end of the current fiscal year (year 0). The company accepts projects with positive *NPV*s, and it uses a 10 percent discount rate to calculate *NPV*.

Up-front costs associated with the investment include \$50,000 in computer equipment (which falls under the MACRS five-year asset class) and \$4,500 in inventory (\$2,500 of which is purchased on credit). For transactions purposes, the firm plans to increase its cash balance by \$1,000 immediately. *The firm does not expect to begin selling CDs until the new fiscal year begins, though it is entitled to take the first half-year of MACRS depreciation in the current fiscal year (year 0).* Currently, the average selling price of Classicaltunes.com's CDs is \$13.50, and company executives believe that CD prices will increase over time at a 2 percent annual rate. Classicaltunes.com knows that some of its suppliers will sell CDs on credit. In addition to relying on this trade credit, the firm expects to finance this investment using cash flow generated from its existing classical-music business.

Like most new business ventures, this one will not be profitable immediately. Managers expect unit sales volume to increase rapidly in the first few years before reaching a long-run stable growth rate. As sales volume increases, the firm expects gross profit margins to widen slightly. The firm does allow credit sales to customers with excellent payment histories. Expanding sales volume will require increases in current assets, as well as additional spending on fixed assets. Classicaltunes.com pays taxes at a 40 percent rate.

Table 9.2 shows various projections for the jazz-music CD project. The top two lines list anticipated selling prices (rounded to the nearest \$0.01) and unit volumes in each of the next six years. Below that appears a series of projected income statements for the next six years. Top-line revenue equals the product of expected selling price (unrounded) and unit volume each year. The figures for cost of goods sold and selling, general, and administrative expenses (SG&A) reflect management's belief that costs as a percentage of sales will fall slightly as volume increases. Depreciation expense each year is determined by spending on fixed assets and the MACRS schedule for five-year equipment.

Beneath the income statement appears a series of abbreviated projected balance sheets. Each shows the project's total asset requirements (including both current and fixed assets) as well as the financing available from suppliers in the form of accounts payable. As mentioned previously, any additional financing the project requires will come from internally generated funds from the classical-music CD side of the business.

To determine whether this is an investment opportunity worth taking, we determine the project's cash flows through time and discount them at 10 percent to calculate the project's *NPV*. As part of this calculation, we have to estimate the value of the endeavor beyond the sixth year. In other words, we have to estimate the project's terminal value.

---

11. Some say that because Classicaltunes.com is a profitable Internet-based firm, it must be fictitious.

Table 9.2
Projections for Jazz-Music CD Proposal

Year	0	1	2	3	4	5	6
Price per unit	$13.50	$13.77	$14.05	$14.33	$14.61	$14.91	$15.20
Units	0	4,000	10,000	16,000	22,000	24,000	25,000
Abbreviated Project Income Statement							
Revenue	$ 0	$55,080	$140,454	$229,221	$321,482	$357,722	$380,080
Less: Cost of goods sold	0	41,861	105,341	169,623	234,682	259,349	273,657
Gross profit	$ 0	$13,219	$ 35,113	$ 59,597	$ 86,800	$ 98,374	$106,422
Less: SG&A expense	0	8,262	19,664	29,799	35,363	35,772	38,008
Less: Depreciation	10,000[a]	18,000	13,800	14,280	23,872	25,208	18,512
Pretax profit	–$10,000	–$13,043	$ 1,649	$ 15,519	$ 27,565	$ 37,393	$ 49,902
Abbreviated Project Balance Sheet							
Cash	$ 1,000	$ 2,000	$ 2,500	$ 3,000	$ 3,200	$ 3,300	$ 3,500
Accounts receivable	0	4,590	11,705	19,102	26,790	29,810	31,673
Inventory	4,500	7,344	18,727	30,563	42,864	47,696	50,678
Current assets	$ 5,500	$13,934	$32,932	$52,665	$ 72,855	$ 80,806	$ 85,851
Gross P&E	$50,000	$60,000	$65,000	$90,000	$130,000	$145,000	$155,000
Less: Accumulated depr.	10,000	28,000	41,800	56,080	79,952	105,160	123,672
Net P&E	$40,000	$32,000	$23,200	$33,920	$ 50,048	$ 39,840	$ 31,328
Total assets	$45,500	$45,934	$56,132	$86,585	$122,903	$120,646	$117,179
Accounts payable	$ 2,500	$ 4,320	$11,016	$17,978	$ 25,214	$ 28,057	$ 29,810

[a] Because the firm makes $50,000 investment in the computer equipment before the end of the current year (year 0), the $10,000 represents the first half-year of MACRS depreciation it is entitled to deduct.

Year 0 Cash Flow

The firm will have cash outlays of $50,000 for computer equipment immediately (year 0). MACRS rules allow the firm to take a depreciation deduction of 20.00 percent, or $10,000, in the first year, which is year 0. Because the company has no other expenses or revenues, the project's incremental pretax profit this year is –$10,000. However, the $10,000 loss does not represent a cash outflow because it derives entirely from a noncash depreciation expense. Assuming that this expense can be deducted from the firm's classical-music CD pretax profits, the expense will save Classicaltunes.com $4,000 in taxes (40% × $10,000). The firm sets up a cash account with an initial balance of $1,000 and purchases $4,500 in inventory. Accounts payable totaling $2,500 are used to finance a portion of these outlays, resulting in an initial net working capital investment of $3,000 ($1,000 cash + $4,500 inventory – $2,500 payables). Therefore, the net cash flow for year 0 is shown as follows:

Increase in gross fixed assets	–$50,000
Tax savings from depreciation	4,000
Initial working capital investment	– 3,000
Net cash flow	–$49,000

Year 1 Cash Flow

Notice in Table 9.2 that gross plant and equipment (P&E) increases by $10,000 in year 1. This means that Classicaltunes.com has purchased $10,000 in additional computer equipment or other fixed assets. Depreciation in the first full year of operation equals $18,000, the difference between accumulated depreciation in year 1 and year 0, ($28,000 – $10,000). That figure results from combining depreciation equal to 32.00 percent of the initial $50,000 investment in fixed assets ($16,000) with depreciation equal to 20 percent of the current-year's $10,000 investment in fixed assets ($2,000).

With sales volume increasing, the firm also makes additional investments in working capital. Cash balances increase by $1,000 ($2,000 – $1,000), receivables rise by $4,590 ($4,590 – $0), and inventories go up by $2,844 ($7,344 – $4,500), partially offsetting the increase in current assets is an increase in accounts payable of $1,820 ($4,320 – $2,500). Therefore, net working capital increases by $6,614 ($1,000 cash + $4,590 receivables + $2,844 inventory – $1,820 payables), a net cash outflow for the firm.

At a sales volume of 4,000 units in its first year of operation, the jazz-music CD business earns a pretax loss of $13,043. To convert this figure into cash flow, we must make two adjustments. First, if Classicaltunes.com can charge this loss against profits in its other operations, then the loss will generate tax savings of $5,217 (40% × $13,043). Second, we need to add depreciation expense back into the pretax loss because depreciation involves no cash outlay. Together, these adjustments result in a net operating cash inflow of $10,174 (–$13,043 + $5,217 + $18,000).

Combining each source of cash flow, we can determine the net cash flow for the project's first full year:

Increase in gross fixed assets	–$10,000
Change in working capital	– 6,614
Operating cash inflow	10,174
Net cash flow	–$ 6,440

Year 2 Cash Flow

We can simply repeat the steps we followed in year 1 to determine cash flow for year 2. First, gross fixed assets increase by $5,000. Depreciation for year 2 is $13,800, again, the difference between accumulated depreciation in year 2 and year 1, ($41,800 – $28,000). The depreciation in year 2 equals the sum of allowable depreciation on assets purchased up front (19.20% × $50,000 = $9,600), assets purchased in year 1 (32% × $10,000 = $3,200), and assets purchased in year 2 (20% × $5,000 = $1,000), which totals $13,800 ($9,600 + $3,200 + $1,000).

Sales continue to rise in year 2, requiring a large investment in working capital. Total current assets increase by $18,998 ($500 cash + $7,115 receivables + $11,383 inventory), but accounts payable rise by $6,696 ($11,016 – $4,320). The increase in net working capital equals $12,302 ($18,998 increase in current assets – $6,696 increase in payables) and results in a cash outflow.

In year 2, the firm earns a small pretax profit of $1,649. After taxes of $660 (40% × $1,649) are deducted, the net earnings amount to $989 ($1,649 – $660). Add

Table 9.3
Annual Net Cash Flow Estimates for Classicaltunes.com

	Year 0	Year 1	Year 2	Year 3	Year 4	Year 5	Year 6
New fixed assets	–$50,000	–$10,000	–$5,000	–$25,000	–$40,000	–$15,000	–$10,000
Change in working capital	– 3,000[a]	– 6,614	–12,302	– 12,771	– 12,953	– 5,109	– 3,291
Operating cash flow	4,000	10,174	14,789	23,591	40,411	47,644	48,454
Net cash flow	–$49,000	–$ 6,440	–$2,513	–$14,180	–$12,542	$27,535	$35,163

[a]Represents the initial working capital investment.

to that figure the depreciation expense of $13,800 to arrive at operating cash inflow of $14,789 ($989 + $13,800). The following are the total net cash flows in year 2:

Increase in fixed assets	–$ 5,000
Change in working capital	– 12,302
Operating cash inflow	14,789
Net cash flow	–$ 2,513

Table 9.3 illustrates the annual net cash flows for the jazz-music CD project all the way through the sixth year. As you can see, project cash flows do not turn from negative to positive until the fifth year. If we calculate the *NPV* (using the 10% discount rate) of the stream of cash flows shown in Table 9.3, it is not surprising that the project generates a negative *NPV*, which equals –$39,206. However, just because the year-by-year cash flow projections end in year 6 does not mean that the project ends at that time. To complete our analysis, we must estimate the project's terminal value.

Terminal Value

We produce two different terminal-value estimates for this project. In the first, we assume that by year 6 the project has reached a steady state, meaning that cash flows continue to grow at 2 percent per year indefinitely. In the second, we assume that the firm sells its investment at the end of year 6 and receives a cash payment equal to the project's book value.

In year 6, the project generates a net cash inflow of $35,163. Assuming that cash flows beyond the sixth year grow at 2 percent per year, and discounting those cash flows at 10 percent, we can use the equation for a growing perpetuity (Equation 3.11) to determine the terminal value of the project *as of the end of year 6*, as follows:

$$\text{Terminal value} = \frac{\$35{,}866}{0.10 - 0.02} = \$448{,}325$$

Notice that the numerator of $35,866 in the expression above is 2 percent greater than the cash flow in year 6 (i.e., 1.02 × $35,163 = $35,866). Remember (from Chapter 3, Equation 3.11, and Chapter 5, Equation 5.4), when valuing a stream of cash flows that grows at a perpetual rate, the *value today* equals *next year's cash flow* divided by the difference between the discount rate and the growth rate. Thus, to determine the terminal value in year 6, we must use the cash flow in year 7 in the numerator.

As a second approach, assume that the terminal value of the project simply equals the book value at the end of year 6. At that time, the firm owns fixed assets worth $31,328 (see Table 9.2 Net P&E for year 6). In this case, because the project is assumed to be terminated and liquidated at the end of year 6, the firm will *recover its net working capital investment* (i.e., liquidate its current assets and pay off outstanding trade credit), which will generate an additional \$56,041 (from Table 9.2 for year 6: \$85,851 current assets – \$29,810 accounts payable) in cash. The terminal value equals the sum of these two items, \$87,369 (\$31,328 net fixed assets + \$56,041 net working capital recovery). Notice that this value is only about one fifth of the \$448,325 value we obtained using the perpetual growth model. The magnitude of that difference should not surprise us too much. In general, as noted in Chapter 5, a profitable, growing business will have a market value that exceeds its book value.

Jazz-Music CD Project *NPV*

Putting all this together, we arrive at two different estimates of the project's *NPV*, depending on which estimate of terminal value we use. Assuming that this business will continue to increase profits forever, we arrive at the following *NPV*:

$$NPV = -\$49{,}000 - \frac{\$6{,}440}{1.10^1} - \frac{\$2{,}513}{1.10^2} - \frac{\$14{,}180}{1.10^3} - \frac{\$12{,}542}{1.10^4} + \frac{\$27{,}535}{1.10^5} + \frac{\$35{,}163 + \$448{,}325}{1.10^6} = \$213{,}862$$

On the other hand, if we assume that the terminal value is only equal to book value after six years, then we arrive at the following *NPV*:

$$NPV = -\$49{,}000 - \frac{\$6{,}440}{1.10^1} - \frac{\$2{,}513}{1.10^2} - \frac{\$14{,}180}{1.10^3} - \frac{\$12{,}542}{1.10^4} + \frac{\$27{,}535}{1.10^5} + \frac{\$35{,}163 + \$87{,}369}{1.10^6} = \$10{,}112$$

In this example, the project yields a positive *NPV*, no matter which terminal-value estimate we choose, so investing in the jazz-music CD project will increase shareholder wealth. However, in many real-world situations, especially those involving long-lived investments, the "go" or "no-go" decision will depend critically on terminal-value assumptions. It is not at all uncommon for the perpetual growth approach to yield a positive *NPV*, while the book value approach shows a negative *NPV*. In that case, managers have to think more deeply about the long-run value of their enterprise.

SMART PRACTICES VIDEO

David Nickel, Controller for Intel Communications Group, Intel Corp.

"Capital budgeting is the key theme for deciding which programs get funded."

See the entire interview at **SMARTFinance**

CONCEPT REVIEW QUESTIONS

7. Embedded in the analysis of the jazz-music CD proposal is an assumption about how Classicaltunes.com's customers will behave when they are able to choose from a new set of CDs. What is that assumption?

8. What other ways might Classicaltunes.com estimate the *terminal value* of this project?

9. Suppose that Congress passes a new MACRS schedule that reclassifies computers as three-year equipment rather than five-year equipment. In general, what impact would this legislation have on the project's *NPV*?

9.4 SPECIAL PROBLEMS IN CAPITAL BUDGETING

Though our objective in writing this book was to give it the most real-world focus possible, real business situations are more complex and occur in more varieties than any textbook can reasonably convey. In this section, we examine common business decisions with special characteristics that make them a little more difficult to analyze than the examples we have covered thus far. We will see that whereas the analysis may require a little more thinking, the principles involved are the same ones discussed throughout this chapter and Chapter 8.

Capital Rationing

In Chapter 8, we asked the following question: If a firm must choose between several investment opportunities, all worth taking, how does it prioritize projects? We learned that the *IRR* and *PI* methods sometimes rank projects differently than the *NPV* does, although all three techniques generate the same accept or reject decisions.

The Fundamental Question. There is a fundamental question that we have avoided until now. If the firm has many projects with positive *NPV*s (or investments with acceptable *IRR*s), why not accept all of them? One possibility is that the company may be constrained by the availability of trained and reliable personnel—especially managers. This prevents the firm from growing extremely rapidly, especially because adding a new product or project would require managerial talent of the highest order. Another possibility is that the firm simply does not have enough money to finance all its attractive investment opportunities. But surely couldn't a large, publicly traded firm raise money by issuing new shares to investors and using the proceeds to undertake any and all appealing investments?

If you watch firms closely over a period of time, you notice that most do not often issue new shares. As Chapter 11 discusses more fully, firms seem to prefer to finance investments with internally generated cash flow and will only infrequently raise money in the external capital markets by issuing new equity. There are several possible reasons for this apparent reluctance to issue new equity. First, when firms announce their intention to raise new equity capital, they may send an unintended negative signal to the market. Perhaps investors may interpret the announcement as a sign that the firm's existing investments are not generating acceptable levels of cash flow. Perhaps investors may see the decision to issue new shares as an indication that managers believe the firm's stock is overvalued. In either case, investors may react negatively to this announcement, causing the stock price to fall. Undoubtedly, managers try to persuade investors that the funds being raised will be invested in profitable projects, but convincing investors that this is the true motive for the issue is an uphill struggle.

A second reason why managers may avoid issuing new equity is that by doing so, they dilute their ownership stake in the firm (unless they participate in the offering by purchasing some of the new shares). A smaller ownership stake means that managers control a shrinking block of votes, raising the potential of a corporate takeover or other threat to their control of the firm.

In conversations with senior executives, we often hear a third reason why firms do not fund every investment project that looks promising. Behind every idea for a new investment is a person, someone who may have an emotional attachment to the idea, or a career-building motivation for proposing the idea in the first place. Upper-level managers are wise to be a little skeptical of the cash flow forecasts they see on projects with favorable *NPVs* or *IRRs*. It is a given that every cash flow forecast will prove to be wrong. If the forecasting process is unbiased, half the time forecasts will be too pessimistic, and half the time they will be too optimistic. Which half is likely to surface on the radar screen of a CFO or CEO in a large corporation? Establishing an annual budget constraint on capital expenditures to ration capital is one mechanism by which senior managers impose discipline on the capital budgeting process. By doing so, they hope to weed out some of the investment proposals with an optimistic bias built into the cash flow projections.

capital rationing
The situation where a firm has more positive *NPV* projects than its available budget can fund. It must choose a combination of those projects that maximizes shareholder wealth.

Selecting the Best Projects Under Rationing. Regardless of their motivation, managers cannot always invest in every project that offers a positive *NPV*. In such an environment, **capital rationing** occurs. Given a set of attractive investment opportunities, managers must choose a combination of projects that maximizes shareholder wealth, subject to the constraint of limited funds. In this environment, ranking projects using the profitability index (*PI*) can be very useful. Once managers rank projects, they select the investment with the highest *PI*. If the total amount of capital available has not been fully exhausted, then managers invest in the project with the second-highest *PI*, and so on, until no more capital remains to invest. By following this routine, managers select a portfolio of projects that in aggregate generates a higher *NPV* than any other combination of projects.[12] The following example demonstrates the application of this approach for selecting investments under capital rationing.

APPLYING THE MODEL

Assume that a particular firm has five projects to choose from as shown in Table 9.4. Note that all of the projects require an initial cash outflow in year 0 that is followed by four years of cash inflows. All of the projects have positive *NPVs*, *IRRs* that exceed the firm's 12 percent required return, and *PIs* greater than 1.0. Notice that the first project has the highest *IRR* and the highest *PI*, but project 5 has the largest *NPV*. This is again the familiar *scale problem* discussed in Chapter 8. Suppose that this firm can invest no more than $300 million this year. What portfolio of investments maximizes shareholder wealth?

Table 9.4
Capital Rationing and the Profitability Index (12% required return)

	Projects				
Year	1	2	3	4	5
0	-$70	-$80	-$100	-$150	-$200
1	30	30	40	50	90
2	40	35	50	55	80
3	50	55	60	60	80
4	55	60	65	90	110
NPV	$59.2	$52.0	$59.6	$38.4	$71.0
IRR	44%	36%	36%	23%	28%
PI	1.8	1.6	1.6	1.3	1.4

12. We are simplifying a bit here. Sorting projects according to the *PI* and selecting from that list until capital runs out may not maximize shareholder wealth when capital is rationed, not only at the beginning of an investment's life but also in all subsequent periods. This method can also lead to suboptimal decisions when projects are interdependent—that is, when one investment is contingent on another. In these situations, more complex decision tools, such as integer programming, may be required.

Notice that there are several combinations of projects that satisfy the constraint of investing no more than $300 million. If we begin by accepting the project with the highest *PI*, then continue to accept additional projects until we bump into the $300 million capital constraint, we will invest in projects 1, 2, and 3. With these three projects, we have invested just $250 million, but that does not leave us with enough capital to fund either project 4 or 5. The total *NPV* obtainable from the first three projects is $170.8 ($59.2 + $52.0 + $59.6) million. No other combination of projects that satisfies the capital constraint yields a higher aggregate *NPV*. For example, investing in projects 3 and 5, thereby using up the full allotment of $300 million in capital, generates a total *NPV* of just $130.6 ($59.6 + $71.0) million. Likewise, investing in projects 1, 2, and 4, another combination that utilizes all $300 million in capital, generates an aggregate *NPV* of $149.6 ($59.2 + $52.0 + $38.4) million.[13]

Equipment Replacement and Equivalent Annual Cost

Assume that a firm must purchase an electronic control device to monitor its assembly line. Two types of devices are available. Both meet the firm's minimum quality standards, but they differ in three dimensions. First, one device is less costly than the other. Second, the cheaper device requires higher maintenance expenditures. Third, the less expensive device (three-year life) does not last as long as the more expensive one (four-year life), so it will have to be replaced sooner. The sequence of expected *cash outflows* (we have omitted the negative signs for convenience) for each device are as follows:

	End of Year (all values are *outflows*)				
Device	0	1	2	3	4
A	$12,000	$1,500	$1,500	$1,500	
B	14,000	1,200	1,200	1,200	1,200

Notice that the maintenance costs do not rise over time. This means either that the expected rate of inflation equals zero or that we have ignored inflation in making the projections.[14] Suppose this firm uses a discount rate of 7 percent. Following is the *NPV* of each stream of cash outflows:

Device	*NPV*
A	$15,936
B	18,065

Purchasing and operating device A seems to be much cheaper than using device B (remember that we are looking for a lower *NPV*, because these are *cash outflows*). But this calculation ignores the fact that using device A will necessitate a large replacement expenditure in year 4, one year earlier than device B must be replaced. We need a way to capture the value of replacing device B less frequently than device A.

13. Reviewing Table 9.4, we see that the *IRR* and *PI* result in identical project rankings. Therefore, had we used the *IRR* rather than the *PI* we would have selected the same set of projects. These two decision techniques generally result in similar, but not necessarily identical, project rankings. We favor the *PI* because of its close link to *NPV*.

14. To simplify the analysis, we are intentionally ignoring inflation. Of course, if we want to recognize inflation, we could restate the cash flows, based on an inflation assumption.

One way to do this is to look at both machines over a twelve-year time horizon. Over the next twelve years, the firm will replace device A four times (4 × 3 years = 12 years) and device B three times (3 × 4 years = 12 years). At the end of the twelfth year, both machines have to be replaced, and thus begins another twelve-year cycle. Table 9.5 shows the streams of cash flows over the cycle, assuming that when either control device wears out it can be replaced and maintained at the same costs that initially applied (i.e., all future costs remain the same). Notice that in the replacement years, the firm must pay both the maintenance cost on the old device (to keep it running through the year) and the purchase price of the new device. The present value (using a 7% discount rate) of the cash outflows for the devices over the entire twelve-year period follows:

Device	*NPV*
A	$48,233
B	42,360

Taking into account the greater longevity of device B, it is the better choice. Remember, *our objective is to find the minimum-cost alternative*, which, in this case, is device B.

equivalent annual cost (EAC) method
Represents the annual expenditure over the life of each asset that has a present value equal to the present value of the asset's annual cash flows over its lifetime.

An alternative approach to this problem is called the **equivalent annual cost (EAC) method.** The EAC method begins by calculating the present value of cash flows for each device over its lifetime. We have already seen that the *NPV* for operating device A for three years is $15,936, and the *NPV* for operating device B for four years is $18,065. Next, the EAC method asks, what annual expenditure over the life of each machine would have the same present value? That is, the EAC solves each expression as follows:

$$\$15{,}936 = \frac{X}{1.07^1} + \frac{X}{1.07^2} + \frac{X}{1.07^3} \qquad X = \$6{,}072$$

$$\$18{,}065 = \frac{Y}{1.07^1} + \frac{Y}{1.07^2} + \frac{Y}{1.07^3} + \frac{Y}{1.07^4} \qquad Y = \$5{,}333$$

Table 9.5
Operating and Replacement Cash Flows for Two Devices (all values are *outflows*)

	Device	
Year	A	B
0	$12,000	$14,000
1	1,500	1,200
2	1,500	1,200
3	13,500	1,200
4	1,500	15,200
5	1,500	1,200
6	13,500	1,200
7	1,500	1,200
8	1,500	15,200
9	13,500	1,200
10	1,500	1,200
11	1,500	1,200
12	1,500	1,200
NPV (@7%)	**$48,233**	**$42,360**

Note: At the end of twelve years, the firm has to replace equipment, regardless of whether it chooses device A or B; thus, a new twelve-year cycle begins.

In the first equation, the variable X represents the annual cash flow from a three-year annuity that has the same present value as the actual purchase and operating costs of device A. If the firm purchases device A and keeps replacing it every three years for the indefinite future, the firm will incur a sequence of cash flows over time with the same present value as a perpetuity of $6,072. In other words, $6,072 is the *equivalent annual cost (EAC)* of device A. Likewise, in the second equation, Y represents the annual cash flow from a four-year annuity with the same present value as the purchase and operating costs of device B. If the firm buys device B and replaces it every four years, then the firm will incur a sequence of cash flows having the same present value as a perpetuity of $5,333. The firm should choose the alternative with the lower EAC, which is device B.

Our approaches for solving the problem of choosing between equipment with unequal lives both assume that the firm will continue to replace worn-out equipment with similar machines for a long period of time. That may not be a bad assumption in some cases, but new technology often makes old equipment obsolete. For example, suppose that the firm in our example believes that in three years a new electronic device will be available that is more reliable, less costly to operate, and longer lived. If this new device becomes available in three years, the firm will replace whatever device it is using at the time with the newer model. Furthermore, the superior attributes of the new model imply that the salvage value for the old device will be zero. How should the firm proceed?

Knowing that it will replace the old device with the improved device in three years, the firm can simply discount cash flows for three years:

$$NPV_A = \$12,000 + \frac{\$1,500}{1.07^1} + \frac{\$1,500}{1.07^2} + \frac{\$1,500}{1.07^3} = \$15,936$$

$$NPV_B = \$14,000 + \frac{\$1,200}{1.07^1} + \frac{\$1,200}{1.07^2} + \frac{\$1,200}{1.07^3} = \$17,149$$

In this case, the best device to purchase is A rather than B. Remember that B's primary advantage was its longevity. In an environment in which technological developments make old machines obsolete, longevity is not much of an advantage.

Excess Capacity

Firms often operate at less than full capacity. In such situations, managers encourage alternative uses of the excess capacity because they view it as a free asset. Although it may be true that the marginal cost of using excess capacity is zero in the very short run, using excess capacity today may accelerate the need for more capacity in the future. When that is so, managers should charge the cost of accelerating new capacity development against the current proposal for using excess capacity. This procedure can be demonstrated by the following example.

APPLYING THE MODEL

Imagine a retail department store chain with a regional distribution center in the southeastern United States. At the moment, the distribution center is not fully utilized. Managers know that in two years, as new stores are built in the region, the firm will have to invest \$2 million (cash outflow) to expand the distribution center's warehouse. A proposal surfaces to lease all the excess space in the warehouse for the next two years at a price that would generate beginning-of-year cash inflow of \$125,000 per year. If the firm accepts this proposal, it will have no excess capacity. In order to hold inventory for new stores coming on line in the next few months, the firm will have to begin expansion immediately. The incremental investment in this expansion is the difference between investing \$2 million now versus investing \$2 million two years from today. The incremental cash inflow is, of course, the \$125,000 lease cash flows that are received today and one year from today. Should the firm accept this offer? Assuming a 10 percent discount rate, the *NPV* of the project is shown as follows:

$$NPV = \$125,000 - \$2,000,000 + \frac{\$125,000}{1.1^1} + \frac{\$2,000,000}{1.1^2} = -\$108,471$$

Notice that we treat the \$2 million investment in the second year as a cash inflow in this expression. By building the warehouse today, the firm avoids having to spend the money two years later. Even so, the *NPV* of leasing excess capacity is negative. However, a clever analyst could propose a counteroffer derived from the follow equation:

$$NPV = X - \$2,000,000 + \frac{X}{1.1^1} + \frac{\$2,000,000}{1.1^2} = \$0$$

The value of X represents the amount of the lease cash inflow (one received today and the other received in one year) that would make the firm indifferent to the proposal. Solving the equation, we see that if the lease cash inflows are \$181,818, the project *NPV* equals zero. Therefore, if the firm can lease its capacity for a price above \$181,818, it should do so.

CONCEPT REVIEW QUESTIONS

10. When a firm is faced with *capital rationing,* how can the *profitability index (PI)* be used to select the best projects? Why does choosing the projects with the highest *PI* not always lead to the best decision?

11. Under what circumstance is the use of the *equivalent annual cost (EAC) method* to compare substitutable projects with different lives clearly more efficient computationally than using multiple investments over a common period where both projects terminate in the same year?

12. In almost every example so far, firms must decide to invest in a project immediately or not at all. But suppose that a firm could invest in a project today or it could wait one year before investing. How could you use *NPV* analysis to decide whether to invest now or later?

13. Can you articulate circumstances under which the cost of excess capacity is zero? Think about why the cost of excess capacity normally is not zero.

9.5 THE HUMAN FACE OF CAPITAL BUDGETING

This chapter illustrates which cash flows analysts should discount and which cash flows they should ignore when valuing real investment projects. There are relatively simple rules of thumb that guide managers in this task; however, executing these rules fittingly in practice is an obvious challenge. Deciding which costs are incremental and which are not, incorporating the myriad of tax factors that influence cash flows, and measuring opportunity costs properly are much more complex maneuvers than we or anyone else can convey in a textbook. The nuances of capital budgeting are best learned through practice.

There is another factor that makes real-world capital budgeting more complicated than textbook examples—the *human element*. Neither the ideas for capital investments nor the financial analysis used to evaluate them occurs in a vacuum. Almost any investment proposal important enough to warrant a thorough financial analysis has a champion behind it, someone who believes that the project is a good idea and perhaps will advance the individual's own career. When companies allocate investment capital across projects or divisions, they must recognize the potential for an optimistic bias to creep into the numbers. This bias can arise through intentional manipulation of the cash flows to make an investment look more attractive, or it may simply arise if the analyst calculating the *NPV* is also the cheerleader advocating the project in the first place.

SMART IDEAS VIDEO

Raghu Rajan, University of Chicago

"Capital budgeting is not just about estimating cash flows and discount rates, but is also a lot about horse trading."

See the entire interview at **SMARTFinance**

One way that companies attempt to control this bias is by putting responsibility for analyzing an investment proposal under an authority independent from the individual or group proposing the investment. For example, it is common in large firms for a particular group to have the responsibility of conducting the financial analysis required to value any potential acquisition targets. In this role, financial analysts play a gatekeeper role, protecting shareholders' interests by steering the firm away from large, negative *NPV* investments. Naturally, these independent analysts face intense pressure from the advocates of each project to portray the investment proposal in its best possible light. Consequently, financial experts need to know more than just which cash flows count in the *NPV* calculation. They also need to have a sense of what is reasonable when forecasting a project's profit margin and its growth potential. Analysts must also prepare to defend their assumptions, explaining why their (often more conservative) projections do not line up with those offered by the managers advocating a given investment.

Many experienced managers say that they have never seen an investment with a negative *NPV*. They do not mean that all investments are good investments, but rather that all analysts know enough about *NPV* analysis to recognize how to make any investment look attractive. Small adjustments to cash flow projections and discount rates can often sway a project's *NPV* from negative to positive. In this environment, another skill comes into play in determining which project receives funding. We refer to this skill as storytelling, as opposed to number crunching. Most good investments have a compelling story behind them, a reason, based on sound economic logic, that the *investment's NPV should be positive*. The best financial analysts not only provide the numbers to highlight the value of a good investment but also explain why the investment makes sense, highlighting the competitive opportunity that makes one investment's *NPV* positive and another one's negative. We return to this storytelling element of capital budgeting in Chapter 10.

14. What role does the *human element* play in the capital budgeting decision process? Could it cause a negative *NPV* project to be accepted?

CONCEPT REVIEW QUESTION

9.6 SUMMARY AND CONCLUSIONS

- To estimate an investment's relevant cash flows, the analyst focuses on incremental cash flows, ignores financing costs, considers taxes, and adjusts for any noncash expenses such as depreciation.
- The costs of financing an investment, such as interest paid to lenders and dividends paid to shareholders, should not be counted as part of a project's cash outflows. The discount rate captures the financing costs, so deducting interest expense and dividends from a project's cash flows would be double counting.
- Certain types of cash flow are common to many different kinds of investments. These include fixed asset cash flow, working capital cash flow, operating cash flow, and terminal cash flow.
- To find working capital cash flow, calculate the change in net working capital from one period to the next. Increases in net working capital represent cash outflows, whereas decreases in net working capital represent cash inflows.
- To find operating cash flow, calculate after-tax net income and add back any noncash expenses.
- To find terminal value, or terminal cash flow, employ one of several methods, including the perpetual growth model and the use of book value.
- Only the incremental cash flows (marginal benefits and marginal costs) associated with a project should be included in *NPV* analysis. The analyst should avoid including sunk costs in estimates of incremental cash flows.
- Opportunity costs and any cannibalization should be reflected in an investment's cash flow projections.
- The profitability index (*PI*) is useful in making investment decisions that maximize *NPV* when capital rationing exists.
- When evaluating alternative equipment purchases with unequal lives, determine the equivalent annual cost (*EAC*) of each type of equipment and choose the one that is least expensive.
- When confronted with proposals to use excess capacity, think carefully about the true cost of that capacity. It is rarely zero.
- When analyzing capital budgeting projects, it is important to consider human factors and make sure that the project, in addition to having a positive *NPV*, makes sense.

SELF-TEST PROBLEMS

Answers to Self-Test Problems appear in Appendix D at back of book. Answers to the Concept Review Questions throughout the chapter appear at http://megginson.swlearning.com.

ST9-1. Claross, Inc. wants to determine the relevant operating cash flows associated with the proposed purchase of a new piece of equipment that has an installed cost of $10 million and falls into the five-year MACRS asset class. The firm's financial analyst estimated that the relevant time horizon for analysis is six years. She expects the revenues attributable to the equipment to be $15.8 million in the first year and to increase at 5 percent per year through year 6. Similarly, she estimates all expenses, other than depreciation attributable to the equipment, to total $12.2 million in the first year and to increase by 4 percent per year through year 6. She plans to ignore any cash flows after year 6. The firm has a marginal tax rate of 40 percent and its required return on the equipment investment is 13 percent. (Note: Round all cash flow calculations to the nearest $0.01 million.)

a. Find the *relevant incremental cash flows* for years 0 through 6.

b. Using the cash flows found in part (a), determine the *NPV* and *IRR* for the proposed equipment purchase.
c. Based on your findings in part (b), would you recommend that Claross, Inc. purchase the equipment? Why?

ST9-2. Atech Industries wants to determine whether it would be advisable for it to replace an existing, fully depreciated machine with a new one. The new machine will have an after-tax installed cost of $300,000 and will be depreciated under a three-year MACRS schedule. The old machine can be sold today for $80,000, after taxes. The firm is in the 40 percent marginal tax bracket and requires a minimum return on the replacement decision of 15 percent. The firms' estimates of its revenues and expenses (excluding depreciation) for both the new and the old machine (in $ thousands) over the next four years are given below.

	New Machine		Old Machine	
Year	Revenue	Expenses (excluding depreciation)	Revenue	Expenses (excluding depreciation)
1	$ 925	$740	$625	$580
2	990	780	645	595
3	1,000	825	670	610
4	1,100	875	695	630

Atech also estimates the values of various current accounts that could be impacted by the proposed replacement. They are shown below for both the new and the old machine over the next four years. Currently (at time 0), the firm's net investment in these current accounts is assumed to be $110,000 with the new machine and $75,000 with the old machine.

New Machine

	Year			
	1	2	3	4
Cash	$20,000	$25,000	$ 30,000	$ 36,000
Accounts Rec.	90,000	95,000	110,000	120,000
Inventory	80,000	90,000	100,000	105,000
Accounts Pay	60,000	65,000	70,000	72,000

Old Machine

	Year			
	1	2	3	4
Cash	$15,000	$15,000	$15,000	$15,000
Accounts Rec.	60,000	64,000	68,000	70,000
Inventory	45,000	48,000	52,000	55,000
Accounts pay.	33,000	35,000	38,000	40,000

Atech estimates that after four years of detailed cash flow development, it will assume, in analyzing this replacement decision, that the year 4 incremental cash flows of the new machine over the old machine will grow at a compound annual rate of 2 percent from the end of year 4 to infinity.

a. Find the incremental *operating cash flows* (including any working capital investment) for years 1 to 4, for Atech's proposed machine-replacement decision.
b. Calculate the *terminal value* of Atech's proposed machine replacement at the end of year 4.
c. Show the *relevant cash flows* (initial outlay, operating cash flows, and terminal cash flow) for years 1 to 4, for Atech's proposed machine replacement.
d. Using the relevant cash flows from part (c), find the *NPV* and *IRR* for Atech's proposed machine replacement.
e. Based on your findings in part (d), what recommendation would you make to Atech regarding its proposed machine replacement?

ST9-3. Performance, Inc. is faced with choosing between two mutually exclusive projects with differing lives. It requires a return of 12 percent on these projects. Project A requires an initial outlay at time 0 of $5,000,000 and is expected to require annual maintenance cash outflows of $3,100,000 per year over its two-year life. Project B requires an initial outlay at time 0 of $6,000,000 and is expected to require annual maintenance cash outflows of $2,600,000 per year over its three-year life. Both projects are acceptable investments and provide equal quality service. The firm assumes that the replacement and maintenance costs for both projects will remain unchanged over time.

a. Find the *NPV* of each project over its life.
b. Which project would you recommend, based on your finding in part (a)? What is wrong with choosing the best project, based on its *NPV*?
c. Use the *equivalent annual cost (EAC) method* to compare the two projects.
d. Which project would you recommend, based on your finding in part (c)? Compare and contrast this recommendation with the one you gave in part (b).

INTERNET RESOURCES

Note: *For updates to links, please go to the book's Web site at* http://megginson.swlearning.com

http://www.ifad.net/content/ie/ie_f_gaap_frameset.htm—An excellent comparison of accounting standards for different countries.

http://clinton3.nara.gov/pcscb/—An interesting report, prepared in 1999 for President Clinton, outlining capital budgeting trends and practices in both the public and private sectors.

http://www.quicken.com/taxes/investing/marginal/yahoo—Site can be used for personal investment decisions by calculating your own marginal tax rate.

http://www.secondarymarket.com—Site can be searched by registered users for used equipment in many different industrial sectors; can use market prices of used equipment to form estimates of salvage value or terminal value for a long-lived project.

KEY TERMS

cannibalization
capital rationing
equivalent annual cost (EAC) method
incremental cash flows
marginal tax rate
modified accelerated cost recovery system (MACRS)
net working capital
noncash expenses
opportunity costs
relevant cash flows
sunk cost
terminal value
working capital

QUESTIONS AND PROBLEMS

Q9-1. In capital budgeting analysis, why do we focus on *cash flow* rather than *accounting profit?*

Q9-2. To finance a certain project, a company must borrow money at 10 percent interest. How should it treat interest payments when it analyzes the project's cash flows?

Q9-3. Does depreciation affect cash flow in a positive or negative manner? From a net present-value perspective, why is accelerated depreciation preferable? Is it acceptable to utilize one depreciation method for tax purposes and another for financial reporting purposes? Which method is relevant for determining project cash flows?

Q9-4. In what sense does an increase in accounts payable represent a cash inflow?

Q9-5. List several ways to estimate a project's *terminal value*.

Q9-6. What are the tax consequences of selling an investment asset for more than its book value? Does this have an effect on project cash flows that must be accounted for in *relevant cash flows*? What is the effect if the asset is sold for less than its book value?

Q9-7. Why must *incremental, after-tax, cash flows*, rather than total cash flows, be evaluated in project analysis?

Q9-8. Differentiate between *sunk costs* and *opportunity costs*. Which of these costs should be included in incremental cash flows and which should be excluded?

Q9-9. Why is it important to consider *cannibalization* in situations where a company is considering adding substitute products to its product line?

Q9-10. Before entering graduate school, a student estimated the value of earning an MBA at $300,000. Based on that analysis, the student decided to go back to school. After completing the first year, the student ran the *NPV* calculations again. How would you expect the *NPV* to look after the student has completed one year of the program? Specifically, what portion of the analysis must be different than it was the year before?

Q9-11. Punxsutawney Taxidermy Inc. (PTI) operates a chain of taxidermy shops across the Midwest, with a handful of locations in the South. A rival firm, Heads Up Corp., has a few Midwestern locations, but most of its shops are located in the South. PTI and Heads Up decide to consolidate their operations by trading ownership of a few locations. PTI will acquire four Heads Up locations in the Midwest, and will relinquish control of its southern locations in exchange. No cash changes hands up front. Does this mean that an analyst working for either company can evaluate the merits of this deal by assuming that the project has no initial cash outlay? Explain.

Q9-12. What is the only relevant decision for independent projects if an unlimited capital budget exists? How does your response change if the projects are mutually exclusive? How does your response change if the firm faces *capital rationing*?

Q9-13. Explain why the *equivalent annual cost (EAC) method* helps firms evaluate alternative investments with unequal lives.

Q9-14. Why isn't excess capacity free?

PROBLEMS

SMART SOLUTIONS

See the problem and solution explained step-by-step at SMARTFinance

Types of Cash Flows

P9-1. Calculate the present value of depreciation tax savings on a depreciable asset with a purchase price of $5 million and zero salvage value, assuming a 10 percent discount rate, a 34 percent tax rate, and the following type of depreciation:

a. The asset is depreciated over a three-year life, according to Table 9.1.
b. The asset is depreciated over a seven-year life, according to Table 9.1.
c. The asset is depreciated over a twenty-year life, according to Table 9.1.

P9-2. A certain piece of equipment costs $32 million, plus an additional $2 million to install. This equipment qualifies under the five-year MACRS category. For a firm that discounts cash flows at 12 percent and faces a tax rate of 34 percent, what is the present value of the depreciation tax savings associated with this equipment? By how much would that number change if the firm could treat the $2-million installation cost as a deductible expense rather than include it as part of the depreciable cost of the asset?

P9-3. The government is considering a proposal to allow even greater accelerated depreciation deductions than those specified by MACRS.

a. For which type of company would this change be more valuable, a company facing a 10 percent tax rate or one facing a 30 percent tax rate?

b. If companies take larger depreciation deductions in the early years of an investment, what will be the effect on reported earnings? On cash flows? On project *NPVs*? How do you think the stock market might respond if the tax law changes to allow greater accelerated depreciation?

P9-4. Taylor United is considering overhauling its equipment to meet increased demand for its product. The cost of equipment overhaul is $3.8 million, plus $200,000 in installation costs. The firm will depreciate the equipment modifications under MACRS using a five-year recovery period. Additional sales revenue from the overhaul should amount to $2.2 million per year, and additional operating expenses and other costs (excluding depreciation) will amount to 35 percent of the additional sales. The firm has an ordinary tax rate of 40 percent. Answer the following questions about Taylor United, for each of the next six years.

a. What additional earnings, before depreciation and taxes, will result from the overhaul?

b. What additional earnings after taxes will result from the overhaul?

c. What incremental operating cash flows will result from the overhaul?

P9-5. Wilbur Corporation is considering replacing a machine. The replacement will cut operating expenses by $24,000 per year for each of the five years that the new machine is expected to last. Although the old machine has a zero book value, it has a remaining useful life of five years. The depreciable value of the new machine is $72,000. Wilbur will depreciate the machine under MACRS using a five-year recovery period, and is subject to a 40 percent tax rate on ordinary income. Estimate the incremental operating cash flows attributable to the replacement. Be sure to consider the depreciation in year 6.

P9-6. Advanced Electronics Corporation is considering purchasing a new packaging machine to replace a fully depreciated packaging machine that will last five more years. The new machine is expected to have a five-year life and depreciation charges of $4,000 in year 1; $6,400 in year 2; $3,800 in year 3; $2,400 in both year 4 and year 5; and $1,000 in year 6. The firm's estimates of revenues and expenses (excluding depreciation) for the new and the old packaging machines are shown in the following table. Advanced Electronics is subject to a 40 percent tax rate on ordinary income.

	New Packaging Machine		Old Packaging Machine	
Year	Revenue	Expenses (excluding depreciation)	Revenue	Expenses (excluding depreciation)
1	$50,000	$40,000	$45,000	$35,000
2	$51,000	$40,000	$45,000	$35,000
3	$52,000	$40,000	$45,000	$35,000
4	$53,000	$40,000	$45,000	$35,000
5	$54,000	$40,000	$45,000	$35,000

a. Calculate the operating cash flows associated with each packaging machine. Be sure to consider the depreciation in year 6.

b. Calculate the incremental operating cash flows resulting from the proposed packaging machine replacement.

c. Depict on a time line the incremental operating cash flows found in part (b).

P9-7. Premium Wines, a producer of medium-quality wines, has maintained stable sales and profits over the past eight years. Although the market for medium-quality wines has been growing by 4 percent per year, Premium Wines has been unsuccessful in sharing this growth. To increase its sales, the firm is considering an aggressive marketing campaign that centers on regularly running ads in major food and wine magazines and airing TV commercials in large metropolitan areas. The campaign is expected to require an *annual* tax-deductible expenditure of $3 million over the next five years. Sales revenue, as noted in the following income statement for 2006, totaled $80 million. If the proposed marketing campaign is not initiated, sales are expected to remain at this level in each of the next five years, 2007–2011. With the marketing campaign, sales are expected to rise to the levels, shown in the sales forecast table, for each of the next five years. The cost of goods sold is expected to remain at 75 percent of sales; general and administrative expense (exclusive of any marketing campaign outlays) is expected to remain at 15 percent of sales; and annual depreciation expense is expected to remain at $2 million. Assuming a 40 percent tax rate, find the *relevant cash flows* over the next five years associated with Premium Wines' proposed marketing campaign.

Premium Wines Income Statement for the Year ended December 31, 2006

Sales revenue		$80,000,000
Less: Cost of goods sold (75%)		60,000,000
Gross profits		$20,000,000
Less: Operating expenses		
General and administrative expense (15%)	$12,000,000	
Depreciation expense	2,000,000	
Total operating expense		14,000,000
Net profits before taxes		$ 6,000,000
Less: Taxes (rate = 40%)		2,400,000
Net profits after taxes		$ 3,600,000

Premium Wines Sales Forecast

Year	Sales Revenue
2007	$82,000,000
2008	$84,000,000
2009	$86,000,000
2010	$90,000,000
2011	$94,000,000

The Relevant Cash Flows

P9-8. Identify each of the following situations as involving *sunk costs*, *opportunity costs*, and/or *cannibalization*. Indicate what amount, if any, of these items would be relevant to the given investment decision.

a. The investment requires use of additional computer storage capacity to create a data warehouse containing information on all your customers. The storage space you will use is currently leased to another firm for $37,500 per year, under a lease that can be canceled without penalty by you at any time.

b. An investment that will result in producing a new lighter-weight version of one of the firm's best-selling products. The new product will sell for 40 percent more than the current product. Because of its high price, the firm expects the old product's sales to decline by about 10 percent from its current level of $27 million.

c. An investment of $8 million in a new venture that is expected to grow sales and profits. To date, you have spent $135,000 researching the venture and performing feasibility studies.

d. Subleasing 100 parking spaces in your firm's parking lot to the tenants in an adjacent building that has inadequate off-street parking. You pay $20 per month for each space under a noncancelable fifty-year lease. The sublessee will pay you $15 per month for each space. You have advertised the spaces for over a year with no other takers, and you do not anticipate needing the 100 spaces for many years.

e. The firm is considering launching a completely new product that can be sold by your existing sales force, which is already overburdened with a large catalog of products to sell. On average, each sales rep sells about $2.1 million per year. You expect that, given the extra time involved in selling the new product, your sales reps will likely devote less time to selling existing products. Although you forecast that the average sales rep will sell about $300,000 of the new product annually, you project a decline of about 7 percent per year in existing product sales.

P9-9. Barans Manufacturing is developing the incremental cash flows associated with the proposed replacement of an existing stamping machine with a new, technologically advanced one. Given the following costs related to the proposed project, explain whether each would be treated as a *sunk cost* or an *opportunity cost* in developing the incremental cash flows associated with the proposed replacement decision.

a. Barans could use the same dies and other tools (with a book value of $40,000) on the new stamping machine that it used on the old one.
b. Barans could link the new machine to its existing computer system to control its operations. The old stamping machine did not have a computer control system. The firm's excess computer capacity could be leased to another firm for an annual fee of $17,000.
c. Barans needs to obtain additional floor space to accommodate the new, larger stamping machine. The space required is currently being leased to another company for $10,000 per year.
d. Barans can use a small storage facility, built by Barans at a cost of $120,000 three years earlier, to store the increased output of the new stamping machine. Because of its unique configuration and location, it is currently of no use to either Barans or any other firm.
e. Barans can retain an existing overhead crane, which it had planned to sell for its $180,000 market value. Although the crane was not needed with the old stamping machine, it can be used to position raw materials on the new stamping machine.

P9-10. Blueberry Electronics is exploring the possibility of producing a new handheld device that will serve both as a basic PC, with Internet access, and as a cell phone. Which of the following items are relevant for the project's analysis?

a. Research and development funds that the company has spent while working on a prototype of the new product.
b. The company's current-generation product has no cell phone capability. The new product may therefore make the old one obsolete in the eyes of many consumers. However, Blueberry expects that other companies will soon bring to market products combining cell phone and PC features, which will also reduce sales on Blueberry's existing products.
c. Costs of ramping up production of the new device.
d. Increases in receivables and inventory that will occur as production increases.

Cash Flows for Classicaltunes.com

P9-11. New York Pizza is considering replacing an existing oven with a new, more sophisticated oven. The old oven was purchased three years ago at a cost of $20,000, and this amount was being depreciated under MACRS using a five-year recovery period. The oven has five years of usable life remaining. The new oven being considered costs $30,500, requires $1,500 in installation costs, and would be depreciated under MACRS using a five-year recovery period. The old oven can currently be sold for $22,000, without incurring any removal or cleanup costs. The firm pays taxes at a rate of 40 percent on both ordinary income and capital gains. The revenues and expenses (excluding depreciation) associated with the new and the old machines for the next five years are given in the following table.

	New Oven		Old Oven	
Year	Revenue	Expenses (excluding depreciation)	Revenue	Expenses (excluding depreciation)
1	$300,000	$288,000	$270,000	$264,000
2	300,000	288,000	270,000	264,000
3	300,000	288,000	270,000	264,000
4	300,000	288,000	270,000	264,000
5	300,000	288,000	270,000	264,000

a. Calculate the initial cash outflow associated with replacement of the old oven by the new one.

b. Determine the incremental cash flows associated with the proposed replacement. Be sure to consider the depreciation in year 6.

c. Depict on a time line the relevant cash flows found in parts (a) and (b), associated with the proposed replacement decision.

P9-12. Speedy Auto Wash is contemplating the purchase of a new high-speed washer to replace the existing washer. The existing washer was purchased two years ago at an installed cost of $120,000; it was being depreciated under MACRS using a five-year recovery period. The existing washer is expected to have a usable life of five more years. The new washer costs $210,000 and requires $10,000 in installation costs; it has a five-year usable life and would be depreciated under MACRS using a five-year recovery period. The existing washer can currently be sold for $140,000, without incurring any removal or cleanup costs. To support the increased business resulting from purchase of the new washer, accounts receivable would increase by $80,000, inventories by $60,000, and accounts payable by $116,000. At the end of five years, the existing washer is expected to have a market value of zero; the new washer would be sold to net $58,000 after removal and cleanup costs, and before taxes. The firm pays taxes at a rate of 40 percent on both ordinary income and capital gains. The estimated *profits before depreciation and taxes* over the five years for both the new and the existing washer are shown in the following table.

	Profits Before Depreciation and Taxes	
Year	New Washer	Existing Washer
1	$86,000	$52,000
2	86,000	48,000
3	86,000	44,000
4	86,000	40,000
5	86,000	36,000

a. Calculate the initial cash outflow associated with the replacement of the existing washer with the new one.

b. Determine the incremental cash flows associated with the proposed washer replacement. Be sure to consider the depreciation in year 6.

c. Determine the terminal cash flow expected at the end of year 5 from the proposed washer replacement.

d. Depict on a time line the relevant cash flows associated with the proposed washer-replacement decision.

P9-13. TransPacific Shipping is considering replacing an existing ship with one of two newer, more efficient ones. The existing ship is three years old, cost $32 million, and is being depreciated under MACRS using a five-year recovery period. Although the existing ship has only three years (years 4, 5, and 6) of depreciation remaining under MACRS, it has a remaining usable life of five years. Ship A, one of the two possible replacement ships, costs $40 million to purchase and $8 million to outfit for service. It has a five-year usable life and will be depreciated under MACRS using a five-year recovery period. Ship B costs $54 million to purchase and $6 million to outfit. It also has a five-year usable life and will be depreciated under MACRS using a five-year recovery period. Increased investments in net working capital will accompany the decision to acquire ship A or ship B. Purchase of ship A would result in a $4-million increase in net working capital; ship B would result in a $6-million increase in net working capital. The projected *profits before depreciation and taxes* for each alternative ship and the existing ship are given in the following table.

	Profits Before Depreciation and Taxes		
Year	Ship A	Ship B	Existing Ship
1	$21,000,000	$22,000,000	$14,000,000
2	21,000,000	24,000,000	14,000,000
3	21,000,000	26,000,000	14,000,000
4	21,000,000	26,000,000	14,000,000
5	21,000,000	26,000,000	14,000,000

The existing ship can currently be sold for $18 million and will not incur any removal or cleanup costs. At the end of five years, the existing ship can be sold to net $1 million before taxes. Ships A and B can be sold to net $12 million and $20 million before taxes, respectively, at the end of the five-year period. The firm is subject to a 40 percent tax rate on both ordinary income and capital gains.

a. Calculate the initial outlay associated with each alternative.
b. Calculate the operating cash flows associated with each alternative. Be sure to consider the depreciation in year 6.
c. Calculate the terminal cash flow at the end of year 5, associated with each alternative.
d. Depict on a time line the relevant cash flows associated with each alternative.

P9-14. The management of Kimco is evaluating replacing their large mainframe computer with a modern network system that requires much less office space. The network would cost $500,000 (including installation costs) and due to efficiency gains, would generate $125,000 per year in operating cash flows (accounting for taxes and depreciation) over the next five years. The mainframe has a remaining book value of $50,000 and would be immediately donated to a charity for the tax benefit. Kimco's cost of capital is 10 percent and the tax rate is 40 percent. On the basis of *NPV*, should management install the network system?

P9-15. Pointless Luxuries Inc. (PLI) produces unusual gifts targeted at wealthy consumers. The company is analyzing the possibility of introducing a new device designed to attach to the collar of a cat or dog. This device emits sonic waves that neutralize airplane engine noise, so that pets traveling with their owners can enjoy a more peaceful ride. PLI estimates that developing this product will require up-front capital expenditures of $10 million. These costs will be depreciated on a straight-line basis for five years. PLI believes that it can sell the product initially for $250. The selling price will increase to $260 in years 2 and 3, before falling to $245 and $240 in years 4 and 5, respectively. After five years the company will withdraw the product from the market and replace it with something else. Variable costs are $135 per unit. PLI forecasts sales volume of 20,000 units the first year, with subsequent increases of 25 percent (year 2), 20 percent (year 3), 20 percent (year 4), and 15 percent (year 5). Offering this product will force PLI to make additional investments in receivables and inventory. Projected end-of-year balances appear in the following table.

	Year 0	Year 1	Year 2	Year 3	Year 4	Year 5
Accounts receivable	$0	$200,000	$250,000	$300,000	$150,000	$0
Inventory	0	500,000	650,000	780,000	600,000	0

The firm faces a tax rate of 34 percent. Assume that cash flows arrive at the end of each year, except for the initial $10-million outlay.

a. Calculate the project's contribution to net income each year.
b. Calculate the project's cash flows each year.
c. Calculate two *NPV*s, one using a 10 percent discount rate and the other using a 15 percent discount rate.
d. A PLI financial analyst reasons as follows: "With the exception of the initial outlay, the cash flows from this project arrive in more or less a continuous stream rather than at the end of each year. Therefore, by discounting each year's cash flow for a full year, we are understating the true *NPV*. A better approximation is to move the discounting six months forward (e.g., discount year 1 cash flows for six months, year 2 cash flows for eighteen months, and so on), as if all the cash flows arrive in the middle of each year rather than at the end." Recalculate the *NPV* (at 10 percent and 15 percent) maintaining this assumption. How much difference does it make?

P9-16. TechGiant Inc. (TGI) is evaluating a proposal to acquire Fusion Chips, a young company with an interesting new chip technology. This technology, when integrated into existing TGI silicon wafers, will enable TGI to offer chips with new capabilities to companies with automated manufacturing systems. TGI analysts have projected income statements for Fusion five years into the future. These projections appear in the income statements below, along with estimates of Fusion's asset requirements and accounts payable balances each year. These statements are designed assuming that Fusion remains an independent, stand-alone company. If TGI acquires Fusion, analysts believe that the following changes will occur.

1. TGI's superior manufacturing capabilities will enable Fusion to increase its gross margin on its existing products to 45 percent.
2. TGI's massive sales force will enable Fusion to increase sales of its existing products by 10 percent above current projections (for example, if acquired, Fusion will sell $110 million, rather than $100 million, in 2007). This increase will occur as a consequence of regularly scheduled conversations between TGI salespeople and existing customers and will not require added marketing expenditures. Operating expenses as a percentage of sales will be the same each year as currently forecasted (ranges from 10 percent to 12 percent). The fixed asset increases currently projected through 2011 will be sufficient to sustain the 10 percent increase in sales volume each year.
3. TGI's more efficient receivables and inventory management systems will allow Fusion to increase its sales as previously described, without making investments in receivables and inventory beyond those already reflected in the financial projection. TGI also enjoys a higher credit rating than Fusion, so after the acquisition, Fusion will obtain credit from suppliers on more favorable terms. Specifically, Fusion's accounts payable balance will be 30 percent higher each year than the level currently forecast.
4. TGI's current cash reserves are more than sufficient for the combined company, so Fusion's existing cash balances will be reduced to $0.
5. Immediately after the acquisition, TGI will invest $50 million in fixed assets to manufacture a new chip that integrates Fusion's technology into one of TGI's best-selling products. These assets will be depreciated on a straight-line basis for eight years. After five years, the new chip will be obsolete, and no additional sales will occur. The equipment will be sold at the end of year 5 for $1 million. Before depreciation and taxes, this new product will generate $20 million in (incremental) profits the first year, $30 million the second year, and $15 million in each of the next three years. TGI will have to invest $3 million in net working capital up front, all of which it will recover at the end of the project's life.
6. Both companies face a tax rate of 34 percent.

Fusion Chips Income Statements ($ in thousands for Years ended December 31)

	2007	2008	2009	2010	2011
Sales	$100,000	$150,000	$200,000	$240,000	$270,000
– Cost of goods sold	60,000	90,000	120,000	144,000	162,000
Gross profit	$ 40,000	$ 60,000	$ 80,000	$ 96,000	$108,000
– Operating expenses	12,000	17,250	22,000	25,200	27,000
– Depreciation	12,000	18,000	24,000	28,800	32,400
Pretax income	$ 16,000	$ 24,750	$ 34,000	$ 42,000	$ 48,600
– Taxes	5,440	8,415	11,560	14,280	16,524
Net income	$ 10,560	$ 16,335	$ 22,440	$ 27,720	$ 32,076

Fusion Chips Assets and Accounts Payable ($ in thousands on December 31)

	2006	2007	2008	2009	2010	2011
Cash	$ 400	$ 400	$ 525	$ 600	$ 600	$ 600
Accounts receivable	6,000	7,000	10,500	14,000	16,800	18,900
Inventory	10,000	12,500	18,750	25,000	30,000	33,750
Total current assets	$16,400	$ 19,900	$ 29,775	$ 39,600	$ 47,400	$ 53,250
Plant and equipment						
Gross	$80,000	$113,000	$166,500	$226,000	$283,200	$336,900
Net	$50,000	$ 71,000	$106,500	$142,000	$170,400	$191,700
Total assets	$66,400	$ 90,900	$136,275	$181,600	$217,800	$244,950
Accounts payable	$ 7,500	$ 13,500	$ 20,250	$ 27,000	$ 32,400	$ 36,450

Note: The 2006 figures represent the balances currently on Fusion's balance sheet.

a. Calculate the cash flows generated by Fusion as a stand-alone entity in each year from 2007 to 2011.

b. Assume that by 2011, Fusion reaches a "steady state," which means that its cash flows will grow by 5 percent per year in perpetuity. If Fusion discounts cash flows at 15 percent, what is the present value as of the end of 2011 of all cash flows that Fusion will generate from 2012 forward?

c. Calculate the present value, as of 2006, of Fusion's cash flows from 2007 forward. What does this *NPV* represent?

d. Suppose TGI acquires Fusion. Recalculate Fusion's cash flows from 2007 to 2011, making all the changes previously described in items 1–4 and 6.

e. Assume that after 2011, Fusion's cash flows will grow at a steady 5 percent per year. Calculate the present value of these cash flows, as of 2011, if the discount rate is 15 percent.

f. Ignoring item 5 in the list of changes, what is the *PV*, as of 2006, of Fusion's cash flows from 2007 forward? Use a discount rate of 15 percent.

g. Finally, calculate the *NPV* of TGI's investment to integrate its technology with Fusion's. Considering this in combination with your answer to part (f), what is the maximum price that TGI should pay for Fusion? Assume a discount rate of 15 percent.

P9-17. A project generates the following sequence of cash flows over six years:

Year	Cash Flow ($ in millions)
0	–59.00
1	4.00
2	5.00
3	6.00
4	7.33
5	8.00
6	8.25

a. Calculate the *NPV* over the six years. The discount rate is 11 percent.

b. This project does not end after the sixth year, but instead will generate cash flows far into the future. Estimate the *terminal value,* assuming that cash flows after year 6 will continue at $8.25 million per year in perpetuity, and then recalculate the investment's *NPV.*

c. Calculate the *terminal value,* assuming that cash flows after the sixth year grow at 2 percent annually in perpetuity, and then recalculate the *NPV.*

d. Using market multiples, calculate the *terminal value* by estimating the project's market value at the end of year 6. Specifically, calculate the terminal value under the assumption that at the end of year 6, the project's market value will be 10 times greater than its most recent annual cash flow. Recalculate the *NPV.*

Special Problems in Capital Budgeting

P9-18. You have a $10-million capital budget and must make the decision about which investments your firm should accept for the coming year. Projects 1, 2, and 3 are mutually exclusive, and Project 4 is independent of all three. The firm's cost of capital is 12 percent.

	Project 1	Project 2	Project 3	Project 4
Initial cash outflow	–$4,000,000	–$5,000,000	–$10,000,000	–$5,000,000
Year 1 cash inflow	1,000,000	2,000,000	4,000,000	2,700,000
Year 2 cash inflow	2,000,000	3,000,000	6,000,000	2,700,000
Year 3 cash inflow	3,000,000	3,000,000	5,000,000	2,700,000

a. Use the information on the *three mutually exclusive projects* to determine which of those three investments your firm should accept on the basis of *NPV?*

b. Which of the *three mutually exclusive projects* should the firm accept on the basis of *PI?*

c. If the *three mutually exclusive projects* are the only investments available, which one do you select?

d. Now given the availability of Project 4, the independent project, which of the mutually exclusive projects do you accept? (Note: Remember, there is a $10 million budget constraint.) Is the better technique in this situation the *NPV* or the *PI*? Why?

P9-19. Semper Mortgage wishes to select the best of three possible computers, each expected to meet the firm's growing need for computational and storage capacity. The three computers—A, B, and C—are equally risky. The firm plans to use a 12 percent cost of capital to evaluate each of them. The initial outlay and the annual cash outflows over the life of each computer are shown in the following table.

	Computer A	Computer B	Computer C
Initial Outlay (CF_0)	$50,000	$35,000	$60,000
Year (t)		Cash Outflows (CF_t)	
1	$ 7,000	$ 5,500	$18,000
2	7,000	12,000	18,000
3	7,000	16,000	18,000
4	7,000	23,000	18,000
5	7,000	—	18,000
6	7,000	—	18,000

a. Calculate the *NPV* for each computer over its life. Rank the computers in descending order, based on *NPV*.
b. Use the *equivalent annual cost (EAC) method* to evaluate and rank the computers in descending order, based on the EAC.
c. Compare and contrast your findings in parts (a) and (b). Which computer would you recommend that the firm acquire? Why?

P9-20. Seattle Manufacturing is considering the purchase of one of three mutually exclusive projects for improving its assembly line. The firm plans to use a 14 percent cost of capital to evaluate these equal-risk projects. The initial outlay and the annual cash outflows over the life of each project are shown in the following table.

	Project X	Project Y	Project Z
Initial Outlay (CF_0)	$156,000	$104,000	$132,000
Year (t)		Cash Outflows (CF_t)	
1	$ 34,000	$ 56,000	$ 30,000
2	50,000	56,000	30,000
3	66,000	—	30,000
4	82,000	—	30,000
5	—	—	30,000
6	—	—	30,000
7	—	—	30,000

a. Calculate the *NPV* for each project over its life. Rank the projects in descending order based on *NPV*.
b. Use the *equivalent annual cost (EAC) method* to evaluate and rank the projects in descending order based on the EAC.
c. Compare and contrast your findings in parts (a) and (b). Which project would you recommend that the firm purchase? Why?

SMART SOLUTIONS

See the problem and solution explained step-by-step at

SMARTFinance

P9-21. As part of a hotel renovation program, a company must choose between two grades of carpet to install. One grade costs $22 per square yard, and the other, $28. The costs of cleaning and maintaining the carpets are identical, but the less expensive carpet must be replaced after six years, whereas the more expensive one will last nine years before it must be replaced. The relevant discount rate is 13 percent. Which grade should the company choose?

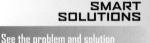

P9-22. Gail Dribble is a financial analyst at Hill Propane Distributors. Gail must provide a financial analysis of the decision to replace a truck used to deliver propane gas to residential customers. Given its age, the truck will require increasing maintenance expenditures if the company keeps it in service. Similarly, the market value of the truck declines as it ages. The current market value of the truck, as well as the market value and the required maintenance expenditures for each of the next four years, appears below.

Year	Market Value	Maintenance Cost
Current	$7,000	$ 0
1	5,500	2,500
2	3,700	3,600
3	0	4,500
4	0	7,500

The company can purchase a new truck for $40,000. The truck will last fifteen years and will require end-of-year maintenance expenditures of $1,500. At the end of fifteen years, the new truck's salvage value will be $3,500.

a. Calculate the *equivalent annual cost (EAC)* of the new truck. Use a discount rate of 9 percent.

b. Suppose the firm keeps the old truck one more year and sells it then rather than now. What is the opportunity cost associated with this decision? What is the present value of the cost of this decision as of today? Restate this cost in terms of year-1 dollars.

c. Based on your answers to (a) and (b), is it optimal for the company to replace the old truck immediately?

d. Suppose the firm decides to keep the truck for another year. Gail must analyze whether replacing the old truck after one year makes sense or whether the truck should stay in use another year. As of the end of year 1, what is the present value of the cost of using the truck and selling it at the end of year 2? Restate this answer in year-2 dollars. Should the firm replace the truck after two years?

e. Suppose the firm keeps the old truck in service for two years. Should it replace it rather than keep it in service for the third year?

P9-23. A firm that manufactures and sells ball bearings currently has excess capacity. The firm expects that it will exhaust its excess capacity in three years. At that time, it will spend $5 million, which represents the cost of equipment as well as the value of depreciation tax shields on that equipment, to build new capacity. Suppose that this firm can accept additional manufacturing work as a subcontractor for another company. By doing so, the firm will receive net cash inflows of $250,000 immediately, and in each of the next two years. However, the firm will also have to spend $5 million two years earlier than originally planned to bring new capacity on line. Should the firm take on the subcontracting job? The discount rate is 12 percent. What is the minimum cash inflow that the firm would require (per year) to accept this job?

For instructions on using Thomson ONE, refer to the instructions provided with the Thomson ONE problems at the end of Chapters 1–6 or to "A Guide for Using Thomson ONE."

THOMSON ONE Business School Edition

P9-24. Compute the annual depreciation tax savings for BASF (ticker: D:BAS) over the last five years. Use an average tax rate (income taxes divided by pretax income from the income statement) for each year. How has depreciation tax savings changed for BASF over these years?

P9-25. Calculate changes in net working capital for Circuit City Stores, Inc. (ticker: CC) over the last five years. For each year, determine if the change represents a cash inflow or a cash outflow for the company. From the balance sheet, identify source(s) for this change.

Since these exercises depend upon real-time data, your answers will change continuously depending upon when you access the Internet to download your data.

MINICASE

Cash Flow and Capital Budgeting

ACE Rental Cars, Incorporated (ACE) is analyzing whether to enter the discount used rental car market. This project would involve the purchase of 100 used, late-model, mid-sized automobiles at the price of $9,500 each. In order to reduce their insurance costs, ACE will have a LoJack Stolen Vehicle Recovery System installed in each automobile at a cost of $1,000 per vehicle. ACE will also utilize one of their abandoned lots to store the vehicles. If ACE does not undertake this project they could sublease this lot to an auto repair company for $80,000 per year. The $20,000 annual maintenance cost on this lot will be paid by ACE whether the lot is subleased or used for this project. In addition, if this project is undertaken, net working capital will increase by $50,000.

The automobiles will qualify as a 3-year class asset under the modified accelerated cost recovery system (MACRS). Each car is expected to generate $4,800 a year in revenue and have operating costs of $1,000 per year. Starting 4 years from now, one-quarter of the fleet is expected to be replaced every year with a similar fleet of used cars. This is expected to result in a net cash flow (including acquisition costs) of $100,000 per year continuing indefinitely. This discount rental car business is expected to have a minimum impact on ACE's regular rental car business where the net cash flow is expected to fall by only $25,000 per year. ACE expects to have a marginal tax rate of 32%.

Based on this information, answer the following questions.

ASSIGNMENT

1. What is the initial cash flow (fixed asset expenditure) for this discount used rental car project?
2. Is the cost of installing the LoJack System relevant to this analysis?
3. Are the maintenance costs relevant?
4. Should you consider the change in net working capital?
5. Estimate the depreciation costs incurred for each of the next 4 years.
6. Estimate the net cash flow for each of the next 4 years.
7. How are possible cannibalization costs considered in this analysis?
8. How does the opportunity to sublease the lot affect this analysis?
9. What do you estimate as the terminal value of this project at the end of year 4 (use a 12% discount rate for this calculation)?
10. Using the standard discount rate of 12% that ACE uses for capital budgeting, what is the *NPV* of this project? If ACE adjusts the discount rate to 14% to reflect higher project risk, what is the *NPV*?

Smart *Excel* Appendix

Appendix Contents

Excel prerequisites
- No new *Excel* prerequisites

Learn to create models to solve for
- *NPV*
- Internal rate of return
- Equivalent annual cost

Use the Smart *Excel* spreadsheets and animated tutorials at http://smartfinance.swlearning.com.

EXCEL PREREQUISITES

There are no new *Excel* prerequisites in this chapter.

CAPITAL BUDGETING ANALYSIS

Problem: Evaluate the capital budgeting decision faced by Classicaltunes.com, described in Chapter 9.

Chapter 9 described the decision faced by Classicaltunes.com. The firm is considering a proposal to expand its music selection to include jazz recordings. We will create a model in *Excel* to analyze the decision. The emphasis here is on creating a model that allows the user to easily change input assumptions and to view the effect of these changing assumptions on net present value and internal rate of return.

CREATE A MODEL

Approach: Create a capital budgeting model to find *NPV* and *IRR* that allows inputs to be easily changed.

Open the Chapter 9 *Excel* file located at the Smart Finance Web site. Open the *Classictunes* tab.

Look at the setup of the model.

Notice:

1. The format uses blue-shaded cells to denote inputs that can be changed and green shading for calculations and output that should not be changed.
2. The price per unit beginning in year 1 is shaded in green—the result of a calculation rather than an input.
3. There is an input for growth in price.
4. Inputs are organized into three categories: income statement projections, balance-sheet projections, and other.
5. Before completing the cash flow projection, there are separate calculations for investment in net working capital and fixed assets.

Step 1: Enter the input information for years 0 through 6 and enter the year 0 price per unit of $13.50. In the text, there is a footnote that states that the price is assumed to grow at 2 percent per year. Thus, the price in year 1 = $13.50 * (1.02) = $13.77. In year 2, the price is $13.77* (1.02) = $14.045. In the text table, this is rounded to $14.05, but the revenue calculation is based on the price of $14.045, NOT the rounded $14.05. To match the text revenue numbers, we create a formula for price, based on the 2 percent annual increase.

Step 2: Fill in the assumptions on growth in price as 2% for each year. Next create a formula for year 1 price in cell E18.

Price = year 0 price *(1+growth in price)
= D18*(1+E19)

Copy the formula across through year 6.

Step 3: Complete the remaining input assumptions.

Step 4: Now begin the calculations section. The first calculation is working capital.

Investment in working capital calcs

Current assets

Net working capital

NEW investment in working capital

Create a formula for current assets equal to the sum of cash, accounts receivable, and inventory.

Net working capital is current assets minus accounts payable.

NEW investment in working capital is the change from one year to another in net working capital. For year 0, the new investment is the total investment. In year 1, the new investment is the net working capital in year 1 minus the net working capital in year 0. The year-1 formula can be copied across.

Your results should match:

Current assets	5,500	13,934	32,932	52,665	72,854	80,806	85,850
Net working capital	3,000	9,614	21,916	34,687	47,640	52,749	56,040
NEW investment in working capital	3,000	6,614	12,302	12,771	12,953	5,109	3,291

Step 5: Complete the calculations on investment in fixed assets. The year 0 figures are:

Change in gross fixed assets	50,000
Accumulated depreciation	10,000
Net PP&E	40,000

Step 6: Find the operating cash flows. Do you find these results?

Operating cash flow	(6,000)	(7,826)	989	9,311	16,539	22,436	29,942

Step 7: Now use a cell reference to pull through the subtotals for New investment in net working capital, new investment in fixed assets, operating cash flow, and depreciation. Then create a formula for total project cash flow. Don't forget to include depreciation, since this was deducted in the operating cash flows but is a noncash expense.

Total Project Cash Flow	(49,000)	(6,440)	(2,513)	(14,180)	(12,542)	27,535	35,163

The total project cash flows represent all cash flows related to the project during years 0 through 6. We have not yet considered the project cash flows after year 6.

Step 8: Find the project's terminal value. The text describes two approaches for incorporating project cash flows after year 6: find a terminal value based on the project continuing at a steady state of growth, or find a terminal value, based on asset book value. Both approaches are included in the model. Complete this now. Remember, using either approach, this is the project value at the end of year 6.

If valued as an ongoing project,
the terminal value at year 6 = Project Cash Flow in year 7 / (Discount rate minus growth rate)

= year 6 Cash Flow *(1 + growth rate) / Discount rate minus growth rate)
= **448,324**

If book value is used,
The terminal value at year 6 = Book value of PP&E plus current assets minus current liabilities

= 87,368

Step 9: Total the cash flows to value the firm, using each approach. The cash flows in years 0 through 5 remain as above but the year 6 cash flow must include the terminal value.

Project cash flows – ongoing	(49,000)	(6,440)	(2,513)	(14,180)	(12,542)	27,535	438,487
Project cash flows – project assets sold	(49,000)	(6,440)	(2,513)	(14,180)	(12,542)	27,535	122,531

Step 10: Find NPV and IRR.

Assuming project continues with 2% growth rate

NPV	$213,862
IRR	42.4%

Assuming project assets sold at book value

NPV	$10,112
IRR	12.9%

Apply it

- ***How important is the assumption about terminal value?***
  The approach used to estimate terminal value has a very significant effect on *NPV* and *IRR*.

EXAMINE PROJECTION ASSUMPTIONS

Problem: Analyze the assumptions embedded in the projections for Classicaltunes.com.

The projection information provided by Classicaltunes.com contains estimates about growth in unit sales and new investments in assets, as well as assumptions regarding future expenditures for production. Let us examine these embedded assumptions to evaluate the reasonableness of the assumptions.

Approach: Find the assumptions embedded in the projection so that a user can more easily understand and change assumptions.

Open the Chapter 9 *Excel* file located at the Smart Finance Web site. Open the *Proj Calcs* tab.

The input information has been entered for you.

Examine price per unit in row 20. Create a formula in row 21 to find the growth rate implied by the prices listed for year 1.

The growth rate is = Price year 1 / Price year 0–1

The result is about 2 percent in each year. It is not exactly 2 percent because, in the input assumptions, we used rounded numbers for price.

Perform the same analysis on unit growth to find the implied growth rate of units sold. You must begin in year 2, since there were no year 0 sales.

The result is:

Year 2	Year 3	Year 4	Year 5	Year 6
150.0%	60.0%	37.5%	9.1%	4.2%

Management may or may not believe this is accurate. Viewing the implied growth rate often provides valuable information. If the results appear unlikely, the input assumptions can be altered.

Complete the projection calculations.

Apply it

- *Which projection assumptions seem most reasonable?*
- *Which assumptions might you question?*

Unit growth would be expected to be highest early on, with slower growth rates in later years. It is difficult to assess the accuracy of the estimates. The projections imply cost of goods sold and SG&A will decrease moderately as a percent of revenues over the six years, whereas accounts receivable, inventory, and accounts payable are assumed to maintain a constant relationship with revenues. The PP&E values might be questioned, since there is not a clear relationship between the values and revenues.

CHANGE KEY ASSUMPTIONS

Problem: Based on your analysis of the assumptions embedded in the projections for Classicaltunes.com, alter some key assumptions and examine the impact on *NPV* and *IRR*.

The original solution is provided on the ***Classictunes (2)*** tab of the file. Use this tab and alter some key assumptions.

Apply it

- *Hold all else constant and assume units sold start at 4000 and increase by 4000 each year.*
  Your result should be:

Assuming project continues with 2% growth rate

NPV	$45,158
IRR	17.4%

Assuming project assets sold at book value

NPV	($92,942)
IRR	#NUM!

NPV is much lower. For the second approach to terminal value, *NPV* is negative and there is no result for *IRR*. The #NUM! message results because *Excel* cannot calculate the *IRR* for this series of cash flows. A glance at the cash flows indicates that there is no positive discount rate that will yield an *NPV* of 0. Therefore, it is clear the project is undesirable.

The solution is provided on the ***Classic units*** tab.

- ***Now begin with the original inputs but assume growth in price is 3 percent.***
  Now the *NPV*s are $337,206 and $34,513. The project looks more attractive.
  The solution is provided on the ***Classic price*** tab.
- ***What if COGS remains at 76 percent of revenues all six years?***
  Now the NPVs are $131,681 and ($6,417). The project looks less attractive. It should only be undertaken if the project is expected to be ongoing.
  The solution is provided on the ***Classic COGS*** tab.

This analysis points out that changes in key assumptions can quickly make an attractive project look far more or far less attractive.

EQUIVALENT ANNUAL COST

Problem: Solve Problem 9-19 in the text.

Approach: Create a capital budgeting model to find *NPV* and equivalent annual cost.

Open the Chapter 9 *Excel* file located at the Smart Finance Web site. Open the *EAC* tab.

First, find each project's net present value.

Next, find each equivalent annual cost.

The equivalent annual cost is the annual expenditure that, if made in each year of the project's life, leads to the net present value. The payment function in *Excel* can calculate equivalent annual cost.

The format of the payment function is: = – pmt(rate,nper,pv,fv,type)

When using the function to find *EAC*, fv and type are left out or set at 0. Nper is the number of years in the project's life, and pv is the project net present value. The negative sign is inserted before the pmt function to handle *Excel's* treatment of cash inflows and outflows.

For this problem,

= –pmt(discount rate, # years, npv)

The costs of the computers are:

***NPV* A**	$ (78,780)	Middle
***NPV* B**	$ (75,482)	Best
***NPV* C**	$(124,886)	Worst
***EAC* A**	$ (19,161)	Best
***EAC* B**	$ (24,851)	Middle
***EAC* C**	$ (34,645)	Worst

Apply it

- *Which project would you recommend?*

Because our goal is to minimize cost, select computer A—it has the lowest annual cost.

Risk and Capital Budgeting

OPENING FOCUS

Alcoa Publicly Discusses Its Cost of Capital

Quick—what do you think the cost of capital should be for the typical large, publicly traded American corporation? Since these firms routinely finance massive capital investment programs by raising capital through public issues of debt and equity securities, virtually all public companies have a "weighted average cost of capital" that their managers use in deciding whether to accept specific investment projects. However, very few of these companies publicly state their cost of capital. Alcoa Inc. is different. Not only did this company specify that its cost of capital was 9 percent in early 2004, it also went to great lengths to measure how efficiently it employs its capital by benchmarking its own return on capital against the return earned by the most profitable 100 members of the Standard and Poors 500 Industrial Stock Index. Alcoa's publicly stated goal is to meet the return on capital performance of these top S&P 500 companies.

Unfortunately for Alcoa, having a goal and reaching it are two different things. The company's actual return on capital during 2001–2003 averaged about 7 percent, versus over 14 percent for the 100 best-performing S&P 500 firms. But by focusing on earning a satisfactory return on its capital investments, Alcoa's mangers are clearly trying to maximize the wealth of the company's shareholders. As the world's largest producer of aluminum and aluminum products, Alcoa's capital investment spending routinely tops $1 billion per year, so the company has good reason to approach capital budgeting decisions carefully.

But how did Alcoa come up with a 9 percent cost of capital? As we discuss in this chapter, a company should determine a *weighted average cost of capital* (*WACC*) by finding the after-tax cost of each major source of financing the company plans to tap for funds, and then by computing an average cost based on the fraction of total funding it wants to draw from each source. Though Alcoa did not describe how it computed its *WACC* to be 9.0 percent, we can present a quick computation to show that this is very reasonable—by noting that the market value of Alcoa's common stock at year-end 2003 was about $32 billion, and its long-term debt was worth about $7 billion. This means that common stock accounted for about 82 percent of

Alcoa's total capital [\$32 billion ÷ (\$32 billion + \$7 billion)], whereas long-term debt accounted for the remaining 18 percent. The average pre-tax cost of the long-term debt was right at 6 percent during 2003. The company stated that its effective corporate tax rate was about 25 percent, so the after-tax cost of debt was 4.5 percent [6% × (1 – 0.25)]. Since debt, with an after-tax cost of 4.5 percent, accounts for 18 percent of Alcoa's total capital, and the *WACC* is 9.0 percent, we can calculate that the cost of Alcoa's equity—which makes up 82 percent of the firm's total capital—must be 10.0 percent. We do this by solving for the cost of equity (r_{equity}) in the formula for the weighted average cost of capital [$WACC = 9.0\% = (0.82 \times r_{equity}) + (0.18 \times 4.5\%)$]. This means that if Alcoa can earn 9.0 percent or more on its capital investments, the company will be able to fully repay its creditors and earn the required 10.0 percent or more on its common equity. This, in turn, should cause the stock price to rise, and Alcoa's managers will have done their proper financial duty.

Sources: Alcoa Inc. news release (January 24, 2004) and 2003 Annual Report, downloaded from company Web site (http://www.alcoa.com).

LEARNING OBJECTIVES

After studying this chapter you should be able to:

- Understand operating leverage and financial leverage, and the potential effect each of them has on a firm's cost of capital;
- Estimate the firm's weighted average cost of capital, both with and without the allowed tax-deductibility of interest payments to bondholders;
- Review the roles of breakeven analysis and sensitivity analysis in evaluating investment opportunities;
- Explain how scenario analysis, Monte Carlo simulation, and decision trees can be used to assess an investment's risk;
- Describe real options and their role in more precisely valuing potential investments; and
- Discuss the strategic aspects of capital budgeting with regard to competition and the role of real options in improving the quality of decisions.

This chapter concludes our coverage of capital budgeting. Chapter 8 preached the virtues of *NPV* analysis, and Chapter 9 showed how to generate the cash flow estimates required to calculate a project's *NPV*. This chapter focuses on the risk dimension of project analysis. Remember, that to accurately measure marginal costs (MCs) and marginal benefits (MBs) in financial decisionmaking, we must incorporate risk factors into the analysis. To achieve this objective with regard to *NPV*, an analyst must evaluate the risk of a project and decide what discount rate adequately reflects the *opportunity costs* of investors who are willing to invest in the project. In many cases, the best place to discover clues for solving this problem is the market for the firm's securities.

The chapter begins with a discussion of how managers can look to the market to calculate a discount rate that properly reflects the risk of firms' investment projects. Even when managers are confident that they have estimated project cash flows carefully and have chosen a proper discount rate, they want to perform additional analysis to understand the sources of a project's risk. Such tools include breakeven analysis, sensitivity analysis, scenario analysis, simulation, and decision trees, all covered in the middle part of this chapter. The chapter concludes with two sections—one on real options and the other on strategy—that describe the sources of value in investment projects and illustrate how *NPV* analysis can sometimes understate the value of certain kinds of investments.

10.1 CHOOSING THE RIGHT DISCOUNT RATE

Cost Of Equity

What discount rate should managers use to calculate a project's *NPV*? This is a very difficult question indeed, undoubtedly the source of heated discussions when firms evaluate capital investment proposals. Conceptually, when a firm establishes a project's discount rate, the rate should reflect the opportunity costs of investors who can choose to invest either in the firm's project or in similar projects undertaken by other firms. This is a rather roundabout way of saying that *a project's discount rate must be high enough to compensate investors for the project's risk*. One implication of this statement is that if a firm undertakes many different kinds of investment projects, each of which may have a different degree of risk, managers go astray if they apply a single, firm-wide discount rate to each investment. In principle, the appropriate discount rate to use in *NPV* calculations can vary from one investment to another as long as risks vary across investments.

To simplify things a little, we consider a firm that finances its operations using only equity and invests in only one industry. Because the firm has no debt, its investments must provide returns sufficient to satisfy just one type of investor, common stockholders. Because the firm invests in only one industry, we may assume that all its investments are *equally risky*. Therefore, when calculating the *NPV* of any project that this firm might undertake, its managers can use the required return on equity, often called the *cost of equity*, as the discount rate. If the firm uses the cost of equity as its discount rate, by definition, any project with a positive *NPV* will generate returns that exceed shareholders' required returns.

To quantify shareholders' expectations, managers must look to the market. Recall from Chapter 7 that, according to the CAPM, the expected or required return on any security equals the risk-free rate plus the security's beta times the expected market risk premium:

$$E(R_i) = R_f + \beta_i(E(R_m) - R_f) \qquad \textbf{(Eq. 10.1)}$$

Managers can estimate the return that shareholders require if they know (1) their firm's stock beta, (2) the risk-free rate, and (3) the expected market risk premium. Research has shown that managers actually do use the CAPM to compute their firm's cost of equity this way.

APPLYING THE MODEL

Carbonlite Inc. manufactures bicycle frames that are both extremely strong and very light. Carbonlite, which finances its operations 100 percent with equity, is evaluating a proposal to build a new manufacturing facility that will enable the firm to double its frame output within three years. Because Carbonlite sells a luxury good, its fortunes are very sensitive to macroeconomic conditions, and its stock has a beta of 1.5. Carbonlite's financial managers observe that the current interest rate on risk-free government bonds is 5 percent, and they believe that the expected return on the overall stock market will be about 11 percent per year in the future. Substituting this information into the CAPM, we find that Carbonlite should calculate the *NPV* of the expansion proposal using a discount rate of 14 percent:

$$E(R) = 5\% + 1.5(11\% - 5\%)$$
$$= 14\%$$

To reiterate, Carbonlite can use its cost of equity capital, 14 percent, to discount cash flows because we have assumed that (1) the company has no debt on its balance sheet and (2) undertaking any of Carbonlite's investment proposals will not alter the firm's risk. If either assumption is invalid, then the cost of equity is not the appropriate discount rate.

In the preceding example, Carbonlite's stock beta is 1.5 because sales of premium bicycle frames are highly correlated with the state of the economy. Carbonlite's investment in new capacity is therefore riskier than an investment in new capacity by a firm that produces a product with sales that are relatively insensitive to economic conditions. For example, managers of a food-processing company may apply a lower discount rate to an expansion project than Carbonlite's managers would because the stock of a food processor would have a lower beta. The general lesson is that the same type of capital investment project (such as capacity expansion, equipment replacement, or new product development) may require different discount rates in different industries. The level of *systematic (nondiversifiable) risk* varies from one industry to another, and so too should the discount rate used in capital budgeting analysis.

Cost Structure and Operating Leverage. Several other factors affect betas, which, in turn, affect project discount rates. One of the most important factors is a firm's cost structure, specifically its mix of fixed and variable costs. In general, holding all other factors constant, the greater the importance of fixed costs in a firm's overall cost structure, the more volatile will be its cash flows and the higher will be its stock beta. **Operating leverage** measures the effect of fixed operating costs on the responsiveness of the firm's *earnings before interest and taxes (EBIT)* to changes in the level of *sales*. Mathematically, the definition of operating leverage can be expressed as follows:

operating leverage
Measures the tendency of the volatility of operating cash flows to increase with fixed operating costs.

$$\text{Operating leverage} = \frac{\Delta EBIT}{EBIT} \div \frac{\Delta \text{sales}}{\text{sales}} \qquad \text{(Eq. 10.2)}$$

where the symbol Δ means "change in." In accounting, *operating profits* typically equal the firm's *EBIT*. Operating leverage equals the percentage change in earnings before interest and taxes, divided by the percentage change in sales. When a small percentage increase (decrease) in sales leads to a large percentage increase (decrease) in *EBIT*, the firm has high operating leverage. The connection between operating leverage and the relative importance of fixed and variable costs is easy to see in the following example.

APPLYING THE MODEL

Carbonlite Inc. uses robotic technology to paint its finished bicycle frames, whereas its main competitor, Fiberspeed Corp., offers customized, hand-painted finishes to its customers. Robots represent a significant fixed cost for Carbonlite, but its variable costs

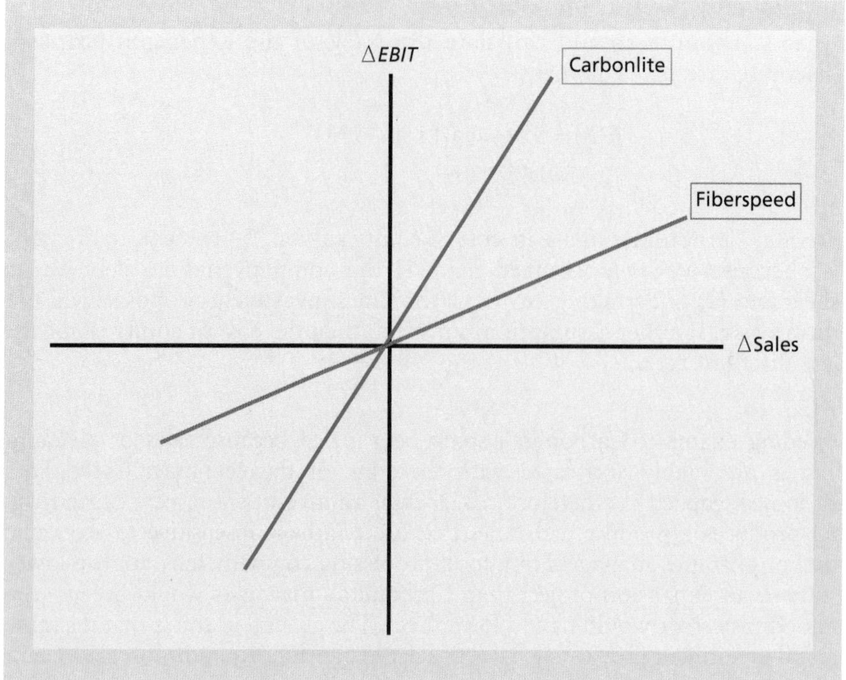

Figure 10.1
Operating Leverage for Carbonlite and Fiberspeed

The higher operating leverage of Carbonlite is reflected in its steeper slope, demonstrating that its EBIT *is more responsive to changes in sales than is the* EBIT *of Fiberspeed.*

are quite low. Fiberspeed has very low fixed costs, but it has high variable costs due to the time and effort that is expended painting frames by hand. Both firms sell their bike frames at an average price of $1,000 apiece. Last year each firm made a profit of $1 million on sales of 10,000 bicycle frames, as shown in Table 10.1. Suppose next year both firms experience a 10 percent increase in sales volume to 11,000 frames, holding constant all the other figures. Carbonlite's fixed costs do not change, and its *EBIT* increases by $600 ($1,000 price minus $400 variable costs) per additional frame sold. Carbonlite's total *EBIT* increases by $600,000 (1,000 additional frames × *EBIT* of $600 per frame), or 60 percent (from $1 million to $1.6 million), whereas Fiberspeed's total *EBIT* increases by $300,000 [1,000 additional frames × ($1,000 price minus $700 variable cost)], or just 30 percent (from $1 million to $1.3 million).

Because Carbonlite has higher fixed costs and lower variable costs, its *EBIT* increases more rapidly in response to a given increase in sales than does Fiberspeed's *EBIT*. Of course, this works both ways: Carbonlite's *EBIT* will decrease more rapidly in response to a given decrease in sales than will Fiberspeed's *EBIT*. *The magnification of changes in sales on* EBIT *occurs equally in both directions.* In short, Carbonlite has more operating leverage. Figure 10.1 shows this graphically. The figure shows two lines, one line tracing out the relationship between sales growth (from the base of 10,000 bicycles per year) and *EBIT* growth (from the $1 million *EBIT* base) for Carbonlite, and the other line illustrating the same linkage for Fiberspeed.[1] Because of its higher operating leverage, Carbonlite has a much steeper line than Fiberspeed does. Even though Carbonlite and Fiberspeed compete in the same industry, they may use different discount rates in their capital budgeting analysis because its greater operating leverage increases the risk of Carbonlite's cash flows relative to Fiberspeed's.

[1] These comparisons are based on a reference point of 10,000 bikes per year sold at a price of $1,000 per bike and *EBIT* of $1 million. All changes described and shown in Figure 10.1 assume these points of reference in each case. Clearly, the sensitivity of these values to change will vary depending on the point of reference utilized.

Table 10.1
Financial Data for Carbonlite Inc. and Fiberspeed Corp.

Item	Carbonlite	Fiberspeed
Fixed cost per year	\$5 million	\$2 million
Variable cost per bike frame	\$ 400	\$ 700
Sale price per bike frame	\$1,000	\$1,000
Contribution margin[a] per bike frame	\$ 600	\$ 300
Last year's sales volume	10,000 frames	10,000 frames
EBIT[b]	\$1 million	\$1 million

[a]*Contribution margin* is the sale price per unit minus the variable cost per unit. In this case:
Carbonlite: \$1,000 – \$400 = \$600 per bike
Fiberspeed: \$1,000 – \$700 = \$300 per bike
[b]*EBIT* equals sales volume times the contribution margin minus fixed costs. In this case:
Carbonlite: (10,000 × \$600) – \$5,000,000 = \$1,000,000
Fiberspeed: (10,000 × \$300) – \$2,000,000 = \$1,000,000

Financial Structure and Financial Leverage. We have seen that Carbonlite's sales are very sensitive to the business cycle because the firm produces a luxury item. We have also observed that Carbonlite's *EBIT* is quite sensitive to sales changes due to high operating leverage. Both of these factors contribute to Carbonlite's relatively high stock beta of 1.5 and its correspondingly high cost of equity of 14 percent. One other factor looms large in determining whether firms have high or low stock betas. Remember that Carbonlite's financial structure is 100 percent equity. In practice, it is much more common to see both debt and equity on the right-hand side of a firm's balance sheet. When firms finance their operations with debt and equity, the presence of debt creates **financial leverage**, which leads to a higher stock beta. The effect of financial leverage on stock betas is much the same as the effect of operating leverage. When a firm borrows money, it creates a fixed cost that it must repay whether sales are high or low.[2] As was the case with operating leverage, an increase (decrease) in sales will lead to sharper increases (decreases) in earnings for a firm with financial leverage compared with a firm that has only equity on its balance sheet.

financial leverage
Using debt to magnify both the risk and expected return on a firm's investments. Also, the result of the presence of debt when firms finance their operations with debt and equity, leading to a higher stock beta.

Table 10.2 on page 428 illustrates the effect of financial leverage on the volatility of a firm's cash flows, and hence on its beta. The table compares two firms, A and B, which are identical in every respect except that Firm A finances its operations with 100 percent equity, and Firm B uses 50 percent long-term debt with an interest rate of 8 percent and 50 percent equity. For simplicity, we assume that neither firm pays taxes. Firms A and B sell identical products at the same price, they both have \$100 million in total assets, and they face the same operating cost structure. Suppose over the next year both firms generate *EBIT* equal to 20 percent of total assets, or \$20 million. Firm A pays no interest, so it can distribute all \$20 million to its shareholders, a 20 percent return on their \$100-million investment. Firm B pays 8 percent interest on \$50 million for a total interest cost of \$4 million (0.08 × \$50 million). After paying interest, Firm B can distribute \$16 million to shareholders, but that represents a 32 percent return on their investment of \$50 million. Conversely, suppose that the firm earns *EBIT* equal to just 5 percent of its assets, or \$5 million. Firm A pays out all \$5 million to its shareholders, a return of 5 percent. Firm B pays \$4 million in interest, leaving just \$1 million to pay out to its shareholders, a

2. Note that even if a firm enters a loan agreement with a variable interest rate, the cost of repaying the debt does not generally vary with sales. In that sense, even a loan with a variable interest rate creates a fixed expense with respect to sales.

Table 10.2
The Effect of Financial Leverage on Shareholder Returns

Account	Firm A	Firm B
Assets	$100 million	$100 million
Debt (interest rate = 8%)	$ 0 (0%)	$ 50 million (50%)
Equity	$100 million (100%)	$ 50 million (50%)
When Return on Assets Equals 20 Percent		
EBIT	$ 20 million	$ 20 million
Less: Interest	0	4 million (0.08 × $50 million)
Cash to equity	$ 20 million	$ 16 million
ROE	$ 20 million/$100 million = 20%	$ 16 million/$50 million = 32%
When Return on Assets Equals 5 Percent		
EBIT	$ 5 million	$ 5 million
Less: Interest	0	4 million (0.08 × $50 million)
Cash to equity	$ 5 million	$ 1 million
ROE	$ 5 million/$100 million = 5%	$ 1million/$50million = 2%

return of only 2 percent. Therefore, in periods when business is very good, shareholders of Firm B earn higher returns than shareholders of Firm A, and the opposite happens when business is bad.

The inclusion of debt as part of a firm's capital structure complicates discount-rate selection in two ways. First, as just shown, debt creates financial leverage, which increases a firm's stock beta relative to the value that it would be if the firm financed investments only with equity. Second, when a firm issues debt, it must satisfy two groups of investors rather than one. Cash flows generated from capital investment projects must be sufficient to meet the return requirements of both bondholders and stockholders. Therefore, a firm that issues debt cannot discount project cash flows using only its cost of equity capital. It must choose a discount rate that reflects the expectations of both investor groups. Fortunately, finance theory offers a way to find that discount rate.

Weighted Average Cost of Capital (*WACC*)

In Chapter 7, we learned that the expected return on a portfolio of two assets equaled the weighted average of the expected returns of each asset in the portfolio. We can apply that idea to the problem of selecting an appropriate discount rate for a firm that has both debt and equity in its capital structure. Imagine that Lox-in-a-Box Inc., a chain of kosher fast-food stores, has outstanding $100 million worth of common stock on which investors require a return of 15 percent. In addition, the firm has outstanding $50 million in bonds that offer a 9 percent return.[3] To simplify our discussion, we hold the firm's overall risk constant by *assuming that the investments being considered do not change either the firm's cost structure or financial structure.* Using this information, we can answer the question: What rate of return must the firm earn on its investments to satisfy both groups of investors?

3. The return we have in mind here is the yield to maturity (*YTM*)—developed in Chapter 4—on the firm's bonds. Unless the bonds sell at par, the coupon rate and the *YTM* will be different, but the *YTM* provides a better measure of the return that investors who purchase the firm's debt can expect.

The Basic Formula. The answer lies in a concept known as the **weighted average cost of capital (*WACC*)**. Let the letters D and E represent the *market value* of the firm's debt-and-equity securities, respectively, and let r_d and r_e represent the rate of return that investors require on bonds and shares. The *WACC* is the simple weighted average of the required rates of return on debt and equity, where the weights equal the percentage of each type of financing in the firm's overall financial structure.[4]

weighted average cost of capital (*WACC*)
The after-tax weighted-average required return on all types of securities issued by a firm, in which the weights equal the percentage of each type of financing in a firm's overall financial structure.

$$WACC = \left(\frac{D}{D+E}\right) r_d + \left(\frac{E}{D+E}\right) r_e \qquad \text{(Eq. 10.3)}$$

Plugging in the values from our example, we find that the *WACC* for Lox-in-a-Box equals 13 percent:

$$WACC = \left(\frac{\$50}{\$50+\$100}\right) \times 9\% + \left(\frac{\$100}{\$50+\$100}\right) \times 15\% = 13\%$$

How can Lox-in-a-Box managers be sure that a 13 percent return on its investments will satisfy the expectations of both bondholders and shareholders? There are two ways to see the answer. First, imagine that a wealthy investor decides to purchase all the outstanding debt-and-equity securities of Lox-in-a-Box. One-third of the portfolio would contain the firm's bonds, with an expected return of 9 percent, and two-thirds of the investor's portfolio would consist of Lox-in-a-Box stock, with an expected return of 15 percent. Relying on the portfolio theory concepts covered in Chapter 7, we can conclude that the expected return on this wealthy investor's portfolio would be 13 percent. If the firm invests (1) only in projects that do not alter the firm's overall risk and (2) in the projects that have positive *NPV*s (i.e., projects offering returns in excess of 13 percent), it will generate returns that exceed the investor's expectations.

Here's a second way to verify that the *WACC* is the proper hurdle rate for Lox-in-a-Box. Suppose the company invests in a project that does not alter the firm's overall risk and earns exactly 13 percent. It therefore has a zero *NPV* if the company uses the *WACC* as its hurdle rate. Lox-in-a-Box has $150 million in assets. A project that offers a 13 percent return will generate $19.5 million in cash flow each year (13% × $150 million). Suppose that the company distributes this cash flow to its investors. Will they be satisfied? Table 10.3 illustrates that the cash flow the company

Table 10.3
Cash Distributions to Lox-in-a-Box Investors

Total cash flow available to distribute (13% × $150 million)	$19.5 million
Less: Interest owed on bonds (9% × $50 million)	4.5 million
Cash available to shareholders ($19.5 million – $4.5 million)	$15.0 million
Rate of return earned by shareholders ($15 million ÷ $100 million)	15%

4. As a practical matter, firms in many countries, including the United States, can deduct interest payments to bondholders when they calculate taxable income. If a firm's interest payments are tax deductible, and if the corporate tax rate equals T_c, we have the following:

$$WACC = \left(\frac{D}{D+E}\right)(1-T_c) r_d + \left(\frac{E}{D+E}\right) r_e$$

We address this important adjustment later in this chapter, after we have fully developed the key concepts.

generates is just enough to meet the expectations of bondholders and stockholders. Bondholders receive \$4.5 million, or exactly the 9 percent return they expected when they purchased bonds. Shareholders receive \$15 million, representing a 15 percent return on their \$100-million investment in the firm's shares.

The *WACC* is a figure of critical importance to almost all firms. Firms that use the *WACC* to value real investments know that a higher *WACC* means that investments have to pass a higher hurdle before they generate shareholder wealth. If an event beyond the firm's control increases the firm's *WACC*, both its existing assets and its prospective investment opportunities become less valuable. The Comparative Corporate Finance insert describes what happens to the corporate cost of capital when a nation that has been closed to inflows of foreign investment from abroad decides to open up to foreign investors.

Modifying the Basic *WACC* Formula. Firms can modify the *WACC* formula to accommodate more than two sources of financing. For instance, suppose a firm raises money by issuing equity, *E*, long-term debt, *D*, and preferred stock, *P*. Denoting the required return on each security with r_e, r_d, and r_p, we can determine the following *WACC* for this firm (still ignoring taxes):

$$WACC = \left(\frac{D}{D+E+P}\right) r_d + \left(\frac{E}{D+E+P}\right) r_e + \left(\frac{P}{D+E+P}\right) r_p$$

APPLYING THE MODEL

The S. D. Williams Company has 1-million shares of common stock outstanding, which currently trade at a price of \$50 per share. The market value of the common stock is therefore \$50 million (\$50 per share × 1-million shares). The company believes that its stockholders require a 15 percent return on their investment. The company also has \$47.1 million (par value) in five-year, fixed-rate notes with a coupon rate of 8 percent and a yield to maturity of 7 percent. Because the yield on these bonds is less than the coupon rate, they trade at a premium. The current market value of the five-year notes is \$49 million. Finally, the company has 200,000 outstanding preferred shares, which pay an \$8 annual dividend and currently trade at their \$80 per share par value. The market value of the preferred stock is therefore \$16 million (\$80 per share × 200,000 shares) and the rate of return on the preferred stock is 10 percent (\$8 annual dividend ÷ \$80 par value). What is the company's *WACC*? Begin by calculating the market value of each security. S. D. Williams has \$50 million in common stock, \$49 million in long-term debt, and \$16 million in preferred stock, for a total capitalization of \$115 million. Next, determine the required rate of return on each type of security. The rates on common stock, long-term debt, and preferred stock are 15 percent, 7 percent, and 10 percent, respectively. Plug all these values into the *WACC* equation to obtain 10.9 percent:

$$WACC = \left(\frac{\$49}{\$115}\right) \times 7\% + \left(\frac{\$50}{\$115}\right) \times 15\% + \left(\frac{\$16}{\$115}\right) \times 10\% = 10.9\%$$

An Important Proviso. Now we have seen two approaches for determining the correct discount rate to apply to capital budgeting problems. An all-equity firm should discount project cash flows using the cost of equity, and a firm that uses both

COMPARATIVE CORPORATE FINANCE

Does Opening Up to the World Reduce the Corporate Cost of Capital?

What happens to the corporate cost of capital when a nation that has been closed to inflows of financial investment from abroad decides to open up to foreign investors? Finance theory suggests that *capital account liberalization*—the process of allowing in foreign capital—should reduce the overall cost of external financing for the country's publicly traded companies by increasing the supply of potential lenders and equity investors from which domestic firms can obtain external financing. Empirical evidence now strongly supports this idea.

A recent academic study by Peter Blair Henry found that three economically important things happen when emerging economies open their stock markets to foreign investors. First, the average cost of equity capital, as measured by the aggregate dividend yield on publicly traded stocks, falls by 240 basis points (2.4 percent). The figure below demonstrates how dividend yields change in the five years before (–5 to –1) and five years after (+1 to +5) capital account liberalization, which is year 0 in the figure. Second, the nation's overall stock of capital increases by an average of 1.1 percentage point per year, meaning that companies invest more in productive assets. Third, the growth rate of output per worker rises by 2.3 percentage points per year. Because the cost of capital falls, the amount of investment increases sharply, and the productivity of workers rises rapidly when countries open their stock markets. The policy is clear: let foreign capital in!

The Cost of Capital Falls When Countries Liberalize the Capital Account.

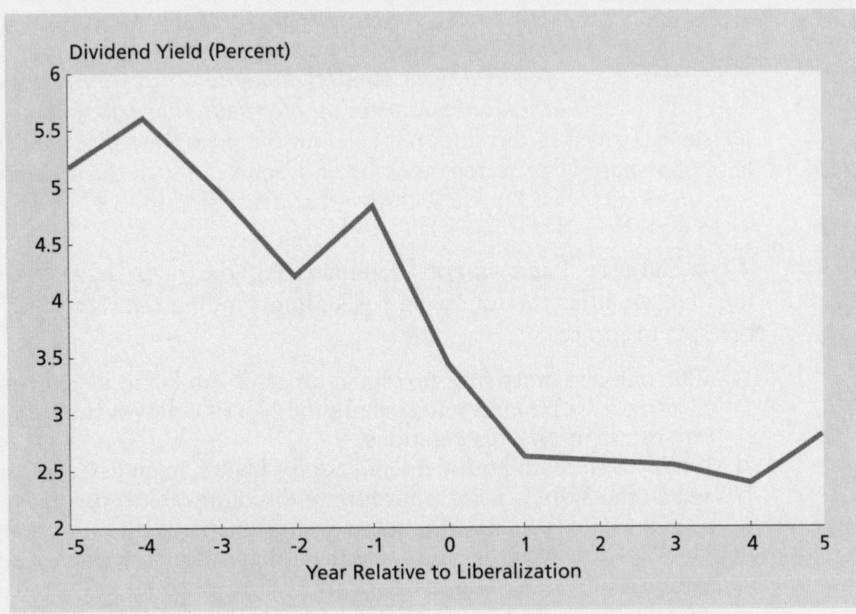

Source: Peter Blair Henry, "Capital Account Liberalization, The Cost of Capital, and Economic Growth," *American Economic Review, Papers and Proceedings* 93 (May 2003), pp. 91–96.

debt and equity (common and possibly preferred stock) should discount cash flows using the *WACC*. Both recommendations are subject to the important proviso (noted earlier) that *the firm makes investments that do not change either its cost or financial structure*. Restated, the firm discounts cash flows using the *WACC* only when the project under consideration is very similar to the firm's existing assets, and the firm's

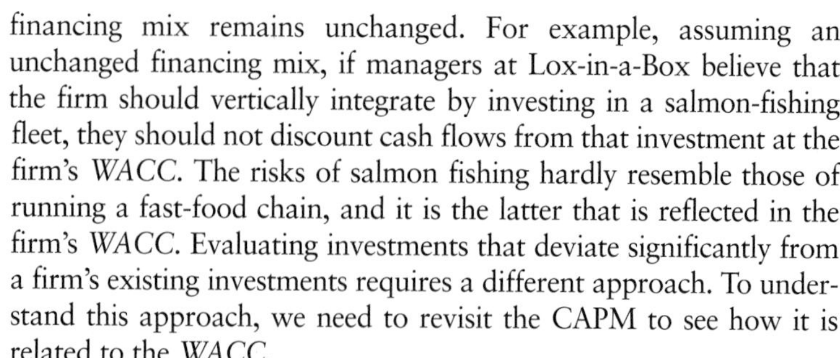

SMART PRACTICES VIDEO

Beth Acton, Vice President and Treasurer of Ford Motor Co. (former),
"For us, it's a very critical calculation because we use it to assess product programs, to assess other capital investments, and to analyze acquisitions."

See the entire interview at **SMARTFinance**

financing mix remains unchanged. For example, assuming an unchanged financing mix, if managers at Lox-in-a-Box believe that the firm should vertically integrate by investing in a salmon-fishing fleet, they should not discount cash flows from that investment at the firm's *WACC*. The risks of salmon fishing hardly resemble those of running a fast-food chain, and it is the latter that is reflected in the firm's *WACC*. Evaluating investments that deviate significantly from a firm's existing investments requires a different approach. To understand this approach, we need to revisit the CAPM to see how it is related to the *WACC*.

The *WACC*, CAPM, and Taxes

SMART IDEAS VIDEO

Kenneth Eades, University of Virginia
"Some of the big things that are hard to convince students to do in fact are widely used in practice."

See the entire interview at **SMARTFinance**

The CAPM states that the required return on any asset is directly linked to the asset's beta. By now we are used to thinking about betas of shares of common stock, but there is nothing about the CAPM that restricts its predictions to shares. When a firm issues preferred stock and bonds, the required returns on those securities should reflect their systematic risks (i.e., their betas) just as the required returns on the firm's common shares do. Because both preferred stock and bonds generally make fixed, predictable cash payments over time, measuring the rate of return that investors require on these securities is relatively easy, even without knowing their betas. *For preferred stock, the dividend yield (annual dividend ÷ price) provides a good measure of required returns, and for debt, the yield to maturity* (YTM) *does the same.* However, this does not rule out the possibility that we could estimate the beta of a share of preferred stock or of a bond in much the same manner as we do for common stocks. But we will save that discussion for a more advanced course.

The Main Lessons. Summarizing the main lessons we have learned thus far, we offer the following rules about finding the right discount rate for an investment project:

1. When an all-equity firm invests in an asset similar to its existing assets (i.e., its cost structure remains unchanged), the cost of equity is the appropriate discount rate to use in *NPV* calculations.
2. When a firm with both debt and equity invests in an asset similar to its existing assets, the *WACC* is the appropriate discount rate to use in *NPV* calculations, as long as its financial structure remains unchanged.
3. The *WACC* reflects the return that the firm must earn on average across all its assets to satisfy investors, but using the *WACC* to discount cash flows of a particular investment can lead to mistakes. The reason for this is that a particular investment may be more or less risky than the firm's average investment, requiring a higher or lower discount rate than the *WACC*, assuming an unchanged financial structure.

Considering Taxes. Nothing in the real world is as simple as it is portrayed in textbooks. One important item that we have neglected thus far is the effect of taxes on project discount rates. In the United States and many other countries, corporations must pay taxes on their earnings, but interest payments to bondholders are tax deductible. The opportunity to deduct interest payments reduces the after-tax cost of debt and changes the *WACC* formula:

$$WACC = \left(\frac{D}{D+E}\right)(1-T_c)r_d + \left(\frac{E}{D+E}\right)r_e \qquad \text{(Eq. 10.4)}$$

where T_c is the marginal corporate tax rate.

Fortunately, the three main lessons listed previously do not change when we add taxes to the picture. Only the calculations change. When a firm is making an "ordinary" investment, it can use Equation 10.4 to determine its after-tax *WACC*, which serves as the discount rate in *NPV* calculations.

CONCEPT REVIEW QUESTIONS

1. Why is using the cost of equity to discount project cash flows inappropriate when a firm uses both debt and equity in its capital structure?

2. Two firms in the same industry have very different equity betas. Offer two reasons why this could occur.

3. For a firm considering expansion of its existing line of business, why is the *WACC*, rather than the cost of equity, the preferred discount rate if the firm has both debt and equity in its capital structure?

4. The cost of debt, r_d, is generally less than the cost of equity, r_e, because debt is a less risky security. A naive application of the *WACC* formula may suggest that a firm could lower its cost of capital (thereby raising the *NPV* of its current and future investments) by using more debt and less equity in its capital structure. Give one reason why using more debt may not lower a firm's *WACC*, even if $r_d < r_e$.

10.2 A CLOSER LOOK AT RISK

Thus far, the only consideration we have given to risk when performing capital budgeting analysis is selecting the right discount rate. But it would be simplistic to say that, given a set of project cash flows, once an analyst has discounted those cash flows using a risk-adjusted discount rate to determine the *NPV*, the analyst's work is done. Managers generally want to know more about a project than just its *NPV*. They want to know the sources of uncertainty in the project as well as the quantitative importance of each source. Managers need this information to decide whether a project requires additional analysis, such as market research or product testing. Managers also want to identify a project's key value drivers, so they can closely monitor them after an investment is made. In this section, we explore several techniques that give managers deeper insights into the uncertainty structure of capital investments.

Breakeven Analysis

When firms make investments, they do so with the objective of making a profit. But another objective that sometimes enters the decision process is avoiding losses. Managers often want to know what is required for a project to break even. **Breakeven analysis** can be formulated in many different ways. For instance, when a firm introduces a new product, it may want to know the level of sales at which incremental net income turns from negative to positive. Evaluating a new product launch over several years,

breakeven analysis The study of what is required for a project's profits and losses to balance out.

breakeven point (BEP) The level of sales or production that a firm must achieve in order to avoid losses by fully covering all costs. Calculated by dividing total fixed costs (FC) by the *contribution margin*.

contribution margin The sale price per unit (SP) minus variable cost per unit (VC).

managers may ask what growth rate in sales the firm must achieve to reach a project *NPV* of zero. When considering a decision to replace old production equipment, a firm may calculate the level of production volume needed to generate cost savings equal to the cost of the new equipment. The standard equation for the **breakeven point (BEP)** is found by dividing the fixed costs (FC) by the **contribution margin**, which is the sale price per unit (SP) minus variable cost per unit (VC).

$$BEP = \frac{\text{fixed costs}}{\text{contribution margin}} = \frac{\text{fixed costs}}{SP - VC} \quad \text{(Eq. 10.5)}$$

APPLYING THE MODEL

Take another look at Table 10.1 on page 427, which shows price and cost information for Carbonlite Inc. and Fiberspeed Corp. How many bicycle frames must each firm sell to achieve a breakeven point with *EBIT* equal to zero? We can obtain the answer by substituting the data for each firm into Equation 10.5.

Carbonlite breakeven point = \$5,000,000 ÷ (\$1,000–\$400) = 8,333 frames
Fiberspeed breakeven point = \$2,000,000 ÷ (\$1,000–\$700) = 6,667 frames

Figures 10.2a and 10.2b illustrate the breakeven point (BEP) for each firm. Despite its \$600 contribution margin, Carbonlite's high fixed costs result in a breakeven point at higher sales volume than Fiberspeed's breakeven point. This should not surprise us, as we already know that Carbonlite's production process results in higher operating leverage than Fiberspeed's.

The popularity of breakeven analysis among practitioners arises, in part, because it gives managers very clear targets. From breakeven calculations, managers can derive specific targets for different functional areas in the firm (e.g., produce at least 10,000 units, gain at least a 5 percent market share, hold variable costs to no more than 65 percent of the selling price). As always, we encourage managers to use breakeven analysis in the context of net present values rather than earnings. A project that reaches the breakeven point in terms of net income may destroy shareholder value because it does not recover the firm's cost of capital.

Sensitivity Analysis

sensitivity analysis A tool that allows exploration of the impact of individual assumptions on a decision variable, such as a project's net present value, by determining the effect of changing one variable while holding all others fixed.

Most capital budgeting problems require analysts to make many different assumptions before arriving at a final *NPV*. For instance, forecasting project cash flows may require assumptions about the selling price of output, costs of raw materials, market share, and many other unknown quantities. In **sensitivity analysis**, managers have a tool that allows them to explore the impact of each individual assumption, holding all other assumptions fixed, on the project's *NPV*. To conduct a sensitivity analysis, firms establish a "base-case" set of assumptions for a particular project and calculate the *NPV* based on those assumptions. Next, managers allow one variable to change while holding all others fixed, and they recalculate the *NPV* based on that change. By repeating this process for all the uncertain variables in an *NPV* calculation, managers can see how sensitive the *NPV* is to changes in baseline assumptions. An example can be used to illustrate this procedure.

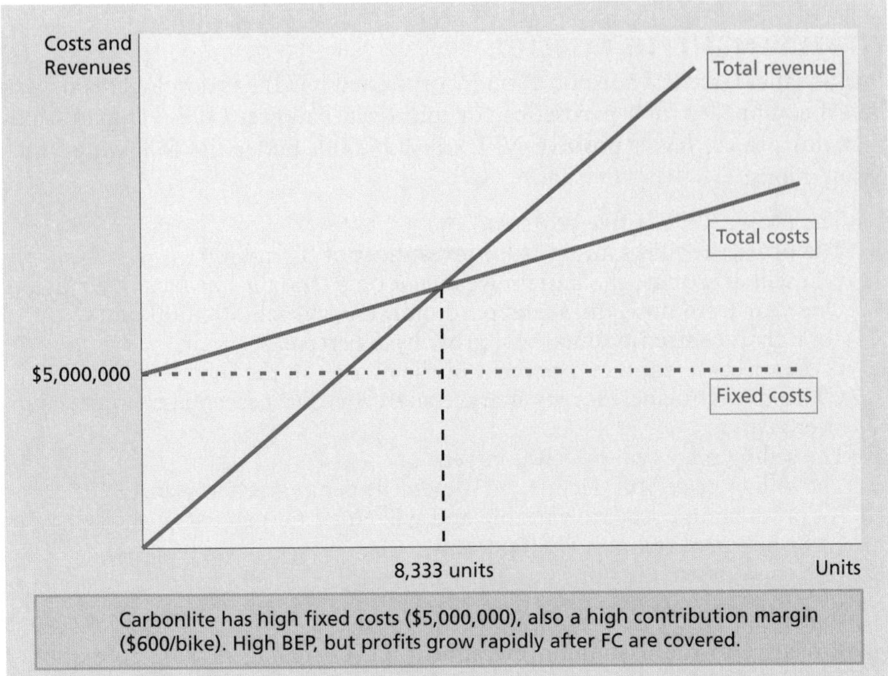
Costs and Revenues
Total revenue
Total costs
$5,000,000
Fixed costs
8,333 units
Units
Carbonlite has high fixed costs ($5,000,000), also a high contribution margin ($600/bike). High BEP, but profits grow rapidly after FC are covered.

Figure 10.2a
Breakeven Point for Carbonlite

The breakeven point (BEP) for Carbonlite is 8,333 units, which occurs at the point where its total costs equal its total revenue.

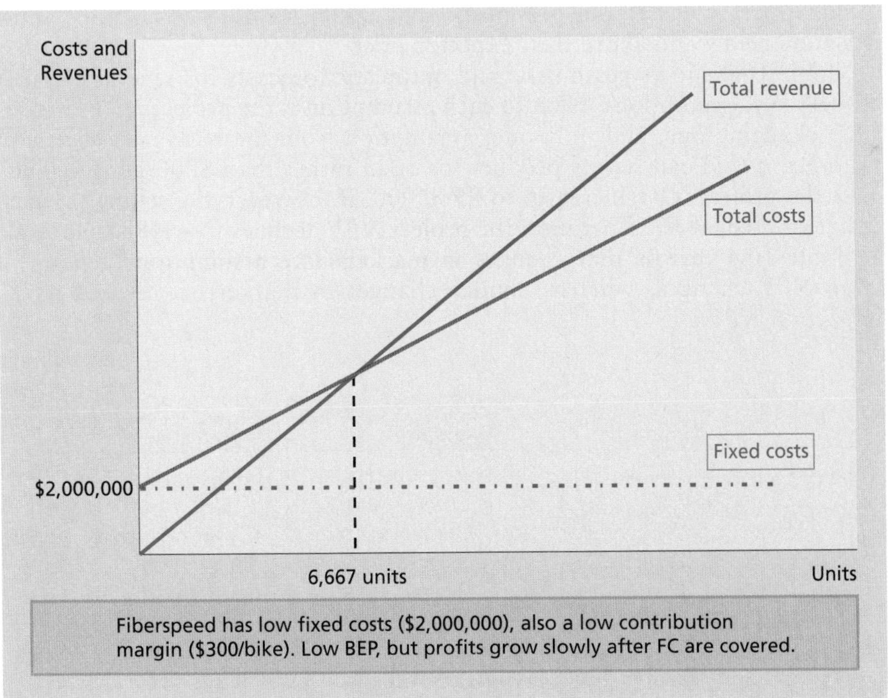
Costs and Revenues
Total revenue
Total costs
Fixed costs
$2,000,000
6,667 units
Units
Fiberspeed has low fixed costs ($2,000,000), also a low contribution margin ($300/bike). Low BEP, but profits grow slowly after FC are covered.

Figure 10.2b
Breakeven Point for Fiberspeed

The breakeven point (BEP) for Fiberspeed is 6,667 units, which occurs at the point where its total costs equal its total revenue.

APPLYING THE MODEL

Imagine that Greene Transportation Incorporated (GTI) has developed a new skateboard equipped with a gyroscope for improved balance. GTI's estimates indicate that **this project has a positive *NPV* of $236,000**, under the following base-case assumptions:

1. The project's life is five years.
2. The project requires an up-front investment of $7 million.
3. GTI will depreciate the initial investment on a straight-line basis over five years.
4. One year from now, the skateboard industry will sell 500,000 units.
5. Total market size (in units) will grow by 5 percent per year.
6. GTI expects to capture 5 percent of the market in the first year.
7. GTI expects to increase its market share by one percentage point each year after year 1.
8. The selling price will be $200 in year 1.
9. The selling price will decline by 10 percent per year after year 1.
10. All production costs are variable and will equal 60 percent of the selling price.
11. GTI's marginal tax rate is 30 percent.
12. The appropriate discount rate is 14 percent.

Under the base-case assumptions, the project's positive *NVP* of $236,000 is small relative to the $7-million investment. GTI's managers want to explore how sensitive the *NPV* is to changes in the assumptions. Analysts often begin a sensitivity analysis by developing both pessimistic and optimistic forecasts for each of the model's important assumptions. These forecasts may be based on subjective judgments about the range of possible outcomes or on historical data drawn from the firm's past investments. For example, a firm with historical data available on output prices may set the pessimistic and optimistic forecasts at one standard deviation below and above their expected price.

Table 10.4 shows pessimistic and optimistic forecasts for several of the *NPV* model's key assumptions. Next to each assumption is the project *NPV* that results from changing one, and only one, assumption from the base-case scenario. For example, if GTI can sell its product for $225 rather than $200 per unit the first year, the project *NPV* increases to $960,000. If, however, the selling price is less than expected, at $175 per unit, the project *NPV* declines to –$488,000. A glance at Table 10.4 reveals that changes in market-share assumptions generate very large *NPV* changes, whereas similar changes in market-size figures have less impact on *NPV*s.

Table 10.4
Sensitivity Analysis of the Gyroscope Skateboard Project (Base-case *NPV* = $236,000) (dollar values in thousands, except price)

NPV	Pessimistic	Assumption	Optimistic	*NPV*
–$ 558	$8,000	initial investment	$6,000	$1,030
–$ 343	450,000 units	market size in year 1	550,000 units	$ 815
–$ 73	2% per year	growth in market size	8% per year	$ 563
–$1,512	3%	initial market share	7%	$1,984
–$1,189	0%	growth in market share	2% per year	$1,661
–$ 488	$ 175	initial selling price	$ 225	$ 960
–$ 54	62% of sales	variable costs	58% of sales	$ 526
–$ 873	–20% per year	annual price change	0% per year	$1,612
–$ 115	16%	discount rate	12%	$ 617

Scenario Analysis and Monte Carlo Simulation

Scenario analysis is just a more complex form of sensitivity analysis. Rather than adjust one assumption up or down, analysts conduct scenario analysis by calculating the project *NPV* when a whole set of assumptions changes in a particular way. For example, if consumer interest in GTI's new skateboard is low, the project may achieve a lower market share and a lower selling price than originally anticipated. If production volume falls short of expectations, cost as a percentage of sales may also be higher than expected.

scenario analysis
A more complex form of *sensitivity analysis* that provides for calculating the decision variable, such as net present value, when a whole set of assumptions changes in a particular way.

Developing realistic scenarios requires a great deal of thinking about how an *NPV* model's assumptions are related to each other. Analysts must ask questions such as, if the market doesn't grow as fast as we expect, which other of our assumptions will also probably be wrong? As with sensitivity analysis, firms often construct a base-case scenario along with more pessimistic and optimistic ones. For instance, consider a worst-case scenario for GTI's new skateboard. Suppose Murphy's Law is manifested, and every pessimistic assumption from Table 10.4 becomes a reality. In that case, the project *NPV* is a disastrous negative $4.9 million. On the other hand, if all the optimistic assumptions turn out to be correct, then the *NPV* rises to $11.7 million. Neither of these outcomes is particularly surprising. If everything goes wrong, the company should expect an extremely negative *NPV*, and it should expect just the opposite if the project does better than predicted in every possible way. These scenarios are still useful because they illustrate the range of possible *NPV*s.

SMART CONCEPTS
See the concept explained step-by-step at SMARTFinance

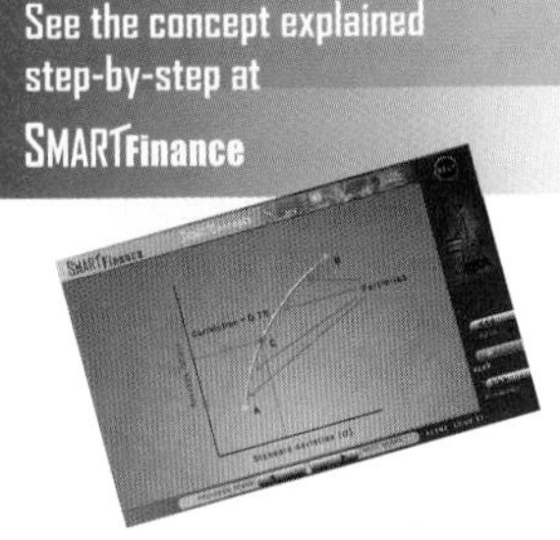

An even more sophisticated variation on this theme is **Monte Carlo simulation.** In a simulation, analysts specify a range or a probability distribution of potential outcomes for each of the model's assumptions. For example, a simulation could specify that GTI's skateboard price is a random variable drawn from a normal distribution with a mean of $200 and a standard deviation of $30. Similarly, the analyst could dictate that the skateboard could achieve an initial market share anywhere between 1 percent and 10 percent, with each outcome being equally likely (i.e., a uniform distribution). It is even possible to specify the degree of correlation between key variables. The model could be structured in such a way that when the demand for skateboards is unusually high, the likelihood of obtaining a high price increases.

Monte Carlo simulation
A sophisticated risk assessment technique that provides for calculating the decision variable, such as net present value, using a range or probability distribution of potential outcomes for each of a model's assumptions.

Analysts enter all the assumptions about distributions of possible outcomes into a spreadsheet. Next, a simulation software package begins to take random "draws" from these distributions, calculating the project's cash flows (and perhaps its *NPV*) over and over again, perhaps thousands or tens of thousands of times. After completing these calculations, the software package produces a large amount of statistical output, including the probability distribution of project cash flows (and *NPV*s) as well as sensitivity figures for each of the model's assumptions.

The use of Monte Carlo simulation has grown dramatically in the last decade because of steep declines in the costs of computer power and simulation software.[5] The bottom line is that simulation is a powerful, effective tool when used properly. Its fundamental appeal is that it provides decision makers with a probability distribution of *NPV*s rather than a single point estimate of the *expected NPV*. This improves the information available to decision makers by allowing them to consider the risk (probability distribution) as well as the expected value of *NPV*. Using simulation to explore the distribution of a project's cash flows and *NPV*s, and the major sources of uncertainty driving that distribution, is very sensible, and is expected to result in better investment decisions.

SMART PRACTICES VIDEO
David Nickel, Controller for Intel Communications Group, Intel Corp.
"One of the key things we try to do is to try to understand key scenarios."
See the entire interview at SMARTFinance

[5]. A few of the companies which have used Monte Carlo simulation include Merck, Intel, Procter & Gamble, General Motors, Pfizer, Owens-Corning, and Cummins Engine.

Decision Trees

SMART PRACTICES VIDEO

Pam Roberts, Executive Director of Corporate Services, Cummins Inc.

"We recognize that we can't predict each parameter with great accuracy."

See the entire interview at **SMARTFinance**

Most important investment decisions involve much more complexity than simply forecasting cash flows, discounting at the appropriate rate, and investing if the *NPV* exceeds zero. In the real world, managers face a sequence of future decisions that influence an investment's value. These decisions may include whether to expand or abandon a project, whether to alter a marketing program, when to upgrade manufacturing equipment, and, most important, how to respond to actions of competitors. A **decision tree** is a visual representation of the sequential choices that managers face over time with regard to a particular investment. Sketching out a decision tree is somewhat like thinking several moves ahead in a game of chess. The value of decision trees is that they force analysts to think through a series of "if-then" statements that describe how they will react as the future unfolds. The following example illustrates the use of decision trees.

decision tree
A visual representation of the sequential choices that managers face over time with regard to a particular investment.

APPLYING THE MODEL

Imagine that Trinkle Foods Limited of Canada has invented a new salt substitute, branded Odessa, which it plans to use to flavor consumer snack foods such as potato chips and crackers. The company is trying to decide whether to spend 5-million Canadian dollars (C$) to test-market a new line of potato chips flavored with Odessa, in Vancouver, British Columbia. Depending on the outcome of that test, Trinkle may spend an additional C$50 million one year later to launch a full line of snack foods across Canada. If consumer acceptance in Vancouver is high, the company predicts that its full product line will generate net cash inflows of C$12 million per year for ten years.[6] If consumers in Vancouver respond less favorably, Trinkle expects cash inflows from a nationwide launch to be just C$2 million per year for ten years. Trinkle's cost of capital equals 15 percent.

Figure 10.3 shows the decision tree for this problem. Initially, the firm can choose to spend the C$5 million on test-marketing or not. If Trinkle goes ahead with

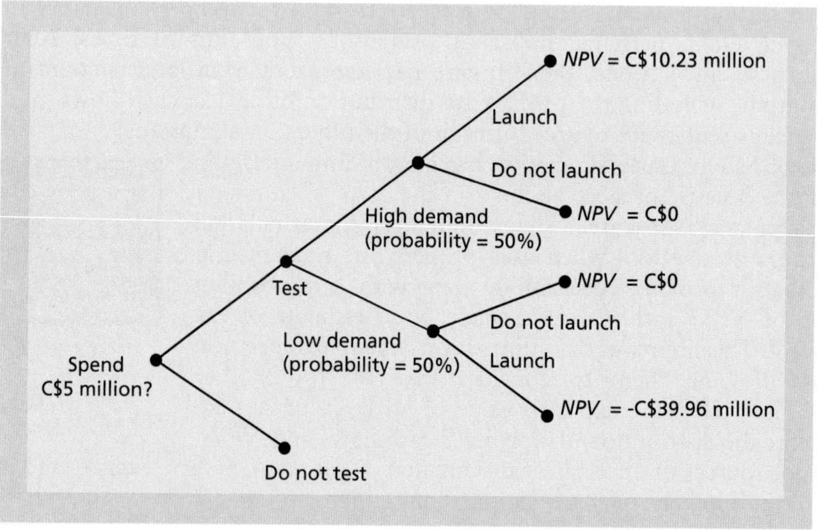

Figure 10.3
Decision Tree for Odessa Investment

The decision tree depicts the sequence of decisions facing Trinkle Foods' decision whether to spend C$5 million to test market Odessa, a new salt substitute. If the test market is successful, the NPV of launching the product is C$10.23 million; if the initial test results are negative, and it launches the product, it will have an NPV of –C$39.96 million.

6. Note that the test begins immediately, the C$50-million investment starts one year later, and the stream of C$12-million annual cash inflows begins one year after that.

the market test, it estimates the probability of high-and low-consumer acceptance to be 50 percent. Once the company sees the test results, it can decide whether to invest C$50 million for a major product launch.

The proper way to work through a decision tree is to begin at the end and work backward to the initial decision. Suppose one year from now, Trinkle learns that the Vancouver market test was successful. At that point, the *NPV* (in millions of Canadian dollars) of launching the product can be determined as follows:

$$NPV = -C\$50 + \frac{C\$12}{1.15^1} + \frac{C\$12}{1.15^2} + \frac{C\$12}{1.15^3} + \ldots + \frac{C\$12}{1.15^{10}} = C\$10.23$$

Clearly, Trinkle will invest if it winds up in this part of the decision tree, but what if initial test results are unfavorable and it launches the product? In that situation, the following *NPV* (in millions of Canadian dollars) results:

$$NPV = -C\$50 + \frac{C\$2}{1.15^1} + \frac{C\$2}{1.15^2} + \frac{C\$2}{1.15^3} + \ldots + \frac{C\$2}{1.15^{10}} = -C\$39.96$$

The best decision to make if the initial test does not go well is to walk away. After the test has been done, its cost is a *sunk cost*. Therefore, as of time 1, the *NPV* of doing nothing is zero.

Now we have a set of simple "if-then" decision rules that come from the decision tree. If initial test results indicate high consumer acceptance of Odessa, Trinkle should go ahead with the full product launch to capture a positive *NPV* of C$10.23 million. On the other hand, if initial results show that consumers do not particularly like foods flavored with Odessa, Trinkle should not invest the additional C$50 million.

Finally, with this information in hand, we can evaluate today's decision about whether to spend the C$5 million on testing. Recall that we calculated the *NPV*s in terms of year-1 dollars—that is, as of the date of the decision whether or not to launch the product nationwide. In terms of today's Canadian dollars (in millions), the expected *NPV* of conducting the market test is determined as follows:

$$NPV = -C\$5 + 0.5\left(\frac{C\$10.23}{1.15}\right) + 0.5\left(\frac{C\$0}{1.15}\right) = -C\$0.55$$

Spending the money for market testing does not appear to be worthwhile.

Evaluating the Role of Decision Trees. There is a very subtle flaw in the preceding analysis of Trinkle's proposed Odessa investment. Can you spot it? At the present time, when Trinkle must decide whether to invest in test-marketing, it does not know what the results of the test will be. One year later, when the firm chooses whether to invest C$50 million for a major product launch, it knows a great deal more. If Odessa is a big success in Vancouver, the risk that it will flop elsewhere in Canada may be very low. If so, does it make sense to use a discount rate of 15 percent when calculating the *NPV* of the product-launch decision? Even a one-point reduction in the discount rate, from 15 percent to 14 percent, would be sufficient to change Trinkle's decision about test-marketing.

Though decision trees are useful tools for sharpening strategic thinking, the previous example illustrates their most serious flaw. The risk of many investments changes as you move from one point in the decision tree to another. Worse, analysts have no obvious way to make adjustments to the discount rate to reflect these risk changes. That makes it very difficult to know whether the final *NPV* obtained from a decision tree is the correct one.

Another practical difficulty in using decision trees is determining the probabilities for each branch of the tree. Unless firms have a great deal of experience making similar "bets" over and over again, estimating these probabilities is more an art than a science. How does Trinkle Foods know that the probability of a successful Vancouver market test equals 50 percent? Why not 80 percent, or 10 percent? The only way to form even remotely reliable estimates of these probabilities is to rely on experience—your experience or the experience of others. For example, large pharmaceutical companies have enough experience investing in potential drug compounds to make reasonable estimates of the odds that any particular drug will ever make it to market.

CONCEPT REVIEW QUESTIONS

5. Why would a project that reaches the *breakeven point (BEP)* in terms of net income be potentially bad for shareholders?

6. Which variable do you think would be more valuable to examine in a project *sensitivity analysis*—the growth rate of sales or the allowable depreciation deductions each year? Explain.

7. You work for an airline that is considering a proposal to offer a new, nonstop flight between Atlanta and Tokyo. Senior management asks a team of analysts to run a *Monte Carlo simulation* of the project. Your job is to advise the group on what assumptions they should put in the simulation regarding the distribution of the ticket price your airline will be able to charge. How would you go about this task?

8. Why might the discount rate vary as you move through a *decision tree?*

10.3 REAL OPTIONS

Why *NPV* Doesn't Always Give the Right Answer

Only a few decades ago, the net present-value method was essentially absent from the world of corporate practice. Today, it has become the standard tool for evaluating capital investments, especially in very large firms. Even so, *NPV* can systematically overstate or understate the value of certain types of investments. These systematic errors occur because the *NPV* method is essentially static. That is, *NPV* calculations do not take into account actions by managers to increase the value of an investment once it has been made. When managers can react to changes in the environment in ways that alter an investment's value, we say that the investment has an embedded **real option.** A real option is the right, but not the obligation, to take a future action that changes an investment's value. We present an in-depth analysis of how option-pricing techniques can be used to improve capital budgeting processes in Chapter 15, so only an overview is presented here. Hopefully, this will be enough to convince you that identifying and valuing—even if only conceptually—the real options embedded in most capital investment projects can help managers make better investment decisions.

real option
The right, but not the obligation, to take a future action that changes an investment's value.

A simple example shows where *NPV* can go wrong. Suppose that you are bidding on the rights to extract oil from a proven site over the next year. You expect extraction costs from this field to run about \$33 per barrel. Currently, oil sells for \$30 per barrel. You know that oil prices fluctuate over time, but you do not possess any unique ability to predict where the price of oil is headed next. Accordingly, you assume that the price of oil follows a **random walk**, meaning that your best estimate of the future price of oil is just today's price. How much would you bid?

random walk
A description of the movement of the price of a financial asset over time. When prices follow a random walk, future and past prices are statistically unrelated, and the best forecast of the future price is simply the current price.

An *NPV* analysis would tell you not to bid at all. If your best forecast of the future price of oil is $30 per barrel, then you cannot make money when extraction costs are $33 per barrel. The expected *NPV* of this investment is negative, no matter how much oil you can pump out of the ground.

A real options approach to the problem yields a different answer. If you own the rights to extract oil, you are not obligated to do so without regard to the price of your output. You reason that you will pump oil only when the market price is high enough to justify incurring the extraction costs. Predicting exactly when the price of oil will be high enough to make pumping profitable is impossible, but historical price fluctuations persuade you that the price of oil will be higher than extraction costs at least some of the time. Therefore, extraction rights at this site are worth more than zero.[7]

The oil-extraction problem is analogous to the test-marketing problem in the previous section on decision trees. In both cases, managers have an option to choose whether to spend additional resources at a future date. These options add to a project's value in a way that *NPV* analysis, because of its static approach to decision making, cannot capture. In general, we can say that the value of a project equals the sum of two components—the part captured by *NPV* and the remaining value of real options.

$$\text{Project value} = NPV \pm \text{option value}$$

The *NPV* may either understate or overstate a project's value depending on whether the proposed investment creates or destroys future options for the firm. In the oil drilling example, buying extraction rights creates an option, the option to pump or not to pump oil in the future, and the *NPV* understates the investment's value. It is easy to imagine projects that eliminate options rather than create them. For instance, if the firm signs a long-term contract to supply a refinery with a certain quantity of crude oil each month, then it loses flexibility in the extraction decision.

Like Monte Carlo simulation, real-options analysis is growing in popularity in many industries. We defer a complete discussion of the real options approach to capital budgeting to Chapter 15. Instead, we now turn to a description of common types of real options encountered in capital budgeting decisions.

Types of Real Options

Expansion Options. What do companies do when one of their investments becomes a huge success? They look for new markets in which to expand that investment. For instance, in recent years DVD technology has gained enormous popularity. Not surprisingly, consumers can rent DVDs in video stores, grocery stores, and many other places where they were recently unavailable. The same is true for DVD players. The number of retail outlets selling DVD players has expanded dramatically. It is even possible in many major airports to rent a DVD player and a movie to watch during your flight.

Naturally, companies invest in expansion only for their most successful investments. As mentioned in the decision-tree problem, the risk of expanding an already-successful project is much less than the risk when the project begins. An *NPV* calculation misses both of these attributes—the *option to expand,* or not, depending on initial success, and the change in risk that occurs when the initial outcome is favorable.

7. To determine exactly how much these rights are worth, we have to use techniques that are presented later in Chapter 15.

Abandonment Options. Just as firms have the right to invest additional resources to expand projects that enjoy early success, they also can withdraw resources from projects that fail to live up to short-run expectations. In an extreme case, a firm may decide to withdraw its entire commitment to a particular project and exercise its *option to abandon.*

In legal systems that provide limited liability to corporations, shareholders have the ultimate abandonment option. A firm may borrow money to finance its operations, but if it cannot generate cash flow sufficient to pay back its debts, shareholders can declare bankruptcy, turn over the company's assets to lenders, and walk away. Although declaring bankruptcy is not what shareholders hope for when they invest, it offers shareholders considerable protection against personal liability for a firm's debts. Put another way, investors who buy shares are willing to pay a little more because of the option to abandon (in this case, the *default option*) than they would be willing to pay without that option.

$$\text{Share value} = NPV + \text{value of default option}$$

Consider the same situation from the perspective of lenders. When they commit funds to a corporation, lenders know that the borrower may default, and their ability to recover their losses does not extend to shareholders' personal assets. We could even say that when an investor buys a bond from a corporation, the investor is simultaneously selling an option to the firm—the option to default. Notice that this option to default is essentially absent in U.S. Treasury securities. Suppose that a Treasury bond and a corporate bond offer the same interest payments to investors. Which one would sell at a higher price?

$$\text{Corporate bond value} = \text{Treasury bond value} - \text{value of firm's default option}$$

Abandonment options crop up in unexpected places, and it is important for managers to recognize whether a given investment has an attached abandonment option or grants another party the right to abandon. Consider refundable and nonrefundable airline tickets. With a refundable ticket, the traveler has the right to abandon travel plans without incurring a penalty. Such a ticket is more valuable than one that requires a traveler to pay a penalty if plans change.

Follow-On Investment Options. A *follow-on investment option* is similar to an expansion option. It entitles a firm to make additional investments should earlier investments prove to be successful. The difference is that the subsequent investments are more complex than a simple expansion of the earlier ones.

Hollywood offers an excellent example of follow-on options. Did you know that the rights to movie sequels are sometimes bought and sold before the original movie is completed? By purchasing the right to produce a sequel, a studio obtains the opportunity to make an additional investment should the first film become a commercial success.

Flexibility Options. The final types of options that have recently come to prominence in capital budgeting analyses are collectively known as *flexibility options.* Three examples illustrate the nature of flexibility options. First, the ability to use multiple production inputs has been shown to create option value. An example of this *input flexibility* is a boiler that can switch between oil or gas as a fuel source, enabling managers to switch from one type of fuel to another as prices change. Second, the value of a flexible production technology, capable of producing (and switching between) a variety of outputs using the same basic plant and equipment, has been demonstrated. This type of *output/operating flexibility* creates value when output prices are volatile. Finally, the option value of maintaining excess production capacity that managers can utilize quickly to meet peaks in demand has been documented. Though costly to purchase and maintain, this *capacity flexibility* can be quite valuable in capital-intensive industries that are subject to wide swings in demand and long lead times for building new capacity.

The Surprising Link Between Risk and Real Option Values

Up to now, every valuation problem covered in this text satisfies the following statement: Holding other factors constant, an increase in an asset's risk decreases its price. If two bonds offer the same coupon, but investors perceive one to be riskier than the other, the safer bond will sell at a higher price. If two investment projects have identical cash flows, but one is riskier, analysts will discount the cash flows of the riskier project at a higher rate, resulting in a lower *NPV*.

SMART PRACTICES VIDEO

Andy Bryant, Executive Vice President of Finance and Enterprise Systems, Chief Financial Officer, Intel Corp.

"Option theory was always used to show why we should do something. I never saw an analysis that said why we should not do something."

See the entire interview at SMARTFinance

A surprising fact is that this relationship does not hold for options. For an explanation, we go back to the oil-extraction problem. The current price of oil is $30 per barrel, and extraction costs at a particular site are $33. The expected future price of oil is the same as the current price, $30, so an *NPV* calculation would say that this investment is worthless.

Consider two different scenarios regarding the future price of oil. In the low-risk scenario, the price of oil in the future will be $33 or $27, each with probability of one half. This means that the expected price of oil is still $30. However, both an *NPV* and an options analysis would conclude that bidding on the rights to this site is not a good idea because the price of oil will never be above the extraction cost of $33.

Next, think about the high-risk scenario. The price of oil may be $38 or $22 with equal probability, so again we have an expected price of $30. If the price turns out to be $22, extracting the oil clearly does not make sense. But if the price turns out to be $38, extracting oil generates a profit of $5 per barrel ($38 sale price – $33 extraction cost). Therefore, a real-options analysis would say that bidding low for the right to extract the oil is a sensible decision.

Why does more risk lead to higher option values? Notice in the two previous scenarios that the payoff from extracting oil is the same, no matter how low the price goes. At a price of $22 and at a price of $27, an oil producer would simply decline to incur extraction costs. A huge decline in the price of oil is no more costly than a small decline. On the other hand, the payoffs on the upside increase, the higher the price of oil goes. In other words, *options are characterized by unequal payoffs*. When the price of oil is extremely volatile, the potential benefits are quite large if prices rise. At the same time, if oil prices fall precipitously, there is no additional cost relative to a slight decline in prices. In either case, the payoff is zero.

CONCEPT REVIEW QUESTIONS

9. Give a real-world example of an *expansion option* and an *abandonment option.*

10. Use the language of *real options* to explain why riskier firms must pay higher interest rates when they borrow money.

10.4 STRATEGY AND CAPITAL BUDGETING

Competition and *NPV*

Finance textbooks tend to focus on the mechanics of project evaluation—how to calculate an *NPV* or *IRR*, how to estimate cash flows, how to select the right discount rate, and so on. This emphasis on technique is not entirely misplaced. Knowing how to apply quantitative discipline to the project selection process is very important. Nevertheless, experienced managers rarely make major investment decisions solely on the basis of *NPV* calculations. The best managers have a well-honed intuition that tells them why a particular project should or should not be a good investment. Their business acumen helps them recognize projects that will create shareholder value, even if the *NPV*s calculated by financial analysts are negative, and to avoid investments that will destroy value, even when the *NPV*s are positive.[8]

No textbook can adequately substitute for the invaluable experience of making many investment decisions over several years, watching some of them succeed and some of them fail. However, there are certain common characteristics shared by projects that enhance shareholder value, and in this section we give you some guidance on how to identify these characteristics.

SMART ETHICS VIDEO

Jon Olson, Vice President of Finance, Intel Corp.

"Our job at the company is to test the limits, not just create financial analysis that ratifies peoples' intuition."

See the entire interview at **SMARTFinance**

Recall some of the most basic lessons from microeconomics about a perfectly competitive market. In such a market, there are many buyers and sellers trading a homogeneous product or service. Because every agent in the market is small relative to the market as a whole, everyone behaves as a price taker. Competition and the lack of entry or exit barriers for sellers ensures that the product's market price equals the marginal cost of producing it, and no firm earns pure economic profit.[9] In a market with zero economic profits, the *NPV* of any investment equals zero because every project earns just enough to recover the cost of capital—no more and no less.

Therefore, if we want to form an intuitive judgment about whether or not an investment proposal should have a positive *NPV* (before actually calculating the *NPV*), we have to identify ways in which the project deviates from the perfectly competitive ideal. For instance, if the proposal calls for production of a new good, is there something about this good that clearly differentiates it from similar goods already in the market? If the new product is genuinely unique, will the firm producing this good be able to erect some kind of entry barrier that will prevent other firms from producing their own nearly identical versions of the product, thereby competing away any pure economic profits?

Competitive advantages of this sort can come in many forms. One firm may have superior engineering or R&D talent that generates a continuous stream of innovative products. Another may excel at low-cost manufacturing processes. Still another may create a sustainable competitive advantage through its unique marketing programs.

---

8. One of the authors of this textbook had a humbling (but also awe-inspiring) lesson in the intuitive powers of good managers. On a consulting assignment for a Fortune 100 corporation, the author was asked to evaluate the assumptions of a firm's *NPV* calculations for a major acquisition. After gathering thousands of data points and running a week or two of simulations, the author was prepared to present his work to the chief financial officer (CFO). "From my work, I can tell you what the probability is that this acquisition will never be profitable for your company," claimed the intrepid author. "But I already know that," the CFO responded. In a fit of hubris, the author challenged, "OK, tell me what you think that probability is." After hearing the CFO's response, the author had to admit that after several weeks of work, he had arrived at exactly the same probability estimate that the CFO had reached intuitively.

9. Remember that the notion of "economic profit" is very different from accounting profit. If a firm makes a *zero economic profit*, it earns just enough to pay competitive prices for the labor, materials, and capital that it uses to produce a good or service.

The main point is that *if any project is to have a positive NPV, advocates of that project ought to be able to articulate the project's competitive advantage even before "running the numbers."* No matter how positive the project's *NPV* appears to be on paper, if no one can explain its main competitive advantage in the market, the firm should probably think twice about investing. Similarly, when an investment proposal has a compelling story explaining its competitive edge but the *NPV* numbers come out negative, it may be worth sending the financial analysts back to their desks to take a second look at their assumptions.[10]

Strategic Thinking and Real Options

We conclude this chapter with a return to the topic of real options. The technical aspects of calculating the real-option value of a given project (which we cover in Chapter 15) can be quite complex. Real-options techniques are still relatively new and are used extensively by only a handful of firms in a few industries. Though we expect an increasing number of firms to include real-options analysis as part of their standard capital budgeting approach, we believe that just thinking about a project from a real-options perspective can be valuable, even if coming up with a dollar value for a real option proves to be elusive.

Investments generally have real-option value as long as they are not "all-or-nothing" bets. Almost all investments fit this description. Managers usually have opportunities to make decisions subsequent to the initial investment that can increase or decrease its value. These decisions can create (or perhaps destroy) an investment's option value. To maximize an investment's option value, or at least to recognize that value, managers should try to describe up front, before the firm commits to an investment, all the subsequent decisions they will make as events unfold. In other words, managers must articulate their strategy for a given investment. This strategy should consist of a series of statements like these:

- If sales in the first year exceed our expectations, then we will commit another $50 million to increase production.
- If consumers enjoy sending and receiving e-mail on their cell phones, then we will be prepared to invest additional resources so that our cell phones will be capable of performing other tasks on the Internet.
- If our MP3 player cannot hold as many songs as the leading model, the unit must weigh at least two ounces less than the market leader, or we will not commit the resources necessary to manufacture it.

This series of "if-then" statements is necessary to value a real option. But it also has intangible value because it forces managers to think through their strategic options before they invest. Identifying a real option is tantamount to identifying future points at which it may be possible for managers to create and sustain competitive advantages.

11. Why must manager intuition be part of the investment-decision process regardless of a project's *NPV* or *IRR?* Why is it helpful to think about *real options* when making an investment decision?

CONCEPT REVIEW QUESTION

[10] We want to emphasize here that we still believe the numbers are extremely important. Our point is that *the numbers and the intuition should line up*. When they are in conflict, managers need to think hard about whether the NPV model is in error or whether the project lacks a true competitive advantage. These conflicts can also result from human factors, as explained in Chapter 9, Section 9.5.

10.5 SUMMARY AND CONCLUSIONS

- All-equity firms can discount their "standard" investment projects at the cost of equity. Managers can estimate the cost of equity using the CAPM.
- The cost of equity is influenced by a firm's cost structure (operating leverage) as well as by its financial structure (financial leverage).
- Firms with both debt and equity in their capital structures can use the weighted-average cost of capital, or *WACC*, to discount the cash flows of investments that do not change the firm's cost structure or financial structure.
- The *WACC* equals the weighted average of the cost of each source of financing used by a firm, with the weights equal to the proportion of the market value of each source of financing.
- The *WACC* and the CAPM are connected in that the cost of debt and equity (and any other financing source) are driven by the betas of the firm's debt and equity. Rather than calculate betas for preferred stock and debt, we can estimate their returns using dividend yield for preferred stock and yield-to-maturity (YTM) for debt.
- The *WACC* can be calculated on both a pretax and an after-tax basis. Because in the United States interest payments to bondholders are tax deductible, we typically focus on the after-tax *WACC* formula.
- A variety of tools exist to assist managers in understanding the sources of uncertainty in a project's cash flows. These tools include breakeven analysis, sensitivity analysis, scenario analysis, Monte Carlo simulation, and decision trees.
- The value of many investments includes not just the *NPV*, but also the investment's option value. As a static analytical tool, *NPV* misses the value of management's ability to alter an investment's value in response to environmental changes that may occur after an investment is made.
- Types of real options include the option to expand, the option to abandon, the option to make follow-on investments, and flexibility options related to production items such as inputs, outputs, and capacity.
- An investment's option value, unlike its *NPV*, increases as risk increases.
- For an investment to have a positive *NPV*, it should have a competitive advantage, something that distinguishes it from the economic ideal of perfect competition.
- Determining an investment's option value requires strategic thinking. Articulating the strategy may be as important as calculating the option value.

SELF-TEST PROBLEMS

Answers to Self-Test Problems appear in Appendix D at back of book. Answers to the Concept Review Questions throughout the chapter appear at http://megginson.swlearning.com.

ST10-1. A financial analyst for Quality Investments, a diversified investment fund, has gathered the following information for the years 2005 and 2006 on two firms—A and B—that it is considering adding to its portfolio. Of particular concern are the operating and financial risks of each firm.

	2005		2006	
	Firm A	Firm B	Firm A	Firm B
Sales ($ million)	10.7	13.9	11.6	14.6
EBIT ($ million)	5.7	7.4	6.2	8.1
Assets ($ million)			10.7	15.6
Debt ($ million)			5.8	9.3
Interest ($ million)			0.6	1.0
Equity ($ million)			4.9	6.3

a. Use the data provided to assess the *operating leverage* of each firm (using 2005 as the point of reference). Which firm has more operating leverage?

b. Use the data provided to assess each firm's *ROE* (Cash to equity/Equity), assuming the firm's Return on Assets is 10 percent and 20 percent in each case. Which firm has more *financial leverage?*

c. Use your findings in parts (a) and (b) to compare and contrast the operating and financial risks of Firms A and B. Which firm is more risky? Explain.

ST10-2. Sierra Vista Industries (SVI) wishes to estimate its cost of capital for use in analyzing projects that are similar to those that already exist. The firm's current capital structure, in terms of market value, includes 40 percent debt, 10 percent preferred stock, and 50 percent common stock. The firm's debt has an average yield-to-maturity of 8.3 percent. Its preferred stock has a $70 par value, an 8 percent dividend, and is currently selling for $76 per share. SVI's beta is 1.05, the risk-free rate is 4 percent, and the return on the S&P 500 (the market proxy) is 11.4 percent. SVI is in the 40 percent marginal tax bracket.

a. What are SVI's pretax costs of debt, preferred stock, and common stock?

b. Calculate SVI's weighted average cost of capital (*WACC*) on both a pretax and an after-tax basis. Which *WACC* should SVI use when making investment decisions?

c. SVI is contemplating a major investment that is expected to increase both its operating and financial leverage. Its new capital structure will contain 50 percent debt, 10 percent preferred stock, and 40 percent common stock. As a result of the proposed investment, the firm's average yield-to-maturity on debt is expected to increase to 9 percent, the market value of preferred stock is expected to fall to its $70 par value, and its beta is expected to rise to 1.15. What effect will this investment have on SVI's *WACC?* Explain your finding.

INTERNET RESOURCES

Note: *For updates to links, please go to the book's Web site at* http://megginson.swlearning.com

http://www.quicken.com—Contains information relevant to calculating the *WACC*, including equity betas, total market value of equity, and debt-to-equity ratios

http://valuation.ibbotson.com—A fee-based site with cost-of-capital estimates for more than 300 industries.

http://www.stern.nyu.edu/~adamodar—Web site of NYU professor Aswath Damodaran; contains downloadable data sets with levered and unlevered industry betas, as well as industry-level estimates of the cost of capital.

KEY TERMS

breakeven analysis
breakeven point (BEP)
contribution margin
decision tree
financial leverage
Monte Carlo simulation
operating leverage
random walk
real option
scenario analysis
sensitivity analysis
weighted average cost of capital (*WACC*)

QUESTIONS AND PROBLEMS

Q10-1. Explain when firms should discount projects using the cost of equity. When should they use the *WACC* instead? When should they use neither?

Q10-2. If a firm takes actions that increase its *operating leverage,* we can expect to see an increase in its equity beta. Why?

Q10-3. Firm A and Firm B plan to raise $1 million to finance identical projects. Firm A finances the project with 100 percent equity, whereas firm B uses a 50-50 mix of debt and equity. The interest rate on the debt equals 7 percent. At what rate of return on the investment (i.e., assets) will the rate of return on equity be the same for Firms A and B? (Hint: Think through Table 10.2.)

Q10-4. Why do you think it is important to use the market values of debt and equity, rather than book values, to calculate a firm's *WACC?*

Q10-5. Assuming that there are no corporate income taxes, how can the costs of preferred stock and debt be estimated without finding a preferred stock and a bond beta?

Q10-6. What are the three main lessons learned about choosing the right discount rate for use in evaluating capital budgeting projects?

Q10-7. How does the calculation of the after-tax *WACC* differ from that of the before-tax *WACC?* Which method is typically applied in the United States? Why?

Q10-8. In what sense could one argue that if managers make decisions using *breakeven analysis,* they are not maximizing shareholder wealth? How can breakeven analysis be modified to solve this problem?

Q10-9. Explain the differences between *sensitivity analysis* and *scenario analysis.* Offer an argument for the proposition that scenario analysis offers a more realistic picture of a project's risk than sensitivity analysis does.

Q10-10. In Chapter 9, we discussed how one can calculate the *NPV* of earning an MBA. Suppose that you are asked to do a sensitivity analysis on the MBA decision. Which of the following factors do you think would have a larger impact on the degree's *NPV?*

a. The ranking of the school you choose to attend
b. Your choice of a major
c. Your GPA
d. The state of the job market when you graduate

Q10-11. Suppose you want to use a *decision tree* to model, based on economic considerations, the decision of whether to pursue an MBA degree. What would such a decision tree look like?

Q10-12. If you decide to invest in pursuing an MBA degree, what is your *abandonment option*? What is your *follow-on investment option?*

Q10-13. Your company is selling the mineral rights to several hundred acres of land that it owns and believes to contain silver deposits. The current price of silver is $5 per ounce, but of course, future prices are uncertain. If investors believe that silver prices will be more volatile in the future than they have been in the past, would you expect the mineral rights to sell for more or less? Explain.

PROBLEMS

Choosing the Right Discount Rate

P10-1. Krispy Kreme Doughnuts (KKD) has a capital structure consisting almost entirely of equity.

a. If the beta of KKD stock equals 1.6, the risk-free rate equals 6 percent, and the expected return on the market portfolio equals 11 percent, what is KKD's cost of equity?

b. Suppose that a 1 percent increase in expected inflation causes a 1 percent increase in the risk-free rate. Holding all other factors constant, what will this do to the firm's cost of equity? Is it reasonable to hold all other factors constant? What other part of the calculation of the cost of equity is likely to change if expected inflation rises?

P10-2. Fournier Industries, a publicly traded waste disposal company, is a highly leveraged firm with 70 percent debt, 0 percent preferred stock, and 30 percent common equity financing. Currently the risk-free rate is about 4.5 percent, and the return on the *S&P* 500 (the market proxy) is 12.7 percent. The firm's beta is currently estimated to be 1.65.

a. What is Fournier's current cost of equity?

b. If the firm shifts its capital structure to a less highly leveraged position by selling preferred stock and using the proceeds to retire debt, it expects its beta to drop to 1.20. What is its cost of equity in this case?

c. If the firm shifts its capital structure to a less highly leveraged position by selling additional shares of common stock and using the proceeds to retire debt, it expects its beta to drop to 0.95. What is its cost of equity in this case?

d. Discuss the potential impact of the two strategies discussed in parts (b) and (c) above on Fournier's weighted-average cost of capital (*WACC*).

P10-3. In its 2001 annual report, The Coca-Cola Company reported sales of $20.09 billion for fiscal year 2001 and $19.89 billion for fiscal year 2000. The company also reported operating income (roughly equivalent to *EBIT*) of $5.35 billion, and $3.69 billion in 2001 and 2000, respectively. Meanwhile, arch-rival PepsiCo, Inc. reported sales of $26.94 billion in 2001 and $25.48 billion in 2000. PepsiCo's operating profit was 4.03 billion in 2001 and $3.82 billion in 2000. Based on these figures, which company had higher operating leverage?

SMART SOLUTIONS

See the problem and solution explained step-by-step at SMARTFinance

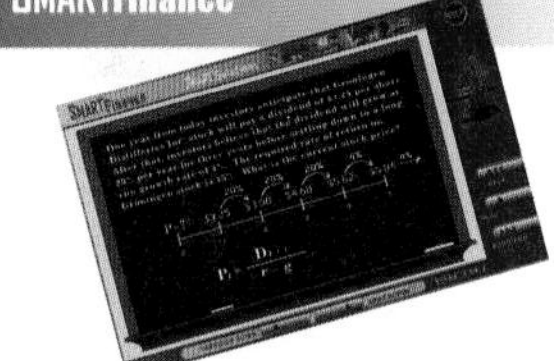

P10-4. Gail and Company had the following sales and *EBIT* during the years 2004 through 2006.

	2004	2005	2006
Sales ($ million)	75.2	82.7	95.1
EBIT ($ million)	26.3	30.5	36.0

a. Use the data provided to assess Gail and Company's operating leverage over the following periods

(1) 2004–2005
(2) 2005–2006
(3) 2004–2006

b. Compare, contrast, and discuss the firm's operating leverage between the 2004–2005 period and the 2005–2006 period. Explain any differences.

c. Compare the operating leverage for the entire 2004–2006 period to the values found for the 2005–2006 and 2005–2006 periods and explain the differences.

P10-5. Firm 1 has a capital structure with 20 percent debt and 80 percent equity. Firm 2's capital structure consists of 50 percent debt and 50 percent equity. Both firms pay 7 percent annual interest on their debt. Finally, suppose both firms have invested in assets worth $100 million. Calculate the *return on equity* (*ROE*) for each firm, assuming the following:

a. The return on assets is 3 percent.
b. The return on assets is 7 percent.
c. The return on assets is 11 percent.

What general pattern do you observe?

P10-6. Firm A's capital structure contains 20 percent debt and 80 percent equity. Firm B's capital structure contains 50 percent debt and 50 percent equity. Both firms pay 7 percent annual interest on their debt. The stock of Firm A has a beta of 1.0, and the stock of Firm B has a beta of 1.375. The risk-free rate of interest equals 4 percent, and the expected return on the market portfolio equals 12 percent.

a. Calculate the *WACC* for each firm, assuming there are no taxes.
b. Recalculate the *WACC* figures, assuming that the firms face a marginal tax rate of 34 percent.
c. Explain how taking taxes into account in part (b) changes your answer found in part (a).

P10-7. A firm has a capital structure containing 60 percent debt and 40 percent common stock equity. Its outstanding bonds offer investors a 6.5 percent yield-to-maturity. The risk-free rate currently equals 5 percent, and the expected risk premium on the market portfolio equals 6 percent. The firm's common stock beta is 1.20.

a. What is the firm's required return on equity?
b. Ignoring taxes, use your finding in part (a) to calculate the firm's *WACC*.
c. Assuming a 40 percent marginal tax rate, recalculate the firm's *WACC* found in part (b).
d. Compare and contrast the values for the firm's *WACC* found in parts (b) and (c).

P10-8. Dingel Inc. is attempting to evaluate three alternative capital structures—A, B, and C. The following table shows the three structures along with relevant cost data. The firm is subject to a 40 percent marginal tax rate. The risk-free rate is 5.3 percent and the market return is currently 10.7 percent.

	Capital Structure		
Item	A	B	C
Debt ($ million)	35	45	55
Preferred Stock ($ million)	0	10	10
Common Stock ($ million)	65	45	35
Total Capital ($ million)	100	100	100
Debt (yield-to-maturity)	7.0%	7.5%	8.5%
Annual Preferred Stock Dividend	—	$ 2.80	$ 2.20
Preferred Stock (Market Price)	—	$30.00	$21.00
Common Stock Beta	0.95	1.10	1.25

a. Calculate the after-tax cost of debt for each capital structure.
b. Calculate the cost of preferred stock for each capital structure.
c. Calculate the cost of common stock for each capital structure.
d. Calculate the weighted average cost of capital (*WACC*) for each capital structure.
e. Compare the *WACC*s calculated in part (d) and discuss the impact of the firm's financial leverage on its *WACC* and its related risk.

P10-9. A firm has a capital structure containing 40 percent debt, 20 percent preferred stock, and 40 percent common stock equity. The firm's debt has a yield-to-maturity of 8.1 percent, its annual preferred stock dividend is $3.10, and the preferred stock's current market price is $50.00 per share. The firm's common stock has a beta of 0.90, and the risk-free rate and the market return are currently 4.0 percent and 13.5 percent, respectively. The firm is subject to a 40 percent marginal tax rate.

a. What is the firm's cost of preferred stock?
b. What is the firm's cost of common stock?
c. Calculate the firm's after-tax *WACC*.
d. Recalculate the firm's *WACC*, assuming that its capital structure is deleveraged to contain 20 percent debt, 20 percent preferred stock, and 60 percent common stock.
e. Compare, contrast, and discuss your findings from parts (c) and (d).

A Closer Look at Risk

P10-10. Alliance Pneumatic Manufacturing, a specialty machine-tool producer, has fixed costs of $200 million per year. Across all the firm's products, the average contribution margin equals $1,200. What is Alliance's breakeven point in terms of units sold?

P10-11. Turn to the values in Table 10.4 on page 436. Determine which of the following has the greater effect on the *NPV* of the gyroscope skateboard project—an increase in the selling price of 12.5 percent (compared to the base case) or an increase in the size of the market of 10 percent in year 1.

P10-12. JK Manufacturing is considering a new product and is unsure about its price as well as the variable cost associated with it. JK's marketing department believes that the firm can sell the product for $500 per unit, but feel that if the initial market response is weak, the price may have to be 20% lower in order to be competitive with exisiting products. The firm's best estimates of its costs are fixed costs of $3.6 million and variable cost of $325 per unit. Concern exists with regard to the variable cost per unit due to currently volatile raw material and labor costs. Although the firm expects this cost to be about $325 per unit, it could be as much as 8 percent above that value. The firm expects to sell about 50,000 units per year.

a. Calculate the firm's volume *breakeven point* (*BEP*) assuming its initial estimates are accurate.
b. Perform a sensitivity analysis by calculating the breakeven point for all combinations of the sale price per unit and variable cost per unit. (Hint: There are four combinations.)
c. In the best case, how many units will the firm need to sell to break even?
d. In the worst case, how many units will the firm need to sell to break even?
e. If each of the possible price/variable cost combinations is equally probable, what is the firm's expected breakeven point?
f. Based on your finding in part (e), should the firm go forward with the proposed new product? Explain why.

P10-13. Consumer Products, Inc. (CPI) is considering performing a feasibility study for a new product available from one of its foreign suppliers. Because CPI will have to make an initial investment of $20 million to obtain exclusive U.S. marketing rights to the product, the firm is contemplating performing a feasibility study of the product's market potential. The cost of the study, which will take two years to complete, is an up-front fee of $2 million. Included in this cost is an exclusive option that gives CPI two years in which to make the decision to pay the foreign supplier the $20 million. If CPI performs the feasibility study, its preliminary estimates indicate that there is a 50 percent chance of strong product demand, which will result in cash inflows of $5.2 million per year for eight years; there is a 20 percent chance of moderate product demand, which will result in cash inflows of $4.5 million per year for eight years; and there is a 30 percent chance of weak demand, which will result in cash inflows of $4.0 million per year for eight years. Note that the $20 million would be paid at the end of year 2, immediately after the feasibility study is completed and that all outcomes will provide only eight years of cash inflows. CPI's cost of capital applicable to the proposed new product decision is 12 percent.

a. Draw the *decision tree* associated with CPI's proposed feasibility study.
b. Calculate the *NPV* associated with each of the possible product demand outcomes—strong, moderate, and weak.
c. Find the expected *NPV* of performing the feasibility study.
d. Based on your findings in part (c), what recommendation would you give CPI about the proposed feasibility study? Explain.

Real Options

P10-14. Stanley Marcus, a financial intern at Mega Manufacturing Company (MMC), was asked by the CFO to review the *NPV* calculations on a major new product investment. After analyzing the cash flows and other calculations, Stanley confirmed that the *NPV* was $1.5 million. In the process of investigating all aspects of the project and its cash flows, Stanley learned that should the new product be successful, it would open the door to a number of opportunities to further expand the firm's product line. Using option-valuation techniques that he learned in an advanced finance course, he estimated the value of these expansion options to be $0.45 million.

a. Based on Stanley's analysis, what is the value of the proposed new product investment?

b. How can Stanley explain the value found in part (b) to the CFO, who is unfamiliar with the concept of *real options?*

P10-15. Tech Industries, a contract manufacturer of circuit boards, is evaluating an investment in a new production line to handle the growing demand from its customers, who produce consumer electronic products. Based on reasonable growth assumptions, the *NPV* of the new production line was found to be –$2.3 million. Management feels obligated to therefore reject the project. It recognizes that the production line would provide a high degree of output flexibility because it could be repurposed easily and inexpensively to produce circuit boards for numerous other applications. The firm's project analyst estimated the value of this *output flexibility option* to be $3.3 million.

a. Based on the information provided, what is the true value of Tech Industries's proposed new production line?

b. What recommendation would you give Tech Industries regarding the proposed new production line? Explain.

THOMSON ONE Business School Edition

For instructions on using Thomson ONE, refer to the instructions provided with the Thomson ONE problems at the end of Chapters 1–6 or to "A Guide for Using Thomson ONE."

P10-16. Compare the *operating leverage* of Toyota Motor Corp. (ticker: J:TYMO) with that of Nissan Motor Company Limited (J:NR@N), using financial information from the last five years. Which company has the higher operating leverage and why? Which company do you expect will have the higher beta? Check the reported betas on Thomson ONE to see if they match your expectations.

P10-17. Conduct a similar analysis on *financial leverage* for the same two companies in Problem 10-16.

Since these exercises depend upon real-time data, your answers will change continuously depending upon when you access the Internet to download your data.

MINICASE

Risk and Capital Budgeting

The Chief Executive Officer (CEO) of Blankson Manufacturing, Incorporated asks to meet with you, the firm's Financial Analyst. The intention of this meeting is for you to answer her questions regarding how the firm assesses project risk. She will use this information when she presents some major capital budgeting recommendations to the Board of Directors for their approval. To assist you in preparing for this meeting your Management Assistant took it upon himself to ask for a list of possible questions. As a result, the CEO has submitted the following questions for you to answer.

ASSIGNMENT

1. How do the concepts of *marginal benefits* (*MB*) and *marginal costs* (*MC*) relate to the evaluation of project risk and capital budgeting decisions?
2. In what case would the cost of equity be the appropriate discount rate to use to calculate a project's *NPV*?
3. How would managers estimate the cost of equity?
4. How would the mix of a company's fixed and variable costs (cost structure) affect the firm's beta?
5. How might managers assess or measure how the firm's cost structure affects its risk?
6. How would *financial leverage* affect company risk?
7. When a company adds debt to its capital structure, how does it affect its discount rate?
8. How do taxes affect the *WACC*?
9. What other techniques might managers use to gauge the risk associated with possible capital investments?

Smart *Excel* Appendix

Appendix Contents

Use the Smart *Excel* spreadsheets and animated tutorials at http://smartfinance.swlearning.com.

EXCEL PREREQUISITES

You need to be familiar with the following *Excel* features to use this appendix:

- Move or Copy a worksheet
- Delete a worksheet
- Rename a worksheet

If this is new to you be sure to complete the ***Excel Prereqs*** tab in the Chapter 10 *Excel* file located **at the Smart Finance Web site** before proceeding.

RISK AND CAPITAL BUDGETING

Chapter 10 considers the risk dimension of project analysis. This appendix explains how to apply *Excel* to use three tools commonly used to analyze the sources of uncertainty of a project's cash flows: breakeven analysis, sensitivity analysis and scenario analysis.

One reason we have emphasized building models in the *Excel* appendices is that often input assumptions are not known with certainty. A well-built model enables the user to easily change the input assumptions and analyze the effect on output. This provides valuable information and can enhance decision making.

Now consider a common tool for analysis of risk: breakeven.

BREAKEVEN ANALYSIS

Problem: Consider the data provided on Carbonlite and Fiberspeed in Table 10.1. Create a model to find *EBIT* for each firm. Carbonlite management also wants to know how many units each firm must sell to reach *EBIT* equal to zero or breakeven.

Approach: Create a simple model to calculate *EBIT* and breakeven.

Try it yourself in a blank *Excel* file. Think about what to include in the input section and how to set up your calculations and output.

Find *EBIT* and breakeven quantity for Carbonlite and Fiberspeed.

Breakeven = Fixed costs / (Sales price per unit – Variable cost per unit)

Be sure to use the parentheses in your equation to ensure the correct order of mathematical operations.

Alternatively, you can use the setup file provided on the ***Breakeven*** tab of the Chapter 10 *Excel* file located at the Smart Finance Web site.

You should get the following results:

Calculations and Output

	Carbonlite	Fiberspeed
Revenues	10,000,000	10,000,000
Fixed costs	5,000,000	2,000,000
Variable costs	4,000,000	7,000,000
EBIT	1,000,000	1,000,000
Breakeven quantity	8,333	6,667

Apply it

- ***What is the significance of breakeven to Carbonlite and Fiberspeed?***
  Breakeven is calculated here by setting *EBIT* to zero. The breakeven shows the number of units each firm must sell to cover fixed and variable costs. Breakeven is significantly higher for Carbonlite than for Fiberspeed due to the higher operating leverage of Carbonlite.

Breakeven provides useful information to firms contemplating new projects. Often, in project analysis, many input assumptions are unknown. As you saw in Chapter 9, changing key input assumptions can have a significant effect on net present value and internal rate of return. Breakeven provides additional information for use in project analysis, because the firm can estimate the number of units that must be sold to cover fixed and variable costs. Management can then assess the probability of reaching breakeven sales.

SENSITIVITY ANALYSIS

Another tool for analyzing risk is sensitivity analysis. In sensitivity analysis, one variable is changed, while all others are held constant. This can be repeated for all uncertain variables. The exercise illustrates which variables the output is sensitive to. We have conducted sensitivity analysis throughout these appendices, but look at this technique in more detail here.

You can conduct sensitivity analysis in our models in several ways.

1. Simply change one input assumption and note the effect on output.
2. Create a formula to analyze the effect of different input values on output.
3. Create a data table to analyze the effect of different input values on output.

Apply Approach 1

- ***Suppose Carbonlite management is uncertain about future unit sales.***
  Use the first approach to analyze the sensitivity of **EBIT** ***to unit sales. Simply change the input assumption on sales volume.***

  What if sales are only 9,000 units?
  What if sales are 11,500 units?

	Carbonlite *EBIT*	Fiberspeed *EBIT*
9,000 units	$400,000	$700,000
11,500 units	$1,900,000	$1,450,000

Carbonlite's *EBIT* is more sensitive than Fiberspeed's *EBIT* to changes in sales due to the firm's higher operating leverage.

Apply Approach 2

- *Now use the second approach to analyze the sensitivity of Carbonlite* EBIT *to sales volume. Allow volume to vary between 5,000 and 15,000 units.*

To use this approach:

First, use the fill-series feature to set up a range of sales volume from 5,000 to 15,000 on the ***Sensitiv*** tab of the Chapter 10 file.

Next, create a formula for *EBIT* that can be copied down the column of sales volume inputs.

The result is:

Unit Sales	*EBIT*
5,000	(2,000,000)
6,000	(1,400,000)
7,000	(800,000)
8,000	(200,000)
9,000	400,000
10,000	1,000,000
11,000	1,600,000
12,000	2,200,000
13,000	2,800,000
14,000	3,400,000
15,000	4,000,000

Apply Approach 3

- *Use Approach three: create a data table to analyze the sensitivity of Carbonlite* EBIT *to sales volume. Allow volume to vary between 5,000 and 15,000 units.*

This is an example of a one-variable data table: the variable is sales volume. Data tables were introduced in Chapter 3. See the Chapter 3 ***Excel Prereqs*** tab if you need to review.

1. The data table is controlled by cell D56. Enter a cell reference to *EBIT* in this cell.
2. Either copy the various sales assumptions from approach 2 or use the fill-series feature in cells C57 through C67.
3. Select the cells in the data table, cells C56:D67.
4. Create the data table by accessing the data menu and selecting table.
5. Do not use the row input cell because this is a one-variable data table with the data in the column. The column input cell is the sales assumption in cell C22. Press OK.

The result is a data table showing *EBIT* at various sales levels. The solution yields the same results as approach 2.

Which approach is best? *It depends. Approach 1 is easy and allows you to simply and quickly perform sensitivity analysis. You also see all calculations and output. Approaches 2 and 3 allow you to see at once the output for more possible input values. With complex calculations, data tables may be simpler to use than Approach 2 and may allow for two-variable analysis.*

Sensitivity analysis may be applied to other input assumptions as well.

SCENARIO ANALYSIS

A third tool for analyzing risk is scenario analysis. In scenario analysis, multiple input assumptions are changed to create likely scenarios. Often scenario analysis includes a base case, best case and worst case, though any number of scenarios can be created.

Scenarios can be created in our models in three ways.

1. Simply change the relevant input assumptions in the model and note the effect on output.
2. Copy the model elsewhere on the sheet and change the input assumptions to create alternative scenarios that are all visible.
3. Copy the sheet to create a separate sheet for each scenario.

Which approach is best? *It depends. Approach 1 is easy and allows you to simply and quickly perform scenario analysis, but you can only view the results of one scenario at a time. Approach 2 is not as fast but allows you to view all results at once and on the same sheet. This works well if the model is not too large. Approach 3 is fairly quick to create and also allows you to have multiple scenarios at once, but only one sheet is visible at a time. Use Approach 3 if your model is too large to view multiple scenarios on the same sheet.*

Apply it

- ***Assume Carbonlite management is fairly confident about its estimate of fixed costs but is concerned about the uncertainty in its estimates of variable cost per unit, sales price, and sales volume. You have been asked to analyze the following three possible scenarios for operations next year. The base case corresponds to the original analysis.***

	Best-Case Scenario	*Base-Case Scenario*	*Worst-Case Scenario*
Variable cost per unit	*350*	*400*	*450*
Sales price	*1,250*	*1,000*	*850*
Sales volume	*13,500*	*10,000*	*8,000*

Apply Approach 1: Carbonlite

- ***Simply change the input assumptions.***
  Note that *EBIT* is negative in the worst-case scenario, and the breakeven is much higher.

Your results should match:

Inputs

	Carbonlite	Solution – Best Carbonlite	Solution – Worst Carbonlite
Fixed costs per year	5,000,000	5,000,000	5,000,000
Variable cost per bike frame	400	350	450
Sales price per bike frame	1,000	1,250	850
Sales volume	10,000	13,500	8,000
Calculations and Output			
Revenues	10,000,000	16,875,000	6,800,000
Fixed costs	5,000,000	5,000,000	5,000,000
Variable costs	4,000,000	4,725,000	3,600,000
EBIT	1,000,000	7,150,000	(1,800,000)
Breakeven quantity	8,333	5,556	12,500

Apply Approach 2: Carbonlite

- *Copy the model elsewhere on the sheet, label the scenarios and change the input assumptions to reflect the scenario.*
  The results are the same as in Approach 1.

  See the solution provided on the Scenario *tab.*

Apply Approach 3: Classicaltunes.com

- *Copy the sheet to create a separate sheet for each scenario.*

The Carbonlite model is so simple that approach 3 is not worthwhile. Instead, apply Approach 3 to scenario analysis of the jazz-recording project considered by Classicaltunes.com in Chapter 9.

For this illustration, we have changed some of the input assumptions. As a result, the *NPV* and *IRR* differ from the chapter 9 results.

Examine the base case-solution on the ***ClassicBase*** tab. Note the new assumptions driving the model. In this example, units sold are derived from a formula that depends upon an assumed unit growth rate. Cost of goods sold is a percent of revenues.

Base-Case Assumptions

The price is $13.50 in year 0, and price grows at 2 percent per year.
Units sold start at 10,000 and grow 20 percent per year.
COGS is 74 percent of Revenues.
All other assumptions remain as in Chapter 9.

Best-Case Assumptions

The price is $15 in year 0 and price grows at 3.5 percent per year.
Units sold start at 12,000 and grow 25 percent per year.
COGS is 72 percent of Revenues.
All other assumptions remain as in Chapter 9.

Worst-Case Assumptions

The price is $12.75 in year 0 and price grows at 1 percent per year.
Units sold start at 9,000 and grow 15 percent per year.

COGS is 75 percent of Revenues.
All other assumptions remain as in Chapter 9.

To create the best-and worst-case scenarios, copy the ***ClassicBase*** tab sheet and rename. (See the ***Excel Prereqs*** tab for instructions on copying and renaming sheets.)

Then change the input assumptions to fit the scenario. The solution files appear on tabs ***ClassicBest*** and ***ClassicWorst***. The base-case solution is on the ***ClassicBase*** tab.

Our results are:

	Best-Case Scenario	*Base-Case Scenario*	*Worst-Case Scenario*
NPV – 2% growth	*677,048*	*174,882*	*(31,844)*
NPV – assets sold	*116,408*	*5,952*	*(40,531)*

Approach 3 is an easy way to create scenarios for more complex models.

PART 4

Capital Structure and Dividend Policy

The previous chapters provided a framework for deciding how a firm should invest its money. Next, we examine at the opposite side of that question. How should managers finance the investments that they undertake? Should managers pay for new investments by using cash that the firm generates internally or should external sources of funds be tapped? Is it better to finance with equity or with debt? If the firm's investments are successful, should the company reward its shareholders by paying a dividend or should it repurchase shares instead? To answer these questions, managers have to assess the marginal benefits and costs of alternative actions. Unfortunately, the advice we have to offer managers who are asking these questions is not as clear-cut as our advice on capital budgeting matters. Nevertheless, there are some important general principles to convey.

Chapter 11 describes some of the trade-offs firms face when they choose between internal or external financing or between debt and equity. The chapter explains how firms work with investment bankers to issue equity. Because investment bankers serve two masters—the firms that want to sell securities and the investors who must be persuaded to buy them—the investment banking business is fraught with potential conflict-of-interest problems. Chapter 11 describes some of the conflicts that arise in this industry and summarizes some of the recent scandals that have plagued it.

In Chapter 12, we explore to the question of whether managers can increase the value of a firm by financing its operations with an optimal mix of debt and equity. A classic and important line of argument in finance suggests that finding an optimal capital structure may be impossible, but the chapter offers useful guidelines that managers can consult when deciding what type of funding to raise for their companies.

Chapter 13 examines the related question of how managers can affect the value of a firm through dividend policy. In Chapter 5, we presented a model that claimed that the value of any stock should equal the present value of all dividends that the stock will pay through time (or more broadly, the value of all cash payments that the stock will make). The surprising message of this chapter is that although dividends are clearly important, dividend policy may or may not affect the value of a firm.

Note: Solutions available in a booklet called *Solutions to Concept Review Questions and Self-Test Problems.*

Raising Long-Term Financing

OPENING FOCUS

Investors Welcome China Life's IPO

At the start of 2003, the China Life Insurance Company hardly seemed a likely candidate to execute the world's largest and most successful share offering of the year. But its $3.47 billion initial public offering (IPO) in New York and Hong Kong indeed earned that title. The company, which was wholly owned by the government of the People's Republic of China and by state-owned financial institutions, prior to its offering, controlled about 45 percent of China's life insurance market and needed additional equity capital to fund its continued rapid growth. Fortunately, international investors developed a strong appetite for Chinese share offerings during 2003, with several smaller offerings to be enthusiastically received before China Life's scheduled IPO in December.

Three international investment banks—Credit Suisse First Boston (CSFB), Citigroup, and Deutsche Bank—combined forces with China International Capital Corporation (CICC) to manage China Life's IPO. These banks not only advised China Life as the company prepared its offering, but they also "underwrote" the IPO, or guaranteed China Life that it would receive a fixed amount from the offering. The company planned to sell a total of 6.47 billion "H shares," or foreign shares, in the offering—with 6.147 billion shares to be sold on the New York Stock Exchange, and 323 million to be sold on the Hong Kong Stock Exchange—to raise $3.02 billion. The shares sold in the United States would be in the form of American Depositary Receipts (ADRs), with each ADR representing forty H shares. Based on information the investment banks had gathered during their pre-offering marketing activities, the underwriters set an offer price of $18.68 per ADR. The offering was launched first in New York and then later in Hong Kong on December 11, 2003.

Investor response to China Life's offering was electrifying. Demand for shares by retail investors was *172 times* greater than the number initially supplied. Hence, in financial terms, the retail portion (or "tranche") of China Life's IPO was 172 times "oversubscribed." Not surprisingly, given this frantic desire for the company's stock, the ADRs began trading in the secondary market well above the offer price and closed the day's trading at $23.72. This was $5.04 higher than the offer price. Investors lucky enough to buy ADRs at the offer price and sell them by the close of the first day's trading earned a one-day return of 27.0 percent. In the terms we define in this chapter, China Life's ADRs were "underpriced" by 27.0 percent.

The news was very good for China Life's underwriters, because the banks had retained a "Green Shoe option," giving them the right to insist that China Life sell additional shares equal to 15 percent of the planned offering. The underwriters exercised this option, so China Life provided an additional 922 million H shares, which the underwriters packaged as 23.1 million ADRs and sold to investors in New York and Hong Kong. As a result, China Life's IPO raised $3.47 billion rather than the $3.02 billion expected. Based on the underwriting agreement negotiated between China Life and the investment banks, the banks received 3.5 percent of the money raised, or $121 million, as their "underwriting discount," or fee. The remaining proceeds of $3.35 billion were paid to China Life.

This IPO turned out to be at least partially successful for all concerned. The company raised a great deal of money to support its continued growth, even though the large initial returns (underpricing) implied that the company could have sold the shares for significantly more. The investment banks earned a very handsome fee, as well as substantial glory, though they clearly underestimated investor demand. The initial investors were the biggest winners, since they received a quick capital gain. Even those investors who purchased shares in the secondary market gained because China Life shares were selling for over $26 per ADR, three months after the issue in March 2004. As we soon discover, this positive outcome is not always assured when firms raise capital by selling securities to investors. ■

LEARNING OBJECTIVES

After studying this chapter you should be able to:

- Discuss the basic choices that corporations face in raising long-term financing;
- Describe the costs and benefits of raising long-term funds by issuing securities on capital markets rather than by borrowing from a financial intermediary;
- Understand how investment banks help corporations issue securities, and describe the services investment banks provide before, during, and after a security issue;
- Explain the basic issuance and pricing patterns observed in the initial public offering (IPO) market in the United States;
- Describe the basic issuance and pricing patterns observed in the U.S. market for seasoned equity offerings (SEOs), and explain why so few large companies issue seasoned common stock in any year; and
- Explain what American Depositary Receipts (ADRs) are and discuss why these have proven to be so popular with U.S. investors.

This chapter introduces the primary instruments that companies around the world use for long-term financing, and it examines key patterns observed in corporate financial systems. The basic instruments are similar worldwide and include common stock, preferred stock, and long-term debt. However, significant differences exist across countries in terms of how corporations use these instruments and in the degree to which firms rely on capital markets, rather than financial intermediaries, for funding. For example, countries such as Canada, the United States, Britain, and Australia are characterized by large, highly liquid stock and bond markets. Other industrialized countries, particularly those in continental Europe, have much smaller capital markets and rely primarily on commercial banks for corporate financing. Despite these differences in financial systems, corporations around the world display certain common tendencies. Perhaps the most important of these regularities is the near universal reliance on internally generated cash flow (retained earnings) as the dominant source of new financing.

Debt and equity constitute the two main sources of corporate long-term financing. The basic features of debt securities were described in Chapter 4, while the basics of common and preferred stock were discussed in Chapter 5. Equity capital represents an ownership interest that is junior to debt, while debt capital represents a legally enforceable claim, with cash flows that are either fixed or varied, according to a predetermined formula. These basic financial instruments exist in most countries, and the rights and responsibilities of the holders of these instruments are very similar worldwide.

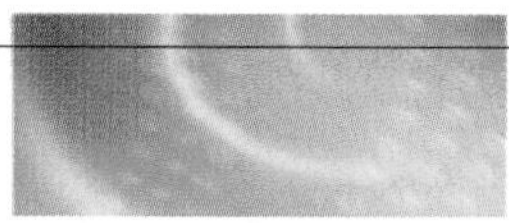

11.1 THE BASIC CHOICES IN LONG-TERM FINANCING

Companies around the world face the same basic financing problem: how to fund those projects and activities that firms need to undertake if they are to grow and prosper. This section examines the choices firms face in selecting among financing alternatives, particularly the choices regarding internal versus external financing. This section also surveys key issues related to the choice between financing via capital markets versus financial intermediaries.

The Need to Fund a Financial Deficit

financial deficit
More financial capital for investment and investor payments than is retained in profits by a corporation.

Corporations everywhere are net dissavers, which is an economic way of saying they demand more financial capital for investment than they supply in the form of retained profits. Corporations must close this **financial deficit** by borrowing or by issuing new equity securities. Every major firm confronts four key financing decisions on an ongoing basis:

1. How much capital must the company raise each year?
2. How much of this must be raised externally rather than through retained profits?
3. How much of the external funding should be raised through borrowing from a bank or another financial intermediary, and how much capital should be raised by selling securities directly to investors?
4. What proportion of the external funding should be structured as common stock, preferred stock, or long-term debt?

The answer to the first question depends on the capital budgeting process of a particular firm, as discussed in Chapters 8–10. A company must raise enough capital to fund all its positive-*NPV* investment projects and to cover its working capital needs. The true financing decision begins with Question 2, the choice between internal versus external financing.

The Choice between Internal Versus External Financing

cash flow from operations
Cash inflows and outflows directly related to the production and sale of a firm's products or services. Calculated as net income plus depreciation and other noncash charges.

At first glance, the internal/external choice seems to be a decision that firms can make mechanically. Managers may approximate external funding needs by subtracting cash dividend payments from their firms' **cash flow from operations** (net income plus depreciation and other noncash charges). The difference between this internally generated funding and the firms' total financing needs equals the external financing requirement. The decision is not simple, however. Management may want to build up or reduce working capital stocks over time, and besides, dividend policy is not fixed, except in the very short term. Additionally, there are obviously higher legal and transactions costs to raising capital externally than by retaining internal cash flow. Managers should choose to raise capital externally whenever the benefits of doing so—such as the ability to raise greater sums of money, or to raise new capital in the form of debt—exceed the additional transactions and other costs of raising external funds. This is another practical application of the *marginal benefits equals marginal costs* decision rule. Not surprising, the residual nature of external funding needs implies that this figure will be highly variable from year to year for individual companies.

External funding is also a highly variable figure for the U.S. corporate sector as a whole, and the same is true for most other developed economies. Internal cash flow is the dominant source of corporate funding in the United States, with businesses regularly financing two thirds to three quarters of all their capital spending needs internally. Over time, other countries have also moved in the same direction. Whereas European corporations relied quite heavily on external funding, as recently as the 1970s, the corporate sectors of Western European nations now meet the majority of their total funding needs internally. Japanese corporations still meet up to half of their total financing needs externally, primarily through bank borrowing. But even this level implies far lower dependence on external funding than was the case prior to the 1980s.

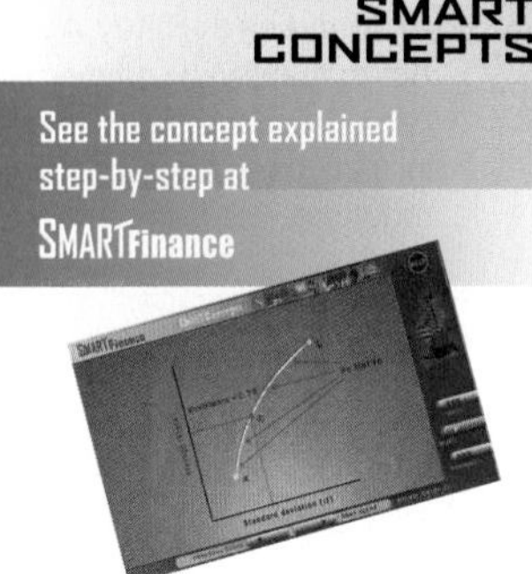

Raising Capital from Financial Intermediaries or on Capital Markets

Should a corporation care whether it raises capital by selling securities to investors in public capital markets or by dealing more directly with a financial intermediary such as a commercial bank? Before analyzing this issue, we should formally define what a financial intermediary is and briefly describe what services it provides. A **financial intermediary (FI)** is an institution that raises capital by issuing liabilities against itself—for example, in the form of demand or savings deposits. The intermediary then pools the funds raised and uses these to make loans to borrowers or, where allowed, to make equity investments in nonfinancial firms. Borrowers repay the intermediary and have no direct contact with the individual savers who actually funded the loans. In other words, both borrowers and savers deal directly with the intermediary, which specializes in credit analysis and collection, while it offers financial products tailored to the specific needs of both borrowers and savers.

financial intermediary (FI) An institution that raises capital by issuing liabilities against itself. Also, a commercial bank or other entity that lends to corporations.

In many countries, intermediaries also play an extremely important corporate governance role, distinct from their activities in granting credit and monitoring loan repayment. Commercial banks, in particular, frequently help set operating and financial policies of firms they have invested in, by serving on corporate boards and monitoring the performance of senior managers. As we now discuss, banks in the United States have long been prohibited from playing any meaningful corporate governance role.

The Role of Financial Intermediaries in U.S. Corporate Finance. Americans have a long history of distrusting concentrated, private economic power, and this has dramatically influenced U.S. financial regulations. In response to public opinion, policymakers discouraged the growth of large intermediaries (especially commercial banks), in part, by imposing on them severe geographical restrictions. Existing restrictions were codified into national law when Congress passed the **McFadden Act** in 1927, which prohibited interstate banking. After numerous failed attempts to repeal the McFadden Act over the years, a bill allowing full interstate branch banking was finally approved by Congress in July 1994.

McFadden Act Congressional act of 1927 that prohibited interstate banking.

Glass-Steagall Act
Congressional act of 1933 mandating the separation of investment and commercial banking.

The second pivotal law affecting American FIs was the **Glass-Steagall Act**, which was passed in 1933 in response to perceived banking abuses during the Great Depression. This legislation mandated the separation of investment and commercial banking. Commercial banks were thereby prohibited from underwriting corporate security issues, providing security brokerage services to their customers, or even owning voting equity securities on their own account. Banking's corporate financing role was thus effectively restricted to making commercial loans and to providing closely related services, such as leasing.

Gramm-Leach-Bliley Act
Act that allowed commercial banks, securities firms, and insurance companies to join together.

As with the McFadden Act, there were repeated attempts to repeal Glass-Steagall, and these finally succeeded when Congress passed the **Gramm-Leach-Bliley Act** in November 1999. This act allows commercial banks, securities firms, and insurance companies to join together in a new *financial holding company* structure, also defined by the act. However, the act still prohibits nonfinancial companies from owning commercial banks. The act also mandates "functional regulation" for banks, insurance companies, securities firms, and other financial companies. This means that regulation applies to specific financial services (i.e., brokerage services, deposit-taking) that are provided by all types of financial companies. Previously, regulators had been assigned based on institutional form. All the activities of commercial banks were regulated by the Federal Reserve Board. The activities of securities firms were regulated by the SEC. All the products and services offered by insurance companies were overseen by state insurance boards.[1]

Finally, nonbank FIs, such as insurance companies, pension funds, and specialized finance companies such as General Electric Credit Corporation and General Motors Acceptance Corporation play important roles in American corporate finance, both as creditors and as equity investors.

The Corporate Finance Role of Non-U.S. Financial Intermediaries. In markets outside the United States, commercial banks typically play much larger roles in corporate finance. In most countries, a relative handful of very large banks service most large firms, and the size and competence of these banks give them tremendous influence over corporate financial and operating policies. This power is further strengthened by the ability of most non-U.S. banks to underwrite corporate security issues and to make direct equity investments in commercial firms. Most Western countries allow commercial banks to act as true **merchant banks**, capable of providing the full range of financial services. Most non-U.S. banks also have far greater power as compared with corporate borrowers than American banks do, and they play a more central role in the resolution of client-firm bankruptcy or financial distress.

merchant bank
A bank capable of providing a full range of financial services.

The Expanding Role of Securities Markets in Corporate Finance

primary security issues
Security offerings that raise capital for firms.

secondary offering
An offering whose purpose is to allow an existing shareholder to sell a large block of stock to new investors. This kind of offering raises no new capital for the firm.

No trend in modern finance is as clear or as transforming as the worldwide shift toward corporate reliance on securities markets rather than intermediaries for external financing. Table 11.1 presents summary information from the *Investment Dealers' Digest* on **primary security issues** worldwide, and for the United States alone, for the years 1990–2003. Primary issues actually raise capital for firms and are thus distinct from **secondary offerings**, in which investors sell their holdings of existing securities. The total value of primary issues around the world in 2003 was a record

[1] A concise but informative summary of the Gramm-Leach-Bliley Act is provided by the Securities Industry Association at http://www.sia.com/gramm_leach_bliley/. A somewhat longer, but more definitive, summary is provided on a United States Senate Web site at http://banking.senate.gov/conf/grmleach.htm.

Type of Security Issue	1990	1995	2000	2003
Worldwide offerings	$ 504	$1,066	$ 3,268	$ 5,327
[debt and equity]	(7,574)	(9,305)	(14,659)	(19,729)
Global debt (2000–01)	184	385	2,624	4,939
International debt (1990–99)	(1,376)	(2,548)	(10,827)	(17,309)
Eurobonds	172	280	946	1,743
	(1,213)	(1,840)	(3,858)	(6,139)
Yankee bonds (2000–01)	13	45	47	94
Foreign bonds (1990–99)	(81)	(237)	(112)	(441)
International common	7	21	335	145
stock [excluding U.S.][a]	(132)	(242)	(2,662)	(1,412)
U.S. Issuers worldwide[b]	313	700	1,958	3,397
[debt and equity]	(6,141)	(6,807)	(15,686)	(12,341)
All debt[c]	--	--	1,726	3,210
			(7,824)	(11,470)
Straight corporate debt[d]	109	417	744	1,248
	(1,016)	(4,562)	(2,986)	(4,231)
High-yield corporate debt	1	28	43	134
	(7)	(153)	(196)	(491)
Collateralized securities	175	155	488	1,481
	(4,542)	(709)	(1,201)	(2,378)
Convertible debt and	5	9	56	96
preferred stock	(43)	(57)	(161)	(282)
Common stock[e]	14	82	223	90
	(362)	(1,159)	(955)	(589)
Initial public offerings[e]	5	30	60	16
	(174)	(572)	(386)	(88)

Note: [a] Capital-raising, private-sector offers; does not include privatization issues.
[b] For 2000 and 2003, all figures include Rule 144A offers on U.S. markets.
[c] Includes mortgage-backed securities (MBS), asset-backed securities (ABS), and municipal bonds.
[d] Years 2000 and 2003 are long-term straight debt only. Before 1999, figures are for investment-grade debt.
[e] Excludes closed-end fund. Data for 1990–2000 are not comparable to 2003 due to definition change.

Table 11.1
Worldwide Securities Issues, 1990–2003

This table details the total value, in billions of U.S. dollars, and the number (in parentheses) of securities issues worldwide (including the United States) for selected years in the period 1990–2003. The data are taken from early January issues of the Investment Dealers' Digest.

Source: Investment Dealer's Digest, *early Jan. issues 2004.*

$5.33 trillion. Worldwide security offerings were $1.82 trillion in 1997 and less than $400 billion as recently as 1988. The thirteen-fold increase in the value of security market financing between 1988 and 2003 was not matched by a remotely comparable increase in world trade, investment, or economic activity. Instead, it is a reflection of the power of the trend toward the "securitization" of corporate finance. **Securitization** involves the repackaging of loans and other traditional bank-based credit products into securities that can be sold to public investors.

securitization
The repackaging of loans and other traditional bank-based credit products into securities that can be sold to public investors.

Besides rapid recent growth, another major trend that can be observed from these data is the relatively steady fraction of worldwide security offerings accounted for by U.S. issuers. American issues represented 63.8 percent ($3,397 billion of $5,327 billion) of the worldwide total value of security offerings in 2003. U.S. issuers have sold between 62 percent and 74 percent of the global total every year since 1990. Looking more closely at the statistics for the United States alone, we can identify several other trends that are working to transform American finance. First, companies issue far more debt than

SMART IDEAS VIDEO
Ben Esty, Harvard University
"The syndicated loan market is now the largest single source of corporate funds."

See the entire interview at **SMARTFinance**

equity each year. During 2003, American corporations issued $3,210 billion in straight (nonconvertible) debt, $96 billion in convertible debt and preferred stock, $116 billion in common-stock (initial public offers and seasoned equity issues), and a mere $36 billion in nonconvertible preferred stock (not listed in Table 11.1). Straight debt therefore represented almost 95 percent of the total capital raised by U.S. companies through public security issues during 2003. The $116 billion in common stock issued in 2003 represented a mere 3.4 percent of the capital-raising total. Although this fraction is unusually small, equity issues always account for a very small share of the total amount of capital raised through public security issues in the United States. And remember that these are all gross issue amounts; once the value of stock removed from public markets through mergers and stock repurchases is accounted for, net equity issues are often negative. Add in the roughly $2 trillion in syndicated bank loans that American companies arrange each year, and it becomes clear that firms needing to raise capital externally greatly prefer to issue debt rather than common or preferred stock.

SMART PRACTICES VIDEO

Frank Popoff, Chairman of the Board (retired), Dow Chemical

"A Samurai bond is just an exercise in matching exposure and income."

See the entire interview at **SMARTFinance**

Second, the relative insignificance of new equity issues as a financing source for U.S. corporations is further emphasized considering that *initial public offerings (IPOs)* accounted for over one seventh ($16 billion of the $116 billion total) of common stock issued by companies in 2003 (and accounted for almost one third of the total issues in previous years). Initial public offerings involve the first public sale of stock to outside investors and are discussed in depth in Section 11.3. IPOs, as well as subsequent seasoned issues, must be registered with the SEC. Virtually all companies choose to list their stock on one of the organized exchanges so that investors can easily buy or sell the stock. America's IPO market is easily the world's largest and most liquid source of equity capital for small, rapidly growing firms, and most observers consider it a key national asset.

Eurobond
A bond issued by an international borrower and sold to investors in countries with currencies other than that in which the bond is denominated.

foreign bond
A bond issued in a host country's financial market, in the host country's currency, by a nonresident corporation.

Yankee bonds
Bonds sold by foreign corporations to U.S. investors.

international common stock
Equity issues sold in more than one country by nonresident corporations.

Yankee common stock
Stock issued by foreign firms in the U.S. market.

We can also identify a number of patterns in the international security-issuance data, presented in Table 11.1. First, the Eurobond market is by far the largest security market outside the United States, with the foreign bond market ranking second. A **Eurobond** issue is a single-currency bond that is sold in several countries simultaneously, whereas a **foreign bond** is an issue that is sold by a nonresident corporation in a single foreign country and denominated in the host country's currency. A dollar-denominated bond issued by an American corporation and sold to European investors is an example of a Eurobond; and a Swiss franc-denominated bond sold in Switzerland by a Japanese corporate issuer is an example of a foreign bond. As in most years, **Yankee bonds** sold by foreign corporations to U.S. investors are the single largest category of foreign bond issue, with Swiss (Heidi bonds) and Japanese (Samurai) foreign bonds the next largest.

A second pattern observable in international finance is that **international common stock** issues raised $145 billion in 2003, somewhat less than 2000's $335 billion record, but up dramatically from the $82-billion total in 1995. These are equity issues that are sold in more than one country by nonresident corporations. Although the non-U.S. portion of this amount has grown steadily over the years, it is small by American standards, and over half the total is usually **Yankee common stock** issued by foreign firms in the U.S. market.

To summarize, the growth in international security issues has kept pace with that in the United States, though this growth has probably effected non-U.S. economies to a greater degree because it began from a much smaller base.

CONCEPT REVIEW QUESTIONS

1. What are financial intermediaries, and what role do these firms play in providing long-term capital to publicly traded U.S. nonfinancial corporations?

2. What patterns are observed in U.S. security issues each year? How do these patterns compare to those in international security issues?

11.2 INVESTMENT BANKING AND THE PUBLIC SALE OF SECURITIES

Although internal financing is the dominant source of funding for corporations around the world, many firms raise capital externally in any given year. Managers may or may not enlist the help of an **investment bank** to sell their firms' debt-and-equity securities. If they desire assistance from an investment bank, managers can negotiate privately with individual banks regarding the terms of the security sale, or they can solicit competitive bids for the business. Firms can issue securities to a small group of sophisticated investors in a private placement, or they can execute a public offering to the general population of investors. If companies want to sell new stock, they can issue shares to existing stockholders through a rights offering, or they can engage in a *general cash offering* open to all investors.

investment bank
A bank that helps firms acquire external capital.

league table
Ranks investment banks, based on the total value of securities they underwrote globally during a given year.

bulge bracket
Consists of firms that generally occupy the lead or co-lead manager's position in large, new security offerings, meaning that they take primary responsibility for the new offering (even though other banks participate as part of a syndicate), and as a result they earn higher fees.

prospectus
The first part of a registration statement; it is distributed to all prospective investors.

Table 11.2 presents a **league table** that ranks investment banks, based on the total value of securities they underwrote globally during 2003. The highest-ranked firms in 2003 generally occupied the top rankings in 2002, and these firms are perennial members of investment banking's prestigious **bulge bracket**. Bulge-bracket firms generally occupy the lead or colead manager's position in large, new security offerings, meaning that they take primary responsibility for the new offering (even though other banks participate as part of a syndicate). As a result, they earn higher fees. Investment banks are compensated with an underwriting spread, which is the difference between the offering price per share and the amount per share that the underwriter passes on to the issuing firms. You can readily identify the lead investment bank in a security offering by looking at the offering **prospectus**, the legal document that describes the terms of the offering. The lead bank's name appears on the front page, usually in larger, bolder print than the names of other participating banks.

Table 11.2
Investment Banking League Tables, Global Debt-and-Equity Issues, 2003

Source: Britt Erica Tunick, Christopher O'Leary and Mairin Burns, "The Face-Off," Investment Dealers' Digest (January 12, 2004), pp. 32–61.

Rank	Lead Underwriter	Proceeds ($ Billion)	Number of issues	Disclosed fees ($ Million)
1	Citigroup	$ 542,749	1,872	$ 1,799
2	Morgan Stanley	394,780	1,365	1,203
3	Merrill Lynch	380,319	1,914	1,028
4	Lehman Brothers	354,259	1,266	643
5	J. P. Morgan Chase	353,911	1,418	1,035
6	CSFB	338,768	1,249	923
7	Deutsche Bank	317,428	1,257	638
8	UBS	293,819	1,147	1,008
9	Goldman Sachs	293,310	807	1,015
10	BofA Securities	206,476	739	421
11	Bears Stearns	182,833	512	279
12	Barclays Capital	135,763	484	310
	Industry Total	**$5,327,491**	**19,729**	**15,461**

APPLYING THE MODEL

Figure 11.1 presents the prospectus title page for Orbitz, Inc.'s initial public share offering on December 16, 2003. The lead underwriter was Goldman, Sachs and Company and the colead underwriter was Credit Suisse First Boston (CSFB). These banks were responsible, respectively, for selling 6,029,100 and 3,836,700 of the 12,180,000 shares on offer. Both firms are perennial members of investment banking's bulge bracket. Legg Mason Wood Walker and Thomas Weisel Partners are also important underwriters for this offering—each is responsible for selling 548,100 shares—though these companies are not routinely members of investment banking's bulge bracket. The title page also shows an underwriting discount of $1.625 per share and an offer price of $26.00 per share, for a percentage discount of 6.25 percent ($1.625 ÷ $26.00). The underwriters thus stood to receive total compensation of $19,792,500 for their efforts in this firm commitment underwriting. Given the unusually large size of Orbitz's IPO, this represented a fairly standard underwriting discount.

unseasoned equity offering
An initial offering of shares by a company that does not currently have a public listing for trading its stock.

book building
A process in which underwriters ask prospective investors to reveal information about their demand for the offering. Through conversations with investors, the underwriter tries to measure the demand curve for a given issue, and the investment bank sets the offer price after gathering all the information it can from investors.

fixed-price offer
An offer in which the underwriters set the final offer price for a new issue weeks in advance.

Underwriting spreads vary considerably depending on the type of security being issued. Banks charge higher spreads on equity issues than on debt issues. They also charge higher spreads for **unseasoned equity offerings** (i.e., IPOs) than they do for seasoned equity offerings (SEOs), which are equity issues by firms that already have common stock outstanding. In general, the riskier the security being offered, the higher the spread charged by the underwriter, so spreads on noninvestment-grade ("junk") bonds exceed those on investment-grade bonds. Similarly, securities that have both debt-and-equity-like features, such as convertible bonds or preferred stock, have spreads higher than those of ordinary debt but lower than those of common stock.

Spreads on international IPOs are significantly lower than on U.S. initial offers. In part, this reflects differences in underwriting practices across countries. U.S. underwriters typically use a process, known as **book building**, to assess demand for a company's shares and to set the offer price, in which underwriters ask prospective investors to reveal information about their demand for the offering. Through conversations with investors, the underwriter tries to measure the demand curve for a given issue, and the investment bank sets the offer price after gathering all the information it can from investors. In international markets, book building is common, but so is a method called a **fixed-price offer**. In fixed-price offers, underwriters set the final offer price for a new issue weeks in advance. Since this imposes more risk on the underwriters, they would naturally charge higher spreads if offering prices were set the same as under book-building. To protect themselves, underwriters thus set share offering prices significantly lower in fixed price offering, and thus observed spreads are actually lower than in book-built offerings.

Conflicts of Interest Facing Investment Banks

The institutional arrangements for selling securities to the public, as described above, confront investment banks with many potential conflicts of interest. Banks are providing advice and underwriting services to companies that want to issue securities and that are naturally eager to sell those securities for the highest possible price. On the other hand, investment banks are selling these securities to their own clients—retail and institutional investors—who naturally want to purchase securities at bargain prices. Furthermore, research analysts working for investment banks produce reports which are supposed to advise clients on whether securities are fairly priced.

Figure 11.1
Title Page from Orbitz's IPO Prospectus

12,180,000 Shares

Orbitz, Inc.

Class A Common Stock

This is an initial public offering of shares of Class A common stock of Orbitz, Inc. Orbitz is offering 4,000,000 shares of the shares to be sold in the offering. The selling stockholders identified in this prospectus are offering an additional 8,180,000 shares. Orbitz will not receive any of the proceeds from the sale of the shares by the selling stockholders.

Prior to this offering, there has been no public market for the Class A common stock. The Class A common stock has been approved for quotation on the Nasdaq Stock Market under the symbol "ORBZ."

See "Risk Factors" beginning on page 9 to read about factors you should consider before buying shares of the Class A common stock.

Neither the Securities and Exchange Commission nor any other regulatory body has approved or disapproved of these securities or passed upon the accuracy or adequacy of this prospectus. Any representation to the contrary is a criminal offense.

	Per Share	**Total**
Initial public offering price	$ 26.00	$ 316,680,000
Underwriting discount	$ 1.625	$ 19,792,500
Proceeds, before expenses, to Orbitz	$ 24.375	$ 97,500,000
Proceeds, before expenses, to the selling stockholders	$ 24.375	$ 199,387,500

To the extent that the underwriters sell more than 12,180,000 shares of Class A common stock, the underwriters have the option to purchase up to an additional 1,827,000 shares from the selling stockholders at the initial public offering price less the underwriting discount.

The underwriters expect to deliver the shares of Class A common stock against payment in New York, New York, on December 19, 2003.

Goldman, Sachs & Co. **Credit Suisse First Boston**

Legg Mason Wood Walker
Incorporated

Thomas Weisel Partners LLC

Prospectus dated December 16, 2003.

Banks cannot "solve" these conflicts of interest; instead, they must price new security issues to strike a balance between the revenue maximization goal of the issuing firms and the profit maximization objective of their investing clients.

SMART IDEAS VIDEO

Tim Jenkinson, Oxford University

"There are basically three ways of doing an IPO."

See the entire interview at **SMARTFinance**

In recent years, various legal actions taken against investment banks suggest that the banks have failed to strike an appropriate balance between the competing interests that they serve. For example, in 2002, ten of the top U.S. investment banking firms agreed to pay fines totaling $1.4 billion to settle an investigation by New York Attorney General Elliot Spitzer. Part of the settlement required investment banks to purchase independent research from third parties. The purpose of this provision is to try to remove any potential bias in investment banks' research that may arise if banks present overly optimistic reports on companies with which they have an underwriting relationship.[2]

More recently, Morgan Stanley, Deutsche Bank, and Bear, Stearns & Co. agreed to pay $15 million as part of an investigation by the National Association of Securities Dealers (NASD). The investigation alleged that these firms were engaged in a kickback scheme in which they would give large allocations of "hot" IPO shares to clients, who, in turn, agreed to pay unusually high commissions to the banks for subsequent trades in other companies. In a hot IPO, the price of the issuing company's shares shoots up dramatically once trading begins in the secondary market. Because the demand for shares in a hot IPO far exceeds the supply, the investment bankers' right to control the initial allocation of shares is quite valuable. Banks may choose to "reward" some of their best customers by giving them large share allocations in hot deals. Sometimes banks may cross an ethical line and use their power to allocate shares in hot IPOs to generate revenue, in addition to the fees paid by the issuing firm. In one such case, a customer of Bear Stearns received a large share allocation in a hot IPO and subsequently paid $2 per share to trade 50,000 shares of a different stock, when the customary commission for a trade of that size might be $0.06 per share. This represented a kind of kickback for Bear Stearns. Interestingly, Google structured its August 2004 IPO as an auction, open to all investors, rather than as an allocated offering specifically in order to prevent investment banks from favoring institutional investors over the ordinary investing public.

Lawmakers and regulators recognize that the investment banking business is fraught with conflict-of-interest problems, and so there is an extensive set of rules that impose constraints on how securities may be sold. Now we turn to a brief overview of the legal environment surrounding security issues.

Securities Act of 1933
The most important federal law governing the sale of new securities.

full disclosure
Requires issuers to reveal all relevant information concerning the company selling the securities and the securities themselves to potential investors.

Legal Rules Governing Public Security Sales in the United States

Security issues in the United States are regulated at both the state and federal levels. The most important federal law governing the sale of new securities is the **Securities Act of 1933**. The basis for federal regulation of the sale of securities is the concept of **full disclosure**, which means that issuers must reveal all relevant information concerning not only the company selling the securities but also the securities themselves, to potential investors. The other major federal law governing securities

2. The French luxury goods maker, LVMH (Moët Hennessy Louis Vitton), recently sued Morgan Stanley successfully in a French court and won a €30 million settlement. The suit alleged that Morgan Stanley's research on one of LVMH's competitors, Gucci, was overly optimistic because Morgan Stanley had other profitable business ties to Gucci. Because Morgan's biased research attracted investors away from LVMH and to Gucci, LVMH successfully persuaded that it had been harmed by the biased research reports.

issues is the **Securities and Exchange Commission Act of 1934**. This act, and its amendments, established the U.S. Securities and Exchange Commission (SEC) and laid out specific procedures for both the public sale of securities and the governance of public companies.

Given the emphasis U.S. securities law places on disclosure, it is no surprise that one of the most important roles investment banks play in the security offering process is performing **due diligence** examinations of potential security issuers. This means that IBs are legally required to search out and disclose all relevant information about an issuer before selling securities to the public. Investors can sue underwriters if they do not perform adequate due diligence, and of course, the underwriter's reputation suffers as well. Because investors understand that the most prestigious investment bankers have the most to lose from inadequate due diligence, the mere fact that these firms are willing to underwrite an issue provides valuable **certification** that the issuing company is, in fact, disclosing all material information. The principal disclosure document for all public security offerings is the **registration statement**. Firms must file this highly detailed document with the SEC before they can solicit investors. Additionally, a final revised version must be approved by the commission before an offering can become **effective**—before any shares can actually be sold to public investors. The first part of the registration statement, the prospectus, must be distributed to all prospective investors. The second part is filed only with the SEC, although investors can obtain a copy from the SEC.

If the purpose of the offering is to allow an existing shareholder to sell a large block of stock to new investors, the issue is a secondary offering and raises no capital for firms. If the shares offered for sale are newly issued shares, which increase the number of outstanding shares and raise new capital for firms, the issue is a **primary offering**. If some of the shares come from existing shareholders and some are new, the issue is a **mixed offering**.

Securities and Exchange Commission Act of 1934
This act, and its amendments, established the U.S. Securities and Exchange Commission (SEC) and laid out specific procedures for both the public sale of securities and the governance of public companies.

due diligence
Examination of potential security issuers in which investment banks are legally required to search out and disclose all relevant information about an issuer before selling securities to the public.

certification
Assurance that the issuing company is in fact disclosing all material information.

registration statement
The principal disclosure document for all public security offerings.

effective
Status of an offering before any shares can actually be sold to public investors.

primary offering
An offering in which the shares offered for sale are newly issued shares, which increases the number of outstanding shares and raises new capital for the firm.

mixed offering
An offering in which some of the shares come from existing shareholders and some are new. Also, a merger financed with a combination of cash and securities.

APPLYING THE MODEL

The Orbitz IPO was a mixed offering. The company itself was issuing 4,000,000 new shares to raise $97,500,000, and planned to use these proceeds for working capital and "general corporate purposes." The four U.S. airlines and one reservation service that founded Orbitz, and which still remain its principal stockholders, were selling 8,180,00 shares. The proceeds from selling these shares, $199,387,500, went to the selling stockholders rather than to Orbitz. Google's August 2004 IPO was also a mixed offering, where the company issued 14,142,135 new shares and a group of existing shareholders sold an additional 5,462,917 shares.

Shelf Registration (Rule 415). As an alternative to filing a lengthy registration statement and awaiting SEC approval, firms with more than $150 million in outstanding common stock can use a procedure, known as **shelf registration (Rule 415)**, for the issue. This procedure allows qualifying companies to file a "master registration statement," which is a single document that summarizes planned financing for a two-year period. Once the SEC approves the issue, it is placed "on the shelf," and the companies can sell the new securities to investors out of inventory (off the shelf), as needed, any time over the next two years. This has proven to be immensely popular with issuing corporations, which previously had to incur the costs (including costs of delay) of filing separate SEC registrations for each new security issue. In addition to saving time and money, shelf registration allows firms to issue securities in response to changes in market conditions.

shelf registration (Rule 415)
A procedure that allows a qualifying company to file a "master registration statement," a single document summarizing planned financing over a two-year period.

Ongoing Regulatory Requirements for a Publicly Traded Firm. Once a company successfully completes an IPO and lists its shares for trading on an exchange, it becomes subject to all the costs and reporting requirements of a public company. These include cash expenses such as exchange-listing fees and the cost of mailing proxies, annual reports, and other documents to shareholders. Additionally, the law requires public companies to hold not only general shareholders' meetings at least once each year but also special meetings, as needed, to obtain shareholder approval for certain types of transactions (i.e., approving a merger, authorizing additional shares of stock, or approving new stock option plans). By far, the most costly regulatory constraints on public companies are the disclosure requirements for firms, their officers and directors, and their principal shareholders. In essence, companies must report any material change in their operations, ownership, or financing. Once firms "go public," life becomes very public indeed.

CONCEPT REVIEW QUESTIONS

3. What does the phrase "bulge bracket" mean?

4. What is the guiding principle behind most of the important U.S. securities legislation? What role does the security registration process play in implementing this philosophy?

5. What is *shelf registration?* Why do you think this has proven to be so popular among issuing firms?

11.3 THE U.S. MARKET FOR INITIAL PUBLIC OFFERINGS (IPOS)

Given its role in providing capital market access for entrepreneurial growth companies, the U.S. initial public offering market is widely considered a vital economic and financial asset. Indeed, a welcoming IPO market has long been a key building block of America's success in high-technology industries. It is thus not surprising that all the U.S. stock markets compete fiercely for IPO listings. The competition is particularly intense between the two largest, the New York Stock Exchange (NYSE) and the Nasdaq electronic market, which merged with the American Stock Exchange in 1998. Although the number of IPOs (usually a few hundred per year) and the total capital they have raised ($30–$75 billion) each year since the mid-1990s does not seem immense in a $10 trillion economy, IPOs generally represent 20–40 percent of all new common equity raised yearly by U.S. corporations. In other words, IPOs collectively raise one-third as much external equity capital each year as do established giants such as IBM, Exxon, and General Motors.

Patterns Observed in the U.S. IPO Market

To the uninitiated, a quick survey of the U.S. IPO market reveals some decidedly odd patterns. For example, it is one of the most highly cyclical securities markets imaginable. As Table 11.3 makes clear, aggregate IPO volume shows a very distinct pattern of boom and bust. Throughout most of the 1990s, the IPO market boomed. The year 1996 set a record for the number of IPOs (666), while 2000 set the record for total proceeds of $65.68 billion. However, as the prices of U.S. stocks tumbled after March 2000, a chill subdued the market. The number of transactions in 2003 was only one tenth of the 1996 total, and the

Year	Number of Offerings[1]	Average First-day Returns, %[2]	Gross Proceeds, $ Millions[3]
1975	12	-1.5%	$ 262
1976	26	1.9	214
1977	15	3.6	127
1978	20	11.2	209
1979	39	8.5	312
1980	75	13.9	934
1981	197	6.2	2,366
1982	82	10.6	1,064
1983	522	9.0	11,323
1984	222	2.6	2,841
1985	216	6.2	5,492
1986	485	5.9	16,349
1987	344	5.6	13,069
1988	129	5.4	4,181
1989	120	7.9	5,402
1990	113	10.4	4,480
1991	288	11.7	15,771
1992	397	10.0	22,204
1993	507	12.7	29,257
1994	416	9.7	18,300
1995	465	21.0	28,872
1996	666	16.5	42,479
1997	484	13.9	33,218
1998	319	20.0	35,112
1999	490	69.1	65,460
2000	385	55.4	65,677
2001	81	13.7	34,368
2002	71	8.5	22,220
2003	67	12.3	10,114
1975–79	112	5.7	1,124
1980–89	2,392	6.8	623,021
1990–99	4,145	20.9	295,153
2000–03	604	39.5	132,379
TOTAL	**14,506**	**17.6%**	**$1,543,354**

1. The number of offerings excludes the following: IPOs with an offer price of less than $5.00, American depositary receipts (ADRs), best efforts offers, unit offers, Regulation A offerings (small issues, raising less than $1.5 million during the 1980s), real estate investment trusts (REITs), partnerships, and closed-end funds.
2. First-day returns are computed as the percentage return from the offering price to the first closing market price.
3. Gross proceeds are from Securities Data Co. and exclude overallotment options, but include the international tranche, if any.

Table 11.3
Number of Offerings, Average First-Day Returns, and Gross Proceeds of U.S. Initial Public Offerings, 1975–2003

Source: Jay R. Ritter, "Some Factoids About the 2003 IPO Market," downloaded from his Web site at http://bear.cba.ufl.edu/ritter/ipodata.htm.

2003 IPOs raised barely $10 billion—only 15 percent of 2000's proceeds. Though this recent cycle was among the most dramatic in history, the general pattern was by no means unprecedented, following boom-and-bust cycles from the 1960s, 1970s, and 1980s. Furthermore, the pace of IPOs during the first half of 2004 suggests another market upswing may be underway.

Another interesting pattern observed in the IPO market is the tendency for firms going public in a certain industry to "cluster" in time. It is common to see bursts of IPO activity in fairly narrow industry sectors, such as energy, biotechnology, and communications, and in the late 1990s, Internet-related companies. Indeed, the latter half of the 1990s saw an incredible boom in both the number of Internet companies going public and the valuations assigned to them by the market. Companies such as Netscape, Yahoo!, Amazon.com, and eBay were able to raise hundreds of millions of dollars in equity, despite their relatively short operating histories and nonexistent profits. Investors were so eager to purchase shares in these firms that their stock prices often doubled the first day they began trading. The recent offering of seven percent of Google raised $1.66 billion, and yielded a significant—but much less frothy—first day return of almost 18 percent.

APPLYING THE MODEL

The short-term stock-price increases for Internet-related IPOs had financial experts scratching their heads in 1999, none more so than the December 9, 1999, debut of VA Linux. The company went public with an offer price of $30 per share, and after one trading day, the stock closed at almost $240 per share. For investors who bought shares at the offer price and sold them as soon as possible, the one-day return was an astronomical *700 percent.* Investors who held on for the long term did not fare as well. After the IPO, the stock closed above $240 only once. By June 2004, the company, now renamed VA Software, saw its stock trading at just over $2.25 per share.

As recently as the early 1980s, investment banks targeted initial offerings almost exclusively at individual investors, more particularly at retail customers of the brokerage firms involved in the underwriting syndicate. Over the past twenty-five years, however, institutional investors have grown in importance. Now they generally receive 50–75 percent of the shares offered in the typical IPOs and up to 90 percent, or more, of the "hot" issues.

A final pattern emerging in the U.S. IPO market is its increasingly international flavor. The largest and most visible of the international IPOs are associated with privatizations of formerly state-owned enterprises. However, both established international companies and non-U.S. entrepreneurial firms are also choosing to make initial stock offerings to U.S. investors, either publicly via a straight IPO or to institutional investors through a **Rule 144A offering.** This special type of offer, which was first approved in April 1990, allows issuing companies to waive some disclosure requirements by selling stock only to sophisticated institutional investors, who may then trade the shares among themselves.

Rule 144A offering
A special type of offer, first approved in April 1990, that allows issuing companies to waive some disclosure requirements by selling stock only to sophisticated institutional investors, who may then trade the shares among themselves.

Advantages and Disadvantages of an IPO

The decision to convert from private to public ownership is not an easy one. The benefits of having publicly traded shares are numerous, but so too are the costs. This section describes the costs and benefits of IPOs for U.S. firms. Interestingly, as we discuss more fully in Section 11.5, the motivations for going public are significantly different for continental European business owners than they are for their U.S. counterparts.

Benefits of Going Public. Chapter 2 of the accounting firm KPMG Peat Marwick's publication *Going Public: What the CEO Needs to Know* (1998) suggests the following advantages of an IPO to an entrepreneur.

1. New capital for the company. An initial public offering gives the typical private firms access to a larger pool of equity capital than is available from any other source. Whereas venture capitalists can provide perhaps $10-$40 million in funding throughout a company's life as a private firm, an IPO allows that same company to raise many times that amount in one offering. Recent academic studies find that the typical U.S. IPO over the past fifteen years raised about $110 million. An infusion of common equity not only permits firms to pursue profitable investment opportunities but also improves their overall financial condition and provides additional borrowing capacity. Furthermore, if the stock of these firms performs well, the companies will be able to raise additional equity capital in the future.

2. Publicly traded stock for use in acquisitions. Unless a firm has publicly traded stock, the only way it can acquire another company is to pay in cash. After going public, a firm has the option of exchanging its own stock for that of the target firm. Not only does this minimize cash outflow for the acquiring firm, but such a payment method may be free from capital gains tax for the target firm's owners. This tax benefit may reduce the price that an acquirer must pay for a target company.

3. Listed stock for use as compensation. Having publicly traded stock allows companies to attract, retain, and provide incentives for talented managers by offering them stock options and other stock-based compensation. Going public also offers liquidity to managers who were awarded options while the firms were private.

4. Personal wealth and liquidity. Entrepreneurship almost always violates finance's basic dictum about diversification: real entrepreneurs generally have most of both their financial wealth and human capital tied up in their companies. Going public allows entrepreneurs to reallocate personal wealth away from their businesses and diversify their portfolios. Entrepreneurial families also frequently execute IPOs during times of transition, when, for example, the company founder wants to retire and therefore provide a method of allocating family assets among those heirs who do and who do not desire to remain active in the business.

In addition to these benefits, the act of going public generally results in a blaze of media attention, which often helps promote a company's products and services. Being a public company also increases a firm's overall prestige. However, the obvious benefits of an IPO must be weighed against the often massive costs of such an offer.

Drawbacks to Going Public. KPMG Peat Marwick's listing also includes the drawbacks of an IPO for a firm's managers.

1. The financial costs of an IPO. Few entrepreneurs are truly prepared for just how costly the process of going public can be in terms of out-of-pocket cash expenses and opportunity costs. Total cash expenses of an IPO, such as printing, accounting, and legal services, frequently approach $1 million, and most of these must be paid even if the offering is postponed or canceled. Additionally, the combined costs associated with the underwriter's discount (usually 7 percent) and the initial underpricing of a firm's stock (roughly 15 percent on average) represent a very large transfer of wealth from current owners to the underwriters and to the new stockholders.

2. The managerial costs of an IPO. As costly as an IPO is financially, many entrepreneurs find the unending claims made on their time during the IPO planning and execution process to be even more burdensome. Rarely, if ever, can CEOs and other top managers delegate these duties, which grow increasingly intense as the offering date approaches. There are also severe restrictions on what an executive can say or do during the immediate pre-offering period. Because the IPO process can take many months (or more) to complete, the cost of going public in terms of managerial distraction is very high. Top executives must also take time to meet with important potential stockholders before the IPO is completed, and forever thereafter.

3. Stock-price emphasis. Owners/managers of private companies frequently operate their firms in ways that balance competing personal and financial interests. This includes seeking profits, but frequently also includes employing family members in high positions and other forms of personal consumption. Once a company goes public, however, external pressures build to maximize a firm's stock price. Furthermore, as managerial shareholdings fall, managers become vulnerable to losing their jobs, either through takeover or through dismissal by the board of directors.

4. Life in a fishbowl. Public shareholders have the right to a great deal of information about a firm's internal affairs. Releasing this information to stockholders also implies releasing it to competitors and potential acquirers as well. Managers must disclose, especially in the IPO prospectus, how and in what markets they intend to compete—information that is obviously valuable to competitors. Additionally, managers who are also significant stockholders are subject to binding disclosure requirements and face serious constraints on their ability to buy or sell company stock.

In spite of these drawbacks, we have seen that several hundred management teams each year decide that the benefits of going public outweigh the costs, and they begin the process of planning for an IPO. In addition to these "standard" IPOs, there are four "special" types of IPOs that warrant additional attention.

Specialized IPOs: Equity Carve-Outs, Spin-Offs, Reverse LBOs, and Tracking Stocks

The four special types of IPOs are equity carve-outs (ECOs), spin-offs, reverse LBOs, and tracking stocks. An **equity carve-out** occurs when a parent company sells shares of a subsidiary corporation to the public through an initial public offering. The parent company may sell some of the subsidiary shares that it already owns, or the subsidiary may issue new shares. In any event, the parent company almost always retains a controlling stake in the newly public company.

equity carve-out
Occurs when a parent company sells shares of a subsidiary corporation to the public through an initial public offering. The parent company may sell some of the subsidiary shares that it already owns, or the subsidiary may issue new shares.

A **spin-off** occurs when a public parent company "spins off" a subsidiary to the parent's shareholders by distributing shares on a pro rata basis. Thus, after the spin-off, there are two public companies rather than one. Conceptually, the total stock value of the parent should drop by approximately the same amount that the market values the shares of the newly public spin-off. Instead, however, academic research finds significantly positive price reactions for the stock of divesting parent companies, at the time that spin-offs are announced, perhaps indicating that the market expects that the two independent companies will be managed more effectively than they would have been had they remained together.

spin-off
A parent company creates a new company with its own shares to form a division or subsidiary, and existing shareholders receive a pro rata distribution of shares in the new company.

In a **reverse LBO** (or **second IPO**), a formerly public company that has previously gone private, through a leveraged buyout, goes public again. Reverse LBOs are easier to price than traditional IPOs because information already exists about how the market valued the company when it was publicly traded. Empirical research indicates the LBO partners earn very high returns on these transactions. One reason for this is obvious: only the most successful LBOs can subsequently go public again.

reverse LBO (or second IPO)
A formerly public company that has previously gone private through a leveraged buyout and then goes public again. Also called a second IPO.

The final type of specialized equity offering, **tracking stocks**, is a very recent innovation. These are equity claims based on (and designed to mirror, or *track*) the earnings of wholly owned subsidiaries of diversified firms. They are hybrid securities, because the tracking stock "firm" is not separated from the parent company in any way.

tracking stocks
Equity claims based on (and designed to mirror, or track) the earnings of wholly owned subsidiaries of diversified firms.

Instead, it remains integrated with the parent, legally and operationally. In contrast, both carve-outs and spin-offs result in legally separate firms. AT&T conducted the largest common-stock offering in U.S. history, when it issued $10.6 billion in AT&T Wireless tracking stock in April 2000. As has been true for most other tracking stock offerings, AT&T's stock rose significantly when it announced the Wireless offering. Unfortunately, both parent and tracking stock performed abysmally during the months after the issue. Thus, in July 2001, AT&T spun off the Wireless division as a separate company. In March 2004, Sprint also announced plans to eliminate its tracking stock, which the company issued in 1998.

flip
To buy shares at the offer price and sell them on the first trading day.

The Investment Performance of IPOs

Are IPOs good investments? The answer seems to depend on the investment horizon of the investor and whether the investor can purchase IPO shares at the offer price. If an investor can buy shares at the offer price and **flip** them (sell them on the first trading day), then the returns on IPOs are substantial. If, instead, the investor buys shares in the secondary market and holds them for the long term, the returns are much less rewarding.

IPO underpricing
Occurs when the offer price in the prospectus is consistently lower than what the market is willing to bear.

initial return
The gain when an allocation of shares from an investment banker is sold at the first opportunity because the offer price is consistently lower that what the market is willing to bear.

Positive Initial Returns for IPO Investors (Underpricing).

Year in and year out, in virtually every country around the world, the very short-term returns on IPOs are surprisingly high. In the United States, the share price in the typical IPO closes roughly 15 percent above the offer price after just one day of trading. Researchers refer to this pattern as **IPO underpricing**, meaning that the offer price in the prospectus is consistently lower than what the market is willing to bear. To capture this **initial return**, an investor must be fortunate enough to receive an allocation of shares from the investment banker and to sell those shares at the first opportunity. Therein lies a problem. Not all investors are allowed to participate in the investment bank's allocations. Bankers discourage those investors who do participate from immediately selling (i.e., flipping) the shares they received on the open market. For investors who buy IPO shares when they begin trading in the open market, in the hope of making a quick profit, the rewards are much smaller, and the risks much greater, than those faced by investors who participate in the initial offering.

SMART PRACTICES VIDEO
Jay Ritter, University of Florida
"Every single country in the world has IPOs underpriced on average."

See the entire interview at **SMARTFinance**

APPLYING THE MODEL

On February 19, 2002, shares of the pioneer in Internet payment methods, Paypal Inc. (ticker symbol, PYPL), began trading for the first time. According to the IPO prospectus, Paypal offered its shares for $13.00 to participating investors. At the close of the first day, Paypal shares were worth $18.20, for a one-day return of 40 percent. However, for investors who could not buy shares from the syndicate but instead bought shares once trading began, the first-day results were not as good. Paypal shares opened the first day of trading at $19.29 before falling 5.7 percent by the day's end. Seven months later, Paypal was acquired by eBay in a stock deal worth $1.37 billion, or $22.68 per share.

Clearly, underpricing is a pervasive phenomenon. However, the long-run performance of IPOs presents a different puzzle.

Figure 11.2
The Long-Run Performance of U.S. Initial Public Offerings (IPOs) and Seasoned Equity Offerings (SEOs) Versus Matching Firms That Did Not Issue New Equity

These figures describe the average annual raw returns for 4,753 IPOs and their capitalization-matched nonissuing firms (top), and the average annual raw returns for 3,702 SEOs and their capitalization-matched nonissuing firms (bottom), during the five years after the issue. The sample period covers 1970–1990.

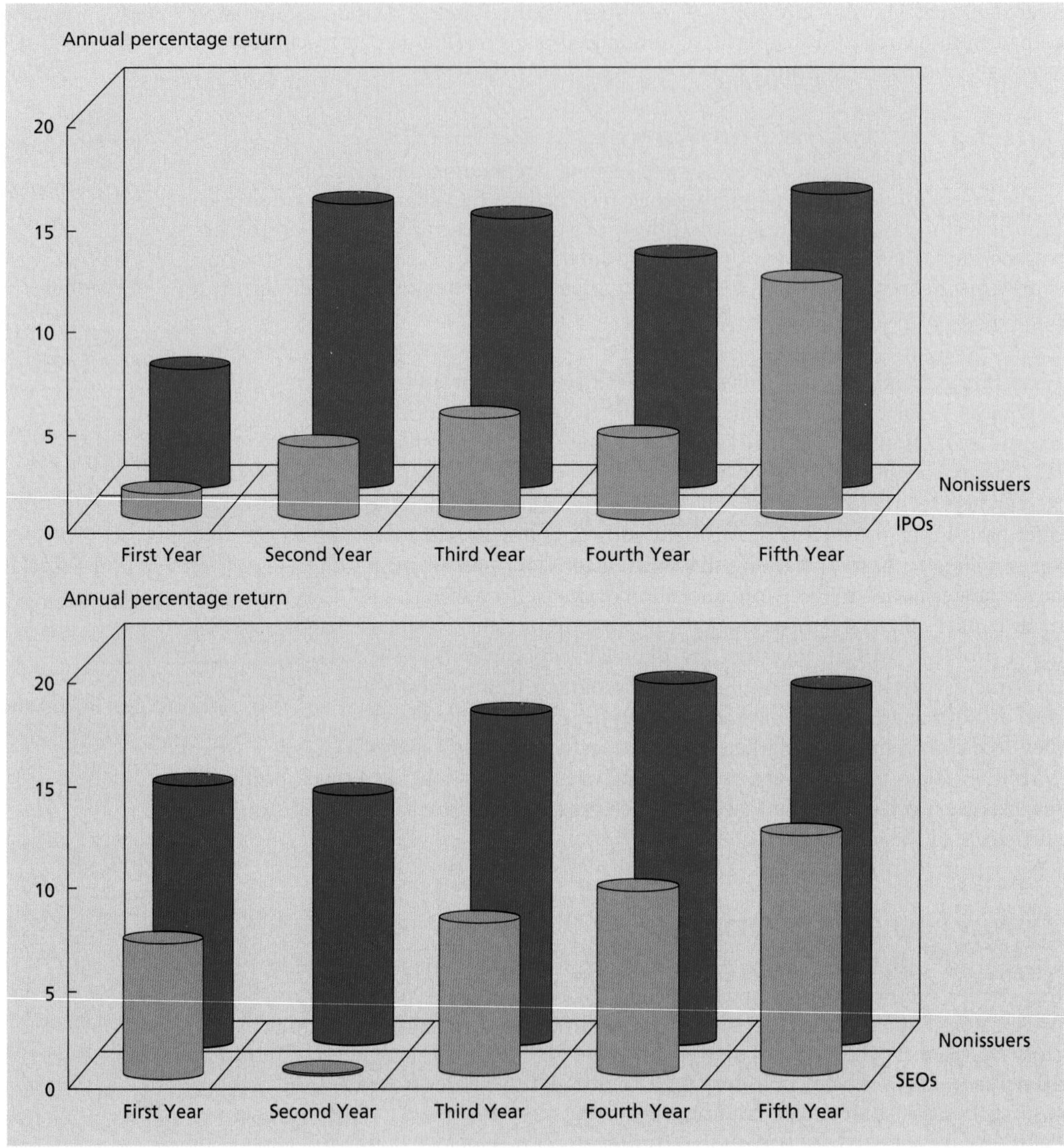

Source: Figure 2 of Tim Loughran and Jay R. Ritter, "The New Issues Puzzle," Journal of Finance *50, March 1995, pp. 23–51.*

Negative Long-Term IPO Returns. Early research on the long-run performance of IPOs was not encouraging for investors. The top graph in Figure 11.2 describes how badly investors fare, if they buy IPO shares at the end of the first month of trading and then hold these shares for five years thereafter, compared to the returns these investors would have earned by purchasing the shares of comparable-sized firms. On average, investors' net returns are over 40 percent below what they would have earned after five years on alternative equity investments.

Because these findings challenge the notions that investors are rational and that financial markets efficient, they are quite controversial. More recent research casts doubt on this long-run underperformance for IPO shares. Given these conflicting findings, we cannot yet draw firm conclusions about the long-run return on IPO shares.

SMART PRACTICES VIDEO

Jay Ritter, University of Florida

"By the middle of 2001, 97% of Internet companies were trading below the offer price."

See the entire interview at **SMARTFinance**

CONCEPT REVIEW QUESTIONS

6. What patterns have been observed in the types of firms going public in the United States? Why do you think that certain industries become popular with investors at different times?

7. What are the principal benefits of going public? What are the key drawbacks?

8. Distinguish between an *equity carve-out* and a *spin-off.* How might a spin-off create value for shareholders?

9. What does the term "underpricing" refer to? If the average IPO is underpriced by about 15 percent, how could an unsophisticated investor, who regularly invests in IPOs, earn an average return less than 15 percent?

10. How does underpricing add to the cost of going public?

11.4 SEASONED EQUITY OFFERINGS IN THE UNITED STATES

Seasoned equity offerings (SEOs) are surprisingly rare for both U.S. and non-U.S. companies. In fact, the typical large U.S. companies will not sell new common stock, even as frequently as once per decade. Nevertheless, when an SEO is launched, it tends to be much larger than the typical IPO. Seasoned common-stock issues must generally follow the same regulatory and underwriting procedures as unseasoned offerings. The company must prepare a registration statement, including a preliminary prospectus, and file it with the SEC. After the SEC approves the registration statement, a final prospectus is printed and the securities can then be sold to investors. Besides its larger-than-average size, a seasoned offering is principally different from an unseasoned offering in that the seasoned securities have an observable market price when the offering is made. Obviously, this makes pricing seasoned offers much easier. Academic studies show that American SEOs tend to be priced very near the current market price. However, ease of pricing does not mean that investors welcome new equity offering announcements, as we now discuss.

Stock Price Reactions to Seasoned Equity Offerings

One reason that corporations very rarely issue seasoned equity is that stock prices usually fall when firms announce plans to conduct SEOs. On average, the price decline is about 3 percent. In the United States, the average dollar value of this price decline is equal to almost one third of the dollar value of the issue itself. Clearly, the announcement of seasoned equity issues conveys negative information to investors, though precisely what information is transmitted is not always clear. The message may be that management, which is presumably better informed about a company's true prospects than are outside investors, believes the firm's current stock price is too high. Alternatively, the message may be that the firm's earnings will be lower than expected in the future, and management is issuing stock to make up for this internal cash flow shortfall.

There is some evidence that SEOs are bad news for shareholders not only at the time they are announced but also over longer holding periods of one to five years. Negative long-run returns, following seasoned equity offerings, are documented, as shown in the bottom graph in Figure 11.2. Whether long-run returns, following SEOs, are unusually low, however, depends somewhat on the comparison benchmark.

general cash offerings Most equity sales in the United States fall under this category.

rights offerings A special type of seasoned equity offering that allows the firm's existing owners to buy new shares at a bargain price or to sell that right to other investors.

preemptive rights These hold that shareholders have first claim on anything of value distributed by a corporation.

Most equity sales in the United States fall under the category of **general cash offerings**, meaning that shares are offered for sale to any and all investors. However, there is a special type of seasoned equity offering that allows firms' existing owners to buy new shares at a bargain price or to sell that right to other investors. These **rights offerings** are relatively scarce in the United States but are more common in other developed countries.

Rights Offerings

One of the basic tenets of English common law, and thus of U.S. commercial laws derived from it, is that shareholders have first claim on anything of value distributed by a corporation. These **preemptive rights** give common stockholders the right to maintain their proportionate ownership in the corporation, by purchasing shares whenever the firm sells new equity. The laws of most American states grant shareholders the preemptive right to participate in new issues, unless this right is removed by shareholder consent. However, most publicly traded U.S. companies have removed preemptive rights from their corporate charters, with shareholder consent, so rights offerings by large American companies are quite rare today. Rights offerings are still quite common in other countries, as the following Applying the Model indicates.

APPLYING THE MODEL

It is often said that "the threat of disaster concentrates the mind," which was certainly true for the world's largest telecommunications firms, during the bleak period after the steep decline in high-tech stocks in March 2000. After a decade of extremely rapid growth in capital spending, fueled primarily by unprecedented borrowing from banks and bond markets, many telecom companies found themselves teetering on the brink of bankruptcy by late 2002. The slower-than-expected revenue growth, coupled with the higher-than-expected costs incurred, to roll out "third-generation" cellular telephone networks, had left most of the large European operators with dangerously high debt levels. Without reducing their outstanding debts, firms risked seeing their credit ratings plummet.

To avert the prospect of financial meltdown, three of the largest European telecoms—British Telecom (BT), the Netherlands' KPN, and France Telecom (FT)—took the highly unusual step of launching immense rights offerings of common stock. BT raised £5.9 billion ($8.5 billion) in June 2001, and KPN issued €5 billion ($4.5 billion) six months later, briefly making these the two largest rights offerings in history. In March 2003, FT shattered all previous records with an enormous €15 billion ($15.8 billion) rights offering. Because this strategy keeps all the gains and losses on share issues "within the family" of current shareholders, firms usually price rights offerings well below the current market price to assure that the offerings sell out, and firms raise the funds needed. All three companies followed this pattern. For example, BT priced its shares, which were selling for 435 pence ($7.54) each, at the time of the rights issue, for 300 pence ($5.20) each. FT also priced its rights issue at about a 30 percent discount to the stock's pre-offer closing price, while KPN priced its new shares at a 4.5 percent discount.

Though all three companies saw their stock prices fall sharply when they announced their rights offerings, the rights issues themselves were successful, and all three issues met with excess demand (in investment banking terms, the issues were "oversubscribed"). After the offerings however, all three stocks underperformed their national stock market indices. In the summer of 2004, all three stocks were more than 75 percent below their March 2000 peaks. Although U.S. telecom firms have also suffered since early 2000, none have announced plans for a rights issue.

Private Placements in the United States

As noted earlier, a **private placement** involves the sale of securities in a transaction that is exempt from the registration requirements imposed by federal securities law. A private placement occurs when an investment banker arranges for the direct sale of a new security issue to an individual, several individuals, an institutional investor, or a group of institutions. The investment banker is then paid a commission for acting as an intermediary in the transaction. To qualify for a private-placement exemption, the sale of the securities must be restricted to a small group of **accredited investors**, who are individuals or institutions that meet certain income and wealth requirements. The reasoning for the private-placement exemption is that accredited investors are financially sophisticated players, who do not need the protection afforded by the registration process. Typical accredited institutional investors include insurance companies, pension funds, mutual funds, and venture capitalists.

private placements
Unregistered security offerings sold directly to accredited investors.

accredited investors
Individuals or institutions that meet certain income and wealth requirements.

Traditional Private Placements Versus Rule 144A Issues. While the private-placement exemption allows securities to be issued privately, this same exemption requires that the securities must be registered before they can be resold, or the subsequent sale must also qualify as a private placement. Rule 144A, adopted in 1990, provides a private-placement exemption for institutions with assets exceeding $100 million (known as **qualified institutional buyers**) and allows them to freely trade privately placed securities among themselves. The principal reasons for instituting Rule 144A were to increase liquidity and to reduce issuing costs in the private-placement market. Another reason was to attract large foreign issuers who were unable or unwilling to conform to U.S. registration requirements for public offerings.

qualified institutional buyers
Institutions with assets exceeding $100 million.

Private placements have several advantages over public offerings. They are less costly, in terms of time and money, than registering with the SEC, and the issuers do not have to reveal confidential information. Also, because there typically are far fewer investors, the terms of a private placement are easier to renegotiate, if necessary. The disadvantage of private placements is that the securities have no readily available market price, they are less liquid, and there is a smaller group of potential investors than in the public market. Two features stand out in any analysis of private placements in recent years. First, debt offerings are much more common than equity offerings, though stock issues raise significantly larger amounts on average. Second, Rule 144A offerings account for about two thirds of the $400–600 billion raised each year through private placements in the United States.

CONCEPT REVIEW QUESTIONS

11. What happens to a company's stock price when the firm announces plans for a seasoned equity offering? What are the long-term returns to investors, following an SEO?

12. Why do you think that rights offerings have largely disappeared in the United States?

13. What is a *qualified institutional buyer?* How does this differ from an *accredited investor?*

14. What are the relative advantages and disadvantages of private placements, compared to those of public offerings of stock and bond issues?

11.5 INTERNATIONAL COMMON-STOCK OFFERINGS

The international market for equity offerings can be broken down into two parts: each nation's market for domestic stock offerings and the international, or cross-border, market for equity offerings. We briefly look at each, in turn, beginning with an overview of national markets.

Non-U.S. Initial Public Offerings

Any nation with a well-functioning stock market must have some mechanism for taking private firms public. The total number of IPOs outside the United States each year usually exceeds the American total by a wide margin. However, far less money is raised in aggregate by private-sector issuers on non-U.S. markets, as these international IPOs are, on average, very much smaller than those on the Nasdaq or NYSE. Yet, many of the same investment anomalies documented in the United States are also observed internationally. First, non-U.S. private-sector IPOs also demonstrate significant first-day returns that are often much higher than for U.S. IPOs. The Comparative Corporate Finance figure summarizes IPO underpricing studies from thirty-eight different countries; all show significant underpricing, and twenty of these countries have mean initial returns greater than the U.S. average.

A second empirical regularity, common to both U.S. and international IPOs, is that unseasoned international offers also appear to yield negative long-term returns. However, studies of non-U.S. long-run returns are subject to all the methodological problems bedeviling U.S. studies (perhaps even more), so it is unclear whether SEOs truly underperform or not. Third, popular non-U.S. issues also tend to be heavily oversubscribed, and the allocation rules mandated by national law or exchange regulations largely determine who captures the IPO initial returns. Fourth, hot-issue markets are as prevalent internationally as in the United States. Finally, taxation issues (particularly capital gains tax rules) significantly effect how issues are priced and which investors the offers target.

International IPO markets do, however, differ in important ways from U.S. markets. For example, many governments impose politically inspired mandates on firms wanting to go public, requiring them to allocate minimum fractions of the issue to their employees or to other targeted groups. Furthermore, the net effect of pricing restrictions in many countries is to ensure that IPOs are severely underpriced; this is especially common in countries where shares must be priced on a par value basis and where minimum dividend payouts may be mandated. Some governments (including those as advanced as Japan's) routinely prohibit firms from making IPOs during

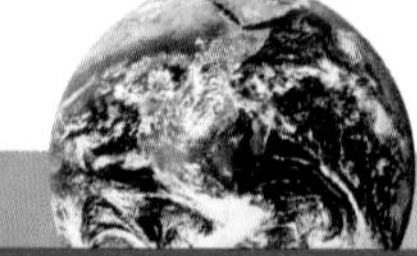

COMPARATIVE CORPORATE FINANCE

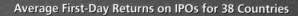

Average First-Day Returns on IPOs for 38 Countries

Significantly positive initial returns on initial public offerings are observed in many other countries besides the United States. As this figure shows, IPO underpricing is observed in at least 38 countries, though the average level varies greatly—from less than 5 percent in Denmark, Canada, and Austria to over 100 percent in Malaysia to an amazing 250 percent in China.

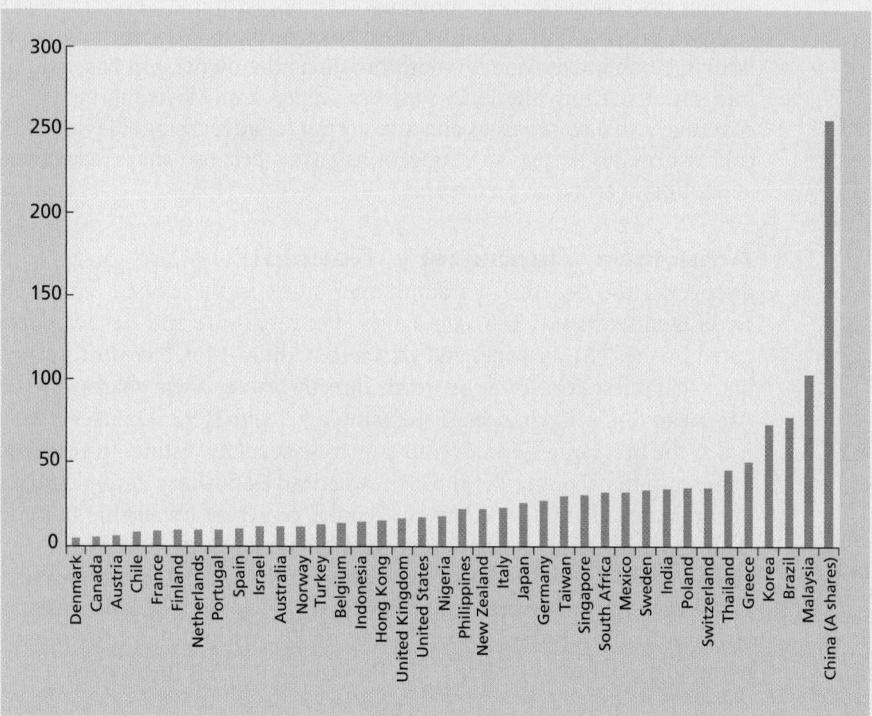

Source: Studies cited in Tim Loughran, Jay R. Ritter and Kristian Rydqvist, "Initial Public Offerings: International Insights," *Pacific-Basin Finance Journal* 2, June 1994, pp. 165–1999; plus updates on Ritter's Web site at http://bear.cba.ufl.edu/ritter/ipodata.htm.

periods when market conditions are "unsettled." They may require explicit permission to be obtained before an IPO can be launched. Many countries require that initial offering prices be set far in advance of the issue, which usually means that offerings, which actually proceed, tend to be highly underpriced. Non-U.S. entrepreneurs often have different motivations for taking firms public than do owner/managers of U.S. private companies. Whereas many U.S. companies go public to acquire the equity capital needed to finance rapid growth, continental European entrepreneurs (specifically, Italian) go public mainly to rebalance their firms' capital structures and to achieve personal liquidity. On a more balanced note, most other countries place fewer restrictions on pre-offer marketing and discussion than do U.S. regulators.

International Common-Stock Issues

Although the international market for common stock is not, and probably never will be, as large as the international market for debt securities, cross-border trading and issuance of common stock have increased dramatically during the past fifteen years. Much of this increase can be accounted for by a growing desire on the part of institutional and individual investors to diversify their investment portfolios internationally. Because foreign stocks currently account for a small fraction of U.S. institutional holdings—as is true in other developed economies—this total will surely grow rapidly in the years ahead.

Besides issuing stock to investors, corporations have also discovered the benefits of issuing stock outside their home markets. For example, several top U.S. multinational companies have chosen to list their stock in half a dozen, or more, stock markets. Issuing stock internationally both broadens the ownership base and helps a company integrate itself into the local business scene. A stock listing increases the local press coverage and also serves as effective corporate advertising. Having locally traded stock can also make corporate acquisitions easier because shares can then be used as an acceptable method of payment.

American Depositary Receipts. Many foreign corporations have discovered the benefits of trading their stock in the United States, although they do so differently than do U.S. companies. The disclosure and reporting requirements mandated by the U.S. Securities and Exchange Commission have historically discouraged all but the largest foreign firms from directly listing their shares on the New York or American Stock Exchanges. For example, in mid-1993, Daimler Benz announced that it was the first large German company to seek such a listing. Instead, most foreign companies tap the U.S. market through **American Depositary Receipts (ADRs).** These dollar-denominated claims, issued by U.S. banks, represent ownership of a foreign company's shares that are held on deposit by the U.S. bank in the issuing firm's home country.

American Depositary Receipts (ADRs) Dollar-denominated claims, issued by U.S. banks, that represent ownership of shares of a foreign company's stock held on deposit by the U.S. bank in the issuing firm's home country.

ADRs have proven to be very popular with U.S. investors, partly because they allow investors to diversify internationally. However, because the shares are covered by American securities laws and pay dividends in dollars (dividends on the underlying shares are converted from the local currency into dollars before being paid

Figure 11.3
Trading Volume in Public American Depositary Receipt (ADR) Issues, 1993–2003

Sources: The Bank of New York, "Depositary Receipt Market Review 2003" and "Depositary Receipts (ADRs and GDRs) 2002 Year-End Market Review," downloaded from the company's Web site at http://adrbny.com.

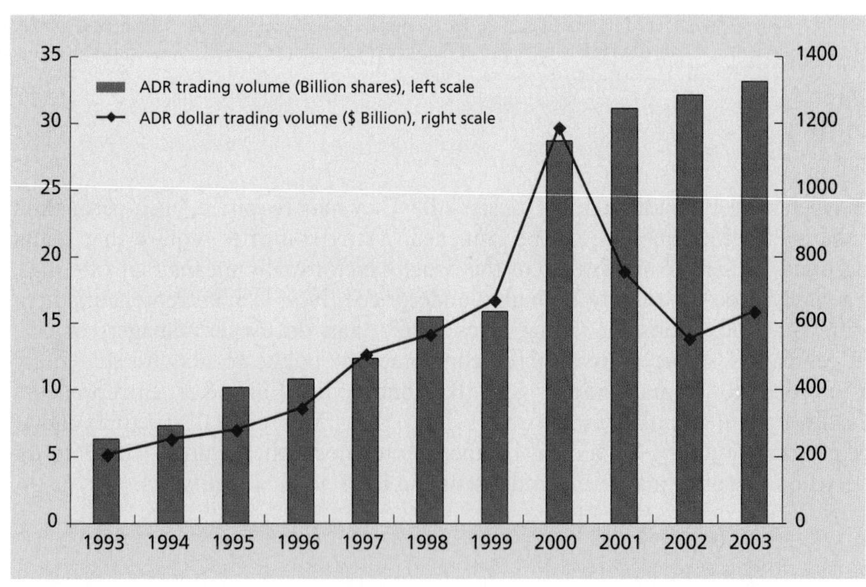

out), U.S investors are able to diversify at very low cost. Figure 11.3 details the rapid growth in market value and trading volume of ADRs on the three major U.S. stock exchanges over the period 1993–2003.

The shares of over 1,400 foreign companies are traded in the United States in the form of sponsored and unsponsored ADRs. The New York Stock Exchange alone has 464 ADRs from fifty countries, listed as of March 2004. A **sponsored ADR** is one for which the issuing (foreign) company absorbs the legal and financial costs of creating and trading the security. In this case, the companies pay a U.S. depositary bank to create an ADR issue. An **unsponsored ADR** is one in which issuing firms are not involved with the issue at all and may even oppose it. Historically, unsponsored ADRs typically resulted from U.S. investor demand for shares of particular foreign companies. Since 1983, however, the SEC has required that all new ADR programs be sponsored, so less than 200 unsponsored ADRs still exist. There are also four different levels of ADR programs, corresponding to different levels of required disclosure and tradeability.

sponsored ADR
An ADR for which the issuing (foreign) company absorbs the legal and financial costs of creating and trading the security.

unsponsored ADR
An ADR in which the issuing firm is not involved with the issue at all and may even oppose it.

APPLYING THE MODEL

To demonstrate how ADRs are created, assume that the Dutch Tulip Company (DTC) wants to set up an ADR program for its shares on the New York Stock Exchange. Suppose that DTC's shares are trading on Euronext Amsterdam (formerly the Amsterdam Stock Exchange) at €21.00 per share, and the U.S. dollar/euro exchange rate is $1.2500/€. If DTC wants to establish an ADR program worth about $100 million, the firm could ask Bank of New York (ticker symbol, BK), one of the two leading ADR issuers, to handle the issue and could offer to pay all of BK's issuing and listing expenses—including underwriting fees. Assume further that BK believes the ideal price for shares to trade on the NYSE is about $50 per share. BK can implement this ADR program by taking the following steps:

1. Purchase 4 million shares of DTC on Euronext Amsterdam at €21.00/share, paying €84 million. This represents an investment worth $105,000,000 by Bank of New York (€84,000,000 × $1.2500/€).
2. Create 2.0 million ADRs for listing on the NYSE, with each ADR representing ownership of two DTC shares.
3. Sell the 2.0 million ADRs to American investors at a price of $52.50 per ADR. This is the dollar price implied by DTC's price in euros, the current $/€ exchange rate, and considering that each ADR is worth two DTC shares (€21.00/share × 2 shares/ADR × $1.2500/€ = $52.50/ADR).

The total proceeds of this offering are $105,000,000, which is exactly equal to the amount BK paid for the shares originally. Holders of these ADRs have a security that is denominated in dollars, but which perfectly reflects both DTC's share price in euros and fluctuations in the dollar/euro exchange rate.

To demonstrate how ADRs reflect changes in DTC's stock price, assume that DTC's shares increase by €1.00 per share in early-morning trading in the Netherlands. We can compute that the ADRs should rise by $2.50 each (€1.00/share × 2 shares/ADR × $1.2500/€) to $55.00 per share when they begin trading in New York later that day. To demonstrate how ADRs reflect exchange rate movements, assume that DTC's price remains unchanged at €21 per share, but that the euro appreciates from $1.2500/€ to $1.3095/€ immediately before trading begins in New York. The ADRs should begin trading at $55.00 per share (€21.00/share × 2 shares/ADR × $1.3095/€) when the NYSE opens. In other words, either an increase in DTC's stock price from €21.00 to €22.00 per share, while holding exchange rates constant, or an appreciation of the euro from $1.2500/€ to $1.3095/€ (holding DTC's stock price unchanged) can cause the price of each Dutch Tulip Company ADR to rise by $2.50, from $52.50 to $55.00 per ADR.

There have been numerous high-profile ADR offerings in recent years. For example, Deutsche Bank established an American Depositary Receipt program on the New York Stock Exchange on October 1, 2001. Citibank sponsored the company's ADRs, each of which represents five ordinary shares and trades under the symbol TSM. China Life Insurance Company, spotlighted in this chapter's Opening Focus, was not only the largest ADR issue of 2003 but also the largest share offering of any kind that year. The two ADR programs with the highest dollar-value trading volume during 2003 were Finland's Nokia ($46.8 billion) and the Britain's BP ($34.2 billion).

Share Issue Privatizations

share issue privatization (SIP)
A government executing one of these will sell all or part of its ownership in a state-owned enterprise to private investors via a public share offering.

Anyone who examines international share offerings is soon struck by the size and importance of share issue privatizations in non-U.S. stock markets. A government executing a **share issue privatization (SIP)** sells all or part of its ownership in a state-owned enterprise to private investors, via a public share offering. The words *public* and *private* can become confusing in this context, because a SIP involves the sale of shares in a state-owned company to *private* investors, via a *public* capital market share offering. Since Britain's Thatcher government first popularized privatizations in the early 1980s, there have been more than 850 privatizing share offerings by almost 100 national governments. Prompted by the British success, governments around the world launched privatization programs that have, to date, raised over $1.25 trillion. Virtually, all this money flowed to the selling governments rather than to the firms being privatized. Figure 11.4 shows how much money governments raised through privatization programs between 1988 and 2003.

For our purposes, the most important aspect of privatization programs is the transforming role they have played in developing many national stock markets, in general, and IPO markets, in particular. Share issue privatizations are particularly important for market development because of their size and the way their shares are allocated to potential investors. As Table 11.4 makes clear, SIPs tend to be vastly larger than their private-sector counterparts; in fact, the eleven largest (and twenty-four of the twenty-five largest) share offerings in history have all been either share issue privatizations or rights offerings by partially privatized companies. Almost without exception, SIPs have been the largest share offerings in the histories of individual countries. The first several large privatization IPOs generally yield a dramatic increase in a national stock market's trading volume and liquidity. In addition to size, SIPs differ from private-sector share issues in being almost exclusively secondary offerings. In other words, the proceeds from SIPs go to the government

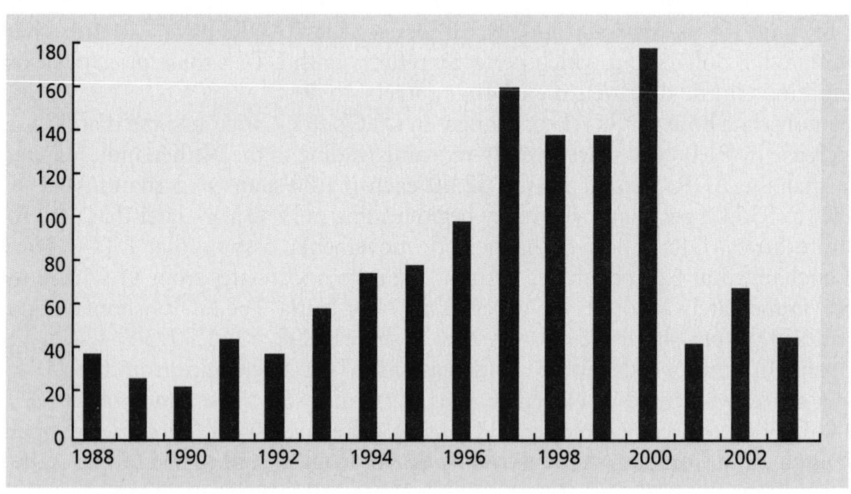

Figure 11.4
Annual Privatization Revenues for Divesting Governments Worldwide, 1988–2003 (in $U.S. Billions)

Source: Data through 1999 from Privatisation International, *as reported in William L. Megginson and Jeffry M. Netter, "From State to Market: A Survey of Empirical Studies on Privatization,"* Journal of Economic Literature *39, June 2001, pp. 321–389. Data for 2000–2003 are from the IFR Thomson database.*

Table 11.4
Details of the World's Largest Share Offerings

With one exception (the AT&T Wireless tracking stock issue in April 2000), the 24 largest share offerings in history have either been share issue privatizations or share offerings by partially privatized companies.

Date	Company	Country	Amount ($ mil)	IPO/SEO
Nov 87	Nippon Telegraph & Telephone	Japan	$40,260	SEO
Oct 88	Nippon Telegraph & Telephone	Japan	22,400	SEO
Nov 99	ENEL	Italy	18,900	IPO
Oct 98	NTT DoCoMo	Japan	18,000	IPO
Mar 03	France Telecom	France	15,800	SEO[a]
Oct 97	Telecom Italia	Italy	15,500	SEO
Feb 87	Nippon Telegraph & Telephone	Japan	15,097	IPO
Nov 99	Nippon Telegraph & Telephone	Japan	15,000	SEO
Jun 00	Deutsche Telekom	Germany	14,760	SEO
Nov 96	Deutsche Telekom	Germany	13,300	IPO
Oct 87	British Petroleum	United Kingdom	12,430	SEO
Apr 00	*ATT Wireless (tracking stock)*	*United States*	*10,600*	*IPO*
Nov 98	France Telecom	France	10,500	SEO
Nov 97	Telstra	Australia	10,530	IPO
Oct 99	Telstra	Australia	10,400	SEO
Jun 99	Deutsche Telekom	Germany	10,200	SEO
Dec 90	Regional Electricity Companies[b]	United Kingdom	9,995	IPO
Dec 91	British Telecom	United Kingdom	9,927	SEO
Jun 00	Telia	Sweden	8,800	IPO
Dec 89	U.K. Water Authorities[b]	United Kingdom	8,679	IPO
Feb 01	NTT DoCoMo	Japan	8,200	SEO
Dec 86	British Gas	United Kingdom	8,012	IPO
Jun 98	Endesa	Spain	8,000	SEO
Jul 97	ENI	Italy	7,800	SEO

a. Rights offering, in which the French government participated proportionately, so not a SIP in the traditional sense. Though a share offering by a state-owned firm, government ownership did not decline.
b. Indicates a group offering of multiple companies that trade separately after the IPO.

Source: Table 12 of William L. Megginson and Jeffry M. Netter. 2001. "From State to Market: A Survey of Empirical Studies on Privatization," Journal of Economic Literature *39, pp. 321–389. Updated through June 2004 by author, using data reported in the* Financial Times.

rather than to the firm being privatized. The sole major exception to this rule to date has occurred in China; almost all Chinese SIPs have been primary offerings.

The importance of SIPs in creating new shareholders derives from the way these issues are typically priced and allocated. Governments almost always set offer prices well below their expected open-market value (they deliberately underprice), thereby ensuring great excess demand for shares in the offering. The issuing governments then allocate shares in a way that ensures maximum political benefit. Invariably, governments favor employees and other small domestic investors (who typically have never purchased common stock before) with relatively large share allocations, whereas domestic institutions and foreign investors are allocated far less than they desire. The net result of this strategy is to guarantee that most of the short-term capital gains of privatization IPOs are captured by the many citizen investors (who vote) rather than by institutional and foreign investors (who do not). Furthermore, the long-run excess returns to investors who purchase privatizing share issues are significantly positive. All these features help promote popular support for privatization and other economic reform measures that the government wants to enact. In all, privatization share offerings have done as much to promote the development of international stock markets during the last twenty-five years as any other single factor.

CONCEPT REVIEW QUESTIONS

15. In what ways are non-U.S. (private-sector) initial public offerings similar to U.S. IPOs, and in what ways are they different?

16. What are *American Depositary Receipts (ADRs),* and how are these created? Why do you think ADRs have proven to be so popular with U.S. investors?

17. In what key ways do *share issue privatizations (SIPs)* differ from private-sector share offerings? Why do you think governments deliberately underprice SIPs?

11.6 SUMMARY AND CONCLUSIONS

- In almost all market economies, internally generated funds (primarily retained earnings) are the dominant source of funding for corporate investment. External financing is used only when needed, and then debt is almost always preferred to equity financing. The difference between a firm's total funding needs and its internally generated cash flow is referred to as its financial deficit.
- Financial intermediaries are institutions that raise funds by selling claims on themselves (often in the form of demand deposits or checking accounts) and then use those funds to purchase the debt-and-equity claims of corporate borrowers. They thus break—or intermediate—the direct link between final savers and borrowers that exists when companies fund their investment needs by selling securities directly to investors.
- Though financial intermediaries are essential to the smooth running of the U.S. economy, FIs play a relatively small direct role in financing American corporations. This is especially true of large, multinational firms. However, intermediaries remain very important in the corporate financial systems of most other nations.
- The total volume of security issues has surged eight-fold in eleven years—reaching $5.33 trillion worldwide in 2003—but U.S. corporate issuers routinely account for two thirds of the worldwide total.
- Companies wanting to raise capital externally must make a series of decisions, beginning with whether to issue debt or equity, and whether to employ an investment bank to assist with the securities' sale. This chapter focuses on common-stock offerings, but the decisions and issuing procedures are very similar for preferred stock and debt securities.
- Firms wanting to raise new common-stock equity must decide whether to sell stock to public investors through a general cash offering, or to rely on sales to existing stockholders in a rights offering. Rights issues are now fairly rare in the United States, though they remain common in other developed countries.
- In the United States, common stock can be sold through private placements to accredited investors, or it can be sold to the public if the securities are registered with the SEC. A company's first public offering of common stock is known as its initial public offering, or IPO. The typical American IPO is underpriced, on average, by about 15 percent, and this has held true for several decades. International IPOs are also underpriced. It is unclear whether IPOs are poor long-term investments.

- Subsequent offerings of common stock are known as seasoned equity offerings, or SEOs. The announcement of a seasoned equity issue tends to decrease a company's stock price. There is strong evidence that firms issuing seasoned equity underperform over the long term.
- Investment banks assist companies in selling new securities by underwriting security offerings. Underwriting a security offering involves three tasks: (1) managing the offering, which includes advising companies about the type and amount of securities to sell, (2) underwriting the offering, by purchasing the securities from the issuer at a fixed price to shift the price risk from the issuer to the investment bank, and (3) selling the securities to investors.
- The largest share offerings in world history have all been share issue privatizations, or SIPs. Since 1981, governments have raised over $850 billion through these share offerings, and they have transformed stock market capitalization, trading volume, and the number of citizens who own shares in many countries.

SELF-TEST PROBLEMS

Answers to Self-Test Problems appear in Appendix D at back of book. Answers to the Concept Review Questions throughout the chapter appear at http://megginson.swlearning.com.

ST11-1. Last year Guaraldi Instruments Inc. conducted an IPO, issuing 2 million common shares with a par value of $0.25 to investors, at a price of $15 per share. During its first year of operation, Guaraldi earned net income of $0.07 per share and paid a dividend of $0.005 per share. At the end of the year, the company's stock was selling for $20 per share. Construct the equity account for Guaraldi at the end of its first year in business and calculate the firm's market capitalization.

ST11-2. The Bloomington Company needs to raise $20 million of new equity capital. Its common stock is currently selling for $42 per share. The investment bankers require an underwriting spread of 7 percent of the offering price. The company's legal, accounting, and printing expenses associated with the seasoned offering are estimated to be $450,000. How many new shares must the company sell to net $20 million?

ST11-3. Assume that Zurich Semiconductor Company (ZSC) wants to create a sponsored ADR program, worth $75 million, to trade its shares on the NASDAQ stock market. Assume that ZSC is currently selling on the SWX Swiss Exchange for SF25.00 per share, and the current dollar/Swiss franc exchange rate is $0.8000/SF. American Bank and Trust (ABT) is handling the ADR issue for ZSC and has advised the company that the ideal trading price for high-technology shares on the NASDAQ is about $60 per share (or per ADR).

a. Describe the precise steps ABT must take to create an ADR issue that meets ZSC's preferences.

b. Assume that ZSC's stock price declines from SF25.00 to SF22.50 per share. If the exchange rate does not also change, what will happen to ZSC's ADR price?

c. If the Swiss franc depreciates from $0.8000/SF to $0.7500/SF, but the price of ZSC's shares remains unchanged in Swiss francs, how will ZSC's ADR price change?

INTERNET RESOURCES

Note: *For updates to links, please go to the book's Web site at*
http://megginson.swlearning.com

http://www.ipohome.com—Site operated by Renaissance Capital, offers up-to-date information on three types of new equity financing: venture capital, IPOs, and seasoned equity offerings; has a calendar of upcoming financing events http://marketrac.nyse.com/mt/index.html—A portion of the NYSE site, offering an exceptional virtual tour of the exchange floor that shows which stocks trade at each "post" and gives numerous up-to-date trading statistics for each stock

http://www.sec.gov/edgar.shtml—The U.S. Securities and Exchange Commission's EDGAR database, from which can be downloaded all registration statements and other required filings by companies with securities that are publicly traded on U.S capital markets

http://www.investorhome.com/ipo.htm—A site full of links to other sites, which include IPO data, research articles, and other information

http://adrbny.com—The Bank of New York's ADR Web site provides detailed information about ADR listing and trading patterns. This site also makes available the Bank's semiannual ADR Market Summary report.

KEY TERMS

accredited investors
American Depositary Receipts (ADRs)
book building
bulge bracket
cash flow from operations
certification
due diligence
effective
equity carve-out
Eurobond
financial deficit
financial intermediary (FI)
fixed-price offer
flip
foreign bond
full disclosure
general cash offerings
Glass-Steagall Act
Gramm-Leach-Bliley Act
initial return
IPO underpricing
international common stock
league table
McFadden Act
merchant banks
mixed offering
preemptive rights
primary offering
primary security issues
private placement
prospectus
qualified institutional buyers
registration statement
reverse LBO (or second IPO)
rights offerings
Rule 144A offering
secondary offerings
Securities Act of 1933
Securities and Exchange Commission Act of 1934
securitization
share issue privatization (SIP)
shelf registration (Rule 415)
spin-off
sponsored ADR
tracking stocks
unseasoned equity offerings
unsponsored ADR
Yankee bonds
Yankee common stock

QUESTIONS AND PROBLEMS

Q11-1. How can a corporation estimate the amount of financing that must be raised externally during a given year? Once that amount is known, what other decision must be made?

Q11-2. What is the dominant source of capital funding in the United States? Given this result, and knowing that most corporations are net dissavers, what decisions do most managers face in order to address this financial deficit?

Q11-3. Define the term "financial intermediary." What role do financial intermediaries play in U.S. corporate finance? How does this compare with the role of non-U.S. financial intermediaries?

Q11-4. Discuss the U.S. banking system regulations that have had a major effect on the development of the U.S. financial system. In what ways has the U.S. system been positively and negatively affected by these regulations?

Q11-5. Differentiate between a U.S. commercial bank and the merchant banks found in other developed countries. How have these differences affected the securities markets in the United States versus those in other developed countries?

Q11-6. What are the general trends regarding public security issuance by U.S. corporations? Specifically, which security type is most often sold to the public? What is the split between initial and seasoned equity offerings?

Q11-7. Distinguish between a Eurobond, a foreign bond, and a Yankee bond. Which of these three represents the greatest volume of security issuance?

Q11-8. What do you think are the most important costs and benefits of becoming a publicly traded firm? If you were asked to advise an entrepreneur whether to take his or her firm public, what are the key questions you would ask before making your recommendation?

Q11-9. If you were an investment banker, how would you determine the offering price of an IPO?

Q11-10. Are the significantly positive short-run returns and the significantly negative long-run returns, earned by IPO shareholders, compatible with market efficiency? If not, why not?

Q11-11. List and briefly describe the key services that investment banks provide to firms which are issuing securities, before, during, and after the offering.

Q11-12. What are *American Depositary Receipts (ADRs)*, and why have they proven to be so popular with U.S. investors?

Q11-13. How do you explain why the underwriting spread on IPOs averages about 7 percent of the offering price, whereas the underwriting spread on a seasoned offering of common stock averages less than 5 percent?

Q11-14. Discuss the various issues that must be considered in selecting an investment banker for an IPO. Which type of placement is usually preferred by the issuing firm?

Q11-15. In terms of IPO investing, what does it mean to "flip" a stock? According to the empirical results regarding short- and long-term returns that follow equity offerings, is flipping a wise investment strategy?

Q11-16. What materials are presented in an IPO prospectus? In general, what result is documented regarding sales of shares by insiders and venture capitalists?

Q11-17. How do you explain the highly politicized nature of *share issue privatization (SIP)* pricing and share allocation policies? Are governments maximizing offering proceeds, or are they pursuing primarily political and economic objectives?

PROBLEMS

P11-1. Meltzer Electronics estimates that its total financing needs for the coming year will be $34.5 million. During the coming fiscal year, the firm's required financing payments on its debt-and-equity financing will total $12.9 million. The firm's financial manager estimates that operating cash flows for the coming year will total $33.7 million and that the following changes will occur in the accounts noted.

Account	Forecast Change
Gross fixed assets	$8.9 million
Change in current assets	+2.3 million
Change in accounts payable	+1.3 million
Change in accrued liabilities	+0.8 million

a. Use Equation 2.3 and the data provided to estimate Meltzer's *free cash flow* in the coming year.
b. How much of the free cash flow will the firm have available as a source of new internal financing in the coming year?
c. How much external financing will Meltzer require during the coming year to meet its total forecast financing need?

P11-2. West Coast Manufacturing Company (WCMC) is executing an initial public offering with the following characteristics. The company will sell 10 million shares at an offer price of $25 per share, the underwriter will charge a 7 percent underwriting fee, and the shares are expected to sell for $32 per share by the end of the first-day's trading. Assuming this IPO is executed as expected, answer the following:

a. Calculate the initial return earned by investors who are allocated shares in the IPO.
b. How much will WCMC receive from this offering?
c. What is the total cost (underwriting fee and underpricing) of this issue to WCMC?

P11-3. Suppose you purchase shares of a company that recently executed an IPO at the post-offering market price of $32 per share, and you hold the shares for one year. You then sell your shares for $35 per share. The company does not pay dividends, and you are not subject to capital gains taxation. During this year, the return on the overall stock market was 11 percent. What net return did you earn on your share investment? Assess this return compared with the overall market return.

P11-4. Norman Internet Service Company (NISC) is interested in selling common stock to raise capital for capacity expansion. The firm has consulted First Tulsa Company, a large underwriting firm, which believes that the stock can be sold for $50 per share. The underwriter's investigation found that its administrative costs will be 2.5 percent of the sale price, and its selling costs will be 2.0 percent of the sale price. If the underwriter requires a profit, equal to 1 percent of the sale price, how much, in dollars, will the spread have to be to cover the underwriter's costs and profit?

P11-5. The Norman Company needs to raise $50 million of new equity capital. Its common stock is currently selling for $50 per share. The investment bankers require an underwriting spread of 3 percent of the offering price. The company's legal, accounting, and printing expenses, associated with the seasoned offering, are estimated to be $750,000. How many new shares must the company sell to net $50 million?

P11-6. LaJolla Securities Inc. specializes in the underwriting of small companies. The terms of a recent offering were as follows:

Number of shares	2 million
Offering price	$25 per share
Net proceeds	$45 million

LaJolla Securities' expenses, associated with the offering, were $500,000. Determine LaJolla Securities' profit on the offering if, immediately after the offering began, the secondary market price of each share was as follows:

a. $23 per share
b. $25 per share
c. $28 per share

P11-7. SMG Corporation sold 20 million shares of common stock in a seasoned offering. The market price of the company's shares, immediately before the offering, was $14.75. The shares were offered to the public at $14.50, and the underwriting spread was 4 percent. The company's expenses associated with the offering were $7.5 million. How much new cash did the company receive?

The U.S. Market for Initial Public Offerings

P11-8. Go to http://www.ipohome.com, and find (under IPO Marketwatch, then Pricings) information about firms that went public in the first few weeks of 2005. Write down the ticker symbols and offer prices for the firms you select; then go to Yahoo! and download daily price quotes since the IPO date. For each firm, calculate the following:

a. The first-day percentage return, measured from the offer price to the closing price
b. The first-day percentage return, measured from the opening price to the closing price

P11-9. Four companies conducted IPOs last month: Hot.Com, Biotech Pipe Dreams Corp., Sleepy Tyme Inc., and Bricks N Mortar International. All four companies went public at an offer price of $10 per share. The first-day performance of each stock (measured as the percentage difference between the IPO offer price and the first-day closing price) appears below:

Company	First-Day Return
Hot.Com	45%
Biotech Pipe Dreams	30%
Sleepy Tyme	5%
Bricks N Mortar	0%

a. You submit a bid through your broker for 100 shares of each company. Your orders were filled completely, and you cashed out of each deal after one day. What was your average return on these investments?
b. Next, suppose your orders were not all filled completely because of excess demand for "hot" IPOs. After ordering 100 shares of each company, you were able to buy only 10 shares of Hot.Com, 20 shares of Biotech Pipe Dreams, 50 shares of Sleepy Tyme, and 100 shares of Bricks N Mortar. Recalculate your average return, taking into account that your orders were only partially filled.

Seasoned Equity Offerings in the United States

P11-10. After a banner year of rising profits and positive stock returns, the managers of Raptor Pharmaceuticals Corporation (RPC) decided to launch a seasoned equity offering to raise new equity capital. RPC currently has 10 million shares outstanding, and yesterday's closing market price was $75.00 per RPC share. The company plans to sell 1 million newly issued shares in its seasoned offering. The investment banking firm Robbum and Blindum (R&B) has agreed to underwrite the new stock issue for a 2.5 percent discount from the offering price, which RPC and R&B have agreed should be $0.75 per share lower than RPC's closing price the day before the offering is sold.

a. What is likely to happen to RPC's stock price when the plan for this seasoned offering is publicly announced?
b. Assume that RPC's stock price closes at $72.75 per share the day before the seasoned offering is launched. What net proceeds will RPC receive from this offering?
c. Calculate the return earned by RPC's *existing* stockholders on their shares from the time preceding the announcement of the seasoned offering through the time it was actually sold for $72.75 per share.
d. Calculate the total cost of the seasoned equity offering to RPC's existing stockholders as a percentage of the offering proceeds.

International Common-Stock Offerings

P11-11. The Rome Electricity Company (REC) wants to create a sponsored ADR program, worth $300 million, to trade its shares on the New York Stock Exchange. Assume that REC is currently selling on the Borsa Italiana (the Italian Stock Exchange, in Milan) for €30.00 per share, and the current dollar/euro exchange rate is $1.2500/€. American Bank and Trust (ABT) is handling the ADR issue for REC and has advised REC that the ideal trading price for utility company shares on the NYSE is about $75 per share (or per ADR).

a. Describe the precise steps ABT must take to create an ADR issue that meets REC's preferences.

b. Suppose REC's stock price rises from €30.00 to €33.00 per share. If the exchange rate does not change, what will happen to REC's ADR price?

c. If the euro appreciates from $1.2500/€ to $1.2900/€, but the price of REC's shares remains unchanged in euros, what will happen to REC's ADR price?

P11-12. Nippon Computer Manufacturing Company (NCM) wants to create a sponsored ADR program, worth $250 million, to trade its shares on NASDAQ. Assume that NCM is currently selling on the Tokyo Stock Exchange for ¥1,550 per share, and the current dollar/yen exchange rate is $0.008089/¥ or, equivalently, ¥123.62/$. Metropolis Bank and Trust (MBT) is handling the ADR issue for NCM and has advised NCM that the ideal trading price for high-technology shares on the NASDAQ is about $20 per share (or per ADR).

a. Describe the precise steps MBT must take to create an ADR issue that meets NCM's preferences.

b. Suppose NCM's stock price rises from ¥1,550 to ¥1,650 per share. If the exchange rate does not change, what will happen to NCM's ADR price?

c. If the yen depreciates from $0.008089/¥ to $0.008050/¥, but the price of NCM's shares remains unchanged in yen, what will happen to NCM's ADR price?

THOMSON ONE Business School Edition

For instructions on using Thomson ONE: Business School Edition, refer to the instructions provided with the Thomson ONE: Business School Edition problems at the end of Chapters 1–6 or to "A Guide for Using Thomson ONE: Business School Edition."

P11-13. Determine the sources of capital for Canon Inc. (ticker: J:CN@N) in each of the last five years. How much capital was raised through internal sources, and how much was raised through external sources? Compare the sources of capital for Canon to those of Xerox Corp. (U:XRX). Does one company appear to depend more heavily on internal sources rather than external sources, or vice versa? What are some possible reasons for this?

Since these exercises depend upon real-time data, your answers will change continuously depending upon when you access the Internet to download your data.

MINICASE

Raising Long-Term Financing

Since graduation from college, you have worked at Precision Manufacturing, Incorporated, as a financial analyst. You have recently been promoted to the position of Senior Financial Manager, with responsibilities that include capital budgeting decisions and the raising of long-term financing. Therefore, you decide to investigate the various alternatives for raising funds. You understand that your goal is to ascertain that the marginal benefits received from undertaking long-term projects should be greater than the marginal costs of raising the long-term funds needed to finance those projects. With this goal in mind, you decide to answer the following questions.

ASSIGNMENT

1. What should managers consider when making the decision whether to finance internally or externally?
2. What services does an investment banker offer to corporations that choose to raise funds in the capital market?
3. What legal rules govern the issue of securities to the public in the United States?
4. What are the benefits to the corporation of going public?
5. What are the drawbacks to the corporation of going public?
6. What returns can investors in the common stock expect on the first day of trading if they commit to purchase shares through the IPO issue? What factors may affect the relative amount of these first-day returns?
7. Describe the following offers: (a) seasoned equity offer; (b) rights offer, and (c) private placement. In what circumstances would a company use each of these offerings to raise funds?
8. Discuss the differences between international public offerings and domestic (U.S.) public offerings.

Capital Structure

OPENING FOCUS

Capital Structures of America's Most Admired Companies

Each spring, *Fortune* magazine publishes a list of the most admired public companies in the United States, as well as a comparable listing of international firms. Wal-Mart tops the U.S. list in 2004, followed, in order, by Berkshire Hathaway (Warren Buffet's company), Southwest Airlines, General Electric, Dell, Microsoft, Johnson & Johnson, Starbucks, FedEx and IBM. Nine of these companies were also in the 2003 Top Ten list, and most have been enshrined on the list for several years.

What characteristics do these ten companies have in common that allow them to prosper and impress, year after year? All ten companies have achieved stellar sales growth rates, at least over the past decade, all are solidly profitable, and as a group, they have turned in a long-term stock performance that stomps the S&P 500 index. Seven of the ten companies pay dividends. All but two, Berkshire Hathaway and GE, have price-to-earnings ratios over 20 (the average P/E ratio is 27.44). This list includes the world's largest company in terms of sales, Wal-Mart, as well as the most valuable, GE (market capitalization of $306 billion).

The purpose of this chapter is to help you understand why some firms use a great deal of debt, while other firms use very little. For some people, the strategies of firms like Microsoft and Starbucks, which issue almost no debt, are intuitively appealing. These firms have adopted a relatively conservative financing strategy and are simply following William Shakespeare's advice, "neither a borrower nor a lender be." On the other hand, readers who have a basic understanding of the U.S. tax code will see a benefit to the high-debt capital structure chosen by GE. The tax law treats interest payments as a tax-deductible business expense, but the same treatment does not apply to dividends. Therefore, by using a significant amount of debt, GE shelters more of the cash flow that it generates from taxation.

In each chapter of this text, we have explained how managers weigh marginal benefits and costs to create value for shareholders. When it comes to financing decisions, our framework suggests that managers should trade off the benefits of debt (e.g., tax deductibility) with its costs (e.g., risk of default and bankruptcy) to arrive at an "optimal" capital structure that maximizes the wealth of shareholders. However, if all the "most admired companies" can prosper, while taking such different approaches to financing their operations, then we may wonder whether the decision to use debt or equity has any influence at all on how they perform. Almost 50 years ago, Franco Modigliani and Merton Miller, two economists who later received the Nobel Prize, reached a controversial and counterintuitive conclusion—a firm's decision to finance its operations with debt or with equity has no affect on its total market value. In this chapter, we explore the factors that determine whether managers can increase the values of their firms by choosing an optimal capital structure or whether they should focus their attention on something other than financing decisions.

	Debt-to-equity ratio, % (Book value)	Debt-to-equity ratio, % (Market value)
Wal-Mart	40	7
Berkshire Hathaway	0	0
Southwest Airlines	26	12
General Electric	215	55
Dell	9	0.6
Microsoft	0	0
Johnson & Johnson	14	2
Starbucks	0.2	0
FedEx	26	9
IBM	61	11

Source: "The 2004 List: America's Most Admired Companies," *Fortune* (March 8, 2004).

LEARNING OBJECTIVES

After studying this chapter you should be able to:

- Explain how financial leverage increases both a firm's risk and its returns;
- Understand how the Modigliani-Miller model proves that capital structure is irrelevant in a world without taxes and other market frictions, but the use of debt is favored when companies are subject to corporate income taxes;
- Discuss how corporate and personal taxes affect capital structure;
- Explain how the costs of bankruptcy and financial distress affect capital structure decisions and explore the questions raised by the agency cost/tax shield trade-off model of corporate leverage; and
- Describe the most important capital structure patterns observed around the world and explain what factors may be driving leverage choices.

The Opening Focus poses a series of questions about capital structure decisions. The most important is: Why do some firms choose to issue large amounts of long-term debt, while other companies issue little or no debt? This question has transfixed financial economists for half a century. Although we still do not have a completely satisfactory answer, experience and research have taught us much about how companies set their leverage ratios. This chapter describes the key influences on managers' decisions to finance with debt or with equity. We begin by showing why firms may choose to substitute debt for equity capital, even in a world without corporate income taxes. We then show that the common practice of allowing companies to deduct interest payments, from taxable income, provides a strong incentive for corporations to substitute debt for equity.

12.1 WHAT IS FINANCIAL LEVERAGE AND WHY DO FIRMS USE IT?

When firms in the U.S. have debt in their capital structures, we say that they are using financial leverage. In Britain, the common term for debt is gearing. Both terms imply that the effect of debt is to magnify a firm's financial performance in some way. In this section, we show how debt can dramatically affect the returns that firms can deliver to their shareholders. That effect can be either positive or negative, depending on the cash flow that firms can generate on their invested capital. A simple example illustrates this principle.

Consider the decision facing Susan Smith, chief financial officer of the High-Tech Manufacturing Corporation (HTMC), a publicly listed corporation that currently has no debt. HTMC has 200,000 shares of common stock outstanding, and shares trade in the secondary market for $50 each. This implies that HTMC's total market capitalization is $10,000,000. Ms. Smith agrees with this valuation, because she expects HTMC to generate total profits of $1,000,000 per year, for the foreseeable future. Financial analysts, who follow the firm, state that HTMC's required return on assets *(ROA)* equals 10 percent. Treating the $1,000,000 annual earnings stream as a perpetuity, then the HTMC's total value equals $10,000,000 ($1,000,000÷0.10=$10,000,000). Note that because HTMC has no debt, the return on assets and the return on equity are equal.

Ms. Smith is weighing a proposal that was presented to her by one of HTMC's largest and most important shareholders. The shareholder suggested that HTMC should issue $5,000,000 in long-term debt, at an interest rate of 6.0 percent, and then use the proceeds of this debt issue to repurchase half the company's common stock. That would leave HTMC with 100,000 shares of stock. For now, let's assume that the shares remaining will still sell for $50 each. This **recapitalization** changes the mix of HTMC's debt-and-equity financing, but it does not change the total amount of financing available to the company. It would change HTMC's capital structure from being entirely equity ($10,000,000 worth of stock and no debt) to one that was 50 percent debt and 50 percent equity. In other words, this strategy would convert HTMC's debt-to-equity ratio from its current level of 0 to 1.0, after the recapitalization. Table 12.1 summarizes HTMC's current and proposed capital structures.

recapitalization
Alteration of a company's capital structure to change the relative mix of debt and equity financing, leaving total capitalization unchanged.

Table 12.1
The Current and Proposed Capital Structures for High-Tech Manufacturing Corporation

	Current	Proposed
Assets	$10,000,000	$10,000,000
Equity	$10,000,000	$ 5,000,000
Debt	$ 0	$ 5,000,000
Debt-to-equity ratio	0	1.0
Shares outstanding	200,000	100,000
Share price	$ 50.00	$ 50.00
Interest rate on debt	—	6.0%

The shareholder suggests that this strategy will increase the expected return to HTMC's stockholders, as measured by earnings per share. Though initially dubious of this proposal, Ms. Smith creates Tables 12.2 and 12.3 to test the shareholder's prediction. As noted, she thinks that HTMC's earnings, before interest and taxes *(EBIT)*, will be \$1,000,000 next year, if the economy continues to grow at a normal rate.[1] However, if the country falls into a recession next year, High-Tech's sales will fall, and *EBIT* will be only \$500,000. On the other hand, if the economy booms, HTMC will enjoy rising sales, and *EBIT* will be \$1,500,000. Ms. Smith believes that the probability of each outcome is one third, so the expected value of *EBIT* equals \$1,000,000:

$$\text{Expected } (EBIT) = (1/3)\ \$1{,}500{,}000 + (1/3)\ \$1{,}000{,}000 + (1/3)\ \$500{,}000 = \$1{,}000{,}000$$

Table 12.2 describes the payoffs to HTMC and to its security-holders, for the current and proposed capital structure, assuming that the economy grows at a normal rate and that *EBIT* equals \$1,000,000. If the current capital structure is retained, earnings per share *(EPS)* will be \$5.00. Because HTMC stock is currently worth \$50 per share, and the company pays out all net profits as dividends, HTMC's stockholders will earn a return on equity of 10 percent (\$5.00 ÷ \$50.00) over the coming year. If HTMC instead adopts the proposed recapitalization, the firm will have to pay \$300,000 interest on the \$5,000,000 debt (0.06 × \$5,000,000), leaving \$700,000 in net income (\$1,000,000 *EBIT* – \$300,000 interest). Only 100,000 shares remain outstanding after the recapitalization, so *EPS* will be \$7.00. In this scenario, the return on equity enjoyed by shareholders is 14 percent (\$7 ÷ \$50).

So far, the recapitalization plan looks rather attractive. But what happens if the economy either falls into a recession or booms? Table 12.3 demonstrates the payoffs to HTMC's stockholders and bondholders in all three economic states next year—recession, normal growth, and boom. If the economy booms, High-Tech's *EBIT* will be \$1,500,000. With the existing capital structure, *EPS* will be \$7.50, and *ROE* will be 15.0 percent. HTMC's shareholders will truly benefit if the company recapitalizes and the economy booms. In this case, *EPS* will be \$12.00, and *ROE* will be an impressive 24.0 percent!

So what's the catch? What could possibly argue against HTMC adopting the recapitalization plan and increasing *EPS* and *ROE?* The answer is that the national economy may well fall into a recession next year, in which case High-Tech's *EBIT* will only be \$500,000. With the existing all-equity capital structure, the company would achieve an *EPS* of \$2.50, yielding a 5.0 percent *ROE* for stockholders. However, if

Table 12.2
Cash Flows to Stockholders and Bondholders Under the Current and Proposed Capital Structure for High-Tech Manufacturing Corporation

Assuming EBIT = *\$1,000,000*

	Current capital structure: All-equity financing	Proposed capital structure: 50% debt: 50% equity
EBIT	\$1,000,000	\$1,000,000.00
– Interest (6.0%)	\$ 0	(\$ 300,000)
Net income	\$1,000,000	\$ 700,000
Shares outstanding	200,000	100,000
Earnings per share	\$ 5.00	\$ 7.00
Return on equity		
(P_0 = \$50.00/share)	**10.0%**	**14.0%**

1. For now, we assume that there are no taxes. Therefore, there is no difference between *EBIT* and net income for an unlevered company like HTMC. We relax this no-tax assumption in Section 12.3.

Table 12.3
Expected Cash Flows to Stockholders and Bondholders Under the Current and Proposed Capital Structure for High-Tech Manufacturing Corporation

For Three Equally Likely Economic Outcomes

	Recession		Normal Growth		Boom	
EBIT	$500,000		$1,000,000		$1,500,000	
	all-equity financing	50% debt: 50% equity	all-equity financing	50% debt: 50% equity	all-equity financing	50% debt: 50% equity
– Interest (6.0%)	$ 0	($300,000)	$ 0	($300,000)	$ 0	($ 300,000)
Net income	$500,000	$200,000	$1,000,000	$700,000	$1,500,000	$1,200,000
Shares outstanding	200,000	100,000	200,000	100,000	200,000	100,000
Earnings per share	$ 2.50	$ 2.00	$ 5.00	$ 7.00	$ 7.50	$ 12.00
% Return on shares (P_0 = $50.00/share)	5.0%	4.0%	10.0%	14.00%	15.0%	24.0%

HTMC recapitalizes and the economy falls into a recession, net income will only be $200,000, after paying $300,000 in interest. Thus, *EPS* will be $2.00 and *ROE* only 4.0 percent. In other words, whether the recapitalization plan generates a higher or a lower *ROE* for shareholders depends on the level of *EBIT.*

Recall that Ms. Smith believes that each of the three economic scenarios is equally likely. Based on that view, we already calculated the expected level of *EBIT*. But what about expected *EPS* and expected *ROE?* As HTMC's major shareholder claimed, the expected return to shareholders rises if HTMC adds debt to its capital structure.

$$\text{Expected } EPS \text{ (no debt)} = (1/3)\ \$7.50 + (1/3)\ \$5 + (1/3)\ \$2.50 = \$5$$

$$\text{Expected } EPS \text{ (with debt)} = (1/3)\ \$12 + (1/3)\ \$7 + (1/3)\ \$2 = \$7$$

$$\text{Expected } ROE \text{ (no debt)} = (1/3)\ 15\% + (1/3)\ 10\% + (1/3)\ 5\% = 10\%$$

$$\text{Expected } ROE \text{ (with debt)} = (1/3)\ 24\% + (1/3)\ 14\% + (1/3)\ 4\% = 14\%$$

How Leverage Increases the Risk of Expected Earnings per Share

Figure 12.1 graphically describes the relationship between *EBIT* and *EPS* for High-Tech's stockholders, under both the current and proposed capital structures. For both the normal-growth and economic-boom scenarios, with *EBIT* of $1,000,000 and $1,500,000, respectively, the company will have higher *EPS* with the proposed 50 percent debt/50 percent equity capital structure than with the current all-equity capitalization. In a recession, with *EBIT* of $500,000, High-Tech's shareholders will earn higher *EPS* with the current all-equity capitalization than with the proposed capital structure. In fact, for any *EBIT* above $600,000, HTMC's shareholders earn a higher *EPS* with the 50 percent debt/50 percent equity capitalization than they would with the current all-equity capital structure. For any *EBIT* below $600,000,

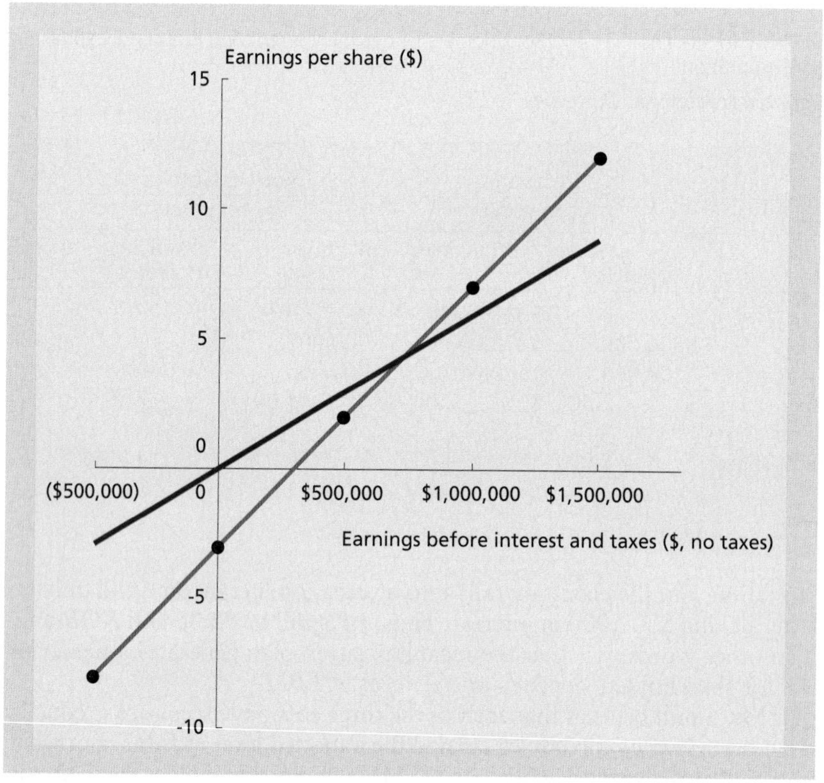

Figure 12.1
Using Debt to Increase Expected Earnings per Share (red line) for High-Tech Manufacturing Corporation (HTMC), versus All-equity Capital Structure (blue line)

the reverse is true—shareholders earn higher *EPS* with an all-equity capitalization than they would if debt is used.

The $600,000 level of *EBIT* is thus the *break-even level of operating profits* for the proposed recapitalization. If the firm's *EBIT* is $600,000 and it has no debt, its return on equity will be 6 percent. This is also the assumed interest rate HTMC would pay if it issued debt. Therefore, if the firm can issue debt at 6 percent and earn more than 6 percent with the money, then *EPS* goes up, relative to the all-equity case. If *EBIT* is less than $600,000, the firm's *ROE* is less than 6 percent, and *EPS* goes down, relative to the all-equity case. Additionally, the proposed capital structure magnifies the effect on *EPS* of any change in *EBIT* away from $600,000. If *EBIT* increases by 25 percent (from $600,000 to $750,000), then *EPS* increases by 50 percent (from $3.00 to $4.50) under the proposed half-debt and half-equity capital structure. However, *EPS* increases by only 25 percent (from $3.00 to $3.75) under the current all-equity capital structure. On the other hand, if *EBIT* declines by 25 percent (from $600,000 to $450,000), the decline in *EPS* will be far greater under the proposed capital structure (–50 percent) than under the existing all-equity structure (–25 percent). If the economy falls into a truly deep recession next year, to the point where HTMC just breaks even on an operating basis (*EBIT* = 0), the shareholders will also break even (*EPS* = 0) under the current all-equity capitalization. But they will suffer losses of $3.00 per share under the proposed capital structure (–$300,000 net income ÷ 100,000 shares outstanding).

financial leverage
Using debt to magnify both the risk and expected return on a firm's investments. Also, the result of the presence of debt when firms finance their operations with debt and equity, leading to a higher stock beta.

The Fundamental Principle of Financial Leverage

The simple example using the High-Tech Manufacturing Corporation shows why employing long-term debt financing is called applying **financial leverage**. Just as a lever is used in the physical world to magnify the effect of a given force on an object, debt financing is used to magnify the impact of a change in *EBIT* on earnings per share. If High-Tech's realized *EBIT* comes in next year at $600,000, or higher, employing debt financing will increase earnings per share for the firm's shareholders. However, the reverse also holds true. If *EBIT* falls below $600,000, HTMC's earnings per share will be lower than they would have been with an all-equity capital structure. This yields a basic and important result:

The **fundamental principle of financial leverage:** *substituting long-term debt for equity in a company's capital structure increases both the level of expected returns to shareholders—measured by earnings per share or* ROE*—and the risk (dispersion) of those expected returns.*

fundamental principle of financial leverage
States that substituting long-term debt for equity in a company's capital structure increases both the level of expected returns to shareholders—measured by earnings per share or *ROE*—and the risk (dispersion) of those expected returns.

Although the addition of debt to HTMC's balance sheet increases expected returns to shareholders, it also increases the risk that HTMC shareholders must bear. As a consequence, we should expect that HTMC shareholders will demand a higher return on their investment. Therefore, if the underlying question is whether the recapitalization is good for shareholders (i.e., whether it increases the total market value of HTMC), then we have to consider two offsetting effects. On average, the cash flows that HTMC can distribute to shareholders increase with debt, but so does the discount rate at which HTMC shareholders discount those cash flows.

Leverage Increases Expected Return—But Does It Increase Value?

Though we have demonstrated the effect that financial leverage should have on HTMC's shareholders, we haven't yet helped Ms. Smith decide whether to adopt the 50 percent debt/50 percent equity recapitalization or to retain the company's existing all-equity capital structure. In Tables 12.1 and 12.2, and in Figure 12.1, she documents that employing debt can increase expected *EPS* and *ROE* for HTMC's shareholders, but the added risk associated with debt makes her uncertain about the net benefit of the recapitalization.

In creating Table 12.1, we assumed that immediately after HTMC's recapitalization, the remaining shares would still sell for $50. If that assumption is valid, then the total market value of HTMC equals $10 million, whether the firm finances with all equity, or with some debt and some equity. Recall that if HTMC recapitalizes, its expected *EPS* increases from $5 to $7. Likewise, expected *ROE* increases from 10 percent to 14 percent. Because of the added risk that they must bear, suppose HTMC shareholders increase their required return from 10 percent to 14 percent. If shareholders believe that HTMC's earnings will be $7 per share in perpetuity, then the stock price will remain at $50, and the recapitalization will have no net impact on HTMC's total value:

SMART IDEAS VIDEO
Mitchell Petersen, Northwestern University
"When firms structure their business, they need to think about trading off operating and financial leverage."
See the entire interview at **SMARTFinance**

$$P = \frac{\$7}{0.14} = \$50$$

From this analysis, Ms. Smith concludes that there is no unique, *optimal capital structure* for her company that maximizes firm value. Substituting debt for equity will increase expected *EPS*, but only at the cost of higher variability. With higher *EPS* volatility, shareholders will expect a higher return, meaning that they will discount future earnings at a higher rate. These two effects essentially cancel each other out, so shareholders are just as happy with a capital structure that includes no debt as they are with one that consists of equal proportions of debt and equity.[2]

CONCEPT REVIEW QUESTIONS

1. What is a recapitalization? Why is this considered a pure capital structure change?
2. What is the fundamental principle of financial leverage? How does it pertain to the reasons why managers may choose to substitute debt for equity in their firm's capital structure?

12.2 THE MODIGLIANI AND MILLER CAPITAL STRUCTURE IRRELEVANCE PROPOSITIONS

business risk
Refers to the variability of a firm's cash flows, as measured by the variability of *EBIT*.

financial risk
Refers to how a firm chooses to distribute the business risk affecting a firm's cash lows between stockholders and bondholders.

Though she doesn't realize it yet, Susan Smith has reached the same capital structure irrelevance conclusion proposed by two economists almost half a century ago. In 1958, Franco Modigliani and Merton Miller showed that in a world with "perfect capital markets," capital structure cannot influence firm value and is thus irrelevant![3] In this context, perfect capital markets are those without frictions such as taxes, trading costs, or any problems transferring information between managers and investors. These two economists, subsequently referred to as M&M, made an important distinction between a firm's **business risk** and its **financial risk.** Business risk refers to the variability of a firm's cash flows, whereas financial risk refers to how a firm chooses to distribute that risk between stockholders and bondholders. HTMC's business risk is determined by how its earnings, before interest and taxes, fluctuate with the state of the economy. Notice that the volatility of *EBIT* is the same, whether HTMC recapitalizes or whether it finances with 100 percent equity. In either case, *EBIT* will be $500,000; $1,000,000; or $1,500,000; depending on the state of the economy.

If HTMC retains its all-equity structure, then the financial risk that shareholders bear equals HTMC's underlying business risk. With no debt, the variations in *EBIT* translate directly into variations in *EPS*. However, under the 50-50 recapitalization, HTMC's leverage magnifies the financial risk borne by shareholders. With debt, HTMC issues a claim to bondholders that insulates them entirely from the firm's business risk. Whether the economy booms, grows normally, or falls into a recession, bondholders receive the $300,000 interest payment they are promised. In this example, because bondholders bear no risk, even though HTMC's business risk hasn't changed, the shareholders remaining after the recapitalization have to shoulder even more risk than they did before.

Modigliani and Miller pointed out that leverage changes neither the total cash flows generated by a firm, nor the variability of those cash flows. Therefore, changing leverage cannot change the overall value of a firm. Leverage simply determines how firms divide their cash flows (and their risk) between stockholders and bondholders.

2. This result holds for any other mix of debt and equity. The total market value of HTMC is the same, whether the firm uses 100 percent equity, 75 percent equity and 25 percent debt, or any other capital structure.

3. See Franco Modigliani and Merton Miller (1958), "The Cost of Capital, Corporation Finance, and the Theory of Investment," *American Economic Review* 48, pp. 261–297.

Proposition I: The Capital Structure Irrelevance Proposition

M&M's famous **Proposition I**, the "irrelevance proposition," asserts the following: *The market value of any firm is independent of its capital structure and is given by capitalizing its expected net operating income* (EBIT) *at the rate* r. Equation 12.1 expresses this simple relationship mathematically.

Proposition I
The famous "irrelevance proposition," which imagines that a company is operating in a world of frictionless capital markets, and in a world where there is uncertainty about corporate revenues and earnings.

$$V = (E + D) = \frac{EBIT}{r} \quad \text{(Eq. 12.1)}$$

where V = total market value of the firm
E = market value of equity
D = market value of debt
$EBIT$ = earnings before interest and taxes
r = required return on a firm's assets

According to M&M, investors will generate an expectation about the long-run level of operating profits that a firm's assets will yield. They will capitalize this stream of profits by dividing *EBIT* by a discount rate *r*, appropriate to the business risk of the company. The discount rate *r* is the required return on assets and is based on the variability of expected *EBIT*. This is exactly what Ms. Smith did for HTMC. She generated an expected level of operating profits for HTMC ($1,000,000 *EBIT* per year), and then discounted this stream of expected earnings, using a discount rate (r = 10%), appropriate to the business risk that HTMC faces. Firm value is thus determined by the level of HTMC's operating profits and by the firm's degree of business risk, not by whether the *EBIT* stream is then allocated entirely to shareholders in the all-equity capital structure or split between debt-and-equity security-holders under the proposed capitalization.

Under HTMC's current, all-equity capital structure, the return on equity is the same as the return on the firm's assets. Both *ROA* and *ROE* are 10 percent. But what happens if HTMC issues low-risk debt and uses the proceeds to repurchase half the firm's outstanding equity? The company's business risk (the variability of expected *EBIT*) is unchanged by this transaction, and all this risk is still borne by shareholders. However, the risk for shareholders is now magnified, because there is only half as much equity outstanding as before. By how much will the risk to HTMC's shareholders be magnified if the company adopts the proposed 50 percent debt/50 percent equity capital structure? It turns out that M&M also provided an answer to this question, with their Proposition II.

Proposition II: How Increasing Leverage Affects the Cost of Equity

Modigliani and Miller's **Proposition II** states that if we hold the required return on assets (r) and the required return on debt (r_d) constant, the required return on levered equity (r_l) rises as the debt-to-equity ratio rises:

Proposition II
Asserts that the expected return on a levered firm's equity is a linear function of that firm's debt-to-equity ratio.

$$r_l = r + (r - r_d)\frac{D}{E} \quad \text{(Eq. 12.2)}$$

Does this formula yield the same expected returns on equity for HTMC's shareholders that Susan Smith had calculated earlier under the current all-equity and the proposed 50 percent debt/50 percent equity capital structures? Remember that the firm's underlying business risk justifies a return, r, of 10 percent and that its cost of debt, r_d, is 6 percent. Clearly, under the current all-equity structure, there is no debt outstanding, and the *D/E* ratio is zero. Therefore, the term to the right of the plus sign is also zero. Equation 12.2 says that the return on equity equals the return on assets, or 10 percent:

$$r_l = 0.10 + (0.10 - 0.06)\frac{\$0}{\$10{,}000{,}000} = 0.10 = 10\%$$

The proposed 50 percent debt/50 percent equity capital structure yields a debt-to-equity ratio of 1.0. We can use Equation 12.2 to calculate that the return on levered equity must be 14 percent, just as Ms. Smith had calculated previously.

$$r_l = 0.10 + (0.10 - 0.06) \times \frac{\$5{,}000{,}000}{\$5{,}000{,}000} = 0.10 + 0.04 = 0.14 = 14\%$$

Proposition II has another important interpretation. Let's rearrange the equation so that r, the return on assets, appears by itself, on the left-hand side. This results in the following expression:

$$r = r_l\left(\frac{E}{D+E}\right) + r_d\left(\frac{D}{D+E}\right)$$

Does this look familiar? It should. It's the expression for a firm's weighted average cost of capital (*WACC*) that we introduced in Chapter 10. We have already said the value of r depends on a firm's business risk and is independent of the firm's capital structure. This equation appears to contradict that claim because it seems that changing the values of E and D on the right-hand side might change r. But remember, Proposition II says that as leverage increases, so does the required return on equity. If a firm replaces equity with debt in its capital structure, the term $E/(D+E)$ falls and the term $D/(D+E)$ rises. However, r_l goes up because of the added financial risk borne by shareholders. The net effect of all this is to leave the *WACC* unchanged. For example, when HTMC uses all debt, we know that the required return on equity is 10 percent, so the *WACC* is 10 percent, too:

$$r = 10\%\ (1.0) + 6\%\ (0) = 10\%$$

If HTMC recapitalizes, then it pays 6 percent to bondholders, shareholders demand a 14 percent return, and the *WACC* remains unchanged at 10 percent:

$$r = 14\%\ (0.50) + 6\%\ (0.50) = 10\%$$

See the concept explained step-by-step at SMARTFinance

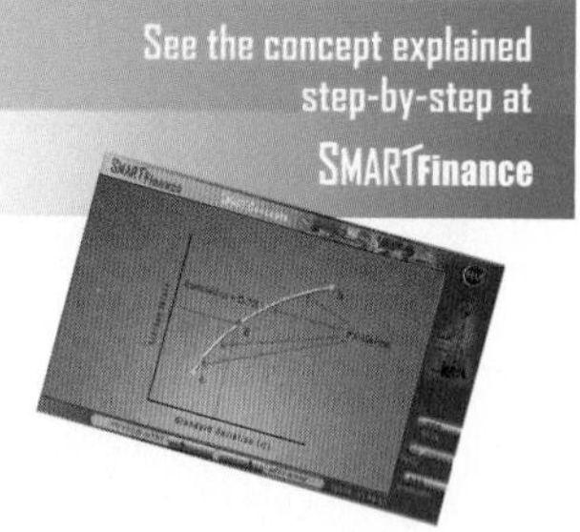

If capital structure is irrelevant (if Proposition I holds), Proposition II tells us what the required return on levered equity must be to maintain the same total firm value (or the same *WACC*). As Figure 12.2 shows, the cost of equity will rise continuously as firms substitute debt for equity, but the weighted average cost of capital remains the same.

Remember that the value of a firm equals its cash flows discounted by its cost of capital. If managers could adjust capital structure to achieve a lower overall *WACC* (while leaving cash flows unchanged), then that would also increase the value of the firm. Propositions I and II illustrate why this can't happen in perfect markets. Proposition I says that there is no capital structure that maximizes the

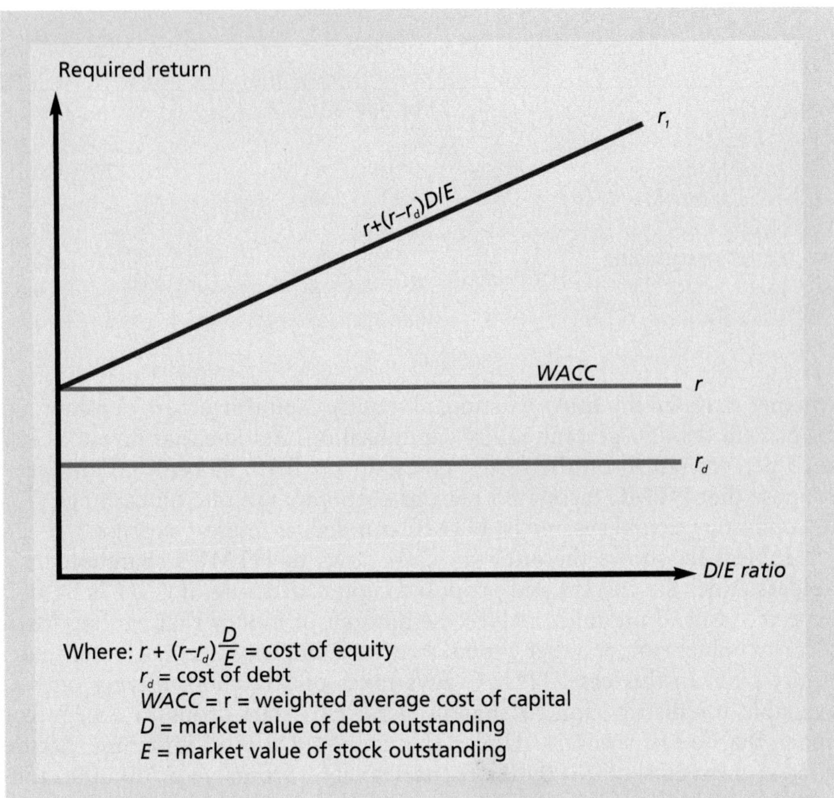

Figure 12.2
M&M Proposition II Illustrated—The Cost of Equity, Cost of Debt, and Weighted Average Cost of Capital for a Firm in a World Without Taxes

value of a firm, while Proposition II says that there is no capital structure that minimizes the *WACC*.

CONCEPT REVIEW QUESTIONS

3. Explain how *Propositions I* and *II* are different and how they are similar.

4. What is the difference between levered and unlevered equity? What effect does substituting debt for equity have on the required return on (levered) equity?

12.3 THE M&M CAPITAL STRUCTURE MODEL WITH CORPORATE AND PERSONAL TAXES

You should now understand why capital structure choices are irrelevant in a world without market frictions, but that is not the world in which we live. One real-world market friction that could change the irrelevance result is corporate taxes. Because interest payments are tax deductible, whereas dividend payments to shareholders are not, perhaps adding debt to the HTMC capital structure could increase the firm's value by reducing the government's tax claim on HTMC's cash flows.

The M&M Model with Corporate Taxes

Let's begin our analysis by assuming, as before, that the High-Tech Manufacturing Corporation's *EBIT* will be \$1,000,000 next year and that we are trying to decide

Table 12.4
Cash Flows to Stockholders and Bondholders Under the Current and Proposed Capital Structure for High-Tech Manufacturing Corporation—with Corporate Taxation

Assuming EBIT = $1,000,000 and T_C = 0.35

	Current capital structure: All-equity financing	Proposed capital structure: 50% debt: 50% equity
EBIT	$1,000,000	$1,000,000
– Interest (6.0%)	$ 0	($ 300,000)
Taxable income	$1,000,000	$ 700,000
– Corporate taxes (T_C = 0.35)	($ 350,000)	(245,000)
Net income	$ 650,000	$ 455,000
Shares outstanding	200,000	100,000
Earnings per share	$ 3.25	$ 4.55

whether to retain the firm's existing, all-equity capital structure or adopt a proposed 50 percent debt/50 percent equity capitalization. Assume that investors still require a 10 percent return on the firm's assets, so r = 0.10, as before. However, we now propose that HTMC faces a 35 percent corporate tax rate on earnings (T_C = 0.35). In computing taxable earnings, HTMC can deduct interest expense.[4]

Table 12.4 shows the after-tax cash flows to HTMC's shareholders and debt holders under the current and proposed capital structure, if *EBIT* is $1,000,000, as expected. Corporate taxes reduce the amount of money that can be distributed to security holders under either capital structure, but the effect is greater under the all-equity plan. In this case, HTMC pays taxes of $350,000, leaving only $650,000 available for distribution to shareholders. *EPS* thus drops to $3.25 from $5.00 under the no-tax scenario. Under the proposed capital structure, tax-deductible interest payments of $300,000 reduce taxable profits to $700,000, and HTMC only pays $245,000 in corporate taxes. This leaves $455,000 in net income that can be distributed to shareholders, yielding an *EPS* of $4.55 from $7.00 under the no-tax scenario. Note that under the proposed capital structure, HTMC is able to distribute $755,000 to private investors ($300,000 interest to debt holders and $455,000 in dividends to shareholders). Under the all-equity capitalization, HTMC can only distribute $650,000 to private investors (dividends to shareholders).

We can now compute the value of both the unlevered and levered versions of HTMC, and define these values as V_U and V_L, respectively. The basic valuation formula (Equation 12.1) used in the absence of taxes to discount *EBIT* must now be modified to discount after-tax net income (*NI*), yielding the following formula for the value of an unlevered HTMC:

$$V_U = \frac{[EBIT(1-T_c)]}{r} = \frac{NI}{r} = \frac{\$650{,}000}{0.10} = \$6{,}500{,}000 \qquad \text{(Eq. 12.3)}$$

The introduction of a 35 percent corporate profits tax causes an immediate $3,500,000 reduction (from $10,000,000 to $6,500,000) in the market value of the current all-equity version of HTMC.

Determining the Present Value of Debt Tax Shields

Equation 12.3 reveals that corporate taxes cause a reduction in the value of an unlevered firm, compared with its value in a zero-tax environment. How can we modify

4. This is the same logic Modigliani and Miller used in their 1963 "modified" capital structure model, which explicitly incorporated a tax on corporate profits. See Franco Modigliani and Merton Miller, "Corporate Income Taxes and the Cost of Capital," *American Economic Review* 53 (June 1963), pp. 433–443.

this valuation formula to reflect the increase in firm value that results from adding leverage to HTMC's capital structure? If the new debt which HTMC will issue under the proposed 50 percent debt/50 percent equity plan, is assumed to be *permanent*—meaning that the firm will always reissue maturing debt—the interest deduction represents a perpetual tax shield of \$105,000 per year. This is equal to the tax rate times the amount of interest paid ($T_c \times r_d \times D = 0.35 \times 0.06 \times \$5,000,000 = \$105,000$ each year). To find the present value of this perpetuity, capitalize this stream of benefits at r_d, the 6 percent rate of interest charged on HTMC's debt. With these assumptions, the present value of HTMC's interest tax shields is:

$$PV \text{ Interest Tax Shields} = \frac{(T_c \times r_d D)}{r_d} = T_c \times D = 0.35(\$5,000,000) = \$1,750,000 \quad \text{(Eq. 12.4)}$$

In other words, the present value of interest tax shields on (perpetual) debt is equal to the tax rate times the face value of the debt outstanding. Therefore, the value of the levered version of HTMC, V_L, is equal to the value of the unlevered company plus the present value of the interest tax shields:

$$V_L = V_U + PV \text{ tax shield} = V_U + T_C D = \$6,500,000 + \$1,750,000 = \$8,250,000 \quad \text{(Eq. 12.5)}$$

What a deal! In essence, the government has given HTMC's shareholders a \$1,750,000 subsidy to employ debt financing rather than equity.

Figure 12.3 illustrates the effect of taxes on firm value by using a series of pie charts. Panel A represents the situation in the original M&M world of no taxes. In this case, capital structure is irrelevant, because no matter how you slice up the value of firms (the overall pie) between debt-and-equity claimants, their overall size (value) remains constant. When we introduce corporate income taxes into the M&M model, the value of firms to private investors is not independent of capital structure. The amount of debt that firms issue determines the size of the government's tax slice of the pie. The more firms borrow, the smaller is the government's claim, and therefore, the larger are the claims held by private investors. Panel B of Figure 12.3 illustrates this point.

The M&M Model with Corporate and Personal Taxes

Clearly, accounting for corporate income taxes leads us to favor the proposed 50 percent debt/50 percent equity capital structure for HTMC. However, this isn't the best possible outcome. If a 50 percent debt-to-capital ratio increases HTMC's total firm value by \$1,750,000 more than that of the unlevered version of HTMC, and if each additional dollar of debt increases the value by \$0.35, then shouldn't the *optimal* leverage ratio for the company be 100 percent debt? This is the result derived by M&M in 1963, though they never quite said so. This result, more than any other, lessened the initial acceptance of their propositions. How could the theory be correct if it predicted that all firms should be highly levered, and yet, in the real world, many companies use little or no debt? Part of the answer to this question is that non-tax factors, such as the debt-related costs of financial distress that we discuss in Section 12.4, partly offset the tax benefits of debt usage. Another part of the answer is that personal income taxes can cancel out some or all of the corporate-level tax benefits of debt usage.

Figure 12.3
Pie Chart Models of Capital Structure With and Without Corporate Income Taxes

Panel A: No taxes, corresponding to the original M&M (1958) model. In this case, how the pie—representing the value of a firm's cash flows from operations—is divided between debt and equity does not affect the size of the pie, and thus capital structure is irrelevant.

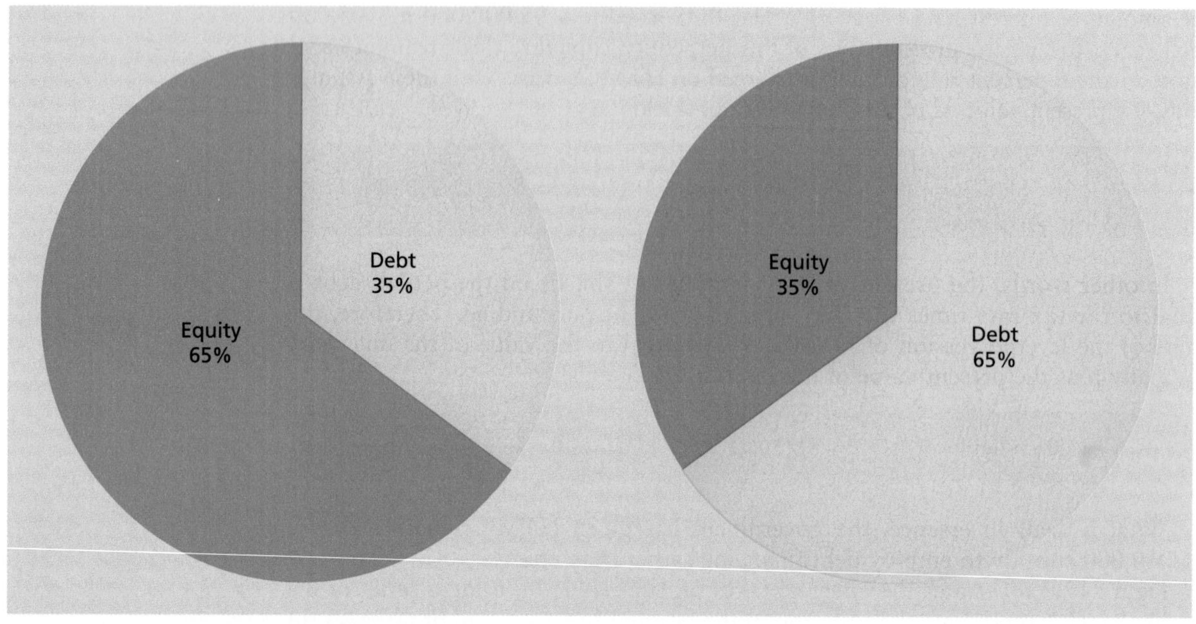

Panel B: Corporate income is subject to taxes at a constant rate T_c, corresponding to the M&M (1963) "modified" model. In this case, the government's tax claim represents a deadweight drain on a firm's cash flows. By issuing debt and deducting interest payments from taxable income, firms minimize the tax claim and maximize the fraction of their cash flows that go to private investors. In this case, capital structure matters and the use of debt maximizes a firm's market value.

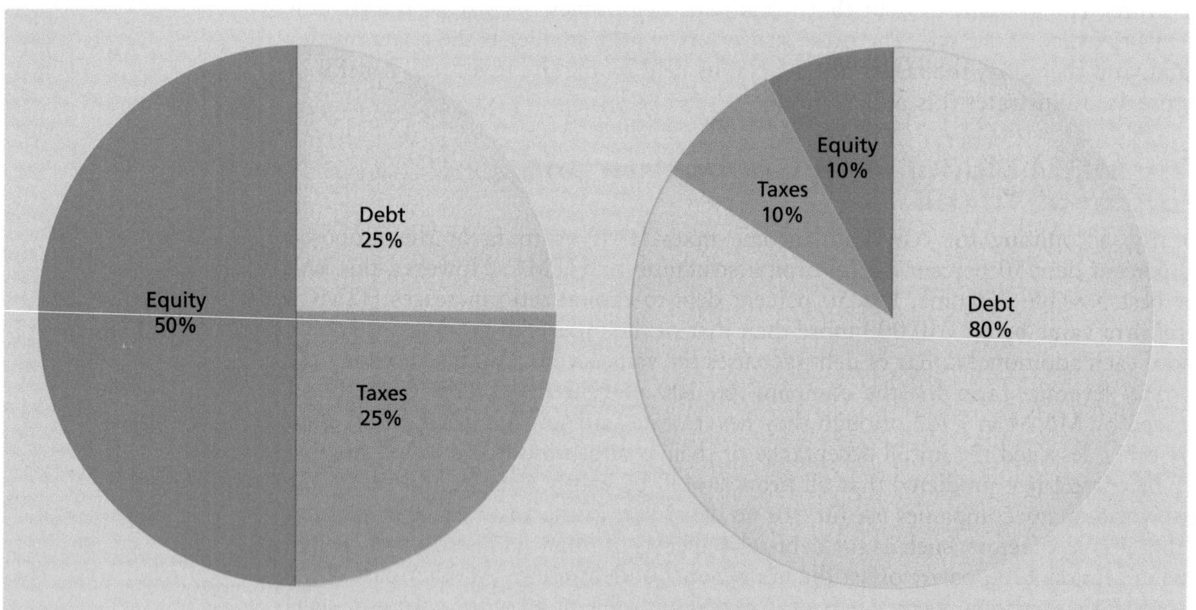

In 1977, Merton Miller developed a valuation model that incorporated both corporate and personal taxes. [5] From this model, Miller provided a formula for computing the gains from using leverage, G_L, both for individual companies and for the corporate sector as a whole:

$$G_L = \left[1 - \frac{(1 - T_c)(1 - T_{ps})}{(1 - T_{pd})}\right] \times D \quad \text{(Eq. 12.6)}$$

where T_c = tax rate on corporate profits, as before
T_{ps} = personal tax rate on income from stock (capital gains and dividends)
T_{pd} = personal tax rate on income from debt (interest income)
D = market value of a firm's outstanding debt

This is, in fact, a very general formulation. In a no-tax world ($T_c = T_{ps} = T_{pd} = 0$), the gains from leverage equal zero, and the original M&M irrelevance proposition holds. (See if you can verify this yourself.) In a world with only corporate income taxes ($T_c = 0.35$; $T_{ps} = T_{pd} = 0$), the 100 percent optimal debt result again obtains. If, however, personal tax rates on interest income are sufficiently high, and personal tax rates on equity income are sufficiently low, the gains to corporate leverage can be dramatically reduced, or even offset entirely. To see this, assume for a moment, as Miller did, that personal taxes on equity income are zero ($T_{ps} = 0$). This is not as wild as it may sound, as U.S. investors pay capital gains taxes only upon realization, and taxes on some equity investments can be skipped entirely with careful estate planning. Investors can also choose non-dividend-paying stocks to avoid personal taxes on equity income. Additionally, as described in Chapter 1, the Jobs and Growth Tax Relief Reconciliation Act of 2003 dramatically reduced the effective personal tax rates on dividend income for most U.S. investors. Assuming that personal taxes on equity income are zero, we can plug the (approximate) top U.S. corporate and personal income tax rates ($T_c = 0.35$ and $T_{pd} = 0.40$) into the gain-from-leverage formula:

$$G_L = \left[1 - \frac{(1-0.35)(1-0)}{(1-0.4)}\right] \times D = \left[1 - \frac{(0.65)(1.0)}{(0.6)}\right] \times D = -0.0833D$$

Using this set of tax rates, the "gain" from leverage is actually negative! In some cases, the effects of corporate and personal taxes may exactly offset each other. If the personal tax rate on equity income is 7.7 percent, the gain from leverage is zero, and capital structure is again irrelevant.

CONCEPT REVIEW QUESTIONS

5. What effect does incorporating corporate income taxation have on the M&M capital structure irrelevance hypothesis? Why?

6. The Jobs and Growth Tax Relief Reconciliation Act of 2003 significantly reduced the effective personal tax rates on dividend income for most U.S. investors. What effect do you expect this act to have on corporate incentive to use debt?

[5] See Merton Miller, "Debt and Taxes," *Journal of Finance* 32 (May 1977), pp. 261–276.

12.4 THE AGENCY COST/TAX SHIELD TRADE-OFF MODEL OF CORPORATE LEVERAGE

We have now seen that the corporate capital structure choice is irrelevant in a world without taxes or other market frictions. We have learned not only that corporate income taxes, by themselves, give corporations a strong incentive to employ financial leverage, but also that things are much less clear-cut when personal income taxes are considered. On balance, corporate and personal taxes seem to influence, but not solely explain, the variation in leverage ratios observed in the United States and in other modern economies. But if taxes do not explain why firms and investors pay attention to capital structure, then what does? One possibility is that the costs of bankruptcy and financial distress may discourage corporate managers from adopting "maximum leverage" capital structures. This section considers the likely effect of bankruptcy and financial distress costs on capital structure choice.

Costs of Bankruptcy and Financial Distress

The threat of bankruptcy may well discourage debt financing. High leverage makes it more likely that firms will be unable to make interest and principal payments when cash flows are low. This could cause companies to default on their debts, which, in turn, could force companies into bankruptcy. Between 35,000 and 70,000 businesses (and nearly one million individuals) file for bankruptcy protection in the United States each year. In the United States, a firm becomes bankrupt when it comes under the supervision of the federal government's bankruptcy courts and ceases to operate as a separate, independently contracting legal entity. The court can then choose either to liquidate the firm and distribute the money received to the firm's creditors to satisfy their claims, or to reorganize the firm's operations and finances, thereby allowing it to reemerge from bankruptcy as a new company. The firm's original shareholders generally lose their entire investment either way, and the ownership of the firm (or the firm's remaining assets) passes to bondholders and other creditors. **Bankruptcy costs** are the direct and indirect costs (defined below) of the bankruptcy process itself.

bankruptcy costs
The direct and indirect costs of the bankruptcy process.

direct costs of bankruptcy
Out-of-pocket cash expenses directly related to bankruptcy filing and administration.

indirect bankruptcy costs
Expenses or economic losses that result from bankruptcy but are not cash outflows spent on the process itself.

Direct costs of bankruptcy are out-of-pocket cash expenses directly related to bankruptcy filing and administration. Document printing and filing expenses, as well as professional fees paid to lawyers, accountants, investment bankers, and court personnel, are all examples of direct bankruptcy costs. These can run to several million dollars per month for complex cases. However, empirical research indicates that direct costs are much too small, relative to the pre-bankruptcy market value of large firms, to truly discourage the use of debt financing. **Indirect bankruptcy costs**, as the name implies, are economic losses that result from bankruptcy but are not cash outlays spent on the process itself. These include the diversion of management's time while bankruptcy is underway, lost sales during and after bankruptcy, constrained capital investment and R&D spending, and the loss of key employees after a firm declares bankruptcy. Even though indirect bankruptcy costs are inherently difficult to measure, empirical research clearly suggests they are significant—significant enough, in many cases, to lessen the incentive for corporate managers to employ financial leverage. This allows us to expand the basic valuation formula, first presented in Section 12.3, to express the value of a levered firm, V_L, relative to the value of an

COMPARATIVE CORPORATE FINANCE

How Important Is R&D Spending to Modern Economies?

This chapter discusses the influence of a firm's research and development spending on its capital structure and shows that, all things being equal, firms which invest large sums of money in research and development typically employ relatively little debt. Casual observation suggests that R&D spending is an extremely important source of innovation and growth for many American corporations, as well as for the United States as a nation. In fact, American corporations, governments, and universities spent some $277.1 billion on R&D in 2002, or about 2.82 percent of GDP. This chart puts that into international perspective, by showing the R&D spending to GDP ratio for the thirty nations that are members of the Organization of Economic Cooperation and Development. These countries collectively spent $638.4 billion on R&D, or about 2.3 percent of overall GDP. Though the U.S. ranks first in the total amount of R&D spending, it ranks only sixth among industrialized economies in the fraction of GDP spent on R&D. Not surprisingly, developing and transition economies invest relatively less in R&D than do developed countries.

4.5
4.0
3.5
3.0
2.5
2.0
1.5
1.0
0.5
0

Sweden
Finland
Iceland
Japan
Korea
United States
Switzerland
Germany
Total OECD
France
Denmark
Belgium
Austria
Netherlands
European Union
Britain
Canada
Norway
Australia
Czech Republic
New Zealand
Ireland
Italy
Spain
Hungary
Portugal
Poland
Greece
Slovak Republic
Turkey
Mexico

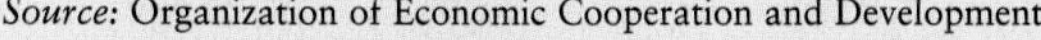

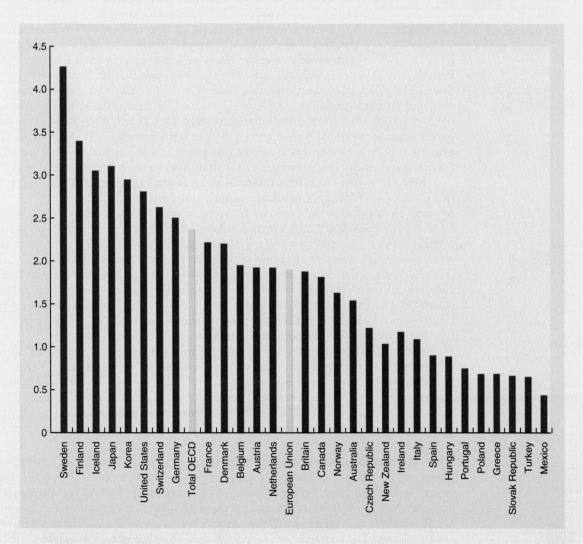

Source: Organization of Economic Cooperation and Development

unlevered firm, V_U, the present value of the benefits from debt tax shields, and the present value of expected bankruptcy costs:

$$V_L = V_U + PV \text{ tax shields} - PV \text{ bankruptcy costs} \quad \text{(Eq. 12.7)}$$

Asset Characteristics and Bankruptcy Costs. Intuitively, it seems that certain firms should be able to weather financial distress better than others. As a general rule, producers of sophisticated products or services have an incentive to use less debt than firms producing simple goods or basic services. It is very important for producers of high-value, durable goods to assure customers that their firms are able to provide ongoing service, warranty and repair work, as well as product improvements. Based on this logic, it is not surprising that the Opening Focus shows that technology-based companies such as Dell and Microsoft use leverage very sparingly.

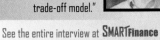

SMART IDEAS VIDEO

John Graham, Duke University

"The majority of companies follow the trade-off model."

See the entire interview at **SMARTFinance**

A firm's asset characteristics also influence its willingness to risk financial distress by using large amounts of debt. Companies with mostly tangible assets and well-established secondary markets should be more willing to use debt than companies with mostly intangible assets. Therefore, trucking companies, airlines, construction firms, pipeline companies, and railroads can all employ more debt than can companies with fewer tangible assets, such as pharmaceutical manufacturers, food distributors (what is the collateral value of week-old tomatoes?), and pure service companies. Once again, the examples in the Opening Focus verify this logic; Southwest Airlines and General Electric have much higher leverage ratios than Johnson & Johnson or Starbucks.

There are two reasons why financial distress can be particularly damaging to firms, such as HTMC, that produce research-and-development-intensive goods and services. First, most of the expenses incurred in production are sunk costs, which have already been made and which can be recovered only with a long period of profitable sales. Second, a financially distressed company is unable to finance the research-and-development spending required to produce "cutting-edge" goods and services. Further, intangible assets such as patents and trademarks are extremely valuable and are unlikely to survive financial distress or bankruptcy intact. Microsoft and Johnson & Johnson are classic examples of companies that invest massive sums in R&D in order to produce cutting-edge products and services. The Opening Focus shows that both of these firms are essentially debt free!

Another major problem associated with financial distress is that it provides otherwise trustworthy managers with perverse, but rational, incentives to play a variety of financial and operating "games," mostly at bondholders' expense. Two such games, asset substitution and underinvestment, are particularly important and potentially damaging. Both typically begin when a company first encounters financial difficulties, and its managers realize that the firm will probably not fulfill its obligations to creditors.

asset substitution
An investment that will increase firm value but does not earn a return high enough to fully redeem the maturing bonds.

The Asset Substitution Problem. To illustrate how **asset substitution** works, assume that a firm has bonds, with a face value of $10 million outstanding, that mature in 30 days. These bonds were issued years ago when the firm was prospering, but since then, the firm has fallen on hard times. In spite of its difficulties, the firm still has $8 million in cash on hand, and the company's managers still make the firm's investment decisions. The company can invest this cash in either of two available projects, both which require a cash investment of $8 million. Otherwise, the firm can simply hold the cash in reserve to partially repay the bond issue in 30 days. The first investment opportunity is a low-risk project (called project *Boring*, by company insiders) that will return a near certain $8.15 million in 30 days. This is a monthly return of 1.88 percent, or an annual return of almost 25 percent. In other words, it is a positive-*NPV* project that will increase firm value, but it does not earn enough to fully pay off the maturing bonds.

The second investment opportunity (called project *Vegas*) is basically a gamble. It offers a 40 percent chance of a $12 million payoff and a 60 percent chance of a $4 million payoff. Because its expected value is only $7.2 million (0.4 × $12,000,000 + 0.6 × $4,000,000), project *Vegas* is a negative-*NPV* "investment" that the firm's managers would reject if the firm did not have debt outstanding. However, if project *Vegas* is successful, the project's $12 million payoff will allow the company to fully pay off the bonds and pocket a $2 million profit.

Consider the incentives facing this company's managers. Clearly, bondholders want the managers to either select the low-risk project or retain the firm's cash in reserve. But because shareholders will lose control of the firm unless they can pay off the creditors' claims in full, when they mature, shareholders want the company's managers to accept project *Vegas*. If successful, the project will yield enough for shareholders to pay off the creditors and to retain ownership of the firm. On the other hand, if project *Vegas* is unsuccessful, the shareholders will simply hand over the firm and any remaining assets to bondholders, after defaulting on the maturing bonds. (Because of limited liability, the corporation's shareholders do not have to repay the bonds themselves.) This is also what will happen if the firm plays it safe by either retaining cash in the firm or accepting project *Boring*. Shareholders therefore have everything to gain and nothing to lose from accepting project *Vegas*, and their agents (the managers) control the firm's investment policy until default actually occurs.

The Underinvestment Problem. The second game set up by financial distress is **underinvestment**. To demonstrate this, assume that the firm described above gains access to a very profitable, but short-lived, investment opportunity. Specifically, a longtime supplier offers to sell its excess inventory to the company at a sharply discounted price, but only if the company will pay for the inventory immediately with cash. The additional supplies will cost $9 million today but will allow the firm to increase production and profitability dramatically over the next thirty days. In fact, the firm will be able to sell the additional production so profitably that, in thirty days time, it will build up the $10 million cash needed to pay off the maturing bond issue. However, because the firm has only $8 million in cash on hand today, the firm's shareholders must contribute the additional $1 million needed to buy the supplier's inventory. Accepting this project would maximize overall firm value and would clearly benefit the bondholders. But the shareholders would rationally choose *not* to accept the project because the shareholders would have to finance the investment, and all the investment's payoff would accrue to the bondholders.

underinvestment
A situation of financial distress in which default is likely, yet a very profitable but short-lived investment opportunity exists.

An all-equity firm is not vulnerable to either of these two games that are associated with financial distress. Managers, acting in the interests of shareholders, have the incentive to choose the project which maximizes firm value, in the first example, and the shareholders' incentive is to choose to contribute cash for positive-*NPV* projects, in the second example. Because these costs of financial distress are related to conflicts of interest between the two groups of security holders, they are also referred to as *agency costs* of the relationship between bondholders and stockholders.

Agency Costs and Capital Structure

In addition to taxes and the costs of financial distress, several other forces influence the corporate capital structure choice. Some thirty years ago, Michael Jensen and William Meckling proposed an *agency cost model of financial structure*.[6] Jensen and Meckling observed that when entrepreneurs own 100 percent of the stock of a company, there is no separation between corporate ownership and control. Entrepreneurs bear all the costs and reap all the benefits of their actions. Once entrepreneurs sell a fraction of their stock to outside investors, they bear only a fraction of the cost of any actions they take that reduce the value of the firm. This gives entrepreneurs a clear incentive to, in Jensen and Meckling's tactful phrasing, "consume perquisites" (goof off, purchase a corporate jet, frequently tour the firm's plant in Hawaii, become a regular "business commentator" on television, etc.).

By selling off a stake in the company, entrepreneurs lower the cost of consuming perquisites (or perks), but this does not come free of charge. In an efficient market, investors expect entrepreneurs' performance to change after they sell stakes in their firms, so investors reduce the price they will pay for these shares. In other words, entrepreneurs are charged *in advance* for the perks they are expected to consume after the equity sale, so entrepreneurs bear the full costs of their actions. Society also suffers because these **agency costs of (outside) equity** reduce the market value of corporate assets. We are therefore at an impasse. Selling stock to outside investors creates agency costs of equity, which are borne solely by the entrepreneur, but which also harm society, by reducing the value of corporate assets and discouraging additional entrepreneurship. On the other hand, selling external equity is vital for entrepreneurs and for society at large, because this allows firms to pursue growth opportunities that would exhaust an entrepreneur's personal wealth.

agency costs of (outside) equity
In an efficient market, informed investors only pay a price per share that fully reflects the perks an entrepreneur is expected to consume after the equity sale, so the entrepreneur bears the full costs of her or his actions.

Using Debt to Overcome the Agency Costs of Outside Equity. Jensen and Meckling show how using debt financing can help overcome the agency costs of external equity, in two ways. First, using debt, by definition, means that less external equity will have to be sold to raise a given dollar amount of external financing. Second, and more important, the effect of employing outside debt rather than equity financing is a reduction in the amount and value of perquisites that managers can consume. The burden of having to make regular debt-service payments serves as a very effective tool for disciplining corporate managers. With debt outstanding, the cost of excessive perk consumption may well include managers losing control of their companies following default. Because taking on debt shows a manager's willingness to risk losing control of her firm, if she fails to perform effectively, shareholders are willing to pay a higher price for a firm's shares.

Agency Costs of Outside Debt. If debt is such an effective disciplining device, then why don't firms use "maximum debt" financing? The answer is that there are also **agency costs of debt**. To understand these, keep in mind that, as the fraction of debt in a firm's capital structure increases, bondholders begin taking on more of the company's business and operating risk. However, shareholders and managers still control the firm's investment and operating decisions. This gives managers a variety of incentives to effectively steal bondholder wealth for themselves and other shareholders. The easiest way to do this is to float a bond issue and then pay out the money raised to shareholders as a dividend. After default, the

agency costs of debt
Costs that must be weighed against the benefits of leverage in reducing the agency costs of outside equity.

[6] See Michael C. Jensen and William H. Meckling, "Theory of the Firm: Managerial Behavior, Agency Costs, and Ownership Structure," *Journal of Financial Economics* 3 (October 1976), pp. 305–360.

bondholders are left with an empty corporate shell, and limited liability prevents them from trying to collect directly from shareholders.

Bondholders are generally sophisticated enough to take steps to prevent managers from playing these games with their money. The most effective, preventive step that bond investors can take is to write very detailed covenants into bond contracts, which limit borrowers' ability to expropriate bondholder wealth. We discussed bond covenants in Chapter 4. The downside of covenants is that they make bond agreements costly to negotiate and to enforce. In any case, the agency costs of debt are real, and they become more important as a firm's leverage ratio increases.

The Agency Cost/Tax Shield Trade-Off Model of Corporate Leverage

Our discussion thus far has shown that certain real-world factors—such as corporate income taxes and agency costs of outside equity—give corporate managers an incentive to substitute debt for equity in their firms' capital structure. Other factors such as personal income taxes, bankruptcy, and agency costs of outside debt give managers an incentive to favor equity financing. We are now ready to tie together all these influences and present the **agency cost/tax shield trade-off model of corporate leverage.** This model expresses the value of a levered firm as the value of an unlevered firm, plus the present values of tax shields and the agency costs of outside equity, minus the present value of bankruptcy costs and the agency costs of debt, as follows:

agency cost/tax shield trade-off model of corporate leverage
This model expresses the value of a levered firm as the value of an unlevered firm, plus the present values of tax shields and the agency costs of outside equity, minus the present value of bankruptcy costs and the agency costs of debt.

$$V_L = V_U + \begin{matrix} PV \text{ Tax} \\ \text{Shields} \end{matrix} - \begin{matrix} PV \text{ Bankruptcy} \\ \text{Costs} \end{matrix} + \begin{matrix} PV \text{ Agency Costs} \\ \text{of Outside Equity} \end{matrix} - \begin{matrix} PV \text{ Agency Costs} \\ \text{of Outside Debt} \end{matrix} \quad \text{(Eq. 12.7b)}$$

Figure 12.4 describes how agency costs, bankruptcy costs, and tax benefits of leverage interact to determine a typical firm's optimal debt level. Starting from a capital structure with no debt, managers can increase firm value by replacing equity with

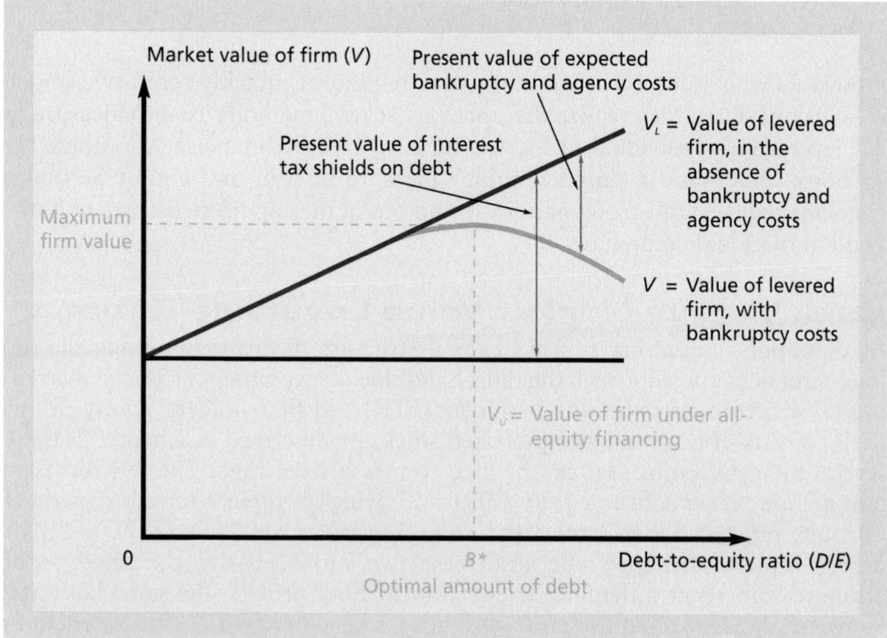

Figure 12.4
The Agency Cost/Tax Shield Trade-Off Model of Corporate Leverage

This model describes the optimal level of debt for a given firm as a trade-off between the tax benefits of corporate borrowing and the increasing agency and bankruptcy costs that come from additional borrowing.

debt, thus shielding more cash flow from taxation. In the absence of bankruptcy costs and the agency costs of debt, managers would maximize firm value by borrowing as much as possible, a situation represented by the green line in Figure 12.4. The red line shows how bankruptcy and agency costs alter this conclusion. As a firm borrows more, it increases the probability that it will go bankrupt. Therefore, expected bankruptcy costs and agency costs of debt rise with leverage. At some point, the additional tax benefit from issuing more debt is exactly offset by the increase in expected bankruptcy and agency costs. When that occurs, the red line reaches a maximum, and managers have found the mix of debt and equity that maximizes the value of the firm.

As we see in the next section, empirical research in finance offers much support for the agency cost/tax-shield trade-off model. It explains many of the key patterns that are observed in corporate capital structures around the world.

CONCEPT REVIEW QUESTIONS

7. What are the important direct and indirect costs of bankruptcy? Which of these, do you think, are the most important for discouraging maximum debt use by corporate managers?

8. Suppose an individual borrows from a bank to buy a new car. Later on, the borrower realizes that in a few months, he will have to default on this loan and the bank will repossess the car. What kind of underinvestment problem could occur here?

9. Suppose a commercial bank experiences losses on some of its loans. As a result, it approaches bankruptcy. What kinds of asset-substitution problems may arise?

10. Think of the gaudy corporate perks given to managers, such as a plush office, a company jet, or luxury box seats at professional sporting events. How can managers justify these as value-maximizing corporate expenditures that benefit the shareholders?

12.5 PATTERNS OBSERVED IN CORPORATE CAPITAL STRUCTURES

Observers who study actual capital structure patterns quickly reach two important conclusions. First, they realize that there are several methods used to measure financial leverage for individual firms, and for each specific financial ratio, there is both a "book-value" and a "market-value" measure of debt and equity. Second, they conclude that several strong patterns stand out in the capital structures of both U.S. and international companies.

Book Versus Market Value Leverage Ratios

By definition, measuring a firm's capital structure means determining the mix of long-term debt and equity on the right-hand side of a company's balance sheet. Thus, capital structure refers to long-term debt (LTD) and shareholders' equity (E), which itself consists of common and preferred stock. As described in Chapter 2, there are several financial ratios that can be used to measure leverage. The two most important are *long-term debt-to-equity* (LTD ÷ E), which is often referred to as the debt-to-equity ratio, and *long-term debt to total capitalization* [LTD ÷ (LTD + E)], or the debt-to-total capital ratio. Because these two ratios involve the same variables, arranged somewhat differently, they naturally both provide the same basic results. However, the debt-to-equity ratio must always be either greater than or equal to the debt-to-total capitalization ratio (can you see why?).

Yet, leverage ratios, which are computed by using either the book values of long-term debt and equity, or market values, often differ dramatically. Because the market value of a typical firm's common stock is usually much higher than its book value, market-value debt ratios tend to be much *lower* than book-value ratios. The debt-to-equity ratios of the most admired U.S. companies, described in the Opening Focus, illustrate this point. The book-value D/E ratios of those companies, with significant debt outstanding, are from two to seven times higher than the corresponding market-value D/E ratios. Economists prefer using market-value leverage ratios, because they measure how investors value corporate securities and so indicate on what terms companies can issue new securities. Corporate practitioners, however, tend to use book-value leverage ratios because these are the measures specified in the contracts governing security issues (indentures) and in bank loan agreements.

Are Capital Structures Randomly Selected?

If capital structure choices have no effect on firm values, then we may not expect to see any predictable patterns in leverage ratios across companies. When we examine different firms in different industries, however, we can quickly conclude that capital structures are not randomly generated. Instead, they show the following patterns:

Capital structures show strong industry patterns. In all developed countries, certain industries have high debt-to-equity ratios, whereas other industries employ little or no long-term debt financing. Highly leveraged industries include utilities, transportation companies (trucking, airlines, railroads), real estate, and many capital-intensive manufacturing sectors. Firms in the service, mining, oil and gas exploration, and high-technology industries generally use little or no debt. These patterns are observed in almost all countries, suggesting that an industry's asset mix and operating environment significantly influence the capital structures that are chosen by firms in that industry, worldwide. Table 12.5 presents median book-value, debt-to-equity

Table 12.5
Book-Value Leverage Ratios for Selected U.S. Industries, 2004

Industry	Long-Term Debt-to-Equity, %	Long-Term Debt-to-Total Capital, %
Metal mining	0	0
Computers and communications equipment	0	0
Software	0	0
Programming and data processing	0	0
Semiconductors	0	0
Motion pictures	1	1
Pharmaceuticals	3	3
Motor vehicles	38	28
Oil and gas	31	28
Steel	44	34
Hotels and motels	71	51
Hospitals	82	45
Airlines	83	60
Chemicals	90	52
TV Broadcast stations	90	54
Natural gas	102	51

Source: Compustat

ratios and debt-to-total capital ratios for eighteen key U.S. industries, in 2004. A glance at the table reveals a clear tendency for firms in technology-based industries to use almost no debt, whereas firms in asset-rich industries such as steel, airlines, and natural gas distribution tend to have much higher leverage ratios.

Economy-wide average leverage ratios vary across countries. Although the same industries have high and low leverage ratios in all countries, national average debt ratios also differ systematically from each other. Firms in Japan, France, Germany, Italy, and South Korea tend to have higher book-value debt ratios than do companies headquartered in the United States, Britain, Canada, Brazil, Mexico, and many other countries. If leverage is measured using market values, however, German companies typically use less long-term debt than firms in any other developed economy. Why leverage ratios vary so much across countries remains an unsolved puzzle. In part, differences in leverage may reflect differences in the industrial composition of national economies. Indeed, historical, institutional, and even cultural factors all probably play a part, as does a nation's reliance on capital markets versus banks for corporate financing. In particular, market-value leverage ratios tend to be low in those countries where creditors have the greatest power to seize assets and to force corporate borrowers to liquidate, when they default on loans. Therefore, borrowing firm managers have a very strong incentive not to issue too much debt.

Leverage ratios are negatively related to the costs of financial distress. Across both industries and countries, the larger the perceived costs of bankruptcy and financial distress, the less debt firms use. For example, when the principal assets of a company are intangible (e.g., patents, brands, copyrights, and other intellectual property), the costs of financial distress are much higher than when the principal assets are tangible structures and equipment. These can be pledged as collateral and easily sold by lenders if a borrower defaults. Companies with valuable intangible assets thus tend to use less debt than do tangible, asset-rich companies.

Within industries, the most profitable companies borrow the least. Regardless of the industry in question, the most profitable companies have the lowest leverage ratios, suggesting that observed leverage ratios are partly the result of past decisions, made by managers, to retain high profits. This is a surprising (though robust) observation, since debt financing enjoys a tax advantage in most countries because firms can deduct interest payments before paying taxes. The implication is that, other things being equal, profitable firms should use *more* leverage than unprofitable firms should use. By borrowing money, profitable companies shelter a larger proportion of their cash flows from taxes.

Corporate and personal income taxes influence capital structures, but taxes alone cannot explain differences in leverage across firms, industries, or countries. Taxes certainly influence corporate leverage usage, but they are not decisive. For example, American corporations apparently used no less debt prior to the introduction of the income tax in 1913 than they did either after its introduction or when corporate and personal income tax rates peaked during World War II. In fact, U.S. book-value debt ratios reached their lowest point in modern history during World War II. They have risen slowly, but surely ever since. The fraction of equity in the capital structures of U.S. firms declined steadily during the second half of the twentieth century, whereas debt continuously rose. In contrast, market-value leverage ratios show no similar long-term trend. The market-value share of debt in the capital structures of American corporations rose from 1951 to 1973, but the trend reversed after 1973. These gradual changes in leverage seem at odds with the sudden changes in tax laws (and hence, sudden changes in the tax advantages of debt) that have occurred over the last fifty years. On the other hand, research has shown that increasing the corporate income tax rates generally causes firms to issue more debt, and that decreasing the personal tax rates on equity income, relative to those on interest income, prompts corporations to issue less debt. Figure 12.5 compares year 2002 statutory corporate income tax rates, in ten OECD countries, versus the rates in those countries during 1986.

SMART PRACTICES VIDEO

Keith Woodward, Vice President of Finance, General Mills

"In General Mills we have lots of discussions about what is the optimal capital structure."

See the entire interview at **SMARTFinance**

Shareholders consider leverage-increasing events to be "good news" and leverage-decreasing events to be "bad news." Almost every published empirical study shows that stock prices rise when a company announces leverage-increasing events such as debt-for-equity exchange offers, debt-financed share repurchase programs, and debt-financed cash tender offers to acquire control of another company. On the other hand, leverage-decreasing events such as equity-for-debt exchange offers, new stock offerings, and acquisition offers, involving payment with a firm's own shares, almost always yield share price declines.

CONCEPT REVIEW QUESTIONS

11. In most countries, firms in high-tech industries are almost all intangible asset-rich rather than fixed asset-rich. What effect do you think the continued growth of these industries will have on average leverage ratios in the future?

12. What happens to stock prices when corporate managers announce leverage-increasing transactions such as debt-for-equity exchange offers? What happens to stock prices, in response to leverage-decreasing announcements? How do you interpret these findings?

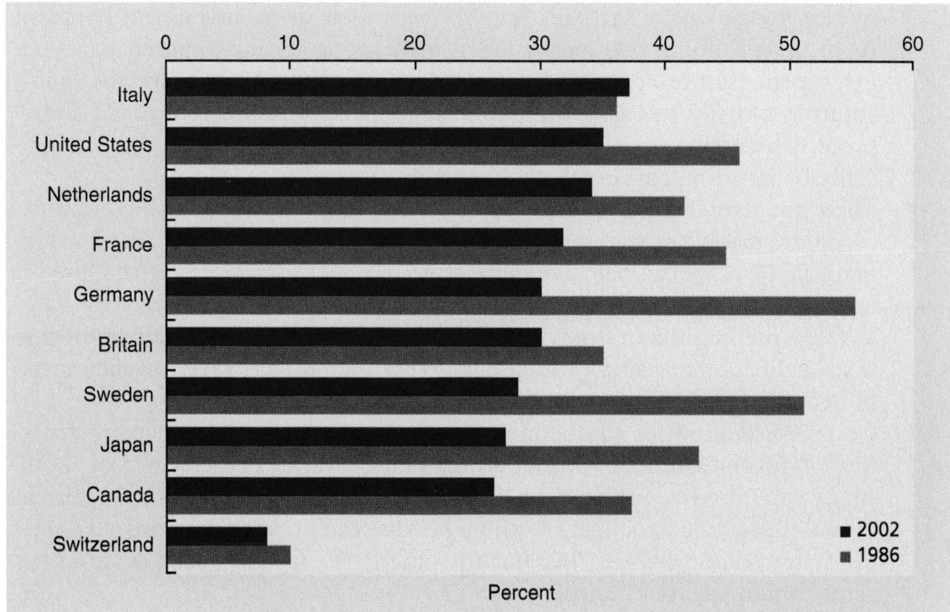

Figure 12.5
Corporate Income Tax Rates in Selected OECD Countries

2002 versus 1986

Source: Organization for Economic Cooperation and development

12.8 SUMMARY AND CONCLUSIONS

- Financial leverage means using fixed-cost debt financing to increase expected earnings per share. Unfortunately, financial leverage also increases the dispersion of expected earnings per share.
- Franco Modigliani and Merton Miller showed that capital structure is irrelevant in a world of frictionless capital markets. This means that the leverage choice cannot affect firm valuation.
- In a world with only company-level taxation of operating profits and tax-deductible interest payments, the optimal corporate strategy is to use the maximum possible leverage. This minimizes the government's claim on profits, in the form of taxes, and maximizes the amount of income flowing to private investors.
- When corporate profits are taxed at both the corporate and personal levels (with taxes on interest and dividends received), the benefits to high levels of corporate leverage are much reduced and may be completely negated. In this more "realistic" world of multiple taxes and other market imperfections, such as transactions costs to issuing securities, it is unclear whether an "optimal" debt level exists for the average firm in any given nation.
- In addition to corporate and personal taxation of income, several characteristics of a firm's asset structure, operating environment, investment opportunities, and ownership structure significantly influence the level of debt that the firm will choose to have.
- Firms with large amounts of tangible assets, such as buildings, transportation equipment, and general-purpose machine tools, tend to use a large amount of debt in their capital structures. These assets can pass fairly easily through bankruptcy, with their values intact. In contrast, firms that rely more on intangible assets, such as brand names and research-and-development spending, tend to use very little financial leverage.
- Creditors know that corporate managers, who operate their firms in the interests of shareholders, have incentives to try to expropriate creditor wealth, by playing a series of "games" with their firms' investment policies. Asset substitution is one such game. It involves promising to purchase a safe investment asset to obtain an interest rate that reflects this risk, and then substituting a higher risk asset that promises a higher expected return. Creditors protect themselves from these games through a variety of techniques, especially by inserting covenants into loan agreements.
- There are several important agency costs inherent in the relationship between corporate managers and outside investors and creditors. In some cases, using financial leverage can help overcome these agency problems; in others, use of leverage exacerbates the problems. The modern trade-off theory of corporate leverage predicts that a firm's optimal debt level will be set by trading off the tax benefits of increasing leverage against the increasingly severe agency costs of heavy debt usage.
- Corporate debt ratios can be measured in various ways, but "capital structure" ratios measure the ratio of a firm's long-term or permanent debt to its equity capital. More problematic is the need to express leverage ratios in terms of both book value and market value, because each type of measure is appropriate for some purposes, but not for others. We usually focus on market-value capital structure ratios.

- Several regularities are observed in capital structure patterns around the world. In general, industries rich in fixed assets and those with assets that retain their value in bankruptcy, tend to have high leverage, whereas industries rich in intangible assets tend to have low levels of indebtedness. This is particularly true for industries in which research-and-development spending is important.
- Though firms in the same industries tend to exhibit similar debt levels in all countries, there are also significant differences in average leverage levels between countries. In those countries where bankruptcy laws favor creditors, especially Britain and Germany, market-value leverage levels tend to be lower than in nations where debtors enjoy greater bankruptcy protection.

SELF-TEST PROBLEMS

Answers to Self-Test Problems appear in Appendix D at back of book. Answers to the Concept Review Questions throughout the chapter appear at http://megginson.swlearning.com.

ST12-1. As Chief Financial Officer of the Uptown Service Corporation (USC), you are considering a recapitalization plan that would convert USC from its current all-equity capital structure to one including substantial financial leverage. USC now has 150,000 shares of common stock outstanding, which are selling for $80.00 each. The recapitalization proposal is to issue $6,000,000 worth of long-term debt, at an interest rate of 7.0 percent, and use the proceeds to repurchase 75,000 shares of common stock worth $6,000,000. USC's earnings in the next year will depend on the state of the economy. If there is normal growth, *EBIT* will be $1,200,000. *EBIT* will be $600,000 if there is a recession, and *EBIT* will be $1,800,000 if there is an economic boom. You believe that each economic outcome is equally likely. Assume there are no market frictions such as corporate or personal income taxes.

a. If the proposed recapitalization is adopted, calculate the number of shares outstanding, the per-share price, and the debt-to-equity ratio for USC.

b. Calculate the earnings per share (*EPS*) and the return on equity for USC shareholders, under all three economic outcomes (recession, normal growth, and boom), for both the current all-equity capitalization and the proposed mixed debt/equity capital structure.

c. Calculate the breakeven level of *EBIT*, where earnings per share for USC stockholders are the same, under the current and proposed capital structures.

d. At what level of *EBIT* will USC shareholders earn zero *EPS*, under the current and the proposed capital structures?

ST12-2. An unlevered company operates in perfect markets and has net operating income (*EBIT*) of $2,000,000. Assume that the required return on assets for firms in this industry is 8 percent. The firm issues $10 million worth of debt, with a required return of 6.5 percent, and uses the proceeds to repurchase outstanding stock. There are no corporate or personal taxes.

a. What is the market value and required return of this firm's stock before the repurchase transaction, according to M&M Proposition I?

b. What is the market value and required return of this firm's remaining stock after the repurchase transaction, according to M&M Proposition II?

ST12-3. Westside Manufacturing has *EBIT* of $10 million. There is $60 million of debt outstanding, with a required rate of return of 6.5 percent. The required rate of return on the industry is 10 percent. The corporate tax rate is 30 percent. Assume there are corporate taxes but no personal taxes.

a. Determine the present value of the interest tax shield of Westside Manufacturing, as well as the total value of the firm.

b. Determine the gain from leverage, if personal taxes of 10 percent on stock income and 35 percent on debt income exist.

ST12-4. You are the manager of a financially distressed corporation, with $10 million in debt outstanding, which will mature in one month. Your firm currently has $7 million cash on hand. Assume that you are offered the opportunity to invest in either of the two projects described below.

Project 1: the opportunity to invest $7 million in risk-free Treasury bills, with a 4 percent annual interest rate (or a 0.333% per month interest rate)

Project 2: a high-risk gamble, which will pay off $12 million in one month, if it is successful (probability = 0.25), but will only pay $4,000,000, if it is unsuccessful (probability = 0.75).

a. Compute the expected payoff for each project and state which one you would adopt if you were operating the firm in the shareholders' best interests? Why?
b. Which project would you accept if the firm was unlevered? Why?
c. Which project would you accept if the company was organized as a partnership rather than a corporation? Why?

ST12-5. Run-and-Hide Detective Company currently has no debt and expects to earn $5 million in *EBIT* each year, for the foreseeable future. The required return on assets for detective companies of this type is 10.0 percent, and the corporate tax rate is 35 percent. There are no taxes on dividends or interest at the personal level. Run-and-Hide calculates that there is a 5 percent chance that the firm will fall into bankruptcy in any given year. If bankruptcy does occur, it will impose direct and indirect costs, totaling $8 million. If necessary, they will use the industry required return for discounting bankruptcy costs.

a. Compute the present value of bankruptcy costs for Run-and-Hide.
b. Compute the overall value of the firm.
c. Recalculate the value of the company, assuming that the firm's shareholders face a 15 percent personal tax rate on equity income.

INTERNET RESOURCES

Note: *For updates to links, please go to the book's Web site at* http://megginson.swlearning.com.

http://www.quicken.com; http://www.yahoo.com; http://www.sec.gov—Three sites from which you can download leverage figures for specific companies and compare them to figures for firms in the same industry as well as firms in other industries

http://www.taxsites.com/international.html—A site that provides country-specific tax information for dozens of countries, as well as links to a wide variety of tax-related sites

http://www.bondsonline.com—A site that offers a wealth of information about bonds

http://www.standardandpoors.com—A site with information on bond ratings as well as the latest changes to ratings on outstanding bonds

KEY TERMS

agency cost/tax shield trade-off model of corporate leverage
agency costs of (outside) equity
agency costs of debt
asset substitution
bankruptcy costs
business risk
direct costs of bankruptcy
financial leverage
financial risk

fundamental principle of financial leverage
indirect bankruptcy costs
Proposition I
Proposition II
recapitalization
underinvestment

QUESTIONS AND PROBLEMS

Q12-1. Why is the use of long-term debt financing referred to as using *financial leverage?*

Q12-2. What is the fundamental principle of financial leverage?

Q12-3. What is the basic conclusion of the original Modigliani and Miller *Proposition I?*

Q12-4. Deriving from the conclusion of Proposition I, what is the crux of M&M *Proposition II?* What is the natural relationship between the required returns on debt and on equity that results from Proposition II?

Q12-5. In what way did M&M change their conclusion, regarding capital structure choice, with the additional assumption of corporate taxes? In this context, what composes the difference in value between levered and unlevered firms?

Q12-6. By introducing personal taxes into the model for capital structure choice, how did Miller alter the previous M&M conclusion that 100 percent debt is optimal? What happens to the gains from leverage if personal tax rates on interest income are significantly higher than those on stock-related income?

Q12-7. Why do a firm's stockholders hold a valuable "default option"? How could this option induce stockholders to employ high levels of financial leverage?

Q12-8. All else equal, which firm would face a greater level of financial distress, a software-development firm or a hotel chain? Why would financial distress costs affect the firms so differently?

Q12-9. Describe how managers whose firms have debt outstanding and face financial distress, could jeopardize the investments of creditors with the "games" of asset substitution and underinvestment.

Q12-10. Differentiate between direct and indirect costs of bankruptcy. Which of the two is generally more significant?

Q12-11. How can restrictive covenants in bonds be both an agency cost of debt and a way to prevent agency costs of debt?

Q12-12. What are the trade-offs in the agency cost/tax shield trade-off model? How is the firm's optimal capital structure determined under the assumptions of this model? Does empirical evidence support this model?

Q12-13. What industrial and national capital structure patterns are exhibited globally? What factors seem to be driving these patterns?

Q12-14. What is the observed relationship between debt ratios and profitability, and the perceived costs of financial distress? Why does the relationship between leverage and profitability imply that capital structure choice is residual in nature?

Q12-15. How influential are corporate and personal taxes on capital structure? Historically, have changes in American tax rates greatly affected debt ratios?

Q12-16. How do stock prices generally react to announcements of firms' changes in leverage? Why is this result perplexing and seemingly contradictory, given your answer to Question 12-3?

PROBLEMS

What Is Financial Leverage and Why Do Firms Use It?

P12-1. As Chief Financial Officer of the Magnificent Electronics Corporation (MEC), you are considering a recapitalization plan that would convert MEC from its current all-equity capital structure to one including substantial financial leverage. MEC now has 500,000 shares of common stock outstanding, which are selling for $60 each, and you expect the firm's *EBIT* to be $2,400,000 per year, for the foreseeable future. The recapitalization proposal is to issue $15,000,000 worth of long-term debt, at an interest rate of 6.0 percent, and use the proceeds to repurchase 250,000 shares of common stock worth $15,000,000. Assuming there are no market frictions such as corporate or personal income taxes, calculate the expected return on equity for MEC shareholders, under both the current all-equity capital structure and under the recapitalization plan.

P12-2. The All-Star Production Corporation (APC) is considering a recapitalization plan that would convert APC from its current all-equity capital structure to one including some financial leverage. APC now has 10,000,000 shares of common stock outstanding, which are selling for $40.00 each, and you expect the firm's *EBIT* to be $50,000,000 per year, for the foreseeable future. The recapitalization proposal is to issue $100,000,000 worth of long-term debt, at an interest rate of 6.50 percent, and use the proceeds to repurchase as many shares as possible, at a price of $40.00 per share. Assume there are no market frictions such as corporate or personal income taxes. Calculate the expected return on equity for APC shareholders, under both the current all-equity capital structure and under the recapitalization plan.

a. Calculate the number of shares outstanding, the per-share price, and the debt-to-equity ratio for APC if the proposed recapitalization is adopted.

b. Calculate the earnings per share (*EPS*) and the return on equity for APC shareholders, under both the current all-equity capitalization and the proposed mixed debt/equity capital structure.

c. Calculate the breakeven level of *EBIT*, where earnings per share for APC stockholders are the same, under the current and proposed capital structures.

d. At what level of *EBIT* will APC shareholders earn zero *EPS*, under the current and the proposed capital structures?

P12-3. As Chief Financial Officer of the Campus Supply Corporation (CSC), you are considering a recapitalization plan that would convert CSC from its current all-equity capital structure to one including substantial financial leverage. CSC now has 250,000 shares of common stock outstanding, which are selling for $60.00 each, and the recapitalization proposal is to issue $7,500,000 worth of long-term debt at an interest rate of 6.0 percent and use the proceeds to repurchase 125,000 shares of common stock worth $7,500,000. USC's earnings next year will depend on the state of the economy. If there is normal growth, *EBIT* will be $2,000,000; *EBIT* will be $1,000,000 if there is a recession and *EBIT* will be $3,000,000 if there is an economic boom. You believe that each economic outcome is equally likely. Assume there are no market frictions such as corporate or personal income taxes.

a. Calculate the number of shares outstanding, the per-share price and the debt-to-equity ratio for CSC if the proposed recapitalization is adopted.

b. Calculate the expected earnings per share (*EPS*) and return on equity for CSC shareholders under all three economic outcomes (recession, normal growth and boom), for both the current all-equity capitalization and the proposed mixed debt/equity capital structure.

c. Calculate the break-even level of *EBIT* where earnings per share for CSC stockholders are the same under the current and proposed capital structures.

d. At what level of *EBIT* will CSC shareholders earn zero *EPS* under the current and the proposed capital structures?

The Modigliani & Miller Capital Structure Irrelevance Propositions

P12-4. An unlevered company operates in perfect markets and has a net operating income (*EBIT*) of $250,000. Assume that the required return on assets for firms in this industry is 12.5 percent. The firm issues $1 million worth of debt, with a required return of 5 percent, and uses the proceeds to repurchase outstanding stock.

a. What is the market value and required return of this firm's stock before the repurchase transaction?
b. What is the market value and required return of this firm's remaining stock after the repurchase transaction?

P12-5. Assume that capital markets are perfect. A firm finances its operations with $50 million in stock, with a required return of 15 percent, and $40 million in bonds, with a required return of 9 percent. Assume that the firm could issue $10 million in additional bonds, at 9 percent. Using the proceeds to retire $10 million worth of equity, what would happen to the firm's *WACC*? What would happen to the required return on the company's stock?

P12-6. A firm operates in perfect capital markets. The required return on its outstanding debt is 6 percent, the required return on its shares is 14 percent, and its *WACC* is 10 percent. What is the firm's debt-to-equity ratio?

P12-7. Assume that two firms, U and L, are identical, in all respects, except that Firm U is debt free, and Firm L has a capital structure that is 50 percent debt and 50 percent equity, by market value. Further suppose that the assumptions of the Modigliani and Miller capital structure irrelevance proposition hold (no taxes or transactions costs, no bankruptcy costs, etc.) and that each firm will have net operating income (*EBIT*) of $800,000. If the required return on assets, r, for these firms is 12.5 percent, and risk-free debt yields 5 percent, calculate the following values for both Firm U and Firm L: (1) total firm value, (2) market value of debt and equity, and (3) required return on equity.

SMART SOLUTIONS

See the problem and solution explained step-by-step at SMARTFinance

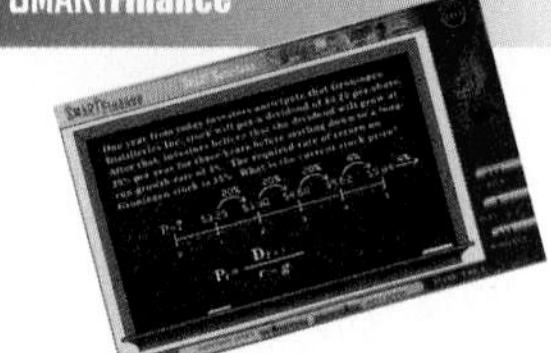

P12-8. Hearthstone Corp. and The Shaky Image Co. are companies that compete in the luxury consumer goods market. The two companies are virtually identical, except that Hearthstone is financed entirely with equity, and The Shaky Image uses equal amounts of debt and equity. Suppose each firm has assets with a total market value of $100 million. Hearthstone has 4 million shares of stock outstanding worth $25 each. Shaky has 2 million shares outstanding, and it also has publicly traded debt, with a market value of $50 million. Both companies operate in a world with perfect capital markets (no taxes, etc.). The *WACC* for each firm is 12 percent. The cost of debt is 8 percent.

a. What is the price of Shaky stock?
b. What is the cost of equity for Hearthstone? For Shaky?

P12-9. In the mid-1980s, Michael Milken and his firm, Drexel Burnham Lambert, made the term "junk bonds" a household word. Many of Drexel's clients issued junk bonds (bonds with low credit ratings) to the public to raise money to conduct a leveraged buyout (LBO) of a target firm. After the LBO, the target firm would have an extremely high debt-to-equity ratio, with only a small portion of equity financing remaining. Many politicians and members of the financial press worried that the increase in junk bonds would bring about an increase in the risk of the U.S. economy because so many large firms had become highly leveraged. Merton Miller disagreed. See if you can follow his argument, by assessing whether each of the statements below is true or false:

a. The junk bonds issued by acquiring firms were riskier than investment-grade bonds.
b. The remaining equity in highly leveraged firms was more risky than it had been before the LBO.

c. After an LBO, the target firm's capital structure would consist of very risky junk bonds and very risky equity. Therefore, the risk of the firm would increase after the LBO.
d. The junk bonds issued to conduct the LBO were less risky than the equity they replaced.

The M&M Capital Structure Model with Corporate and Personal Taxes

P12-10. Herculio Mining has net operating income of $5 million; there is $50 million of debt outstanding, with a required rate of return of 6 percent; the required rate of return on the industry is 12 percent; and the corporate tax rate is 40 percent. Assume there are corporate taxes but no personal taxes.

a. Determine the present value of the interest tax shield of Herculio Mining, as well as the total value of the firm.
b. Determine the gain from leverage if personal taxes of 20 percent on stock income and 30 percent on debt income exist.

P12-11. An all-equity firm is subject to a 30 percent tax rate. Its total market value is initially $3,500,000. There are 175,000 shares outstanding. The firm announces a program to issue $1 million worth of bonds, at 10 percent interest, and to use the proceeds to buy back common stock. Assume that there is no change in costs of financial distress and that the debt is perpetual.

a. What is the value of the tax shield that the firm acquires through the bond issue?
b. According to Modigliani & Miller, what is the likely increase in the firm's market value per share, after the announcement, assuming efficient markets?
c. How many shares will the company be able to repurchase?

P12-12. Intel Corp. is a firm that uses almost no debt and had a total market capitalization of about $179 billion in April 2004. Assume that Intel faces a 35 percent tax rate on corporate earnings. Ignore all elements of the decision, except the corporate tax savings.

a. By how much could Intel managers increase the value of the firm by issuing $50 billion in bonds (which would be rolled over in perpetuity) and simultaneously repurchasing $50 billion in stock? Why do you think that Intel has not taken advantage of this opportunity?
b. Suppose the personal tax rate on equity income, faced by Intel shareholders, is 10 percent, and the personal tax rate on interest income is 40 percent. Recalculate the gains to Intel from replacing $50 billion of equity with debt.

P12-13. Soonerco has $15 million of common stock outstanding, net operating income of $2.5 million per year, and $15 million of debt outstanding, with a required return (interest rate) of 8 percent. The required rate of return on assets in this industry is 12.5 percent, and the corporate tax rate is 35 percent. Within the M&M framework of corporate taxes but no personal taxes, determine the present value of the interest tax shield of Soonerco, as well as the total value of the firm. Finally, determine the gain from leverage if personal taxes are levied at the rates of 15 percent on stock income and 25 percent on debt income.

Costs of Bankruptcy and Financial Distress

P12-14. Assume that you are the manager of a financially distressed corporation, with $1.5 million in debt outstanding, which will mature in two months. Your firm currently has $1 million cash on hand. Assuming that you are operating the firm in the shareholders' best interests and that debt covenants prevent you from simply paying out the cash to shareholders as cash dividends, what should you do?

P12-15. You are the manager of a financially distressed corporation, with $1.5 million in debt outstanding, which will mature in three months. Your firm currently has $1 million cash on hand. Assume that you are offered the opportunity to invest in either of the two projects described below.

Project 1: the opportunity to invest \$1 million in risk-free Treasury bills, with a 4 percent annual interest rate (a quarterly interest rate of 1 percent = 4% per year ÷ 4 quarters per year)

Project 2: a high-risk gamble, which will pay off \$1.6 million in two months, if it is successful (probability = 0.4), but will only pay \$400,000, if it is unsuccessful (probability = 0.6).

a. Compute the expected payoff for each project and state which one you would adopt if you were operating the firm in the shareholders' best interests? Why?
b. Which project would you accept if the firm was unlevered? Why?
c. Which project would you accept if the company was organized as a partnership rather than a corporation? Why?

P12-16. A firm has the choice of investing in one of two projects. Both projects last for one year. Project 1 requires an investment of \$11,000 and yields \$11,000, with a probability of 0.5, and \$13,000, with a probability of 0.5. Project 2 also requires an investment of \$11,000 and yields \$5,000, with a probability of 0.5, and \$20,000, with a probability of 0.5. The firm is capable of raising \$10,000 of the required investment through a bond issue that carries an annual interest rate of 10 percent. Assuming that the investors are concerned only about expected returns, which project would stockholders prefer? Why? Which project would bondholders prefer? Why?

P12-17. An all-equity firm has 100,000 shares outstanding worth \$10 each. The firm is considering a project that requires an investment of \$400,000 and has an *NPV* of \$50,000. The company is also considering financing this project with a new issue of equity.

a. What is the price at which the firm needs to issue the new shares so that the existing shareholders are indifferent to whether the firm takes on the project with this equity financing or does not take on the project?
b. What is the price at which the firm needs to issue the new shares so that the existing shareholders capture the full benefit associated with the new project?

P12-18. You are the manager of a financially distressed corporation that has \$5 million in loans, which come due in 30 days. Your firm has \$4 million cash on hand. Suppose that a longtime supplier of materials to your firm is planning to exit the business but has offered to sell your company a large supply of material at a bargain price of \$4.5 million—but only if payment is made immediately in cash. If you choose not to acquire this material, the supplier will offer it to a competitor. Your firm will then have to acquire the materials at market prices, totaling \$5 million, over the next few months.

a. Assuming that you are operating the firm in the shareholders' best interests, would you accept the project? Why or why not?
b. Would you accept this project if the firm were unlevered? Why or why not?
c. Would you accept this project if the company were organized as a partnership? Why or why not?

Agency Costs and Capital Structure

P12-19. Magnum Enterprises has net operating income of \$5 million. There is \$50 million of debt outstanding, with a required rate of return of 6 percent. The required rate of return on the industry is 12 percent. The corporate tax rate is 40 percent. There are corporate taxes but no personal taxes. Compute the value of Magnum, assuming that the present value of bankruptcy costs are \$10 million.

P12-20. Slash and Burn Construction Company currently has no debt and expects to earn \$10 million in net operating income each year, for the foreseeable future. The required return on assets for construction companies of this type is 12.5 percent, and the corporate tax rate is 40 percent. There are no taxes on dividends or interest at the personal level. Slash and Burn calculates that there is a 10 percent chance that the firm will fall into bankruptcy in any given year. If bankruptcy does occur, it will impose direct and indirect costs, totaling \$12 million. If necessary, use the industry required return for discounting bankruptcy costs.

a. Compute the present value of bankruptcy costs for Slash and Burn.
b. Compute the overall value of the firm.
c. Recalculate the value of the company, assuming that the firm's shareholders face a 25 percent personal tax rate on equity income.

P12-21. Slash and Burn Construction Company currently has no debt and expects to earn \$10 million in net operating income each year, for the foreseeable future. The required return on assets for construction companies of this type is 12.5 percent, and the corporate tax rate is 40 percent. There are no taxes on dividends or interest at the personal level. Slash and Burn calculates that there is a 10 percent chance that the firm will fall into bankruptcy in any given year. If bankruptcy does occur, it will impose direct and indirect costs, totaling \$12 million. If necessary, use the industry required return for discounting bankruptcy costs. Assume that the managers of this company are weighing two capital structure alteration proposals.

Proposal 1 involves borrowing \$20 million, at an interest rate of 6 percent, and using the proceeds to repurchase an equal amount of outstanding stock. With this level of debt, the likelihood that Slash and Burn will fall into bankruptcy in any given year increases to 15 percent. If bankruptcy occurs, it will impose direct and indirect costs, totaling \$12 million.

Proposal 2 involves borrowing \$30 million, at an interest rate of 8 percent, and also using the proceeds to repurchase an equal amount of outstanding stock. With this level of debt, the likelihood of Slash and Burn falling into bankruptcy in any given year rises to 25 percent. The associated direct and indirect costs of bankruptcy, if it occurs, increase to \$20 million. For each proposal, calculate both the present value of the interest tax shields and the overall value of the firm, assuming that there are no personal taxes on debt or on equity income.

Capital Structure Patterns Observed Worldwide

P12-22. Go to Yahoo! and download recent balance sheets for Microsoft, Merck, Archer Daniels Midland, and General Mills (ticker symbols MSFT, MRK, ADM, and GIS, respectively). Calculate several debt ratios for each company and comment on the differences that you observe in the use of leverage. What factors do you think account for these differences?

THOMSON ONE Business School Edition

For instructions on using Thomson ONE: Business School Edition, refer to the instructions provided with the Thomson ONE: Business School Edition problems at the end of Chapters 1–6 or to "A Guide for Using Thomson ONE: Business School Edition."

P12-23. How does the value of an unlevered firm change if it takes on debt in a perfect capital market? Abercrombie & Fitch (ticker: ANF) is an all-equity firm. Using the latest year's net operating income (*EBIT*) and its weighted average cost of capital (*WACC*), calculate the value of ANF. If the company decides to change its debt-to-equity ratio to 0.5, by issuing debt and by using the proceeds to repurchase stock, what will ANF's value be after the change in capital structure? Assume that its cost of debt is one quarter of its cost of equity and that markets are perfect. What happens to its cost of equity after the new debt is issued? What is likely to happen to ANF's equity beta after debt is issued?

P12-24. How does the value of an unlevered firm change if it takes on debt in the presence of corporate taxes? Repeat the analysis for ANF from the previous problem, after relaxing only the "no corporate tax" assumption of perfect capital markets. Use the average tax rate (income taxes divided by pretax income from the income statement) for the latest available year. What is the value of ANF after it issues debt? What is the benefit of issuing debt when there are corporate taxes? How will the beta for a levered ANF, in the presence of corporate taxes, compare to that of an all-equity ANF and that of a levered ANF, in perfect capital markets? When capital markets are perfect, except for corporate taxes, what is the optimal level of debt the company should issue? In reality, do we observe firms that maintain this optimal level of debt? Why or why not?

Since these exercises depend upon real-time data, your answers will change continuously depending upon when you access the Internet to download your data.

MINICASE

Capital Structure

A few years after being appointed financial manager at Sedona Fabricators, Inc., you are asked by your boss to prepare for your first presentation to the Board of Directors. This presentation will pertain to issues associated with capital structure. It is intended to ensure that some of the newly appointed, independent board members understand certain terminology and issues. As a guideline for your presentation, you are provided with the following outline of questions.

ASSIGNMENT

1. What is capital structure?
2. What is financial leverage?
3. How does financial leverage relate to firm risk and expected returns?
4. Modigliani and Miller demonstrated that capital structure policy is irrelevant. What is the basis for their argument? What are their Propositions I and II?
5. How does the introduction of corporate taxes affect the M&M model?
6. How do the costs of bankruptcy and financial distress affect the M&M model?
7. What are agency costs? How can the use of debt reduce agency costs associated with equity?

CHAPTER 13

Dividend Policy

OPENING FOCUS

British Airways Cuts Dividend to Preserve Cash During Airline Crisis

To say that the period immediately following the September 11, 2001, terrorist attacks on the World Trade Center and the Pentagon was a difficult one for the world's airlines would be a serious understatement. Traffic on all the major airlines fell precipitously, and almost all were forced to cut both staff and schedules quite severely. Within weeks of the attack, two major European carriers—Swissair and Sabena—filed for bankruptcy protection, and several other international carriers appeared on the brink of following suit. The threat to the viability of the U.S. airline industry was so severe, in fact, that the major carriers successfully lobbied the U.S. Congress for an unprecedented $15 billion bailout package. Even with this financial lifeline, U.S. carriers announced job cuts of more than 120,000 people in the weeks following September 11.

British Airways (London Stock Exchange ticker symbol BAY) faced these same pressures, and more, during the fall of 2001. Most of BAY's scheduled flights were international rather than domestic, and these had suffered the largest decline in demand following the attacks. In early October 2001, in response to the financial pressures weighing on the firm, British Airways took the unprecedented step of suspending its interim (semiannual) dividend payment, which it normally paid in December. The company also announced that its full-year dividend payment for fiscal year 2002 was in serious jeopardy. This dividend suspension was very traumatic for BAY because the company had taken great pride in paying a dividend every six months, since its privatization in 1987. Over the years, its dividend payment had increased steadily and stood at 17.8 pence per share for fiscal year 2001. In line with industry norms, this payment represented over 57 percent of BAY's net profits for 2001. But with massive financial losses looming and job cuts of 7,000 employees already announced, BAY's managers felt there was no alternative but to eliminate dividend payments. The chief executive officer had already announced he would take a salary cut and the firm had told the British government it might need a bailout package, similar to the one given to the American airline industry. The firm was clearly fighting for financial survival.

Though traumatic for BAY and its shareholders, the dividend cut allowed the company to retain £193 million, which it otherwise would have paid out each year. This, in turn, helped BAY weather the next two turbulent years, during which the number of passengers carried by BAY declined by 15 percent, and revenue passenger kilometers fell by almost one fifth. The company suffered a net loss of £142 million during the fiscal year that ended in March 2002, but was able to rebound to a net profit of £72 million for fiscal year 2003. The company's share price, which had been above 300 pence per share in August 2001, fell to less than 150 pence per share, immediately after the World Trade Center attacks. It then declined even further, to 95 pence per share, in March 2003. By early September 2004, BAY's share price had more than doubled, to 237 pence per share, and the company was regaining its financial health—though company officials were not yet promising to resume dividend payments anytime soon.

Sources: Kevin Done and Cathy Newman, "BA's Dividend Warning Signals Trouble," *Financial Times* (October 7, 2001), p. 10; company information at the British Airways' Web site (http://www.britishairways.com); September 9, 2004, stock price data from the *Financial Times'* Web site (http://mwprices.ft.com/custom/ft-com/html-marketsDataTools.asp). ■

LEARNING OBJECTIVES

After studying this chapter you should be able to:

- Discuss the fundamentals of dividends, including payment procedures, types of policies, and other forms of dividends;
- Describe the observed patterns of dividend policies on a worldwide basis;
- Understand the agency cost model of dividends;
- Explain the argument for dividend irrelevance in a world with perfect capital markets;
- Review the real-world influences on dividend policy such as taxes, transactions costs, and uncertainty; and
- Summarize the predictions of the agency cost model, regarding expected dividend payout.

SMART PRACTICES VIDEO

Andy Bryant, Executive Vice President of Finance and Enterprise Systems, Chief Financial Officer, Intel Corp.

"Dividends are probably not the most effective way to return cash to shareholders."

See the entire interview at **SMARTFinance**

A firm's *dividend policy* refers to the choices the firm makes about whether to pay shareholders a cash dividend, about how large the cash dividend should be, and about how frequently it should be distributed. In a broader sense, dividend policy also encompasses decisions such as whether to distribute cash to investors via share repurchases or specially designated dividends, rather than regular dividends, and whether to rely on stock or on cash distributions. Though there are numerous elements in the dividend decision, modern corporations still struggle with the same issues that occupied managers in the 1950s. Managers must decide if firms should maintain their current dividends or change them. Managers tend to increase regular dividends only when they expect that future cash flow is sufficient to pay the dividends and to meet their firm's other financial needs. Firms must also weigh the stock market's reaction to changes in dividend policy. Influencing that reaction are factors such as the level of a firm's dividends, the volatility of the dividend stream over time, and the income taxes that investors must pay when they receive dividends. As you can see, the many dimensions of this problem make dividend policy decisions quite difficult, at least for some firms.

In addition to these firm-level issues regarding dividend policy, two recent trends in the aggregate dividend decisions of U.S. firms are interesting. The first of these is the phenomenal growth in both the number of firms implementing **share repurchase programs** and in the total value of these programs. Companies that

share repurchase program A company announcing this kind of program states that it will buy some of its own shares over a period of time.

Figure 13.1
The Fractions of Publicly Traded U.S. Firms Paying Cash Dividends, 1926–1999

This figure details the percentage of all publicly traded firms in the United States that paid regular cash dividends over the period 1926–1999. The top figure shows this for all publicly traded firms, whereas the bottom figure breaks this out by exchange, from 1962 (AMEX) and 1972 (NASDAQ) onward.

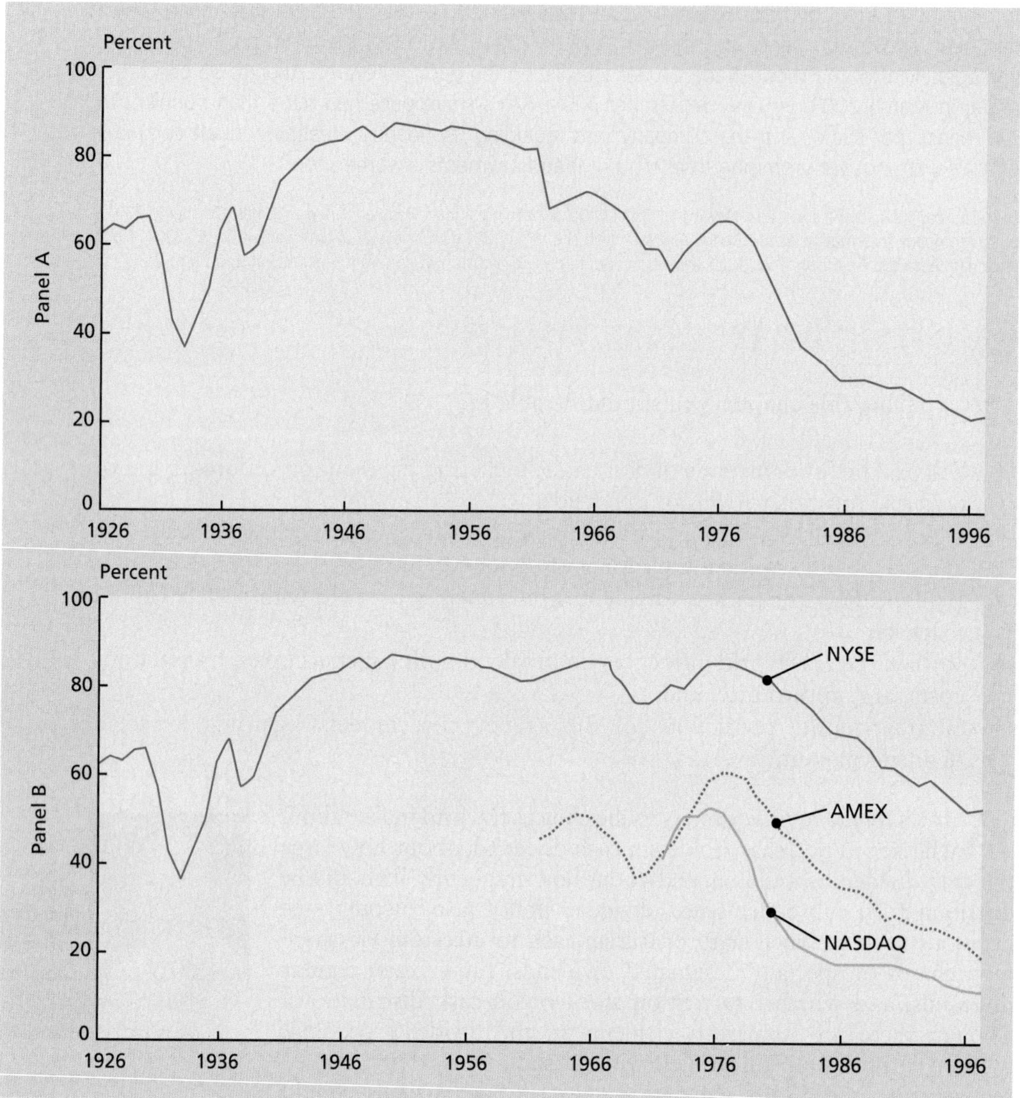

Source: Eugene F. Fama and Kenneth R. French, "Disappearing Dividends: Changing Firm Characteristics or Lower Propensity to Pay?" Journal of Applied Corporate Finance *14 (Spring 2001), pp. 67–79.*

announce a share repurchase program state that they will buy some of their own shares over a period of time. In executing a repurchase program, firms distribute some of the cash, which they have accumulated, to investors who want to sell their shares. Therefore, dividends and share repurchases are alternative means by which firms distribute cash to investors. In fact, the annual value of share repurchases in the United States sometimes exceeds that of cash dividends.

The second dramatic trend in corporate dividend policy is the very sharp decline in the percentage of publicly traded U.S. companies that pay any dividends at all.

As Panel A of Figure 13.1 demonstrates, the percentage of all publicly traded firms paying dividends was four times greater in the 1950s than it is today. Panel B breaks this out by exchange. Additionally, those firms that do pay dividends now pay out a lower fraction of their earnings than they did before. In other words, companies have a lower *propensity* to pay dividends today than they had in years past. As we will see, both of these patterns reflect the changing nature of publicly listed companies in the United States, as increasing numbers of young, rapidly growing technology companies, which consume more cash than they generate, have "gone public" over the past three decades. The average **dividend yield**, defined as annual dividend per share divided by stock price, of U.S. stocks has also declined over the past five decades, and now stands at less than two percent.

dividend yield
Annual dividend per share divided by stock price.

Our objective in this chapter is to answer two basic questions. First, does dividend policy matter? (Can managers increase or decrease the total market value of a firm's securities by changing its dividend payments?) Second, if dividend policy does matter, what factors determine a firm's optimal dividend policy? Before attacking these questions, however, we provide a brief overview of the fundamentals of dividend payments, which defines the key terms and discusses the basic issues that corporate managers everywhere must face in setting dividend policies. Section 13.2 provides an overview of dividend payment patterns around the world. These are the patterns that a modern theory of dividend policy should be able to explain. Section 13.3 shows that dividends are irrelevant in a world of perfect (frictionless) capital markets, which suggests that dividends exist because of some flaw in markets or human nature. Section 13.4 describes various real-world market imperfections that affect actual dividend policy decisions. Finally, Section 13.5 presents both a summary of the predictions of the current "mainstream" model of dividend policy and a checklist that practicing managers can use to set dividend policies for their firms.

13.1 DIVIDEND FUNDAMENTALS

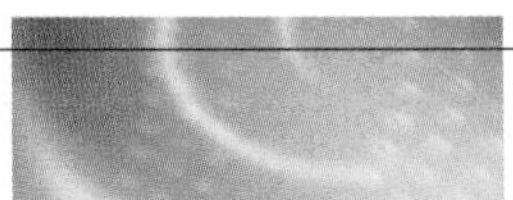

In Chapter 4, we argued that the value of a share of stock equals the present value of cash flows that the shareholder receives over time. Even though a company is not paying dividends (or repurchasing shares) today, its market value reflects the likelihood that the firm will either pay dividends in the future or be acquired by another company, at a price that reflects a higher stream of dividend payments. To provide an understanding of the fundamentals of dividend policy, we discuss the procedures for paying cash dividends and the factors affecting dividend policy.

Cash Dividend Payment Procedures

In the United States, as in most countries, shareholders do not have a legal right to receive dividends. Instead, a firm's board of directors must decide whether to pay dividends. The directors usually meet to evaluate the firm's recent financial performance and future outlook and to determine whether, and in what amount, dividends should be paid. The payment date of the cash dividend, if one is declared, must also be established.

Most U.S. firms that pay cash dividends do so once every quarter, whereas corporations in other industrialized countries generally pay dividends annually or semiannually. Firms adjust the size of their dividends periodically, but not necessarily every quarter. For example, among the roughly 1,300 U.S. firms that paid dividends continuously from 1999 to 2003, just over 36 percent changed their dividend once per year, on average. About 14 percent of these firms maintained a constant dividend during this five-year span, and about 23 percent changed their dividend more frequently than once per year. Only five of the 1,300 firms changed their dividend every quarter.[1] These figures suggest that firms maintain a constant dividend until significant increases or decreases in earnings justify changing it.

announcement date
The day a firm releases the dividend record and payment dates to the public.

date of record
The date on which the names of all persons who own shares in a company are recorded as stockholders and thus eligible to receive a dividend.

ex-dividend
A purchaser of a stock does not receive the current dividend.

payment date
The actual date on which a firm mails the dividend payment to the holders of record.

Relevant Dates. If a firm's directors declare a dividend, they also set the dividend record and the payment dates. The day on which firms release this information to the public is the **announcement date**. All persons whose names are recorded as stockholders on the **date of record** receive the declared dividend at a specified future time. The stockholders who own shares on this *record date* are often referred to as *shareholders of record*. Because of the time it takes to make bookkeeping entries when a stock is traded, the stock begins selling **ex-dividend** several business days prior to the date of record. Purchasers of a stock selling ex-dividend do not receive the current dividend. Ignoring normal market fluctuations, the stock's price should drop by approximately the amount of the declared dividend on the ex-dividend date. For example, suppose a stock that pays a $1 dividend sells for $51 just before going ex-dividend. Once the ex-dividend date passes, the price should drop to $50, in the absence of any other news affecting the stock. However, the average ex-dividend-day price drop, in the United States and many other countries, is significantly less than 100 percent of the value of the dividend payment, partly due to what appears to be a personal tax effect. The **payment date** is generally set a few weeks after the record date. The payment date is the actual date on which the firm mails the dividend payment to the holders of record.

APPLYING THE MODEL

In a move that surprised almost all commentators, Microsoft Corporation announced on January 16, 2003, that it would pay a cash dividend to shareholders for the first time ever. The company declared an annual dividend of $0.08 per share, which would be out of earnings for fiscal year 2003, ending June 30, 2003. In contrast to standard practice for most U.S. corporations, dividends would be paid only once per year rather than quarterly. Microsoft's earnings per share were $0.92 for fiscal year 2003, implying a payout ratio of 8.7 percent. Though the total amount of the dividend, $870 million, would only make a small dent in Microsoft's holdings of cash and marketable securities (worth more than $56 billion in March 2004), investors generally applauded the company's announcement. In September 2003, Microsoft announced that fiscal year 2004 dividends per share would be doubled, to $0.16 per share. Ten months later, Microsoft shocked investors by announcing plans to pay a one-time $32 billion special cash dividend and also to once again double the annual dividend payment.

External Factors Affecting Dividend Policy

Before discussing the basic types of dividend policies, we should briefly consider some of the practical issues related to formulating a value-maximizing policy (theoretical issues are discussed in later sections). These include legal constraints, contractual constraints, internal constraints, the firm's growth prospects, and owner considerations.

Most U.S. states prohibit corporations from paying out as cash dividends any portion of their "legal capital," which is measured by the par value of common stock. Other states define legal capital to include not only the par value of the

1. Author's calculations using data from the Center for Research on Securities Prices (CRSP), excluding closed-end mutual funds, real estate investment trusts (REITs), and other investment companies.

Omega Corporation's Stockholders' Equity	
Common stock at par	$100,000
Paid-in capital, in surplus of par	200,000
Retained earnings	140,000
Total stockholders' equity	$440,000

In states where a firm's legal capital is defined as the par value of its common stock, the firm could pay out a maximum of $340,000 ($200,000 + $140,000) in cash dividends without impairing its capital. In states where a firm's capital includes all paid-in capital, the firm could pay out only $140,000 in cash dividends.

Table 13.1
Calculating the Maximum Amount a Firm Can Pay in Cash Dividends

The stockholders' equity account of the Omega Corporation is presented in the table to the left.

common stock but also any paid-in capital in excess of par. States establish these *capital-impairment restrictions* to provide a sufficient equity base to protect creditors' claims. The example presented for the Omega Corporation in Table 13.1 clarifies the varying definitions of capital.

An earnings requirement limiting the amount of dividends to the sum of a firm's present and past earnings is sometimes imposed. In other words, Omega cannot pay more in cash dividends than the sum of its most recent and historic retained earnings. However, *laws do not prohibit a firm from paying more in dividends than its current earnings.*

If a firm has overdue liabilities or is legally insolvent (if the fair market value of its assets is less than its liabilities), most states prohibit cash dividends. In addition, the Internal Revenue Service prohibits firms from accumulating earnings to reduce the owners' taxes. A firm's owners must pay income taxes on dividends when they are received, but the owners pay no tax on capital gains until they sell the stock. A firm may retain a large portion of earnings to delay the payment of taxes by its owners. If the IRS can determine that a firm has accumulated excess earnings to allow owners to delay paying ordinary income taxes, it may levy an **excess earnings accumulation tax** on any retained earnings above a specified amount. This rarely occurs in practice, however.

excess earnings accumulation tax
A tax levied by the IRS on a firm that has accumulated sufficient excess earnings to allow owners to delay paying ordinary income taxes.

Restrictive provisions in loan agreements sometimes constrain a firm's ability to pay cash dividends. Generally, these constraints prohibit cash dividends until the firm achieves a certain level of earnings, or they may limit dividends to a certain dollar amount or percentage of earnings. Constraints on dividend payments help protect creditors from losses due to insolvency. If a firm violates one of these contractual restrictions, creditors generally have the right to demand immediate repayment on their loans.

Types of Dividend Policies

The following sections describe three basic dividend policies, but bear in mind that the constant nominal dividend policy predominates in every major economy. A particular firm's cash dividend policy may incorporate elements of each policy type.

dividend payout ratio
The percentage of current earnings available for common stockholders paid out as dividends. Calculated by dividing the firm's cash dividend per share by its earnings per share.

Constant Payout Ratio Policy. One type of dividend policy that is rarely adopted by firms is a constant payout ratio. The **dividend payout ratio**, calculated by dividing the firm's cash dividend per share by its earnings per share, indicates the percentage of each dollar earned that is distributed to the owners. With a **constant payout ratio dividend policy**, the firm establishes that a certain percentage of earnings is paid to owners in each dividend period. The problem with this policy

constant payout ratio dividend policy
Used by a firm to establish that a certain percentage of earnings is paid to owners in each dividend period.

is that if the firm's earnings drop, or if a loss occurs in a given period, the dividends may be low or even nonexistent, making them as volatile as the firm's earnings.

constant nominal payment policy
Based on the payment of a fixed-dollar dividend in each period.

target dividend payout ratio
Under this policy, the firm attempts to pay out a certain percentage of earnings, but rather than let dividends fluctuate, it pays a stated dollar dividend and adjusts it toward the target payout slowly as proven earnings increases occur.

Constant Nominal Payment Policy. Another type of dividend policy, the **constant nominal payment policy**, is based on the payment of a fixed-dollar dividend in each period. Using this policy, firms often increase the regular dividend once a *proven* increase in earnings has occurred. Under this policy, firms almost never cut dividends unless they face a true crisis.

Firms that pay a steady dividend may build their policy around a **target dividend payout ratio**. Under this policy, the firm attempts to pay out a certain percentage of earnings. Rather than let dividends fluctuate, however, it pays a stated dollar dividend and slowly adjusts it toward the target payout, as proven earnings increases occur. This is known as a *partial-adjustment strategy*, and it implies that at any given time, firms may be in a transition between two dividend payment levels.

low-regular-and-extra policy
Policy of a firm paying a low regular dividend supplemented by an additional cash dividend when earnings warrant it.

extra dividend / special dividend
The additional dividend that a firm pays if earnings are higher than normal in a given period.

Low-Regular-and-Extra Policy. Some firms establish a **low-regular-and-extra policy** that pays a low regular dividend, supplemented by an additional cash dividend when earnings warrant it. If earnings are higher than normal in a given period, the firm may pay this additional dividend, which is designated an **extra dividend** or a **special dividend**. By designating the amount—by which the dividend exceeds the regular payment—as an extra dividend, the firm avoids giving shareholders false hopes. The use of the "extra" or the "special" designation is more common among companies that experience temporary shifts in earnings. For example, interest rates on residential mortgages declined to the lowest level in thirty-five years, during 2003. As a result, many homeowners refinanced their loans. The refinancing boom resulted in a sharp increase in fees earned by banks and other financial institutions that were active in the mortgage market. Many of these companies paid special dividends as a way to distribute some of this cash to investors.

Other Forms of Dividends

In addition to paying cash dividends, firms often employ three other methods of distributing either cash or securities to investors: stock dividends, stock splits, and share repurchases.

stock dividend
The payment to existing owners of a dividend in the form of stock.

Stock Dividends. A **stock dividend** is the payment to existing owners of a dividend in the form of stock. For example, if a firm declares a 20 percent stock dividend, it will issue twenty new shares for every one hundred shares that an investor owns. Often, firms pay stock dividends as a replacement for, or a supplement to, cash dividends. Remember that a stock dividend does not necessarily increase the value of an investor's holdings. If a firm pays a 20 percent stock dividend, and nothing else about the firm changes, then the number of outstanding shares increases by 20 percent, and the stock price drops by 20 percent. The net effect on shareholder wealth is neutral. Shareholders receiving stock dividends also maintain a constant proportional share in the firm's equity.

stock split
Involves a company splitting the par value of its stock and issuing new shares to existing investors. For example, in a 2-for-1 split, the firm doubles the number of shares outstanding.

Stock Splits. Stock splits have an effect on a firm's share price, similar to that of stock dividends. When a firm conducts a **stock split**, its share price declines because the number of outstanding shares increases. For example, in a 2-for-1 split, the firm doubles the number of shares outstanding. As in the case of a stock dividend, intuition suggests that stock splits should not create value for shareholders. After all, if someone offers to give you two $5 bills in exchange for one $10 bill, you are no better off. A stock split also has no effect on the firm's capital structure; it simply increases the number of shares outstanding and reduces the stock's per-share par value.

We have often stated that managers should strive to increase stock prices, not decrease them. In the case of a stock split (or stock dividend), if the decrease in share prices is proportional to the change in shares outstanding, the net effect on shareholder wealth is zero (ignoring the administrative costs of doing the split). Managers nevertheless decide to engage in stock splits because, they believe, that if the price per share gets too high, some investors (especially individual investors) will no longer trade the stock.

APPLYING THE MODEL

Since going public in March 1986, Microsoft has split its stock nine times, most recently on February 14, 2003. An investor who purchased a single Microsoft share in its IPO in 1986 would own 288 Microsoft shares today. Look at this another way. Microsoft's stock price at the end of June 2004 was close to $28. But that price reflected the cumulative 288-for-1 splits that took place since 1986. Taking Microsoft's stock performance since its IPO as a given, had Microsoft never split its stock, the price in June 2004 would have been about $8,064 per share.

Though most stock splits increase the number of shares outstanding, firms sometimes conduct **reverse stock splits**, in which firms replace a certain number of outstanding shares with just one new share. For example, in a 1-for-2 split, one new share replaces two old shares; in a 2-for-3 split, two new shares replace three old shares; and so on. Firms initiate reverse stock splits when their stock is selling at a very low price, possibly so low that the exchange, which lists the stock, threatens to remove it.

reverse stock split
Occurs when a firm replaces a certain number of outstanding shares with just one new share. This is done to increase the stock price.

Share Repurchases. U.S. firms have dramatically increased repurchases of their own outstanding common stock in recent years, particularly since 1982. In that year, an SEC ruling clarified when companies could and could not repurchase their shares, without fear of being charged with insider dealing or price manipulation. Figure 13.2 illustrates the dramatic growth in repurchases between 1972 and 2001, especially since 1982. The practical motives for stock repurchases include obtaining shares to be used in acquisitions, having shares available for employee stock-option plans, and retiring shares. From a broader perspective, the rising importance of share repurchases implies that they enhance shareholder value, perhaps because they have traditionally been a tax-advantaged method of distributing cash. Though it is not clear exactly what managers are trying to achieve through repurchases, frequently mentioned rationales include this one: sending a *positive signal* to investors in the marketplace that management believes that the stock is undervalued, thus reducing the number of shares outstanding and thereby raising earnings per share (*EPS*). A recent study argues convincingly that share repurchases have grown rapidly since the early 1990s, largely to offset the dilution effects of the exercise of stock options.[2] As the number and the value of options, granted to (and exercised by) top executives, have increased in importance, companies have been buying back shares to keep the total number outstanding from rising too sharply, thus reducing earnings per share.

---

2. See J. Fred Weston and Juan A. Siu (2003) "Changing Motives for Share Repurchases," *Finance* Paper 3 (2003), Anderson Graduate School of Management, UCLA.

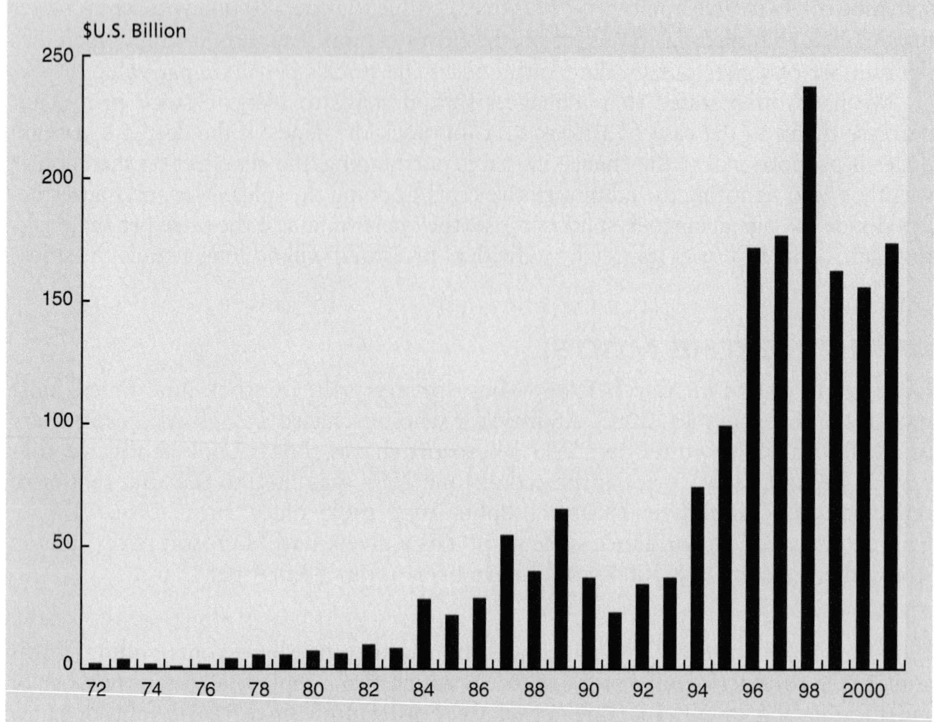

Figure 13.2
Market Value of Share Repurchases by U.S. Corporations, 1972–2001

Source: Table B-90, Economic Report of the President (2002) and Thomson Financial Securities Data, as reported in Table 1 of J. Fed Weston and Juan A. Siu (2003) "Changing Motives for Share Repurchases," Finance *Paper 3 (2003), Anderson Graduate School of Management, UCLA.*

Prior to the passage of the Jobs and Growth Tax Relief Reconciliation Act of 2003, there was a substantial tax advantage to American corporations that distributed cash to shareholders, using share repurchases rather than by paying dividends. The reason is that cash dividends were taxable as ordinary income for the shareholder in the year received, whereas only the capital gains component of share repurchases were subject to taxation—and then only for stockholders who actually sold their shares. Additionally, gains were taxed at the stockholders' capital gains tax rates, which were generally lower than the rates on ordinary income. To see the tax advantages of share repurchases implied by this tax treatment, consider a firm that was weighing the choice of distributing \$2 million as a cash dividend or as a share repurchase. If the firm paid a cash dividend, the shareholders were required to pay ordinary income taxes on the dividend. However, if the firm bought back \$2 million worth of its shares, the total tax bite would almost certainly be much lower, for the three reasons noted above. Only the shareholders who chose to sell had to pay taxes, only the capital gain portion of the proceeds from the stock sale was taxable, and the tax rate on capital gains was less than that on dividends for almost all shareholders. If the share repurchase resulted in an increase in the firm's stock price, shareholders who did not sell out could defer paying taxes on their gains indefinitely.

The Jobs and Growth Tax Relief Reconciliation Act of 2003 dramatically reduced tax rates on cash dividends received by individuals. Dividends are now taxed at either 5 or 15 percent—the same rates that apply to capital gains income. Capital gains tax rates were themselves also lowered from 10 and 20 percent, to 5 and 15 percent, by the 2003 tax reform. Although too little time has elapsed since the passage of this act, to tell what effect it will have on the total level of share repurchases, it seems clear that the tax incentive for American corporations to favor repurchases over cash dividends has been reduced. The tax benefits have not, however, been eliminated entirely. Repurchase programs still give investors the option to participate or not (to sell or to retain their shares). Therefore, capital gains taxes can be deferred, whereas taxes on cash dividends must be paid in the year the dividends are received.

There are several methods that companies use to repurchase shares. The most common approach is called an "open-market share repurchase," in which, as the name implies, firms buy back their shares by transacting in the open market. A second share-repurchase method is called a "tender offer," or "self-tender." Firms using this approach announce their intentions to buy back a certain number of their outstanding shares at a premium above the current market price. The market reaction to self-tender announcements is generally quite positive.

SMART IDEAS VIDEO

Scott Lee, Texas A&M University

"Generally associated with repurchase announcements is a fairly strong market response."

See the entire interview at **SMARTFinance**

The phenomenal recent growth in repurchases in the United States significantly complicates our discussion in this chapter, as it blurs exactly what we mean by "dividend payout." Repurchases today are equal to between one third and one half the total value of ordinary cash dividend payments. Therefore, we should probably talk about corporate payout policy as encompassing both dividends and share repurchases because both represent regular cash distributions from corporations to their shareholders.[3] Additionally, empirical research documents that dividends and repurchases are complements—companies paying high cash dividends also tend to be the companies most likely to repurchase their shares. In the following sections, we thus adopt the convention of referring to "payout policy" when we are talking about both types of cash distributions; we use the narrower term, "dividend policy," when we are discussing just the payment of cash dividends.

Having surveyed the basic mechanics and issues surrounding dividend payments, we can now look more closely at the economically interesting questions about dividends, such as why firms pay dividends at all and how capital markets value dividends.

CONCEPT REVIEW QUESTIONS

1. What policies and payments comprise a firm's "dividend policy"? Why is determining dividend policy more difficult today than in decades past?

2. What do you think the typical stock market reaction is to the announcement that a firm will increase its dividend payment? Why?

3. Assume you are the sole owner of a profitable, private U.S. corporation. What do you think would be the most tax-efficient method of receiving ownership income (via salary, perks, retained earnings, or dividends)?

4. Why should we expect a firm's stock price to decline by approximately the amount of the dividend payment on the ex-dividend date? Why do U.S. stock prices generally fall by less than the amount of the dividend payment?

[3] Professors Roni Michaely and Franklin Allen point out that an even broader definition of "payout" encompasses cash payments for shares acquired by bidding firms in mergers and acquisitions. Because the acquired firm disappears as a separate entity after the merger, cash payments by the acquirer to the target's stockholders are effectively the same as a liquidating cash dividend. In recent years, cash payments in mergers have exceeded the combined value of share repurchases and ordinary cash dividends, which means that the total cash payout from the corporate sector significantly exceeds the total net profits of U.S. companies every year. This "excess payout" must be financed by new security issues (roughly one-third equity, two-thirds debt) and net borrowing from financial institutions. See Roni Michaely and Franklin Allen, "Payout Policy," in George Constantinides *et al.*, eds., *Handbook of Economics* (North Holland, 2002).

13.2 PATTERNS OBSERVED IN PAYOUT POLICIES WORLDWIDE

Similar to our discussion of capital structure, we find that observation of worldwide dividend payment and share repurchase patterns clarifies exactly what a robust theory of payout policy suggests. The following stylized facts reveal remarkable similarities in the dividend policies observed around the world, but there are equally fascinating differences as well.

Payout Patterns Observed

1. Payout policies show distinct national patterns. As shown in Table 13.2, companies that are headquartered in countries with legal systems based on English common law generally have higher cash dividend payout ratios than do companies that are headquartered in countries with civil-law systems. British, Australian, Singaporean, and South African firms have especially high payout ratios, whereas U.S. firms are nearer the global average.[4] French and Italian firms tend to have lower payouts than do other Western companies. Companies that are headquartered in developing countries typically have very low dividend payouts, if they pay dividends at all. Many factors influence these patterns, but clearly the nation's legal system is an important factor. This factor also underlies other differences, such as differences in capital market size and efficiency. Common-law countries that rely heavily on capital markets for corporate financing tend to observe higher dividend payments than do continental European and other countries, which rely more on financing by banks and other financial intermediaries. Not surprisingly, countries with either a strong socialist tradition or a long history of state involvement in the economy are inclined to discourage dividend payments to private investors.

2. Payout policies show pronounced industry patterns, and these are the same worldwide. In general, large, profitable firms, in mature industries, tend to pay out much larger fractions of their earnings than do firms in younger, rapidly growing industries. Utility companies have very high dividend payouts in almost every country. The most important influences on payout decisions appear to be industry growth rate, capital investment needs, profitability, earnings variability, and asset characteristics (the mix between tangible and intangible assets). In the United States, an industry's average payout ratio (dividends plus repurchases) is negatively related to the richness of its investment opportunities and positively related to the degree to which the industry is regulated. Table 13.3 lists average dividend payout ratios for several U.S. industries.

---

4. Having the United States fall in the mid-range of national payout policies actually represents a very significant change from the traditional pattern. American companies have historically ranked near the top of the dividend payout league, but this has changed over the past decade for three reasons. First, as noted above, share repurchases have grown dramatically in recent years. Second, as shown by Professors Eugene Fama and Ken French, a far lower fraction of publicly traded U.S. firms pay dividends today than in the past—and those that do pay dividends pay out less than in previous eras. Third, European and Japanese companies have significantly increased their payout ratios since the early 1990s. This picture is significantly different when one looks at payout policy (including share repurchases) rather than just dividends. Though these are now legal in most developed countries, only the United States has witnessed a dramatic surge in the total value of repurchases. When both dividends and repurchases are included, the United States once more becomes a high-payout country; in fact, by this definition the payout ratio of the U.S corporate sector has been increasing, rather than decreasing, since the early 1990s. See Eugene F. Fama and Kenneth R. French, "Disappearing Dividends: Changing Firm Characteristics or Lower Propensity to Pay?" *Journal of Financial Economics* 60 (April 2001), pp. 3–43.

Country	Number of Firms	Dividends to Cash Flow (%)	Dividends to Earnings (%)	Dividends to Sales (%)
Belgium	33	11.77%	39.38%	1.09%
Denmark	75	6.55	17.27	0.71
Finland	39	8.08	21.27	0.77
France	246	9.46	23.55	0.63
Germany	146	12.70	42.86	0.83
Italy	58	9.74	21.83	0.92
Japan	149	13.03	52.88	0.72
Netherlands	96	11.29	30.02	0.74
Norway	50	10.74	23.91	0.98
Spain	33	15.77	30.45	1.04
Sweden	81	5.59	18.33	0.78
Switzerland	70	10.38	25.30	0.98
Civil Law Median	**33**	**9.74%**	**25.11%**	**0.83%**
Australia	103	22.83%	42.82%	2.22%
Canada	236	8.00	19.78	0.78
Hong Kong	40	35.43	45.93	7.51
Malaysia	41	15.29	37.93	3.12
Singapore	27	22.28	41.04	2.14
South Africa	90	16.16	35.62	1.90
United Kingdom	799	16.67	36.91	1.89
United States	1,588	11.38	22.11	0.95
Common Law Median	**40**	**18.28%**	**37.42%**	**2.02%**
Sample Median	**39**	**11.77%**	**30.02%**	**0.98%**

Table 13.2
Dividend Payout Measures for OECD and Selected Developing Countries

This table classifies countries by legal origin (Civil Law versus Common Law) and presents three measures of average dividend payout for the firms from each country.

Source: Rafael LaPorta, Florencio Lopez-de-Silanes, Andrei Shleifer and Robert W. Vishny, "Agency Problems and Dividend Policies Around the World," Journal of Finance *55 (February 2000), pp. 1–33.*

Industry	Simple average payout ratio (%)	Weighted-average payout ratio (%)
Biotechnology	0	0
Airlines	0	0
Computer software	0	0
Semiconductors	8.3[a]	14.1[a]
Computer hardware	14.3	19.9
Transportation: Commercial	21.0	22.6
Insurance: Property and casualty	22.3	18.5
Pharmaceuticals	24.3	23.1
Aerospace and defense	29.3[a]	35.7[a]
Natural gas distribution	35.3[a]	36.1[a]
Foods and nonalcoholic beverages	36.5	37.2
Autos and auto parts	40.7[a]	40.2[a]
Electric utilities	41.4	44.5
Banking	41.7[a]	33.7[a]
Household nondurables	43.0	44.2
Alcoholic beverages and tobacco	49.5	47.6
Paper and forest products	49.5[a]	62.8[a]
Telecommunications: Wireless	51.0[a]	49.8[a]
Oil and gas production, and marketing	52.0	52.5
Metals: Industrial	57.0	77.1
Telecommunications: Wireline	63.0	68.37
Basic chemicals	73.7	74.1

[a] Average based on three firms instead of four, due to extremely high payout ratios (over 125%) resulting from very low (or negative) levels of earnings for one firm.

Table 13.3
Dividend Payout Ratios for Selected U.S. Industries

This table describes the average dividend payout ratios for the four largest (based on sales) companies in selected American industries, using data presented in Standard and Poors' Industry Reports, *from July to December 2003. The simple average ratio gives equal weight to all four firms in an industry, whereas the weighted average weighs firms by their most recent annual sales.*

Source: Standard and Poors Corporation, Industry Reports, *various issues (July–December 2003).*

Table 13.4
Dividend Ratios for Selected U.S. Corporations in 2003

This table presents the annual dividend payment, as well as dividend yield and payout ratios, for the thirty-five most valuable publicly traded U.S. corporations in May 2003, as reported in "The Business Week Global 1000," Business Week *(July 14, 2003). Companies are listed beginning with the industry having the lowest leverage (computer software) to the industry having the highest leverage (telecommunications).*

Company	Industry	Annual Dividend per Share ($)	Dividend Yield (%)	Payout Ratio (%)	Market-to-Book Ratio[1]
Cisco Systems	Computer systems	0	0	0	6.07
Oracle	Computer software	0	0	0	10.31
Microsoft	Computer software	$0.16	0.50%	17.4%	5.54
Dell Computer	Computer hardware	0	0	0	14.74
IBM	Computer hardware	0.64	0.69	15.7	5.84
HP	Computer hardware	0.32	1.43	38.4	1.80
Intel	Semiconductors	0.08	0.26	11.6	5.40
Berkshire Hathaway	Insurance, conglomerate	0	0	0	1.79
Wal-Mart	Retailing	0.36	0.69	17.5	5.42
Home Depot	Retailing	0.28	0.81	14.2	3.54
UPS	Transportation	1.00	1.36	7.3	6.01
AOL Time Warner	Entertainment, media	0	0	0*	1.43
Viacom	Entertainment, media	0.24	0.57	17.1	1.14
American Intl Group	Financial	0.26	0.42	8.3	2.38
Fannie Mae	Financial	1.80	2.57	24.1	5.07
Citigroup	Financial	1.40	2.94	30.6	2.61
Wells Fargo	Financial	1.80	3.16	37.0	2.96
Bank of America	Financial	3.20	4.22	38.0	2.24
J. P. Morgan Chase	Financial	1.36	3.88	61.8	1.63
Exxon Mobil	Integrated petroleum	1.00	2.63	35.6	3.00
ChevronTexaco	Integrated petroleum	2.92	3.64	44.4	2.43
Pepsico	Consumer products	0.64	1.37	29.5	7.37
Coca-Cola	Consumer products	0.88	1.78	48.8	8.95
Procter & Gamble	Consumer products	1.82	1.88	40.9	7.94
Altria Group	Consumer products	2.72	5.12	58.62	4.73
Amgen	Pharmaceuticals	0	0	0	3.94
Johnson & Johnson	Pharmaceuticals	0.96	1.94	37.7	5.70
Eli Lilly	Pharmaceuticals	1.34	1.86	55.5	8.55
Merck	Pharmaceuticals	1.48	3.39	47.1	6.36
Abbott Laboratories	Pharmaceuticals	0.98	2.14	62.2	6.04
Pfizer	Pharmaceuticals	0.60	1.74	90.3	3.84
General Electric	Conglomerate	0.76	2.52	53.8	4.17
Comcast	Telecommunications, cable	0	0	0	1.73
SBC Communications	Telecommunications	1.53	6.23	61.3	2.15
Verizon Communications	Telecommunications	1.54	4.61	58.6	2.63

* Indicates that the company had a negative net income for the fiscal year in question.
1. Per-share price of company stock, divided by the per-share book value of shareholders' common equity.

Sources: Dividend data taken from each company's financial information at http://money.cnn.com *(December 20, 2003).*

3. Asset-rich, regulated, and slow-growing companies tend to have high dividend payout ratios. Companies in which tangible assets make up a large fraction of total value tend to have higher dividend payouts, whereas companies in which intangible assets are more important tend to have low payouts. Furthermore, regulated companies (particularly utilities) pay out more of their earnings than do unregulated companies. The relationship between dividend payout and growth rate is equally clear. Rapidly growing firms hoard cash and select zero or very low dividend payouts. As these companies mature, dividend payouts typically increase. Table 13.4 reports dividend payout ratios and dividend yields for the thirty-five most valuable (largest market capitalization) U.S. companies in mid-2003. *Dividend yield* is computed by dividing a firm's annual dividend per share by its stock price. Rapidly growing and/or high-technology companies, such as Cisco and Dell, pay no dividends; slower-growing, less-high-technology firms, such as J. P. Morgan Chase, Altria Group (formerly Philip Morris), and SBC Communications, pay out more than half their net profits and have relatively high dividend yields.

4. Firms maintain constant nominal dividend payments per share for significant periods of time. Put another way, companies everywhere tend to "smooth" dividend payments. These payments show far less variability than do the corporate profits on which they ultimately are based. In the terminology introduced in Section 13.1, firms follow a policy of constant nominal dividend payments (regular dividends), with partial adjustments made as earnings change over time. Managers will not increase per-share dividends until they believe that "permanent" earnings have increased enough to support a higher dividend level. Even then, managers will gradually increase dividend payments to reach a new equilibrium payment. Likewise, corporate managers will try to maintain constant per-share dividend payments, even in the face of temporary net losses, until it becomes clear that earnings will not revive. Managers will then reduce, but rarely eliminate, dividend payments, and they will make the full downward adjustment in one large cut.

SMART IDEAS VIDEO
Kenneth Eades, University of Virginia
"It's an earnings story, not a dividend story."

See the entire interview at **SMARTFinance**

5. Whereas the number (and fraction) of publicly traded companies that pay dividends has been declining over the past three decades, the aggregate payout ratio of the U.S corporate sector has been increasing. Figure 13.3 shows the aggregate dividend payout ratio for the U.S. corporate sector from 1972 to 2001. This figure also shows the "payout ratio" for share repurchases as a fraction of the total net income of the corporate sector. In other words, American corporations have been steadily increasing their payout ratios over the past three decades. This

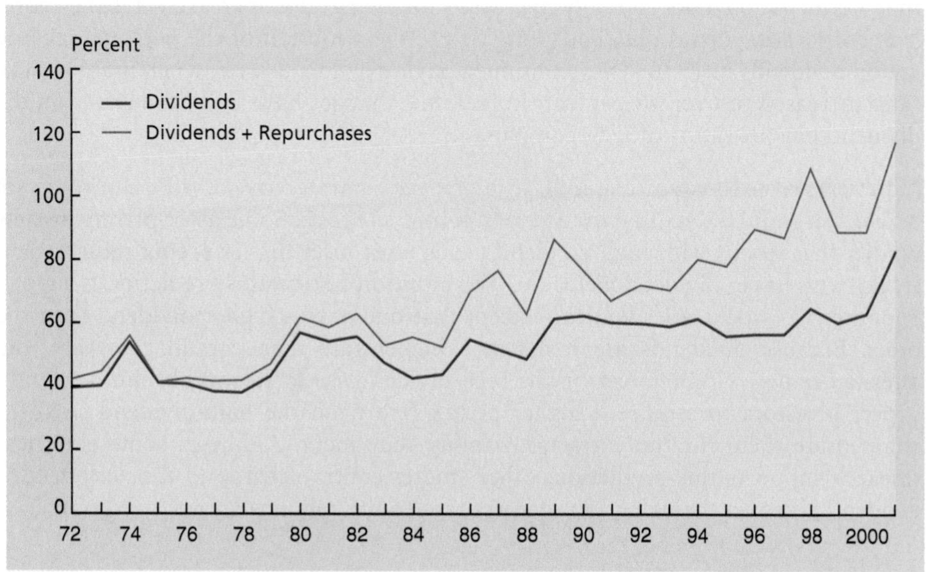

Figure 13.3
Aggregate Payout Ratio (Dividends and Share Repurchases) for the U.S. Corporate Sector, 1972–2001

Source: Table B-90, Economic Report of the President (2002) and Thomson Financial Securities Data, as reported in Table 2 of J. Fed Weston and Juan A. Siu (2003) "Changing Motives for Share Repurchases," Finance *Paper 3 (2003), Anderson Graduate School of Management, UCLA.*

seemingly contradictory finding can be rationalized by observing that relatively few very large companies account for the bulk of cash dividend payments each year. However, these companies account for a large fraction of the annual net profits earned by U.S. businesses.

6. Investors react positively to dividend (and share repurchase) initiations and increases, but react negatively to dividend decreases or eliminations. When a company announces either its first regular cash dividend payment (an initiation) or an increase in its existing per-share dividend, that company's stock price typically increases by 1 to 3 percent. A similar response occurs when firms announce share repurchase programs. Investors appear to believe that dividend increases imply that management expects higher earnings in the future. On the other hand, the markets punish firms that cut or eliminate their dividends, often shaving 25 percent, or more, from the company's stock price, following the announcement. Because the market reaction is so spiteful, managers only cut dividends when a firm is in serious financial trouble.

APPLYING THE MODEL

On February 18, 2003, the NorthWestern Corporation announced that it was suspending its common stock dividend to free up $48 million to help pay down its $2.2 billion debt burden. NorthWestern thus became the eleventh publicly traded electric utility to cut its dividend as a result of the industry-wide credit crunch that followed Enron Corporation's collapse in late 2001. The firm also announced plans to sell off non-core assets to raise cash. Following the news of the dividend cut, NorthWestern's shares fell by 7 percent.

7. Taxes influence payout policies, but taxes neither cause nor prevent companies from initiating dividend payments or share repurchases. It appears obvious that levying income taxes on investors who receive dividend payments would reduce the demand for dividends and thus prompt corporations to retain a larger share of their profits. In the extreme, very high tax rates should cause corporations to stop paying dividends entirely. Plausible though these arguments may be, they are not supported by empirical evidence; in fact, some studies show that dividend payouts actually increase, following tax increases. Furthermore, U.S. corporations paid dividends long before the adoption of the personal income tax on dividends in 1936. They continued paying dividends even when marginal tax rates increased to over 90 percent. In fact, tax changes have had little effect on the dividend payout ratios of U.S. companies.

8. In spite of intensive research, it is unclear exactly how dividend payments affect the required return on a firm's common stock. Some asset-pricing models predict that stocks with high dividend yields must offer higher pretax returns than stocks with lower dividend yields do. The intuition behind this prediction is simple. Suppose two stocks are identical, except that one pays a higher dividend than the other. Because dividends are taxed at a higher rate than capital gains are, the after-tax return will be lower on the high-dividend stock. In equilibrium, we could expect investors to require a higher pretax return on the high-dividend stock to compensate them for the extra tax liability they incur. Although some empirical research supports this prediction, other studies contradict it, and the net effect of dividend taxes on the valuation of corporate equity remains an unsolved puzzle.

9. Changes in transactions costs or in the technical efficiency of capital markets seem to have very little effect on dividend payments. Some theories suggest that the presence of transactions costs causes investors to value dividends. Dividends put cash in investors' hands, without requiring them to pay brokerage commissions or other transactions costs. If transactions costs do create an investor preference for dividends, the steep decline in transactions costs, in recent years, should have been accompanied by a steep decline in dividends. It is true that the percentage of companies paying dividends has recently declined, whereas aggregate dividend payments have not. If we broaden our focus to include all forms of cash payments to shareholders, then corporations today pay out an even higher fraction of total profits than in the past.

10. Ownership matters. One of the most enduring dividend regularities, both in the United States and around the world, is that private or closely held companies rarely pay any dividends at all. Yet publicly traded companies are likely to pay out substantial fractions of their earnings as dividends each year. In almost every country and every industry, firms with tight ownership structures, composed of a few controlling shareholders, tend to have very low dividend payouts; widely held companies with diffuse ownership tend to have higher payouts.

Introduction to the Agency Cost/Contracting Model of Dividends

As was true for capital structure, it is hard to conceive of a single theoretical model that can explain all the empirical regularities previously described. Nonetheless, several theoretical models have been developed, and each has garnered some empirical support. In this chapter, we concentrate on one of these, the **agency cost/contracting model of dividends** (or simply, the agency cost model). We also briefly introduce the agency cost model's principal competitor, the signaling model of dividend payments.

agency cost/contracting model of dividends
A theoretical model that explains empirical regularities in dividend payment and share repurchase patterns, based on agency problems between managers and shareholders.

The agency cost model assumes that dividend payments arise as an attempt to overcome the agency problems that result when there is a separation of corporate ownership and control. In privately held companies with tight ownership coalitions, there is little or no separation between ownership and control. Because agency problems in these firms are minimal, dividends are unnecessary. Even after a company goes public, it rarely commences dividend payments immediately. Ownership tends to remain quite concentrated for a number of years after the IPO. Eventually, however, ownership becomes widely dispersed, as firms raise new equity capital and as original stockholders/owners diversify their holdings. As ownership becomes more dispersed, few investors have the incentive or the ability to monitor and control corporate managers. Agency problems become more important and especially severe in large, slowly growing firms that generate large quantities of free cash flow. The natural tendency of corporate managers is to spend this cash flow (calling it "investment," of course) rather than to pay it out to shareholders. Investors understand these incentives and will pay a low price for manager-controlled firms that hoard cash. On the other hand, shareholders are willing to pay higher prices for stock in companies with more responsive management teams. Managers who want to maximize firm value will thus begin paying dividends, committing to paying out free cash flow. By doing this, managers overcome the agency costs related to retaining excess cash in the firm. This model thus explains why announcements of dividend initiations or increases are related to stock-price increases. Other aspects of the model help explain cross-sectional variations in dividend payments, based on industry growth rates, firm size, or asset characteristics.

APPLYING THE MODEL

The agency cost model predicts that dividend-paying firms are older and larger than firms which do not pay dividends. It also predicts that dividend payers have fewer growth opportunities. The data for U.S. firms confirm these predictions. If we compare U.S. firms that pay dividends with firms that do not, we find that dividend payers are more than 7 times larger in size and grow more slowly than nonpayers. The average age of dividend payers is more than twice the average age of nonpayers.

Dividend	Payers	Nonpayers
Market cap ($ in millions)	$8,998	$1,222
Sales growth (%)	3.2%	5.1%
Firms age (years)	27.4	11.9

Note: Figures determined by author's calculations and Compustat. Dividend payers are firms that paid dividends in 1999, and nonpayers are those that did not. Market capitalization is as of 1999. Sales growth is the compound annual growth rate in sales, from 1999 to 2002, for the median firm in each group. Firm age is calculated based on the number of years of data available.

Recent research shows that firms that increase dividends become less profitable and less risky, whereas the opposite happens to firms that cut dividends. Similarly, dividend-increasing firms cut back on capital spending after raising payouts, whereas dividend-decreasing firms increase capital expenditures. These results are broadly consistent with the agency cost model. When a firm has many profitable investment opportunities on hand, it reinvests more cash and distributes less to investors. When a firm's investment opportunities dim, it pays higher dividends, rather than reinvesting its cash in negative-*NPV* projects.

signaling model of dividends
Assumes that managers use dividends to convey positive information to poorly informed shareholders.

The competing **signaling model of dividends** assumes that managers use dividends to convey positive information to poorly informed shareholders. Cash dividend payments are costly, both to the paying firms, as this reduces the amount of money the firm can use for investment, and to shareholders receiving the dividends, as they will have to pay taxes on the dividends received. This means that only the "best" (most profitable) firms can afford to pay dividends, in the sense that they can bear the cost of these payments. Weaker firms cannot mimic the dividend payments of strong firms, so dividends help investors solve an asymmetric information problem—distinguishing between high-quality and low-quality firms. Like the agency cost model, the signaling model predicts that stock prices should rise (fall) in response to dividend increases (cuts). However, the signaling model also predicts that firms with high-growth opportunities will pay higher dividends, contrary to the empirical evidence. Finally, many observers think that the "tax cost" of signaling with dividends is implausibly high. That is, when firms distribute cash by paying dividends rather than by repurchasing shares, they impose an additional tax burden on investors.

Before describing a model that explains why managers may choose to pay cash dividends—and why investors may demand them—we must ask whether dividends "matter" in a world of perfect and frictionless capital markets. In other words, would investors demand and managers pay dividends if there were no taxes at the corporate and personal level, if there were no costs of trading or issuing securities, and if managers and investors all had the same information. Our old friends from the capital structure chapter, Merton Miller and Franco Modigliani, examined this question in 1961, and they came to a similar conclusion—in a world of perfect markets, dividend policy is irrelevant.[5]

CONCEPT REVIEW QUESTIONS

5. How do average dividend payout ratios for companies headquartered in English common-law countries compare with those of companies headquartered in civil law countries? What explains this difference?

6. If high-dividend stocks offer a higher expected (and required) return than low-dividend stocks, due to the higher personal taxes levied on the former, why don't corporations simply reduce dividend payments and thus lower their cost of capital?

7. Which U.S. industries are characterized by relatively high dividend payout ratios? Are these same industry patterns observed in other industrialized countries? What explains these industry patterns?

8. What is the basis of the argument that transactions costs provide a reason for firms to pay dividends, and how has the steep decline in transactions costs in recent years affected this argument?

13.3 DIVIDEND IRRELEVANCE IN A WORLD WITH PERFECT CAPITAL MARKETS

In a world of frictionless capital markets, payout policy cannot affect the market value of the firm. Value derives solely from the inherent profitability of the firm's assets and the competence of its management team. Even though markets are not perfect, describing how dividend payments or share repurchases affect firm valuation in frictionless markets allows us to more conclusively say under what conditions dividend policy *will* matter in a world with frictions such as taxes, transactions costs, information asymmetries, and other market imperfections. In a frictionless world, there is little difference between cash dividends and share repurchases. In the interest of simplicity, we analyze only cash dividend payments in this section.

The notion that dividends are irrelevant appears to be a contradiction. After all, we argued in Chapter 5 that the value of stock was equal to the present value of the dividends that the stock would pay over time. If cash dividends are the only source of value to market participants, how do we arrive at a dividend-irrelevance result? As was the case for capital structure, the answer to this question is that the economic value of a firm is always derived solely from the operating profits that the firm is currently generating and will continue to generate in the future, as its investments unfold. As long as the firm accepts all positive-*NPV* investment projects and has *costless* access to capital markets, it can pay any level of dividends it desires, each period. But if a firm pays out its earnings as dividends, it must issue new shares to raise the cash required to finance its ongoing investment projects. So a company can choose to retain all its profits and to finance its investments with internally generated cash flow, or that same company can pay out all its earnings as dividends and raise the cash needed for investment by selling new shares. As usual, this principle is best explained with an example.

[5] See Merton Miller and Franco Modigliani, "Dividend Policy, Growth, and the Valuation of Shares," *Journal of Business* 34 (October 1961), pp. 411–433.

Consider two firms, Retention and Payout, which are the same size today (January 1, 2006), are in the same industry, and have access to the same investment opportunities. Suppose both companies have assets worth $20 million, generating a net cash inflow of $2 million continuously during 2006, and thus providing a return on investment of 10 percent. Furthermore, assume that the return required by investors, r, is 10 percent per year for both companies and that each company is presented with the opportunity to invest $2 million in a positive-*NPV* project during 2006. Each firm currently has 1 million shares outstanding, implying that each firm's share price is $20 ($P_{\text{Jan06}}$ = $20). The managers of firm Payout want to distribute all the firm's earnings as dividends, but they also intend to finance the company's $2 million investment opportunity by issuing as many new shares as necessary. The managers of firm Retention would rather not pay dividends, preferring instead to retain the firm's net cash inflow for use in funding the planned $2 million investment program. Can each management team pursue its preferred strategy and still have identical market values at the end of the period?

Yes. To see how, we first examine Retention's strategy. Retention's managers decide to retain the $2 million ($2 per share) profit, which the firm earns during 2006, to internally finance the $2 million investment project. Therefore, the total dividends paid (and dividends per share) during 2006 are zero. The market value of the firm on December 31, 2006, is equal to the $20 million beginning value, plus the $2 million in reinvested earnings, plus the net present value of the investment opportunity. For simplicity, assume that the project's *NPV* is positive but small enough to be ignored. The value of Retention at year-end 2006 is therefore equal to $22 million ($20 million + $2 million), which is equal to $22 per share ($P_{\text{Dec06}}$ = $22), because the firm did not have to issue any new shares to finance its investment opportunity. Plugging these values into our basic valuation equation (Chapter 5) verifies that Retention shareholders indeed earn the 10 percent return on investment that they expected:

$$r = \frac{D_{2006} + P_{Dec06} - P_{Jan06}}{P_{Jan06}} = \frac{\$0 + \$22 - \$20}{\$20} = 10\%$$

We can extend this example indefinitely into the future. In each period, firm Retention commits to reinvesting all its annual profits (10% return on assets) in new productive assets. Shareholders earn their return by seeing the value of their shares increase by 10 percent each year. No new shares are ever issued, so the number of outstanding shares remains fixed at 1 million over time.

So far, so good, but what about firm Payout? This firm's managers decide to pay out, as dividends, the net cash flow of $2 million, as it is received during 2006, so they must raise the $2 million needed to finance the investment project by selling new shares today (January 1, 2006). But how many shares must they sell? To answer that, we must reason through what the price of Payout's shares will be on December 31, 2006. After it distributes the dividend during 2006, Payout will have assets worth $20 million, exactly the amount that it started with on January 1. With 1 million shares outstanding, the share price will still be $20, so Payout must issue 100,000 new shares, at $20 each, to raise the $2 million it needs to undertake its investment opportunity. After the company issues new shares and invests the proceeds, Payout's total market value will equal $22 million ($20 per share × 1.1 million shares outstanding). Therefore, on December 31, 2006, the market value of Payout, $22 million, is identical to the market value of Retention. Once again, we can verify that Payout's original shareholders earned exactly the rate of return that they expected, the same return earned by Retention's investors:

$$r = \frac{D_{2006} + P_{Dec06} - P_{Jan06}}{P_{Jan06}} = \frac{\$2 + \$20 - \$20}{\$20} = 10\%$$

As was the case earlier, we can repeat this process indefinitely. Each year, Payout distributes all of its net cash flow as a dividend, and the firm issues new shares to finance new investment opportunities.

We have shown that the market capitalization of Retention equals that of Payout on December 31, 2006, even though they follow radically different dividend policies. Retention has 1,000,000 shares outstanding, worth $22 each, while Payout has 1,100,000 shares outstanding, worth $20 each. Because both companies have an aggregate value of $22 million, we can conclude that dividend policy is irrelevant in determining the value of a firm, at least when markets are frictionless. But what if investors in Retention prefer that the company pay out earnings rather than reinvest them, or what if shareholders in Payout prefer that the company reinvest earnings rather than issue new shares? We can reinforce the notion that dividend policy is irrelevant, by demonstrating that investors can "unwind" the dividend policy decisions of firms. In the end, what is true for the firm, as a whole, is true for each investor: dividend policy is irrelevant.

SMART CONCEPTS

See the concept explained step-by-step at SMARTFinance

APPLYING THE MODEL

Consider two investors, Burt and Ernie. On January 1, 2006, Burt owns an 11 percent (110,000 shares) stake in Retention, whereas Ernie holds an 11 percent stake (also 110,000 shares) in Payout. By the end of 2006, Burt has received no dividend, but he still owns 11 percent of Retention's outstanding shares, which are now worth $22 each. Ernie, however, receives a dividend payment of $220,000 during 2006, but because Payout issues 100,000 shares to finance its investment opportunity, the shares Ernie owns now represent only a 10 percent ownership stake in Payout (110,000 ÷ 1,100,000).

If either Burt or Ernie is unhappy with the dividend policy of the firm in which he has invested, either can "unwind" that policy. For example, suppose Burt would like to receive a dividend. At the end of 2006, Burt could sell 10,000 of his shares for $22 each, generating a cash inflow of $220,000, exactly equal to the dividend that Ernie received on his investment. After selling a portion of his shares, Burt would own just 10 percent of the outstanding equity of Retention, exactly equal to the ownership stake that Ernie holds in Payout.

Conversely, suppose that Ernie prefers that Payout did not pay dividends. The solution to Ernie's problem is simple. As he receives the $220,000 dividend during 2006, he could simply reinvest the money by purchasing 11,000 new shares in Payout. That would bring his total ownership stake to 121,000, or 11 percent, of Payout's outstanding shares (121,000 ÷ 1,100,000). In other words, Ernie's position is just like Burt's.

This may seem complex, but the essential points of these examples are really quite simple. Investors are indifferent about whether (1) the firm retains earnings to fund positive-*NPV* investments, or (2) the firm distributes cash dividends and sells new shares to finance new investments. In either case, shareholders' returns are determined by the cash flows generated by the firm's investments, not by how the firm distributes those cash flows. In the absence of taxes, transactions costs, or any other market friction, investors do not care whether they earn returns in the form of dividends (as Payout's shareholders do) or capital gains (as Retention's shareholders do).

CONCEPT REVIEW QUESTIONS

9. What does it mean to say that dividends are "irrelevant" in a world without taxes or other market frictions?

10. Managers of slow-growing, but profitable, firms (i.e., tobacco companies) *should* pay out these high earnings as dividends. What can they choose to do instead?

11. How do Miller and Modigliani (M&M) arrive at their conclusion that dividend policy is irrelevant in a world of frictionless capital markets? Why is the assumption of fixed investment policy crucial to this conclusion?

13.4 REAL-WORLD INFLUENCES ON DIVIDEND POLICY

Few of us have ever traded in frictionless capital markets, so our next task is to examine whether dividend policy continues to be irrelevant when we account for "real-world" factors such as taxes, trading costs and information differences between managers and investors. Our final goal for this section is to determine whether a given firm has an "optimal" (value-maximizing) dividend policy and, if so, how that policy should be set. As we proceed, you may notice a puzzling fact: almost all the real-world issues we incorporate—such as taxes, transactions costs for issuing new securities, and uncertainty about a firm's investment opportunities—argue *against* the payment of cash dividends. Yet, U.S. corporations pay out over half their annual earnings in most years, and non-U.S. firms also regularly pay out substantial fractions of their earnings. We show that accounting for agency costs and conflicts between managers and investors does a better job of explaining dividend policies than do arguments based on taxes or market frictions such as trading costs. In other words, dividends do not exist to overcome changing technical problems with markets and tax regimes; dividends exist to overcome unchanging human problems with trust, communication, and commitment.

Personal Income Taxes

When the personal tax rate on dividends is higher than the tax rate on capital gains, we have a clear-cut result: firms should not pay any cash dividends. Instead, profitable companies should retain all their earnings, and shareholders should earn their investment returns by selling stock, after it has increased in value. To see this, note that personal taxes reduce the after-tax value of dividends, relative to capital gains, so firms should not pay dividends as long as dividends are taxed at a higher rate. Any distribution from the firm should be through a share repurchase program. This offers investors the choice of either receiving cash in a tax-favored form (as a capital gain) or foregoing the cash altogether by not selling shares, and thus seeing their share values increase as their fractional ownership increases.

What if a large capital gains tax is imposed? Will that reestablish dividend-policy irrelevance? (Before reading on, see if you can reason through to an answer.) Apparently, imposing a capital gains tax at a rate equal to the dividend tax rate will again make investors indifferent to whether they receive taxable dividends or taxable capital gains. But this will happen only if the tax on stock appreciation is levied every period, regardless of whether the shares are sold or not. Such a levy is called a **wealth tax**. Although never used in the United States, such a tax has been tried in Norway and some other Western European countries. Capital gains taxes are almost always paid only at *realization*, when the shares are actually sold, and a tax payment delayed is a tax payment rendered less painful. Furthermore, in the United States and other countries, stock-related capital gains taxes can often be avoided entirely, if shares are bequeathed to an investor's heirs. Therefore, investors generally have a tax preference for capital gains over cash dividends, even if the nominal tax rates for both types of income are the same. Debt financing enjoys a tax advantage, relative to equity, in most industrialized countries, but retained earnings almost always enjoy a significant tax preference, relative to dividend payments. In summary, almost all real-world dividend taxation systems discourage the payment of cash dividends. We must look elsewhere for a reason for dividends to exist.

wealth tax
A tax levied on stock appreciation every period, regardless of whether the shares are sold or not.

What is the empirical evidence regarding the effect of taxes on dividend payments? Researchers have employed two principal methodologies to study tax effects. The first method is to employ a variant of the capital asset pricing model (CAPM) to see whether investors demand a higher pretax return on high-dividend-paying stocks than they do on stocks paying a low dividend, as is expected if investors paid a higher effective tax rate on cash-dividend income than on capital gains income. Studies using this approach show mixed results. Despite the empirical findings, proponents of a tax-effect model have great difficulty explaining why rational corporate managers would ever pay cash dividends when doing so results in a higher pretax required return. Apparently, managers could increase stock prices and thus lower the firm's cost of capital simply by cutting dividend payouts. The survival of dividend payments in modern economies therefore suggests that the tax-effect model of dividend valuation must be missing something important.

The second method used to study tax effects is to examine the average change in a firm's stock price on its ex-dividend day. Prior to this day, an investor who owns the stock is entitled to receive the next dividend payment. If an investor buys the stock after it goes ex-dividend, the dividend is paid to the former owner. Consider the problem faced by a taxable investor who holds a stock and wants to sell it near an ex-dividend date. The investor faces a choice between selling the stock before the ex-dividend date, at the higher *cum-dividend* (with dividend) price, thus earning a return in the form of a capital gain, or waiting until the stock goes *ex-dividend*, selling the stock at a lower price, and receiving a return in the form of cash dividends. If stock prices fall by the full amount of the dividend payment, the investor would prefer to sell shares before they go ex-dividend. By selling the shares and realizing a capital gain, rather than receiving a dividend, the investor earns a higher after-tax return. The only circumstances under which this investor would be indifferent about whether to take the dividend or the capital gain is if the ex-dividend price drop is less than the dividend payment. In that case, the higher pretax return from receiving the dividend offsets the tax disadvantage of dividends. The empirical observation that, on ex-dividend day, stock prices fall by significantly less than the amount of the dividend (on average, by about sixty to seventy cents on the dollar) has often been interpreted as evidence of a tax effect in dividend valuation.

APPLYING THE MODEL

Three months ago, you purchased a share of stock for \$20. Today that share sells for \$22, a gain of 10 percent. The stock will pay a \$2 dividend in a few days, and the ex-dividend date is tomorrow. Suppose you want to sell the stock, and you face a

33 percent tax rate on dividend income and a 20 percent tax rate on capital gains. If you sell today, you earn an after-tax profit of $1.60 ($2 capital gain minus $0.40 in taxes). That represents an 8 percent return on your original $20 investment. If you sell tomorrow, your after-tax return depends on how far the price drops when the stock goes ex-dividend. If the price drops by the full $2, then you earn no capital gain, and your after-tax profit equals $1.34 ($2 dividend minus $0.66 in taxes), or 6.7 percent. Clearly, in this scenario, your after-tax return is higher if you sell the stock before it goes ex-dividend. However, suppose the stock price drops by just $1, when it goes ex-dividend. In that case, if you wait to sell the stock, you receive a $1 capital gain (worth $0.80 after taxes) and a $2 dividend (worth $1.34 after taxes), for an after-tax return of $2.14, or 10.7 percent. In that case, it pays to wait for the dividend. Only when the stock price falls by $1.675, on the ex-dividend date, would you be indifferent about whether to sell immediately or wait until the dividend is paid.

Although ex-dividend-day studies show plausible average results, there is reason to be suspicious about whether these studies are definitive evidence of differential tax effects, particularly because transactions costs must be very high for a pure tax effect to occur. The reason is that tax-free traders have an incentive to buy stocks just before they go ex-dividend, if the traders expect the price to decline by less than the dividend. For example, suppose the stock described above is about to pay a $2 dividend, and traders expect the price to drop $1.675, on the ex-dividend date, because of differential tax rates applied to capital gains and dividends. As the example demonstrated, a taxable investor, presented with these figures, would be indifferent between selling the stock immediately or waiting until it goes ex-dividend. But a tax-free investor would be anything but indifferent. Such an investor could purchase the stock at $22, receive the $2 dividend, and then resell the stock immediately afterward for $20.33, generating a one-day profit of $0.33. If the transactions costs associated with this strategy are greater than $0.33 per share, then "dividend arbitrage" is not profitable. The differential tax treatment of capital gains and dividends determines the size of the ex-dividend-day price decline. However, currently in U.S. markets, the per-share cost of a round-trip trade can be as low as a few pennies. In that case, the actions of tax-free investors should increase the ex-dividend-day price decline to almost the full amount of the dividend.

Perhaps we may soon be able to determine, once and for all, if the ex-dividend-day price effect is indeed a tax effect. Since the Jobs and Growth Tax Relief Reconciliation Act of 2003 made the federal tax rate on cash dividends, received by an individual, equal to the investor's marginal capital gains tax rate, there is now little tax reason to forego dividends. If taxes were driving the effect historically, the average ex-dividend-day stock-price drop should move closer to the nominal cash dividend. If the average ex-dividend-day price drop continues to be significantly less than the amount of the dividend, then it will be clear that differential personal tax rates were never the key influence on ex-day price changes.

Why do we not see more companies substituting share repurchase programs for cash dividend payments? There are three answers to this question. First, as we have seen, many U.S. companies *have* been repurchasing their shares for several years. Increasing numbers of non-U.S. companies are beginning to do so as their national laws allow. Second, the firms that initiate share repurchase programs are the same companies that also make large cash dividend payments. In the language of economics, this means that firms seem to treat repurchases and cash dividends as *complements* rather than *substitutes*. Finally, the IRS has the power to rule that a given company's share repurchase program is merely an attempt to avoid taxes. Under the program, it can impose the higher personal income tax rates on all income received by investors.

In other words, companies that adopt routine share repurchase programs, in lieu of dividend payments, can theoretically be imposing large supplemental tax liabilities on their shareholders. The actual importance of this rule in deterring repurchases is questionable, however, because the IRS almost never invokes it.

On balance, incorporating personal taxes into our model does not help us understand why firms pay dividends. However, tax effects may account for some of the patterns we observe, such as the rise in share repurchase programs in the United States and other industrialized countries.

Trading and Other Transactions Costs

If personal taxes cannot explain observed dividend payments, what about transactions costs of issuing and trading stocks? Positive trading costs affect expected dividend payouts in two potentially offsetting ways. First, if investors find it costly to sell just a few shares to generate cash (i.e., to create homemade dividends), then they could pay a premium for stocks that habitually pay dividends. Regular cash dividend payments are a costless way to receive a cash return on an investor's stock portfolio. This cash could be used either for consumption or for rebalancing the investor's portfolio. A serious flaw in this argument, however, is the suggestion that dividend payments should be highest in undeveloped markets with very high transactions costs. In reality, dividend payments are highest in countries with liquid, low-cost stock markets—such as Britain, Germany, and Australia—and are lowest or nonexistent in most developing countries. Furthermore, a transactions-cost argument cannot easily explain why aggregate dividend payouts in the United States have remained fairly high, even as U.S. stock markets have become vastly more efficient, and the costs of trading have declined dramatically.

The second effect of transactions costs on dividend payments is completely negative. This relates to a corporation's need to replace cash paid out as dividends with cash obtained through new share sales. Remember that our dividend-irrelevance result depends critically on a company being able to fund its investment, either by retaining corporate profits or by paying out profits as dividends, and to replace this cash by issuing new shares. As long as share issues are costless, investors are indifferent about whether to receive returns in the form of capital gains (on non-dividend-paying shares) or as cash dividends on shares. If issuing securities entails large costs, however, all parties should prefer a full-retention strategy. No corporation should ever both pay dividends and raise funds for investment by issuing new stock. Because many large corporations do just that, it is obvious that transactions costs alone do not explain observed dividend policy.[6]

The Residual Theory of Dividends

The previous discussion suggests another possible explanation of observed dividend payments. Might they simply be a residual, the cash left over after corporations have funded all their positive-*NPV* investments? This would help explain why firms in rapidly growing industries retain almost all their profits, whereas firms in mature, slow-growing industries tend to have very high dividend payouts. It would also explain the "life-cycle" pattern of dividend payments for individual firms, where young, fast-growing companies rarely pay any dividends. But those same companies typically change to a high-payout strategy once they mature and their growth rate slows.

SMART PRACTICES VIDEO

Frank Popoff, Chairman of the Board (retired), Dow Chemical

"The decision specific to dividends is one that boards wrestle with on a regular basis."

See the entire interview at **SMARTFinance**

6. Interestingly, at least one academic researcher suggests that corporations pay dividends precisely because this forces them into the capital market for financing (rather than relying solely on internal financing), where investors have the incentive and the ability to monitor and discipline corporate management. See Frank H. Easterbrook, "Two Agency-Cost Explanations of Dividends," *American Economic Review* 74 (September 1984), pp. 650–659.

residual theory of dividends
States that observed dividend payments will simply be a residual, the cash left over after corporations have funded all their positive-*NPV* investments.

The **residual theory of dividends** probably has some merit, but it suffers from one massive empirical problem. Dividend payments are not as variable as they would be if firms were viewing them as residuals from cash flow. In fact, dividend payments are the most stable of any cash flow, into or out of a firm. All available evidence suggests that corporate managers smooth dividends, and they are very cautious about changing established dividend-payout levels. Clearly, the residual theory is not the sole explanation of observed dividend payments.

Paying Dividends as a Means of Communicating Information

Sooner or later, many who study the dividend puzzle recognize that firms may pay dividends to convey information to investors. Managers, who have a better understanding of the firm's true financial condition than shareholders do, can convey this information to shareholders through the dividend policy which managers select. Dividend payments have what accountants call "cash validity," meaning that these payments are believable and are harder for weaker firms to duplicate. Phrased in economic terms, in a world that is characterized by informational asymmetries between managers and investors, cash dividend payments serve as a credible conduit of information from corporate insiders (officers and directors) to the company's shareholders. Viewed this way, every aspect of a firm's dividend policy conveys significant new information.

What Type of Information Is Being Communicated?

When a company begins paying dividends (a dividend initiation), the company is conveying management's confidence that the firm is now profitable enough to both fund its investment projects and pay out cash. Investors and managers know that cutting or eliminating dividend payments, once they begin, results in a very negative market reaction. Therefore, dividend initiations send a strong signal to the market about management's assessment of the firm's long-term ability to generate cash.

The same logic applies to dividend increases. Because everyone understands that dividend cuts are to be avoided at almost all costs, management's willingness to increase dividend payments clearly implies confidence that its profits will remain high enough to support the new payment level. Dividend increases suggest a *permanent* increase in a firm's normal level of profitability. In other words, dividends change only when the level of *permanent earnings* changes. Unfortunately, this logic applies even more strongly to dividend decreases. Dividend cuts are viewed as very bad news. Managers reduce dividend payments only when they have no choice, such as when there is a cash flow crisis or when the financial health of the firm is declining, and no turnaround is in sight. Therefore, it is no surprise that when managers do cut dividends, the market reaction is often severe.

Dividend Payments as Solutions to Agency Problems

The free cash flow hypothesis offers yet another solution to the dividend puzzle. This hypothesis is based squarely on the agency problems that result from the separation of ownership and control, as observed in large public companies. When firms are small and growing rapidly, they not only have tight ownership structures but also tend to have many profitable investment opportunities. These growth firms can profitably use all the cash flow that they generate internally. Thus, they have no reason to pay cash dividends. In time, successful growth firms establish secure, often dominant, market positions. They begin to generate operating cash flows that are much larger than the remaining positive-*NPV* investment opportunities open to them. Michael Jensen defines free cash flow as any cash flow in excess of that needed to fund all positive-*NPV* projects.[7] Managers of firms with free cash flow *should* begin to pay dividends to ensure that they will not invest the free cash flow in negative-*NPV* projects. However, managers may prefer to retain cash and spend it, because of the increased status attained from running a larger (though not necessarily more valuable) company.

Jensen asserts that if managers are given the proper incentives, they will initiate dividend payments, as soon as the firm begins generating free cash flow. Managerial contracts that tie compensation to the firm's stock-price performance are designed to ensure that managers pay out free cash flow rather than invest it unwisely. The larger the free cash flow generated, the larger the dividend payout should be. This is the essential prediction of what is known as the agency cost/contracting model of dividend payments, which was introduced in Section 13.2. The central predictions of this model are threefold. First, it predicts that dividend initiations and increases should be viewed as good news by investors and thus should lead to stock-price increases upon announcement. Second, the agency cost model predicts that firms (and industries) that generate the largest amounts of free cash flow should also have the highest dividend payout ratios. Finally, this model predicts that managerial compensation contracts will not only be designed to entice managers to pursue a value-maximizing dividend policy but will also be effective. The empirical patterns observed in dividend payment policies worldwide, described in Section 13.2, are all consistent with these predictions.

CONCEPT REVIEW QUESTIONS

12. During the late 1960s, the top marginal personal income tax rate on dividends, received by British investors, reached 98 percent, yet dividend payouts actually *increased*. How can you justify this empirical fact?

13. In what way can managers use dividends to convey pertinent information about their firms in a world of informational asymmetry? Why would a manager choose to convey information via a dividend policy? Does empirical evidence support or refute the informational role of dividends?

14. Why is it difficult for a firm with weaker cash flows to mimic a dividend increase undertaken by a firm with stronger cash flows?

15. According to the residual theory of dividends, how does a firm set its dividend? With which dividend policy is this theory most compatible? Does it appear to be empirically validated?

13.5 A CHECKLIST FOR DIVIDEND PAYMENTS

As we have seen, the agency cost model explains cash dividend payments as value-maximizing attempts by managers of certain companies to minimize the agency costs that result from the separation of ownership and control. The severity of these agency problems is, in turn, a function of a firm's *investment opportunity set* and its *ownership structure*. The investment opportunity set encompasses the industry in which the firm operates, the company's size, the capital intensity of the firm's production process, the free cash flow generated, and the availability of positive-*NPV* investment opportunities to the firm. Ownership structure refers to the number of

SMART IDEAS VIDEO
John Graham, Duke University
"Why do companies hesitate to initiate a dividend or to increase a dividend?"

See the entire interview at **SMARTFinance**

[7]. See Michael C. Jensen, "Agency Costs of Free Cash Flow, Corporate Finance and Takeovers," *American Economic Review* 76 (May 1986), pp. 323–329.

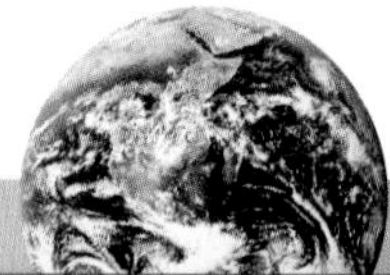

COMPARATIVE CORPORATE FINANCE

Dividend Policies of the Twenty-five Most Valuable Non-U.S. Public Companies

Company name	Country	Industry	Market Value May 31, 2003 (US Billions)	Dividend Payout ratio (%)	Dividend yield (%)	P/E ratio
Royal Dutch Shell	Netherlands/UK	Petroleum	$158.48	71.0%	4.2%	16.8
BP	*Britain*	*Petroleum*	*153.24*	120.7	*3.7*	*32.7*
Vodafone Group	Britain	Telecommunications	147.99	29.1	1.3	22.4
HSBC Holdings	Britain	Banking	126.97	63.5	4.5	14.1
GlaxoSmithKline	Britain	Pharmaceuticals	118.96	50.8	3.3	15.4
Novartis	Switzerland	Pharmaceuticals	113.09	37.4	1.9	19.7
NTT DoCoMo	*Japan*	*Telecommunications*	*105.31*	11.9	*0.2*	*59.3*
Total	*France*	*Petroleum*	*103.78*	67.1	*4.9*	*13.7*
Toyota Motor	Japan	Automobiles	86.32	14.2	1.3	10.9
Nokia	Finland	Mobile phone mfrg	86.09	38.7	1.8	21.5
Nestle	Switzerland	Food and Beverages	83.00	38.0	2.6	14.6
Royal Bank of Scotland Group	Britain	Banking	75.13	30.8	2.8	11
Roche Holdings	Switzerland	Pharmaceuticals	72.61	31.6	0.9	35.1
AstraZeneca	Britain	Pharmaceuticals	69.67	36.7	1.7	21.6
UBS	Switzerland	Banking	67.64	53.9	2.9	18.6
Deutsche Telekom	*Germany*	*Telecommunications*	*62.85*	0	*0*	–2
Telecom Italia	*Italy*	*Telecommunications*	*60.12*	43.2	4	*10.8*
Unilever	Netherlands/UK	Consumer products	59.36	24.4	3.4	12.6
France Telecom	*France*	*Telecommunications*	*57.45*	0	*0*	*–3.2*
Telefonica	*Spain*	*Telecommunications*	*56.80*	0	*0*	*25.2*
Nippon Telegraph & Telephone	*Japan*	*Telecommunications*	*55.58*	34.2	*1.2*	*28.5*
L'Oreal	France	Cosmetics, Luxury goods	49.06	45.9	1.6	28.7
Sanofi-Synthelabo	*France*	*Pharmaceuticals*	*46.81*	*18.7*	*2.3*	*22.6*
Barclays	Britain	Banking	46.19	44.8	4.3	10.5
Orange	France	Telecommunications	45.58	0	0	61.2
China Mobile (Hong Kong)	*China*	*Telecommunications*	*44.90*	*20.4*	*1.8*	*11.4*

As this table shows, the dividend policies of the world's most valuable companies are becoming increasingly similar, regardless of the country in which they are headquartered. Privatized companies, which are indicated with *italics*, have lead the way in promoting high dividend payments by publicly traded, non-U.S. firms, especially since these are usually some of the largest and most valuable companies in most national markets.

Source: "The Business Week Global 1000," *Business Week* (July 14, 2003).

shareholders, the size of each investor's holdings, and the presence or absence of an active investor, willing and able to directly monitor corporate management. Other factors that influence dividend payments include transactions costs, taxes, and two characteristics of a firm's home country: its legal system and the importance of capital markets, relative to financial intermediaries.

Developing a Checklist for Dividend Policy

In this section, we summarize what managers need to know about dividends. The following lists provide the predictions of the agency cost model about the relationship between corporate-level variables and expected dividend payout. The second column shows the effect on dividend payout of an increase in each firm-level variable in the first column.

Firm-Level Variable	Effect of Increase on Dividend Payout
Asset growth rate	Reduce
Positive-*NPV* investment opportunities	Reduce
Capital intensity of the production process	Increase
Free cash flow generated	Increase
Number of individual shareholders	Increase
Relative "tightness" of ownership coalition	Reduce
Size of largest block holder	Reduce

In addition to firm-level variables, macroeconomic and national financial variables also influence equilibrium dividend payments. The predictions of the agency cost/contracting model, concerning these variables, are detailed in the following list. Again, the second column shows the effect on dividend payout of an increase in each macroeconomic variable in the first column.

Macroeconomic Variable	Effect of Increase on Dividend Payout
Transactions costs of security issuance	Increase
Personal tax rates on dividend income	Reduce
Personal tax rates on capital gains income	Increase
Importance of institutional investors	Reduce
Corporate governance power of institutional investors	Reduce
Capital market, relative to intermediated (bank) financing	Increase

13.6 SUMMARY AND CONCLUSIONS

- One of the most enduring features of corporate finance worldwide is that large publicly traded corporations almost invariably choose to pay regular cash dividends to their shareholders. Furthermore, these payments are generally a constant, absolute amount per period ($0.25 per share), rather than a constant fraction (20 percent) of the firm's profits. In the United States, dividends are usually paid on a quarterly basis but are paid annually or semiannually in most other countries.
- There are striking regularities in the patterns of dividend payments, as observed across countries and industries. Among developed countries, dividend payout ratios (dividends as a fraction of corporate profits) tend to be highest in British Commonwealth countries, whereas payouts are much smaller in France and Italy.

Payouts by U.S. and other continental European companies tend to fall between these two extremes. However, the same industries (utilities, transportation firms) have high dividend payouts in all countries, and certain other industries (high-technology, health sciences) have low dividend payouts in all countries.

- In the United States, and increasingly in other countries, corporations frequently choose to repurchase shares on the open market rather than to pay (or in addition to paying) ordinary cash dividends, partly because repurchases are subject to lower effective tax rates for most individual investors. In recent years, repurchases by U.S. corporations have exceeded $100 billion per year, and ordinary (cash) dividend payments have been around $250 billion annually.
- Stock splits and stock dividends are used by companies that want to reduce the per-share price of their stock in the open market. In a 2-for-1 stock split, for example, one new share is distributed for every existing share an investor holds, and the price of the stock falls by roughly half.
- In a world without market imperfections, dividend policy is irrelevant, in the sense that it cannot affect the value of a firm. However, the fact that many firms pay dividends is something of a puzzle because most real market imperfections (such as taxes) argue against paying cash dividends.
- One theory of dividend policy assumes that dividend payments serve to reduce agency costs between corporate managers and external investors by committing the firm to pay out excess profits. Managers are prevented from consuming the profits as perquisites or wasting them on unwise capital investments (such as unrelated corporate acquisitions). Most of the empirical evidence supports this agency cost model of dividends over the competing signaling model, which predicts that managers use dividend payments to convey information to investors about the firm's expected future earnings.
- In addition to ownership considerations, several other aspects of a firm's operating and regulatory environment seem to influence dividend payouts. Other things being equal, closely held corporations, which operate in a high-growth industry where large ongoing capital investments are needed to compete, have lower dividend payouts than do widely held firms in slow-growing or highly regulated industries.

SELF-TEST PROBLEMS

Answers to Self-Test Problems appear in Appendix D at back of book. Answers to the Concept Review Questions throughout the chapter appear at http://megginson.swlearning.com.

ST13-1. What do record date, ex-dividend date, and payment date mean, related to dividends? Why would you expect the price of a stock to drop by the amount of the dividend on the ex-dividend date? What rationale has been offered for why this does not actually occur?

ST13-2. What has happened to the total volume of share repurchases announced by U.S. public companies since 1982? Why did that year mark such an important milestone in the history of share repurchase programs in the United States?

ST13-3. What has happened to the average cash dividend payout ratio of U.S. corporations over time? What explains this trend? How would your answer change if share repurchases were included in calculating U.S. dividend payout ratios?

ST13-4. What does it mean to say that corporate managers "smooth" cash dividend payments? Why do managers do this?

ST13-5. What are the key assumptions and predictions of the signaling model of dividends? Are these predictions supported by empirical research findings?

ST13-6. What is the expected relationship between dividend payout levels and the growth rate and availability of positive-*NPV* projects, under the agency cost model of dividends? What about the expected relationship between dividend payout and the diffuseness of firm shareholders? Free cash flow? Consider a firm, such as Microsoft, awash in free cash flow, available positive-*NPV* projects, and a relatively diffuse shareholder base in an industry with increasing competition. Does either the agency model or the signaling model adequately predict the dividend policy of Microsoft? Which does the better job?

INTERNET RESOURCES

Note: *For updates to links, please go to the book's Web site at* http://megginson.swlearning.com.

http://www.tenpercentdividends.com—Describes how to identify and to invest in companies with high dividend yields

http://www.ex-dividend.com—Lists recent stock splits and dividend changes; includes record dates, ex-dividend dates, and payment dates

http://www.dripcentral.com—Describes what a dividend reinvestment plan (DRIP) is and how it works; lists the companies that offer these plans, which allow shareholders to automatically use the cash they receive in dividends to purchase additional shares of company stock

KEY TERMS

agency cost/contracting model of dividends
announcement date
constant nominal payment policy
constant payout ratio dividend policy
date of record
dividend payout ratio
dividend yield
ex-dividend
excess earnings accumulation tax
extra dividend
low-regular-and-extra policy
payment date
residual theory of dividends
reverse stock splits
share repurchase programs
signaling model of dividends
special dividend
stock dividend
stock split
target dividend payout ratio
wealth tax

QUESTIONS AND PROBLEMS

Q13-1. What fraction of U.S. public companies pays regular cash dividends today? How has this changed over the past fifty years?

Q13-2. How does the fraction of NASDAQ-listed companies that regularly pay cash dividends compare with the fraction of NYSE-listed firms that do the same? What accounts for this difference?

Q13-3. Compare and contrast the constant payout ratio dividend policy and the constant nominal dividend payment policy. Which policy do most public companies actually follow? Why?

Q13-4. What is a low-regular-and-extra dividend policy? Why do firms pursuing this policy explicitly label some cash dividend payments as "extra"?

Q13-5. What is a stock dividend? How does this differ from a stock split?

Q13-6. What factors have contributed to the growth in share repurchase programs by American public companies over the past fifteen years? What is the expected effect on share repurchase programs from the passage of the Jobs and Growth Tax Relief Reconciliation Act of 2003?

Q13-7. How do the industrial patterns observed for dividend payouts compare with the patterns observed for capital structures? For example, are industries characterized by high dividend payouts also characterized by high leverage?

Q13-8. What is a firm's dividend yield? How does this compare with that firm's dividend payout ratio?

Q13-9. What is the average stock market reaction to: (a) a dividend initiation; (b) a dividend increase; (c) a dividend termination; and (d) a dividend decrease (cut)? Are these reactions logically consistent?

Q13-10. What are the key assumptions and predictions of the agency cost/contracting model of dividend payments? Are these predictions supported by empirical research findings?

Q13-11. Around the world, utilities generally have the highest dividend payouts of any industry, yet they also tend to have massive investment programs to finance through external funding. How do you reconcile high payouts and large-scale security issuance?

Q13-12. Why do firms with diverse shareholder bases typically pay higher dividends than private firms or public firms with concentrated ownership structures? How are fixed dividends used as a bonding (commitment) mechanism by managers of firms with dispersed ownership structures and large amounts of free cash flow?

PROBLEMS

Dividend Fundamentals

P13-1. Beta Corporation has the following shareholders' equity accounts:

Common stock at par	\$ 5,000,000
Paid-in capital in excess of par	\$ 2,000,000
Retained earnings	\$25,000,000
Total stockholders' equity	\$32,000,000

a. What is the maximum amount that Beta Corporation can pay in cash dividends, without impairing its legal capital, if it is headquartered in a U.S. state where capital is defined as the par value of common stock?

b. What is the maximum amount that Beta Corporation can pay in cash dividends, without impairing its legal capital, if it is headquartered in a U.S. state where capital is defined as the par value of common stock, plus paid-in capital in excess of par?

P13-2. What are alternative ways in which investors can receive a cash return from their investment in the equity of a company? From a tax standpoint, which of these would be preferred, assuming that investors pay a 35 percent tax rate on dividends and a 15 percent tax rate on capital gains? What if investors faced the same 15 percent tax on income and capital gains? What are the pros and cons of paying out cash dividends?

P13-3. Delta Corporation earned \$2.50 per share during fiscal year 2005 and paid cash dividends of \$1.00 per share. During the fiscal year that just ended on

December 31, 2006, Delta earned \$3.00 per share, and the firm's managers expect to earn this amount per share during fiscal years 2007 and 2008, as well.

a. What was Delta's payout ratio for fiscal year 2005?
b. If Delta's managers want to follow a constant nominal dividend policy, what dividend per share will they declare for fiscal year 2006?
c. If Delta's managers want to follow a constant payout ratio dividend policy, what dividend per share will they declare for fiscal year 2007?
d. If Delta's managers want to follow a partial-adjustment strategy, with a target payout ratio equal to FY 2005's, how could they change dividend payments during 2006, 2007 and 2008?

P13-4. General Manufacturing Company (GMC) follows a policy of paying out 50 percent of its net income as cash dividends to its shareholders each year. The company plans to do so again this year, during which GMC earned \$100 million in net profits after tax. The company has 40 million shares outstanding and pays dividends annually.

a. What is the company's nominal dividend payment per share each year?
b. Assuming that GMC's stock price is \$54 per share immediately before its ex-dividend date, what is the expected price of GMC stock on the ex-dividend date if there are no personal taxes on dividend income received?

P13-5. General Manufacturing Company (GMC) follows a policy of paying out 50 percent of its net income as cash dividends to its shareholders each year. The company plans to do so again this year, during which GMC earned \$100 million in net profits after tax. The company has 40 million shares outstanding and pays dividends annually. Assume that an investor purchased GMC stock a year ago at \$45. The investor, who faces a personal tax rate of 15 percent on both dividend income and on capital gains, plans to sell the stock very soon. Transactions costs are negligible.

a. Calculate the after-tax return this investor will earn if she sells GMC stock at the current \$54 stock price prior to the ex-dividend date.
b. Calculate the after-tax return the investor will earn if she sells GMC stock on the ex-dividend date, assuming that the price of GMC stock falls by the dividend amount on the ex-dividend date.
c. Calculate the after-tax return the investor will earn if she sells GMC stock on the ex-dividend date, assuming that the price of GMC stock falls by one half the dividend amount on the ex-dividend date.

P13-6. General Manufacturing Company (GMC) pays out 50 percent of its net income as cash dividends to its shareholders once each quarter. The company plans to do so again this year, during which GMC earned \$100 million in net profits after tax. If the company has 40 million shares outstanding and pays dividends quarterly, what is the company's nominal dividend payment per share each quarter?

P13-7. Twilight Company's stock is selling for \$60.25 per share, and the firm's managers have just announced a \$1.50 per share dividend payment.

a. What should happen to Twilight Company's stock price on the ex-dividend date, assuming that investors do not have to pay taxes on dividends or capital gains and do not incur any transactions costs in trading shares?
b. What should happen to Twilight Company's stock price on the ex-dividend date, assuming that it follows the historical performance of U.S. stock prices on ex-dividend days?
c. If the historical "ex-dividend-day-price effect," observed in U.S. stock markets, was indeed a tax effect, what should happen to Twilight Company's stock price on the ex-dividend date, given the tax changes embodied in the Jobs and Growth Tax Relief Reconciliation Act of 2003?

P13-8. Global Financial Corporation (GFC) has 10 million shares outstanding, each currently worth \$80 per share. The firm's managers are considering a 2-for-1 stock split, but they are concerned with the effect this split announcement will have on the firm's stock price.

a. If GFC's managers announce a 2-for-1 stock split, what exactly will the company do, and what will GFC's stock price likely be after the split?
b. How many total shares of GFC stock will be outstanding after the stock split?
c. If GFC's managers believe the "ideal" stock price for the firm's shares is $20 per share, what should they do? How many shares would be outstanding after this action?
d. Why do you think GFC's managers are considering a stock split?

P13-9. Maggie Fiduciary is a shareholder in the Superior Service Company (SSC). The current price of SSC's stock is $33 per share, and there are 1 million shares outstanding. Maggie owns 10,000 shares, or 1 percent of the stock, which she purchased one year ago for $30 per share. Assume that SSC makes a surprise announcement that it plans to repurchase 100,000 shares of its own stock, at a price of $35 per share. In response to this announcement, SSC's stock price increases $1 per share, from $33 to $34, but this price is expected to fall back to $33.50 per share after the repurchase is completed. Assume that Maggie faces marginal personal tax rates of 15 percent on both dividend income and capital gains.

a. Calculate Maggie's (realized) after-tax return from her investment in SSC shares, assuming that she chooses to participate in the repurchase program and that all of the shares she tenders are purchased at $35 per share.
b. How many shares will Maggie be able to sell if all SSC's shareholders tender their shares to the firm, as part of this repurchase program, and the company purchases shares on a pro rata basis?
c. What fraction of SSC's total common equity will Maggie own after the repurchase program is completed if she chooses not to tender her shares?

Patterns Observed in Payout Policies Worldwide

P13-10. Go to the home page of Cisco Systems, Inc. (http://www.cisco.com) and link to its financial reports page. Download the most recent annual report and observe the capital investment and dividend policies of Cisco Systems. Now, do the same for ChevronTexaco (http://www.chevrontexaco.com). Which of the two firms appears to have more high-growth, positive-*NPV* investment opportunities? Which pays the higher relative dividend? Do these results support the agency cost/contracting model? The signaling model?

P13-11. Go to the home page of ExxonMobil Corporation (http://www.cisco.com) and link to its financial reports page. Now, do the same for Royal Dutch Petroleum Company (http://www.shell.com), BP plc (http://www.bp.com), and Total Group (http://www.total.com/ho/en). Compare the dividend and the capital investment policies of these four major international oil companies. How do the dividend payment policies of the three European-based companies differ from the U.S.-based company, regarding payout percentages, absolute amount, and payment frequency? Why do you think that BP's accounts are denominated in dollars, even though the group is headquartered in London?

P13-12. Go to the home page for Dogs of the Dow (http://www.dogsofthedow.com), look at the year-to-date figures, and observe the dividend yields of the thirty stocks of the Dow Jones Industrial Average. Which industries contain the higher-dividend-yielding stocks, and which contain the lower-yielding stocks? Are there differences in the growth prospects between the high- and low-yielding stocks? Is this what you expected? Explain.

P13-13. A publicly traded firm announces an increase in its dividend, with no other material information accompanying the announcement. What information is this announcement likely to convey, and what is the expected stock-price effect, as the market assimilates this information?

P13-14. Stately Building Company's shares are selling for $75 each, and its dividend yield is 2.0 percent. What is the amount of Stately's dividend per share?

P13-15. The stock of Up-and-Away Inc. is selling for $80 per share, and it is currently paying a quarterly dividend of $0.25 per share. What is the dividend yield on Up-and-Away stock?

P13-16. Well-Bred Service Company earned $50,000,000 during 2005 and paid $20,000,000 in dividends to the holders of its 40 million shares. If the current market price of Well-Bred's stock is $31.25, calculate the following: (a) the company's dividend payout ratio; (b) the nominal dividend per share, assuming Well-Bred pays dividends annually; (c) the nominal dividend per share, assuming Well-Bred pays dividends in equal quarterly payments; and (d) the current dividend yield on Well-Bred stock.

Dividend Irrelevance in a World with Perfect Capital Markets

P13-17. It is January 1, 2006. Boomer Equipment Company (BEC) currently has assets of $250 million and expects to earn a 10 percent return on assets during the year. There are 20 million shares of BEC stock outstanding. The firm has an opportunity to invest in a (minimally) positive-*NPV* project that will cost $25 million over the course of 2006. BEC needs to determine whether it should finance this investment by retaining profits over the course of the year or pay the profits earned as dividends and issue new shares to finance the investments. Show that the decision is irrelevant in a world of frictionless markets.

P13-18. Swelter Manufacturing Company (SMC) currently has assets of $200 million and a required return of 10 percent on its 10 million shares outstanding. The firm has an opportunity to invest in (minimally) positive-*NPV* projects that will cost $20 million. SMC needs to determine whether it should withhold this amount from dividends payable to finance the investments or pay out the dividends and issue new shares to finance the investments. Show that the decision is irrelevant in a world of frictionless markets. What happens to the dividend-irrelevance result if a personal income tax of 15 percent is introduced into the model?

P13-19. On January 1, 2006, you examine two unlevered firms that operate in the same industry, have identical assets worth $80 million that yield a net profit of 12.5 percent per year, and have 10 million shares outstanding. During 2006, and all subsequent years, each firm has the opportunity to invest an amount equal to its net income in (slightly) positive-*NPV* investment projects. The Beta Company wants to finance its capital spending through retained earnings. The Gamma Company wants to pay out 100 percent of its annual earnings as cash dividends and to finance its investments with a new share offering each year. There are no taxes or transactions costs to issuing securities.

a. Calculate the overall and per-share market value of the Beta Company at the end of 2006 and each of the two following years (2007 and 2008). What return on investment will this firm's shareholders earn?

b. Describe the specific steps that the Gamma Company must take today (1/1/2006), and at the end of each of the next three years (year-end 2006, 2007, and 2008), if it pays out all of its net income as dividends and still grows its assets at the same rate as that of the Beta Company.

c. Calculate the number and per-share price of shares that the Gamma Company must sell today, and at the end of 2006, 2007, and 2008, if it pays out all of its net income as dividends and still grows its assets at the same rate as that of the Beta Company.

d. Assuming that you currently own 100,000 shares (1 percent) of Gamma Company stock, compute the fraction of the company's total outstanding equity that you will own three years from now if you do not participate in any of the share offerings the firm will make during this holding period.

P13-20. Investors anticipate that Sweetwater Manufacturing Inc.'s next dividend, due in one year, will be $4 per share. Investors also expect earnings to grow at 5 percent in perpetuity, and they require a return of 10 percent on their shares. Use the Gordon growth model (see Equation 5.6) to calculate Sweetwater's stock price today.

P13-21. Super-Thrift Pharmaceuticals Company traditionally pays an annual dividend equal to 50 percent of its earnings. Earnings this year are $30,000,000. The company has 15 million shares outstanding. Investors expect earnings to grow at a 5 percent annual rate in perpetuity, and they require a return of 12 percent on their shares.

a. What is Super-Thrift's current dividend per share? What is it expected to be next year?

b. Use the Gordon growth model (see Equation 4.6) to calculate Super-Thrift's stock price today.

P13-22. Casual Construction Corporation (CCC) earned $60,000,000 during 2006. The firm expects to earn $63,000,000 during 2007, in line with its long-term earnings growth rate. There are 20 million CCC shares outstanding, and the firm has a policy of paying out 40 percent of its earnings as cash dividends. Investors require a 10 percent return on CCC shares.

a. What is CCC's current dividend per share? What is it expected to be next year?

b. Use the Gordon growth model (see Equation 5.6) to calculate CCC's stock price today.

Real World Influences on Dividend Policy

P13-23. Universal Windmill Company (UWC) currently has assets worth $50 million and a required return of 10 percent on its 2 million shares outstanding. The firm has an opportunity to invest in (minimally) positive-*NPV* projects that will cost $5 million. UWC needs to determine whether it should withhold this amount from dividends payable to finance the investments or pay out the dividends and issue new shares to finance the investments. Show that the decision is irrelevant in a world of frictionless markets. What happens if a personal income tax of 15 percent on dividends (but not capital gains) is introduced into the model?

P13-24. Sam Sharp purchased 100 shares of Electric Lighting Inc. (ELI) one year ago for $60 per share. He also received cash dividends totaling $5 per share over the past twelve months. Now that ELI's stock price has increased to $64.50 per share, Sam has decided to sell his holdings. What is Sam's gross (pre-tax) and net (after-tax) return on this investment, assuming that he faces a 15 percent tax rate on dividends and capital gains?

THOMSON ONE | Business School Edition

For instructions on using Thomson ONE, refer to the instructions provided with the Thomson ONE problems at the end of Chapters 1–6 or to "A Guide for Using Thomson ONE."

P13-25. Compare the dividend policies of Novartis AG (ticker: S:NOVN), Astrazeneca PLC (AZN), Aventis SA (F:RPP), and Merck and Company Inc. (U:MRK) over the last five years. Determine the annual dividend payout ratios and the dividend yield for the four firms in each year. What do the dividend payout ratios tell you about investment opportunities available to each company? Do the payout ratios change significantly over time? Which of these firms, if any, follows a constant payout ratio policy or a constant nominal payment policy? Did any of these firms pay out an extra or special dividend over the last five years? Was it paid in a year with higher than normal earnings?

P13-26. Do any of the four companies in Problem 25 change dividends over the last five years? Do dividends change (in the same direction) every time earnings change? What does this say about a manager's expectations of changes in company earnings?

Since these exercises depend upon real-time data, your answers will change continuously depending upon when you access the Internet to download your data.

MINICASE

Dividend Policy

After working for the past four years as a financial analyst for Nevada Power Corporation, you receive a well-deserved promotion. You have been appointed to work on special projects for Mr. Watkins, the chief financial officer (CFO). Your first assignment is to gather information on dividend theory and policy, because the CFO wants to reassess the firm's current dividend policy.

ASSIGNMENT

1. What are the different types of dividend policies? Provide examples of situations in which each of these dividend policies could be used.
2. Describe the difference between cash dividends, stock dividends, stock splits, and share repurchases. Provide examples when each of these forms of dividends can be used.
3. Discuss the theory of dividend irrelevance. How do taxes affect the dividend-irrelevance theory?
4. How do managers use dividend policy to convey information to the marketplace? Why is dividend policy, instead of a press release, used to communicate information?

CHAPTER 14

Entrepreneurial Finance and Venture Capital

OPENING FOCUS

Amazon.com Redefines Electronic Commerce and Stock Volatility

Since its founding in July 1994, Amazon.com has emerged as one of the prototypical companies of the Internet age. Billed from the beginning as "Earth's Biggest Bookstore," Amazon.com quickly established itself as the premier on-line marketer of published materials, offering several million titles in a variety of languages. After it began expanding its on-line offerings in 1999, to include music, auctions, toys, electronics, travel, and other products and services, Amazon.com changed its slogan to claim that it had Earth's Biggest Selection™. Few could doubt this claim. Amazon.com's customers in 220 countries set a one-day record by ordering 2.1 million items on-line during the 2003 Christmas season alone. In the twelve months ending on December 31, 2003, the company's sales reached $5.26 billion. Sales during the first quarter of 2004 were running 50 percent ahead of prior-year levels.

In addition to becoming a poster child for savvy electronic marketing, Amazon.com offers a classic example of creative corporate finance. Launched with a $10,000 cash investment and a $15,000 loan from Jeffrey Bezos, the company's founder and CEO, Amazon.com's early growth was fueled, in part, by credit card loans drawn on Mr. Bezos's personal account. In July 1995, one year after Amazon.com went "on-line," the company secured private equity funding from Silicon Valley's top venture capital firm (Kleiner Perkins Caufield & Byers). In May 1997, the firm executed one of the splashiest initial public offerings of a very splashy decade. Within one year of its IPO, and less than four years after its inception, Amazon.com had annual revenues of $175 million and a market capitalization of over $7 billion. Investors who purchased Amazon's stock at its IPO price of $18 per share experienced a one-year return of more than 400 percent. The private equity investors (whose weighted average share purchase price was a mere $0.56 per share) received an astronomical total return of more than 15,000 percent!

Amazon.com's stock peaked in December 1999 at $107 per share ($1,280 per share after adjusting for three stock splits). This gave the firm a market capitalization of over $33 billion, in spite of never having reported a single quarterly profit since inception (and did not until the fourth quarter of 2001). The stock price then began a long slide. It hit bottom at $5.51 per share in late September 2001, before rebounding to $61 in October 2003. It then fell by one third over the next four months, only to recover to $50 per share in July 2004. The chart below describes Amazon.com's stock return versus that of the S&P 500 Index over the seven-year period following the company's IPO in 1997. Compared to the extreme volatility of Amazon's return (maroon line), the S&P 500's return (black line) appears almost unchanging.

The brief, but exciting, history of Amazon.com offers a classic case study of the promise and perils of financing entrepreneurial growth companies. Venture capitalists facilitated Amazon.com's rapid early development. The company later obtained a large chunk of pure-risk capital, through a very successful IPO. Nevertheless, Amazon.com's evolution as a public company has been marked by an extremely high level of stock-price volatility. The company faces the ongoing challenge of sustaining and financing rapid growth.

Cumulative Percentage Return on Amazon.com Stock (top line) versus Return on S&P 500 Index (bottom line), January 1988 to July 2004

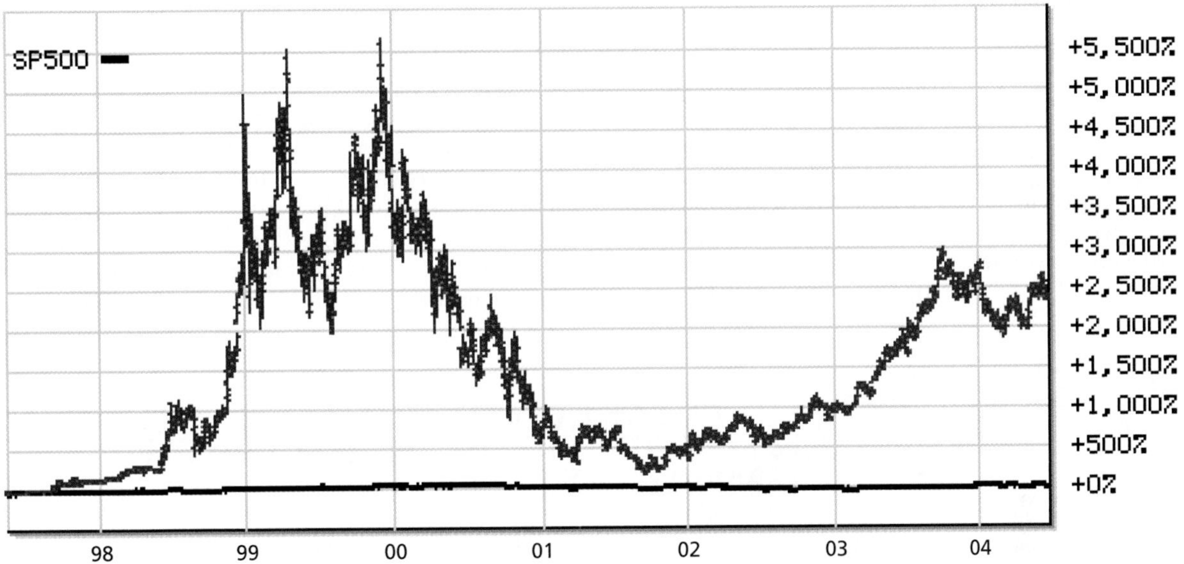

Sources: The information on Amazon.com cited is drawn from the prospectus for the company's IPO, the firm's now-famous Web site (http://www.amazon.com), the Web sites of CNN Money (http://money.cnn.com), Quicken (http://www.quicken.com), and various published reports. The chart is from the *Financial Times'* Web site (http://www.ft.com). ■

LEARNING OBJECTIVES

After studying this chapter you should be able to:

- Describe how the financing of entrepreneurial growth companies differs from the financing techniques used by more mature, publicly traded corporations;
- Discuss the four main types of institutional venture capitalists operating in the United States today and explain how these differ in terms of organization, financing, and investment objectives;

- Explain why venture capitalists almost always use convertible preferred stock as their investment vehicle and employ staged financing techniques to fund a developing company;
- Discuss how western European venture capital processes, practices, funding sources, and target industries differ from those in the United States, and describe the profitability of venture capital investments in these two major economies; and
- Describe why a vibrant market for initial public offerings is a vital prerequisite for a healthy venture capital industry.

entrepreneurial finance
Study of the special challenges and problems involved with investment in and financing of entrepreneurial growth companies.

entrepreneurial growth companies (EGCs)
Rapidly growing private companies that are usually technology-based and which offer both high returns and high risk to equity investors. These are the companies typically funded by venture capitalists.

The past three decades have been kind to finance generally, but no area of our profession has prospered quite as much as the field of **entrepreneurial finance.** From the proliferation of venture capital investors, to the boom and bust in Internet-related IPOs, the financial performance of **entrepreneurial growth companies (EGCs)** has offered spectacular theater over the past thirty years. In this chapter, we examine the particular challenges faced by financial managers of EGCs and the ways that venture capitalists (VCs) help meet these challenges. The topic is an important one, even for students who are not aspiring venture capitalists. Formerly the near-exclusive domain of small, highly specialized venture capital limited partnerships, the financing of EGCs now affects professionals working for mutual funds, pension funds, and even Fortune 500 manufacturing concerns. Increasingly, large corporations have internal venture capital units which finance, nurture, and grow new business opportunities. Companies such as Intel, Microsoft, Cisco Systems, Pfizer, and General Electric spend billions each year investing in EGCs. Deciding which EGCs to invest in, as well as how to structure and monitor those investments, presents a difficult problem. By studying how VCs approach these issues, we can learn lessons that extend well beyond the venture capital industry.

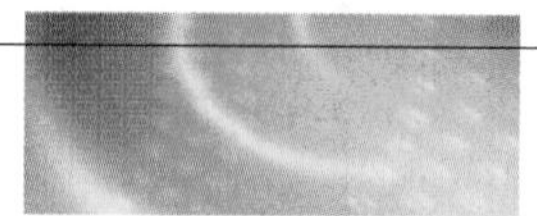

14.1 THE CHALLENGES OF FINANCING ENTREPRENEURIAL GROWTH COMPANIES

How does entrepreneurial finance differ from "ordinary" finance? Entrepreneurial growth companies differ from large, publicly traded firms in four important ways. First, EGCs often achieve compound annual growth rates of 50 percent, or more, in sales and assets. Though it is somewhat counterintuitive, companies growing that rapidly usually consume more cash than they generate. Growth requires ongoing investments in fixed assets and working capital. In fact, there is an old saying that the leading causes of death for young firms are (1) not enough customers and (2) too many customers. Too many customers, or very rapid growth, can lead to bankruptcy if firms do not have adequate financing in place. Privately owned EGCs almost always plan to convert to public ownership, either through an initial public offering (IPO) or by selling out to a larger firm. Once they become publicly traded, EGCs tend to rely on external equity funding much more than do older, larger firms. In other words, EGCs grow rapidly and require a great deal of cash, much of which must be obtained externally.

SMART IDEAS VIDEO
Greg Udell, Indiana University
"Firms that access venture capital finance typically have loads of intangible assets on their balance sheets and very little in the way of tangible assets."

See the entire interview at **SMARTFinance**

Second, the most valuable assets of many of these firms are often patents and other (intangible) intellectual property rights. We know these are inherently difficult to finance externally. This poses a huge challenge to those professionals who must obtain adequate funding on attractive terms. Amazon.com demonstrates this point

Capital Sources[1]	Mean Percent	Standard Deviation
Equity:		
Personal equity	35.6	40.8
Partnerships	5.2	17.9
Issuance of stock	3.2	14.5
Miscellaneous	2.7	13.6
	46.7	
Debt:		
Institutional loans	43.8	40.5
Loans from individuals	5.3	19.1
Issuance of bonds	1.1	8.6
Miscellaneous	2.7	12.8
	52.9	

1. Capital sources are stated as percentages of the total start-up capital. Means do not add to 100%, due to rounding.

Table 14.1
Sources of Start-Up Capital for a Sample of 132 Small Companies

Source: Richard B. Carter and Howard E. Van Auken, "Personal Equity Investment and Small Business Financial Difficulties," Entrepreneurship: Theory and Practice *15 (Winter 1990), pp. 51–60.*

very well. The company has total assets of only $1.74 billion, but it boasts a stock market capitalization of over $19.7 billion. Third, many entrepreneurial growth companies seek to commercialize highly promising, but untested, technologies. This inevitably means that both the risk of failure and the potential payoff from success are dizzyingly high. Fourth, EGCs must attract, motivate, compensate, and retain highly skilled technical and entrepreneurial talent—but must do so in a way that minimizes cash outflow, since EGCs are often severely cash constrained. Not surprisingly, these companies rely very heavily on stock-option grants for compensation.

The distinctive features of entrepreneurial finance imply that EGCs rely heavily on equity financing and that financial contracting between these companies and their financiers will always be plagued with information problems. As we saw in Chapter 12, growth opportunities cannot easily be financed with borrowed money. Instead, they must be funded with equity capital. Whereas almost all technology- and knowledge-based companies struggle to finance growth opportunities with equity, mature firms can obtain the bulk of the equity funding they need each year by reinvesting profits. EGCs, by definition, grow very rapidly. They must rely on *external* equity financing to fund investments, which vastly exceed the amount of internal funding the companies can generate. Finally, because most EGCs are privately held, they lack access to public stock markets and rely instead on private-equity financing. Private equity generally means either capital investments by current owners or funding by professional venture capitalists.

We should point out that the vast majority of firms, even those that subsequently emerge as EGCs, begin life on a modest scale, often with little or no external equity financing besides that provided by the founder's friends and family. This is what Professor Amar Bhide calls "bootstrap finance."[1] Only after entrepreneurs exhaust these sources of personal equity can they expect to obtain debt financing from banks or other financial institutions. Table 14.1 describes the results of an empirical study that examines the sources of start-up capital for a sample of 132 companies founded during 1987. The table shows that personal-equity financing and loans from financial institutions constitute the two most important sources of start-up capital, accounting

1. See Amar Bhide, "Bootstrap Finance: The Art of Start-ups," *Harvard Business Review* (November/December 1992), pp. 109–117. A reader, interested in a recent survey article on entrepreneurial finance, should also see David J. Denis, "Entrepreneurial Finance: An Overview of the Issues and Evidence," *Journal of Corporate Finance* 10 (March 2004), pp. 301–326. Finally, a potential entrepreneur, seeking guidance to determine how much money he or she needs to raise before starting a new venture, should refer to the classic article by James McNeill Stancill, "How Much Money Does Your New Venture Need?" *Harvard Business Review* (May/June 1986), pp. 122–139.

for almost 80 percent of funds raised. This study does not explicitly examine whether the institutions are personally guaranteed by the entrepreneurs (rather than being limited liability loans directly to the company). However, this is almost always the only way that entrepreneurs can borrow money for newly formed businesses.

CONCEPT REVIEW QUESTIONS

1. What are the most important ways that entrepreneurial finance differs from "ordinary" finance? What special burdens confront financial managers of EGCs?
2. Why do firms usually finance intangible assets with equity rather than with debt?

14.2 VENTURE CAPITAL FINANCING IN THE UNITED STATES

venture capital
A professionally managed pool of money raised for the sole purpose of making actively managed direct equity investments in rapidly growing private companies.

Defined broadly, *venture capital* has been a fixture of Western civilization for many centuries. In this context, the decision by Spain's Ferdinand and Isabella to finance the voyage of Christopher Columbus can be considered one of history's most profitable venture capital investments (at least for the Spanish). However, modern **venture capital**—defined as a professionally managed pool of money that is raised for the sole purpose of making actively managed direct equity investments in rapidly growing private companies—is a recent financial innovation. Until recently, only the United States had an active venture capital market. This is changing rapidly, as many countries have experienced rapid growth in venture capital financing over the past ten years.

The birth of America's venture capital industry can be traced to the American Research and Development Company (ARDC) that began operating in Boston shortly after the end of World War II.[2] As often happens with pioneers, ARDC had to invent the practices of modern venture capital and made many unprofitable investments in its early years. However, ARDC more than made up for its early mistakes with a single, spectacularly successful $70,000 investment in Digital Equipment in 1957, which grew in value to $355 million over the next fifteen years. Through the late 1970s, the total pool of venture capital was quite small. Most of the active funds were sponsored either by financial institutions (e.g., Citicorp Venture Capital) or nonfinancial corporations (e.g., Xerox). Most of the money raised by these funds came from their corporate backers and from wealthy individuals or family trusts. There are two features of early venture capital funds that we still observe today: (1) these funds' investments were mostly intermediate-term, equity-related investments targeted at technology-based private companies and (2) the venture capitalists played a unique role as active investors, contributing both capital and expertise to portfolio companies. Also, from the very start, VCs looked to invest in those rare companies which not only had the potential of going public or being acquired at a premium within a few years, but offered investment returns of 25–50 percent per year.

A fundamental change in the U.S. venture capital market occurred during the late 1970s. Two seemingly unrelated public policy innovations contributed to this change. First, Congress lowered the top personal income tax rate on capital gains from 35 percent to 28 percent in 1978, thereby increasing the return to entrepreneurship. Second, the Labor Department adopted its "Prudent Man Rule" in 1979, effectively authorizing pension fund managers to allocate a moderate fraction of fund assets to private-equity investments. Neither of these changes appears revolutionary, but their effect on venture capital funding was dramatic. There was an increase in the

[2] Many of the facts cited in this section are presented in the excellent survey article by Paul Gompers and Josh Lerner, "The Venture Capital Revolution," *Journal of Economic Perspectives* 15 (Spring 2001), pp. 145–168.

total venture capital funds raised, from $68.2 million in 1977 to $978.1 million in 1978 (both figures are in 1987 dollars). In 1981, a further capital gains tax reduction contributed to venture capital funding growth, from $961.4 million in 1980 to $5.1 billion in 1983. Fund-raising then remained in the $2–$5 billion range for the rest of the 1980s. After falling to $1.3 billion in 1991, venture capital fund-raising began a steady climb to a record $105.4 billion in 2000, before falling all the way back to $10.8 billion during 2003. Because the Jobs and Growth Tax Relief Reconciliation Act of 2003 significantly lowered the effective tax rate on personal investment income, this recent tax law change could well promote venture capital investment over the next few years, just as the 1978 capital gains tax reduction did.

Types of Venture Capital Funds

In discussing venture capital, we must carefully differentiate between institutional venture capital funds and angel capitalists. **Institutional venture capital funds** are formal business entities in which full-time professionals seek out and fund promising ventures, whereas **angel capitalists** (or *angels*) are wealthy individuals who make private-equity investments on a more ad hoc basis. A vibrant market for "angel capital" exists and routinely provides over $50 billion per year in total equity investment to private businesses in the United States. Apart from the boom years of 1998–2000, angel capitalists have generally provided far more total investment to entrepreneurial companies each year than have institutional venture capital firms. Nonetheless, we focus on the latter group throughout this text because these firms operate nationally and provide the performance benchmark against which all private equity investment is compared.

institutional venture capital funds
Formal business entities with full-time professionals dedicated to seeking out and funding promising ventures.

angel capitalists
Wealthy individuals who make private equity investments on an ad hoc basis.

There are four categories of institutional venture capital funds. First, **small business investment companies (SBICs)** are federally chartered corporations established as a result of the Small Business Administration Act of 1958. Since then, SBICs have invested over $14 billion in approximately 80,000 small firms. Historically, these venture capitalists have relied on their unique ability to borrow money from the U.S. Treasury, at very attractive rates. SBICs were the only types of VCs that structured their investments as debt rather than equity. This feature seriously hampered their flexibility. But a revision of the law in 1992 has made it possible for SBICs to obtain equity capital from the Treasury in the form of preferred equity interests and also to organize themselves as limited partnerships. Recent evidence suggests that this change, by itself, has not been enough for SBICs to regain venture capital market share.

small business investment companies (SBICs)
Federally chartered corporations established as a result of the Small Business Administration Act of 1958.

Second, **financial venture capital funds** are subsidiaries of financial institutions, particularly commercial banks. These are generally set up both to nurture portfolio companies, which will ultimately become profitable customers of the corporate parent, and to earn high investment returns, by leveraging the financial expertise and contacts of existing corporate staff. Though many financial venture capital funds are organized as SBICs, their orientation is sufficiently specialized that they are generally classified separately. Third, **corporate venture capital funds** are subsidiaries or stand-alone firms, established by nonfinancial corporations, which are eager to gain access to emerging technologies by making early-stage investments in high-tech firms. Finally, **venture capital limited partnerships** are funds that are established by professional venture capital firms. These firms act as the general partners—organizing, investing, managing, and ultimately liquidating the capital raised from the limited partners. Most limited partnerships have a single-industry focus that is determined by the expertise of the general partners.

financial venture capital funds
Subsidiaries of financial institutions, particularly commercial banks.

corporate venture capital funds
Subsidiaries or stand-alone firms established by nonfinancial corporations eager to gain access to emerging technologies by making early-stage investments in high-tech firms.

venture capital limited partnerships
Funds established by professional venture capital firms, and organized as limited partnerships.

Limited partnerships dominate the venture capital industry, partly because they make their investment decisions free from outside influences. The SBICs have been hampered by their historical reliance on inappropriate funding sources and by the myriad regulations that apply to government-sponsored companies. The financial and corporate funds tend to suffer because their ultimate loyalty rests with their corporate parents rather than their portfolio companies. Divided loyalties lead to conflicts of interest between financier and entrepreneur, and between the corporate funds and other venture capital investors. Compensating employees who work in corporate venture capital funds also frequently poses a challenge. The compensation of venture capitalists is likely to be much higher and more directly related to performance than is the case for most corporate employees. Finally, corporate funds have histories of only intermittent commitment to venture capital investing. Corporate funds tend to scale back dramatically when business conditions sour. For all these reasons, limited partnerships now control over 75 percent of total industry resources, and their sway over fund-raising seems to be increasing.

Investment Patterns of U.S. Venture Capital Firms

Given the media attention lavished on venture capital in the United States, most people are surprised to learn just how small the industry actually was before 1998. Figure 14.1 plots the total amount of capital invested each year, from 1990 through the first quarter of 2004. Annual disbursements naturally differ from total fund-raising. The total amount of money available for investment is the sum of realized investment returns (from IPOs and mergers of portfolio companies) as well as new fund inflows from investors. Figure 14.1 reveals that total investments by VCs never exceeded \$6 billion until 1996. Total investment spending then surged to an astonishing \$102.3 billion (spread over 5,608 companies) in 2000, before declining very sharply thereafter. The average investment of \$18.24 million per company during 2000 was over four times larger than the \$4.5 million average investment per company in 1995. Even with the dramatic three-year falloff in venture spending, 2004 was on a pace (as this book was going to press) to register the fifth-highest venture investment year ever.

The bulk of venture capital funding once came either from corporate sponsors (in the case of financial or corporate funds) or wealthy individuals. However, institutional investors have become the dominant sources of funding today. Pension funds alone typically account for 25–40 percent of all new money raised

Figure 14.1
Annual Venture Capital Investments in the United States, 1990–2004

In \$ Billion current dollars

Note: *The \$18.4 billion figure for 2004 is based on annualizing the first-quarter figure of \$4.60 billion.*

Source: National Venture Capital Association http://www.nvca.com

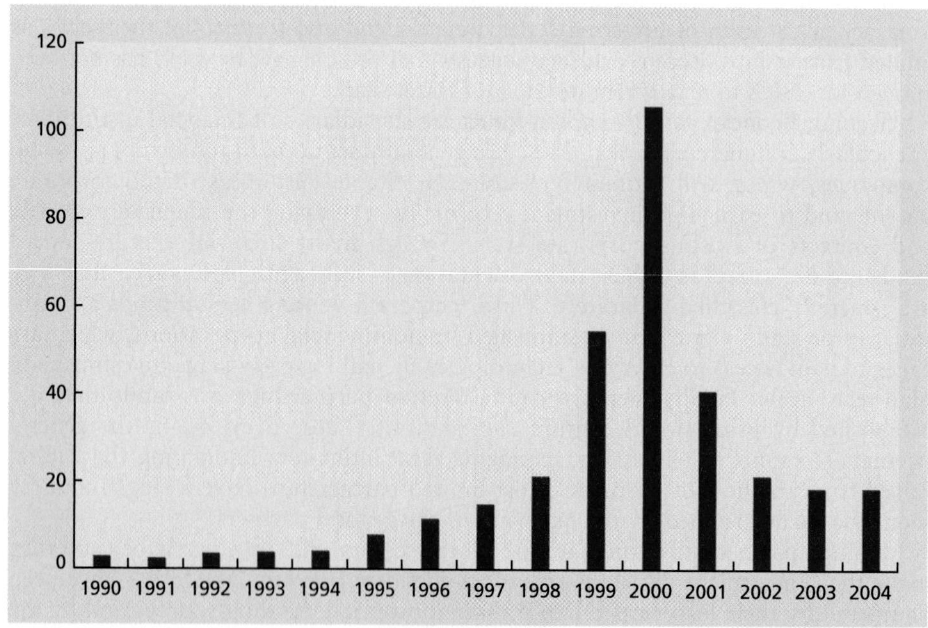

by institutional venture capital firms. Even though few pension funds allocate more than 5 percent of their total assets to private-equity funding, their sheer size makes them extremely important investors. Their long-term investment horizons make them ideal partners for venture capital funds. Financial and nonfinancial corporations usually represent the second-largest contributors of capital to venture funds, accounting for 10–30 percent of the total. Foundations (endowments) are the third important source of venture capital funding, usually accounting for 10–25 percent of the total. Foreign investors have recently become more important. In combination with "other" investors, they now account for about one fifth of total funding. Individuals and family trusts are the final major group of venture capital investors. These two groups together generally contribute 10–20 percent of the total venture capital funding.

Industrial and Geographic Distribution of Venture Capital Investment. One reason for the success enjoyed by institutional VCs is that they usually invest only in those industries where they have some competitive advantage and where their involvement in portfolio-company management can create real economic value. Table 14.2 lists the industries that received the most venture capital funding in 1998, 2000, and 2003. Typical of the history of venture capital, the majority of investment flowed into information-technology industries (communications and computers) during all three periods. Internet-specific investments accounted for a whopping 46.4 percent of the total in year 2000, but for much lower fractions in 1998 and 2003. Reductions in venture capital spending in this sector made room for expanded investments in 2003, in industries such as biotechnology, telecommunications, and medical devices and equipment.

Another striking regularity in venture capital investment patterns concerns the geographical distribution of portfolio companies. Firms located in California consistently receive more venture capital backing than firms in any other state. For instance, in the first quarter of 2004, California firms captured 40.5 percent of total funding, almost three times the funding received by firms in New England (15.7%). The flow of money into California dwarfed those in other large, populous states such as New York (5.8%) and Texas (4.5%).

Table 14.2
U.S. Venture Capital Investment by Industry: 1998, 2000, and 2003

In $ US Millions

Industry	1998	2000	2003
Computer software and services	21.6%	14.0%	19.6%
Biotechnology	5.2	2.7	18.5
Other products and services	12.7	5.1	11.2
Telecommunications	17.6	17.1	10.9
Networking and equipment [a]	13.4	46.4	9.3
Medical devices and equipment	12.8	3.5	8.1
Semiconductor	4.2	5.9	6.5
Computer hardware	3.1	2.2	<5
Industrial/energy	2.4	1.4	<5
Consumer related	6.9	1.6	<5
Total ($ Million)	**$18,705**	**$102,976**	**$18,352**

[a] This category was called "Internet specific" in 1998 and 2000.

Source: Data for years 2000 and 2003 are from the PricewaterhouseCoopers/VentureEconomics/National Venture Capital Association Moneytree™ quarterly description of venture capital investment in the United States (http://www.pwcmoneytree.com). Data for 1998 are drawn from the NVCA Web site (http://www.nvca.com).

Venture Capital Investment by Stage of Company Development. The popular image of VCs holds that they specialize in making investments in start-up or very early-stage companies. This is only partly true. In fact, as Figure 14.2 documents, early-stage financing accounted for only 18 percent of total investment in 2003, down from 25 percent in 2000 and 24 percent in 1997. Truly early-stage (start-up and seed-stage) financing represented a mere 2.0 percent in 2003, and similarly small fractions were allocated in prior years. Being rational investors, venture capitalists are as leery as anyone else of backing extremely risky new companies. They will do so only if the entrepreneur/founder is well known to the venture capitalists or the venture is exceptionally promising, or both. Later-stage investments in more mature private companies accounted for 26 percent of total venture capital investment in 2003, 15 percent in 2000, and 16 percent in 1997. Finally, expansion financing accounted for over 50 percent of the total investment in all three years.

Although the distribution between early- and later-stage funding varies from year to year, one principle of venture capital funding never changes—the earlier the development stage of the portfolio company, the higher must be the expected return on the venture capitalist's investment. Professional VCs typically demand compound annual investment returns in excess of 50 percent on start-up investments. But they will accept returns of 20–30 percent per year on later-stage deals because the risk is far lower in more established companies. VCs extract a higher expected return on early-stage investments, in part, by requiring entrepreneurs to sell them a higher ownership stake for a given investment amount in these deals.

Usually, there is not a stark choice between early- and later-stage investments. Most VC funds that invest in a company during its early years remain committed to the firm as it develops. VCs typically participate in many financing rounds as the portfolio company matures. On average, the prices venture capitalists pay to acquire additional shares in portfolio companies rise in each subsequent round of financing.

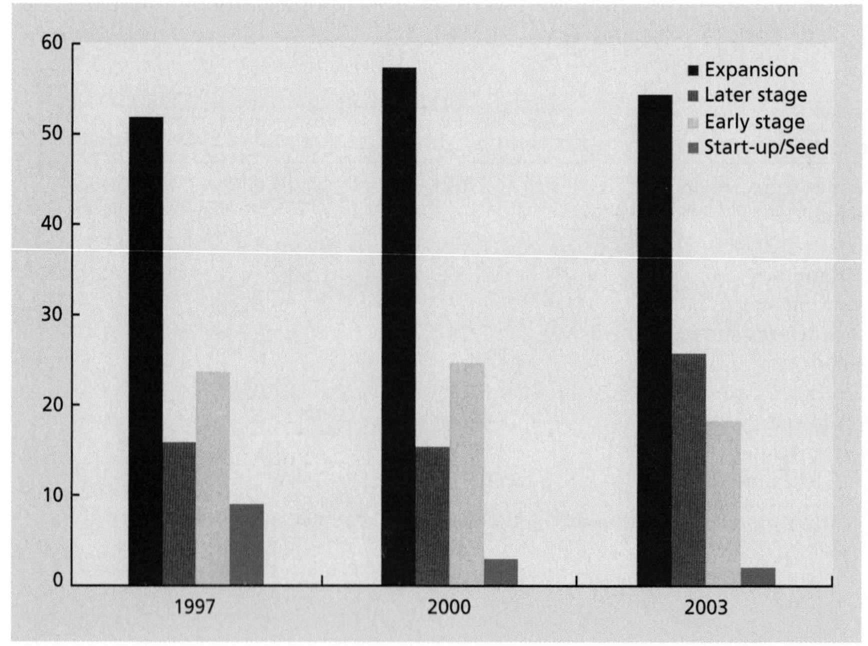

Figure 14.2
U.S. Venture Capital Investments by Stage of Company Development: 1997–2003

Source: PricewaterhouseCoopers/ Venture Economics/ National Venture Capital Association Moneytree[TM] *quarterly description of venture capital investment in the United States (http://www.pwcmoneytree.com).*

Table 14.3
The Economic Effect of Three Decades of U.S. Venture Capital Funding, 1970–2000

Cumulative Investment (1970–2000); Year 2000 Sales and Employment of Venture-Backed Companies, Year 2001 VC Investment and Growth Rate

State	Cumulative VC Invested, 1970–2000 ($ millions)	Sales of VC-Backed Firms, 2000 ($ millions)	Employment by VC-Backed Firms, 2000 (# of workers)	Venture Capital Invested, 2001 ($ millions) [Est]	5-Yr Compound Annual VC Growth Rate, 1996–2001
California	$108,810	$ 207,616	1,415,748	$14,431	24.3%
Massachusetts	25,986	48,848	381,433	4,456	35.7
Texas	17,189	158,183	676,158	2,679	29.8
New York	16,070	65,848	369,314	2,080	33.1
Colorado	9,881	14,565	62,971	1,227	32.1
New Jersey	9,138	38,151	260,114	1,207	23.3
Washington	7,383	75,392	263,585	908	20.9
Virginia	7,215	35,689	207,777	972	14.5
Pennsylvania	7,187	58,037	424,652	na	na
Georgia	6,435	62,797	338,188	996	34.5
U.S. Total	$273,300	$1,300,000	7,600,000	—	—

Source: Jeanne Metzger and Channa Brooks, "Three Decades of Venture Capital Investment Yields 7.6 Million Jobs and $1.3 Trillion in Revenue," National Venture Capital Association (October 22, 2001) http://www.nvca.com.

The Economic Effect of Venture Capital Investment

Before turning to an examination of the organizational structure of the U.S. venture capital industry, we should briefly assess whether venture capital investments have really been as large and influential as is generally believed. A recent study published by the National Venture Capital Association documented the scale and economic effect of thirty years of VC investment in the United States.[3] The key results of that study are presented in Table 14.3. Over the period 1970–2000, American venture capitalists invested $273.3 billion into 16,278 companies in all 50 states. No less than $192 billion of that investment occurred during the six-year period of 1995–2000. Venture capital-backed firms employed 7.6 million people and generated $1.3 trillion in sales during 2000, representing 5.9 percent of the nation's jobs and 13.1 percent of America's GDP for that year. The study also found that, over the thirty-year period, "venture capital-financed companies had approximately twice the sales, paid almost three times the federal taxes, generated almost twice the exports, and invested almost three times as much in R&D per $1,000 in assets as did the average non-venture capital-backed companies." Finally, the study documented that, on average, every $36,000 in VC investment created one new job.

Much the same pattern is observed in Western Europe, the other major international market for venture capital. A study by the European Private Equity and Venture Capital Association found that VC-backed European companies generated significantly higher growth rates in sales, research spending, exports, and job creation during the 1990-1995 period than did otherwise comparable non-VC-backed companies.[4] Recent updates

[3] See Jeanne Metzger and Channa Brooks, "Three Decades of Venture Capital Investment Yields 7.6 Million Jobs and $1.3 Trillion in Revenue," National Venture Capital Association (October 22, 2001), downloaded at http://www.nvca.com.

[4] The study is entitled "The Economic Impact of Venture Capital in Europe," and is available for downloading at http://www.evca.com. Updates of this study include the *Survey of the Economic and Social Impact of Venture Capital in Europe*, published by EVCA on June 20, 2002, and the *EVCA Final Survey of Pan-European Private Equity and Venture Capital Activity 2002*, published by EVCA on June 4, 2003.

of this study show that European private-equity funds invested €8.4 billion in 8,399 VC-stage companies during 2003. Roughly one fourth the total investment was in early-stage companies. Finally, an astonishing 95 percent of European venture-backed companies said that they either would not exist or would not have developed as quickly without VC investment.

CONCEPT REVIEW QUESTIONS

3. What is an *angel capitalist,* and how does this type of investor differ from a professional (institutional) venture capitalist?

4. Why do you think that private limited partnerships have come to dominate the U.S. venture capital industry? Can you think of any weaknesses this organizational form may have as a vehicle for financing entrepreneurial growth companies?

14.3 THE ORGANIZATION AND OPERATIONS OF U.S. VENTURE CAPITAL FIRMS

Organization and Funding of Venture Capital Limited Partnerships

Most of the top venture capital firms are organized as general partnerships. Many of these are concentrated in California's Silicon Valley, south of San Francisco. These firms usually begin the venture financing process by creating a distinct limited partnership fund, typically with a dedicated investment target, such as funding biotechnology start-ups.

Some venture funds are created by public offerings of limited partnership interests, which can then be freely traded. Most are organized and capitalized by private negotiation between the fund's sponsor and a well-established group of institutional investors. To say that a fund is "capitalized" at its inception is something of a misnomer. In practice, the limited partners make capital commitments, which the general partner then draws on over time as the fund becomes fully invested. In addition to organizing the limited partnership, the sponsoring firm acts as the general partner (and has unlimited liability) over the fund's entire life, typically seven to ten years. As general partner, the VC is responsible for (1) seeking out investment opportunities and negotiating the terms on which these investments will be made; (2) monitoring the performance of the portfolio companies and providing additional funding and expertise, as necessary; (3) finding an attractive exit opportunity, such as an IPO or a merger, that will allow the fund to liquidate its investments; and (4) distributing the realized cash returns from these exit opportunities to the limited partners and then terminating the fund. For its services, the general partner usually receives a percentage claim, called *carried interest,* on the realized return (almost always 20 percent) as well as an annual management fee, equal to 1 to 3 percent of the fund's total committed capital.

The relationship between VCs and investors is fraught with agency problems. Investors must commit large amounts of money for long-term, illiquid, nontransparent investments in private partnerships, over which they can exercise no direct control without forfeiting their limited liability. Venture capitalists have many opportunities to expropriate the limited partners' wealth. They can set up new funds, which exclude the old limited partners, to finance the most promising companies, and they can make side deals with the best portfolio companies. Reputational concerns largely control these problems, but contractual covenants also play a role in curtailing agency problems. These include limiting the VC's ability to establish new funds, without granting existing investors equal access, mandating that existing investors be included in any equity sale contracts the VC negotiates, and restricting the VC's freedom to invest in foreign and in publicly traded securities, or in leveraged buyouts. These covenants restrict the VC's ability to expropriate the limited partners' wealth through side deals, as well as ensure that the VC will not make investments outside the fund manager's area of expertise.

Many senior partners at top venture capital firms are well known for their skills in finding, nurturing, and bringing to market high-tech companies. Examples include John Doerr of Kleiner Perkins Caufield & Byers, William Hambricht of Hambricht and Quist, and Sam Rosen of Rosen Partners. These industry leaders have become extraordinarily wealthy, but even "ordinary" venture capitalists did quite well during the 1995–2000 boom. The industry's financial rewards attract numerous wanna-be VCs, but jobs in the industry are notoriously difficult to obtain, particularly for newly minted business school graduates. Partners and associates in venture capital firms often are engineers or other technically trained professionals who themselves worked in high-tech companies before becoming full-time VCs. This experience gives them in-depth knowledge of both the technological and business aspects of the industries in which they invest. It is this expertise, along with capital and contacts, which entrepreneurs look for when they approach a VC for funding. For example, John Doerr of Kleiner Perkins Caufield & Byers has bachelor's and master's degrees in electrical engineering, plus an MBA from Harvard Business School. He worked for Intel Corporation for five years before becoming a venture capitalist.

SMART IDEAS VIDEO

Manju Puri, Stanford University

"Venture capital does have a positive role for innovative companies in helping to push their product out quickly."

See the entire interview at **SMARTFinance**

How Venture Capitalists Structure Their Investments

SMART IDEAS VIDEO

Steve Kaplan, University of Chicago

"It's not just about what fraction of the company the venture capitalists are getting."

See the entire interview at **SMARTFinance**

As unique as a venture capital investment contract is, most agreements between VCs and entrepreneurs share certain characteristics. First and foremost, venture capital contracts allocate risk, return, and ownership rights between the entrepreneur (and other existing owners of a portfolio company) and the fund. The distribution of rights and responsibilities depends on (1) the experience and reputation of the entrepreneur, (2) the attractiveness of the portfolio company as an investment opportunity, (3) the stage of the company's development, (4) the negotiating skills of the contracting parties, and (5) the overall state of the market. If, at a time of fierce competition among VCs, a respected and experienced entrepreneur approaches a fund with an opportunity to invest in an established company with a promising technology, the entrepreneur will secure financing on relatively attractive terms. However, if an inexperienced entrepreneur asks for start-up funding at a time when venture capital is scarce (such as the early 1990s), the entrepreneur will have to accept fairly onerous contract terms to attract funding.

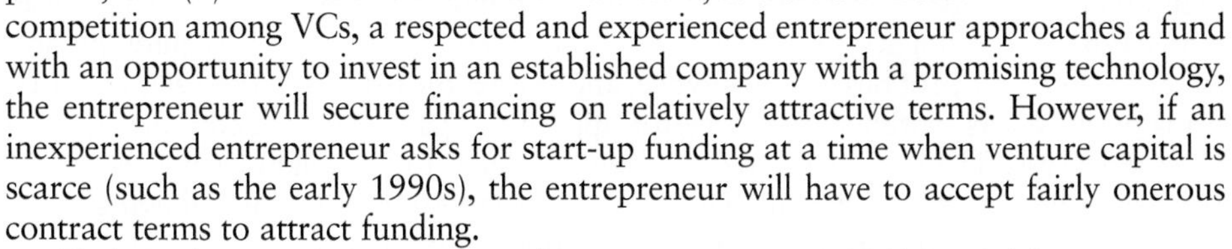

Early in the negotiation process, the parties must estimate the portfolio company's value. The company's past R&D efforts, its current and prospective sales revenue, its tangible assets, and the present value of its expected net cash flows all enter into the valuation equation. In large measure, the valuation will determine what fraction of the firm the entrepreneur must exchange for venture backing. Next, the parties must agree on the amount of new funding the venture capitalist will provide and the required return on that investment. Naturally, the higher the perceived risk, the higher the required return.

staged financing
Method of investing venture capital in a portfolio company in stages, over time, with additional funding being provided each stage only if the company is achieving satisfactory results. Used by venture capitalists to minimize their risk exposure.

Venture capitalists use **staged financing** to minimize their risk exposure. To illustrate how staged financing works, assume that a company needs $25 million in private funding to fully commercialize a promising new technology. Rather than invest the entire amount at once, the venture capitalist initially advances only enough (say, $5 million) to fund the company to its next development stage. Both parties agree to specific performance objectives (e.g., building a working product prototype) as a condition for more rounds of financing. If the company succeeds in reaching those goals, the venture capitalist will provide funding for the next development stage, usually on terms more favorable to the entrepreneur. Staged financing is not only a very efficient way to minimize risk for the venture capitalist, but it also gives the venture fund an extremely valuable option to deny or delay additional funding. This **cancellation option** places the maximum feasible amount of financial risk on the entrepreneur. In return, it allows the entrepreneur to obtain funding at a less onerous price than would otherwise be possible. Staged financing also provides tremendous incentives for the entrepreneur to create value. At each new funding stage, the VC provides capital on increasingly attractive terms.

cancellation option Option held by the venture capitalist to deny or delay additional funding for a portfolio company.

APPLYING THE MODEL

Paul Gompers provides two classic examples of how staged financing should work in the development of private companies: Apple Computer and Federal Express.[5] Apple received three rounds of private-equity funding. In the first round, venture capitalists purchased stock at $0.09 per share. This rose to $0.28 per share in the second round and then $0.97 per share in the third round. Needless to say, all these investments proved spectacularly profitable when Apple went public, at $22.00 per share, in 1980. Investors in Federal Express, however, used staged financing with more telling effect, during their three rounds of private-equity financing. The investors purchased stock for $204.17 per share in the first round, but the firm's early performance was much poorer than anticipated. In the second round, shares were purchased for $7.34 each. But the company's finances continued to deteriorate, so a third financing round, at $0.63 per share, was required. As we know, FedEx eventually became a roaring success and went public, at $6.00 per share, in 1978. Staged financing allowed venture capitalists to intervene decisively during the firm's problematic early development.

A distinguishing characteristic of venture capital investment contracts is their extensive and sophisticated covenants. These are contract clauses that mandate certain things that the portfolio firm's managers must do (**positive covenants**) and must not do (**negative covenants**). Some of these covenants appear in many standard bond- and loan-financing contracts. For example, venture capital contracts often contain clauses that specify maximum acceptable leverage and dividend payout ratios, require the firm to carry certain types of business insurance, and restrict the firm's ability to acquire other firms or sell assets, without prior investor approval. Again, Amazon.com provides an illustrative case. The firm's bank required Jeffrey Bezos to personally guarantee all the company's borrowing, prior to its IPO. Other covenants, including the following types, occur almost exclusively in private-equity investment contracts.

positive covenants Requirements a borrower must meet to secure a loan. What a company must do.

negative covenants Restrictions a borrower must accept in order to secure a loan. What a company must not do.

ownership right agreements Agreements between venture capital investors and portfolio-company managers allocating ownership stakes and voting rights to venture capitalists, and usually mandating that the VCs will vote together on all contested issues.

1. **Ownership right agreements** not only specify the distribution of ownership but also allocate board seats and voting rights to the participating VC. Special voting rights, often given to VCs, include the right to veto major corporate actions and to remove the management teams if firms fail to meet performance goals.

2. **Ratchet provisions** protect the venture group's ownership rights if firms sell new equity under duress. Generally, these provisions ensure that the venture capital

[5] See Paul A. Gompers, "Optimal Investment, Monitoring, and the Staging of Venture Capital," *Journal of Finance* 50 (December 1995), pp. 1,461–1,489.

group's share values adjust so that entrepreneurs bear the penalty of selling low-priced new stock. For example, if the venture fund purchased shares initially for $1 each, and the start-up later sells new stock at $0.50 per share, a "full ratchet" provision mandates that the venture group receives one new share for each old share. Thus, the value of the VC's initial stake is protected (a "partial ratchet" only partially protects the venture group). Obviously, it would not take many rounds of financing, at reduced prices, to completely wipe out a management team's ownership stake.

ratchet provisions
Contract terms that adjust downward the par value of the stock venture capitalists have purchased in a company in case the firm must sell new stock at a lower price than the VC originally paid. This preserves the venture capitalists' ownership stake in portfolio companies, at the expense of the company's managers.

3. **Demand registration rights**, **participation rights**, and **repurchase rights** preserve exit opportunities for VCs. *Demand registration rights* give the venture fund the right to compel the firm to register shares with the SEC for a public offering—at the firm's expense. The venture capital investors in Amazon.com had such a demand registration right, though they never exercised it. *Participation rights* give VCs the option to participate in any private stock sale that the firm's managers arrange for themselves. If a portfolio company does not conduct an IPO or sell out to another firm, within a specified time period, *repurchase rights* give VCs the option to sell their shares back to the firm.

demand registration rights
Agreements giving the venture capitalists the right to demand that a portfolio company's managers arrange for a public offering of shares in the company, to be paid for by the company itself.

4. **Stock option plans** provide incentives for portfolio-company managers, in virtually all venture capital deals. As part of these plans, the firm sets aside a large pool of stock to compensate current managers for superior performance and to attract talented new managers as the company grows.

APPLYING THE MODEL

Amazon.com provides an example of using stock options to motivate and compensate managers. At the time of the firm's IPO, no less than 10.8 million shares were reserved under two stock option plans. Over 4 million had already been allocated to the firm's executives.

This listing of covenants is by no means comprehensive. Other common provisions describe the conditions for additional financing and the payoffs to entrepreneurs, if the VCs decide to hire new managers. However, the most fascinating and distinguishing feature of venture capital contracts is unquestionably their almost exclusive reliance on convertible securities (particularly convertible preferred stock) as the investment vehicle of choice.

participation rights
Agreements giving the venture capitalists the right to participate, on equal terms, in any sale of portfolio-company stock to third parties that the company's managers might arrange for themselves.

Why Venture Capitalists Use Convertible Securities

Most people assume that when VCs invest in a firm, they receive shares of common stock in exchange for their capital. In fact, venture capitalists almost always receive some type of convertible security instead, either convertible debt or, more frequently, convertible preferred stock. There are several reasons for this marked preference. First, it allows venture capitalists to exercise effective voting control over a portfolio company, without having to purchase a majority of that firm's common stock, which would be extremely expensive and would place far more of the firm's business risk on the venture group than on the entrepreneur. Because convertible debt or preferred stock is a distinct security class, contract terms and covenants, specific to that issue, are negotiable. Furthermore, because firms can create multiple classes of convertible debt or preferred stock, they can use these securities to construct extremely complex, sophisticated contracting arrangements with different investor groups.

repurchase rights
Give the venture capitalists the right to force the company to buy back (repurchase) the shares held by the VC.

stock option plans
Plans set up to provide stock options to newly-hired managers of portfolio companies in order to give them incentives to manage the company to create value.

Seniority offers a second reason why venture capitalists generally demand convertible debt or preferred stock rather than common stock. This places the VC ahead of the entrepreneur in a line of claimants on the firm's assets, should the firm not succeed. However, preferred stock or subordinated debt leaves the firm the option to issue senior debt, thereby preserving its borrowing capacity and making it easier for the firm to arrange trade credit or bank loans. The convertible securities held by VCs typically pay a very low dividend, suggesting that VCs use these securities for control reasons, rather than to generate steady cash flows.

Most important, convertible securities give VCs the right to participate in the upside when portfolio companies succeed, just as common shareholders do. In fact, VCs usually convert their convertible debt and preferred stock to common equity before venture-backed companies execute initial public offerings, to lock in their equity stakes and to present an uncluttered balance sheet to prospective investors.

APPLYING THE MODEL

The venture capitalists backing Amazon.com structured their entire investment (in June 1996) as convertible preferred stock, for which they paid $14.05 per share. Two of the firm's directors, who purchased convertible preferred stock in a much smaller subsequent financing round, in early 1997, paid $40 per share.

The Pricing of Venture Capital Investments

As you might expect, valuing the types of young, rapidly growing companies that venture capital firms finance presents a huge challenge. How do VCs value portfolio companies? The empirical evidence suggests that VCs use a wide variety of valuation methods, and valuations can be rather idiosyncratic from one deal to the next. As in all other areas of financial valuation, however, venture capitalists employ the basic valuation process of investing in those ventures where the expected marginal benefit exceeds the marginal cost. The key distinction of VC investment is that the expected return must be quite high because the risk of most VC investments is also much higher than in other areas. The following example illustrates one common valuation approach. Assume that the president and founder of a start-up company, Internet Concepts Corporation (ICC), approaches a technology-oriented venture capital fund, for $5 million in new funding, to support her firm's rapid growth. After intense negotiations, the parties agree that ICC is currently worth $10 million. The risk of the firm is such that the venture capitalist is entitled to a 50 percent compound annual (expected) return. To arrive at the $10 million estimate, the VC may compare the portfolio company's sales (or earnings, if there are any) with those of similar public companies and apply a pricing multiple. Both parties agree that ICC should plan to execute an IPO in five years. At that time, the firm is expected to have net profits of $4 million and to sell at a price/earnings ratio of 20, which will put the company's value (*Exp MV*) at $80 million. To calculate the value of its stake in the portfolio company, as of the IPO date, the VC uses basic future-value techniques, as described in Equation 14.1. The initial investment, $\$A$, equals $5 million; the required rate of return, r, is 50 percent; and the time horizon, n, is five years.

$$FV = A(1+r)^n = \$5,000,000(1.50)^5 = \$5,000,000(7.6) = \$38,000,000 \quad \text{(Eq. 14.1)}$$

To determine what fraction of ICC's equity that it will receive now, the VC divides the future value of its stake by ICC's expected IPO market valuation:

$$Equity\ fraction = FV \div Exp\ MV = \$38{,}000{,}000 \div \$80{,}000{,}000 = 0.475 \quad \text{(Eq. 14.2)}$$

This means that the venture capital fund will receive 47.5 percent of ICC's equity in exchange for its $5 million investment. If the VC agrees to accept a lower return, about 40 percent, the VC's expected IPO payoff will be $26.9 million, and the VC would require a 33.6 percent equity stake up front to achieve this return. When the VC requires a higher return, the entrepreneur must relinquish a larger fraction of the firm.

The Profitability of Venture Capital Investments

The data on venture capital returns are rather sketchy, but clearly, investments made by venture capital funds during the middle 1990s earned average compound annual returns of up to 30 percent. There have been repeated examples of boom-and-bust investment cycles, in which high realized returns prompt excessive new capital inflows into venture capital funds, which in turn cause returns to drop sharply over the next harvest cycle. Although 30 percent annual returns were typical for venture capital funds during the late 1970s and early 1980s, Figure 14.3 shows that returns fell short of 30 percent every year from 1984 to 1994. Returns were again at target levels in 1995 and 1996, and then surged to nearly 150 percent in 1999. However, as Table 14.4 demonstrates, returns for the three years that followed the collapse of the Nasdaq market in March 2000 were negative; they only turned positive again during 2003. The first column of the table shows the one-year returns on various types of venture capital investments during 2003. The other columns list average annual returns over longer horizons, ending December 31, 2003. A key question is whether the massive influx of new venture capital that occurred during the 1998–2000 period will have the same negative impact on returns over the next few years.

SMART IDEAS VIDEO

Antoinette Schoar, MIT

"We find that there's a very large amount of variation in returns of different funds."

See the entire interview at **SMARTFinance**

A strong positive correlation exists between venture returns and returns on small stock mutual funds. It highlights the importance of a healthy public stock market for new ventures, in general, and for initial public offerings, in particular.

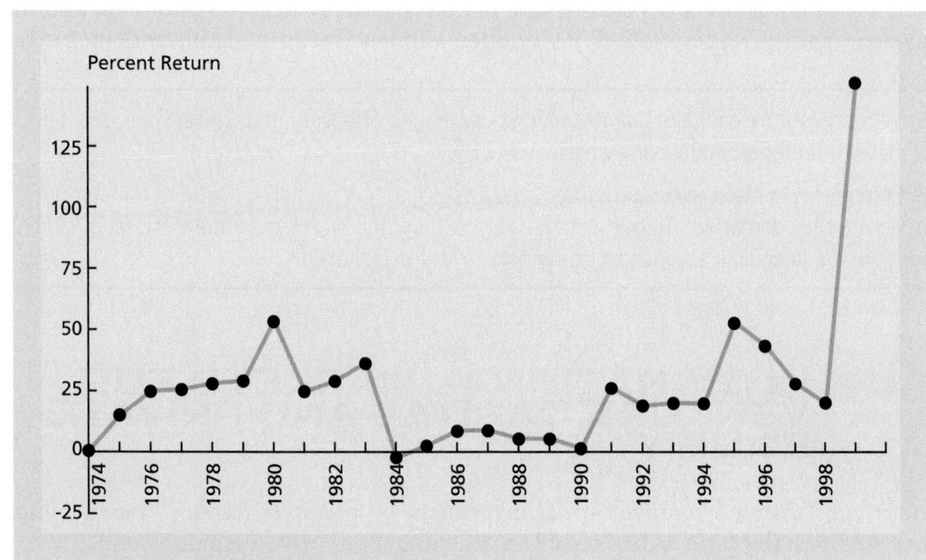

Figure 14.3
Average Annual Rate of Return to Investors in U.S Venture Capital Funds, 1974–1999

Source: Data from Venture Economics, as reported in Figure 2 of Paul Gompers and Josh Lerner, "The Venture Capital Revolution," Journal of Economic Perspectives *15 (Spring 2001), pp. 145–168.*

Table 14.4
U.S. Venture Capital and Private-Equity Returns by Fund Type and Investment Horizons

Investment Horizon Returns (Average Annual Pooled IRR), as of December 30, 2003

Source: National Venture Capital Association http://www.nvca.com.

Fund Type	1 year	3 year	5 year	10 year	20 year
Early/seed stage	−7.0%	−23.3%	54.9%	37.0%	19.1%
Balanced	11.0	−13.9	19.4	20.4	13.3
Later stage	25.4	−18.8	3.5	17.0	13.8
All venture	**8.1%**	**−18.9%**	**22.8%**	**25.4%**	**15.5%**
All buyouts	24.1	−2.1	2.2	7.8	12.4
Mezzanine	5.7	1.1	5.6	7.3	9.6
All private equity	**18.3%**	**−7.0%**	**6.8%**	**12.7%**	**13.6%**
NASDAQ	50.0%	−6.7%	−1.8%	9.9%	12.4%
S&P 500	26.4	−5.6	−2.0	9.1	12.9

Because VCs prefer to exit via an IPO, and because "recycled" returns partially flow into new venture investments, any decline in the stock market's appetite for new issues has an immediate negative effect on the venture capital industry.

Exit Strategies Employed by Venture Capitalists

redemption option
Option for venture capitalists to sell a company back to its entrepreneur or founders.

VCs are not long-term equity investors. They seek to add value to a private company and then to harvest their investment. VCs use three principal methods to exit an investment: (1) through an initial public offering of shares to outside investors; (2) through a sale of the portfolio company directly to another company; or (3) through selling the company back to the entrepreneur/founders, known as the **redemption option**. IPOs are by far the most profitable and visible option for the venture capitalists. During 1990–2000, IPOs were executed on U.S. capital markets by 5,803 companies and raised $419.5 billion. The annual volume of all kinds of IPOs declined dramatically during 2001–2003, but the IPO market showed some flickers of life during the first quarter of 2004. Thirteen venture-capital-backed IPOs raised $2.72 billion during that three-month period, the highest total since the third quarter of 2000.

SMART PRACTICES VIDEO

David Haeberle, Chief Executive Officer, Command Equity Group

"If you make 10 investments as a fund, you're probably going to see 5 write-offs."

See the entire interview at **SMARTFinance**

Perhaps surprisingly, VCs do not exit immediately at the time of an IPO. Instead, they retain shares for several months, or even years, and then typically distribute shares back to the limited partners, rather than sell the shares on the open market. The distributions usually occur after a period of sharply rising stock prices, and the average stock-price response to distribution announcements is significantly negative.

CONCEPT REVIEW QUESTIONS

5. Why do venture capitalists almost always use *staged financing* and convertible securities to finance entrepreneurial companies?

6. Entrepreneurs often refer to venture capitalists as "vulture capitalists," due to the amount of equity they demand before investing. Do you think the standard venture capital pricing formula is a justifiable compensation for risk, or is it exploitative?

14.4 INTERNATIONAL MARKETS FOR VENTURE CAPITAL AND PRIVATE EQUITY

Although "classic" venture capital investment by privately financed partnerships has traditionally been a distinctly U.S. phenomenon, private-equity financing has long been an established financial specialty in other developed countries, especially in Western Europe. Because Europe is the birthplace of both the industrial revolution and modern capitalism, it is not surprising that a highly sophisticated method of funneling growth capital to private (often family-owned) businesses evolved there. In fact, private-equity fund-raising in Europe compared quite well with that in the United States, until 1997, and showed far less annual variability. The chief differences between European and American venture capital lie in (1) the principal sources of funds for venture capital investing, (2) the organization of the venture funds themselves, (3) the development stage of the portfolio companies able to attract venture financing, and (4) the principal method of harvesting venture capital investments. These differences are all related and help explain why the volatility of venture capital investment in the United States is so much higher than in Europe.

There is a difference in the definition of the term "venture capital" in Europe, as opposed to the United States. American commentators tend to refer to all professionally managed, equity-based investments in private, entrepreneurial growth companies as venture capital. European commentators apply the term only to early- and expansion-stage financing. Later-stage investments and funding for management buyouts are called "private-equity investment" in Europe. Where necessary, we maintain this distinction. In general, we refer to both venture capital and private-equity investment as simply "European venture capital."

European Venture Capital and Private-Equity Fund-Raising and Investment

As in the United States, venture capital fund-raising and investment in Europe has grown rapidly since the mid-1990s. Figure 14.4 describes the growth in total private-equity investment over the period 1989–2003. According to a

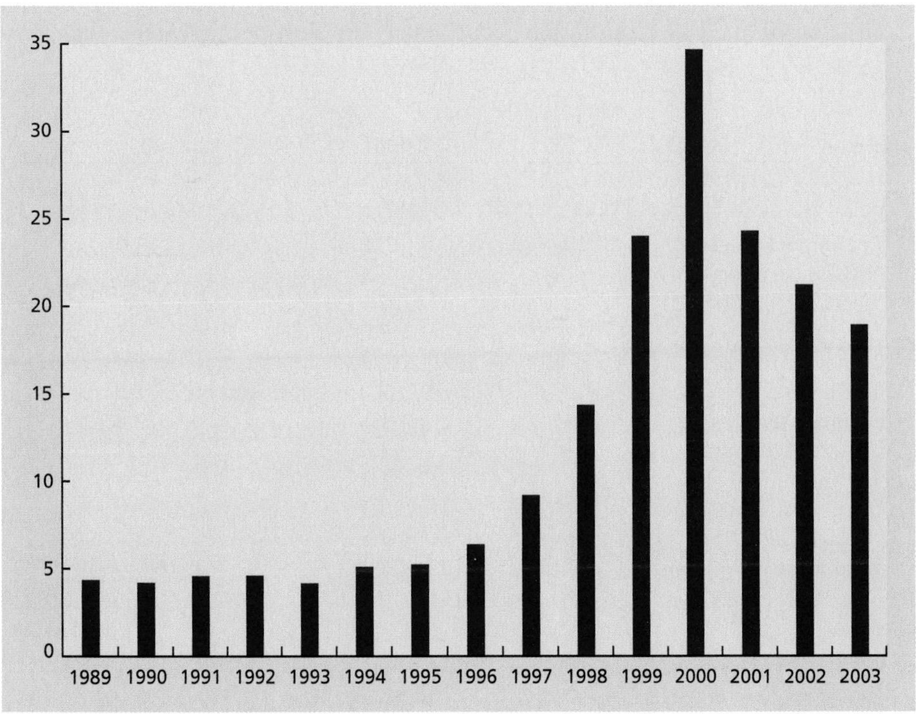

Figure 14.4
European Private-Equity Investment, 1989–2003

In € Billions

Source: European Private Equity and Venture Capital Association Web site http://www.evca.com.

survey of pan-European private-equity and venture capital activity, conducted for the European Private Equity & Venture Capital Association by PricewaterhouseCoopers, total investment grew from a stable level of about €5 billion per year, during the 1989–1996 period, to €25 billion in 1999 and €34.9 billion (invested in some 10,440 companies) in 2000. Disbursements dropped significantly to €19.0 billion during 2003. But this 46 percent decline was far less than the 82 percent decline in U.S. venture capital investment between 2000 and 2003. Fund-raising has grown even more dramatically over the past seven years—rising from about €5 billion during 1995, to nearly €48 billion in 2000, before falling to €17.3 billion in 2003. Since the early 1980s, a cumulative total of more than €175 billion has been raised for investment in European private equity.

Historically, European venture capital has been funneled to different industries and different types of companies than is the norm for the United States, though this has been changing lately. As recently as 1996, less than one fourth of European venture capital went into high-technology investments. In 2001, the fraction allocated to high-tech industries topped 55 percent, but this dropped back to about one third in 2003. Table 14.5 describes the industry breakdown of European private-equity investments in technology, for the years 2000 and 2003. As in the United States, over two thirds of European high-tech venture capital investment is funneled into computers and communications businesses.

In one important respect, venture capital funding patterns in Europe and in the United States have long been similar. Both are highly concentrated geographically. Some 38 percent of year-2002's total investment was targeted at British companies. After Britain came France, Italy, and Germany, which received 22, 10.5, and 9.7 percent of European venture capital investment, respectively.

The Changing Sources of Funding for European Venture Capital. The sourcing of European venture capital funds differs from that of its U.S. counterparts, primarily in Europe's greater reliance on

Table 14.5
European Private-Equity Investment by Industry, 2000 and 2003

Source: European Venture Capital Association http://www.evca.com.

Sector	2000	2003
Consumer related	18.5%	19.4%
Industrial products and services	10.0	6.8
Communications	13.8	16.9
Nonfinancial services	5.6	9.8
Medical/health related	7.9	6.0
Other manufacturing	9.3	7.7
Computer related	13.3	6.0
Biotechnology	2.9	2.3
Financial services	1.8	2.4
Chemicals and materials	2.9	2.3
Transportation	1.2	5.3
Other electronics related	3.9	1.9
Construction	1.8	3.4
Total value (€ Millions)	**€34,926**	**€29,096**

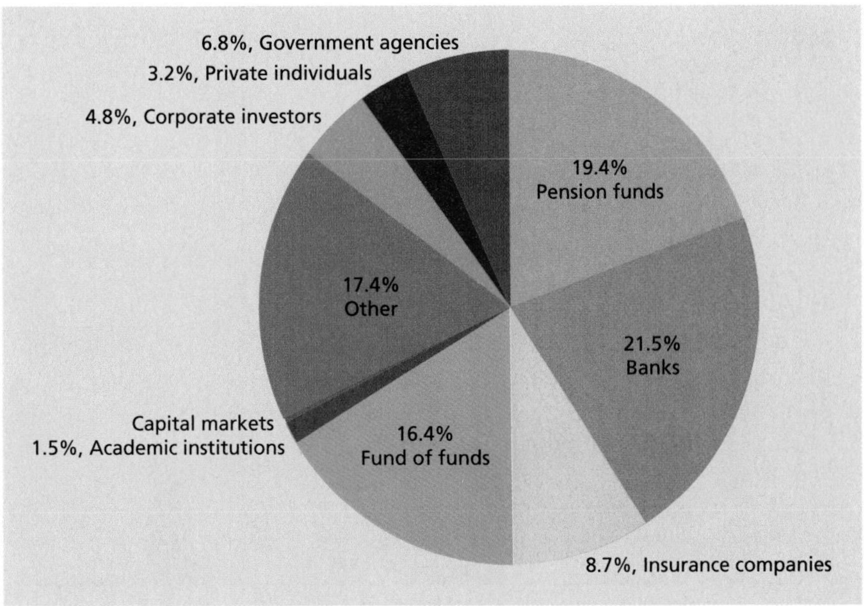

Figure 14.5
European Private-Equity Raised by Type of Investor, Year 2003

€29.096 Billion Total Investment

Source: PriceWaterhouseCoopers and European Private Equity and Venture Capital Association, as reported on the EVCA Web site http://www.evca.com.

financial institutions. As shown in Figure 14.5, banks, insurance companies, and other corporate investors accounted for almost half (35.0%) of all European venture funding in 2003, whereas pension fund money represents less than one fifth (19.4%) of total fund-raising. Government agencies account for 6.8 percent of total capital raised.

For a mix of cultural and legal reasons, European venture capital funds are rarely, if ever, organized according to the U.S. model. Instead, funds are generally organized as investment companies under various national laws. Their approach to dealing with portfolio companies is much more akin to the reactive style of U.S. mutual fund managers than to the proactive style of America's venture capitalists. The relative lack of a vibrant entrepreneurial high-technology sector in Europe also hampers continental VCs' efforts to attract technologically savvy fund managers or entrepreneur/founders who want to use their expertise to grow new firms.

European Venture Capital Investment by Stage of Company Development. Partly for the reasons previously detailed, European venture capital has historically been less focused on early-stage investments than has America's. As in other areas, however, this is changing fast. The breakdown of European venture capital investment by stage of portfolio-company development for the years 1997, 2000, and 2003 is presented in Figure 14.6. Buyouts accounted for more than 40 percent of European private-equity investment during 1997 and 2000, and then surged to 73.6 percent of 2003's total investment. After spiking upwards during the 1997–2001 period, early-stage companies now attract less than 10 percent of total investment. This figure is roughly half the fraction of U.S. venture capital investment targeted at early-stage companies.

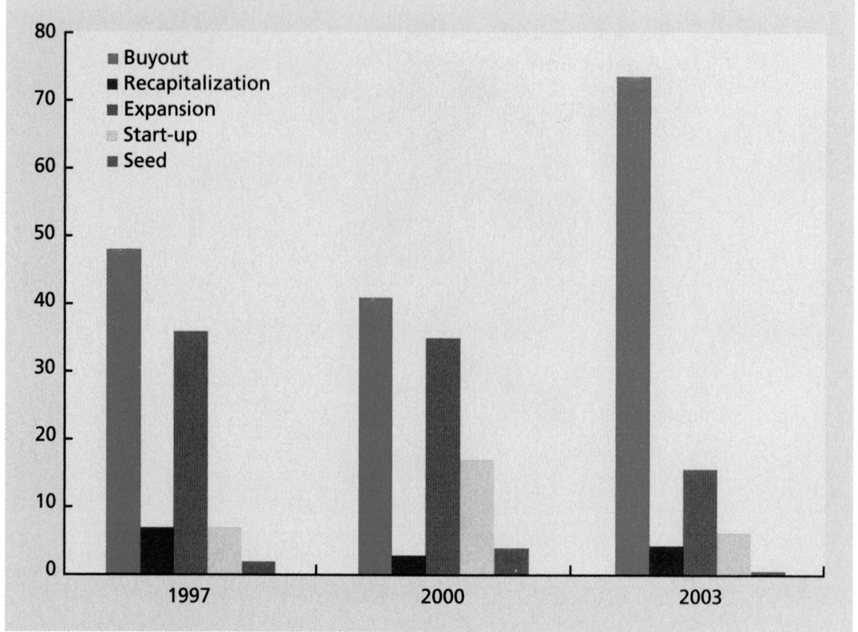

Figure 14.6
Distribution of European Private-Equity Investment by Stage of Company Development, as Percent of Total Investment, 1997–2003

Source: European Private Equity and Venture Capital Association http://www.evca.com.

Investment Returns for European Venture Capital Investments. Yet another historical difference between U.S. and European venture capital was in the mostly disappointing returns European private-equity investors earned. Figure 14.7 clearly shows that European venture funds performed abysmally over the 1984–1994 period, except during 1987. After 1995, however, European venture fund returns steadily rose and were truly stellar during the period from 1997 to year-end 2000. During this period, venture fund returns beat all other types of private-equity funds. They were much higher than the returns earned by investors in publicly traded European stocks, which had a dismal 2000. Unfortunately, the collapse of Europe's public stock markets, after March 2000, hurt measured returns, an ill omen for future venture capital returns.

Exit Strategies of European Venture Capitalists. One of the greatest disappointments of European policymakers, wanting to duplicate the success of the United States in high-technology development, has been the continent's failure, until very recently, to establish a large liquid market for the stock of entrepreneurial growth firms. Many national stock markets exist, and these collectively rival U.S. exchanges in total capitalization of listed companies. However, no European market emerged as a serious alternative to the Nasdaq or the NYSE in the United States. There was no market for initial public offerings until the German Neuer Markt, the pan-European Easdaq, and other markets, such as France's Nouveau Marche, reached critical mass in the late 1990s. This had a direct effect on the exit strategies that European venture capitalists followed in harvesting their investments in portfolio companies.

Whereas IPOs have long been the preferred method of exit for U.S. venture funds, public offerings accounted for only 21 percent of European venture capital divestments in 1996, with comparable fractions in earlier years. The number of European IPOs surged after these markets matured, especially the Neuer Markt,

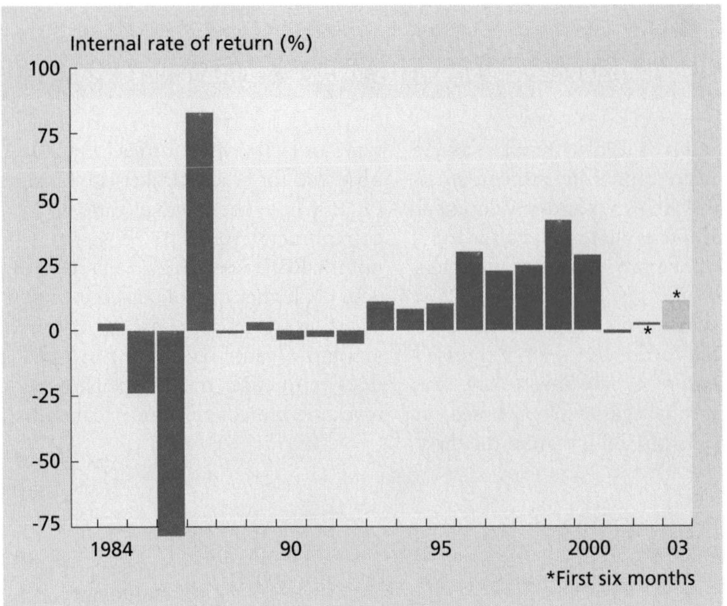

Figure 14.7
Investment Returns to Categories of European Private-Equity Investment, 1984–2003

Five-Year Rolling Internal Rate of Return

Source: Thomson Financial and Ernst & Young, as reported in Deborah Brewster, "Google IPO Offers Hope for Private Equity Funds, Financial Times *(December 1, 2003), p. 27.*

which had attracted over 300 listings by early 2000. Unfortunately, the Neuer Markt collapsed almost as fast as it took off. By January 2003, the market's total capitalization had fallen by over 95 percent from its March 2000 peak, amid a series of accounting scandals and great acrimony between entrepreneurs, exchange officials, and investors. The Neuer Markt was officially shut down in June 2003. The European IPO market is now effectively closed to all but the most profitable and established firms. A few European (and many Israeli) technology companies have been able to execute IPOs on U.S markets. Unfortunately, this is not an option for most entrepreneurial companies.

Venture Capital Markets Outside the United States and Western Europe

The key venture capital markets outside the United States and Western Europe are Canada, Israel, Japan, China, and India.[6] The venture capital industries of Israel and Canada differ dramatically from other advanced countries. Canadian government policies led to its venture capital system being based on funds sponsored by labor unions. Rapid growth in Canada's VC market during the late 1990s, however, weakened the union funds' grip on VC funding. Total investment grew at a compound annual rate of 60 percent between 1994 and 2000. In 2000, Canada was the world's fifth largest recipient of VC financing and attracted almost as much investment ($4.3 billion versus $4.4 billion) as Germany, a nation five times larger. This preeminence was not to last, however. By 2002, Canada had fallen to ninth place overall, having attracted only $1.57 billion in total private-equity investment, though it still ranked fourth in high-tech investment. As the Comparative Corporate Finance feature discusses, the fact that Canada has an English common law legal system is a key reason why its venture capital industry has prospered historically.

---

6. This section draws heavily on material presented by one of the authors in a recently published paper. See William L. Megginson, "Towards a Global Model for Venture Capital?" *Journal of Applied Corporate Finance* 16 (Winter 2004), pp. 89–107. This article is currently (July 2004) also posted on the PriceWaterhouseCoopers *MoneyTree*™ Web site at http://www.pwcmoneytree.com/moneytree/index.jsp.

COMPARATIVE CORPORATE FINANCE

Does a Nation's Legal System Influence the Size of Its Venture Capital Industry?

This table details how a country's legal system effects the relative importance of venture capital investment, stock market capitalization, and research-and-development spending for the twenty countries that received the most VC investment during 2002. Family of legal origin refers to the four main legal families (English common law, French civil law, German law, and Scandinavian law) that the nation's commercial code is based on. Expressed as a fraction of GDP, venture capital investment was much higher in countries with legal systems, based on English common law (0.47% of GDP), than in the three types of civil law countries (0.26%). A similar pattern is observed for stock market capitalization as a percent of GDP, where the average ratio is 110.64% of GDP, in common law, versus 68.65%, in civil law countries, but not for R&D spending as a percent of GDP. This ratio is actually higher in civil law countries, which suggests that a nation's legal system does not influence the relative amount of national output invested in research, but it does influence the propensity to channel research investment through venture capitalists.

Country	Family of legal origin	Venture capital and private-equity investment: $US Billion	Venture capital and private-equity investment: % of GDP	Stock market capitalization as a % of GDP	R&D spending as a % of GDP
Israel	English common law	$ 0.98	0.951	39.59	2.72
United Kingdom	English common law	9.58	0.616	115.80	1.90
United States	English common law	62.68	0.600	105.84	2.82
Sweden	Scandinavian law/Civil	1.39	0.584	75.26	4.27
Hong Kong SAR	English common law	0.75	0.460	284.08	0.21
Korea	German law/Civil	1.95	0.416	45.98	2.96
France	French civil law	5.53	0.390	104.02	2.20
Netherlands	French civil law	1.63	0.388	165.87	1.94
South Africa	English common law	0.37	0.356	112.06	0.70
Finland	Scandinavian law/Civil	0.43	0.326	105.17	3.40
Indonesia	French civil law	0.56	0.324	17.38	0.65
Australia	English common law	1.21	0.308	96.71	1.53
India	English common law	1.05	0.228	52.79	0.50
Canada	English common law	1.57	0.215	78.22	1.94
Italy	French civil law	2.48	0.209	40.23	1.07
Spain	French civil law	0.92	0.140	70.57	0.96
Belgium	French civil law	0.34	0.137	74.90	1.96
Germany	German law/Civil	2.37	0.120	34.53	2.49
Japan	German law/Civil	2.38	0.060	52.44	3.09
China	German law/Civil	0.35	0.028	37.44	4.85
Average, English common law countries		—	0.47%	110.64%	**1.60%**
Average, all civil law countries		—	0.26%	68.65%	**2.10%**

Sources: 1. GDP data, Institute for International Management World Competitiveness 2003 (http://www01.imd.ch/documents/wcy/content/GDP.pdf). 2. Venture Capital Investment data, PricewaterhouseCoopers (http://www.pwcmoneytree.com/moneytree/pdfs/gpe_report_2003.pdf).3. Stock Market Capitalization data, World Federation of Exchanges (http://www.world-echanges.org), except France, Netherlands, and Belgium, whose data are the estimates from Euronext. 4. R&D Spending data, OECD Statistics (http://www.oecd.org), except India, Israel, Hong Kong, Indonesia, South Africa, and China, whose data are from national statistical agencies.

In a relative sense, Israel has achieved the greatest success in venture capital and private equity. It was the sixth largest recipient of PE funding in 2000 (receiving $3.2 billion). It was the world's largest recipient, if VC financing is expressed as a percent of GDP (3.17%). Even during 2002, Israel attracted almost $1 billion and remained the leader, if private-equity investment is expressed as a percentage of GDP (0.95%). Part of Israel's success can be traced to deliberate policy decisions in the early 1990s by the Likud government, which took concrete steps to commercialize defense-related technology developed with public funding. The influx of trained engineers and scientists from the former Soviet Union also helped, as did the pioneering steps taken by Israeli entrepreneurs to go public in the United States, opening a path to public markets others could and did follow.

Venture capital fund-raising and investment in Asia grew significantly between 1995 and 2000, though much less rapidly than in Europe or the United States because of a moribund VC industry in Japan. Elsewhere in Asia, growth was more robust, although from a low base. Japan has a financial specialty referred to as "venture capital," but most of the firms involved are commercial or investment bank subsidiaries that make few truly entrepreneurial investments. Venture capital shows no real sign of taking root in Japan, and the world's second largest economy attracted only $2.38 billion (0.06% of GDP) in venture funding in 2002. Although China is the fastest-growing major economy in the world, venture capital and private equity play very little role in its development. The country lacks the basic legal infrastructure needed to support a vibrant VC market, and the Chinese stock markets remain inefficient and politicized.

In many ways, India is the most interesting and promising private-equity market in the world today. It ranked twelfth overall in total investment during 2002, up from nineteenth in 2000. The total amount invested ($1.05 billion) was more than twice that of 2000. India's history, as a former British colony, gave it a common law legal system, multiple stock exchanges, and a heritage of English as the native tongue of its educated classes. Since 1991, India's rapid economic development has been propelled both by the macroeconomic and market opening reforms adopted that year and by relatively large inflows of foreign investment, which were, in turn, attracted by India's vast potential and by the quality of the graduates of its elite universities and technical institutes. Crucially, much of India's growth has been in the IT sector, which is the traditional target of true venture capital investment. For all these reasons, India should become one of the five leading venture capital markets by the end of this decade.

What about venture capital investment in emerging markets, besides China and India? A recent study by Josh Lerner and Antoinette Schoar presents an empirical analysis of the transaction structures employed by private-equity investors in developing countries.[7] From a sample of 210 transactions, they find that convertible securities are rarely used in developing countries. Investors are much more likely to invest in traditional, low-tech industries in emerging markets than are American venture capitalists. Lerner and Schoar also find that a nation's legal system significantly effects the transaction structure chosen for investments. Investors in countries with French or socialist legal systems show much greater determination to achieve majority voting control than do investors in English common law countries.

---

7. See Josh Lerner and Antoinette Schoar, "Transaction Structures in the Developing World: Evidence from Private Equity," Working Paper, Harvard University and MIT (December 2003).

CONCEPT REVIEW QUESTIONS

7. Why do you think European governments and stock exchanges want to promote a vibrant entrepreneurial sector? Can you think of any competitive advantages that may accrue to Europe, due to its relatively late start in developing IPO markets?

8. Compare some of the competitive strengths and weaknesses of venture capital, as practiced in Europe, Japan, and Canada, with those of the United States.

9. How has the European venture capital industry changed over the past five years? Do you think these changes have made it more or less competitive and efficient?

10. What type of growth in venture capital funding and investment have China and India experienced during recent years? What is their future outlook for venture capital growth?

14.5 SUMMARY AND CONCLUSIONS

- Entrepreneurial finance requires specialized financial management skills because entrepreneurial growth companies are unlike other private or publicly traded companies. In particular, EGCs must finance much higher asset growth rates than other firms and tap external financial markets much more frequently.
- In addition to providing risk capital to entrepreneurial growth firms, professional venture capitalists (VCs) provide managerial oversight, coupled with technical and business advice, assistance in developing and launching new products, and valuable help recruiting experienced management talent.
- U.S. venture capital investments are highly concentrated, both geographically and industrially. Furthermore, the most successful venture capital funds are almost always organized as limited partnerships and follow distinctive investment strategies (staged investment) using unique financial instruments (convertible preferred stock).
- U.S. venture capitalists endeavor to make intermediate-term (3–7 years), high-risk investments in entrepreneurial growth firms. Then, they exit these investments, either by selling the portfolio companies to another firm or (preferably) by executing an initial public offering. During recent years, VCs have, on average, achieved their target compound annual returns of over 30 percent.
- Phenomenal growth in venture capital fund-raising and investment has occurred over the past decade in the United States, Western Europe, and in certain Asian countries, but not in Japan or in most developing countries. In recent years, the two largest venture capital markets, the United States and Europe, have seen significant convergence in contracting practices, investment patterns, and returns.
- The funding of European venture capital is moving rapidly toward greater reliance on pension funds (rather than commercial banks). Today, a higher fraction of European venture capital investment is being targeted toward early-stage investment than in the past. More of Europe's total funding is also being directed toward high technology, rather than management buyouts, again mirroring practices in the United States.

- After a long period of relative underperformance, returns on European private-equity investment have increased steadily in recent years. However, the recent collapse of Germany's Neuer Markt has temporarily closed what once was the most promising exit route for European venture capitalists.
- Although Canada and Israel successfully promoted venture capital funding and investment, growth in venture capital in Asia, Latin America, and Africa has lagged behind that of Europe and North America. Venture capital funding and investment in developing countries has been growing from its low base during recent years.

SELF-TEST PROBLEMS

Answers to Self-Test Problems appear in Appendix D at back of book. Answers to the Concept Review Questions throughout the chapter appear at http://megginson.swlearning.com.

ST14-1. You are seeking $1.5 million from a venture capitalist to finance the launch of your on-line financial search engine. You and the VC agree that your venture is currently worth $3 million. When the company goes public in an IPO in five years, it is expected to have a market capitalization of $20 million. Given the company's stage of development, the VC requires a 50 percent return on investment. What fraction of the firm will the VC receive in exchange for its $1.5 million investment in your company?

ST14-2. An entrepreneur seeks $12 million from a VC fund. The entrepreneur and fund managers agree that the entrepreneur's venture is currently worth $30 million and that the company is likely to be ready to go public in four years. At that time, the company is expected to have a net income of $9 million. Comparable firms are expected to be selling at a price/earnings ratio of 25. Given the company's stage of development, the venture capital fund managers require a 40 percent compound annual return on their investment. What fraction of the firm will the fund receive in exchange for its $12 million investment?

ST14-3. Suppose that six out of ten investments, made by a VC fund, are a total loss, meaning that the return on each of them is –100 percent. Of the remaining investments, three break even, earning a 0 percent return. One investment pays off spectacularly and earns a 650 percent return. What is the realized return on the VC fund's overall portfolio?

INTERNET RESOURCES

Note: *For updates to links, please go to the book's Web site at* http://megginson.swlearning.com.

http://www.nvca.com—Web site of the National Venture Capital Association, which presents a wide range of data and provides reports about the U.S. venture capital industry, much of it current

http://www.pwcmoneytree.com—Web site of PricewaterhouseCoopers *MoneyTree*™, which presents details about the company's quarterly and annual venture capital surveys, and offers the company's electronic publication, *Global Private Equity Report,* which can be downloaded

http://www.evca.com—Web site of the European Venture Capital & Private Equity Association, which presents detailed information about Europe's venture capital industry and provides numerous reports about the European venture capital scene

KEY TERMS

angel capitalists
cancellation option
corporate venture capital funds
demand registration rights
entrepreneurial finance
entrepreneurial growth companies (EGCs)
financial venture capital funds
institutional venture capital funds
negative covenants
ownership right agreements
participation rights
positive covenants
ratchet provisions
redemption option
repurchase rights
small business investment companies (SBICs)
staged financing
stock option plans
venture capital
venture capital limited partnerships

QUESTIONS AND PROBLEMS

Q14-1. List and describe the key financial differences between entrepreneurial growth companies and large publicly traded firms?

Q14-2. How does the financing of entrepreneurial growth companies differ from that of most firms in mature industries? How does the concept of "bootstrap finance" relate to this difference?

Q14-3. What is an *angel capitalist?* How do the financing techniques used by angels differ from those used by professional venture capitalists?

Q14-4. Distinguish between the four basic types of venture capital funds. Which type has emerged as the dominant organizational form? Why?

Q14-5. What are some of the common characteristics of those entrepreneurial growth companies that are able to attract venture capital investment? In which industries and states is the majority of venture capital invested?

Q14-6. What is meant by early-stage and later-stage venture capital investment? What proportions of venture capital have been allocated between the two in recent years? Which stage requires a higher expected return? Why?

Q14-7. What are the responsibilities and typical payoff for a general partner in a venture capital limited partnership?

Q14-8. Distinguish between *positive covenants* and *negative covenants* in venture capital investment contracts. List and describe some of the more popular covenants found in these contracts.

Q14-9. What is the most popular form of financing (or security type) required by venture capitalists in return for their investment? Why is this form of financing optimal for both the entrepreneur and the venture capitalist?

Q14-10. List the major differences between venture capital financing in the United States and in Western Europe. What major changes have been occurring recently in the European venture capital industry?

Q14-11. Why is a vibrant IPO market considered vital to the success of a nation's venture capital industry? What effect is the collapse of Germany's Neuer Markt likely to have on the European venture capital industry?

Q14-12. Describe the recent levels of venture capital activity in Canada, Israel, Asia, and developing countries. What is the outlook for each of them?

PROBLEMS

P14-1. Access the National Venture Capital Association Web site at http://www.nvca.com. Update Tables 14.2 and 14.4, as well as Figures 14.1 and 14.2, using the most recent data available. What general trends, do you see, regarding sources of venture capital funding and patterns of investing from this Web site and its links?

P14-2. An entrepreneur seeks $4 million from a venture capitalist. They agree that the entrepreneur's venture is currently worth $12 million. When the company goes public in an IPO in three years, it is expected to have a market capitalization of $70 million. Given the company's stage of development, the VC requires a 40 percent return on investment. What fraction of the firm will the VC receive in exchange for its $4 million investment?

P14-3. An entrepreneur seeks $10 million from a VC fund. The entrepreneur and fund managers agree that the entrepreneur's venture is currently worth $25 million and that the company is likely to be ready to go public in five years. At that time, the company is expected to have a net income of $7.5 million. Comparable firms are expected to be selling at a price/earnings ratio of 30. Given the company's stage of development, the venture capital fund managers require a 50 percent compound annual return on their investment. What fraction of the firm will the fund receive in exchange for its $10 million investment?

P14-4. Five years ago, the venture capital fund Techno Fund II made a $4 million investment in Optical Fibers Corporation and in return received 1 million shares representing 20 percent of Optical Fibers' equity. Optical Fibers is now planning an initial public offering in which it will sell 1 million newly created shares for $50 per share. Techno has chosen to exercise its demand registration rights and will sell its shares—alongside the newly created shares—in Optical Fibers' IPO. The investment banks underwriting Optical Fibers' IPO will charge a 7 percent underwriting spread, so both the firm and Techno Fund II will receive 93 percent of the $50 per-share offer price. Assuming the IPO is successful, calculate the compound annual return that Techno will have earned on its investment.

P14-5. Six years ago, High-Tech Fund III made a $3 million investment in Internet Printing Company (IPC) and received 2 million shares of series A convertible preferred stock. Each of these shares is convertible into two shares of IPC common stock. Three years later, High-Tech III participated in a second round of financing for IPC and received 3 million shares of series B convertible preferred stock in exchange for a $15 million investment. Each series B share is convertible into one share of IPC common stock. Internet Printing Company is now planning an IPO, but prior to this announcement, the company will convert all its outstanding convertible preferred shares into common stock. After conversion, IPC will have 20 million common shares outstanding and will create another 2 million common shares for sale in the IPO. The underwriter handling IPC's initial offering expects to sell these new shares for $45 each but has prohibited existing shareholders from selling any of their stock in the IPO. The underwriter will keep 7 percent of the offer as an underwriting discount. Assume that the IPO is successful and that IPC shares sell for $60 each, immediately after the offering.

a. Calculate the total number of IPC common shares that High-Tech III will own after the IPO. What fraction of IPC's total outstanding common stock does this represent?

b. Using the post-issue market price for IPC shares, calculate the (unrealized) compound annual return that High-Tech III earned on its original, and subsequent investments, in IPC stock.

c. Now assume that the second-round IPC financing had been made under much less favorable conditions and that High-Tech III paid only $1 million, instead of $15 million, for the 3 million series B shares. Assuming that all the other features of IPC's initial offering, described above, hold true, calculate the (unrealized) compound annual return that High-Tech III earned on this second investment in IPC stock.

P14-6. Suppose that five out of ten investments made by a VC fund are a total loss, meaning that the return on each of them is –100 percent. Of the ten investments, three break even, earning a 0 percent return. If the VC fund's expected return equals 50 percent, what rate of return must it earn on the two most successful deals to achieve a portfolio return equal to expectations?

P14-7. Access the European Private Equity & Venture Capital Association Web site at http://www.evca.com. Update Table 14.5 and Figures 14.4, 14.5, and 14.6, using the most recent data available. What general trends, do you see, regarding sources of venture capital funding and patterns of investing from this Web site and its links?

MINICASE

Entrepreneurial Finance and Venture Capital

Through your financial services firm, Vestin Capital, Incorporated, you have raised a pool of money from clients. You intend to invest it in new business opportunities. To prepare for this endeavor, you decide to answer the following questions.

ASSIGNMENT

1. What are some of the challenges of financing entrepreneurial growth companies?
2. What are the different types of venture capital funds?
3. What are some choices for organizing a venture capital firm?
4. In what ways should a venture capital firm structure its investments?
5. Should venture capital firms use convertible securities?
6. What are some of the exit strategies that may be available to a venture capital firm?

Options, International Finance, and Risk Management

In the last three decades, no part of finance has witnessed as much innovation or explosive growth as the area covered in Part 5. In 1973, two economists published a paper which, for the first time, provided a formula for pricing an exotic financial instrument called an option. Almost immediately, an options exchange opened where traders could buy and sell these instruments. In just a few years, the number of venues trading options and the variety of options available exploded.

Over the same period, countries around the world began lowering trade barriers, resulting in a tremendous increase in exports and imports. Multinational corporations expanded their operations and their brands all over the world. But as a result of their expansion into foreign countries, which required firms to do business in many different currencies, these companies faced exposure to a new set of risks. Fortunately, options and other exotic securities provided just the tools that multinational corporations needed to manage these risks.

Chapter 15 provides an introduction to options. We begin with a simple explanation of option contracts, illustrating how option payoffs depend on, or derive from, the performance of an underlying stock. We explain how traders can use options to take risk or to reduce it, and we show how the price of an option depends on five key factors. Chapter 15 concludes with an introduction to the famous option-pricing model developed way back in 1973.

Chapter 16 deals with the unique financial issues that arise when firms do business in multiple currencies. The chapter starts with an explanation of how different countries establish an exchange rate policy. Next, the chapter illustrates how exchange rates are quoted and how exchange rates are linked across countries. Many factors influence currency values, including differences in inflation rates and interest rates in different countries. Chapter 16 shows how inflation and interest rates affect exchange rates and how smart traders may find profit opportunities when markets are not in equilibrium.

Chapter 17 addresses the issue of risk management. The risks that firms face on a daily basis are not limited to the exchange rate fluctuations discussed in Chapter 16, but include changes in the prices of commodities such as oil and changes in interest rates. Financial markets offer managers a vast array of instruments to help them reduce their firms' exposures to all of these sources of risk. Chapter 17 describes some of these instruments and illustrates how firms use them to reduce or eliminate exposure to certain risks.

Note: Solutions available in a booklet called *Solutions to Concept Review Questions and Self-Test Problems.*

CHAPTER 15

Options

OPENING FOCUS

Cuban Collars Yahoo!

In the late 1990s, newspapers were littered with stories of entrepreneurs who had made and lost huge fortunes throughout the rise and fall of "dot-com" stocks. One such story involved college classmates, Mark Cuban and Todd Wagner, who came up with the idea to broadcast sports events over the Internet so that fans, no matter where they lived, could track their favorite teams. Dubbing their company Broadcast.com, Cuban and Wagner quickly expanded their product offerings beyond sports, capturing media attention with events such as a Victoria's Secret Web cast and President Clinton's grand jury testimony. In just a few years, the company's revenues grew to almost $25 million. However, like most Internet stocks, Broadcast.com was not profitable. In 1998, the company lost $16.4 million, even though it attracted millions of "viewers" to its premier events.

In April 1999, Yahoo! agreed to acquire Broadcast.com for $5.7 billion in a stock swap. The deal's terms called for an exchange of each Broadcast.com common share for 0.77 Yahoo! shares. At the time, Yahoo! stock was worth nearly $200 per share. But in just one year, the stock market turned sour for Internet stocks. In September 2001, Yahoo! shares began a long slide that bottomed out at about $8. Many Yahoo! executives saw their wealth evaporate, but not Mark Cuban.

Sensing that the market values of Internet stocks had reached their peak, Cuban engaged in a little financial engineering. Cuban purchased put options on Yahoo! shares and simultaneously sold Yahoo! call options. The put options would enable Cuban to sell Yahoo! shares at a fixed price, at any time during the next three years, effectively providing him with an insurance policy against a collapse of Yahoo!'s stock price. To pay for the put options, Cuban sold call options, which would obligate him to sell his Yahoo! shares if the price rose high enough. In essence, Cuban was placing a "collar" around the value of his shares. If Yahoo! stock dropped, Cuban's put options would allow him to sell his shares at an above-market price. But if Yahoo! stock rose, Cuban would have to part with his shares for less than their full value. The collar allowed Cuban to eliminate downside risk, at the cost of giving up future gains on

Yahoo! shares. As it turned out, Cuban's move may have saved him more than $1 billion. With the cash he obtained as he sold his holdings of Yahoo! stock, Cuban purchased the NBA's Dallas Mavericks franchise, invested in high-definition TV, and pursued other business opportunities. Though Yahoo! stock rebounded from its all-time low, by early 2004, the shares were only worth about one quarter of their value when Cuban sold out.

Sources: http://www.akllp.com/EventsMediaCenter/ClientAlerts/Deriv/Deriv0802.html After Hitting It Big on Internet, Cuban Is Scoring in Basketball, *The Wall Street Journal*, April 22, 2003.

LEARNING OBJECTIVES

After reading this chapter you should be able to:

- Describe the basic features of call and put options;
- Construct payoff diagrams for individual options as well as portfolios of options and other securities;
- Explain qualitatively what factors are important in determining option prices;
- Calculate the price of an option, using the binomial model; and
- List several corporate finance applications of option pricing theory.

A bit of folk wisdom says, "Always keep your options open." This implies that choices have value. Having the right to do something is better than being obligated to do it. This chapter shows how to apply that intuition to financial instruments called options. In their most basic forms, options allow investors to buy or to sell an asset at a fixed price, for a given period of time. As the opening focus illustrates, having the right to sell shares at a fixed price can be extremely valuable, provided the price of the underlying stock moves in the right direction.

Many commentators see options merely as a form of legalized gambling for the rich. We strongly disagree with that perspective. Options exist because they provide real economic benefits that come in many different forms. First, options provide incentives for managers to take actions that increase their firms' stock prices, thereby increasing the wealth of shareholders. Abuses may occur when firms award excessive option grants, but we see this as a corporate governance problem, not a problem with options, per se.

Second, a wide variety of options exist, which allow holders the right to buy and to sell many different types of assets, not just shares of stock in a single company. Sometimes, trading the option is more cost effective than trading the underlying asset. For example, trading a stock index option, which grants the right to buy or to sell a portfolio of stocks such as the S&P 500, enables investors to avoid paying all of the transactions costs that would result from trading 500 individual stocks.

Third, firms use options to reduce their exposure to certain types of risk. Firms regularly buy and sell options to shelter their cash flows from movements in exchange rates, interest rates, and commodity prices. In that function, options resemble insurance much more than they resemble gambling.

Fourth, options facilitate the creation of innovative trading strategies, like the one adopted by Mark Cuban. If Yahoo! executives insisted on paying for their acquisition of Broadcast.com with Yahoo! stock rather than with cash, Mark Cuban and other Broadcast.com shareholders faced several alternatives. They could hold their Yahoo! shares, but doing so would subject them to the risk of a decline in Yahoo! stock. They could sell their shares, but selling would trigger capital gains taxes and maybe put downward pressure on Yahoo! stock. Alternatively, they could use options to protect their gains and sell their Yahoo! shares at a more leisurely pace.

SMART PRACTICES VIDEO

Myron Scholes, Stanford University and Chairman of Oak Hill Platinum Partners

"Options markets have grown dramatically over the last 30 years."

See the entire interview at **SMARTFinance**

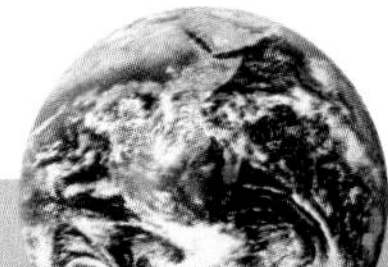

COMPARATIVE CORPORATE FINANCE

International Derivatives Trading

Since options began trading in the United States in 1973, the growth in options (and other derivatives) trading has been remarkable, and not only in the U.S. In 1978, call options on ten stocks began trading on the London Traded Options Market, and that same year, the European Options Exchange opened in Amsterdam. Today, equity-linked derivatives such as stock options, stock index options, and index futures contracts trade in roughly thirty countries, including most of the largest economies of North America, Europe, and Asia. Even Brazil, which formed its Bolsa de Mercadorias and Futuros exchange in 1985, now ranks among the world's top ten equity derivative markets, in terms of annual trading volume. Other nations with derivative markets that rank in the top ten include the United States, the United Kingdom, Germany, and France.

In many of these markets, trading in equity derivatives exceeds the volume of trading in the underlying stocks. The figure below shows the volume of trading in equity options and equity futures contracts, each relative to trading in stocks, in thirteen countries. Using the combined trading volume of options and futures contracts, we see that trading in derivatives is greater than trading in the underlying shares in every country except Canada and Sweden.

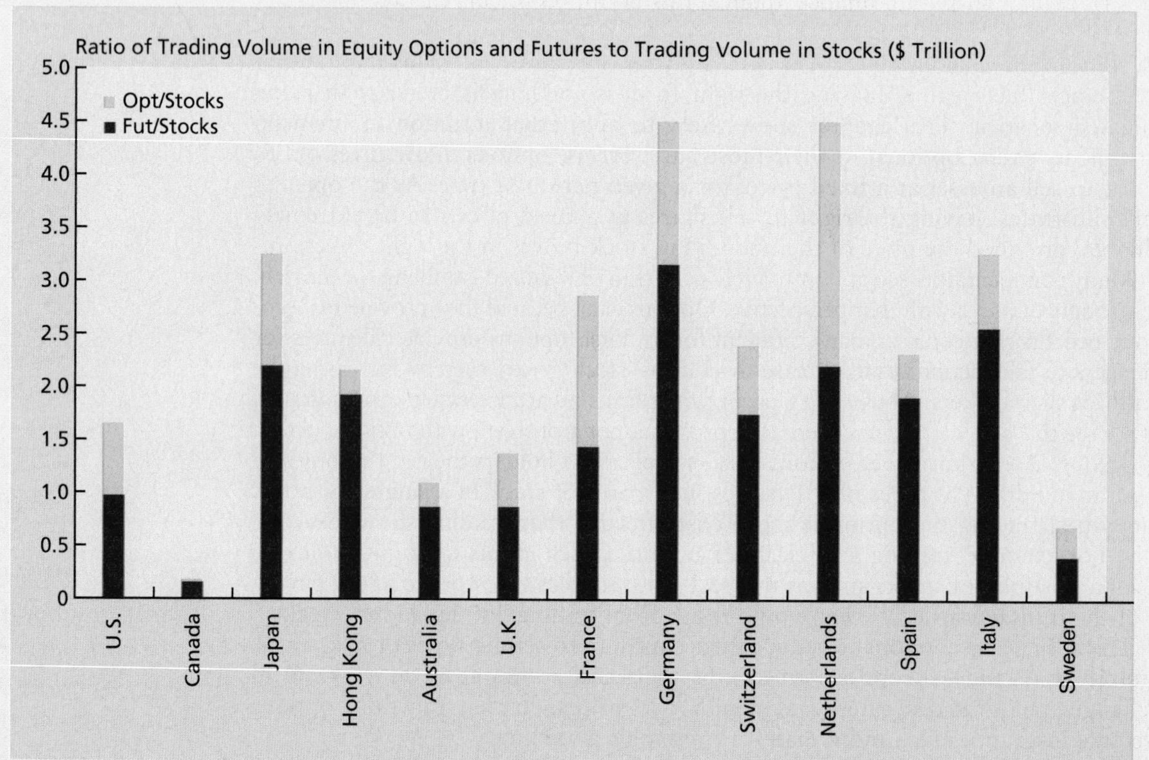

Source: Francis, Jack C., William W. Toy, and J. Gregg Whittaker, eds. (2000) *Handbook of Equity Derivatives (revised edition)* New York: John Wiley & Sons, Inc.

The growth in options trading and trading in other exotic financial instruments such as futures contracts offers some evidence of our claim that options provide real economic benefits to society. As the Comparative Corporate Finance insert explains, the growth in options markets has been a worldwide phenomenon for roughly the past twenty-five years. In many of the world's largest economies, trading in stock options exceeds the trading volume in the underlying stocks themselves.

Why does a chapter on options belong in a corporate finance textbook? We offer three answers. First, employees of large and small corporations regularly receive options as part of their compensation. It is valuable for both the employees and the employers to understand the value of this component of pay packages. In early 2004, as this text was going to press, it appeared that the Financial Accounting Standards Board (FASB) would require firms to deduct a charge for employee stock options when calculating net income. Clearly, it is necessary to understand how to determine the value of options to calculate the proper expense for employee stock option grants. Second, firms often raise capital by issuing securities with embedded options. For example, firms can issue debt that is convertible into shares of common stock, at a lower interest rate than ordinary, nonconvertible debt. To evaluate whether the interest savings is worth giving bondholders the opportunity to convert their bonds into shares requires an understanding of option pricing. Third, many capital budgeting projects have characteristics similar to options. The net present value method, discussed in Chapters 8–10, can generate incorrect accept/reject decisions for projects with downstream options. The best way to develop the ability to recognize which real investment projects have embedded options and which ones do not is to become an expert on ordinary financial options.

We begin this chapter with a brief description of the most common types of stock options and their essential characteristics. Next, we turn our attention to portfolios of options, illustrating how options can be used to construct unique trading strategies and gaining insight into how prices of different kinds of options are linked together in the market. The rest of the chapter examines factors that influence option prices, and we introduce a simple, yet powerful, tool for pricing many different kinds of options.

15.1 OPTIONS VOCABULARY

An option is one of the three main types of **derivative securities**, a class of financial instruments that derive their value from other assets.[1] An option fits this description because its value depends on the price of the underlying stock that the option holder can buy or sell. The asset from which a derivative security obtains its value is called the **underlying asset**. A **call option** grants the right to purchase a share of stock at a fixed price, on or before a certain date. The price at which a call option allows an investor to purchase the underlying share is called the **strike price** or the **exercise price**. It is not too hard to see how a call option's value derives from the value of the underlying stock. For example, if a particular call option has an exercise price of \$25, then the holder of the option can purchase one share of underlying stock for \$25. If the market price of the stock rises above \$25, the call option's value will increase because it allows the option holder to purchase the stock at a bargain price. On the other hand, if the underlying stock's price stays below \$25, then the call option holder will not exercise the right to buy the stock for \$25. Because it is cheaper to buy the stock at the market price than at the exercise price, the call option's value is low (perhaps even zero).

derivative securities
Securities such as options, futures, forwards, and swaps that derive their value from some underlying asset.

underlying asset
The asset from which an option or other derivative security derives its value.

call option
An option that grants the right to buy an underlying asset at a fixed price.

strike price
The price at which an option holder can buy or sell the underlying asset.

exercise price
The price at which an option holder can buy or sell the underlying asset.

---

1. The other main types of derivatives are futures contracts (and their close cousins, forward contracts) and swaps. A futures contract is an agreement between two parties to trade an asset at a fixed price on a specific future date. Unlike an option, a futures contract obligates both parties to fulfill their end of the bargain. A swap is an agreement between two parties to exchange streams of cash flows over time. For instance, a currency swap might involve one company paying British pounds to another in exchange for Japanese yen. We discuss other types of derivatives in more detail in Chapter 17.

Call options grant investors the right to purchase a share for a fairly short time period, usually just a few months.[2] The point at which this right expires is called the option's **expiration date.** An **American call option** gives holders the right to purchase stock at a fixed price, on or before its expiration date, whereas a **European call option** grants that right only on the expiration date. If we compare the prices of two options that are identical in every respect, except that one is American and one is European, the price of the American option should be at least as high as the European option because of the American option's greater flexibility.

expiration date
The date on which the right to buy or to sell the underlying asset expires.

American call option
An option that grants the right to buy an underlying asset, on or before the expiration date.

European call option
An option that grants the right to buy the underlying asset only on the expiration date.

put option
An option that grants the right to sell an underlying asset at a fixed price.

A **put option** grants the right to sell a share of stock at a fixed price, for a specific period of time. The right to sell stock at a fixed price becomes more and more valuable as the price of the underlying stock decreases. Thus, we have the most basic distinction between put and call options—put options rise in value as the underlying stock price goes down, whereas call options increase in value as the underlying stock price goes up. Just like call options, put options specify both an exercise price at which investors can sell the underlying stock and an expiration date at which the right to sell vanishes. Also, put options come in American and in European varieties, just as call options do.

The most distinctive feature of options, both puts and calls, can be deduced from the term "option." Investors who own calls and puts have the right to buy or sell shares, but they are not obligated to do so. We have already said that having the option to do something is better than being obligated to do it, and that intuition is important in understanding options. Because option holders can choose whether to exercise their option, an asymmetry exists in option payoffs. This means that an option behaves very differently, depending on whether the underlying stock price is above or below the option's strike price. This trait is central to understanding how to use options effectively and how to price them.

An important feature distinguishing calls and puts from other securities we've studied, such as stocks and bonds, is that options are not necessarily issued by firms.[3] Rather, an option is a contract between two parties, neither one having any connection to the company whose stock serves as the underlying asset for the contract. For example, suppose Tony and Oscar, neither one working for General Electric, decide to enter into an option contract. Tony agrees to pay Oscar $5 for the right to purchase one share of General Electric stock for $50 at any time during the next month. As the option buyer, Tony has a **long position** in a call option. He can decide at any point whether he wants to **exercise the option.** If he chooses to exercise his option, he will pay Oscar $50, and Oscar will deliver one share of GE stock to Tony. Naturally, Tony will choose to exercise the option only if GE stock is worth more than $50. If GE stock is worth less than $50, Tony will let the option expire worthless and will lose his $5 investment.

long position
To own an option or another security.

exercise the option
Pay (receive) the strike price and buy (sell) the underlying asset.

short position
To sell an option or another security.

option premium
The market price of the option.

Now let's look at Oscar's side of this transaction. As the seller of the option, Oscar has a **short position** in a call option.[4] If Tony decides to exercise his option, Oscar's *obligation* is to follow through on his promise to deliver one share of GE for $50. If Oscar does not already own a share of GE stock, he can buy one in the market. Oscar agrees to this arrangement because he receives the **option premium,** the $5 payment that Tony made at the beginning of their agreement. If GE's stock rises above $50, Oscar will lose part or all of the option premium because he must

---

2. Employee stock options, which typically give workers the right to buy stock at a fixed price for up to ten years, are an important exception to this rule. Some publicly traded options have long expiration dates, too, such as the Long-Term Equity AnticiPation Securities (LEAPS) introduced by the American Stock Exchange in 1990.

3. This is not to say that firms cannot issue options if they want to. Firms do issue options to employees and may also sell options, as part of their risk management activities, or bundle options with other securities such as bonds and preferred shares that they sell to raise capital.

4. We may also say that Oscar **writes an option** when he sells the option to Tony.

sell Tony an asset for less than what it is worth. On the other hand, if GE's stock price does not rise above $50, then Tony will not attempt to buy the asset, and Oscar can keep the $5 option premium.

Options trades do not usually occur in face-to-face transactions between two parties. Instead, options trade either on an exchange such as the Chicago Board Options Exchange in the U.S. or on the over-the-counter market. Exchanges list options on a limited number of stocks, with a limited set of exercise prices and expiration dates. By limiting the number and the variety of listed options, the exchange expects greater liquidity in the option contracts that are available for trading. Furthermore, an options exchange may serve as a guarantor, fulfilling the terms of an option contract if one party defaults. In contrast, over-the-counter (OTC) options come in seemingly infinite varieties. They are less liquid than exchange-traded options. A trader of OTC options faces **counterparty risk**, the risk that their counterparty on a specific trade will default on their obligation.

counterparty risk
The risk that the counterparty in an over-the-counter options transaction will default on its obligation.

Most investors who trade options never exercise them. An investor who holds an option and wants to convert that holding into cash can do so in several ways. First, one investor can simply sell the option to another investor, as long as there is some time remaining before expiration. Second, an investor can receive a **cash settlement** for the option. To illustrate this idea, go back to Tony's call option to buy GE stock for $50. Suppose the price of GE is $60 per share when the option expires. Rather than having Tony pay Oscar $50 in exchange for one share of GE, Oscar may agree to simply pay Tony $10, the difference between the market price of GE and the option's strike price. Settling in cash avoids the potential need for Oscar to buy one share of GE to give to Tony and the need for Tony to sell that share if he wants to convert his profit into cash. Avoiding these unnecessary trades saves transactions costs.

cash settlement
An agreement between two parties, in which one party pays the other party the cash value of its option position, rather than forcing it to exercise the option by buying or selling the underlying asset.

Table 15.1 shows a set of option-price quotations for Opti-Tech Corp.[5] The first column indicates that the quoted options are on Opti-Tech common stock. On the day that these option prices were obtained, the closing price of Opti-Tech was $30.00. The second column illustrates the range of expiration dates available for Opti-Tech options. The prices we've chosen to illustrate in the table are for options expiring either in April, May, or July. The third column shows the range of option strike prices available, from $27.50 to $35. The fourth and fifth columns give the most recent trading prices for

Table 15.1
Option Price Quotes for Opti-Tech Corp.

The table lists prices for call and put options that expire in April, May, and July, with strike prices of $27.50, $30.00, $32.50, and $35.00.

Company	Expiration	Strike	Calls	Puts	
OPTI	April	27.50	3.26	0.67	When X = $27.50, calls are in the money and puts are out of the money (X = strike price).
30.00	May	27.50	3.91	1.23	
30.00	July	27.50	4.91	2.04	
30.00	April	30.00	1.77	1.67	When X = $30, calls and puts are both at the money.
30.00	May	30.00	2.53	2.33	
30.00	July	30.00	3.62	3.23	
30.00	April	32.50	0.85	3.24	When X = $32.50 or $35, calls are out of the money and puts are in the money.
30.00	May	32.50	1.55	3.83	
30.00	July	32.50	2.62	4.69	
30.00	April	35.00	0.36	5.24	
30.00	May	35.00	0.90	5.67	
30.00	July	35.00	1.86	6.40	

5. This table shows only a handful of the option contracts that you may find trading at the Chicago Board Options Exchange http://www.cboe.com for an actively traded stock like Microsoft or General Electric. We have also chosen to exclude from the table the daily trading volume figures that are usually included.

calls and puts.[6] For instance, an investor who wanted to buy a call option on Opti-Tech stock, with a strike price of $27.50 and an expiration date in May, would pay $3.91. For a May put, with the same strike price, an investor would pay just $1.23. Remember, we also refer to the price of an option as the option's premium.

in the money
A call (put) option is in the money when the stock price is greater (less) than the strike price.

out of the money
A call (put) option is out of the money when the stock price is less (greater) than the strike price.

at the money
An option is at the money when the stock price equals the strike price.

intrinsic value
For a call, intrinsic value equals $S - X$ or zero, whichever is greater. For a put, it equals $X - S$ or zero, whichever is greater.

time value
The difference between an option's market price and its intrinsic value.

When a call option's strike price is less than the current stock price, options traders say that the option is **in the money**. For puts, an option is in the money if the strike price exceeds the stock price. Using these definitions, we can say that the call options in the upper three rows of Table 15.1 are in the money, whereas the put options in the lower six rows are in the money. Similarly, options traders say that a call option is **out of the money** when the strike price exceeds the current stock price. Puts are out of the money when the strike price falls short of the stock price. Finally, an option is **at the money** when the stock price and the strike price are equal. In Table 15.1, the Opti-Tech options, with a strike price of $30, are at the money because the stock price is $30.00.

Take one more look at the May call option, with a strike price of $27.50. If an investor who owned this option exercised it, she could buy Opti-Tech stock for $27.50 and resell it at the market price of $30.00, a difference of $2.50. But the current price of this option is $3.91, or $1.41 more than the value the investor would obtain by exercising it. In this example, $2.50 is the option's **intrinsic value**.[7] For a call option, the intrinsic value equals either zero or the stock price minus the option's strike price (S-X), whichever is greater. For a put option, the intrinsic value equals either zero or the option's strike price minus the stock price (X-S), whichever is greater. You can think of intrinsic value as measuring the cash flow an investor receives from exercising an in-the-money option (ignoring transactions costs as well as the option premium). If an option is out of the money, its intrinsic value is zero. The difference between an option's intrinsic value and its market price ($1.41, for the May call) is called the option's **time value**. At the expiration date, the time value equals zero.

Suppose you purchase the May call, with a $30 strike price for $2.53. On the option's expiration date, the price of Opti-Tech stock has grown from $30 to $35, an increase of $5, or 16.7 percent. What would the option be worth at that time? Because the option holder can buy stock at $30 and then immediately resell it for $35, the option should be worth $5. If the option sells for $5, that's an increase of $2.47, or a percentage increase of almost 98 percent from the $2.53 purchase price! Similarly, if Opti-Tech's stock price is just $25 when the option expires, then the option will be worthless. If you purchased the call for $2.53, your return on that investment would be –100 percent, even though Opti-Tech's stock fell just $5, or –16.7 percent, from the date of your purchase.

This example illustrates what may be the most important fact to know about options. *When the price of a stock moves, the dollar change of the stock is generally more than the dollar change of the option price, but the percentage change in the option price is greater than the percentage change in the stock price.* We have heard students argue that buying a call option is less risky than buying the underlying share because the maximum dollar loss that an investor can experience is much less on the option. That's only true when we compare the $30 investment required to

6. Two minor institutional details are worth mentioning here. First, at the CBOE, options expire on the third Saturday of the month. Second, an option contract grants the right to buy or to sell 100 shares of the underlying stock, even though the price quotes in the table are on a "per-share" or "per-option" basis. That is, the call price of $3.91 for the May option, with a $27.50 strike, means that for $391, an investor can purchase the right to buy 100 shares of Opti-Tech at $27.50 per share. All the examples in this chapter are constructed as if an investor can trade one option to buy or to sell one share. We make that assumption to keep the numbers simple, but it does not affect any of the main lessons of the chapter.

7. The intrinsic value of each of the three call options, with a strike price of $30, is $0. For put options, the intrinsic value equals either X–S or $0, whichever is greater. For example, the intrinsic value of each of the three put options, with a strike price of $35, is $5 ($35–$30).

buy one share of Opti-Tech with the $2.53 required to buy one May call. It is accurate to say that the call investor can lose, at most, $2.53, whereas an investor in Opti-Tech stock may lose $30. But there are two problems with this comparison. First, the likelihood that Opti-Tech will go bankrupt and that its stock will fall to $0 in a short time frame is negligible. The likelihood that the stock could dip below $30, resulting in a $0 value for the call option, is much greater. Second, it is better to compare an equal dollar investment in Opti-Tech stock and calls than to compare one stock to one call. An investment of $30 would purchase almost twelve Opti-Tech call options. Which position, do you think, is riskier? One share of stock or twelve call options?

CONCEPT REVIEW QUESTIONS

1. Explain the difference between the stock price, the exercise price, and the option premium. Which of these are market prices determined by the forces of supply and demand?

2. Explain the difference between a long position and a short position. Considering call options, what is the maximum gain and loss possible for an investor who holds the long position? What is the maximum gain and loss for the investor on the short side of the transaction?

3. Suppose an investor holds a call option on Nestlé stock and decides to exercise the option. What will happen to the total shares of common stock outstanding for Nestlé?

4. Which of the following would increase the value of a put option—an increase in the stock price or an increase in the strike price?

15.2 OPTION PAYOFF DIAGRAMS

So far, our discussion of options has been mostly descriptive. Now we turn to the problem of determining an option's market price. Valuing an option is an extraordinarily difficult problem, so difficult in fact that the economists who solved the problem won a Nobel Prize for their efforts. In earlier chapters, when we studied the pricing of stocks and bonds, we began by describing their cash flows. We do the same here, focusing initially on the relatively simple problem of outlining options' cash flows on the expiration date. Eventually, that will help us understand the intuition behind complex option pricing models.

Call Option Payoffs

We define an option's **payoff** as the price an investor would be willing to pay for the option the instant before it expires.[8] An option's payoff is distinct from its price, or premium, because the payoff only refers to the price of the option at a particular instant in time, the expiration date. Graphs that illustrate an option's payoff as a function of the underlying stock price are called **payoff diagrams.** Payoff diagrams are extremely useful tools for understanding how options behave and how they can be combined to form portfolios with fascinating properties.

payoff
The value received from exercising an option on the expiration date (or zero), ignoring the initial premium required to purchase the option.

payoff diagrams
A diagram that shows how the expiration date payoff from an option or a portfolio varies, as the underlying asset price changes.

Suppose an investor purchases a call option, with a strike price of $75, and an expiration date in three months. To acquire this option, the investor pays a premium of $8. When the option expires, what will it be worth? If the underlying stock price is less than $75 on the expiration date, the option will be worthless. No one would pay anything for the right to buy this stock for $75 when they can easily buy it for less in the market. What if the stock price equals $76 on the expiration date? In that case,

[8] Alternatively, we could define the payoff as the value an investor would receive, ignoring transactions costs, if he or she exercised the option when it expired. If it did not make sense to exercise the option when it expired, the payoff would be zero.

owning the right to buy the stock at $75 is worth $1, the difference between the stock's market price and the option's exercise price. Ignoring transactions costs, an investor who owns the option can buy the stock for $75 and immediately sell it in the market for $76, earning a $1 payoff. In general, the payoff of this option will equal the greater of

- $0, if the stock price is less than $75 at expiration or
- the difference between the stock price and $75, if the stock price is more than $75 at expiration.

net payoff
The difference between the payoff received when the option expires and the premium paid to acquire the option.

The top line in Figure 15.1 shows a payoff diagram for the option buyer, or the long position. This picture is a classic in finance, known as the *hockey-stick diagram*. It shows that the option, at worst, will be worth $0, and at best, the option's value is unlimited. The lower line in the figure represents the investor's **net payoff**. The net payoff line appears $8 lower than the solid line, reflecting the $8 premium the investor paid to acquire the option. On a net basis, the holder of the call option makes a profit when the price of the stock exceeds $83.[9]

Figure 15.1 also shows the call's payoff from the seller's perspective, or the short position. Options are a zero-sum game, meaning that profits on the long position

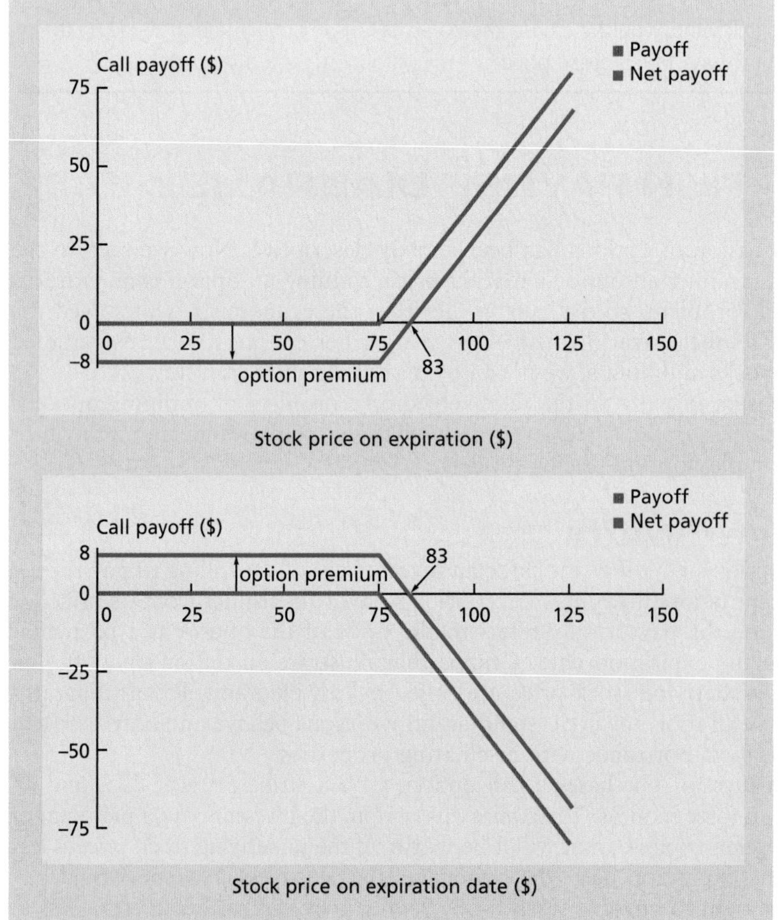

Figure 15.1
Payoff of a Call Option with X = $75

The top graph illustrates, from the option buyers' point of view, how a call option's payoff varies as the underlying stock price changes. The lower graph shows the seller's perspective. The payoff line shows that a call option, with a strike price of $75, will be worthless on the expiration date, if the stock price is $75, or less. For the buyer, the call's value rises dollar for dollar with the stock price, as long as the stock is worth more than $75. For the seller, the payoff falls as the stock price rises above $75. The net payoff line reflects the $8 option premium that the call buyer must pay (or that the seller receives). The buyer and seller break even when the stock price is $83. At higher stock prices, the buyer earns a net gain at the seller's expense. At stock prices below $83, the seller realizes a net gain, at the buyer's expense.

9. Notice that when the stock price is above $75 but below $83, it still makes sense for the investor to exercise his option, or to sell it, because it reduces the investor's losses. For example, if the stock price at expiration equals $80, the option payoff is $5, reducing the net loss to –$3. The careful reader may notice that we are committing a major sin, for finance professors anyway, by comparing the $8 premium paid up front to the payoff received three months later. At this point, ignoring the time value of money, in the graphs, is relatively harmless, but rest assured, we take that into account later when we determine the price of an option.

represent losses on the short side, and vice versa. In this part of the figure, the lower line illustrates that the seller's payoff equals $0 when the stock price is below $75. It decreases as the stock price rises above $75. The incentive for the seller to engage in this transaction is the $8 premium, as shown in the figure's upper line. If the option expires out of the money, the seller earns an $8 profit. If the option expires in the money, the seller may realize a net profit or a net loss, depending on how high the stock price is at that time. Whereas the call option buyer enjoys the potential for unlimited gains, the option seller faces exposure to the risk of unlimited losses. Rationally, if $8 is sufficient to induce someone to sell this option and thereby face the potential of huge losses, it must be the case that the seller perceives the probability of a large loss to be relatively low.

Put Option Payoffs

Figure 15.2 shows payoffs for put option buyers (long) and sellers (short). We maintain the assumption that the strike price equals $75, but, in this figure, the option premium is $7. For an investor holding a put option, the payoff rises as the stock price falls below the option's strike price. However, unlike a call option, a put option's potential gains are limited by a stock price that cannot fall below zero (because the law provides limited liability for a firm's shareholders). The maximum gain on this particular put equals $75 (or $68 on a net basis after subtracting the premium), whereas the maximum loss is the $7 option premium.

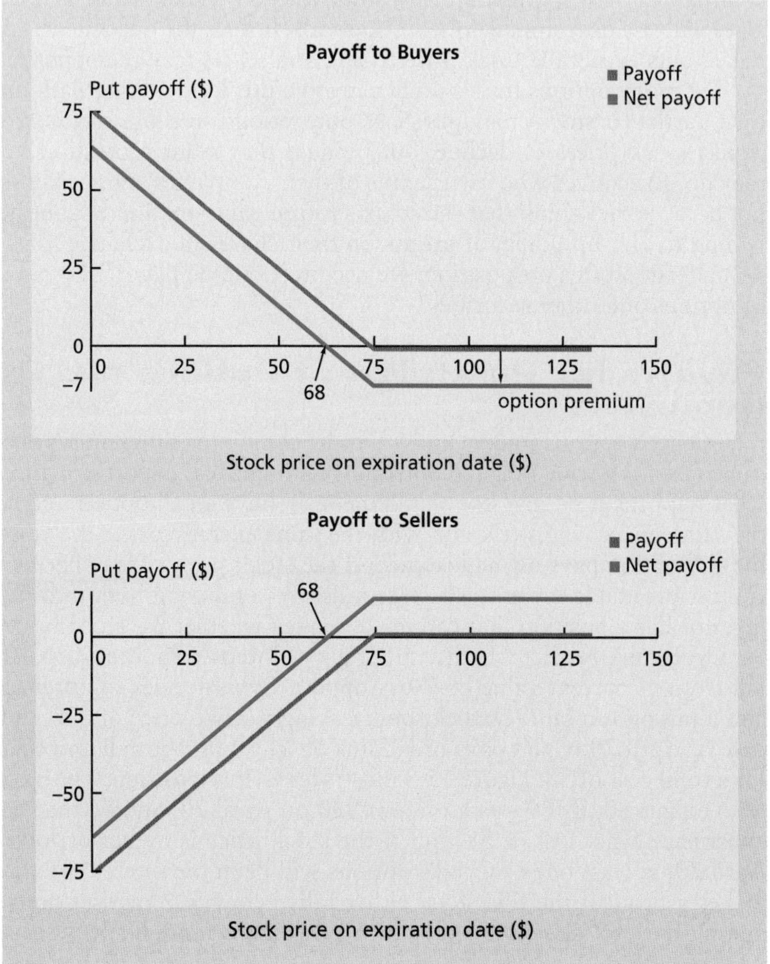

Figure 15.2
Payoff of a Put Option with X = $75

The top graph illustrates, from the option buyers' point of view, how a put option's payoff varies as the underlying stock price changes. The lower graph shows the seller's perspective. The payoff line shows that a put option, with a strike price of $75, will be worthless on the expiration date, if the stock price is $75 or more. For the buyer, the put's value rises as the stock price falls, as long as the stock is worth less than $75. For the seller, the payoff falls as the stock price falls below $75. The net payoff line reflects the $7 option premium that the put buyer must pay (or that the seller receives). The buyer and seller break even when the stock price is $68. At higher stock prices, the seller earns a net gain at the buyer's expense. At stock prices below $68, the buyer realizes a net gain, at the seller's expense.

Again, the seller's perspective is just the opposite of the buyer's. The seller earns a maximum net gain of $7, if the option expires worthless, because the stock price exceeds $75 on the expiration date, and the seller faces a maximum net loss of $68, if the firm goes bankrupt and its stock becomes worthless.

APPLYING THE MODEL

Jennifer sells a put option on Electro-Lighting Systems Inc. (ELS) stock to Jason. The option's strike price is $65, and it expires in one month. Jason pays Jennifer a premium of $5 for the option. One month later, ELS stock sells for $45 per share. Jason purchases a share of ELS in the open market for $45 and immediately exercises his option to sell it to Jennifer for $65 (or Jennifer and Jason could agree to settle their contract by having Jennifer pay Jason $20). The payoff on Jason's option is $20, or $15 on a net basis. Jennifer loses $20 on the deal, or just $15, taking into account the $5 premium she received up front.

naked option position
To buy or to sell an option, without a simultaneous position in the underlying asset.

This is a good time for us to clarify an important point. Thus far, all our discussions about options payoffs have assumed that each option buyer or seller had what traders refer to as a **naked option position**. A naked call option, for example, occurs when an investor buys or sells an option on a stock, without already owning the underlying stock. Similarly, when a trader buys or sells a put option, without owning the underlying stock, the trader creates a naked put position. Buying or selling naked options is an act of pure speculation. Investors who buy naked calls believe that the stock price will rise. Investors who sell naked calls believe the opposite. Similarly, buyers of naked puts expect the stock price to fall, and sellers take the opposite view.

But many options trades do not involve this kind of speculation. Investors who own particular stocks may purchase put options on those stocks, not because they expect stock prices to decline, but because they want protection in the event that they do. Executives who own shares of their companies' stock may sell call options, not because they think that the stock's future gains are limited, but because they are willing to give up potential profits on their shares in exchange for current income. To understand this proposition, we need to examine payoff diagrams for portfolios of options and other securities.

Payoffs for Portfolios of Options and Other Securities

Experienced options traders know that by combining different types of options, they can construct a wide range of portfolios with unusual payoff structures. Think about what happens if an investor simultaneously buys a call option and a put option on the same underlying stock and with the same exercise price. We've seen before that the call option pays off handsomely if the stock price rises, whereas the put option is most profitable if the stock price falls. By combining both into one portfolio, an investor has a position that can make money whether the stock price rises or falls.

Cybil can't predict whether the stock of Internet Phones Corp. (IPC) will rise or fall from its current value of $30. Suppose Cybil decides to purchase a call option and a put option on IPC stock, both having a strike price of $30 and an expiration date of April 20. Cybil pays premiums of $4.50 for the call and $3.50 for the put, for a total cost of $8. Figure 15.3 illustrates Cybil's position. The payoff of her portfolio equals $0, if IPC stock price is $30 on April 20. Should that occur, Cybil will experience a net loss of $8. But if the stock price is higher or lower than $30 on April 20, at least one of Cybil's options will be in the money. On a net basis, Cybil makes a profit if the IPC stock either falls below $22 or rises above $38, but she doesn't have to take a view on which outcome is more likely.

Figure 15.3
Payoff to Portfolio Containing 1 Call and 1 Put (X = $30)

By purchasing a call and a put option, each with a strike price of $30, an investor creates a position that can be profitable whether the stock price rises or falls. Because the total cost of the call and put options is $8, the stock price must either fall below $22 or rise above $38 before the trader makes a net profit.

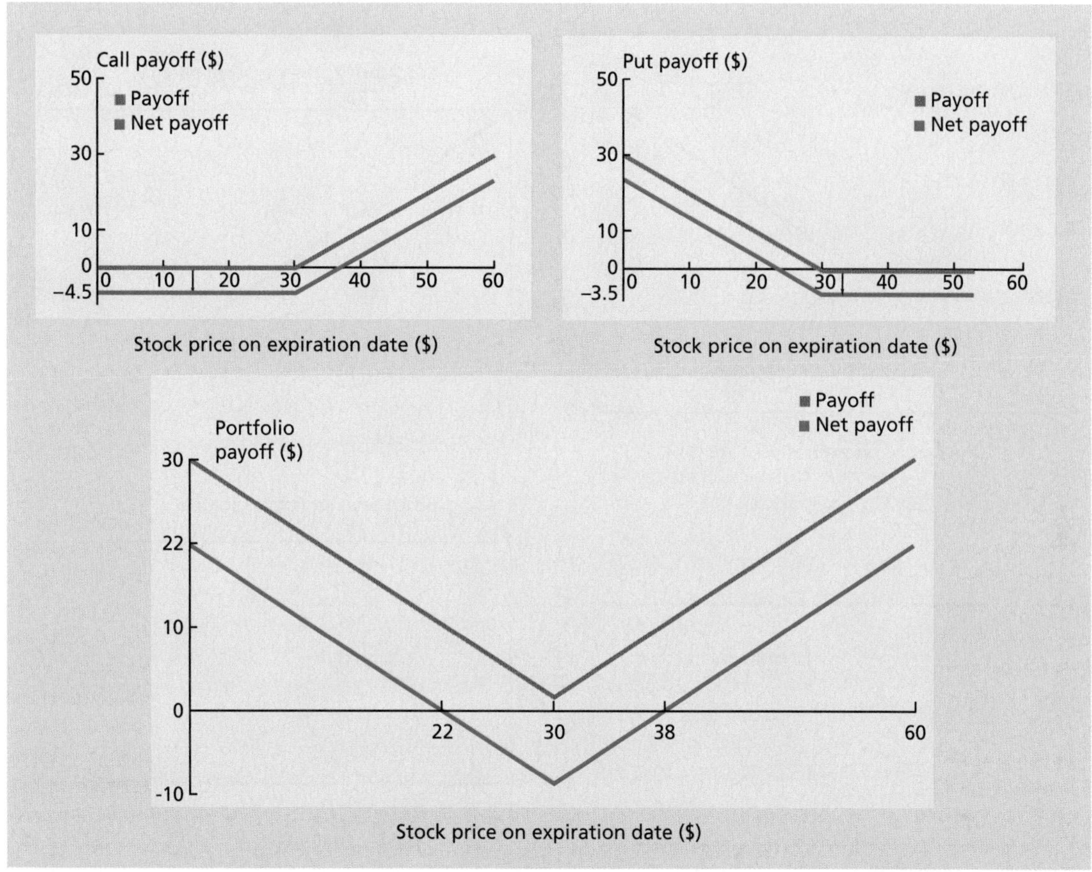

In this example, Cybil is speculating, but not on the direction of IPC stock. Rather, Cybil's gamble is on the volatility of IPC shares. If the shares move a great deal, either up or down, she makes a net profit. If the shares do not move much by April 20, she experiences a net loss. Options traders refer to this type of position as a *long straddle*, a portfolio consisting of long positions in calls and puts on the same stock with the same strike price and expiration date. Naturally, creating a *short straddle* is possible, too. If Cybil believed that IPC stock would not move far from its current value, she could simultaneously sell a put and a call option on IPC stock, with a strike price of $30. She would receive $8 in option premiums from this trade. If IPC stock was priced at $30 on April 20, both of the options she sold would expire worthless. On the other hand, if IPC stock moved up or down from $30, one of the options would be exercised, reducing Cybil's profits from the options sale.

Now let's look at what happens when investors form portfolios by combining options with other securities such as stocks and bonds. To begin, examine Figure 15.4 which displays payoff diagrams for a long position in common stocks and bonds.[10]

10. In Figure 15.4, we do not plot the net payoff, meaning that the diagram ignores the initial cost of buying stocks or bonds, or the revenue obtained from shorting them.

Figure 15.4
Payoff Diagrams for Bonds and Stocks

The graphs show the payoff for long and short positions in common stock and in risk-free, zero-coupon bonds. The payoff diagram for stock is a 45-degree line (upward sloping for the buyer and downward sloping for the seller) because the payoff of the stock simply equals the price of the stock. Similarly, the bond payoff lines are horizontal because the bond pays $75 to the buyer (or requires the seller to pay $75) with certainty. The bond's payoff is not affected by changes in the stock price.

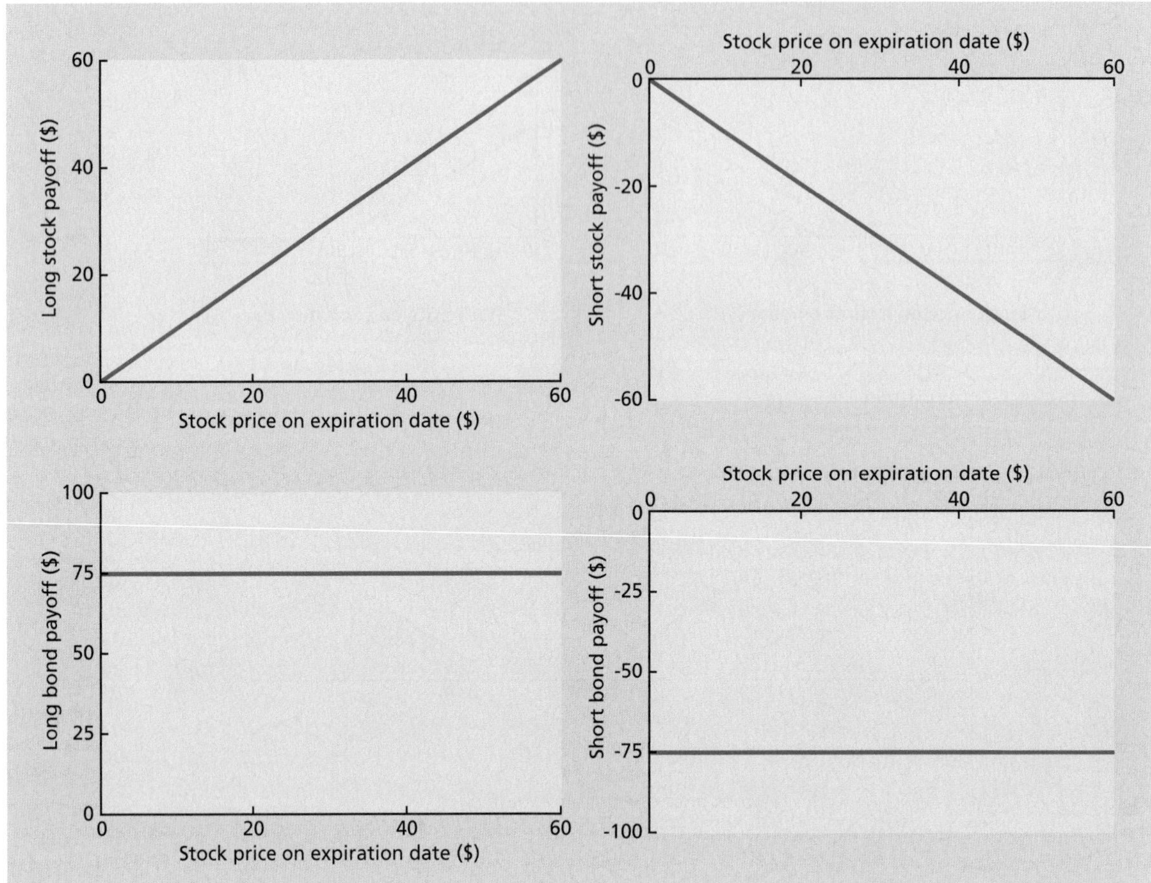

Remember, a payoff diagram shows the total value of a security (in this case, one share of common stock or one bond) on a specific future date on the *y*-axis, and the value of a share of stock on that same date on the *x*-axis. In Figure 15.4, the payoff diagram from holding a share of stock is a 45-degree line emanating from the origin because both axes of the graph are plotting the same thing—the value of the stock on a future date.[11]

The payoff diagram for the bond requires a little more explanation. The type of bond in this example is very special. It is a risk-free, zero-coupon bond with a face value of $75. The payoff for an investor who purchases this bond is simply $75, no matter what the price of the stock underlying the put and call options turns out to be. That's why the diagram shows a horizontal line at $75 for the long bond's payoff.[12]

---

11. Figure 15.4 also shows the payoff diagram for a short position in stock, and as always, it is just the opposite of the long payoff diagram. When investors short sell stocks, they borrow shares from other investors, promising to return the shares at a future date. Short selling therefore creates a liability. The magnitude of that liability is just the price of the stock that the short seller must return on a future date.

12. Is it really possible to buy a risk-free bond with a face value of $75? Perhaps not, but an investor could buy 75 Treasury bills, each with a face value of $1,000, resulting in a risk-free bond portfolio with a face value of $75,000. The assumption that investors can buy risk-free bonds with any face value is just a simplification to keep the numbers in our examples manageable.

Next, consider a portfolio consisting of one share of stock and one put option on that share, with a strike price of \$40. If, on the expiration date of the option, the stock price is \$40, or more, the put option will be worthless. Therefore, the portfolio's total value will equal the value of the stock. What happens if the stock price is less than \$40 on the option's expiration date? In that case, the put option has a positive payoff, which insures that the portfolio's value cannot drop below \$40, even if the stock price does. Imagine that the stock price falls to \$30. At that point, the put option's payoff is \$10, leaving the combined portfolio value at \$40 (\$30 from the stock + \$10 from the put). Simply stated, the put option provides a kind of portfolio insurance, for it guarantees that the share of stock can be sold for at least \$40. However, if the price of the stock rises, the portfolio value will rise right along with it. Though the put option will be worthless, any increase in the stock price beyond \$40 increases the portfolio's value as well, as shown in Figure 15.5. This strategy is known as a **protective put.**

protective put
A portfolio containing a share of stock and a put option on that stock.

Figure 15.5
Payoff from One Long Share and One Long Put (X = \$40)

The graph shows the payoff on a protective put, a portfolio that combines a long position in the underlying stock and a long position in a put option on that stock, with a strike price of \$40. If the stock price increases above \$40, the investor's portfolio goes up. However, if the stock falls below \$40, the put option gives the investor the right to sell the stock at \$40, essentially putting a floor on the portfolio's value.

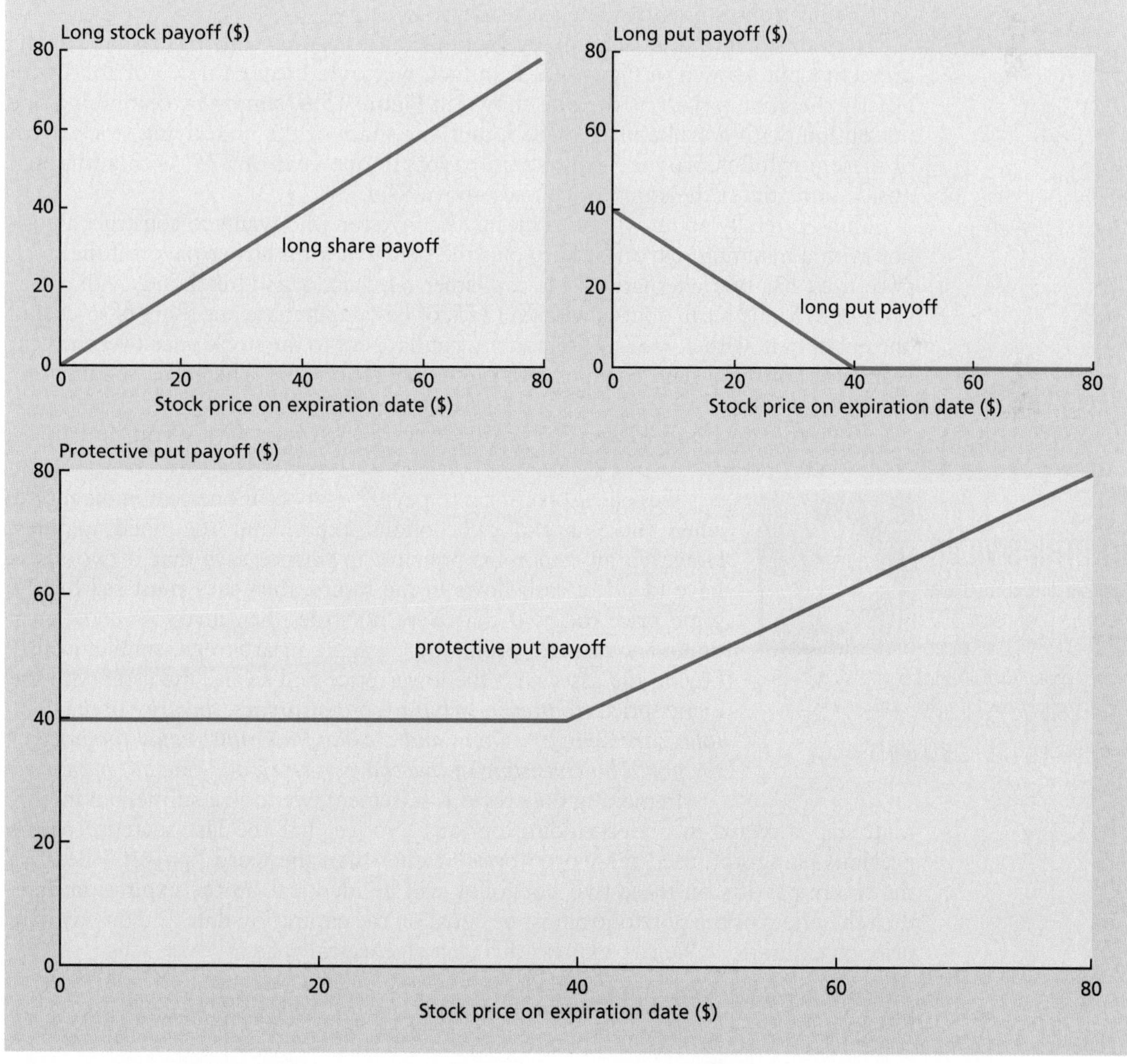

Investors can construct portfolios containing options, stocks, and bonds in ways that generate a wide range of interesting payoffs. We have illustrated how investors could construct a portfolio not only to profit from a stock's volatility, but to protect themselves from that volatility, using put options. As we see in the next section, no matter what kind of payoff structure an investor wants to create, there is always more than one way to form a portfolio that generates the desired payoffs.

Put-Call Parity

In the payoff diagrams we have studied thus far, the vertical axis shows the value of an option at a particular point in time—the expiration date. Knowing what an option is worth when it expires is important, but option traders need to know the value of options at any time, not just on the expiration date. We explore option pricing in greater depth in the next two sections, but we can gain some basic insights into the process of valuing option by examining payoff diagrams.

Suppose an investor forms a portfolio containing one risk-free, zero-coupon bond, with a face value of $75, and one call option, with a strike price of $75. The bond matures in one year, which is also when the call option expires. Figure 15.6 shows that in one year, this portfolio's payoff will be at least $75. Even if the call option expires out of the money, the bond will pay $75. In addition, if the price of the underlying stock is high enough, the call option will have a positive payoff, too, and the portfolio's payoff will exceed $75.

Does this diagram look familiar? Notice that it has the same basic shape as the protective put, shown in Figure 15.5. In fact, we could create a new portfolio with exactly the same payoff as the one shown in Figure 15.6, simply by combining one put option, with a strike price of $75, and one share of the underlying stock. Both of these portfolios provide a minimum payoff in one year of $75, with additional upside potential if the stock price rises above $75.

Think carefully about what this means. An investor who wants to construct a position with a minimum payoff of $75, plus the potential for a higher payoff if the stock price rises, has two alternatives. He can either purchase a risk-free bond, with a face value of $75, and a call option, with $X = \$75$, or he can purchase one share of stock and one put option, with $X = \$75$. No matter what happens to the stock price over the next year, these portfolios have equal payoffs on the expiration date. Therefore we can write:

$$\text{Payoff on bond} + \text{Payoff on call} = \text{Payoff on stock} + \text{Payoff on put}$$

SMART ETHICS VIDEO

John Eck, President of Broadcast and Network Operations, NBC

"That allowed us to create some doubt around the transaction and allowed us not to have to book the gain up front but to book it as the cash came in."

See the entire interview at **SMARTFinance**

This equation applies to payoffs that occur one year in the future, when the put and call options expire and the bond matures. However, an important principle in finance says that if two assets have identical cash flows in the future, then they must sell for the same price today. If that were not true, then investors could earn unlimited risk-free profits by engaging in arbitrage, simultaneously buying the asset with the lower price and selling the asset with the higher price. *To prevent arbitrage opportunities, the price of the portfolio consisting of a bond and a call option must equal the price of the portfolio consisting of one share of stock and one put option.*

In making the previous statement, we took a subtle, but important, step forward in understanding options. Notice that the last sentence of the previous paragraph used the word "price" rather than the word "payoff." Because the future payoffs on these two portfolios will be identical on the expiration date, then the prices of the portfolios must be equal on the expiration date and on any date prior to expiration. We can express this idea algebraically, as follows:

$$S + P = B + C \quad \text{(Eq. 15.1)}$$

Figure 15.6
Payoff on Portfolio of One Bond (FV = \$75) and One Call (X = \$75)

The diagram illustrates the payoff of a portfolio containing a risk-free bond and a call option. The bond ensures that the portfolio's payoff will never be less than \$75. However, if the underlying stock's price is greater than \$75 on the expiration date, then the portfolio's payoff will be greater than \$75 because both the bond and the call option will have a positive payoff.

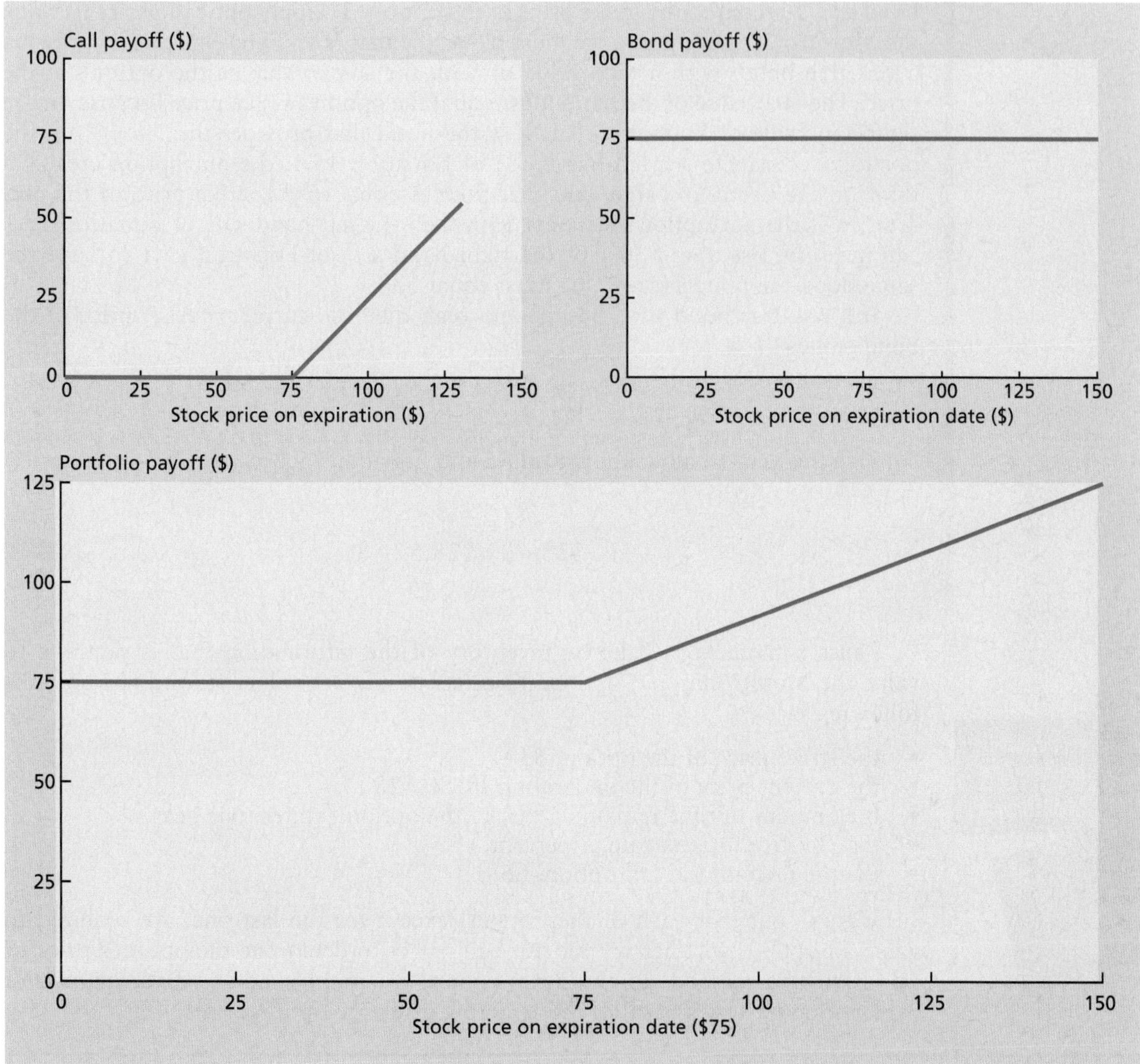

In this equation, S stands for the current stock price, P and C represent the current market prices (premiums) of the put and call options, respectively, and B equals the current price of the risk-free, zero-coupon bond. Equation 15.1 describes one of the most fundamental ideas in option pricing, known as **put-call parity.** Put-call parity says that the prices of put and call options on the same underlying stock, with the same strike price and the same expiration date, must be related to each other.

put-call parity
A relationship that links the market prices of stock, risk-free bonds, call options, and put options.

APPLYING THE MODEL

Mototronics Inc. stock currently sells for \$28 per share. Put and call options on Mototronics shares are available, with a strike price of \$30 and an expiration date of one year. The price of the Mototronics call option is \$6, and the risk-free interest rate equals 5 percent. What put option price satisfies put-call parity?

Examine Equation 15.1. We know that the stock price equals \$28, and the call price is \$6. To find the put price, we also need to know the market price of a risk-free bond. Refer once again to Figure 15.6. In that example, the face value of the bond is \$75, equal to the strike price of the option. To apply put-call parity to value the Mototronics put option, we must recognize that B, in Equation 15.1, represents a risk-free bond, with a face value of \$30, the same value as the option's strike price. The face value of the bond must equal the option's strike price because on the right-hand side of Equation 15.1, it is the bond that provides the "floor" on the portfolio value. On the left-hand side of Equation 15.1, the put option creates a floor on the portfolio value, and that floor is equal to the strike price of the put. That is, if the put option's strike is \$30, then the left-hand side of Equation 15.1 can never be less than \$30. For the right-hand side of Equation 15.1 to have the same floor, the bond's face value must equal \$30.

If a risk-free bond pays \$30 in one year, then the current market price of the bond equals

$$B = \$30 \div (1.05) = \$28.57$$

Plug this and the other known values into Equation 15.1 to solve for the put price:

$$S + P = B + C$$
$$\$28 + P = \$28.57 + \$6$$
$$P = \$6.57$$

SMART CONCEPTS

See the concept explained step-by-step at SMARTFinance

Pause a moment to take an inventory of the information that is required to value the Mototronics put option. To calculate the put value, we had to know the following facts:

- the strike price of the option, \$30
- the current price of the underlying stock, \$28
- the amount of time remaining before the option expires, one year
- the risk-free interest rate, 5 percent
- the the price of the call option, \$6

It turns out that each of these items, except for the last one, are required to value an option, whether we use put-call parity to determine the option's price or an alternative method. In the next section, we provide an intuitive, qualitative explanation of how several of these factors influence option prices.

CONCEPT REVIEW QUESTIONS

5. What would happen if an investor who owned a share of a particular stock also bought a put option, with a strike price of \$50, and sold a call option, with a strike price of \$50? Try to draw the payoff diagram for this portfolio.

6. Is selling a call the same thing as buying a put? Explain why or why not.

7. A major corporation is involved in high-profile antitrust litigation with the government. The firm's stock price is somewhat depressed due to the uncertainty of this case. If the company wins, investors expect its stock price to shoot up. If it loses, the stock price will decline even more than it already has. If investors expect a resolution to the case in the near future, what affect do you think that resolution will have on put and call options on the company's stock? Hint: think about Figure 15.3.

15.3 QUALITATIVE ANALYSIS OF OPTION PRICES

Factors That Influence Option Values

Before getting into the rather complex quantitative aspects of pricing options, let's cultivate the intuition needed to understand the factors which influence option prices. We begin by taking a look at recent price quotes for options on Yahoo! stock. Table 15.2 shows prices of several Yahoo! option contracts, as taken from the Chicago Board Options Exchange Web site (http://www.cboe.com) on April 13, 2004.

You should notice a striking pattern here. The prices of both calls and puts rise the longer the time before expiration. To understand why, think about the call option that expires in May, roughly one month in the future (as of the date that we gathered the option prices). Currently, this option is out of the money because it grants the right to purchase Yahoo! stock for $60, but investors can buy Yahoo! in the open market for $54.14. Buying the May call option requires an investment of just $0.60. The option is inexpensive because there is only a small chance that, before the option expires in one month, Yahoo's stock price will increase enough to make exercising the option worthwhile. No investor would exercise this option until Yahoo! stock reached at least $60.01, representing an increase of more than ten percent from its current price. Investors aren't willing to pay more than a few pennies for this option because they doubt that the stock will rise that much in just one month.

However, the price of the July option, with a strike price of $60, is more than three times greater than the price of the May call. The July option expires in about three months, so investors must think that the probability of a 10 percent increase, or more, in Yahoo! stock over that time period is much higher than the probability of seeing the same move by May. The same pattern holds for puts. The July put option sells for $1.30 more than the May put option because investors recognize that the chance of a significant drop in Yahoo! stock over a one-month period is much lower than the chance of a large decrease over the next three months. In general, *holding other factors constant, call and put option prices increase as the time to expiration increases.*[13]

Next, let's examine the prices of several Yahoo! puts and calls, all which expire in May. Table 15.3 lists the market prices of these options, as of April 13, 2004. Once again, a clear pattern emerges. Call option prices fall as the strike price increases, and put option prices rise as the strike price increases. This relationship is quite intuitive. A call option grants the right to buy stock at a fixed price. That

Table 15.2
Prices of Option Contracts on Yahoo! Stock, April 13, 2004

The table shows the market prices of various call and put options on Yahoo! stock, as of April 13, 2004. Both call and put prices increase as the expiration date moves from May to July to October.

Yahoo price	Expiration	Strike	Call	Put
$54.14	May	$60	$0.60	$6.35
$54.14	July	$60	$1.95	$7.65
$54.14	October	$60	$3.40	$9.05

13. There are a few exceptions to this rule. Suppose you hold a European put option on a company that is about to go bankrupt. The firm's stock price will be nearly zero, and it cannot drop much farther. In this case, you would prefer to exercise your option immediately, rather than having to wait to sell it, so the value of the option will decline as the time to expiration lengthens.

Table 15.3
Prices of May Option Contracts on Yahoo! Stock

The table shows the market prices of various call and put options on Yahoo! stock, as of April 13 and April 15, 2004. The table illustrates that call prices increase and put prices decrease when the difference between the stock price and the exercise price (S–X) increases.

		April 13, 2004 Yahoo! = $54.14		April 15, 2004 Yahoo! = $53.90	
Expiration	Strike	Call	Put	Call	Put
May	$47.50	$7.05	$0.35	$6.85	$0.40
May	$50	$5.00	$0.90	$4.90	$0.95
May	$55	$1.95	$2.75	$1.85	$2.85
May	$60	$0.60	$6.35	$0.50	$6.50

right is more valuable the cheaper the price at which the option holder can buy the stock. Conversely, put options grant the right to sell shares at a fixed price. That right is more valuable the higher the price at which investors can sell.

We can see a similar relationship by looking at the last two columns of Table 15.3, which show what happened to the prices of May Yahoo! options two days later, on April 15, 2004. From April 13 to April 15, Yahoo! shares dropped $0.24. All the call prices in Table 15.3 declined over those two days, but all the put prices increased. In response to the $0.24 decline in Yahoo! stock, call prices dropped between ten and twenty cents, and put prices rose between five and fifteen cents. Combining the lessons of the last few paragraphs, we can say that *call prices increase and put prices decrease when the difference between the underlying stock price and the exercise price (S–X) increases.*

Finally, to isolate the most important, and the most subtle, influence on option prices, examine Table 15.4, which compares the prices of May options, with a $50 strike price, on two different stocks, Yahoo! and the bank holding company, Fifth Third Bancorp. On April 13, 2004, Fifth Third stock was worth $0.88 more than Yahoo! stock, $55.02 compared to $54.14. We have already seen that higher stock prices lead to higher call values and lower put values. Therefore, when we compare similar options (similar meaning that the options have the same strike price and expiration date) on Yahoo! and Fifth Third stock, we expect higher prices on Fifth Third calls and lower prices on Fifth Third puts, compared to Yahoo! option prices. Table 15.4 confirms this intuition for puts because the Yahoo! put option sells for $1.25 more than Fifth Third's May put option. However, despite the fact that the

Table 15.4
Prices of Option Contracts on Two Stocks, April 13, 2004

On April 13, 2004, Yahoo! puts and calls were trading for more than Fifth Third puts and calls (all having the same strike price and expiration date). Yahoo! options were more valuable, in part, because Yahoo! stock was more volatile.

	Expiration	Strike	Call	Put
Yahoo! stock price = $54.14	May	$55	$1.95	$2.75
Fifth Third Bancorp stock price = $55.02	May	$55	$1.55	$1.50

Figure 15.7
Daily Percentage Change in Fifth Third Bancorp and Yahoo!
During the first quarter of 2004, Yahoo! stock exhibited larger day-to-day fluctuations than did Fifth Third Bancorp shares.

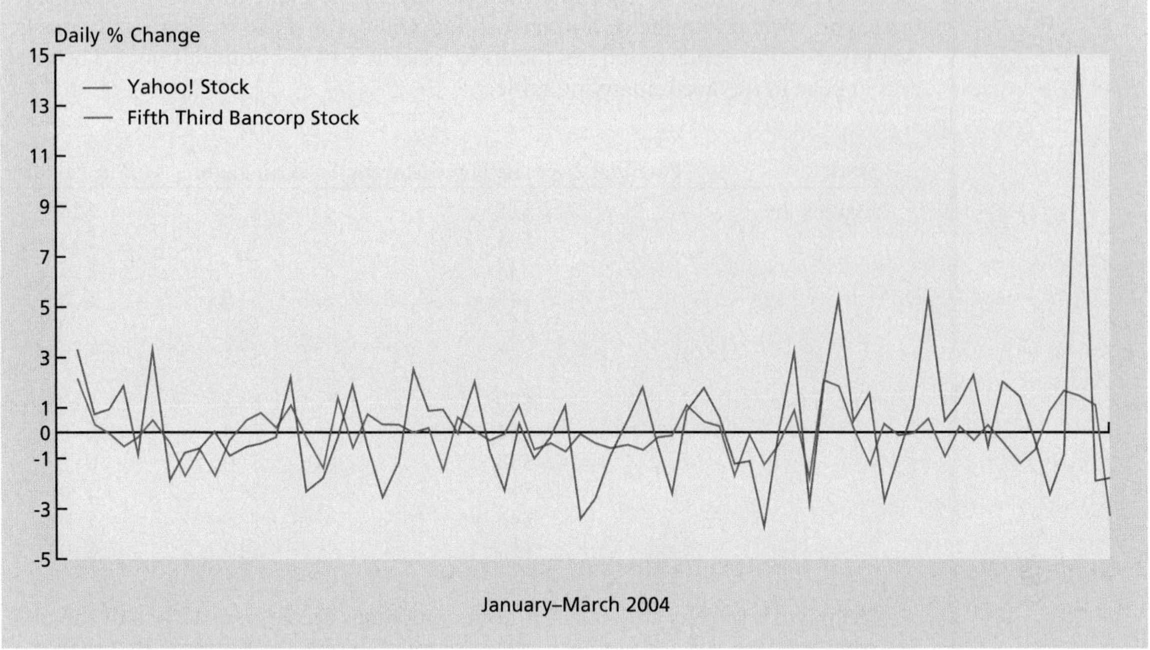

Fifth Third call option is in the money and the Yahoo! call is out of the money, the Yahoo! call commands a $0.40 higher premium. There must be another factor that makes Yahoo! options more valuable than Fifth Third Bancorp options, if influences such as the strike price and expiration date are held constant.

Figure 15.7 offers a clue about what makes Yahoo! options so valuable. The figure charts daily price movements in the two stocks through the first quarter of 2004. Notice that the daily fluctuations in Yahoo! are usually larger than Fifth Third's movements. It should not be too surprising that Yahoo! shares exhibit more volatility than the shares of a large financial institution. But why should Yahoo!'s higher volatility lead to higher call and put prices?

The answer lies in the asymmetry of option payoffs. When a call option expires, its payoff is zero, for a wide range of stock prices. Whether the stock price falls below the option's strike price by $1, $10, or $100, the call payoff is zero. On the other hand, as the stock price rises above the strike price, the call option's payoff increases. A similar relationship holds for puts. The value of a put at expiration is zero if the stock price is greater than the strike price. Whether the stock price is just above the strike price or far above it does not change the payoff. However, the put option has a larger payoff the lower the stock price falls, once it falls below the strike price. In summary, *call and put option prices increase as the volatility of the underlying stock increases.*

APPLYING THE MODEL

Suppose you are tracking two stocks. One exhibits much more volatility than the other. Call the more volatile stock Extreme Inc. and the less volatile one Steady Corp.

At present, shares of both companies sell for about $40. At-the-money put and call options are available on both stocks, with an expiration date in three months. Based on the historical volatility of each stock, you estimate a range of prices that you think the shares may attain by the time the options expire. Next to each possible stock price, you write down the option payoff that will occur if the stock actually reaches that price on the expiration date (the strike price is $40 for both options). The numbers appear in the accompanying table.

Stock	Potential Prices in Three Months	Call Payoff	Put Payoff
Extreme Inc.	$15	$ 0	$25
	$25	$ 0	$15
	$35	$ 0	$ 5
	$45	$ 5	$ 0
	$55	$15	$ 0
	$65	$25	$ 0
Steady Corp.	$30	$ 0	$10
	$34	$ 0	$ 6
	$38	$ 0	$ 2
	$42	$ 2	$ 0
	$46	$ 6	$ 0
	$50	$10	$ 0

The payoffs of puts and calls for both companies are zero, exactly half the time. But when the payoffs are not zero, they are much larger for Extreme Inc. than they are for Steady Corp. That makes options on Extreme Inc. shares much more valuable than options on Steady Corp. stock.

Summing up, we now know that option prices usually increase as time to expiration increases. Option values also rise as the volatility of the underlying asset increases. Call option prices increase as the difference between the stock price and the strike price (S-X) grows larger, whereas put prices increase as this difference decreases. We are finally ready to tie all this together and calculate market price of puts and calls. Fortunately, simple, but powerful, tools exist for valuing options. We examine two approaches for valuing options, the binomial model and the Black and Scholes model.

CONCEPT REVIEW QUESTIONS

8. Throughout most of this book, we have shown that if an asset's risk increases, its price declines. Why is the opposite true for options?

9. Put options increase in value as stock prices fall, and call options increase in value as stock prices rise. How can the same movement in an underlying variable (e.g., an increase either in time before expiration or in volatility) cause both put and call prices to rise at the same time?

15.4 OPTION PRICING MODELS

The Binomial Model

Earlier in this chapter, we studied an important relationship linking the prices of puts, calls, shares, and risk-free bonds. Put-call parity establishes a direct link between the prices of these assets, a link which must hold to prevent arbitrage opportunities. A similar logic drives the binomial option pricing model. The binomial model recognizes investors can combine options (either calls or puts) with shares of the underlying asset to construct a portfolio with a risk-free payoff. Any asset with a risk-free payoff is relatively easy to value—just discount its future cash flows at the risk-free rate. But if we can value a portfolio containing options and shares, then we can also calculate the value of the options by subtracting the value of the shares from the value of the portfolio.

Let's work through an example that shows how to price an option, using the binomial method. The example proceeds in three distinct steps. First, we must find a portfolio of stock and options which generates a risk-free payoff in the future. Second, given that the portfolio offers a risk-free cash payment, we can calculate the present value of that portfolio by discounting its cash flow at the risk-free rate. Third, given the portfolio's present value, we can determine how much of the portfolio's value comes from the stock and how much comes from the option. By subtracting the value of the underlying shares from the value of the portfolio, we obtain the option's market price.

Step 1: Create a Risk-Free Portfolio. Suppose the shares of Financial Engineers Ltd. currently sell for $55. We want to determine the price of a call option on Financial Engineers stock, with an exercise price of $55 and an expiration date in one year. Assume the risk-free rate is 4 percent.

The binomial model begins with an assumption about the volatility of the underlying stock. Specifically, the model assumes that by the time the option expires, the stock will have increased or decreased to a particular dollar value. In this problem, we assume that one year from now, Financial Engineers stock price will have risen to $70 or it will have fallen to $40. Figure 15.8 provides a simple diagram of this assumption.[14]

The call option we want to price has a strike of $55. Therefore, if the underlying stock reaches $70 in one year, the call option will be worth $15. However, if Financial Engineers stock falls to $40, the call option will be worthless.

Now here is the crux of Step 1. We want to find some combination of Financial Engineers stock and the call option which yields the same payoff, whether the stock goes up or down over the next year. In other words, we want to create a risk-free combination of shares and calls. Here's how to do it. Suppose we purchase one share of

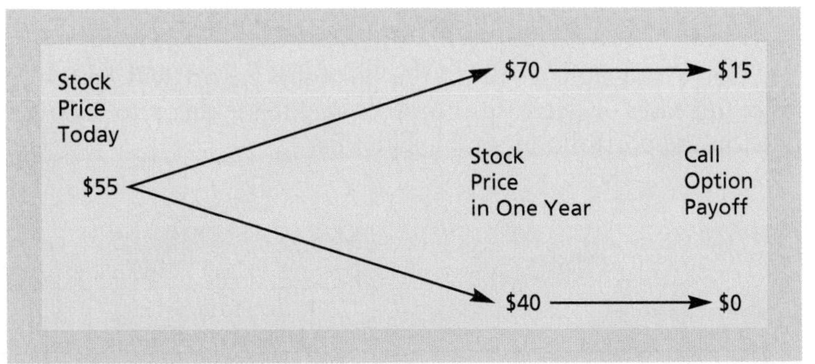

Figure 15.8
Binomial Option Pricing

The figure shows that in one year, Financial Engineers stock will be worth $70 or $40. If there is a call option on this stock, with a strike price of $55, then it will be worth $15 or $0 when that option expires in one year.

[14] How can we possibly know that the price of Financial Engineer's stock will be either $70 or $40? Of course we cannot know that. Almost any price is possible one year in the future. Soon, we will illustrate that this assumption, which seems completely ridiculous now, isn't really necessary in a more complex version of the binomial model. But let's get the simple version down first.

stock and h call options. At the moment, we do not know the value of h, but we can solve for it. Because our portfolio objective is to generate the same cash payment one year from now, whether our share of stock rises or falls, we can write down the portfolio's payoffs in each possible scenario and then choose h so that the payoffs are equal:

	Cash Flows One Year from Today	
	If the stock price goes up to \$70	If the stock price drops to \$40
One share of stock is worth	\$70	\$40
h options are worth	\$15h	\$0h
Total portfolio is worth	\$70 + \$15h	\$40 + \$0h

A portfolio that contains one share of stock and h call options will have the same cash value in one year if we choose the value of h that solves this equation:

$$70 + 15h = 40 + 0h$$
$$h = -2$$

The value of h represents the number of call options in our risk-free portfolio. Because h equals –2, we must *sell two call options* and combine that position with our single share of stock to create a risk-free portfolio. Why do we wind up selling options to achieve this objective? Remember that the value of a call option rises as the stock price rises. If we own a share of stock and a call option (or several call options) on that stock, the assets in our portfolio will move together, rising and falling at the same time. To create a portfolio that behaves like a risk-free bond, we need the movements in the stock and the call option to offset each other. If the stock's movements exactly cancel out fluctuations in the call, then the portfolio's payout will not move at all, just like a risk-free bond. Therefore, if we buy a share we must sell call options to create offsetting movements between the assets in our portfolio.

What happens to our portfolio if we buy one share and sell two calls? You can see the answer in two ways. First, just plug the value, –2, back into the equation that we used to solve for h and you get:

$$40 = 40$$

This expression says that the portfolio payoff will be \$40, whether the stock price increases or decreases. Another way to see this is to lay out the payoffs of each asset in the portfolio in a table like this.

	Cash Flows One Year from Today	
	If the stock price goes up to \$70	If the stock price drops to \$40
One share of stock is worth	\$70	\$40
Two short options are worth	–\$30	\$ 0
Total portfolio is worth	\$40	\$40

The first line of the table is self-explanatory. The second line indicates that if we sell two call options and the stock price equals \$70 next year, then we will owe the holder of the calls \$15 per option, or \$30 total. On the other hand, if one year from now the stock price equals \$40, then the call options we sold will be worthless, and we will have no cash outflow. In either case, the total cash inflow from the portfolio will be \$40.

Because this portfolio pays \$40 in one year, no matter what happens, we call it a perfectly hedged portfolio. The value of *h* is called the **hedge ratio** because it tells us what combination of stocks and calls results in a perfectly hedged position.

hedge ratio
A combination of stock and options that results in a risk-free payoff.

Step 2: Calculate the Present Value of the Portfolio. Because the portfolio, consisting of one share of stock and two short call options, pays \$40 for certain next year, we can say that the portfolio behaves like a risk-free bond. Step 2 requires us to calculate the present value of the portfolio. Because we already know that the risk-free rate equals 4 percent, the present value of the portfolio equals:

$$PV = \frac{\$40}{1.04} = \$38.46$$

It is crucial at this step to understand the following point. Buying one share of stock and selling two calls yields the same future payoff as buying a risk-free, zero-coupon bond, with a face value of \$40. Because both of these investments offer \$40 in one year, with certainty, they should both sell for the same price today. That's the insight that allows us to determine the option's price in Step 3.

Step 3: Determine the Price of the Option. If a risk-free bond, paying \$40 in one year, costs \$38.46 today, then the net cost of buying one share of Financial Engineers stock and selling two call options must also be \$38.46. Why? Both investment strategies offer the same future cash flows, so they must both sell for the same price. Therefore, to determine the price of the option, we need to write down an expression for the cost of our hedged portfolio and set that expression equal to \$38.46.

From the information given in the problem, purchasing one share of stock costs \$55. Partially offsetting this cost will be the revenue from selling two call options. Denoting the price of the call option, C, we can calculate the total cost of the portfolio as follows:

$$\text{Total portfolio cost} = \$55 - 2C = \$38.46$$

Solving for C, we obtain a call value of \$8.27.

At this point, it is worth reviewing what we've accomplished. We began with an assumption about the future movements of the underlying stock. Next, given the type of option we wanted to value and its characteristics, we calculated the payoffs of the option for each of the two possible future stock prices. Given those payoffs, we discovered that by buying one share and selling two calls, we could generate a certain payoff of \$40 in one year. Because the present value of that payoff is \$38.46, the net cost of buying the share and selling the calls must also equal \$38.46. That implies that we received revenue of \$11.54 from selling two calls, or \$8.57 each. Let's repeat the process to value an identical put option on the same underlying stock.

APPLYING THE MODEL

We begin this problem with the same set of assumptions from the last problem. Financial Engineers stock sells for \$55, and it may increase to \$70 or decrease to \$40 in one year. The risk-free rate equals 4 percent. We want to use the binomial model to calculate the value of a one-year put option, with a strike price of \$55. We begin by finding the composition of a perfectly hedged portfolio. As before, let's write down the payoffs of a portfolio that contains one share of stock and h put options:

Cash Flows One Year from Today		
	If the stock price goes up to \$70	If the stock price drops to \$40
One share of stock is worth	\$70	\$40
h options are worth	\$0h	\$15h
Total portfolio is worth	\$70 + \$0h	\$40 + \$15h

Notice that the put option pays \$15 when the stock price drops, and it pays nothing when the stock price rises. Set the payoffs in each scenario equal to each other and solve for h:

$$70 + 0h = 40 + 15h$$
$$h = 2$$

To create a perfectly hedged portfolio, we must buy one share of stock and two put options. In this problem, notice that we are buying options rather than selling them. Remember that put option prices move in the opposite direction of the underlying stock. Therefore, it is possible to simultaneously purchase stock and put options in such a combination that the movements in the stock and the options exactly offset. By plugging the value of $h = 2$ back into the equation, we see that an investor who buys one share of stock and two put options essentially creates a synthetic bond, with a face value of \$70:

$$70 + 0(2) = 40 + 15(2)$$
$$70 = 70$$

Given a risk-free rate of 4 percent, the present value today of \$70 is \$67.31. It would cost \$67.31 to buy a one-year, risk-free bond paying \$70, so it must also cost \$67.31 to buy one share and two puts. Given that the current share price is \$55, and letting P stand for the price of the put, we find that the put option is worth \$6.15 (rounding to the nearest penny):

$$\text{Cost of one share} + 2\text{ puts} = \$67.31 = \$55 + 2P$$
$$\$12.31 = 2P$$
$$\$6.15 = P$$

Take a moment to look over the last two examples of pricing options that use the binomial approach. Make a list of the data needed to price these options.

1) the current price of the underlying stock
2) the amount of time remaining before the option expires
3) the strike price of the option
4) the risk-free rate
5) the possible values that the underlying stock could take in the future

On this list, the only unknown is the fifth item. You can easily find the other four necessary values by looking at current market data.

At this point, we want to pause and ask one of our all-time favorite exam questions. Look back at Figure 15.8. What assumption do we make there about the probability of an up and down move in Financial Engineers stock? Most people see that the figure shows two possible outcomes and guess that the probabilities must be 50-50. That is not true. At no point in our discussion of the binomial model did we make any assumption about the probabilities of up and down movements in the stock. We don't have to know what those probabilities are to value the option. That's convenient because estimating them could be very difficult.

Why are the probabilities of no concern to us? There are two answers to this question. The first answer is that the market sets the current price of the stock at a level that reflects the probabilities of future up and down movements. In other words, the probabilities are embedded in the stock price, even though no one can see them directly.

The second answer is that the binomial model prices an option through the principle of "no arbitrage." Because it is always possible to combine a share of stock with options (either calls or puts) into a risk-free portfolio, the binomial model says that the value of that portfolio must be the same as the value of a risk-free bond. Otherwise, an arbitrage opportunity would exist—identical assets would be selling at different prices. Because the portfolio containing stock and options offers a risk-free payoff, the probabilities of up and down movements in the stock price do not enter the calculations. An investor who holds the hedged portfolio doesn't need to worry about movements in the stock because they do not affect the portfolio's payoffs.

Almost all students object to the binomial model's assumption that the price of a stock can take just two values in the future. Fair enough. It is certainly true that one year from today, the price of Financial Engineers may be $70, $40, or almost any other value. However, it turns out that more complex versions of the binomial do not require analysts to specify just two final prices for the stock. The binomial model can accommodate a wide range of final prices. To see how this works, consider a slight modification to our original problem.

Rather than presuming that Financial Engineers stock will rise or fall by $15 over a year's time, suppose it may rise or fall by $7.50 every six months. That's still a big assumption, but if we make it, we find that the list of potential prices of Financial Engineers stock, one year from today, has grown from two values to three. Figure 15.9 proves this claim. After one year, the price of the stock may be $40, $55, or $70. Now let's modify the assumption one more time. Suppose the price of the stock can move up or down $3.75 every three months. Figure 15.9 shows that in this case, the number of possible stock prices one year in the future grows to five.

Given a tree with many branches like the one in Figure 15.9, it is possible to solve for the value of a call or put option by applying the same steps we followed to value options using the simple two-step tree. Now imagine a much larger tree, one in which the stock moves up or down every few minutes, or even every few seconds. Each change in the stock price is very small, perhaps a penny or two, but as the tree unfolds and time passes, the number of branches rapidly expands, as does the number of possible values of the stock at the option's expiration date. If you imagine what this tree would look like, you can see that when the option expires in a year, the price of Financial Engineers stock can take any one of hundreds, or even thousands, of different values. Therefore, the complaint about the binomial model's artificial assumption of just two possible stock prices no longer applies. Though extremely tedious, solving for the call value involves working all the way through the tree, applying the same steps over and over again.

The binomial model is an incredibly powerful and flexible tool that analysts can use to price all sorts of options, from ordinary puts and calls, to complex real options

Figure 15.9
Multistage Binomial Trees

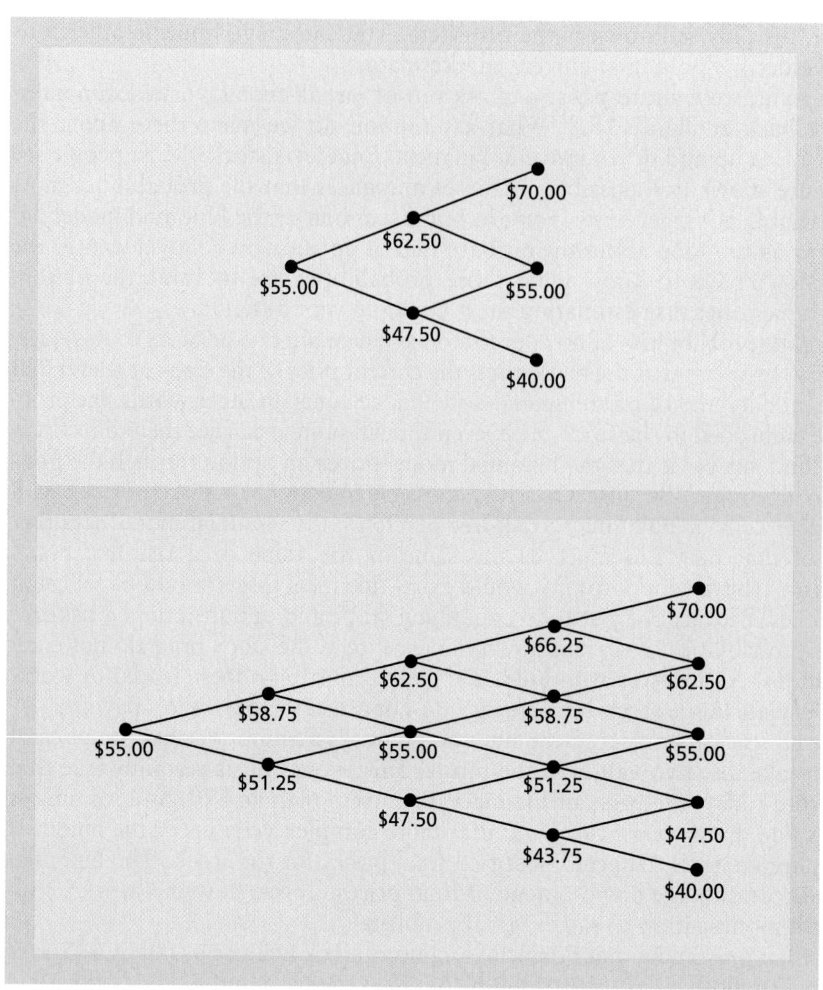

which are embedded in capital investment projects. The genius of the model is in its recognition of the opportunity to use stock and options to mimic the payoffs of risk-free bonds, the easiest of all securities to price. That insight is also central to the second option pricing model that we discuss, the Black and Scholes Model.

The Black and Scholes Model

In 1973, Myron Scholes and Fisher Black published what might fairly be called a trillion-dollar research paper. Their research produced for the first time a formula that traders could use to calculate the value of call options, a path-breaking discovery, which had eluded researchers for decades. Black and Scholes did not have to wait long to see whether their formula would have an effect in financial markets. That same year, options began trading in the United States on the newly formed Chicago Board Options Exchange (CBOE). Traders on the floor of the options exchange used handheld calculators that were programmed with the Black-Scholes formula. From that beginning, trading in options exploded over the next two decades, hence, the trillion-dollar moniker given to the original research paper.[15]

15. For this achievement, Myron Scholes won the Nobel Prize in economics in 1997, an honor he shared with Robert Merton, another researcher who made seminal contributions to options research. Fisher Black undoubtedly would have been a corecipient of the award had he not died in 1995.

When you first encounter it, the Black and Scholes option pricing equation looks rather intimidating. As a matter of fact, their paper was originally rejected by the editor at the prestigious academic journal in which Black and Scholes published their prize-winning formula. He felt it was too technical and not of interest to a wide audience. Although it is true that the derivation of the formula requires a rather high level of mathematics, the intuition behind the equation is fairly straightforward. In fact, the logic of the Black and Scholes model mirrors that of the binomial model.

Black and Scholes began their research by asking a question. Suppose investors can buy and sell shares of stock, options on those shares, and risk-free bonds. Does a combination of options and shares exist that provides a risk-free payoff? This should sound familiar, because this is exactly how you begin when you price an option, using the binomial model. However, Black and Scholes' approach to valuing an option differs from the binomial method in several important ways.

First, recall that the binomial model assumes that over a given period of time, the stock price will move up or down by a known amount. In Figure 15.9, we showed that by shortening the length of the period during which the stock price moves, we increase the number of different prices that the stock may reach by the option's expiration date. Black and Scholes take this approach to its logical extreme. Their model presumes that stock prices can move at every moment in time. If we were to illustrate this assumption by drawing a binomial tree like the ones in Figure 15.9, the tree would have an infinite number of branches, and on the option's expiration date, the stock price could take on almost any value.

Second, Black and Scholes did not assume that they knew precisely what the up and down movements in stock would be at every instant. They recognized that these movements were essentially random, and therefore unpredictable. Instead, they assumed that the volatility, or standard deviation, of a stock's movements was known. As we shall see, the challenge for practitioners, using the Black and Scholes model, is to find a reliable way to estimate the volatility of the stock underlying an option.

With these assumptions in place, Black and Scholes determined that the price of a European call option (on a nondividend-paying stock) must be:

$$C = SN(d_1) - Xe^{-rt}N(d_2) \qquad \text{(Eq. 15.2)}$$

$$d_1 = \frac{\ln\left(\frac{S}{X}\right) + \left(r + \frac{\sigma^2}{2}\right)t}{\sigma\sqrt{t}} \qquad \text{(Eq. 15.3)}$$

$$d_2 = d_1 - \sigma\sqrt{t}$$

Let's dissect this carefully. We have seen most of the terms in the equation before:

S = current market price of underlying stock
X = strike price of option
t = amount of time before option expires (in years)
r = annual risk-free interest rate
σ = annual standard deviation of underlying stock's returns
e = 2.718 (approximately)
$N(X)$ = the probability of drawing a value less than or equal to X from the standard normal distribution

Does this list of variables sound familiar? It should because it is nearly identical to the list of inputs required to use the binomial model. The stock price (S), the strike price (X), the time until expiration (t), and the risk-free rate (r) are all variables that we used before to price options with the binomial method. As mentioned above, one difference between this model and the binomial is the assumption that analysts know the standard deviation of a stock's returns (σ).

What about the term Xe^{-rt}? Recall from our discussion about continuous compounding, in Chapter 3, that the term e^{-rt} reflects the present value of $1, discounted at r percent for t years. Therefore, Xe^{-rt} simply equals the present value of the option's strike price.[16] With this in mind, look again at Equation 15.2. The first term equals the stock price, multiplied by a quantity labeled $N(d_1)$. The second term is the present value of the strike price, multiplied by a quantity labeled $N(d_2)$. Therefore, we can say that the call option value equals the "adjusted" stock price, minus the present value of the "adjusted" strike price, where $N(d_1)$ and $N(d_2)$ represent some kind of adjustment factors. Earlier in this chapter, we saw that call option values increase as the difference between the stock price and the strike price, S-X, increases. The same relationship holds here, although we must now factor in the terms $N(d_1)$ and $N(d_2)$.

In the Black and Scholes equation, d_1 and d_2 are simply numerical values (calculated using Equation 15.3) that depend on the model's inputs: the stock price, the strike price, the interest rate, the time to expiration, and volatility. The expressions $N(d_1)$ and $N(d_2)$ convert the numerical values of d_1 and d_2 into probabilities, using the standard normal distribution.[17] Figure 15.10 shows that the value, $N(d_1)$, equals the area under the standard normal curve to the left of value d_1. For example, if we calculate the value of d_1 and find that it equals 0, then $N(d_1)$ equals 0.5 because half of the area under the curve falls to the left of zero. The higher the value of d_1, the closer $N(d_1)$ gets to 1.0. The lower the value of d_1, the closer $N(d_1)$ gets to zero. The same relationship holds between d_2 and $N(d_2)$. Given a particular value of d_1 (or d_2), to calculate $N(d_1)$ you need a table showing the cumulative standard

Figure 15.10
Standard Normal Distribution

The expression $N(d_1)$ equals the probability of drawing a particular value, d_1, or a lower value, from the standard normal distribution. In the figure, $N(d_1)$ is represented by the shaded portion under the bell curve. Because the normal distribution is symmetric about the mean, we can write, $N(d_1) = 1 - N(-d_1)$.

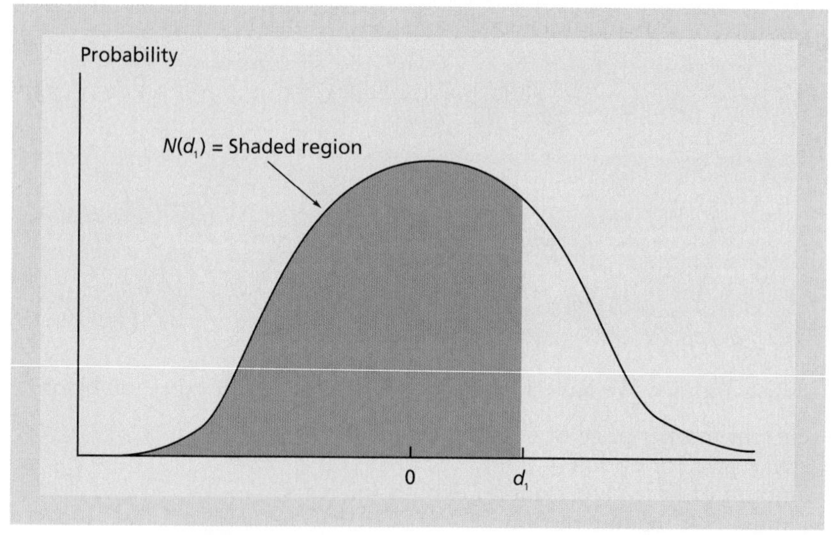

[16] Remember, this expression can be written in two ways: $Xe^{-rt} = \frac{X}{e^{rt}}$. Assuming that the continuously compounded risk-free rate of interest equals r and the amount of time before expiration equals t, this is simply the present value of the strike price.

[17] Recall from the statistics that the standard normal distribution has a mean equal to zero and a standard deviation equal to one.

normal probabilities, or you can plug d_1 into the *Excel* function, =normsdist(d_1). A common intuitive interpretation of $N(d_1)$ and $N(d_2)$ is that they represent the risk-adjusted probabilities that the call will expire in the money. Therefore, a verbal description of Equation 15.10 is:

> *The call option price equals the stock price, minus the present value of the exercise price, adjusted for the probability that when the option expires, the stock price will exceed the strike price (i.e., the probability that the option expires in the money).*

APPLYING THE MODEL

The stock of Cloverdale Food Processors currently sells for \$40. A European call option on Cloverdale stock has an expiration date six months in the future, and a strike price of \$38. The estimate of the annual standard deviation of Cloverdale stock is 45 percent, and the risk-free rate is 6 percent. What is the call worth?

$$d_1 = \frac{\ln\left(\frac{40}{38}\right) + \left(0.06 + \frac{0.45^2}{2}\right)\frac{1}{2}}{0.45\sqrt{\frac{1}{2}}} = \frac{(0.0513) + (0.0806)}{0.3182} = 0.4146$$

$$d_2 = d_1 - \sigma\sqrt{t} = 0.4146 - 0.45\sqrt{\frac{1}{2}} = 0.0964$$

$$N(0.4146) = 0.6608 \qquad N(0.0964) = 0.5384$$

$$C = 40(0.6608) - 38(2.718^{-(.06)(0.5)})(0.5384) = \$6.58$$

By experimenting with Equations 15.2 and 15.3, we can study the effect of changes in each of the key input variables on the price of a call option. For example, suppose we recalculate the value of the Cloverdale call option, described earlier, by adjusting just one of the required inputs each time to see the resulting effect on the option's price. After just a few experiments, we could reach the following conclusions:

- the call value increases as the price of Cloverdale stock (S) increases
- the call value increases as the time to expiration (t) increases
- the call value increases as the standard deviation of Cloverdale stock (σ) increases
- the call value increases as the strike price (X) decreases
- the call value increases as the risk-free interest rate (r) increases

SMART CONCEPTS

See the concept explained step-by-step at SMARTFinance

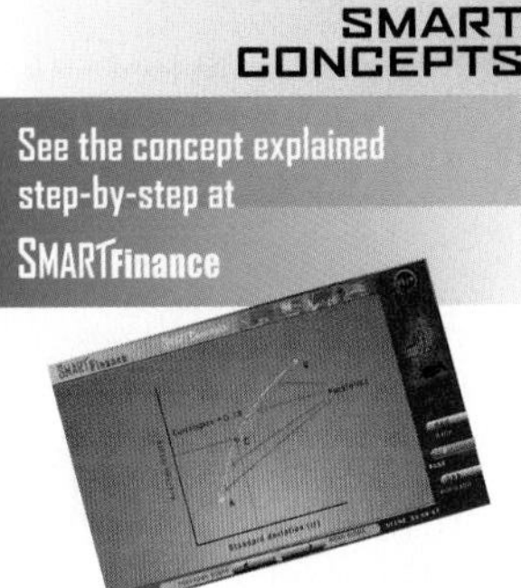

We have already discussed the first four relationships above. Call values generally increase with increases in the underlying stock price, the time to expiration, or the volatility of the underlying stock, and calls are more valuable when the strike price is lower. The finding that call values increase when the interest rate increases is new. Here is an intuitive explanation for that relationship. The call option grants the holder the right to buy something and to pay for it at a later date. The right to defer payment is more valuable when the interest rate is high, so call values increase when interest rates do.

Though the Black and Scholes model and the binomial model look very different at first glance, they share the same underlying logical principles. Both models calculate option values, based on the notion that combinations of options and underlying shares can mimic the payoffs of risk-free bonds. Both models require essentially the same inputs (S, X, r, t, and some assumption about volatility) to calculate option values. And both models produce the same predictions about how changes in the input variables affect option prices.

CONCEPT REVIEW QUESTIONS

10. To value options, using the binomial method, is it necessary to know the expected return on the stock? Why or why not?

11. There is an old saying that nature abhors a vacuum. The financial equivalent is "markets abhor arbitrage opportunities." Explain the central role this principle plays in the binomial model.

15.5 OPTIONS IN CORPORATE FINANCE

Thus far, our emphasis has been on stock options that trade in financial markets. The principles we've developed to understand those options can be applied more broadly in a wide range of corporate finance problems. We conclude this chapter with a brief overview of the applications of option pricing techniques to the problems that corporate financial managers encounter on a regular basis.

Employee Stock Options

Many firms use employee stock option grants (ESOs) as part of their compensation packages. ESOs are essentially call options that give employees the right to buy shares in the company they work for, at a fixed price. When firms distribute ESOs to their employees, they typically set the strike price equal to the current market price, so ESOs are typically at the money when they are issued. Like the ordinary call options that trade in financial markets, ESOs are most valuable when the price of the underlying stock is well above the strike price. Thus, granting ESOs gives employees an incentive to take actions that increase the firm's stock price. Aligning the interests of employees with those of shareholders is one of the primary reasons that firms compensate their people with options. Options do not result in a perfect alignment of interests, however. For example, we know that option values increase if the volatility of the underlying stock increases, so paying managers in options creates at least some incentive for them to take added risk. That added risk may or may not be in the interests of shareholders.

ESOs differ from ordinary call options in several important ways. Whereas the majority of options traded in financial markets expire within a few months, ESOs grant employees the right to buy stock for as long as ten years. We know that call option values increase as the time toward expiration grows longer, so the long life of ESOs makes them particularly attractive to employees. However, many firms do not allow employees to exercise their options until a vesting period has passed. For example, a common requirement is that the employee must work for the firm for five years after receiving an ESO grant, before the option can be exercised. In a sense, ESOs are a blend of American and European options. Like European options, ESOs cannot be exercised immediately, but like American options, ESOs can be exercised at any time after the vesting period has passed.

Besides using options to give employees an incentive to increase the stock price, firms issue options because they require no immediate cash outlay. Small firms, rapidly growing firms, and firms that do not have an abundance of cash may elect to pay employees with options as a way of conserving cash.

A related motivation for firms to grant ESOs has to do with the accounting treatment of options. As this book was going to press, the Financial Accounting Standards Board (FASB) was in the process of revising its standards for reporting the cost of stock options. At that time, the rules allowed firms to disclose the value of their ESOs in the footnotes to their financial statements. In early 2004, the FASB proposed a new rule that would require firms to deduct the "fair value" of ESOs on their income statement. To calculate the fair value of a particular option, the FASB recommended using a version of the binomial model that we discussed in the previous section.

Opponents of this change argued that forcing companies to create an expense category for options didn't make sense because firms paid no cash to employees at the time that ESOs were issued. Those opposed to the proposed rule also said that the binomial model was too complex and required too many assumptions to generate reliable estimates of the cost of option grants. Furthermore, they argued that many firms would restrict their option grants to senior executives, if the FASB forced companies to report a charge against income for ESOs. Intel, which historically granted options to nearly all of its more than 70,000 employees, joined other high-tech firms in an intense lobbying effort to persuade Congress not to require option expensing.

SMART IDEAS VIDEO

Myron Scholes, Stanford University and Chairman of Oak Hill Platinum Partners

"I think that companies should expense executive stock option grants."

See the entire interview at **SMARTFinance**

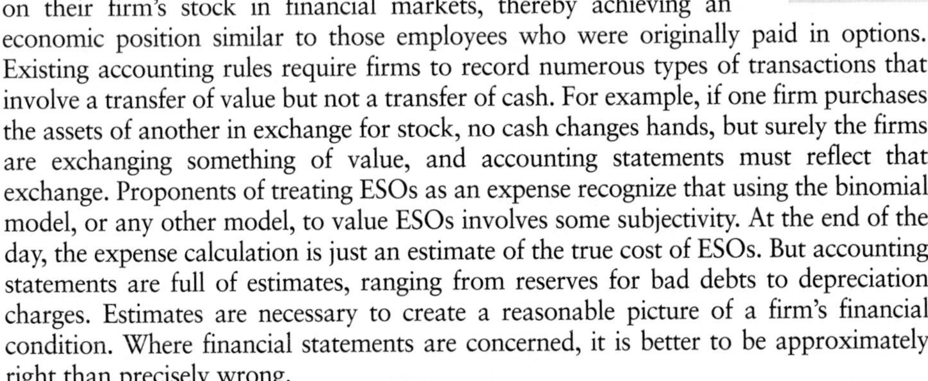

Proponents of expensing options, including business luminaries such as Warren Buffet and Alan Greenspan, point out that ignoring the cost of issuing ESOs when calculating net income defies economic logic. We know that options have value, even when they are not in the money. Even if a company pays employees in options rather than cash, that option-based compensation still constitutes an expense because options have value. For example, imagine that one firm pays employees in cash, whereas another firm pays in options. Employees who receive cash compensation can use that cash to purchase options on their firm's stock in financial markets, thereby achieving an economic position similar to those employees who were originally paid in options. Existing accounting rules require firms to record numerous types of transactions that involve a transfer of value but not a transfer of cash. For example, if one firm purchases the assets of another in exchange for stock, no cash changes hands, but surely the firms are exchanging something of value, and accounting statements must reflect that exchange. Proponents of treating ESOs as an expense recognize that using the binomial model, or any other model, to value ESOs involves some subjectivity. At the end of the day, the expense calculation is just an estimate of the true cost of ESOs. But accounting statements are full of estimates, ranging from reserves for bad debts to depreciation charges. Estimates are necessary to create a reasonable picture of a firm's financial condition. Where financial statements are concerned, it is better to be approximately right than precisely wrong.

Warrants and Convertibles

Warrants are securities that are issued by firms and that grant investors the right to buy shares of stock at a fixed price, for a given period of time. Warrants bear a close resemblance to call options, and the same factors that influence call option values affect warrant prices, too (stock price, risk-free rate, strike price, expiration date, and volatility). However, there are some important differences between warrants and calls.

warrants
Securities that grant rights similar to a call option, except that when a warrant is exercised, the firm must issue a new share, and it receives the strike price as a cash inflow.

1) Warrants are issued by firms, whereas call options are contracts between investors who are not necessarily connected to the firm whose stock serves as the underlying asset.
2) When investors exercise warrants, the number of outstanding shares increases and the issuing firm receives the strike price as a capital inflow. When investors exercise call options, no change in outstanding shares occurs, and the firm receives no cash.

3) Warrants are often issued with expiration dates that are several years in the future, whereas most options expire in just a few months.
4) Whereas call and put options trade as stand-alone securities, firms frequently attach warrants to public or privately-placed bonds, preferred stock, and sometimes even common stock. When warrants are attached to other securities, they are called **equity kickers**, implying that they give additional upside potential to the security to which they are attached. When firms bundle warrants together with other securities, they may or may not grant investors the right to unbundle them and sell the warrants separately.

equity kickers
Warrants attached to another security offering (usually a bond offering) that give investors more upside potential.

For example, on October 23, 2003, SureBeam Corporation announced that it had issued preferred stock and warrants, worth $4.5 million, to a group of institutional investors. The warrants would allow the investors to purchase up to 2.7 million shares of SureBeam common stock for $1 per share at any time over the next five years. If $1 seems like a bargain price, consider that SureBeam, the maker of food radiation systems, had fallen on hard times by late 2003. Because the company had failed to file quarterly financial statements, as required by the S.E.C., Nasdaq officials warned the company that its stock might be delisted. Surebeam desperately needed capital to stay afloat, hence, the $1 strike price on its warrants. In fact, even that price turned out to be too high, as SureBeam's stock was delisted in late October, and it filed for bankruptcy in January 2004.

In contrast, the warrants issued by Canadian firm Dundee Precious Metals, in 1994, turned out to be quite valuable for investors. These warrants allowed investors to purchase Dundee shares for $25 over ten years. When the warrants were exercised in February 2004, Dundee's shares were worth $36.57. Because the warrant holders decided to exercise their right to purchase 2,432,323 Dundee shares, the company received additional capital of more than $60.8 million.

In each case, firms receive capital from warrants, once when they are issued and again if they are exercised. This stands in sharp contrast to the buying, selling, and exercising of call options, which occurs without having any direct cash flow effect on the underlying firms.

convertible bond
A bond that gives investors the right to convert their bonds into shares.

A **convertible bond** grants investors the right to receive payment in the shares of an underlying stock rather than in cash. Usually, the stock, which investors have the right to "purchase" in exchange for their bonds, is the stock of the firm that issued the bonds. In some cases, however, a firm that owns a large amount of common stock in a different firm will use those shares as the underlying asset for a convertible bond issue. In either case, a convertible bond is essentially an ordinary corporate bond with an attached call option or warrant.

In February 2002, the biotech giant, Amgen Inc., announced a sale of thirty-year, zero-coupon bonds, which would generate proceeds for the company of approximately $2.5 billion. Amgen's bonds offered investors a yield to maturity of just 1.125 percent, well below the yields on long-term government bonds at the time. How could a biotech firm borrow money at a lower rate than the government? Investors were willing to buy Amgen's bonds, despite the low yield, because the bonds were convertible into Amgen common stock. Specifically, each Amgen bond that had a face value of $1,000 could be converted into 8.8601 shares of Amgen common stock.

Convertible bonds offer investors the security of a bond and the upside potential of common stock. If Amgen's shares increase in value, its convertible bondholders will redeem their bonds for Amgen shares rather than cash. To see how far Amgen's shares would have to rise before bondholders would want to convert, we must first calculate the market price of Amgen's bonds:

$$\text{Price} = \frac{\$1{,}000}{(1.01125)^{30}} = \$714.90$$

The **conversion ratio** defines how many Amgen shares bondholders will receive if they convert. In this case, the conversion ratio is 8.8601. Therefore, if bondholders choose to convert immediately, they will effectively be paying a **conversion price** for Amgen of:

conversion ratio
The number of shares bondholders receive if they convert their bonds into shares.

$$\text{Conversion price} = \frac{\$714.90}{8.8601} = \$80.69$$

conversion price
The market price of a convertible bond, divided by the number of shares of stock that bondholders receive if they convert.

At the time Amgen issued these bonds, its stock was selling for approximately \$57 per share. Holding the price of the bond constant, Amgen's shares would have to rise more than 41 percent before bondholders would want to convert their bonds into Amgen's shares. This 41 percent figure equals the bond's **conversion premium.**

conversion premium
The percentage increase in the underlying stock that must occur before it is profitable to exercise the option to convert a bond into shares.

At a stock price of \$57, it does not make sense for holders of Amgen's convertible bonds to trade them for shares of stock. Nevertheless, we can still ask, what value will bondholders receive if they do convert? If Amgen stock sells for \$57 and each bond can be exchanged for 8.8601 shares, then the **conversion value** of one bond equals \$505.03 (8.8601 × \$57).

conversion value
The market price of the stock, multiplied by the number of shares of stock that bondholders receive if they convert.

Conversion value is important because it helps define a lower bound on the market value of a convertible bond. For example, suppose interest rates jump suddenly, and the yield on Amgen's bonds goes from 1.125 percent to 2.5 percent. Ignoring the opportunity to convert the bonds, the price would drop to:

$$\text{Price} = \frac{\$1{,}000}{(1.025)^{30}} = \$476.74$$

However, the price of Amgen's cannot dip this low if Amgen's stock remains at \$57. If it did, investors could exploit an arbitrage opportunity by purchasing one bond for \$476.74 and immediately converting it into 8.8601 shares of stock, worth \$505.03.

In general, we can say that the price of a convertible bond will be, at a minimum, the higher of (1) the value of an identical bond without conversion rights, or (2) the conversion value. Figure 15.11 demonstrates this pattern for a generic convertible bond with a par value of \$1,000 and a conversion ratio of 20. The horizontal line represents the present value of the convertible bond's scheduled interest and principal payments, which we simplify to be \$1,000. The upward sloping line shows the bond's conversion value at different stock prices, and the curve shows the

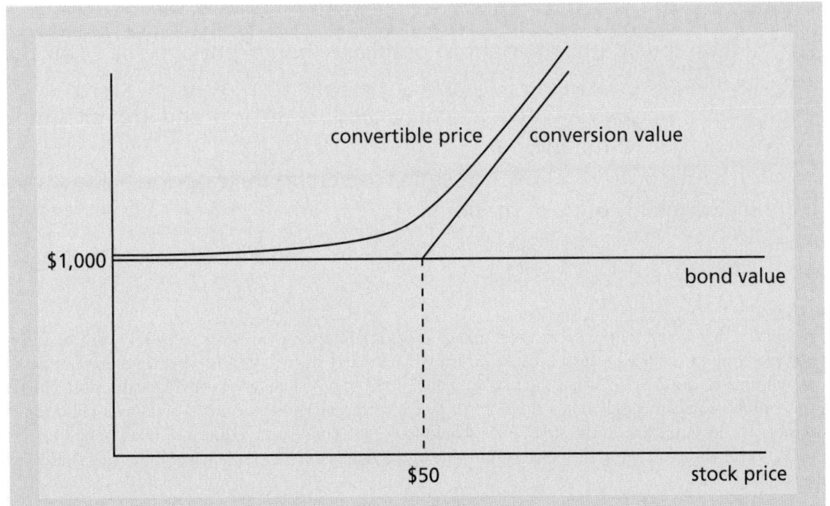

Figure 15.11
The Value of a Convertible Bond

The convertible bond must sell for at least its value as a straight bond, or its conversion value, whichever is greater. If the bond's value is \$1,000, and the conversion ratio is 20, then the conversion price equals \$50. For each \$1 increase in the stock price beyond \$50, the bond's conversion value rises by \$20.

convertible bond's price. When the stock price is very low, so is the probability that the bonds will ever be worth converting into shares, so the convertible bond sells at a price comparable to an ordinary bond. As the share price rises, the value of the conversion option increases.

Most convertible bonds have another feature that slightly complicates matters. When firms issue convertibles, they almost always retain the right to call back the bonds. When firms call their outstanding bonds, bondholders can choose, within 30 days of the call, to receive either the call price in cash or a quantity of shares equal to the conversion ratio. Effectively, the call option that firms retain allows them to shorten the conversion option held by bondholders. If a firm calls its bonds, investors will choose cash if the call price exceeds conversion value, and they will choose shares if the opposite is true.

Under what circumstances should a firm call its convertible bonds? If managers are acting in the interests of shareholders, they will never call bonds that are worth less than the call price. Doing so would transfer wealth from shareholders to bondholders. Similarly, if the price of a bond rises above the call price, because the underlying stock has increased in value, then firms should call the bonds. If firms do not call the bonds and the stock price continues to increase, then when investors ultimately choose to convert their bonds into shares, firms will be selling stock at a bargain. Again, the result is a transfer of wealth from shareholders to bondholders. Therefore, the optimal policy is to call the bonds when their market value equals the call price.[18]

CONCEPT REVIEW QUESTIONS

12. How are employee stock options different from the options that trade on the exchanges and in the over-the-counter market?

13. What is the most important reason why firms should be required to show an expense on their income statement for employee stock options?

14. Suppose a warrant and a call option have the same strike price, the same expiration date, and the same underlying asset. Which is more valuable, the warrant or the call? Why?

15.6 SUMMARY AND CONCLUSIONS

- Options are contracts that grant the buyer the right to buy or sell stock at a fixed price.
- Call options grant the right to purchase shares; put options grant the right to sell shares.
- Options provide a real economic benefit to society and are not simply a form of legalized gambling.
- American options allow investors to exercise their options before they expire, but European options do not.

[18] Actually, this would be the optimal call policy if firms could force investors to choose cash or shares immediately upon receiving the call. However, because investors have thirty days to decide whether they want cash or shares, the optimal time to call may be when the market value of the bonds slightly exceeds the call price. The reason is that if firms call the bonds precisely when the market price hits the call price, the stock price may fall during the thirty-day decision period. A decline in the stock price would lower the conversion value, and firms would be forced to redeem the bonds for cash. Allowing the conversion value of the bonds to rise a little beyond the strike price gives firms a little "slack."

- Payoff diagrams show the value of options or portfolios of options on the expiration date. Payoff diagrams can be used to illustrate how portfolios of options and other securities perform as the underlying stock price moves.
- Put-call parity establishes a link between the market prices of calls, puts, shares, and bonds.
- Call option prices rise and put option prices fall as (S-X) increases.
- Calls increase in value when there is time left before expiration, whereas the effect of a longer expiration period on the value of a put can be positive or negative.
- An increase in the volatility of the underlying asset increases the values of puts and calls.
- The binomial model uses the principle of "no arbitrage" to determine the market prices of puts and calls.

SELF-TEST PROBLEMS

Answers to Self-Test Problems appear in Appendix D at back of book. Answers to the Concept Review Questions throughout the chapter appear at http://megginson.swlearning.com.

ST 15-1. Several call options on Cuban Cigars Inc. are available for trading. The expiration date, strike price, and current premium for each of these options appears below.

Strike	Expiration	Premium
\$40	July	\$6
\$45	July	\$3.50
\$50	July	\$1.75

An investor decides to purchase one call, with a \$40 strike, and one, with a \$50 strike. At the same time, the investor sells two of the calls, with a \$45 strike price. Draw a payoff diagram for this portfolio of options. Your diagram should have two lines, one showing the portfolio's payoff on a gross basis, and one showing the payoff net of the cost of forming the portfolio.

ST 15-2. A stock currently sells for \$36. In the next six months, the stock will either go up to \$42 or it will fall to \$31. If the risk-free rate is 4 percent per year, calculate the current market price of a call option on this stock, with an expiration date in six months and a strike price of \$35.

INTERNET RESOURCES

Note: *For updates to links, please go to the book's Web site at* http://megginson.swlearning.com.

http://www.cboe.com—Offers price quotes for many options and provides several tutorials that explain the characteristics of options and how they are traded

KEY TERMS

American call option
at the money
call option
cash settlement
conversion ratio
conversion premium
conversion price
conversion value
convertible bond
counterparty risk
derivative securities
equity kickers
European call option
exercise price
exercise the option
expiration date

hedge ratio
in the money
intrinsic value
long position
naked option position
net payoff
option premium
out of the money
payoff
payoff diagrams
protective put
put-call parity
put option
short position
strike price
time value
underlying asset
warrants

QUESTIONS AND PROBLEMS

Q15-1. Explain why an option is a derivative security.

Q15-2. Is buying an option more or less risky than buying the underlying stock?

Q15-3. What is the difference between an option's price and its payoff?

Q15-4. List five factors that influence the prices of calls and puts.

Q15-5. What are the economic benefits which options provide?

Q15-6. What is the primary advantage of settling options contracts in cash?

Q15-7. Suppose you want to invest in a particular company. What are the pros and cons of buying the company's shares versus buying their options?

Q15-8. Suppose you want to make an investment that will be profitable if a company's stock price falls. What are the pros and cons of buying a put option on the company's stock versus short selling the stock?

Q15-9. Suppose you own an American call option on Pfizer stock. Pfizer stock has gone up in value considerably since you bought the option, so your investment has been profitable. There is still one month to go before the option expires, but you decide to go ahead and take your profits in cash. Describe two ways that you could accomplish this goal. Which one is likely to leave you with the highest cash payoff?

Q15-10. Look at the Opti-Tech call option prices in Table 15.1. Holding the expiration month constant, call prices increase as the strike price decreases. The strike prices decrease in increments of $2.50. Do the call option prices increase in constant increments? That is, does the call price increase by the same amount as the strike price drops, from $35 to $32.50 to $30, and so on?

PROBLEMS

Options Vocabulary

P15-1. If the underlying stock price is $25, indicate whether each of the options below is in the money, at the money, or out of the money.

Strike	Call	Put
$20		
$25		
$30		

P 15-2. The stock of Spears Entertainment currently sells for \$28. A call option on this stock has a strike price of \$25, and it sells for \$5.25. A put option on this stock has a strike price of \$30, and it sells for \$3.10. What is the intrinsic value of each option? What is the time value of each option?

Option Payoff Diagrams

P15-3. Draw payoff diagrams for each of the positions below (X = strike price).

a. Buy a call, with X = \$50
b. Sell a call, with X = \$60
c. Buy a put, with X = \$60
d. Sell a put, with X = \$50

P15-4. Draw payoff diagrams for each of the portfolios below (X = strike price).

a. Buy a share of stock and short a call, with X = \$35.
b. Buy a risk-free zero-coupon bond with a face value of \$35 and sell a put, with X = \$35.
c. Explain how these payoff diagrams relate to the concept of put-call parity.

P15-5. Draw payoff diagrams for each of the following portfolios (X = strike price):

a. Buy a call, with X = \$50, and sell a call, with X = \$60.
b. Buy a bond with a face value of \$10, short a put, with X = \$60, and buy a put, with X = \$50.
c. Buy a share of stock, buy a put option, with X = \$50, sell a call, with X = \$60, and short a bond (i.e., borrow) with a face value of \$50.
d. What principle do these diagrams illustrate?

P15-6. Draw a payoff diagram for the following portfolio. Buy two call options, one with X = \$20 and one with X = \$30, and sell two call options, both with X = \$25.

P15-7. Refer to the data in the table below.

Strike price	Put price
\$30	\$1.00
\$35	\$3.50
\$40	\$6.50

Suppose an investor purchases one put, with X = \$30, and one put, with X = \$40, and sells two puts, with X = \$35. Draw a payoff diagram for this position. In your diagram, show the gross payoff (ignoring the costs of buying and selling the options) and the net payoff. In what range of stock prices does the investor make a net profit? What is the investor's maximum potential dollar profit and maximum potential dollar loss?

P15-8. Draw a payoff diagram for the following portfolios:

a. Buy a bond with a face value of \$80, buy a call, with X = \$80, and sell a put, with X = \$80.
b. Buy a share of stock, buy a put, with X = \$80, and sell a call, with X = \$80.
c. Buy a share of stock, buy a put, with X = \$80, and sell a bond with a face value of \$80.

SMART SOLUTIONS

See the problem and solution explained step-by-step at

SMARTFinance

P15-9. Suppose that Lisa Emerson owns a share of Zytex Chemical stock, which is worth \$100 per share. Lisa purchases a put option on this stock, with a strike price of \$95, and she sells a call option, with a strike price of \$105. Plot the payoff diagram for Lisa's new portfolio and explain how it relates to this chapter's Opening Focus.

P15-10. Imagine that a stock sells for \$33. A call option, with X = \$35 and an expiration date in six months, sells for \$4.50. The annual risk-free rate is 5 percent. Calculate the price of a put option that expires in six months and has a strike price of \$35.

Qualitative Analysis of Option Prices

P15-11. Examine the data in the table below. Given that both stocks trade for $50 and both options have a $45 strike price and a July expiration date, can we say that the option of Company A is overvalued or that the option of Company B is undervalued? Why or why not?

Company	Stock price	Expiration	Strike price	Call price
A	$50	July	$45	$7.50
B	$50	July	$45	$6.75

P15-12. Examine the data in the table below. The call option on Company #1 is out of the money by $1 and so is the call option on Company #2. Given that the options expire at the same time, is it surprising that their prices are so different? Why or why not?

Company	Stock price	Expiration	Strike price	Call price
#1	$49	August	$50	$6
#2	$19	August	$20	$3.75

P15-13. Suppose an American call option is in the money, so $S > X$. Demonstrate that the market price of this call (C) cannot be less than the difference between the stock price and the exercise price. That is, explain why this must be true: $C \geq S - X$. (Hint: consider what would happen if $C < S - X$).

Option Pricing Models

P15-14. **a.** A call option expires in three months and has $X = \$40$. The underlying stock is worth $42 today. In three months, the stock may increase by $7 or decrease by $6. The risk-free rate is 2 percent per year. Use the binomial model to value the call option.

b. A put option expires in three months and has $X = \$40$. The underlying stock is worth $42 today. In three months, the stock may increase by $7 or decrease by $6. The risk-free rate is 2 percent per year. Use the binomial model to value the put option.

c. Given the call and the put prices you calculated in parts (a) and (b), check to see if put-call parity holds.

P15-15. A stock is worth $20 today, and it may increase or decrease $5 over the next year. If the risk-free rate of interest is 6 percent, calculate the market price of the at-the-money put and call options on this stock that expire in one year. Which option is more valuable, the put or the call? Is it always the case that a call option is worth more than a put if both are tied to the same underlying stock, have the same expiration date, and are at the money? (Hint: use the put-call parity to prove the statement true or false.)

P15-16. Explain the following paradox. A put option is a highly volatile security. If the underlying stock has a positive beta, then a put option on that stock will have a negative beta (because the put and the stock move in opposite directions). According to the CAPM, an asset with a negative beta, such as the put option, has an expected return below the risk-free rate. How can an equilibrium exist in which a highly risky security such as a put option offers an expected return below a much safer security such as a Treasury bill?

P15-17. A particular stock sells for $27. A call option on this stock is available, with a strike price of $28 and an expiration date in four months. If the risk-free rate equals 6 percent and the standard deviation of the stock's return is 40 percent, what is the price of the call option? Next, recalculate your answer assuming that the market price of the stock is $28. How much does the option price change in dollar terms? How much does it change in percentage terms?

P15-18. Temex Foods stock currently sells for $48. A call option on this stock is available, with a strike price of $45 and an expiration date six months in the future. The standard deviation of the stock's return is 45 percent, and the risk-free interest rate is 4 percent. Calculate the value of the call option. Next, use the put-call parity to determine the value of a Temex put option that also has a $45 strike price and six months until expiration.

Options in Corporate Finance

P15-19. A convertible bond has a par value of $1,000 and a conversion ratio of 20. If the underlying stock currently sells for $40 and the bond sells at par, what is the conversion premium? The conversion value?

MINICASE

Options

You have recently spent one of your Saturday afternoons at an options seminar presented by Derivatives Traders Incorporated. Interested in putting some of your new knowledge to work, you start by thinking about possible returns from an investment in the volatile common stock of PurchasePro.com, Incorporated (PPRO). Four options currently trade on PPRO. Two are call options, one with a strike price of $35 and the other with a strike price of $45. The other two are put options, which also have strike prices of $35 and $45, respectively. To help you decide which options strategies might work, evaluate the following option positions.

ASSIGNMENT

1. You believe the price of PPRO will rise and are therefore considering either (a) taking a long position in a $45 call by paying a premium of $3, or (b) taking a short position in a $45 put for which you will receive a premium of $3. If the stock price is $50 on the expiration date, which position makes you better off?
2. You believe the price of PPRO will fall and are therefore considering either (a) taking a long position in a $35 put, paying a premium of $2, or (b) taking a short position in a $35 call, receiving a premium of $2. If the stock price is $30 on the expiration date, which position makes you better off?
3. Assume you can buy or sell either the call or the put options, with a strike price of $35. The call option has a premium of $3, and the put option has a premium of $2. Which of these option contracts can be used to form a long straddle? What is the payoff if the stock price closes at $38 on the option expiration date? What is the payoff if the stock price closes at $28 on the option expiration date?
4. Assume you can buy or sell either the call or the put options, with a strike price of $35. The call option has a premium of $3, and the put option has a premium of $2. Which of these option contracts can be used to form a short straddle? What is the payoff if the stock price closes at $38 on the option expiration date? What is the payoff if the stock price closes at $28 on the option expiration date?

Smart *Excel* Appendix

Appendix Contents

Use the Smart *Excel* spreadsheets and animated tutorials at http://smartfinance.swlearning.com.

EXCEL PREREQUISITES

You need to be familiar with the following *Excel* features to use this appendix:

- If function
- Max function

If this is new to you, be sure to complete the ***Excel Prereqs*** tab in the Chapter 15 *Excel* file located at the **Smart Finance Web site** before proceeding.

OPTION PRICING

In this appendix, we'll determine option prices, using put-call parity and the binomial option pricing model.

CALCULATE OPTION PAYOFFS

Option Payoffs

Problem: Calculate the payoff to a long call position, assuming the stock price at expiration is $75, the strike price is $72, and the call premium is $6.

Approach: Create a simple model to find the call payoff and net call payoff.

Open the Chapter 15 *Excel* file located at the Smart Finance Web site. Turn to the *Payoff1* tab.

Fill in the inputs and then create the formula for call payoff and net payoff. The net figure reduces the call's payoff by the premium paid by the buyer.

Your results should match:

Inputs	
Stock price at expiration	$75.00
Strike price of call option	$72.00
Call premium	$6.00
Calculations and Output	
Call payoff at expiration	$3.00
Net call payoff at expiration	($3.00)

If the stock price is $75 on the expiration date, but the payoff net of the $6 call premium is –$3.

Apply it

- *Create a table of call payoffs for various stock prices on the expiration date.*
- *Graph the results.*
  The table can be quickly created by using the fill-series feature to enter various stock prices. Then create a formula for the payoff that can be copied down.
  Use the chart wizard to select a line graph and plot the results. To match our solutions, you will need to format your graph, especially the fonts.
- *You can also include the net payoff in your table and plot the results on the same graph.*

Problem: Now calculate the payoff to a short call position, assuming the stock price at expiration is $75, the strike price is $72, and the call premium is $6.

Approach: Create a simple model to find the call payoff and the net call payoff.

Try it on your own or turn to the *Payoff2* tab.

Fill in the inputs and then create the formula for the call payoff and the net payoff. This time, the net figure is higher than the payoff by the amount of the premium received by the seller. Your results should look like this:

Inputs	
Stock price at expiration	$75.00
Strike price of call option	$72.00
Call premium	$6.00
Calculations and Output	
Call payoff at expiration	($3.00)
Net call payoff at expiration	$3.00

If the stock price is $75 on the expiration date, the short call payoff equals –$3, but the seller's net payoff is a $3 gain.

Apply it

- *Create a table of call payoffs for various stock prices on the expiration date.*
- *Graph the results.*
- *Our solution appears in the file.*
- *You can evaluate put payoffs similarly.*

Apply it

Go to the *Payoff3* tab.

This tab allows you to examine option payoffs in more detail. You can also see payoffs on portfolios of different options. The spreadsheet allows you to form a portfolio containing any number of long or short positions in call or put options. You can adjust the number of options, the stock price on the expiration date, and the options' strike prices and premiums.

PRICING EUROPEAN OPTIONS USING PUT-CALL PARITY

Pricing Put Options

Problem: SnackHappy Foods stock currently sells for $45 per share. European put and call options on the shares are available, with a strike price of $50 and an expiration of one year. If the price of the call option is $5 and the risk-free rate of interest is 3.5 percent, what is the appropriate price of the put option according to the put-call parity theory?

Approach: Create a simple model to find the price of the put option.

Open the Chapter 15 *Excel* file located at the Smart Finance Web site. Turn to the ***Put*** tab.

Equation 15.1 states: $S + P = B + C$

Where S = stock price, P = put premium, B = market price of a risk-free, zero-coupon bond with a face value equal to the options' strike price, and C = call premium

Recognize that the bond's market price equals the present value of the options' strike price, this can be rewritten to solve for the put premium as:

$P = PV(X) + C - S$

Enter the inputs. Then use this equation to create a formula to solve for the put price. The solution follows.

Inputs	
Stock price	$45.00
Price of call option	$5.00
Strike price of option	$50.00
Risk-free rate	3.5%
Expiration (# of years)	1.00
Calculations and Output	
Price of risk-free zero-coupon bond	$48.31
Price of put option	$8.31

Apply it

- ***Perform sensitivity analysis on the risk-free rate.***
- ***Perform sensitivity analysis on the stock price.***
- ***Perform sensitivity analysis on the strike price.***

  Holding all other inputs constant:

  As the risk-free rate rises, the value of the put falls.

As the stock price rises, the value of the put falls.
As the strike price rises, the value of the put rises.

Apply Put-Call Parity

Confirm that put-call parity holds

Find the value of the total cash inflows and outflows to the portfolio and confirm that put-call parity holds.

The portfolio cash flows are calculated as:

Cash Inflows	
Sell put	$8.31
Sell stock	$45.00
Total Cash Inflows	$53.31
Cash Outflows	
Buy bond	($48.31)
Buy call	($5.00)
Total Cash Outflows	($53.31)
Net Cash Flow	$0.00

A net cash flow of $0 confirms that put-call parity holds.

Use the IF function to alert you to arbitrage opportunities.

If the net cash flow is not zero, there is an arbitrage opportunity. We'll use the If function for this. If you have not yet worked with the If function, see the ***Excel Prereqs*** tab.

Write an If statement that returns **Put-Call Parity Holds** when the net cash flow is zero and otherwise returns **Arbitrage Opportunity.**

The IF statement in cell B53 will be: =IF(C51=0,"Put-Call Parity Holds","Arbitrage Opportunity")

The result is:

Put-Call Parity Holds

Pricing Call Options

Problem: SnackHappy Foods stock currently sells for $45 per share. European put and call options on the shares are available, with a strike price of $52 and an expiration of one year. If the price of the put option is $6.50, and the risk-free rate of interest is 3.5 percent, what is the appropriate price of the call option, according to put-call parity theory?

Approach: Create a simple model to find the price of the call option.

Open the Chapter 15 Excel file located at the Smart Finance Web site. Turn to the *Call* tab.

Equation 15.1 states: $S + P = B + C$

Where S *= stock price,* P *= put premium,* B *= present value of risk-free zero-coupon bond, and* C *= call premium*

This can be rewritten to solve for the call premium as:
$C = S + P - PV(X)$
Complete the model and find the call premium. You should get $1.26.

Apply it

- *Perform sensitivity analysis on the risk-free rate.*
- *Perform sensitivity analysis on the stock price.*
- *Perform sensitivity analysis on the strike price.*

  Holding all other inputs constant:
  As the risk-free rate rises, the value of the call rises.
  As the stock price rises, the value of the call rises.
  As the strike price rises, the value of the call falls.

Complete the put-call parity check, again using the IF function to alert you to arbitrage opportunities.

PRICING OPTIONS USING THE BINOMIAL OPTION PRICING MODEL

Pricing Put Options

Problem: SnackHappy Foods stock currently sells for $45 per share. Use the binomial option pricing model to find the price of a put option, with a strike price of $50 and an expiration of one year. Assume the price of the stock in one year will either be $66 or $38. The risk-free rate of interest is 3.5 percent.

Approach: Create a risk-free portfolio and use it to find the price of the put option.

Open the Chapter 15 *Excel* file located at the Smart Finance Web site. Turn to the *Binom Put* tab.

Recall from the chapter the three steps in the binomial pricing model.

1. Find a portfolio of stocks and options that generates a risk-free payoff in the future.
2. Find the present value of the portfolio by discounting at the risk-free rate.
3. Determine how much value comes from the stock and how much from the option, to obtain the option's market price.

Apply Step 1

Start by entering the input information.

Next, find a combination of stock and put options that yields the same payoff, whether the stock goes up or down over the next year.

To value a put option, create a riskless portfolio that is long both stock and put options. Why? Because the two securities are negatively correlated. If stock prices rise, the value of the stock increases, and the value of the put decreases.

To find the appropriate number of put options to create the riskless portfolio, first find the value of the share and the option, under both possible future stock prices.

Calculations and Output

	Cash flows one year from today	
	If stock price UP	If stock price DOWN
One share is worth		
Each LONG put option is worth		
Number of options for hedge		
Total portfolio is worth		

Find the share value in one year.

If the stock price goes up, it is equal to \$66. Use a cell reference to pull this from the inputs.

If the stock price goes down, it is equal to \$38. Use a cell reference to pull this from the inputs.

Find the option value in one year.

If the stock price goes down, the value of the option is the difference between the strike price and the future stock price. If the stock price goes up above the strike price, the option is worthless at expiration.

You can create one formula to find the value of the option if you use the max function.

The value of the option is the maximum of:

The strike price minus the future stock price OR zero.

Create the following max statement in cell C32. =max(C24-C31,0)

Copy the formula across.

Find the number of options to create a hedge.

The number of options required for the riskless portfolio is:

options = (stock price if UP – stock price if DOWN) / (option value if UP + option value if DOWN)

Create a formula for this in cell C30. The formula is =(C31–D31) / (C32 + D32)

Find the portfolio value.

The value of the portfolio in one year equals the share price, plus the number of options, multiplied by the option value.

Your results should match:

	Cash flows one year from today	
	If stock price UP	If stock price DOWN
One share is worth	\$66.00	\$38.00
Each LONG put option is worth	\$0.00	\$12.00
Number of options for hedge	2.3	
Total portfolio is worth	\$66.00	\$66.00

This shows the portfolio value, in one year, under the future stock prices of $66 and $38.

Apply Step 2

Find the present value of the portfolio by discounting at the risk-free rate for the appropriate number of years (here, one year).

The present value = Portfolio value /(1 + risk-free rate) ^ #years
= $63.77

Apply Step 3

The put price can be found as:

(*PV* of portfolio – current share price) / # options in portfolio
=($63.77 – $45) / 2.333 = $8.04

Price of put option

Present value of portfolio	$63.77
Put price	$8.04

Apply it

- *Perform sensitivity analysis on the risk-free rate.*
- *Perform sensitivity analysis on the stock price.*
- *Perform sensitivity analysis on the strike price.*

Again, holding all other inputs constant:
As the risk-free rate rises, the value of the put falls.
As the stock price rises, the value of the put falls.
As the strike price rises, the value of the put rises.

Pricing Call Options

Problem: SnackHappy Foods stock currently sells for $45 per share. Use the binomial option pricing model to find the price of a call option, with a strike price of $50 and an expiration of one year. Assume that the price of the stock in one year will either be $66 or $38. The risk-free rate of interest is 3.5 percent.

Approach: Create a risk-free portfolio and use it to find the price of the call option.

Open file and turn to the ***Binom Call*** tab.

Solve as with the put option above. Remember, first find a combination of stock and call options that yields the same payoff, whether the stock goes up or down over the next year.

To value a call option, create a riskless portfolio that is long stock but short call options. Why? Because the two securities are positively correlated. If stock prices rise, the value of both the stock and the call option increases.

The solution is provided in the file. It should match:

Inputs

Stock price (current)	$45.00
Stock price (if UP in one year)	$66.00
Stock price (if DOWN in one year)	$38.00
Strike price of call option	$50.00
Risk-free rate	3.5%
Expiration (# years)	1.00

Calculations and Output

	Cash flows one year from today	
	If stock price UP	**If stock price DOWN**
One share is worth	$66.00	$38.00
Each SHORT call option is worth	$16.00	$0.00
Number of options for hedge	(1.8)	
Total portfolio is worth	$38.00	$38.00
Price of call option		
Present value of portfolio	$36.71	
Call price	$4.73	

Apply it

- *Perform sensitivity analysis on the risk-free rate.*
- *Perform sensitivity analysis on the stock price.*
- *Perform sensitivity analysis on the strike price.*

Holding all other inputs constant:
As the risk-free rate rises, the value of the call rises.
As the stock price rises, the value of the call rises.
As the strike price rises, the value of the call falls.

International Financial Management

OPENING FOCUS

Dollar's Fall Creates Winners and Losers

Shares in the Hong Kong apparel maker Esprit Holdings Ltd. closed up almost 3.7 percent on Tuesday, July 2, 2002, despite weakness in Hong Kong's Hang Seng stock index, which fell 1.3 percent the same day. Analysts pointed to the recent decline in the U.S. dollar (US$) against the euro (€), among other factors, as the reason for the gain. Just five months earlier, currency traders could exchange $1 for roughly €1.16, but by early July the dollar and the euro traded almost one for one. The sharp decline in the dollar (rise in the euro) benefited Esprit for two reasons. First, since October 1983, the value of the Hong Kong dollar (HK$) had been pegged to the US$ by a mechanism known as a currency board, a system in which Hong Kong monetary authorities stood ready to exchange HK$ for US$ at a fixed exchange rate of HK$7.8 for US$1. Therefore, as the value of the US$ fell against the euro, so did the value of Hong Kong's currency. This allowed Esprit to charge lower euro prices for their clothing in Europe than competing producers. The lower prices helped Esprit gain market share in Europe, and the strength of the euro meant that even though Esprit cut prices in Europe, it would still earn a substantial profit once the euro revenues were converted back into dollars. Second, the benefit Esprit gained from a rising euro was significant because almost 70 percent of its revenues originated in Europe. Put simply, as Esprit sold clothing in European markets, it earned revenues denominated in euros, and the value of those revenues in HK$ terms had been rising along with the euro.

Just three weeks later, shares in the world's fifth-largest insurance company, Aegon NV, dropped 28.2 percent in two days on the Amsterdam Stock Exchange after the Dutch company issued a statement that its profits for the year would be 30–35 percent lower than previously anticipated. The reason? The company blamed several factors, but topping the list was the decline in the US$, which slid another 1 percent during mid-July. Aegon generated roughly 65 percent of its profits from the United States, in part because of its $10 billion acquisition of Transamerica in 1999. The falling dollar hurt Aegon's bottom line because the company's dollar-denominated business was high volume, and Aegon had chosen not to hedge this exposure.

Making matters even worse, the company disclosed that it held $200 million in bonds issued by WorldCom, which had filed for bankruptcy just two days earlier.

The lessons here are twofold. First, though the media reports changes in currency values as though they were somehow a symbol of national vigor or lack thereof, currency movements are neither unambiguously good nor unambiguously bad. Rather, major swings in currency values create winners and losers. The decline in the US$ was a boon for Esprit, and for any other company that sold goods in Europe and then converted those revenues back into a depreciating home currency. Conversely, the dollar's value created serious problems for Aegon, and for any other company that earned revenues in US$ and converted them back into an appreciating home currency. Second, because currency fluctuations of this magnitude occur frequently and have a large impact on profits, companies often choose to hedge their currency exposures. Understanding the factors that cause currency values to move and the mechanisms by which firms can hedge against those movements is the primary purpose of this chapter.

Sources: "Aegon's Warning Sparks Fears for Other Insurers," *Financial Times* (July 23, 2002); "Esprit Closes Morning Higher on U.S. Strategy Hopes; Euro Exposure," *AFX Asia* (July 2, 2002).

LEARNING OBJECTIVES

After studying this chapter you should be able to:

- Describe the difference between fixed and floating exchange rates, and interpret exchange rate quotes taken from the Web or financial newspapers;
- Explain how the four parity relationships in international finance tie together forward and spot exchange rates, interest rates, and inflation rates in different countries;
- List the types of risks that multinational corporations face when they conduct business in different countries and currencies; and
- Revise the *NPV* decision rule for capital budgeting analysis to incorporate the added complexity that arises when an investment is undertaken in a foreign currency.

Walk down the aisle of a grocery store, visit a shopping mall, go hunting for a new automobile, or check the outstanding balance of your credit card. In each of these activities, chances are that you will be dealing with products and services provided by **multinational corporations (MNCs)**, businesses that operate in many countries around the world. In recent decades, international trade in goods and services has expanded dramatically, and so too have the size and scope of MNCs. Although all the financial principles covered in this text thus far apply to MNCs, companies operating across national borders also face unique challenges. Primary among them is coping with exchange rate risk. An **exchange rate** is simply the price of one currency in terms of another, and for the past thirty years, the exchange rates of major currencies have fluctuated daily. These movements create uncertainty for firms that earn revenues and pay operating costs in more than one currency. Currency movements also add to the pressures faced by wholly domestic companies that face competition from foreign firms.

multinational corporations (MNCs) Businesses that operate in many countries around the world.

exchange rate The price of one currency in terms of another currency.

This chapter focuses on the problems and opportunities firms face as a result of globalization, with special emphasis on currency-related issues. First, we explain the rudimentary features of currency markets, including how and why currencies trade and the rules governments impose on trading in their currencies. Second, we describe factors that drive currency values, at least for those countries that allow their currencies to float in response to market forces. Third, we discuss the special risks faced by MNCs and the strategies they employ to manage those risks. We conclude by illustrating how operating across national borders affects capital budgeting analysis.

16.1 EXCHANGE RATE FUNDAMENTALS

We begin our coverage of exchange rate fundamentals by describing the "rules of the game" as dictated by national governments.

Fixed Versus Floating Exchange Rates

floating exchange rate
An exchange rate system in which a currency's value is allowed to fluctuate in response to market forces.

fixed exchange rate
An exchange rate system in which the price of one currency is fixed relative to all other currencies by government authorities.

Since the mid-1970s, the major currencies of the world have had a **floating exchange rate** relationship with respect to the U.S. dollar and to one another, which means that forces of supply and demand continuously move currency values up and down. The opposite of a floating exchange rate regime is a **fixed exchange rate** system. Under a fixed-rate system, governments fix (or *peg*) their currency's value, usually in terms of another currency such as the U.S. dollar. Once a government pegs the currency at a particular value, it must stand ready to pursue economic and financial policies necessary to maintain that value. For example, if demand for the currency increases, the government must stand ready to sell currency so that the increase in demand does not cause the currency to appreciate. If demand for the currency falls, the government must buy its own currency to prevent the currency from depreciating. In many countries with fixed exchange rates, governments impose restrictions on the free flow of currencies into and out of the country. Even so, maintaining a currency peg can be quite difficult. For example, in response to mounting economic problems, the government of Argentina allowed the peso, which had been linked to the U.S. dollar, to float freely for the first time in a decade on January 11, 2002. After one day, the peso lost more than 40 percent of its value relative to the dollar.

managed floating rate system
A hybrid currency system in which a government loosely fixes the value of the national currency.

currency board arrangement
An exchange rate system in which each unit of the domestic currency is backed by a unit of some foreign currency.

Some countries have adopted hybrid currency systems in which the currency is neither pegged nor allowed to float freely. A **managed floating rate system** is a hybrid in which a nation's government loosely "fixes" the value of the national currency in relation to that of another currency, but does not expend the effort and resources that would be required to maintain a completely fixed exchange rate regime. Other countries simply choose to use another nation's currency as their own, and a handful of nations have adopted a **currency board arrangement**. In such an arrangement, the national currency continues to circulate, but every unit of the currency is fully backed by government holdings of another currency—usually the U.S. dollar.

The International Monetary Fund, in its April 2003 issue of *International Financial Statistics,* detailed the exchange rate systems in place for 186 countries. Forty-one countries had independently floating exchange rates, 40 had conventional fixed exchange rates, 33 had managed floats, 39 used another currency as their country's legal tender (including the 12 Western European countries using the euro), 8 maintained currency boards, and 15 maintained some other type of hybrid system. In terms of trading volume, the major currencies in international finance today are (in no particular order) the British pound sterling (£), the Swiss franc (SF), the Japanese yen (¥), the Canadian dollar (C$), the U.S. dollar (US$, or simply $), and the euro (€).

Exchange Rate Quotes

direct quote
An exchange rate quoted in terms of units of domestic currency per unit of foreign currency.

Figure 16.1 shows exchange rate values quoted in *The Wall Street Journal* in April 2004. Note that the figure states each exchange rate in two ways. The first two columns of numbers report the "US $ Equivalent" value of a given currency. In this column, exchange rates are quoted in terms of dollars per unit of foreign currency. This type of quote is called a **direct quote**. The numbers in these columns show the dollar cost of one unit of foreign currency. In row 1, for example, we see that on Wednesday, April 21, 2004, one Argentine peso cost $0.3506. One day earlier, one peso

Exchange Rates

April 21, 2004

The foreign exchange mid-range rates below apply to trading among banks in amounts of $1 million and more, as quoted at 4 p.m. Eastern time by Reuters and other sources. Retail transactions provide fewer units of foreign currency per dollar.

	U.S. $ EQUIVALENT		CURRENCY PER U.S. $	
Country	**Wed**	**Tue**	**Wed**	**Tue**
Argentina (Peso)	**.3506**	**.3525**	**2.823**	**2.8369**
Australia (Dollar)	.7297	.7343	1.3704	1.3618
Bahrain (Dinar)	2.6525	2.6526	.3770	.3770
Brazil (Real)	.3415	.3414	2.9283	2.9291
Canada (Dollar)	**.7353**	**.7371**	**1.3600**	**1.3567**
1-month forward	**.7347**	**.7365**	**1.3611**	**1.3578**
3-months forward	**.7336**	**.7353**	**1.3631**	**1.3600**
6-months forward	**.7322**	**.7340**	**1.3657**	**1.3624**
Chile (Peso)	.001631	.001661	613.12	602.05
China (Renminbi)	.1208	.1208	8.2781	8.2781
Colombia (Peso)	.0003812	.0003824	2623.29	2615.06
Czech. Rep. (Koruna)				
Commercial rate	.03643	.03654	27.450	27.367
Denmark (Krone)	.1590	.1594	6.2893	6.2735
Ecuador (US Dollar)	1.0000	1.0000	1.0000	1.0000
Egypt (Pound)-y	.1614	.1612	6.1950	6.2050
Hong Kong (Dollar)	.1282	.1282	7.8003	7.8003
Hungary (Forint)	.004729	.004751	211.46	210.48
India (Rupee)	.02272	.02280	44.014	43.860
Indonesia (Rupiah)	.0001156	.0001160	8651	8621
Israel (Shekel)	.2187	.2192	4.5725	4.5620
Japan (Yen)	**.009138**	**.009203**	**109.43**	**108.66**
1-month forward	**.009147**	**.009213**	**109.33**	**108.54**
3-months forward	**.009165**	**.009231**	**109.11**	**108.33**
6-months forward	**.009199**	**.009263**	**108.71**	**107.96**
Jordan (Dinar)	1.4104	1.4104	.7090	.7090
Kuwait (Dinar)	3.3921	3.3921	.2948	.2948
Lebanon (Pound)	.0006601	.0006601	1514.92	1514.92
Malaysia (Ringgit)-b	.2632	.2632	3.7994	3.7994
Malta (Lira)	2.7847	2.7950	.3591	.3578
Mexico (Peso)				
Floating rate	.0885	.0882	11.3007	11.3404
New Zealand (Dollar)	.6200	.6316	1.6129	1.5833
Norway (Krone)	.1430	.1432	6.9930	6.9832
Pakistan (Rupee)	.01742	.01745	57.405	57.307
Peru (new Sol)	.2880	.2883	3.4722	3.4686
Philippines (Peso)	.01791	.01796	55.835	55.679
Poland (Zloty)	.2488	.2506	4.0193	3.9904
Russia (Ruble)-a	.03464	.03461	28.868	28.893
Saudi Arabia (Riyal)	.2666	.2667	3.7509	3.7495
Singapore (Dollar)	.5916	.5950	1.6903	1.6807
Slovak Rep. (Koruna)	.02956	.02957	33.830	33.818
South Africa (Rand)	.1475	.1533	6.7797	6.5232
South Korea (Won)	.0008654	.0008662	1155.54	1154.47
Sweden (Krona)	.1292	.1293	7.7399	7.7340
Switzerland (Franc)	**.7607**	**.7617**	**1.3146**	**1.3129**
1-month forward	**.7612**	**.7623**	**1.3137**	**1.3118**
3-months forward	**.7623**	**.7634**	**1.3118**	**1.3099**
6-months forward	**.7641**	**.7651**	**1.3087**	**1.3070**
Taiwan (Dollar)	.03037	.03044	32.927	32.852
Thailand (Baht)	.02524	.02539	39.620	39.386
Turkey (Lira)	.00000072	.00000073	1388889	1369863
U.K. (Pound)	**1.7733**	**1.7877**	**.5639**	**.5594**
1-month forward	**1.7686**	**1.7828**	**.5654**	**.5609**
3-months forward	**1.7593**	**1.7735**	**.5684**	**.5639**
6-months forward	**1.7453**	**1.7593**	**.5730**	**.5684**
United Arab (Dirham)	.2723	.2723	3.6724	3.6724
Uruguay (Peso)				
Financial	.03380	.03370	29.586	29.674
Venezuela (Bolivar)	.000521	.000521	1919.39	1919.39
SDR	1.4466	1.4562	.6913	.6867
Euro	1.1831	1.1860	.8452	.8432

Special Drawing Rights (SDR) are based on exchange rates for the U.S., British, and Japanese currencies. Source: International Monetary Fund.

a-Russian Central Bank rate. b-Government rate. y-Floating rate.

Figure 16.1
Exchange Rate Quotes

The figure shows direct (dollars per unit of foreign currency) and indirect (units of foreign currency per dollar) exchange rate quotes.

Source: The Wall Street Journal *(April 22, 2004).*

cost $0.3525. Because the value of one peso in terms of U.S. currency fell slightly from Tuesday to Wednesday, we say that the peso **depreciated** against the dollar.

depreciate
A currency depreciates when it buys less of another currency than it did previously.

The third and fourth columns of Figure 16.1 present the same information in a slightly different way. These columns show the value of each foreign currency relative to one U.S. dollar. That is, the numbers show how many units of a foreign currency you can buy with $1. This way of stating exchange rates is called an

indirect quote
An exchange rate quoted in terms of foreign currency per unit of domestic currency.

appreciate
A currency appreciates when it buys more of another currency than it did previously.

indirect quote. Again, in row 1 we see that on Tuesday, April 20, it cost 2.8369 pesos to purchase one dollar, but on the next day, one dollar was worth a little more, 2.8523 pesos. Because the value of one dollar in terms of pesos rose from Tuesday to Wednesday, we say that the dollar **appreciated** against the peso. Of course, the exchange rate quotes in the first two columns reveal exactly the same information as the quotes in the second two columns. Each of these methods of quoting exchange rates is simply the reciprocal of the other:

$$\frac{\text{dollars}}{\text{pesos}} = \frac{1}{\text{pesos}/\text{dollars}} \qquad 0.3506 = \frac{1}{2.8523}$$

Figure 16.1 also reveals that many currencies do not float freely against the dollar, because the exchange rates did not move at all from Monday to Tuesday. These currencies include the dinar (Bahrain), the renminbi (China), the Hong Kong dollar, and several others.

spot exchange rate
The exchange rate that applies to immediate currency transactions.

forward exchange rate
The exchange rate quoted for a transaction that will occur on a future date.

Notice that for a few countries, Figure 16.1 lists several different exchange rates rather than just one. For each currency, the first exchange rate listed is the **spot exchange rate**. The spot exchange rate is just another word for the current exchange rate. That is, if you are going to trade currencies right now, the relevant exchange rate is the spot exchange rate. In many currencies, it is possible to enter a contract today to trade foreign currency at a fixed price at some future date. The price at which that future trade will take place is called the **forward exchange rate**. For example, a U.S. trader wishing to exchange dollars for British pounds could do so on Wednesday, April 21, at the spot exchange rate of $1.7733/£ (or equivalently, £0.5639/$). Alternatively, that trader could enter into an agreement to trade dollars for pounds one month later at the forward rate of $1.7686/£ (or equivalently, £0.5654/$). If the trader chooses to transact through a forward contract, no cash changes hands until the date specified by the contract. Though the figure only quotes forward contracts at maturities of one, three, and six months, a much richer set of forward contracts is available in the foreign exchange market.

forward premium
When one currency buys more of another on the forward market than it buys on the spot market.

Just as we compared movements in the spot exchange rate from Tuesday to Wednesday, we can also examine differences in the spot exchange rate for current transactions and the forward rate for future transactions. For example, look at the rate quotes for Japanese yen. On the spot market, one yen costs $0.009138/¥, but the exchange rate for trades that will take place six months later is $0.009199/¥. One yen buys slightly more dollars on the forward market than on the spot market. When one currency buys more of another on the forward market than it does on the spot market, traders say that the first currency trades at a **forward premium**. The forward premium is usually expressed as a percentage relative to the spot rate, so for the yen, we can calculate the six-month forward premium as follows:

$$\frac{F-S}{S} = \frac{\$0.009199/¥ - \$0.009138/¥}{\$0.009138/¥} = 0.0067 = 0.67\%$$

forward discount
When one currency buys less of another on the forward market than it buys on the spot market.

where F is the symbol for the forward rate and S stands for the spot rate, both quoted in terms of $/¥. Recognizing that the yen's 0.67 percent forward premium refers to a six-month contract, we could restate the premium in annual terms by multiplying the premium times 2, which would yield an annualized forward premium of 1.34 percent.

If the yen trades at a forward premium relative to the dollar, then the dollar must trade at a **forward discount** relative to the yen, meaning that one dollar buys fewer yen on the forward market than it does on the spot market. To calculate the forward discount on the dollar, we use the same equation as above, but we express the exchange rate in terms of yen per dollar:

$$\frac{F-S}{S}=\frac{¥108.71/\$-¥109.43/\$}{¥109.43/\$}=-0.0066$$

The dollar trades at a –0.66 percent forward discount for a six-month contract, or about –1.32 percent per year. In other words, the forward discount on the dollar is opposite in sign and similar in magnitude to the forward premium on the yen, though the discount is always smaller in absolute value than the premium. In general, to calculate the annualized forward premium or discount on a currency, based on a forward contract to be executed in N days, use the following equation:

$$\frac{F-S}{S}\times\frac{360}{N} \qquad \text{(Eq. 16.1)}$$

APPLYING THE MODEL

Using the exchange rate quotes in Figure 16.1, we can calculate the annualized forward discount (or premium) on the Swiss franc (SF) relative to the \$. We will calculate this based on the rate for a three-month forward contract. The spot rate equals \$0.7607/SF, and the three-month (or ninety-day) forward rate equals \$0.7623/SF. Notice that the franc buys more dollars on the forward market than it does on the spot market, so it trades at a forward premium. We can determine the annualized premium as follows, given that we are using a ninety-day contract:

$$\frac{\$0.7623/SF-\$0.7607/SF}{\$0.7607/SF}\times\frac{360}{90}=0.0084=0.84\%$$

The forward discount or premium gives traders information about more than just the price of exchanging currencies at different points in time. The forward premium is tightly linked to differences in interest rates on short-term, low-risk bonds across countries. We explore that relationship in depth in the next section.

One last lesson remains to be gleaned from Figure 16.1. In its daily exchange rate table, *The Wall Street Journal* quotes the value of the world's major currencies relative to the U.S. dollar. But what if someone wants to know the exchange rate between British pounds and Canadian dollars? In fact, all the information needed to calculate this exchange rate appears in the figure. We simply need to calculate a **cross exchange rate** by dividing the dollar exchange rate for one currency by the dollar exchange rate for the other currency. For example, using Tuesday's spot rates, we can determine the £/C\$ exchange rate:

$$\frac{\$1.7733/£}{\$0.7353/C\$}=C\$2.4117/£$$

How can we be sure that one pound buys 2.4117 Canadian dollars simply by taking this ratio? The answer is that if the exchange rate between pounds and Canadian dollars was any other number, then currency traders could engage in **triangular arbitrage**, trading currencies simultaneously in different markets to earn

cross exchange rate
An exchange rate between two currencies calculated by taking the ratio of the exchange rate of each currency, expressed in terms of a third currency.

triangular arbitrage
A trading strategy in which traders buy a currency in a country where the value of that currency is too low and immediately sell the currency in another country where the currency value is too high.

a risk-free profit. Because currency markets operate virtually twenty-four hours per day, and because currency trades take place with lightning speed and with very low transactions costs, arbitrage maintains actual currency values in different markets relatively close to this theoretical ideal.

APPLYING THE MODEL

Suppose that on Wednesday, April 21, 2004, a trader learns that the exchange rate offered by a London bank is C$2.5000/£ rather than C$2.4117/£ as calculated previously. What is the arbitrage opportunity? First, note that the figure C$2.5000/£ is "too high" relative to the theoretically correct rate. This means that in London, one pound costs too much in terms of Canadian dollars. In other words, the pound is overvalued, and the Canadian dollar is undervalued. Therefore, a trader could make a profit by executing the following steps.

1. Convert U.S. dollars to British pounds in New York at the prevailing spot rate as given in Figure 16.1. Assume that the trader starts with $1 million, which will convert to £563,920 ($1,000,000 ÷ $1.7733/£).
2. Simultaneously, the trader sells £563,920 in London (because pounds are overvalued there) at the exchange rate of C$2.5000/£. The trader will then have C$1,409,800.
3. Convert the Canadian dollars back into U.S. currency in New York. Given the spot rate of $0.7353/C$ in Figure 16.1, the trader will receive $1,036,626 (C$1,409,800 × $0.7353/C$).

After making these trades, all of which can occur with the touch of a keystroke, the trader winds up $36,626 richer, all without taking risk. As long as the exchange rates do not change, the trader can keep making a profit over and over again.

The preceding example shows that a trader can repeatedly make a profit if the exchange rates do not change. Of course exchange rates do change, and they change in a way that brings the market back into equilibrium. Figure 16.2 illustrates what happens as arbitrage takes place. As traders in New York sell U.S. currency in exchange for pounds, the pound appreciates vis-à-vis the U.S. dollar, and the exchange rate will rise from $1.7733/£ to some new, higher level. Likewise, as traders in London sell pounds in exchange for Canadian dollars, the pound will depreciate against the Canadian currency, and the exchange rate will fall below C$2.5000/£ to a lower level. Finally, as traders reap profits in New York by selling Canadian and buying U.S. currency, the exchange rate between Canadian and U.S. dollars will fall from $0.7353/C$. Though we cannot say exactly how much each of these exchange rates will move, we can say that, collectively, they will move enough to reach a new equilibrium in which the cross exchange rate in New York and the exchange rate quoted in London will be virtually identical.

With this basic understanding of foreign exchange rates in place, let us now turn to some important institutional features of the foreign exchange market.

The Foreign Exchange Market

The foreign exchange (forex) "market" is not actually a physical exchange but a global telecommunications market. In fact, it is the world's largest financial market, with total volume of almost $2 trillion *per day!* The forex market operates continuously during the business week, with trading beginning each calendar day in Tokyo. As the day evolves, trading moves westward as major dealing centers in Singapore, Bahrain

Figure 16.2
Triangular Arbitrage

The exchange rates in New York imply that one British pound should buy 2.4117 Canadian dollars. If a bank in London offers to sell C$2.5000 for one pound, then traders can make an instant profit by selling dollars for pounds in New York, converting those to Canadian dollars in London, and then selling the Canadian dollars for U.S. dollars back in New York. The effect of these trades in New York will be to raise the dollar-pound exchange rate above 1.7733 and to push the exchange rate between U.S. and Canadian dollars below 0.7353. In London, the value of the pound will fall below C$2.5000.

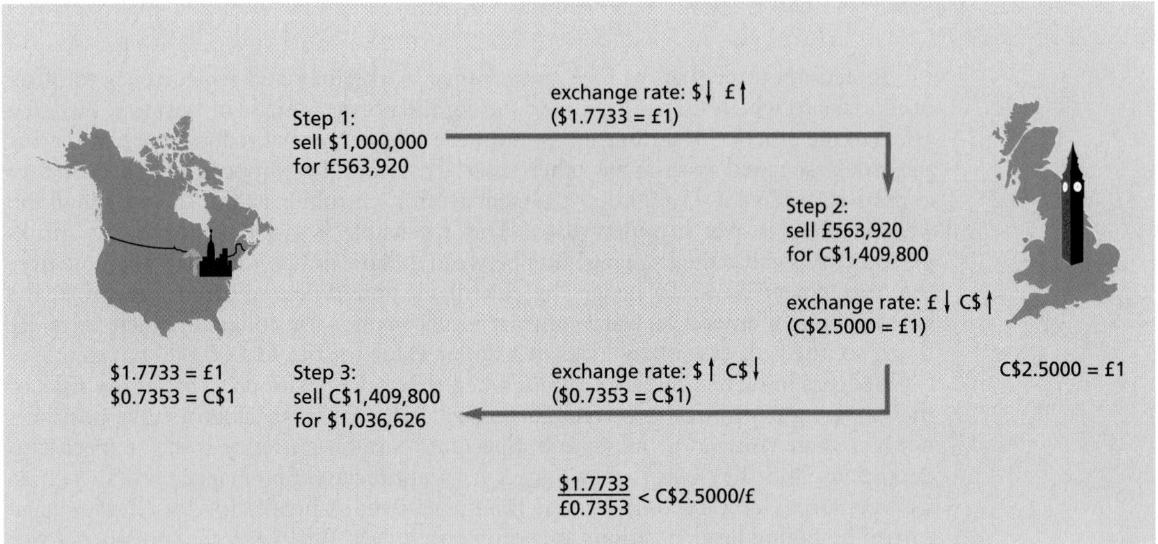

(Persian Gulf), continental Europe, London, and finally North America (particularly New York and Toronto) come on-line. Prices for all the floating currencies are set by global supply and demand. Trading in fixed-rate currencies is more constrained and regulated and frequently involves a national government (or a state-owned bank) as counterparty on one side of the trade.

The players in the forex market are numerous, as are their motivations for participating in the market. We can break market participants into six distinct (but not mutually exclusive) groups: (1) exporters and importers, (2) investors, (3) hedgers, (4) speculators, (5) dealers, and at times, (6) governments.

Businesses that export goods to or import goods from a foreign country need to enter the foreign exchange market to pay bills denominated in foreign currency or to convert foreign currency revenues back into the domestic currency. Along with all the other players in the market, exporters and importers influence currency values. For instance, if Europeans develop a taste for California wines, then European importers will exchange euros (or perhaps pounds, kroner, francs, etc.) for dollars to purchase wine. Other factors held constant, these trades would tend to put upward pressure on the value of the dollar and downward pressure on European currencies.

Investors also trade foreign currency when they seek to buy and sell financial assets in foreign countries. For example, when foreign investors want to buy U.S. stocks or bonds, they must first sell their home currencies and buy dollars. Buying pressure from investors causes the dollar to appreciate against foreign currencies. In general, the pressures exerted on currencies by investors are much larger than those exerted by exporters and importers because investors account for a larger fraction of currency trading volume. For example, the total value of goods and services traded internationally each year is about $10 trillion, whereas the aggregate value of currency trading is 50 times that, some $500 trillion annually.

APPLYING THE MODEL

In his testimony to the U.S. Senate Banking Committee on April 20, 2004, Fed Chairman Alan Greenspan hinted that the Federal Reserve might raise U.S. interest rates to fight inflation. Higher rates in the United States would attract money from foreign investors who would have to buy dollars to purchase U.S. investments. In response to Greenspan's comments, the dollar rose 1.3 percent in a single day.

Sometimes traders in the foreign exchange market buy and sell currency to offset other risks to which they are exposed during the normal course of business. Hedging refers to the practice of trading an asset for the sole purpose of reducing or eliminating the risk associated with some other asset. For example, suppose that a U.S. firm expects to receive a £1,000,000 payment from a customer in the United Kingdom. The payment is due in ninety days. This receivable is risky from the U.S. firm's perspective because the exchange rate between dollars and pounds may fluctuate over the next ninety days. To hedge the risk of its pound-denominated receivable, the U.S. firm might enter a forward contract to sell pounds for dollars in ninety days. By doing so, the firm essentially locks in a dollar value for the £1,000,000 payment.

Hedgers influence currency values when they take positions to offset the risks of their existing exposures to certain currencies. In contrast, speculators take positions not to reduce risk but to increase it. Speculators sell a currency if they expect it to depreciate, and they buy if they expect it to appreciate. Some speculators, such as George Soros, have become famous for the enormous profits (or losses) they have earned by taking large positions in certain currencies. When external pressures force a country with a pegged currency to devalue its currency, speculators often take the blame. Whether they deserve blame for causing, accelerating, or exacerbating currency crises or not, speculators can play a useful economic role by taking the opposite side of a transaction from that of hedgers. Speculators help make the foreign currency market more liquid and more efficient.

As in all financial markets, dealers play a crucial role in the foreign exchange business. Most foreign currency trades go through large, international banks in the leading financial centers around the globe. These banks provide a means for buyers and sellers to come together, and as their reward they earn a small fee, the bid-ask spread, on each round-trip buy-and-sell transaction they facilitate. The ask price is the price at which a currency dealer is willing to sell foreign currency, and the bid price is the price at which the dealer is willing to buy currency. Because the ask price is slightly higher than the bid (hence the term, bid-ask spread), dealers make a small profit each time they buy and sell currency.

Finally, governments intervene in financial markets to put upward or downward pressure on currencies as circumstances dictate. Governments that attempt to maintain a fixed exchange rate must generally intervene more frequently than those that intervene only in times of crisis. As this chapter's Opening Focus illustrates, currency movements create winners and losers, not only across national boundaries but also within a given country. For example, a rise in the value of the U.S. dollar makes U.S. exports more expensive and foreign imports cheaper. Remember, an exchange rate is simply a price, the price of trading one currency for another. Though the financial press dramatizes changes in exchange rates by attaching adjectives such as *strong* or *weak* to a given currency, this practice is rather odd when you recognize that they are just talking about a price. For instance, if the price of apples rises and the price of bananas falls, we do not refer to apples as being strong and bananas as being weak! If the price of apples is high, that is good for apple producers and bad for apple consumers. In the same way, a rise in the value of a particular currency benefits some and harms others. Therefore, at least for the major, free-floating currencies, governments are reluctant to intervene because doing so does not unambiguously improve welfare across the board.

Even when governments want to intervene in currency markets, intervention is complicated by the fact that currency values are not set in a vacuum but are linked to other economic variables such as interest rates and inflation. In the next section, we discuss four parity relationships that illustrate the linkages that should hold in equilibrium between exchange rates and other macroeconomic variables.

CONCEPT REVIEW QUESTIONS

1. Explain how a rise in the euro might affect a French company exporting wine to the United States, and compare that with the impact on a German firm importing semiconductors from the United States.

2. Holding all other factors constant, how might an increase in interest rates in Britain affect the value of the pound?

3. If someone says, "The exchange rate between dollars and pounds increased today," can you know with certainty which currency appreciated and which depreciated? Why or why not?

4. Define spot and forward exchange rates. If a trader expects to buy a foreign currency in one month, can you explain why the trader might prefer to enter into a forward contract today rather than simply wait a month and transact at the spot rate prevailing then?

16.2 THE PARITY CONDITIONS IN INTERNATIONAL FINANCE

In this section, we discuss the major forces that influence the values of all the world's free-floating currencies. Theory suggests that when markets are in equilibrium, spot and forward exchange rates, interest rates, and inflation rates should be linked across countries. Market imperfections, such as trade barriers and transactions costs, may prevent these parity conditions from holding precisely at all times, but they are still powerful determinants of exchange rate values in the long run.

Forward-Spot Parity

If the spot rate governs foreign exchange transactions in the present and the forward rate equals the price of trading currencies at some point in the future, intuition suggests that the forward rate might be useful in predicting how the spot rate will change over time. For example, suppose that a British firm intends to import U.S. wheat, for which it must pay $1.5 million in one month. Imagine that the pound currently trades at a forward premium, and the prevailing spot and forward exchange rates are as follows:

$$\text{Spot} = \$1.4/£ \quad \text{1-month forward} = \$1.50/£$$

The U.K. firm faces a choice. Either it can lock in the forward rate today, guaranteeing that it will pay £1 million for its wheat ($1.5 million ÷ $1.50/£), or it can wait a month and transact at the spot rate prevailing then. Let us suppose that the U.K. firm in this example does not care about exchange rate risk per se, so it will enter the forward contract only if it believes that trading at the forward rate will be less expensive than trading at the spot rate in thirty days.[1]

1. This is clearly an abstraction. Firms may decide to enter a forward contract, even if they think that transacting later at the spot rate might be more profitable, because they value the certainty that the forward contract gives them. In this example, we are considering the hypothetical case of a firm that does not care about uncertainty and makes currency-trading decisions solely on the basis of expected profitability.

This results in a simple decision rule for the U.K. importer. First, it must form a forecast of what the spot exchange rate will be in one month. Let's call that the expected spot rate and denote it with the symbol $E(S)$. We can now determine the U.K. firm's decision rule:

1. Enter the forward contract today if $E(S) < \$1.50/£$.
2. Wait and buy dollars at the spot rate if $E(S) > \$1.50/£$.

For example, assume that the firm's forecast is that the spot rate will not change from its current level of \$1.40/£. Given this forecast, the expected cost of purchasing \$1.50 million in thirty days is £1,071,429 (\$1.5 million ÷ \$1.40/£); and given that the firm will need only £1 million if it locks in the forward rate, it does not pay to wait. Conversely, assume that the U.K. firm believes that over the next thirty days, the pound will appreciate to \$1.60/£. In that case, the expected cost of paying for the wheat is just £937,500 (\$1.5 million ÷ \$1.60/£), and the firm should wait. Only if the firm's forecast of the expected spot rate is \$1.50/£, equal to the current forward rate, will it be indifferent to whether it locks in the forward contract now or waits thirty days to transact.

If we look at this problem from the perspective of a U.S. firm that must pay in pounds in thirty days to import some good from the United Kingdom, we get just the opposite decision rule. For the U.S. firm, entering a forward contract to buy pounds makes sense if the expected spot rate in thirty days is greater than the current forward rate ($E(S) > \$1.50/£$). Appreciation in the pound increases the cost of importing from Britain, so if a U.S. firm expects the pound to appreciate above the current forward rate, it will lock in a forward contract immediately. On the other hand, if the U.S. firm expects the spot rate to be less than \$1.50/£ in thirty days, it will choose to wait rather than lock in at the forward rate.

Now we broaden the example to include all U.S. and U.K. firms who face a future need to buy foreign currency. Ideally, U.S. firms who need to buy pounds to import British goods could trade with U.K. firms who must sell pounds and buy dollars to import U.S. goods. However, there is a problem because the circumstances under which firms in each country prefer to trade in the spot market rather than the forward market are mirror images of each other:

1. If $E(S) > F$, the U.K. firms do not want the forward contract, but U.S. firms do.
2. If $E(S) < F$, the U.K. firms want the forward contract, but U.S. firms do not.

forward–spot parity
An equilibrium relationship that predicts that the current forward rate will be an unbiased predictor of the spot rate on a future date.

Equilibrium will occur in this market only when the forecast of the spot rate is equal to the current forward rate. In that case, U.S. and U.K. firms are indifferent to whether they transact in the spot or the forward market. This yields our first parity condition, known as **forward-spot parity**. It says that the forward rate should be an unbiased predictor of where the spot rate is headed:

$$E(S) = F \quad \text{(Eq. 16.2)}$$

It would certainly be convenient for currency traders if the forward exchange rate provided a reliable forecast of future spot rates. Unfortunately, most studies suggest that this is not the case. Changes in spot exchange rates are not closely tied to the forward exchange rate. For that matter, most researchers and practitioners agree that it is nearly impossible to predict how most exchange rates will move most of the time, at least in the short run.

If forward rates do not accurately predict movements in currency values over time, perhaps something else does. Economists have long observed a correlation between currency movements and inflation rate differentials across countries. To illustrate, Table 16.1 reports the cumulative inflation that occurred in the United

Table 16.1
Inflation and Exchange Rate Movements

Source: Authors calculations using data from 1984–1996.

	% Cumulative Inflation	% U.S. Inflation – Foreign Inflation	% Appreciation/Depreciation Against the $
United States	51	NA	NA
Japan	17	+34	+46
Germany	52	–1	–4.5
France	100	–49	–50

States, Japan, Germany, and France from 1984 to 1996. Beside those figures we show the difference between the U.S. inflation and that which occurred in the other countries, as well as the cumulative change in the values of the yen, the German mark, and the French franc against the dollar over the same period.

Notice the remarkable correspondence between the numbers in the third and fourth columns. Japan's was the only currency that appreciated against the dollar from 1984 to 1996, and it was the only country on the list with less inflation than the United States. German and U.S. inflation was about equal, and the dollar-mark exchange rate was about the same in 1996 as it was in 1984. French inflation was roughly 50 percentage points higher than U.S. inflation, about equal to the decline in the franc.

These figures suggest that differences in inflation do a good job of explaining currency movements, at least over a long period of time. The second parity relationship reveals why.

Purchasing Power Parity

One of the simplest ideas in economics is that identical goods trading in different markets should sell at the same price, absent any barriers to trade. This **law of one price** has a natural application in international finance. Suppose that a DVD of a hit movie retails in the United States for $20, and the identical DVD can be purchased in Tokyo for ¥2,000. Does the law of one price hold? It depends on the exchange rate. If the spot rate of exchange equals ¥100/$, then the answer is yes. A U.S. consumer can spend $20 to purchase the DVD in the United States, or he can convert $20 to ¥2,000 and purchase the item in Tokyo. We can generalize this example as follows. Suppose that the price of an item in domestic currency is P_{dom} and the price of the identical item in foreign currency is P_{for}. If the spot exchange rate quoted in foreign currency per domestic is $S^{for/dom}$, then the law of one price holds if the following is true:

law of one price
A theory that says that the identical good trading in different markets must sell at the same price.

$$\frac{P_{for}}{P_{dom}} = S^{for/dom} \quad \text{(Eq. 16.3)}$$

Naturally, the law of one price extends to any pair of countries, not just the United States and Japan. When Equation 16.3 does not hold, traders may engage in arbitrage to exploit price discrepancies across national boundaries.

APPLYING THE MODEL

Suppose that a pair of Maui Jim sunglasses sells for $200 in the United States and for €180 in Italy. The exchange rate between dollars and euros is €0.95/$. Does the law of one price hold? Apparently not, because the following is true:

$$€180 \div \$200 < €0.95/\$$$

Figure 16.3
Arbitrage and the Law of One Price

If sunglasses sell for $200 in the US and €180 in Italy, then the law of one price holds only if the exchange rate equals €0.90/$. If the exchange rate is €0.95, then traders can make a profit by purchasing the sunglasses in Italy, shipping them to the U.S. and selling them there, and converting the proceeds back into euros.

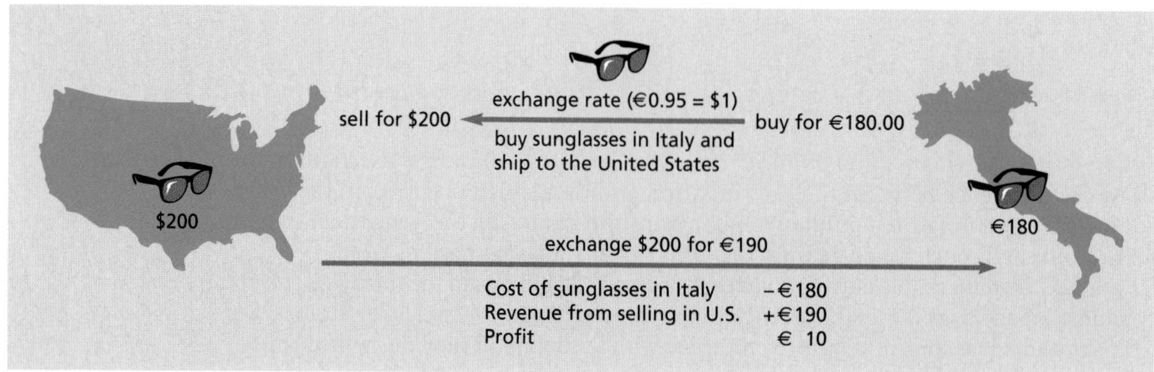

How can arbitrageurs exploit this violation of the law of one price? The previous equation reveals that the price of sunglasses in Italy is too low, or the price in the United States is too high, relative to the current exchange rate. Therefore, suppose that a trader buys sunglasses in Italy for €180 and ships them to the United States. After selling them for $200, the trader can convert back to euros, receiving €190 ($200 × €0.95/$). The arbitrage profit is €10. As long as the transactions costs of making these trades is less than €10, and as long as there are no other barriers to trade, then the process will continue until the market reaches equilibrium. Figure 16.3 illustrates how the trades of arbritragers push the market back toward an equilibrium in which the law of one price holds.

Now we will add a new wrinkle to the law of one price. Suppose that prices in different countries satisfy Equation 16.3 not just at one moment in time, but all the time. We do not necessarily expect this to be the case for every type of good sold in two countries, but if price discrepancies for similar goods become too large, the forces of arbitrage should push them back into line. Of course, the prices of goods and services change every day due to inflation (or deflation), and there is no reason to expect the inflation rate in one country to be the same as in another. If different countries are subject to different inflation pressures, how can the law of one price hold on an ongoing basis? The answer is that the exchange rate adjusts to maintain equilibrium.

APPLYING THE MODEL

Suppose that the forces of arbitrage have influenced the prices of Maui Jim sunglasses in the United States and in Italy so that the law of one price now holds. Specifically, the U.S. price is $195 and the Italian price is €185.25. If the exchange rate is still €0.95/$, then the law of one price holds because the following is true:

$$€185.25 \div \$195 = €0.95 / \$$$

Now suppose that the expected rate of inflation in Italy over the next year is 12 percent, but no inflation is expected in the United States. One year from today, Maui Jim sunglasses will still sell for $195 in the United States, but with 12 percent inflation, the price in Italy will rise to €207.48 (185.25 × 1.12). If these forecasts are correct, then in a year the exchange rate must rise to €1.064/$ for the law of one price to hold:

$$€207.48 \div \$195 = €1.064/\$$$

Remember that this exchange rate is expressed in euros per dollar, so an increase from €0.95/$ to €1.064/$ represents appreciation of the dollar and depreciation of the euro.

Purchasing power parity is an extension of the law of one price. Purchasing power parity says that if the law of one price holds at all times, then differences in expected inflation between two countries are associated with expected changes in currency values. Mathematically, we can express this idea as follows:

purchasing power parity An equilibrium relationship that predicts that currency movements are tied to differences in inflation rates across countries.

$$\frac{E(S^{for/dom})}{(S^{for/dom})} = \frac{[1+E(i_{for})]}{[1+E(i_{dom})]} \quad \text{(Eq. 16.4)}$$

where, as before, the expected spot rate is $E(S)$, the current spot rate is S, the expected rate of inflation in the foreign country is $E(i_{for})$, and the expected rate of inflation in the domestic country is $E(i_{dom})$. Notice that the left-hand side of this equation exceeds 1.0 if traders expect the domestic currency to appreciate, and it is less than 1.0 if traders expect the foreign currency to appreciate. Likewise, the right-hand side of the equation exceeds 1.0 when expected inflation is higher abroad than it is at home, and the ratio falls below 1.0 when the opposite is true. Therefore, the equation produces the already familiar prediction that if inflation is higher in one country than another, then the currency of the country with higher inflation will depreciate. The equation advises traders who want to forecast currency movements to invest resources in forecasting inflation rates.

How accurately does purchasing power parity predict exchange rate movements? As we have already seen, over the long term there is a strong relationship between currency values and inflation rates. Countries with high inflation see their currencies depreciate over time, whereas the opposite happens for countries with lower inflation. This is no accident. If we did not observe this pattern in the data, it would signal gross violations of the law of one price and indicate that arbitrage was not working to bring prices back into line.

But purchasing power parity does not fare as well in the short run. Violations of the law of one price do occur frequently, and many studies suggest that they persist from three to four years on average. Again, arbitrage, or in this case, limits to arbitrage explain why. When goods prices in different countries are out of equilibrium, arbitrageurs must trade the goods, moving them across national borders, to earn a profit. This process cannot occur without investments in time and money, and for certain goods, trade may be impossible due to legal restrictions or the physical impediments to transporting goods. Accordingly, there is no reason to expect goods to flow from one market to the other instantaneously at any moment when the law of one price does not hold. Only if price discrepancies across markets are large enough and persistent enough will arbitrageurs find it profitable to trade. Hence, purchasing power parity does a good job of explaining long-run movements in currencies, but not day-to-day, or even year-to-year, fluctuations.

Interest Rate Parity

Although it is both time-consuming and expensive to move goods across borders, the same cannot generally be said about purely financial transactions. Large institutional investors can buy and sell currencies very rapidly and at low cost, and they can buy and sell financial assets denominated in different currencies just as quickly. Interest rate parity applies the law of one price to financial assets, specifically to risk-free assets denominated in different currencies.

To illustrate, assume that a U.S. institution has \$10 million that it wants to invest for 180 days in a risk-free government bill. The current annual interest rate on 180-day U.S. Treasury bills is 2 percent per year (1 percent for six months), so if the institution chooses this investment, it will have \$10.1 million six months later:

$$\$10{,}000{,}000\left(1+\frac{R_{US}}{2}\right)=\$10{,}000{,}000\left(1+\frac{0.02}{2}\right)=\$10{,}100{,}000$$

Alternatively, the institution might choose to convert its \$10 million into another currency and invest abroad. However, even if it invests in a risk-free government bill issued by a foreign government, the institution must enter into a forward contract to convert back into dollars when the investment matures. Otherwise, the return on the foreign investment is not risk-free and will depend on changes in currency values over the next six months.

For example, suppose that the annual interest rate on a six-month British government bill is 5.26 percent per year (2.63 percent for six months). Suppose also that the spot and six-month forward exchange rates are £0.5639/\$ and £0.5730/\$, respectively, as given in Figure 16.1. The U.S. institution converts \$10 million into £5,639,000 at the spot rate. It invests the pounds for six months at the U.K. interest rate and enters into a forward contract to convert those pounds back into dollars when the U.K. bill matures. At the end of six months, the institution has the following:[2]

$$\$10{,}000{,}000(S^{£/\$})\left(1+\frac{R_{UK}}{2}\right)\left(\frac{1}{F^{£/\$}}\right)=\$10{,}000{,}000(£0.5639)\left(1+\frac{0.0526}{2}\right)\left(\frac{1}{£0.5730/\$}\right)=\$10{,}100{,}010$$

Given the prevailing interest rates on short-term, risk-free U.S. and U.K. bonds, and given current spot and forward exchange rates between dollars and pounds, investors are more or less indifferent to whether they invest in the United States or the United Kingdom. In other words, with respect to short-term, risk-free financial assets, the law of one price holds. This relationship is called **interest rate parity**, which simply means that risk-free investments should offer the same return (after converting currencies) everywhere. As usual, we can express interest rate parity in mathematical terms. Letting R_{for} and R_{dom} represent the risk-free rate on foreign and domestic government debt, we obtain the following equation:[3]

interest rate parity
An equilibrium relationship that predicts that differences in risk-free interest rates in two countries must be tied to differences in currency values on the spot and forward markets.

$$\frac{F^{for/dom}}{S^{for/dom}}=\frac{(1+R_{for})}{(1+R_{dom})} \quad \text{(Eq. 16.5)}$$

[2] There is a \$10 difference between the return that our investor earns in the U.S. and the return earned in the U.K. This \$10 is really nothing more than a rounding error because we do not carry exchange rates past the fourth decimal place. Also, note that we first multiply the \$10,000,000 times the spot exchange rate to determine the quantity of pounds available for investing. Next, we increase this amount by multiplying times one plus the U.K. interest rate. Finally, we have to divide the total by the forward rate to convert the currency back into dollars.

[3] Be careful to match the term of the forward rate to the term of the interest rate in this expression. For example, if you are comparing interest rates on 180-day government bills, you must use a 180-day forward rate. You can see this by going back to the example of the institution with \$10 million to invest. If you set the equation representing the institution's U.S. return equal to the equation representing its U.K. return, the following equation results:

$$\frac{F^{£/\$}}{S^{£/\$}}=\frac{\left(1+\frac{R_{UK}}{2}\right)}{\left(1+\frac{R_{US}}{2}\right)}$$

What is the intuitive interpretation of this expression? Observe that if the left-hand side of the equation is greater than 1.0, the domestic currency trades at a forward premium. If domestic investors send money abroad, when they convert back to domestic currency, they will realize an exchange loss because the foreign currency buys less domestic currency than it did at the spot rate. Domestic investors know this, so they require an incentive in the form of a higher foreign interest rate before they will send money abroad. To maintain equilibrium, the right-hand side must also be greater than 1.0, which means that the foreign interest rate must exceed the domestic rate. The bottom line is that when a nation's currency trades at a forward premium (discount), risk-free interest rates in that country should be lower (higher) than they are abroad.

As is the case with purchasing power parity, deviations from interest rate parity create arbitrage opportunities. However, these arbitrage opportunities involve buying and selling financial assets rather than physical commodities. Naturally, trade in securities can occur rapidly and much less expensively than trade in goods, so the forces of arbitrage are more powerful in maintaining interest rate parity.

APPLYING THE MODEL

Suppose that the six-month, risk-free rate in the United States is 2 percent, and in Canada it is 6 percent. The spot exchange rate is C$1.5855/$, and the 180-day forward rate is C$1.5937/$. Interest rate parity does not hold, as shown in the following equation:

$$\frac{C\$1.5937/\$}{C\$1.5855/\$} < \frac{\left(1+\frac{0.06}{2}\right)}{\left(1+\frac{0.02}{2}\right)}$$

Because the right-hand side of this equation is "too large" relative to parity, the interest rate in Canada is "too high" or the rate in the United States is "too low." The arbitrage opportunity is as follows. An investor borrows money (say $1 million) at 2 percent in the United States, then converts the proceeds into Canadian dollars, and invests them at 6 percent. Six months later, the investor converts the Canadian dollars back into U.S. currency to repay the loan. Anything left over is pure arbitrage profit.

Borrow $1 million in the U.S. at 2 percent for six months → must repay $1,010,000
$1 million → converted at spot rate → C$1,585,500
C$1,585,500 invested for six months at 6 percent → (C$1,585,500)(1.03) → C$1,633,065
C$1,633,065 converted to US$ at the forward rate → $1,024,700
$1,010,000 needed to repay U.S. loan → leaves $14,700 arbitrage profit

The effect of all these transactions, repeated again and again, is to push exchange rates and interest rates back toward parity. As investors borrow in the United States, the U.S. interest rate will rise from 2 percent to a higher level. Similarly, as investors purchase Canadian government bonds, the bond prices will rise and the risk-free rate in Canada will fall. When investors sell U.S. dollars to buy Canadian dollars on the spot market, the spot rate (in terms of Canadian dollars per U.S. dollar) will rise, and just the opposite happens on the forward market as investors sell Canadian dollars to buy U.S. dollars. In terms

SMART CONCEPTS

See the concept explained step-by-step at SMARTFinance

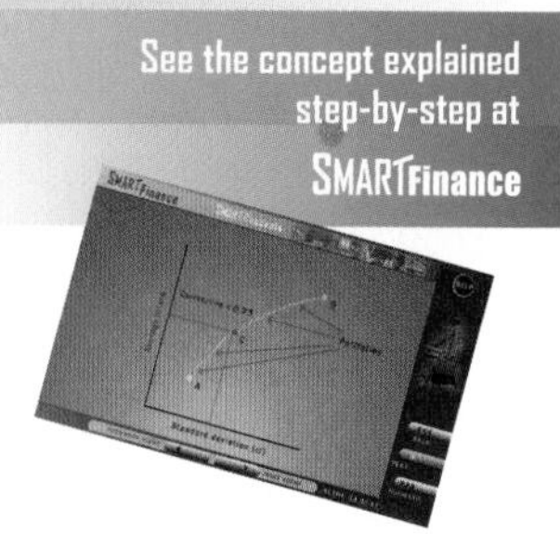

of the interest rate parity equation, we can see how these forces drive markets to equilibrium:

$$\text{This ratio is increasing} \leftarrow \frac{\text{C\$}1.5937/\$\uparrow}{\text{C\$}1.5855/\$\downarrow} < \frac{\left(1+\frac{0.06\downarrow}{2}\right)}{\left(1+\frac{0.02\uparrow}{2}\right)} \rightarrow \text{This ratio is decreasing}$$

$$\downarrow$$

New equilibrium occurs when inequality becomes an equality

covered interest arbitrage A trading strategy designed to exploit deviations from interest rate parity to earn an arbitrage profit.

The process illustrated in the preceding example is known as **covered interest arbitrage** because traders attempt to earn arbitrage profits arising from differences in interest rates across countries, and they "cover" their currency exposures with forward contracts. Implicit in this example was the assumption that investors could borrow and lend at the risk-free rate in each country. Not all investors can do this, but large, creditworthy institutions can get very close to this ideal. Moreover, they can execute the trades described in the example at very high speed and at low cost. In the real world, deviations from interest rate parity are small and transitory.

Real Interest Rate Parity (the Fisher Effect)

real interest rate parity An equilibrium relationship that predicts that the real interest rate will be the same in every country.

If nominal rates of return on risk-free investments are equalized around the world, after adjusting for currency translation, perhaps real rates of return are also equalized. **Real interest rate parity** means that investors should earn the same real rate of return on risk-free investments no matter the country in which they choose to invest. Recall from Chapter 5 that the real rate of interest is defined as follows:

$$1+\text{real} = \frac{1+R}{1+E(i)}$$

If market forces equalize real rates across national borders, then the ratio on the right-hand side should be the same in every country. Continuing to use the notation for foreign and domestic nominal interest rates and expected inflation rates, we can write the following equation:

$$\frac{1+R_{\text{for}}}{1+E(i_{\text{for}})} = \frac{1+R_{\text{dom}}}{1+E(i_{\text{dom}})}$$

Then by cross multiplying we obtain

$$\frac{1+R_{\text{for}}}{1+R_{\text{dom}}} = \frac{1+E(i_{\text{for}})}{1+E(i_{\text{dom}})} \quad \text{(Eq. 16.6)}$$

This equation says that if real rates are the same in the domestic and the foreign country, then the ratio of (1 plus) nominal interest rates in the two countries must equal the ratio of (1 plus) expected inflation rates. If expected inflation is higher in one country than in another, then the country with higher inflation must offer higher interest rates to give investors the same real return.

APPLYING THE MODEL

Suppose that expected inflation in the United States equals zero and expected inflation in Italy is 12 percent. Suppose also that the one-year, risk-free rate in the United States is 3 percent. What would the one-year, risk-free rate have to be in Italy to maintain real interest rate parity?

$$\frac{1+R_{\text{Italy}}}{1+0.03}=\frac{1+0.12}{1+0.0} \qquad R_{\text{Italy}}=15.36\%$$

As with purchasing power parity, real interest rate parity need not hold at all times, because when deviations from parity occur, limits to arbitrage prevent market forces from quickly reaching a new equilibrium. In the long run, we expect that real interest rate parity will hold, at least approximately, but that will not necessarily be the case in the short run.

We conclude this section with a quick review of the four parity relationships, highlighting how they are linked together. If we combine Equations 16.2, 16.4, 16.5, and 16.6, we have the following relationships:[4]

$$\frac{E(S)}{S}=\frac{F}{S}=\frac{1+R_{\text{for}}}{1+R_{\text{dom}}}=\frac{1+E(i_{\text{for}})}{1+E(i_{\text{dom}})}=\frac{E(S)}{S} \qquad \text{(Eq. 16.7)}$$

The first equality simply restates the forward-spot parity relationship. The second equality is the expression for interest rate parity, and the third and fourth equalities define real interest rate parity and purchasing power parity, respectively. Here we see for the first time that if markets are in equilibrium, spot and forward exchange rates, nominal interest rates, and expected inflation rates are all linked internationally. If we want to understand why currency values change, Equation 16.7 gives us a number of clues. The equation also illustrates how difficult it can be for countries to manage their exchange rates. Attempts to push the exchange rate in a particular direction invariably lead to changes in other macroeconomic variables that policy makers may not desire.[5]

CONCEPT REVIEW QUESTIONS

5. Explain the logic behind each of the four parity relationships.

6. Explain the role of arbitrage in maintaining the parity relationships.

7. In what sense is interest rate parity an application of the law of one price?

8. An investor who notices that interest rates are much lower in Japan than in the United States borrows in Japan and invests the proceeds in the United States. This is called uncovered interest arbitrage, but is it really arbitrage? Why or why not?

4. Notice that to create this equation we divided equation 16.2 by S, the spot rate. This does no harm to the equality, and it allows us to highlight the connection between the four parity relationships.

5. In October 1997, market pressure was building for a devaluation of the Hong Kong dollar. Hong Kong's currency board reacted by purchasing vast amounts of Hong Kong currency. One consequence of their activity was that overnight interest rates in Hong Kong briefly reached 280 percent. A year later a similar spike in short-term interest rates occurred in Russia as the government there unsuccessfully tried to prevent a sharp drop in the value of the ruble.

16.3 MANAGING FINANCIAL AND POLITICAL RISK

Transactions Risk

Any firm that might experience an adverse change in the value of any of its cash flows as a result of exchange rate movements faces exposure to exchange rate risk. Almost every firm is exposed to exchange rate risk to some degree, even if it operates strictly in one country and has cash flows in only one currency. Such a firm will face exchange rate risk if (1) it produces a good or service that competes with imports in the home market, or (2) it uses as a production input an imported product or service.

Nonetheless, some types of companies face greater exchange rate risk than do others. MNCs obviously face this risk in all aspects of their business, but they also have many opportunities to minimize that risk by, for example, moving production facilities to the countries where their products are sold so that costs and revenues can be in the same currency. The greatest exchange rate exposure occurs when a firm's costs and revenues are largely denominated in different currencies.

As usual, it is easiest to describe the importance of exchange rate risk to an exporter with an example. Assume that the Boeing Co. has just sold an airplane to a Japanese buyer, with the following details. First, when Boeing sells to Japanese customers, it prices its planes in yen. Boeing wants to set the yen price high enough so that the payment it receives converts back into at least $1 million. This allows Boeing to cover costs and earn an acceptable profit. Second, assume that the current yen/dollar exchange rate is ¥100.00/$. Boeing therefore negotiates a price of ¥100 million for the airplane. However, the company is primarily concerned with how many dollars it will collect when payment is made in yen and then converted into dollars on the foreign exchange market.

If Boeing negotiates the terms of this sale at the same time that it receives payment, it does not face any foreign exchange risk. The company will simply exchange ¥100 million for $1 million on the spot market. In reality, Boeing will probably negotiate payment terms months before it expects payment from the Japanese customer. This simple fact creates exchange rate risk, because between the dates when Boeing sets the price in yen for the plane and when it receives payment, the exchange rate can move. Because the contract is denominated in yen, Boeing bears this exchange rate risk, but the risk would not be eliminated by denominating the sales contract in dollars—the risk would simply be shifted to the Japanese buyer.

Suppose that after Boeing agrees to a price, it must wait six months for payment. In that time, the exchange rate changes to ¥110.00/$, meaning that the dollar has appreciated and the yen has depreciated. Boeing will still receive the same ¥100 million, but now that converts to just $909,091. Appreciation in the dollar results in Boeing realizing an exchange rate loss of $90,909. If the yen appreciates, say to ¥90.00/$, Boeing will receive $1,111,111 and will realize an exchange rate gain of $111,111.

This exchange rate risk cannot be eliminated, but it can be hedged (transferred to a third party) using financial contracts. Assume that immediately after Boeing agrees to sell the plane for ¥100 million it enters a six-month forward contract to sell yen in exchange for dollars. Boeing's forward contract is not with its Japanese customer, but rather with a money-center bank, such as Citigroup, that serves as a dealer in the foreign exchange market. If the forward rate that Boeing agrees to equals ¥99/$, Boeing promises to deliver ¥100 million in exchange for $1,010,101 exactly six months from now. Once this forward contract is executed, Boeing is no longer exposed to exchange rate risk. The risk has not disappeared; it has simply been transferred from Boeing to Citigroup. But why would Citigroup be willing to assume this risk?

International banks—and, increasingly, other types of financial institutions—are uniquely positioned to bear exchange rate risk because they can create what amounts to a natural hedge, or offsetting risk exposure, as a normal course of their business. Offsetting risk means they are able to easily arrange mirror-image positions with other customers. To see this, consider what type of foreign exchange contract Toyota Motors might demand from Citigroup. The exchange rate risk problem for Toyota (one of Japan's biggest exporters) is the opposite of Boeing's: Toyota exports many automobiles from Japan and sells these in the United States. The company receives U.S. dollars as payment, but its costs are in yen, so it would need to *sell dollars forward* (locking in a yen price) in order to cover its costs and make an acceptable profit. Citigroup can buy dollars forward (sell yen) from Toyota and simultaneously sell dollars forward (buy yen) to Boeing, and thus net out the exchange rate exposure on its own books. This is a simplified example because Citigroup may not have a perfectly offsetting exposure for Boeing's needs, but in that case it would simply execute its own forward contract with another bank—perhaps with Toyota's main bank.

We have discussed how to measure exchange rate risk as it applies to specific transactions and have briefly discussed one method of dealing with it using a forward market hedge. However, this **transactions exposure** is but one of many types of exchange rate risk.

transactions exposure The risk that movements in exchange rates will adversely affect the value of a particular transaction.

Translation and Economic Risk

MNCs must deal with additional complexities if they have affiliates or subsidiaries on the ground in a foreign country. One such complication arises when MNCs translate costs and revenues denominated in foreign currencies to report on their financial statements, which, of course, are denominated in the home currency. This type of risk is called **translation exposure** or **accounting exposure.** In other words, foreign exchange rate fluctuations affect individual accounts in the financial statements. A more important risk element concerns **economic exposure**, which is the overall impact of foreign exchange rate fluctuations on the firm's value. A firm faces economic exposure when exchange rate changes affect its cash flows, even those cash flows not specifically tied to transactions in other currencies. For example, a rise in the value of the dollar against the euro makes European wines less expensive to U.S. consumers, and it makes U.S. wine more expensive for European consumers. A winery operating in the United States, even one that does not sell directly to foreign customers, may realize a decline in cash flows due to competition from suddenly less expensive European vintners.

translation exposure or accounting exposure The risk that exchange rate movements will adversely impact reported financial results on a firm's financial statements.

economic exposure The risk that a firm's value will fluctuate due to exchange rate movements.

What can managers do about these risks? Hedging economic exposure is more difficult than hedging transactions exposure, in part because measuring the exposure is more difficult. For instance, a U.S. winery concerned about the declining prices of foreign wines could engage in currency trades that would result in a profit if the dollar appreciates against the euro. In theory, these profits could offset the decline in earnings that occurs when European wines become less expensive, but exactly how large will these losses be for a given change in the exchange rate? Increasingly, MNCs manage their economic exposures both by using sophisticated currency derivatives and by matching costs and revenues in a given currency. For instance, a foreign company exporting to Japan might issue yen-denominated bonds, so-called **Samurai bonds,** to create a yen-based liability that would partially or fully offset the exposure resulting from yen-based receivables. However, it is important to emphasize that unless the cash inflows and outflows match exactly, some residual yen exposure will remain.

Samurai bonds Yen-denominated bonds issued by non-Japanese corporations.

Political Risk

political risk
The risk that a government will take an action that negatively affects the values of firms operating in that country.

Another important risk facing MNCs is **political risk**, which refers to actions taken by a government that have a negative impact on the value of foreign companies operating in that country, such as raising taxes on a firm's activities or erecting barriers that prevent a firm from repatriating profits back to the home country. In its most extreme form, political risk can mean confiscation of a corporation's assets by a foreign government.

Political risk has two basic dimensions: *macro* and *micro*. *Macro political risk* means that *all* foreign firms in the country will be subject to political risk because of political change, revolution, or the adoption of new policies by a host government. In other words, no individual country or firm is treated differently. An example of macro political risk occurred when communist regimes came to power in China in 1949 and in Cuba in 1959–1960. More recently, the near collapse of Indonesia's currency in late 1997 and early 1998, plus the attendant political and economic turmoil elsewhere in Asia, highlights the real and present danger that macro political risk can pose to MNCs and international investors alike. *Micro political risk*, on the other hand, refers to a foreign government targeting punitive action against an individual firm, a specific industry, or companies from a particular foreign country. Examples include the nationalization by a majority of the oil-exporting countries of the assets of the international oil companies in their territories during the 1970s.

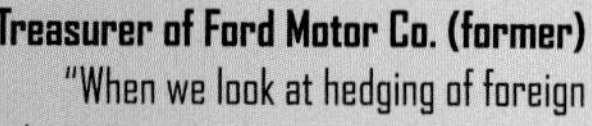

Beth Acton, Vice President and Treasurer of Ford Motor Co. (former)

"When we look at hedging of foreign exchange exposures, we make an assessment of what kinds of risks we want to take in the business, and we are not out to second-guess the market."

Although political risk can take place in any country, even in the United States, the political instability of many developing countries generally makes the positions of multinational companies most vulnerable there. At the same time, some of the countries in this group have the most promising markets for the goods and services being offered by MNCs. The main question, therefore, is how to engage in operations and foreign investment in such countries and yet avoid or minimize the potential political risk.

MNCs may adopt both positive and negative approaches to cope with political risk. Negative approaches include taking a trade dispute with a host country to the World Trade Organization (described later) or threatening to withhold additional investments from a country unless an MNC's demands are met. Firms may also negotiate agreements with host governments that build in costs that the host government must bear if it breaches the terms of the original agreement. Positive approaches for MNCs include working proactively to develop environmental and labor standards in a country, and generally attempting to become perceived as a domestic company by the host country's citizenry.

European Monetary Union and the Rise of Regional Trading Blocks

euro
The currency used throughout the countries that make up the European Union.

monetary union
An agreement between many European countries to integrate their monetary systems including using a single currency.

As a result of the Maastricht Treaty of 1991, eleven of the fifteen European Union (EU) nations adopted a single currency, the **euro**, as a continent-wide medium of exchange beginning January 2, 1999. In early 2002, the national currencies of the twelve (now including Greece) countries participating in **monetary union** disappeared and were completely replaced by the euro. At the same time that the European Union is struggling to implement monetary union (which also involved creating a new European Central Bank), the EU must also deal with a wave of new applicants from Eastern Europe and the Mediterranean region. Whatever its final shape, the new community of Europe will offer both challenges and opportunities to a variety of players, including multinational firms. MNCs, especially those based in the United States, will face heightened levels of competition when operating inside the EU.

COMPARATIVE CORPORATE FINANCE

How Risky Are Different Countries

How much risk do companies face when they decide to do business in a particular country? Twice each year, the magazine *Euromoney* tries to answer this question when it publishes its semiannual country risk rankings. The rankings, which range from 0 to 100 with higher numbers indicating less risk, evaluate several elements of the risk of investing in each country. The factors that *Euromoney* considers in its rankings include the expected economic growth rate, political risk, various measures related to the country's indebtedness, and measures indicating the access to capital from banks and capital markets in the country. The following table lists some of the results from the March 2004 rankings.

The rankings contain few surprises. The top 10 (safest) countries are primarily European and North American nations. At the bottom of the list are hot spots such as Iraq and Afghanistan, lingering communist regimes in Cuba and North Korea, and troubled African nations like Libya, Somalia, Liberia, and Sudan.

Country	Score	Country	Score	Country	Score	Country	Score
Norway	98.93	Greece	80.32	India	55.58	Venezuela	36.49
Switzerland	97.04	Slovenia	76.73	Costa Rica	53.81	Uganda	36.28
U.S.	95.79	Malta	76.20	Bulgaria	52.66	Kenya	36.25
Denmark	94.09	Kuwait	75.81	Panama	50.28	Paraguay	36.24
U.K.	93.49	U.A.E.	72.53	Russia	50.12	Benin	35.32
Austria	93.45	Brunei	69.52	Romania	49.62	Honduras	34.59
Netherlands	93.24	Hungary	67.74	El Salvador	49.23	Nigeria	34.58
Canada	92.76	South Korea	67.21	Philippines	48.77	Ecuador	34.37
Sweden	92.73	Czech Republic	66.45	Colombia	47.34	Ethiopia	31.66
Ireland	92.24	Saudi Arabia	65.93	Vietnam	47.31	Argentina	31.57
Germany	91.69	Bahrain	65.73	Turkey	46.87	Nicaragua	30.86
Finland	91.58	Israel	65.70	Brazil	46.59	Rwanda	27.72
France	91.46	Chile	65.01	Peru	46.57	Haiti	25.94
Japan	91.19	China	62.86	Jordan	45.27	Sudan	24.75
Singapore	89.63	Poland	62.76	Iran	43.79	Libya	23.02
Australia	89.51	Mexico	62.39	Guatemala	42.33	Zimbabwe	21.66
Belgium	89.34	South Africa	60.52	Indonesia	41.48	Somalia	20.32
Spain	87.75	Botswana	60.48	Pakistan	40.50	Liberia	15.60
Italy	85.77	Oman	60.46	Ukraine	40.15	Cuba	12.14
New Zealand	85.22	Thailand	60.21	Jamaica	40.11	North Korea	9.28
Portugal	84.55	Lithuania	59.29	Ghana	37.00	Iraq	8.27
Hong Kong	82.05	Latvia	58.74	Lebanon	36.96	Afghanistan	4.11

Another major trading block that arose during the 1990s is the Mercosur group of countries in South America. Beginning in 1991, the nations of Brazil, Argentina, Paraguay, and Uruguay began removing tariffs and other barriers to intraregional trade. The second stage of Mercosur's development began at the end of 1994 and involved the development of a customs union to impose a common tariff on external trade while enforcing uniform and lower tariffs on intragroup trade. To date, Mercosur has been even more successful than its founders had imagined, though the economic collapse of Argentina in early 2002 obviously places Mercosur's near-term viability at risk. The long-term importance of Mercosur will likely depend on whether the U.S. Congress overcomes its reluctance to extend the North American Free Trade Agreement (NAFTA) throughout Latin America. In any case, the Mercosur countries represent well over half of total Latin American GDP, and thus will loom large in the plans of any MNC wishing to access the growth markets of this region.

General Agreement on Tariffs and Trade (GATT)
A trade treaty that extends free trade principles to broad areas of economic activity in many countries.

World Trade Organization (WTO)
An organization established by GATT to police world trading practices and to settle disputes between GATT member countries.

Although it may seem that the world is splitting into a handful of trading blocs, this is less dangerous than it may appear because many international treaties are in force that guarantee relatively open access to at least the largest economies. The most important such treaty is the **General Agreement on Tariffs and Trade (GATT)**, which celebrated its fiftieth anniversary in May 1998. The current agreement extends free-trading rules to broad areas of economic activity—such as agriculture, financial services, and intellectual property rights—that had not previously been covered by international treaty and that were thus effectively off-limits to foreign competition. The 1994 revised GATT treaty also established a new international body, the **World Trade Organization (WTO)**, to police world trading practices and to mediate disputes between member countries. The WTO began operating in January 1995, and one extremely important nation, the People's Republic of China, became a member in 2002.

CONCEPT REVIEW QUESTIONS

9. Distinguish between transactions, translation, and economic exposure.

10. Describe how a domestic firm might use a forward contract to hedge an economic exposure. Why does uncertainty about the magnitude of the exposure make this difficult?

11. Consider a U.S. firm that has for many years exported to European countries. How does the creation of the euro simplify or complicate the management of transactions exposure for this firm?

16.4 LONG-TERM INVESTMENT DECISIONS

SMART IDEAS VIDEO
Ike Mathur, University of Southern Illinois at Carbondale
"What I find very interesting is that for a long time in international finance we have talked about the first mover advantage."
See the entire interview at **SMARTFinance**

In Chapters 8–10, we emphasized the importance of sound capital budgeting practices for a corporation's long-term survival. The same lessons covered in those chapters apply to multinational corporations. Whether investing at home or abroad, MNCs should evaluate investments based on their incremental cash flows and should discount those cash flows at a rate that is appropriate given the risk of the investment. However, when a company makes investments denominated in many different currencies, this process becomes a bit more complicated. First, in what currency should the firm express a foreign project's cash flows? Second, how does one calculate the cost of capital for an MNC, or for a given project?

Capital Budgeting

Suppose that a U.S. firm is weighing an investment that will generate cash flows in euros. The company's financial analysts have estimated the project's cash flows in euros as follows:

Initial Cost	Year 1	Year 2	Year 3
–€2 million	€900,000	€850,000	€800,000

To calculate the project's *NPV*, the U.S. firm can take either of two approaches. First, it can discount euro-denominated cash flows using a euro-based cost of capital. Having done this, the firm can then convert the resulting *NPV* back to dollars at the spot rate. For example, assume that the risk-free rate in Europe is 5 percent, and the firm estimates that the cost of capital (expressed as a euro rate) for this project is 10 percent (in other words, there is a 5 percent risk premium associated with the investment). The *NPV*, rounded to the nearest thousand euros, equals €122,000:

$$NPV = -2{,}000{,}000 + \frac{900{,}000}{1.10^1} + \frac{850{,}000}{1.10^2} + \frac{800{,}000}{1.10^3} = 121{,}713$$

Assume that the current spot rate equals \$0.95/€. Multiplying the spot rate times the *NPV* yields a dollar-based *NPV* of \$116,000 (rounded to the nearest thousand dollars).

In this example, we did not make specific year-by-year forecasts of the future spot rates. Doing so is unnecessary because the firm can choose to hedge its currency exposure through a forward contract. Hedging the currency exposure allows the firm to separate the decision to accept or reject the project from projections of where the dollar-to-euro exchange rate might be headed. Of course, the firm may have a view on the exchange rate question, but even so, it is wise to first consider the investment on its own merits. For instance, suppose that this project has a negative *NPV*, but managers believe that the euro will appreciate over the life of the project, increasing the project's appeal in dollar terms. Given that belief, there is no need for the firm to undertake the project. Instead, it could purchase euros directly, invest them in safe financial assets in Europe, and convert back to dollars several years later. That is, if the firm wants to speculate on currency movements, it need not invest in physical assets to accomplish that objective.

A second approach for evaluating the investment project is to calculate the *NPV* in dollar terms, assuming that the firm hedges the project's cash flows using forward contracts. To begin this calculation, we must know the risk-free rate in the United States. Suppose that this rate is 3 percent. Recognizing that interest rate parity must hold, we can use Equation 16.5 to calculate the one-year forward rate:

$$\frac{F^{\$/euro}}{S^{\$/euro}} = \frac{1+R_{US}}{1+R_{euro}} \qquad \frac{F}{0.95} = \frac{1.03^1}{1.05^1} \qquad F = \$0.9319/€$$

Similarly, we can calculate the two-year and three-year forward rates as follows:

$$\frac{F}{0.95} = \frac{1.03^2}{1.05^2} \qquad F = \$0.9142/€ \qquad \frac{F}{0.95} = \frac{1.03^3}{1.05^3} \qquad F = \$0.8967/€$$

Next, multiply each period's cash flow in euros times the matching spot or forward exchange rate to obtain a sequence of cash flows in dollars (rounded to the nearest thousand dollars):

Currency	Initial Investment	Year 1	Year 2	Year 3
€	2,000,000 × 0.95	900,000 × 0.9319	850,000 × 0.9142	800,000 × 0.8967
$	1,900,000	839,000	777,000	717,000

All that remains is to discount this project's cash flows at an appropriate risk-adjusted U.S. interest rate. But how do we determine that rate? Recall that the European discount rate used to calculate the euro-denominated *NPV* was 10 percent, 5 percent above the European risk-free rate. Intuitively, we might expect that the comparable U.S. rate is 8 percent, representing a 5-percent risk premium over the current risk-free rate in the United States. That intuition is more or less correct. To be precise, use the following formula to solve for the project's required return in U.S. dollar terms:

$$(1+r)=(1+0.10)\frac{(1+0.03)}{(1+0.05)} \qquad R=7.9\%$$

This equation takes the project's required return in euro terms, 10 percent, and rescales it to dollar terms by multiplying by the ratio of risk-free interest rates in each country. We can verify that discounting the dollar-denominated cash flows using this rate results in the same *NPV* (again, rounding to the nearest thousand dollars) that we obtained by discounting the cash flows in euros and converting to dollars at the spot rate.

$$NPV=-\$1{,}900{,}000+\frac{\$839{,}000}{1.079^1}+\frac{\$777{,}000}{1.079^2}+\frac{\$717{,}000}{1.079^3}=\$116{,}000$$

These calculations demonstrate that a company does not have to "take a view" on currency movements when it invests abroad. Whether the company hedges a project's cash flows using forward contracts, or whether it calculates a project's *NPV* in local currency before converting to the home currency at the spot exchange rate, future exchange rate movements need not cloud the capital budgeting decision.

Cost of Capital

In the preceding example, we assumed that the project's cost of capital in Europe was 10 percent, which translated into a dollar-based discount rate of 7.9 percent. But where did the 10 percent come from? We return to the lessons of Chapter 10, namely that the discount rate should reflect the project's risk. One way to assess that risk is to calculate a beta for the investment. However, calculating the beta for an international project raises some questions for which finance as yet has no definitive answers.

For example, suppose that shareholders of the U.S. firm investing in Europe hold mostly U.S. stocks in their portfolios. Perhaps the costs of diversifying internationally are prohibitively expensive for many investors. In that case, when a firm diversifies internationally, it creates value for its shareholders. That stands in sharp contrast to the case when a firm diversifies domestically. Because U.S. investors can diversify their domestic investments at very low cost, they will not realize any benefit if a firm diversifies on their behalf.

If a firm's shareholders cannot diversify internationally, when the firm invests abroad, it should calculate a project's beta by measuring the movement of similar European investments in relation to the U.S. market, not the European market. The reason is that from the perspective of U.S. investors, the project's systematic risk depends on its relationship with the other assets that U.S. investors already own. A U.S. firm planning to build an electronics manufacturing facility in Germany might compare the returns of existing German electronics firms with returns on a U.S. stock index to estimate a project beta.

In contrast, if the firm's shareholders do hold internationally diversified portfolios, the firm should calculate the project's beta by comparing the relationship between its returns (or returns on similar investments) with returns on a worldwide stock index. This generates the project's "global beta." Next, to estimate the project's required return, the firm should apply the CAPM, multiplying the global market risk premium times the project's beta, and adding the risk-free rate. In all likelihood, because a globally diversified portfolio is less volatile than a portfolio containing only domestic securities, the risk premium on the global market will be less than the domestic risk premium.

APPLYING THE MODEL

A Japanese auto manufacturer decides to build a plant to make cars for the North American market. The firm estimates two project betas. The first calculation takes returns on U.S. auto stocks and calculates their betas relative to those on the Nikkei stock index. Based on these calculations, the Japanese firm decides to apply a beta of 1.1 to the investment. The risk-free rate of interest in Japan is 2 percent, and the market risk premium on the Nikkei index is 8 percent, so the project's required return is calculated as follows:

$$R_{\text{project}} = 2\% + 1.1(8\%) = 10.8\%$$

The second calculation takes the returns on U.S. auto manufacturers and determines their betas relative to those on a world stock index. It turns out that U.S. auto stocks are more sensitive to movements in the world market than they are to the Nikkei. This leads to a higher estimate of the project beta, say 1.3. However, offsetting this effect is the fact that the risk premium on the world market portfolio is just 5 percent. Therefore, the second estimate of the project's required return is calculated as follows:

$$R_{\text{project}} = 2\% + 1.3(5\%) = 8.5\%$$

CONCEPT REVIEW QUESTIONS

12. Why does discounting the cash flows of a foreign investment using the foreign cost of capital, then converting that to the home currency at the spot rate, yield the same *NPV* as converting the project's cash flows to domestic currency at the forward rate and then discounting them at the domestic cost of capital?

13. Why is it not surprising to find that the risk premium on the world market portfolio is lower than the domestic risk premium?

16.5 SUMMARY AND CONCLUSIONS

- Though the major currencies of the world float freely against each other, many countries have adopted exchange rate policies that fix the value of their currency relative to the currencies of other nations.
- A currency appreciates when it buys more of another currency over time. A currency depreciates when it buys less of another currency over time.
- The spot exchange rate applies to immediate currency transactions, whereas the forward exchange rate applies to trades that take place at some future time.
- The foreign exchange market is the world's largest financial market and attracts many types of participants including exporters and importers, investors, hedgers, speculators, governments, and dealers.

- The four parity relationships in international finance spell out how spot and forward exchange rates are linked to inflation and interest rates in different countries.
- When firms conduct business in other countries and currencies, they face exposure to transactions risk, translation risk, economic risk, and political risk.
- When a firm analyzes a capital investment in a foreign currency, it can either discount the foreign currency cash flows using a foreign cost of capital, or it can calculate the domestic currency equivalent of those cash flows using forward rates and discount them at the domestic cost of capital.

SELF-TEST PROBLEMS

Answers to Self-Test Problems appear in Appendix D at back of book. Answers to the Concept Review Questions throughout the chapter appear at http://megginson.swlearning.com.

ST16-1. Use Figure 16.1 to determine whether the British pound trades at a forward discount or a forward premium relative to the Japanese yen. Use the six-month forward rate in your calculations.

ST16-2. Suppose the spot exchange rate equals ¥100/$, and the six-month forward rate equals ¥101/$. An investor can purchase a U.S. T-bill that matures in six months and earns an annual rate of return of 3 percent. What would be the annual return on a similar Japanese investment?

INTERNET RESOURCES

Note: *For updates to links, please go to the book's Web site at* http://megginson.swlearning.com.

http://www.economist.com—At this site for the British publication, *The Economist*, click on the "Markets and Data" link and then launch the foreign exchange map. The map provides a wealth of information such as the name of each nation's currency and (using color codes) how the value of each currency has changed relative to a base currency (which you can choose).

http://www.bis.org—This is the site of the Bank for International Settlements. It offers a wide range of information related to the banking industry as well as interest data on international financial markets.

http://www.oanda.com—This site offers an enormous amount of information on the foreign exchange markets.

http://www.securities.com—The site for ISI Emerging Markets specializes in providing data on emerging markets around the world.

http://www.euribor.org—This site provides data on the Euribor (Euro Interbank Offered Rate), a rate on loans between prime banks within the European Monetary Union.

http://www.x-rates.com—At this site you can create charts and graphs showing historical data on most of the world's major currencies

http://www.euroland.com—This site provides data on eleven different European stock exchanges.

KEY TERMS

accounting exposure
appreciate
covered interest arbitrage
cross exchange rate
currency board arrangement
depreciate
direct quote
economic exposure
euro
exchange rate
fixed exchange rate
floating exchange rate
forward discount
forward exchange rate
forward premium
forward-spot parity
General Agreement on Tariffs and Trade (GATT)
indirect quote
interest rate parity
law of one price
managed floating rate system
monetary union
multinational corporations (MNCs)
political risk
purchasing power parity
real interest rate parity
Samurai bonds
spot exchange rate
transactions exposure
translation exposure
triangular arbitrage
World Trade Organization (WTO)

QUESTIONS AND PROBLEMS

Q16-1. Define a multinational corporation (MNC). What additional factors must be considered by the manager of an MNC that a manager of a purely domestic firm is not forced to face?

Q16-2. Who are the major players in foreign currency markets, and what are their motivations for trading?

Q16-3. Suppose that an exchange rate is quoted in terms of euros per pound. In what direction would this rate move if the euro appreciated against the pound?

Q16-4. Explain how triangular arbitrage ensures that currency values are essentially the same in different markets around the world at any given moment.

Q16-5. In what sense is it a misnomer to refer to a currency as weak or strong? Who benefits and who loses if the yen appreciates against the pound?

Q16-6. What does a spot exchange rate have in common with a forward rate, and how are they different?

Q16-7. What does it mean to say that a currency trades at a forward premium?

Q16-8. Explain how the law of one price establishes a relationship between changes in currency values and inflation rates.

Q16-9. Why does purchasing power parity appear to hold in the long run but not in the short run?

Q16-10. In terms of risk, is a U.S. investor indifferent about whether to buy a U.S. government bond or a U.K. government bond? Why or why not?

Q16-11. If the euro trades at a forward premium against the yen, explain why interest rates in Japan would have to be higher than they are in Europe.

Q16-12. Suppose that the U.S. Federal Reserve suddenly decides to raise interest rates. Trace out the potential impact that this action might have on (1) interest rates abroad, (2) the spot value of the dollar, and (3) the forward value of the dollar.

Q16-13. Interest rates on risk-free bonds in the United States are about 2 percent, whereas interest rates on Swiss government bonds are 6 percent. Can we conclude that investors around the world will flock to buy Swiss bonds? Why or why not?

Q16-14. A Japanese investor decides to purchase shares in a company that trades on the London Stock Exchange. The investor's plan is to hold these shares for one year, sell them and convert the proceeds to yen at year's end. During the year, the pound appreciates against the yen. Does this enhance or diminish the investor's return on the stock?

Q16-15. Suppose that the dollar trades at a forward discount relative to the yen. A U.S. firm must pay a Japanese supplier ¥10 million in three months. A manager in the U.S. firm reasons that because the dollar buys fewer yen on the forward market than it does on the spot market, the firm should not enter a forward hedge to eliminate its exchange rate exposure. Comment on this opinion.

PROBLEMS

Exchange Rate Fundamentals

P16-1. One month ago, the Mexican peso (Ps) – U.S. dollar exchange rate was Ps9.0395/$ ($0.1107/Ps). This month, the exchange rate is Ps9.4805/$ ($0.1055/Ps). State which currency appreciated and which depreciated over the last month, and then calculate both the percentage appreciation of the currency that rose in value and the percentage depreciation of the currency that declined in value.

P16-2. Using the data presented in Figure 16.1, calculate the spot exchange rate on Wednesday between Canadian dollars and British pounds (in pounds per Canadian dollar).

P16-3. Using the data presented in Figure 16.1, specify whether the following currencies appreciated or depreciated (against the dollar) from Tuesday to Wednesday: the yen, the Swiss franc, and the Brazilian real. (Focus only on spot rates.)

P16-4. Go to http://www.economist.com. Under the "Markets & Data" section, activate the foreign exchange map. On the menu at the far left, choose the U.S. dollar as the base currency.

a. Click on the "1-month" selection to show the appreciation or depreciation of the world's currencies relative to the dollar. Does the dollar appear to be appreciating or depreciating against most of the world's currencies, or is the answer mixed?

b. Next, choose the "1-year" option, and identify two or three countries whose currencies have depreciated the most against the U.S. dollar and two or three whose currencies have appreciated the most. Search the Web to try to find out those countries' most recent inflation figures. What lesson does this reveal?

SMART EXCEL

See this problem explained in Excel at SMARTFinance

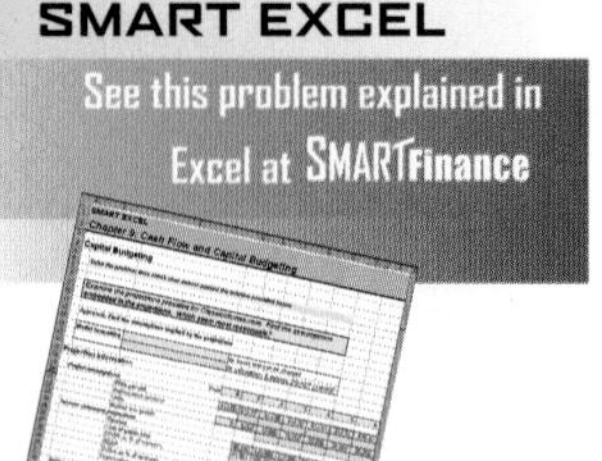

P16-5. Recently, a financial newspaper reported the following spot and forward rates for the Japanese yen (¥).

Spot:	$0.007556/¥ (¥132.34/$)
1-month:	$0.007568/¥ (¥132.14/$)
3-month:	$0.007593/¥ (¥131.71/$)

Supply the forward yen premium or discount (specify which it is) for both the one- and three-month quotes as an annual percentage rate.

P16-6. Using the data presented in Figure 16.1, specify whether the U.S. dollar trades at a forward premium or discount relative to the Canadian dollar, the Japanese yen, and the Swiss franc. Use the three-month forward rates to determine the answer.

P16-7. Using the data presented in Figure 16.1, determine the forward premium or discount on the Canadian dollar relative to the British pound, the Japanese yen, and the Swiss franc. Use the six-month forward rates to determine the answer, and express your answer as an annual rate.

P16-8. You are quoted the following series of exchange rates for the U.S. dollar ($), the Canadian dollar (C$), and the British pound (£):

$0.6000/C$	C$1.6667/$
$1.2500/£	£0.8000/$
C$2.5000/£	£0.4000/C$

Assuming that you have $1 million in cash, how can you take advantage of this series of exchange rates? Show the series of trades that would yield an arbitrage profit, and calculate how much profit you would make.

SMART SOLUTIONS

See the problem and solution explained step-by-step at SMARTFinance

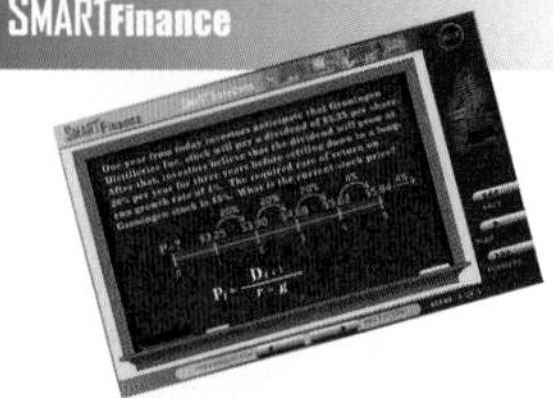

The Parity Conditions in International Finance

P16-9. Use the data presented in Figure 16.1 to answer this problem. A particular commodity sells for $5,000 in the United States and ¥600,000 in Japan.

a. Does the law of one price hold? If not, explain how to profit through arbitrage.
b. If it costs ¥60,000 to transport the commodity from the United States to Japan, is there still an arbitrage opportunity? At what exchange rate (in yen per dollar) would buying the commodity in the United States and shipping it to sell in Japan become profitable?
c. Given shipping costs of ¥60,000, at what exchange rate would it be profitable to buy the commodity in Japan and ship it to the United States to sell? Comment on the general lesson from parts (a)–(c).
d. Taking the commodity prices in the United States and Japan as given, at what exchange rate (in terms of yen per dollar) would the law of one price hold ignoring shipping costs?

SMART EXCEL

See this problem explained in Excel at SMARTFinance

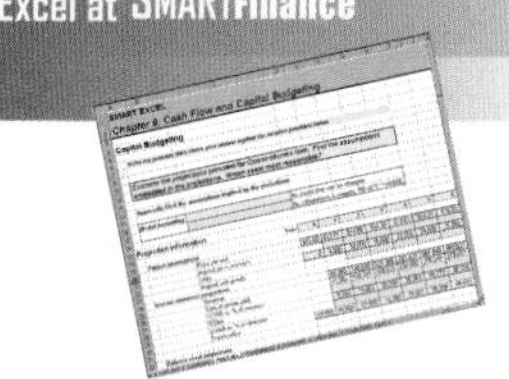

P16-10. If the expected rate of inflation in the United States is 1 percent, the one-year risk-free interest rate is 2 percent, and the one-year risk-free rate in Britain is 4 percent, what is the expected inflation rate in Britain? Use the data presented in Figure 16.1 to answer this problem.

P16-11. Go to http://www.economist.com. Under the "Markets & Data" section, find the link for the "Big Mac index." After exploring this part of the site, explain why the Big Mac index might foreshadow changes in exchange rates. What features of the Big Mac would suggest that Big Macs may not satisfy the law of one price?

P16-12. Assume that the annual interest rate on a six-month U.S. Treasury bill is 5 percent, and use the data presented in Figure 16.1 to answer the following:

a. Calculate the annual interest rate on six-month bills in Canada and Japan.
b. Suppose that the annual interest rate on a six-month bill in Japan is 0.5 percent. Illustrate how to exploit this via covered interest arbitrage.
c. Suppose that the annual interest rate on a three-month U.K. government bond is 4 percent. What is the annual interest rate on a three-month government bond in Switzerland?
d. Suppose that the actual Swiss interest rate is 0.5 percent. Illustrate how to conduct covered interest arbitrage to exploit this situation.

P16-13. Shortly after it was introduced, the euro traded just below parity with the dollar, meaning that one dollar purchased more than one euro. This implies

a. that U.S. inflation was lower than European inflation
b. that U.S. interest rates were lower than European rates
c. that the law of one price does not hold
d. none of the above

P16-14. Assume that the following information is known about the current spot exchange rate between the U.S. dollar and the British pound (£), inflation rates in Britain and the United States, and the real rate of interest—which is assumed to be the same in both countries:

Current spot rate, S = \$1.4500/£ (£0.6897/\$)
U.S. inflation rate, i_{US} = 1.5 percent per year (0.015)
British inflation rate, i_{UK} = 2.0 percent per year (0.020)
Real rate of interest, *real* = 2.5 percent per year (0.025)

Based on this data, use the parity conditions of international finance to compute the following:

a. expected spot rate next year
b. U.S. risk-free rate (on a one-year bond)
c. British risk-free rate (on a one-year bond)
d. one-year forward rate

Finally, show how you can make an arbitrage profit if you are offered the chance to sell or buy pounds forward (for delivery one year from now) at the current spot rate of \$1.4500/£ (£0.6897/\$). Assuming that you can borrow \$1 million or £689,700 at the risk-free interest rate, what would your profit be on this arbitrage transaction?

Managing Financial and Political Risk

P16-15. Suppose that the spot exchange rate follows a random walk, which means that the best forecast of the spot rate at some future date is simply its current value. Now suppose that a U.S. firm owes €1 million to a Spanish supplier. If the U.S. firm wants to minimize the expected dollar cost of paying its Spanish supplier (without regard to currency risk), describe the circumstances under which the firm will or will not enter into a forward contract to hedge its exposure.

P16-16. Classic City Exporters (CCE) recently sold a large shipment of sporting equipment to a Swiss company—the goods will be sold in Zurich. The sale was denominated in Swiss francs (SF) and was worth SF500,000. Delivery of the sporting goods and payment by the Swiss buyer are due to occur in six months. The current spot exchange rate is \$0.6002/SF (SF1.6661/\$), and the six-month forward rate is \$0.6020/SF (SF1.6611/\$). What risk would CCE run if it remained unhedged, and how could it hedge that risk with a forward contract? Assuming that the actual exchange rate in six months is \$0.5500/SF (SF1.8182/\$), compute the profit or loss—and state which it is—CCE would experience if it had chosen to remain unhedged.

P16-17. A British firm will receive \$1 million from a U.S. customer in three months. The firm is considering two strategies to eliminate its foreign exchange exposure. The first strategy is to pledge the \$1 million as collateral for a three-month loan from a U.S. bank at 4 percent interest. The U.K. firm will then convert the proceeds of the loan to pounds at the spot rate. When the loan is due, the firm will pay the \$1 million balance due by handing its U.S. receivable over to the bank. This strategy allows the U.K. firm to "monetize" its receivable immediately. The spot exchange rate is 0.6550 pounds per dollar.

The second strategy is to enter a forward contract at an exchange rate of 0.6450 pounds per dollar. This ensures that the U.K. firm will receive £645,000 in three months. If the firm wanted to monetize this payment immediately, it could take out a three-month loan from a U.K. bank at 8 percent, pledging the proceeds of the forward contract as collateral.

Which of these strategies should the firm follow?

Long-Term Investment Decisions

P16-18. A German company manufactures a specialized piece of manufacturing equipment and leases it to a U.K. enterprise. The lease calls for five end-of-year payments of £1 million. The German firm spent €3.5 million to produce the equipment, which is expected to have no salvage value after five years. The current spot rate is €1.5/£. The risk-free interest rate in Germany is 3 percent, and in the United Kingdom it is 5 percent. The German firm reasons that the appropriate (German) discount rate for this investment is 7 percent. Calculate the *NPV* of this investment in two ways.

a. First, convert all cash flows to pounds, and discount at an appropriate (U.K.) cost of capital. Convert the resulting *NPV* to euros at the spot rate.

b. Second, calculate forward rates for each year, convert the pound-denominated cash flows into euros using those rates, and discount at the German cost of capital. Verify that the *NPV* obtained from this approach matches (except perhaps for small rounding errors) that obtained in part (a).

THOMSON ONE Business School Edition

For instructions on using Thomson ONE, refer to the instructions provided with the Thomson ONE problems at the end of Chapters 1–6 or to "A Guide for Using Thomson ONE."

P16-19. How do changes in exchange rates affect the consolidation of financial statements of a multinational corporation? BP PLC (ticker: BP) has operations all over the world. Look at BP's sales and operating income from U.S. operations for the last five years.[6] The default currency for all figures is BP's home currency, British pounds. Convert these numbers to U.S. dollars.[7] The bottom of the page gives you the exchange rate at which the numbers have been converted from British pounds to U.S. dollars in each year. Has the U.S. dollar strengthened or weakened over the last five years? Convert U.S. sales and operating income for each of the last five years to British pounds using both the minimum and maximum of the five exchange rates. Which of the two exchange rates gives BP the larger sales and operating income in British pounds in each year? As a multinational corporation, does BP prefer a stronger or a weaker U.S. dollar relative to the British pound?

P16-20. How do changes in exchange rates affect an international investor's returns? Calculate Deutsche Telekom's (ticker: D:DTE) annual stock returns using the closing stock price in euros at the end of each of the last five fiscal years. Convert the closing stock price to U.S. dollars (to determine the exchange rate at the end of each fiscal year see footnote 7 in the previous problem). Calculate the annual stock returns using U.S. dollar prices. Which years have a higher return in U.S. dollars and which years in euros? As a U.S. investor, do you prefer a strong or a weak U.S. dollar relative to the euro?

Since these exercises depend upon real-time data, your answers will change continuously depending upon when you access the Internet to download your data.

---

6. Geographic segment data can be found under the Financial tab. Click on "More," go to Worldscope Reports & Charts, and select "Geographic Segment Review."

7. You can change currency by clicking on the dollar sign ($) on the right side of the menu at the top and then selecting "US Dollar."

MINICASE

International Financial Management

Five years after completing your college degree you accept an exciting new job with the multinational firm Rangsit Trading Incorporated. This new position will involve a great deal of travel, along with some other challenging responsibilities. Part of your job function is to set company policy to manage exchange rate risk. As such, you decide that you need to become fluent in the following topics.

ASSIGNMENT

1. First, you decide to review basic exchange rate terminology.
   A. Describe fixed and floating exchange rate systems. What are some problems with these systems?
   B. Describe a managed floating rate system.
   C. Describe a currency board arrangement system.
2. Next, you review the following parity relationships.
   A. Describe forward-spot parity.
   B. Describe purchasing power parity.
   C. Describe interest rate parity.
   D. Describe real interest rate parity.
   E. Describe how these four parity relationships link together.
3. Finally, you review the following risks that are relevant to multinational firms.
   A. Describe transactions risk and how this risk can be alleviated.
   B. Describe translation and economic risks and how these risks can be alleviated.
   C. Describe political risk and how this risk can be alleviated.

Smart *Excel* Appendix

Use the Smart *Excel* spreadsheets and animated tutorials at http://smartfinance.swlearning.com.

EXCEL PREREQUISITES

You need to be familiar with the following *Excel* features to use this appendix:

- If function—introduced in Chapter 15 and repeated here

If this is new to you be sure to complete the ***Excel Prereqs*** tab in the Chapter 16 *Excel* file located at the Smart Finance Web site before proceeding.

FORWARD PREMIUM OR DISCOUNT

Problem: Solve Problem 16-5 in the text. Supply the forward yen premium or discount (specify which it is) for the given one- and three-month quotes as an annual percentage rate.

Approach: Create a simple model to find the forward premium or discount

Try it yourself in a blank *Excel* file. Think about what to include in the input section and how to set up your calculations and output.

Or, Open the Chapter 16 *Excel* file located at the Smart Finance Web site. Turn to the ***ForwPrem*** tab.

Enter the input information from Problem 16-5.

The forward premium or discount on a currency is:

$= (F - S) / S$

This must then be annualized.

Apply it

Find the forward premium.

To annualize the one-month premium, multiply by 12. To annualize the three-month premium, multiply by 12/3, or 4.

Your results should match:

Annualized 1-month forward premium	1.91%
Annualized 3-month forward premium	1.96%

Appendix Contents

PURCHASING POWER PARITY

The law of one price states that identical goods trading in different markets should sell at the same price, absent any barriers to trade.

Law of one price holds if $P_{for} / P_{dom} = S_{for/dom}$

This concept is applied in Problem 16-9.

Problem: Solve Problem 16-9 in the text. A particular commodity sells for $5,000 in the United States and ¥600,000 in Japan. Assume the current spot rate is ¥109.43 per dollar.

Approach: Create a model to analyze purchasing power parity.

Open the Chapter 16 Excel file located at the Smart Finance Web site. Turn to the *PPP* tab.

Apply it

- *Solve Part (a): Does the law of one price hold?*
  Fill in the inputs. Then compare the cost in Japan to the cost in the United States. To do so, translate the cost in the United States into yen.

  The cost in yen in the United States equals the cost in dollars multiplied by the spot rate. You should get ¥547,150 in the United States compared with ¥600,000 in Japan. Since the two are not equal, the law of one price does not hold.

  Option: Use an IF statement to answer Part (a).
  You can set up an IF statement that returns **Yes** if the law of one price holds and **No** if it does not.

- *Solve Part (b): Is arbitrage possible if shipping costs are ¥60,000? At what exchange rate (in yen per dollar) would buying the commodity in the United States and shipping to Japan become profitable?*

  To solve this, first include shipping costs. Simply add the ¥60,000 yen shipping cost to the cost of ¥547,150. The result is ¥607,150. Arbitrage is NOT possible because this exceeds the cost in Japan of ¥600,000.

  Again, you can use an IF statement to answer this question. Compare the cost including shipping with the cost in Japan.

  Now find the exchange rate at which buying the commodity in the United States and shipping to Japan becomes profitable.

  Buying in the United States and shipping to Japan becomes profitable when the cost in the United States (in yen) plus the ¥60,000 cost of shipping is less than the Japanese cost of ¥600,000.

  Or, find the exchange rate that solves:

  $5,000 + ¥60,000 < ¥600,000
  ¥/$ such that $5,000 < ¥540,000
  ¥/$ <108.00

  If the current exchange rate fell to below 108.00, arbitrage becomes possible. **In the model you can easily find this:**

  = (Price in Japan – Shipping costs) / Price in $

- ***Solve Part (c): At what exchange rate (in yen per dollar) would buying the commodity in Japan and shipping to the United States become profitable?***

  Buying in Japan and shipping to the United States becomes profitable when the cost in Japan, including the ¥60,000 cost of shipping, is less than the United States cost of $5,000.

  Or, find the exchange rate that solves:

  $5,000 > ¥600,000 + ¥60,000
  ¥/$ such that $5,000 > ¥660,000
  ¥/$ > 132.00

  If the current exchange rate rises above 132.00, arbitrage becomes possible.

  In the model you can easily find this:

  = (Price in Japan + Shipping costs) / Price in $

- ***Solve Part (d): At what exchange rate does the law of one price hold?***
  At the rate = Price in yen / Price in dollars

  = 120.00

  Your model results should match:

Inputs		
Price in ¥		600,000.00
Price in $		5,000.00
Spot rate ¥/$		109.43
Shipping costs—¥		600,000.00
Calculations		
US Cost in ¥		547,150.00
Cost with shipping		607,150.00
Output		
Part (a)	*Does law of one price hold?*	**No**
Part (b)	*Is arbitrage possible if buy in U.S. and ship to Japan?*	**No**
	To profit by buying in U.S. and shipping to Japan, spot rate must be below:	108.00
Part (c)	*To profit by buying in Japan and shipping to U.S., spot rate must be above:*	132.00
Part (d)	*Spot rate for Law of one price:*	120.00

Apply it

- ***In this problem, when is arbitrage possible?***
  At an exchange rate of ¥120/$, the price is the same in Japan and the United States. Ignoring shipping costs, arbitrage is therefore possible at rates above or below ¥120/$. However, arbitrage would involve buying in one country and

shipping to another. The cost of shipping is significant. It leads to a band of exchange rates within which arbitrage is impossible. At exchange rates below 108¥/$, buying in the United States and shipping to Japan leads to profits. At exchange rates above 132¥/$, buying in Japan and shipping to the United States is profitable. Between 108¥/$ and 132¥/$ arbitrage is not possible because any potential gains from differential pricing of the commodity between the two countries is eliminated by the shipping costs.

Risk Management

OPENING FOCUS

The Fred Hutchinson Cancer Research Center Uses Derivatives to Fight Cancer

The Fred Hutchinson Cancer Research Center in Seattle, Washington, is the world's largest bone-marrow transplant center. In 1991, the center issued $72 million in fixed-rate bonds to finance the construction of research laboratories on the center's new campus. The bond covenants included a ten-year call deferment so the bonds could not be called until January 2001. In addition, the bonds paid an annual coupon between 6.6 percent and 7.4 percent.

By 1999, interest rates on comparable bonds had dropped well below 6 percent, and Randy Main, the CFO for the Hutchinson Center, was concerned that interest rates would increase again before the center was able to refinance (or "refund") the high-coupon-rate bonds. The solution was to enter into an interest rate swap with the investment bank Lehman Brothers. Beginning in January 2001, the center began paying Lehman Brothers a fixed rate of 5.19 percent per year based on a principal of $72 million. In return, Lehman Brothers would pay the center a variable rate of interest. This type of swap is called a forward swap because the exchange of interest payments did not begin until January 2001 even though Hutchinson and Lehman entered the agreement in 1999. At the same time the center began exchanging interest payments with Lehman Brothers, the center issued new variable-rate bonds to pay off the old fixed-rate bonds. The center uses the variable-rate cash inflows from the swap to pay the variable-rate coupon payments on the bonds. Both the swap and the new floating-rate bonds will mature in 2029.

The net result of this transaction was that the Hutchinson Center was able to lock in lower fixed-rate borrowing costs. Regardless of what happened to interest rates between 1999 and 2001, the Hutchinson Center was assured that its net borrowing costs would be a fixed rate of 5.19 percent beginning in January 2001. The center estimates that the cost savings from entering into the swap will be about $13 million, money that can be spent on cancer research rather than interest payments.

By entering into the swap agreement, the Hutchinson Center was able to minimize its exposure to the risk of an increase in interest rates between 1999 and 2001. If interest rates declined between 1999 and 2001, however, the Center would not enjoy any reduction in its borrowing costs. The question Randy Main faced was whether to hedge the center's interest rate risk exposure. Ultimately, Randy Main decided it was better to lock in a reduced borrowing cost rather than risk $13 million on the hope that interest rates would decline.

Source: "Interest Swap Saves Hutch Money," *Seattle Post-Intelligencer* (August 9, 1999), p. C2.

LEARNING OBJECTIVES

After studying this chapter you should be able to:

- Describe the types of risks that can adversely affect a firm's cash flows and explain why firms might choose to hedge those risks;
- Calculate the price of a forward contract and illustrate how to use such a contract to hedge a risk exposure;
- Explain the differences between forward and futures contracts; and
- Describe the basic features of options and swaps and explain how they can be used to hedge risk exposure.

Trading in virtually all types of financial instruments has increased over the past two decades, but no markets have experienced growth rates as explosive as those for the financial instruments used for hedging and risk management. Since the collapse of the Bretton Woods fixed exchange rate regime in 1973, corporations have been exposed to extreme fluctuations in interest rates, in exchange rates, and in the prices of important raw materials. This increased risk has led to a mushrooming demand for financial instruments and strategies that corporations can use to hedge, or offset, their underlying operating and financial exposures.

This chapter discusses *risk management* and *financial engineering* in the modern corporation. Traditionally, **risk management** has meant the process of identifying firm-specific risk exposures and managing those risk exposures. In recent years, however, the risk-management function has expanded to include identifying, measuring, and managing all types of risk exposures, including interest rate, commodity, and currency risk exposures. There are three ways to minimize a firm's risk exposures—diversifying, insuring, and hedging; this chapter focuses on hedging. Derivative securities, including forwards, futures, options, and swaps, are the financial instruments commonly used for hedging and risk management. Figure 17.1 illustrates the growth in the market for these types of products. Currency and interest rate swaps have experienced especially rapid growth.

risk management
The process of identifying firm-specific risk exposures and managing those exposures by means of insurance products. Also includes identifying, measuring, and managing all types of risk exposures.

Though the financial press often portrays derivatives in a negative light, these securities can be an effective means of hedging risk exposures. We will discuss each of these instruments, but we begin with an overview of risk management. Next, we describe each of the major types of derivative securities and discuss how each can be used to manage a firm's risk exposures. Finally, we discuss financial engineering, which is the application of finance principles to design securities and strategies that help firms manage their risk exposures.

Figure 17.1
Selected Over-the-Counter Derivatives Contracts Outstanding (Year-End Notional Amounts)

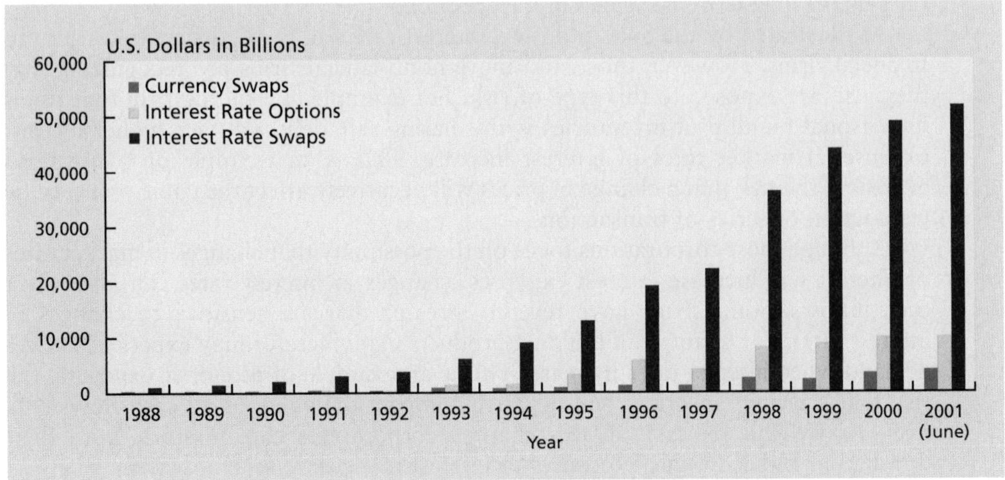

Source: International Swaps and Derivatives Association, ISDA Market Survey, *1988–1997, and the Bank for International Settlements,* BIS Quarterly Review, *various issues, 1998–2001.*

17.1 OVERVIEW OF RISK MANAGEMENT

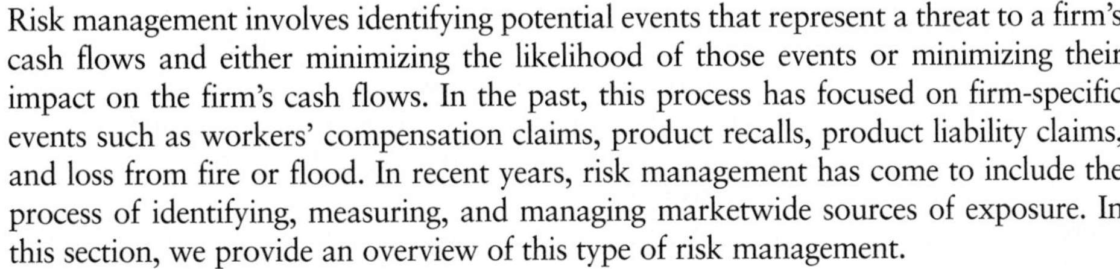

Risk management involves identifying potential events that represent a threat to a firm's cash flows and either minimizing the likelihood of those events or minimizing their impact on the firm's cash flows. In the past, this process has focused on firm-specific events such as workers' compensation claims, product recalls, product liability claims, and loss from fire or flood. In recent years, risk management has come to include the process of identifying, measuring, and managing marketwide sources of exposure. In this section, we provide an overview of this type of risk management.

Risk Factors

Chapters 6 and 7 introduced the concepts of systematic and unsystematic risk. Systematic risks affect a broad class of securities simultaneously and cannot be eliminated through diversification. The underlying forces that drive systematic risks are largely out of the control of managers, but managers can take certain actions to minimize the impact of these risks on their firms' cash flows.

SMART PRACTICES VIDEO

David Childress, Asset Liability Manager, Ford Motor Co.

"Interest rate risk really comes down to how assets and liabilities on the balance sheet reprice."

See the entire interview at **SMARTFinance**

If a change in the level of interest rates will adversely affect the cash flows of a company (perhaps by raising its cost of borrowing), that firm is exposed to **interest rate risk**. This is the single most common concern among managers engaged in risk management. Interest rate risk is the risk of suffering losses as a result of unanticipated changes in market rates of interest. The most often cited example of losses caused by interest rate risk is the experience of the savings and loan (S&L) industry in the 1980s. S&Ls suffered from a mismatch in terms of the maturity of their assets and liabilities because they funded long-term assets (e.g., thirty-year, fixed-rate mortgages) with short-term liabilities (e.g., passbook savings deposits and short-term certificates of deposit). When interest rates spiked in the

interest rate risk
The risk that changes in market interest rates will cause fluctuations in a bond's price. Also, the risk of suffering losses as a result of unanticipated changes in market interest rates.

late 1970s and early 1980s, firms in the industry suffered tremendous losses because they were paying high rates on their short-term deposits while continuing to earn low rates on the long-term mortgages in their portfolio.

As illustrated by the S&L industry, interest rate risk is of particular concern to financial firms. However, more and more nonfinancial firms are recognizing that they also are exposed to this type of risk. For example, a retailing firm that funds its seasonal buildup of inventories with floating-rate debt will face higher interest expenses if market rates of interest increase. This is an example of **transactions exposure**, the risk that a change in prices will negatively affect the value of a specific transaction or series of transactions.

transactions exposure
The risk that a change in prices will negatively affect the value of a specific transaction or series of transactions.

Although most corporations focus on the possibility that changes in market rates of interest will increase interest expenses, changes in interest rates can also affect cash inflows. Some firms have revenue streams that are sensitive to changes in interest rates. For example, a building products manufacturer may experience lower demand when interest rates increase. This is an example of **economic exposure**, the risk that a change in prices will negatively impact the value of all cash flows of a firm. As we will see later in this chapter, corporations can minimize both their transaction and economic exposures to interest rate risk in several ways.

economic exposure
The risk that a change in prices will negatively impact the value of all cash flows of a firm.

At the same time that currency exchange rates were becoming more volatile, world economies were becoming more integrated. In recent years, currency exchange rates have remained volatile, and the pace of global integration has continued to accelerate. This means ever increasing exposure to foreign exchange risk, as discussed in Chapter 16. Consider another example of a transactions exposure. A U.S.-based company with manufacturing operations in Canada denominates the products it sells in international markets in the buyer's home currency. Suppose that it books a sale, denominated in euros, to a buyer in Germany, requiring delivery and payment in three months. If the euro depreciates in value relative to the Canadian dollar (C$) over the next three months, this company will receive fewer C$ than expected when it converts the euros received in payment into C$ to cover its own production costs.

As another example of economic exposure, if this U.S. manufacturing firm faces stiff competition from a Japanese manufacturer and the value of the yen declines, the Japanese firm may be able to reduce the prices it charges in European markets, thereby hurting demand for the products manufactured by the U.S. firm. Again, most firms concentrate on minimizing transactions exposure, but economic exposures are usually much more important. Unfortunately, these exposures are also much harder to hedge, or otherwise manage, because they are systemic.

Although most discussions of risk management focus on interest rate risk and foreign exchange risk, commodity price risk is also very important for many firms. Any firm that uses a commodity as a production input is potentially exposed to losses if the price of the commodity increases. Likewise, the commodity producers are also exposed to the risk that the price of the commodity could decline.

APPLYING THE MODEL

A significant source of risk for Hershey Foods Corporation is the price of cocoa. Cocoa is an important commodity input for Hershey. If the price of cocoa increases, Hershey may be able to pass the increase to consumers by charging higher prices for Kisses and other confections. However, an increase in the price of Kisses is bound to hurt the demand for them. Consider the consequences of not hedging this risk exposure, especially if competitors such as Nestlé and Mars do hedge their exposure by locking in the price they pay for cocoa. Hershey could be faced with having to increase the price of its products in response to an increase in the price of cocoa, while the price of Nestlé and Mars products remains the same. Of course, if

COMPARATIVE CORPORATE FINANCE

International Differences in Foreign Exchange Risk Management Emphasis

The two charts summarize the concerns of managers in multinational corporations in the United Kingdom, the United States, and Asia/Pacific countries. Generally, U.S. companies seem to be more concerned with transaction exposures than companies in the U.K. or Asia. Asia/ Pacific companies, on the other hand, are more concerned about economic exposure than managers in the United States or the United Kingdom.

The differences in emphasis can be attributed, in part, to differences in product markets and the location of production facilities. For example, U.S. multinationals often have product markets that are primarily domestic, but their production facilities are commonly in other countries. Consequently, U.S. multinationals tend to focus more on how changes in exchange rates affect their cost structure and less on how changes in exchange rates affect their revenue stream. Asia/Pacific multinationals, on the other hand, often have domestic production facilities and foreign product markets. Therefore, they tend to worry less about the impact of exchange rates on their cost structures and more about the impact of exchange rates on their revenue stream.

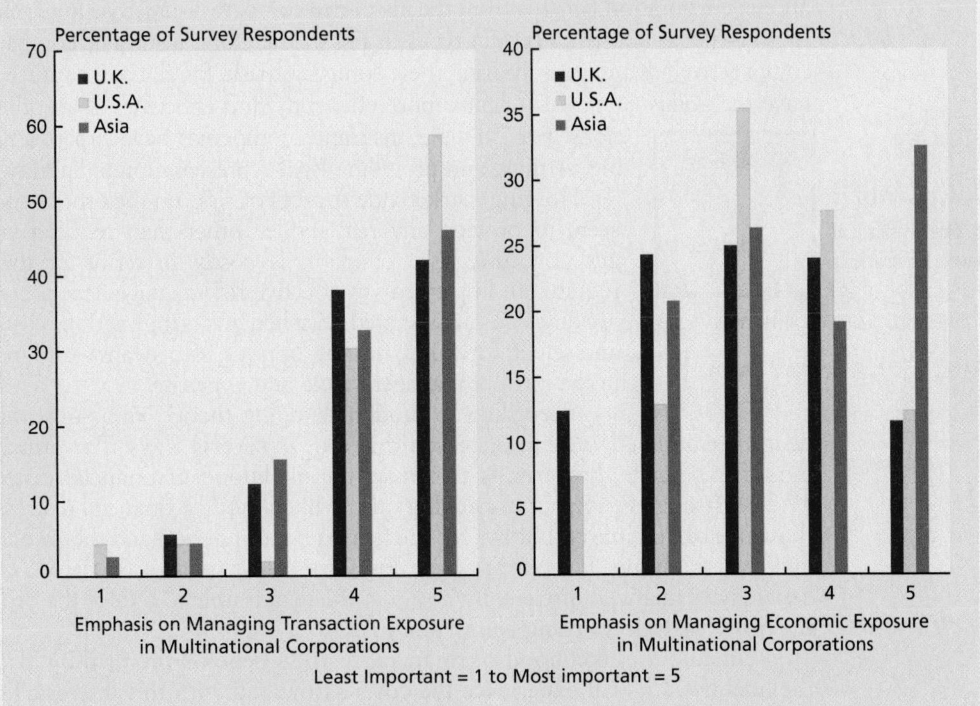

Source: Andrew P. Marshall, "Foreign Exchange Risk Management in UK, USA, and Asia Pacific Multinational Companies," *Journal of Multinational Financial Management* 10 (2000), pp. 185–211.

the price of cocoa declines, Hershey would benefit from the lower price, while Nestlé and Mars are committed to paying a higher price.[1]

[1] Hershey takes its hedging activities so seriously that it has expressed concerns over Financial Accounting Standards Board proposals to require greater disclosure of a firm's activities in derivative markets. Hershey's major competitors, Nestlé and Mars, would not be subject to these requirements because Nestlé is a Swiss-based firm and Mars is privately held. Hershey is concerned because it believes the new requirements would put it at a competitive disadvantage in terms of its derivative positions. See *Investment Dealers' Digest* (1997).

The Hedging Decision

Although it is clear that the corporate demand for hedging and risk-management products has grown dramatically in recent years, it is less clear why a public company would choose to hedge at all. In Chapters 12 and 13, we learned that, in perfect markets, investors can effectively unwind managers' decisions regarding capital structure and dividends. Modigliani and Miller (1958) showed that managers could not increase firm value by choosing an optimal capital structure or dividend policy. The same conclusion applies to risk management when markets are perfect. If managers use derivative securities to hedge a particular risk, investors can trade on their own to undo what managers have done. The explanation for firms' hedging activities could be either that markets are imperfect or that managers hedge for their own benefit rather than for the benefit of shareholders. This section discusses the various potential motivations for hedging and possible hedging strategies.

Motivations for Hedging. The motivations for buying insurance are similar to those for hedging. However, there are some crucial differences. By purchasing insurance, a corporation benefits from the insurance company's expertise in terms of its ability to evaluate and price certain types of risks. Therefore, insurance companies have a comparative advantage in bearing these sources of risk. Similarly, insurance companies have the ability to process claims more efficiently and effectively than other corporations. For example, insurance companies have expertise in negotiating, settling, and providing legal representation in liability suits.

SMART PRACTICES VIDEO

Keith Woodward, Vice President of Finance, General Mills

"For General Mills, hedging and commodities is core to our business."

See the entire interview at **SMARTFinance**

Hedging marketwide sources of risk, on the other hand, does not seem to provide any real service other than reduced volatility. In addition, this risk reduction is costly in terms of the resources required to implement an effective risk-management program. There are direct costs associated with hedging—transactions costs of buying and selling forwards, futures, options, and swaps—and indirect costs in the form of managers' time and expertise.

According to modern hedging theory, value-maximizing firms hedge because hedging can increase firm value in several ways. The principal reason most firms hedge, however, is to reduce the likelihood of financial distress. Figure 17.2 illustrates the impact of hedging on the likelihood of financial distress, showing the range of possible cash flows for the firm in a given period and the associated probability distribution. If the firm's cash flows are below point A on the x-axis, the firm experiences financial distress. By hedging, the firm is able to reduce the probability of the firm's cash flows being below point A.

Reducing the likelihood of financial distress benefits the firm by also reducing the likelihood it will experience the costs associated with this distress. Direct costs

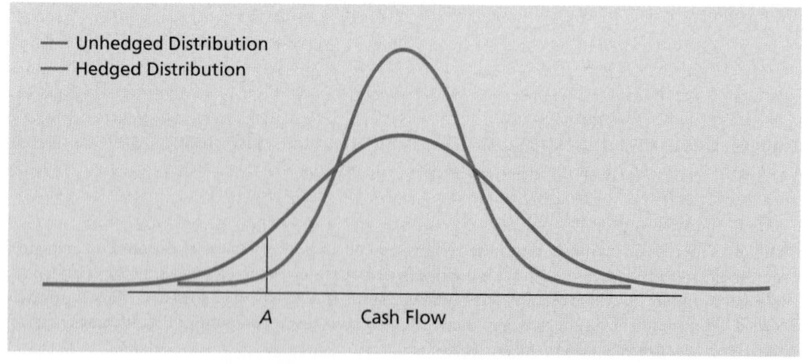

Figure 17.2
Probability Distribution of Possible Cash Flows for a Corporation

of distress include out-of-pocket cash expenses that must be paid to third parties (lawyers, auditors, consultants, court personnel, etc.) in the event of bankruptcy or severe financial distress. Many of the indirect costs are contracting costs involving relationships with creditors, suppliers, and employees. For example, a credible promise to hedge can sometimes entice creditors to lend the firm money on more favorable terms than they would be willing to lend to an unhedged borrower. Similarly, suppliers are more likely to extend trade credit when the likelihood of financial distress is low. In addition to potential cost savings, hedging may increase revenue for firms that sell products with warranties or service contracts. Warranties or service contracts are more likely to be honored, and customers will place a higher value on them, if the firm has a lower likelihood of financial distress. Similarly, if the products will require replacement parts or if there is the possibility of future upgrades, minimizing the likelihood of financial distress can promote sales.

Hedging can also reduce a firm's expected tax liability. If a firm's tax rate increases as income increases, hedging can reduce the expected tax liability and increase expected after-tax earnings. For example, suppose that a firm thinks its taxable earnings over the coming year will be one of three equally likely levels, depending on the actual realized price of a key input. If the input price is very high, the firm will generate no earnings at all. If the input price is very low, then earnings will be $20,000. In the intermediate case with a medium price for the key input, the firm's earnings are $10,000. Managers believe that each of these outcomes is equally likely (i.e., probability = 1/3). To highlight the tax incentive to hedge, we will make two assumptions. First, assume that by hedging the firm can lock in the price of its key input at the medium level and thereby ensure that its pre-tax earnings will be $10,000. Second, assume that the firm pays a 10 percent tax rate on the first $10,000 in earnings and a 20 percent tax rate on all earnings above $10,000. Table 17.1 illustrates how the firm's hedging decision can affect its value.

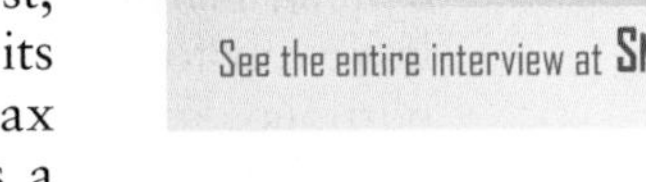

SMART IDEAS VIDEO
John Graham, Duke University
"There can be a tax incentive to hedge."

See the entire interview at SMARTFinance

If the firm hedges to lock in the key input price, then its after-tax earnings equal $9,000. The tax schedule drives the difference in the two scenarios. When the firm does not hedge, it pays a higher tax rate when the input price is low and earnings are high than at other times. As a result, the expected tax bill is higher and earnings

Table 17.1
The Tax Incentive to Hedge

Table 17.1 illustrates that when firms face higher tax rates as their earnings increase, the tax schedule creates an incentive to hedge. If the firm does not hedge, its expected after-tax earnings equal $8,667, but if it does hedge, it can lock in after-tax earnings of $9,000.

No Hedging Scenario			
Input Price	High	Medium	Low
Taxable Earnings	$0	$10,000	$20,000
Taxes Due	0	1,000	3,000
After-tax Earnings	0	9,000	17,000
Expected After-tax Earnings	1/3($0) + 1/3($9,000) + 1/3($17,000) = $8,667		

Hedging Scenario (Input Price Locked in at Medium)	
Taxable Earnings	$10,000
Taxes Due	1,000
After-tax Earnings	9,000

Tax Schedule	
Tax Rate on First $10,000	10%
Tax Rate on Earnings > $10,000	20%

are lower than when the firm hedges and earns $10,000 before taxes. Hedging can also reduce expected tax liabilities by smoothing the profit stream and reducing the likelihood that the firm will pay high taxes in one period while having to forgo (or delay) the benefits of tax shields in another period. Current tax laws limit the extent to which corporations can use losses in one period to offset gains in another period. For this reason, it is in the interest of some corporations to hedge their risk exposures, otherwise they could lose some of the tax benefits associated with losses experienced in periods of poor performance.

Closely held firms are more likely to hedge risk exposures because owners have a greater proportion of their wealth invested in the firm. Because the owners of these firms are less diversified, they generally seek to minimize the risk exposures faced by the firm. Similarly, if the managers of the firm are risk averse, the firm is more likely to pursue strategies that minimize risk exposures. Research studies confirm these expectations. The hedging activities of firms increase as share ownership by managers increases.

Another benefit of hedging is that it makes it easier for the board of directors and outsiders to evaluate the performance of managers. Absent an effective risk-management program, it is difficult to disentangle firm performance due to the manager's performance from firm performance due to external factors. A manager can make his or her performance more observable by minimizing the firm's exposure to external risk factors. For this reason, superior managers may be more inclined to hedge, whereas inferior managers may prefer to disguise their performance behind the firm's unhedged performance.

Finally, even though shareholders can hedge the exposures they face as a result of owning shares in a risky firm, there are some circumstances under which it may be less costly for the firm to minimize risk than for the shareholders to hold a diversified portfolio. For some firms, however, the costs of hedging outweigh the benefits. There are substantial fixed costs associated with hedging, including the costs of acquiring the necessary expertise to implement a successful risk-management program, and small firms are therefore less likely to hedge than large firms.

Hedging Strategies. In some circumstances, a firm may not hedge a risk exposure if it is confident that the risk factor will be changing in a positive direction or that it has a comparative advantage in bearing the risk. For example, if a silver-mining company is convinced that the price of silver will increase in the coming months, it may choose not to hedge its exposure to changes in the price of silver. When the price of silver increases, the mining company will benefit from the higher price it will receive for silver. In other circumstances, a firm may overhedge if it is certain that a risk factor will be changing in a negative direction. For example, if the mining company is convinced that the price of silver will decrease in the coming months, it may overhedge by taking a position in a derivative security that will more than offset the reduced price it receives for silver, thereby generating a profit on the price decrease. These examples illustrate that derivatives are an effective means for managers to take a position in a risk factor based on their expectations. It is important to note that if a firm chooses *not* to hedge a risk exposure, or chooses to overhedge, it is speculating on changes in the risk factor.

How a firm chooses to hedge a given risk exposure will depend on the costs of the alternative hedging strategies. The firm needs to consider transactions costs, the effectiveness and accuracy of alternative strategies in offsetting underlying risk exposures, and the liquidity and default risks associated with those strategies. Customized hedging strategies, especially those that are financially engineered, are effective and accurate but suffer from greater transactions costs and low liquidity. Off-the-shelf solutions, such as exchange-traded derivative securities, while attractive because of their low transactions costs, high liquidity, and low default risk, may not effectively and accurately offset the risk exposure.

CONCEPT REVIEW QUESTIONS

1. Recently, a U.S. senator described the markets for derivative securities as an electronic pyramid scheme. How do you respond?

2. Contrast hedging and speculation.

17.2 FORWARD CONTRACTS

As discussed in Chapter 16, a forward contract involves two parties agreeing today on a price, called the **forward price,** at which the purchaser will buy a specified amount of an asset from the seller at a fixed date sometime in the future. This is in contrast to a cash market transaction in which the buyer and seller conduct their transaction today at the **spot price**. The buyer of a forward contract has a long position and has an obligation to pay the forward price for the asset. The seller of a forward contract has a short position and has an obligation to sell the asset to the buyer in exchange for the forward price. The future date on which the buyer pays the seller (and the seller delivers the asset to the buyer) is referred to as the **settlement date**. It is important to note that, unlike options, which were discussed in Chapter 15, forward contracts are obligations, and failure to make or take delivery of the underlying asset represents default. In addition, no cash changes hands in a forward contract until the contract settlement date. For these two reasons, default risk is a concern in forward contracts, and market participants enter into such contracts only with parties that they know and trust.

Most forward contracts are individually negotiated between corporations and financial intermediaries, but there are active markets for standard denomination and maturity forward contracts on several currencies and raw materials that institutions (including the bank market-makers themselves) can use to hedge their own exposures.

forward price
The price to which parties in a forward contract agree. The price dictates what the buyer will pay to the seller on a future date.

spot price
The price that the buyer pays the seller in a current, cash market transaction.

settlement date
The future date on which the buyer pays the seller and the seller delivers the asset to the buyer.

arbitrage
The process of buying something in one market at a low price and simultaneously selling it in another market at a higher price to generate an immediate, risk-free profit.

Forward Prices

The forward price is the price that makes the forward contract have zero net present value. The key to determining a security's fair forward price is being able to form an alternative to the forward contract that has identical cash flows. For example, consider an asset that pays no income (e.g., a discount bond) and does not cost anything to store (e.g., financial assets). Rather than buy the asset six months forward, we could borrow the current price of the asset and buy it today. Six months from now, we would repay the loan plus interest. Whether we buy the asset six months forward or borrow and buy it today, we end up in the same position—owning the asset in six months. Because both strategies have identical cash flows in all circumstances, we can make the argument that the value of both strategies must be the same. This argument is based on **arbitrage**, which involves generating a riskless profit by simultaneously buying the strategy with the low value and selling the strategy with the high value. In a well-functioning market, these opportunities are quickly eliminated. Therefore, the forward price, F, for an asset that pays no income and does not cost anything to store should be the following:

$$F = S_0(1+R_f)^n \qquad \textbf{(Eq. 17.1)}$$

where S_0 is the current spot price of the asset, R_f is the current risk-free rate, and n is the number of years until the forward contract is to be settled. If Equation 17.1 does not hold and F is greater than $S_0(1 + R_f)^n$, we can make a riskless profit by simultaneously borrowing an amount equal to S_0, using the borrowed funds to buy the asset, and selling the asset forward. On the settlement date, assuming we are able to borrow at the risk-free rate, we would sell the asset for F by delivering on the forward contract and pay our debt (including interest) of $S_0(1 + R_f)^n$. This arbitrage strategy would generate $F - S_0(1 + R_f)^n > 0$ in riskless profits on the settlement date without requiring any up-front investment.

Alternatively, if F is less than $S_0(1+ R_f)^n$, we would simultaneously short-sell the asset for S_0, lend the proceeds from the short sale at the risk-free rate, and buy the asset forward. On the settlement date, we would collect $S_0(1 + R_f)^n$ from the loan, pay F for the asset, and close out our short-sale position. This arbitrage strategy would generate $S_0(1 + R_f)^n - F > 0$ in riskless profits on the settlement date without requiring any up-front investment.

APPLYING THE MODEL

Helen Clemons is a portfolio manager who plans to buy one-month Treasury bills in two months with a total face amount of \$5 million. The current price for three-month Treasury bills is \$985,149 per \$1 million face amount. The current risk-free rate is 6.17 percent. The fair forward price is calculated as follows:

$$F = \$985,149(1+0.0617)^{2 \div 12} = \$995,029$$

Therefore, the total forward price Helen should pay is \$4,975,145 (\$995,029 × 5). If this is not the forward rate quoted to her, Helen or another arbitrageur has an opportunity to earn a riskless profit.

A similar approach can be used to determine the forward price for an asset that pays income (e.g., a coupon bond) or is costly to store (e.g., commodities). In this case, we must account for the receipt of income and/or the payment of storage cost before the contract matures. If an investor purchases an asset through a forward contract rather than through a spot market transaction, the investor incurs certain costs and benefits. If the asset generates any income, then an investor who owns the asset receives the income whereas the investor who owns the futures contract does not. Similarly, if the asset is costly to store, then the owner of the asset must bear those costs and the futures contract holder avoids them. Therefore, a fair future contract price strikes a balance between the marginal benefits and costs of owning the asset. We determine the appropriate forward price for these assets as follows:

$$F = (S_0 - I + W)(1 + R_f)^n \qquad \text{(Eq. 17.2)}$$

where I is the present value of income to be paid by the asset during the life of the forward contract, and W equals the present value of the cost of storing the asset for the life of the contract.

APPLYING THE MODEL

Consider a forward contract to purchase a ten-year bond in one year. Currently, an eleven-year bond has a coupon rate of 8 percent and a price of \$1,100, and will thus make two \$40 coupon interest payments over the coming year. The current effective annual risk-free rate of interest over the next year is 5 percent. The fair forward price is calculated as follows:

$$F = \left[\$1,100 - \frac{\$40}{(1+0.05)^{0.5}} - \frac{\$40}{(1+0.05)}\right](1+0.05) = \$1,074.01$$

Of course, we have made a number of assumptions to arrive at Equations 17.1 and 17.2. First, we have assumed that market participants are able to borrow and lend at the risk-free rate, though most individual and institutional investors are unable to do so. However, a sufficiently large number of institutional investors can borrow at or near the risk-free rate, such that Equations 17.1 and 17.2 should hold. Second, we have assumed that there are no transactions costs associated with establishing these positions, which will tend to widen the bounds on futures prices. Third, we have assumed that we can use the proceeds from short-selling and that short-selling does not involve any costs. In reality, only institutional investors can use all the proceeds from short-selling, and there are transactions costs associated with short-selling. These costs can be incorporated into the model by discounting the right-hand side of Equations 17.1 and 17.2.

SMART CONCEPTS

See the concept explained step-by-step at SMARTFinance

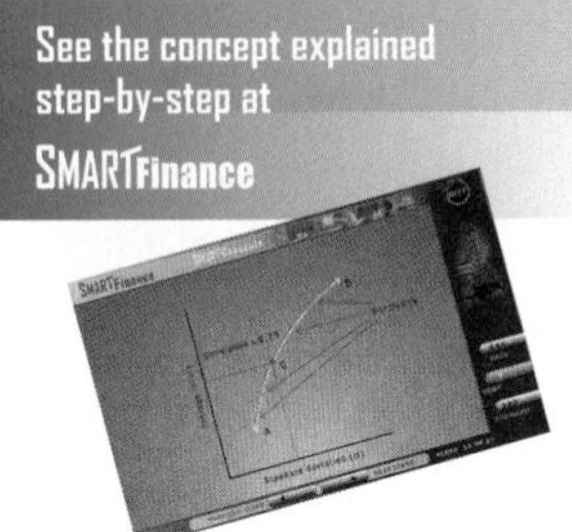

Currency Forward Contracts

Currency forward contracts, which involve exchanging one currency for another at a fixed date in the future, express the forward price as a **forward rate**. Table 17.2 presents hypothetical spot and forward exchange rates between the U.S. dollar, the British pound, and the euro. For example, the spot rate between pounds and dollars is \$1.6450/£ (or equivalently £0.6079/\$), and the spot rate between euros and dollars is \$1.1100/€ (or €0.9009/\$).

currency forward contract
Exchange of one currency for another at a fixed date in the future.

forward rate
In a currency forward contract, the forward price.

Figures 17.3 and 17.4 show payoff diagrams for the buyer and seller of a one-month forward contract on the British pound where the forward rate, which is agreed upon at contract origination, is \$1.6845/£. The *x*-axis of these diagrams represents possible spot rates for the British pound on the settlement date (one month in the future). The *y*-axis represents the profit or loss to the parties involved in the transaction. The buyer's profit is the spot rate for the British pound on the settlement date minus the forward rate. The seller's profit is the forward rate minus the spot rate on the settlement date. For example, if the spot rate is \$1.7500/£ in one month, the buyer's profit is \$0.0655/£ (\$1.7500/£ – \$1.6845/£). The seller would have a loss of \$0.0655/£.[2]

Table 17.2
Spot and Forward Exchange Rates

Currency	U.S. \$ Equivalent	Currency per U.S. \$
Pound	1.6450	0.6079
1-month fwd	1.6516	0.6055
3-month fwd	1.6647	0.6007
6-month fwd	1.6845	0.5936
Euro	1.1100	0.9009
1-month fwd	1.1144	0.8973
3-month fwd	1.1233	0.8902
6-month fwd	1.1366	0.8798

2. To understand why the profit or loss from a forward position depends on the spot rate at the settlement date, consider the following. If we pay \$1.6845/£ on the settlement date and immediately sell the British pounds in the spot market, we will receive \$1.7500/£. The net effect of this transaction is a cash inflow of \$0.0655/£. On the other hand, if we have the short position, we would be selling British pounds for \$0.0655/£ less than they are worth, thus experiencing a loss.

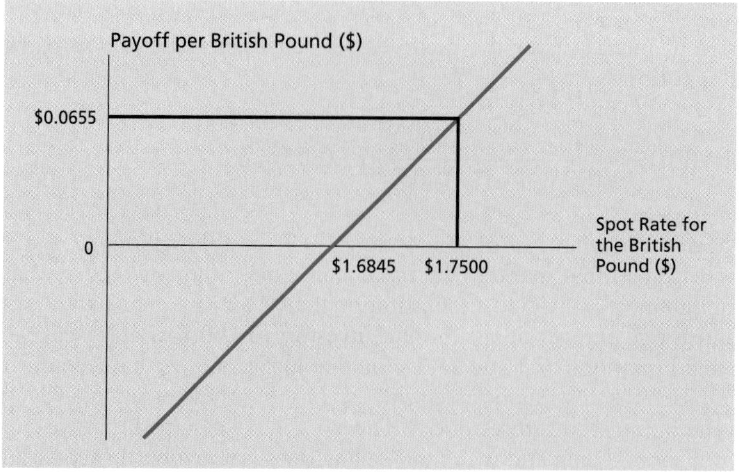

Figure 17.3
Payoff Diagram for the Buyer of a 1-Month Forward Contract on the British Pound

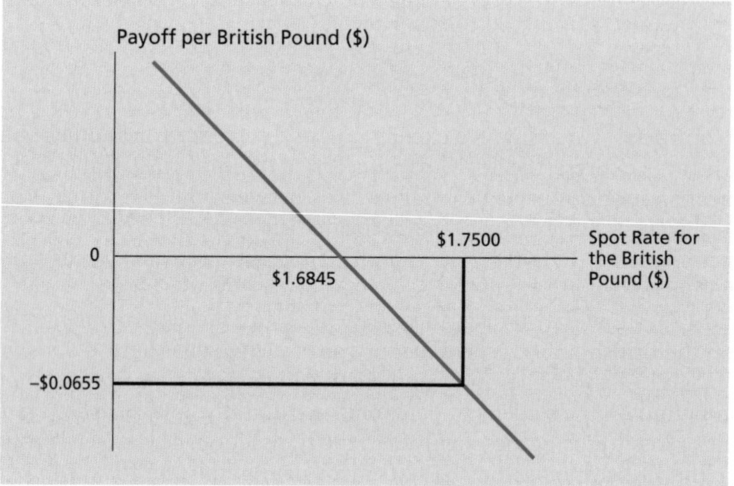

Figure 17.4
Payoff Diagram for the Seller of a 1-Month Forward Contract on the British Pound

Currency Forward Rates. Determining the fair forward rate in a currency contract is slightly more complicated than for a financial asset that pays no income. Unlike the financial asset discussed previously, currencies generate income in the form of interest earned from investing the currency. However, the principle of how we determine the fair forward price still applies. For example, rather than buy British pounds three months forward, we could borrow dollars, convert the dollars to British pounds at the spot rate, and invest the pounds in Britain at the risk-free rate. These transactions guarantee a fixed amount of British pounds in three months, just as a forward contract does.

In fact, we have already studied a pricing relationship for forward exchange rates. In Chapter 16, we saw that interest rate parity established conditions under which an investor was indifferent between investing in a risk-free asset at home or abroad. These conditions are expressed mathematically as follows:

$$\frac{F}{S} = \frac{1 + R_{\text{for}}}{1 + R_{\text{dom}}}$$

This equation says that the ratio of the forward rate to the spot rate (expressed in foreign currency per unit of domestic currency) must equal the ratio of one plus the foreign risk-free rate divided by one plus the domestic risk-free rate. If this equation does not hold, then an arbitrage opportunity exists, and traders can borrow in one country and simultaneously invest in another country to make a quick profit. Rearranging this equation slightly, we can derive the formula for the fair price of a forward exchange contract:

$$F = (S)\left(\frac{1+R_{\text{for}}}{1+R_{\text{dom}}}\right) \qquad \text{(Eq. 17.3)}$$

APPLYING THE MODEL

Suppose that the current spot exchange rate on the Swiss franc (SF) is \$0.5800/SF, or SF1.7241/\$. The one-year risk-free rate for borrowing in dollars is 6 percent, and the rate for borrowing in Swiss francs is 5 percent. According to Equation 17.3, the following is the one-year forward exchange rate on the Swiss franc:

$$F = (1.7241)\left(\frac{1+0.05}{1+0.06}\right) = \text{SF}1.7078/\$$$

Hedging with Currency Forward Contracts. To see how forward contracts can be used to hedge foreign exchange risk, consider a multinational company's treasurer who expects to receive a 10 million Swiss franc (SF) payment in ninety days. Suppose the spot rate is currently \$0.6050/SF. In ninety days, however, the spot rate may be lower. For example, if the spot rate declines to \$0.5800/SF, then the SF10 million payment will be worth only \$5,800,000 (\$0.5800/SF × SF10,000,000) rather than the \$6,050,000 (\$0.6050/SF × SF10,000,000) it would be worth today.

This type of foreign exchange risk can be hedged by selling the payment forward. Suppose the three-month forward rate for exchanging Swiss francs into dollars is \$0.6051/SF. In three months, after receiving the SF10 million payment, the company will deliver SF10 million to the counterparty in the forward contract and receive in exchange \$6,051,000 (\$0.6051/SF × SF10,000,000), regardless of what the spot rate happens to be at that time. The treasurer has hedged the company's foreign exchange risk associated with this payment by locking in the dollar price the company will receive for its foreign currency cash flow.

Interest Rate Forward Contracts

The underlying asset in an interest rate forward contract is either an interest rate or a debt security. Contracts involving an interest rate as the underlying security are cash settled, which simply means that the underlying security is not transferred from the seller to the buyer. Instead, the buyer and seller exchange the cash value of the contract. Either way, interest rate forward contracts are used to hedge an interest rate risk exposure in much the same way that currency forward contracts are used to hedge a currency risk exposure.

forward rate agreement (FRA)
A forward contract in which the underlying asset is not an asset at all but an interest rate.

Forward Rate Agreements. A **forward rate agreement (FRA)** is an example of a forward contract where the underlying asset is not an asset at all but an interest rate. An FRA is an agreement between two parties to exchange cash flows based on a reference interest rate and principal amount at a single point in time in the future. In an FRA, the first party will pay the second party if the market rate of interest at a specified future time is greater than the forward rate specified in the contract. If, however, the market rate of interest is less than the forward rate, the second party will pay the first party. The size of the payment will depend on the hypothetical principal amount, called the notional principal, and the difference between the market rate of interest and the forward rate. Equation 17.4 shows how to determine the cash flow in an FRA (CF_{FRA}). Note that, by convention, this computation uses a 360-day year.

$$CF_{\text{FRA}} = \frac{np \times (r_s - r_f) \times (D/360)}{1 + [r_s \times (D/360)]} \quad \text{(Eq. 17.4)}$$

In this equation, np stands for the contract's notional principal, r_s is the reference rate on the contract settlement date (e.g., the three-month Treasury bill rate), r_f is the forward rate established at the beginning of the contract, and D is the number of days in the contract period.

Hedging with Interest Rate Forward Contracts. To see how FRAs can be used to hedge interest rate risk, consider CFE Manufacturing (CFE). The company is planning to borrow \$10 million in six months at LIBOR plus 100 basis points and is concerned that LIBOR will increase before the company borrows.[3] To hedge this exposure, CFE and Bankamerica enter into a six-month FRA with a notional principal of \$10 million. The terms of the contract are such that CFE will pay Bankamerica if the three-month LIBOR six months from now is less than the forward rate of 6 percent. If the three-month LIBOR exceeds 6 percent, Bankamerica must pay CFE. The size of the cash flow is determined by Equation 17.4. For example, if the three-month LIBOR six months from now is 7 percent, Bankamerica must pay CFE the following:

$$\frac{\$10{,}000{,}000 \times (0.07 - 0.06) \times (92/360)}{1 + [0.07 \times (92/360)]} = \$25{,}106.43$$

However, if the three-month LIBOR six months from now is 5 percent rather than 7 percent, CFE must pay Bankamerica \$25,233.14.

CONCEPT REVIEW QUESTIONS

3. If Equation 17.2 does not hold, how might an arbitrageur earn a riskless profit?

4. What is the difference in the timing of cash flows in a forward contract and a spot market transaction?

[3] LIBOR, the London Interbank Offered Rate, is the rate of interest charged for Eurodollar borrowing between banks. Most large bank loans are priced with reference to LIBOR.

17.3 FUTURES CONTRACTS

For firms trying to hedge risk exposures, forward contracts suffer from two important problems: default risk and liquidity. Futures contracts solve these problems. Like a forward contract, a **futures contract** involves two parties agreeing today on a price at which the purchaser will buy a given amount of a commodity or financial instrument from the seller at a fixed date sometime in the future. In fact, the contracts are so similar that, for most purposes, we can use the same pricing formulas to price futures contracts that we used for forward contracts. Similarly, we can use the same payoff diagram for futures that we used for forwards.

Although futures and forwards serve the same economic function, there are differences in the characteristics of the two contracts. In contrast to a forward contract, a futures contract is an exchange-traded contract that promises the delivery of a specified volume of a commodity or financial instrument on a standardized date of the month in which the contract expires. The futures exchange acts as a guarantor for all transactions, eliminating the forward contract's problem of counterparty risk. Because futures exchanges offer a limited set of contracts for trading, futures contracts are relatively liquid compared with forward contracts.

For example, gold futures contracts are traded on the New York Mercantile Exchange. The standard gold futures contract size is 100 troy ounces. Contracts are available for delivery in the current month; the next two months; any February, April, August, and October falling within the next two years; and any June and December falling within the next five years.

Table 17.3 provides data on the prices of gold futures contracts on May 17, 2004. The first trade of the day, called the **opening futures price**, was $378.10 per troy ounce for delivery in June 2004. The highest price for the day was $383.70/oz. The low for the day was $376.80/oz. The last June 2004 futures price for the day was $379.60/oz. This **closing futures price** is the result of a $2.50/oz increase in the settle price from the previous day, as indicated by the change column. The closing price is also known as the **settlement price** and is used to settle all contracts at the end of each day's trading, in a process called "marking-to-market" (described below). Also shown are the **lifetime high** and **lifetime low prices** for this contract, which are the highest and lowest settlement prices recorded for this contract since its inception—perhaps several months (or even a year or more) before. The **open interest** represents the number of contracts that are currently outstanding. This number changes every day as contracts are bought and sold. If a trader were to take a long position in gold futures contracts at the settle price of $280.40/oz, the total futures price of one contract would be $28,040 ($280.40/oz × 100 troy ounces).

futures contract
Involves two parties agreeing today on a price at which the purchaser will buy a given amount of a commodity or financial instrument from the seller at a fixed date sometime in the future.

opening futures price
Price on the first trade of the day.

closing futures price
The price used to settle all contracts at the end of each day's trading.

settlement price
The average price at which a contract sells at the end of a trading day.

lifetime high prices
The highest settlement prices recorded for a contract since its inception.

lifetime low prices
The lowest settlement prices recorded for a contract since its inception.

open interest
The number of contracts that are currently outstanding.

Table 17.3
Gold Futures Prices, May 2004

						Lifetime		
	Open	High	Low	Settle	Change	High	Low	Open Int
Gold (COMEX) 100 troy oz; $ per troy oz								
June	378.10	383.70	376.80	379.60	2.50	433.00	287.00	147,694
Aug	378.50	384.70	378.40	380.60	2.50	433.00	324.70	27,992
Oct	381.50	385.00	381.50	381.70	2.50	432.00	332.00	6,565
Dec	381.40	386.80	380.50	382.90	2.50	436.50	290.00	30,148
Feb 05	387.50	388.50	383.50	384.30	2.50	435.00	331.50	3,072
June 05	391.20	392.00	387.50	387.50	2.50	436.60	302.00	13,637

Table 17.4 provides a few examples of the types of available futures contracts and the exchanges on which they are traded. All the contracts traded on these exchanges are standardized with respect to size and delivery date. The economic rationale for designing futures contracts in this way is that it provides a standardized, high-trading-volume (hence low transactions cost) financial instrument that can be used by both individuals and businesses to hedge underlying commercial risks, as well as by speculators wishing to place a highly leveraged bet on the direction of commodity prices. Contract sizes are small enough for individuals to be able to participate in futures markets, and the volume is high enough for businesses to take significant positions by buying or selling multiple contracts.

Table 17.4
Examples of Exchange-Traded Futures Contracts

Contract	Exchange	Face Amount
Grains and oilseeds		
Corn	Chicago Board of Trade	5,000 bushels
Oats	Chicago Board of Trade	5,000 bushels
Wheat	Chicago Board of Trade	5,000 bushels
Canola	Winnipeg Commodity Exchange	20 metric tons
Livestock and meat		
Cattle—feeder	Chicago Mercantile Exchange	50,000 lbs
Cattle—live	Chicago Mercantile Exchange	40,000 lbs
Pork bellies	Chicago Mercantile Exchange	40,000 lbs
Food and fiber		
Cocoa	Coffee, Sugar, & Cocoa Exchange, New York	10 metric tons
Coffee	Coffee, Sugar, & Cocoa Exchange, New York	37,500 lbs
Sugar—world	Coffee, Sugar, & Cocoa Exchange, New York	112,000 lbs
Sugar—domestic	Coffee, Sugar, & Cocoa Exchange, New York	112,000 lbs
Cotton	New York Cotton Exchange	50,000 lbs
Orange juice	New York Cotton Exchange	15,000 lbs
Metals and petroleum		
Copper	Comex, New York Mercantile Exchange	25,000 lbs
Gold	Comex, New York Mercantile Exchange	100 troy oz
Platinum	New York Mercantile Exchange	50 troy oz
Silver	Comex, New York Mercantile Exchange	5,000 troy oz
Crude oil	New York Mercantile Exchange	1,000 bbls
Natural gas	New York Mercantile Exchange	10,000MMBtu
Interest rate		
Treasury bonds	Chicago Board of Trade	$100,000
5-year Treasury notes	Chicago Board of Trade	$100,000
30-day federal funds	Chicago Board of Trade	$5 million
LIBOR	Chicago Mercantile Exchange	$3 million
Eurodollars	Chicago Mercantile Exchange	$1 million
Index		
Dow Jones Industrial Average	Chicago Board of Trade	$10 × average
S&P 500	Chicago Mercantile Exchange	$250 × average
Nikkei 225	Chicago Mercantile Exchange	$5 × average
Currency		
Japanese yen (¥)	Chicago Mercantile Exchange	¥12.5 million
British pound (BP)	Chicago Mercantile Exchange	BP62,500
Swiss franc (SF)	Chicago Mercantile Exchange	SF125,000

Source: Futures Prices, Wall Street Journal, *(January 7, 2002), p. C13.*

Although both futures and forwards impose obligations on their holders, the default risk of a futures contract is much lower, for two reasons. First, every major futures exchange operates a clearinghouse that acts as the counterparty to all buyers and sellers. This means that traders need not worry about the creditworthiness of the party they trade with (as forward market traders must), but only about the creditworthiness of the exchange itself. Second, futures contracts feature daily cash settlement of all contracts, called **marking-to-market**. By its very nature, a futures contract is a zero-sum game because whenever the market price of a commodity changes, the underlying value of a long (purchase) or short (sale) position also changes—and one party's gain is the other party's loss. By requiring each contract's loser to pay the winner the net amount of this change each day, futures exchanges eliminate the possibility that large, unrealized losses will build up over time. In a forward contract, on the other hand, there are no cash flows until termination of the contract.

marking-to-market
Daily cash settlement of all futures contracts.

APPLYING THE MODEL

As an example of marking-to-market, consider the gold futures discussed previously. Recall that the settle price for the June 2004 contract was \$379.60 per troy ounce. If the settle price on the next business day is \$380.20/oz, the person with the long position will receive \$0.60/oz (the new futures price minus the original futures price), or a total of \$60.00 per contract (\$0.60/oz × 100 troy ounces). The person with the short position must pay \$0.60/oz. In effect, the new contract with a futures price of \$380.20/oz replaces the original contract. The party with the long position is compensated (and the person with the short position must pay) for the increase in the futures price. This type of daily settlement takes place on every trading day until delivery takes place. It is important to note that the party with the long position ultimately ends up paying a total of \$379.60/oz, and the party with the short position receives a total of \$379.60/oz upon delivery if each party holds his or her contract until maturity.

When taking a position in a futures contract, the investor must deposit a minimum dollar amount called the **initial margin**, which varies by contract, in a **margin account**. The investor deposits gains in or withdraws losses from this account. Each exchange has margin requirements, and brokerage firms may require additional margin above the minimum specified. If losses deplete the margin below the level needed to maintain an open position, the **maintenance margin**, the investor must deposit additional funds in the account to bring the account back to the initial margin. Failure to deposit additional funds before the next day's trading results in the position being closed out by the exchange.

initial margin
The minimum dollar amount required of an investor when taking a position in a futures contract.

margin account
The account into which the investor must deposit the initial margin.

maintenance margin
Margin level required to maintain an open position.

In addition to these distinctions, futures differ from forward contracts in two other important respects. First, futures contracts are designed to have a value (usually around \$100,000) that will appeal to a "retail" market of individuals and smaller companies, whereas most actively traded forward contracts have minimum denominations of \$1 million or more. This small contract size is rarely a problem for futures traders, however, as those wishing to hedge large exposures can simply purchase multiple contracts. Second, most forward contracts are settled by actual delivery, but this rarely occurs with futures contracts. Instead, futures market hedgers will execute an offsetting trade to close out their position in the futures market whenever they have closed out their underlying commercial risk through delivery in the normal course of business.

The ability to close out a position by taking an offsetting position is referred to as **fungibility**. Fungibility is made possible because the counterparty in a futures contract is the clearinghouse and because futures contracts are settled daily. If an

fungibility
The ability to close out a position by taking an offsetting position.

investor were to take a long position in a futures contract and subsequently take a short position in the same contract, the contracts would cancel each other out for two reasons: (1) after marking-to-market, the futures prices of the two contracts would be the same, and (2) the clearinghouse is the counterparty to both contracts. It is important to note that unless buyers or sellers close out their positions, they are required to make or take delivery of the underlying asset.

Hedging with Futures Contracts

Futures contracts are a very effective mechanism for hedging. In addition to futures markets for metals, there are futures markets for foreign currencies, interest rates, stock indexes, and commodities. *Long hedges* involve buying a futures contract to offset an underlying short (sold) position. *Short hedges* involve selling a futures contract to offset an underlying long (purchased) position.

Hedging with Foreign Currency Futures. The multinational company with the SF10 million exposure discussed earlier could have chosen to hedge that exposure in the futures market rather than with a forward contract by selling 80 Swiss franc futures contracts (each mandating delivery of SF125,000). Recall that the multinational company will be receiving a payment of 10 million Swiss francs in ninety days. By selling 80 SF futures contracts that expire after the date on which it will receive the SF payments (because futures contracts have fixed delivery periods, they will only rarely exactly match a trader's desired payment date), the company can hedge this exposure using futures rather than forwards. Suppose that the current settle price for Swiss franc futures is $0.6057/SF. When the SF payment is received, the company will exchange it for dollars at whatever the spot $/SF exchange rate happens to be at the time and will simultaneously buy 80 SF futures contracts with the same delivery date as the contracts purchased earlier—thereby offsetting, or closing out, its futures position. If the dollar value of the Swiss franc declines from $0.6050/SF to, say, $0.5000/SF during the sixty days in question, then the company will lose $0.1050/SF, or a total of $1,050,000, on its spot market sale of the SF payment. But this loss will be offset by the profit the company will achieve on its futures position. If the futures price declines from $0.6057/SF to $0.5007/SF, the profit in the futures position will be $0.1050/SF, or a total of $1,050,000, exactly offsetting the loss in the cash market position. If the Swiss franc appreciates rather than depreciates against the dollar, then the company will gain on its cash market transaction and lose on its futures contracts. Either way, hedgers can use a futures contract to hedge an underlying commercial risk without actually having to take physical delivery on the futures contract.

Hedging with Interest Rate Futures. We can use futures contracts to hedge interest rate risk in much the same way that we hedged foreign exchange risk. Consider a corporate treasurer who anticipates borrowing $1 million in five months. The loan will be at 100 basis points over the three-month LIBOR at the time of borrowing. LIBOR is currently at 5 percent. Eurodollar futures contracts for delivery in six months are trading at a yield of 5.2 percent. By selling one Eurodollar futures contract, the treasurer can effectively lock in a borrowing rate of 6.2 percent (5.2 percent plus 100 basis points) for the three months beginning in six months. As in the currency contract, the treasurer would close out the position in Eurodollar futures and borrow at the same time.

Concerns When Using Futures Contracts

In the previous examples, we ignored several potential problems associated with using futures markets to hedge. We discuss some of these problems in the following sections.

Basis Risk. The basis in a futures contract is the difference between the futures price and the spot price. **Basis risk** arises from the possibility of unanticipated changes in the basis. As the maturity date approaches, the basis goes to zero. This simply means that when a futures contract is about to expire, the futures price must equal the spot price. If this were not the case, a trader could easily make an instant profit. For example, if the futures price is greater than the spot price, then a trader could buy the underlying asset on the spot market and sell it at the higher futures price.

basis risk
The possibility of unanticipated changes in the difference between the futures price and the spot price.

If a futures contract is closed out prior to maturity, as in the previous examples, basis risk can cause gains (losses) in the underlying risky position to differ from the offsetting losses (gains) in the futures position. In the currency hedging example, if the futures price had not changed by exactly the amount as the spot price, the loss in the cash position would have differed from the gain in the futures position.

Cross-Hedging. The underlying securities in the futures contracts were identical to the assets being hedged in the two previous examples. However, the underlying securities in the futures contract and the assets being hedged often have different characteristics. This practice is called **cross-hedging**. For example, a farmer who uses orange juice futures to hedge his crop of grapefruits is cross-hedging. Some traders use cross-hedging strategies because there is no futures contract available that precisely matches the asset exposure that the trader wants to hedge, or because one futures contract is more liquid than another one that matches the underlying asset being hedged. To minimize basis risk in a cross hedge, we need to determine the relation between changes in the value of the asset being hedged and changes in the value of the asset in the futures contract. It is possible to estimate this relation using historical data. Once we measure the sensitivity of the asset being hedged to changes in the price of the underlying asset in the futures contract, we can use that information to adjust the number of futures contracts to buy or sell in order to achieve an effective hedge.

cross-hedging
The underlying securities in a futures contract and the assets being hedged have different characteristics.

Tailing the Hedge. Because of the marking-to-market feature of futures contracts, interest is earned on gains to the futures position as they are paid in and interest is lost on losses as they are paid out. This causes gains on a long position in futures to be slightly greater than the losses on a short position in the underlying asset because of the interest earned on the gains. To avoid overhedging, we can **tail the hedge**, or purchase enough futures contracts to hedge the risk exposure, but not so many that we overhedge. To achieve a perfect hedge in the currency hedging example, we would need to sell slightly fewer than 80 Swiss franc futures contracts.

tailing the hedge
Purchasing enough futures contracts to hedge risk exposure, but not so many as to cause overhedging.

Delivery Options. The deliverable instrument in some futures contracts can take a variety of forms. For example, the underlying security in a Treasury bond futures contract is a twenty-year Treasury bond. However, the contract allows for the delivery of any Treasury bond that has a maturity date of at least fifteen years from the first day of the delivery month. If the bond is callable, it must not be callable for at least fifteen years from the first day of the delivery month. When delivery occurs, a conversion factor is used to account for differences in the characteristics of the deliverable instruments. See the Chicago Board of Trade's Web site (http://www.cbot.com) for information on current conversion factors.

Another delivery option is the timing option. Many futures contracts allow delivery to take place at any time during the delivery month. In fact, several futures contracts allow for delivery to take place several days after the last trading day for a contract. For example, the delivery process for Treasury bond futures contracts is as follows: (1) Sometime during the delivery month, the seller notifies the clearinghouse of the intent to deliver on the futures contract; (2) the clearinghouse notifies the party with the oldest long position that delivery will take place in two days; (3) the seller delivers Treasury bonds to the individual with the long position; and (4) the seller receives the futures price (adjusted by the conversion factors associated with the bonds).

Because delivery rarely takes place in a futures contract, delivery options are not generally a major concern for the manager who is using futures to hedge risk. However, these delivery options do affect futures prices and are important for those market participants who are planning to make or take delivery of the underlying asset in the futures market.

CONCEPT REVIEW QUESTIONS

5. What is the difference in the cash flows for a forward contract and a futures contract?

6. What features of a futures contract tend to reduce default risk?

17.4 OPTIONS AND SWAPS

Options and swaps can also be used to hedge risk exposures. This section discusses both these instruments and describes how they can be used to hedge risk exposures.

Options

As discussed in Chapter 15, options contracts are pervasive in modern financial systems. There are exchange-traded options contracts on individual common stocks, on stock indexes, on numerous currencies and interest rates, on a bewildering number of industrial and agricultural commodities, and even on futures contracts. Financial institutions custom-design even more options to meet the needs of their customers (these are often called over-the-counter, or OTC options). A call option gives its holder the right to buy a fixed amount of a commodity at a fixed price, on (with a European option) or by (with an American option) a fixed date in the future, whereas a put option entails a similar right to sell that commodity. The valuation of, and payoff patterns for, options are discussed in depth in Chapter 15.

For our purposes, the key feature of an option as a hedging tool is that it provides protection against adverse price risk (an investor has the right to exercise the option if price changes make it optimal to do so) without having to forfeit the right to profit if the price on the underlying commodity moves in the investor's favor (in which case, the investor allows the option to expire unexercised). Of course, this one-sided protection against risk comes at a price. To acquire an option, unlike a forward contract, a trader must first pay the premium to the option seller.

Hedging with Currency Options. Recall the multinational corporation that is expecting to receive a payment of SF10 million. Earlier, we demonstrated how this foreign exchange risk could be hedged using forwards or futures. We can also hedge this risk using options. The multinational company could have purchased 160 Swiss franc put options (each granting the right to deliver SF62,500) that expire after the date on which it will receive the SF payments (like futures contracts, exchange-traded options have fixed expiration dates and will only rarely exactly match a trader's desired payment date). When the SF payment is received, the company will exchange it for dollars at the current spot $/SF exchange rate and will simultaneously sell 160 SF put options with the same delivery date as the contracts purchased earlier—thereby offsetting, or canceling out, its options position. If the dollar value of the Swiss franc has declined from $0.6050/SF to, say, $0.50/SF during the sixty days in question, then the company will lose on its cash market transaction and gain on its options contract. If the Swiss franc appreciates against the dollar, the company will gain on its cash market transaction, and its losses on the options contract will be limited to the premium paid for the option. By using an option to hedge this foreign exchange risk, the multinational corporation minimizes its downside risk without giving up its upside potential. The cost of this hedge is the premium paid for the option.

Hedging with Interest Rate Options. In addition to hedging foreign exchange risk, options are commonly used to hedge interest rate risk. For example, a retailer that has borrowed using a variable-rate loan is probably concerned about interest rates rising. If the loan rate is tied to Treasury bill rates, the firm could hedge this interest rate risk by purchasing a call option on the thirteen-week T-bill yield. Call options on interest rates are called **interest rate caps**.

interest rate cap
A call option on interest rates.

The Chicago Board Options Exchange (CBOE) offers options on the thirteen-week T-bill rate and other, longer-term Treasury rates. See the CBOE's Web site (http://www.cboe.com) for more information on interest rate options traded on that exchange. The underlying instruments in CBOE interest rate options are yields rather than prices, as in stock options. The underlying values for these options are 10 times the underlying Treasury yields, and the contracts are cash settled at $100 times the difference between the underlying value at option expiration and the strike price. For the retailer, the underlying value would be 10 times the yield to maturity (YTM) on thirteen-week T-bills. If the retailer paid 1.00 for a July 55 call, the total price of one contract is $100 (1.00 × $100). If the YTM on thirteen-week T-bills is 6 percent on the option expiration date, the cash settlement will be $500 [(60 – 55) × $100]. The net profit for the hedge will be $400 ($500 settlement – $100 premium). This profit will offset the higher interest costs of the variable-rate loan. If the YTM on thirteen-week T-bills declines to 5 percent, however, the option will expire worthless, and the retailer will have lost only the $100 premium paid for the option. The advantage of using options to hedge the retailer's interest rate risk is that the retailer retains the potential for lower interest costs if interest rates decline but is able to offset the potential for higher interest costs if interest rates increase.

Just as an interest rate cap is a call option on interest rates, an **interest rate floor** is a put option on interest rates. Recall from Chapter 15 that a put option represents the right to sell an asset for a specified price within a specified period of time. In the case of interest rate options, which involve cash settlement, a put option will generate a positive payoff for the buyer when the underlying value ($100 times the YTM) declines below the strike price.

interest rate floor
A put option on interest rates.

One common strategy, called an **interest rate collar**, is to buy an interest rate cap and simultaneously sell an interest rate floor. The purpose of this strategy is to use the proceeds from selling the floor to purchase the cap. Of course, by selling the floor, an investor forgoes some upside potential. If our intrepid retailer sold a July 50 put for 0.75 and bought the July 55 call at the same time, the retailer would receive $75 (0.75 × $100) for the put. This would offset all but $25 of the premium

interest rate collar
A strategy involving the purchase of an interest rate cap and the simultaneous sale of an interest rate floor, using the proceeds from selling the floor to purchase the cap.

paid for the call. The result of this strategy would be the same as just purchasing the cap for all yields above 5.0 percent. Below 5.0 percent, however, gains from the lower interest costs will be offset by losses from selling the put.

Swaps

swap contract
Agreement between two parties to exchange payment obligations on two underlying financial liabilities that are equal in principal amount but differ in payment patterns.

In a **swap contract**, two parties agree to exchange payment obligations on two underlying financial liabilities that are equal in principal amount but differ in payment patterns. Investors use swaps to change the characteristics of cash flows, most often to change the characteristics of cash outflows. We will concentrate on the most common types, *interest rate swaps* and *currency swaps*. According to a survey by the Bank for International Settlements, the total notional volume of over-the-counter derivative contracts outstanding totaled more than $197 trillion at the end of 2003, with interest rate swaps accounting for more than half ($111 trillion) of this total.[4] It is important to note that, like forward contracts, swap contracts are over-the-counter instruments and subject to default risk. For this reason, swap market participants enter into contracts only with parties that they know and trust.

interest rate swap
A swap contract in which two parties exchange payment obligations involving different interest payment schedules.

fixed-for-floating interest rate swap
Typically one party will make fixed-rate payments to another party in exchange for floating-rate payments.

interest differential
In an interest rate swap, only the differential is exchanged.

Interest Rate Swaps. An **interest rate swap** is the most common type of swap transaction. In a typical interest rate swap, one party will make fixed-rate payments to another party in exchange for floating-rate payments. This is often called a **fixed-for-floating interest rate swap**. As in the FRAs discussed earlier, the interest payments on a fixed-for-floating swap will be based on a hypothetical principal amount called the *notional principal*.

Figure 17.5 illustrates the structure of a fixed-for-floating swap. The party making fixed-rate payments, Company A, promises to make fixed-rate payments based on some notional principal amount to a financial intermediary in exchange for floating-rate payments. In this example, as in many swap transactions, an intermediary has arranged the swap and is acting as the counterparty to both contracts. The contract calls for Company A to pay the intermediary 8 percent per year based on a notional principal of $10 million. In return, the intermediary will pay Company A the six-month LIBOR applied to the same $10 million notional principal amount. In practice, only the **interest differential** is exchanged between the intermediary and Company A.

At the same time that the intermediary and company agree to swap interest payments, the intermediary enters into an agreement to pay a fixed rate of interest to the floating-rate payer, Company B, in exchange for a floating rate. In this example, the intermediary agrees to pay Company B 7.85 percent in exchange for the six-month LIBOR. The intermediary's compensation is the spread between the fixed rate received from Company A and the fixed rate paid to Company B.

Figure 17.5
Typical Structure of a Fixed-for-Floating Swap

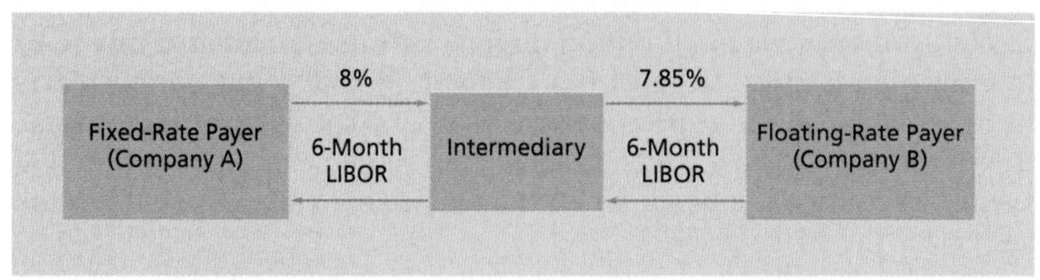

[4] These figures were obtained at http://www.bis.org.

Figures 17.6 and 17.7 show payoff diagrams for Company A and Company B in the interest rate swap. The *x*-axis of these diagrams represents possible spot rates for the six-month LIBOR at the end of each six-month period. The *y*-axis represents the cash flow to the parties involved in the transaction. If the contract calls for semiannual payments, the cash flow for Company A is [$10,000,000 × (LIBOR – 0.08) ÷ 2]. The cash flow for Company B is [$10,000,000 × (0.0785 – LIBOR) ÷ 2]. If the six-month LIBOR is 7 percent at the end of the first six-month period, Company A will pay the intermediary $50,000 [$10,000,000 × (0.07 – 0.08) ÷ 2]. The intermediary will pay Company B $42,500 [$10,000,000 × (0.0785 – 0.07) ÷ 2]. Six months later, if the six-month LIBOR is 8.5 percent, the intermediary will pay Company A $25,000 [$10,000,000 × (0.085 – 0.08) ÷ 2]. Company B will pay the intermediary $32,500 [$10,000,000 × (0.0785 – 0.085) ÷ 2]. These exchanges will take place every six months until the termination date.

SMART IDEAS VIDEO

Betty Simkins, Oklahoma State University

"The most common interest rate swap is the fixed for floating swap."

See the entire interview at **SMARTFinance**

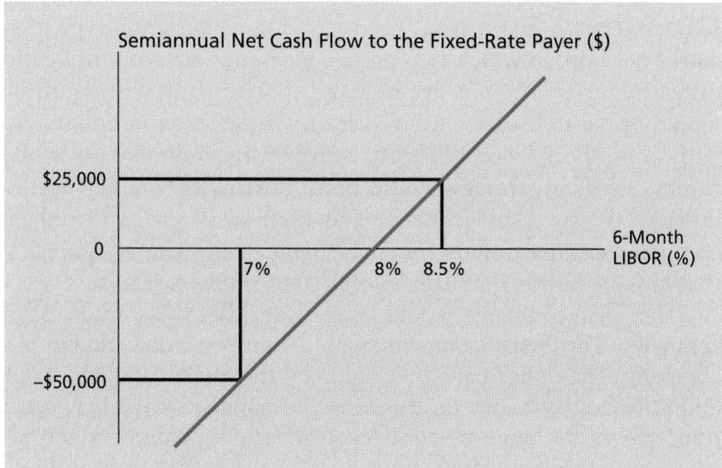

Figure 17.6
Semiannual Net Cash Flow for the Fixed-Rate Payer in a Fixed-for-Floating Swap with a Notional Principal of $10,000,000

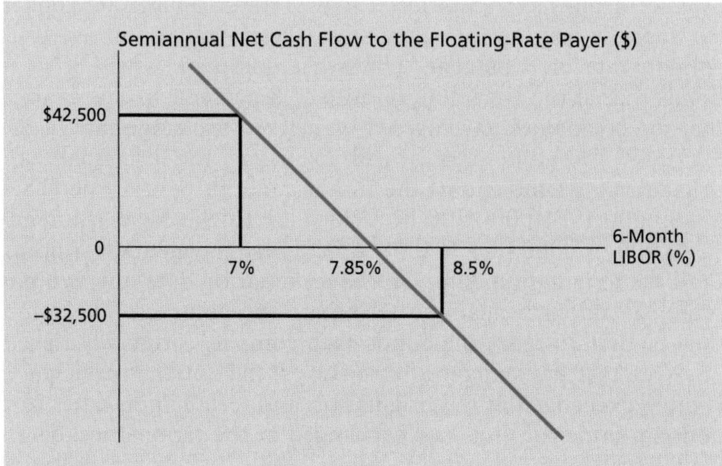

Figure 17.7
Semiannual Net Cash Flow for the Floating-Rate Payer in a Fixed-for-Floating Swap with a Notional Principal of $10,000,000

Typically, these interest rate swaps arise because one party wanted to issue fixed-rate debt but chose instead to issue floating-rate debt, either because the fixed-rate market was closed to this issuer or was more costly. By entering a swap agreement, the floating-rate issuer can effectively obtain a fixed-rate payment obligation. By paying a fixed rate and receiving a floating rate, this firm can use the cash inflows in the form of floating-rate payments to make the floating-rate payments on the debt that is outstanding. The net effect of the swap agreement is to offset the floating-rate payments being paid on the floating-rate debt with the floating-rate payments received on the swap. The fixed-rate payments being made on the swap are all that remain. The counterparty in the swap contract (who has better access to fixed-rate debt markets) achieves a preferred floating-rate pattern of payments. As mentioned previously, rather than exchange gross amounts, the two parties will exchange only the net difference between the two payment obligations, the interest differential; therefore, the party that has swapped a fixed-rate payment obligation for one with a floating rate will lose (have to increase payment amounts) if market rates rise and will benefit if market rates fall.

currency swap
A swap contract in which two parties exchange payment obligations denominated in different currencies.

Currency Swaps. The second most common type of swap contract is the **currency swap**, in which two parties exchange payment obligations denominated in different currencies. For example, a U.S. company wishing to invest in Switzerland would prefer to borrow in Swiss francs rather than in dollars. If, however, the company could borrow on more attractive terms in dollars (as is often the case) than in francs, a logical strategy would be to borrow the money needed for investment in dollars, say, by issuing bonds, and then swap payment obligations with a Swiss company seeking dollars for investment in the United States. The Swiss company would issue bonds that are denominated in Swiss francs.

The U.S. company would make periodic Swiss franc payments to the Swiss company. The Swiss company would make periodic dollar payments to the U.S. company. The dollar payments made by the Swiss company would cover the interest and principal payments on the dollar borrowing by the U.S. company, and the Swiss franc payments made by the U.S. company would cover the interest and principal payments on the Swiss franc borrowing by the Swiss company. By engaging in the swap, the U.S. company has transformed its dollar liabilities into Swiss franc liabilities, and the Swiss company has transformed its Swiss franc liabilities into dollar liabilities.

Suppose that the U.S. company issues $7 million in ten-year bonds that have a coupon rate of 8 percent. The Swiss company issues SF10 million in ten-year bonds that also have a coupon rate of 8 percent. In this example, we will assume that the companies have agreed on a fixed exchange rate in the swap contract of $0.70/SF. The two parties will exchange the principal amounts at contract origination. At the end of the first six-month period, the U.S. company will pay SF400,000 (SF10,000,000 × 0.08 ÷ 2) to the Swiss company in exchange for $280,000 ($7,000,000 × 0.08 ÷ 2). These payments will occur every six months until the termination date. On the termination date, the two parties will exchange principal amounts again to terminate the contract. The principal amounts will then be used to retire the bonds each company originally issued.

Note that unlike interest rate swaps, the notional principal in a currency swap is often exchanged at the origination and termination dates of the contract. If the notional principal were not exchanged at the termination date, the U.S. company would still be faced with a dollar liability when the dollar-denominated bonds mature, and the Swiss company would be faced with a Swiss franc liability.

fixed-for-floating currency swap
A combination of a currency swap and an interest rate swap.

Another variant of the currency swap is the **fixed-for-floating currency swap.** This is simply a combination of a currency swap and an interest rate swap. In this transaction, the first party pays a fixed rate of interest denominated in one currency to the second party in exchange for a floating rate of interest denominated in another currency. For example, if the U.S. company in the previous example preferred to borrow in Swiss francs at a floating rate of interest, and the Swiss company preferred to borrow in dollars at a fixed rate of interest, the two firms could engage in a fixed-for-floating currency swap.

Suppose that the U.S. company was able to borrow $7 million in ten-year bonds with a coupon rate of 8 percent. The Swiss company borrows SF10 million in ten-year bonds with a coupon rate of LIBOR + 100 basis points. As in the currency swap, the two parties will exchange the principal amounts at contract origination. At the end of the first six-month period, if LIBOR is 6.5 percent, the cost of the loan will be 7.5 percent (0.065 + 0.01). The U.S. company will pay SF375,000 [SF10,000,000 × (0.065 + 0.01) ÷ 2] to the Swiss company in exchange for $280,000 ($7,000,000 × 0.08 ÷ 2). For both parties, the semiannual cash inflows from the swap contract are used to make the interest payments on the bonds that were issued in the cash market. Upon termination of the swap contract, the principal amounts are exchanged again and the bonds are retired.

CONCEPT REVIEW QUESTIONS

7. Describe how an interest rate swap is just a portfolio of FRAs.

8. Why would any corporation hedge with forwards, futures, or swaps if it can keep its upside potential by hedging with options?

17.5 FINANCIAL ENGINEERING

The key to a successful hedging strategy is the ability to identify and offset the underlying risk exposure that has the largest impact on the firm's value. For many firms, however, the underlying risk exposure is unique because the risk exposure is based on an asset whose value is not easily hedged. **Financial engineering**, at least for our purposes here, can be defined as the process of using the principles of financial economics to design and price financial instruments. In particular, financial engineering has meant combining the risk-management building blocks—forwards, futures, options, and swaps—in complex patterns in order to achieve specific risk profiles that benefit corporate issuers or to offer investors unique payoff structures that help complete the capital markets, or both. For example, some firms are not able to use off-the-shelf hedging instruments because those instruments do not have payoff structures that will offset the firm's underlying risk exposures. Similarly, an institutional investor may desire an investment security that has specific payoff structures, but no such security is currently available.

financial engineering
The process of using the principles of financial economics to design and price financial instruments.

By combining elements of forwards, futures, options, and swaps, however, it is often possible to create a financial instrument that meets the needs of the corporation trying to hedge its risk exposure or that offers the institutional investor an investment opportunity with a unique payoff structure. Modern corporations, and the financial institutions that cater to them, have become extremely adept at this process. For example, Chidambaran, Fernando, and Spindt describe how Freeport-McMoRan used financial engineering to finance an expansion of its mining facilities in Indonesia. Rather than issue fixed-rate bonds, Freeport-McMoRan issued depository shares that act like bonds with principal and interest payments that are directly tied to the price of gold. This built-in hedge actually enhanced the credit quality of Freeport-McMoRan because of the reduced risk of default.

Given that the returns to successful financial innovation can be very high, a great many new financial products are developed every year. Enough of these products succeed that we can identify certain trends that are likely to continue for the foreseeable future. First, longer-maturity risk-management products will continue to be developed. Standard futures, forwards, and options are all short-term contracts, but recent years have seen the introduction of contracts with much longer dates, as well as the development of intermediate- and long-term securities that effectively perform hedging roles. Second, even more complex securities will be developed to hedge multiple interest rate, currency, and input/output pricing risks, particularly in the international arena. Third, new techniques for hedging pricing and underwriting risks in the issuance of new securities will continue to arise as the securitization trend accelerates around the world. Finally, it seems inevitable that new methods of hedging the strategic and currency risks of investing in small, politically unstable or financially underdeveloped countries will emerge in the coming decade as Western capital is committed to the transformation of the formerly socialist or mixed economies of China, India, Russia, and Eastern Europe.

The practice of risk management and financial engineering is evolving, and we have only touched on the basic strategies here. As the markets for derivative securities grow and the practice of risk management develops, it is likely that we will see increasingly complex financially engineered instruments. However, it is important to remember that even the most complex instrument includes elements of the securities we described here.

CONCEPT REVIEW QUESTION

9. Under what circumstances might a corporation prefer a financially engineered solution for a risk-management problem to an off-the-shelf solution?

17.6 SUMMARY AND CONCLUSIONS

- Increased volatility in interest rates, currency exchange rates, and commodity prices has led to mushrooming demand for financial instruments that corporations can use to hedge their exposure to these risk factors.
- It is not always in the corporation's best interest to hedge. However, hedging can reduce the likelihood of financial distress, thereby reducing the expected costs of financial distress.
- A forward contract is an over-the-counter instrument that involves two parties agreeing on a price at which the purchaser will buy a specified amount of an asset from the seller at a fixed date sometime in the future. A futures contract is similar to a forward contract but is traded on an organized exchange.
- The fair forward price (or rate) in a forward contract is the price that eliminates the possibility of an arbitrageur generating riskless profits by trading in the forward contract.
- Unlike forward contracts, which are customized instruments, futures are standardized. Several issues to consider when using futures to hedge include basis risk, cross-hedging, tailing the hedge, and delivery options.
- Options offer a corporation the opportunity to hedge its downside risk without giving up its upside potential. However, this comes at a cost in the form of the premium paid for the option. Swap contracts are longer-term hedging instruments that allow corporations to change the characteristics of their periodic cash flows.

- In some cases, a corporation may not be able to hedge its risk exposure using off-the-shelf forwards, futures, options, or swaps. In these cases, the corporation may turn to financial engineering in an effort to create a specialized financial instrument that will hedge the exposure.

SELF-TEST PROBLEMS

Answers to Self-Test Problems appear in Appendix D at back of book. Answers to the Concept Review Questions throughout the chapter appear at http://megginson.swlearning.com.

ST17-1. A certain commodity sells for \$150 today. The present value of the cost of storing this commodity for one year is \$10. The risk-free rate is 4 percent. What is a fair price for a one-year forward contract on this asset?

ST17-2. The spot exchange rate is \$1.6666/£. The risk-free rate is 4 percent in the United States and 6 percent in the United Kingdom. What is the forward exchange rate (assume a one-year contract)?

INTERNET RESOURCES

Note: *For updates to links, please go to the book's Web site at* http://megginson.swlearning.com

http://www.cbot.com—Web site of Chicago Board of Trade (CBOT), the oldest major futures exchange, which lists futures contracts for both commodities (corn, wheat, soybeans, gold) and financial instruments (two-, five-, ten-, and thirty-year Treasury bonds, Eurodollars).

http://www.cme.com—This is the site of the Chicago Mercantile Exchange, another leading market for derivative securities.

http://www.eurexchange.com—Web site of the Eurex futures exchange, which began in December 1996 as a joint venture between the Swiss Exchange and the Deutsche Börse, and within an amazingly short period of time emerged as the leading international futures market.

KEY TERMS

arbitrage
basis risk
closing futures price
cross-hedging
currency forward contracts
currency swap
economic exposure
financial engineering
fixed-for-floating currency swap
fixed-for-floating interest rate swap
forward price
forward rate
forward rate agreement (FRA)
fungibility
futures contract
initial margin
interest differential
interest rate caps
interest rate collar
interest rate floor
interest rate risk
interest rate swap
lifetime high price
lifetime low price
maintenance margin
margin account
marking-to-market
opening futures price
open interest
risk management
settlement date
settlement price
spot price
swap contract
tailing the hedge
transactions exposure

QUESTIONS AND PROBLEMS

Q17-1. Historically, what types of risk were the focus of most firms' risk-management practices?

Q17-2. Distinguish between the motivations for purchasing insurance and the motivations for hedging marketwide sources of risk.

Q17-3. Distinguish between transactions exposure and economic exposure.

Q17-4. In what way can hedging reduce the risk of financial distress? How might reducing the risk of financial distress increase firm value?

Q17-5. Explain how hedging can reduce a firm's tax liability.

Q17-6. Why do closely held firms tend to hedge more than firms with diffuse ownership?

Q17-7. How can hedging make it easier to evaluate a manager's performance?

Q17-8. What are the advantages of using exchange-traded derivatives to hedge a risk exposure? What are the advantages of over-the-counter derivatives?

Q17-9. Conceptually, how do we determine the fair forward price for an asset? What are the necessary assumptions to arrive at a fair forward price?

Q17-10. Conceptually, what are the differences between Equations 17.1, 17.2, and 17.3? Which equation would you use to determine the fair forward price for an asset that does not earn any income but is costly to store, such as gold or silver? How would you modify the equation?

Q17-11. Describe the features of a futures contract that make it more liquid than a forward contract.

Q17-12. Explain the features of a futures contract that make it have less credit risk than a forward contract.

Q17-13. Why is fungibility an important feature of futures contracts?

Q17-14. Describe the delivery process for futures contracts. Why does delivery rarely take place in futures contracts?

Q17-15. Why is a call option on an interest rate called an interest rate cap and a put option called an interest rate floor?

Q17-16. Explain how a fixed-for-floating swap can be considered a portfolio of forward contracts on six-month discount bonds.

Q17-17. Go to the CBOT Web site (http://www.cbot.com), and determine the contract specifications for soybean meal futures and ten-year U.S. Treasury note futures. Apart from the difference in the type of asset, what is the difference between the two contracts in terms of what qualifies as deliverable grades?

Q17-18. Go to the CBOT Web site (http://www.cbot.com), and determine the minimum initial margin requirements for speculators in the contracts traded on that exchange. Which contracts have the smallest margin requirements? Which contracts have the largest requirements? Why do you suppose these contracts have such different margin requirements?

PROBLEMS

P17-1. Suppose that an investor has agreed to pay $94,339.62 for a one-year discount bond in one year. Two years from now, the investor will receive the bond's face value of $100,000. The current effective annual risk-free rate of interest is 5.8 percent, and the current spot price for a two-year discount bond is $88,999.64. Has the investor agreed to pay too much or too little? How might an arbitrageur capitalize on this opportunity?

P17-2. Company A's stock will pay a dividend of $5 in three months and $6 in six months. The current stock price is $200, and the risk-free rate of interest is 7 percent per year with monthly compounding for all maturities. What is the fair forward price for a seven-month forward contract?

SMART SOLUTIONS

See the problem and solution explained step-by-step at SMARTFinance

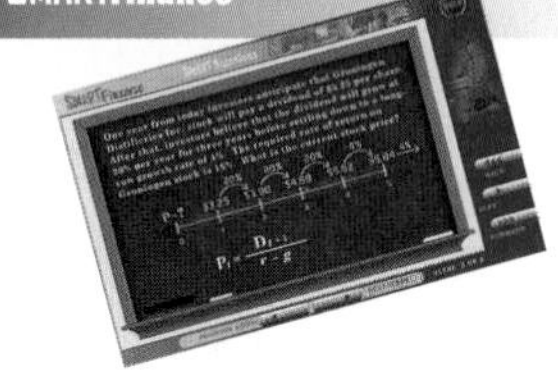

P17-3. The current price of gold is $288 per troy ounce. The cost of storing gold is $0.03/oz per month. Assuming an annual risk-free rate of interest of 12 percent compounded monthly, what is the approximate futures price of gold for delivery in four months?

P17-4. Following is the current yield to maturity on Treasury bills of various maturities:

Time to Maturity Months	Yield %
1	5.0
3	5.2
6	5.4
9	5.8

Assuming monthly compounding, what should the forward interest rate of a three-month T-bill be if it is to be delivered at the end of three months? What if it is to be delivered at the end of six months?

P17-5. Using the information in Table 17.2, determine whether the three-month forward rate on euros is fair if the annualized yield for risk-free borrowing over the next three months is 8 percent in Europe and 5 percent in the United States. If the price is not fair, how could you capitalize on the arbitrage opportunity? What is the potential profit? Assume monthly compounding for borrowing and lending.

P17-6. A U.S. automobile importer is expecting a shipment of custom-made cars from Britain in six months. Upon delivery, the importer will pay for the cars in pounds. Using the information in Table 17.2, suggest a hedging strategy for the importer. Explain the consequences for the spot market transaction and the forward market transaction if the $/£ spot exchange rate increases over the next six months.

P17-7. Suppose that KF Exports enters into an FRA with Interfirst Bank with a notional principal of $50 million and the following terms: in six months, if LIBOR is above 6 percent, KF will pay Interfirst according to the standard FRA formula. On the other hand, if LIBOR is less than 6 percent, Interfirst will pay KF. If LIBOR is 5.5 percent in six months, who pays and how much will the company pay? What if LIBOR is 6.5 percent?

P17-8. An investor purchases one gold futures contract for delivery in August 2004. Using the information in Table 17.3, determine the settle price for the contract in May 2004. What is the total futures price for the contract? If the settle price on the next trading day is $380/oz, will the investor have money deposited into his margin account or withdrawn? How much? Suppose that the investor eventually closes out the position by selling at $384/oz. How much is his profit or loss?

P17-9. Consider the following scenarios, determine how to hedge each scenario using bond futures, and comment on whether it would be appropriate to hedge the exposure.

a. A bond portfolio manager will be paid a large bonus if her $10 million portfolio earns 6 percent in the current fiscal year. She has done very well through the first nine months. However, she is concerned that interest rates might increase over the next few months.

b. The manager of a company is selling one of its warehouses. The deal will close in two months. The manager plans to buy six-month Treasury bills when the company receives payment for the warehouse space, but the manager is worried that interest rates might decline in the next two months.

c. Sam Blackwell plans to retire in a year. Upon retirement, he will be paid a lump sum based on the value of the securities in his defined-contribution retirement plan. Sam's portfolio consists largely of Treasury bonds, and he is worried that interest rates will be increasing in the coming year.

Options and Swaps

P17-10. Chipman Products Company will suffer an increase in borrowing costs if the thirteen-week Treasury bill rate increases in the next six months. Chipman Products is willing to accept the risk of small changes in the thirteen-week T-bill rate but wishes to avoid the potential losses associated with large changes. The company plans to hedge its risk exposure using an interest rate collar. If the company buys a call option on the thirteen-week T-bill rate with a strike price of 60 and sells a put option with a strike price of 50, describe how this strategy will limit the company's exposure to changes in the T-bill rate. The premium on the call is 0.75, and the premium on the put is 0.85. What is the company's profit (or loss) in the option market if the T-bill rate is 4.5 percent in five months? If the T-bill rate is 5.5 percent? If the T-bill rate is 6.5 percent?

P17-11. Go to the CBOT Web site (http://www.cbot.com), and determine the contract specifications for Dow Jones Industrial Average futures. Determine the current futures price for the next available contract month. What would your profit or loss be if you bought one contract today, and the Dow Jones Industrial Average increased by 100 points before the last settlement date?

P17-12. Company A, based in Switzerland, would like to borrow $10 million at a fixed rate of interest. Because the company is not well known, however, it has been unable to find a willing U.S. lender. Instead, the company can borrow SF17,825,000 at 11 percent per year for five years. Company B, based in the United States, would like to borrow SF17,825,000 for five years at a fixed rate of interest. It has not been able to find a Swiss lender. However, it has been offered a loan of $10 million at 9 percent per year. Five-year government bonds are yielding 9.5 percent and 8.5 percent in Switzerland and the United States, respectively. Suggest a currency swap that would net the financial intermediary 0.5 percent per year.

P17-13. Citibank and ABM Company enter into a five-year interest rate swap with a notional principal of $100 million and the following terms: every year for the next five years, ABM agrees to pay Citibank 6 percent and receive from Citibank LIBOR. Using the following information about LIBOR at the end of each of the next five years, determine the cash flows in the swap.

Year	LIBOR (%)
1	5.0
2	5.5
3	6.2
4	6.0
5	6.4

P17-14. Based on the type of swap ABM entered into in the previous problem, what type of liabilities do you think ABM has? Long-term or short-term?

THOMSON ONE Business School Edition

For instructions on using Thomson ONE, refer to the instructions provided with the Thomson ONE problems at the end of Chapters 1–6 or to "A Guide for Using Thomson ONE."

P17-15. Review Coca-Cola Company's (ticker: U:KO) most recent 10K filing. What types of risk does Coca-Cola hedge with derivative instruments? What does the filing say about the types of derivative instruments Coca-Cola uses to hedge these risks? If the filing does not say anything about the types of derivative instruments used, what would your choice of derivative instruments be?

Since these exercises depend upon real-time data, your answers will change continuously depending upon when you access the Internet to download your data.

MINICASE

Risk Management

Basic International Group Incorporated has been involved in international trade for the past four years. Recently, the CEO has come to realize that Basic needs better risk management, and he asks you to investigate ways to manage risk through hedging. You remember that derivative securities, including forwards, futures, options, and swaps, are the financial instruments commonly used for hedging and risk management. However, to gain more insight into risk management, you decide to answer the following questions.

ASSIGNMENT

1. What are the types of risk factors that a company faces?
2. If risk aversion cannot explain why firms choose to hedge, then what are their motivations?
3. Explain how a firm's management can limit risk exposure through using a forward contract. What types of forward contracts are available?
4. What are the differences between forward and futures contracts?
5. How do managers use futures contracts to limit risk exposure?
6. How do managers use options to limit risk exposure?
7. How do managers use swaps to limit risk exposure?

P A R T 6

Financial Planning and Management

A big part of what financial managers do in large corporations might be called "the control function." By this we mean that financial managers are responsible for making sure that the firm has sufficient cash balances to operate each day. This involves checking to see that the firm pays its bills on time (but not too early) and following up on credit sales to ensure that customers pay on time as well. These are the issues that we address in Part 6.

Chapter 18 describes the financial planning process. Financial planning methods vary widely, but almost all firms' financial plans have certain characteristics in common. Most firms plan over several horizons, with the detail of the plan decreasing as the planning horizon increases. That is, firms have very detailed plans that they use to project inflows and outflows of cash, as well as earnings, over the next year or two. Most companies also develop plans that look ahead two to five years or more. Financial plans help firms identify problems before they arise, and they help managers line up financing before cash shortfalls become critical.

Chapter 19 takes a closer look at how cash moves through a firm. Before a manufacturing firm makes a sale, it must purchase raw materials and begin manufacturing its product. It must also maintain work-in-process as well as finished goods inventories. Most firms sell to customers on credit, so even after making a sale, no cash comes in immediately. The cash conversion cycle illustrates how managers can track the length of time that it takes a firm to generate cash from selling its goods. Clearly, the amount of time a firm's goods spend in inventory, and how long the firm must wait before its customers pay for their orders play central roles in determining how quickly a firm generates cash. As with other financial decisions, when managers determine how much to invest in items such as inventories and receivables, they must weigh the marginal costs and benefits of those investments. Over time, information technology has enabled firms to invest less and less in these types of assets.

Firms hold cash balances for many reasons, and Chapter 20 examines the factors that firms consider when they decide how much cash to hold. Part of that decision revolves around the timing of the firm's cash disbursements, and that in turn depends on the terms under which the firm's suppliers grant it credit. Chapter 20 illustrates how the credit terms granted by suppliers contain an implicit interest rate, and when the firm decides to pay its suppliers determines its effective borrowing costs.

Financial Planning

OPENING FOCUS

LG Philips Plans to Spend $21.6 Billion for New Complex

Late in March 2004, LG Philips LCD Inc. announced its plan to spend $21.6 billion over the following ten years on a factory complex for flat-screen production. This announcement increased the firm's stake in the ongoing battle with Samsung Electronics Co. to lead worldwide flat-screen production. The company is a joint venture of LG Electronics, Inc. of South Korea and Philips Electronics NV of the Netherlands. Several components producers will also contribute to the complex, which will be located in Paju, north of Seoul.

The expansion was in response to Samsung's 2003 announcement that it planned to spend about $17 billion over seven years on factories to produce liquid-crystal display (LCD) screens that are used for computer monitors, cell phones, and TV sets. While the exact amounts of spending would likely change, the announcement seemed to signal that the South Korean giants, which controlled about half of the worldwide LCD-panel production, were planning to solidify the lead they had taken over Japan several years earlier.

LG Philips officials envisioned the Paju complex to eventually include a research center, several more factories, and room for suppliers to operate. "This will be the core site for the LCD industry," said Bon Joon Koo, chief executive for LG Philips. The aggressive production expansion plans were driven by the rocketing demand for LCD panels. During 2003, more LCD-based monitors were sold than conventional tube-based models. Future worldwide sales of LCD-based TV sets were expected to grow at a combined annual rate of 74 percent through 2007, when they would account for 14 percent of overall TV sales, according to iSuppli Corp., a research firm based in El Segundo, California.

The production capacity plans of LG Philips LCD Inc. demonstrate the importance of financial plans in allowing firms to achieve their growth potential and maintain their competitive position in a fast-growing and highly competitive product market. Without their announced new complex in Paju, it's unlikely that LG Philips would be able to maintain its share of the rapid growth predicted for LCD panels, and remain competitive with Samsung, its key rival. Although well-developed financial plans do not guarantee success, their absence can result in lost opportunities and competitiveness. Clearly, financial planning is an important perquisite to business success.

Source: Evan Ramstad, "LG Philips Raises the Stakes in Production of Flat Screens," *The Wall Street Journal* (March 19, 2004), p. B4.

LEARNING OBJECTIVES

After studying this chapter you should be able to:

- Understand the relationship between a firm's strategy and its plans and the roles that finance plays in constructing strategic plans;
- Describe the impact of growth on the firm's balance sheet and the role of the sustainable growth model as a planning device;
- Discuss the role of pro forma financial statements in the financial planning process and the shorthand approach for estimating external funds required;
- Explain the "plug figure" used in constructing a pro forma balance sheet and the information it provides in the financial planning process;
- Review the conservative, aggressive, and matching financing strategies that a firm might employ to fund the long-term trend and seasonal fluctuations in its business; and
- Describe the role of the cash budget in planning and monitoring the firm's cash inflows and outflows on a short-term basis.

In our experience, almost everyone working in a large corporation encounters two areas of corporate finance on a regular basis. The first area is justification of spending plans, or capital budgeting. Chapters 8 through 10 covered the essential elements of capital budgeting analysis that business professionals in any discipline should know. The second part of corporate finance that touches almost all functional groups in a firm is financial planning. Financial planning encompasses a wide array of activities: setting long-run strategic goals, preparing quarterly and annual budgets, and managing day-to-day fluctuations in cash balances. Financial planning is an additional cost of doing business that most firms believe is easily justified by the benefit of an improved chance of achieving its goal of creating value for its shareholders. No one with corporate work experience is completely unfamiliar with budgeting processes, but how budgets and other financial plans are compiled at the corporate level, how they tie together sometimes competing interests within the firm, and how they interact with the firm's strategic objectives can be something of a mystery.

In this chapter, we discuss various elements of a firm's financial planning processes. We emphasize both long-term and short-term financial planning. In Chapters 19 and 20, we consider the operational aspects of short-term financial decisions. The three chapters in Part 6 will demonstrate how firms' financial plans must balance the interests and objectives of different business units and functional areas. For example, in setting long-term strategic and financial goals, a firm must prioritize its desires to increase sales and market share; to increase, decrease, or maintain its exposure to financial risk; to achieve production efficiencies; to attract and retain capable employees; and to distribute cash to shareholders. In almost every instance, making incremental progress on one of these objectives means an incremental sacrifice on one or more of the other goals. Simply stated, these trade-offs are driven by the need to act only when the marginal benefits from greater progress on one objective exceed the marginal costs of sacrificing the achievement of another objective. Only when there is a *net benefit* from shifting resources between competing objectives will the firm's actions contribute toward achieving its goal of creating value for its shareholders. In Part 6, you will also learn how to make effective short-term financial decisions by considering the cost-benefit trade-offs with regard to the management of inventory, receivables, cash, payables, and liquidity.

SMART PRACTICES VIDEO

Jackie Sturm, Director of Finance for Technology and Manufacturing, Intel Corp.

"Once the product line business plan is completed, we move into our annual planning process, which is more of a tactical exercise."

See the entire interview at SMARTFinance

For better or worse, financial planning, particularly long-term planning, is more art than science—the connection between most financial planning models and the objective of shareholder wealth maximization is tenuous at best. The Comparative Corporate Finance insert on page 722 provides data that confirms the difficulty of making accurate macroeconomic forecasts. At one level, the advice we would give to a firm constructing a long-term plan is trivial—do whatever is necessary to invest in all positive-*NPV* projects. In practice, a variety of factors make following that advice a major challenge. CFOs usually tell us that they have many more projects with *NPV*s that appear to be positive than they can possibly undertake. Limits on capital, production capacity, human resources, and many other inputs make the planning process more complex than simply accepting all projects that look promising. In this chapter, we concede that the theoretical underpinnings of planning models are weak, and therefore we focus as much as possible on practice. That is, we attempt to describe how firms actually build both long-term and short-term financial plans rather than argue about how they should plan.

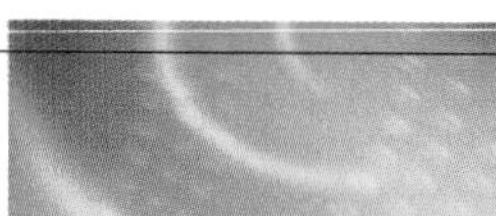

18.1 OVERVIEW OF THE PLANNING PROCESS

A long-term financial plan begins with strategy. Typically, the senior management team conducts an analysis of the markets in which the firm competes. Managers try to identify ways to protect and increase the firm's competitive advantage in those markets. For example, the first priority of a firm that competes by achieving the lowest production cost in an industry might be to determine whether it should make additional investments in manufacturing facilities to achieve even greater production efficiencies. Of course, being the low-cost producer is difficult if the firm's fixed assets are chronically underutilized. This type of firm, therefore, will spend a great deal of time and energy trying to forecast market demand and developing contingency plans for the possibility that the expected demand does not materialize. If a firm's competitive advantage derives from the value of its brand, it might begin by assessing whether new or expanded marketing programs might increase the value of its brand relative to those of its competitors.

Successful Long-Term Planning

Long-term planning requires more than paying close attention to a firm's existing markets. Even more important is the ability to identify and prioritize new market opportunities. Successful long-term planning means asking and answering questions such as the following:

- In what emerging markets might we have a sustainable competitive advantage?
- How can we leverage our competitive strengths across existing markets in which we currently do not compete?
- What threats to our current business exist, and how can we meet those threats?
- Where in the world should we produce? Where should we sell?
- Can we deploy resources more efficiently by exiting certain markets and using those resources elsewhere?

As the firm's senior managers develop answers to these questions, they construct a **strategic plan**, a multiyear action plan for the major investments and competitive initiatives that they believe will drive the future success of the enterprise.

strategic plan
A multiyear action plan for the major investments and competitive initiatives that a firm's senior managers believe will drive the future success of the enterprise.

The Role of Finance in Long-Term Planning

Finance plays several roles in this discussion. First, financial managers draw on a broad set of skills to assess the likelihood that a given strategic objective can be achieved. With respect to a major new investment proposal, the first question to ask is probably not "What does it cost?" or "Can we afford it?" Rather, drawing on their experience and knowledge outside the realm of finance, managers should ask, "Does this investment make sense?" or "Is there a good reason to expect this proposal to generate wealth for our shareholders?"

Second, the responsibility to assess the feasibility of a strategic action plan given a firm's existing and prospective sources of funding falls primarily to the finance function. Though some corporate giants, such as Microsoft or Intel, hold such vast amounts of cash that they are nearly unconstrained in terms of their ability to make large, new investments, for most companies financial constraints are more binding. Given a broad set of strategic objectives, financial managers must determine whether the firm's ability to generate cash internally plus its ability to raise cash externally will be sufficient to fund new spending initiatives. As we have seen, firms that pay dividends are extremely reluctant to cut them, so financial analysts generally treat expected dividend payments as a factor that limits a firm's ability to make new investments. Similarly, if fulfilling strategic objectives will require that a firm accept a significant increase in leverage, it is finance's role to communicate that trade-off to the top management team. We will see in the next section that financial managers have several tools at their disposal that enable them to highlight the trade-offs firms face when setting growth targets.

Third, finance clearly plays an important control function as firms implement their strategic plans. Financial analysts prepare and update cash budgets to make sure that firms do not unknowingly slip into a liquidity crisis. The frequency with which these budgets are constructed and monitored depends on several factors, including the firm's current level of liquidity, its access to external funding sources, and the volatility of demand for its products. At an even more detailed level, analysts monitor individual items in the cash budget, such as changes in inventories and receivables (our focus in Chapter 19) and changes in payables (our focus in Chapter 20). Here, too, financial managers must evaluate trade-offs. For example, a firm's sales force generally prefers that the firm maintain sufficient inventories to ensure that no customer has to wait for an order to be filled. Managers responsible for production want the firm to hold inventories of raw materials to minimize interruptions in manufacturing. But in both cases, holding higher inventories involves additional costs that may lower the firm's profitability.

Fourth, a major contribution of finance to the strategic planning process involves risk management. When a firm's strategy calls for making new investments in overseas markets (either producing or selling abroad), the firm faces a new set of risk exposures. The finance function is charged with managing these exposures and ensuring, to the extent possible, that the firm takes those risks that it believes it has a comparative advantage in taking and that it hedges risks for which it has no advantage. Similarly, more than in any other functional area, the job of finance is to identify problems that could develop in the future if the firm's strategic plans unfold in unexpected ways. Developing these "problem scenarios" and options for dealing with them when they occur is an important part of finance's risk-management responsibility.

In this chapter, we focus primarily on the second and third roles just described. The next section discusses the financial tools that help managers determine the trade-offs they face when setting growth objectives for the future.

COMPARATIVE CORPORATE FINANCE

Public Versus Private Forecasts

In corporate finance, many planning processes begin with a sales forecast. One of the more important pieces of information that firms use to develop their forecasts is an overall assessment of how the macroeconomy will perform. Managers especially worry about the prospect of an economic recession, and so many firms track economic forecasts produced both by governmental bodies and by private economic research firms. Some have argued that forecasts produced by private entities should be more accurate than those produced in public institutions. Forecasts generated in the public sector might be influenced by political factors, but private sector predictions should be unbiased.

A recent study produced at the International Monetary Fund (IMF) tests that claim by comparing the ability of private and public sector forecasts to predict recessions in sixty-three different countries. The study tabulates a "consensus forecast" by collecting numerous private sector forecasts and averaging them. The study then compares the consensus to a variety of forecasts published by organizations such as the IMF, the World Bank, and other public institutions. Two important conclusions emerge from this research.

First, private sector forecasts perform no better or worse than forecasts produced by the IMF and other similar agencies. Second, and more troubling for managers putting together their financial planning models, both public and private sector forecasts are much too optimistic, especially leading up to recessions. Pooling together the data from all countries in the study, there were sixty recessions that economic forecasters might have predicted. Forecasters managed to predict just two of these episodes as early as April the year before they occurred, and only twenty of the recessions were predicted as late as April of the year in which the recession actually started. As the accompanying table shows, virtually all of the forecasts, including those that were calling for a recession, were too optimistic and predicted a growth rate higher than what the economy ultimately produced. For example, in April of the year prior to a recession, the average forecast predicted that the economy would grow 5.76 percent faster than it actually did grow the following year. The good news, if you can call it that, is that the bias toward optimism in these forecasts was smaller for forecasts that were looking less than one year ahead. Knowing that professional forecasters can foresee a recession only when one is imminent is of little comfort to managers who must build long-range plans around their sales forecasts.

Performance of Forecasts Prior to 60 Recessions in 63 Countries

	Year Prior to Recession		Year Recession Began	
	April	October	April	October
Number of recessions predicted	2	3	20	47
Number of optimistic forecasts	60	60	59	50
Average forecast error—all countries	5.76%	4.87%	2.91%	0.89%
For industrial countries	3.77%	3.15%	1.84%	0.81%
For developing countries	10.31%	8.62%	4.89%	1.05%

Source: "How accurate are private sector forecasts? Cross-country evidence from consensus forecasts of output growth," by Prakash Loungani, *International Journal of Forecasting*, Vol. 17, No. 3 (July–Sept 2001), pp. 419–432.

CONCEPT REVIEW QUESTIONS

1. A company decides to compete by making a major investment to modernize production facilities. Describe two ways in which meeting this objective might force a firm to sacrifice other objectives.

2. Firm A competes in a market in which the demand for its product and its selling price are highly unpredictable. Firm B competes in a market in which these factors are much more stable. Which firm probably creates and monitors cash budgets more frequently?

18.2 PLANNING FOR GROWTH

Sustainable Growth

Most firms strive to grow over time, and most firms prefer rapid growth to slow growth. Of course, rapid growth is not wealth maximizing for all firms at all times, and a great deal of financial research has studied why firms place so much emphasis on growth, even at times to the detriment of shareholders. For the moment, we lay aside the question of whether growth creates or destroys shareholder value. Instead, we want to demonstrate a simple model that highlights the trade-offs that firms must weigh when they choose to grow. These trade-offs depend on several factors, including how rapidly the firm plans to grow, how profitable its existing business is, how much of its earnings it retains and how much it pays out to shareholders, how efficiently it manages its assets, and how much financial leverage it is willing to bear.

Defining Growth. First, let us define what we mean by "growth." A firm's growth could be measured by increases in its market value, its asset base, the number of people it employs, or any number of other values. For now, let us imagine that a firm establishes a growth target in terms of sales. That is, when we say that a firm plans to grow next year by 10 percent, we mean that it hopes to achieve a 10 percent increase in sales. Our experience suggests that *most firms define and measure growth targets in terms of sales*, so we will adopt that convention as well.

With that definition in mind, think about what growth means for a firm in terms of its balance sheet. An increase in sales probably requires additional investments in assets. Certainly, we would anticipate that increased sales volume would require additional investments in current assets, such as inventories and receivables; but over time, increases in sales will also require new investments in fixed assets, such as production capacity and office space. As a shortcut, let us assume that a firm's total asset turnover ratio, the ratio of sales (S) divided by total assets (A), remains constant through time. In other words, any increase in sales will be matched by a comparable percentage increase in assets.

Because the balance sheet equation must hold, increases in liabilities and shareholders' equity must equal the increase in assets. In what forms do we expect increases in liabilities and shareholders' equity to occur? In previous chapters, we learned that most companies issue new common shares very infrequently, so we will rule that out as a potential source of new financing. As with inventories and receivables, accounts payable should increase because higher sales volume means higher purchases. We might also expect to see higher accruals and higher short-term liabilities of other types. Similarly, if a firm's business is profitable, its equity account will increase, even if it does not issue any new stock, by the amount of earnings it retains. Figure 18.1 illustrates that the growth in assets must equal growth in these liability and equity accounts over time.

Developing the Sustainable Growth Model. The **sustainable growth model** takes the balance sheet identity, adds to it a few assumptions, and derives an expression that determines how rapidly a firm can grow while maintaining a balance between its outflows (increases in assets) and inflows (increases in liabilities and equity) of cash. Specifically, the sustainable growth model assumes the following:

sustainable growth model Derives an expression that determines how rapidly a firm can grow while maintaining a balance between its outflows (increases in assets) and inflows (increases in liabilities and equity) of cash.

1. The firm has only common stock equity (E) and will issue no new shares of common stock next year.
2. The firm's total asset turnover ratio, S/A, remains constant.
3. The firm pays out a constant fraction, d, of its earnings as dividends.
4. The firm maintains a constant assets-to-equity ratio, A/E.
5. The firm's net profit margin, m, is constant.

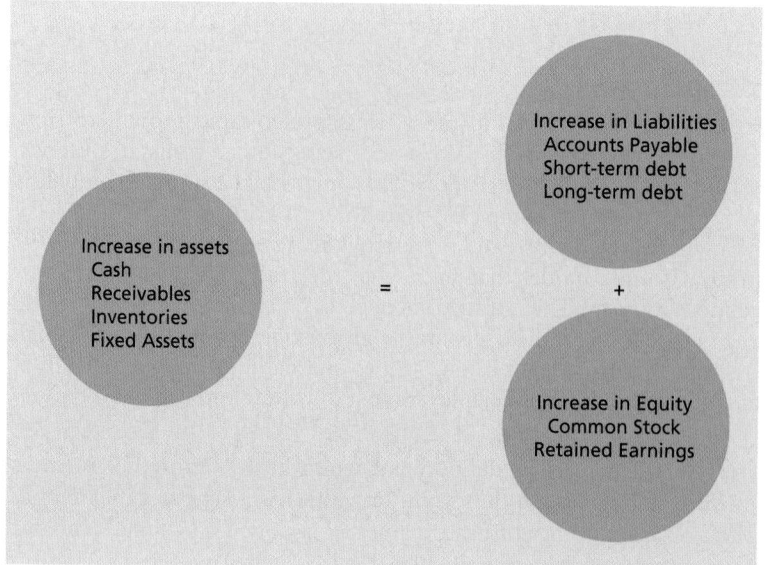

Figure 18.1
Sustainable Growth Equality

As a firm grows, it must invest in new assets to support increased sales volume. The investments in new assets must be financed with some combination of increased liabilities and increased equity.

Consider a firm that wants to increase sales next period by g percent. If total assets in the current period equal A, and if the total asset turnover ratio remains constant, then assets must increase in the next period by gA. This represents the change in the left-hand side of the firm's balance sheet next period. That change must be met with an equal change on the right-hand side.

Given sales this period of S, a net profit margin (in this case, defined as net income/sales) equal to m, and a dividend payout ratio of d, we can determine the firm's retained earnings next period:

$$S(m)(1+g)(1-d)$$

The product of S and m yields net profits in the current year. Multiplying this product times $(1 + g)$ results in next year's profits, and multiplying this result times $(1 - d)$ gives next year's retained earnings. This is the amount by which the equity component of the balance sheet will grow. Next, observe that the ratio of assets to equity (total assets to common stock equity) equals 1 plus the ratio of total liabilities, L, to shareholders' equity:

$$A = E + L$$

$$\frac{A}{E} = \frac{E+L}{E} = 1 + \frac{L}{E}$$

The assumption that the firm maintains a constant assets-to-equity ratio is therefore equivalent to an assumption that the ratio of liabilities to equity remains constant. Therefore, for each dollar of earnings that the company retains, it can borrow an additional L/E dollars to keep the mix of debt and equity constant. For example, if a firm finances half of its assets with debt and half with equity, then the ratio L/E equals 1.0. If the firm retains \$1 million in earnings in a given year, it can afford to borrow an additional \$1 million to maintain the desired mix of debt and equity. Therefore, the increase in liabilities next year simply equals the product of next year's retained earnings and the ratio of liabilities to equity:

$$[S(m)(1+g)(1-d)](L/E)$$

Finally, if the increase in assets must match the increase in the sum of liabilities and equity, we can write the following:

$$\underset{\uparrow \text{assets}}{gA} = \underset{\uparrow \text{ret. earnings}}{S(m)(1+g)(1-d)} + \underset{\uparrow \text{liabilities}}{[S(m)(1+g)(1-d)](L/E)}$$

$$= \underset{\uparrow (\text{equity} + \text{liabilities})}{[S(m)(1+g)(1-d)](1+L/E)}$$

The insight of the sustainable growth model is that there will be some rate of growth, g^*, that keeps the outflows and inflows of funds in balance. This *sustainable growth rate,* calculated from the preceding equation, is represented as follows:

$$g^* = \frac{m(1-d)\dfrac{A}{E}}{\dfrac{A}{S} - m(1-d)\dfrac{A}{E}} \qquad \text{(Eq. 18.1)}$$

Notice how each of the key variables in Equation 18.1 affects the sustainable growth rate. If a firm's net profit margin (m) increases, the numerator rises and the denominator falls, so g^* increases. Therefore, generating a higher quantity of profits per dollar of sales provides fuel for a higher growth rate. Similarly, an increase in the ratio of assets to equity (*A/E*), which can occur only if the firm is willing to accept higher financial leverage, also increases the sustainable growth rate. Firms willing to borrow more can grow more rapidly. If a firm can increase its total asset turnover ratio (*S/A*), then the ratio of *A/S* falls and the sustainable growth rate rises. Firms that manage assets more efficiently and generate higher sales volume per dollar of assets can achieve more rapid growth. Finally, a reduction in dividend payouts (d) also tends to increase g^*. When firms retain more earnings, they can finance faster growth.

APPLYING THE MODEL

In 2002, Yahoo! Inc. reported the following financial data:

Sales	\$ 953.1 million
Net income	\$ 42.8 million
Total assets	\$2,790.2 million
Total equity	\$2,262.3 million
Dividends	\$ 0

From these figures, we can determine that Yahoo!'s net profit margin was 4.49 percent, its assets-to-equity ratio was 1.23, its asset turnover ratio was 0.342 (which implies an assets-to-sales ratio of 2.93), and its dividend payout ratio was 0.0. Plugging these values into Equation 18.1 yields a sustainable growth rate of 1.92 percent. For Yahoo! this meant that the company could increase sales by 1.92 percent without issuing new shares of common stock and without changing asset turnover, dividend policy, profit margins, or leverage.

Interpreting the Sustainable Growth Model. It is as important to understand what the sustainable growth model *does not* say as it is to grasp what it does say. From the previous calculation, should we assume that Yahoo! managers should set as their firm's growth target an increase in sales of 1.92 percent, equal to the sustainable growth rate? Not at all. Yahoo! managers should decide what rate of growth maximizes shareholder wealth, and then they should use the sustainable growth model as a planning device to help them prepare for the consequences of their growth plans. For example, suppose that Yahoo! decides that it is best for their shareholders if the firm grows more rapidly than 1.92 percent. To do so, Yahoo! must alter one or more of the baseline assumptions of the model. Yahoo! could try to find ways to raise its profit margin, to increase its asset turnover, or to increase leverage. Yahoo! does not pay dividends, so it cannot use a dividend cut to increase growth.

APPLYING THE MODEL

In fact, from 2002 to 2003, Yahoo!'s sales increased by roughly 71 percent, almost 37 times (71 percent ÷ 1.92 percent) the sustainable rate. The sustainable growth model would suggest that to finance this rapid growth, Yahoo! must have achieved some combination of higher profit margins, faster asset turnover, and increased financial leverage. Indeed, by the end of 2003, Yahoo!'s net profit margin had increased by 226 percent (from 4.49% to 14.64%), and its assets-to-equity ratio increased by nearly 11 percent (from 1.23 to 1.36). These two changes provided the fuel for rapid growth, even though Yahoo!'s asset turnover ratio decreased by roughly 20 percent (from 0.342 to 0.274).

The sustainable growth model gives managers a kind of shorthand projection that ties together growth objectives and financing needs. It provides hints about the levers that managers must pull to achieve growth above the sustainable rate. It also identifies some of the financial benefits of growing more slowly than the sustainable rate. A firm that expects to grow at a rate below g^* can plan to reduce leverage or asset turnover, or it can increase dividends. Again, we emphasize that the model does not say anything about how fast the firm *should* grow.

The sustainable growth concept also highlights tensions that can develop as firms pursue multiple objectives simultaneously. For example, the compensation of the vice president (VP) of marketing may be tied to generating additional sales volume, whereas the CFO's compensation may depend on maintaining the firm's credit rating. We have seen that one way to finance faster growth is to increase leverage, so the goals of increasing sales while maintaining the current degree of leverage may be difficult to achieve simultaneously. For the firm to achieve faster sales growth, the marketing function may indicate that the firm should offer a wider array of products, but doing so may result in lower inventory turns and hence reduced total asset turnover. If the firm is unwilling to increase leverage, and if expanding the product line means reducing asset turnover, then meeting the sales target will depend on improving profit margins or cutting dividend payouts.

The primary advantage of the sustainable growth model is its simplicity. However, the financial planning process generally involves more complex projections. These projections are usually embodied in a set of pro forma income statements and balance sheets that firms use to provide a benchmark against which future performance will be judged. Let us now turn to the creation of these statements.

Pro Forma Financial Statements

pro forma financial statements
A forecast of what a firm expects its income statement and balance sheet to look like a year or two ahead.

Periodically, firms produce **pro forma financial statements**, which are forecasts of what they expect their income statement and balance sheet to look like a year or two ahead. Occasionally, firms use these statements to communicate their plans to outside investors (such as at the time of an IPO or earnings announcement), but most of the time managers construct these statements for internal planning and control purposes.

By making projections of sales volume, profits, fixed asset requirements, working capital needs, and sources of financing, the firm can establish goals to which compensation may be tied, and it can predict any liquidity problems with enough lead time to have additional financing sources available when needed.

The Sales Forecast. The process of creating pro forma financial statements varies from firm to firm, but there are some common elements. For example, most pro forma statements begin with a sales forecast. The sales forecast may be derived in either a "top-down" or "bottom-up" approach. **Top-down sales forecasts** rely heavily on macroeconomic and industry forecasts. Some firms use complex statistical models or subscribe to forecasts produced by firms specializing in econometric modeling. In the top-down approach, senior managers establish a firmwide objective for increased sales. Next, individual divisions or business units receive targets that may not be identical but that collectively aggregate to achieve the firm's overall growth target. Division heads pass down sales targets to product line managers and other smaller-scale units. Again, the sales targets will vary across units within the division, but they must add up to achieve the divisional goal.

top-down sales forecast
A sales forecast that relies heavily on macroeconomic and industry forecasts.

Firms that use a **bottom-up sales forecast** begin by talking with customers. Sales personnel try to assess demand in the coming year on a customer-by-customer basis. These figures are added up across sales territories, product lines, and divisions to arrive at the overall sales forecast for the company. Bottom-up forecasting approaches generally do not rely on mathematical and statistical models.

bottom-up sales forecast
A sales forecast that relies on the assessment by sales personnel of demand in the coming year on a customer-by-customer basis.

Not surprisingly, many firms use a blend of these two approaches. For example, a firm may generate a set of assumptions regarding the macroeconomic environment to which all divisions must adhere, but forecasts can still be generated from the customer level and aggregated up. Some firms produce two sets of forecasts, one that uses a statistical approach and another that relies on customer feedback. Senior managers then compare the two forecasts to see how far apart they are before setting a final sales objective.

Constructing Pro Forma Statements. Starting with the sales forecast, financial analysts construct pro forma income statements and balance sheets using a mix of facts and assumptions. For example, if a firm's strategic plan calls for major investments in fixed assets, the analyst will incorporate those projections in the forecast of the firm's total fixed asset requirements, as well as in the forecast of depreciation expense on the income statement. In the absence of any specific knowledge of capital spending plans, an analyst may assume that total fixed assets will remain at a fixed percentage relative to sales or total assets, and that assumption in turn would drive the depreciation line item on the income statement.

SMART PRACTICES VIDEO

John Eck, President of Broadcast and Network Operations, NBC

"We put together assumptions . . . that we believe the whole company should follow, and then we leave it up to each division to give us their forecast."

See the entire interview at **SMARTFinance**

In a similar fashion, an analyst can make projections for line items that vary with sales volume. For example, by assuming a constant gross profit margin, the analyst can estimate cost of goods sold directly from the sales forecast. When firms construct pro forma statements by extending that logic to all income statement and balance sheet accounts, assuming that all items grow in proportion to sales, they are using the **percentage-of-sales method**. This is a convenient way to construct pro forma statements, and it is usually a good starting point when making financial projections. However, on the balance sheet, items such as receivables, inventory, and payables typically increase with sales, though not always in a linear fashion. For example, a company with $100 billion in sales may not need 100 times as much inventory as a firm with $1 billion in sales.

percentage-of-sales method
Constructing pro forma statements by assuming that all items grow in proportion to sales.

plug figure
A line item on the pro forma balance sheet that represents an account that can be adjusted after all other projections are made, so that the balance sheet balances.

In constructing pro forma statements, analysts usually leave one line item on the balance sheet as a **plug figure**, and they adjust this account after making all their other projections so that the balance sheet will balance. For example, the analyst may make projections for all asset, liability, and equity accounts except for the cash balance. When the projections are complete, the analyst simply adjusts the cash account to make the balance sheet balance. Alternatively, the analyst might leave a short-term liability account open to serve as the plug figure. The line item representing the amount borrowed on a bank line of credit, for instance, could be used to bring the right-hand and left-hand sides of the balance sheet into equality once the projections are complete.

APPLYING THE MODEL

Table 18.1 shows the 2006 income statement and balance sheet for Zinsmeister Shoe Corporation. We will use this historical information plus the following assumptions to generate pro forma financial statements for 2007.

1. Zinsmeister plans to increase sales by 30 percent in 2007.
2. The company's gross profit margin will remain at 35 percent.
3. Operating expenses will equal 10 percent of sales as they did in 2006.
4. Zinsmeister pays 10 percent interest on both its long-term debt and its credit line.
5. Zinsmeister will invest an additional $20 million in fixed assets in 2007, which will increase depreciation expense from $10 million to $15 million in 2007.
6. The company faces a 35 percent tax rate.
7. The company plans to increase cash holdings by $1 million next year.
8. Accounts receivable equal 8.5 percent of sales.
9. Inventories equal 10 percent of sales.
10. Accounts payable equal 12 percent of cost of goods sold.
11. The company will repay an additional $5 million in long-term debt in 2007.
12. The company will pay out 50 percent of its net income as a cash dividend.
13. The company plans to use its credit line as the *plug figure*.

From this set of assumptions and the data in Table 18.1, we can construct the pro forma statements for 2007 shown in Table 18.2. First, Zinsmeister's sales increase to $325 million. Cost of goods sold and operating expenses increase 30 percent over the prior year (hitting the percentage-of-sales assumptions above). Interest expense is a tricky item. To begin, assume that Zinsmeister will maintain its $5 million balance on its credit line and will retire the current portion of long-term debt. This means that its total outstanding debt will be $25 million. At 10 percent, interest expense should equal $2.5 million. As we will see, that assumption may change as we continue to build the statements.

Putting these figures together in the pro forma income statement, we see that Zinsmeister earns a net profit of just over $41 million, half of which it pays out to shareholders. Next, build the pro forma balance sheet. Cash is given at $11 million ($10 million in 2006 plus $1 million increase). Accounts receivable and inventory increase with sales as stated, so current assets increase to $71.125 million. With the additional investment in fixed assets of $20 million, less 2007's depreciation expense, net fixed assets grow to $65 million, so total assets equal $136.125 million.

On the right-hand side, accounts payable increases with sales, the current portion of long-term debt remains at $5 million, total long-term debt declines $5 million, and common stock does not change. The retained earnings figure for 2007 equals the 2006 figure plus half of 2007's net income. Zinsmeister uses its

Table 18.1
Financial Statements of Zinsmeister Shoe Corporation for 2006 ($ in thousands)

Zinsmeister Shoe Corporation Balance Sheet as of December 31, 2006

Assets		Liabilities and Equity	
Cash	$ 10,000	Accounts payable	$ 19,500
Accounts receivable	21,250	Credit line	5,000
Inventory	25,000	Current long-term debt	5,000
Current assets	$ 56,250	Current liabilities	$ 29,500
Gross fixed assets	$ 80,000	Long-term debt	$ 20,000
Less: Accumulated depreciation	20,000	Common stock	$ 20,200
Net fixed assets	$ 60,000	Retained earnings	$ 46,550
Total assets	$116,250	Total liabilities and equity	$116,250

Zinsmeister Shoe Corporation Income Statement for the Year Ended December 31, 2006

Sales	$250,000
Less: Cost of goods sold	162,500
Gross profit	$ 87,500
Less: Operating expenses	25,000
Less: Interest expense	3,000
Less: Depreciation expense	10,000
Pretax income	$ 49,500
Less: Taxes	17,325
Net income	$ 32,175

Table 18.2
Pro Forma Financial Statements for Zinsmeister Shoe Corporation for 2007 ($ in thousands)

Zinsmeister Shoe Corporation Pro Forma Balance Sheet as of December 31, 2007

Assets		Liabilities and Equity	
Cash	$ 11,000	Accounts payable	$ 25,350
Accounts receivable	27,625	Credit line	3,306
Inventory	32,500	Current long-term debt	5,000
Current assets	$ 71,125	Current liabilities	$ 33,656
Gross fixed assets	$100,000	Long-term debt	$ 15,000
Less: Accumulated depreciation	35,000	Common stock	$ 20,200
Net fixed assets	$ 65,000	Retained earnings	$ 67,269
Total assets	$136,125	Total liabilities and equity	$136,125

Zinsmeister Shoe Corporation Pro Forma Income Statement for the Year Ended December 31, 2007

Sales	$325,000
Less: Cost of goods sold	211,250
Gross profit	$113,750
Less: Operating expenses	32,500
Less: Interest expense	2,500
Less: Depreciation expense	15,000
Pretax income	$ 63,750
Less: Taxes	22,312
Net income	$ 41,438
Dividends	$ 20,719

credit line as the *plug figure*. That is, given all the assumptions so far, the credit line will decline from $5 million to $3.306 million because that is the figure necessary to keep assets in balance with liabilities and equity. However, because the credit line declines, our estimate of interest expense in the income state-ment is too high. Recall that we predicted interest expense of $2.5 million based on a 10 percent interest rate on total outstanding debt of $25 million. The pro forma balance sheet now shows long-term and short-term debt of just $23.306 million, so interest expense falls to $2.33 million. A decline in interest expense leads to an increase in profits and retained earnings. Higher retained earnings means that the line of credit can be reduced even more, and the cycle repeats. To find the amount of borrowing on the credit line and the corresponding interest expense that reconciles the balance sheet with the income statement, an analyst would need to use an iterative approach, such as *Excel*'s Solver function.

Nonetheless, the bottom line for Zinsmeister is that its pro forma outlook is quite good. If the company achieves its sales growth target and keeps expenses and working capital accounts in line with historical norms, it can simultaneously invest $20 million in new fixed assets and reduce its outstanding interest-bearing debt. In one sense, that conclusion is hardly surprising. If we take the 2006 data for Zinsmeister and plug it into Equation 18.1, we find that the company's sustainable growth rate is 31.8 percent. Therefore, the firm's target growth rate of 30 percent should leave it with some "financial slack." Going through the added steps to build pro forma statements provides the firm with a lot more information than the sustainable growth rate does. With the figures in Tables 18.1 and 18.2 programmed into a spreadsheet, analysts could easily study the effects of changes in any of the assumptions on Zinsmeister's ability to pay down debt or perhaps identify a need to increase the credit line balance.

A Shorthand Approach for Estimating External Funds Required. Equation 18.2 uses the notation defined earlier to present another shorthand approach for estimating the amount of external financing that a firm will require in the future. The equation states that the *external funds required*, *EFR*, are a function of three factors. The first term in the equation, $(A \div S)\Delta S$, indicates the additional investment in assets required for a firm if it plans to maintain its total asset turnover ratio and increase the dollar volume of sales by ΔS. The second term measures the inflow of funds available to finance this growth, assuming that the relationship between a firm's sales and its spontaneous liabilities (in this case, simply accounts payable) remains constant. The third term captures the additional financing inflows that the firm creates internally through retained earnings:

$$EFR = \frac{A}{S}\Delta S - \frac{AP}{S}\Delta S - mS(1+g)(1-d) \qquad \text{(Eq. 18.2)}$$

If we apply this shorthand calculation to Zinsmeister, we can determine its external funds required (in thousands of dollars):

$$EFR = \frac{\$116{,}250}{\$250{,}000}(\$75{,}000) - \frac{\$19{,}500}{\$250{,}000}(\$75{,}000) - \left(\frac{\$32{,}175}{\$250{,}000}\right)\$250{,}000(1+0.30)(1-0.50) = \$8{,}111$$

SMART PRACTICES VIDEO

Daniel Carter, Chief Financial Officer of Charlotte Russe

"We use information on our expectations to manage expectations of investors."

See the entire interview at SMARTFinance

Under the assumptions of this model, Zinsmeister will require additional external funding of \$8.1 million. In the pro forma projections in Table 18.2, Zinsmeister's total external financing actually declined by \$6.7 million.[1] Why the discrepancy? Closer examination of the pro forma statements reveals that several of the assumptions in Equation 18.2 do not hold when we conduct a more complete analysis. For instance, from 2006 to 2007, Zinsmeister's ratio of assets to sales is not constant, as the equation assumes; instead, the ratio declines from 0.465 to 0.419. Zinsmeister is increasing sales more rapidly than assets, so its funding needs are actually less than Equation 18.2 assumes. The apparent need for external funding revealed by Equation 18.2 turns into a financial surplus when we build projections on an account-by-account basis as in Table 18.2.

Some Concluding Comments. This discussion has presented two important points. First, shorthand approaches such as the sustainable growth model or the equation for determining **external funds required** help managers look ahead to determine whether they should expect a scarcity or a surplus of financial resources given the firm's growth objectives. Second, a more complete picture of a firm's funding requirements can be constructed by building pro forma balance sheets and income statements, leaving one variable on the balance sheet as a plug figure. Managers can use any of these models to avoid unpleasant financial surprises a year or two ahead.

external funds required The expected shortage or surplus of financial resources, given the firm's growth objectives.

Besides planning for growth that will occur over a period of years, companies also construct financial plans with shorter time horizons. These plans generally focus on temporary cash surpluses or deficits that firms face because of seasonal fluctuations in transactions volume. The next section examines this dimension of financial planning.

CONCEPT REVIEW QUESTIONS

3. Explain the difference between a firm's *sustainable growth rate* and its optimal growth rate. In what circumstances is a firm's optimal growth rate likely to exceed its sustainable rate, and under what conditions would you expect the opposite to be true?

4. Current asset accounts, especially cash and inventory, usually increase at a rate slightly less than the growth rate in sales. Why? If true, what is the implication of this fact for the *sustainable growth model*?

18.3 PLANNING AND CONTROL

Short-Term Financing Strategies

Several factors cause a firm's sales volume to fluctuate over time. In the previous section, we observed that most firms establish growth as one of their long-term objectives. Therefore, when we look at the sales volume generated by a particular company historically, it is not unusual to observe a distinct upward trend. However, during a single year, many firms experience sharp quarter-to-quarter sales changes due to seasonal factors. Construction-related businesses generate much higher volume in the summer than they do in the winter. In contrast, toy companies experience peak volume in the winter.

Therefore, because sales volume tends to fluctuate around a long-term upward trend, we expect to observe the same pattern when we examine a firm's total assets over time. As sales volume grows, so does the firm's need for current and fixed

1. The figure in Table 18.2 includes a \$5 million reduction in long-term debt and a \$1.7 million (\$5.0 million – \$3.3 million) reduction in the line of credit. The figure in this equation is still imprecise because the interest expense and outstanding debt figures in Table 18.2 are not fully reconciled.

assets. During the year, a firm's investment in current assets will tend to rise and fall with sales, and this seasonal pattern creates temporary cash surpluses and deficits that the firm must manage. In the remainder of this section, we use relevant data for Hershey Foods to demonstrate alternative financing strategies.

Hershey Foods' Quarterly Sales and Total Current Assets. Panel A of Figure18.2 plots quarterly sales figures for Hershey Foods from 1992 through the fourth quarter of 2003. Hershey's fiscal year matches the calendar year, so its quarterly income statements report sales for quarters ending in March, June, September, and December each year. For Hershey, sales usually peak in the third or fourth quarter of each year, whereas sales troughs typically occur in the second quarter. Panel A of Figure 18.2 also reveals a gradual upward trend in Hershey sales, at least from 1992 to 1999. That growth trend leveled off from 2000 to 2003 with the U.S. economic recession.

Panel B of Figure 18.2 plots Hershey's quarterly total current assets over the same period. The patterns closely match those in Panel A. Hershey's current assets show the same seasonal pattern (with a lag of one quarter) and the same upward trend that the company's sales follow. Hershey builds current assets, mostly inventory and receivables, during the third and fourth quarters of each year, and it draws down these items during the first and second quarters.

Because Hershey's current assets fluctuate around a long-term upward trend, we can think of the company's current assets as containing both a temporary and a permanent component. The temporary component reflects the differences between the seasonal peaks and troughs of Hershey's business, and the permanent component represents the sizeable investment in current assets that Hershey maintains, even during the quarters when business is slow. Hershey's fixed assets (not shown in the figure) do not exhibit the seasonal pattern that sales and current assets do, but fixed assets do follow the long-term upward trend, essentially following the long-term growth in Hershey's sales.

Alternative Financing Strategies. What financing strategies might Hershey employ to fund both the long-term trend and the seasonal fluctuations in its business? First, Hershey might adopt a **conservative strategy**, making sure that it has enough long-term financing to cover both its permanent investments in fixed and current assets and the additional seasonal investments in current assets that it makes during various quarters each year. For example, Hershey might issue long-term bonds to generate enough cash to cover all its cash needs for several years. If Hershey followed this type of strategy, represented graphically by the yellow line in Panel B of Figure 18.2, it would typically have a cash surplus, drawing down that surplus only when business volume reaches its peak during the third and fourth quarters each year. Hershey will invest its excess cash balances in marketable securities. We describe this strategy as conservative because it minimizes the risk that Hershey will experience a liquidity crisis during peak quarters. However, keep in mind that large investments in cash and marketable securities are not likely to make Hershey shareholders rich.[2] Furthermore, because the term structure of interest rates (the *yield curve*) is typically upward sloping, Hershey will generally pay higher interest rates on its long-term debt than it would pay if it were willing to borrow on a short-term basis.

conservative strategy
When a company makes sure that it has enough long-term financing to cover its permanent investments in fixed and current assets as well as the additional seasonal investments in current assets that it makes during the various quarters each year.

[2] Companies sometimes argue that a large cash reserve is a strategic asset because it enables the firm to make acquisitions quickly as opportunities arise. We agree that, in principle, a cash reserve could have strategic value, but it also enables managers to make value-reducing investments without facing the discipline of raising money in the capital markets. As you will learn in Chapter 22, research suggests that managers of acquiring firms generally do not create wealth for their shareholders.

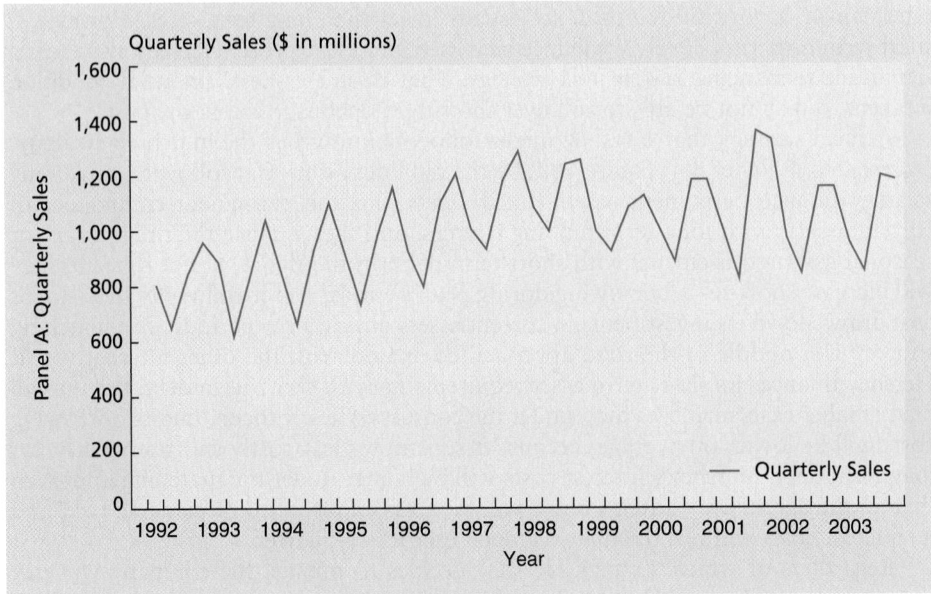

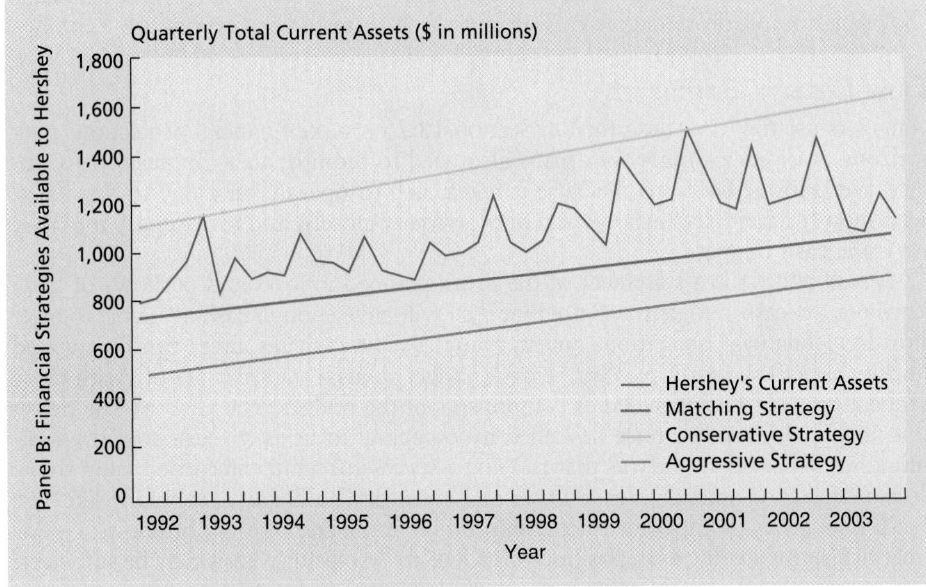

Figure 18.2
Quarterly Sales and Total Current Assets for Hershey Foods (1992 through the fourth quarter of 2003)

Panel A shows the seasonal pattern in Hershey's sales, and Panel B shows a similar pattern for current assets. Panel B assumes that Hershey finances all of its fixed assets and a portion of its current assets with long-term financing, with the straight lines representing the amount of current assets covered by Hershey's long-term financing. The purple line represents an aggressive strategy in the sense that Hershey does not secure enough long-term financing to cover the permanent component of the growth in current assets. The yellow line is a conservative strategy because Hershey has sufficient long-term financing to pay for both the permanent upward trend and the seasonal fluctuations in assets. The red line is a matching strategy, a middle-of-the-road approach in which Hershey finances permanent assets (fixed assets plus the permanent component of current assets) with long-term funding sources, and finances temporary or seasonal asset requirements with short-term debt.

The second strategy that Hershey might adopt is much more aggressive. In this **aggressive strategy**, Hershey relies heavily on short-term borrowing, not only to meet the seasonal peaks each year but also to finance a portion of the long-term growth in sales and assets. In Panel B of Figure 18.2, the purple line represents the aggressive strategy. The difference between that line and the one representing Hershey's current assets indicates how much short-term debt Hershey has outstanding at any moment in time. During peak quarters, Hershey increases its short-term borrowings, but even during the first and second quarters, when business is relatively slow, Hershey continues to finance at least part of its operations with short-term debt. This implies that Hershey uses short-term financing to fund a portion of its long-term, or permanent, growth in assets. In this strategy, Hershey takes advantage of short-term interest

aggressive strategy
When a company relies heavily on short-term borrowing, not only to meet the seasonal peaks each year but also to finance a portion of the long-term growth in sales and assets.

rates, which, as previously noted, are usually lower than long-term rates. However, if short-term rates rise, Hershey will face increased interest expense. Hershey also faces a significant refinancing risk in this strategy. That is, if Hershey's financial condition weakens, it may not be able to roll over short-term debt as it had in the past.

matching strategy
When a company finances permanent assets (fixed assets plus the permanent component of current assets) with long-term funding sources and finances its temporary or seasonal asset requirements with short-term debt.

A third strategy that Hershey might follow is known as the **matching strategy**, represented in Panel B of Figure 18.2 by the red line. Firms that follow the matching strategy finance permanent assets (fixed assets plus the permanent component of current assets) with long-term funding sources, and they finance their temporary or seasonal asset requirements with short-term debt. In the figure, notice that Hershey will increase short-term borrowing during peak periods, and it will repay those loans as it draws down its investments in current assets during slow periods. The matching strategy is a middle-of-the-road approach compared with the other alternatives. If Hershey finances its short-term asset requirements with short-term debt, then it will have smaller cash surpluses than under the conservative approach, but its borrowing costs will be lower, on average, because it substitutes less costly short-term debt for long-term debt. Hershey's interest costs will be higher under the matching approach than in the aggressive strategy, but it will face less exposure to refinancing risk, and its interest costs will not fluctuate as much quarter-to-quarter.

SMART CONCEPTS

See the concept explained step-by-step at SMARTFinance

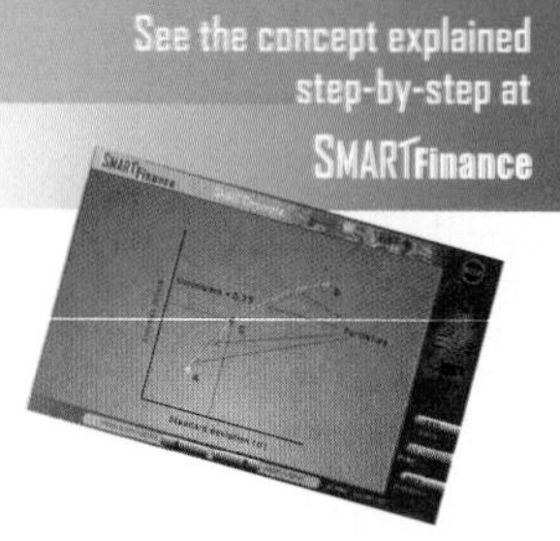

Regardless of which strategy Hershey decides to pursue, the company will pay very careful attention to short-term inflows and outflows of cash. Doing so will allow the company to invest unanticipated cash surpluses and cover unexpected deficits. The primary tool for managing cash flow on a short-term basis is the cash budget.

The Cash Budget

Managers use the tools described in Section 18.2 to make financial projections over horizons of a year or more, but firms also need to monitor their financial performance over shorter horizons. Because it takes cash to operate on a day-to-day basis, firms monitor their cash inflows and outflows very closely, and the primary tool they use is the cash budget.

cash budget
A statement of a firm's planned inflows and outflows of cash.

A **cash budget** is a statement of the firm's planned inflows and outflows of cash. Firms use the cash budget to ensure that they will have enough cash available to meet short-term financial obligations and that any surplus cash resources can be invested quickly and efficiently. Typically, the cash budget spans a one-year period, with more frequent breakdowns provided as components of the budget. The CFO of The Finish Line, a specialty retailer, once described his company to us as a "cash and inventory business." What he meant was that running a successful retail enterprise requires very close attention to managing cash flows and inventory holdings. A company like The Finish Line needs to know its exact cash position at the end of every business day. For other firms, monitoring cash positions on a weekly or monthly basis may be sufficient. Besides the volume of cash transactions that a business must process, other factors that determine the frequency with which cash budgets are constructed include the volatility of prices and volume and the importance of seasonal fluctuations.

Running out of cash is an ever-present threat at small and medium-size companies, especially those that are growing rapidly. However, astonishing changes in cash reserves can occur over just a few years, even in large corporations. For example, in December 1999, Boeing Co. reported cash and marketable security holdings in excess of $4.4 billion. Just two years later, that figure had fallen to $0.6 billion. Over the same two years, cash holdings at Phillip Morris, United Parcel Service, and Sears Roebuck fell $4.7 billion, $4.6 billion, and $2.8 billion, respectively. With the possibility of dramatic swings in cash holdings such as these, even large firms have to monitor their cash positions closely.

As was the case with pro forma financial statements, the key input required to build a cash budget is the firm's sales forecast. On the basis of the forecast, the financial manager estimates the monthly cash inflows that will result from cash sales and receivable collections. Naturally, a complete cash budget also contains estimates of cash outflows, some of which vary directly with sales and some of which do not. Cash outlays include purchases of raw materials, labor and other production expenses, selling expenses, fixed asset investments, and so on. A cash budget usually presents projected inflows first, then projected outflows, and the net cash inflow or outflow for the period. Depending on the firm's cash balance at the start of the period, the cash budget will either reveal a need for additional financing or demonstrate that the firm will have surplus cash to invest in short-term securities.

SMART PRACTICES VIDEO

Beth Acton, Vice President and Treasurer of Ford Motor Co. (former)

"Because there is a long cycle of developing product from concept to customer, it is critical that we understand what the business implications are for the business planning period."

See the entire interview at **SMARTFinance**

Cash Receipts. **Cash receipts** include all the firm's cash inflows in a given period. The most common components of cash receipts are cash sales, collections of accounts receivable, and other cash receipts. The collections of accounts receivable are estimated using the payment patterns of the firm's customers.[3]

cash receipts
All of a firm's cash inflows in a given period.

APPLYING THE MODEL

Consider the cash receipts projections of Farrell Industries, a candy manufacturer, which is developing a cash budget for October, November, and December. Farrell's sales in August and September were \$300,000 and \$600,000, respectively. Sales of \$1,200,000, \$900,000, and \$600,000 have been forecast for October, November, and December, respectively. Typically, 90 percent of Farrell's sales are on credit, and 10 percent are cash sales. Farrell collects about 60 percent of each month's sales in the next month, and it has to wait two months to collect the remaining 30 percent of sales. Bad debts for Farrell have been negligible. In December, the firm expects to receive a \$90,000 dividend from stock it holds in a subsidiary.

Table 18.3 presents the schedule of receipts. The first row shows total sales in each month. Remember, the figures for October–December are projections. The second row lists cash sales in each month, which, by assumption, equal 10 percent of total monthly sales. The third and fourth rows report the expected cash inflows from collecting receivables from the previous two months' sales. The next line reports cash receipts not related to sales, and the final line shows total cash receipts each month.

For example, consider the month of November. Projected sales are \$900,000, which implies that expected cash sales equal \$90,000 (0.10 × \$900,000). During November, Farrell expects to collect receivables equal to 60 percent of October's \$1,200,000 sales, or \$720,000. Farrell also expects to collect the 30 percent of September's \$600,000 sales still on the books as receivables, or \$180,000. No other cash receipts are expected in November, so total cash receipts equal \$990,000 (\$90,000 + \$720,000 + \$180,000).

Table 18.3
Schedule of Projected Cash Receipts for Farrell Industries (\$ in thousands)

	August	September	October	November	December
Forecast sales	\$300	\$600	\$1,200	\$900	\$ 600
Cash sales (10%)	30	60	120	90	60
Collection of accounts receivable					
Previous month (60%)		180	360	720	540
Two months prior (30%)			90	180	360
Other cash receipts					90
Total cash receipts			\$ 570	\$990	\$1,050

[3] We discuss payment patterns more fully in Chapter 19.

cash disbursements
All outlays of cash by a firm in a given period.

Cash Disbursements. **Cash disbursements** include all outlays of cash by the firm during the period. The most common cash disbursements are cash purchases, fixed asset outlays, payments of accounts payable, wages, interest payments, taxes, and rent and lease payments, but cash disbursements may also include items such as dividends paid and share repurchases. It is important to remember that depreciation and other non-cash expenses are *not* included in the cash budget because they merely represent a scheduled write-off of an earlier cash outflow. Depreciation does have a cash outflow effect through its impact on tax payments.

APPLYING THE MODEL

To demonstrate a schedule of cash disbursements, we continue with Farrell Industries, which has gathered the following data needed for the preparation of a cash disbursements schedule for October, November, and December.

Purchases: The firm's purchases average 70 percent of sales. Of this amount, Farrell pays 20 percent in cash, 60 percent in the month following the purchase, and the remaining 20 percent two months following the purchase. Thus, October purchases are $840,000 (0.70 × $1,200,000) with $168,000 (0.20 × $840,000) paid in cash, $504,000 (0.60 × $840,000) paid on account in November, and $168,000 (0.20 × $840,000) paid on account in December.
Rent payments: Rent of $20,000 will be paid each month.
Wages and salaries: The firm's wages and salaries equal 10 percent of monthly sales plus $30,000. Thus, October's wages and salaries will be $150,000 [(0.10 × $1,200,000) + $30,000]. The figures for November and December are calculated in the same manner.
Tax payments: Taxes of $75,000 must be paid in December.
Fixed asset outlays: New machinery costing $390,000 will be purchased and paid for in November.
Interest payments: An interest payment of $30,000 is due in December.
Cash dividend payments: Cash dividends of $60,000 will be paid in October.
Principal payments: A $60,000 principal payment is due in December.

Table 18.4 presents the firm's disbursement schedule, based on the preceding data.

Table 18.4
Schedule of Projected Cash Disbursements for Farrell Industries ($ in thousands)

	August	September	October	November	December
Purchases (70% of sales)	$210	$420	$840	$ 630	$420
Cash purchases (20%)	$ 42	$ 84	$168	$ 126	$ 84
Payments of accounts payable					
Previous month (60%)		126	252	504	378
Two months prior (20%)			42	84	168
Rent payments			20	20	20
Wages and salaries			150	120	90
Tax payments					75
Fixed asset outlays				390	
Interest payments					30
Cash dividend payments			60		
Principal payments					60
Total cash disbursements			$692	$1,244	$905

Net Cash Flow, Ending Cash, Financing Needs, and Excess Cash. We can calculate the firm's net cash flow by subtracting its cash disbursements from its cash receipts for each period. By adding the beginning cash balance to the firm's net cash flow, we determine the ending cash balance for each period. Like most companies, Farrell does not want its cash balance to dip below some minimum level at any time. Therefore, by subtracting the desired minimum cash balance from the ending cash balance, we arrive at the required total financing or the excess cash balance. If the ending cash balance is less than the desired minimum cash balance, then the firm has a short-term financing need. This need is met using notes payable. If the ending cash balance exceeds the desired minimum cash balance, then the firm has an excess cash balance that it can invest in short-term marketable securities.

APPLYING THE MODEL

Table 18.5 presents the cash budget for Farrell Industries based on the cash receipt and cash disbursement schedules developed in earlier examples and the following additional information: (1) Farrell's cash balance at the end of September is $200,000, (2) notes payable and marketable securities are $0 at the end of September, and (3) the desired minimum cash balance is $50,000.

For Farrell to maintain its desired minimum ending cash balance of $50,000, it will have notes payable (short-term borrowing) balances of $226,000 in November and $81,000 in December. In October, the firm will have excess cash of $28,000, which it can invest in marketable securities. The required total financing figures in the cash budget refer to *how much will be owed at the end of each month,* but the figures do not represent the monthly change in borrowing. For Farrell, the monthly financial activities are as follows:

October: Invest $28,000 of excess cash.
November: Liquidate $28,000 of excess cash and borrow $226,000. Net cash flow of –$254,000 uses all the available cash reserves ($50,000 minimum cash balance from October + $28,000 excess cash), leaving an ending cash balance of –$176,000. To cover the negative balance ($176,000) and the desired minimum cash balance ($50,000), Farrell must borrow $226,000.
December: Repay $145,000 of amount borrowed. Net cash flows of $145,000

Table 18.5
Cash Budget for Farrell Industries ($ in thousands)

	October	November	December
Total cash receipts[a]	$570	$ 990	$1,050
Less: Total cash disbursements[b]	692	1,244	905
Net cash flow	–$122	–$ 254	$ 145
Add: Beginning cash	200	78	– 176
Ending balance cash	$ 78	–$ 176	–$ 31
Less: Minimum cash balance	50	50	50
Required total financing (notes payable)[c]		$ 226	$ 81
Excess cash balance (marketable securities)[d]	$ 28		

[a] From Table 18.3.
[b] From Table 18.4.
[c] Values are placed on this line when the ending cash balance is *less than* the desired minimum cash balance. These amounts are typically financed short-term, and therefore are represented by notes payable.
[d] Values are placed on this line when the ending cash balance is *greater than* the desired minimum cash balance. These amounts are typically invested in short-term vehicles and therefore are represented by marketable securities.

reduced Farrell's end-of-month borrowing needs to $81,000, which is a reduction from November's borrowing needs of $226,000. Thus, Farrell repays $145,000 of the amount borrowed.

The cash budget provides the firm with figures indicating whether a cash shortage (financing need) or a cash surplus (short-term investment opportunity) is expected in each of the months covered by the forecast. Farrell Industries can expect a cash surplus of $28,000 in October, followed by cash shortages of $226,000 in November and $81,000 in December. Each of these values is based on the internal constraint of a minimum cash balance of $50,000.

Because the firm expects to borrow as much as $226,000 during the three-month period, the financial manager should establish a line of credit to ensure the availability of the necessary funds. The maximum amount of borrowing available on the line of credit should exceed the $226,000 forecast to allow for errors in the forecast.

Dealing with Uncertainty in the Cash Budget. Because the cash budget provides only month-end totals, it does not ensure that the firm has sufficient credit to cover intramonth financing needs. For example, if a firm's disbursements occur before its receipts during a month, then its intramonth borrowing needs will exceed the monthly totals shown in its cash budget. To assure sufficient credit, the firm may forecast its expected receipts and disbursement on a daily basis and use these estimates along with its cash budget to request adequate credit to cover its maximum expected cash deficit.

Though it is usually the responsibility of the finance group to create a firm's cash budget, the monthly cash surpluses and deficits predicted in the budget are affected by virtually all facets of a firm's operations. For example, changes in receivables collection or payment patterns and changes in inventory turnover can have a dramatic impact on financing needs. Any action that slows collections from customers or accelerates payments to suppliers will increase monthly financial deficits (or reduce surpluses). In that sense, almost any functional area in the firm can affect, or be affected by, the cash budget.

APPLYING THE MODEL

Consider the effect of a change in customer payment patterns on Farrell Industries. In the original example, Farrell Industries had a collection pattern on its accounts receivable as follows: (1) 10 percent cash sales, (2) 60 percent collected one month after sale, and (3) 30 percent collected two months after sale. This pattern resulted in (1) a $28,000 cash surplus in October, (2) $226,000 total borrowing in November, and (3) $81,000 total borrowing in December.

Now assume that Farrell Industries has a slowdown in its collection pattern, perhaps due to the effects of an economic recession. The new pattern is (1) 5 percent cash sales, (2) 40 percent collected after one month, (3) 50 percent collected after two months, and (4) 5 percent uncollectible. This collection pattern changes Farrell's cash receipts to (1) $450,000 in October, (2) $825,000 in November, and (3) $1,080,000 in December. If Farrell's cash disbursements remain unchanged, the cash budget will show the following: (1) $92,000 total borrowing in October, (2) $511,000 total borrowing in November, and (3) $336,000 total borrowing in December. Comparing these values to the initial collection pattern, it is clear that Farrell's short-term financing requirements have increased.

Two important points were demonstrated in the preceding example. First, changes in a firm's collection or payment pattern alter the timing and magnitude of its financing needs. Second, a slowdown in collections increases the firm's short-term financing needs. Conversely, one would expect a speedup in collections to decrease the firm's financing needs. With regard to payment patterns, a speedup in payments would likely increase the firm's financing needs, whereas a slowdown in payments would reduce financing needs. The next two chapters focus on the management of working capital accounts such as inventory, receivables, cash, and payables. By managing these items carefully, firms can increase the profitability of their enterprises and lower the need for external financing.

In this chapter, we have emphasized the importance of financial planning and illustrated a few of the most widely used tools of the trade. We end with a word of caution. When firms construct financial plans, they clearly hope to meet the plans' goals. But the value of planning is not just in attaining established goals. Rather, its importance derives from the thinking it forces managers to do, not only about what they expect to occur in the future, but what they will do if their expectations are not realized.

CONCEPT REVIEW QUESTIONS

5. Suppose that a firm follows the *matching strategy*. Does this imply that the firm's current assets will equal its current liabilities?

6. Why do firms prepare *cash budgets*? How do (a) collection patterns and (b) payment patterns impact the cash budget?

7. What can be done to deal with uncertainty in the cash budgeting process? Why might an intramonth view of the firm's cash flows cause a well-prepared cash budget to fail?

18.4 SUMMARY AND CONCLUSIONS

- Strategic (long-term) financial plans act as a guide for preparing operating (short-term) financial plans. For most firms, strategic plans are driven by competitive forces that are not always explicitly financial in nature. However, strategic plans have important financial consequences.
- Finance acts as a business partner with other functional units in developing the firm's strategic plan. Once the plan is established, it is the job of finance to ensure that the plan is feasible given the firm's financial resources. Finance also plays a crucial role both in monitoring progress and in managing risks associated with the plan.
- The sustainable growth model is a tool that managers can use to determine the feasibility of a target growth rate under certain conditions. When the growth rate that maximizes shareholder value does not match the sustainable rate, the firm must make adjustments to the model's assumptions, such as altering leverage or dividend policy, to achieve the desired growth rate.
- Pro forma financial statements are projected, or forecast, financial statements, typically based on the historical financial relationships within the firm. The preparation process begins with a sales forecast that can be developed using either a top-down or a bottom-up approach, or a blend of these two approaches. The key inputs to pro forma statements are a mix of facts and assumptions.

- Pro forma statements can be prepared by using the percentage-of-sales method, which assumes that all items grow in proportion to sales. Using this approach on the balance sheet requires recognizing that certain accounts such as receivables, inventory, and payables do not typically increase in a linear fashion. As a result, analysts typically use one line item on the balance sheet as a "plug figure" that can be used to make sure the pro forma balance sheet balances. The plug figure provides useful information with regard to the firm's ability to internally fund its anticipated growth.
- The amount of external financing required to fund a firm's anticipated growth can be estimated directly using the equation for external funds required (EFR). This approach, like the preparation of pro forma statements, helps managers look ahead to determine whether they should expect a scarcity or surplus of financial resources given the firm's growth objectives.
- During the year, a firm's investment in current assets will tend to rise and fall with sales, and this seasonal pattern creates temporary cash surpluses and deficits that the firm must manage. Three basic financing strategies—a conservative strategy, an aggressive strategy, and a matching strategy—can be used to fund both the long-term trend and seasonal fluctuations in a business. The conservative strategy is the least risky and least profitable, the aggressive strategy is the most risky and most profitable, and the matching strategy falls between the conservative and aggressive strategies in terms of risk and profits.
- A cash budget forecasts the short-term cash inflows and outflows of a firm. For a firm with significant seasonal variations in the flow of business, the financial manager typically prepares the cash budget month by month for an entire year. This allows the firm to determine peak borrowing needs and peak short-term investment opportunities, typically over a one-year period.
- The financial manager often applies sensitivity analysis to the cash budget to assess financing needs under the most adverse situations. Attention must also be given to intramonth cash flows to assure that sufficient credit is available. Changes in collection and payment periods, which change the cash conversion cycle, can significantly impact the magnitude and timing of the firm's cash flows and the resulting financing reflected in its cash budget.

SELF-TEST PROBLEMS

Answers to Self-Test Problems appear in Appendix D at back of book. Answers to the Concept Review Questions throughout the chapter appear at http://megginson.swlearning.com.

ST18-1. Use this key financial data from the most recent annual report of Rancho, Inc. to answer the questions that follow.

Sales	\$12.7 million
Net income	\$ 1.3 million
Total assets	\$ 7.6 million
Total equity	\$ 5.2 million
Dividends	\$ 0.3 million

The firm's CFO wishes to use this data to estimate the firm's sustainable growth rate.

a. Use the data provided to calculate Rancho's net profit margin, assets-to-equity ratio, total asset turnover ratio, and its dividend payout ratio.

b. Use your findings in part (a) to find Rancho's *sustainable growth rate*.

c. Interpret the sustainable growth rate calculated in part (b). Does this rate of growth assure shareholder wealth maximization? Explain.

d. If the firm's Board feels that it is best for its shareholders if the firm grows more slowly, what alterations in each of the baseline assumptions would be necessary to achieve this objective?

ST18-2. Planet Inc. wishes to construct a pro forma income statement and a pro forma balance sheet for the coming year using the following data.

1. Sales are forecast to grow by 5 percent from $809.5 million last year to $850 million in the coming year.
2. Cost of goods sold is expected to represent 72 percent of forecast sales.
3. Operating expenses are expected to represent 11 percent of forecast sales.
4. Depreciation expense on the firm's existing net fixed assets, which currently total $275 million, is expected to remain at $55 million per year for at least four more years.
5. Planet's marginal tax rate is expected to remain at 40 percent.
6. Planet is expected to continue its policy of paying out 10 percent of net income as dividends.
7. Planet's net profit margin last year was 5.2 percent.
8. Planet wishes to maintain a minimum cash balance of $8 million in the coming year.
9. The firm's accounts receivable are expected to equal about 15 percent of sales.
10. The firm's inventory has historically averaged about 12 percent of cost of goods sold.
11. Planet is planning to invest an additional $35 million in fixed assets that will be depreciated on a straight-line basis over a seven-year life.
12. The firm's accounts payable, which totaled $63.5 million at the end of last year, is expected to equal about 11 percent of cost of goods sold in the coming year.
13. Planet plans to maintain its notes payable of $42 million requiring annual interest of 5 percent, which totals $2.1 million.
14. The firm has $80 million of long-term debt that matures as a lump sum due and payable in full in five years. Annual interest of $4.8 million must be paid on this debt.
15. Planet has no preferred stock outstanding, and its retained earnings and common stock currently total $250 million.
16. Planet's total assets at the end of last year were $435 million.

   a. Use the preceding data to prepare Planet's pro forma income statement for the coming year.

   b. Use the data provided and your findings in part (a) to prepare Planet's pro forma balance sheet for the coming year. Use notes payable as the balancing figure and ignore any change in annual interest expense caused by the change in notes payable.

   c. Explain the amount of notes payable used as the balancing figure in part (b). Indicate the resulting amount of the *plug figure* needed to create the balancing figure. Will Planet be able to fund its planned growth internally? Explain.

   d. Use Equation 18.2 along with Planet's relevant data to determine its *external funds required* (*EFR*). Compare this value with the *plug figure* you found in part (c), and explain in general terms why differences between these two values might result.

ST18-3. Sportif, Inc.'s financial analyst has compiled sales and total cash disbursement estimates for the coming months of January through May. Historically, 60 percent of sales are for cash with the remaining 40 percent collected in the following month. The ending cash balance in January is $1,000. The firm's minimum cash balance is $1,000. The analyst plans to use this data to prepare a cash budget for the months of February through May.

Sportif, Inc.

Month	Sales	Total Cash Disbursements
January	$ 5,000	$6,000
February	6,000	8,000
March	10,000	8,000
April	10,000	6,000
May	10,000	5,000

a. Use the data provided to prepare Sportif's cash budget for the four months February through May.

b. How much total financing will Sportif need to meet its financial requirements for the period February to May?

c. If a pro forma balance sheet dated at the end of May was prepared from the information presented, how much would Sportif have in accounts receivable?

INTERNET RESOURCES

Note: *For updates to links, please go to the book's Web site at* http://megginson.swlearning.com

http://www.sba.gov (Small Business Administration)—Provides useful resources for managing small businesses.

http://www.toolkit.cch.com—Provides a number of interesting resources, including a cash budgeting spreadsheet template.

http://www.cfo.com/magazine—Web site for *CFO Magazine*, a publication devoted to issues facing corporate CFOs, including corporate planning.

http://www.acg.org—Web site of the Association for Corporate Growth.

http://www.gtnews.com—An excellent site for news regarding cash and treasury management functions.

KEY TERMS

aggressive strategy
bottom-up sales forecast
cash budget
cash disbursements
cash receipts
conservative strategy
external funds required
matching strategy
percentage-of-sales method
plug figure
pro forma financial statements
strategic plan
sustainable growth model
top-down sales forecast

QUESTIONS AND PROBLEMS

Q18-1. What is the financial planning process? What is a *strategic plan*? Describe the roles that financial managers play with regard to strategic planning.

Q18-2. What does the word *sustainable* mean in "sustainable growth model"?

Q18-3. In what ways can the sustainable growth model highlight conflicts between a firm's competing objectives?

Q18-4. With reference to Equation 18.1, explain how each of the variables influences the firm's sustainable growth rate. If high leverage allows a firm to increase its sustainable growth rate, does that mean that higher leverage is necessarily good for the firm?

Q18-5. A firm chooses to grow at a rate above its sustainable rate. What changes might we expect to see on the firm's financial statements in the next year? What changes would result from growing at a rate below the firm's sustainable rate?

Q18-6. Describe the differences between top-down and bottom-up sales forecasting methods. Describe advantages and disadvantages of each. Do you think one approach is likely to be more accurate than the other?

Q18-7. What is the logic of the *percentage-of-sales method* for constructing *pro forma financial statements?*

Q18-8. On a year-to-year basis, which balance sheet and income statement items do you think will fluctuate most closely with sales, and which items are not likely to vary as directly with sales volume?

Q18-9. Why does it make sense to let the firm's cash balance or a short-term liability account serve as the *plug figure* in pro forma projections? Why not use gross fixed assets as the plug figure?

Q18-10. Why might pro forma statements and the equation for *external funds required* yield different projections for a firm's financing needs?

Q18-11. What is the difference between the *conservative strategy*, the *aggressive strategy*, and the *matching strategy* for funding the long-term trend and the seasonal fluctuations in a business? Which strategy is most risky? Which is least profitable?

Q18-12. How is a *cash budget* different from a set of pro forma financial statements? Why do you think that firms typically create cash budgets at higher frequencies than they create pro forma financial statements?

Q18-13. Explain how slower inventory turns, slower receivables collections, or faster payments to suppliers would influence the numbers produced by a cash budget.

PROBLEMS

Planning for Growth

P18-1. Go to http://finance.yahoo.com or another financial Web site, and download the most recent two years' balance sheets and income statements for a firm of your choice. Do not choose a firm that issued or retired a significant amount of common stock in either year.

a. Calculate the actual percentage change in sales from two years ago to last year.
b. Using the balance sheet and income statement from two years ago, calculate the firm's sustainable growth rate.
c. If the sustainable growth rate does not equal the actual growth rate in sales, explain how changes in the firm's financial ratios in the second year reflected the firm's decision in the previous year to grow at a rate other than the sustainable rate.

P18-2. Eisner Amusement Parks reported the following data in its most recent annual report:

Sales	$42.5 million
Net income	$ 3.8 million
Dividends	$ 1.1 million
Assets	$50.0 million

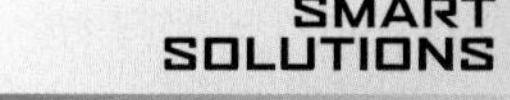

See the problem and solution explained step-by-step at SMARTFinance

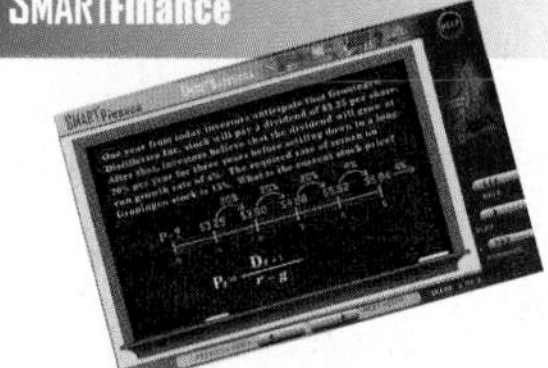

Eisner is financed 100 percent with equity. What is the company's *sustainable growth rate*? Suppose that Eisner issued bonds to the public and used the proceeds to repurchase half of its outstanding shares. This new capital structure would create additional interest expenses of $2 million. Assuming that the company faces a 35 percent tax rate, what impact would this restructuring have on its sustainable growth rate?

P18-3. Review the abbreviated financial statements for the last two years for the Norne Energy Corp. All values are expressed in billions of dollars.

Norne Energy Corp.

Balance Sheet

	2007	2006
Current assets	$2.7	$2.5
Fixed assets	3.5	3.4
Total assets	$6.2	$5.9
Current liabilities	$1.9	$1.8
Long-term debt	2.1	2.2
Shareholders' equity	2.2	1.9
Total liabilities and equity	$6.2	$5.9

Norne Energy Corp.

Income Statement

	2007	2006
Sales	$7.5	$7.1
Net income	0.5	0.4
Dividends	0.2	0.1

a. What was Norne's *sustainable growth rate* at the end of 2006?
b. How rapidly did Norne actually grow in 2007?
c. What changes in Norne's financial condition from 2006 to 2007 can you trace to the difference between the actual and sustainable growth rates?

P18-4. The 2007 sales forecast for Clearwater Development Co. is $150 million. Interest expense will not change in the coming year. Use Clearwater's 2006 income statement ($ in thousands) presented below to answer the questions that follow.

Clearwater Development Co.

Income Statement

Sales	$125,000
Less: Cost of goods sold	80,000
Gross profit	$ 45,000
Less: Operating expenses	30,000
Less: Interest	10,000
Pretax profit	$ 5,000
Less: Taxes (35%)	1,750
Net income	$ 3,250

a. Use the *percentage-of-sales method* to construct a pro forma income statement for 2007.
b. You learn that 25 percent of the cost of goods sold and operating expense figures for 2006 are fixed costs that will not change in 2007. Reconstruct the pro forma income statement.
c. Compare and contrast the statement prepared in parts (a) and (b). Which statement will likely provide the better estimate of 2007 income? Explain.

See this problem explained in Excel at SMARTFinance

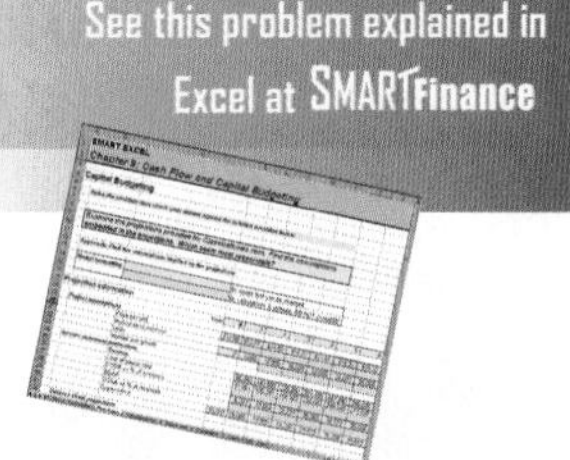

P18-5. Hill Propane Distributors wants to construct a pro forma balance sheet for 2007. Build the statement using the following data and assumptions:

1. Projected sales for 2007 are $35 million.
2. Hill's gross profit margin is 35 percent.
3. Operating expenses average 10 percent of sales.
4. Depreciation expense last year was $5 million.
5. Hill faces a tax rate of 35 percent.
6. Hill distributes 20 percent of its net income to shareholders as a dividend.
7. Hill wants to maintain a minimum cash balance of $3 million.
8. Accounts receivable equal 8.5 percent of sales.
9. Inventory averages 10 percent of cost of goods sold.
10. Last year's balance sheet lists net fixed assets of $30 million. All these assets are depreciated on a straight-line basis, and none of them will be fully depreciated for at least three years.
11. Hill plans to invest an additional $1 million in fixed assets that it will depreciate over a five-year life on a straight-line basis.
12. In 2006, Hill reported common stock and retained earnings of $20 million.
13. Accounts payable averages 9 percent of sales.

Will Hill Propane's cash balance at the end of 2007 exceed its minimum requirement of $3 million?

P18-6. Review the following 2006 balance sheet and income statement for T. F. Baker Cosmetics, Inc. The numerical values are in thousands of dollars.

T. F. Baker Cosmetics, Inc.

Balance Sheet

Cash	$ 5,000	Accounts payable	$10,000
Accounts receivable	12,500	Short-term bank loan	15,000
Inventory	10,000	Long-term debt	10,000
Current assets	$27,500	Common stock	15,000
Gross fixed assets	$65,000	Retained earnings	12,500
Less: accum. depr.	30,000	Total liabilities and equity	$62,500
Net fixed assets	$35,000		
Total assets	$62,500		

T. F. Baker Cosmetics, Inc.

Income Statement

Sales	$150,000
Less: Cost of goods sold	120,000
Gross profit	$ 30,000
Less: Operating expenses	15,000
Less: Depreciation	5,000
Less: Interest expense	2,000
Pretax profit	$ 8,000
Less: Taxes (35%)	2,800
Net income	$ 5,200

At a recent board meeting, the firm set the following objectives for 2007:

1. The firm would increase liquidity. For competitive reasons, accounts receivable and inventory balances were expected to continue their historical relationships with sales and cost of goods sold, respectively, but the Board felt that the company should double its cash holdings.
2. The firm would accelerate payments to suppliers. This would have two effects. First, by paying more rapidly, the firm would be able to take advantage of early payment discounts, which would increase its gross margin from 20 percent to 22 percent. Second, by paying earlier, the firm's accounts payable balance, which historically averaged about one twelfth of cost of goods sold, would decline to 4 percent of cost of goods sold.
3. The firm would expand its warehouse, which would require an investment in fixed assets of $10 million. This would increase projected depreciation expense from $5 million in 2006 to $7 million in 2007.
4. The firm would issue no new common stock during the year, and it would initiate a dividend. Dividend payments in 2007 would total $1.2 million.
5. Operating expenses would remain at 10 percent of sales.
6. The firm did not expect to retire any long-term debt, and it was willing to borrow up to the limit of its current credit line with the bank, $20 million. The interest rate on its outstanding debts would average 8 percent.
7. The firm set a sales target for 2007 of $200 million.

Develop a set of pro forma statements to determine whether or not T. F. Baker Cosmetics can achieve all these goals simultaneously.

SMART SOLUTIONS

See the problem and solution explained step-by-step at SMARTFinance

Planning and Control

P18-7. A firm has actual sales of $50,000 in January and $70,000 in February. It expects sales of $90,000 in March and $110,000 in both April and May. Assuming that sales are the only source of cash inflow, and that 60 percent of these are for cash and the rest are collected evenly over the following two months, what are the firm's expected cash receipts for March, April, and May?

P18-8. Bachrach Fertilizer Corp. had sales of $2 million in March and $2.2 million in April. Expected sales for the next three months are $2.4 million, $2.5 million, and $2.7 million. Bachrach has a cash balance of $200,000 on May 1 and does not want its balance to dip below that level. Prepare a cash budget for May, June, and July given the following information:

1. Of total sales, 30 percent are for cash, 50 percent are collected in the month after the sale, and 20 percent are collected two months after the sale.
2. Bachrach has cash receipts from other sources of $100,000 per month.
3. The firm expects to purchase items for $2 million in each of the next three months. All purchases are paid for in cash.
4. Bachrach has fixed cash expenses of $150,000 per month and variable cash expenses equal to 5 percent of the previous month's sales.
5. Bachrach will pay a cash dividend of $300,000 in June.
6. The company must make a $250,000 loan payment in June.
7. Bachrach plans to acquire fixed assets worth $500,000 in July.
8. Bachrach must make a tax payment of $225,000 in June.

P18-9. The actual sales and purchases for White Inc. for September and October 2006, along with its forecast sales and purchases for November 2006 through April 2007, follow.

Year	Month	Sales	Purchases
2006	September	$310,000	$220,000
2006	October	350,000	250,000
2006	November	270,000	240,000
2006	December	260,000	200,000
2007	January	240,000	180,000
2007	February	280,000	210,000
2007	March	300,000	200,000
2007	April	350,000	190,000

The firm makes 30 percent of all sales for cash and collects 35 percent of its sales in each of the two months following the sale. Other cash inflows are expected to be $22,000 in September and April, $25,000 in January and March, and $37,000 in February. The firm pays cash for 20 percent of its purchases. It pays for 40 percent of its purchases in the following month and for 40 percent of its purchases two months later.

Wages and salaries amount to 15 percent of the preceding month's sales. Lease expenses of $30,000 per month must be paid. Interest payments of $20,000 are due in January and April. A principal payment of $50,000 is also due in April. The firm expects to pay a cash dividend of $30,000 in January and April. Taxes of $120,000 are due in April. The firm also intends to make a $55,000 cash purchase of fixed assets in December.

a. Assuming that the firm has a cash balance of $42,000 at the beginning of November and its desired minimum cash balance is $25,000, prepare a *cash budget* for November through April.
b. If the firm is requesting a line of credit, how large should the line be? Explain your answer.

P18-10. Berlin Inc. expects sales of $300,000 during each of the next three months. It will make monthly purchases of $180,000 during this time. Wages and salaries total $30,000 per month plus 5 percent of monthly sales. The firm expects to make a tax payment of $60,000 in the first month and a $45,000 purchase of fixed assets in the second month and to receive $24,000 in cash from the sale of an asset in the third month. All sales and purchases are for cash. Beginning cash and the minimum cash balance equal zero.

a. Construct a cash budget for the next three months.

b. Berlin is unsure of the level of sales, but all other figures are certain. If the most pessimistic sales figure is $240,000 per month and the most optimistic is $360,000 per month, what are the monthly minimum and maximum ending cash balances that the firm can expect for each month?

c. Discuss how the financial manager can use the data in parts (a) and (b).

THOMSON ONE Business School Edition

For instructions on using Thomson ONE, refer to the instructions provided with the Thomson ONE problems at the end of Chapters 1–6 or to "A Guide for Using Thomson ONE."

P18-11. Calculate Kroger's (ticker: U:KR) *sustainable growth rate* at the end of each of the last five fiscal years. Compare the sustainable growth rate to its actual growth rate each year and, if different, identify changes in Kroger's financial condition each year that explain the differences in growth rates.

P18-12. Construct a pro forma balance sheet and income statement for the next year for Novell Inc. (ticker: @NOVL). Estimate the *sustainable growth rate* using the latest fiscal year-end data. Assume that sales grow at this sustainable growth rate over the next year. Use the *percentage-of-sales method* to prepare the pro forma statements. Do you need a *plug figure* to make the pro forma balance sheet balance? If so, what plug figure do you use?

Since these exercises depend upon real-time data, your answers will change continuously depending upon when you access the Internet to download your data.

MINICASE

Financial Planning

Burrito Brothers, Incorporated, a regional restaurant chain, has decided to expand nationwide and, consequently, expects rapid growth. As Burrito Brothers' new CFO, you are in charge of planning for this growth. Before starting to plan, you decide to refresh your knowledge of financial planning by answering the following questions.

ASSIGNMENT

1. One method of estimating the effects of growth is the *sustainable growth model.* What assumptions are inherent with this model?
2. Another method of estimating growth is for firm managers to forecast *pro forma financial statements.* How are the sales forecasts that are necessary to create pro forma statements derived?
3. Why might the estimates for *external funds required* differ between using the *percentage-of-sales method* to estimate pro forma statements and using the shorthand approach in Equation 18.2?
4. If sales volume fluctuates in the short-term around the long-term estimated trend, what alternative financing strategies might be considered?
5. Discuss how managers might monitor a company's cash inflows and cash outflows on a day-to-day basis?

Smart *Excel* Appendix

Appendix Contents

Use the Smart *Excel* spreadsheets and animated tutorials at http://smartfinance.swlearning.com.

EXCEL PREREQUISITES

You need to be familiar with the IF function to use this appendix. This has been covered in other appendices but is repeated in the ***Excel Prereqs*** tab in the Chapter 18 *Excel* file located at the Smart Finance Web site.

PRO FORMA STATEMENTS

Problem: Solve Problem 18-5 in the text.

Approach: Create a simple model of pro forma statements

Try it yourself in a blank *Excel* file. Think about what to include in the input section and how to set up your calculations and output.

Or, open the Chapter 18 *Excel* file located at the Smart Finance Web site. Turn to the ***Pro forma*** tab.

The sales forecast drives the pro forma statements since most assumptions are related to sales.

Step 1: To create a flexible model, determine and enter the key assumptions captions and values in the input section.
Step 2: Create the pro forma income statement
Step 3: Create the pro forma balance sheet
Step 4: Determine if there is excess cash or a funding gap
Step 5: Change your assumptions and note the impact

Apply it:

Step 1: Enter the input information from Problem 18-5

Tip: Maximize the flexibility of the model so that input assumptions can be altered easily.

SMARTFinance
Use the learning tools at
http://smartfinance.swlearning.com

Create clear input captions so that other users understand your model. For example, list operating expenses as "% of Sales". We included a comment in the caption for new investment in fixed assets to describe the method of depreciation.

Our input captions follow:

Projected Sales
Gross profit margin
Operating expenses as % Sales
Depreciation expense – last year $
Tax rate
Dividends as % net income
Minimum cash balance – $
Accounts receivable – % sales
Inventory – % COGS
Fixed assets – prior year
Accounts payable – % sales
New investment in fixed assets
Common stock & RE – prior year

Step 2: Create formulas for the pro forma income statement. Most are straightforward. Based on the assumptions in the problem, depreciation expense is equal to last year's value plus 20% of the new investment in fixed assets (since these assets were assumed to be depreciated straight line over 5 years).

Below the income statement, calculate the values for dividends and retained earnings. Retained earnings is equal to net income minus dividends.

Your results should match:

Income Statement	
Revenues	$35,000,000
Cost of goods sold	$22,750,000
Gross profit	$12,250,000
Operating expenses	$3,500,000
Depreciation	$5,200,000
Pretax profit	$3,550,000
Taxes	$1,242,500
Net income	$2,307,500
Dividends	$461,500
Retained earnings	$1,846,000

Step 3: Create formulas to complete the pro forma balance sheet.

Step 4: Then find Total liabilities plus Equity minus Total assets. This gap indicates whether the firm is expected to generate excess cash or a funding gap.

The result is:

Balance sheet	
Cash	$3,000,000
Accounts receivable	$2,975,000
Inventory	$2,275,000
Net fixed assets	$25,800,000
Total assets	$34,050,000
Accounts payable	$3,150,000
Equity	$21,846,000
Total liabilities & Equity	$24,996,000
Total Liabilities & Equity minus Total assets	
Gap	$(9,054,000)

Optional: Use the IF function to create a statement that identifies the result as excess cash or a financing gap and provides the value of the gap.

We designed the output section to display either "Amount of Funding Required" or "Amount of Excess Cash" in cell B59 and the value of the required funding or excess cash in cell C59.

The IF statement in cell B59 compares the gap between total liabilities and equity and total assets (in cell C55).

=IF(C55>0, "Amount of Excess Cash", "Amount of Funding Required")

When the gap is positive this will display as "Amount of Excess Cash", when negative, "Amount of Funding Required".

Then in cell C59, show the value of the gap as a positive number whether there is excess cash or funding required since a negative value for financing can be confusing.

We accomplished this with another IF statement.

=IF(C55>0,C55,–C55)

In this problem, the result is:

Output

Based on pro forma statement:	
Amount of Funding Required	$9,054,000

Step 5: Analyze the impact of changes in input assumptions.

- *What is the result if projected sales are $30,000,000?*
  The funding required rises to $9,404,000.
- *The operating expenses fall to 9.5% of sales?*
  The funding required falls to $8,963,000.
- *The new investment in fixed assets falls to $250,000?*
  The funding required falls to $8,376,000.

Changes in input assumptions will affect the amount of funding required. After changing several key inputs, we found there is still a significant funding gap in this example.

PRO FORMA STATEMENTS

Problem: Solve Problem 18-8 in the text.

Approach: Create a simple model to create the cash budget

Try it yourself in a blank *Excel* file. Think about what to include in the input section and how to set up your calculations and output.

Or, Open the Chapter 18 *Excel* file located at the Smart Finance Web site. Turn to the *CashBudget* tab.

The sales forecast and collection and expenditure assumptions drive the cash budget. Many of these assumptions are just guesses so a model that allows you to see the impact of changing the assumptions is valuable.

Step 1: To create a flexible model, determine and enter the key assumptions captions and values in the input section.
Step 2: Enter the starting cash balance and create the calculations for cash inflows and total cash receipts. Then create the calculations for cash outflows and total cash outflows.
Step 3: Calculate the desired output.
Step 4: Change your assumptions and note the impact.

Apply it:

Step 1: Enter the input information from Problem 18-8. Remember to use clear input captions.

Maximize the flexibility of the model by allowing for changes in the collection policy, receipts, and for all cash outflows so that inflows and expenditures can occur in any month.

We set up our inputs as:

Inputs	*Historical Info* **March**	*Historical Info* **April**	*Projection* **May**	*Projection* **June**	*Projection* **July**
Sales					
Sales	$2,000,000	$2,200,000	$2,400,000	$2,500,000	$2,700,000
Cash sales – %	30%	30%	30%	30%	30%
Sales collected within 30 days	50%	50%	50%	50%	50%
Sales collected 31-60 days	20%	20%	20%	20%	20%
Cash					
Starting cash balance			$200,000		
Required cash balance			$200,000	$200,000	$200,000
Cash receipts from other sources			$100,000	$100,000	$100,000
Cash purchases			$2,000,000	$2,000,000	$2,000,000
Fixed cash expenses			$150,000	$150,000	$150,000
Variable cash expenses – % prior month's sales			5%	5%	5%
Cash dividend				$300,000	
Loan payments				$250,000	
Fixed asset expenditures					$500,000
Tax payments				$225,000	

Step 2: Use a cell reference to pull through the starting cash balance in the calculations section FOR MAY ONLY. June and July can only be determined after further calculations.

Find the cash receipts and outflows.

Your results should match:

Calculations	**May**	**June**	**July**
Starting cash balance	$200,000		
Cash sales	$720,000	$750,000	$810,000
Collections on credit from prior month	$1,100,000	$1,200,000	$1,250,000
Collections on credit from 2 months prior	$400,000	$440,000	$480,000
Other cash receipts	$100,000	$100,000	$100,000
Total cash receipts	$2,320,000	$2,490,000	$2,640,000
Purchases	$2,000,000	$2,000,000	$2,000,000
Fixed expenses	$150,000	$150,000	$150,000
Variable expenses	$110,000	$120,000	$125,000
Cash dividend	$0	$300,000	$0
Loan payments	$0	$250,000	$0
Fixed asset expenditures	$0	$0	$500,000
Tax payments	$0	$225,000	$0
Total cash outflows	$2,260,000	$3,045,000	$2,775,000

Notice that we made the model flexible and allowed for cash dividends, tax payments and fixed asset expenditures to occur in any month.

Step 3: Calculate the desired output, here:

Output
Net cash flow
Cash balance
Borrowing required
Ending cash balance after borrowing

Net cash flow is the total cash receipts minus total cash outflows.

Cash balance is the starting cash balance plus net cash flow.

Borrowing required is the total borrowing to meet the assumed required cash balance (in inputs).

This will be zero if the cash balance is above the required value ($200,000 in this problem). If the cash balance is below the required value, the borrowing is the amount of borrowing to provide the required cash balance.

We use an IF statement in cell E54 to find this. The statement is:

=IF(E53>E22,0,E22–E53)

The statement compares the cash balance in cell E53 to the required cash (from inputs) and returns zero if the balance exceeds the required value. If not, it returns the required value minus the cash balance.

The ending cash balance after borrowing is the sum of the cash balance plus any borrowing. This balance then becomes the starting cash balance for the next month. Use a cell reference to pull through the ending cash balance after borrowing in May to the beginning cash balance for June (cell F33) then copy across for July.

Our results are:

Output	May	June	July
Net cash flow	$60,000	$(555,000)	$(135,000)
Cash balance	$260,000	$(295,000)	$65,000
Borrowing required	$0	$495,000	$135,000
Ending cash balance after borrowing	$260,000	$200,000	$200,000

In June and July when the cash balance is below the required balance, borrowing is required. When the cash balance is below the required balance, the ending balance is therefore equal to the required balance since the firm borrows just enough to meet the minimum cash requirement.

Step 4: Analyze the impact of changes in input assumptions.

- *What is the result if projected sales are only $2,000,000 in May?*
  Then borrowing of $60,000 is required in May, $735,000 in June and $215,000 in July. This has a significant impact on financing needs.
- *The collections within 30 days fall to 45% and cash sales rise to 35% in each month?*
  The borrowing requirements drop to $480,000 in June and $125,000 in July.
- *Some payments arrive after 60 days?*

Changes in input assumptions will affect the cash balance and borrowing requirements. To allow for payments after 60 days, you must edit the model to include an assumption on payments from days 61–90 and incorporate this change into the calculations. This is illustrated on the ***CashBudget2*** tab. In this example, we allow for later payments and change the assumptions on collections. Without information on the February sales, the collections from 61–90 days begin in May. The result of the slower collections assumed here is higher required borrowing in all months.

Cash Conversion, Inventory, and Receivables Management*

OPENING FOCUS

Effective Short-Term Financial Management at Dell Computer

Dell Computer Corp. is one of the personal computer industry's biggest success stories. Founded by a nineteen-year-old college dropout, Michael Dell, in the mid-1980s, Dell has become a leader in the manufacturing and distribution of personal computers. Increased demand, lower cost, greater competition, and standardization have transformed the PC market into a commodity business. Dell's competitive advantage comes not from building better computers, but from building them faster and consuming fewer resources in the process. Dell's business model emphasizes minimizing short-term investment, maintaining tight cost controls, generating high sales turnover, and owning few fixed assets.

Dell uses a direct marketing approach in which the company takes orders directly from customers. This allows Dell to build its PCs to demand rather than to an inexact sales forecast. As a result, customers get what they want. Dell strives to deliver PCs quickly, often in a few days with all of the customer's software preloaded. Also, Dell is not saddled with unwanted inventory, and it does not have to pay a distribution fee to any middlemen, such as retailers.

Dell's manufacturing strategy uses a just-in-time production process that requires the company to hold just four days of inventory. In contrast, its main competitor, Compaq (now part of Hewlett-Packard), holds about twenty-three days of inventory. A network links suppliers to Dell's worldwide manufacturing facilities and provides hourly feedback on inventory levels. This is a huge edge in an industry where the price of chips, drives, and other parts typically declines by 1 percent per week. By taking advantage of the latest prices in components, Dell lowers its production costs, which gives it the enviable choice of either taking a higher profit or undercutting its rivals' prices. Dell's inventory turnover, on average, is three times faster than the industry average, and its total asset turnover is typically a little less than twice the industry norm.

Besides keeping only four days of inventories, Dell collects its receivables in about twenty-seven days and pushes its payables out about

* A large part of this chapter was prepared with the assistance of Professor Dubos J. Masson, CCM, CertCM, of The Resource Alliance and the University of West Florida. The authors very much appreciate D.J.'s important contribution.

seventy-nine days. This means that Dell typically receives payment on the sale of a PC long before it pays suppliers for the component parts, giving the company another significant financial advantage. One sign of this advantage is Dell's high level of liquidity. Dell's cash and marketable securities are three times larger than the industry average. In a sense, this underscores Dell's short-term financial management efforts, which allows the company to respond rapidly to changes in the business environment. Industry competitors typically are cash squeezed and have to be more aggressive in reducing costs and staffing or deferring technology enhancements in order to respond to changes in the business environment.

Sources: Andrew Parks, "How Dell Keeps from Stumbling," *Business Week* (May 14, 2001), pp. 38B–38D; Peter Burrows, "Dell, the Conqueror," *Business Week* (September 24, 2001), pp. 92–102. Data for Dell updated to 2003 by the authors. ■

LEARNING OBJECTIVES

After studying this chapter you should be able to:

- Describe the cash conversion cycle, the firm's objectives with regard to it, and the actions the firm can use to accomplish these objectives;
- Explain the cost trade-offs the firm must consider when finding the optimum levels of both operating assets and short-term financing;
- Discuss the key concerns of the financial manager with regard to inventory and some of the popular techniques used to manage it;
- Review the key aspects of a firm's credit standards, including the five C's of credit and the role of credit scoring;
- Analyze proposed changes in a firm's credit standards and its credit terms using both descriptive and quantitative techniques; and
- Understand the collection policy procedures used by firms, the techniques firms use in credit monitoring, and the cash application process.

SMART PRACTICES VIDEO

Vern LoForti, Chief Financial Officer, Overland Storage Inc.

"Working capital management is extremely important because it results in good cash flow."

See the entire interview at **SMARTFinance**

The focus in the preceding chapter was primarily on financial planning with regard to sustainable growth rates and using pro forma financial statements and the cash budget. In this chapter, we switch our focus from planning to operations and focus on the firm's cash conversion and key operating assets—inventory and accounts receivable. Other **operating assets**, current assets needed to support a firm's day-to-day operations, including cash and marketable securities, are the focus of Chapter 20. Although it is difficult to directly measure their contribution to a firm's profitability, a firm's operating assets are needed to grow a business. For example, effective inventory and credit policies are necessary to grow the business by maintaining adequate inventory to meet demand quickly with infrequent stockouts and offering attractive credit terms to stimulate sales. Because investments in operating assets consume the firm's scarce cash resources, they should be efficiently managed and controlled.

operating assets
Cash, marketable securities, accounts receivable, and inventories that are necessary to support the day-to-day operations of a firm.

Similarly, as explained in Chapter 18, **short-term financing**, which includes accounts payable, commercial paper, and various types of short-term loans discussed in Chapter 20, is used by the firm to finance seasonal fluctuations in current asset investments and provide the firm with adequate liquidity to achieve its growth objectives and meet its obligations in a timely manner. Therefore, the objective for managing current assets and liabilities is to be as efficient as possible, which means the firm should minimize unnecessary operating assets and maximize the use of inexpensive short-term financing, typically accounts payable. A number of liquidity and activity ratios introduced in Chapter 2 can be used to gain insight into important aspects of the firm's short-term financial management activities.

short-term financing
Accounts payable, commercial paper, and various types of short-term loans that are used by a firm to finance seasonal fluctuations in current asset investments and provide adequate liquidity to achieve its growth objectives and meet its obligations in a timely manner.

Table 19.1
Current Assets and Current Liabilities as a Percentage of Total Assets for U.S. Companies, 1981 and 2002

Note: This table shows the investments made in current assets and current liabilities, expressed as a percentage of total assets, for two groups of firms. The first group is made up of the 200 largest U.S. manufacturing firms with continuous operating histories from 1981 through 2002. The second group includes all U.S. manufacturing firms listed on Compustat in 1981 and 2002.

For a Sample of 200 Large Firms (median)			
Year	Current Assets	Current Liabilities	
1981	37.4%	22.8%	
2002	25.3%	21.7%	
For the Aggregate Manufacturing Corporate Sector			
Year	Current Assets	Current Liabilities	Current Ratio
1981	32.2%	22.6%	1.42
2002	24.1%	19.3%	1.25

Source: Compustat and authors' calculations.

What evidence can we cite suggesting that firms spend time and effort trying to economize on their investments in current (operating) assets while taking advantage of relatively inexpensive current liabilities (short-term financing)? Table 19.1 reports the median investment, expressed as a percentage of total assets, in current assets and current liabilities for a sample of 200 large U.S. companies in existence from 1981 to 2002. In 1981, current assets accounted for 37.4 percent of total assets for the median firm in this group, but by 2002 that figure had dropped to just 25.3 percent. Over the same period, the importance of current liabilities in financing these firms decreased from 22.8 percent in 1981 to 21.7 percent in 2002. Table 19.1 also shows the aggregate investment in current assets and current liabilities for all U.S. manufacturing firms, expressed as a percentage of the aggregate assets of these firms. In 1981, current assets accounted for 32.2 percent of aggregate corporate assets, whereas current liabilities made up 22.6 percent of the financing for those assets. By 2002, those figures had changed to 24.1 percent and 19.3 percent, respectively. Put another way, the aggregate *current ratio* of U.S. manufacturing corporations declined from 1.42 in 1981 to 1.25 in 2002. These figures illustrate both the importance of and the advances in short-term financial management by U.S. firms.

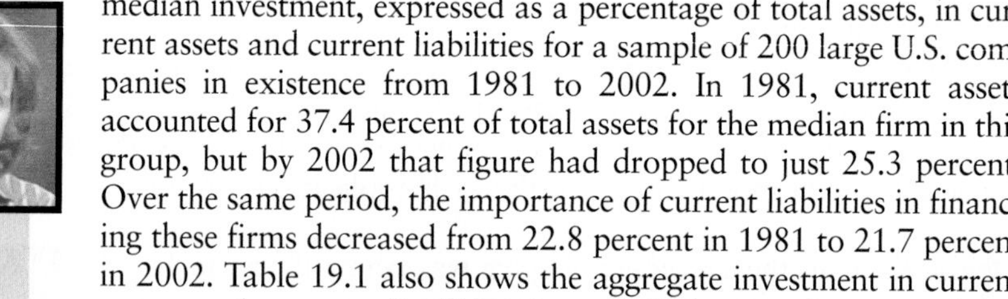

SMART PRACTICES VIDEO
Jackie Sturm, Director of Finance for Technology and Manufacturing, Intel Corp.
"Inventory loses value every day you hold it."
See the entire interview at SMARTFinance

A variety of forces prompted firms to find efficiencies in short-term financial management. For example, high inflation in the late 1970s and early 1980s gave firms a tremendous incentive to reduce their investments in non-interest-bearing operating assets. Perhaps even more important, developments in information technology allowed firms to become much more efficient in managing cash, investing short-term cash surpluses, monitoring receivables, managing inventories, managing payables, and establishing and monitoring short-term loans. With better access to information and the ability to move and dispatch funds electronically, firms today can operate with lower levels of operating asset investment.[1]

[1] A popular professional certification in the field of treasury and financial management is the Certified Treasury Professional (CTP) credential offered by the Association for Financial Professionals (http://www.afponline.org). The more than 15,500 CTPs have passed an exam reflecting the required expertise in the field of treasury and financial management, and they have agreed to participate in ongoing professional education to maintain the CTP credential.

This chapter focuses on the cash conversion cycle and the efficient management of two key operating assets—inventory and accounts receivable. We begin with a description of the cash conversion cycle, the goal for managing it, and the actions that can be used to accomplish the goal. Next, we describe the cost trade-offs in short-term financial management. Evaluation of these trade-offs involves measurement and comparison of their marginal costs and marginal benefits. Then, we briefly consider the key concerns of the financial manager with regard to inventory, and review some popular inventory management techniques. We next review two important aspects of accounts receivable management—credit standards and credit terms. Finally, we briefly discuss some other receivables management activities—collection policy, credit monitoring, and cash application.

19.1 THE CASH CONVERSION CYCLE

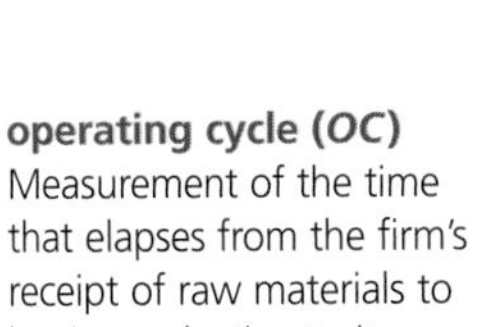

Operating Cycle

A central concept in short-term financial management is the notion of the operating cycle. A firm's **operating cycle (*OC*)** measures the time that elapses from the firm's receipt of raw materials to begin production to its collection of cash from the sale of the finished product. As you might expect, operating cycles vary widely by industry. For instance, a bakery, which uses fresh ingredients, keeps finished goods in inventory for only a day or two, and generally sells its products for cash, will have a very short operating cycle. In contrast, semiconductor manufacturers take several months to convert raw materials into finished products, which are sold on credit. The operating cycle for such a firm may extend to six months or longer.

operating cycle (*OC*) Measurement of the time that elapses from the firm's receipt of raw materials to begin production to its collection of cash from the sale of the finished product.

The operating cycle influences a company's need for internal or external financing. In general, the longer a firm's operating cycle, the greater its need for financing. For example, a bakery might pay its suppliers and its employees using the revenues generated each week, but the semiconductor manufacturer probably cannot persuade suppliers and employees to wait the months it takes to earn cash from chip sales. Therefore, the semiconductor firm has a greater need for financing day-to-day operations.

The operating cycle encompasses two major short-term asset categories, inventory and accounts receivable. To measure the operating cycle, we will use two ratios covered in Chapter 2. First, calculate the *average age of inventory* (*AAI*) and the *average collection period* (*ACP*). Next, take the sum of these two items to determine the length of the operating cycle. Table 19.2 presents the actual operating cycles for some well-known computer manufacturers and a number of other firms. The raw data and given for fiscal-year 2003 is given in lines 1 through 5, and the time periods for *AAI*, *ACP*, and average payment period (*APP*) are calculated from the raw data and given on lines 6 through 8, respectively. Using the *AAI* and *ACP* calculated in lines 6 and 7, the OCs are calculated for each firm and given in line 9. Note that among the five computer manufacturers—IBM, Dell, Gateway, Apple, and Hewlett-Packard—the make-to-order firms, Dell and Gateway, have the shortest operating cycles, closely followed by Apple. IBM and Hewlett-Packard's operating cycles of 148 and 136 days, respectively, are far longer than the 26- to 61-day range of operating cycles for Dell, Gateway, and Apple, probably as a result of their diversified computer businesses. The final four columns show the operating cycles for four noncomputer firms. Clearly, the operating cycle varies greatly across industries as well as across different types of companies within a given industry.

Table 19.2
Operating Cycles (*OC*) and Cash Conversion Cycles (*CCC*) for Selected Companies, Fiscal Year 2003

Data ($ in billions)	Computer Companies					Other Companies			
	IBM (IBM)	DELL (DELL)	Gateway (GTW)[a]	Apple (APPL)	Hewlett-Packard (HPQ)	Albertsons (ABS)	Polo Ralph Lauren (RL)	GM (GM)	McDonald's (MCD)
(1) Sales	89.131	35.404	4.171	6.207	73.061	35.626	2.439	186.763	17.141
(2) Cost of sales	56.113	29.055	3.605	4.499	53.648	25.242	1.232	153.344	11.944
(3) A/P	21.091	6.282	0.700	2.053	21.893	2.009	0.181	69.517	2.098
(4) A/R	31.465	2.586	0.198	0.956	19.030	0.647	0.376	18.223	0.735
(5) Inventory	2.942	0.306	0.089	0.056	6.065	3.093	0.364	15.272	0.129
Time Periods (in days)									
(6) *AAI* {[5] ÷ [(2) ÷ 365]}	19.14	3.84	9.01	4.54	41.26	44.72	107.84	36.35	3.94
(7) *ACP* {[4] ÷ [(1) ÷ 365]}	128.85	26.66	17.33	56.22	95.07	6.63	56.27	35.61	15.65
(8) *APP* {[3] ÷ [(2) ÷ 365]}[b]	137.19	78.92	70.87	166.56	148.95	29.05	53.62	165.47	64.11
Cycles (in days)									
(9) *OC* [(6) + (7)]	147.99	30.50	26.34	60.76	136.33	51.35	164.11	71.96	19.59
(10) *CCC* [(9) – (8)]	10.80	–48.42	–44.53	–105.80	–12.62	22.30	110.49	–93.51	–44.52

[a] FY 2002

[b] Note that because "annual purchases" cannot be found in published financial statements, this value is calculated using "cost of sales" (line 2), which is an approach external analysts commonly use. Because annual purchases are likely to be smaller than the cost of sales, these *APP*s may be understated.

Cash Conversion Cycle

Most firms obtain a significant amount of the financing they need through trade credit, represented by accounts payable. By taking advantage of trade credit, a firm reduces the amount of financing it needs from other sources to make it through the operating cycle. The elapsed time between the points at which a firm pays for raw materials and at which it receives payment for finished goods is called the **cash conversion cycle (CCC)**. The difference between the operating cycle and the cash conversion cycle is simply the amount of time that suppliers are willing to extend credit. In other words, to calculate the cash conversion cycle, start with the operating cycle and then subtract the *average payment period* (*APP*) on accounts payable. The formula for the cash conversion cycle follows:

cash conversion cycle (CCC)
The elapsed time between the points at which a firm pays for raw materials and at which it receives payment for finished goods.

$$CCC = OC - APP = AAI + ACP - APP \quad \text{(Eq. 19.1)}$$

As Equation 19.1 shows, the cash conversion cycle has three main components: (1) average age of the inventory, (2) average collection period, and (3) average payment period. It also shows that if a firm changes any of these time periods, it changes the amount of time resources are tied up in the day-to-day operation of the firm. Again referring to Table 19.2, we can see that the cash conversion cycles for each firm are calculated in line 10 by subtracting the average payment periods in line 8 from the operating cycles calculated in line 9. Reviewing the CCC for the computer manufacturers, we see that Dell, Gateway, Apple, and Hewlett-Packard have negative CCCs, which means that these firms effectively receive cash inflows ahead of having to make the cash outflows needed to generate those inflows. This very desirable CCC is in effect a pay-up-front-and-we'll-manufacture-and-ship-the-product-to-you-later type of business. The other top computer manufacturer, IBM, has a positive but relatively short CCC, reflecting very effective current account management. It is interesting to note that two of the other firms, GM and McDonald's, also have negative CCCs. Looking at the time periods for their *AAI*, *ACP*, and *APP* in lines 6 through 8, respectively, we can see that their vendors are effectively financing their operations given that their high *APP*s more than cover their time delays in inventory and accounts receivable. Albertsons and Polo Ralph Lauren also have positive CCCs, primarily due to their somewhat lengthy inventory periods. The cash conversion cycles shown demonstrate both inter- and intra-industry differences in the amount of time firms have their money tied up.

SMART PRACTICES VIDEO

Keith Woodward, Vice President of Finance, General Mills

"What we expect of financial analysts is to be able to manage all of the complexity and moving parts of working capital utilizing different ratios."

See the entire interview at SMARTFinance

APPLYING THE MODEL

Reese Industries, which has annual sales of $5 billion, a cost of goods sold of 70 percent of sales, and purchases that are 60 percent of cost of goods sold, can be used to demonstrate the cash conversion cycle. Reese has an *AAI* of 70 days, *ACP* of 45 days, and *APP* of 40 days. Also, the 45-day *ACP* can be broken into 37 days until the customer places the payment in the mail and an additional 8 days before the funds are available to the firm in a spendable form. Thus, Reese's operating cycle is 115 days (70 + 45), and its cash conversion cycle is 75 days (70 + 45 − 40). Figure 19.1 on page 760 presents Reese's operating and cash conversion cycles on a time line.

Figure 19.1
Time Line for the Operating and Cash Conversion Cycles for Reese Industries
Reese Industries has an operating cycle of 115 days, and because it takes on average 40 days to pay its accounts payable, the firm's cash conversion cycle is 75 days.

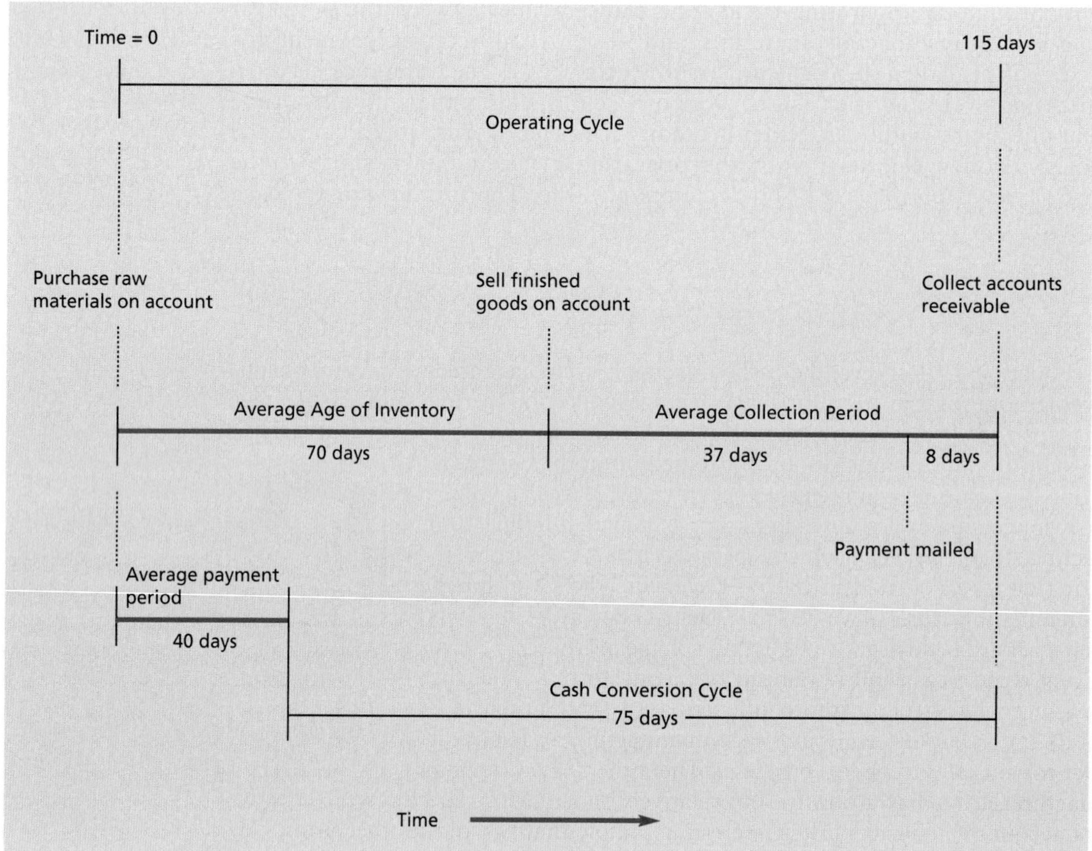

Reese has invested the following resources in its cash conversion cycle:

$$\begin{aligned}
& \text{inventory} = (\$5 \text{ billion} \times 0.70) \times (70/365) = \$671.2 \text{ million} \\
+\; & \text{accounts receivable} = (\$5 \text{ billion}) \times (45/365) = \$616.4 \text{ million} \\
-\; & \text{accounts payable} = (\$5 \text{ billion} \times 0.70 \times 0.60) \times (40/365) \\
& \qquad = \$230.1 \text{ million} \\
=\; & \text{resources invested of } \$1{,}057.5 \text{ million}
\end{aligned}$$

If Reese could reduce from 8 days to 3 days the amount of time it takes to receive, process, and collect payments after they are mailed by the firm's customers, it would reduce its average collection period to 40 days (37 + 3). This would shorten the cash conversion time line by 5 days (8 – 3) and thus reduce the amount of resources Reese has invested in operations. For Reese, a 5-day reduction in the average collection period would reduce the resources invested in the cash conversion cycle by \$68.5 million [\$5 billion × (5 ÷ 365)].

Shortening The Cash Conversion Cycle

Simply stated, in order *to positively contribute to the shareholder value-maximization goal, the financial manager should manage the firm's short-term activities in a manner that shortens the cash conversion cycle.* This will allow the firm to operate effectively with minimum cash investment. Cash that is not used to fund the cash conversion cycle can be deployed to more productive long-term investments, can be used to pay down expensive long-term financing, or can be distributed to owners as dividends. A positive cash conversion cycle means that trade credit does not provide enough financing to cover the firm's entire operating cycle. In that case, the firm must seek out other forms of financing, such as bank lines of credit, term loans, and so on. The costs of these financing sources tend to be higher than the costs of trade credit, so the firm benefits by finding ways to shorten its operating cycle or to lengthen its payment period. Actions that accomplish these objectives include the following:

1. *Turn over inventory as quickly as possible* without stockouts that result in lost sales.
2. *Collect accounts receivable as quickly as possible* without losing sales from high-pressure collection techniques.
3. *Pay accounts as slowly as possible* without damaging the firm's credit rating.
4. *Manage mail, processing, and clearing time* to reduce them when collecting from customers and increase them when paying vendors.

Techniques for implementing the first two strategies are the focus of the remainder of this chapter. Chapter 20 focuses on strategies 3 and 4.

CONCEPT REVIEW QUESTIONS

1. What does the firm's *cash conversion cycle* represent? What is the financial manager's goal with regard to it? Why?

2. How should the firm manage its inventory, accounts receivable, and accounts payable in order to reduce the length of its cash conversion cycle?

19.2 COST TRADE-OFFS IN SHORT-TERM FINANCIAL MANAGEMENT

When attempting to manage the firm's short-term accounts in a manner that minimizes cash while adequately funding the firm's operations, the financial manager must focus on competing costs. Decisions with regard to the optimum levels of both operating assets and short-term financing involve cost trade-offs. For convenience, we will view the current account decision strategies as revenue neutral and therefore examine their cost trade-offs solely with the *goal of minimizing total cost.* Although these decisions focus on cost trade-offs, they are yet another example of the cost-benefit trade-offs involved in financial decisions. In this case the reduction in one cost is the *marginal benefit* (a negative cost) and the increase in the other cost is the *marginal cost.* The firm will only act when the reduction in one cost—the marginal revenue—is greater than the increase in the other cost—the marginal cost. This approach should result in a net benefit that should contribute to the creation of additional shareholder value.

The optimum levels of the key operating assets—cash and marketable securities, accounts receivable, and inventory—involve trade-offs between the cost of holding the operating asset and the cost of maintaining too little of the asset. Figure 19.2 on page 762 depicts the cost trade-offs and optimum level of a given operating asset. Cost 1 is the holding cost, which increases (the *marginal cost*) with larger operating asset account balances, and cost 2 is the cost of holding too little of the operating asset, which decreases (the *marginal benefit*) with larger operating asset account balances. The total cost is the sum of cost 1 and cost 2 associated with a given account balance for the operating asset. As noted, the optimum balance occurs at the point where total cost is minimized.[2] (Note: In microeconomic terms, the optimum [minimum total cost] occurs where the marginal cost just equals the marginal benefit.)

Figure 19.2
Trade-off of Short-Term Financial Costs

Decisions with regard to the balance of both operating assets and short-term financing involve trade-offs between certain costs that increase with increasing balances (Cost 1) and other costs that decrease with increasing balances (Cost 2). The increasing costs are the marginal costs, *and the decreasing costs are the* marginal benefits. *The optimum balance occurs at the point where total cost is minimized.*

Cost ($)

— Total cost (cost 1 + cost 2)
— Cost 1*
— Cost 2**

Optimum Balance

Account Balance ($)

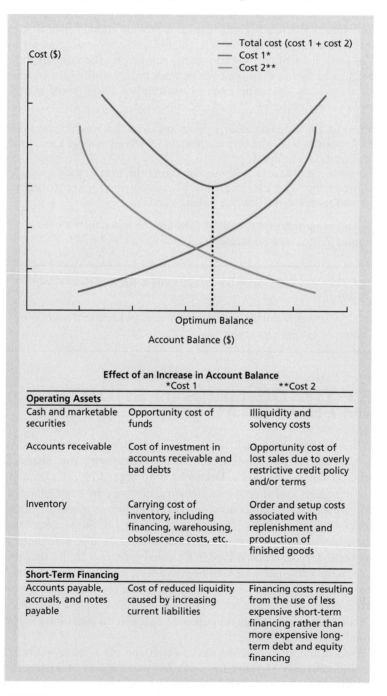

Effect of an Increase in Account Balance

	*Cost 1	**Cost 2
Operating Assets		
Cash and marketable securities	Opportunity cost of funds	Illiquidity and solvency costs
Accounts receivable	Cost of investment in accounts receivable and bad debts	Opportunity cost of lost sales due to overly restrictive credit policy and/or terms
Inventory	Carrying cost of inventory, including financing, warehousing, obsolescence costs, etc.	Order and setup costs associated with replenishment and production of finished goods
Short-Term Financing		
Accounts payable, accruals, and notes payable	Cost of reduced liquidity caused by increasing current liabilities	Financing costs resulting from the use of less expensive short-term financing rather than more expensive long-term debt and equity financing

SMART CONCEPTS

See the concept explained step-by-step at SMARTFinance

2. Figure 19.2 shows that the account balance that minimizes total cost occurs where cost 1 andcost 2 are equal. In fact, the optimum point does not necessarily occur where these two lines intersect. The minimum occurs where the marginal increase in cost 1 exactly offsets the marginal decrease in cost 2.

The table at the bottom of Figure 19.2 provides more detail on the specific costs for each operating asset. For example, consider cash and marketable securities. As the balance of these accounts increases, the opportunity costs (cost 1) of the funds held in the firm rise (the marginal cost). At the same time, the illiquidity and solvency costs (cost 2) fall (the marginal benefit) because the higher the cash and marketable securities balance, the greater the firm's liquidity and the lower its likelihood of becoming insolvent. The optimum balance of cash and marketable securities is therefore the one that minimizes the total of these two competing costs. The cost trade-offs for accounts receivable and inventory can be evaluated similarly using the cost descriptions given in the table and relating them to the two cost functions in the figure. Clearly, in all cases a decrease in the operating asset account balance would have the opposite effect.

The optimum level of short-term financing (accounts payable, accruals, and notes payable) involves the same type of cost trade-offs as demonstrated in Figure 19.2 for operating assets. As noted in the table, as the short-term financing balance increases, the firm faces an increasing cost of reduced liquidity (cost 1—the marginal cost). At the same time, the firm's financing costs (cost 2) decline (the marginal benefit) because short-term financing costs are lower than the alternative of using long-term debt and equity financing. Again, the optimum amount of short-term financing is that which minimizes total cost, as shown in the graph in Figure 19.2. A decrease in the short-term financing balance would have the opposite effects on the competing costs.

It should be clear from the preceding discussion that the financial manager's primary focus when managing current accounts is to minimize total cost and thereby increase shareholder value. Each of these account balances can be evaluated quantitatively using decision models much like the often-cited *economic order quantity (EOQ) model* (described in the next section), which focuses on determining the inventory order quantity that minimizes total cost. The remainder of this chapter and the following chapter emphasize effective techniques and strategies for actively managing the current accounts over which the financial manager has direct responsibility.

CONCEPT REVIEW QUESTIONS

3. What general cost trade-offs must the financial manager consider when managing the firm's operating assets? How do these costs behave as a firm considers reducing its accounts receivable by offering more restrictive credit terms? How can the optimum balance be determined?

4. What general cost trade-offs are associated with the firm's level of short-term financing? How do these costs behave when a firm substitutes short-term financing for long-term financing? How would you quantitatively model this decision to find the optimal level of short-term financing?

19.3 INVENTORY MANAGEMENT

Inventory is an important current asset that for the typical U.S. manufacturer represents between 10 percent and 20 percent of total assets—a sizable investment. It is made up of the firm's stock of raw materials, work in process, and finished goods. Although inventory management is the responsibility of production and operations managers, given its large investment, it is a major concern of the financial manager.

The firm's goal should be to move inventory quickly in order to minimize its investment, but it must be careful to maintain adequate inventory to meet demand and minimize stockouts, which can result in lost sales. The financial manager must therefore make sure that the firm maintains "optimal" inventory levels that reconcile these conflicting objectives. Also, because obsolescence can severely reduce the value of inventories, careful control of inventory is needed to avoid potential major losses in asset values. Here we consider the aspects of inventory that concern the financial manager, that is, the amount invested in inventory and several popular techniques for controlling inventory.

Investing in Inventory

A firm's investment in inventory must be evaluated in terms of associated revenues and costs; simply stated, additional investment must be justified by additional returns. From a financial point of view, constraining inventory levels improves returns by releasing funds that can be placed in more profitable investments. However, from production and marketing perspectives, expanding inventories provides for uninterrupted production runs, good product selection, and prompt delivery schedules. A balancing of the conflicting preferences of finance, production, and marketing managers is required in order to implement an effective inventory management system.

The financial manager should consider several specific factors in evaluating an inventory system. On the asset side of the balance sheet, inventories represent an important short-term investment. The smaller the level of inventory needed to support the firm's sales, the faster the total asset turnover, and the higher the returns on total assets. (Note: This is consistent with the basic DuPont formula discussed in Chapter 2.) More rapid inventory turnover also reduces the potential for obsolescence and resulting price concessions. On the liability side, smaller inventories reduce the firm's short-term financing requirements and thereby lower financing costs and improve profits. The key financial trade-off associated with inventory investment can be illustrated by the following example.

APPLYING THE MODEL

Kerry Manufacturing is contemplating larger production runs to reduce the high setup costs associated with a major product. The total annual savings in setup costs are estimated to be $120,000. The firm currently turns this product's inventory six times a year; with the proposed larger production runs, its inventory turnover is expected to drop to five. If the firm's cost of goods sold for this product of $30.0 million is unaffected by this proposal, and assuming the firm's required return on similar-risk investments is 15 percent, the analysis would be performed as follows.

Analysis:

Average investment in inventory = cost of goods sold ÷ inventory turnover

Proposed system	= $30.0 million ÷ 5 =	$6.0 million
Less: Present system	= 30.0 million ÷ 6 =	5.0 million
Increased inventory investment		$1.0 million
× required return		× 0.15
Annual cost of increased inventory investment		$ 150,000
Less: Annual savings in setup costs		120,000
Net loss from proposed plan		$ 30,000

Decision:

Don't do it; an annual loss of $30,000 will result from the proposed plan.

Techniques for Controlling Inventory

Although inventory control is a production/operations management responsibility, the financial manager serves as a "watchdog" over this activity. This oversight is quite important given the firm's typically sizable investment in inventory. A variety of techniques, such as an ABC system, the basic economic order quantity (EOQ) model, reorder points and safety stock, material requirements planning (MRP), and the just-in-time (JIT) system, are commonly used to control inventory. A good financial manager should understand them.

ABC System. A firm using the **ABC system** segregates its inventory into three groups, A, B, and C. The A items are those in which it has the largest dollar investment. In Figure 19.3, which depicts a typical distribution of inventory items, this group consists of 20 percent of the inventory items but accounts for 90 percent of the firm's dollar investment. These are the most costly inventory items. The B group consists of the items accounting for the next largest investment. In Figure 19.3, the B group consists of 30 percent of the items accounting for about 8 percent of the firm's dollar investment. The C group typically consists of a large number of items accounting for a small dollar investment. In Figure 19.3, the C group consists of approximately 50 percent of all items of inventory, but accounts for only about 2 percent of the firm's dollar investment. Such items as screws, nails, and washers would be in this group.

ABC system
An inventory control system that segregates inventory into three groups—A, B, and C. The A items require the largest dollar investment and the most intensive control, the B items require the next largest investment and less intensive control, and the C items require the smallest investment and the least intensive control.

Separating its inventory into A, B, and C groups allows the firm to determine the level and types of inventory control procedures needed. Control of the A items should be most intensive due to the high dollar investments involved, whereas the B and C items would be subject to correspondingly less sophisticated procedures.

Basic Economic Order Quantity (EOQ) Model. One of the most commonly mentioned tools for determining the optimal order quantity for an item of inventory is the **economic order quantity (EOQ) model.** This model could be used to control the firm's big-ticket inventory items such as those included in the A group of an ABC system. The EOQ model considers operating and financial costs and determines the order quantity that minimizes overall inventory costs. Here we will briefly review the key costs, study a graphic view, and develop a mathematical approach for finding the EOQ.

economic order quantity (EOQ) model
A common tool used to estimate the optimal order quantity for big-ticket items of inventory. It considers operating and financial costs and determines the order quantity that minimizes overall inventory costs.

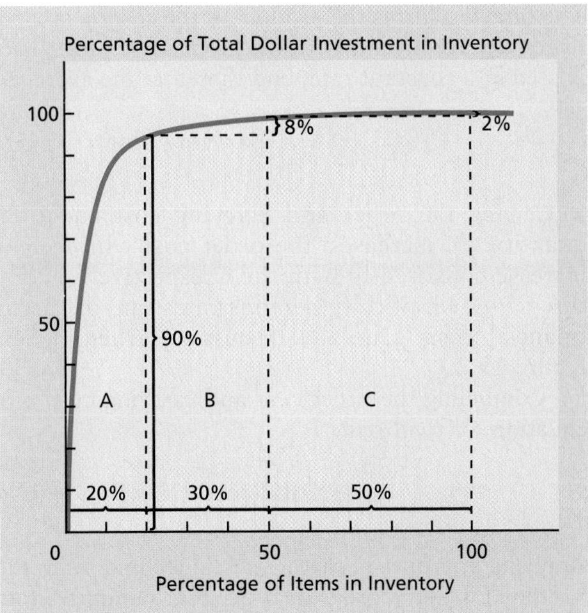

Figure 19.3
The ABC System Applied to a Typical Distribution of Inventory Items

Under the ABC system, the inventory is divided into three groups—A, B, and C. Because the A items are a small number of items requiring a large dollar investment, they would be most carefully controlled; whereas the B and C items because they require relatively small dollar investments would be less carefully controlled.

The Key Costs. Excluding the actual cost of the merchandise, the key costs associated with inventory include order costs, carrying costs, and total costs.

order cost
The *fixed dollar amount per order* that covers the costs of placing and receiving an order, which includes the cost of preparing, processing, and transmitting a purchase order, and the cost of receiving an order and checking it against the invoice. Used in calculating the EOQ.

carrying cost
The *variable cost per unit* of holding an item in inventory for a specified period of time. Used in calculating the EOQ.

total cost
The sum of the *order costs* and the *carrying costs* that is minimized at the *economic order quantity (EOQ) model.*

- **Order costs** include the fixed clerical costs of placing and receiving an order, which includes the cost of preparing, processing, and transmitting a purchase order, and the cost of receiving an order and checking it against the invoice. Order costs are normally viewed as a *fixed dollar amount per order.*
- **Carrying costs** are the *variable cost per unit* of holding an item in inventory for a specified period of time. They are typically stated as dollars per unit per period and represent about 25 percent of the dollar value of the inventory. Carrying costs include storage costs, insurance costs, deterioration and obsolescence costs, and most important, the opportunity cost of the funds tied up in inventory. The opportunity cost is the financial component, which represents the value of the returns that have been forgone in order to maintain the current inventory investment.
- **Total cost** is the sum of the *order costs* and *carrying costs.* Total cost is the focus of the EOQ, which represents the order quantity that minimizes this cost.

A Mathematical Approach. The following notation can be used to develop a formula for calculating the EOQ for a given inventory item.

$$S = \text{inventory usage per period (typically one year)}$$
$$O = \text{order cost per order}$$
$$C = \text{carrying cost per unit per period}$$
$$Q = \text{order quantity in units}$$

Using this notation, *order cost* can be expressed as the product of the cost per order (O) and the number of orders, which is merely the usage per period divided by the order quantity (S/Q).

$$\text{Order cost} = O \times S / Q$$

The *carrying cost* is the product of the cost of carrying a unit per period (C) and the firm's average inventory of the given item ($Q/2$). The model assumes that inventory is used at a constant rate, and therefore the average inventory is $Q/2$.

$$\text{Carrying cost} = C \times Q / 2$$

Reviewing the order and carrying cost equations, we see that as the order quantity, Q, increases, the order cost will decrease and the carrying cost will increase consistently with their respective functions in Figure 19.4. (Note that this figure specifically demonstrates one of the many trade-offs of short-term financial costs generally discussed earlier in Section 19.2 and illustrated in Figure 19.2.)

Combining the order cost and carrying cost expressions, we get the following equation for *total cost.*

$$\text{Total cost} = (O \times S / Q) + (C \times Q / 2)$$

Applying appropriate mathematical techniques to the total cost function[3], we solve for the EOQ—the order quantity that minimizes total cost:

[3] The total cost equation can be solved for the EOQ either by setting the order cost equal to the carrying cost and solving for Q, or by taking the first derivative of the total cost equation and setting it equal to 0 and solving for Q.

$$\text{EOQ} = \sqrt{\frac{2SO}{C}} \quad \text{(Eq. 19.2)}$$

APPLYING THE MODEL

Garrison Industries currently uses 16,000 units of an expensive inventory item each year. The firm estimates order cost to be \$500 per order and carrying cost for this item to be \$100 per unit per year. Garrison wishes to estimate the optimal quantity in which to order this item. By substituting S = 16,000, O = \$500, and C = \$100 into Equation 19.2, we can calculate the EOQ for this item as:

$$\text{EOQ} = \sqrt{\frac{2 \times 16{,}000 \times \$500}{\$100}} = \sqrt{160{,}000} = 400 \text{ units}$$

If Garrison Industries orders this item in quantities of 400 units, it should minimize its total inventory cost for this item.

A Graphic View. The objective of the EOQ model is to find the order quantity that minimizes total cost. The model can be viewed graphically by plotting order quantities on the x-axis and costs on the y-axis. Figure 19.4 shows the general behavior of these costs. Given the mathematical assumptions of the EOQ model, the minimum total cost occurs at the point labeled EOQ, which occurs at the point where the order cost and the carrying cost lines intersect. Note that the order cost varies inversely with the order quantity—as the order quantity increases, the order cost for the period decreases, and vice versa. Given the assumed fixed annual usage, as larger amounts are ordered, fewer orders are placed, resulting in lower order costs per unit. The carrying costs are directly related to the size of the order—the larger the order quantity, the larger the average inventory and therefore the higher the firm's carrying cost, and vice versa.

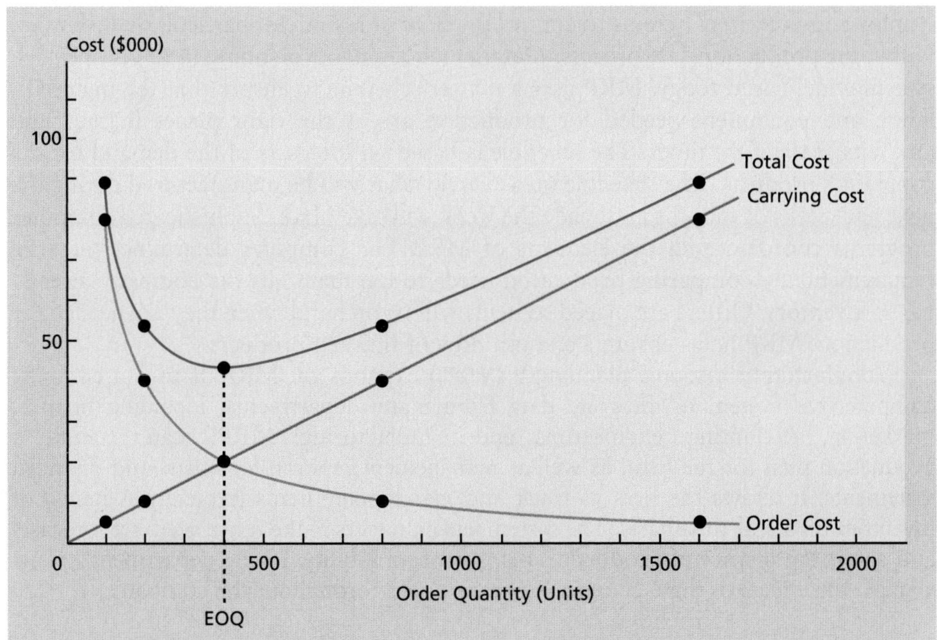

Figure 19.4
A Graphic View of an EOQ

Because the order costs decline and the carrying costs rise as the order quantity increases in size, the total of the two costs tends to be U-shaped. The order quantity for which the total cost is minimized is the economic order quantity (EOQ).

The total cost line, which represents the sum of the order costs and carrying costs, exhibits a U shape, indicating that the function has a minimum value. Research has shown that in a range of ±20 percent of the EOQ, the total cost function is relatively flat, suggesting that total cost is relatively insensitive to small deviations from the EOQ.

Reorder Points and Safety Stock. The simple EOQ model just presented assumes that inventory is instantaneously replenished with the receipt of a new order precisely at the time the inventory is exhausted. This model implies perfect certainty with regard to the rate of usage and the timing of receipt from suppliers. Assuming a constant rate of usage, a *reorder point* can be easily estimated as follows:

SMART PRACTICES VIDEO

Vern LoForti, Chief Financial Officer of Overland Storage Inc.

"You have to have a high level of confidence in those suppliers who are holding that inventory at their warehouse."

See the entire interview at SMARTFinance

$$\text{Reorder point} = \text{lead time in days} \times \text{daily usage}$$

For example, if Garrison Industries, noted previously, uses about 44 units per day (16,000 units per year ÷ 365 days), and it typically takes the firm 4 days to place and receive an order, the firm should place an order when its inventory falls to 176 units (4 days × 44 units).

To allow for faster-than-anticipated rates of usage and delayed deliveries, many firms maintain *safety stocks* of inventory. The size of these stocks would be determined by management's analysis of the probabilities of both increased usage rates and delivery delays. For example, if Garrison Industries estimates that a safety stock equal to 2 percent of its annual usage of the given item will adequately protect against stockouts due to faster-than-anticipated usage and order fulfillment delays, it will maintain a safety stock of 320 units (0.02 × 16,000 units). Clearly, a variety of more sophisticated models are available for both setting reorder points and safety stocks.

material requirements planning (MRP)
A computerized system used to control the flow of resources, particularly inventory, within the production-sale process. Uses a master schedule to ensure that the materials, labor, and equipment needed for production are at the right places in the right amounts at the right times.

manufacturing resource planning II (MRPII)
Expands on MRP by using a complex computerized system to integrate data from many departments and generate a production plan for the firm along with management reports, forecasts, and financial statements.

Material Requirements Planning. Many manufacturing firms employ computerized systems to control the flow of resources, particularly inventory, within the production-sale process. **Material requirements planning (MRP)** is one such system widely used today. MRP uses a master schedule to ensure that the materials, labor, and equipment needed for production are at the right places in the right amounts at the right times. The schedule is based on forecasts of the demand for the company's products. The schedule says exactly what will be manufactured during the next few weeks or months and when the work will take place. Sophisticated computer programs coordinate all the elements of MRP. The computer determines material requirements by comparing production needs to the materials the company already has in inventory. Orders are placed so items will be on hand when they are needed for production. MRP helps ensure a smooth flow of finished products.

Manufacturing resource planning II (MRPII) expands on MRP. It uses a complex computerized system to integrate data from many departments, including finance, marketing, accounting, engineering, and manufacturing. MRPII can generate a production plan for the firm, as well as management reports, forecasts, and financial statements. It allows the firm to track and manage key items (typically A items) of inventory on a real-time basis. The system lets managers make more accurate forecasts and assess the impact of production plans on profitability. If one department's plans change, the effects of these changes are transmitted throughout the company.

Just-in-Time System. An important and widely adopted inventory management technique, imported from Japan, is the **just-in-time (JIT) system**. JIT is based on the belief that materials should arrive exactly when they are needed for production, rather than being stored on-site. Relying closely on computerized systems such as MRP and MRPII, manufacturers determine what parts will be needed and when, and then order them from suppliers so they arrive "just in time." Under the JIT system, inventory products are "pulled" through the production process in response to customer demand. JIT requires close teamwork among vendors and purchasing and production personnel because any delay in deliveries of supplies could bring production to a halt. Clearly unexpected events, such as 9/11, can cause problems for firms using a JIT system. In spite of such risks, a properly employed JIT system can significantly reduce inventory levels and carrying costs, thereby freeing funds for more productive uses.

just-in-time (JIT) system
An inventory management technique used to make sure that materials arrive exactly when they are needed for production, rather than being stored on-site. To work effectively it requires close teamwork among vendors and purchasing and production personnel.

CONCEPT REVIEW QUESTIONS

5. How might the financial manager's view of inventory differ from that of managers in production and marketing? What is the relationship between inventory turnover and inventory investment? Explain.

6. What is the *ABC system*? What role does the *EOQ model* play in controlling inventory? How does it capture the opportunity costs associated with inventory investment?

7. From the financial manager's perspective, describe the role of reorder points, safety stock, MRP, MRPII, and a *just-in-time system* in managing a firm's inventory.

19.4 ACCOUNTS RECEIVABLE STANDARDS AND TERMS

Accounts receivable (A/R) result from a company selling its products or services on cred it and are represented in the cash conversion cycle by the **average collection period (*ACP*)**. This period is the average length of time from a sale on credit until the payment becomes usable funds for the firm. The average collection period has two parts. The first, and generally the longest, is the credit period, measured as the time from the sale (or customer invoicing) until the customers place their payments in the mail. The second is the time from when the customers place their payments in the mail to when the firm has spendable funds in its bank account. The first part of the average collection period involves managing the credit available to the firm's customers; the second part involves receiving, processing, and collecting payments. This section discusses customer credit, and Chapter 20 presents discussions of receiving, processing, and collecting payments.

average collection period (*ACP*)
The average length of time from a sale on credit until the payment becomes usable funds for a firm. Also *known as days' sales outstanding (DSO).*

As with all current accounts, receivables management requires managers to balance competing interests. On the one hand, managers (generally the cash or treasury managers) would prefer to receive cash payments sooner rather than later, and that leads toward strict credit terms and strict enforcement of those terms. On the other hand, firms can use credit terms as a marketing tool to attract new customers (or to keep current customers from defecting to another firm). This objective argues for easier credit terms and more flexible enforcement. For many companies, in order to be competitive, credit terms are a very necessary part of determining the ultimate sales price for their products and services.

Effective Accounts Receivable Management

Effectively managing the credit and accounts receivable process involves cooperation among sales, customer service, finance, and accounting staffs. The key areas of concern involve:

1. Setting and communicating the company's general credit and collections policies;
2. Determining who is granted credit and how much credit is allowed for each customer;
3. Managing the billing and collection process in a timely and accurate manner;
4. Applying payments and updating the accounts receivable ledger;
5. Monitoring accounts receivable on both an individual and aggregate basis; and
6. Following up on overdue accounts and initiating collection procedures, if required.

In the typical company, the credit and accounts receivable departments handle most of these tasks, but the cash management or treasury area will usually be responsible for managing the actual receipt of payments. As part of this process, the cash manager will usually also have to collect and organize the remittance data that is sent along with the payments so that the A/R department will be able to determine what invoices have been paid. This *cash application* process will be covered in greater detail later in the chapter.

The first decision a company must make is whether it will offer trade credit at all. There are many reasons for offering credit, including increasing or facilitating sales, meeting terms offered by competitors, attracting new customers, or providing general convenience. In a typical business-to-business environment, a company may have to offer trade credit just to generate sales. This is especially the case for a large company selling to smaller companies, where the smaller company literally needs the credit period to sell merchandise so that it can pay its supplier. The small company would not usually have access to other types of credit, so if the supplier did not offer credit, there would be no sale.

As mentioned earlier, many companies see trade credit and credit terms as simply an extension of the sales price and may use credit terms to motivate customers or compete with other suppliers. In many cases, industry practices may dictate whether credit is offered and what the terms are. The Comparative Corporate Finance insert on page 771 compares the level of trade credit in the United States to that in other major countries throughout the world. In today's financial environment, there are also many opportunities for companies to outsource part or all of the credit and accounts receivable process, including use of credit cards, third-party financing, or **factoring**, which involves the outright sale of receivables to a third-party *factor* at a discount.

factoring
The outright sale of receivables to a third-party *factor* at a discount.

Once the decision has been made to offer trade credit, a company must then (1) determine its credit standards (Who gets offered credit and how much?), (2) set its credit terms (How long do customers have to pay, and are any discounts offered for early payment?), (3) develop its collection policy (How should delinquent accounts be handled?), and (4) monitor its accounts receivable on both an individual and aggregate basis (What is the status of each customer and the overall quality of its receivables?). In addition, the firm must have effective cash application procedures in place.

Credit Standards

The first, and most important, aspect of accounts receivable management is setting credit standards, which involves applying techniques for determining which customers should receive credit and how much credit should be granted. Although much of the focus is on making sure that a company does not accept substandard customers (i.e., potential defaulters on trade credit), there is also the risk that the standards will be set too high and that potential good customers will be rejected. Accounts receivable default rates for a given company should generally be in line with those of other companies in the same industry if it wants to remain competitive.

Granting Credit to Customers. In analyzing credit requests and determining the level of credit to be offered, the company can gather information

COMPARATIVE CORPORATE FINANCE

Trade Credit Practices Around the World

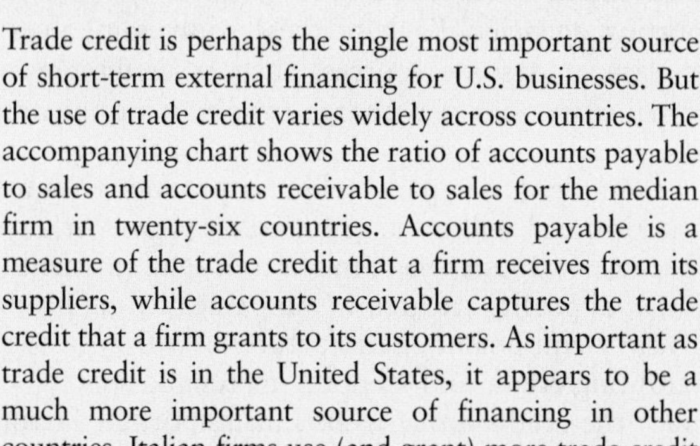

Trade credit is perhaps the single most important source of short-term external financing for U.S. businesses. But the use of trade credit varies widely across countries. The accompanying chart shows the ratio of accounts payable to sales and accounts receivable to sales for the median firm in twenty-six countries. Accounts payable is a measure of the trade credit that a firm receives from its suppliers, while accounts receivable captures the trade credit that a firm grants to its customers. As important as trade credit is in the United States, it appears to be a much more important source of financing in other countries. Italian firms use (and grant) more trade credit than firms in any other country. Heavy trade credit usage is common among the Mediterranean countries of Europe, while in northern Europe (e.g. Finland and Germany), firms use trade credit at a rate similar to that seen in the United States.

The use of trade credit varies across countries for many reasons. Probably the most important factor is whether or not a given country has well-developed markets for external capital, including a thriving banking sector. When sources of external funds are few, firms may rely more heavily on trade credit as a means of financing operations. Another factor that helps to explain cross-country differences in trade credit is firm size. Large firms have access to broader capital sources than small firms do, so in a country where firms are relatively small (e.g., Italy), trade credit may be more important.

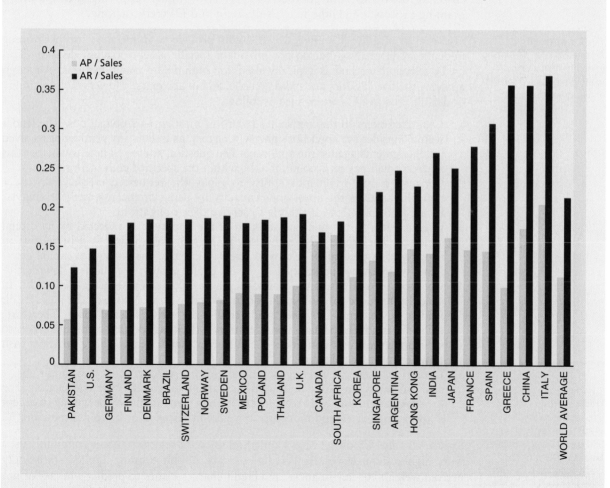

Source: Data from Worldscope; calculations by Inessa Love.

from both internal and external sources. The usual internal sources of credit information are the credit application and agreement submitted by the applicant and, if available, the company's own records of that applicant's payment history. External sources typically include financial statements, trade references, banks or other creditors, and credit reporting agencies. Each of these sources involves the internal costs of analyzing the data, and some sources, such as credit reporting agencies, also have explicit external costs, that is, a charge for obtaining the data.

The company must also take into account the variable costs of the products it would be selling on credit. For example, a company selling a product with a low variable cost (i.e., magazine subscriptions) will often grant credit to almost anyone without a credit check simply because it doesn't have much to lose if payment isn't made, but on the other hand potential profits are great. Companies selling products with high variable costs (i.e., heavy-equipment manufacturers) will typically do extensive credit checks before granting credit and shipping merchandise.

The amount of credit offered (the credit limit) is also an important factor. In order to reduce some of the credit decision costs, a company may routinely grant small levels of credit to new customers, allowing the credit limit to rise as the customer proves to be a good credit risk. Two popular approaches to the credit granting process are (1) the five C's of credit and (2) credit scoring.

five C's of credit
A framework for performing in-depth credit analysis without providing a specific accept or reject decision.

Five C's of Credit. The **five C's of credit** provide a framework for performing in-depth credit analysis but do not provide a specific accept or reject decision. This credit selection method is typically used for high-dollar credit requests. Although applying the five C's does not speed up collection of accounts, it lowers the probability of default. The five C's are defined as follows:

1. *Character* refers to the applicant's record of meeting past obligations. The lender would consider the applicant's payment history, as well as any pending or resolved legal judgments against the applicant. The question addressed here is whether this applicant will pay its account, if able, within the specified credit terms.
2. *Capacity* is the applicant's ability to repay the requested credit. The lender typically assesses the applicant's capacity by using financial statement analysis focused on cash flows available to service debt obligations.
3. *Capital* refers to the financial strength of the applicant as reflected by its capital structure. The lender frequently uses analysis of the applicant's debt relative to equity and its profitability ratios to assess its capital. The analysis of capital determines whether the applicant has sufficient equity to survive a business downturn.
4. *Collateral* is the assets the applicant has available for securing the credit. In general, the more valuable and more marketable these assets are, the more credit lenders will extend. However, trade credits are rarely secured loans. Therefore, collateral is not the primary consideration in deciding to grant credit but serves to strengthen the creditworthiness of a customer that appears to have sufficient cash flows to meet its obligation.
5. *Conditions* refer to current general and industry-specific economic conditions. It also considers any unique conditions surrounding a specific transaction. For example, a firm that has excess inventory of a given item may be willing to accept a lower price or extend more attractive credit terms in order to sell the item.

credit scoring
Applies statistically derived weights for key financial and credit characteristics to predict whether or not a credit applicant with specific scores for each characteristic will pay the requested credit in a timely fashion.

Credit Scoring. Credit scoring is a method of credit selection that is commonly used with high-volume–low-dollar credit requests. **Credit scoring** applies statistically derived weights for key financial and credit characteristics to predict whether or not a credit applicant with specific scores (assigned either subjectively by an analyst or by a computer using an expert system) for each characteristic will pay the requested

Table 19.3
Consumer Credit Application Credit Score by WEG Oil

Note: Column (1): Scores assigned by analyst or computer based on information supplied on credit application. Scores range from 0 (lowest) to 100 (highest). Column (2): Weights based on the company's analysis of the relative importance of each characteristic in predicting whether a customer will pay its account in a timely fashion. The weights must add up to 1.00.

Financial and Credit Characteristics	Score (0 to 100) (1)	Predetermined Weight (2)	Weighted Score [(1) × (2)] (3)
Credit references	80	0.15	12.00
Home ownership	100	0.15	15.00
Income range	75	0.25	18.75
Payment history	80	0.25	20.00
Years at address	90	0.10	9.00
Years on job	85	0.10	8.50
	Totals	1.00	Credit score 83.25

credit in a timely fashion. It uses a weighted average score derived as the sum of the products of the applicant's score and the associated predetermined weight for each characteristic to determine whether to accept or reject the credit applicant. Simply stated, the procedure results in a score that measures the applicant's overall credit strength, and the score is used to make the accept or reject decision for granting the applicant credit. Credit scoring is most commonly used by large credit card operations, such as those of banks, oil companies, and department stores.

APPLYING THE MODEL

WEG Oil, a major oil company, uses credit scoring to make its consumer credit decisions. Each applicant fills out a credit application. Data from the application are input into an expert system, and a computer generates the applicant's final credit score, creates a letter indicating whether the application was approved, and if approved, issues the credit card. Table 19.3 demonstrates the scoring of a consumer credit application, and Table 19.4 describes WEG's predetermined credit standards. Because the applicant in Table 19.3 has a credit score of 83.25, it will receive WEG's standard credit terms (referring to Table 19.4).

Changing Credit Standards. As a practical matter, the vast majority of sales by U.S. corporations is made on credit, so it is important to understand how

Table 19.4
WEG Oil's Credit Standards

Credit Score	Action
Higher than 75	Extend standard credit terms
65 to 75	Extend limited credit; if account is properly maintained, convert to standard credit terms after one year
Lower than 65	Reject application

establishing and changing credit standards impact sales, costs, and overall cash flows for a given company. As we discussed earlier, it is essential that firms accurately assess the creditworthiness of individual customers who buy on credit, but this does not mean that a firm should extend credit only to those customers who are certain to repay their debts. Following such an excessively conservative strategy will cost the company many profitable sales, especially if industry practice is to be more generous in extending credit. Instead, the firm should accept a degree of default risk in order to increase sales, but obviously not so much that the additional profit from sales is overwhelmed by the need to invest huge amounts in accounts receivable and absorb bad debts. The financial manager is typically responsible for estimating the cash flow and financial impact of a proposed change in credit standards.

Fortunately, measuring the overall financial impact of either tightening or relaxing credit standards is fairly straightforward. Any change will likely yield both benefits and costs; the decision to change standards will naturally depend on whether or not the marginal benefits exceed the marginal costs. In general, *relaxing credit standards* will yield the benefit of increased unit sales and (assuming each unit is sold at a positive contribution margin) additional profits, but it will also yield higher costs from additional investment in accounts receivable and additional bad debt expense. The **contribution margin** is defined as a product's price per unit minus variable costs per unit, and is thus a direct measure of gross profit per unit sold. *Tightening credit standards* will generally yield the benefits of reduced investment in accounts receivable and lower bad debt expense at the cost of lower sales and profits. It is easiest to demonstrate how to calculate the net effect of changing credit standards using an example.

contribution margin
The sale price per unit minus variable cost per unit.

APPLYING THE MODEL

Yeoman Manufacturing Company (YMC) produces and sells a CD organizer to music stores nationwide. YMC charges $20/unit, and all of its sales are on credit, with customers selected for credit on the basis of a scoring process. If these credit standards are left unchanged, YMC expects to sell 120,000 units (un) over the coming year, yielding total sales of $2,400,000 (120,000 units × $20/unit). Variable costs are $12/unit, and YMC has fixed costs of $240,000 per year.

The company is contemplating a relaxation of its credit standards and expects the following effects: a 5 percent increase in sales to 126,000 units; an increase in the average collection period from 30 days (the current level) to 45 days; and an increase in bad debt expense from 1 percent (the current level) to 2 percent of sales. YMC plans to keep the product's sale price unchanged at $20/unit, which implies that total sales will increase to $2,520,000 (126,000 units × $20/unit). If the firm's required return on investments of equal risk is 12 percent, should YMC relax its credit standards?

YMC's managers must calculate (1) how much profits will increase from the additional sales that relaxing credit standards are expected to generate, (2) how much the additional investment in accounts receivable will cost, (3) how much the additional bad debt expense will cost, and (4) whether the financial benefits exceed the costs.

1. **Additional profit contribution from sales.** Because we are assuming that a 5 percent increase in sales volume will not cause YMC's fixed costs to increase, we need only account for changes in revenues and variable costs. Specifically, we

can compute the marginal increase in profits as the increased unit sales volume times the contribution margin per unit sold, as in Equation 19.3:

$$\text{Marginal profit from increased sales} = \Delta\text{Sales} \times CM = \Delta\text{Sales} \times (\text{Price} - VC) \quad \text{(Eq. 19.3)}$$

where ΔSales = change in unit sales resulting from the change in credit policies
CM = contribution margin
Price = price per unit
VC = variable cost per unit

Using the assumptions just detailed for YMC, we can use Equation 19.3 to determine that relaxing credit standards as suggested will yield a marginal profit of $48,000:

$$\begin{aligned}\text{Marginal profit from increased sales} &= 6{,}000 \text{ un} \times (\$20/\text{un} - \$12/\text{un}) = 6{,}000 \text{ un} \times (\$8/\text{un}) \\ &= \$48{,}000\end{aligned}$$

2. **Cost of the marginal investment in accounts receivable.** To determine the cost of the additional investment in accounts receivable, we must calculate the cost of financing the current level of accounts receivable and compare it to the expected cost under the new credit standards. This is more complicated than it sounds, as we must first calculate how much YMC currently has invested in accounts receivable—based on its current annual sales, variable costs, and accounts receivable turnover—and then repeat this process for the level of sales expected to result from a change in credit standards. The steps required are presented in Equations 19.4, 19.5, and 19.6. *Note that we use variable costs in calculating investment in accounts receivable because this is the firm's actual cash expense incurred (and tied up in receivables).*

$$\text{Average investment in accounts receivable } (AIAR) = \frac{\text{total variable cost of annual sales}}{\text{turnover of accounts receivable}} \quad \text{(Eq. 19.4)}$$

$$\text{Total variable cost of annual sales } (TVC) = \text{annual unit sales} \times \text{variable cost/unit} \quad \text{(Eq. 19.5)}$$

$$\text{Turnover of accounts receivable } (TOAR) = \frac{365}{\text{average collection period } (ACP)} \quad \text{(Eq. 19.6)}$$

average investment in accounts receivable (*AIAR*)
An estimate of the actual amount of cash tied up in accounts receivable at any time during the year.

total variable cost of annual sales (*TVC*)
Calculated by multiplying the annual sales in units by the variable cost per unit and used to estimate the average investment in accounts receivable under a stated policy.

We can use these equations to compute the **average investment in accounts receivable (*AIAR*)** for the current, $AIAR_{CURRENT}$, and proposed, $AIAR_{PROPOSED}$, credit standards. First, we compute the **total variable cost of annual sales (*TVC*)** under the current credit standards, $TVC_{CURRENT}$, and the proposed plan, $TVC_{PROPOSED}$, using Equation 19.5:

$$TVC_{CURRENT} = 120{,}000 \text{ un} \times \$12/\text{un} = \$1{,}440{,}000$$
$$TVC_{PROPOSED} = 126{,}000 \text{ un} \times \$12/\text{un} = \$1{,}512{,}000$$

turnover of accounts receivable (*TOAR*)
Three-hundred-sixty-five divided by the *average collection period (ACP)*. Used to calculate the *average investment in accounts receivable (AIAR)* when evaluating accounts receivable policies.

Next, we note that the average collection period under the current plan, $ACP_{CURRENT}$, is 30 days, but this is expected to rise to 45 days under the proposed plan, $ACP_{PROPOSED}$. This allows us to use Equation 19.6 to compute the **turnover of accounts receivable (*TOAR*)** under the current, $TOAR_{CURRENT}$, and proposed, $TOAR_{PROPOSED}$, credit terms:

$$TOAR_{CURRENT} = \frac{365}{ACP_{CURRENT}} = \frac{365}{30 \text{ days}} = 12.2 \text{ times/year}$$

$$TOAR_{PROPOSED} = \frac{365}{ACP_{PROPOSED}} = \frac{365}{45 \text{ days}} = 8.1 \text{ times/year}$$

These turnover measures suggest that if YMC relaxes its credit standards, the turnover of its accounts receivable will slow down from 12.2 times per year to 8.1 times per year. Clearly, this slowing is attributable to the generally slower paying of the additional credit customers generated by the relaxed credit standards.

We now have all the inputs required to use Equation 19.4 to compute the $AIAR_{CURRENT}$ and $AIAR_{PROPOSED}$:

$$AIAR_{CURRENT} = \frac{TVC_{CURRENT}}{TOAR_{CURRENT}} = \frac{\$1,440,000}{12.2} = \$118,033$$

$$AIAR_{PROPOSED} = \frac{TVC_{PROPOSED}}{TOAR_{PROPOSED}} = \frac{\$1,512,000}{8.1} = \$186,667$$

cost of marginal investment in accounts receivable
The marginal investment in accounts receivable required to support a proposed change in credit policy multiplied by the required return on investment.

With these measures, we can now determine the **cost of the marginal investment in accounts receivable**, which is equal to the marginal investment in accounts receivable required to support the proposed change in credit policy multiplied by the required return on investment, r_a:

$$\text{Cost of marginal investment in accounts receivable} = \text{additional investment} \times \text{required return} \qquad \textbf{(Eq. 19.7)}$$

$$= (AIAR_{PROPOSED} - AIAR_{CURRENT}) \times r_a$$

$$= (\$186,667 - \$118,033) \times 0.12 = \$68,634 \times 0.12 = \$8,236$$

This value of \$8,236 is properly considered a cost of adopting the relaxed credit standards because it represents the opportunity cost of investing an additional \$68,634 in accounts receivable rather than investing these funds in another earning asset.

3. **Cost of marginal bad debt expense.** Relaxing YMC's credit standards is expected to increase the firm's bad debt expense by 1 percent, from 1 percent to 2 percent of sales. The cost of this is calculated quite easily by subtracting the current level of bad debt expense, $BDE_{CURRENT}$ (computed as the bad debt expense rate, $\%BDE_{CURRENT}$, times the current annual sales level, $Sales_{CURRENT}$), from the expected level of bad debt expense under the proposed new credit standards, $BDE_{PROPOSED}$ (computed similarly using the

bad debt expense rate, $\%BDE_{PROPOSED}$, and the annual sales level, $Sales_{PROPOSED}$, under the proposed new credit standards). Equations 19.8 and 19.9 demonstrate the calculations required:

$$\text{Bad debt expense } (BDE) = \text{annual sales (Sales)} \times \text{bad debt expense rate } (\%BDE) \quad \text{(Eq. 19.8)}$$

$$BDE_{PROPOSED} = (Sales_{PROPOSED}) \times (\%BDE_{PROPOSED}) = \$2{,}520{,}000 \times 0.02 = \$50{,}400$$

$$BDE_{CURRENT} = (Sales_{CURRENT}) \times (\%BDE_{CURRENT}) = \$2{,}400{,}000 \times 0.01 = \$24{,}000$$

$$\text{Cost of marginal bad debts} = BDE_{PROPOSED} - BDE_{CURRENT} = \$50{,}400 - \$24{,}000 = \$26{,}400 \quad \text{(Eq. 19.9)}$$

4. **Net profit for the credit decision.** Now that we have calculated the individual financial benefits and costs of changing YMC's credit standards, we can use Equation 19.10 to compute the overall net profit for the credit decision:

$$\text{Net profit for the credit decision} = \text{Marginal profit from increased sales} - \text{Cost of marginal investment in accounts receivable} - \text{Cost of marginal bad debts} \quad \text{(Eq. 19.10)}$$

$$= \$48{,}000 - \$8{,}236 - \$26{,}400 = \underline{\underline{\$13{,}364}}$$

Because relaxing YMC's credit standards is expected to yield $13,364 in increased profit, the firm should implement the proposed change. The profit from additional sales will more than offset the total cost of additional investment in accounts receivable and the increased bad debt expense.

Credit Terms

credit terms The terms of sale for customers.

Credit terms are the terms of sale for customers. Terms of *net 30* mean the customer has 30 days from the beginning of the credit period (typically *end of month [EOM]* or *date of invoice*) to pay the full invoice amount. Some firms offer cash discounts with terms, such as *2/10 net 30*. These terms mean the customer can take a 2 percent *cash discount* from the invoice amount if the payment is made within the 10-day *cash discount period*, or the customer can pay the full amount of the invoice within the 30-day *credit period*.

A firm's regular credit terms are strongly influenced by the nature of its business. For example, a firm selling perishable items will have very short credit terms because its items have little long-term collateral value. These types of firms will typically offer short terms, where the buyer has 7–10 days to make payment. A firm in a seasonal business may tailor its terms to fit the industry cycles with terms known as *seasonal dating*. Most managers want their company's regular credit terms to be consistent with industry standards because if the company's terms are more restrictive than those of its competitors, it will lose business; if its terms are less restrictive than those of its competitors, it will attract customers of poor quality that probably could not pay under the standard industry term.

cash discount
A method of lowering investment in accounts receivable by giving customers a cash incentive to pay sooner.

A popular method used by the firm to lower its investment in accounts receivable is to include a **cash discount** in the credit terms. The cash discount provides a cash incentive for customers to pay sooner. The discount, by speeding collections, will decrease the firm's investment in accounts receivable, which is the objective, but it will also decrease the per-unit profit because the customer pays less than the full invoice amount. Additionally, initiating a cash discount should reduce bad debts, because customers will pay sooner, and increase sales volume, because the customers that take the cash discount pay a lower price for the product. Accordingly, firms considering offering a cash discount must perform a cost-benefit analysis to determine if a cash discount is profitable enough to be included in their credit terms.

APPLYING THE MODEL

Consider Masson Industries, which has an average collection period of 45 days—37 days until the customers place their payments in the mail and a further 8 days to receive, process, and collect payments. Masson is contemplating changing its credit terms from *net 30* to *2/10 net 30*. The change should reduce the average collection period to 26 days.

Masson currently sells 1,200 units of its product for $2,500 per unit. Its variable cost per unit is $2,000. Masson estimates that 70 percent of its customers will take the 2 percent discount, offering the discount will increase sales by 50 units per year, and offering the discount will not alter its bad debt percentage for this product. Masson's opportunity cost of funds invested in accounts receivable is 13.5 percent per year. Should Masson offer the proposed cash discount? The cost-benefit analysis, presented in Table 19.5, shows that the *net cost* of the cash discount is $2,846. Thus, *Masson should not implement the proposed cash discount.*

Table 19.5
Analysis of Offering a Cash Discount at Masson Industries

Marginal profit from increased sales [50 units × ($2,500 – $2,000)]		$25,000
Current investment in accounts receivable ($2,000[a] × 1,200 units) × (45/365)	$295,890	
New investment in accounts receivable ($2,000[a] × 1,250 units) × (26/365)[b]	178,082	
Reduction in accounts receivable investment	$117,808	
Cost savings from reduced investment in accounts receivable (0.135 × $117,808)[c]		15,904
Cost of cash discount (0.02 × $2,500 × 1,250 × 0.70)		43,750
Net profit (cost) from proposed cash discount		($ 2,846)

[a] In analyzing the investment in accounts receivable, we use the $2,000 variable cost of the product sold instead of its $2,500 sales price, because the variable cost represents the firm's actual cash expense incurred and tied up in receivables.
[b] The new investment in accounts receivable is tied up for 26 days instead of the 45 days under the original terms. The 26 days is calculated as [(0.70 × 10 days + 0.30 × 37 days) + 8 days] = 26.1 days, which is rounded to 26 days.
[c] Masson's opportunity cost of funds is 13.5% per year.

CONCEPT REVIEW QUESTIONS

8. Why do a firm's regular credit terms typically conform to industry standards? On what basis other than credit terms should the firm compete?

9. How are the *five C's of credit* used to perform in-depth credit analysis? Why is this framework typically used only on high-dollar credit requests?

10. How is *credit scoring* used in the credit selection process? In what types of situations is it most useful?

11. What are the key variables to consider when evaluating the benefits and costs *of changing credit standards*? How do these variables differ when evaluating the benefits and costs of changing *credit terms*?

12. Why do we include only the variable cost of sales when estimating the average investment in accounts receivable? Why do we apply an opportunity cost to this investment to estimate its cost?

13. What are the key elements of a firm's *credit terms*? What is a key determinant of the credit terms offered by a firm?

19.5 COLLECTING, MONITORING, AND APPLYING CASH TO RECEIVABLES

In addition to establishing the firm's accounts receivable standards and terms, the financial manager's responsibilities include collecting and monitoring receivables. Whereas decisions with regard to standards and terms tend to involve periodic policy actions, the collection and monitoring process is an ongoing operating activity that is also the responsibility of finance personnel. Here we briefly consider collection policy, credit monitoring, and cash application.

SMART PRACTICES VIDEO

Jon Olson, Vice President of Finance, Intel Corp.

"Because cash is king, we want to make sure that we have a high quality collections organization."

See the entire interview at **SMARTFinance**

Collection Policy

A company must determine what its **collection policy** will be and how it will be implemented. As in the case of the credit standards and terms, the approach to collections may be a function of the industry and the competitive environment. For many delinquent accounts, a reminder, form letter, telephone call, or visit may facilitate customer payment. At a minimum, the company should generally suspend further sales until the delinquent account is brought current. When these actions fail to generate customer payment, it may be necessary to negotiate with the customer for past-due amounts and report the customer to credit bureaus. It is possible that the goods were sold with a lien attached, collateral was pledged against the account, or additional corporate or personal guarantees were given. In these cases, the company should utilize these options for obtaining payment. Generally as a last resort, the account can be turned over to a collection agency or referred to an attorney for direct legal action. Obviously, a cost-benefit analysis should be made at each stage to compare the cost of further collection actions against the cost of simply writing off the account as a bad debt.

collection policy
The procedures used by a company to collect overdue or delinquent accounts receivable. The approach used is often a function of the industry and the competitive environment.

Credit Monitoring

Credit monitoring involves the ongoing review of a firm's accounts receivable to determine if customers are paying according to the stated credit terms. If customers

credit monitoring
The ongoing review of a firm's accounts receivable to determine if customers are paying according to the stated credit terms.

are not paying on time, credit monitoring will alert the firm to the problem. Credit must be monitored on both an individual and an aggregate basis. Individual monitoring is necessary to determine if each customer is paying in a timely manner and to assess if the customer is within its credit limits.

Credit monitoring on an aggregate basis is also important because it indicates the overall quality of the company's accounts receivable. Slow payments are costly to a firm because they increase the average collection period and thus the firm's investment in accounts receivable. If a company is also using its accounts receivable as collateral for a loan, the lending institution will generally exclude any past-due accounts from those used as backup for the credit line. Changes in accounts receivable over time could impact the company's overall liquidity and the need for additional financing. Analysis of accounts receivable payment patterns can also be essential for forecasting future cash receipts in the cash budget.

The three most frequently cited techniques for monitoring the overall quality of accounts receivable are (1) the average collection period, (2) aging of accounts receivable, and (3) payment pattern monitoring.

Average Collection Period. The *average collection period (ACP)*, also known as *days' sales outstanding (DSO)*, is the second component of the cash conversion cycle. As noted in Chapter 2, it represents the average number of days credit sales are outstanding. The average collection period has two components: (1) the time from sale until the customer places the payment in the mail; and (2) the time to receive, process, and collect the payment once it has been mailed by the customer. Equation 19.11 gives the formula for determining the average collection period:

$$\text{Average collection period} = \frac{\text{accounts receivable}}{\text{average sales per day}} \qquad \text{(Eq. 19.11)}$$

Assuming that receipt, processing, and collection time is constant, the average collection period tells the firm, on average, when its customers pay their accounts. In applying this formula, the analysts must be sure to be consistent in the use of the sales period and to adjust for known seasonal fluctuations.

APPLYING THE MODEL

P. Scofield Enterprises has an accounts receivable balance of $1.2 million. Sales during the past 90 days were $3.6 million, for an average daily sales figure of $40,000. Dividing $1.2 million by $40,000 yields Scofield's average collection period, 30 days.

However, a diligent analyst at Scofield notices that sales have been increasing recently, with average daily sales over the last 30 days of $45,000 per day. Using this figure in the denominator of Equation 19.11 results in an average collection period of 26.7 days.

The average collection period allows the firm to determine whether there is a general problem with its accounts receivable, but the *ACP* is also prone to sending misleading signals when daily sales fluctuate. In the example shown in the Applying the Model, suppose that Scofield's credit terms are net 25. Using the most recent month to calculate average daily sales results in an average collection period of 26.7 days, which is right on target given Scofield's credit terms. However, using average daily sales over the past three months yields the higher 30-day collection period. Therefore, when using this ratio to assess the performance of the collections department, analysts have to be wary of the impact of sales fluctuations on their calculations.

If a firm believes it has a collections problem, a first step in analyzing the problem is to age the accounts receivable. By aging its accounts receivable, the firm can determine if the problem exists in its accounts receivable in general or is attributable to a few specific accounts or to a given time period.

Aging of Accounts Receivable. The **aging of accounts receivable** results in a schedule that indicates the portions of the total accounts receivable balance that have been outstanding for specified periods of time. Aging requires the firm's accounts receivable to be broken down into groups based on the time of origin. The breakdown is typically made on a month-by-month basis, going back three or four months. The purpose is to allow the firm to pinpoint problems.

aging of accounts receivable
A schedule that indicates the portions of the total accounts receivable balance that have been outstanding for specified periods of time.

If a firm with terms of net 30 has an average collection period (minus receipt, processing, and collection time) of 50 days, the firm will want to age its accounts receivable. If the majority of accounts are two months old, then the firm has a general problem and should review its accounts receivable operations. If the aging shows that most accounts are collected in about 35 days and a few accounts are significantly past due, then the firm should analyze and pursue collection of those specific past-due accounts. If the firm has an abnormally high percentage of outstanding accounts initiated in a given month, it may be attributable to a specific event during that time period, such as hiring a new credit manager or selling a substandard product whose quality is being disputed by customers who are withholding payment. Table 19.6 provides an example of an *aging schedule.* If the stated credit terms for the company in this example were net 60 days, then the aging schedule would tell us that 80 percent of the company's receivables are current and 20 percent are considered past due.

Payment Pattern Monitoring. The average collection period and the aging of accounts receivable are excellent monitoring techniques when sales are relatively constant. However, for cyclical or growing firms, both techniques provide potentially misleading results. For example, the average collection period divides the accounts receivable balance by the average daily sales. If the accounts receivable balance is measured during a cyclical firm's high sales period, then the average collection period is distorted by the cyclical sales peak. Use of the firm's customer payment pattern avoids the problems of cyclical or growing sales when monitoring accounts receivable. The **payment pattern** is the normal timing in which a firm's customers pay their accounts, expressed as the percentage of monthly sales collected in each month following the sale. Every firm has a pattern in which its credit sales are paid. This pattern is not affected by changes in sales levels and therefore should be constant across time. If the payment pattern changes, the firm should review its credit policies.

payment pattern
The normal timing in which a firm's customers pay their accounts, expressed as the percentage of monthly sales collected in each month following the sale.

One approach to determining this pattern is to analyze a company's sales and resulting collections on a monthly basis. That is, for each month's sales, the amount collected in the month of sale and each of the following months must be computed.

Table 19.6
Sample Aging Schedule for Accounts Receivable

Age of Accounts	Accounts Receivable	Percentage of Accounts Receivable
0–30 days	$1,200,000	50%
31–60 days	720,000	30
61–90 days	336,000	14
91+ days	144,000	6
Total accounts receivable	$2,400,000	100%

By tracking these patterns over a period of time, the company can determine the average pattern of its collections using either a spreadsheet or regression analysis. For most companies, these patterns tend to be fairly stable over time, even as sales volumes might be fluctuating.

APPLYING THE MODEL

To demonstrate the payment pattern, consider DJM Manufacturing, which has determined that, on average, 10 percent of credit sales are collected in the month of sale, 60 percent are collected in the month following the sale, and the remaining 30 percent are collected in the second month following the sale. Thus, if sales for the month of January were $200,000, the company would expect to collect $20,000 in January, $120,000 in February, and the remaining $60,000 in March. Table 19.7 shows an example of this approach, which can be extended to develop the cash receipts portion of the cash budget.

Cash Application

cash application
The process through which a customer's payment is posted to its account and the outstanding invoices are cleared as paid.

Cash application is the process through which a customer's payment is posted to its account and the outstanding invoices are cleared as paid. In most business-to-business environments, the typical application method is known as *open item.* In this approach, each invoice sent to a customer is recorded in the A/R journal, and received payments must be "matched" to the invoices in order to clear them. This task is complicated by the usual practice of paying multiple invoices with a single check and remittance information. Ideally, the remittance information accompanying the check should clearly indicate any adjustments, discounts, or allowances taken related to each invoice in that remittance. Unfortunately, the remittance information is sometimes no more than barely legible copies of the invoices with handwritten notes on the adjustments stapled to the check. One of the critical tasks of the accounts receivable department, therefore, is to figure out what has been paid for so the outstanding invoices can be closed out.

Some types of companies are able to use an alternative approach called *balance forward.* In this type of system, customer payments are applied to outstanding

Table 19.7
Forecasted Collections for DJM Manufacturing

Note: This table is created using the assumption that 10 percent of each month's sales are collected in the month of sale, 60 percent are collected in the month following sale, and the remaining 30 percent are collected in the second month following sale. The forecasted sales for each month are provided in the first column, the remaining columns total up the actual cash flows for each month. In an actual application, the remaining collections from the prior year's last quarter would be included to complete the projected cash flows in January and February.

	Forecasted Collections for DJM Manufacturing				
Sales Forecast	January	February	March	April	May
January: $200,000	$20,000	$120,000	$ 60,000		
February: 150,000		15,000	90,000	$ 45,000	
March: 300,000			30,000	180,000	$ 90,000
April: 400,000				40,000	240,000
May: 250,000					25,000
Total projected collections for cash budget			$180,000	$265,000	$355,000

balances, and any unpaid amounts are simply carried forward to the next billing period. Examples are credit card companies and utilities, where the only remittance information needed is the customer's account number, the amount of payment, and the date received. These systems also generally utilize a scannable remittance document, which allows for automated capture of payment and account information. Automated processing reduces the costs of the cash application process.

CONCEPT REVIEW QUESTIONS

14. What is a *collection policy*? What is the typical sequence of actions taken by a firm when attempting to collect an overdue account?

15. Why should a firm actively monitor the accounts receivable of its credit customers? How does each of the following credit monitoring techniques work: (a) average collection period, (b) aging of accounts receivable, and (c) payment pattern monitoring?

19.6 SUMMARY AND CONCLUSIONS

- The cash conversion cycle has three main components: (1) the average age of inventory (*AAI*), (2) the average collection period (*ACP*), and (3) the average payment period (*APP*). The operating cycle (*OC*) is the sum of the *AAI* and *ACP*. The cash conversion cycle (*CCC*) is $OC - APP$. The length of the cash conversion cycle determines the amount of resources the firm must invest in its operations.
- The financial manager's focus in managing the firm's short-term activities is to shorten the cash conversion cycle. The basic strategies are to turn inventory quickly; collect accounts receivable quickly; pay accounts slowly; and manage mail, processing, and clearing time efficiently.
- When managing the firm's short-term accounts, the financial manager must focus on competing costs. These cost trade-offs apply to managing cash and marketable securities; accounts receivable; inventory; and accounts payable, accruals, and notes payable. The goal is to balance the cost trade-offs in a fashion that minimizes the total cost of each of these accounts.
- The large inventory investment made by most firms makes inventory a major concern of the financial manager, who must make sure that the amount of money tied up in inventory—raw materials, work in process, and finished goods—is justified by the returns generated from such investment.
- A number of techniques are used by production/operations managers to control inventory. Included are the ABC system, the basic economic order quantity (EOQ) model, reorder points and safety stock, material requirements planning, and the just-in-time (JIT) system. Financial managers tend to serve a "watchdog" role over these activities.
- The objective for managing accounts receivable is to balance the competing interests of financial managers who prefer to receive cash payments sooner and sales personnel who wish to use liberal credit terms to attract new customers. The key aspects of accounts receivable management include credit standards, credit terms, collection policy, credit monitoring, and cash application.
- To analyze credit applicants, the firm can gather information from both internal and external sources. Two popular approaches to granting credit to customers are the use of the five C's of credit and, for high-volume–low-dollar requests, credit scoring.

- A cost-benefit analysis of credit standard, credit term, and other accounts receivable changes can be performed to make sure such policy actions are profitable. Key variables involved in such an analysis include the additional profit contribution from sales, the cost of the marginal investment in accounts receivable, and the cost of marginal bad debts.
- The firm's collection policy involves a planned sequence of actions aimed at collecting delinquent accounts; typically, reminders, form letters, telephone calls, or personal visits. If these actions are ineffective, negative reports are sent to credit bureaus, and the account is turned over to a collection agency or an attorney for collection.
- The three most popular techniques for credit monitoring are the average collection period, aging of accounts receivable, and payment pattern monitoring. Cash application of customer payments by the firm is typically made using either the open item method or the balance forward method.

SELF-TEST PROBLEMS

Answers to Self-Test Problems appear in Appendix D at back of book. Answers to the Concept Review Questions throughout the chapter appear at http://megginson.swlearning.com.

ST19-1. Aztec Products wishes to evaluate its cash conversion cycle (*CCC*). One of the firm's financial analysts has discovered that on average the firm holds items in inventory for 65 days, pays its suppliers 35 days after purchase, and collects its receivables after 55 days. The firm's annual sales (all on credit) are about $2.1 billion, its cost of goods sold represent about 67 percent of sales, and purchases represent about 40 percent of cost of goods sold. Assume a 365-day year.

a. What is Aztec Products' operating cycle (*OC*) and cash conversion cycle (*CCC*)?
b. How many dollars of resources does Aztec have invested in (1) inventory, (2) accounts receivable, (3) accounts payable, and (4) the total *CCC*?
c. If Aztec could shorten its cash conversion cycle by reducing its inventory holding period by 5 days, what effect would that have on its total resource investment found in part (b)?
d. If Aztec could shorten its *CCC* by 5 days, would it be best to reduce the inventory holding period, reduce the receivable collection period, or extend the accounts payable period? Why?

ST19-2. Vargas Enterprises wishes to determine the economic order quantity (EOQ) for a critical and expensive inventory item that it uses in large amounts at a relatively constant rate throughout the year. The firm uses 450,000 units of the item annually, has order costs of $375 per order, and its carrying costs associated with this item are $28 per unit per year. The firm plans to hold safety stock of the item equal to 5 days of usage, and it estimates that it takes 12 days to receive an order of the item once placed. Assume a 365-day year.

a. Calculate the firm's EOQ for the item of inventory described above.
b. What is the firm's total cost based upon the EOQ calculated in part (a)?
c. How many units of safety stock should Vargas hold?
d. What is the firm's reorder point for the item of inventory being evaluated? (Hint: Be sure to include the safety stock.)

ST19-3. Belton Company is considering relaxing its credit standards to boost its currently sagging sales. It expects its proposed relaxation will increase sales by 20 percent from the current annual level of $10 million. The firm's average collection period is expected to increase from 35 days to 50 days, and bad debts are expected to increase from 2 percent of sales to 7 percent of sales as a result of relaxing the firm's credit standards as proposed. The firm's variable costs equal 60 percent of sales and its fixed costs total

$2.5 million per year. Belton's opportunity cost is 16 percent. Assume a 365-day year.

a. What is Belton's *contribution margin*?

b. Calculate Belton's *marginal profit from increased sales*.

c. What is Belton's *cost of the marginal investment in accounts receivable*?

d. What is Belton's *cost of marginal bad debts*?

e. Use your findings in parts (b), (c), and (d) to determine the net profit (cost) of Belton's proposed relaxation of credit standards. Should it relax credit standards?

INTERNET RESOURCES

Note: *For updates to links, please go to the book's Web site at* http://megginson.swlearning.com

http://www.bankone.com—A large Chicago-based bank—the sixth-largest U.S. bank—that offers numerous commercial banking services, including cash management and lending.

http://www.dunandbradstreet.com—A site that sells mercantile credit reports on thousands of companies; opening a D&B account is required for full access.

KEY TERMS

ABC system
aging of accounts receivable
average collection period (*ACP*)
average investment in accounts receivable (*AIAR*)
carrying cost
cash application
cash conversion cycle (*CCC*)
cash discount
collection policy
contribution margin
cost of the marginal investment in accounts receivable
credit monitoring
credit scoring
credit terms
economic order quantity (EOQ) model
factoring
five C's of credit
just-in-time (JIT) system
manufacturing resource planning II (MRPII)
material requirements planning (MRP)
operating assets
operating cycle (*OC*)
order cost
payment pattern
short-term financing
total cost
total variable cost of annual sales (*TVC*)
turnover of accounts receivable (*TOAR*)

QUESTIONS AND PROBLEMS

Q19-1. If you randomly chose a sample of firms and then calculated the operating cycle (*OC*) of each firm, what is likely to be the key cause of differences in their operating cycles? What goal should these firms attempt to achieve with regard to their *OC*s? How and why?

Q19-2. Why would a firm wish to minimize its cash conversion cycle (*CCC*) even though each of its components is important to the operation of the business? What key actions should the firm pursue to achieve this objective?

Q19-3. What impact would aggressive action aimed at minimizing a firm's cash conversion cycle (*CCC*) have on the following financial ratios: inventory turnover, average collection period, and average payment period? What are the key constraints on aggressive pursuit of these strategies with regard to inventory, accounts receivable, and accounts payable?

Q19-4. What are some of the key cost trade-offs that the financial manager must focus on when attempting to manage short-term accounts in a manner that minimizes cash? Prepare a graph describing the general nature of these cost trade-offs and the optimal level of total cost.

Q19-5. Assume that the financial manager is considering stretching the firm's accounts payable by paying its vendors at a later date. What key cost trade-offs would be involved when making this stretching decision? How would you quantitatively model this decision?

Q19-6. What is the financial manager's primary goal with regard to inventory management? How does this goal compare with the inventory goals of production and marketing?

Q19-7. What trade-off confronts the financial manager with regard to inventory turnover, inventory cost, and stockouts? In what way is inventory viewed as an investment?

Q19-8. Why is it important for the financial manager to understand the inventory control techniques used by production/operations managers? How does controlling inventory impact a firm's profitability?

Q19-9. What role does the *ABC system* play in inventory control? What group of inventory items does the *EOQ model* focus on controlling? Describe the objective and cost trade-off addressed by the EOQ model.

Q19-10. Why would a firm extend credit to its customers given that such an action would lengthen its cash conversion cycle? What key cost trade-offs would be involved in this decision? What typically dictates the actual credit terms the firm extends to its customers?

Q19-11. Why is using the *five C's of credit* appropriate for evaluating high-dollar credit requests but not high-volume–low-dollar requests, such as department store credit cards?

Q19-12. What is *credit scoring*? In what types of situations is it most useful? If you were developing a credit scoring model, what factors might be most useful in predicting whether or not a credit customer would pay in a timely manner?

Q19-13. What are the key variables to consider when evaluating potential changes in a firm's credit standards? Why are only variable costs of sales included when estimating the firm's *average investment in accounts receivable*?

Q19-14. If a firm were contemplating increasing the cash discount it offers its credit customers for early payment, what key variables would need to be considered when quantitatively analyzing this decision? How do the variables used in this analysis differ from those considered when analyzing a potential change in the firm's credit standards?

Q19-15. What is *credit monitoring*? How can each of the following techniques be used to monitor accounts receivable? What are their attributes?

a. Average collection period
b. Aging of accounts receivable
c. Payment pattern monitoring

PROBLEMS

The Cash Conversion Cycle

P19-1. Canadian Products is concerned about managing its operating assets and liabilities efficiently. Inventories have an average age of 110 days, and accounts receivable have an average age of 50 days. Accounts payable are paid approximately 40 days after they arise. The firm has annual sales of $36 million, its cost of goods sold represents 75 percent of sales, and its purchases represent 70 percent of cost of goods sold. Assume a 365-day year.

a. Calculate the firm's operating cycle (OC).
b. Calculate the firm's cash conversion cycle (CCC).
c. Calculate the amount of total resources Canadian Products has invested in its CCC.
d. Discuss how management might be able to reduce the amount of total resources invested in the CCC.

P19-2. The cash conversion cycle is an important tool for the financial manager in managing day-to-day operations of the firm. As an investor, knowing how the firm manages its CCC would provide useful insights about management's effectiveness in managing the firm's resource investment in the CCC. Access Microsoft's annual statement at http://www.microsoft.com, and calculate Microsoft's CCC. Discuss any difficulties you had in obtaining adequately detailed data from Microsoft's Web site for use in calculating its CCC. Evaluate Microsoft's CCC in light of your calculations.

P19-3. A firm is weighing five plans that affect several current accounts. Given the five plans and their probable effects on inventory, receivables, and payables, as shown in the following table, which plan would you favor? Explain.

SMART EXCEL

See this problem explained in Excel at SMARTFinance

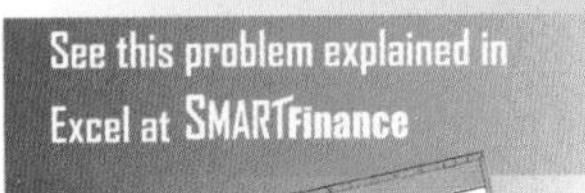

		Change	
Plan	Average age of inventory (days)	Average collection period (days)	Average payment period (days)
A	+35	+20	+10
B	+20	−15	+10
C	−10	+5	0
D	−20	+15	+5
E	+15	−15	+20

P19-4. King Manufacturing turns its inventory 9.1 times each year, has an average payment period of 35 days, and has an average collection period of 60 days. The firm's annual sales are $72 million, its cost of goods sold represents 50 percent of sales, and its purchases represent 80 percent of cost of goods sold. Assume a 365-day year.

a. Calculate the firm's operating cycle (OC) and cash conversion cycle (CCC).
b. Calculate the firm's total resources invested in its CCC.
c. Assuming that the firm pays 14 percent to finance its resource investment in its CCC, how much would it save annually by reducing its CCC by 20 days if this reduction were achieved by shortening the average age of inventory by 10 days, shortening the average collection period by 5 days, and lengthening the average payment period by 5 days?
d. If the 20-day reduction in the firm's CCC could be achieved by a 20-day change in only one of the three components of the CCC, which one would you recommend? Explain.

P19-5. Bradbury Corporation turns its inventory five times each year, has an average payment period of 25 days, and has an average collection period of 32 days. The firm's annual sales are $3.6 billion, its cost of goods sold represents 80 percent of sales, and its purchases represent 50 percent of cost of goods sold. Assume a 365-day year.

a. Calculate the firm's operating cycle (OC) and cash conversion cycle (CCC).
b. Calculate the total resources invested in the firm's CCC.
c. Assuming that the firm pays 18 percent to finance its resource investment, how much would it increase its annual profits by reducing its CCC by 12 days if this reduction were solely the result of extending its average payment period by 12 days?
d. If the 12-day reduction in the firm's CCC in part (c) could have alternatively been achieved by shortening either the average age of inventory or the average collection period by 12 days, would you have recommended one of those actions

rather than the 12-day extension of the average payment period specified in part (c)? Which change would you recommend? Explain.

P19-6. Use the following firms to complete this problem:

Anheuser-Busch Companies, Inc. (BUD)
Coca-Cola Company (KO)
Adolph Coors Company (RKY)
PepsiCo, Inc. (PEP)

Go to http://finance.yahoo.com, and input the ticker symbols noted in parentheses following each company name above. Under the Financials heading in the left-hand column, click on "Income Statement" and then "Balance Sheet" to obtain the most recent income statement and balance sheet for each firm. Use the appropriate financial statement data for each firm to respond to the following instructions and questions.

a. Use the formulas given in the chapter to calculate the following time periods (in days) for each of the firms:
(1) Average age of inventory (*AAI*)
(2) Average collection period (*ACP*)
(3) Average payment period (*APP*)

b. Use the time periods calculated in part (a) to calculate each firm's operating cycle (*OC*) and cash conversion cycle (*CCC*).

c. Compare, contrast, and evaluate the *OC* and *CCC* calculated in part (b) for each of the following combinations:
(1) The two soft drink companies (KO and PEP)
(2) The two beer companies (BUD and RKY)
How would you describe the differences found for each pair of firms?

d. Compare and contrast the *OC* and *CCC* for the two soft drink companies to those of the two beer companies. Explain any differences you observe.

Cost Trade-offs in Short-Term Financial Management

P19-7. Geet Industries wants to install a just-in-time (JIT) inventory system in order to significantly reduce its in-process inventories. The annual cost of the system is gauged to be $95,000. The financial manager estimates that with this system, the firm's average inventory investment will decline by 40 percent from its current level of $2.05 million. All other costs are expected to be unaffected by this system. The firm can earn 14 percent per year on equal-risk investments.

a. What is the annual cost savings expected to result from installation of the proposed JIT system?

b. Should the firm install the system?

P19-8. Sheth and Sons Inc. is considering changing its pay period for its salaried management from paying salaries every two weeks to paying salaries monthly. The firm's CFO, Ken Smart, believes that such action will free up cash that can be used elsewhere in the business, which currently faces a cash crunch. In order to avoid a strong negative response from the salaried managers, the firm will simultaneously announce a new health plan that will lower managers' cost contributions without cutting benefits. Ken's analysis indicates that the salaried managers' bimonthly payroll is $1.8 million and is expected to remain at that level for the foreseeable future. With the bimonthly system, there were 2.2 pay periods in a month. Because the managers will be paid monthly, the monthly payroll will be about $4.0 million (2.2 × $1.8 million). The annual cost to the firm of the new health plan will be $180,000. Ken believes that because managers' salaries accrue at a constant rate over the pay period, the average salaries over the period can be estimated by dividing the total amount by 2. The firm believes that it can earn 15 percent annually on any funds made available through the accrual of the managers' salaries.

a. How much additional financing will Sheth and Sons obtain as a result of switching the pay period for managers' salaries from every two weeks to monthly?

b. Should the firm implement the proposed change in pay periods?

Inventory Management

P19-9. Calculate the average investment in inventory for each of the following situations. Assume a 365-day year.

a. The firm's annual sales were \$18 million, its gross profit margin was 32 percent, and its average age of inventory is 45 days.

b. The firm's annual sales were \$325 million, its cost of goods sold are 80 percent of sales, and it turns its inventory 10 times per year.

c. The firm's annual cost of goods sold total \$120 million, and it turns its inventory about every 70 days.

P19-10. GEP Manufacturing is mulling over a plan to rent a proprietary inventory control system at an annual cost of \$4.5 million. The firm predicts its sales will remain relatively stable at \$585 million and its gross profit margin will continue to be 28 percent. It expects that as a result of the new inventory control system its average age of inventory (*AAI*) will drop from its current level of 83 days to about 46 days. The firm's required return on similar-risk investments is 12 percent. Assume a 365-day year.

a. Calculate GEP's average inventory investment both currently and assuming it rents the inventory control system.

b. Use your findings in part (a) to determine the annual savings expected to result from the proposed inventory control system.

c. Based on your finding in part (b), would you recommend that GEP rent the inventory control system? Explain your recommendation.

P19-11. Iverson Industries uses 80,000 units of an "A" item of raw material inventory each year. The firm maintains level production throughout the year given the steady demand for its finished products. The raw material order cost is \$225 per order and carrying costs are estimated to be \$10.50 per unit per year. The firm wishes to maintain a safety stock of 10 days of inventory, and it takes 5 days for the firm to receive an order once it is placed. Assume a 365-day year.

a. Calculate the economic order quantity (EOQ) for Iverson's raw material.

b. How large a *safety stock* (in units) of inventory should the firm maintain?

c. What is Iverson's *reorder point* for this item of inventory? (Hint: Be sure to include the safety stock.)

P19-12. Litespeed Products buys 200,000 motors per year from a supplier that can fulfill orders within two days of receiving them. Litespeed transmits its orders to this supplier electronically so the lead time to receive orders is two days. Litespeed's order cost is about \$295 per order and its carrying cost is about \$37 per motor per year. The firm maintains a safety stock of motors equal to six days of usage. Assume a 365-day year.

a. What is Litespeed's economic order quantity (EOQ) for the motors?

b. What is its *total cost* at the EOQ?

c. How large a *safety stock* (in units) of motors should Litespeed maintain?

d. What is Litespeed's *reorder point* for motors? (Hint: Be sure to include the safety stock.)

e. If Litespeed has an opportunity to reduce by 10 percent either its order cost or its carrying cost, which would result in the lowest total cost at the associated new EOQ?

f. How much total cost savings will result from the lowest-cost strategy found in part (e) relative to the total cost found in part (b)?

Accounts Receivable Standards and Terms

P19-13. International Oil Company (IOC) uses credit scoring to evaluate gasoline credit card applications. The following table presents the financial and credit characteristics and weights (indicating the relative importance of each characteristic) used in the credit decision. The firm's credit standards are to accept all applicants with credit scores of 80 or higher, to extend limited credit on a probationary basis to applicants with scores higher than 70 and lower than 80, and to reject all applicants with scores below 70.

Financial and Credit Characteristics	Predetermined Weight
Credit references	0.25
Education	0.10
Home ownership	0.10
Income range	0.15
Payment history	0.30
Years on job	0.10

The firm needs to process three applications that were recently scored by one of its credit analysts. The scores for each of the applicants on each of the financial and credit characteristics are summarized in the following table.

Financial and	Applicants' Scores (0 to 100)		
Credit Characteristics	X	Y	Z
Credit references	60	90	80
Education	75	80	80
Home ownership	100	90	60
Income range	70	70	80
Payment history	60	85	70
Years on job	50	60	90

a. Use the data presented to find the credit score for each of the applicants.
b. Recommend the appropriate action that the firm should take for each of the three applicants.

SMART SOLUTIONS

See the problem and solution explained step-by-step at SMARTFinance

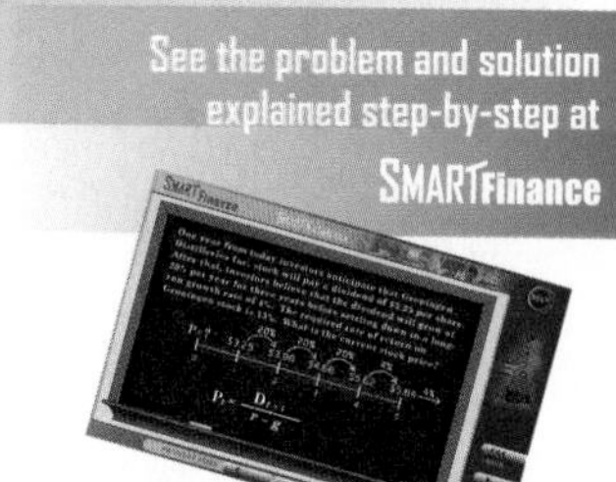

P19-14. Barans Company currently has an average collection period of 55 days and annual sales of $1 billion. Assume a 365-day year.

a. What is the firm's average accounts receivable balance?
b. If the variable cost of each product is 65 percent of sales, what is the *average investment in accounts receivable*?
c. If the equal-risk opportunity cost of the investment in accounts receivable is 12 percent, what is the total annual cost of the resources invested in accounts receivable?

P19-15. Melton Electronics currently has an average collection period of 35 days and annual sales of $72 million. Assume a 365-day year.

a. What is the firm's average accounts receivable balance?
b. If the variable cost of each product is 70 percent of sales, what is the firm's *average investment in accounts receivable*?
c. If the equal-risk opportunity cost of the investment in accounts receivable is 16 percent, what is the total annual cost of the resources invested in accounts receivable?
d. If the firm can shorten the average collection period to 30 days by offering a cash discount of 1 percent for early payment, and 60 percent of the customers take this discount, should the firm offer this discount assuming its cost of bad debts will rise by $150,000 per year?

SMART EXCEL

See this problem explained in Excel at SMARTFinance

P19-16. Davis Manufacturing Industries (DMI) produces and sells 20,000 units of a machine tool each year. All sales are on credit, and DMI charges all customers $500 per unit. Variable costs are $350 per unit, and the firm incurs $2 million in fixed costs each year. DMI's top managers are evaluating a proposal from the firm's CFO that the firm relax its credit standards to increase its sales and profits. The CFO believes this change will increase unit sales by 4 percent. Currently, DMI's average collection period is 40 days, and the CFO expects this to increase to 60 days under the new policy. Bad debt expense is also expected to increase from 1 percent to 2.5 percent of annual sales. The firm's board of directors has set a required return of 15 percent on investments with this level of risk. Assume a 365-day year.

a. What is DMI's *contribution margin*? By how much will profits from increased sales change if DMI adopts the new credit standards?

b. What is DMI's *average investment in accounts receivable* under the current credit standards? Under the proposed credit standards? What is the cost of this additional investment?

c. What is DMI's *cost of marginal bad debt expense* resulting from the relaxation of its credit standards?

d. What is DMI's net profit/loss from adopting the new credit standards? Should DMI relax its credit standards?

P19-17. Jeans Manufacturing thinks that it can reduce its high credit costs by tightening its credit standards. However, as a result of the planned tightening, the firm believes its annual sales will drop from $38 million to $36 million. On the positive side, the firm expects its average collection period to fall from 58 to 45 days and its bad debts to drop from 2.5 percent to 1 percent of sales. The firm's variable cost per unit is 70 percent of its sale price, and its required return on investment is 15 percent. Assume a 365-day year. Evaluate the proposed tightening of credit standards, and make a recommendation to the management of Jeans Manufacturing.

P19-18. Webb Inc. currently makes all sales on credit and offers no cash discounts. The firm is considering a 2 percent cash discount for payments within 10 days. The firm's current average collection period is 65 days, sales are 400,000 units, selling price is $50 per unit, and variable cost per unit is $40. The firm expects that the changes in credit terms will result in an increase in sales to 410,000 units, that 75 percent of the sales will take the discount, and that the average collection period will fall to 45 days. Bad debts are expected to drop from 1.0 to 0.9 percent of sales. If the firm's required rate of return on equal-risk investments is 25 percent, assuming a 365-day year, should the firm offer the proposed discount?

P19-19. Microboard, Inc., a major computer chip manufacturer, is contemplating lengthening its credit period from net 30 days to net 50 days. Presently, its average collection period is 40 days, and the firm's CFO believes that with the proposed new credit period, the average collection period will be 65 days. The firm's sales are $900 million, and the CFO believes that with the new credit terms, sales will increase to $980 million. At the current $900 million sales level, the firm's total variable costs are $630 million. The firm's CFO estimates that with the proposed new credit terms, bad debt expenses will increase from the current level of 1.5 percent of sales to 2.0 percent of sales. The CFO also estimates that due to the increased sales volume and accompanying receivables, the firm will have to add additional facilities and personnel to its credit and collections department. The annual cost of the expanded credit operations resulting from the proposed new credit period is estimated to be $10 million. The firm's required return on similar-risk investments is 18 percent. Assume a 365-day year. Evaluate the economics of Microboard's proposed credit-period lengthening, and make a recommendation to the firm's management.

SMART EXCEL

See this problem explained in Excel at SMARTFinance

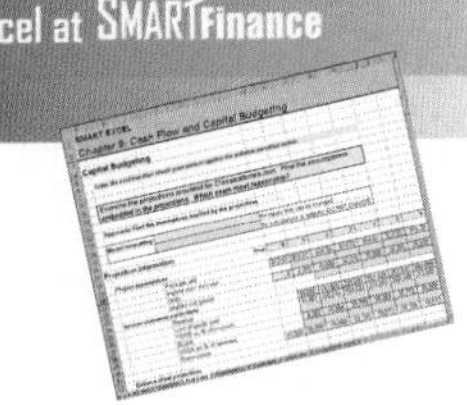

Collecting, Monitoring, and Applying Cash to Receivables

P19-20. United Worldwide's accounts receivable totaled $1.75 million on August 31, 2006. A breakdown of these outstanding accounts on the basis of the month in which the credit sale was initially made follows. The firm extends *net 30, EOM* credit terms to its credit customers.

Month of Credit Sale	Accounts Receivable
August 2006	$ 640,000
July 2006	500,000
June 2006	164,000
May 2006	390,000
April 2006 or before	56,000
Total (August 31, 2006)	$1,750,000

a. Prepare an *aging schedule* for United Worldwide's August 31, 2006, accounts receivable balance.
b. Using your findings in part (a), evaluate the firm's credit and collection activities.
c. What are some probable causes of the situation discussed in part (b)?

P19-21. Big Air Board Company, a global manufacturer and distributor of both surfboards and snowboards, is in a seasonal business. Although surfboard sales are only mildly seasonal, the snowboard sales are very seasonal, driven by peak demand in the first and fourth calendar quarters of each year. The following table gives the firm's monthly sales for the immediate past quarter (October through December 2006) and its forecast monthly sales for the coming year (calendar-year 2007).

Month	Sales ($ in millions)
Historic	
October 2006	$3.7
November 2006	3.9
December 2006	4.3
Forecast	
January 2007	$3.8
February 2007	2.6
March 2007	2.2
April 2007	1.6
May 2007	1.8
June 2007	1.9
July 2007	2.0
August 2007	2.2
September 2007	2.4
October 2007	4.1
November 2007	4.6
December 2007	5.1

The firm extends *2/10 net 30, EOM* credit terms to all customers. It collects 98 percent of its receivables; the other 2 percent is typically written off as bad debts. Big Air Board's historic collection pattern, which is expected to continue through 2007, is 5 percent collected in the month of the sale, 65 percent collected in the first month following the sale, and 28 percent collected in the second month following the sale. Using the data given, calculate the *payment pattern* of Big Air Board's accounts receivable, and comment on the firm's monthly collections during calendar-year 2007.

THOMSON ONE Business School Edition

For instructions on using Thomson ONE, refer to the instructions provided with the Thomson ONE problems at the end of Chapters 1–6 or to "A Guide for Using Thomson ONE."

P19-22. Compare and contrast the cash conversion cycles (*CCC*) of Caterpillar Inc. (ticker: U:CAT), Ingersoll-Rand Company Limited (U:IR), and Terex Corp. (U:TEX). Calculate the average age of inventory (*AAI*), average collection period (*ACP*), average payment period (*APP*), operating cycle (*OC*), and cash conversion cycle (*CCC*) at the end of each of the last five fiscal years for the three companies. Also calculate the resources invested in the cash conversion cycle in each year for the three companies. How has the *CCC* changed over the last five years for each firm? What are the reasons for the changes? Compare the *CCC* of the three firms in each of the five years and identify sources for the difference in each year. Which company has the lowest resources invested in the cash conversion cycle each year? Assume a 365-day year.

P19-23. Calculate 3M's (ticker: U:MMM) total annual cost of resources invested in accounts receivable in each of the last five years. Assume that there are no fixed costs, that is, all costs are variable costs (use COGS and SG&A). Calculate 3M's *average investment in accounts receivable* in each year. Using 3M's *WACC* as a measure of equal-risk opportunity cost of the investment in accounts receivable, calculate the total annual cost of resources invested in accounts receivable. Has this cost decreased or increased over the years?

Since these exercises depend upon real-time data, your answers will change continuously depending upon when you access the Internet to download your data.

MINICASE

Cash Conversion, Inventory, and Receivables Management

Upon graduation you receive a job offer from Pronto Manufacturing Incorporated. In this position, you will be responsible for implementing the policy and management of cash conversion, inventory, and receivables. To get ready for the start of this job, you decide to review the following topics.

ASSIGNMENT

1. What is the *cash conversion cycle*, and what is the difference between it and the *operating cycle*?
2. What are some ways of shortening the cash conversion cycle?
3. Discuss techniques for controlling inventory.
4. What aspects must managers consider when deciding on a trade credit policy for the firm?
5. Describe the *five C's of credit*.
6. What factors should managers consider when determining the company's collection policy?

Smart *Excel* Appendix

Appendix Contents

Use the Smart *Excel* spreadsheets and animated tutorials at http://smartfinance.swlearning.com.

EXCEL PREREQUISITES

There are no new *Excel* prerequisites in this chapter.

Chapter 19 analyzes the speed with which a firm converts operating assets to cash and considers management of inventory and accounts receivable. In this appendix, we create models to analyze the cash conversion cycle, alternative credit policies and accounts receivable aging.

CASH CONVERSION CYCLE

Problem: Solve Problem 19-3 in the text.

Approach: Create a simple model to determine the cash conversion cycle

Try it yourself in a blank *Excel* file. Think about what to include in the input section and how to set up your calculations and output.

Or, Open the Chapter 19 *Excel* file located at the Smart Finance Web site. Turn to the *CCC* tab.

The cash conversion cycle measures the time elapsed between the purchase of raw materials and the time payment is received. It is calculated as

$$CCC = AAI + ACP - APP$$

Where AAI is the age of inventory, ACP is the average collection period and APP is the average payment period.

Step 1: Enter the inputs for the 5 plans in problem 19-3.
Step 2: Find the impact of each plan on the cash conversion cycle. The plan that most reduces the cash conversion cycle is optimal.

Your results should match:

Calculations & Output

Plan	Change in CCC
A	45
B	−5
C	−5
D	−10
E	−20

Optional: Use the IF function to create a statement that identifies the optimal result.

See our solution. We used an IF statement to return "Optimal" for the plan with the largest negative impact on the cash conversion cycle. If you choose to use this, create the IF statement for the first plan (using absolute references as needed) that compares the value for plan A to the minimum of the plans.

The statement is:

=IF(C25=MIN($C$25:$C$29),"Optimal"," ")

C25 is the change in cash conversion cycle for plan A. If this is the minimum of the 5 plans, the statement returns "Optimal", otherwise the statement returns a blank space. You need to absolute reference the range of cells in the minimum function to copy the statement down for the other plans.

Apply it

- Since Plan E reduces the cash conversion cycle most significantly, it should be adopted.

ALTERNATIVE CREDIT POLICIES

Problem: Solve Problem 19-16 in the text.

Approach: Create a model to analyze the impact of a change in credit policy

Try it yourself in a blank *Excel* file. Think about what to include in the input section and how to set up your calculations and output.

Or, Open the Chapter 19 *Excel* file located at the Smart Finance Web site. Turn to the *Credit* tab.

When analyzing the impact of a change in credit policy, you must consider the marginal costs and benefits of the proposed policy. Often, there is an impact on sales, accounts receivable levels, and bad debt expense. You must estimate each impact and then calculate the net impact of the policy.

Step 1: Identify the sources of potential costs and benefits that will arise from adoption of the proposed policy.

Step 2: Enter the input information on the current situation and the proposed policy.

Step 3: Calculate each expected cost and benefit if the new policy is adopted.
Step 4: Find the net impact.

Apply it

Step 1: The new policy is expected to affect the level of sales, the level of accounts receivable and bad debt expense.

Step 2: Enter all inputs using clear captions and an organized presentation. Our input design is:

Inputs	
Current situation	
Unit sales	20,000
% sales on credit	100%
Unit price	$500
Variable cost per unit	$350
Fixed costs	$2,000,000
Avg collection period	40
Bad debt expense as % sales	1.0%
Required return on investment	15.0%
Expected values under new policy	
Increase in Unit Sales	4.0%
Avg collection period	60
Bad debt expense as % sales	2.5%

Step 3: Calculate each expected cost and benefit if the new policy is adopted. Remember it is the CHANGE in costs and benefits that is relevant.

The impact on sales is determined by multiplying the current sales by one plus the growth rate to get the sales under the proposed policy. Then measure the change in sales.

The impact on receivables is due to the cost of financing receivables. If the level of receivables rises, the associated financing costs increase. To calculate the impact, find the expected level of receivables. Then determine the change in the level of accounts receivable and multiply the change by the cost of financing.

Find the level of bad debt expense under the current situation and compare it to the level under the proposed policy.

Step 4: Find the net impact.
The result is:

Calculations

Impact on profit	
Current sales – $	$10,000,000
Contribution margin	$150
Current operating profit	$3,000,000
Expected unit sales	20,800
Expected sales – $	$10,400,000
Expected operating profit	$3,120,000
Increase in profits	**$120,000**

Impact on receivables	
Current investment in receivables	$767,123
Expected investment in receivables	$1,196,712
Increase in receivable financing cost	$64,438

Impact on bad debt expense	
Current bad debt expense	$100.000
Expected bad debt expense	$260,000
Increase in bad debt expense	$160,000

Output	
Net impact of proposed policy	($104,438)
Should proposal be adopted?	**No**

Optional: We use an IF statement to indicate if the proposal should be adopted. The statement returns "Yes" if the net impact is positive and "No" otherwise.

Apply it

The proposal has a negative net impact so should not be adopted. ***But suppose,***

- *Bad debt expense only increases to 1.5%?*
  The net impact is –$54,438.
- *Sales increase by 10%?*
  The net impact is $50,205 and the proposed policy is attractive.

ACCOUNTS RECEIVABLE AGING

Problem: Solve Problem 19-20 in the text.

Approach: Create a model to analyze the accounts receivable aging

Try it yourself in a blank *Excel* file. Think about what to include in the input section and how to set up your calculations and output.

Or, Open the Chapter 19 *Excel* file located at the Smart Finance Web site. Turn to the ***AR* aging** tab.

An accounts receivable aging shows the portion of receivables of different ages. To prepare an accounts receivable aging, show the dollar and percent value of receivables of different ages. This is fairly simple to prepare.

Step 1: Prepare the input section, entering the receivable values for each month.
Step 2: In the calculations and output section, find the percent of receivables in each age category.

Our results follow.

Inputs

Month of Sale	*Age of Accounts*	*Accounts Receivable*
August	0–30 days	$640,000
July	31–60 days	$500,000
June	61–90 days	$164,000
May	91–120 days	$390,000
April	121+ days	$56,000

Calculations & Output

Month of sale	*Age of Accounts*	*Accounts Receivable*	*Percent of A/R*
August	0–30 days	$640,000	36.6%
July	31–60 days	$500,000	28.6%
June	61–90 days	$164,000	9.4%
May	91–120 days	$390,000	22.3%
April	121+ days	$56,000	3.2%
Total		$1,750,000	100.0%

CHAPTER 20

Cash, Payables, and Liquidity Management*

OPENING FOCUS

The Electronic Payment Revolution?

Many believe that moving money by wire was the original form of e-business, given that its roots can be traced back nearly 100 years. Yet, today many aspects of cash management involve the same manual process that was used 40 years ago. During the 1960s, a firm was considered efficient if it could process an order in 4–7 days, have the product delivered in 14–21 days, get the invoice within a week, and pay within 45–60 days. Today, a firm is considered "old school" if its customers can't order today, have it shipped to their door tomorrow, get the invoice that same day, but still pay in 45–60 days!

To address this issue in today's e-everything world, some firms are embracing e-invoicing when making business-to-business transactions. The clunky technical term for this process, which involves sending bills and payments electronically, is *electronic invoice presentment and payment*, or simply EIPP. Big-name enterprise software developers such as PeopleSoft, Oracle, and SAP are expected to roll out sophisticated packages that tie payments to procurement and make it easier for firms to use EIPP.

It's not surprising that the lack of incentive for firms to speed their payments to vendors has slowed the adoption of EIPP. Clearly, paying faster is contrary to the firm's goal of shortening the cash conversion cycle (*CCC*) and thereby reducing its resource investment. The strategy for increasing the adoption of EIPP being pushed by Xign Corp., a leader in on-demand order-to-pay business software, is for the buyer to agree to pay quickly in exchange for an attractive early-pay discount from the vendor. They believe a cash discount of around 2 percent for payments made within 10 days adequately reduces the buyer's cost enough to compensate it for the earnings lost by paying sooner than would otherwise have been the case. In addition, by making the transaction and payment electronically, the buyer and seller will reduce their manual labor costs.

---

* A large part of this chapter was prepared with the assistance of Professor Dubos J. Masson, CCM, CertCM, of The Resource Alliance and the University of West Florida. The authors very much appreciate D.J.'s important contribution.

As testimony to EIPP, Bill Dvorak, CFO of Cimco Communications, an Oakbrook Terrace, Illinois, telecommunications service firm, puts the cost of receiving, auditing, processing, and paying a paper invoice at $100 or more. As part of its services, the firm now mails clients a printed summary of charges but relies on EIPP to do most of the heavy lifting, keeping overhead low. Cimco says it also fields fewer customer service calls about bills now that customers can get a full range of details using the Internet to look into the EIPP system.

In spite of the fact that some major companies such as Dell Inc., Wells Fargo & Co., Office Depot Inc., and Pacific Care Health Systems have adopted EIPP, to date, its universal adoption has been relatively slow. The problem is that each company that adopts it must convince its customers to sign on. Beth Robertson, a senior research analyst at research and advisory firm TowerGroup, suggests the growth in EIPP will be gradual. She predicts a quadrupling of the number of invoices sent electronically between 2003 and 2007 from 30 million to about 130 million. She suggests that broad technical standards need to be established and security issues resolved before there will be widespread adoption of EIPP.

Sources: Julie Sturgeon, "Electronic Payments," *CFO* (Winter 2003), pp. 52–53; Doug Roberts, "Giving Cash Management a Technology Boost," *Financial Executive* (December 2003), pp. 62–63. ■

LEARNING OBJECTIVES

After studying this chapter you should be able to:

- Understand float, its components, and the financial manager's responsibilities with regard to cash position management;
- Review the objective of cash collections, the key types of collection systems, and the role of lockbox systems in cash collections;
- Describe the role of cash concentration and various mechanisms used by firms to transfer funds from depository banks to concentration banks;
- Explain accounts payable management with regard to the average payment period and the effect of cash discounts on timing the payment of accounts payable;
- Discuss popular disbursement products and methods and recent developments in accounts payable and disbursements; and
- Describe popular investment vehicles for short-term surpluses and the key sources of borrowing used to meet short-term deficits.

Chapter 19 described the operating and cash conversion cycles and then focused on management of the two key components of the operating cycle—inventory and accounts receivable. Here we shift focus to the management of cash, accounts payable, and liquidity. Clearly, cash is the lifeblood of the firm and the primary focus of the financial manager, who must conserve it by gathering cash receipts and making cash disbursements in a cost-effective manner. Additionally, the financial manager's cash conservation efforts are enhanced through the use of efficient mechanisms for transferring it within and between the firm's operating units. As noted in Chapter 19, short-term financing decisions should result from a comparison of the marginal costs and the marginal benefits associated with the proposed action. Clearly, only those actions for which the marginal benefits exceed the marginal costs are consistent with the firm's overriding goal of enhancing shareholder wealth.

Accounts payable, as noted in Chapter 19, are an important component of the cash conversion cycle. The firm needs to manage them in a fashion that lengthens the payment period while preserving the firm's credit reputation. This strategy will help shorten the cash conversion cycle and reduce the firm's resource requirements. Similarly, the financial manager will use other strategies and tools to slow down disbursements. Of course, all of these cash management strategies are predicated on the firm's ability to maintain adequate liquidity to preserve the firm's solvency. Specifically, the firm must be able to both earn a positive return on idle excess cash balances and obtain low-cost financing for meeting unexpected needs and seasonal cash shortages. This important activity is commonly called "liquidity management."

This chapter emphasizes the key procedures for managing cash, payables, and liquidity. We begin with a discussion of cash management that focuses on float in the cash collection–payment system and the principles of managing the firm's cash position. Next, we consider cash collection, placing emphasis on the types of collection systems, lockbox systems, cash concentration, and various funds transfer mechanisms. Then we review some key aspects of accounts payable and disbursements—the accounts payable process, cash discounts, disbursement products and methods, and developments in accounts payable and disbursements. Finally, we briefly consider the firm's use of short-term investing and borrowing to maintain adequate liquidity.

20.1 CASH MANAGEMENT

Many companies employ financial specialists known as cash managers. One of the primary roles of these specialists is to manage the cash flow time line related to collection, concentration, and disbursement of funds for the company. More specifically, their job typically starts when a customer (the payer) initiates payment to the company (the payee) in any format (cash, check, or electronic). Because most business-to-business payments are still effected by sending a check in the mail, the collections process usually involves trying to reduce mail, processing, and check-collection delays. The cash manager is also responsible for concentrating cash from remote collection points into a central account and for initiating payments from the company to its suppliers. The final stage of this process usually involves reconciling the company's various bank accounts and managing all the banking relationships. Any delay in timing on either the collection or disbursement side is generally referred to as *float*.

Float

Float refers to funds that have been sent by the payer but are not yet usable funds to the payee. Float is important in the cash conversion cycle because its presence increases both the firm's average collection period and its average payment period. The primary role of the cash manager on the collections side is to *minimize collection float* wherever possible. On the payments side, trying to *maximize disbursement float* is a common practice that raises an important ethical question: Is it ethical to intentionally pay a supplier late, beyond the term within which a firm agreed to pay? This topic will be discussed in greater detail later in this chapter.

float
Funds that have been sent by the payer but are not yet usable funds to the payee.

Float must be viewed from either the receiving party's perspective (the payee) or the paying party's perspective (the payer). The following list points out that both mail and processing float are generally the same from both perspectives, but the final component is different. The four components of float are defined as follows:

mail float
The time delay between when payment is placed in the mail and when payment is received.

1. **Mail float** is the time delay between when payment is placed in the mail and when payment is received. This float component can range from one day to as much as five days or more depending on location and other factors.
2. **Processing float** is the time between receipt of the payment and its deposit into the firm's account. In a mail-based system, this involves opening the envelope, separating the check from the remittance advice, preparing the check for deposit, and actual deposit at the company's bank. This float component can range from less than one day to three or more days depending on any processing delays the company may have.

processing float
The time that elapses between the receipt of a payment by a firm and its deposit into the firm's account.

availability float
The time between deposit of a check and availability of the funds to a firm.

3. **Availability float** is the time between deposit of the check and availability of the funds to the firm. Although this may be related to the actual clearing time of the check, it is ultimately a function of the availability schedule offered by the deposit bank. For most business checks, this ranges from same day up to three business days depending on where the check is drawn.

clearing float
The time between deposit of the check and presentation of the check back to the bank on which it is drawn.

4. **Clearing float** is the time between deposit of the check and presentation of the check back to the bank on which it is drawn. This component of float is attributable to the time required for a check to clear the banking system and to have funds debited from the payer's account. In today's clearing system for business checks, availability float and clearing float are generally the same, but there are some exceptions when checks are drawn on small, geographically remote banks.

In addition to managing the collection, concentration, and disbursement of funds, the cash manager is also responsible for the following areas:

- *Financial relationships:* Managing relationships with banks and other providers of cash management services
- *Cash flow forecasting:* Determining future cash flows to predict surpluses or deficits (see Chapter 18)
- *Investing and borrowing:* Managing the investing of short-term surpluses or the borrowing for short-term deficits
- *Information management:* Developing and maintaining information systems to gather and analyze cash management data

The cash manager typically resides in the treasury area of a firm along with such functions as external financing and risk management. In smaller companies, accounting or clerical staffs may perform the cash management function. The specific cash management tasks related to collection, concentration, and disbursement of funds are described in the following sections.

Cash Position Management

cash position management
The collection, concentration, and disbursement of funds for the company.

On a daily basis, the primary cash management tasks related to the collection, concentration, and disbursement of funds for the company is generally referred to as **cash position management**. That is, each day the cash manager must determine the amount of funds to be collected, move balances to the appropriate accounts, and fund the projected disbursements. The cash position can be managed with some degree of accuracy many weeks into the future with proper forecasting of future cash flows. Most of the cash management products and services offered by banks and other financial institutions are associated with some part of this process.

At the end of the day, the cash manager must determine (1) whether the company will have a surplus or a deficit of funds in each checking account and (2) how to manage the difference. If the company has a surplus of funds, then the money may be placed in some type of short-term investment, such as an interest-bearing account at its bank or a portfolio of marketable securities. If, however, the firm will have a deficit, then the cash manager must make arrangements either to transfer funds from investment accounts or to draw on a short-term credit agreement with the firm's bank. The management of these short-term investing and borrowing arrangements is typically the responsibility of the cash manager.

target cash balance
A cash total that is set for checking accounts to avoid engaging in *cash position management*.

Many companies, especially smaller ones, do not actively engage in cash position management, but rather set a **target cash balance** for their checking accounts. The primary approach to determining these target cash balances is based on transactions requirements or a minimum balance set by the bank. The transactions requirement is determined simply by how much cash a firm needs to fund its day-to-day operations. Firms with a high volume of daily inflows and outflows will find that some balances remain in non-interest-bearing checking accounts, regardless of their forecasting ability. Many banks also require a specified minimum balance in customer checking accounts.

For smaller companies and banks, this minimum balance is designed to provide adequate compensation to the bank for the services it provides. For larger companies, most banks perform *account analysis,* which compares the value of the balances a firm leaves on deposit to the value of the services it receives from the bank.

A **bank account analysis statement** is a report (usually monthly) provided to a bank's commercial customers that specifies all services provided, including items processed and any charges assessed. It is basically a detailed invoice that lists all checks cleared, account charges, lockbox charges, electronic transactions, and so on. The statement also lists all balances held by the firm at the bank, and includes a computation of the credit earned by the firm on those balances. Although, under current federal regulations, a bank is not allowed to pay actual interest on corporate checking account balances, it can offer an *earnings credit* on these balances that is used to offset service charges. Most companies on account analysis will receive some credit for the transaction balances they leave in the account, and the credit typically will only partially offset the service fees. The balance of fees owed the bank will then be deducted as a service charge for the month in question.

bank account analysis statement
A regular report (usually monthly) provided to a bank's commercial customers that specifies all services provided, including items processed and any charges assessed.

CONCEPT REVIEW QUESTIONS

1. What is *float*? What are its four components? What is the difference between *availability float* and *clearing float*?

2. What activities are involved in *cash position management*? How does the cash manager monitor and take actions with regard to the end-of-day checking account balances?

3. How do smaller firms that do not engage in cash position management typically set their *target cash balance*? What is typically detailed in a *bank account analysis statement*?

20.2 COLLECTIONS

The primary objective of the collections process is to quickly and efficiently collect funds from customers and others. This process includes gathering and disseminating information related to the collections, and in some cases, the information may be as important as the money itself. One key requirement is to make sure that the accounts receivable department has the remittance information needed to properly post receipts and update customer files. A secondary requirement is to provide audit trails for the company's internal and external auditors.

As discussed earlier, a major delay in the collections process results from *collection float,* which is a function of the mail float, processing float, and availability float. The primary goal of collections is to reduce each of these float components as much as possible. Collection float is typically measured in "dollar-days," the number of dollars in the process of collection multiplied by the number of days of float. For example, \$10 million of checks with an average of five days of float would represent \$50 million dollar-days of float.

It is also important to understand the various payment practices in the U.S. business environment. In the United States, most business-to-business payments are still made via a check in the mail. Many consumer payments are also made via check, whereas retail establishments must handle cash, debit, and credit cards in addition to checks. The U.S. business environment is also characterized by a large number of financial institutions (approximately 20,000 according to recent FDIC statistics) and a lack of true nationwide branch banking. The Comparative Corporate Finance insert on page 804 provides insight into the cost to those working abroad of sending money back to Latin American countries. Clearly, funds transfers of this type can be costly, although these costs are declining.

COMPARATIVE CORPORATE FINANCE

Please Send Money

Over the past two decades, U.S. corporations and firms in other countries have dramatically reduced their cash holdings. As with other financial decisions, the decision to reduce cash holdings results from an analysis of the marginal costs and marginal benefits of holding a specified cash balance. The primary cost of holding a large cash balance is the opportunity cost of the funds. Corporations earn very low returns on cash balances and short-term marketable securities, and stockholders expect firms to invest all of their assets, including cash, to maximize shareholder wealth. On the other hand, maintaining a large cash balance gives the firm flexibility to meet fluctuating daily operating needs. When cash needs are uncertain, a firm may decide that the benefit of having a cash buffer is worth the cost of holding a cash balance earning a low return.

As financial institutions developed innovative cash management tools and new technology enabled firms to maintain almost up-to-the-minute monitoring of their cash position, the benefits of a large cash buffer declined, and so did cash balances of large companies. The same trend at work in the corporate finance world is also having its impact in the personal finance realm. The accompanying chart shows how changes in the cost of handling cash have affected people working abroad that send money back to their home country. Since 1999, competition among banks and technological innovation pushed the cost of remitting money to one's home country from more than 15 percent to less than 8 percent. In no part of the world is this effect more pronounced than in Latin America, which received more than $38 billion in remittances in 2003. Within the region, the cost of sending money home varies widely, from about $12 per $200 payment in Ecuador and Peru, to almost $25 in Cuba. If the cost of sending money home continues to decline, we should expect to see increases in remittances, especially in those countries that achieve the greatest cost reductions.

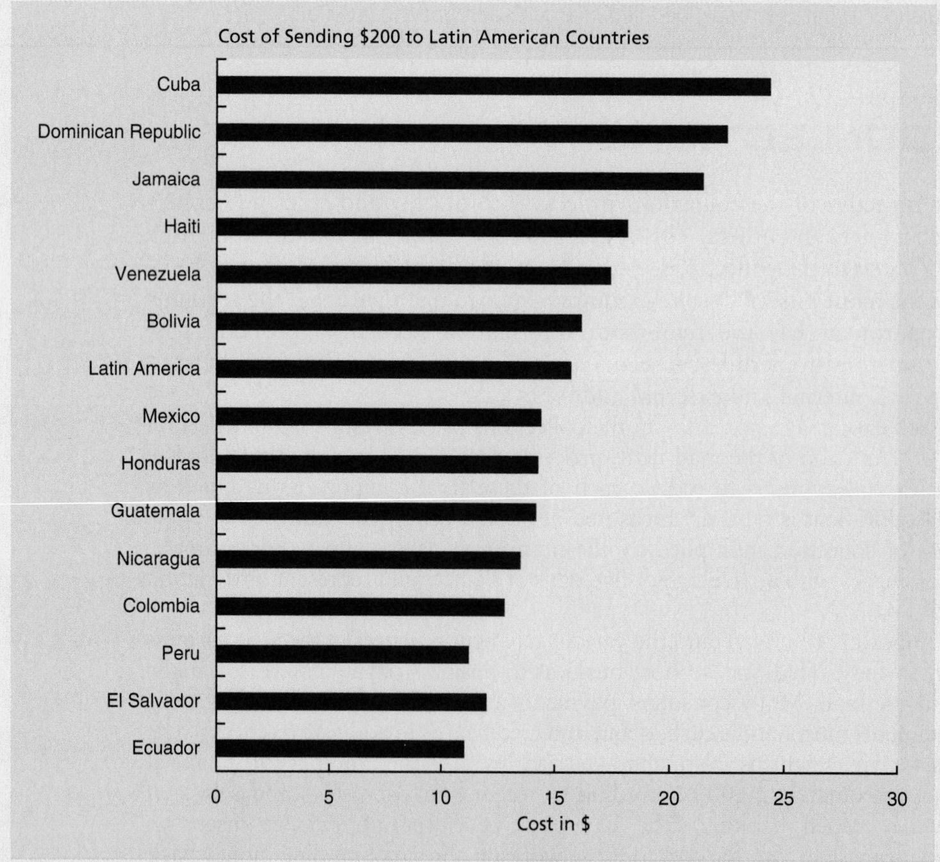

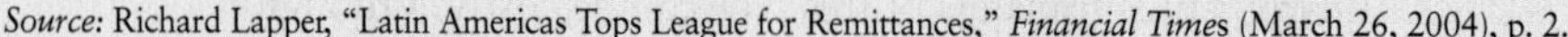

Source: Richard Lapper, "Latin Americas Tops League for Remittances," *Financial Times* (March 26, 2004), p. 2.

Speeding up collections reduces the firm's *average collection period,* which, in turn, reduces the investment the firm must make in its cash conversion cycle. In our example of the *cash conversion cycle* in Chapter 19 (Section 19.1), Reese Industries had annual sales of $5 billion and 8 days of total collection float (mail, processing, and availability time). If Reese can reduce its collection float time by 3 days (to 5 days), it reduces its investment in the cash conversion cycle by $41.1 million [$5 billion × (3 days/365 days)]. A number of popular collection systems and techniques can be implemented to speed up collections.

Types of Collection Systems

The nature of its business primarily determines a firm's collection system. Many high-volume retail establishments, such as fast-food restaurants or convenience stores, receive the bulk of their payments in cash. Other types of retail operations, such as department and variety stores, will collect most of their payments by credit card, debit card, or check.

As noted earlier, the typical business-to-business payment mechanism is a check that is mailed in response to an invoice received for products or services. What can complicate the collection process is that one check is often used to pay multiple invoices, and there may be adjustments or partial payments related to those invoices. This makes the information collected by the cash manager of critical importance to the accounts receivable department. Collection systems must take into account the information management requirements related to the payment application process.

Some types of time-critical transactions, such as real estate closings or high-dollar payments, may be received via wire transfers with same-day value. Other forms of high-volume-low-dollar receipts, especially those of a recurring nature (utility payments, insurance premiums, etc.), may come through the *automated clearinghouse (ACH) system,* which generally offers next-day settlement with fairly low transaction costs. The important thing to understand is that the type of collection system used by a company is usually a function of both the type of business and the customary methods of payment used by that type of business.

field-banking system
System characterized by many collection points, each of which may have a depository account at a local bank.

Field-Banking System. In a **field-banking system**, most collections are made either over the counter (as at a retail store) or at a collection office (often used by utilities). These systems are characterized by many collection points, each of which may have a depository account at a local bank. The main collection problem in this type of system involves transferring the funds from the local (often small) banks to the main account at the company's primary bank. Given the lack of an effective nationwide branch banking system, many large national retailers find they must maintain hundreds or even thousands of bank relationships as part of their collections system.

Typically, the collections in a field-banking system are local checks, cash, debit cards, and credit cards. Although the debit card and credit card processing is usually highly automated and efficient, the checks and cash must be processed and deposited at the local deposit bank. The funds must then be concentrated into the company's main account before the money can be used. The backbone of this type of system is information management—that is, the company needs to know where the money is before the company can make use of it. Most large retailers utilize *point-of-sale (POS) information systems* that allow them to know on a daily basis how much money has been collected, in what formats (cash, check, debit card, or credit card) it was received, and how much of it was deposited at the local bank. The task of moving this money into a concentration account is discussed in the section on cash concentration.

mail-based collection system
Processing centers receive the mail payments, open the envelopes, separate the check from the remittance information, prepare the check for deposit, and send the remittance information to the accounts receivable department for application of payment.

Mail-Based Collection System. In a **mail-based collection system**, the company typically has one or more collection points that process the incoming mail payments. These processing centers will receive the mail payments, open the envelopes, separate the check from the remittance information, prepare the check for deposit, and send the remittance information to the accounts receivable department for application of payment. Companies, such as utilities and credit-card processors that utilize standardized, scannable remittance information, can often process the payments they receive quickly and efficiently using automated equipment. Although many high-volume processors can justify the cost of the equipment needed for automated processing, other companies may find that using a *lockbox* (discussed later) is more cost effective. However, recent developments in payment processing equipment have made automated processing available to smaller companies at a reasonable price.

electronic invoice presentment and payment (EIPP)
A system in business-to-business transactions under which business customers are sent bills in an electronic format and then can pay them via electronic means.

electronic bill presentment and payment (EBPP)
A system in the business-to-consumer market under which consumers are sent bills in an electronic format and can then pay them via electronic means.

Electronic Systems. Electronic collection systems are still fairly new but are developing rapidly as both businesses and consumers begin to understand the benefits. One of the key developments in this area is **electronic invoice presentment and payment (EIPP)** in the business-to-business market and **electronic bill presentment and payment (EBPP)** in the business-to-consumer market. In EIPP and EBPP systems, customers are sent electronic bills and then can pay them electronically. Most of these systems are Internet-based and are beginning to gain some acceptance in the marketplace. The most successful of the consumer systems offer a consolidator-type service, where customers can go to one site to view and pay all their bills rather than visiting individual billing sites. Electronic payment systems are only slowly gaining acceptance in the business-to-business environment.

Some of the primary advantages of using a system such as the EIPP for business-to-business payments are (1) reduced float to the receiving party, (2) lower cost of both receivables processing for the receiver and payment initiation and reconciliation costs for the payer, and (3) better forecasting for both parties. Though there may be a need for negotiation of payment dates and possible discounts for changed payment timing, companies that have implemented electronic payments report significant overall savings as a result.

Lockbox Systems

lockbox system
A technique for speeding up collections that is popular because it affects all three components of float. Instead of mailing payments to the company, customers mail payments to a post office box, which is emptied regularly by the firm's bank.

A **lockbox system** is a popular technique for speeding up collections because it affects all three components of float. It works like this: instead of mailing payments to the company, customers mail payments to a post office box, which is emptied regularly by the firm's bank. The bank processes each payment and deposits the payments into the firm's account. The bank sends (or transmits electronically by computer) deposit slips and enclosures to the firm so the firm can properly credit its customers' accounts.

Lockboxes are typically geographically dispersed to match the locations of the firm's customers. As a result of being near the firm's customers, lockboxes reduce mail time, and clearing time is reduced because the payer's bank is often close to the payee's depository bank. They reduce processing time to nearly zero because the bank deposits payments before the firm processes them. Obviously, a lockbox system reduces collection float, but not without a cost; therefore, a firm must perform a cost-benefit analysis to determine if a lockbox system should be implemented. Equation 20.1 presents a simple formula for the cost-benefit analysis of a lockbox system:

$$\text{Net benefit (cost)} = (FVR \times r) - LC \qquad \text{(Eq. 20.1)}$$

where FVR = float value reduction in dollars,
r = cost of capital,
LC = annual operating cost of the lockbox system.

Thus, if the return on the float reduction exceeds the cost of the lockbox system, the firm should implement the lockbox system.

APPLYING THE MODEL

To demonstrate, consider Reese Industries, which has $5 billion in annual sales and 8 days of customer collection float in its cash conversion cycle. Reese wants to determine if it should implement a lockbox system that reduces customer collection float to 5 days. The reduction in float value from decreasing customer float from 8 days to 5 days is $41.1 million [$5 billion × (3 days/365 days)]. Reese has a cost of capital of 13.5 percent per year. Thus, the value to Reese of reducing customer float by 3 days is $5.55 million (0.135 × $41.1 million). If the annual cost of the lockbox system is less than $5.55 million, it would be beneficial to implement the system.

Although large firms whose customers are geographically dispersed commonly use lockbox systems, smaller firms may also find a lockbox system advantageous. The benefit to small firms often comes primarily from transferring the processing of payments to the bank.

Lockboxes are typically classified as either retail or wholesale. A *retail lockbox* utilizes standardized, scannable remittance documents in order to highly automate the processing of incoming payments. These types of systems are characterized by very high volumes of low-dollar payments, and the key issue is processing these payments at a minimum cost per dollar collected. Given the low-dollar amounts of the payments, availability float is generally not a big issue. *Wholesale lockboxes,* on the other hand, primarily process high-dollar payments with nonstandard remittance information. The key issues in this type of system are (1) reducing the availability float related to the large checks and (2) quickly forwarding the remittance information to the accounts receivable department for application of payment. The current practice for wholesale lockboxes is to make extensive use of imaging technology to quickly and accurately relay copies of the remittance information back to the A/R department.

Cash Concentration

In the previous section, lockbox systems were discussed as a means to reduce collection float. With a lockbox system, the firm has deposits in each lockbox bank. **Cash concentration** is the process of bringing the lockbox and other deposits together into one bank, commonly called the *concentration bank.*

cash concentration
The process of bringing the lockbox and other deposits together into one bank, often called the *concentration bank.*

Cash concentration has three main advantages. First, it creates a large pool of funds for use in making short-term cash investments. Because there is a fixed-cost component in the transaction cost associated with making marketable security investments, investing a single pool of funds reduces the firm's transaction costs. The larger investment pool also allows the firm to choose from a larger variety of marketable securities. Second, concentrating the firm's cash in one account improves the tracking and internal control of the firm's cash. Third, having one concentration bank allows the firm to more effectively implement payment strategies that preserve its invested balances for as long as possible.[1]

SMART PRACTICES VIDEO

Daniel Carter, Chief Financial Officer of Charlotte Russe

"Each of our stores makes deposits into a local account which are concentrated back into our corporate account."

See the entire interview at **SMARTFinance**

The configuration of a company's cash concentration system is generally a function of the collection system. That is, a company with a *field-banking system* will need a way to move money quickly and efficiently from many small deposit banks into its concentration account, whereas a

[1] In the process of transferring deposits between banks, it is possible that balances may exist at two banks simultaneously. These dual balances are created by "slippage" in the clearing system. *Clearing system slippage* is often cited as an advantage of cash concentration. However, rarely can a firm concentrating its cash take advantage of the slippage, so we therefore ignore slippage in our discussions.

company with several collection centers or lockboxes will typically use wire transfers to quickly move large balances from a limited number of collection points into its concentration account. The type of disbursement system (discussed in a later section) is also an important consideration, because these accounts must be funded either by internal transfer or wire transfer.

Funds Transfer Mechanisms

There are a variety of mechanisms for transferring cash from the depository banks to the concentration bank. These mechanisms include (1) depository transfer checks, (2) ACH debit transfers, and (3) wire transfers.

depository transfer check (DTC)
A method for transferring cash from the depository banks to the concentration bank. An unsigned check is drawn on one of the firm's bank accounts and deposited in another of the firm's bank accounts.

Depository Transfer Checks. The first method is a **depository transfer check (DTC)**, which is an unsigned check drawn on one of the firm's bank accounts and deposited in another of the firm's bank accounts. For cash concentration, a DTC is drawn on each deposit bank account and deposited in the concentration bank account. Once the DTC has cleared the bank on which it is drawn, the actual transfer of funds is completed. Most firms currently provide deposit information by telephone to the concentration bank, which then prepares and deposits into its account the DTC drawn on the collecting bank account. Because these paper-based items are subject to normal check-clearing delays, today most companies utilize faster, electronic methods to concentrate funds.

automated clearinghouse (ACH) debit transfer
A preauthorized electronic withdrawal from the payer's account.

electronic depository transfer (EDT)
The term used in the cash management trade for an *automated clearinghouse (ACH) debit transfer.*

Automated Clearinghouse Debit Transfers. The second mechanism is an **automated clearinghouse (ACH) debit transfer**, which is a preauthorized electronic withdrawal from the payer's account, and is generally known in the cash management trade as an **electronic depository transfer (EDT)**. An ACH can be thought of as an electronic DTC and is generally slightly cheaper to use than a paper-based DTC. The ACH, a computerized clearing facility, makes a paperless transfer of funds between the payer and payee banks. An ACH settles accounts among participating banks; individual accounts are settled by respective bank balance adjustments. ACH transfers of this type generally clear in one day, offering significant advantages over the paper-based DTC.

For cash concentration, an ACH debit is initiated by the concentration bank and sent to each deposit bank, with funds then moving from the deposit bank into the concentration bank. These transfers can be automatically created from deposit information and can then be centrally initiated from the company's headquarters through its concentration bank. A large nationwide retailer can easily concentrate deposits from many small deposit banks into its concentration account by using the daily deposit information gathered from its stores' point-of-sale (POS) systems.

wire transfer
In the United States, the primary wire transfer system, known as *Fedwire*, is run by the Federal Reserve System and is available to all depository institutions.

Wire Transfers. The third funds transfer mechanism is a **wire transfer**. In the United States, the primary wire transfer system, known as *Fedwire,* is run by the Federal Reserve System and is available to all depository institutions. A Fedwire transfer is an electronic communication that removes funds from the payer's bank and deposits the funds in the payee's bank on a same-day basis via bookkeeping entries in the financial institution's Federal Reserve account.

Wire transfers can eliminate mail float and clearing float and may provide processing float reductions as well. For cash concentration, the firm moves funds using a wire transfer from each deposit account to its concentration account. Wire transfers are a substitute for DTC and ACH debit transfers, but they are generally much more expensive, with both the sending and receiving banks charging significant fees for the transaction. Wire transfers are usually used only for high-dollar transfers where the investment value of the funds outweighs the cost of the transfer.

Selecting the Best Transfer Mechanism. The firm must balance the marginal benefits and marginal costs of concentrating cash to determine the type and timing of transfers from its lockbox accounts to its concentration account. The transfer mechanism selected should be the one that is most profitable (i.e., profit per period equals earnings on the increased funds' availability [the *marginal benefit*] minus the cost of the transfer system [the *marginal cost*]). In general practice, most companies use wire transfers for large transfers of funds from lockbox deposits and use EDTs for high-volume, low-dollar transfers from small deposit banks.

APPLYING THE MODEL

To demonstrate alternative transfer methods, consider DJM Manufacturing, which needs to transfer $120,000 from its deposit account to its concentration account. It has two choices: an EDT with a total cost of $1 or a wire transfer with a total cost of $15. Because this would be a midweek transfer, the funds would be accelerated by one day. (Note: A Friday transfer would represent three days of funds' acceleration.) The firm's opportunity cost for these funds is 7 percent.

In this example, the value of moving the funds via wire transfer is the one day of interest (the *marginal benefit*) that could be earned if the funds arrived in the concentration account today rather than tomorrow. This amount is calculated to be $23.01 (0.07/365 × $120,000). Because the differential cost (the *marginal cost*) of wire transfer versus an EDT is $14 ($15 – $1), the company should use a wire in this case because it would result in a net benefit of $9.01 ($23.01 – $14.00).

We could also determine the *minimum transfer amount* for which a wire transfer would be beneficial given the opportunity cost and transfer fees. We take the differential cost of a wire ($14.00) and divide by the daily interest rate (0.07/365). In this case, it would be $73,000 [$14.00 ÷ (0.07/365)]. If we were transferring funds on a Friday and thus could earn three days of interest, the minimum transfer amount would be one third of the standard amount, or $24,333 ($73,000 ÷ 3).

CONCEPT REVIEW QUESTIONS

4. What is the firm's objective with regard to *collection float*? What are the common types of collection systems?

5. What are the benefits of using a *lockbox system*? How does it work? How can the firm assess the economics of a lockbox system?

6. Why do firms employ *cash concentration* techniques? What are some of the popular transfer mechanisms used by firms to move funds from depository banks to their concentration banks?

7. How can the cash manager model the benefits and costs of various funds transfer mechanisms to assess their economics? How can this analysis be used to determine the *minimum transfer amount*?

20.3 ACCOUNTS PAYABLE AND DISBURSEMENTS

Overview of the Accounts Payable Process

The final component of the cash conversion cycle is the **average payment period (*APP*)**, which has two parts: (1) the time from the purchase of raw materials until the firm places the payment in the mail and (2) payment float time (disbursement float), the

average payment period (*APP*)
The average length of time it takes a firm to pay its suppliers, calculated by dividing the firm's accounts payable balance by its average daily purchases.

time it takes after the firm places its payment in the mail until the supplier has withdrawn funds from the firm's account. Section 20.1 discussed issues related to payment float time. In this section, we discuss the management of the time that elapses between the purchase of raw materials and mailing the payment to the supplier. This activity is called **accounts payable management**.

accounts payable management
A short-term financing activity that involves managing the time that elapses between the purchase of raw materials and mailing the payment to the supplier.

Purpose of the Accounts Payable Function. The primary purpose of the accounts payable (A/P) function is to examine all incoming invoices and determine the proper amount to be paid. As part of this process, the cash manager matches the invoice to both the purchase order and receiving information to ensure that the goods/services were ordered by an authorized person and that they were actually received. The accounts payable clerk may make adjustments to the invoiced amount for price or quantity differences. Companies usually pay multiple invoices with a single check. A company has the right to make full use of any credit period offered, but intentionally delaying payments or increasing disbursement float is considered an unethical cash management practice. Once payment has been authorized (sometimes referred to as "vouchering"), the cash manager is often responsible for the actual payment itself, either managing the preparation and mailing of the checks or initiating the electronic transfer of funds.

Types of Payment Systems. The other issue involved with managing disbursements is the choice of a centralized or decentralized payables and payments system. In a *centralized system,* all invoices are sent to a central accounts payable department where payment is authorized and checks or other forms of payment are initiated. Centralized systems offer many advantages, including easier concentration of funds, improved access to cash position information, better control, and reduced transaction and administrative costs. There are, however, several problems with centralized payables, such as slow payment times (which could damage relationships with vendors or cause missed opportunities for cash discounts) and the need to coordinate between central payables and field offices/managers to resolve any disputes.

Some companies utilize a more *decentralized system* to the payables and disbursement process, wherein payments are authorized and, in some cases, initiated at the local level. Although this approach generally helps to improve relationships with vendors and enhance local management autonomy, it makes it harder to concentrate funds and obtain daily cash position information, and it increases the chance of unauthorized disbursements.

Cash Discounts

When suppliers offer *cash discounts* to encourage their customers to pay before the end of the credit period, it may not be in the firm's best financial interest to pay on the last day of the credit period. Accounts payable with cash discounts have stated credit terms, such as *2/10 net 30,* which means the purchaser can take a *2 percent discount* from the invoice amount if the payment is made within *10 days* of the beginning of the credit period; otherwise, it must pay the full amount within *30 days* of the beginning of the credit period. The credit period begins at a specific date set by the supplier, typically either the end of the month in which the purchase is made (noted as *EOM*) or on the *date of the invoice*. Taking the discount is at the discretion of the purchaser.

When a firm is extended credit terms that include a cash discount, it has two options: (1) pay the full invoice amount at the end of the credit period or (2) pay the invoice amount less the cash discount at the end of the cash discount period. In either case, the firm purchases the same goods. Thus, the difference between the payment amount without and with taking the cash discount is, in effect, the interest payment made by the firm to its supplier. The firm in need of short-term funds must therefore compare the interest rate charged by its supplier to the best rate charged by purveyors of short-term financing (typically banks) and choose the lowest-cost option. This comparison is important, because if the firm takes the cash discount, it will shorten its average payment period and thus increase the amount of resources it has invested in operating assets, which will require additional negotiated short-term financing.

To calculate the relevant cost, we assume that the firm will always render payment on the *final day of the specified payment period*—credit period or cash discount period. Equation 20.2 presents the formula for calculating the interest rate, r_{discount}, associated with *not taking the cash discount and paying at the end of the credit period* when cash discount terms are offered:

SMART CONCEPTS

See the concept explained step-by-step at SMARTFinance

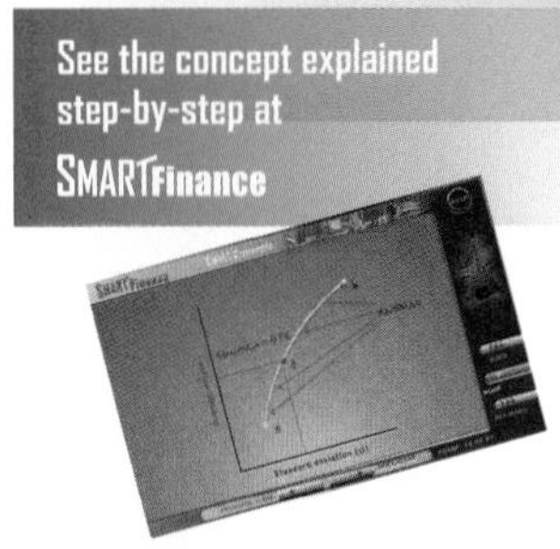

$$r_{\text{discount}} = \frac{d}{(1-d)} \times \frac{365}{(CP-DP)} \qquad \text{(Eq. 20.2)}$$

where d = percent discount (in decimal form),
CP = credit period,
DP = cash discount period.

APPLYING THE MODEL

Assume that a supplier to Masson Industries has changed its terms from *net 30* to *2/10 net 30*. Masson has a line of credit with a bank, and the current interest rate on the line of credit is 6.75 percent per year. Should Masson take the cash discount or continue to use 30 days of credit from its supplier? The interest rate from the supplier is calculated using Equation 20.2:

$$r_{\text{discount}} = \frac{0.02}{(1-0.02)} \times \frac{365}{(30-10)} = 0.372 = 37.2\% \text{ per year}$$

Thus, the annualized rate charged by the supplier to those customers not taking the cash discount is 37.2 percent, whereas the bank charges 6.75 percent. Masson should take the cash discount and obtain needed short-term financing by drawing on its bank line of credit.

Disbursement Products and Methods

Zero-Balance Accounts. **Zero-balance accounts (ZBAs)** are disbursement accounts that always have an end-of-day balance of zero. The purpose is to eliminate nonearning cash balances in corporate checking accounts. A ZBA is often used as a disbursement account under a cash concentration system.

zero-balance accounts (ZBAs)
Disbursement accounts that always have an end-of-day balance of zero. The purpose is to eliminate nonearning cash balances in corporate checking accounts.

A ZBA is designed as follows. Once all of a given day's checks are presented to the firm's ZBA for payment, the bank notifies the firm of the total amount to be drawn, and the firm transfers funds into the account to cover the amount of that day's checks. This leaves an end-of-day balance of $0 (zero dollars). The ZBA allows the firm to keep all operating cash in an interest-earning account, thereby eliminating idle cash balances. Thus, a firm that uses a ZBA in conjunction with a cash concentration system would need two accounts. The firm would concentrate its cash from the lockboxes into an interest-earning account and write checks against its ZBA. The firm would cover the exact dollar amount of checks presented against the ZBA with transfers from the interest-earning account, leaving the end-of-day balance in the ZBA at $0. In many cases, the funding of the ZBA is made automatically and only involves an accounting entry on the part of the bank.

A ZBA is a disbursement management tool that allows the firm to *maximize the use of float on each check*. The firm accomplishes this by keeping all its cash in an interest-earning account instead of leaving nonearning balances in its checking account to later cover the checks the firm has written. This allows the firm to maximize earnings on its cash balances by capturing the full float time on each check it writes.

We have discussed only ZBAs in this section. However, banks offer a variety of similar products. Another common product that achieves the same goal as a ZBA is a *sweep account*, in which the bank "sweeps" account surpluses into the appropriate interest-earning vehicle and liquidates similar vehicles in order to cover account shortages when they occur. Many banks also offer *multitiered ZBAs* that may be used by multidivisional companies or to segregate different types of payments (payrolls, dividends, accounts payable, etc.). This type of account allows the cash manager to better control balances and funding of the master account and associated ZBAs, thus reducing excess balances and transfers.

controlled disbursement
A bank service that provides early notification of checks that will be presented against a company's account on a given day.

Controlled Disbursement. **Controlled disbursement** is a bank service that provides early notification of checks that will be presented against a company's account on a given day. For most large cash management banks, the Federal Reserve Bank makes two presentments of checks to be cleared each day. A bank offering controlled disbursement accounts would get advance electronic notification from the Fed several hours prior to the actual presentment of the items. This allows the bank to let its controlled disbursement customers know what will be presented to their accounts as early as possible in the day. This, in turn, allows the customers to determine their cash position and make any necessary investment/borrowing decisions in the morning, before the checks are presented for payment. Controlled disbursement accounts are often set up as ZBAs to allow for automatic funding through a company's concentration account.

positive pay
A bank service used to combat the most common types of check fraud. A company transmits a check-issued file, designating the check number and amount of each item, to the bank when the checks are issued. The bank matches the presented checks against this file and rejects any items that do not match.

Positive Pay. **Positive pay** is a bank service used to combat the most common types of check fraud. Given the availability of inexpensive computers, scanners, and printers, it is very easy to create excellent copies of corporate checks or change payees or amounts. The risk to a company issuing checks is that the bank might pay fraudulent items and the fraud would not be revealed until the account is reconciled. When using a positive pay service, the company transmits a check-issued file, designating the check number and amount of each item, to the bank when the checks are issued. The bank matches the presented checks against this file and rejects any items that do not match. It is important to note that several courts have ruled that positive pay is a "commercially reasonable" measure to prevent check fraud. This means that a company that does not use this service when available may find itself liable for fraudulent items accepted by its bank.

Developments in Accounts Payable and Disbursements

integrated accounts payable
Provides a company with outsourcing of its accounts payable or disbursement operations. The outsourcing may be as minor as contracting with a bank to issue checks and perform reconciliations or as major as outsourcing the entire payables function.

Integrated Accounts Payable. **Integrated accounts payable**, also known as *comprehensive accounts payable*, provides a company with outsourcing of its accounts payable or disbursement operations. The outsourcing may be as minor as contracting with a bank to issue checks and perform reconciliations or as major as outsourcing the entire payables function. One of the most typical approaches to A/P outsourcing is to send a bank (or other financial service provider) a data file containing a listing of all payments to be made. The bank will maintain a vendor file for the company and send each vendor payment (in the preferred format) in accordance with the company's remittance advice.

Purchasing/Procurement Cards. Many companies are implementing **purchasing** (or **procurement**) **card programs** as a means of reducing the cost of low-dollar indirect purchases. Though companies have been using credit cards for travel and related expenses for many years, they have only recently begun using them to make routine purchases of supplies, equipment, or services. The purchasing cards are issued to designated employees, and both dollar amounts and vendors where they can be used are limited. Companies that have implemented such programs report significant cost savings from streamlining the purchasing process for low-cost items. The other advantage is that the firm can pay the issuer of the purchasing card in a single, large payment that consolidates many small purchases.

purchasing card programs
Implemented by companies as a means of reducing the cost of low-dollar indirect purchases. Also called *procurement card programs*.

Imaging Services. Many disbursement services offered by banks and other vendors incorporate **imaging services** as part of the package. This technology allows both sides of the check, as well as remittance information, to be converted into digital images. The images can then be transmitted via the Internet or easily stored for future reference. Imaging services are especially useful when incorporated with *positive pay* services.

imaging services
Disbursement services offered by banks and other vendors to allow both sides of the check, as well as remittance information, to be converted into digital images. The images can then be transmitted via the Internet or easily stored for future reference. Imaging services are especially useful when incorporated with *positive pay* services.

Fraud Prevention in Disbursements. In recent years, disbursement fraud, especially related to check payments, has increased significantly. Fraudulent checks can be easily created using inexpensive scanners, computers, and laser printers. As a result, fraud prevention and control have become even more important in the accounts payable and disbursement functions. Some of the common fraud prevention measures include the following:

- Written policies and procedures for creating and disbursing checks
- Separating check-issuance duties (approval, signing, and reconciliation)
- Using safety features on checks (microprinting, watermarks, tamper resistance, etc.)
- Setting maximum dollar limits and/or requiring multiple signatures on checks
- Using positive pay services
- Increasing the use of electronic payment methods

CONCEPT REVIEW QUESTIONS

8. What is the primary purpose of the accounts payable function? Describe the procedures used to manage accounts payable. What are the key differences between *centralized* and *decentralized* payables and payment systems?

9. When is it advantageous for a company to pay early and take an offered cash discount? Under what circumstance would the firm be advised to always take any offered cash discounts?

10. What is the difference between a *ZBA* and a *controlled disbursement* account? Are they direct substitutes?

11. What are some of the recent developments in the accounts payable and disbursements area? What role does new technology play in fraud prevention in disbursements?

20.4 SHORT-TERM INVESTING AND BORROWING

After determining the company's cash position, the cash manager will generally have either surplus funds to invest or deficit funds creating a need for short-term borrowing. Clearly, the goal is to earn relatively safe returns on short-term surpluses and to borrow at reasonable cost to meet short-term deficits. This section reviews some of the key options available to the financial manager for investing short-term surpluses and borrowing to meet short-term deficits.

Short-Term Investing

Making sure that the company has access to liquid assets when and where they are needed is one of the critical tasks for the cash manager. Although the primary form of liquidity will generally be a company's checking or demand deposit accounts at its banks, these accounts usually do not earn interest, and the company should not hold excess balances in these accounts. To earn some type of short-term return, a company will hold some "near-cash" assets in the form of short-term investments, often labeled *marketable securities*. These investments may be either a source of reserve liquidity or a place to maintain temporary surplus funds.[2]

Because the short-term investments are essentially a substitute for cash, *providing liquidity* and *preserving principal* should be the primary concerns. Earning a competitive return is also a consideration; however, care must be taken not to place the underlying principal at risk. Remember that the primary purpose of short-term investments is to maintain a pool of liquid assets as a substitute for cash, not to generate profits for the company. To this end, it is important that a company establish policies and guidelines for the management of short-term investments, which should clearly specify the purpose of the investment portfolio and provide recommendations and/or restrictions on acceptable investments and the amount of diversification.

money market mutual funds
Professionally managed short-term investment portfolios used by many small companies and some large companies.

Money Market Mutual Funds. Many large companies will manage their own portfolios of short-term investments, but most companies (especially smaller ones) use money market mutual funds as an alternative. The **money market mutual funds** are professionally managed portfolios that invest in the same types of short-term instruments that cash managers invest in. They may, in fact, offer even more flexibility and stability than a self-managed fund. Using these types of funds makes sense, especially when the costs of running and managing a short-term portfolio are considered.

In most cases, these funds set their *net asset value (NAV)* at a fixed $1 per share in order to preserve the principal value of the fund. As the value of the fund increases, the fund pays investors in additional shares rather than allowing the share price to increase. Commercial money market mutual funds are available from independent companies, as well as from most large banks.

Money Market Financial Instruments. Short-term financial instruments are primarily fixed-income securities generally issued in registered form rather than bearer form, yet they are often called "marketable securities." Many of these securities are also issued in *discount form*, meaning the investor pays less than face value for the security at the time of purchase and receives the face value at maturity. Table 20.1 lists the more common securities used for money market investments.

2. *Temporary surplus funds* may result from ongoing operations, seasonal performance, sales of large assets, or proceeds from a large securities issue.

Table 20.1
Money Market Financial Instruments

U.S. Treasuries	Interest Basis	Maturity
Treasury bills (T-bills)	Discount	Less than 1 year
Treasury notes (T-notes)	Interest bearing	1–10 years
Treasury bonds (T-bonds)	Interest bearing	10–30 years
Federal Agency Issues	**Underlying Assets**	**Backing**
Government National Mortgage Association (Ginnie Mae)	Home mortgages	Full faith and credit
Department of Veterans Affairs (Vinnie Mac)	VA home loans	Full faith and credit
Federal National Mortgage Association (Fannie Mae)	Home mortgages	GSE-implied federal backing
Federal Home Loan Mortgage Corporation	Home mortgages	GSE-implied federal backing
SLM Holding Corporation (Sallie Mae)	Student loans	Quasi-GSE-implied federal backing
Federal Farm Credit Banks Funding Corporation	Agricultural loans	GSE-implied federal backing
Farm Credit System Insurance Corporation	Insurer of Farm Credit banks	GSE-implied federal backing
Central Bank for Cooperatives (CoBank)	Loans to agricultural cooperatives	GSE-implied federal backing
Federal Agricultural Mortgage Corporation (Farmer Mac)	Agricultural loans, rural real estate, and home mortgages	GSE-implied federal backing
Bank Financial Instruments	**Special Features**	
Certificates of deposit – CDs (domestic)	Interest-bearing deposits at financial institutions in the U.S.; may be fixed rate or floating rate with maturities from 7 days to several years	
Overnight sweep accounts	Interest-bearing accounts used for investing end-of-day surplus funds	
Yankee CDs	Dollar-denominated CDs issued by U.S. branches of foreign banks	
Eurodollar CDs	Dollar-denominated CDs issued by banks outside the U.S.	
Eurodollar time deposits	Nonnegotiable, fixed-rate time deposits issued by banks outside the U.S., with maturities ranging from overnight to several years	
Banker's acceptances	Negotiable short-term instruments used for trade finance	
Bank notes	Unsecured or subordinated debt of the bank (not insured)	
Corporate Obligations	**Special Features**	
Commercial paper	Unsecured promissory notes issued by corporations; maturities from 1 to 270 days; usually sold on a discount basis and backed by a credit guarantee from a bank	
Adjustable rate preferred stock	Tax advantaged for corporate holders due to dividend exclusion rule; dividend rate adjusts to maintain stable pricing	
Other Short-Term Investments	**Special Features**	
Money market mutual funds	Available directly from funds or through banks	
Asset-backed securities	Debt obligations issued by companies that are secured by assets such as receivables, credit card obligations, consumer finance loans, major retailers, and automobile companies	
International money market investments	Short-term bills or notes issued by foreign governments, foreign commercial paper, or other types of interest-bearing deposits in foreign currencies	
Repurchase agreements (repos)	A collateralized transaction between a securities dealer or bank and an investor; generally backed by Treasuries or agency securities	

U.S. Treasuries: U.S. T-bills are the benchmark of money market financial instruments. The U.S. government issues these short-term securities to finance its activities, and they appeal to a wide range of investors, both domestic and foreign. They are backed by the "full faith and credit" of the U.S. government (making them essentially free of default risk) and have a very active secondary market. They are issued in weekly auctions on a discount basis with maturities of less than one year (usually 13 or 26 weeks). T-bills are available in minimum denominations of $1,000 but are generally traded in round lots of $1 million. Other Treasury instruments such as *Treasury notes* (*T-notes*) and *Treasury bonds* (*T-bonds*) are initially issued as long-term securities but may be suitable for a short-term portfolio as they approach maturity. All treasury securities are registered and issued in book entry form and are exempt from state income taxes.

Federal agency issues: These instruments have some degree of federal government backing and are issued by either federal agencies or private, shareholder-owned companies known as *government-sponsored enterprises* (*GSEs*). Most of the agencies are securitized investments backed by home mortgages, student loans, or agricultural lending. Two of the agencies (Ginnie Mae and Vinnie Mac) are backed by the "full faith and credit" of the U.S. government, whereas the rest are backed by the implied intervention of the government in the event of a crisis.

Bank financial instruments: U.S. and foreign banks issue short-term *certificates of deposit (CDs)* as well as *time deposits* and *banker's acceptances*. Many banks also offer money market mutual funds and sweep accounts in which their customers can invest short-term cash.

Corporate obligations: The primary corporate obligation in the short-term market is **commercial paper**. Highly rated corporations typically issue this investment, which is structured as an unsecured promissory note with a maturity of less than 270 days. The short maturity allows for issuance without SEC registration, and commercial paper is usually sold to other corporations rather than the general public. Most issues are also backed by credit guarantees from a financial institution and sold on a discount basis, similar to T-bills. The other corporate obligation used for short-term investments is **adjustable rate preferred stock**. These stocks take advantage of the dividend exclusion (of 70 percent or more) for stock in one corporation held by another corporation. In order to make this investment suitable for short-term holdings, the dividend rate paid on the stock is adjusted according to some rate index. This will stabilize the price, even if interest rates change during the forty-five-day holding period required to qualify for the dividend exclusion.

commercial paper
The primary corporate obligation in the short-term market. Typically structured as an unsecured promissory note with a maturity of less than 270 days and sold to other corporations and individual investors. Most issues are also backed by credit guarantees from a financial institution and are sold on a discount basis.

adjustable rate preferred stock
A corporate obligation used for short-term investments. These stocks take advantage of the dividend exclusion (of 70 percent or more) for stock in one corporation held by another corporation. In order to make this investment suitable for short-term holdings, the dividend rate paid on the stock is adjusted according to some rate index. This will stabilize the price, even if interest rates change during the forty-five-day holding period required to qualify for the dividend exclusion.

discount investment
An investment vehicle for which the investor pays less than face value at the time of purchase, and then receives the face value of the investment at its maturity date.

Yield Calculations for Discount Instruments (T-Bills or Commercial Paper)[3]. The yield for short-term *discount investments* such as T-bills and commercial paper is typically calculated using algebraic approximations rather than more precise present value methods. In the case of a **discount investment**, the investor pays less than face value at time of purchase, and then receives the face value of the investment at its maturity date. There are generally no interim interest or coupon payments during the course of holding such an investment.

Determining the yield of T-bills or commercial paper generally involves a two-step process. In most cases, the rate on the investment is expressed as the discount rate, which is used to compute the "dollar discount" and selling price for the instrument. For example, a one-year, $100,000 T-bill sold at a 5 percent discount would sell for $95,000 [$100,000 × (1 – 0.05)]. The investor would pay $95,000 today and receive $100,000 in one year at the maturity date. The yield on this investment would be approximately 5.26 percent ($5,000/$95,000). Though the calculations for a

3. The calculations demonstrated in this section are the same ones we introduced in our discussion of bond prices and interest rates in Section 4.2 of Chapter 4. For convenience as well as custom, we present these formulas a bit differently here.

shorter-term investment are slightly more complicated, they follow the same basic approach. **Money market yield (*MMY*)** for discount instruments is calculated on a 360-day basis but must be converted to **bond equivalent yield (*BEY*)** to compare discount instruments to interest-bearing investments, such as bank CDs. Yield calculations are illustrated in the following example.

money market yield (*MMY*)
The yield for short-term discount instruments such as T-bills and commercial paper is typically calculated using algebraic approximations rather than more precise present value methods.

bond equivalent yield (*BEY*)
The percentage return on zero-coupon bonds calculated as the difference between the par value and the purchase price.

APPLYING THE MODEL

We can use two steps to determine the yield on a 91-day, $1 million T-bill that is selling at a discount of 3.75 percent. Note that the convention in the discount market is to use 360 days when calculating the purchase price and money market yield.

Step 1: Calculate the dollar discount and purchase price.

$$\text{Purchase price} = \text{face value} - \text{dollar discount}$$

$$\text{Dollar discount} = (\text{face value} \times \text{discount rate}) \times (\text{days to maturity}/360)$$

$$= (\$1{,}000{,}000 \times 0.0375) \times (91/360) = \$9{,}479.17$$

$$\text{Purchase price} = \$1{,}000{,}000 - \$9{,}479.17 = \$990{,}520.83$$

Step 2: Calculate *MMY* and *BEY*.

$$\text{Money Market Yield } (MMY) = (\text{dollar discount/purchase price}) \times (360/\text{days to maturity})$$

$$= (\$9{,}479.17/\$990{,}520.83) \times (360/91) = \underline{\underline{3.786\%}}$$

$$\text{Bond Equivalent Yield } (BEY) = \text{Money Market Yield} \times (365/360)$$

$$= 3.786\% \times (365/360) = \underline{\underline{3.839\%}}$$

Short-Term Borrowing

For many companies, a primary source of liquidity is access to short-term lines of credit or commercial paper programs to provide needed funds. This is especially the case for companies in seasonal businesses where large amounts of operating capital may be needed for only a few months of the year. The role of the cash manager in establishing short-term borrowing arrangements is to ensure that the company has credit facilities sufficient to meet short-term cash requirements. Obviously, these arrangements should provide maximum flexibility at a minimum cost.

SMART CONCEPTS

See the concept explained step-by-step at SMARTFinance

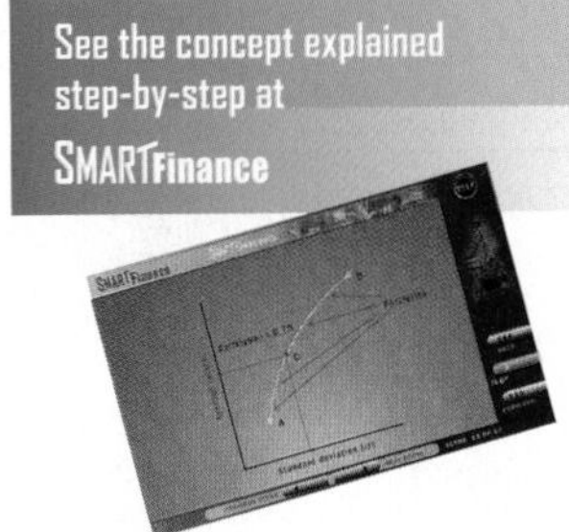

Most short-term borrowing is done on a variable rate basis, with rates quoted in terms of a base rate plus a spread. The spread is essentially an adjustment for the estimated riskiness and overall creditworthiness of the borrower. The base rate and the spread are referred to as the **all-in-rate**. Typical base rates include the *prime rate* and *LIBOR* (*London Interbank Offered Rate*). The **prime rate** is the rate of interest charged by the largest U.S. banks on short-term loans to the best business borrowers. **LIBOR** is the rate that the most creditworthy international banks that deal in Eurodollars charge on interbank loans.

all-in rate
The base rate and the spread.

prime rate
The rate of interest charged by the largest U.S. banks on short-term loans to the best business borrowers.

LIBOR
The London Interbank Offered Rate. The rate that the most creditworthy international banks that deal in Eurodollars charge on interbank loans.

For bank lines of credit, lending agreements may require *commitment fees* (fees paid for the bank's agreement to make money available) and/or *compensating balance requirements* (minimum deposit balances that must be maintained by the borrower at the lending bank). These agreements may also be set up on a multiyear, revolving basis and may use current assets such as receivables or inventory as collateral. In any type of bank lending, most of the terms and conditions result from negotiations between the borrower and the bank.

effective borrowing rate (*EBR*) Generally determined as the total amount of interest and fees paid, divided by the average usable loan amount.

The **effective borrowing rate (*EBR*)** on a bank line of credit is generally determined as the total amount of interest and fees paid, divided by the average usable loan amount. This rate is then adjusted for the actual number of days the loan is outstanding. A demonstration of this calculation follows.

APPLYING THE MODEL

We can determine the *effective borrowing rate, EBR,* on a one-year line of credit with the following characteristics:

CL = total credit line, \$500,000
AL = average loan outstanding, \$200,000
CF = commitment fee, 0.35 percent (35 basis points) on the *unused portion* of the line
IR = interest rate, 2.5 percent over LIBOR (LIBOR is currently 5.75 percent), which equals 8.25 percent
No compensating balances required
Year basis, 365 days

$$EBR = \frac{(IR \times AL) + [CF \times (CL - AL)]}{AL} \times \frac{365}{\text{days loan is outstanding}}$$

$$= \frac{(0.0825 \times \$200{,}000) + [0.0035 \times (\$500{,}000 - \$200{,}000)]}{\$200{,}000} \times \frac{365}{365}$$

$$= \frac{(\$16{,}500) + (\$1{,}050)}{\$200{,}000} \times \frac{365}{365} = \frac{\$17{,}550}{\$200{,}000} \times 1 = \underline{\underline{8.775\%}}$$

The effective borrowing rate of 8.775 percent is about 50 basis points (0.50 percent) above the 8.25 percent interest rate as a result of the commitment fee paid on the unused portion of the line.

CONCEPT REVIEW QUESTIONS

12. Why are *providing liquidity* and *preserving principal* the primary concerns in choosing short-term investments? What guidelines should be included in a short-term investment policy?

13. What securities are considered the benchmark for money market financial instruments, and why? What are some of the popular non-U.S. Treasury money market instruments?

14. What are the key base rates used in variable rate short-term borrowing, and how do they factor into the *all-in-rate*? What other charges might be applicable to short-term borrowing? How do they impact the *effective borrowing rate* (*EBR*)?

20.5 SUMMARY AND CONCLUSIONS

- The cash manager's job is to manage the cash flow time line related to collection, concentration, and disbursement of the company's funds. Float can be viewed from the perspective of either the receiving party or the paying party. Mail float and processing float are viewed the same from both perspectives. The third float component is availability float (to the receiving party) and clearing float (to the paying party). The receiving party's goal is to minimize collection float, whereas the paying party's goal is to maximize disbursement float.

- Cash managers are also responsible for financial relationships, cash flow forecasting, investing and borrowing, and information management. In large firms, they must manage the firm's cash position. In smaller firms, they set target cash balances based on transactions requirements and minimum balances set by their bank.
- In managing collections, the cash manager attempts to reduce collection float using various collection systems, such as field-banking systems, mail-based systems, and electronic systems. Large firms whose customers are geographically dispersed commonly use lockbox systems, although small firms can also benefit from them.
- Firms use cash concentration to bring lockbox and other deposits together into one bank, often a concentration bank. Firms often use depository transfer checks, automated clearinghouse (ACH) debit transfers [also known as electronic depository transfer (EDT)], and wire transfers to transfer funds from the depository bank to the concentration bank.
- The objective for managing the firm's accounts payable is to pay accounts as slowly as possible without damaging the firm's credit rating. If a supplier offers a cash discount, the firm in need of short-term funds must determine the interest rate associated with not taking the discount and paying at the end of the credit period, and then compare it with its lowest-cost, short-term borrowing alternative. If it can borrow elsewhere at a lower cost, the firm should take the discount; otherwise, it should not take it.
- Financial managers use popular disbursement products and methods such as zero-balance accounts (ZBAs), controlled disbursement, and positive pay. Some of the key developments in accounts payable and disbursements are integrated accounts payable, use of purchasing/procurement cards, imaging services, and a number of fraud prevention measures.
- The cash manager will hold near-cash assets in the form of short-term investments (often labeled *marketable securities*) to earn a return on temporary excess cash balances. Investment policies and guidelines should be established for management of short-term investments.
- Smaller companies are likely to invest their short-term surpluses in money market mutual funds. Larger firms will invest in any of a variety of short-term, fixed-income securities, including U.S Treasuries, federal agency issues, bank financial instruments, and corporate obligations, such as commercial paper and adjustable rate preferred stock. The yield on discount investments, such as T-bills and commercial paper, is typically approximated by calculating the money market yield (*MMY*) and converting it into a bond equivalent yield (*BEY*).
- Short-term borrowing can be obtained through the issuance of commercial paper, primarily by large firms, and through lines of credit. Most short-term borrowing is done at a rate quoted at a base rate—the prime rate or LIBOR—plus a spread reflecting the borrower's relative riskiness. The effective borrowing rate can be calculated to capture both the interest costs and other fees associated with a short-term loan.

SELF-TEST PROBLEMS

Answers to Self-Test Problems appear in Appendix D at back of book. Answers to the Concept Review Questions throughout the chapter appear at http://megginson.swlearning.com.

ST20-1. Gale Supply estimates that its customers' payments are in the mail for 3 days, and once received they are processed in 2 days. After the payments are deposited in the firm's bank, the funds are made available to the firm by the bank in 2.5 days. The firm estimates its total annual collections, received at a constant rate, from credit customers to be $87 million. Its annual opportunity cost of funds is 9.5 percent. Assume a 365-day year.

a. How many days of *collection float* does Gale Supply have?
b. What is the current annual dollar cost of Gale Supply's collection float?
c. If the installation of an *electronic invoice presentment and payment (EIPP) system* would result in a 4-day reduction in Gale's collection float, how much could the firm earn annually on this float reduction?
d. Based on your findings in part (c), should Gale install the *EIPP system* if its annual cost is $85,000? Explain your recommendation.

ST20-2. Derson Manufacturing wishes to evaluate the credit terms offered by its four biggest suppliers of raw materials. The prime rate is currently 7.0 percent, and Derson can borrow short-term funds at a spread of 2.5 percent above the prime rate. Assume a 365-day year and that the firm always pays its suppliers on the last day allowed by their stated credit terms. The terms offered by each supplier are as follows:

Supplier 1: 2/10 net 40
Supplier 2: 1/15 net 60
Supplier 3: 3/10 net 70
Supplier 4: 1/10 net 50

a. Calculate the interest rate associated with not taking the discount from each supplier.
b. Assuming the firm needs short-term financing and considering each supplier separately, indicate whether the firm should take the discount from each supplier.
c. If the firm did not need any short-term financing, when should it pay each of the suppliers?
d. If the firm could not obtain a loan from banks and other financial institutions and needed short-term financing, when should it pay each of the suppliers?
e. What impact, if any, would the fact that Derson could stretch its accounts payable (net period only) from Supplier 1 to day 90 without damaging its credit rating have on your recommendation with regard to Supplier 1 in part (b)? Explain you answer.

ST20-3. Rosa Inc. has arranged a one-year, $2 million credit line with its lead bank. The bank set the interest rate at the prime rate plus a spread of 1.50 percent. The prime rate is expected to remain stable at 5.25 percent during the coming year. In addition, the bank requires Rosa to pay a 0.50 percent commitment fee on the average unused portion of the line. Assume a 365-day year.

a. Calculate the *effective borrowing rate (EBR)* on Rosa's line of credit during the coming year assuming an average loan balance outstanding during the year is $1.8 million.
b. Calculate Rosa's *EBR* on the line of credit during the coming year assuming the average loan balance outstanding during the year is $0.8 million.
c. Compare and contrast the *EBR*s calculated for Rosa Inc. in parts (a) and (b). Explain the causes of the differences in *EBR*s.

INTERNET RESOURCES

Note: *For updates to links, please go to the book's Web site at* http://megginson.swlearning.com

http://www.csfb.com (Credit Suisse First Boston)—Part of the Credit Suisse global banking corporation, which offers numerous cash management, investment, and lending services to its corporate customers.

http://www.phoenixhecht.com—A site that contains a variety of cash and treasury management resources, including links to various areas such as payment systems, cash and treasury management, and electronic commerce.

http://www.wellsfargo.com—The fifth-largest U.S. bank, which offers numerous commercial banking services, including business lending and leasing, cash management and treasury, and institutional investments.

KEY TERMS

accounts payable management
adjustable rate preferred stock
all-in-rate
automated clearinghouse (ACH) debit transfer
availability float
average payment period (*APP*)
bank account analysis statement
bond equivalent yield (*BEY*)
cash concentration
cash position management
clearing float
commercial paper
controlled disbursement
depository transfer check (DTC)
discount investment
effective borrowing rate (*EBR*)
electronic bill presentment and payment (EBPP)
electronic depository transfer (EDT)
electronic invoice presentment and payment (EIPP)
field-banking system
float
imaging services
integrated accounts payable
LIBOR
lockbox system
mail float
mail-based collection system
money market mutual funds
money market yield (*MMY*)
positive pay
prime rate
processing float
procurement card programs
purchasing card programs
target cash balance
wire transfer
zero-balance accounts (ZBAs)

QUESTIONS AND PROBLEMS

Q20-1. What is *float*? What are its four basic components? Which of these components is the same from both a collection and a payment perspective? What is the difference between *availability float* and *clearing float*, and from which perspective—collection or payment—is each relevant?

Q20-2. What is *cash position management*? What types of firms set a *target cash balance*? Why? What is the purpose of a bank's requiring the firm to maintain a minimum balance in its checking account? How does this relate to a *bank account analysis statement*?

Q20-3. What is the firm's goal with regard to cash collections? Describe each of the following types of collection systems:

a. Field-banking system
b. Mail-based collection system
c. Electronic system

Q20-4. What is a *lockbox system*? How does it typically work? Briefly describe the economics involved in performing a cost-benefit analysis of such a system.

Q20-5. Briefly describe each of the following funds transfer mechanisms:

a. Depository transfer check (DTC)
b. Automated clearinghouse (ACH) debit transfer
c. Wire transfer

Why are wire transfers typically used only for high-dollar transfers?

Q20-6. What is the goal with regard to managing accounts payable as it relates to the *cash conversion cycle*? Briefly describe the process involved in managing the accounts payable function.

Q20-7. How can a firm in need of short-term financing decide whether or not to take a *cash discount* offered by its supplier? How would this decision change in the event the firm has no alternative source of short-term financing? How would it change for a firm that needs no additional short-term financing?

Q20-8. Briefly describe each of the following disbursement products/methods:

a. Zero-balance accounts (ZBAs)
b. Controlled disbursement
c. Positive pay

How does a ZBA relate to the firm's *target cash balance*?

Q20-9. Briefly describe each of the following developments in accounts payable and disbursements.

a. Integrated accounts payable
b. Purchasing/procurement cards
c. Imaging services
d. Fraud prevention in disbursements

Q20-10. What is the firm's goal in short-term investing? How does it use *money market mutual funds*? Describe some of the popular money market financial instruments in each of the following groups:

a. U.S. Treasuries
b. Federal agency issues
c. Bank financial instruments
d. Corporate obligations

Q20-11. How is interest paid on a *discount investment*? What is the *money market yield (MMY)*? How can the *MMY* be converted into a *bond equivalent yield* (*BEY*)?

Q20-12. How are the rates on short-term borrowing typically set? What role does either the *prime rate* or *LIBOR* play in this process? What is the *effective borrowing rate* (*EBR*)? How does the *EBR* differ from the stated *all-in-rate*?

PROBLEMS

Cash Management

See the problem and solution explained step-by-step at SMARTFinance

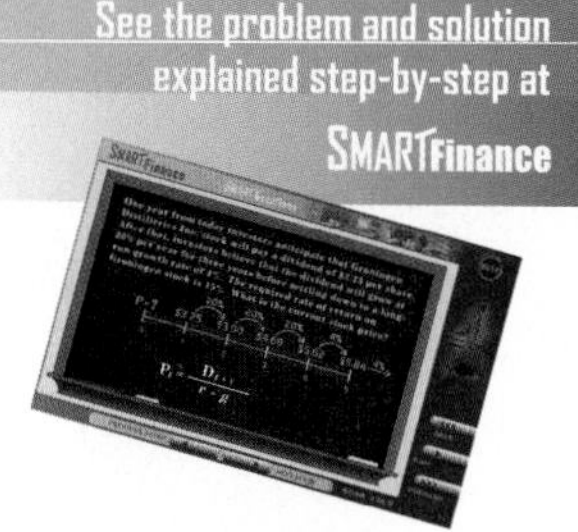

P20-1. Nickolas Industries has daily cash receipts of $350,000. A recent analysis of the firm's collections indicated that customers' payments are in the mail an average of 2 days. Once received, the payments are processed in 1.5 days. After the payments are deposited, the receipts clear the banking system, on average, in 2.5 days. Assume a 365-day year.

a. How much *collection float* (in days) does the firm have?
b. If the firm's opportunity cost is 11 percent, would it be economically advisable for the firm to pay an annual fee of $84,000 for a lockbox system that reduces collection float by 2.5 days? Explain why or why not.

P20-2. NorthAm Trucking is a long-haul trucking company serving customers all across the continental United States and parts of Canada and Mexico. At present, all billing activities, from preparation to collection, are handled by staff at corporate headquarters in Bloomington, Indiana. Payments are recorded and deposits are made once a day in the firm's bank, Hoosier National. You have been hired to recommend ways to reduce collection float and thereby generate cost savings.

a. Suggest and explain at least three specific ways that NorthAm could reduce its *collection float*.
b. Assume your preferred recommendation will cut the collection float by four days. NorthAm bills $108 million per year. If collections are evenly distributed throughout a 365-day year and the firm's cost of short-term financing is 8 percent, what savings could be achieved by implementing the suggestion?
c. If the cost of implementing your recommendation is $100,000 per year, based on your finding in part (b), should NorthAm implement it?

Collections

P20-3. Qtime Products believes that use of a lockbox system can shorten its accounts receivable collection period by four days. The firm's annual sales, all on credit, are $65 million, billed on a continuous basis. The firm can earn 9 percent on its short-term investments. The cost of the lockbox system is $57,500 per year. Assume a 365-day year.

a. What amount of cash will be made available for other uses under the lockbox system?
b. What net benefit (or cost) will the firm receive if it adopts the lockbox system? Should it adopt the proposed lockbox system?

P20-4. Wachovia Corporation is a major (superregional) U.S. bank. The Wachovia corporate Web site is located at http://www.wachovia.com. Among the cash management services available to its business customers are lockboxes. Access Wachovia's cash management and deposit services at http://www.wachovia.com/corp_inst/page/0,,7_17,00.html, and determine the lockbox products available from Wachovia. Discuss the differences between the various lockbox products.

P20-5. Quick Burger Inc., a national chain of hamburger restaurants, has accumulated a $27,000 balance in one of its regional collection accounts. It wishes to make an efficient, cost-effective transfer of $25,000 of this balance to its corporate concentration account, thus leaving a $2,000 minimum balance in the regional collection account. It has the following options:

Option 1: DTC at a cost of $1 and requiring four days to clear
Option 2: EDT at a cost of $2.50 and requiring one day to clear
Option 3: Wire transfer at a cost of $12 and clearing the same day (zero days to clear)

a. If Quick Burger can earn 6 percent on its short-term investments, assuming a 365-day year, which of the options would you recommend to minimize the transfer cost?
b. Compare Options 2 and 3, and determine the minimum amount that would have to be transferred in order for the wire transfer (Option 3) to be more cost-effective than the EDT (Option 2).

Accounts Payable and Disbursements

P20-6. Assume a firm receives the following credit terms from six suppliers and a 365-day year.

Supplier 1: 2/10 net 50
Supplier 2: 1/10 net 30
Supplier 3: 2/10 net 150
Supplier 4: 3/10 net 60
Supplier 5: 1/10 net 45
Supplier 6: 1/20 net 80

a. Determine the interest rate associated with not taking the cash discount and paying at the end of the credit period for each of the six suppliers' credit terms.
b. In part (a), you calculated the interest rate associated with not taking the discount for each supplier's credit terms. Now you must decide whether or not to take the cash discount by paying within the discount period. To pay early, you will need to borrow from your firm's line of credit at the local bank. The interest rate on the line of credit is the prime rate plus 2.5 percent. You can get the most recent prime rate

from the Federal Reserve at http://www.federalreserve.gov/releases/h15/data.htm. For each supplier's terms, use the current prime rate to determine whether the firm should borrow from the bank or borrow from the supplier.

P20-7. Access Enterprises is vetting four possible suppliers of an important raw material used in its production process, all offering different credit terms. The products offered by each supplier are virtually identical. The following table shows the credit terms offered by these suppliers. Assume a 365-day year.

Supplier	Credit Terms
A	1/10 net 40
B	2/20 net 90
C	1/20 net 60
D	3/10 net 75

a. Calculate the interest rate associated with not taking the discount from each supplier.

b. If the firm needs short-term funds, which are currently available from its commercial bank at 11 percent, and if each of the suppliers is viewed *separately*, which, if any, of the suppliers' cash discounts should the firm not take? Explain why.

c. What impact, if any, would the fact that the firm could stretch its accounts payable (net period only) by 20 days from supplier A have on your answer in part (b) relative to this supplier?

P20-8. Union Company is examining its operating cash management. One of the options the firm is considering is a *zero-balance account* (*ZBA*). The firm's bank is offering a *ZBA* with monthly charges of $1,500, and the bank estimates that the firm can expect to earn 8 percent on its short-term investments. Determine the minimum average cash balance that would make this *ZBA* a benefit to the firm. Assume a 365-day year.

P20-9. Wachovia Corporation is a major (superregional) U.S. bank. The Wachovia corporate Web site is located at http://www.wachovia.com. Among the cash management services available to its business customers are various collection and disbursement products.

a. Access Wachovia's cash management and deposit services at http://www.wachovia.com/corp_inst/page/0,,7_17,00.html, and determine the disbursement products available from Wachovia. Compare Wachovia's controlled disbursements and sweep accounts to the text definition for a *ZBA*.

b. Bank of America is the first truly national bank in the United States. Access its corporate Web site at http://www.bankofamerica.com, and compare Bank of America's disbursement products with the products from Wachovia Corporation discussed in part (a).

Short-Term Investing and Borrowing

See the problem and solution explained step-by-step at SMARTFinance

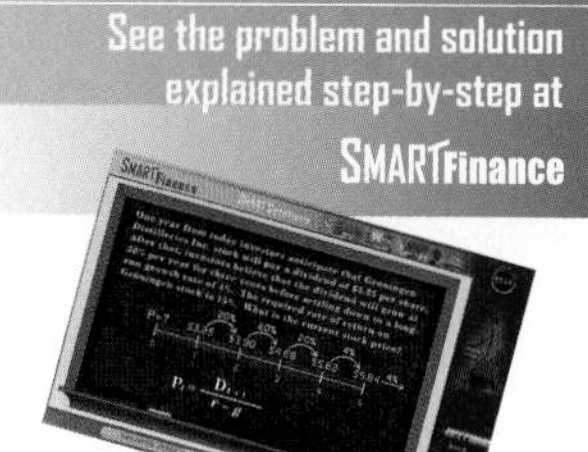

P20-10. Sager Inc. just purchased a 91-day, $1 million T-bill that was selling at a discount of 3.25 percent.

a. Calculate the dollar discount and purchase price on this T-bill.

b. Find the *money market yield* (*MMY*) on this T-bill.

c. Find the *bond equivalent yield* (*BEY*) on this T-bill.

d. Rework parts (a), (b), and (c) assuming the T-bill was selling at a 3.0 percent discount. What effect does this drop of 25 basis points in the T-bill discount have on its *BEY*?

P20-11. Matthews Manufacturing is negotiating a one-year credit line with its bank, Worldwide Bank. The amount of the credit line is $6.5 million with an interest rate set at 1.5 percent above the prime rate. A commitment fee of 0.50 percent (50 basis points) will be charged on the unused portion of the line. No compensating balances are required, and the loan is made on a 365-day basis.

a. If the prime rate is assumed constant at 4.25 percent during the term of the loan and Matthews' average loan outstanding during the year is $5.0 million, calculate the firm's *effective borrowing rate* (*EBR*).

b. What effect would an increase in the prime rate to 4.75 percent for the entire year have on Matthews' *effective borrowing rate* (*EBR*) calculated in part (a)?

c. What effect would a decrease in Matthews' average loan outstanding during the year to $4.0 million have on the *effective borrowing rate* (*EBR*) calculated in part (a)?

d. Using your findings in parts (a), (b), and (c), compare, contrast, and discuss the effects of interest rate changes versus changes in the average loan outstanding on Matthews' effective borrowing rates.

THOMSON ONE Business School Edition

For instructions on using Thomson ONE, refer to the instructions provided with the Thomson ONE problems at the end of Chapters 1–6 or to "A Guide for Using Thomson ONE."

P20-12. Analyze the cash positions of General Electric Company (ticker: GE), General Motors Corp. (GM), Ford Motor Company (F), and Microsoft Corp. (@MSFT) relative to total assets over the last ten years. Use the cash and equivalents item from the balance sheet for the analysis. How large of a cash balance relative to total assets do these companies have? How has the cash balance (relative to total assets) changed over the last ten years?

Since these exercises depend upon real-time data, your answers will change continuously depending upon when you access the Internet to download your data.

MINICASE

Cash, Payables, and Liquidity Management

The company CEO and your direct boss, Otto Stressinbaum, has asked you to take over the direct supervision of the cash, payables, and liquidity management process. Because you have not been directly involved in these processes since your first few years with the company, you decide to review some relevant topics. To assist you in the review, you ask the company's cash manager, Lily Fairchild, to submit a list of questions for you to research and answer. She submits the following questions.

ASSIGNMENT

1. What are the typical cash manager's job duties?
2. What is *cash position management*?
3. Discuss the more popular collection systems and techniques that are utilized for collections.
4. What are the mechanisms for transferring cash from depository banks to concentration banks?
5. What is the purpose of the accounts payable function and what are the general types of payment systems that are available?
6. Why are cash discounts viewed by customers as a method of suppliers charging interest on the purchase of goods?
7. What are some disbursement products and methods?
8. What are some options available to managers for short-term investing?

PART 7

Special Topics

In this section we take a look at three special topics. Chapter 21 examines long-term debt and leasing. It may seem odd to put debt and leasing together, but if you think about it, a lease can be a long-term obligation just like the obligation that firms undertake when they borrow money by issuing bonds. So managers evaluate some of the same marginal costs and benefits when they make decisions about leasing that they evaluate when they decide how much long-term debt to issue.

Chapter 22 covers one of the most exciting areas of finance, mergers and acquisitions. Historically, mergers have come in waves, with some years seeing a huge volume of merger transactions, while in other years very few mergers occur. The same statement can be made looking across countries rather than across time. In the United States, mergers and acquisition are simply part of the economic landscape. Managers know that engaging in a merger is one strategic choice open to them, and they also know that if they do not make choices that increase shareholder wealth, they themselves may become the target of a takeover attempt. In this chapter, we study some of the motivations for mergers and the tactics that firms use to buy other firms or defend against unwanted bids.

In a sense, it is appropriate to end the book with a chapter on bankruptcy, because for some firms, bankruptcy is the end of the line. However, in the United States, bankruptcy laws give firms a chance to reorganize and renegotiate with their creditors. Many firms enter bankruptcy only to emerge later as on-going concerns. Just as managers can attempt to merge with another firm as a strategic choice, they can also use a bankruptcy filing as a strategic option, albeit an extreme one. Chapter 23 explains how the bankruptcy process works in the U.S.

Part 1: Introduction

1 The Scope of Corporate Finance

2 Financial Statement and Cash Flow Analysis

3 Present Value

Part 2: Valuation, Risk, and Return

4 Valuing Bonds

5 Valuing Stocks

6 The Trade-off Between Risk and Return

7 Risk, Return, and the Capital Asset Pricing Model

Part 3: Capital Budgeting

8 Capital Budgeting Process and Techniques

9 Cash Flow and Capital Budgeting

10 Risk and Capital Budgeting

Part 4: Capital Structure and Dividend Policy

11 Raising Long-Term Financing

12 Capital Structure

13 Dividend Policy

14 Entrepreneurial Finance and Venture Capital

Part 5: Options, International Finance, and Risk Management

15 Options

16 International Financial Management

17 Risk Management

Part 6: Financial Planning and Management

18 Financial Planning

19 Cash Conversion, Inventory, and Receivables Management

20 Cash, Payables, and Liquidity Management

Part 7: Special Topics

21 Long-Term Debt and Leasing

22 Mergers, Acquisitions, and Corporate Control

23 Bankruptcy and Financial Distress

CHAPTER 21

Long-Term Debt and Leasing

OPENING FOCUS

The Terminator Sells Economic Recovery Bonds

California has long been called the "golden state," but by early 2004 the state government's finances were in crisis, with a projected two-year budget deficit approaching $45 billion. In response to the deteriorating fiscal situation, California voters in October 2003 recalled the sitting governor, Grey Davis, who had been reelected less than one year earlier, and replaced him with Arnold Schwarzenegger, the Austrian-born actor best known for the swashbuckling roles that earned him the nickname "The Terminator." Schwarzenegger swept to victory on a pledge to right the state's chaotic finances through a combination of budget cuts and new debt issues. In a March 2004 referendum on his plan, California approved the issuance of up to $15 billion worth of new bonds.

In mid-April 2004, the state treasurer announced that the first $9.7 billion portion, or **tranche**, of this bond issue would be priced in late May 2004. This largest-ever bond issue by a U.S. state had originally been planned for late June but was moved forward because state officials feared that delay would significantly increase the overall cost of the offering. U.S. interest rates began rising sharply in April, as signs of a strengthening economy pushed up demands for capital by corporate and government borrowers, and had increased by almost a full percentage point in the month following California's referendum.

The actual sale of these bonds on May 5 was very successful, with investors placing demands for almost twice the amount of the offering. The Economic Recovery bonds were actually assigned an Aa3 bond rating by Moody's Investors Service, several notches higher than the Baa1 bond rating that Moody's assigns to California's existing general obligation bonds. The Baa1 rating is barely investment-grade, and is by far the lowest credit rating of any U.S. state. While this bond issue alone will not solve California's long-term fiscal problems, its successful launch—coupled with news that the state's tax revenues in June 2004 were running 10 percent ahead of the previous year—might well provide the state with the breathing room needed to let The Terminator's financial reforms work their magic.

Source: Jennifer Hughes, "California to Bring Forward Bond Issue," *Financial Times* (April 16, 2004), from the *Financial Times* Web site at http://www.ft.com.

LEARNING OBJECTIVES

After studying this chapter you should be able to:

- Describe the most important characteristics of long-term debt financing, such as the factors that influence its cost and the covenants lenders include to protect their investment;
- Discuss the differences between the two main types of loans arranged by corporate borrowers and explain why syndicated loans have become such an attractive source of debt financing;
- Describe the most important types of corporate bonds issued by U.S. corporations and compare these to bonds issued by international borrowers;
- Explain how corporations decide whether to refund an existing bond issue by exercising a call option;
- Explain the difference between operating leases and capital, or financial, leases; and
- Describe the steps involved in deciding whether to acquire an asset through a lease or by borrowing the money required to purchase the asset (the lease-versus-purchase decision).

Corporations and governments around the world issue long-term debt in order to finance capital investments or to fund current operations. As we saw in Chapter 11, the vast majority of external capital that is raised by companies each year is debt rather than equity, and most of this debt is long-term.[1] This chapter focuses on the two most important sources of debt capital for business: long-term debt and leasing. We examine the key features, costs, advantages, and disadvantages of each of these funding sources, beginning with long-term debt.

21.1 CHARACTERISTICS OF LONG-TERM DEBT FINANCING

Long-term debt is the dominant form of long-term, external financing in all developed economies. On the balance sheet, accountants classify debt as long-term if it matures in more than one year. Firms obtain long-term debt by negotiating with a financial institution for a term loan, or through selling bonds. We discuss each of these in the following sections, as well as *syndicated lending,* which has emerged as one of the most important sources of debt financing for companies located in the thirty member countries of the Organization for Economic Cooperation and Development (OECD)—and especially in the United States. This section first analyzes the choice between public and private debt offerings and then discusses long-term debt covenants and costs.

1. By definition, governments can only issue debt, since few investors would wish to purchase "government equity," even if such a financial creature existed. Although government debt issuance is an extremely important and interesting topic, we henceforth focus exclusively on corporate debt issuance.

The Choice between Public and Private Debt Issues

Once a firm's managers decide to employ long-term debt financing, they face a series of practical choices regarding how best to structure the debt. The first, and arguably the most important, decision managers must make is whether to issue debt publicly or privately. In the United States, public long-term debt offerings involve selling securities (bonds and notes) directly to investors, almost always with the help of investment bankers. Firms must register these offerings with the SEC, and most long-term corporate bond offerings take the form of unsecured debentures, as discussed in Section 21.3. Furthermore, the vast majority of U.S. public debt offerings are **fixed-rate offerings**, meaning they have a coupon interest rate that remains constant throughout the issue's life.

fixed-rate offerings
Issues that have a coupon interest rate that remains constant throughout the issue's life.

Private debt issues take one of two principal forms. **Loans** are private debt agreements arranged between corporate borrowers and financial institutions, especially commercial banks, whereas **private placements** are unregistered security offerings sold directly to *accredited investors*. The best-known and most common form of loan is a *term loan* arranged between a borrower and a single bank. However, the total value of large-denomination, *syndicated* loans arranged for a single borrower but funded by multiple banks exceeds that of single-lender term loans by a wide margin. The overwhelming majority of both term loans and syndicated loans extended to corporate borrowers are **floating-rate issues**, where the loan is priced at a fixed spread above a base interest rate, usually **LIBOR**, the London Interbank Offered Rate, or the U.S. bank **prime lending rate**. As discussed briefly in Chapter 4, the interest rate paid by issuers of floating-rate debt thus adjusts up and down over time as the base interest rate changes.

loans
Private debt agreements arranged between corporate borrowers and financial institutions, especially commercial banks.

private placements
Unregistered security offerings sold directly to accredited investors.

floating-rate issues
Debt issues with an interest (coupon) rate that periodically changes.

LIBOR
The London Interbank Offered Rate.

prime lending rate
The interest rate charged by banks on their most creditworthy borrowers.

Debt Covenants

Long-term debt agreements, whether resulting from a term loan or a bond issue, normally include certain *covenants*. These are contractual clauses that place specific operating and financial constraints on the borrower. There are two types of covenants: *positive covenants* require the borrower to take a specific action, and *negative covenants* prohibit certain actions. Debt covenants do not normally place a burden on a financially sound business and typically remain in force for the life of the debt agreement.

Covenants allow the lender to monitor and control the borrower's activities to protect the creditor's investment. Without these provisions, the borrower could take advantage of the lender by investing in riskier projects without compensating lenders with a higher interest rate on their loans.

Positive Covenants. As noted, positive covenants specify things that a borrower "must do." Some of the most common positive covenants include the following:

1. The borrower is required to maintain satisfactory accounting records in accordance with generally accepted accounting principles (GAAP).
2. The borrower is periodically required to supply audited financial statements that the lender uses to monitor the firm and enforce the debt agreement.
3. The borrower is required to pay taxes and other liabilities when due.
4. The borrower is required to maintain all facilities in good working order, thereby behaving as a going concern.
5. The borrower is required to maintain a minimum level of *net working capital*. Net working capital below the minimum is considered indicative of inadequate liquidity, a common precursor to default.
6. The borrower is required to maintain life insurance policies on certain "key employees" without whom the firm's future would be in doubt. These policies

SMART IDEAS VIDEO
Annette Poulsen, University of Georgia
"The covenant is the promise about what the corporation is going to do or not do."

See the entire interview at **SMARTFinance**

COMPARATIVE CORPORATE FINANCE

Islamic Finance: How Do You Sell Bonds When You Cannot Pay Interest?

The past two decades have seen a handful of Muslim countries modify their commercial banking laws to make them consistent with the principle of *Syariah,* or the prohibition on the charging of interest on loans. Several other countries have allowed banks to operate under the *Syariah* principle, which is similar to the Catholic church's injunction against usury (charging interest) during the Middle Ages in Europe. Needless to say, bankers have found this restriction on a core source of revenue to be a serious challenge, but many have been able to comply with the religious intent of the laws by structuring loans as investment partnerships—where the bank's return comes in the form of a share of profits—or by structuring loan payments as fees or dividends rather than interest.

While Islamic banking has, perhaps unsurprisingly, made few inroads in global markets, it has been relatively successful within the borders of at least some of the countries that have adopted it. But how do you attract international investors to an Islamic bond issue when the same *Syariah*-based restriction on payment of interest applies? As it happens, several governments and one major international development bank have executed successful Islamic finance bond offerings since July 2002. That month, the Malaysian government raised $600 million with the world's first Global Islamic Bond offering targeted primarily at investors in West Asia and the Middle East. The bond issue carried an investment-grade rating, and investors were promised a return (comparable to dividend payments) equal to 0.95 percentage points above LIBOR, funded by rentals from Malaysian government properties.

The second Islamic bond offering was even more intriguing, since the issuer was the government of Iran, and this was its first international capital market offering since the fundamentalist regime came to power in 1979. The €500 million issue was assigned a B+ bond rating by Fitch and was priced at 425 basis points over the reference rate for interest rate swaps of similar risk. Perhaps most surprisingly, the issue was targeted at European investors and sold out very quickly.

The year 2003 saw two even more important Islamic bond offerings. First, the Islamic Development Bank (IDB) executed a $400 million offering, targeted at European investors, while Qatar sold a $700 million offering in October. The Qatari issue was the largest-ever bond offering that met *Syariah* requirements. Intriguingly, non-Muslim investors purchased 70 percent of the IDB issue, according to Saad Ashraf, the head of Citigroup's Global Islamic Finance Group, which managed the sale.

By mid-2004, the worldwide value of the Islamic finance market had reached $230 billion and was growing at a rate of 15 percent per year, according to a study released by the Kuala Lumpur Stock Exchange. Moreover, this study suggested there is over $1.3 trillion worth of untapped Islamic funds worldwide. Given this potential, it is not surprising that virtually every major international investment bank has established an Islamic Finance unit, and that several highly successful Islamic finance mutual funds have sprung up to cater to this wealthy and pious investor clientele.

Sources: Ishun P. Ahmad, "Islamic Bond Investors in for the Long Term," *The New Straits Times Press* [Malaysia] (July 13, 2002) and Arkady Ostrovsky and Bayan Rahman, "Capital Markets: Iran Pays More to Raise €500m," *Financial Times* (July 15, 2002), "Islamic Bond Market Expands with Record Sale by Qatar: Didn't Exist 15 Months ago," *Financial Post* [Canada] (October 1, 2003) and Mark Warner, "Tapping into the Potential of the East," *Lloyds List* (April 16, 2004), all downloaded from the *Financial Times* Web site at http://www.ft.com.

provide the financial resources to hire qualified people quickly in the event that a key person dies or is disabled.

7. The borrower is often considered to be in default on all debts if it is in default on any debt to any lender. This is known as a **cross-default covenant.**
8. Occasionally, a covenant specifically requires the borrower to spend the borrowed funds on a proven financial need.

cross-default covenant In which the borrower is often considered to be in default on all debts if it is in default on any debt.

Negative Covenants. Negative covenants specify what a borrower "must not do." Common negative covenants include the following:

1. Borrowers may not sell accounts receivable to generate cash because doing so could cause a long-run cash shortage if the borrower uses the proceeds to meet current obligations.
2. Long-term lenders commonly impose fixed asset restrictions on the borrower. These constrain the firm with respect to the liquidation, acquisition, and

encumbrance of fixed assets because any of these actions could damage the firm's ability to repay its debt.

3. Many debt agreements prohibit borrowing additional long-term debt or require that additional borrowing be subordinated to the original loan. **Subordination** means that all subsequent or more junior creditors agree to wait until all claims of the senior debt are satisfied in full before having their own claims satisfied.

subordination Agreement by all subsequent or more-junior creditors to wait until all claims of the senior debt are satisfied in full before having their own claims satisfied.

4. Borrowers may not enter into certain types of leases to limit additional fixed-payment obligations.
5. Occasionally, the lender prohibits business combinations by requiring the borrower to agree not to consolidate, merge, or combine in any way with another firm because such an action could significantly change the borrower's business and financial risk.
6. To prevent liquidation of assets through large salary payments, the lender may prohibit or limit salary increases for specified employees.
7. A relatively common provision prohibits the firm's annual cash dividend payments from exceeding 50–70 percent of its net earnings or a specified dollar amount.

In the process of negotiating the terms of long-term debt, the borrower and lender must agree to an acceptable set of covenants. If the borrower violates a covenant, the lender may demand immediate repayment, waive the violation and continue the loan, or waive the violation but alter the terms of the original debt agreement.

Cost of Long-Term Debt

In addition to specifying positive and negative covenants, the long-term debt agreement specifies the interest rate, the timing of interest payments, and the size of principal repayment. The major factors affecting the cost, or interest rate, of long-term debt are loan maturity, loan size, borrower risk, and the basic cost of money.

Loan Maturity. Generally, long-term loans have higher interest rates than short-term loans. Recall from Chapter 4 that the yield curve, which plots the relationship between yield to maturity and time to maturity for bonds having similar risk, typically slopes upward. Factors that can cause an upward-sloping yield curve include (1) the general expectation of higher future inflation or interest rates; (2) lender preferences for shorter-term, more liquid loans; and (3) greater demand for long-term rather than short-term loans relative to the supply of such loans. In a more practical sense, the longer the term, the greater the default risk associated with the loan. To compensate for all these factors, the lender typically charges a higher interest rate on long-term loans.

Loan Size. The size of the loan usually affects the interest cost of borrowing in an inverse manner due to economies of scale. Loan administration costs per dollar borrowed are likely to decrease with increasing loan size. However, the risk to the lender increases, because larger loans result in less diversification. The size of the loan sought by each borrower must therefore be evaluated to determine the net administrative cost and risk trade-off.

Borrower Risk. As noted in Chapter 10, the higher the firm's operating leverage, the greater its business risk. Also, the higher the borrower's debt ratio or the lower its interest coverage ratio, the greater its financial risk. The lender's main concern is with the borrower's ability to fully repay the loan as prescribed in the debt agreement. A lender uses an overall assessment of the borrower's business and financial risk, along with information on past payment patterns, when setting the interest rate on a loan.

Basic Cost of Money. The cost of money is the basis for determining the actual interest rate charged. Generally, the rate on U.S. Treasury securities with equivalent maturities is used as the basic (lowest-risk) cost of money. To determine the actual interest rate to be charged, the lender will add premiums for borrower risk and other factors to this basic cost of money for the given maturity. Alternatively, some lenders determine a prospective borrower's risk class and find the rates charged on loans with similar maturities and terms to firms in the same risk class. Instead of having to determine a risk premium, the lender can use the risk premium prevailing in the marketplace for similar loans.

CONCEPT REVIEW QUESTIONS

1. What factors should a manager consider when deciding on the amount and type of long-term debt to be used to finance a business?

2. What factors should a manager consider when negotiating the covenants in a long-term debt agreement?

3. How can managers estimate their firms' cost of long-term debt prior to meeting with a lender?

21.2 CORPORATE LOANS

Corporations can acquire debt financing either by borrowing money as a loan from a financial or nonfinancial institution or by selling debt securities directly to investors using capital markets. This section describes the two most important types of corporate borrowings: term loans and syndicated loans. In both cases, the primary lenders are commercial banks and other financial institutions, though many nonfinancial institutions also serve as term lenders in special situations.

Term Loans

A **term loan** is made by an institution to a business and has an initial maturity of more than one year, generally five to twelve years. Term loans are often made to finance permanent working capital needs, to pay for machinery and equipment, or to liquidate other loans. Term loans are essentially private placements of debt. However, firms typically negotiate term loans directly with the lender rather than use an investment banker as an intermediary. An advantage of term loans over publicly traded debt is their flexibility. The securities (bonds or notes) in any given public debt issue are usually purchased by many different investors, so it is almost impossible to alter the terms of the borrowing agreement even if new business conditions make such changes desirable. With a term loan, the borrower can negotiate with a single lender for modifications to the borrowing agreement.[2]

term loan
A loan made by a financial institution to a business, with an initial maturity of more than 1 year, generally 5 to 12 years.

Characteristics of Term Loan Agreements. The actual term loan agreement is a formal contract ranging from a few to a few hundred pages. The following items commonly appear in the document: the amount and maturity of the loan, payment dates, interest rate, positive and negative covenants, collateral (if any), purpose of the loan, action to be taken in the event the agreement is violated, and stock purchase warrants. Of these, only payment dates, collateral requirements, and stock purchase warrants require further discussion.

[2] Companies typically arrange loans with commercial banks as part of a larger, ongoing banking relationship. Large companies often have dozens of these bilateral relationships, but a critical decision for smaller firms is whether to maintain one large banking relationship or several smaller bilateral relationships in order to minimize the risk of not being able to arrange financing during an emergency.

Payment Dates. Term loan agreements usually specify monthly, quarterly, semiannual, or annual loan payments. Generally, these equal payments fully repay the interest and principal over the life of the loan. Occasionally, a term loan agreement will require periodic interest payments over the life of the loan followed by a large lump-sum payment at maturity. This so-called **balloon payment** represents the entire loan principal if the periodic payments represent only interest.

balloon payment
A term loan agreement that requires periodic interest payments over the life of the loan followed by a large lump-sum payment at maturity.

Collateral Requirements. Term lending arrangements may be unsecured or secured. Secured loans have specific assets pledged as **collateral.** The collateral often takes the form of an asset such as machinery and equipment, plant, inventory, pledges of accounts receivable, and pledges of securities. Unsecured loans are obtained without pledging specific assets as collateral. Whether lenders require collateral depends on the lender's evaluation of the borrower's financial condition.

collateral
The specific assets pledged to secure a loan.

Term lending is often referred to as asset-backed lending, though term lenders in reality are primarily cash flow lenders. They hope and expect to be repaid out of cash flow, but require collateral both as an alternative source of repayment and as "ransom" to decrease the incentive of borrowing firms to default (because a defaulting borrower would lose the use of valuable corporate assets). Most pledged assets are secured by a **lien**, which is a legal contract specifying under what conditions the lender can take title to the asset if the loan is not repaid, and prohibiting the borrowing firm from selling or disposing of the asset without the lender's consent. The liens serve two purposes: they establish clearly the lender's right to seize and liquidate collateral if the borrower defaults, and they serve notice to subsequent lenders of a prior claim on the asset(s). Some of the more technical aspects of loan default are presented in Chapter 23.

lien
A legal contract specifying under what conditions a lender can take title to an asset if a loan is not repaid, and prohibiting the borrowing firm from selling or disposing of the asset without the lender's consent.

Not all assets make acceptable collateral, of course. For an asset to be useful as collateral, it should (1) be nonperishable, (2) be relatively homogeneous in quality, (3) have a high value relative to its bulk, and (4) have a well-established secondary market where seized assets can be turned into cash without a severe price penalty.

Stock Purchase Warrants. The corporate borrower often gives the lender certain financial benefits, usually **stock purchase warrants,** in addition to the payment of interest and repayment of principal. Stock purchase warrants are instruments that give their holder the right to purchase a certain number of shares of the firm's common stock at a specified price over a certain period. These are designed to entice institutional lenders to make long-term loans, possibly under relatively favorable terms. Warrants are also frequently used as "sweeteners" for corporate bond issues.

stock purchase warrants
Instruments that give their holder the right to purchase a certain number of shares of a firm's common stock at a specified price over a certain period.

Term Lenders. Students are often surprised to learn about the wide array of sources for term loans. The primary lenders making term loans to businesses are commercial banks, insurance companies, pension funds, regional development companies, the U.S. federal government's Small Business Administration, small business investment companies, commercial finance companies, and equipment manufacturers' financing subsidiaries.

Syndicated Loans

A **syndicated loan** is a large-denomination credit arranged by a group (a *syndicate*) of commercial banks for a single borrower. Although syndicated lending has been a fixture of U.S. and international finance for over three decades, syndicated loans have increased dramatically in size, volume, and importance during the last fifteen years. During the 1970s and early 1980s, many syndicated loans were arranged for governments in developing countries. These *petrodollar loans* were funded with the (dollar-denominated) trade surpluses that oil-exporting countries built up following the surge in oil prices in 1974–1975 and 1980–1982. Oil producers deposited their surpluses in global banks, which then "recycled" these funds into petrodollar loans. The "Third World debt crisis" of the early 1980s occurred after developing-country debt loads hit critical levels and the borrowing countries defaulted on some of their interest and principal payments.

syndicated loan
A large loan that is financed by several banks joining together in a syndicate, where each bank provides a small part of the total loan.

The majority of syndicated loans were arranged for Western corporate borrowers even during the 1970s and 1980s, and since that time the market has become overwhelmingly corporate. Today, over $2 trillion worth of syndicated loans are arranged annually, roughly two thirds of which go to corporate borrowers. The syndicated loan market appeals to borrowers who need to arrange very large loans quickly. Loans for top-tier corporate borrowers are floating-rate credits, with very narrow spreads (10–75 basis points) over LIBOR. Typically, lenders structure these loans as lines of credit that borrowers can draw down as needed over four to six years. After that time, the loans generally convert to term credits that firms must repay on a set schedule. One increasingly important use of syndicated lending is as funding for debt-financed acquisitions by U.S. corporate borrowers, where the ability to borrow large sums quickly and (relatively) discreetly is especially valuable.

SMART IDEAS VIDEO

Benjamin Esty, Harvard University

"The syndicated loan market is now the largest single source of corporate funds in the world."

See the entire interview at **SMARTFinance**

Though syndicated loans are used for virtually all types of corporate finance, there are two uses that stand out as so distinct and important that they merit special discussion: Eurocurrency lending and project finance.

Eurocurrency Lending. The **Eurocurrency loan market** consists of a large number of international banks that stand ready to make floating-rate, hard-currency loans (typically, U.S. dollar-denominated) to international corporate and government borrowers. For example, a British bank that accepts a dollar-denominated deposit in London is creating a *Eurodollar deposit,* and if it then relends the deposit to another bank or corporate borrower, it is making a *Eurodollar loan.* These loans are usually structured as lines of credit on which borrowers can draw. Most large loans (over $500 million) are syndicated, thereby providing a measure of diversification to the lenders. Eurocurrency syndicated loans sometimes exceed $10 billion in size, and loans of $1 billion or more are quite common. Furthermore, in total size, the Eurocurrency market dwarfs all other international corporate financial markets.

Eurocurrency loan market
A large number of international banks that stand ready to make floating-rate, hard-currency loans to international corporate and government borrowers.

Project Finance. **Project finance (PF) loans** are typically arranged for infrastructure projects—such as toll roads, bridges, power plants, seaports, tunnels, and airports—that require large sums to construct but which, once built, generate significant amounts of free cash flow for many years. Although project finance lending almost always involves the use of syndicated loans, these differ from other types of syndicated credits in two vital ways. First, PF loans are extended to **stand-alone companies**, sometimes called vehicle companies, created for the sole purpose of constructing and operating a single project. Second, PF loans are almost always limited or nonrecourse credits, backed only by the assets and cash flows of the project, so the sponsors of the project do not guarantee payment of the loan. Project finance loans have been employed in many famous recent projects, such as the Eurotunnel under the English Channel, Euro Disneyland in France, the new Athens International Airport, and the Seoul-Pusan High-Speed Rail Project in Korea.

project finance (PF) loans
Loans usually arranged for infrastructure projects such as toll roads, bridges, and power plants.

stand-alone companies
Companies created for the sole purpose of constructing and operating a single project.

CONCEPT REVIEW QUESTIONS

4. Suppose that a specialty retail firm takes out a term loan from a bank. Which do you think the bank would prefer to receive as collateral, a claim on the firm's inventory or its receivables?

5. A problem with collateral is that its value is positively correlated with the borrower's ability to repay. Explain.

6. What aspect of syndicated lending is most attractive to the lenders?

7. Why are syndicated loans especially useful for financing takeovers?

8. How do project finance loans differ from other types of syndicated loans?

Table 21.1
Characteristics and Priority of Lender's Claims of Traditional Types of Bonds

Bond Type	Characteristics	Priority of Lender's Claim
Debentures	Unsecured bonds that only creditworthy firms can issue. Most convertible bonds are debentures.	Claims are the same as those of any general creditor. May have other unsecured bonds subordinated to them.
Subordinated debentures	Claims are not satisfied until those of the creditors holding certain (senior) debts have been fully satisfied.	Claim is that of a general creditor but not as good as a senior debt claim.
Income bonds	Payment of interest is required only when earnings are available from which to make such payment. Commonly issued in reorganization of a failed or failing firm.	Claim is that of a general creditor. Not in default when interest payments are missed, because they are contingent only on earnings being available.
Mortgage bonds	Secured by real estate or buildings. Can be *open-end* (additional bonds issued against collateral), *limited open-end* (a specified amount of additional bonds can be issued against collateral), or *closed-end*; may contain an *after-acquired clause* (property subsequently acquired becomes part of mortgage collateral).	Claim is on proceeds from sale of mortgaged assets; if not fully satisfied, the lender becomes a general creditor. The *first mortgage* claim must be satisfied before distribution of proceeds to *second mortgage* holders. A number of mortgages can be issued against the same collateral.
Collateral trust bonds	Secured by stock and/or bonds that are owned by the issuer. Collateral value is generally 25 to 35 percent higher than bond value.	Claim is on proceeds from stock and/or bond collateral; if not fully satisfied, the lender becomes a general creditor.
Equipment trust certificates	Used to finance transportation equipment—airplanes, trucks, boats, and railroad cars. A trustee buys such an asset with funds raised through the sale of trust certificates and then leases it to the firm, which, after making the final scheduled lease payment, receives title to the asset. A type of leasing.	Claim is on proceeds from the sale of the asset; if proceeds do not satisfy outstanding debt, trust certificate lenders become general creditors.

21.3 CORPORATE BONDS

A *corporate bond* is a debt instrument indicating that a corporation has borrowed a certain amount of money from institutions or individuals and promises to repay it in the future under clearly defined terms. Firms issue bonds with maturities of ten to thirty years (debt securities with an original maturity of one to ten years are called *notes*) and with a par, or face, value of $1,000. The coupon interest rate on a bond represents the percentage of the bond's par value that the firm will pay to investors each year. In the United States, firms typically pay interest semiannually in two equal coupon payments. Bondholders receive the par value back when the bonds mature.

debentures
Unsecured bonds backed only by the general faith and credit of the borrowing company.

subordinated debenture
An unsecured type of bond.

income bonds
An unsecured type of bond that pays interest only when the debtor company has positive earnings.

mortgage bonds
A type of secured bond, where the security is real estate.

Popular Types of Bonds

Bonds can be classified in a variety of ways. Here we break them into traditional bonds, the basic types that have been around for years, and contemporary, innovative bonds. Table 21.1 summarizes the traditional types of bonds issued by corporations in terms of their key characteristics and priority of lender's claim in the event of default. Note that the first three types, **debentures, subordinated debentures**, and **income bonds**, are unsecured; but the last three, **mortgage bonds, collateral trust bonds**, and **equipment trust certificates**, are secured. As noted, the majority of U.S.

Table 21.2
Characteristics of Contemporary Types of Bonds

Bond Type	Characteristics[a]
Zero (or low) coupon bonds	Issued with no (zero) or very low coupon (stated interest) rate and sold at a large discount from par. A significant portion (or all) of the investor's return therefore comes from gain in value (i.e., par value minus purchase price). Generally callable at par value. Because the issuer can annually deduct the current year's interest accrual without having to actually pay the interest until the bond matures (or is called), its cash flow each year is increased by the amount of the tax shield provided by the interest deduction.
Junk bonds	Debt rated Ba or lower by Moody's or BB or lower by Standard & Poor's. During the 1980s, commonly used by rapidly growing firms to obtain growth capital, most often as a way to finance mergers and takeovers of other firms. High-risk bonds with high yields—typically yielding at least 3 percentage points more than high-quality corporate debt.
Floating-rate bonds	Stated interest rate is adjusted periodically within stated limits in response to changes in specified money or capital market rates. Popular when future inflation and interest rates are uncertain. Tend to sell at close to par as a result of the automatic adjustment to changing market conditions. Some issues provide for annual redemption at par at the option of the bondholder.
Extendible notes	Debt instruments with short maturities, typically 1 to 5 years, that can be redeemed or renewed for a similar period at the option of the holders. Similar to a floating rate bond. An issue might be a series of 3-year renewable notes over a period of 15 years; every 3 years, the notes could be extended for another 3 years, at a new rate that is competitive with market interest rates prevailing at the time of renewal.
Putable bonds	Bonds that can be redeemed at par (typically, $1,000) at the option of their holder either at specified dates, such as 3 to 5 years after the date of issue and every 1 to 5 years thereafter, or when and if the firm takes specified actions such as being acquired, acquiring another company, or issuing a large amount of additional debt. In return for the right to "put the bond" at specified times or actions by the firm, the bond's yield is lower than that of a nonputable bond.

[a] The claims of lenders (i.e., bondholders) against issuers of each of these types of bonds vary, depending on their other features. Each of these bonds can be unsecured or secured.

corporate bonds are debentures, where the debt is backed by the faith and credit of the issuing corporation itself rather than by specific pledged collateral.[3]

In recent years, corporations have developed a profusion of new debt instruments designed to attract a unique clientele of bond investors whose members presumably would be willing to pay a higher price for a given special feature. A detailed discussion of these innovative offerings is beyond the scope of an overview chapter, but Table 21.2 surveys the characteristics of a few of these contemporary types of bonds.

collateral trust bonds
A type of bond secured by stock and/or bonds that are owned by the issuer.

equipment trust certificates
A type of secured bond used to finance transportation equipment.

Legal Aspects of Corporate Bonds

When they issue bonds, corporations raise hundreds of millions of dollars from many unrelated investors. The dispersion in the investor base creates a need for special legal arrangements to protect lenders.

mortgage-backed securities (MBS)
Debt securities that pass through to investors the principal and interest payments that homeowners make on their mortgages.

3. Although not a direct source of financing for individual corporations, the market for **mortgage-backed securities (MBS)** has been growing much faster and now represents a market worth a half-trillion dollars per year in the United States alone. MBS offerings are created by pooling large numbers of home mortgage loans and then selling securities backed by these mortgages directly to investors. This market has revolutionized home mortgage lending in the United States because it allows financial institutions to economize on the use of their capital by originating mortgage loans and then selling these to MBS specialists.

indenture
A legal document stating the conditions under which a bond has been issued.

Bond Indenture. A bond **indenture** is a complex and lengthy legal document stating the conditions under which a bond has been issued. It specifies both the rights of the bondholders and the duties of the issuing corporation. In addition to specifying the interest and principal payment dates and containing various positive and negative covenants, the indenture frequently contains *sinking fund requirements* and provisions with respect to a security interest (if the bond is secured).

sinking fund
An additional positive covenant included in a bond indenture, the objective of which is to provide for the systematic retirement of bonds prior to their maturity.

Sinking Fund Requirements. We have already described the positive and negative covenants for long-term debt and for bond issues in Section 21.1. However, an additional positive covenant often included in a bond indenture is a **sinking fund** requirement. Its objective is to provide for the systematic retirement of bonds prior to their maturity. To carry out this requirement, the corporation makes semiannual or annual payments to a trustee, who uses these funds to retire bonds by purchasing them in the marketplace. This process is simplified by inclusion of a limited call feature, which permits the issuer to repurchase a fraction of outstanding bonds each year at a stated price. The trustee will exercise this limited call option only when sufficient bonds cannot be purchased in the marketplace or when the market price of the bond is above the call price.

Although U.S. corporations (and non-U.S. companies that can issue bonds in U.S. markets) have the opportunity to issue longer-maturity bonds than those of their international competitors, the actual average maturity of the typical U.S. bond issue is far less than its stated maturity would imply. The reasons for this are the ability of companies to call (and then refinance) bonds and the pervasiveness of mandated sinking funds in long-term U.S. debt security issues. Sinking funds work in such a way that the typical bond issue with, say, $100 million principal amount and a fifteen-year maturity will probably have only a few million dollars worth of bonds still outstanding when the last bonds are redeemed a decade and a half after issuance. Depending on the terms of the sinking fund, the actual average maturity of this issue (the weighted average years outstanding) will probably be less than ten years, rather than the fifteen years advertised.

Because sinking funds force the corporation to redeem part of each issue early, they reduce the risk of default on an individual issue, for two reasons. First, sinking funds increase the likelihood that investors will become aware of any financial difficulties an issuing firm encounters (by the firm missing a sinking fund payment) early rather than late. This will trigger the demand for effective corrective action, up to and including the removal of the issuing firm's incumbent management team. Second, because at maturity only a fraction of a given bond issue will remain outstanding, the issuing firm's managers will have less incentive to default on the issue and attempt to expropriate bondholder wealth by filing for bankruptcy protection.

Security Interest. The bond indenture is similar to a loan agreement in that any collateral pledged against the bond is specifically identified in the document. Usually, the title to the collateral is attached to the indenture, and the disposition of the collateral in various circumstances is specifically described. The protection of bond collateral is crucial to increasing the safety, and thus enhancing the marketability, of a bond issue.

trustee
In bankruptcy, someone appointed by a judge to replace a firm's current management team and to oversee liquidation or reorganization.

Trustee. A **trustee** is a third party to a bond indenture and can be an individual, a corporation, or, most often, a commercial bank trust department. The trustee, whose services are paid for by the issuer, acts as a "watchdog" on behalf of the bondholders, making sure that the issuer does not default on its contractual responsibilities. The trustee is empowered to take specified actions on behalf of bondholders if the borrower violates any indenture terms.

Methods of Issuing Corporate Bonds

Public issues of corporate bonds in the United States are sold using the general cash offering procedures described in Chapter 16. Corporate issues sold to public investors must be registered with the Securities and Exchange Commission (SEC), and large offerings are generally underwritten by an investment banking syndicate. However, there is a tremendous variation in actual offering procedures, and this heterogeneity has increased over time as new debt securities have been developed. In particular, two recent financial and regulatory innovations have transformed U.S. bond-issuance patterns. First, the introduction of *shelf registration* in the early 1980s allowed corporations to register large blocks of debt securities, then sell these in discrete pieces over the subsequent two years as market conditions warranted. As discussed in Chapter 11, shelf registration can be used for both debt and equity offerings, but relatively few issuers use this technique for selling stock. In contrast, most companies that can use shelf registration for debt offerings do so.

The second major innovation occurred in 1990, when the SEC created a new private-placement market by implementing *Rule 144A*. This allows institutional investors to trade unregistered securities among themselves, and corporate issuers soon found this was a welcoming market for new equity and, especially, debt issues. Because Rule 144A issues offer investors much greater liquidity than do traditional private placements, and yet are less costly than traditional public offerings, U.S. and international corporations now sell securities worth over $400 billion per year using this rule.

General Features of a Bond Issue

Three features commonly observed in a U.S. bond issue are (1) a call feature, (2) a conversion feature, and (3) stock purchase warrants. Each of these features grants an option, either to the issuer or the investor, that has a significant impact on a bond's value.

Call Feature. The call feature is included in most corporate bond issues and gives the issuer the opportunity to repurchase bonds prior to maturity. The call price is the stated price at which bonds may be repurchased. Sometimes the call privilege is exercisable only during a certain period. Typically, the call price exceeds the par value of a bond by an amount equal to one year's interest. For example, a $1,000 bond with a 10 percent coupon interest rate would be callable for around $1,100 [$1,000 + (0.10 × $1,000)]. The amount by which the call price exceeds the bond's par value is commonly referred to as the *call premium*. This premium compensates bondholders for having the bond called away from them and is the cost to the issuer of calling the bonds.

The call feature is generally advantageous to the issuer because it enables the issuer to retire outstanding debt prior to maturity. Thus, when interest rates fall, an issuer can call an outstanding bond and reissue a new bond at a lower interest rate. When interest rates rise, the call privilege will not be exercised, except possibly to meet sinking fund requirements. Of course, to issue a callable bond, the firm must pay a higher interest rate than that on noncallable bonds of equal risk to compensate bondholders for the risk of having the bonds called away.

Conversion Feature. The conversion feature of **convertible bonds** allows bondholders to change each bond into a stated number of shares of common stock. Bondholders will convert their bonds only when the market price of the stock is greater than the conversion price, hence providing a profit for the bondholder. We discussed the valuation of convertible bonds in detail in Chapter 19.

convertible bonds
Securities that allow bondholder to change each bond into a stated number of shares of common stock.

Stock Purchase Warrants. Like term loans, bonds occasionally have warrants attached as "sweeteners" to make them more attractive to prospective buyers. As we noted earlier, a stock purchase warrant gives its holder the right to purchase a certain number of shares of common stock at a specified price over a certain period of time.

High-Yield Bonds

bond ratings
Grades assigned based on degree of risk.

investment-grade bonds
Bonds rated Baa or higher by Moody's (BBB by S&P).

high-yield bonds
Bonds rated below investment grade (also known as junk bonds).

junk bonds
Bonds rated below investment grade (also known as high yield bonds).

fallen angels
Bonds that received investment-grade ratings when first issued but later fell to junk status.

As discussed in Chapter 4, the risk of publicly traded bond issues is assessed by independent agencies such as Moody's and Standard & Poor's (S&P). Both agencies have ten major **bond ratings** derived by using financial ratio and cash flow analyses. Bonds rated Baa or higher by Moody's (BBB by S&P) are known as **investment-grade bonds.** Bonds rated below investment-grade are known as **high-yield bonds** or **junk bonds.** As the pejorative name suggests, junk bonds carry a much higher default risk than do investment-grade bonds, but they also offer higher yields. Prior to the late 1970s, such issues were quite rare. Historically, most of the sub-investment-grade bonds trading in the market were **fallen angels**, bonds that received investment-grade ratings when they were first issued but later fell to junk status. During the late 1970s, however, Michael Milken and the investment bank he worked for, Drexel Burnham Lambert, began arranging new junk bond issues for companies such as Turner Broadcasting and MCI. Milken and Drexel also helped corporate raiders issue junk bonds to finance their hostile takeover bids.

When junk bond default rates rose sharply during the 1990–1991 recession, many commentators wrote off high-yield debt as a viable financing tool. As Figure 21.1 shows, however, the junk bond market not only survived but prospered after the early 1990s. Junk bond investors recognize that they are assuming much of the issuing firm's business risk when they purchase high-yield debt, but they are willing to do so in return for promised yields that approach the returns earned by stockholders.

Of course, a higher *promised* yield may or may not result in a higher *realized* return, because the higher yield reflects a higher expected likelihood that the borrower will default (in whole or in part) on the bond sometime during its life. For example, as the U.S. economy sagged in 2001, the default rate on junk bonds reached 9.8 percent, and the loss rate reached 7.8 percent. In other words, almost one in ten junk bonds was in some form of default during the year, and this caused a reduction of 7.8 percent in the returns junk bond investors earned (relative to what they would have earned in the absence of defaults). The next year was no better. In 2002, defaults on junk bonds reached a record $96.9 billion for a 12.8 percent default rate.

SMART IDEAS VIDEO
Ed Altman, New York University
"Probably about 75% of the bonds are investment grade; that's BBB or higher."
See the entire interview at **SMARTFinance**

International Corporate Bond Financing

Companies can sell bonds internationally by tapping the *Eurobond* or *foreign bond* markets. Both of these provide established, creditworthy borrowers the opportunity to obtain large amounts of long-term debt financing quickly and efficiently, in their choice of currency and with flexible repayment terms. The following sections briefly describe these markets.

Eurobond
A bond issued by an international borrower and sold to investors in countries with currencies other than that in which the bond is denominated.

Eurobonds. A **Eurobond** is a bond issued by an international borrower and sold to investors in countries with currencies other than the currency in which the bond is denominated. A dollar-denominated bond issued by a U.S. corporation and sold to Western European investors is an example of a Eurobond. The Eurobond

Figure 21.1
Value Outstanding and Default Rates for High-Yield Bonds (Junk Bonds), 1978–2000

Source: Table 1 from Edward I. Altman, "Revisiting the High Yield Bond Market: Mature But Never Dull," Journal of Applied Corporate Finance *13 (Spring 2000), pp. 64–74, plus updates from Professor Altman.*

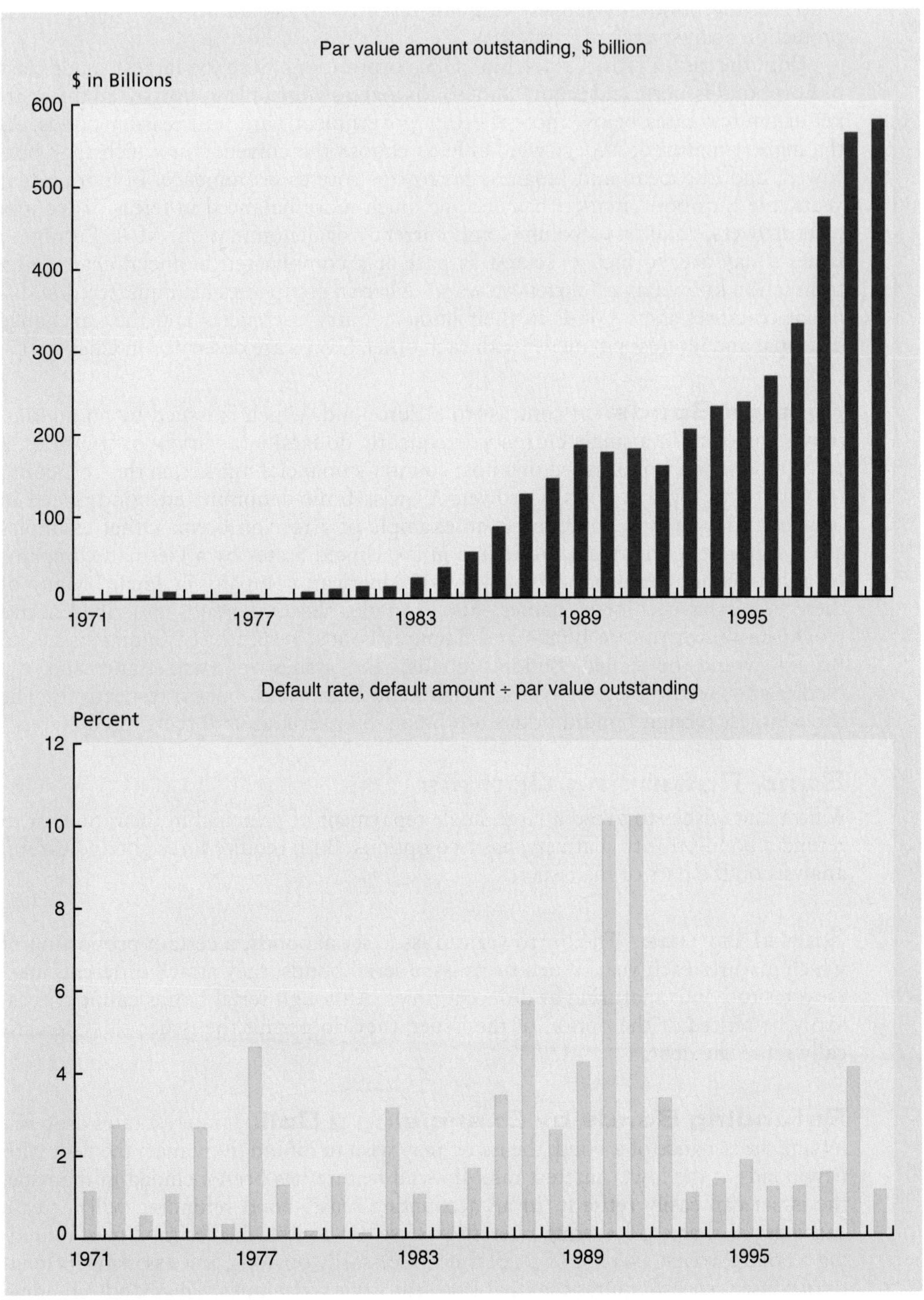

bearer bonds
Bonds that both shelter investment income from taxation and provide protection against exchange rate risk.

market first developed in the early 1960s, when several European and U.S. borrowers discovered that many European investors wanted to hold dollar-denominated, **bearer bonds.** Investors wanted bearer bonds because they would both shelter investment income from taxation—because coupon interest payments were made to the bearer of the bond and names were not reported to tax authorities—and provide protection against exchange rate risk.

Until the mid-1980s, "blue-chip" U.S. corporations were the largest single class of Eurobond issuers, and many of these companies were able to borrow in this market at interest rates below those the U.S. government paid on Treasury bonds. As the market matured, issuers were able to choose the currency in which they borrowed, and European and Japanese borrowers rose to prominence. In more recent years, the Eurobond market has become much more balanced in terms of the mix of borrowers, total issue volume, and currency of denomination. Most Eurobond issues today are, in fact, executed as part of a complicated financial engineering transaction known as a "currency swap," wherein companies headquartered in different countries issue bonds in their home-country currencies and then exchange principal and interest payments with each other. Swaps are described in Chapter 17.

foreign bond
A bond issued in a host country's financial market, in the host country's currency, by a nonresident corporation.

Foreign Bonds. In contrast to a Eurobond, which is issued by an international borrower in a single currency (frequently dollars) in a variety of countries, a **foreign bond** is a bond issued in a host country's financial market, in the host country's currency, by a foreign borrower. A Swiss franc-denominated bond issued in Switzerland by a U.S. company is an example of a foreign bond. Other examples are a dollar-denominated bond issued in the United States by a German company, or a yen-denominated bond issued by an American company in Japan. Many of these issues have colorful names. For example, the two bonds described above would be called Yankee bonds and Samurai bonds, respectively. Similar issues in Britain would be called Bulldog bonds, and issues in Switzerland and the Netherlands would be referred to as Heidi and Rembrandt bonds, respectively. The three largest foreign bond markets are Japan, Switzerland, and the United States.

Bond-Refunding Options

A firm that wishes to avoid a large single repayment of principal in the future, or to refund a bond prior to maturity, has two options. Both require foresight and careful analysis on the part of the issuer.

serial bonds
Bonds of which a certain proportion mature each year.

Serial Issues. The borrower can issue **serial bonds,** a certain proportion of which matures each year. When firms issue serial bonds, they attach different interest rates to bonds maturing at different times. Although serial bonds cannot necessarily be retired at the option of the issuer, they do permit the issuer to systematically retire the debt.

refund
To refinance a debt with new bonds at a lower interest rate.

Refunding Bonds by Exercising a Call. If interest rates drop following the issuance of a bond, the issuer may wish to **refund** (refinance) the debt with new bonds at the lower interest rate. If a call feature has been included in the issue, the issuer can easily retire it. In an accounting sense, bond refunding will increase earnings per share by lowering interest expense. Of course, the desirability of refunding a bond through exercise of a call is not necessarily obvious, and assessing its long-term consequences requires the use of present value techniques. This bond-refunding decision is another application of the capital budgeting techniques we described in Chapters 8 and 9. The basic decision rule is the same we have presented throughout this book: managers should call a bond when the marginal benefit of doing so (the stream of reduced interest payments) equals or exceeds the marginal cost of exercising the call option.

Here the firm must find the net present value (*NPV*) of the bond-refunding cash flows. The initial investment is the incremental after-tax cash outflows associated with calling the old bonds and issuing new bonds, and the annual cash flow savings are the after-tax cash savings that are expected from the reduced debt payments on the new lower-interest bond. These cash flows are the same each year. The resulting cash flow pattern surrounding this decision is "typical": an outflow followed by a series of inflows. The bond-refunding decision can be made using the following three-step procedure.

Step 1. **Find the initial investment** by estimating the incremental after-tax cash outflow required at time 0 to call the old bond, and issue a new bond in its place. Any overlapping interest resulting from the need to pay interest on both the old and new bonds is treated as part of the initial investment.

Step 2. **Find the annual cash flow savings,** which is the difference between the annual after-tax debt payments with the old and new bonds. This cash flow stream will be an annuity, with a life equal to the maturity of the old bond.

Step 3. Use the after-tax cost of the new debt (as the discount rate) to **find the net present value (*NPV*)** by subtracting the initial investment from the present value of the annual cash flow savings. The annual cash flow savings is a certain cash flow stream that represents the difference between two contractual debt-service streams, the old bond and the new bond. Therefore, the decision is virtually risk-free because it does not increase the firm's financial risk (i.e., degree of indebtedness or ability to service debt). Therefore, the after-tax cost of debt is used as the discount rate because it represents the firm's lowest cost of financing. If the resulting *NPV* is positive, the proposed refunding is recommended; otherwise, it should be rejected.

Application of these bond-refunding decision procedures can be illustrated in the Applying the Model below. However, a few tax-related points must be clarified first.

Call Premiums. The amount by which the call price exceeds the par value of the bond is the **call premium**. The issuer pays the bondholder this premium to buy back outstanding bonds prior to maturity. The call premium is treated as a tax-deductible expense in the year of the call.

call premium
The amount by which the call price exceeds the par value of a bond. Paid by corporations to call bonds after a protection period ends.

Bond Discounts and Premiums. When bonds are sold at a discount or at a premium, the firm is required to amortize (write off) the discount or premium in equal portions over the life of the bond. The amortized discount is treated as a tax-deductible expenditure, whereas the amortized premium is treated as taxable income. If a bond is retired prior to maturity, any unamortized portion of a discount or premium is deducted from or added to pretax income at that time.

Floatation or Issuance Costs. Any costs incurred in the process of issuing a bond must be amortized over the life of the bond. The annual write-off is therefore a tax-deductible expenditure. If a bond is retired prior to maturity, any unamortized portion of this cost is deducted from pretax income at that time.

APPLYING THE MODEL

The Davis Corporation, a manufacturer of industrial piping, is contemplating calling $50 million of thirty-year, $1,000 par value bonds (50,000 bonds) issued five years ago with a coupon interest rate of 9 percent. The bonds have a call price of $1,090 and initially netted proceeds of $48.5 million due to a discount of $30 per bond (50,000 bonds × $970 net per bond). The initial floatation cost was $400,000. The company intends to sell $50 million of twenty-five-year, $1,000 par value bonds with a 7 percent (coupon) interest rate to raise funds for retiring the old bonds. The floatation costs on the new issue are estimated to be $450,000. The firm is currently in the 30 percent tax bracket and estimates its after-tax cost of debt to be 4.9 percent [0.07 × (1 – 0.30)]. Because the new bonds must first be sold and their proceeds then used to retire the old bonds, the firm expects a two-month period of overlapping interest during which interest must be paid on both the old and the new bonds.

Step 1. Find the initial investment. Finding the initial investment requires a number of calculations.

a. *Call premium.* The call premium per bond is $90 ($1,090 call price – $1,000 par value). Because the total call premium is deductible in the year of the call, its after-tax cost is calculated as follows:

Before tax ($90 × 50,000 bonds)	$4,500,000
Less: Taxes (0.30 × $4,500,000)	1,350,000
After-tax cost of call premium	$3,150,000

b. *Floatation cost of new bond.* This cost was given as $450,000.

c. *Overlapping interest.*[4] The after-tax cost of the overlapping interest on the old bond is treated as part of the initial investment and calculated as follows:

Before tax (0.09 × 2 ÷12 × $50,000,000)	$750,000
Less: Taxes (0.30 × $750,000)	225,000
After-tax cost of overlapping interest	$525,000

d. *Unamortized discount on old bond.* The firm was amortizing the $1,500,000 discount ($50,000,000 par value – $48,500,000 net proceeds from sale) on the old bond over thirty years. Because only five of the thirty years' amortization of the discount has been applied, the firm can deduct the remaining twenty-five years of unamortized discount as a lump sum, thereby reducing taxes by $375,000 (25 ÷ 30 × $1,500,000 × 0.30).

e. *Unamortized floatation cost of old bond.* The firm was amortizing the $400,000 initial floatation cost on the old bond over thirty years. Because only five of the thirty years' amortization of this cost has been applied, the firm can deduct the remaining twenty-five years of unamortized floatation cost as a lump sum, thereby reducing taxes by $100,000 (25 ÷ 30 × $400,000 × 0.30).

Summarizing these calculations in Table 21.3, we find the initial investment to be $3,650,000. This means that the Davis Corporation must pay out $3,650,000 now to implement the proposed bond refunding.

Step 2. Find the cash flow savings. To find the annual cash flow savings requires a number of calculations.

a. *Interest cost of old bond.* The after-tax annual interest cost of the old bond is calculated as follows:

Before tax (0.09 × $50,000,000)	$4,500,000
Less: Taxes (0.30 × $4,500,000)	1,350,000
After-tax interest cost	$3,150,000

[4] Technically, the after-tax amount of overlapping interest could be reduced by the after-tax interest earnings from investment of the average proceeds available from the sale of the new bonds during the interest overlap period. For clarity, any interest earned on the proceeds from sale of the new bonds during the overlap period is ignored.

Table 21.3
Finding the Initial Investment for the Davis Corporation's Bond-Refunding Decision

a.	**Call premium**		
	Before tax [($1,090 – $1,000) × 50,000 bonds]	$4,500,000	
	Less: Taxes (0.30 × $4,500,000)	(1,350,000)	
	After-tax cost of call premium		$3,150,000
b.	**Floatation cost of new bond**		450,000
c.	**Overlapping interest**		
	Before tax (0.09 × 2 ÷ 12 × $50,000,000)	$ 750,000	
	Less: Taxes (0.30 × $750,000)	(225,000)	
	After-tax cost of overlapping interest		525,000
d.	**Tax savings from unamortized discount on old bond**		
	[25 ÷ 30 × ($50,000,000 – $48,500,000) × 0.30]		(375,000)
e.	**Tax savings from unamortized floatation cost of old bond**		
	(25 ÷ 30 × $400,000 × 0.30)		(100,000)
	Initial investment		$3,650,000

b. *Amortization of discount on old bond.* The firm was amortizing the $1,500,000 discount ($50,000,000 par value – $48,500,000 net proceeds from sale) on the old bond over thirty years, resulting in an annual write-off of $50,000 ($1,500,000 ÷ 30). Because it is a tax-deductible noncash charge, the amortization of this discount results in an annual tax savings of $15,000 (0.30 × $50,000).
c. *Amortization of floatation cost on old bond.* The firm was amortizing the $400,000 floatation cost on the old bond over thirty years, resulting in an annual write-off of $13,333 ($400,000 ÷ 30). Because it is a tax-deductible noncash charge, the amortization of the floatation cost results in an annual tax savings of $4,000 (0.30 × $13,333).
d. *Interest cost of new bond.* The after-tax annual interest cost of the new bond is calculated as follows:

Before tax (0.07 × $50,000,000)	$3,500,000
Less: Taxes (0.30 × $3,500,000)	1,050,000
After-tax interest cost	$2,450,000

e. *Amortization of floatation cost on the new bond.* The firm will amortize the $450,000 floatation cost on the new bond over twenty-five years, resulting in an annual write-off of $18,000 ($450,000 ÷ 25). Because it is a tax-deductible noncash charge, the amortization of the floatation cost results in an annual tax savings of $5,400 (0.30 × $18,000).

Table 21.4 summarizes these calculations. Combining the first three values [(a), (b), and (c)] yields the annual after-tax debt payment for the old bond of $3,131,000. When the values for the new bond [(d) and (e)] are combined, the annual after-tax debt payment for the new bond is $2,444,600.

Subtracting the new bond's annual after-tax debt payment from that of the old bond, we find that implementation of the proposed bond refunding will result in an annual cash flow savings of $686,400 ($3,131,000 – $2,444,600).

Step 3. Find the net present value (*NPV*). Table 21.5 shows the calculations for determining the *NPV* of the proposed bond refunding. The present value of the annual cash flow savings of $686,400 at the 4.9 percent after-tax cost of debt over the twenty-five years is computed (using Equation 3.7) to be $9,771,792. Subtracting the initial investment of $3,650,000 from the present value of the annual cash flow savings results in a net present value of $6,121,792. Because a positive *NPV* results, the proposed bond refunding is recommended.

Table 21.4
Finding the Annual Cash Flow Savings for the Davis Corporation's Bond-Refunding Decision

	Old Bond		
a.	**Interest cost**		
	Before tax (0.09 × $50,000,000)	$4,500,000	
	Less: Taxes (0.30 × $4,500,000)	(1,350,000)	
	After-tax interest cost		$3,150,000
b.	**Tax savings from amortization of discount**		
	[($1,500,000[a] ÷ 30) × 0.30]		(15,000)
c.	**Tax savings from amortization of flotation cost**		
	[($400,000 ÷ 30) × 0.30]		(4,000)
	(1) Annual after-tax debt payment		$3,131,000
	New Bond		
d.	**Interest cost**		
	Before tax (0.07 × $50,000,000)	$3,500,000	
	Less: Taxes (0.30 × $3,500,000)	(1,050,000)	
	After-tax interest cost		$2,450,000
e.	**Tax savings from amortization of floatation cost**		
	[($450,000 ÷ 25) × 0.30]		(5,400)
	(2) Annual after-tax debt payment		$2,444,600
	Annual cash flow savings [(1) – (2)]		$ 686,400

[a] $50,000,000 par value – $48,500,000 net proceeds from sale.

CONCEPT REVIEW QUESTIONS

9. What factors should a manager consider when choosing between a term loan and a bond issue for funding long-term debt?

10. What factors might influence the choice between a bond issue with a sinking fund requirement and a serial bond issue?

11. What factors, other than the current interest rate at which new debt could be sold, should a manager consider when deciding to refund a bond issue?

21.4 LEASING

leasing
Acquiring use of an asset by renting rather than by purchasing the asset.

lessee
The user of the underlying asset who makes regular payments to the lessor.

lessor
The owner of the asset who receives regular payments for its use by the lessee.

Leasing, like long-term debt, requires the firm to make a series of periodic, tax-deductible payments that may be fixed or variable. You can think of a lease as being comparable to secured long-term debt, because in both cases there is an underlying asset tied to the firm's financial obligation. The **lessee** uses the underlying asset and makes regular payments to the **lessor**, who retains ownership of the asset. Leasing can take a number of forms. Here we discuss the basic types of leases, lease arrangements, the lease contract, the lease-versus-purchase decision, the effects of leasing on future financing, and the advantages and disadvantages of leasing.

Basic Types of Leases

The two basic types of leases available to a business are *operating leases* and *financial leases*. Accountants also use the term *capital leases* to refer to financial leases.

Table 21.5
Finding the Net Present Value of the Davis Corporation's Bond-Refunding Decision

Present value of annual cash flow[a]

$$\$686{,}400\times\frac{1}{r}\left[1-\frac{1}{(1+r)^N}\right]=\$686{,}400\times\frac{1}{0.049}\left[1-\frac{1}{(1.049)^{25}}\right]$$

$686,400 × 14.236 =	$9,771,792
Less: Initial investment (from Table 21.3)	(3,650,000)
Net present value (*NPV*) of refunding	$6,121,792

Decision: The proposed refunding is recommended because the *NPV* of refunding of $6,121,792 is greater than $0.

[a] Annual cash flow savings from Table 21.4 multiplied by the present value factor of a twenty-five-year, 4.9 percent annuity (Equation 3.7).

Operating Leases. An **operating lease** is typically a contractual arrangement whereby the lessee agrees to make periodic payments to the lessor, often for five years or less, to obtain an asset's services. The lessee generally receives an option to cancel the lease by paying a cancellation fee. Assets that are leased under operating leases have useful lives that are longer than the lease's term, although as with most assets, the economic usefulness of the assets declines over time. Computer systems are prime examples of assets whose relative efficiency diminishes with new technological developments. The operating lease is a common arrangement for obtaining such systems, as well as for other relatively short-lived assets such as automobiles. When an operating lease expires, the lessee returns the asset to the lessor, who may lease it again or sell it. In some instances, the lease contract will give the lessee the opportunity to purchase the asset. In operating leases, the underlying asset usually has significant market value when the lease ends, and the lessor's original cost generally exceeds the total value of the lessee's payments.

operating lease
A contractual arrangement whereby the lessee agrees to make periodic payments to the lessor, often for five years or less, to obtain an asset's services. The lessee generally receives an option to cancel, and the asset has a useful life longer than the lease.

Financial or Capital Leases. A **financial** (or **capital**) **lease** is longer term than an operating lease. Financial leases are noncancelable and therefore obligate the lessee to make payments over a predefined period. Even if the lessee no longer needs the asset, payments must continue until the lease expires. Financial leases are commonly used for leasing land, buildings, and large pieces of equipment. The noncancelable feature of the financial lease makes it quite similar to certain types of long-term debt. As is the case with debt, failure to make the contractual lease payments can result in bankruptcy for the lessee.

financial (or capital) lease
A noncancelable contractual arrangement whereby the lessee agrees to make periodic payments to the lessor, typically for more than five years, to obtain an asset's services. Same as a capital lease.

Another distinguishing characteristic of the financial lease is that the total payments over the lease period are greater than the lessor's initial cost. In other words, the lessor earns a return by receiving more than the asset's purchase price. Technically, under Financial Accounting Standards Board (FASB) Standard No. 13, "Accounting for Leases," a financial (or capital) lease is defined as having one of the following elements:

1. The lease transfers ownership of the property to the lessee by the end of the lease term.
2. The lease contains an option to purchase the property at a "bargain price." Such an option must be exercisable at a "fair market value" for the lease to be classified as an operating lease.
3. The lease term is equal to 75 percent or more of the estimated economic life of the property (exceptions exist for property leased toward the end of its usable economic life).
4. At the beginning of the lease, the present value of the lease payments is equal to 90 percent or more of the fair market value of the leased property.

The emphasis in this chapter is on financial leases because they result in inescapable long-term financial commitments by the firm.

Lease Arrangements

direct lease
A lessor acquires the assets that are leased to a given lessee.

sale-leaseback arrangement
One firm sells an asset to another for cash, then leases the asset from its new owner.

leveraged leases
The lessor acts as an equity participant, supplying only about 20 percent of the cost of the asset, and a lender supplies the balance.

maintenance clauses
Specifying who is to maintain the assets and make insurance and tax payments.

renewal options
In an operating lease, the lessee often has the option to renew a lease at its expiration.

purchase options
The lessee may have the option to purchase the leased asset when the lease expires.

Lessors use three primary techniques for obtaining assets for leasing. The method selected depends largely on the desires of the prospective lessee. A **direct lease** results when a lessor acquires the assets that are leased to a given lessee. In other words, the lessee did not previously own the assets that it is leasing. In a **sale-leaseback arrangement**, one firm sells an asset to another for cash, then leases the asset from its new owner. You can see the resemblance of this arrangement to a collateralized loan. In such a loan, the lender gives the firm cash up front in exchange for a stream of future payments. If the borrower defaults on those payments, the lender keeps the collateral. In a sale-leaseback, the firm receives cash immediately (giving up ownership of the asset) and effectively repays this loan by leasing back the underlying asset. Sale-leaseback arrangements are therefore attractive to firms that need cash for operations. Leasing arrangements that include one or more third-party lenders are **leveraged leases**. Unlike in direct and sale-leaseback arrangements, the lessor in a leveraged lease acts as an equity participant, supplying only about 20 percent of the cost of the asset, and a lender supplies the balance. In recent years, leveraged leases have become especially popular in structuring leases of very expensive assets.

A lease agreement usually specifies whether or not the lessee is responsible for maintenance of the leased assets. Both operating and financial leases generally include **maintenance clauses** specifying who is to maintain the assets and make insurance and tax payments. Under operating leases these costs are typically the lessor's responsibility, whereas under financial leases, the lessee is typically responsible for these costs. The lessee often has the option to renew a lease at its expiration. **Renewal options** are especially common in operating leases because their term is generally shorter than the useful life of the leased assets. **Purchase options** allowing the lessee to purchase the leased asset at maturity occur in both operating and financial leases.

The lessor can be one of a number of parties. In operating lease arrangements, the lessor is quite likely to be the manufacturer's leasing subsidiary or an independent leasing company. Financial leases are frequently handled by independent leasing companies or by the leasing subsidiaries of large financial institutions such as commercial banks and life insurance companies. Life insurance companies are especially active in real estate leasing. Pension funds, like commercial banks, have also been increasing their leasing activities.

The Lease Contract

The key items in a lease contract generally include a description of the leased assets, the term or duration of the lease, provisions for its cancellation, lease payment amounts and dates, provisions for maintenance and associated costs, renewal options, purchase options, and other provisions specified in the lease negotiation process. Furthermore, lease contracts spell out the consequences of the violation of any lease provision by either the lessee or the lessor.

The Lease-Versus-Purchase Decision

lease-versus-purchase decision
The alternatives available are to (1) lease the assets, (2) borrow funds to purchase the assets, or (3) purchase the assets using available liquid resources. Even if the firm has the liquid resources with which to purchase the assets, the use of these funds is viewed as equivalent to borrowing.

The **lease-versus-purchase** (or lease-versus-buy) **decision** is one that commonly confronts firms contemplating the acquisition of new fixed assets. The alternatives available are to (1) lease the assets, (2) borrow funds to purchase the assets, or (3) purchase the assets using available liquid resources. Similar financial analysis applies to alternatives 2 and 3. Even if the firm has the liquid resources with which to purchase the assets, the use of these funds is viewed as equivalent to borrowing. Therefore, here we need to compare only the leasing and purchasing alternatives.

The lease-versus-purchase decision involves application of the capital budgeting methods we presented in Chapters 8 and 9. We first determine the relevant cash flows and then apply present value techniques. Although the approach we demonstrate here analyzes and compares the present values of the cash flows for the lease and the purchase, an alternative approach would calculate the net present value of the incremental cash flows. The following steps are involved in the analysis.

Step I. Find the after-tax cash flow for each year under the lease alternative. This step generally involves a simple tax adjustment of the annual lease payments. In addition, the cost of exercising a purchase option in the final year of the lease term may be included.[5]

Step 2. Find the after-tax cash flows for each year under the purchase alternative. This step involves adjusting the sum of the scheduled loan-payment and maintenance-cost outlay for the tax shields resulting from the tax deductions attributable to maintenance, depreciation, and interest.

Step 3. Calculate the present value of the cash flows associated with the lease (from Step 1) and purchase (from Step 2) alternatives using the after-tax cost of debt as the discount rate. Although some controversy surrounds the appropriate discount rate, we use the after-tax cost of debt to evaluate the lease-versus-purchase decision because the decision itself involves the choice between two financing alternatives having very low risk. If we were evaluating whether a given machine should be acquired, we would use the appropriate risk-adjusted discount rate or cost of capital, but in this type of analysis, we are attempting to determine only the better financing technique, leasing or borrowing.

Step 4. Choose the alternative with the lower present value of cash outflows from Step 3. This will be the least costly financing alternative.

The application of each of these steps is demonstrated in the following example.

APPLYING THE MODEL

The Portland Company, a small lumber mill, would like to acquire a new machine tool costing $24,000. The firm is in the 40 percent tax bracket and can either lease or purchase the machine.

Lease. The firm obtains a five-year lease requiring annual *beginning*-of-year lease payments of $6,000.[6] The lessor will pay all maintenance costs, and the firm will pay insurance and other costs. The firm exercises its option to purchase the machine for $4,000 at termination of the lease—at the end of year 4 (beginning of year 5).

Purchase. The firm finances the purchase of the machine with a 9 percent, five-year loan requiring end-of-year installment payments of $6,170.[7] The machine will be depreciated under MACRS using a five-year recovery period. The firm pays $1,500 per year for a service contract that covers all maintenance costs and also pays insurance and other costs. The firm plans to keep the machine and use it beyond its five-year recovery period.

Using these data, we can apply the steps presented in the introduction to this model.

---

5. Including the cost of exercising a purchase option in the lease-alternative cash flows ensures that under both the lease and purchase alternatives, the firm owns the asset at the end of the relevant time horizon. The alternative would be to include the cash flows from the sale of the asset in the purchase-alternative cash flows at the end of the lease term. These approaches guarantee avoidance of unequal project lives, which we discussed in Chapter 9. They also make any subsequent cash flows irrelevant because they would either be identical or nonexistent, respectively, under each alternative.

6. Lease payments are generally made at the beginning of the lease period (in this case, a year), and we make that assumption here.

7. The annual loan payment on the 9 percent, five-year loan of $24,000 is calculated by using the loan amortization technique that we described in Chapter 3.

Step 1. The annual after-tax cash outflow from the lease payments can be found by multiplying the before-tax payment of $6,000 by 1 minus the tax rate, T_C, of 40 percent.

$$\text{Annual after-tax cash outflow from lease} = \$6{,}000 \times (1 - T_C) = \$6{,}000 \times (1 - 0.40) = \$3{,}600$$

Therefore, the lease alternative results in annual cash outflows over the five-year lease of $3,600, paid at the beginning of each year. In the final year, the $4,000 cost of the purchase option would be added to the $3,600 lease outflow to get a total cash outflow at the end of year 4 (beginning of year 5) of $7,600 ($3,600 + $4,000).

Step 2. The after-tax cash outflow from the purchase alternative is a bit more difficult to find. First, the interest component of each annual loan payment must be determined, because the Internal Revenue Service allows the deduction from income of interest only, not principal, for tax purposes. Table 21.6 presents the calculations required to split the loan payments into their interest and principal components. Columns 3 and 4 show the annual interest and principal paid in each of the five years. Column 1 lists the annual loan payment.

Next, we find the annual depreciation write-off resulting from the $24,000 machine. Using the applicable MACRS five-year recovery period depreciation percentages from Table 9.1 of 20 percent in year 1, 32 percent in year 2, 19.2 percent in year 3, and 11.52 percent in years 4 and 5 results in the annual depreciation for years 1 through 5 given in column 3 of Table 21.7.[8]

Table 21.7 presents all the calculations required to determine the cash outflows associated with borrowing to purchase the new machine.[9] Column 7 of the table presents the after-tax cash outflows associated with the purchase alternative. A few points should be clarified with respect to the calculations in Table 21.7. The major cash outflows are the total loan payment for each year given in column 1 and the annual maintenance cost, which is a tax-deductible expense, in column 2. The sum of these two outflows is reduced by the tax savings from writing off the maintenance,

Table 21.6
Determining the Interest and Principal Components of the Portland Company Loan Payments

End of Year	Loan Payments (1)	Beginning-of-year Principal (2)	Payments: Interest [0.09 × (2)] (3)	Payments: Principal [(1) − (3)] (4)	End-of-year Principal [(2) − (4)] (5)
1	$6,170	$24,000	$2,160	$4,010	$19,990
2	$6,170	19,990	1,799	4,371	15,619
3	$6,170	15,619	1,406	4,764	10,855
4	$6,170	10,855	977	5,193	5,662
5	$6,170	5,662	510	5,660	—[a]

[a] The values in this table have been rounded to the nearest dollar, which results in a slight difference ($2) between the beginning-of-year-5 principal (in column 2) and the year-5 principal payment (in column 4).

[8] The year-6 depreciation is ignored because we are considering the cash flows solely over a five-year time horizon. Similarly, depreciation on the leased asset when purchased at the end of the lease for $4,000 is ignored. The tax benefits resulting from this depreciation would make the lease alternative even more attractive. Clearly, the analysis would become more precise and more complex if we chose to look beyond the five-year time horizon, though the basic conclusions would remain unchanged.

[9] Although other cash outflows such as insurance and operating expenses may be relevant here, they would be the same under the lease and purchase alternatives and therefore would cancel out in the final analysis.

Table 21.7
After-Tax Cash Outflows Associated with Purchasing for the Portland Company

End of Year	Loan Payments (1)	Maintenance Costs (2)	Depreciation (3)	Interest[a] (4)	Total Deductions [(2) + (3) + (4)] (5)	Tax Shields [0.40 × (5)] (6)	After-tax Cash Outflows [(1) + (2) – (6)] (7)
1	$6,170	$1,500	$4,800	$2,160	$ 8,460	$3,384	$4,286
2	6,170	1,500	7,680	1,799	10,979	4,392	3,278
3	6,170	1,500	4,608	1,406	7,514	3,006	4,664
4	6,170	1,500	2,765	977	5,242	2,097	5,573
5	6,170	1,500	2,765	510	4,775	1,910	5,760

[a] From Table 21.6, column 3.

depreciation, and interest expenses associated with the new machine and its financing, respectively. The resulting cash outflows are the after-tax cash outflows associated with the purchase alternative.

Step 3. The present values of the cash outflows associated with the lease (from Step 1) and purchase (from Step 2) alternatives are calculated in Table 21.8 using the firm's 5.4 percent after-tax cost of debt [0.09 × (1 – 0.40)]. Applying the appropriate present value interest factors given in columns 2 and 5 to the after-tax cash outflows in columns 1 and 4 results in the present values of lease and purchase cash outflows given in columns 3 and 6, respectively. Column 3 presents the sum of the present values of the cash outflows for the leasing alternative, and column 6, the sum for the purchasing alternative.

Step 4. Because the present value of cash outflows for leasing ($19,490) is lower than that for purchasing ($19,942), the leasing alternative is preferable. Leasing results in an incremental savings of $452 ($19,942 – $19,490) and is therefore the less costly alternative.

The techniques described here for comparing lease and purchase alternatives may be applied in different ways. The approach illustrated by using the Portland Company's

Table 21.8
A Comparison of the Cash Outflows Associated with Leasing Versus Purchasing for the Portland Company

	Leasing			Purchasing		
End of Year	After-tax Cash Outflows (1)	Present Value Factors (2)	Present Value of Outflows [(1) × (2)] (3)	After-tax Cash Outflows[a] (4)	Present Value Factors (5)	Present Value of Outflows [(1) × (2)] (6)
0	$3,600	1.000	$ 3,600	0	1.000	0
1	3,600	0.949	3,416	$4,286	0.949	$ 4,066
2	3,600	0.900	3,241	3,278	0.900	2,951
3	3,600	0.854	3,075	4,664	0.854	3,983
4	7,600[b]	0.810	6,158	5,573	0.810	4,514
5	0	0.769	0	5,760	0.769	4,428
	PV of cash outflows		$19,490	PV of cash outflows		$19,942

[a] From Table 21.7, column 7.
[b] After-tax lease payment outflow of $3,600 plus the $4,000 cost of exercising the purchase option.

data is one of the most straightforward. It is important to recognize that the lower cost of one alternative over the other results from factors such as the differing tax brackets of the lessor and the lessee, different tax treatments for leases versus purchases, and differing risks and borrowing costs for the lessor and the lessee. Therefore, when making a lease-versus-purchase decision, the firm will find that inexpensive borrowing opportunities, high required lessor returns, and a low risk of obsolescence increase the attractiveness of purchasing. Subjective factors must also be included in the decision-making process, and, like most financial decisions, the lease-versus-purchase decision requires a certain degree of judgment and/or intuition. In essence, however, the lease-versus-purchase decision is another application of our marginal benefit equals or exceeds marginal cost decision rule.

Effects of Leasing on Future Financing

Because leasing is considered a type of debt funding, it affects a firm's future financing ability. Lease payments are shown as a tax-deductible expense on the firm's income statement. Anyone analyzing the income statement would probably recognize that an asset is being leased, although the actual details of the amount and term of the lease might be unclear. The following sections discuss the lease disclosure requirements established by the Financial Accounting Standards Board (FASB) and the effect of leases on financial ratios.

Lease Disclosure Requirements. Standard No. 13 of the FASB, "Accounting for Leases," requires explicit disclosure of financial (capital) lease obligations on the firm's balance sheet. Such a lease must be shown as a capitalized lease, meaning that the present value of all its payments is included as an asset and corresponding liability on the firm's balance sheet. An operating lease, on the other hand, need not be capitalized, but its basic features must be disclosed in a footnote to the financial statements. Standard No. 13, of course, establishes detailed guidelines to be used in capitalizing leases to reflect them as an asset and corresponding liability on the balance sheet. Subsequent standards have further refined lease capitalization and disclosure procedures.

The following Applying the Model provides an example.

APPLYING THE MODEL

Webster Company, a manufacturer of printing equipment, is leasing an asset under a ten-year lease requiring annual beginning-of-year payments of $15,000. The lease can be capitalized merely by calculating the present value of the lease payments over the life of the lease. However, the rate at which the payments should be discounted is difficult to determine. If 10 percent is used, the present, or capitalized, value of the lease is found by multiplying the annual lease payment by the present value factor of a ten-year, 10 percent annuity due (Equation 3.8). This value of $101,385 ($15,000 × 6.759) would be shown as an asset and corresponding liability on the firm's balance sheet, which should result in an accurate reflection of the firm's true financial position.

Leasing and Financial Ratios. Because the consequences of missing a financial lease payment are the same as those of missing an interest or principal payment on debt, a financial analyst must view the lease as a long-term financial commitment of the lessee. With FASB Standard No. 13, the inclusion of each financial (capital) lease as an asset and corresponding liability (i.e., long-term debt) provides for a balance sheet that more accurately reflects the firm's financial status. It thereby permits various types of financial ratio analyses to be performed directly on the statement by any interested party.

Advantages and Disadvantages of Leasing

Leasing has a number of commonly cited advantages and disadvantages that should be considered when making a lease-versus-purchase decision. Although not all these advantages and disadvantages hold in every case, several of them may apply in any given situation.

Commonly Cited Advantages.

1. Leasing allows the lessee, in effect, to depreciate land, which is prohibited if the land were purchased. Because the lessee who leases land is permitted to deduct the total lease payment as an expense for tax purposes, the effect is the same as if the firm had purchased the land and then depreciated it.
2. The use of sale-leaseback arrangements may permit the firm to increase its liquidity by converting an asset into cash, which can then be used as working capital. A firm short of working capital or in a liquidity bind can sell an owned asset to a lessor and lease the asset back for a specified number of years.
3. Leasing provides 100 percent financing. Most loan agreements for the purchase of fixed assets require the borrower to pay a portion of the purchase price as a down payment. Therefore, the borrower is able to borrow (at most) only 90–95 percent of the purchase price of the asset.
4. When a firm becomes bankrupt or is reorganized, the maximum claim of lessors against the corporation is three years of lease payments, and the lessor, of course, reclaims the asset. If debt is used to purchase an asset, the creditors have a claim that is equal to the total outstanding loan balance.
5. In a lease arrangement, the firm may avoid the cost of obsolescence if the lessor fails to accurately anticipate the obsolescence of assets and sets the lease payment too low. This is especially true in the case of operating leases, which generally have relatively short lives.
6. A lessee avoids many of the restrictive covenants that are usually included as part of a long-term loan. Requirements with respect to minimum net working capital, subsequent borrowing, business combinations, and so on are not generally found in a lease agreement.
7. In the case of low-cost assets that are infrequently acquired, leasing, especially through operating leases, may provide the firm with needed financing flexibility. That is, the firm does not have to arrange other financing for these assets and can obtain them somewhat conveniently through a lease.

Commonly Cited Disadvantages.

1. A lease does not have a stated interest cost. In many leases, the return to the lessor is quite high, so the firm might be better off borrowing to purchase the asset.
2. At the end of the term of the lease agreement, the lessor realizes the salvage value, if any, of an asset. If the lessee had purchased the asset, it could have claimed the asset's salvage value. Of course, in a competitive market, if the lessor expects a higher salvage value, then the lease payments would be lower.
3. Under a lease, the lessee is generally prohibited from making improvements on the leased property or asset without the approval of the lessor. If the property were owned outright, this difficulty would not arise. Of course, lessors generally encourage leasehold improvements when they are expected to enhance the asset's salvage value.
4. If a lessee leases an asset that subsequently becomes obsolete, it still must make lease payments over the remaining term of the lease. This is true even if the asset is unusable.

CONCEPT REVIEW QUESTIONS

12. Why is it considered important whether a lease is classified as an operating lease or as a financial (or capital) lease?

13. What factors should be considered when deciding between leasing an asset and borrowing funds to purchase the asset?

21.5 SUMMARY AND CONCLUSIONS

- Long-term debt and leasing are important sources of capital for businesses. Long-term debt can take the form of term loans or bonds. The characteristics of each can be tailored to meet the needs of both the borrower and the lender.
- The conditions of a term loan are specified in the loan agreement. This agreement specifies the rights and responsibilities of both creditor and borrower, and the agreement typically lists several positive and negative covenants that the borrower must not violate.
- Syndicated loans are large credits arranged by a syndicate of commercial banks for a single borrower. These have been increasing in importance in recent years because very large loans can be arranged quickly and inexpensively and can have very flexible borrowing terms.
- The conditions of a bond issue are specified in the bond indenture and are enforced by a trustee. These legal agreements are highly detailed and not easily modified, because bonds are held by many individual investors. In contrast, privately arranged loan terms can be modified rather easily, because the borrower can negotiate directly with one creditor or a relatively small number of creditors.
- Frequently when interest rates drop, bond issuers make refunding decisions, which involve finding the *NPV* associated with calling outstanding bonds and issuing new, lower-interest coupon bonds to replace the refunded bonds.
- Leasing serves as an alternative to borrowing funds to purchase an asset. Operating leases need not be shown on a firm's balance sheet, whereas capital lease obligations must be shown. Firms often make lease-versus-purchase decisions, which involve choosing the alternative with the lower present value of cash outflows.

SELF-TEST PROBLEMS

Answers to Self-Test Problems appear in Appendix D at back of book. Answers to the Concept Review Questions throughout the chapter appear at http://megginson.swlearning.com.

ST21-1. The initial proceeds per bond, the size of the issue, the initial maturity of the bond, and the years remaining to maturity are shown in the following table for a number of bonds. In each case, the firm is in the 35 percent tax bracket, and the bond has a $1,000 par value.

Bond	Proceeds per Bond	Size of Issue	Initial Maturity of Bond	Years Remaining to Maturity
A	$ 975	50,000 bonds	10 years	5 years
B	1,020	25,000	20	15
C	1,000	100,000	25	12

a. Indicate whether each bond was sold at a discount, at a premium, or at its par value.
b. Determine the total discount or premium for each issue.
c. Determine the annual amount of discount or premium amortized for each bond.

d. Calculate the unamortized discount or premium for each bond.
e. Determine the after-tax cash flow associated with the retirement now of each of these bonds, using the values developed in part (d).

ST21-2. The principal, coupon interest rate, and interest overlap period are shown in the following table for a number of bonds.

Bond	Principal	Coupon Interest Rate	Interest Overlap Period
A	$ 15,000,000	6.5%	2 months
B	20,000,000	7.0	3
C	15,000,000	6.0	4
D	100,000,000	8.0	6

a. Calculate the dollar amount of interest that must be paid for each bond during the interest overlap period.
b. Calculate the after-tax cost of overlapping interest for each bond if the firm is in the 40 percent tax bracket.

ST21-3. Well-Sprung Corporation is considering offering a new $100 million bond issue to replace an outstanding $100 million bond issue. The firm wishes to take advantage of the decline in interest rates that has occurred since the original issue. The two bond issues are described in what follows. The firm is in the 30 percent tax bracket.

Old bonds. The outstanding bonds have a $1,000 par value and an 8.5 percent coupon interest rate. They were issued five years ago with a twenty-year maturity. They were initially sold at a $30 per bond discount, and a $750,000 floatation cost was incurred. They are callable at $1,085.

New bonds. The new bonds would have a fifteen-year maturity, a par value of $1,000, and a 7.0 percent coupon interest rate. It is expected that these bonds can be sold at par for a floatation cost of $600,000. The firm expects a three-month period of overlapping interest while it retires the old bonds.

a. Calculate the initial investment that is required to call the old bonds and issue the new bonds.
b. Calculate the annual cash flow savings, if any, expected from the proposed bond-refunding decision.
c. If the firm uses its after-tax cost of debt of 4.9 percent to evaluate low-risk decisions, find the net present value (*NPV*) of the bond-refunding decision. Would you recommend the proposed refunding? Explain your answer.

ST21-4. Strident Corporation is attempting to determine whether to lease or purchase a new telephone system. The firm is in the 40 percent tax bracket, and its after-tax cost of debt is currently 4.5 percent. The terms of the lease and the purchase are as follows:

Lease. Annual beginning-of-year lease payments of $22,000 are required over the five-year life of the lease. The lessor will pay all maintenance costs; the lessee will pay insurance and other costs. The lessee will exercise its option to purchase the asset for $30,000 paid along with the final lease payment.

Purchase. The $100,000 cost of the telephone system can be financed entirely with a 7.5 percent loan requiring annual end-of-year payments of $24,716 for five years. The firm in this case will depreciate the equipment under MACRS using a five-year recovery period. (See Table 9.1 for applicable MACRS percentages.) The firm will pay $3,500 per year for a service contract that covers all maintenance costs; the firm will pay insurance and other costs. The firm plans to keep the equipment and use it beyond its five-year recovery period.

a. Calculate the after-tax cash outflows associated with each alternative.
b. Calculate the present value of each cash outflow stream using the after-tax cost of debt.
c. Which alternative, lease or purchase, would you recommend? Why?

INTERNET RESOURCES

Note: *For updates to links, please go to the book's Web site at*
http://megginson.swlearning.com
http://www.bondsonline.com—Offers a wealth of information on the bond market.
http://www.investinginbonds.com—A site with statistics on the Treasury, municipal, and corporate bond markets.

KEY TERMS

balloon payment
bearer bonds
bond ratings
call premium
collateral
collateral trust bonds
convertible bonds
cross-default covenant
debentures
direct lease
equipment trust certificates
Eurobond
Eurocurrency loan market
fallen angels
financial (or capital) lease
fixed-rate offerings
floating-rate issues
foreign bond
high-yield bonds
income bonds
indenture
investment-grade bonds
junk bonds
lease-versus-purchase decision
leasing
lessee
lessor
leveraged leases
LIBOR
lien
loans
maintenance clauses
mortgage bonds
mortgage-backed securities (MBS)
operating lease
prime lending rate
private placements
project finance (PF) loans
purchase options
refund
renewal options
sale-leaseback arrangement
serial bonds
sinking fund
stand-alone companies
stock purchase warrants
subordinated debentures
subordination
syndicated loan
term loan
trustee

QUESTIONS AND PROBLEMS

Q21-1. Comment on the following proposition: Using floating-rate debt eliminates interest rate risk (the risk that interest payment amounts will change in the future) for both the borrower and the lender.

Q21-2. What purpose do *covenants* serve in a debt agreement? What factors should a manager consider when negotiating covenants?

Q21-3. List and briefly discuss the key features that distinguish long-term debt issues from each other.

Q21-4. Define the following: term loan, balloon payment, collateral, and stock purchase warrants.

Q21-5. What is a debenture? Why do you think that this is the most common form of corporate bond in the United States but is much less commonly used elsewhere?

Q21-6. How do sinking funds reduce default risk?

Q21-7. What is a trustee? Why do bondholders insist that a trustee be included in all public bond offerings? Why are these less necessary in private debt placements?

Q21-8. What impact has adoption of Rule 144A had on debt-issuance patterns in the United States?

Q21-9. Why are most corporate bonds callable? Who benefits from this feature, and what is the cost of adopting a call provision in a public bond issue?

Q21-10. Why do corporations have their debt rated? Compare the role played by rating agencies and a company's outside auditors.

Q21-11. What does "investment grade" mean in the context of corporate bond issues? How do these bonds differ from junk bonds, and why have the latter proven so popular with investors?

Q21-12. What is a Eurobond? Why did these bonds come into existence? Why do Eurobond investors like the fact that these are typically "bearer bonds"? What risk does an investor run from holding bearer bonds rather than registered bonds?

Q21-13. Explain how uncertainty concerning future interest rates would affect the decision to refund a bond issue.

Q21-14. What is a syndicated loan? Why have these loans proven so popular with corporate borrowers?

Q21-15. What is a project finance loan? What role does a vehicle company play in the typical project finance deal?

Q21-16. Define the following: direct lease, sale-leaseback arrangement, leveraged lease, and financial (capital) lease.

Q21-17. What elements must be included in a lease in order for it to be considered a financial (capital) lease?

Q21-18. Comment on the following statement: A key benefit of leasing is that it allows for the effective depreciation of land.

Q21-19. How would the availability of floating-rate debt rather than fixed-rate debt affect the lease-versus-buy decision?

Q21-20. What are the key advantages of leasing as compared to borrowing to acquire an asset? What are the key disadvantages of leasing?

PROBLEMS

Corporate Bonds

P21-1. The initial proceeds per bond, the size of the issue, the initial maturity of the bond, and the years remaining to maturity are shown in the following table for a number of bonds. In each case, the firm is in the 40 percent tax bracket, and the bond has a $1,000 par value.

Bond	Proceeds per Bond	Size of Issue	Initial Maturity of Bond	Years Remaining to Maturity
A	$ 985	10,000 bonds	20 years	15 years
B	1,025	20,000	25	16
C	1,000	22,500	12	9
D	960	5,000	25	15
E	1,035	10,000	30	16

a. Indicate whether each bond was sold at a discount, at a premium, or at its par value.

b. Determine the total discount or premium for each issue.
c. Determine the annual amount of discount or premium amortized for each bond.
d. Calculate the unamortized discount or premium for each bond.
e. Determine the after-tax cash flow associated with the retirement now of each of these bonds, using the values developed in part (d).

P21-2. For each of the callable bond issues in the following table, calculate the after-tax cost of calling the issue. Each bond has a $1,000 par value, and the various issue sizes and call prices are shown in the following table. The firm is in the 40 percent tax bracket.

Bond	Size of Issue	Call Price
A	12,000 bonds	$1,050
B	20,000	1,030
C	30,000	1,015
D	50,000	1,050
E	100,000	1,045
F	500,000	1,060

P21-3. The floatation cost, the initial maturity, and the number of years remaining to maturity are shown in the following table for a number of bonds. The firm is in the 40 percent tax bracket.

Bond	Floatation Cost	Initial Maturity of Bond	Years Remaining to Maturity
A	$250,000	30 years	22 years
B	500,000	15	5
C	125,000	20	10
D	750,000	10	1
E	650,000	15	6

a. Calculate the annual amortization of the flotation cost for each bond.
b. Determine the tax savings, if any, expected to result from the unamortized floatation cost if the bond were called today.

P21-4. The principal, coupon interest rate, and interest overlap period are shown in the following table for a number of bonds.

Bond	Principal	Coupon Interest Rate	Interest Overlap Period
A	$ 5,000,000	8.0%	3 months
B	40,000,000	7.0	2
C	50,000,000	6.5	3
D	100,000,000	9.0	6
E	20,000,000	5.5	1

a. Calculate the dollar amount of interest that must be paid for each bond during the interest overlap period.
b. Calculate the after-tax cost of overlapping interest for each bond if the firm is in the 40 percent tax bracket.

P21-5. Schooner Company is contemplating offering a new $50 million bond issue to replace an outstanding $50 million bond issue. The firm wishes to take advantage of the decline in interest rates that has occurred since the initial bond issuance. The old and new bonds are described in what follows. The firm is in the 40 percent tax bracket.

Old bonds. The outstanding bonds have a $1,000 par value and a 9 percent coupon interest rate. They were issued five years ago with a twenty-year maturity. They were initially sold for their par value of $1,000, and the firm incurred $350,000 in flotation costs. They are callable at $1,090.

New bonds. The new bonds would have a $1,000 par value, a 7 percent coupon interest rate, and a fifteen-year maturity. They could be sold at their par value. The flotation cost of the new bonds would be $500,000. The firm does not expect to have any overlapping interest.

a. Calculate the tax savings that are expected from the unamortized portion or the old bonds' flotation cost.

b. Calculate the annual tax savings from the floatation cost of the new bonds, assuming the fifteen-year amortization.

c. Calculate the after-tax cost of the call premium that is required to retire the old bonds.

d. Determine the initial investment that is required to call the old bonds and issue the new bonds.

e. Calculate the annual cash flow savings, if any, that are expected from the proposed bond-refunding decision.

f. If the firm has a 4.2 percent after-tax cost of debt, find the net present value (*NPV*) of the bond-refunding decision. Would you recommend the proposed refunding? Explain your answer.

P21-6. High-Gearing Incorporated is considering offering a new $40 million bond issue to replace an outstanding $40 million bond issue. The firm wishes to take advantage of the decline in interest rates that has occurred since the original issue. The two bond issues are described in what follows. The firm is in the 40 percent tax bracket.

Old bonds. The outstanding bonds have a $1,000 par value and a 10 percent coupon interest rate. They were issued five years ago with a twenty-five-year maturity. They were initially sold at a $25 per bond discount, and a $200,000 flotation cost was incurred. They are callable at $1,100.

New bonds. The new bonds would have a twenty-year maturity, a par value of $1,000, and a 7.5 percent coupon interest rate. It is expected that these bonds can be sold at par for a flotation cost of $250,000. The firm expects a three-month period of overlapping interest while it retires the old bonds.

a. Calculate the initial investment that is required to call the old bonds and issue the new bonds.

b. Calculate the annual cash flow savings, if any, expected from the proposed bond-refunding decision.

c. If the firm uses its after-tax cost of debt of 4.5 percent to evaluate low-risk decisions, find the net present value (*NPV*) of the bond-refunding decision. Would you recommend the proposed refunding? Explain your answer.

P21-7. Web Tools Company is considering using the proceeds from a new $50 million bond issue to call and retire its outstanding $50 million bond issue. The details of both bond issues are outlined in what follows. The firm is in the 40 percent tax bracket.

Old bonds. The firm's old issue has a coupon interest rate of 10 percent, was issued four years ago, and had a twenty-year maturity. The bonds sold at a $10 discount from their $1,000 par value, floatation costs were $420,000, and their call price is $1,100.

New bonds. The new bonds are expected to sell at par ($1,000), have a sixteen-year maturity, and have floatation costs of $520,000. The firm will have a two-month period of overlapping interest while it retires the old bonds.

a. What is the initial investment that is required to call the old bonds and issue the new bonds?

b. What are the annual cash flow savings, if any, from the proposed bond-refunding decision if (1) the new bonds have an 8 percent coupon interest rate and (2) the new bonds have a 9 percent coupon interest rate?

c. Calculate the net present value (*NPV*) of refunding under the two circumstances given in part (b) when (1) the firm has an after-tax cost of debt of 4.8 percent [0.08 × (1 – 0.40)] and (2) the firm has an after-tax cost of debt of 5.4 percent [0.09 × (1 – 0.40)].

d. Discuss the circumstances [described in part (c)] when refunding would be favorable and when it would not.

P21-8. For each of the loan amounts, interest rates, loan terms, and annual payments shown in the following table, calculate the annual interest paid each year over the term of the loan, assuming that the payments are made at the *end of each year.*

Loan	Amount	Interest Rate	Term	Annual Payment
A	$ 20,000	8.0%	4 years	$ 6,038
B	35,500	7.0	6	7,448
C	152,500	9.0	5	39,207
D	250,000	7.5	10	36,421
E	575,500	6.0	15	59,204

P21-9. Shredding Pines Company wishes to purchase an asset that costs $750,000. The full amount needed to finance the asset can be borrowed at 9 percent interest. The terms of the loan require equal end-of-year payments for the next eight years. Determine the total annual loan payment, and break it into the amount of interest and the amount of principal paid for each year.

Leasing

P21-10. Given the lease payments and terms shown in the following table, determine the yearly after-tax cash outflows for each firm, assuming that lease payments are made at the *beginning of each year* and that the firm is in the 40 percent tax bracket. Assume that no purchase option exists.

Firm	Annual Lease Payment	Term of Lease
A	$ 250,000	5 years
B	160,000	12
C	500,000	8
D	1,000,000	20
E	25,000	6

P21-11. GMS Corporation is attempting to determine whether to lease or purchase research equipment. The firm is in the 40 percent tax bracket, and its after-tax cost of debt is currently 6 percent. The terms of the lease and the purchase are as follows:

Lease. Annual beginning-of-year lease payments of $93,500 are required over the three-year life of the lease. The lessor will pay all maintenance costs; the lessee will pay insurance and other costs. The lessee will exercise its option to purchase the asset for $25,000 paid along with the final lease payment.

Purchase. The $250,000 cost of the research equipment can be financed entirely with a 10 percent loan requiring annual end-of-year payments of $100,529 for three years. The firm in this case will depreciate the equipment under MACRS using a three-year recovery period. (See Table 9.1 for applicable MACRS percentages.) The firm will pay $9,500 per year for a service contract that covers all maintenance costs; the firm will pay insurance and other costs. The firm plans to keep the equipment and use it beyond its three-year recovery period.

a. Calculate the after-tax cash outflows associated with each alternative.

b. Calculate the present value of each cash outflow stream using the after-tax cost of debt.

c. Which alternative, lease or purchase, would you recommend? Why?

P21-12. Eastern Trucking Company needs to expand its facilities. To do so, the firm must acquire a machine costing $80,000. The machine can be leased or purchased. The firm is in the 40 percent tax bracket, and its after-tax cost of debt is 5.4 percent. The terms of the lease and purchase plans are as follows:

Lease. The leasing arrangement requires beginning-of-year payments of $16,900 over five years. The lessor will pay all maintenance costs; the lessee will pay insurance and other costs. The lessee will exercise its option to purchase the asset for $20,000 paid along with the final lease payment.

Purchase. If the firm purchases the machine, its cost of $80,000 will be financed with a five-year, 9 percent loan requiring equal end-of-year payments of $20,567. The machine will be depreciated under MACRS using a five-year recovery period.

(See Table 9.1 for applicable MACRS percentages.) The firm will pay $2,000 per year for a service contract that covers all maintenance costs; the firm will pay insurance and other costs. The firm plans to keep the equipment and use it beyond its five-year recovery period.

a. Determine the after-tax cash outflows of Eastern Trucking under each alternative.

b. Find the present value of the after-tax cash outflows for each alternative using the after-tax cost of debt.

c. Which alternative, lease or purchase, would you recommend? Why?

P21-13. Given the lease payments, terms remaining until the leases expire, and discount rates shown in the following table, calculate the capitalized value of each lease, assuming that lease payments are made annually at the beginning of each year.

Lease	Lease Payment	Remaining Term	Discount Rate
A	$ 40,000	12 years	10%
B	120,000	8	12
C	9,000	18	14
D	16,000	3	9
E	47,000	20	11

THOMSON ONE Business School Edition

For instructions on using Thomson ONE, refer to the instructions provided with the Thomson ONE problems at the end of Chapters 1–6 or to "A Guide for Using Thomson ONE."

P21-14. Analyze the long-term debt of General Electric Company (ticker: GE), General Motors Corp. (GM), and Ford Motor Company (F) relative to total assets over the last ten years. How has long-term debt changed over this period? Do the companies appear to maintain a certain level of long-term debt?

Since these exercises depend upon real-time data, your answers will change continuously depending upon when you access the Internet to download your data.

Long-Term Debt and Leasing

The CFO of your firm asks you to review the long-term debt position of the company to decide if the company should change borrowing arrangements in any way. Before conducting this review, you decide to bring yourself up-to-date on terminology and types of long-term borrowing arrangements. Therefore, as a start you decide to answer the following questions.

ASSIGNMENT

1. What types of debt covenants might managers consider?
2. What are the major factors that affect the cost or interest rate of a debt instrument?
3. What are term loans and what are their characteristics?
4. What are syndicated loans, and what are their primary applications?
5. What are some of the legal arrangements used to protect lenders related to corporate bonds?
6. What are some of the general features of corporate bonds?
7. What options are available for a firm that wishes to avoid a large single repayment of principal in the future or to refund a bond prior to maturity?
8. In what ways are leases similar to long-term debt?
9. What are the two basic types of leases?
10. What are the advantages and disadvantages of leasing?

Mergers, Acquisitions, and Corporate Control

OPENING FOCUS

Mergers Create Two $1 *Trillion* Banks in a Single Quarter

For most people, $1 trillion is an unimaginably large sum of money. Only seven countries have gross domestic products of $1 trillion or more, and the total value of "world GDP" is about $35 trillion. Yet a pair of mergers announced between late 2003 and early 2004 created the second and third U.S.-based financial services companies with assets of at least $1 trillion, joining America's Citigroup and Japan's Mizuho Holdings as the only companies in the world with assets so vast.

In October 2003, Bank of America announced plans to acquire FleetBoston Financial in a friendly, stock-swap merger where BofA agreed to pay $47 billion to acquire all of FleetBoston's outstanding stock. The merger would give the combined institution total assets of about $1 trillion, as well as a near-nationwide retail banking presence. The banks' executives predicted that the integration of their operations would yield important operating synergies as well as cost savings in excess of $1.1 billion per year. The synergies were expected to result from combining BofA's national reach and strength in international banking with Fleet's strong retail banking presence in New England. The cost savings were expected to come largely from eliminating some 13,000 jobs, or 7 percent of the combined work force, and by consolidating purchasing and other functions. Although analysts generally praised BofA's strategy, they were appalled by the high 42 percent premium BofA offered FleetBoston's shareholders, and BofA's shares promptly dropped by 10 percent the day the merger was announced. Both companies' shareholders approved the merger in April 2004.

A mere three months after the BofA/FleetBoston deal was announced, J. P. Morgan Chase and Bank One announced their own plans to merge to create a banking behemoth with $1.1 trillion in assets. As with the BofA/FleetBoston merger, this would be a friendly, stock-swap deal with J. P. Morgan offering $60 billion worth of its shares to acquire Bank One's outstanding stock. Both companies had much to gain from the merger. J. P. Morgan, already America's second largest bank, was seeking to reduce its dependence on the highly cyclical investment banking business, and also to acquire

Bank One's strong credit card operations, while Bank One (the nation's sixth largest bank) was jumping at the chance to be an equal partner in what would likely become one of the world's premier financial companies. In fact, Bank One's CEO, Jamie Dimon, is tapped to head the combined company after J. P. Morgan's CEO retires in 2006. In a reprise of the motivations announced three months previously, the banks' executives predicted that the J. P. Morgan/Bank One merger would yield major operating synergies as well as cost savings of $2.2 billion over three years, mostly through the elimination of some 10,000 jobs. Analysts praised this merger announcement as well, though the stock market reaction to the announcement was much more balanced than it had been for BofA/FleetBoston. Bank One's stock rose 13 percent on the news, while J. P. Morgan's stock fell by three percent. The merger between J. P. Morgan and Bank One was approved by both companies' shareholders in May 2004.

Mergers and acquisitions play important roles in shaping many industries in the United States, but few industries have been as transformed by takeovers as has commercial banking. Each of the four merging parties detailed above had been created by a series of massive combinations over the previous two decades, as indeed had the country's largest financial company, Citigroup. In fact, mergers and acquisitions have reduced the number of independent banks in the United States from over 15,000 in 1980 to less than 8,500 today.

Source: Multiple articles downloaded from the *Financial Times* Web site (http://www.ft.com). ■

LEARNING OBJECTIVES

After studying this chapter you should be able to:

- Describe the most important forms of corporate control transactions and distinguish between transactions that integrate two businesses and those that split up an existing single business;
- Discuss the differences between horizontal, vertical, and conglomerate mergers;
- Explain the different methods of payment acquirers use to execute mergers and acquisitions, and discuss how returns to target and bidder firm shareholders differ between cash and stock mergers;
- Contrast the motivations of managers who implement value-maximizing mergers and acquisitions to those who execute non-value-maximizing combinations; and
- Describe the most important laws and regulations that govern corporate control activities in the United States, and explain why international corporate control regulations have become much more important recently.

As its name implies, **corporate control** refers to the monitoring, supervision, and direction of a corporation or other business organization. The most common change in corporate control results from the combination of two or more business entities into a single organization, as happens in a merger or acquisition. A change in corporate control also occurs with the consolidation of voting power within a small group of investors, as found in going-private transactions such as leveraged buyouts (LBOs) and management buyouts (MBOs). Transfer of ownership of a business unit with a divestiture and the creation of a new corporation through a spin-off are other ways to bring about such a change.

corporate control
The monitoring, supervision, and direction of a corporation or other business organization.

The forces effecting changes in corporate control and the resulting impact on the business community present some of the most interesting and hotly contested debates in the field of finance. For example, the corporate control contest for RJR Nabisco captivated corporate America in the fall of 1988, spawned a book and a movie about the takeover, and remains a source of debate for academics and politicians over the social benefit of corporate control activities. We address the causes and consequences of changes in corporate control in this chapter, as well as provide real-world examples of the merger/acquisition process and the technical aspects a corporate manager must consider before making decisions regarding corporate control changes.

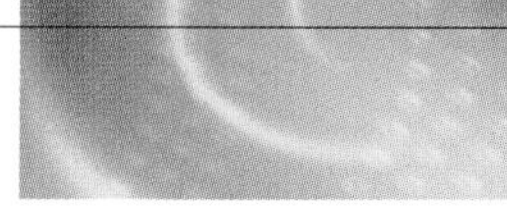

22.1 OVERVIEW OF CORPORATE CONTROL ACTIVITIES

You probably understand what the expressions "mergers and acquisitions" or "M&As" mean in general. However, the terminology of corporate control is far more expansive than these generic terms indicate. For instance, the popular press often uses the term "takeover" to conjure up images of an unwelcome bidder commandeering control of a corporation through the techniques of high finance and the means of great sums of money. A **takeover**, however, simply refers to any transaction in which the control of one entity is taken over by another. Thus, a friendly merger negotiated between the boards of directors and shareholders of two independent corporations is a takeover, as is a successful entrepreneur selling out her enterprise to a corporation. The terminology of corporate control can be easily misconstrued and must be clearly defined to prevent such ambiguities. In the following discussion, we will define the many terms and concepts encountered in the corporate control arena.

takeover
Any transaction in which the control of one entity is taken over by another.

Corporate Control Transactions

Changes in corporate control occur through several mechanisms, most notably via acquisitions. An **acquisition** is the purchase of additional resources by a business enterprise. These resources may come from the purchase of new assets, the purchase of some of the assets of another company, or the purchase of another whole business entity, which is known as a merger. **Merger** is itself a general term applied to a transaction in which two or more business organizations combine into a single entity. Oftentimes, however, the term "merger" is reserved for a transaction in which one corporation takes over another upon the approval of both companies' boards of directors and shareholders after a friendly and mutually agreeable set of terms and conditions and a price are negotiated. Payment is in the form of an exchange of common stock. In actuality, there are many different types of mergers, and they (as well as other corporate control activities) can be differentiated according to several criteria. We define mergers by the mode of target integration used by the acquiring firm, by the level of business concentration created by the merger, and by other transaction characteristics for which mergers are commonly known.

acquisition
The purchase of additional resources by a business enterprise.

merger
A transaction in which two or more business organizations combine into a single entity.

There are a number of ways to integrate the assets and resources of an acquired firm into the acquiring company (the acquirer). The following discussion describes the various forms of resource integration that may be used to combine the resources of an acquirer and target.

Statutory Merger. A **statutory merger** is a form of target integration in which the acquirer can absorb the target's resources directly with no remaining trace of the target as a separate entity. Many intrastate bank mergers are of this form.

statutory merger
A target integration in which the acquirer can absorb the target's resources directly with no remaining trace of the target as a separate entity.

Subsidiary Merger. Conversely, an acquirer may wish to maintain the identity of the target as either a separate subsidiary or division. A **subsidiary merger** is often the integration vehicle when there is brand value in the name of the target, such

subsidiary merger
A merger in which the acquirer maintains the identity of the target as a separate subsidiary or division.

as the case of PepsiCo's merger with Pizza Hut in 1977 (can you imagine eating a Pepsi Pizza?). Sometimes, separate "tracking" or "target" shares are issued in the subsidiary's name. Sometimes, these shares are issued as new common shares in exchange for the target's common shares, as occurred when General Motors issued new Class E and Class H shares to acquire, respectively, Electronic Data Systems and Hughes Electronics during the 1980s. Alternatively, a new class of preferred stock may be issued by the bidding firm to replace the common shares of the target as well.

Consolidation. **Consolidation** is another integrative form used to effect a merger of two publicly traded companies. Under this form, both the acquirer and target disappear as separate corporations and combine to form an entirely new corporation with new common stock. This form of integration is common in mergers of equals where the market values of the acquirer and target are similar. Many of these new corporations adopt a name that is merely a hybrid of the former names, such as the 1985 consolidation of Allied Corporation and Signal Companies to become AlliedSignal. But some managers of newly created companies want a "fresh start" with a company name, as in the case of Sandoz and Ciba-Geigy when they merged in 1997 to form Novartis.

Another type of merger that warrants mention, even though it is not a separate integrative form, is the **reverse merger**. In this transaction, the acquirer has a lesser market value than the target. Differences in size can be substantial in a reverse merger but are often the result of a merger of equals where the *control premium* paid by the acquirer causes the market value of the target to exceed that of the acquirer.[1]

LBOs, MBOs, and Dual-Class Recapitalizations

Changes in corporate control also occur when voting power is concentrated in the hands of one individual or a small group. Going-private transactions are one way to achieve this concentration of control. Just as they sound, **going-private transactions** transform public corporations into private companies through issuance of large amounts of debt used to buy all (or at least a voting majority) of the outstanding shares of the corporation. The acquiring party may be a leveraged-buyout (LBO) firm, such as Kohlberg, Kravis, and Roberts (KKR), which specializes in such deals; the current managers of the corporation (known as a **management buyout** or **MBO**); or even the employees of the corporation itself through an **employee stock ownership plan (ESOP)**. A prime example of both an LBO and an MBO attempt is the 1988 corporate control contest for RJR Nabisco. H. Ross Johnson, the CEO of RJR Nabisco, led a management team that attempted to take the company private but was outbid by KKR in a $29 billion LBO.[2] An LBO that sells shares to the public again is known as a **reverse LBO**.

A **dual-class recapitalization** may also concentrate control. Under this form of organizational restructuring, the parties wishing to concentrate control (usually management) buy all the shares of a newly issued Class B stock, which carries "super" voting rights (100 votes per share, for example). Traditional Class A shareholders generally receive some form of compensation, such as higher dividends, for the dilution of their voting power.

consolidation
A merger in which both the acquirer and target disappear as separate corporations, combining to form an entirely new corporation with new common stock.

reverse merger
A merger in which the acquirer has a lesser market value than the target.

going-private transactions
The transformation of a public corporation into a private company through issuance of large amounts of debt used to buy all (or at least a voting majority) of the outstanding shares of the corporation.

management buyout (MBO)
The transformation of a public corporation into a private company by the current managers of the corporation.

employee stock ownership plan (ESOP)
The transformation of a public corporation into a private company by the employees of the corporation itself.

reverse LBO
A formerly public company that has previously gone private through a leveraged buyout and then goes public again. Also called a second IPO.

dual-class recapitalization
Organizational restructuring in which the parties wishing to concentrate control (usually management) buy all the shares of a newly issued Class B stock, which carries "super" voting rights (100 votes per share, for example).

1. A control premium is the difference between premerger market value and acquisition value. For example, if ABC Company offered to buy XYZ Company for $25 per share for its 100 million shares outstanding when the stock price was $20, then the control premium is $5 per share, $500 million total, or 25 percent.

2. For an insightful and entertaining look at this deal, as well as the LBO/MBO process, see Bryan Burroughs and John Helyar, *Barbarians at the Gate: The Fall of RJR Nabisco* (HarperCollins, New York, 1993).

Tender Offers, Acquisitions, and Proxy Fights

An acquirer can also attain control of a public corporation through a nonnegotiated purchase of the corporation's shares in the open market or through the voting control of other stockholders' shares via proxy. Theoretically, an acquirer can gain control simply through open-market purchases of a target firm's shares, though regulation severely restricts this form of "creeping acquisition" in most developed countries. Generally, an acquirer must explicitly bid for control through a tender offer for shares. A **tender offer** is a structured purchase of the target's shares in which the acquirer announces a public offer to buy a minimum number of shares at a specific price. Interested stockholders may then "tender" their shares at the offer price. If at least the minimum number of shares is tendered, then the acquirer buys those shares at the offer price. The acquirer has the option of buying the shares tendered at the offer price or canceling the offer altogether if the minimum number of shares is not tendered.[3] A two-tiered offer results when the acquirer offers to buy a certain number of shares at one price and then more shares at another price. These offers are especially popular in situations where the acquirer wishes to purchase 100 percent of the shares outstanding as quickly as possible and offers to buy 51 percent at a higher price and the remaining 49 percent at a lower price in an attempt to provide an incentive for shareholders to tender their shares early in order to receive the higher price. A **tender-merger** is a merger that occurs after an acquirer secures enough voting control of the target's shares through a tender offer to effect a merger.

tender offer
The structured purchase of a target's shares in which the acquirer announces a public offer to buy a minimum number of shares at a specific price.

tender-merger
A merger that occurs after an acquirer secures enough voting control of the target's shares through a tender offer to effect a merger.

Tender offers are often associated with hostile takeovers, but these are the highly publicized minority cases. In fact, one academic study shows that target management resisted only 86 of 263 tender offers from 1979 to 1987, and anecdotal evidence suggests that the fraction of resisted offers has declined even further since then.[4] Yet, open-market purchases, tender offers, and proxy fights may all be used in combination to launch a "surprise attack" on an unwitting (and often unwilling) target. In the United States, individuals or corporations may own up to 5 percent of any corporation's stock before facing the requirement of filing a Schedule 13-d form with the Securities and Exchange Commission (SEC) identifying themselves as a significant stockholder in the company. Thus, an interested potential acquirer could accumulate a substantial number of shares (known as a *foothold*) without the knowledge of the target's management and then follow a number of acquisition strategies. First, the interested acquirer could simply initiate a tender offer to purchase the remaining shares of the target required for voting control and then effect a merger (a tender-merger as mentioned previously). Second, the potential acquirer could approach the target with both a merger offer and the threat of a proxy fight and/or hostile tender offer to gain the remaining shares needed to obtain voting control of the target if the merger offer is refused. This tactic is known as a **bear hug**. Third, the acquirer could also threaten the target with a hostile tender offer and/or proxy fight in order to gain initial or greater access to the board of directors or to sell its shares to the target firm at a premium price.[5] Target firms employ defensive measures such as **antitakeover amendments** to their corporate charters (also known as **shark repellents**), **poison pills**, the pursuit of **white knights** ("friendly" acquirers who will top the price of an unwelcome bidder), MBOs, stock buybacks, payment of greenmail (see footnote 5), and other defensive tactics.[6] See Table 22.1 for greater detail on antitakeover mechanisms.

bear hug
The potential acquirer approaches the target with both a merger offer and the threat of a proxy fight and/or hostile tender offer to gain the remaining shares needed to obtain voting control of the target if the merger offer is refused.

antitakeover amendments
Adding defensive measures to corporate charters to avoid a hostile takeover.

shark repellents
Antitakeover measures added to corporate charters.

poison pills
Defensive measures taken to avoid a hostile takeover.

white knights
"Friendly" acquirers who will top the price of an unwelcome bidder to avoid a hostile takeover.

greenmail
Targeted repurchase of shares, at an above-market price, by a company from a potential acquirer, paid to make the "raider" drop the threat of acquiring the company.

---

3. The U.S. tender offer process is strictly regulated by the Williams Act, an amendment to the Securities and Exchange Act. See the discussion of the Williams Act in Section 22.5 for more details on the regulation of tender offers.

4. See Robert Jennings and Michael Mazzeo, "Competing Bids, Target Management Resistance, and the Structure of Takeover Bids," *Review of Financial Studies* 6 (Winter 1993), pp. 883–909.

5. The latter practice is a type of *targeted share repurchase* known as **greenmail**. This was a widespread practice used by corporate raiders in the 1980s, but is now outlawed in many states and taxed heavily by the Internal Revenue Service.

6. *Poison pills* are takeover defenses that can be triggered unilaterally by the target firm's board and effectively make a hostile takeover prohibitively expensive to the potential acquirer. These are typically adopted *without* shareholder approval.

Table 22.1
Commonly Used Antitakeover Measures

Measure	Antitakeover Effect
Fair price amendments	Corporate charter amendments mandating that a "fair price," usually defined as the highest price paid to any shareholder, be paid to all of the target firm's shareholders in the event of a takeover
Golden parachutes	Valuable termination arrangements made for executives that are activated after a takeover
Greenmail	The payment of a premium price for the shares held by a potential hostile acquirer but not paid to all stockholders
Just-say-no defense	Refusal to entertain a takeover offer on the grounds that no consideration offered is sufficient to relinquish control
Pac-Man defense	The initiation of a takeover attempt for the hostile acquirer itself
Poison pills	Dilution of the value of shares acquired by a hostile bidder through the offer of additional shares to all other existing shareholders at a discounted price
Poison puts	Deterrent to hostile takeovers through put options attached to bonds that allow the holders to sell their bonds back to the company at a prespecified price in the event of a takeover
Recapitalization	A change in capital structure designed to make the target less attractive by increasing firm leverage
Staggered director elections	Corporate charter amendments designed to make it more difficult for a hostile acquirer to replace members of the board of directors with persons sympathetic to a takeover
Standstill agreements	Negotiated contracts that prevent a substantial shareholder from acquiring more shares for a defined period of time
Supermajority approvals	Corporate charter amendments that require the approval of large majorities (67% or 80%) for a takeover to occur
White knight defense	The pursuit of a friendly acquirer to take over the company instead of a hostile acquirer
White squire defense	The sale of a substantial number of shares to an entity that is sympathetic to current management but has no intention of acquiring the firm

Obviously, there are many different acquisition strategies and methods for integrating the resources of the acquiring and acquired firms.

SMART IDEAS VIDEO
James Brickley, University of Utah
"Theoretically, antitakeover devices like poison pills might benefit shareholders."

See the entire interview at **SMARTFinance**

Divestitures and Spin-offs

Sometimes, managers prefer to transfer control of certain assets and resources through divestitures, spin-offs, split-offs, equity carve-outs, split-ups, or bust-ups. A **divestiture** occurs when the assets and/or resources of a subsidiary or division are sold to another organization. The sale by Vivendi of its Universal Studios to General Electric in early 2004 is an important recent example of a divestiture.

In a **spin-off**, a parent company creates a new company with its own shares by spinning off a division or subsidiary. Existing shareholders receive a pro rata distribution of shares in the new company. This happened when PepsiCo spun off its restaurant operations (Pizza Hut, Taco Bell, and KFC) in 1997 as a new company named Tricon Global Restaurants (with the catchy ticker symbol YUM). A **split-off** is similar to a spin-off in that a parent company creates a newly independent company from a subsidiary, but ownership of the company is transferred to only certain existing shareholders in exchange for their shares in the parent. *Equity carve-outs* (described more fully in Chapter 11) bring a cash infusion to the parent through the sale of a partial interest in a subsidiary through a public offering to new stockholders. Split-ups and bust-ups are the ultimate transfers of corporate control. As it sounds, the **split-up** of a corporation is the split-up and sale of all its subsidiaries so that it ceases to exist (except possibly as a holding company with no assets). A **bust-up** is the takeover of a company that is subsequently split up.

divestiture
Assets and/or resources of a subsidiary or division are sold to another organization.

spin-off
A parent company creates a new company with its own shares to form a division or subsidiary, and existing shareholders receive a pro rata distribution of shares in the new company.

CONCEPT REVIEW QUESTIONS

1. Why are acquired resources integrated into a company in so many different forms? What transaction-specific circumstances might lead to a preference of one integrative form over another?

2. How does a tender offer differ from a proxy fight? Why might these two corporate control actions be considered different ways to achieve the same objective?

3. What is an equity carve-out? Why do you think these are so popular with corporate issuers?

22.2 MERGERS AND BUSINESS CONCENTRATION

Mergers may also be classified by the relatedness of the business activities of the merging firms. There are several different classification schemes utilized for the business relatedness of the acquiring and acquired firms, but the most commonly applied scheme is the abbreviated classification offered by the Federal Trade Commission (FTC). In the following paragraphs, we define these FTC classifications, as well as others that are used, and introduce their importance to our eventual discussion of antitrust laws.

Horizontal Mergers

In a strict sense, the FTC defines a **horizontal merger** as a combination of competitors within the same geographic market; the Commission defines a **market extension merger** as a combination of firms that produce the same product in different geographic markets. As interstate commerce and technology have rendered geographic market classification less meaningful over time, the common interpretation of a horizontal merger has loosened to become a merger between companies that produce identical or closely related products in any geographic market. For example, a merger between two electric companies, one in Oregon and the other in Oklahoma, would have once been considered a market extension merger but would now be classified as horizontal.

The classification of mergers is important with regard to the regulatory authority of the FTC and the Department of Justice (DOJ), especially in the case of horizontal mergers. The FTC and DOJ have broad regulatory powers that can be used to prevent any merger that is deemed to be anticompetitive in nature, and the combinations that have the greatest potential to be anticompetitive are horizontal mergers.

split-off
A parent company creates a new, independent company with its own shares, and ownership of the company is transferred to certain existing shareholders only, in exchange for their shares in the parent.

split-up
The division and sale of all of a company's subsidiaries, so that it ceases to exist (except possibly as a holding company with no assets).

bust-up
The takeover of a company that is subsequently split up.

horizontal merger
A combination of competitors within the same geographic market.

market extension merger
A combination of firms that produce the same product in different geographic markets.

APPLYING THE MODEL

The failed 1997 merger attempt of Staples and Office Depot illustrates the legal perils facing companies wishing to execute horizontal mergers. Both companies were discount office supply retailers with some overlapping geographic markets and only one major competitor (OfficeMax). FTC and DOJ regulators opposed the merger on the grounds that it would be anticompetitive. Staples and Office Depot countered with an offer to sell all the Office Depot stores sharing the same market as a Staples store and an OfficeMax, making the merger more of a traditional market extension merger than a "strict" horizontal merger. The companies also sought to have their market more broadly defined as general discount retail (such as Target and Wal-Mart) so that the impact of the merger would not appear so anticompetitive. The companies' tactics failed, as did their attempted merger, reflecting the evolving definition of horizontal and anticompetitive mergers.

Horizontal mergers also have the greatest potential for wealth creation. Firms with similar businesses and assets have the ability to benefit from economies of scale and scope from combining their resources. These mergers also have the greatest *possibility* of realizing cost savings through the reduction or elimination of overlapping resources. **Market power** is another obvious benefit that might arise from a horizontal merger. Increased market power results when competition is too weak (or nonexistent) to prevent the merged company from raising prices in a market at will. Of course, this is exactly the kind of anticompetitiveness that the regulators in the Staples-Office Depot merger sought to prevent.

market power
A benefit that might arise from a horizontal merger when competition is too weak (or nonexistent) to prevent the merged company from raising prices in a market at will.

Vertical Mergers

A **vertical merger** occurs when companies with current or potential buyer-seller relationships combine to create a more integrated company. These mergers are easiest to think of in terms of steps in the production process. Consider the process of producing and selling finished petroleum products. Petroleum exploration and production is followed by transportation, refining, and end-use sales. If a company in the drilling business acquires a company that refines crude oil, then the driller is moving forward in the production process by purchasing the potential buyer of its crude oil. This type of vertical merger is a **forward integration**. Had a refiner and distributor acquired a driller, then the merger would be a **backward integration**, as exemplified by the 1984 merger between Texaco and Getty Oil. Texaco needed Getty's drilling operations and reserves to complement its own refineries and distribution and marketing outlets in order to be a fully integrated oil company.

vertical merger
Companies with current or potential buyer-seller relationships combine to create a more integrated company.

forward integration
A merger in which the acquired company provides a later step in the production process.

backward integration
A merger in which the acquired company provides an earlier step in the production process.

There are several obvious potential benefits to vertical integration via merger. One advantage to a vertical merger is that product quality and procurement can be ensured from earlier stages of the production process with backward integration. For instance, a manufacturer of precision surgical devices might wish to ensure the high-quality standards required of an input such as a laser beam by acquiring the company that manufactures the laser beam. Or, a manufacturer with great sensitivity to inventory conversion cycles could more efficiently monitor an orderly inventory flow by acquiring a supplier of raw materials. Another advantage to backward integration is the reduction of input prices. The "middleman" and associated price markup are eliminated.

Forward integration may also offer benefits. Whereas backward integration emphasizes inputs, forward integration focuses on output quality and distribution. Provision of an outlet for a product is an advantage to forward integration. One reason for Disney's merger with Capital Cities/ABC was to gain access to a television network as an outlet for Disney's television entertainment production.[7] Vertical integration can also be used as a marketing tool. Many retail stores and automobile manufacturers have acquired financing subsidiaries to make it easier for a customer to obtain credit to purchase their products (e.g., Ford Motor Credit).

However, there are also disadvantages to vertical mergers. The major disadvantage is the entry into a new line of business. Acquiring managers are likely to have some knowledge of the target firm's business because it is part of the same production process, but similarities do not always imply compatibility. A manager of an automobile manufacturer might find that what works well for manufacturing cars does not work well for renting them, even though both businesses revolve around automobiles (as Chrysler found out with its Thrifty Rent-a-Car unit). Managers might also find that the cost savings from "eliminating the middleman" are not as great as expected. Eliminating the markup might reduce costs for the acquirer, but it also means that the acquired subsidiary is no longer producing profits for the parent company. The acquirer might overlook or underestimate this factor when attempting to value a target. Finally, vertical mergers may also be subject to antitrust regulation, albeit with a smaller probability than with horizontal mergers.

Conglomerate Mergers

product extension mergers
Diversification mergers that combine companies with similar but not identical lines of business.

pure conglomerate mergers
Unrelated diversification mergers that occur between companies in completely different lines of business.

The remaining two types of FTC-defined mergers are diversifying in nature. **Product extension mergers**, or related diversification mergers, are combinations of companies with similar but not exact lines of business. **Pure conglomerate mergers**, or unrelated diversification mergers, occur between companies in completely different lines of business.

Product extension mergers, like market extension mergers, are something of a hybrid classification, in this case a cross between vertical and purely conglomerate mergers. These mergers are not vertical because they are not between firms in different stages of the production process, but their business operations are still related. The 1989 merger of Consolidated Freightways and Emery Air Freight provides an example of a related diversification merger. Consolidated was a major provider of surface freight transportation with a minimal presence in airfreight transportation, the sole business of Emery. Consolidated was experienced in the general business of freight transportation, but not the specific business of airfreight transportation. Managers tend to pursue these types of mergers when searching for a higher-growth business that is not entirely new to them.

Pure conglomerate mergers marry two companies that operate in totally unrelated businesses. Although popular in the 1960s, these mergers have significantly declined in frequency since the 1980s. Based on the principles of portfolio diversification, the purpose of these mergers is to put together two companies that operate in businesses so different that if some systematic or idiosyncratic event has an adverse effect on one business, then the other business will be minimally (or even positively) impacted. Merging these two firms is expected to make earnings and cash flows less volatile. The 1984 merger of automaker General Motors and computer/business service consulting firm Electronic Data Systems is a prime example of a pure conglomerate merger.

7. Interestingly, this forward integration strategy proved largely unsuccessful for Disney, as ABC experienced an extended ratings swoon almost immediately after Disney acquired the network. The failure of this strategy was one reason why Disney appeared vulnerable to a hostile takeover attempt launched by Comcast Corporation in early 2004. The takeover attempt eventually fizzled, though Disney remains "in play" as of September 2004.

Table 22.2
Level of Business Concentration Resulting from Merger—An Example of Various Classifications

	Acquirer			Target			Combined		
Line of Business	Revenues	%	% Squared	Revenues	%	% Squared	Revenue	%	% Squared
Chemicals	$ 500,000,000	50.0	0.2500	$200,000,000	40.0	0.1600	$ 700,000,000	46.7	0.2180
Oil refining	300,000,000	30.0	0.0900	0	0.0	0.0000	300,000,000	20.0	0.0400
Coal mining	200,000,000	20.0	0.0400	0	0.0	0.0000	200,000,000	13.3	0.0178
Retail drugs	0	0.0	0.0000	150,000,000	30.0	0.0900	150,000,000	10.0	0.0100
Plastics	0	0.0	0.0000	150,000,000	30.0	0.0900	150,000,000	10.0	0.0100
Total	$1,000,000,000	100.0	0.3800	$500,000,000	100.0	0.3400	$1,500,000,000	100.0	0.2958

Note: *Abbreviated FTC classification: horizontal*
Business overlap classification: medium overlap
Change in focus classification: focus-decreasing

Other Concentration Classifications

The abbreviated (horizontal/vertical/conglomerate) and full (abbreviated plus market and product extension) FTC merger classifications are not always satisfactory for determining the degree of business concentration created by a merger. Compare the following two hypothetical mergers for an illustration of a possible shortcoming of the FTC classification. The first merger pairs two software companies that operate in no other lines of business. The second merger occurs between the companies in Table 22.2. The acquirer in this merger derives 50 percent of its revenue from chemicals, 30 percent from crude oil refining, and 20 percent from coal-mining operations. Chemicals are also the primary line of business for the target at 40 percent of revenues, followed by 30 percent from retail drugs and 30 percent from plastics. Because the acquirer and target are in the same primary line of business in both mergers, both are classified as horizontal mergers under the abbreviated FTC scheme. But do both mergers have the same level of business concentration? Obviously not—the first merger clearly has more concentration than the second. The need for a finer definition of business concentration in such cases gave rise to the creation of alternative measures, such as degree of overlapping business and change in corporate focus (defined below).

Research initiated in the early 1990s introduced the concept of classifying mergers according to the degree of overlapping business operations between the acquirer and target.[8] Reviewing the lines of business of the acquirer and target, the researchers categorized mergers as having high, medium, and low levels of overlapping business. These categories loosely correspond to (respectively) horizontal, vertical, and conglomerate classifications, but more flexibility exists for assessing the concentration of more complex cases such as our merger in Table 22.2. Although considered a horizontal merger under traditional classification, this merger would fall under medium overlap in the HPR categorization rather than high overlap. You can easily see how the flexibility of the HPR classification allows for a truer account of a merger's business concentration.

An even more finely tuned measure of business concentration revolves around the concept of **corporate focus.** A focused firm concentrates its efforts on its core (primary) business, the opposite end of the spectrum from a diversified firm. A

corporate focus
A focused firm concentrates its efforts on its core (primary) business; the opposite end of the spectrum from a diversified firm.

[8] See especially Paul Healy, Krishna Palepu, and Richard Ruback, "Does Corporate Performance Improve After Mergers?" *Journal of Financial Economics* 31 (April 1992), pp. 135–176 (HPR) and Robert Comment and Gregg Jarrell, "Corporate Focus and Stock Returns," *Journal of Financial Economics* 37 (January 1995), pp. 67–87.

Herfindahl Index (HI)
A measure popularized by Comment and Jarrell (1995) to demonstrate the relationship between corporate focus and shareholder wealth.

measure known as the **Herfindahl Index (HI)** demonstrates the relationship between corporate focus and shareholder wealth. The HI is computed as the sum of the squared percentages, in this case the proportion of revenues derived from each line of business. Thus, the HI exaggerates the difference between focused and diversified firms. A completely focused firm has an HI of 1.00 compared with the diversified acquiring firm in our example, which has an HI of 0.38 ($0.5^2 + 0.3^2 + 0.2^2$). A merger (or divestiture) increases focus if the HI of the merged firm is greater than that of the acquiring firm prior to the merger, preserves focus if the HI does not change, and decreases focus if the HI declines. In our hypothetical mergers, the first merger between the software companies preserves corporate focus whereas the second merger between the diversified companies decreases corporate focus, as the HI declines from 0.380 to 0.296.

CONCEPT REVIEW QUESTIONS

4. What is the purpose of classifying mergers by degree of business concentration? Why do you think these classifications have changed over time?

5. As conglomerate mergers and corporate diversification have proven to be failures in general, why would any manager pursue these objectives? Can you think of any cases where corporate diversification has worked successfully? What distinguishes these cases from the norm?

6. What is a Herfindahl Index, and what is it meant to measure?

22.3 MERGER AND ACQUISITION TRANSACTION CHARACTERISTICS

Corporate control events can be categorized according to certain defining characteristics of the transactions, including the method of payment used to finance a transaction, the attitude or response of target management to a takeover attempt, and the accounting treatment used when the firms combine.

Method of Payment

Just like any other type of investment, a merger must be financed with capital components—including debt, retained earnings, and newly issued common stock. These components comprise the consideration offered in a transaction and sum to the transaction value, the dollar value of all forms of payment offered to the target for control of the company. Cash on hand from retained earnings and/or generated from an issue of debt is used in financing a cash-only deal, where the target's shareholders receive only cash for their shares in a public company or the target's owner(s) receives cash for the private enterprise. More rarely, the target receives a new issue of debt in exchange for control in a debt-only transaction.

pure stock exchange merger
A merger in which stock is the only mode of payment.

Conversely, stock is the only mode of payment in a stock-swap or **pure stock exchange merger.** The general stock-swap merger involves the issuance of new shares of common stock in exchange for the target's common stock, but payment may come in the form of either preferred stock or subsidiary tracking shares. The number of shares of the surviving firm's common stock that target shareholders receive is determined by the exchange ratio. The surviving firm is either the acquiring firm or the new firm created in a consolidation. For instance, an acquirer with a current stock price of $20 that sets an exchange ratio of 0.75 for a target with a current stock price of $12 and 100 million shares outstanding will issue 75 million new shares in exchange for the target's shares. The transaction value of this merger would be $1.5 billion ($20 × 75 million).[9] An individual who owns 100 shares ($1,200) of the target stock would receive acquirer stock worth $1,500 ($20 × 75 shares), a 25 percent control premium.

Mergers may also be financed with a combination of cash and securities, in transactions known as **mixed offerings**. Recent research by Tim Loughran and Anand Vijh reveals that 24.1 percent of U.S. acquisitions are mixed, compared with 33.2 percent for cash-only deals and 42.8 percent for stock-swap mergers.[10] The 1995 Disney-Capital Cities/ABC merger is an example of a mixed offering. Capital Cities/ABC shareholders were offered $65 and one share of Disney stock for each of their shares.

mixed offerings
Offerings in which some of the shares come from existing shareholders and some are new. Also, a merger financed with a combination of cash and securities.

Sometimes, target shareholders are also offered a choice for the medium of exchange. For example, target shareholders could be offered the choice of either $30 cash or 1.25 shares of the surviving company's shares for each share that they hold. This way, the shareholders can decide whether the exchange ratio is sufficient for them to remain shareholders in the surviving company or whether they should "take the money and run" with the cash offer.

Attitude of Target Management

Takeover attempts (successful and unsuccessful) are often classified by the degree of resistance offered by the management of the target firm. Uncontested offers are generally referred to as "friendly" deals, whereas resisted offers are termed "hostile" transactions. As it seems that everyone likes a good fight, hostile deals receive a disproportionate share of attention. However, management resisted only 31 percent of the takeover attempts in the Jennings and Mazzeo study of public targets cited earlier. Considering the more recent corporate trend of adopting antitakeover measures to thwart hostile bidders and the fact that takeovers of private or closely held firms are friendly by nature, hostile deals represent an increasingly smaller (but highly publicized) percentage of all corporate control activities.

Accounting Treatment

Prior to June 30, 2001, two financial accounting procedures existed for recording a merger in the United States: the pooling-of-interests and purchase methods. However, with implementation of Financial Accounting Standards Board (FASB) Statement 141 and the near-concurrent (December 31, 2001) Statement 142, there now exists one standard method of accounting for mergers. Under these new standards, target liabilities remain unchanged, but target assets are "written up" to reflect current market values, and the equity of the target is revised upward to incorporate the purchase price paid. These revised values are then carried over to the surviving firm's financial statements. The intangible asset *goodwill* is created if the restated values of the target lead to a situation in which its assets are less than its liabilities and equity. This **goodwill** reflects the premium that an acquiring firm is willing to pay in excess of net asset market value in order to capture synergies from the merger—goodwill becomes an intangible asset on the balance sheet. Going forward, the value of this intangible asset must be evaluated to determine if it has been "impaired" due to a decline in fair value relative to carrying value. If the value of goodwill is impaired, then the amount of the impairment is "written down" from the goodwill account on the balance sheet and charged off against earnings. Otherwise, it remains unchanged on the balance sheet indefinitely. Many large write-downs were taken soon after FASB 142 went into effect at the beginning of 2002. JDS Uniphase, AOL Time Warner, and Nortel Networks all took multi-billion-dollar

goodwill
An intangible asset created if the restated values of the target in a merger lead to a situation in which its assets are less than its liabilities and equity.

9. This is under the assumption that the acquirer's stock price remains the same—a very optimistic assumption, as we will later see. In most stock-swap mergers, an acceptable range of stock prices and exchange ratios is negotiated from the outset.

10. See Tim Loughran and Anand Vijh, "Do Long-Term Shareholders Benefit from Corporate Acquisitions?" *Journal of Finance* 52 (December 1997), pp. 1765–1790.

write-downs in 2002 for acquisitions completed in prior years, while the newly renamed MCI Inc. took a $75 billion write-down in early 2004 for acquisitions completed by the company when it was named WorldCom. See the following Applying the Model for a mathematical example of accounting for mergers.

APPLYING THE MODEL

Assume that a target firm has 5 million shares outstanding priced at $10 per share. The acquiring firm offers a 20 percent takeover premium ($12 per share) for a transaction value of equity of $60 million. The acquiring firm wants the R&D capabilities of the target firm and is willing to pay a premium to obtain those capabilities and leverage R&D synergies. The market value of the target's fixed assets is $65 million. Along with the $10 million in current assets, the target has a market value of assets of $75 million. Deducting the $5 million in current liabilities and $25 million in long-term liabilities, the target firm has a net asset value of $45 million. Thus, the acquiring firm is willing to pay $15 million ($60 million less $45 million) for intangible assets in the form of R&D.

Current assets	$10,000,000
Restated fixed assets	65,000,000
Less: Liabilities	30,000,000
Net asset value	$45,000,000
Purchase price paid	60,000,000
Less: Net asset value	45,000,000
Goodwill	$15,000,000

Further assume that the target firm is treated as a separate reporting subsidiary after the merger. Going forward, the firm must value its intangible assets (goodwill) to determine if the value of $15 million on the balance sheet represents a fair value. As long as the firm can demonstrate that the goodwill is fairly valued, then it will remain unaffected on the balance sheet. However, if the value is "impaired," then the value loss must be reported, deducted from the balance sheet, and taken as a write-off against earnings. For example, if the R&D of the subsidiary does not turn out as synergistic as hoped for two years later, then the fair market value and net asset value of the subsidiary will be estimated. If the fair market value is estimated at $70 million and the net asset value at $60 million, then the value of goodwill is only $10 million—a $5 million impairment. This $5 million will be deducted from the balance sheet and taken as an intangible asset write-down on the income statement.

	Acquirer ($ in millions)	Target ($ in millions)	Merged ($ in millions)	
			Subsidiary	Consolidated
Assets				
Current	$ 50	$10	$10	$ 60
Fixed	350	50	65	415
Goodwill	0	0	15	15
Total assets	$400	$60	$90	$490
Liabilities				
Current	$ 50	$ 5	$ 5	$ 55
Long-term	250	25	25	275
Total	$300	$30	$30	$330
Owner's equity	100	30	60	160
Total liabilities and equity	$400	$60	$90	$490

Shareholder Wealth Effects and Transaction Characteristics

How do the shareholders of companies involved in mergers and acquisitions generally fare? The consensus result obtained in merger studies is that the common stockholders of target firms in successful takeovers experience large and significant wealth gains. Acquirer returns are much smaller and not as generalized, and we discuss the theories offered to explain the cross-sectional differences in acquirers' returns. We also explore the wealth effects of various transaction characteristics.

Returns to Target and Bidding Firm Shareholders.

Target Returns. As previously noted, target-firm stockholders almost always experience substantial wealth gains due to the premium offered for giving up control of their company.[11] An early survey article by Michael Jensen and Richard Ruback finds that, on average, target-firm common stockholders receive takeover premiums of 29.1 percent in successful tender offers and 15.9 percent in successful mergers, while more recent studies find that the average takeover premium is 31.8 percent in tender offers and that the average premium has risen over time.[12] Target returns are also higher when there are multiple bidders and when managerial resistance leads to a higher offer, but takeover premiums are lost when resistance is too great and prevents a takeover.

Acquirer Returns. Results concerning the common stock returns of acquiring firms are not as conclusive as those for target shareholders. Studies show that, on average, the common stockholders of acquiring firms experience positive returns in successful tender offers and virtually zero returns in successful mergers. However, in contrast to the rising trend of target returns, a negative trend in acquirer returns occurs over time. This joint trend in target and acquirer returns is primarily attributed to implementation of the Williams Act in 1968. The weighted-average return of acquirers and targets has consistently ranged between 7 percent and 8 percent over time, reflecting a constant anticipated synergistic gain from the combination of the two firms. But the protective provisions of the Williams Act seem to have caused a transfer of this consistent gain from acquirer to target-firm shareholders, as acquirer returns were significantly positive prior to the Williams Act and have become slightly negative since.

Mode of Payment. The mode of payment used to finance an acquisition explains much of the cross-sectional variance in acquirers' returns. Multiple studies find higher returns in cash transactions than in stock transactions.[13] These studies also show that the higher returns observed by both acquirers and targets in tender offers relative to negotiated mergers are attributable to the fact that most tender offers are financed by cash, whereas most negotiated mergers are equity financed. Announcement-period target returns are 13 percentage points greater for cash deals, acquirer returns in cash-financed deals are near zero, and those in stock-financed deals are significantly negative. Long-term results are even more startling: common stockholders in cash tender offers outperform those in stock-swap mergers by 123 percent through the fifth post-acquisition year.

---

11. The rare case where a target shareholder receives a negative takeover premium is known as a *takeunder.*

12. See Michael Jensen and Richard Ruback, "The Market for Corporate Control: The Scientific Evidence," *Journal of Financial Economics* 11 (April 1983), pp. 5–50, Michael Bradley, Anand Desai, and Han Kim, "Synergistic Gains from Corporate Acquisitions and Their Division between the Stockholders of Target and Acquiring Firms," *Journal of Financial Economics* 21 (May 1988), pp. 3–40, and Yen-Sheng Huang and Ralph Walkling, "Target Abnormal Returns Associated with Acquisition Announcements: Payment, Acquisition Form, and Managerial Resistance," *Journal of Financial Economics* 19 (December 1987), pp. 329–349.

13. See Nikolaos Travlos, "Corporate Takeover Bids, Method of Payment, and Bidding Firms' Stock Returns," *Journal of Finance* 42 (September 1987), pp. 943–963 and the 1997 Loughran and Vijh article cited in footnote 10.

Researchers have proposed several theories to explain the differential returns between cash and stock offers. The most prominent of these theories revolves around the signaling model first described in Chapter 12. In the context of this model, the mode of payment offered by acquiring firms signals inside information to the capital markets. Managers will finance acquisitions with the cheapest source of capital available. Financing an acquisition with equity signals to the market that managers believe equity is a (relatively) cheap source of capital because they think the acquirer's stock price is overvalued. Receiving this signal, the capital markets will make a downward revision of the value of the acquirer's equity. Other theories concerning the differential returns due to financing method include the tax and preemptive bidding hypotheses. The *tax hypothesis* postulates that target shareholders must be awarded a capital gains tax premium in cash offers, which is not required in a stock offer. The *preemptive bidding hypothesis* asserts that acquirers wishing to ward off other potential bidders for a target offer a substantial initial takeover premium in the form of cash.

Returns to Other Security Holders. Obviously, common stocks are not the only securities affected in corporate control activities. Corporate control events also impact bonds and preferred stocks. Recent empirical research finds that some nonconvertible bondholders experience significant wealth gains, but these gains are driven by the bonds of acquiring firms in nonconglomerate mergers (average gain of 1.9 percent). No financial synergies are realized in conglomerate mergers, and the nonconvertible bondholders in these mergers neither gain nor lose. In general, convertible bond returns are significantly higher than those of nonconvertible bonds. Further research indicates that increased leverage in a merger causes bondholder wealth losses, and also that certain types of restrictive covenants protect bondholder wealth in mergers. No evidence of significant bondholder wealth losses is systematically observed in LBOs, though specific transactions have yielded dramatic bondholder losses. Both convertible and nonconvertible preferred stockholders exhibit significant wealth gains in nonconglomerate mergers.

The validity of the financial synergy motive for conglomerate mergers has also been questioned. Academics contend that the existence of internal capital markets will lead to investment in lines of business with poor investment opportunities and no economic value added. Indeed, academic research has not documented any financial synergies. Performance measures also prove corporate diversification to be a failure in general. Various studies demonstrate the superior operating performance of mergers that occur between companies with high levels of business overlap relative to those that occur between companies with little overlap in their businesses. Research also shows that diversified firms trade at a significant discount in market value relative to their focused counterparts of around 15 percent, and firms increasing focus experience value gains and those decreasing focus suffer wealth losses. Capital markets have also learned of the failure of diversification and now greet the announcements of diversifying mergers with negative stock-price reactions. Empirical evidence strongly supports the notion that mergers that decrease focus cause a loss in firm value.

CONCEPT REVIEW QUESTIONS

7. What are the two most important methods of paying for corporate acquisitions?

8. What is "goodwill" in the context of merger accounting? What must an acquiring company do if the value of an acquired company is revealed to have declined after a merger?

9. Who wins and who loses in corporate takeovers? Why do acquiring firm shareholders generally lose in stock-swap mergers but either benefit or at least break even in acquisitions paid for with cash?

22.4 RATIONALE AND MOTIVES FOR MERGERS AND ACQUISITIONS

As we have seen, the primary objective of any corporation's management team should be the maximization of shareholder wealth. Management should undertake a potential merger or acquisition, like any other investment, as long as its net present value is positive and enhances shareholder value. Mergers may be value enhancing in several ways. However, we know that corporate managers do not always act as proper agents for their shareholders, and agency problems arise when managers engage in non-value-maximizing behavior. In this section, we examine both the value-maximizing and non-value-maximizing motives that lead managers to pursue mergers and acquisitions.

SMART PRACTICES VIDEO

David Baum, Co-head of M&A for Goldman Sachs in the Americas

"Broadly I put M&A opportunities into three distinct buckets."

See the entire interview at SMARTFinance

Value-Maximizing Motives

Mergers create value when managers seek goals such as increasing operating profit, realizing gains from restructuring poorly managed firms, or creating greater barriers to entry in their industry. These and other value-enhancing objectives can be achieved through mergers and acquisitions that garner access to new geographic markets, increase market power, capitalize on economies of scale, or create value through the sale of underperforming target resources.

Expansion. Geographic expansion (both domestic and international) may enhance shareholder wealth if the market entered is subject to little or no competition. Managers considering expansion must first evaluate two mutually exclusive alternatives: internal versus external expansion. Internal expansion into a new market, also known as **greenfield entry**, involves acquiring and organizing all resources required for each stage of the investment. These stages encompass contracting with an engineering firm to build a new plant, hiring new employees to staff the plant, implementing training programs for the new staff, establishing distribution outlets, and so on.

greenfield entry
Internal expansion into a new market.

External expansion is the acquisition of a firm with resources already in place. Acquirers pay a control premium to the owners of the acquired firm for relinquishing control, but the payment of this premium ensures that many of the potential problems of greenfield entry are avoided. For instance, external expansion avoids construction delays in the building of a new plant or the inability to adequately staff a new facility. Usually, external expansion is the better option in situations where rapid expansion is desired or when great uncertainty exists about the success of any stage of greenfield entry. International expansion is another good reason to choose external expansion over internal expansion. The business operations, political climate, and social mores differ so greatly between some countries that an acquisition is often the only viable alternative for international expansion.[14]

SMART IDEAS VIDEO

Claire Crutchley, Auburn University

"Overall, joint ventures are good for shareholders."

See the entire interview at SMARTFinance

Synergy, Market Power, and Strategic Mergers. A **strategic merger** is one that seeks to create a more efficient merged company than the two premerger companies operating independently. This efficiency-enhancing effect is known as **synergy**. Michael Eisner, CEO of Disney, provided the best definition of synergy with his perception of the value created by his company's merger with Capital Cities/ABC: "1 + 1 = 4." There are three types of merger-related synergies—*operational, managerial,* and *financial.*

strategic merger
Seeks to create a more efficient merged company than the two premerger companies operating independently.

synergy
An efficiency-enhancing effect resulting from a strategic merger.

[14] Joint ventures and strategic alliances also allow access to foreign markets through existing resources, but these are partnering relationships in which profits must be shared.

operational synergy Economies of scale, economies of scope, and resource complementarities.

economies of scale Relative operating costs are reduced for merged companies because of an increase in size that allows for the reduction or elimination of overlapping resources.

economies of scope Value-creating benefits of increased size for merged companies.

resource complementarities A firm with a particular operating expertise merges with a firm with another operating strength to create a company that has expertise in multiple areas.

managerial synergies Efficiency gains from combining the management teams of merged companies.

financial synergies A merger results in less-volatile cash flows, lower default risk, and a lower cost of capital.

Synergies. The main sources of **operational synergy** are economies of scale, economies of scope, and resource complementarities. **Economies of scale** result when relative operating costs are reduced because of an increase in size that allows for the reduction or elimination of overlapping resources. For example, the reason given for the elimination of 12,000 positions in the 1995 merger of Chemical Bank and Chase Manhattan Bank was the cost savings generated from the elimination of overlapping jobs. **Economies of scope** are other value-creating benefits of increased size. The ability for a merged firm to launch a national advertising campaign that would not have been feasible for either of the premerger firms is such a benefit. **Resource complementarities** exist when a firm with a particular operating expertise merges with a firm with another operating strength to create a company that has expertise in multiple areas. A good example of such a complementarity is the merger of two pharmaceutical companies, the first a specialist in researching and developing new drugs and the second a master marketer of drug products. Operating synergies are most likely to be achieved in horizontal mergers and least likely to be realized in conglomerate mergers. However, resource complementarities are just as likely to be realized in vertical mergers as horizontal mergers, because vertical combinations pair companies that specialize in different areas.

Managerial synergies, like operating synergies, cause two firms to have greater value when combined than when they are independent. Managerial synergies, however, result in efficiency gains from the combination of management teams. Similar to resource complementarities, managerial synergies arise when management teams with different strengths are paired together. Consider a merger between two retailing firms with differing managerial expertise. The first retailer has a management team that emphasizes revenue growth and excels in recognizing customer trends. The second retailer has a technically oriented management team that excels in cost containment and has perfected inventory control with its superior information systems. A merger between these two firms should benefit from managerial synergies with a joint emphasis on and expertise in revenue growth and cost containment, assuming the two management teams can mesh together smoothly.

Financial synergies occur when a merger results in less volatile cash flows, lower default risk, and a lower cost of capital. As financial synergies are largely the anticipated result of conglomerate mergers, we defer this discussion to the section on the diversification motive for mergers.

Market Power. Other, more controversial, motives support increasing firm size through mergers and acquisitions. As we have seen, horizontal mergers have the potential to create more efficient companies through size-related operational synergies. Horizontal mergers may also profit from size in another fashion: increased market power. As horizontal mergers are those that take place between competitors, the number of competitors in an industry will necessarily decline. Presumably, price competition will also decline if the merger creates a dominant firm that has the power to control prices in a market.

Consider the Staples-Office Depot merger attempt previously mentioned. The two largest competitors in an industry with only three true competitors attempted to merge. The regulatory authorities denied this merger on the grounds that the merged company would have the power to control prices in the office supplies market with only one, much smaller, competitor to provide price competition. Regulatory authorities must balance the corporate benefit of increased efficiency against the consumer cost of increased market power when making decisions on allowing a merger to take place—especially a horizontal merger.

Other Strategic Rationales. Other strategic reasons also motivate managers to pursue mergers. As we mentioned earlier, in vertical mergers, product quality can sometimes be more closely monitored. Another strategic motive is defensive consolidation in a mature or declining industry. As consumer demand declines in an industry, competitors may seek each other out for a merger in order to survive the permanent industry downturn. Not only does the merged firm stand to benefit from economies of scale and scope, but it will also benefit from the reduction of competition. Of course, this does introduce the market power issue for regulators. But recent history has seen regulators adopt a more permissive attitude toward defensive consolidation—for example, the consolidation in the U.S. defense industry in the post-Cold War period.

Cash Flow Generation and Financial Mergers. Financial mergers are motivated by the prospect of uncovering hidden value in a target through a major restructuring or the generation of free cash flow from merger-related tax advantages. Many of the hostile deals of the 1980s were junk bond-financed financial mergers aimed at either "busting up" undervalued firms by selling off the assets of the acquired firm for a value greater than the acquisition price or restructuring the acquired firm to increase its corporate focus. A typical financial merger involves a focused acquirer that acquires a diversified firm with some business operations in the acquirer's line of business. The acquirer then sells the noncore businesses and uses the cash flow to pay down the cost of the acquisition.

Tax considerations may also motivate managers to pursue a particular target for a merger. The asymmetrical nature of the U.S. tax code provides an incentive to merge in certain circumstances. Although taxes must always be paid on positive income, negative income (net losses) creates only tax-loss carrybacks and carryforwards that offset taxes paid (on past income) or due on future income; the government does not pay negative taxes (cash payments) to firms suffering net losses. **Tax-loss carryforwards** can be charged against future income for up to fifteen years. Acquiring a target that has accumulated tax-loss carryforwards could shelter taxable income and redistribute that cash flow to other uses.

tax-loss carryforwards
Negative income (net losses) can be used to offset taxes due on future income.

As junk bond financing of acquisitions has declined since the 1980s, so has the occurrence of financial mergers. This merger motive was further minimized by a change in the tax code in 1986 that limited the extent to which tax-loss carryforwards could be used after a merger. Financial mergers still occur, but their importance in the market for corporate control has declined significantly.

Non-Value-Maximizing Motives

Unfortunately, not all mergers are motivated for the purpose of maximizing shareholder wealth. Although the motives of managers may not be intentionally value reducing, most revolve around agency problems between managers and shareholders. We discuss these improper motives next.

managerialism theory of mergers
Poorly monitored managers will pursue mergers to maximize their corporation's asset size because managerial compensation is usually based on firm size, regardless of whether or not these mergers create value for stockholders.

Agency Problems. Managers will sometimes disguise their attempts to derive personal benefits from creating and managing larger corporations as the need to expand through mergers and acquisitions. Academic research confirms the importance of this motive with findings that merger activity is positively related to growth in sales and assets but not related to increased profits or stock prices. Considering these findings, Dennis Mueller offered the **managerialism theory of mergers.**[15] According to this theory, poorly monitored managers will pursue mergers to maximize their corporation's asset size because managerial compensation is usually based on firm size, regardless of whether or not these mergers create value for stockholders.

Michael Jensen further advanced the managerialism theory with his **free cash flow theory of mergers.**[16] Jensen hypothesizes that managers will use free cash flow to invest

free cash flow theory of mergers
Michael Jensen (1986) hypothesizes that managers will use free cash flow to invest in mergers that have negative net present values in order to build corporate empires from which the managers will derive personal benefits, including greater compensation.

15. See Dennis Mueller, "A Theory of Conglomerate Mergers," *Quarterly Journal of Economics* 83 (1969), pp. 643–659.
16. See Michael Jensen, "Agency Costs of Free Cash Flow, Corporate Finance, and Takeovers," *American Economic Review* 76 (May 1986), pp. 323–329.

in mergers that have negative net present values in order to build corporate empires from which the managers will derive personal benefits, including greater compensation. Obviously, investing in negative-*NPV* projects is not value enhancing for shareholders. Another variation on this theme is the **managerial entrenchment theory of mergers** proposed by Andrei Shleifer and Robert Vishny.[17] Like the free cash flow theory, this theory holds that unmonitored managers will try to build corporate empires through the pursuit of negative-*NPV* mergers. However, the entrenchment theory holds that the motive is to make the management team indispensable to the firm because of its greater size and the team's supposed expertise in managing a large company. All three theories have a common theme: agency problems motivate managers to seek mergers that benefit themselves but not shareholders.

managerial entrenchment theory of mergers Shleifer and Vishny (1989) propose that unmonitored managers will try to build corporate empires through the pursuit of negative-NPV mergers, with the motive of making the management team indispensable to the firm because of its greater size and the team's supposed expertise in managing a large company.

Richard Roll offers a similar rationale with his **hubris hypothesis of corporate takeovers.**[18] Roll contends that some managers overestimate their own managerial capabilities and pursue takeovers with the belief that they can better manage their takeover target than the target's current management team can. Acquiring managers then overbid for the target and fail to realize the gains expected from the merger in the postmerger period, thereby diminishing shareholder wealth. Thus, the intent of the managers is not incongruent with the best interests of shareholders (the managers think they will create value), but the result is nonetheless value decreasing.

hubris hypothesis of corporate takeovers Richard Roll (1986) contends that some managers overestimate their own managerial capabilities and pursue takeovers with the belief that they can better manage their takeover target than the target's current management team can.

Diversification. As recently as the late 1960s, diversification was actually considered a value-maximizing motive for merger. Over time, however, the capital markets have learned of the failure of corporate diversification strategies, especially those emphasizing unrelated diversification. Given these empirical discoveries, we must now consider that diversification is a non-value-enhancing motive for merger.

As previously discussed, corporate diversification and conglomerate mergers were an experiment in portfolio theory applied to corporations. The basic premise of corporate diversification is that the combination of two businesses with less than perfectly correlated cash flows will create a merged firm with less volatile cash flows and inherently lower business risk, where bad outcomes in one business can be offset by good outcomes in another business. Diversification supporters contend that these less volatile cash flows make debt service less risky, lowering default risk and the required return on debt. As described by Wilbur Lewellen, financial synergy is created by this **coinsurance of debt**, as the debt of each combining firm is now insured with cash flows from two businesses.[19] Other proponents of unrelated diversification cite the existence of internal capital markets as another reason to pursue conglomerate mergers. **Internal capital markets** are created when the high cash flows (*cash cow*) businesses of a conglomerate generate enough cash flow to fund the "rising star" businesses. Since this financing is accomplished internally, underwriting costs are avoided and riskier business ventures can be financed with "cheaper" capital generated from more mature and less risky businesses.

coinsurance of debt The debt of each combining firm in a merger is insured with cash flows from two businesses.

internal capital markets Created when the high-cash-flow businesses of a conglomerate generate enough cash to fund the riskier business ventures internally.

Additional research on corporate diversification generated theories describing the flaws in the diversification motive for merger. Realizing that conglomerate mergers are not likely to benefit from any synergies other than financial, researchers showed that the net effect of conglomerate mergers is zero wealth creation and that any wealth gains experienced by bondholders due to financial synergies are merely redistributed from stockholders. Further, internal capital markets fell into disrepute when it became obvious that managerial control over free cash flow created its own, often severe, agency problems. In particular, capital attained and invested without having to pass a market test is often wasted.

17. See Andrei Shleifer and Robert Vishny, "Management Entrenchment," *Journal of Financial Economics* 25 (November 1989), pp. 123–139.

18. See Richard Roll, "The Hubris Hypothesis of Corporate Takeovers," *Journal of Business* 59 (April 1986), pp. 197–217.

19. See Wilbur Lewellen, "A Pure Financial Rationale for the Conglomerate Merger," *Journal of Finance* 26 (May 1971), pp. 531–537.

In the early 1980s, researchers theorized that managers pursue conglomerate mergers for risk reduction motives that were personal instead of corporate. Managers recognize that less volatile cash flows result in a lower probability of a substantially poor performance in any single year and the concomitant threat of management dismissal. Therefore, managers are motivated to pursue conglomerate mergers in order to reduce their employment risk. Given the failing results of diversified firms, the **managerial risk reduction theory** seems to be quite insightful and implies that the diversification motive, once thought to be beneficial to stockholders, must now be viewed as a value-destroying rationale caused by agency problems.

managerial risk reduction theory
Implies that acquiring firms manager acquire other firms primarily to reduce the volatility of the combined firm's earnings, thus reducing the risk that they will be fired due to an unexpected decline in earnings.

CONCEPT REVIEW QUESTIONS

10. What characteristics surrounding a merger would lead you to conclude that it is motivated by value-maximizing managers rather than non-value-maximizing managers? What actions could directors or stockholders take to prevent non-value-maximizing mergers?

11. If you wanted to expand your operations into a foreign country with nebulous laws and an unstable political climate, would you favor internal or external expansion? Why?

12. What is the free cash flow theory of mergers? Why do you think that managers might be tempted to pursue size-increasing mergers even when these do not maximize value?

22.5 HISTORY AND REGULATION OF MERGERS AND ACQUISITIONS

Merger activity in the United States has been defined more by waves of concentrated intensity rather than by continuous activity over time. These waves tend to be positively related to high growth rates in the overall economy and are also related to "industry shocks," or industry-wide events such as deregulation that affect the corporate control activities of whole industries and lead to these merger waves. In this section, we identify the key merger waves in U.S. history and discuss the factors that led to their occurrence, as well as the corporate control regulation that has evolved over time.

The History of Merger Waves

The United States has witnessed five major merger waves in its history, most of which have been similar in nature. They begin with a robust stock market, and the types of mergers occurring in each wave reflect the current regulatory environment. Activity is generally concentrated in industries undergoing changes (shocks), and the merger waves tend to end with large declines in the stock market. The following discussion presents an overview of these waves.

The first major merger wave began in 1897 and was largely the result of a growing emphasis on a truly national economy rather than a grouping of regional economies. When interstate commerce became viable with the completion of transcontinental railroads, corporations sought expansion and market power through market extension mergers. The lax regulatory environment of that period also made in-market horizontal mergers popular. Thus, the first merger wave was primarily a market concentration phase in which monopolies were created in the mining and manufacturing industries. Merger activity peaked in 1899 in this wave and ended with the stock market crash of 1904.

Another merger wave began shortly after World War I with a zeal for consolidation equal to that of the first wave. However, Theodore Roosevelt's administration had strengthened enforcement of antitrust laws in the early 1900s, limiting the ability to create a monopoly through merger in this second wave. Instead, horizontal combinations created oligopolies within industries rather than one dominant monopoly. Heavily concentrated industries, such as mining and manufacturing, turned to vertical mergers in an attempt to benefit from integration, as further consolidation was not possible. Much like the first wave, the second wave was sparked by the desire to create national rather than regional brands. Transportation services improved with the advent of motor vehicles, and the capability of marketing a national brand became a more realistic possibility with the invention and proliferation of the radio. Also like the first wave, the second wave ended with a stock market decline, the infamous 1929 crash.

Conglomerate mergers set the tone for the third merger wave of the 1960s. A combination of two forces led to the preference for diversification over consolidation in this wave. First, the Celler-Kefauver Act of 1950 created a heightened level of antitrust enforcement because it gave the federal government greater ammunition to deny horizontal and vertical mergers. Second, managers began experimenting with the concept of diversification at the firm level. Corporations became portfolios of business units; the diversification across different industries was supposed to reduce the risk of the corporation and the volatility of its cash flows in the same manner as portfolio diversification. These "portfolio" corporations became known as conglomerates. The push for conglomeration was so great during this wave that approximately 70 percent of the mergers that took place in the 1960s were either pure conglomerate or product extension mergers. Conglomerate giants reached their heyday during this era, only to underperform the overall stock market in later years. This wave ended with the stock market decline of 1969.

The most interesting and dramatic merger wave occurred in the 1980s. Initiated by the more lax regulatory emphasis of the Reagan administration, the fourth merger wave saw a shift back to corporate specialization and witnessed such occurrences as junk bond financing, hostile takeovers, corporate raiders, greenmail, LBOs, MBOs, and poison pills. One distinguishing characteristic of this merger wave is how junk bond financing transformed the corporate control market. Prior to the 1980s, acquirers were usually larger firms with greater access to capital than the targets that they acquired. However, Michael Milken led the investment bank Drexel Burnham Lambert into a new era of junk bond financing that enabled previously minor players, who would not otherwise have had the financial resources, to become acquirers. Junk bond financing made LBOs and MBOs an active market and also led to several hostile bust-up takeovers, where junk bonds were used to acquire a firm, and then the proceeds from the sale of the acquired firm's assets were used to pay down the acquisition debt. Many antitakeover measures were adopted in the 1980s to prevent such hostile takeover attempts. This merger wave differs from previous ones in that it did not end with a major stock market decline. Many finance professionals felt that the wave would end with the stock market crash of 1987, yet many of the largest acquisitions of that decade took place between the time of the stock market crash and the end of the decade. Activity did decline at the end of the decade as the proliferation of junk bond financing became a concern (and the ability to obtain such financing waned with the increasing federal scrutiny of the practices of Drexel Burnham Lambert) and as the market players began to digest the magnitude of the $29 billion buyout of RJR Nabisco. This bidding contest culminated in a transaction value almost twice that of the next-largest deal in history at that time.

industry shock theory of takeovers
Explains much of the activity in the wave of mergers as a reaction to some external shock to the industry, such as a change in regulation or the introduction of a fundamentally new technology.

Friendly stock-swap mergers became the transaction method of choice in the fifth and latest wave of mergers, which began in 1993 and ended with the sharp drop in takeovers during 2001. Following the trend of corporate specialization from the fourth wave, the vast majority of mergers in this wave occurred between companies in the same industry. Federal regulators remained relatively open to horizontal mergers as merger activity in other countries also led to larger (and supposedly more efficient) foreign competitors. The **industry shock theory of takeovers** seems to explain much of the activity in this wave. The industries with heavy merger activity were health care, banking, and telecommunications, each having gone through a recent shock. Managed

Acquirer	Target	Transaction Value ($ billions)	Year
Vodafone AirTouch PLC (UK)	Mannesmann AG (Germany)	$202.8	2000
America Online Inc. (US)	Time Warner Inc. (US)	164.7	2001
Pfizer Inc.(US)	Warner-Lambert Co. (US)	89.2	2000
Exxon Corp.(US)	Mobil Corp. (US)	78.9	1999
Glaxo Wellcome PLC (UK)	SmithKline Beecham (UK)	76.0	2000
Travelers Group Inc. (US)	Citicorp (US)	72.6	1998
SBC Communications Inc. (US)	Ameritech Corp. (US)	62.6	1999
NationsBank Corp. (US)	BankAmerica Corp. (US)	61.6	1998
Vodafone Group PLC (UK)	AirTouch Communications (US)	60.3	1999
Pfizer (US)	Pharmacia (US/Europe)	58.0	2003

Table 22.3
Ten Largest Corporate Takeovers, Ranked by Transaction Value (as of March 31, 2004)

Source: Mergers & Acquisitions (SDC Publishing) and Mergers and Acquisitions Report (Thomson Financial).

care affected health care, and deregulation and rapid technological changes transformed the banking and telecommunications industries. Merger activity in this wave surpassed that in all the others, reaching $3.4 trillion in aggregate transaction value in the peak year of 2000. Of this aggregate value, slightly less than $1.8 trillion was generated from deals completed in the United States and about $1.6 billion from deals outside the United States. The total value of mergers worldwide fell by half to $1.7 trillion in 2001, then to $1.21 trillion in 2002 and $1.33 trillion in 2003. During the first quarter of 2004, however, global M&A volume increased sharply to $535 billion. Table 22.3 details the ten largest corporate mergers of all time.

SMART PRACTICES VIDEO

David Baum, Co-head of M&A for Goldman Sachs in the Americas

"Today cross-border transactions are about a quarter of the overall M&A business."

See the entire interview at **SMARTFinance**

Regulation of Corporate Control Activities

The legal environment affecting mergers evolved from a state of virtually no regulation during the first merger wave to what is currently a relatively complex nexus of interrelated legal issues, including antitrust enforcement, tender offer regulation, and laws regarding the actions of managers and directors and even actions of state and international regulators. This section addresses these legal issues and their ramifications for the decision to merge.

Antitrust Regulation. **Antitrust** legislation is intended to prevent an anticompetitive business environment. Obviously, mergers—especially horizontal mergers—often represent the most expedient manner to create corporate giants with the power to control prices in their markets. For this reason, antitrust enforcement encompasses the prevention of mergers that are deemed to have anticompetitive effects. Antitrust regulation began with the loophole-ridden Sherman Antitrust Act of 1890, was reinforced by the Clayton Act of 1914, and then was further strengthened by the Celler-Kefauver Act of 1950. The level of antitrust enforcement, administered in part by the Department of Justice (DOJ), tends to be related to the philosophy of the governing executive administration. Following passage of the Celler-Kefauver Act, antitrust laws were relatively strictly enforced until the Reagan administration took office and relaxed antitrust enforcement. Aside from a few noted cases, antitrust enforcement has remained more lax since the 1980s.[20] The following sections outline the major aspects of various antitrust laws as well as the guidelines established by the regulatory agencies for determining the anticompetitive potential of a merger.

antitrust
Legislation intended to prevent mergers that are deemed to have anticompetitive effects on the business environment.

20. Such exceptions include the DOJ's refusal to allow Microsoft and Intuit to merge in 1994 and its continued pursuit of Microsoft for anticompetitive business practices.

Table 22.4
Major U.S. Antitrust Legislation

Legislation (year)	Purpose of Legislation
Sherman Antitrust Act (1890)	Enacted to prevent the formation of trusts (similar to monopolies) and prohibited "every contract, combination, . . . , or conspiracy in the restraint of trade; allowed aggrieved parties or the federal government to sue violators for triple damages[a]
Clayton Act (1914)	Created to strengthen the Sherman Act after a series of Supreme Court rulings rendered Sherman as unenforceable due to its broad and ambiguous prohibitions against monopolistic actions; outlawed specific business activities such as price discrimination, tying contracts, concurrent service on competitors' boards of directors, and acquisition of a competitor's stock in order to lessen competition
Federal Trade Commission Act (1914)	Established the Federal Trade Commission (FTC) as a regulatory agency to complement the Justice Department (DOJ) as an antitrust watchdog
Celler-Kefauver Act (1950)	Closed the "Section 7 loophole" of the Clayton Act, which did not prohibit the acquisition of a competitor's assets in order to lessen competition; severely limited the possibility of obtaining approval for a horizontal merger
Hart-Scott-Rodino Act (1976)	Allowed the FTC or DOJ to rule on the permissibility of a merger prior to consummation

[a] In an ironic example of the triple damages awarded under the provisions of the Sherman Act, the United States Football League (USFL) won its antitrust case against the National Football League (NFL) in 1986. However, the damage was determined to be $1 and the USFL folded before the next season—despite its gargantuan $3 award.

Antitrust Laws. The Sherman Antitrust Act initiated antitrust regulation in 1890 and has been amended and modified many times since. The last major federal antitrust legislation was enacted in 1976, but the interpretation of antitrust laws is a dynamic process in which regulatory agencies maintain an ongoing dialogue on the application of the laws. Table 22.4 lists the major federal antitrust laws.

Determination of Anticompetitiveness. Much like the business concentration classifications of the Federal Trade Commission (FTC), the measures and determinants of anticompetitiveness have evolved over time. The DOJ established the first set of merger guidelines for determining anticompetitiveness in 1968 and modified them in 1982, 1984, and 1992. The following guidelines are those currently utilized by the DOJ and FTC.

The 1982 guidelines introduced the use of the Herfindahl-Hirschman Index (HHI), a variant of the Herfindahl Index defined earlier, to determine market concentration in the same manner that we used the index to measure business concentration earlier in the chapter. The DOJ determines the anticompetitive effect of a merger by evaluating that merger's impact on the HHI of the industry involved. The HHI is calculated as the sum of the squares of each company's percentage of sales within a market (industry). This HHI is then used to establish a range of concentration levels within a market or industry:

HHI > 1,800	Highly concentrated
HHI = 1,000–1,800	Moderately concentrated
HHI < 1,000	Not concentrated

Table 22.5
Determination of Anticompetiitiveness—An Illustration of the Use of the Herfindahl-Hirschman Index (HHI)

Premerger Concentration			Postmerger Concentration					
Firm	Market Share (%)	Market Share Squared	Firm	Market Share (%)	Market Share Squared	Firm	Market Share (%)	Market Share Squared
1	20%	0.0400	1	20%	0.0400	1 + 2	35%	0.1225
2	15	0.0225	2	15	0.0225	3	15	0.0225
3	15	0.0225	3	15	0.0225	4	15	0.0225
4	15	0.0225	4	15	0.0225	5	15	0.0225
5	15	0.0225	5	15	0.0225	6	10	0.0100
6	10	0.0100	6	10	0.0100	7	5	0.0025
7	5	0.0025	7 + 8	10	0.0100	8	5	0.0025
8	5	0.0025						
Sum		0.1450			0.1500			0.2050
HHI		1,450			1,500			2,050
Concentration		Moderate			Moderate			High

Mergers resulting in an HHI measure in the highly concentrated category are the most likely to be challenged. Consider the example in Table 22.5. The premerger HHI of this industry is 1,450 (moderately concentrated). A merger between Company 7 and Company 8 would reduce the number of competitors in the industry, but the marginal impact of a merger between the two smallest players in the industry would increase the HHI to only 1,500 and would likely not face a challenge. However, a merger between the two largest firms in the industry would result in an HHI of 2,050—moving this industry from moderately to highly concentrated and likely prompting a challenge by the DOJ or FTC.

Realizing the efficiency-enhancing benefits of economies of scale and scope, which come only from increased size, the regulatory authorities developed an alternative measure to determine the anticompetitiveness of a merger. This alternative, an elasticity measure, offers an advantage over the strict use of the HHI: the elasticity measure does not necessarily deem a merger to be anticompetitive because of fewer competitors in a highly concentrated industry. Instead, an elasticity measure determines if a merged firm will have the market power to control prices in its market. The DOJ uses a "5 percent rule" to measure elasticity: if a 5 percent increase in price results in a greater than 5 percent decline in demand in a market, then that market is elastic. Elastic markets are less likely to be adversely impacted by a merger and also less likely to be strictly governed by the HHI measure.

APPLYING THE MODEL

The failed 1997 merger attempt of Staples and Office Depot exemplifies the role of regulatory agencies in preventing what are deemed to be anticompetitive combinations. On September 4, 1996, Staples and Office Depot announced their intent to merge in a $3.4 billion deal. At the time, Office Depot and Staples were the largest and second-largest office supply superstores, respectively. Of the $14.0 billion in sales in this market, Office Depot had a market share of $6.6 billion, followed by Staples with $4.1 billion, and the only other major competitor, OfficeMax, with sales of $3.3 billion.

As permitted under the Hart-Scott-Rodino Act, the Federal Trade Commission (FTC) reviewed the proposed merger for anticompetitive effects and requested more information from the companies at the end of the initial review period. At the end of the second review, the FTC concluded that the proposed merger would have an anticompetitive impact if allowed to be consummated and rejected the merger proposal. One of the key points cited by the FTC in its rejection was the market power that the merged firm would be able to wield in those markets where no stores other than Staples or Office Depot existed (the 5 percent rule). In order to remedy this obstacle, Staples and Office Depot proposed to sell sixty-three stores to OfficeMax in the geographic market where both Staples and Office Depot were located. The FTC again rejected the merger and threatened to sue the companies in federal court if they attempted to pursue their merger. The FTC further threatened that if it could not prevent the merger under the Hart-Scott-Rodino Act through its federal lawsuit, it would continue to pursue the merged firm for antitrust violations.

The managers of both companies continued to fight for their merger, despite the FTC's threats. When presenting their argument to the federal judge assigned to the case, lawyers for the companies presented the companies' willingness to sell off stores in order to satisfy the FTC and enhance competition and also contended that the FTC had improperly defined their industry when determining the Herfindahl-Hirschman Index. The FTC had limited their industry classification to office supply superstores with three competitors and an HHI of 3,634 (already highly concentrated), which would increase to 6,394 after the merger. Lawyers for the companies, however, stated that the appropriate industry classification should be discount retailers and should include such discount retailers as Wal-Mart and Kmart in addition to office supply stores. The judge in the case disagreed with the companies' lawyers and sided with the FTC in barring the merger from taking place. The managers of Staples and Office Depot announced their intentions to abandon their merger plans shortly thereafter.

Although merger guidelines have evolved over time and now seem to be less hostile toward horizontal combinations, the DOJ and FTC remain active enforcers of antitrust laws. One merely needs to ask the managers of Staples and Office Depot about this active enforcement. As we mention above and in the section on horizontal mergers, the managers of these corporations attempted to take advantage of the elasticity measure in 1997 with their contention that their true competitors were all the discount retailers rather than OfficeMax alone, the only other major discount office supply chain. The managers explained that the merger of their two companies would have a negligible impact on prices in the discount retailing market. Although this latter argument was probably true, the DOJ and FTC did not accept the managers' contention that their market was too narrowly defined and disapproved the merger.

Other Antitrust Considerations. Managers contemplating a merger now face antitrust scrutiny from sources other than U.S. federal regulators. Globalization and proactive state regulators have created more recent obstacles to merger approval. Individual states have become more active participants in the oversight of anticompetitive business practices since the 1990s. State attorneys general from fourteen states joined the antitrust lawsuit first lodged against Microsoft by the Justice Department in 1994. Even after the federal government abandoned its case against Microsoft in 2001 in an effort to settle the case out of court, many of the states refused to abandon their status as plaintiffs against Microsoft. Although only California has expressed an open willingness to file suit in opposition to a merger on the grounds of anticompetitiveness, the vigilance of the plaintiff states in the antitrust case against Microsoft indicates that state regulators could become an impediment to future mergers.

The Williams Act. During the conglomerate merger wave of the 1960s, hostile tender offers became an increasingly frequent and controversial means to facilitate takeovers. The controversy over these tender offers revolved around target shareholders' inability to evaluate the terms of the tender offers in the often short periods of time for which they were open and around the abuses of higher takeover premiums being offered to select shareholders. In response to this controversy, the Williams Act passed in 1967 and was enacted in 1968 as an amendment to the Securities and Exchange Commission Act of 1934. Section 13 of the Williams Act introduced ownership disclosure requirements, and Section 14 created rules for the tender offer process.

Ownership Disclosure Requirements. Section 13-d of the Williams Act now requires public disclosure of ownership levels beyond 5 percent.[21] This section of the act mandates that any individual, group of individuals acting in concert, or firm must file a Schedule 13-d form within ten days of acquiring a 5 percent or greater stake in a publicly traded company. This disclosure sends a warning signal to the managers and stockholders of a corporation that a potential acquirer might be lurking about and provides background information on that potential acquirer. Stockholders or managers of the corporation may sue for damages if any material misrepresentation (such as initiating a later takeover attempt when the stated purpose of ownership is for investment purposes) is made on the form.[22]

Tender Offer Regulation. Whereas Section 13 of the Williams Act forces the disclosure of pertinent information regarding a potential acquirer, Section 14 governs stock acquisitions via tender offers. Prior to the passage of the Williams Act, tender offers were largely unregulated open calls to the shareholders of public companies to tender (sell) their shares at offered prices. Tender offers could be completed swiftly and repeated at different offer prices if desired. Section 14 changed this free-form nature of the tender offer market to a much more restrictive and structured process. Any party initiating a tender offer must file a Schedule 14-d-1 form (a tender offer statement). Managers of tender offer targets are then required to file a Schedule 14-d-9 form, which contains their recommendation to shareholders on whether to accept, reject, or refrain from supplying an opinion on the offer.

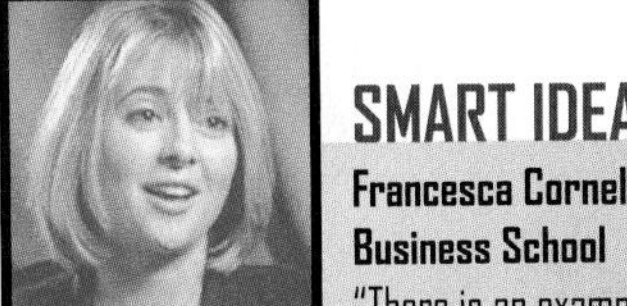

SMART IDEAS VIDEO

Francesca Cornelli, London Business School

"There is an example that shows how crucial risk arbitrage can be to the success of a takeover."

See the entire interview at SMARTFinance

Section 14 provides structural rules and restrictions on the tender offer process in addition to establishing disclosure requirements. These rules include a minimum tender offer period of twenty days, the right of target shareholders to withdraw shares already tendered at any time during the tender offer period, and the requirement that the acquirer accept all shares tendered and that all tendered shares will receive the same price. Again, the intent of these rules is to prevent a "sneak attack" in which target shareholders have no opportunity to evaluate the terms of a tender offer and also to assure fair treatment for all target shareholders who tender their shares.

Other Legal Issues Concerning Corporate Control

Federal securities laws also regulate the actions of managers in corporate control events. The high-profile insider-trading scandals of the 1980s generated a keen interest in these laws. Individual states have also become more interested in promoting corporate control legislation after witnessing business practices that were perceived as detrimental to the welfare of the electorate. In recent years, many states have developed antitakeover and antitrust laws designed to regulate takeovers of corporations located in their states. We describe the major elements of these other federal and state corporate control laws in the following sections.

Laws Affecting Corporate Insiders. A variety of federal securities laws govern the actions of corporate managers and other individuals considered to be

21. The threshold was originally 10 percent but was dropped to 5 percent in 1970.

22. It is also illegal to "park" shares, which means engaging another individual to buy shares for you in order to avoid disclosure requirements.

COMPARATIVE CORPORATE FINANCE

Searching for Effective Corporate Governance and Value-Enhancing Mergers

Enron, WorldCom, Adelphia, Global Crossing, Qwest Communications, Tyco. These are but a few of the high-profile corporate bankruptcies or near failures that have destroyed shareholder wealth and shaken investor confidence in the years after the great 1990s bull market. Underlying the much-publicized accounting scandals and extraordinary executive compensation paid out in these American corporate failures is the ultimate factor that led to their demise—ineffective corporate governance. Stockholders, bondholders, employees, journalists, and politicians (of course) are all demanding to know, "Where were the boards of directors who were supposed to be monitoring the managers?" These same groups are demanding reforms to restore confidence in corporate America, and both domestic and international groups are also seeking corporate reforms.

One domestic reform had already taken place before the spate of corporate failures began. Beginning in 2001, the Financial Accounting Standards Board (FASB) enacted Standards 141 and 142 to update and codify merger and acquisition accounting and the goodwill account created in these transactions. However, these two new standards were promulgated too late to prevent the old tricks being used in merger and acquisition accounting in the 1990s. Before the new standards were enacted, firms could manipulate merger and acquisition accounting rules to overstate their true financial performance. When the merger wave waned and the firms could no longer use their overvalued stock to fund acquisitions, the firms' true financial performance was revealed. Even with the new rules in place, Sam DiPiazza, CEO of accounting firm PricewaterhouseCoopers, has called for even more stringent accounting rules and implementation of international best accounting practices for U.S. corporations.

International proposals for corporate governance reform are also being considered. Governance structures in the United Kingdom and continental Europe are being discussed as possible alternatives to the typical governance structure in place in publicly traded U.S. corporations. In particular, two major British committees issued guidelines for more effective corporate governance during the 1990s. The three basic recommendations of the Cadbury Committee on the Financial Aspects of Corporate Governance (1992) and the Hempel Committee (1998) were that a corporation's chairman of the board and chief executive officer (CEO) always be separate persons, that the board of directors should have a majority of independent directors, and that no corporate insiders should serve on the board's audit committee. The similarity of capital markets in Britain and America appears to make these guidelines implementable as listing policies for either the New York Stock Exchange or Nasdaq.

In many continental European corporations (especially in Germany), management responsibilities are split between two mutually exclusive groups—a management board and a supervisory board consisting of representatives from the government, financial institutions, labor unions, and other interested parties. Corporate managers do not serve on the supervisory board, which is charged with overseeing the management team. However, the continental governance system is much less consistent with the U.S. model than is the British system. First, hostile takeovers are virtually unheard of in continental Europe, whereas these are commonly used as a disciplining device in Great Britain and the United States. Second, unlike U.S. corporations, financial institutions (and oftentimes the government) have substantial ownership stakes in European corporations. On the other hand, the complete separation of a supervisory board and managers offers an appealing alternative for those seeking to reform U.S. corporate governance.

As the search continues for effective corporate governance structures in the United States and abroad, it has become clear that no country or system has perfected a corporate governance structure. Concurrent with the spectacular U.S. corporate failures that occurred during the spring and summer of 2002 were the precipitous declines in shareholder value and CEO ousters witnessed at French conglomerate Vivendi and German telecom giant Deutsche Telekom. These were followed by major scandals at Accord and Parmalat in 2003 and at Royal Dutch Shell in early 2004. Especially disconcerting to the European business community was the saga of Sir Christopher Gent, CEO of British telecom firm Vodafone. Gent had led Vodafone through the takeover of Mannesmann AG, the largest takeover in history. Unfortunately, the merger was ill-advised and led to a significant loss in shareholder wealth, but an increase in Gent's compensation and stock options. While U.S. reformers were looking to the United Kingdom for ideas on more effective corporate governance, British stockholders and institutional investors were complaining of the ineffective corporate governance that had allowed Gent to enhance his own wealth while stockholders continued to lose money. And the search for effective corporate governance goes on.

corporate insiders during corporate control events. The majority of these laws attempt to prevent informed trading on material nonpublic information (inside information), such as an upcoming takeover attempt known only to the insiders of the acquiring firm. Rule 10-b-5 dictated by the Securities and Exchange Commission outlaws material misrepresentation of information used in the sale or purchase of a security. Trading on inside information about a pending merger is such a material misrepresentation because material information (news of the merger) is being withheld. Also, SEC Rule 14-e-3 specifically forbids trading on inside information in tender offers. The Insider Trading Sanctions Act of 1984 strengthened both SEC rules with triple damage awards. Managers are also restricted from issuing misleading information regarding merger negotiations and may be sued if they deny the existence of merger negotiations that are actually taking place.

SMART PRACTICES VIDEO

David Baum, Co-head of M&A for Goldman Sachs in the Americas

"When the poison pill was introduced, it changed the landscape related to hostile takeovers."

See the entire interview at SMARTFinance

The SEC has applied the "misappropriation theory" of trading on inside information to extend the prohibitions of Rules 10-b-5 and 14-e-3 to other individuals who trade on inside information but are not corporate insiders. This theory holds that non-insiders who profit from trading on misappropriated inside information are equally guilty of violations of insider-trading rules. The SEC applied the misappropriation theory in a highly publicized case in which it brought suit against a *Wall Street Journal* columnist who traded in the stocks about which he wrote before his column was published. Because he realized the impact of his column on a stock's price, the columnist was charged with trading on material nonpublic information, even though he was not a corporate insider.

Section 16 of the Securities and Exchange Act establishes a monitoring facility for the trading of corporate insiders. Under Section 16-a, insiders must report the sale or purchase of any shares in their affiliated corporation. Section 16-b, the "short swing rule" section, permits a corporation or its shareholders to sue a corporate insider for any profits garnered from buy-sell transactions occurring within a six-month cycle.

State Laws. Individual states have increasingly regulated corporate control activities over the years. Some states have adopted various antitakeover and anti-bust-up provisions and formed antitrust agencies that restrict corporate control activities in their states beyond the level of federal regulations.

Antitakeover and anti-bust-up provisions include voting initiatives such as super-majority voting, which requires that large majorities (usually 67 percent) approve a takeover, and control share provisions that require the approval of target shareholders before a potential acquirer may even buy a substantial number of shares in the target firm. Fair price provisions and cash-out statutes are also popular measures that further restrict tender offers. **Fair price provisions** ensure that all target shareholders receive the same offer price in any tender offers initiated by the same acquirer, limiting the ability of acquirers to buy minority shares cheaply with a two-tiered offer. **Cash-out statutes** are "all-or-none" rules that disallow a partial tender offer/acquisition of a company and the ability to control that company with less than 100 percent ownership. Business combination rules prevent the bust-up or other major restructuring of a company that is taken over. These provisions are often used in conjunction with each other, and individual state laws must be reviewed when considering a takeover to determine if these provisions are present, and, if so, what impact their presence will have on the value of the takeover. The formation of state-level antitrust regulatory boards is an even more recent trend in state corporate control regulation. California has filed antitrust lawsuits and merger injunctions. Other states are following California's lead and have become more active antitrust monitors as well.

fair price provisions
Antitrust rules that ensure that all target shareholders receive the same offer price in any tender offers initiated by the same acquirer, limiting the ability of acquirers to buy minority shares cheaply with a two-tiered offer.

cash-out statutes
Antitrust "all-or-none" rules that disallow a partial tender offer/acquisition of a company and the ability to control that company with less than 100 percent ownership.

International Regulation of Mergers and Acquisitions

International regulatory authorities, especially in Europe, have become a force to be reckoned with for those companies attempting large-scale mergers. The European Commission (EC) first signaled its more stringent antitrust regulatory authority in 1999, when it vetoed the proposed merger of U.S. communications giants WorldCom and Sprint. The EC expressed concerns about the pricing power that the combined firm could have if the second- and third-largest U.S. communications firms (behind industry leader AT&T) merged to become the first- or second-largest communications firm in many European markets. The managers of both WorldCom and Sprint abandoned their effort to merge after the EC's decision. EC competition commissioner Mario Monti created an international stir in 2001 when he denied the petition to merge filed by General Electric and Honeywell, although the merger had already been approved by U.S. antitrust authorities. Monti's stern defense of his position and denial of the petition on appeal sends a clear message that firms with international operations that are considering a merger must account for antitrust authorities outside the United States, even if the merger is between U.S. firms. Monti caused an even bigger stir when in early 2004 his commission sued Microsoft in an attempt to force the company to uncouple application packages from its operating system (Windows). The commission maintained that this tie gave Microsoft monopoly power. If successful, this lawsuit could seriously undermine Microsoft's global competitive position.

CONCEPT REVIEW QUESTIONS

13. Which industries do you anticipate will experience industry shocks that will spur merger activity in the near future?

14. How does the dynamic interpretation of antitrust laws affect managers' acquisition strategies? What impact does the involvement of individual states have on the acquisition decision?

15. Do you believe that increasing global competition will further heighten merger activity?

22.6 SUMMARY AND CONCLUSIONS

- Mergers and acquisitions are major corporate finance events that, when executed efficiently and with the proper motives, can help managers realize their ultimate goal of maximizing shareholder wealth. Merging firms may be integrated in a number of ways, and the circumstances surrounding the merger determine the means of integration. Transactions may be hostile or friendly; may be financed by cash, stock, debt, or some combination of the three; and may increase, preserve, or decrease the acquirer's level of business concentration.
- Research on corporate control is bountiful. Major empirical findings include the following: target shareholders almost always win but acquirers' returns are mixed. The combined value of merging firms also increases, especially in nonconglomerate combinations. The highest announcement-period returns are found in mergers between well-managed acquirers and poorly managed targets. Long-term performance is highest for focus-increasing deals financed with cash and lowest for diversifying mergers financed with stock.
- Managers have either value-maximizing or non-value-maximizing motives for pursuing mergers. Value-maximizing motives include expansion into new markets, capturing size economies and other synergies, establishing market power, or generating free cash flow to make better investments. Agency problems result in such non-value-maximizing motives as empire building, entrenchment, hubris, and diversification.

- Merger activity occurs in waves spurred by industry-wide events such as deregulation. Domestically, we have witnessed five major merger waves: a turn-of-the-twentieth-century wave of horizontal mergers, a 1920s wave of vertical mergers, the 1960s wave of conglomerate mergers, the 1980s wave that deconstructed many of the 1960s conglomerates, and a recent wave of deregulation-based mergers and consolidations made in preparation for an increasingly global economy. Antitrust enforcement at the time affects activity in each of these waves.
- Corporate control activities are regulated by federal, and increasingly, state and international authorities. Federal antitrust legislation has been developed over the course of the century, but its enforcement ebbs and flows with the executive administration in office. The Williams Act established disclosure requirements for ownership in public corporations, as well as regulation of tender offers. Federal securities laws also prohibit corporate insiders from trading on the nonpublic information of a pending takeover.

SELF-TEST PROBLEMS

Answers to Self-Test Problems appear in Appendix D at back of book. Answers to the Concept Review Questions throughout the chapter appear at http://megginson.swlearning.com.

ST22-1. Mega Service Corporation (MSC) is offering to exchange 2.5 shares of its own stock for each share of target firm Norman Corporation stock as consideration for a proposed merger. There are ten million Norman Corp shares outstanding, and its stock price was $60 before the merger offer. MSC's preoffer stock price was $30. What is the control premium percentage offered? Now suppose that when the merger is consummated eight months later, MSC's stock price drops to $25. At that point, what is the control premium percentage and total transaction value?

ST22-2. You are the director of capital acquisitions for Morningside Hotel Company. One of the projects you are deliberating is the acquisition of Monroe Hospitality, a company that owns and operates a chain of bed-and-breakfast inns. Susan Sharp, Monroe's owner, is willing to sell her company to Morningside only if she is offered an all-cash purchase price of $5 million. Your project analysis team estimates that the purchase of Monroe Hospitality will generate the following after-tax marginal cash flow:

Year	Cash Flow
1	$1,000,000
2	1,500,000
3	2,000,000
4	2,500,000
5	3,000,000

If you decide to go ahead with this acquisition, it will be funded with Morningside's standard mix of debt and equity, at the firm's weighted average (after-tax) cost of capital of 9 percent. Morningside's tax rate is 30 percent. Should you recommend acquiring Monroe Hospitality to your CEO?

INTERNET RESOURCES

Note: *For updates to links, please go to the book's Web site at* http://megginson.swlearning.com

http://www.sec.gov/about/laws.shtml—"The Laws That Govern the Securities Industry" section of the U.S. Securities and Exchange Commission's Web site;

provides a brief overview of the six key laws that the SEC enforces, including those relating to tender offers and M&A regulations.

http://europa.eu.int/pol/comp/index_en.htm—The "Competition" section of the European Union's official Web site; describes the key legislation setting up this Commission, provides an overview of its enforcement philosophy, and describes key ongoing cases.

KEY TERMS

acquisition
antitakeover amendments
antitrust
backward integration
bear hug
bust-up
cash-out statutes
coinsurance of debt
consolidation
corporate control
corporate focus
divestiture
dual-class recapitalization
economies of scale
economies of scope
employee stock ownership plan (ESOP)
fair price provisions
financial synergies
forward integration
free cash flow theory of mergers
going-private transactions
goodwill
greenfield entry
greenmail
Herfindahl Index (HI)
horizontal merger
hubris hypothesis of corporate takeovers
industry shock theory of takeovers
internal capital markets
management buyout (MBO)
managerial entrenchment theory of mergers
managerial risk reduction theory
managerial synergies
managerialism theory of mergers
market extension merger
market power
merger
mixed offerings
operational synergy
poison pills
product extension mergers
pure conglomerate mergers
pure stock exchange merger
resource complementarities
reverse LBO
reverse merger
shark repellents
spin-off
split-off
split-up
statutory merger
strategic merger
subsidiary merger
synergy
takeover
tax-loss carryforwards
tender offer
tender-merger
vertical merger
white knights

QUESTIONS AND PROBLEMS

Q22-1. What is meant by a change in corporate control? List and describe the various ways in which a change of corporate control may occur.

Q22-2. What is a tender offer, and how can it be used as a mechanism to orchestrate a merger?

Q22-3. Differentiate between the different levels of business concentration created by mergers. Explain how the changing business environment has caused an evolution in the classification of concentration from the original FTC classification to the abbreviated FTC classification and now to the measures of overlap and focus.

Q22-4. Elaborate on the significance of the mode of payment for the stockholders of the target firm and their continued interest in the surviving firm. Specifically, which form of payment retains the stockholders of the target firm as stockholders in the surviving firm? Which payment form receives preferential tax treatment?

Q22-5. What is the signaling theory of mergers? What is the relationship between signaling and the mode of payment used in acquisitions? Is there a relationship between the mode of payment used in acquisitions and the level of insider shareholdings of acquiring firms?

Q22-6. Empirically, what are the wealth effects of corporate control activities? Who wins and who loses in corporate control contests? What explanations or theories are offered for the differences in returns of acquiring firms' common stocks? Why are higher takeover premiums paid in cash transactions than in stock transactions? How do other security holders fare in takeovers?

Q22-7. Relate the industry shock theory of mergers to the history of merger waves. What were the motivating factors for increased merger activity during each of the five major merger waves?

Q22-8. Under what conditions would external expansion be preferable to internal expansion? What is the ultimate decision criterion for determining the acceptability of any expansion strategy?

Q22-9. Delineate the value-maximizing motives for mergers. How are these motives interrelated?

Q22-10. Define the three types of synergy that may result from mergers. What are the sources of these synergies?

Q22-11. Explain how agency problems may lead to non-value-maximizing motives for mergers. Discuss the various academic theories offered as the rationale for these agency problem-induced motives.

Q22-12. Describe the relationship between conglomerate mergers and portfolio theory. What is the desired result of merging two unrelated businesses? Has the empirical evidence proven corporate diversification to be successful?

Q22-13. List the federal laws regulating antitrust and anticompetitive mergers. What are the actions governed by each law? How do the regulatory agencies determine anticompetitiveness?

Q22-14. What is the purpose of the Williams Act? What are the specific provisions of the act?

Q22-15. What are the restrictions faced by corporate insiders during corporate control events?

Q22-16. How have individual states become more active monitors of takeover activity?

Q22-17. What is the signaling theory of mergers? What is the relationship between signaling and the mode of payment used in acquisitions? Is there a relationship between the mode of payment used in acquisitions and the level of insider shareholdings of acquiring firms?

PROBLEMS

Overview of Corporate Control Activities

P22-1. Bulldog Industries is offering, as consideration for merger, target Blazerco 1.5 shares of their stock for each share of Blazerco. There are 1 million shares of Blazerco outstanding, and its stock price was $50 before the merger offer. Bulldog's preoffer stock price was $40. What is the control premium percentage offered? Now suppose that when the merger is consummated six months later, Bulldog's stock price drops to $30. At that point, what is the control premium percentage and total transaction value?

P22-2. You are the director of capital acquisitions for Crimson Software Company. One of the projects you are considering is the acquisition of Geekware, a private software company that produces software for finance professors. Dave Vanzandt, the owner of Geekware, is amenable to the idea of selling his enterprise to Crimson, but he has certain conditions that must be met before selling. The primary condition set forth is a nonnegotiable, all-cash purchase price of $20 million. Your project analysis team estimates that the purchase of Geekware will generate the following marginal cash flow:

Year	Cash Flow
1	$1,000,000
2	3,000,000
3	5,000,000
4	7,500,000
5	7,500,000

Of the $20 million in cash needed for the purchase, $5 million is available from retained earnings, with a required return of 12 percent, and the remaining $15 million will come from a new debt issue yielding 8 percent. Crimson's tax rate is 40 percent. Should you recommend acquiring Geekware to your CEO?

P22-3. Firm A plans to acquire Firm B. The acquisition would result in incremental cash flows for Firm A of $10 million in each of the first five years. Firm A expects to divest Firm B at the end of the fifth year for $100 million. The ß for Firm A is 1.1, which is expected to remain unchanged after the acquisition. The risk-free rate, R_f, is 7 percent, and the expected market rate of return, R_m, is 15 percent. Firm A is financed by 80 percent equity and 20 percent debt, and this leverage will also remain unchanged after the acquisition. Firm A pays interest of 10 percent on its debt, which will also remain unchanged after the acquisition.

a. Disregarding taxes, what is the maximum price that Firm A should pay for firm B?

b. Firm A has a stock price of $30 per share and 10 million shares outstanding. If Firm B shareholders are to be paid the maximum price determined in part (a) via a new stock issue, how many new shares will be issued, and what will be the postmerger stock price?

P22-4. Charger Incorporated and Sparks Electrical Company are competitors in the business of electrical components distribution. Sparks is the smaller firm and has garnered the attention of the management of Charger, as Sparks has taken away market share from the larger firm by increasing its sales force over the past few years. Charger is considering a takeover offer for Sparks and has asked you to serve on the acquisition valuation team that will turn into the due diligence team if an offer is made and accepted. Given the following information and assumptions:

a. Make your recommendation about whether or not the acquisition should be pursued.

b. Assume Sparks has accepted the takeover offer from Charger, and now the new subsidiary must be consolidated within Charger's financial statements. Taking Sparks' most recent balance sheet and a restated market value of assets of $295.6 million, calculate the goodwill that must be booked for this transaction.

Sparks Electrical Company
Condensed Balance Sheet
Previous Year
($ in millions)

	2005
Current assets	$ 12.2
Fixed assets	442.5
Total assets	$454.7
Current liabilities	$ 10.1
Long-term debt	150.0
Total liabilities	$160.1
Shareholders' equity	$294.6
Total liab. and equity	$454.7

Sparks Electrical Company
Condensed Income Statement
Previous Five Years
($ in millions)

	2005	2004	2003	2002	2001
Revenues	$1,626.5	$1,614.1	$1,485.2	$1,380.5	$1,373.4
Less: Cost of goods sold	1,488.1	1,490.9	1,359.5	1,271.4	1,268.0
Gross profit	$ 138.4	$ 123.2	$ 125.7	$ 109.1	$ 105.4
Selling, general & administrative expenses (SG&A)	$ 41.1	$ 36.8	$ 41.2	$ 35	$ 36.1
Noncash expense (depreciation & amortization)	7.3	6.7	7.1	6.6	6.4
Less: Operating expense	$ 48.4	$ 43.5	$ 48.3	$ 41.6	$ 42.5
Operating profit (EBIT)	$ 90.0	$ 79.7	$ 77.4	$ 67.5	$ 62.9
Less: Interest expense	11.5	12.0	12.0	12.0	12.0
Earnings before taxes (EBT)	$ 78.5	$ 67.7	$ 65.4	$ 55.5	$ 50.9
Less: Taxes paid	24.3	20.8	19.9	16.8	15.3
Net income	$ 54.2	$ 46.9	$ 45.5	$ 38.7	$ 35.6

Assumptions:

- Sparks would become a wholly owned subsidiary of Charger.
- Revenues will continue to grow at 4.3 percent for the next five years and will level off at 4 percent thereafter.
- Cost of goods sold will represent 95 percent of revenue going forward.
- Sales force layoffs will reduce SG&A expenses to $22 million next year with a 2 percent growth rate going forward.
- These layoffs and other restructuring charges are expected to result in expensed restructuring charges of $30 million, $15 million, and $5 million, respectively, over the next three years.
- Noncash expenses are expected to remain around $7 million going forward.
- Interest expenses are expected to remain around $11.5 million going forward.
- A tax rate of 31 percent is assumed going forward.
- Charger's cost of equity is 12 percent.
- Sparks' current market capitalization is $315.7 million.
- Charger will offer Sparks a takeover premium of 20 percent over current market capitalization.

P22-5. Referring to Problem 22-4, assume it is now two years after the acquisition of Sparks, and you must perform a goodwill impairment test of the subsidiary. Growth expectations have been lowered to 3 percent going forward. Using the following five-year projection of cash flows and a 12 percent cost of equity, estimate the value of the subsidiary beyond year 5, the current value of the subsidiary, the current value of goodwill, and any goodwill impairment. Total assets (excluding intangibles) are now $612.5 million, and total liabilities are $175.0 million.

Cash Flow Projections for Next Five Years

	2008	2009	2010	2011	2012
Revenues	$1,815.2	$1,869.7	$1,925.7	$1,983.5	$2,043.0
Less: Cost of goods sold @ 95% of revenue	1,724.4	1,776.2	1,829.5	1,884.3	1,940.9
Gross profit	$ 90.8	$ 93.5	$ 96.2	$ 99.2	$ 102.1
SG&A expense @ 2% growth rate going forward	$ 23	$ 23.5	$ 23.9	$ 24.4	$ 24.9
Noncash expense (depreciation & amortization)	7.0	7.0	7.0	7.0	7.0

Cash Flow Projections for Next Five Years

	2008	2009	2010	2011	2012
Less: Operating expense	$ 30.0	$ 30.5	$ 30.9	$ 31.4	$ 31.9
Operating profit (EBIT)	$ 60.8	$ 63.0	$ 65.3	$ 67.8	$ 70.2
Less: Interest expense	11.5	11.5	11.5	11.5	11.5
Less: Restructuring charges	5.0	0.0	0.0	0.0	0.0
Earnings before taxes (EBT)	$ 44.3	$ 51.5	$ 53.8	$ 56.3	$ 58.7
Less: Taxes paid	13.7	16.0	16.7	17.4	18.2
Net income	$ 30.6	$ 35.5	$ 37.1	$ 38.9	$ 40.5
Free cash flow	$ 54.1	$ 54.0	$ 55.6	$ 57.4	$ 59.0

THOMSON ONE Business School Edition

For instructions on using Thomson ONE, refer to the instructions provided with the Thomson ONE problems at the end of Chapters 1–6 or to "A Guide for Using Thomson ONE."

P22-6. There were many large write-downs of goodwill on the balance sheet after FASB 142 went into effect at the beginning of 2002. Specifically, this chapter refers to JDS Uniphase Corp. (ticker: @JDSU), AOL Time Warner (U:TWX), and Nortel Networks (C:NT) having to take multi-billion-dollar write-downs in 2002 for acquisitions completed in previous years. Look at the financial statements for the three companies for the fiscal year ending in 2002.[23] How much do intangible assets on the balance sheet change for the companies between 2001 and 2002 (between 2000 and 2001 for Nortel)? How much of a corresponding change do you observe under extraordinary charge—pretax on the income statement? Did the companies perform as badly as suggested by their net incomes in the year they took the extraordinary charge [look at Inc.(Dec.) in Cash & Short Term Investments in the cash flow statement]? Does this tell you if the goodwill write-down is a cash or a noncash expense?

Since these exercises depend upon real-time data, your answers will change continuously depending upon when you access the Internet to download your data.

MINICASE

Mergers, Acquisitions, and Corporate Control

Corporate control activities through merger and acquisition have recently changed the landscape of casino ownership with the acquisition of Mirage Resorts, Incorporated and then Mandalay Resort Group by MGM Grand, Incorporated and the acquisition of Caesars Entertainment Incorporated by Harrah's Entertainment Incorporated. As chief financial officer (CFO) of a competing casino, you feel that you should know all the particulars about corporate control activities, both to protect your company from takeover and to evaluate potential takeover targets. As such, you decide to find the answers to the following questions.

ASSIGNMENT

1. What are the different types of corporate control activities?
2. What are horizontal, vertical, and conglomerate mergers?
3. What returns do target and bidding firm shareholders realize around the announcement of acquisitions?
4. What are some of the motives for value-maximizing mergers and acquisitions?
5. What are some of the motives for mergers and acquisitions that are not value-maximizing?
6. What are the reasons for the various merger waves that have occurred throughout U.S. history?
7. Discuss the regulation of corporate control activities.

23. Look at the financial statements under Worldscope Financials. These financial statements break down items on the financial statements in greater detail.

Bankruptcy and Financial Distress

OPENING FOCUS

WorldCom Emerges from Bankruptcy with a New Name, New Management, and a New Capital Structure

The largest bankruptcy in U.S. history was finally coming to an end. On April 20, 2004, MCI Inc. emerged from Chapter 11 bankruptcy with an announcement that it had begun distributing securities and cash to its creditors according to a court-approved reorganization plan. MCI's chief executive officer, Michael Capellas, heralded a new beginning for his company, which had filed for bankruptcy court protection twenty-one months earlier—when the company was called WorldCom—after disclosing an $11 billion accounting fraud. At the time of its Chapter 11 filing, WorldCom had assets totaling nearly $104 billion and debts of $32 billion.

WorldCom shocked the business world when the company announced in June 2002 that it had fraudulently overstated $3.9 billion of expenses as capital expenditures, which had allowed it to book higher profits during the telecom boom years of 1998–2001. WorldCom chief financial officer Scott Sullivan was fired the day the accounting fraud was disclosed, and his exit followed that of founder and long-time CEO, Bernie Ebbers, who had been forced out in April 2002. Over the next two years, more than $7 billion in additional accounting errors and frauds were uncovered, bringing the total misstatements to $11 billion, and in a March 2004 restatement of its 2001 and 2002 financial results, the company wrote off over $74 billion in previously booked profits and goodwill.

WorldCom's trip through Chapter 11 bankruptcy, while painful, was also remarkably successful. With the bankruptcy court's blessing, creditors installed Michael Capellas (formerly CEO of Compaq Computer) as CEO in November 2002. He submitted a reorganization plan five months later that called for almost all of the company's debt to be converted into equity, and over 90 percent of WorldCom's creditors voted to approve this plan. Soon thereafter, Capellas also announced that the company would change its name from the tainted WorldCom to that of its principal consumer brand, MCI Inc. Therefore, when MCI finally emerged from Chapter 11 in April 2004, the company had a new name, a new management team, and an entirely new capital structure that in some ways gave it a competitive advantage over its more heavily indebted telecom competitors.

Source: "MCI Emerges From Bankruptcy," cnn.com (April 20, 2004), downloaded from http://money.cnn.com/2004/04/20/technology/mci_bankruptcy/index.htm. ■

LEARNING OBJECTIVES

After studying this chapter you should be able to:

- Describe the three major types of business failure, and discuss what each implies for the long-term prospects of the company;
- Explain what a voluntary settlement is, and discuss why these are only occasionally successful;
- Discuss the key differences between Chapter 7 and Chapter 11 bankruptcy filings;
- Explain how a reorganization plan is developed and implemented for a company that is in Chapter 11 bankruptcy;
- Understand how absolute priority rules are applied when a company is liquidated under a Chapter 7 bankruptcy process; and
- Discuss the importance of being able to predict when a firm will file for bankruptcy and discuss how effectively analysts can make these predictions.

A fundamental concept in economics is that competition drives markets toward a state of long-term equilibrium in which surviving companies produce at minimum average cost. This transition process eliminates firms using obsolete technologies, inefficient firms, and firms producing goods and services that are in excess supply. Consumers benefit because, in the long run, products are manufactured and sold at the lowest possible price. The mechanism through which inefficient firms leave the market is frequently bankruptcy, the legal procedure applied to businesses that fail.

In this chapter, we will examine first how and why firms fail. We then look at U.S. bankruptcy law and the ways that a business that has failed can resolve its difficulties, either voluntarily or involuntarily, through bankruptcy.

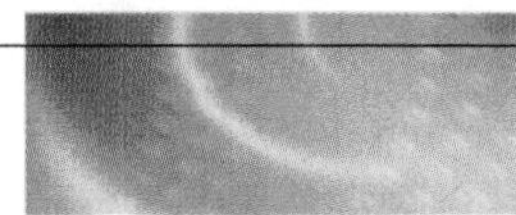

23.1 BUSINESS FAILURE FUNDAMENTALS

business failure
The unfortunate circumstance of a firm's inability to stay in business.

A **business failure** is an unfortunate circumstance. Although the majority of firms that fail do so within the first year or two of life, other firms grow, mature, and fail much later. The failure of a business can be viewed in a number of ways and can result from one or more causes.

Types of Business Failure

economic failure
A firm fails to earn a return that is greater than its cost of capital.

technical insolvency
A firm is unable to pay its liabilities as they come due, although its assets are still greater than its liabilities.

A firm can fail because its returns are negative or low. A firm that consistently reports operating losses will probably experience a decline in market value. If the firm fails to earn a return that is greater than its cost of capital, it can be viewed as having experienced **economic failure**. Negative or low returns, unless remedied, are likely to result eventually in a more serious type of failure.

A second type of failure, **technical insolvency**, occurs when a firm is unable to pay its liabilities as they come due. When a firm is technically insolvent, its assets are still

Company	Bankruptcy Date	Total Assets, Prebankruptcy
WorldCom	July 21, 2002	$103,914,000,000
Enron Corp.	December 2, 2001	63,392,000,000
Conseco	December 18, 2002	61,392,000,000
Texaco, Inc.	April 12, 1987	35,892,000,000
Financial Corp. of America	September 9, 1988	33,864,000,000
Pacific Gas and Electric Co.	April 6, 2001	21,470,000,000
MCorp	March 31, 1989	20,228,000,000
First Executive Corp.	May 13, 1991	15,193,000,000
Gibraltar Financial Corp.	February 8, 1990	15,011,000,000
FINOVA Group, Inc.	March 7, 2001	14,050,000,000
HomeFed Corp.	October 22, 1992	13,885,000,000
Southeast Banking Corporation	September 20, 1991	13,390,000,000
Reliance Group Holdings, Inc.	June 12, 2001	12,598,000,000
Imperial Corp. of America	February 28, 1990	12,263,000,000
Federal-Mogul Corp.	October 1, 2001	10,150,000,000
First City Bankcorp. of Texas	October 31, 1992	9,943,000,000
First Capital Holdings	May 30, 1991	9,675,000,000
Baldwin-United	September 26, 1983	9,383,000,000

Table 23.1
Largest Bankruptcies in U.S. History as of April 20, 2004

Sources: "MCI Emerges from Bankruptcy," CNNMoney.com, April 20, 2004 (available at http://money.cnn.com/2004/04/20/technology/mci_bankruptcy/index.htm) and Bankruptcydata.com, January 3, 2002 (http://www.bankruptcydata.com).

greater than its liabilities, but it is confronted with a **liquidity crisis**. If some of its assets can be converted into cash within a reasonable period, the company may be able to escape complete failure. For example, in February 2001, Amazon.com, the online retailer, had to deny that it was facing a liquidity crisis. "The company has never been in better shape," chief executive Jeff Bezos was quoted as saying. The company indeed survived and prospered, but at least one Amazon supplier said that it had limited the amount of business it does with Amazon. Limiting business with a retailer is a typical first step for a creditor trying to protect itself from loss. Other techniques include shortening the terms under which a creditor will extend credit or even asking for cash in advance.

liquidity crisis
A firm is unable to pay its liabilities as they come due because assets cannot be converted into cash within a reasonable period of time.

If a company cannot convert its assets into cash quickly enough, the result is the third and most serious type of failure, **insolvency bankruptcy**. Insolvency occurs when a firm's liabilities exceed the fair market value of its assets. Because the firm's assets equal the sum of its liabilities and stockholders' equity, the only way a firm that has more liabilities than assets can balance its balance sheet is to have a negative stockholders' equity. This means that the claims of creditors cannot be satisfied unless the firm's assets can be liquidated for more than their book value.

insolvency bankruptcy
A firm's liabilities exceed the fair market value of its assets.

Although an insolvent firm is often said to be "bankrupt," **bankruptcy** technically occurs only when a company enters bankruptcy court and effectively surrenders control of the firm to a bankruptcy judge. The failing firm may file for bankruptcy protection itself, or it may be forced into bankruptcy court (under certain conditions, discussed later in this chapter) by its creditors.

bankruptcy
Occurs only when a company enters bankruptcy court and effectively surrenders control of the firm to a bankruptcy judge.

Table 23.1 shows the largest bankruptcies in U.S. history through April 20, 2004. The largest U.S. bankruptcy was that of WorldCom in July 2002, as discussed in this chapter's Opening Focus. WorldCom followed very closely on the heels of Enron's massive bankruptcy in December 2001, the second largest in American history, and was followed only five months later by Conseco's bankruptcy, the third largest in U.S. history. In other words, the three largest bankruptcies in American financial history occurred within twelve months of each other and involved over $228 billion worth of prebankruptcy assets. Before Enron, the largest U.S. bankruptcies were that of Texaco in 1987 and Financial Corporation of America in September 1988. In December 2003, a massive scandal involving forged documents and fictitious cash accounts in the Cayman Islands forced the Italian milk company Parmalat into bankruptcy and landed key company executives in an Italian jail. Although Parmalat's accounts are still being unwound, it appears that this may well become the single largest bankruptcy in world financial history. Clearly, the early years of the twenty-first century have been interesting times for bankruptcy courts around the world.

Major Causes of Business Failure

Financial distress is the primary cause of business failure (as briefly discussed in Chapter 12). This, in turn, is often the result of mismanagement, which accounts for more than 50 percent of all business failures. Numerous specific managerial faults can cause the firm to fail. Overexpansion, poor financial actions, an ineffective sales force, and high production costs can all singly or in combination cause the ultimate failure of the firm. For example, poor financial actions include bad capital budgeting decisions based on unrealistic sales and cost forecasts, failure to identify all relevant cash flows, failure to assess risk properly, inadequate financial evaluation of the firm's strategic plans prior to making financial commitments, inconsistent or inadequate cash flow planning, and failure to control receivables and inventories. Because all major corporate decisions are eventually measured in terms of dollars, the financial manager may play a crucial role in avoiding or causing a business failure. One of the financial manager's key duties must therefore be to monitor the firm's financial pulse.

Economic activity can contribute to the failure of a firm, especially during economic downturns. The success of some firms runs countercyclical to economic activity, whereas other firms are unaffected by economic activity. For example, sewing machine sales are likely to increase during a recession because people are more willing to make their own clothes and less willing to pay for the labor of others. The sale of boats and other luxury items may decline during a recession, whereas sales of staple items, such as electricity, are likely to be unaffected. In terms of beta, the measure of nondiversifiable risk, a stock with a negative beta would be associated with a firm whose behavior is generally countercyclical to economic activity.

However, the fortunes of most firms are positively tied to the business cycle, so bankruptcy filings always spike upward during economic contractions. If the economy goes into a recession, sales may decrease abruptly, leaving the firm with high fixed costs and insufficient revenues to cover them. In addition, rapid rises in interest rates just prior to a recession can further contribute to cash flow problems and make it more difficult for the firm to obtain and maintain needed financing. If the recession is prolonged, the likelihood of survival decreases even further. A number of major business failures occurring during 2001 and 2002, such as those of the FINOVA Group and Reliance Group Holdings, resulted from overexpansion and the recessionary economy. On the other hand, the bankruptcy of Pacific Gas and Electric in 2001 directly resulted from policies enacted during a flawed deregulation of California's electricity market during the mid-1990s. Several other extremely large bankruptcies occurred during this period, including Adelphia, Global Crossing, Qwest Communications, and, of course, WorldCom, Enron, and Conseco.

A final cause of business failure is corporate maturity. Firms, like individuals, do not have infinite lives. Like a product, a firm goes through the stages of birth, growth, maturity, and eventual decline. The firm's management should attempt to prolong the growth stage through research, the development of new products, and mergers. Once the firm has matured and has begun to decline, it should seek to be acquired by another firm or liquidate before it fails. Effective management planning should help the firm postpone decline and ultimate failure.

APPLYING THE MODEL

Polaroid is an example of a company that has failed because of corporate maturity. Almost a decade ago, digital photography brought with it distant warnings of the demise of instant photography. Before long, computer chips would capture and store images and instant, self-developing film would disappear. That prediction came true most recently in the form of Polaroid's insolvency. The company, which dominated the instant photography business for years, filed for Chapter 11 bankruptcy protection (discussed later) on October 12, 2001. The stock price had fallen from nearly $50 per share in 1998 to 28 cents on October 11. Polaroid, it turns out, was unable to change with the times.

The company's troubles date back to the late 1980s when it went deeply into debt to fight off a hostile takeover bid. A string of strategic errors followed, including its failure to anticipate how much digital photography would cut into its instant film business. The company's latest generation of instant cameras has fallen flat because digital cameras for consumers are just as instant and much more versatile. Although the company tried to reorganize its debts and continue operating, this strategy failed and the firm's remaining assets were purchased by an investment group associated with Bank One of Ohio in an auction conducted by the bankruptcy court in July 2002. As often occurs in bankruptcies, Polaroid's shareholders (including employees) were effectively wiped out by the failed reorganization, and litigation by unsecured creditors against the investment group that acquired the renamed Primary PDC, Inc. was not settled until April 2004. Polaroid's unfunded pension liabilities were taken over by the federal government.

Sometimes the cause of a business failure is difficult to anticipate and can happen quite suddenly in response to an economic or political event. For example, ANC Rental Corp., the owner of the Alamo and National car rental chains, filed for Chapter 11 bankruptcy protection on November 13, 2001, as the downturn in the travel sector worsened the company's troubles. ANC claims to have been the hardest-hit car rental company after the September 11 terrorist attacks, mainly because most of its rental offices were at airports. "The drastic decline in travel after September 11 has taken a tremendous toll on our business, and our current capital and expense structure cannot absorb the shortfall," CEO Michael Egan was quoted as saying. ANC, which listed assets of nearly $6.5 billion, estimated it had more than 1,000 creditors at the time of its filing.

As it happens, ANC's trip through Chapter 11 bankruptcy was quite successful. The company was auctioned to a private investment group in June 2003 and exited the bankruptcy court's protection shortly thereafter. Renamed Vanguard Car Rental, the company announced plans in early 2004 to expand its operations in an effort to double its share of the car rental market back to the 4.5 percent level achieved in mid-2001.

CONCEPT REVIEW QUESTIONS

1. Are the occurrence of operating losses, technical insolvency, and bankruptcy independent, or are they likely to be related?

2. Why do the managers of a business allow its condition to deteriorate to the point where bankruptcy occurs? Why don't the shareholders intervene?

3. Explain how business failures help the economy overall.

23.2 VOLUNTARY SETTLEMENTS

When a firm becomes technically insolvent or bankrupt, it may arrange a **voluntary settlement** or **workout** with its creditors, which enables it to bypass many of the costs involved in legal bankruptcy proceedings. The debtor firm usually initiates the settlement, because such an arrangement may enable it to continue to exist or to be liquidated in a manner that gives the owners the greatest chance of recovering part of their investment. The debtor, possibly with the aid of a key creditor, arranges a meeting between itself and all its creditors. At the meeting, a committee of creditors is selected to investigate and analyze the debtor's situation and recommend a plan of action. The committee discusses its recommendations with both the debtor and the creditors and draws up a plan for sustaining or liquidating the firm.

voluntary settlement
A firm that becomes technically insolvent or bankrupt may make an arrangement with its creditors that enables it to bypass many of the costs involved in legal bankruptcy proceedings.

workout
A firm that becomes technically insolvent or bankrupt may make an arrangement with its creditors that enables it to bypass many of the costs involved in legal bankruptcy proceedings.

Voluntary Reorganization

Generally, the rationale for sustaining a firm is that it is reasonable to believe that the firm's recovery is feasible. By sustaining the firm, the creditor can continue to receive business from it. A number of strategies are commonly used to implement a **voluntary reorganization.** An **extension** is an arrangement wherein the firm's creditors are promised payment in full, although not immediately. Usually, when creditors grant an extension, they require the firm to make cash payments for purchases until all past debts have been paid. By now, you will probably recognize this as another example where the "marginal benefits equal or exceed marginal costs" decision rule will apply to managerial decision-making. Creditors will agree to a voluntary reorganization, rather than pushing for a formal bankruptcy filing, if the expected payoff (net of transactions costs) from voluntary negotiations is higher than the expected payoff after legal bankruptcy proceedings.

voluntary reorganization
A strategy that sustains a firm so that the creditor can continue to receive business from it.

extension
An arrangement wherein a firm's creditors are promised payment in full, although not immediately.

A second arrangement, called a **composition**, is a pro rata cash settlement of creditor claims. Instead of receiving full payment for their claims, as in the case of an extension, creditors receive only a partial payment. A uniform percentage of each dollar owed is paid in satisfaction of each creditor's claim.

composition
A pro rata cash settlement of creditor claims.

A third arrangement is **creditor control**. In this case, the creditor committee may decide that replacing the operating management is the only feasible way to maintain the firm. The committee may then take control of the firm and operate it until all claims have been settled. Sometimes, a plan involving some combination of extension, composition, and creditor control will result. An example of this would be a settlement whereby the debtor agrees to pay a total of 75 cents on the dollar in three annual installments of 25 cents on the dollar. The creditors also agree to sell additional merchandise to the firm on thirty-day terms, if a new management team that is acceptable to them replaces the existing managers.

creditor control
The creditor committee takes control of the firm and operates it until all claims have been settled.

Voluntary Liquidation

After the creditor committee has investigated the firm's situation, made recommendations, and held talks with the creditors and the debtor, the only acceptable course of action may be to liquidate the firm. **Liquidation** involves winding up the firm's operations, selling off its assets, and distributing the proceeds to creditors. Liquidation can be carried out in two ways, privately or through the legal procedures provided by bankruptcy law. If the debtor firm is willing to accept liquidation, legal procedures may not be required. Generally, avoiding litigation enables the creditors to obtain quicker and higher settlements. However, all the creditors must agree to a private liquidation for it to be feasible.

liquidation
Winding up a firm's operations, selling off its assets, and distributing the proceeds to creditors.

The objective of the voluntary liquidation process is to recover as much per dollar owed as possible. Under voluntary liquidation, common stockholders, who are the firm's true owners, cannot receive any funds until the claims of all other parties have been satisfied. A common procedure is a creditors meeting at which they make an **assignment** by passing the power to liquidate the firm's assets to an adjustment bureau, a trade association, or a third party that is designated the *assignee*. The assignee's job is to liquidate the assets, obtaining the best price possible. The assignee is sometimes referred to as **trustee**, because it is entrusted with the title to the company's assets and the responsibility to liquidate them efficiently. Once the trustee has liquidated the assets, it distributes the recovered funds to the creditors and owners (if any funds remain for the owners). The final action in a private liquidation is for the creditors to sign a release attesting to the satisfactory settlement of their claims. If a voluntary settlement for a failed firm cannot be agreed upon, the creditors can force the firm into bankruptcy. Because of bankruptcy proceedings, the firm may be either reorganized or liquidated.

An alternative to liquidation of the firm is for it to be acquired. Merger with a financially sound company may allow the firm suffering from financial distress to return to profitability and continue as a going concern.

assignment
An agreement of the creditors by which they pass the power to liquidate the firm's assets to an adjustment bureau, a trade association, or a third party.

trustee
In bankruptcy, someone appointed by a judge to replace a firm's current management team and to oversee liquidation or reorganization.

Bankruptcy Reform Act of 1978
The governing bankruptcy legislation in the United States today.

CONCEPT REVIEW QUESTIONS

4. If you were a supplier and creditor to a company that had undergone a voluntary reorganization, would you continue to do business with the company?

5. If you were a creditor of a company that was undergoing a voluntary reorganization, what would be the advantages and disadvantages from your perspective of handling it as an extension, composition, or creditor control?

6. Why would a firm's shareholders agree to a voluntary liquidation if the business had a negative net worth, and they could expect to receive nothing?

23.3 BANKRUPTCY LAW IN THE UNITED STATES

As already stated, bankruptcy in the legal sense occurs when the firm cannot pay its bills or when its liabilities exceed the fair market value of its assets and the firm is forced into bankruptcy court. In either of these situations, a firm may be declared legally bankrupt. However, creditors generally attempt to avoid forcing a firm into bankruptcy if it appears to have opportunities for future success.

The governing bankruptcy legislation in the United States today is the **Bankruptcy Reform Act of 1978**, which significantly modified earlier bankruptcy legislation. This law contains eight odd-numbered (1 through 15) and one even-numbered (12) chapters. Several of these chapters would apply in the instance of failure; the two key ones are Chapters 7 and 11.

Chapter 7 of the Bankruptcy Reform Act of 1978 details the procedures for liquidating a failed firm. This chapter typically comes into play once it has been determined that a fair, equitable, and feasible basis for the reorganization of a failed firm does not exist (although a firm may of its own accord choose not to reorganize and may instead go directly into liquidation). Chapter 7 includes the rules, known as **absolute priority rules (APR)**, that determine the order in which creditor claims are to be paid. As described in detail in Section 23.5, the APR specify which claimants are to be paid first, and in full, before any payments can be made to more junior claimants.

Chapter 11 outlines the procedures for reorganizing a failed or failing firm, whether its petition is filed voluntarily or involuntarily. If a workable reorganization

Chapter 7
Section of the Bankruptcy Reform Act of 1978 that details the procedures to be followed when liquidating a failed firm.

absolute priority rules (APR)
Rules contained in Chapter 7 of the Bankruptcy Reform Act of 1978 that specify the procedure by which secured creditors are paid first, then unsecured creditors, then preferred shareholders, and finally common stockholders.

Chapter 11
Section of the Bankruptcy Reform Act of 1978 that outlines the procedures for reorganizing a failed or failing firm, whether its petition is filed voluntarily or involuntarily.

Table 23.2
Business and Nonbusiness Bankruptcy Cases Filed in U.S. Bankruptcy Courts, by Chapter of the Bankruptcy Code, 1980–2003

Source: United States Bankruptcy Courts.

Fiscal Year[a]	Total Filings	Business Filings[b]		Nonbusiness Filings	
		Chapter 7	Chapter 11	Total	Chapter 7
1980	298,492	30,402	5,333	259,160	194,491
1981	362,233	34,356	7,795	315,250	230,139
1982	373,853	41,863	14,696	310,330	219,930
1983	362,051	39,573	17,608	297,835	203,096
1984	346,500	38,649	17,396	283,618	196,541
1985	383,510	41,838	19,864	314,378	216,090
1986	507,557	48,976	21,110	429,334	307,972
1987	568,430	49,471	18,333	482,300	353,087
1988	604,759	39,803	16,025	538,636	391,428
1989	656,980	27,228	15,703	595,511	427,147
1990	749,981	36,687	17,789	685,429	484,671
1991	918,988	38,705	20,394	848,812	599,799
1992	977,478	38,467	20,070	905,753	646,399
1993	897,231	35,807	17,068	832,374	585,264
1994	837,797	30,781	13,379	783,372	541,190
1995	883,457	28,800	11,168	832,415	569,450
1996	1,111,964	30,289	11,358	1,058,444	731,363
1997	1,367,364	31,862	10,092	1,313,112	926,183
1998	1,436,964	29,229	7,884	1,389,839	996,905
1999	1,354,376	23,499	8,238	1,315,751	935,792
2000	1,262,102	20,687	9,135	1,226,037	850,118
2001	1,437,354	22,800	9,787	1,398,860	991,337
2002	1,547,669	22,574	10,702	1,508,578	1,061,762
2003	1,661,996	21,008	9,185	1,625,813	1,156,284

[a] The fiscal year end runs through September 30.
[b] Chapter 7: "Straight Bankruptcy"—Liquidation; Chapter 11: Reorganization

plan cannot be developed, the firm will be liquidated under Chapter 7. Table 23.2 shows how the total number of U.S. corporate bankruptcies was divided between Chapter 7 and Chapter 11 filings for the period from 1980 to 2003. The table shows that in 2003 there were a total of 1,661,996 bankruptcy filings in the United States. These filings consisted of 36,183 business failures and a record 1,625,813 nonbusiness (mostly personal) bankruptcies. Keep in mind that the total population of the United States was about 280 million in 2003, so roughly 1 percent of all American adults filed for bankruptcy in that year alone!

When a company files either to reorganize or liquidate in bankruptcy, a collective legal procedure begins by which all claims against the company are resolved. When a firm declares bankruptcy, individual creditors are prevented (stayed) from beginning or continuing with lawsuits against the debtor. Thus, bankruptcy law is substituted for the commercial and tax laws that normally govern firms.

Without a collective procedure, individual creditors would engage in a costly and unproductive race to be first to sue the company for repayment of their own claims. Creditors that sued first would be paid in full until the firm's resources were exhausted, after which other creditors would receive nothing. Both the creditors' duplicative expenses and the costs of the lawsuits themselves would consume assets. Bankruptcy eliminates the benefit of being the first to sue because all claims against the firm are settled simultaneously, and all creditors having the same type of claim receive the same settlement. Although there is still an incentive for creditors to attempt to sue the firm first, the incentive is diminished because a large number of suits will cause the firm to enter bankruptcy voluntarily.

COMPARATIVE CORPORATE FINANCE

If Companies Can Declare Bankruptcy; Why Not Countries?

On January 6, 2002, Argentina abandoned the decade-old parity between its currency and the U.S. dollar by devaluing the peso. "We are bankrupt," admitted Economy Minister Jorge Remes Lenicov when he announced the devaluation. The government also confirmed that Argentina cannot continue to service its $155 billion of foreign currency debt, and it declared a moratorium on payments. Because of the default, the price of Argentine bonds fell to about 25 percent of their par value.

Argentina's creditors braced themselves for a long fight for their money. The Argentine bondholders formed a committee in November 2001 to communicate some of the large investors' views to the Argentine government. The committee included investment banks that began to pay out on credit-default swaps, derivative securities that guarantee payment should a borrower default. The default swaps totaled almost $4 billion, and the investment banks now own the bonds returned to them under the terms of the swaps.

The questions for bondholders are how vigorously should they react, and how quickly should they call their lawyers? The announcement of a default means that bondholders can now "accelerate" their claims by demanding immediate payment of all principal and interest from the debtor. However, acceleration is unlikely to result in prompt payment because, as the bondholders realize, Argentina has serious problems. Most creditors figure that they will receive more money by negotiation than by confrontation.

While the moratorium gave Argentina room to maneuver, it was clear by spring 2004 that no quick turnaround was in sight. After an extremely severe economic contraction during 2002 and 2003, the Argentine economy began to grow again, but not at a fast enough pace to service their existing debt, much less to begin actual repayment. The Argentine government has also consistently refused to make net payments to creditors (pay more in interest and principal than it receives in new loans). However, if Argentina ignores its creditors, then difficulties might arise with even the simplest trade finance transactions. In the worst case, creditors could seize Argentine assets abroad, such as ships or aircraft. Also, many of the bond covenants do not contain so-called collective action clauses; therefore, each bondholder is free to litigate individually, a frightening scenario for everyone except the lawyers.

The question remains, What should Argentina do? Whereas companies can declare bankruptcy and seek protection from their creditors, countries have no such option. They are faced with the bleak choice between bailouts and chaotic defaults. However, that could change. The International Monetary Fund (IMF) has suggested that a country whose debts are "truly unsustainable" should have a mechanism for restructuring them, in the same way that companies can file for bankruptcy protection and reorganize their obligations.

The idea is that a country in financial distress would get temporary legal protection when it stopped making payments on its debt. In return, it would have to promise to negotiate with its creditors in good faith. Lenders would get an incentive to provide new "working capital" by giving new debt seniority over old. Also, small creditors would have to go along with the reorganization plan if enough creditors agreed.

Sovereign bankruptcy is appealing because it might eliminate the need for IMF bailouts while avoiding the legal quagmire of unilateral default. Both creditors and debtors would benefit from clear rules about the procedure for debt restructuring, if the rules balanced the rights of debtors and creditors. Since Argentina has become the single largest, and by far the most troublesome, borrower from the IMF, this institution is particularly keen to develop alternative workout procedures for heavily indebted countries.

Previous proposals on sovereign bankruptcy have failed, in part, because the details are difficult to work out. Who, for instance, will act as the impartial judge? Also, how do you force a debtor country to negotiate in good faith? After all, countries cannot be threatened with liquidation or a forcible change in "management."

CONCEPT REVIEW QUESTIONS

7. Why are bankruptcy laws necessary? Why is normal contracting under commercial law insufficient?

8. How does society benefit by allowing firms to declare bankruptcy?

9. Why is it important that bankruptcy law eliminate the incentive for creditors to be the first to sue for repayment of claims?

23.4 REORGANIZATION IN BANKRUPTCY

reorganization
The process in bankruptcy designed to allow businesses that are in temporary financial distress but are worth saving to continue operating while the claims of creditors are settled using a collective procedure.

A company's managers typically make the initial decision to attempt to reorganize their firm under the protection of Chapter 11 of the bankruptcy laws. The **reorganization** process in bankruptcy is designed to allow businesses that are in temporary financial distress, but are worth saving, to continue operating while the claims of creditors are settled using a collective procedure. A disadvantage of this procedure is that the managers of the company, and not an outside party, make the decision to file under Chapter 11. Thus, managers have an incentive to choose the bankruptcy procedure that is best for themselves and for equity holders and not the firm's creditors. This sometimes results in firms being reorganized that are not worth saving because of a lack of economic efficiency. Thus, a problem with reorganization is that even though it may allow some efficient firms to continue operating that would otherwise be liquidated, it is also likely to allow some economically inefficient firms to be saved.

Reorganization Procedures

The procedures for initiation and execution of corporate reorganization under Chapter 11 entail five separate steps: filing, appointment, development and approval of a reorganization plan, acceptance of the plan, and payment of expenses.

Filing. A firm must file a reorganization petition under Chapter 11 in a federal bankruptcy court. There are two basic types of bankruptcy reorganization petitions: voluntary and involuntary. Any firm that is not a municipal or financial institution can voluntarily file a petition for reorganization on its own behalf. Firms sometimes file a voluntary petition to obtain temporary legal protection from creditors or from prolonged litigation. Once they have straightened out their legal or financial affairs, prior to further reorganization or liquidation actions, they will have the petition dismissed. Although such actions are not the intent of the bankruptcy laws, difficulty in enforcing the law has allowed this abuse to occur.

involuntary reorganization
A reorganization initiated by an outside party, usually a creditor.

An outside party, usually a creditor, initiates **involuntary reorganization**. An involuntary petition against a firm can be filed if one of three conditions is met:

1. The firm has past-due debts of $5,000 or more.
2. Three or more creditors can prove that they have aggregate unpaid claims of $5,000 against the firm. If the firm has fewer than twelve creditors, any creditor that is owed more than $5,000 can file the petition.
3. The firm is **insolvent**, which means that (a) it is not paying its debts as they come due, (b) within the immediately preceding 120 days a custodian (a third party) was appointed or took possession of the debtor's property, or (c) the fair market value of the firm's assets is less than the stated value of its liabilities.

insolvent
A firm is insolvent when (a) it is not paying its debts as they come due; (b) within the immediately preceding 120 days a custodian (a third party) was appointed or took possession of the debtor's property; or (c) the fair market value of its assets is less than the stated value of its liabilities.

If the debtor challenges an involuntary petition, a hearing must be held to determine whether the firm is insolvent. If it is, the court enters an "Order for Relief" that formally initiates the process.

Appointment. Upon the filing of a reorganization petition, the filing firm becomes the **debtor in possession (DIP)** of the assets, and its existing management usually remains in control. However, one or more creditors' committees are appointed to represent the interests of creditors.

debtor in possession (DIP)
The firm filing a reorganization petition.

If the creditors object to the filing firm being the debtor in possession, they can petition the bankruptcy court to appoint a trustee to replace management. However, the incompetence of the existing management, which is strongly suggested by the fact that the firm is in bankruptcy, is not considered a sufficient reason for replacing management. To replace existing management, the creditors usually must present evidence that the management is making preferential transfers to favored creditors or stealing the company's assets.

Because reorganization activities are largely in the hands of the DIP, it is useful to understand the DIP's responsibilities. The DIP's first responsibility is the valuation of the firm to determine whether reorganization is appropriate. To do this, the DIP must estimate both the liquidation value of the business and its value as a going concern. If the DIP finds that its value as a going concern is less than its liquidation value, it will recommend liquidation. If the opposite is true, the DIP will recommend reorganization. If the DIP recommends reorganization of the firm, a plan of reorganization must be drawn up.

Reorganization Plan. After reviewing its situation, the debtor in possession submits a plan of reorganization to the court and files the plan and a disclosure statement summarizing the plan. A hearing is held to determine whether the plan is fair, equitable, and feasible, and whether the disclosure statement contains adequate information. The court's approval or disapproval is based on its evaluation of the plan in light of these standards. A plan is considered fair and equitable if it maintains the priorities of the contractual claims of the creditors, preferred stockholders, and common stockholders. The court must also find the reorganization plan *feasible,* meaning that it must be workable. The reorganized corporation must have sufficient working capital, sufficient funds to cover fixed charges, sufficient credit prospects, and sufficient ability to retire or refund debts as proposed by the plan.

The key portion of the reorganization plan generally concerns the firm's capital structure. Because most firms' financial difficulties result from high fixed charges, the company's capital structure is generally recapitalized, or altered, to reduce these charges. Under **recapitalization**, debts are generally exchanged for equity or the maturities of existing debts are extended. The DIP, when recapitalizing the firm, places a great deal of emphasis on building a mix of debt and equity that will allow the firm to meet its debts and provide a reasonable level of earnings for its owners.

recapitalization
Alteration of a company's capital structure to reduce high fixed charges.

Once the optimal capital structure has been determined, the DIP must establish a plan for exchanging outstanding obligations for new securities. The guiding principle is to observe priorities. Senior claims are those with higher legal priority that must be satisfied in full before junior claims receive any payment. To comply with this principle, senior suppliers of capital must receive a claim on new capital equal to their previous claim. The common stockholders are the last to receive any new securities, and it is not unusual for them to receive nothing. Security holders do not necessarily have to receive the same type of security they held before; often they receive a combination of securities. Once the debtor in possession has determined the new capital structure and distribution of capital, it will submit the reorganization plan and disclosure statement to the court as described.

The DIP is in a strong bargaining position in negotiations over the reorganization plan. During the first four months after the bankruptcy filing—plus any extensions, which are often granted—managers have the exclusive right to propose a plan. Then an extra two months are allowed for voting on management's plan. Only then, and only if no further extensions have been granted, can creditors propose reorganization plans.

Acceptance of the Reorganization Plan. Once approved by the bankruptcy court, the plan and the disclosure statement are given to the firm's creditors and shareholders for their acceptance. Under the Bankruptcy Reform Act, creditors and owners are separated into groups with similar types of claims. Intense bargaining and litigation often occur concerning the construction of the classes of creditors in a reorganization. Creditors that are in substantially the same position are placed in the same class to assure that they receive the same treatment under the reorganization plan. Creditors in different positions are placed in different classes. However, managers sometimes wish to prevent a particular creditor from defeating a reorganization plan. They accomplish this by arguing that the creditor should be part of a larger class in which the creditor's opposition to the plan will be outvoted.

unanimous consent procedure (UCP) A reorganization plan instituted by consent of all creditors and equity classes.

There are two procedures for instituting a reorganization plan: the unanimous consent procedure and the cramdown procedure. Under the **unanimous consent procedure (UCP),** creditors and equity classes must consent unanimously to the reorganization plan, although not all members of each class are required to consent. The UCP assumes that the company's assets will be worth more if it reorganizes and continues operations than if it liquidates. This difference in value, which under the absolute priority rule (APR) of Chapter 7 would belong entirely to the creditors with senior claims, must be divided up among all the creditors and equity classes by means of a negotiating process, with all classes sharing the difference in value.

A company must be solvent to use the UCP. That is, the value of creditors' claims must be less than the value of the company as a going concern. This implies that the firm's existing equity has some value. If the existing equity is worthless, then the company is considered insolvent, and the UCP cannot be used because equity holders cannot consent to a reorganization plan that eliminates their interest. To make a firm appear solvent, reorganization plans sometimes use inflated valuations of the firm's assets to make them appear to be worth more than the liabilities under the proposed plan.

Reorganization plans using the UCP must be approved by all classes of creditors and by equity as a class. Each class of unsecured creditors must vote for the plan by a two-thirds margin, weighing claims by value, and also by a simple majority, weighing all claims equally. Each secured creditor is a class, and each must vote for the plan if its claims are impaired. (If its claims are not impaired, a secured creditor's consent to the plan is not needed.) Because equity holders must vote for the plan by a two-thirds margin, reorganization plans under the UCP yield a different division of the company's value than would occur under the APR of a Chapter 7 liquidation. Under the UCP, every class, even the equity holders, must receive some value. Under the APR, the equity holders and junior creditors often receive nothing.

Managers can also threaten to transfer the firm's bankruptcy filing from Chapter 11 to Chapter 7 if the creditors do not agree to a plan, a threat that is often effective in prodding unsecured creditors to accept the plan, as they anticipate receiving little or nothing if liquidation occurs. Managers also run the firm during the negotiating process, so secured creditors often fear that the value of their lien assets will decline. Finally, even after their exclusive period for proposing a reorganization plan ends, managers remain in a strong bargaining position. Individual creditors typically are unrepresented except in the largest cases, and severe free-rider problems arise when creditors attempt to form groups and raise funds to take an active part in bargaining.

cramdown procedure Used when a reorganization plan fails to meet the standard for approval by all classes, but at least one class of creditors has voted for a reorganization plan; or when the firm is clearly insolvent and the existing equity has no value.

The **cramdown procedure** is used when a reorganization plan fails to meet the standard for approval by all classes under the UCP or when the firm is clearly insolvent and the existing equity has no value. In a cramdown, if at least one class of creditors has voted for a reorganization plan, the bankruptcy court can approve the plan without the consent of the other classes, as long as each dissenting class is treated fairly and equitably. The fair and equitable standard closely reflects the APR by requiring either that all unsecured creditors receive full payment of their claims over the period of the plan or that all junior classes receive nothing. The cramdown procedure also requires that secured creditors retain their prebankruptcy liens on assets and that they receive periodic cash payments equal to the value of their claims. Cramdowns typically involve higher transaction costs than UCP reorganization plans because the bankruptcy judge often requires asset valuations by outside experts and more court hearings usually occur before the plan is approved.

When no reorganization plan is adopted under either the UCP or cramdown, managers sometimes voluntarily sell the firm as a going concern. In that case, the proceeds of the sale are paid to creditors according to the APR. This liquidating reorganization is similar to a Chapter 7 liquidation, except that the firm is sold as a going concern and is not shut down. Finally, if no progress is being made toward completion of a Chapter 11 reorganization, some creditor usually petitions the bankruptcy judge to order a shift of the firm's bankruptcy filing to a Chapter 7 liquidation.

Payment of Expenses. After the reorganization plan has been approved or disapproved, all parties to the proceedings whose services were beneficial or contributed to the approval or disapproval of the plan file a statement of expenses. If the court finds these claims acceptable, the debtor must pay these expenses within a reasonable period.

APPLYING THE MODEL

Campbell Technologies, a telecommunications equipment manufacturer, has filed Chapter 11 bankruptcy and is seeking to reorganize because it cannot service its debt. The company's current capital structure is as follows:

Debentures (unsecured debt)	$4,000,000
Subordinated debentures	2,000,000
Common stock (100,000 shares)	2,000,000
Total	$8,000,000

The company's book-value leverage is high, with a debt/equity ratio of 3.0 ($6,000,000/$2,000,000). It has been determined that Campbell Technologies is worth $5 million as a going concern. The company can be reorganized as follows:

Debentures (unsecured debt)	$2,000,000
Subordinated debentures	1,000,000
Common stock (200,000 shares)	2,000,000
Total	$5,000,000

The face value of the debt is cut in half, but the debt holders receive 100,000 shares, or half of the company's equity. The debt/equity ratio of Campbell Technologies is now a more reasonable 1.5 ($3,000,000/$2,000,000), and the company's operating profits should be more than sufficient to service the reduced debt burden.

Subsidies to Firms That Reorganize

Reorganization is viewed as a means of providing breathing space to viable firms that are in temporary financial distress in order to save jobs and avoid disruption to local communities. In contrast, liquidation is viewed as the process of winding up the operation of firms that are not viable. Therefore, in order to make reorganization attractive to managers and equity holders, Congress has provided a number of subsidies to firms in reorganization. These subsidies come either from the government or from creditors. They give firms in reorganization advantages relative to firms that continue operating outside of bankruptcy and firms that liquidate. The six major subsidies are as follows:

1. When reorganizing firms settle liabilities for less than their face value, the amount of debt forgiveness is deducted as a loss by the creditor but is not immediately treated as taxable income to the reorganizing firm. The debt forgiveness amount becomes taxable when the reorganized firm becomes profitable by reducing either its tax loss carryforward or its depreciation allowances.

2. Firms reorganizing under Chapter 11 have the right to terminate underfunded pension plans, and the U.S. government picks up the uncovered pension costs. For example, three large firms that filed for bankruptcy in the 1980s, LTV, Wheeling-Pittsburgh Steel, and Allis-Chalmers, terminated their pension funds and together transferred almost $3 billion of uncovered pension liabilities to the government.
3. Firms that reorganize retain most of their accrued tax loss carryforwards, which would be lost if they liquidated. These loss carryforwards shelter the firm from paying taxes on corporate profits for a period in the future, if its operations start to be profitable. They also make reorganized firms attractive merger partners for profitable firms, because the profitable firm can use the tax loss carryforward immediately. This subsidy makes reorganization more attractive than liquidation for a failing firm but has no effect on the choice between reorganization and remaining out of bankruptcy.
4. When firms file for bankruptcy, their obligation to pay interest to prebankruptcy creditors, both secured and unsecured, ceases. They do not have to start paying interest again until a reorganization plan is approved, and the unpaid interest does not become a claim against the firm. This subsidy clearly gives managers of failing firms an incentive to file for bankruptcy earlier and to delay proposing a reorganization plan.
5. Firms in reorganization can reject any of their contracts that are not substantially completed. Thus, they can get out of any unprofitable contracts. Although firms are still liable for damages to other parties to rejected contracts, such damage claims are unsecured and likely to receive a low payoff rate. Thus, the cost to the firm of shedding unprofitable contracts is small.
6. Firms in reorganization can reject their collective bargaining labor agreements. Since 1984, however, this step has required the approval of the bankruptcy judge. This has particularly benefited unionized firms in industries that have a mixture of unionized and non-unionized establishments by enabling them to cut all wages to non-unionized levels. A prominent example is Continental Airlines, which, following airline deregulation, filed to reorganize in bankruptcy in 1983. Continental was allowed to cut wages by 50 percent and cut its workforce by 65 percent.

APPLYING THE MODEL

Although companies are no longer able to unilaterally revoke collective bargaining agreements after they file for bankruptcy protection, the supervising judges allows companies this flexibility frequently enough that the companies are often able to win concessions from their unionized employees by *threatening* to file for bankruptcy. American Airlines used this tactic very successfully in April 2003, when it secured some $1.8 billion in annual cost savings from its eight principal unions by credibly threatening to file for Chapter 11 protection if the wage cuts were not approved. In the previous eight months, no less than three major North American airlines had in fact filed for bankruptcy protection. The second largest U.S. carrier, UAL Corporation, filed for Chapter 11 in December 2002, and seventh largest, US Airways, had filed in August—though US Airways emerged from Chapter 7 a mere seven months later. Air Canada filed for protection from creditors, in the Canadian bankruptcy courts, in early April 2003.

As it happened, all American Airlines' stakeholders were fortunate that the company was able to avoid filing for bankruptcy. As the economy improved, travel picked up and American was able to return to an operating profit by the end of 2003 (though net income was still negative) without having to drastically cut employment levels. Most spectacularly, the parent company's (AMR Corporation) share price increased almost sixfold in eight months, rising from a low of $3.08 per share in April 2003 to over $17 per share in late January 2004, before falling back to $7.62 per share in October 2004.

Prepackaged Bankruptcies

Sometimes companies prepare a reorganization plan that is negotiated and voted on by creditors and stockholders before the company actually files for Chapter 11 bankruptcy. This process, known as a **prepackaged bankruptcy,** shortens and simplifies the process, saving the company money, and frequently generating more for the creditors as there is less spent in legal and related fees, less disruption to the company's business, and less damage to its goodwill.

prepackaged bankruptcy
Companies prepare a reorganization plan that is negotiated and voted on by creditors and stockholders before the company actually files for Chapter 11 bankruptcy.

For example, Regal Cinemas, the largest U.S. movie theater chain, simultaneously filed a voluntary petition for Chapter 11 bankruptcy protection and a prepackaged plan of reorganization on October 12, 2001. The reorganization plan gave effective control of the operation of 3,831 movie screens to Denver billionaire Philip Anschutz, who has used the theater industry's misfortunes to gain control of two other chains, United Artists and Edwards. The reorganization plan gives Regal's senior debt holders 100 percent of the reorganized company's stock. As it turns out, Anschutz owns the majority of the senior debt, having bought it for pennies on the dollar from Regal's bankers earlier in the year. Regal Cinemas emerged from bankruptcy in January 2002, an astonishingly short three months after filing!

CONCEPT REVIEW QUESTIONS

10. Under what circumstances would it make sense for a company to reorganize rather than liquidate?

11. Why is the existing management generally allowed to remain in control when a company files for bankruptcy?

12. Why is a cramdown procedure sometimes necessary when a company reorganizes?

23.5 LIQUIDATION IN BANKRUPTCY

A bankrupt firm is usually liquidated once the courts have determined that reorganization is not feasible. The managers or creditors of the bankrupt firm normally file a petition for reorganization. If no petition is filed, if a petition is filed and denied, or if the reorganization plan is denied, the firm must be liquidated. Three important aspects of liquidation in bankruptcy are the procedures, the priority of claims, and the final accounting.

SMART ETHICS VIDEO
Tom Cole, Deutsche Bank, Leveraged Finance Group
"Obviously companies don't want to go bankrupt and obviously investors don't want to lose money."
See the entire interview at **SMARTFinance**

Procedures

When a firm is adjudged bankrupt, the judge may appoint a trustee to perform the many routine duties required in administering the bankruptcy. The trustee takes charge of the property of the bankrupt firm and protects the interest of its creditors. Between twenty and forty days after the firm has been adjudged bankrupt, the creditors must hold a meeting. The bankruptcy court clerk presides over this meeting, during which the creditors are made aware of the prospects for the liquidation. The trustee is then given the responsibility of liquidating the firm, keeping records, examining creditors' claims, disbursing money, furnishing information as required, and making final reports on the liquidation. In essence, the trustee is responsible for the liquidation of the firm. Occasionally, the court will call subsequent creditor meetings, but only a final meeting for closing the bankruptcy is required.

Priority of Claims

The trustee has the responsibility to liquidate all the firm's assets and to distribute the proceeds to the holders of provable claims. The courts have established certain procedures for determining the provability of claims, known as the absolute priority rules. The priority of claims, which is specified in Chapter 7 of the Bankruptcy Reform Act, must be maintained by the trustee when distributing the funds from liquidation. It is important to recognize that if in a liquidation any **secured creditors** have specific assets pledged as collateral, they receive the proceeds from the sale of those assets. If these proceeds are inadequate to meet their claim, the secured creditors become **unsecured** (or **general**) **creditors** for the unrecovered amount because specific collateral no longer exists. These and all other unsecured creditors will divide up, on a pro rata basis, any funds remaining after all prior claims have been satisfied. If the proceeds from the sale of secured assets are in excess of the claims against them, the excess funds become available to meet claims of unsecured creditors.

secured creditors
Creditors who have specific assets pledged as collateral and who receive the proceeds from the sale of those assets.

unsecured creditors
Creditors who have no specific assets pledged as collateral, or the proceeds from the sale of whose pledged assets are inadequate to cover the debt.

general creditors
Creditors who have no specific assets pledged as collateral, or the proceeds from the sale of whose pledged assets are inadequate to cover the debt.

The complete order of priority of claims is as follows:

1. The expenses of administering the bankruptcy proceedings.
2. Any unpaid interim expenses incurred in the ordinary course of business between filing the bankruptcy petition and the entry of an Order of Relief in an involuntary proceeding. (This step is not applicable in a voluntary bankruptcy.)
3. Wages of not more than $2,000 per worker that have been earned by workers in the 90-day period immediately preceding the commencement of bankruptcy proceedings.
4. Unpaid employee benefit plan contributions that were to be paid in the 180-day period preceding the filing of bankruptcy or the termination of business, whichever occurred first. For any employee, the sum of this claim plus eligible unpaid wages cannot exceed $2,000.
5. Claims of farmers or fishermen in a grain-storage or fish-storage facility, not to exceed $2,000 for each producer.
6. Unsecured customer deposits, not to exceed $900 each, resulting from purchasing or leasing a good or service from the failed firm.
7. Taxes legally due and owed by the bankrupt firm to the federal government, state government, or any other governmental subdivision.
8. Claims of secured creditors, who receive the proceeds from the sale of collateral held, regardless of priorities one through seven. If the proceeds from the liquidation of the collateral are insufficient to satisfy the secured creditors' claims, the secured creditors become unsecured creditors for the unpaid amount.
9. Claims of unsecured creditors. The claims of unsecured, or general, creditors and unsatisfied portions of secured creditors' claims are treated equally.
10. Preferred stockholders, who receive an amount up to the par, or stated, value of their preferred stock.
11. Common stockholders, who receive any remaining funds, which are distributed on an equal per-share basis. If different classes of common stock are outstanding, priorities may exist.

SMART IDEAS VIDEO
Ed Altman, New York University
"The average time in bankruptcy is around 18 months to two years in the U.S."

See the entire interview at **SMARTFinance**

In spite of the priorities listed in items one through seven, secured creditors have first claim on proceeds from the sale of their collateral. The claims of unsecured creditors, including the unpaid claims of secured creditors, are satisfied next, and, finally, the claims of preferred and common stockholders. Also, some unsecured creditors' claims may be subordinated to those of other unsecured creditors. In the event of liquidation, the subordinated creditors do not receive any cash until the claims to which they are subordinated are paid in full.

The following Applying the Model gives a simple example of the application of these priorities by the trustee in bankruptcy liquidation proceedings.

APPLYING THE MODEL

Table 23.3 presents the balance sheet of Oxford Company, a computer drive manufacturer. The trustee has liquidated the firm's assets, obtaining the largest amounts possible. He obtained $2.1 million for the firm's current assets and $1.8 million for the firm's fixed assets. The total proceeds from the liquidation, therefore, were $3.9 million. It is clear that the firm is legally insolvent because its liabilities of $5.5 million exceed the $3.9 million market value of its assets.

The next step is to distribute the proceeds to the various creditors. The only liability that is not shown on the balance sheet is $500,000 in expenses for administering the bankruptcy proceedings and satisfying unpaid bills incurred between the time of filing the bankruptcy petition and the entry of an Order of Relief. Table 23.4 shows the distribution of the $3.9 million among the firm's creditors and illustrates that once all prior claims on the proceeds to liquidation have been satisfied, the unsecured creditors get the remaining funds. Table 23.5 gives the pro rata distribution of the $1 million among the unsecured creditors. The disposition of funds in the Oxford Company liquidation should be clear from Tables 23.4 and 23.5. Because the claims of the unsecured creditors have not been fully satisfied, the preferred and common shareholders receive nothing.

Final Accounting

The trustee, after liquidating the bankrupt firm's assets and distributing proceeds to satisfy all provable claims in the appropriate order of priority, makes a final accounting to the bankruptcy court and creditors. Once the court approves the final accounting, the liquidation is complete.

Table 23.3
Balance Sheet for Oxford Company

Assets		Liabilities and Stockholders' Equity	
Cash	$ 100,000	Accounts payable	$ 200,000
Accounts receivable	1,200,000	Notes payable – bank	1,500,000
Inventories	3,150,000	Accrued wages[a]	100,000
Total current assets	$4,450,000	Unpaid employee benefits[b]	110,000
Land	$2,000,000	Unsecured customer deposits[c]	90,000
Net plant	1,500,000	Taxes payable	300,000
Net equipment	1,100,000	Total current liabilities	$2,300,000
Total fixed assets	$4,600,000	First mortgage[d]	$1,400,000
Total	$9,050,000	Second mortgage[d]	800,000
		Subordinated debentures[e]	1,000,000
		Total long-term debt	$3,200,000
		Preferred stock (7,000 shares)	$ 700,000
		Common stock (20,000 shares)	200,000
		Paid-in capital in excess of par	300,000
		Retained earnings	2,350,000
		Total common stockholders' equity	$2,850,000
		Total	$9,050,000

[a] Represents wages of $2,000 or less per employee earned within 90 days of filing bankruptcy for the firm's employees.
[b] These unpaid employee benefits were due in the 180-day period preceding the firm's bankruptcy filing, which occurred simultaneously with the termination of its business.
[c] Unsecured customer deposits not exceeding $900 each.
[d] The first and second mortgages are on the firm's total fixed assets.
[e] The debentures are subordinated to the bank's note payable.

Table 23.4
Distribution of the Liquidation Proceeds of Oxford Company

Proceeds from liquidation	$3,900,000
Expenses of administering bankruptcy and paying bills	500,000
Wages owed workers	100,000
Unpaid employee benefits	110,000
Unsecured customer deposits	90,000
Taxes owed governments	300,000
Funds available for creditors	$2,800,000
First mortgage, paid from $2 million proceeds of fixed asset sale	1,400,000
Second mortgage, partially paid from the remaining assets	400,000
Funds available for unsecured creditors	$1,000,000

Table 23.5
Pro Rata Distribution of Funds among the Unsecured Creditors of Oxford Company

Unsecured Creditors' Claims	Amount	Settlement at 32%[a]	After Subordination
Unpaid balance on second mortgage	$ 400,000[b]	$ 129,032	$ 129,032
Accounts payable	200,000	64,516	64,516
Notes payable – bank	1,500,000	483,871	806,452
Subordinated debentures	1,000,000	322,581	0
Totals	$3,100,000	$1,000,000	$1,000,000

[a] The 32 percent rate is calculated by dividing the $1 million available for the unsecured creditors by the $3.1 million owed the unsecured creditors. Each is entitled to a pro rata share.

[b] This figure represents the difference between the $800,000 second mortgage and the $400,000 payment on the second mortgage from the proceeds from the sale of the collateral remaining after satisfying the first mortgage.

CONCEPT REVIEW QUESTIONS

13. What is the purpose of the absolute priority rule? Why shouldn't the bankruptcy judge be given more discretion?

14. What is the significance of subordinating a claim if a firm is liquidated?

15. Why is the payment of the expenses of administering the bankruptcy proceeding given the highest priority?

23.6 PREDICTING BANKRUPTCY

Z score
The product of a quantitative model for forecasting bankruptcy that uses a blend of traditional financial ratios and a statistical technique known as multiple discriminant analysis. The Z score has been found to be about 90 percent accurate in forecasting bankruptcy one year in the future and about 80 percent accurate in forecasting it two years in the future.

Predicting bankruptcy with some degree of accuracy is possible using Altman's Z score, named after Professor Ed Altman of New York University. The **Z score** is the product of a quantitative model that uses a blend of traditional financial ratios and a statistical technique known as multiple discriminant analysis. The Z score has been found to be about 90 percent accurate in forecasting bankruptcy one year in the future and about 80 percent accurate in forecasting it two years in the future. The model is as follows:

$$Z = 1.2 \times X_1 + 1.4 \times X_2 + 3.3 \times X_3 + 0.6 \times X_4 + 1.0 \times X_5$$

Where X_1 = working capital ÷ total assets
X_2 = retained earnings ÷ total assets
X_3 = earnings before interest and taxes ÷ total assets
X_4 = market value of equity ÷ book value of equity
X_5 = sales ÷ total assets

The following are guidelines for classifying businesses: Z score less than 1.8, high probability of failure; Z score between 1.81 and 2.99, unsure; and Z score above 3.0, failure unlikely.

APPLYING THE MODEL

Table 23.6 presents the balance sheet and Table 23.7, the income statement, for Poff Industries, a manufacturer of computer power supplies. The company's stock price currently is $3.50 per share. The company's Z score can be calculated as follows:

$$Z = 1.2(0.052) + 1.4(0.095) + 3.3(0.086) + 0.6(0.700) + 1.0(0.431) = 1.330$$

The Z score of 1.330 indicates that the probability that Poff Industries will fail is quite high.

CONCEPT REVIEW QUESTIONS

16. Why is predicting bankruptcy a useful ability?

17. How are the five factors that determine a Z score related to the financial health of a business?

Table 23.6
Balance Sheet for Poff Industries

Assets		Liabilities and Stockholders' Equity	
Cash	$ 100,000	Accounts payable	$ 2,000,000
Accounts receivable	1,000,000	Notes payable – bank	1,500,000
Inventories	3,000,000	Total current liabilities	$ 3,500,000
Total current assets	$ 4,100,000	Mortgage	$ 2,000,000
Land	$ 2,000,000	Debentures	3,000,000
Net plant	2,500,000	Total long-term debt	$ 5,000,000
Net equipment	3,000,000	Preferred stock (100,000 shares)	1,000,000
Total fixed assets	$ 7,500,000	Common stock (1,000,000 shares)	1,000,000
Total	$11,600,000	Paid-in capital in excess of par	1,000,000
		Retained earnings	1,100,000
		Total stockholders' equity	$ 3,100,000
		Total	$11,600,000

Table 22.7
Income Statement for Poff Industries

Sales	$5,000,000
Less: Cost of goods sold	3,000,000
Less: Selling and administrative expenses	1,000,000
Earnings before interest and taxes	$1,000,000
Less: Interest	500,000
Earnings before taxes	$ 500,000
Less: Taxes (40%)	200,000
Net Income	$ 300,000

23.7 SUMMARY AND CONCLUSIONS

- A business can fail in two ways. When it cannot pay its liabilities when they come due, the firm is technically insolvent due to a liquidity crisis. When its liabilities exceed the fair market value of its assets, the firm is insolvent. Bankruptcy occurs once a company comes under the authority of a bankruptcy court, which then exercises ultimate control over the firm.
- Mismanagement is the primary cause of business failure. Managerial faults include overexpansion, poor financial actions, an ineffective sales force, and high production costs. Other causes are economic downturns and corporate maturity.
- The financial distress a pending business failure places on a company and its management can have a profound effect on how the firm behaves and how its suppliers and customers perceive it. When a firm is in financial distress, suppliers are reluctant to extend credit and customers are concerned about service and warranties.
- Companies facing financial distress can voluntarily reorganize or liquidate. By acting voluntarily, firms reduce the legal and administrative expenses associated with a formal bankruptcy filing.
- The Bankruptcy Reform Act of 1978 specifies in Chapter 7 how firms are liquidated and in Chapter 11 how firms are reorganized.
- Firms can reorganize under Chapter 11 by means of the unanimous consent procedure or the cramdown procedure. In a reorganization, the terms of the debt can be relaxed by extending the payment term or lowering the interest rate. Also, debt can be exchanged for equity in the firm, thus reducing the amount of cash flow required to service the debt.
- Firms are liquidated under Chapter 7 by means of the absolute priority rule, which ranks the order for paying creditors from the proceeds of the liquidation of the firm's assets.
- The likelihood of bankruptcy can be predicted with a fair degree of accuracy (at least in the short term) using Altman's Z score.

SELF-TEST PROBLEMS

Answers to Self-Test Problems appear in Appendix D at back of book. Answers to the Concept Review Questions throughout the chapter appear at http://megginson.swlearning.com.

ST23-1. For a firm with outstanding debt of $50 million, classify each of the following voluntary settlements as an extension, a composition, or a combination of the two.

a. Paying a group of creditors in full in six periodic installments and paying the remaining creditors 75 cents on the dollar immediately

b. Paying a group of creditors 50 cents on the dollar immediately and paying the remaining creditors 70 cents on the dollar in five periodic installments

c. Paying all creditors 30 cents on the dollar

ST23-2. A firm has $8 million in funds to distribute to its unsecured creditors. Three possible sets of unsecured creditor claims are presented. Calculate the settlement, if any, to be received by each creditor in each case shown in the following table:

Unsecured Creditors' Claims	Case I	Case II	Case III
Unpaid balance of second mortgage	$ 2,000,000	$ 2,500,000	$ 5,000,000
Accounts payable	2,500,000	3,000,000	4,000,000
Notes payable – bank	3,500,000	3,500,000	1,500,000
Unsecured bonds	4,000,000	5,000,000	5,500,000
Total	$12,000,000	$14,000,000	$16,000,000

ST23-3. Oxygen Filtration Systems recently failed and will be liquidated by a court-appointed trustee who will charge $500,000 for his services. The preliquidation balance sheet follows. Assume that the trustee liquidates the assets for $10.2 million, with $5.8 million coming from the sale of current assets and $4.4 million coming from fixed assets. Also assume that the unsecured bonds are subordinate to the notes payable. Prepare a table indicating the amount to be distributed to each claimant. Do the firm's owners receive any funds?

Oxygen Filtration Systems
Balance Sheet
as of December 31, 2006

Assets		Liabilities and Stockholder's Equity	
Cash	$ 600,000	Accounts payable	$ 2,500,000
Marketable securities	750,000	Notes payable – bank	4,000,000
Accounts receivable	1,750,000	Accrued wages[a]	750,000
Inventories	2,250,000	Unpaid employee benefits[b]	500,000
Prepaid expenses	900,000	Unsecured customer deposits[c]	500,000
Total current assets	$ 6,250,000	Taxes payable	1,000,000
		Total current liabilities	$ 9,250,000
Land	$ 3,000,000	First mortgage[d]	$ 3,000,000
Net plant	5,000,000	Second mortgage[d]	2,000,000
Net equipment	6,250,000	Unsecured bonds	3,500,000
Total fixed assets	$14,250,000	Total long-term debt	$ 8,500,000
Total	$20,500,000	Preferred stock (10,000 shares)	$ 500,000
		Common stock (20,000 shares)	2,000,000
		Retained earnings	250,000
		Total stockholders' equity	$ 2,750,000
		Total	$20,500,000

[a] Represents wages of $2,000 or less per employee earned within 90 days of filing bankruptcy for 400 of the firm's employees.
[b] Unpaid employee benefits that were due in the 180-day period preceding the firm's bankruptcy filing, which occurred simultaneously with the termination of its business.
[c] Unsecured customer deposits not exceeding $900 each.
[d] First and second mortgages on the firm's total fixed assets.

ST23-4. Express Trailers has a working capital/total assets ratio of 0.3, a retained earnings/total assets ratio of 0.15, an earnings before interest and taxes/total asset ratio of 0.20, a market value of equity/book value of equity ratio of 0.5, and a sales/total assets ratio of 0.75. Calculate and interpret the company's Z score.

INTERNET RESOURCES

Note: *For updates to links, please go to the book's Web site at* http://megginson.swlearning.com

http://www.bankruptcydata.com/—Searchable Web site providing data and information on bankruptcies in the United States. Though most of the data are fee-based, a significant amount can be obtained for free.

http://www.uscourts.gov/bankruptcycourts.html—The main Web site for the United States Bankruptcy Courts, offering access to both data and information about bankruptcy filings.

KEY TERMS

absolute priority rules (APR)
assignment
bankruptcy
Bankruptcy Reform Act of 1978
business failure
Chapter 11
Chapter 7
composition
cramdown procedure
creditor control

debtor in possession (DIP)
economic failure
extension
general creditors
insolvency bankruptcy
insolvent
involuntary reorganization
liquidation
liquidity crisis
prepackaged bankruptcy
recapitalization
reorganization
secured creditors
technical insolvency
trustee
unanimous consent procedure (UCP)
unsecured creditors
voluntary reorganization
voluntary settlement
workout
Z score

QUESTIONS AND PROBLEMS

Q23-1. Discuss why it makes sense to offer subsidies to firms that reorganize rather than liquidate.

Q23-2. Explain why the option to delay entering bankruptcy has value for corporate managers.

Q23-3. Why do creditors usually accept a plan for financial rehabilitation rather than demand liquidation of a business?

Q23-4. A certain number of bankruptcies are good for the economy. Discuss why you agree or disagree with this statement.

Q23-5. A business should always be liquidated when the liquidation value exceeds the business's value as a going concern. Discuss why you agree or disagree with this statement.

Q23-6. What are the advantages and disadvantages of a voluntary workout to resolve financial distress? What are the advantages and disadvantages of declaring bankruptcy to resolve financial distress?

Q23-7. A business can be liquidated for $700,000, or it can be reorganized. Reorganization would require an investment of $400,000. If the company is reorganized, earnings are projected to be $150,000 per year, and the company would trade at a price/earnings ratio of 8.0. Should the company be liquidated or reorganized?

Q23-8. Explain why the priorities for liquidation are determined as they are. Do you agree with the order?

Q23-9. What is the difference between economic failure and financial distress? Which situation is likely to lead to liquidation, and which is likely to result in reorganization?

Q23-10. Who would use Altman's Z score to predict bankruptcy? Why would the ability to predict bankruptcy be useful to them?

Q23-11. What is the purpose of a prepackaged bankruptcy? Would a prepackaged bankruptcy be more likely to be used for a liquidation or a reorganization?

Q23-12. Why would some creditors be willing to subordinate their claims to the claims of other creditors?

PROBLEMS

Voluntary Settlements

P23-1. For a firm with outstanding debt of $2.4 million, classify each of the following voluntary settlements as an extension, a composition, or a combination of the two.

a. Paying all creditors 40 cents on the dollar in exchange for complete discharge of the debt
b. Paying all creditors in full in three periodic installments
c. Paying a group of creditors with claims of $1 million in full over two years and immediately paying the remaining creditors 75 cents on the dollar

P23-2. For a firm with outstanding debt of $125,000, classify each of the following voluntary settlements as an extension, a composition, or a combination of the two.

a. Paying a group of creditors in full in four periodic installments and paying the remaining creditors in full immediately
b. Paying a group of creditors 80 cents on the dollar immediately and paying the remaining creditors 70 cents on the dollar in two periodic installments
c. Paying all creditors in full in 270 days

P23-3. For a firm with outstanding debt of $200 million, classify each of the following voluntary settlements as an extension, a composition, or a combination of the two.

a. Paying a group of creditors in full in three periodic installments and paying the remaining creditors 70 cents on the dollar immediately
b. Paying a group of creditors 60 cents on the dollar immediately and paying the remaining creditors 80 cents on the dollar in five periodic installments
c. Paying all creditors 25 cents on the dollar

P23-4. Go to http://www.bankruptcydata.com, and pinpoint the largest public company bankruptcies during the previous year. Compare the list of the largest bankruptcies in U.S. history presented in Table 23.1 with the current list at http://www.bankruptcydata.com. Have any bankruptcies that occurred after April 2004 made the list?

P23-5. Jacobi Supply Company recently ran into financial difficulties that have resulted in the initiation of voluntary settlement procedures. The firm currently has $250,000 in outstanding debts and approximately $100,000 in marketable short-term assets. Indicate, for each of the following plans, whether the plan is an extension, a composition, or a combination of the two. Also indicate the cash payments and timing of the payments required of the firm under each plan.

a. Each creditor will be paid 40 cents on the dollar immediately, and the debts will be considered fully satisfied.
b. Each creditor will be paid 40 cents on the dollar in two quarterly installments of 20 cents and 20 cents. The first installment is to be paid in ninety days.
c. Each creditor will be paid the full amount of its claims in three installments of 50 cents, 25 cents, and 25 cents on the dollar. The installments will be made in sixty-day intervals, beginning in sixty days.

P23-6. Heriot Manufacturing Company recently ran into certain financial difficulties that have resulted in the initiation of voluntary settlement procedures. The firm currently has $2 million in outstanding debts and approximately $1.2 million in marketable short-term assets. Indicate, for each of the following plans, whether the plan is an extension, a composition, or a combination of the two. Also indicate the cash payments and timing of the payments required of the firm under each plan.

a. Each creditor will be paid 60 cents on the dollar immediately, and the debts will be considered fully satisfied.
b. Each creditor will be paid 80 cents on the dollar in two quarterly installments of 50 cents and 30 cents. The first installment is to be paid in ninety days.
c. A group of creditors with claims of $600,000 will be immediately paid in full; the rest will be paid 85 cents on the dollar, payable in ninety days.

Liquidation in Bankruptcy

P23-7. A firm has $450,000 in funds to distribute to its unsecured creditors. Three possible sets of unsecured creditor claims are presented. Calculate the settlement, if any, to be received by each creditor in each case shown in the following table:

Unsecured Creditors' Claims	Case I	Case II	Case III
Unpaid balance of second mortgage	$300,000	$200,000	$ 500,000
Accounts payable	200,000	100,000	300,000
Notes payable – bank	300,000	100,000	500,000
Unsecured bonds	100,000	200,000	500,000
Total	$900,000	$600,000	$1,800,000

P23-8. A firm has $5 million in funds to distribute to its unsecured creditors. Three possible sets of unsecured creditor claims are presented. Calculate the settlement, if any, to be received by each creditor in each case shown in the following table:

Unsecured Creditors' Claims	Case I	Case II	Case III
Unpaid balance of second mortgage	$1,000,000	$2,000,000	$3,000,000
Accounts payable	2,000,000	1,000,000	3,000,000
Notes payable – bank	3,000,000	2,000,000	1,000,000
Unsecured bonds	1,000,000	3,000,000	2,000,000
Total	$7,000,000	$8,000,000	$9,000,000

P23-9. Keck Business Forms recently failed and will be liquidated by a court-appointed trustee who will charge $300,000 for her services. The preliquidation balance sheet follows. Assume that the trustee liquidates the assets for $4.8 million, with $2.6 million coming from the sale of current assets and $2.2 million coming from fixed assets. Also assume that the unsecured bonds are subordinate to the notes payable. Prepare a table indicating the amount to be distributed to each claimant. Do the firm's owners receive any funds?

Keck Business Forms
Balance Sheet
as of December 31, 2006

Assets		Liabilities and Stockholder's Equity	
Cash	$ 100,000	Accounts payable	$1,200,000
Marketable securities	50,000	Notes payable – bank	1,100,000
Accounts receivable	1,100,000	Accrued wages[a]	300,000
Inventories	2,400,000	Unpaid employee benefits[b]	200,000
Prepaid expenses	400,000	Unsecured customer deposits[c]	250,000
Total current assets	$4,050,000	Taxes payable	100,000
		Total current liabilities	$3,150,000
Land	$1,000,000	First mortgage[d]	$1,500,000
Net plant	2,100,000	Second mortgage[d]	1,000,000
Net equipment	2,300,000	Unsecured bonds	2,000,000
Total fixed assets	$5,400,000	Total long-term debt	$4,500,000
Total	$9,450,000	Preferred stock (5,000 shares)	$ 500,000
		Common stock (10,000 shares)	1,000,000
		Retained earnings	300,000
		Total stockholders' equity	$1,800,000
		Total	$9,450,000

[a] Represents wages of $2,000 or less per employee earned within 90 days of filing bankruptcy for 400 of the firm's employees.
[b] Unpaid employee benefits that were due in the 180-day period preceding the firm's bankruptcy filing, which occurred simultaneously with the termination of its business.
[c] Unsecured customer deposits not exceeding $900 each.
[d] First and second mortgages on the firm's total fixed assets.

See the problem and solution explained step-by-step at SMARTFinance

Predicting Bankruptcy

P23-10. Sosbee Foods has a working capital/total assets ratio of 0.2, a retained earnings/total assets ratio of 0.1, an earnings before interest and taxes/total asset ratio of 0.25, a market value of equity/book value of equity ratio of 0.6, and a sales/total assets ratio of 0.8. Calculate and interpret the company's Z score.

P23-11. The following balance sheet and income statement are for Weber Industries. The firm's stock currently is priced at $6.00 per share. Calculate and interpret the company's Z score.

Weber Industries
Balance Sheet
as of December 31, 2006

Assets		Liabilities and Stockholder's Equity	
Cash	$ 400,000	Accounts payable	$ 5,000,000
Accounts receivable	3,000,000	Notes payable – bank	1,000,000
Inventories	4,000,000	Total current liabilities	$ 6,000,000
Total current assets	$ 7,400,000	Mortgage	$ 4,000,000
Land	$ 1,000,000	Debentures	6,000,000
Net plant	5,000,000	Total long-term debt	$10,000,000
Net equipment	8,000,000	Preferred stock (100,000 shares)	$ 1,000,000
Total fixed assets	$14,000,000	Common stock (500,000 shares)	1,000,000
Total	$21,400,000	Paid-in capital in excess of par	2,000,000
		Retained earnings	1,400,000
		Total shareholders' equity	$ 5,400,000
		Total	$21,400,000

Weber Industries
Income Statement
for the Year Ending December 31, 2004

Sales:	$6,000,000
Less: Cost of goods sold	3,500,000
Less: Selling and administrative	1,000,000
Earnings before interest and taxes	$1,500,000
Less: Interest	1,100,000
Earnings before taxes	$ 400,000
Less: Taxes (30%)	120,000
Net Income	$ 280,000

THOMSON ONE Business School Edition

For instructions on using Thomson ONE, refer to the instructions provided with the Thomson ONE problems at the end of Chapters 1–6 or to "A Guide for Using Thomson ONE."

P23-12. Calculate and interpret Altman's Z score for Sun Microsystems Inc. (ticker: @SUNW) using the latest year's financial statements and its current market capitalization. Do you think Sun Microsystems will go bankrupt within the next year?

Since these exercises depend upon real-time data, your answers will change continuously depending upon when you access the Internet to download your data.

MINICASE

Bankruptcy and Financial Distress

You have recently joined the financial planning department of American Steel Works, Incorporated. Along with much of the steel industry, this firm has gone through some difficult economic times the past few years. American Steel Works has been able to survive due to comprehensive financial planning. Therefore, as part of the firm's long-term strategic planning, the chief executive officer (CEO) decides to hold a discussion on bankruptcy and financial distress and asks you to help prepare some background information. To assist you in this information gathering, you are asked to answer the following questions.

ASSIGNMENT

1. What are the types of business failure?
2. What are the causes of business failure?
3. Describe the types of voluntary settlement.
4. What is reorganization? Discuss reorganization procedures.
5. How does liquidation through bankruptcy work?

Appendix A: Financial Tables

Table A1

Future Value Factors for One Dollar Compounded at *r* Percent for *n* Periods

$$FVF_{r\%,n} = (1 + r)^n$$

Period	1%	2%	3%	4%	5%	6%	7%	8%	9%	10%	11%	12%	13%	14%	15%	16%
1	1.010	1.020	1.030	1.040	1.050	1.060	1.070	1.080	1.090	1.100	1.110	1.120	1.130	1.140	1.150	1.160
2	1.020	1.040	1.061	1.082	1.103	1.124	1.145	1.166	1.188	1.210	1.232	1.254	1.277	1.300	1.323	1.346
3	1.030	1.061	1.093	1.125	1.158	1.191	1.225	1.260	1.295	1.331	1.368	1.405	1.443	1.482	1.521	1.561
4	1.041	1.082	1.126	1.170	1.216	1.262	1.311	1.360	1.412	1.464	1.518	1.574	1.630	1.689	1.749	1.811
5	1.051	1.104	1.159	1.217	1.276	1.338	1.403	1.469	1.539	1.611	1.685	1.762	1.842	1.925	2.011	2.100
6	1.062	1.126	1.194	1.265	1.340	1.419	1.501	1.587	1.677	1.772	1.870	1.974	2.082	2.195	2.313	2.436
7	1.072	1.149	1.230	1.316	1.407	1.504	1.606	1.714	1.828	1.949	2.076	2.211	2.353	2.502	2.660	2.826
8	1.083	1.172	1.267	1.369	1.477	1.594	1.718	1.851	1.993	2.144	2.305	2.476	2.658	2.853	3.059	3.278
9	1.094	1.195	1.305	1.423	1.551	1.689	1.838	1.999	2.172	2.358	2.558	2.773	3.004	3.252	3.518	3.803
10	1.105	1.219	1.344	1.480	1.629	1.791	1.967	2.159	2.367	2.594	2.839	3.106	3.395	3.707	4.046	4.411
11	1.116	1.243	1.384	1.539	1.710	1.898	2.105	2.332	2.580	2.853	3.152	3.479	3.836	4.226	4.652	5.117
12	1.127	1.268	1.426	1.601	1.796	2.012	2.252	2.518	2.813	3.138	3.498	3.896	4.335	4.818	5.350	5.936
13	1.138	1.294	1.469	1.665	1.886	2.133	2.410	2.720	3.066	3.452	3.883	4.363	4.898	5.492	6.153	6.886
14	1.149	1.319	1.513	1.732	1.980	2.261	2.579	2.937	3.342	3.797	4.310	4.887	5.535	6.261	7.076	7.988
15	1.161	1.346	1.558	1.801	2.079	2.397	2.759	3.172	3.642	4.177	4.785	5.474	6.254	7.138	8.137	9.266
16	1.173	1.373	1.605	1.873	2.183	2.540	2.952	3.426	3.970	4.595	5.311	6.130	7.067	8.137	9.358	10.748
17	1.184	1.400	1.653	1.948	2.292	2.693	3.159	3.700	4.328	5.054	5.895	6.866	7.986	9.276	10.761	12.468
18	1.196	1.428	1.702	2.026	2.407	2.854	3.380	3.996	4.717	5.560	6.544	7.690	9.024	10.575	12.375	14.463
19	1.208	1.457	1.754	2.107	2.527	3.026	3.617	4.316	5.142	6.116	7.263	8.613	10.197	12.056	14.232	16.777
20	1.220	1.486	1.806	2.191	2.653	3.207	3.870	4.661	5.604	6.727	8.062	9.646	11.523	13.743	16.367	19.461
21	1.232	1.516	1.860	2.279	2.786	3.400	4.141	5.034	6.109	7.400	8.949	10.804	13.021	15.668	18.822	22.574
22	1.245	1.546	1.916	2.370	2.925	3.604	4.430	5.437	6.659	8.140	9.934	12.100	14.714	17.861	21.645	26.186
23	1.257	1.577	1.974	2.465	3.072	3.820	4.741	5.871	7.258	8.954	11.026	13.552	16.627	20.362	24.891	30.376
24	1.270	1.608	2.033	2.563	3.225	4.049	5.072	6.341	7.911	9.850	12.239	15.179	18.788	23.212	28.625	35.236
25	1.282	1.641	2.094	2.666	3.386	4.292	5.427	6.848	8.623	10.835	13.585	17.000	21.231	26.462	32.919	40.874
30	1.348	1.811	2.427	3.243	4.322	5.743	7.612	10.063	13.268	17.449	22.892	29.960	39.116	50.950	66.212	85.850
35	1.417	2.000	2.814	3.946	5.516	7.686	10.677	14.785	20.414	28.102	38.575	52.800	72.069	98.100	133.176	180.314
40	1.489	2.208	3.262	4.801	7.040	10.286	14.974	21.725	31.409	45.259	65.001	93.051	132.782	188.884	267.864	378.721
45	1.565	2.438	3.782	5.841	8.985	13.765	21.002	31.920	48.327	72.890	109.530	163.988	244.641	363.679	538.769	795.444
50	645	2.692	4.384	7.107	11.467	18.420	29.457	46.902	74.358	117.391	184.565	289.002	450.736	700.233	1083.657	1670.704

Table A1 (*continued*)

Period	17%	18%	19%	20%	21%	22%	23%	24%	25%	30%	35%	40%	45%	50%
1	1.170	1.180	1.190	1.200	1.210	1.220	1.230	1.240	1.250	1.300	1.350	1.400	1.450	1.500
2	1.369	1.392	1.416	1.440	1.464	1.488	1.513	1.538	1.563	1.690	1.823	1.960	2.103	2.250
3	1.602	1.643	1.685	1.728	1.772	1.816	1.861	1.907	1.953	2.197	2.460	2.744	3.049	3.375
4	1.874	1.939	2.005	2.074	2.144	2.215	2.289	2.364	2.441	2.856	3.322	3.842	4.421	5.063
5	2.192	2.288	2.386	2.488	2.594	2.703	2.815	2.932	3.052	3.713	4.484	5.378	6.410	7.594
6	2.565	2.700	2.840	2.986	3.138	3.297	3.463	3.635	3.815	4.827	6.053	7.530	9.294	11.391
7	3.001	3.185	3.379	3.583	3.797	4.023	4.259	4.508	4.768	6.275	8.172	10.541	13.476	17.086
8	3.511	3.759	4.021	4.300	4.595	4.908	5.239	5.590	5.960	8.157	11.032	14.758	19.541	25.629
9	4.108	4.435	4.785	5.160	5.560	5.987	6.444	6.931	7.451	10.604	14.894	20.661	28.334	38.443
10	4.807	5.234	5.695	6.192	6.727	7.305	7.926	8.594	9.313	13.786	20.107	28.925	41.085	57.665
11	5.624	6.176	6.777	7.430	8.140	8.912	9.749	10.657	11.642	17.922	27.144	40.496	59.573	86.498
12	6.580	7.288	8.064	8.916	9.850	10.872	11.991	13.215	14.552	23.298	36.644	56.694	86.381	129.746
13	7.699	8.599	9.596	10.699	11.918	13.264	14.749	16.386	18.190	30.288	49.470	79.371	125.252	194.620
14	9.007	10.147	11.420	12.839	14.421	16.182	18.141	20.319	22.737	39.374	66.784	111.120	181.615	291.929
15	10.539	11.974	13.590	15.407	17.449	19.742	22.314	25.196	28.422	51.186	90.158	155.568	263.342	437.894
16	12.330	14.129	16.172	18.488	21.114	24.086	27.446	31.243	35.527	66.542	121.714	217.795	381.846	656.841
17	14.426	16.672	19.244	22.186	25.548	29.384	33.759	38.741	44.409	86.504	164.314	304.913	553.676	985.261
18	16.879	19.673	22.901	26.623	30.913	35.849	41.523	48.039	55.511	112.455	221.824	426.879	802.831	1477.892
19	19.748	23.214	27.252	31.948	37.404	43.736	51.074	59.568	69.389	146.192	299.462	597.630	1164.105	2216.838
20	23.106	27.393	32.429	38.338	45.259	53.358	62.821	73.864	86.736	190.050	404.274	836.683	1687.952	3325.257
21	27.034	32.324	38.591	46.005	54.764	65.096	77.269	91.592	108.420	247.065	545.769	1171.356	2447.530	4987.885
22	31.629	38.142	45.923	55.206	66.264	79.418	95.041	113.574	135.525	321.184	736.789	1639.898	3548.919	7481.828
23	37.006	45.008	54.649	66.247	80.180	96.889	116.901	140.831	169.407	417.539	994.665	2295.857	5145.932	11222.741
24	43.297	53.109	65.032	79.497	97.017	118.205	143.788	174.631	211.758	542.801	1342.797	3214.200	7461.602	16834.112
25	50.658	62.669	77.388	95.396	117.391	144.210	176.859	216.542	264.698	705.641	1812.776	4499.880	10819.322	25251.168
30	111.065	143.371	184.675	237.376	304.482	389.758	497.913	634.820	807.794	2619.996	8128.550	24201.432	69348.978	191751.059
35	243.503	327.997	440.701	590.668	789.747	1053.402	1401.777	1861.054	2465.190	9727.860	36448.688	130161.112	444508.508	*
40	533.869	750.378	1051.668	1469.772	2048.400	2847.038	3946.430	5455.913	7523.164	36118.865	163437.135	700037.697	*	*
45	1170.479	1716.684	2509.651	3657.262	5313.023	7694.712	11110.408	15994.690	22958.874	134106.817	732857.577	*	*	*
50	2566.215	3927.357	5988.914	9100.438	13780.612	20796.561	31279.195	46890.435	70064.923	497929.223	*	*	*	*

* Not shown because of space limitations.

Table A2
Present Value Factors for One Dollar Discounted at *r* Percent for *n* Periods

$$PVF_{r\%,n} = 1/(1 + r)^n$$

Period	1%	2%	3%	4%	5%	6%	7%	8%	9%	10%	11%	12%	13%	14%	15%	16%
1	0.990	0.980	0.971	0.962	0.952	0.943	0.935	0.926	0.917	0.909	0.901	0.893	0.885	0.877	0.870	0.862
2	0.980	0.961	0.943	0.925	0.907	0.890	0.873	0.857	0.842	0.826	0.812	0.797	0.783	0.769	0.756	0.743
3	0.971	0.942	0.915	0.889	0.864	0.840	0.816	0.794	0.772	0.751	0.731	0.712	0.693	0.675	0.658	0.641
4	0.961	0.924	0.888	0.855	0.823	0.792	0.763	0.735	0.708	0.683	0.659	0.636	0.613	0.592	0.572	0.552
5	0.951	0.906	0.863	0.822	0.784	0.747	0.713	0.681	0.650	0.621	0.593	0.567	0.543	0.519	0.497	0.476
6	0.942	0.888	0.837	0.790	0.746	0.705	0.666	0.630	0.596	0.564	0.535	0.507	0.480	0.456	0.432	0.410
7	0.933	0.871	0.813	0.760	0.711	0.665	0.623	0.583	0.547	0.513	0.482	0.452	0.425	0.400	0.376	0.354
8	0.923	0.853	0.789	0.731	0.677	0.627	0.582	0.540	0.502	0.467	0.434	0.404	0.376	0.351	0.327	0.305
9	0.914	0.837	0.766	0.703	0.645	0.592	0.544	0.500	0.460	0.424	0.391	0.361	0.333	0.308	0.284	0.263
10	0.905	0.820	0.744	0.676	0.614	0.558	0.508	0.463	0.422	0.386	0.352	0.322	0.295	0.270	0.247	0.227
11	0.896	0.804	0.722	0.650	0.585	0.527	0.475	0.429	0.388	0.350	0.317	0.287	0.261	0.237	0.215	0.195
12	0.887	0.788	0.701	0.625	0.557	0.497	0.444	0.397	0.356	0.319	0.286	0.257	0.231	0.208	0.187	0.168
13	0.879	0.773	0.681	0.601	0.530	0.469	0.415	0.368	0.326	0.290	0.258	0.229	0.204	0.182	0.163	0.145
14	0.870	0.758	0.661	0.577	0.505	0.442	0.388	0.340	0.299	0.263	0.232	0.205	0.181	0.160	0.141	0.125
15	0.861	0.743	0.642	0.555	0.481	0.417	0.362	0.315	0.275	0.239	0.209	0.183	0.160	0.140	0.123	0.108
16	0.853	0.728	0.623	0.534	0.458	0.394	0.339	0.292	0.252	0.218	0.188	0.163	0.141	0.123	0.107	0.093
17	0.844	0.714	0.605	0.513	0.436	0.371	0.317	0.270	0.231	0.198	0.170	0.146	0.125	0.108	0.093	0.080
18	0.836	0.700	0.587	0.494	0.416	0.350	0.296	0.250	0.212	0.180	0.153	0.130	0.111	0.095	0.081	0.069
19	0.828	0.686	0.570	0.475	0.396	0.331	0.277	0.232	0.194	0.164	0.138	0.116	0.098	0.083	0.070	0.060
20	0.820	0.673	0.554	0.456	0.377	0.312	0.258	0.215	0.178	0.149	0.124	0.104	0.087	0.073	0.061	0.051
21	0.811	0.660	0.538	0.439	0.359	0.294	0.242	0.199	0.164	0.135	0.112	0.093	0.077	0.064	0.053	0.044
22	0.803	0.647	0.522	0.422	0.342	0.278	0.226	0.184	0.150	0.123	0.101	0.083	0.068	0.056	0.046	0.038
23	0.795	0.634	0.507	0.406	0.326	0.262	0.211	0.170	0.138	0.112	0.091	0.074	0.060	0.049	0.040	0.033
24	0.788	0.622	0.492	0.390	0.310	0.247	0.197	0.158	0.126	0.102	0.082	0.066	0.053	0.043	0.035	0.028
25	0.780	0.610	0.478	0.375	0.295	0.233	0.184	0.146	0.116	0.092	0.074	0.059	0.047	0.038	0.030	0.024
30	0.742	0.552	0.412	0.308	0.231	0.174	0.131	0.099	0.075	0.057	0.044	0.033	0.026	0.020	0.015	0.012
35	0.706	0.500	0.355	0.253	0.181	0.130	0.094	0.068	0.049	0.036	0.026	0.019	0.014	0.010	0.008	0.006
40	0.672	0.453	0.307	0.208	0.142	0.097	0.067	0.046	0.032	0.022	0.015	0.011	0.008	0.005	0.004	0.003
45	0.639	0.410	0.264	0.171	0.111	0.073	0.048	0.031	0.021	0.014	0.009	0.006	0.004	0.003	0.002	0.001
50	0.608	0.372	0.228	0.141	0.087	0.054	0.034	0.021	0.013	0.009	0.005	0.003	0.002	0.001	0.001	0.001

Table A2 (*continued*)

Period	17%	18%	19%	20%	21%	22%	23%	24%	25%	30%	35%	40%	45%	50%
1	0.855	0.847	0.840	0.833	0.826	0.820	0.813	0.806	0.800	0.769	0.741	0.714	0.690	0.667
2	0.731	0.718	0.706	0.694	0.683	0.672	0.661	0.650	0.640	0.592	0.549	0.510	0.476	0.444
3	0.624	0.609	0.593	0.579	0.564	0.551	0.537	0.524	0.512	0.455	0.406	0.364	0.328	0.296
4	0.534	0.516	0.499	0.482	0.467	0.451	0.437	0.423	0.410	0.350	0.301	0.260	0.226	0.198
5	0.456	0.437	0.419	0.402	0.386	0.370	0.355	0.341	0.328	0.269	0.223	0.186	0.156	0.132
6	0.390	0.370	0.352	0.335	0.319	0.303	0.289	0.275	0.262	0.207	0.165	0.133	0.108	0.088
7	0.333	0.314	0.296	0.279	0.263	0.249	0.235	0.222	0.210	0.159	0.122	0.095	0.074	0.059
8	0.285	0.266	0.249	0.233	0.218	0.204	0.191	0.179	0.168	0.123	0.091	0.068	0.051	0.039
9	0.243	0.225	0.209	0.194	0.180	0.167	0.155	0.144	0.134	0.094	0.067	0.048	0.035	0.026
10	0.208	0.191	0.176	0.162	0.149	0.137	0.126	0.116	0.107	0.073	0.050	0.035	0.024	0.017
11	0.178	0.162	0.148	0.135	0.123	0.112	0.103	0.094	0.086	0.056	0.037	0.025	0.017	0.012
12	0.152	0.137	0.124	0.112	0.102	0.092	0.083	0.076	0.069	0.043	0.027	0.018	0.012	0.008
13	0.130	0.116	0.104	0.093	0.084	0.075	0.068	0.061	0.055	0.033	0.020	0.013	0.008	0.005
14	0.111	0.099	0.088	0.078	0.069	0.062	0.055	0.049	0.044	0.025	0.015	0.009	0.006	0.003
15	0.095	0.084	0.074	0.065	0.057	0.051	0.045	0.040	0.035	0.020	0.011	0.006	0.004	0.002
16	0.081	0.071	0.062	0.054	0.047	0.042	0.036	0.032	0.028	0.015	0.008	0.005	0.003	0.002
17	0.069	0.060	0.052	0.045	0.039	0.034	0.030	0.026	0.023	0.012	0.006	0.003	0.002	0.001
18	0.059	0.051	0.044	0.038	0.032	0.028	0.024	0.021	0.018	0.009	0.005	0.002	0.001	0.001
19	0.051	0.043	0.037	0.031	0.027	0.023	0.020	0.017	0.014	0.007	0.003	0.002	0.001	*
20	0.043	0.037	0.031	0.026	0.022	0.019	0.016	0.014	0.012	0.005	0.002	0.001	0.001	*
21	0.037	0.031	0.026	0.022	0.018	0.015	0.013	0.011	0.009	0.004	0.002	0.001	*	*
22	0.032	0.026	0.022	0.018	0.015	0.013	0.011	0.009	0.007	0.003	0.001	0.001	*	*
23	0.027	0.022	0.018	0.015	0.012	0.010	0.009	0.007	0.006	0.002	*	*	*	*
24	0.023	0.019	0.015	0.013	0.010	0.008	0.007	0.006	0.005	0.002	0.001	*	*	*
25	0.020	0.016	0.013	0.010	0.009	0.007	0.006	0.005	0.004	0.001	0.001	*	*	*
30	0.009	0.007	0.005	0.004	0.003	0.003	0.002	0.002	0.001	*	*	*	*	*
35	0.004	0.003	0.002	0.002	0.001	0.001	0.001	0.001	*	*	*	*	*	*
40	0.002	0.001	0.001	0.001	*	*	*	*	*	*	*	*	*	*
45	0.001	0.001	*	*	*	*	*	*	*	*	*	*	*	*
50	*	*	*	*	*	*	*	*	*	*	*	*	*	*

* *PVF* is zero to three decimal places.

Table A3
Future Value Factors for a One-Dollar Ordinary Annuity Compounded at *r* Percent for *n* Periods

$$FVFA_{r\%,n} = PMT \times \frac{(1+r)^n - 1}{r}$$

Period	1%	2%	3%	4%	5%	6%	7%	8%	9%	10%	11%	12%	13%	14%	15%	16%
1	1.000	1.000	1.000	1.000	1.000	1.000	1.000	1.000	1.000	1.000	1.000	1.000	1.000	1.000	1.000	1.000
2	2.010	2.020	2.030	2.040	2.050	2.060	2.070	2.080	2.090	2.100	2.110	2.120	2.130	2.140	2.150	2.160
3	3.030	3.060	3.091	3.122	3.153	3.184	3.215	3.246	3.278	3.310	3.342	3.374	3.407	3.440	3.473	3.506
4	4.060	4.122	4.184	4.246	4.310	4.375	4.440	4.506	4.573	4.641	4.710	4.779	4.850	4.921	4.993	5.066
5	5.101	5.204	5.309	5.416	5.526	5.637	5.751	5.867	5.985	6.105	6.228	6.353	6.480	6.610	6.742	6.877
6	6.152	6.308	6.468	6.633	6.802	6.975	7.153	7.336	7.523	7.716	7.913	8.115	8.323	8.536	8.754	8.977
7	7.214	7.434	7.662	7.898	8.142	8.394	8.654	8.923	9.200	9.487	9.783	10.089	10.405	10.730	11.067	11.414
8	8.286	8.583	8.892	9.214	9.549	9.897	10.260	10.637	11.028	11.436	11.859	12.300	12.757	13.233	13.727	14.240
9	9.369	9.755	10.159	10.583	11.027	11.491	11.978	12.488	13.021	13.579	14.164	14.776	15.416	16.085	16.786	17.519
10	10.462	10.950	11.464	12.006	12.578	13.181	13.816	14.487	15.193	15.937	16.722	17.549	18.420	19.337	20.304	21.321
11	11.567	12.169	12.808	13.486	14.207	14.972	15.784	16.645	17.560	18.531	19.561	20.655	21.814	23.045	24.349	25.733
12	12.683	13.412	14.192	15.026	15.917	16.870	17.888	18.977	20.141	21.384	22.713	24.133	25.650	27.271	29.002	30.850
13	13.809	14.680	15.618	16.627	17.713	18.882	20.141	21.495	22.953	24.523	26.212	28.029	29.985	32.089	34.352	36.786
14	14.947	15.974	17.086	18.292	19.599	21.015	22.550	24.215	26.019	27.975	30.095	32.393	34.883	37.581	40.505	43.672
15	16.097	17.293	18.599	20.024	21.579	23.276	25.129	27.152	29.361	31.772	34.405	37.280	40.417	43.842	47.580	51.660
16	17.258	18.639	20.157	21.825	23.657	25.673	27.888	30.324	33.003	35.950	39.190	42.753	46.672	50.980	55.717	60.925
17	18.430	20.012	21.762	23.698	25.840	28.213	30.840	33.750	36.974	40.545	44.501	48.884	53.739	59.118	65.075	71.673
18	19.615	21.412	23.414	25.645	28.132	30.906	33.999	37.450	41.301	45.599	50.396	55.750	61.725	68.394	84.141	75.836
19	20.811	22.841	25.117	27.671	30.539	33.760	37.379	41.446	46.018	51.159	56.939	63.440	70.749	78.969	88.212	98.603
20	22.019	24.297	26.870	29.778	33.066	36.786	40.995	45.762	51.160	57.275	64.203	72.052	80.947	91.025	102.444	115.380
21	23.239	25.783	28.676	31.969	35.719	39.993	44.865	50.423	56.765	64.002	72.265	81.699	92.470	104.768	118.810	134.841
22	24.472	27.299	30.537	34.248	38.505	43.392	49.006	55.457	62.873	71.403	81.214	92.503	105.491	120.436	137.632	157.415
23	25.716	28.845	32.453	36.618	41.430	46.996	53.436	60.893	69.532	79.543	91.148	104.603	120.205	138.297	159.276	183.601
24	26.973	30.422	34.426	39.083	44.502	50.816	58.177	66.765	76.790	88.497	102.174	118.155	136.831	158.659	184.168	213.978
25	28.243	32.030	36.459	41.646	47.727	54.865	63.249	73.106	84.701	98.347	114.413	133.334	155.620	181.871	212.793	249.214
30	34.785	40.568	47.575	56.085	66.439	79.058	94.461	113.283	136.308	164.494	199.021	241.333	293.199	356.787	434.745	530.312
35	41.660	49.994	60.462	73.652	90.320	111.435	138.237	172.317	215.711	271.024	341.590	431.663	546.681	693.573	881.170	1120.713
40	48.886	60.402	75.401	95.026	120.800	154.762	199.635	259.057	337.882	442.593	581.826	767.091	1013.704	1342.025	1779.090	2360.757
45	56.481	71.893	92.720	121.029	159.700	212.744	285.749	386.506	525.859	718.905	986.639	1358.230	1874.165	2590.565	3585.128	4965.274
50	64.463	84.579	112.797	152.667	209.348	290.336	406.529	573.770	815.084	1163.909	1668.771	2400.018	3459.507	4994.521	7217.716	10435.649

Table A3 (*continued*)

Period	17%	18%	19%	20%	21%	22%	23%	24%	25%	30%	35%	40%	45%	50%
1	1.000	1.000	1.000	1.000	1.000	1.000	1.000	1.000	1.000	1.000	1.000	1.000	1.000	1.000
2	2.170	2.180	2.190	2.200	2.210	2.220	2.230	2.240	2.250	2.300	2.350	2.400	2.450	2.500
3	3.539	3.572	3.606	3.640	3.674	3.708	3.743	3.778	3.813	3.990	4.173	4.360	4.553	4.750
4	5.141	5.215	5.291	5.368	5.446	5.524	5.604	5.684	5.766	6.187	6.633	7.104	7.601	8.125
5	7.014	7.154	7.297	7.442	7.589	7.740	7.893	8.048	8.207	9.043	9.954	10.946	12.022	13.188
6	9.207	9.442	9.683	9.930	10.183	10.442	10.708	10.980	11.259	12.756	14.438	16.324	18.431	20.781
7	11.772	12.142	12.523	12.916	13.321	13.740	14.171	14.615	15.073	17.583	20.492	23.853	27.725	32.172
8	14.773	15.327	15.902	16.499	17.119	17.762	18.430	19.123	19.842	23.858	28.664	34.395	41.202	49.258
9	18.285	19.086	19.923	20.799	21.714	22.670	23.669	24.712	25.802	32.015	39.696	49.153	60.743	74.887
10	22.393	23.521	24.709	25.959	27.274	28.657	30.113	31.643	33.253	42.619	54.590	69.814	89.077	113.330
11	27.200	28.755	30.404	32.150	34.001	35.962	38.039	40.238	42.566	56.405	74.697	98.739	130.162	170.995
12	32.824	34.931	37.180	39.581	42.142	44.874	47.788	50.895	54.208	74.327	101.841	139.235	189.735	257.493
13	39.404	42.219	45.244	48.497	51.991	55.746	59.779	64.110	68.760	97.625	138.485	195.929	276.115	387.239
14	47.103	50.818	54.841	59.196	63.909	69.010	74.528	80.496	86.949	127.91	187.954	275.300	401.367	581.859
15	56.110	60.965	66.261	72.035	78.330	85.192	92.669	100.815	109.687	167.286	254.738	386.420	582.982	873.788
16	66.649	72.939	79.850	87.442	95.780	104.935	114.983	126.011	138.109	218.472	344.897	541.988	846.324	1311.682
17	78.979	87.068	96.022	105.931	116.894	129.020	142.430	157.253	173.636	285.014	466.611	759.784	1228.170	1968.523
18	93.406	103.740	115.266	128.117	142.441	158.405	176.188	195.994	218.045	371.518	630.925	1064.697	1781.846	2953.784
19	110.285	123.414	138.166	154.740	173.354	194.254	217.712	244.033	273.556	483.973	852.748	1491.576	2584.677	4431.676
20	130.033	146.628	165.418	186.688	210.758	237.989	268.785	303.601	342.945	630.165	1152.210	2089.206	3748.782	6648.513
21	153.139	174.021	197.847	225.026	256.018	291.347	331.606	377.465	429.681	820.215	1556.484	2925.889	5436.734	9973.770
22	180.172	206.345	236.438	271.031	310.781	356.443	408.875	469.056	538.101	1067.280	2102.253	4097.245	7884.264	14961.655
23	211.801	244.487	282.362	326.237	377.045	435.861	503.917	582.630	673.626	1388.464	2839.042	5737.142	11433.182	22443.483
24	248.808	289.494	337.010	392.484	457.225	532.750	620.817	723.461	843.033	1806.003	3833.706	8032.999	16579.115	33666.224
25	292.105	342.603	402.042	471.981	554.242	650.955	764.605	898.092	1054.79	2348.803	5176.504	11247.199	24040.716	50500.337
30	647.439	790.948	966.712	1181.882	1445.151	1767.081	2160.491	2640.916	3227.174	8729.985	23221.570	60501.081	154106.618	383500.118
35	1426.491	1816.652	2314.214	2948.341	3755.938	4783.645	6090.334	7750.225	9856.761	32422.868	104136.251	325400.279	987794.463	*
40	3134.522	4163.213	5529.829	7343.858	9749.525	12936.535	17154.046	22728.803	30088.655	120392.883	466960.385	*	*	*
45	6879.291	9531.577	13203.424	18281.310	25295.346	34971.419	48301.775	66640.376	91831.496	447019.389	*	*	*	*
50	15089.502	21813.094	31515.336	45497.191	65617.202	94525.279	135992.154	195372.644	280255.693	*	*	*	*	*

* Not shown because of space limitations.

Table A4
Present Value Factors for a One-Dollar Ordinary Annuity Discounted at *r* Percent for *n* Periods

$$PVFA_{r\%,n} = \frac{PMT}{r} \times \left[1 - \frac{1}{(1+r)^n}\right]$$

Period	1%	2%	3%	4%	5%	6%	7%	8%	9%	10%	11%	12%	13%	14%	15%	16%
1	0.990	0.980	0.971	0.962	0.952	0.943	0.935	0.926	0.917	0.909	0.901	0.893	0.885	0.877	0.870	0.862
2	0.980	0.961	0.943	0.925	0.907	0.890	0.873	0.857	0.842	0.826	0.812	0.797	0.783	0.769	0.756	1.605
3	0.971	0.942	0.915	0.889	0.864	0.840	0.816	0.794	0.772	0.751	0.731	0.712	0.693	0.675	0.658	2.246
4	0.961	0.924	0.888	0.855	0.823	0.792	0.763	0.735	0.708	0.683	0.659	0.636	0.613	0.592	0.572	2.798
5	0.951	0.906	0.863	0.822	0.784	0.747	0.713	0.681	0.650	0.621	0.593	0.567	0.543	0.519	0.497	3.274
6	0.942	0.888	0.837	0.790	0.746	0.705	0.666	0.630	0.596	0.564	0.535	0.507	0.480	0.456	0.432	3.685
7	0.933	0.871	0.813	0.760	0.711	0.665	0.623	0.583	0.547	0.513	0.482	0.452	0.425	0.400	0.376	4.039
8	0.923	0.853	0.789	0.731	0.677	0.627	0.582	0.540	0.502	0.467	0.434	0.404	0.376	0.351	0.327	4.344
9	0.914	0.837	0.766	0.703	0.645	0.592	0.544	0.500	0.460	0.424	0.391	0.361	0.333	0.308	0.284	4.607
10	0.905	0.820	0.744	0.676	0.614	0.558	0.508	0.463	0.422	0.386	0.352	0.322	0.295	0.270	0.247	4.833
11	0.896	0.804	0.722	0.650	0.585	0.527	0.475	0.429	0.388	0.350	0.317	0.287	0.261	0.237	0.215	5.029
12	0.887	0.788	0.701	0.625	0.557	0.497	0.444	0.397	0.356	0.319	0.286	0.257	0.231	0.208	0.187	5.197
13	0.879	0.773	0.681	0.601	0.530	0.469	0.415	0.368	0.326	0.290	0.258	0.229	0.204	0.182	0.163	5.342
14	0.870	0.758	0.661	0.577	0.505	0.442	0.388	0.340	0.299	0.263	0.232	0.205	0.181	0.160	0.141	5.468
15	0.861	0.743	0.642	0.555	0.481	0.417	0.362	0.315	0.275	0.239	0.209	0.183	0.160	0.140	0.123	5.575
16	0.853	0.728	0.623	0.534	0.458	0.394	0.339	0.292	0.252	0.218	0.188	0.163	0.141	0.123	0.107	5.668
17	0.844	0.714	0.605	0.513	0.436	0.371	0.317	0.270	0.231	0.198	0.170	0.146	0.125	0.108	0.093	5.749
18	0.836	0.700	0.587	0.494	0.416	0.350	0.296	0.250	0.212	0.180	0.153	0.130	0.111	0.095	0.081	5.818
19	0.828	0.686	0.570	0.475	0.396	0.331	0.277	0.232	0.194	0.164	0.138	0.116	0.098	0.083	0.07	05.877
20	0.820	0.673	0.554	0.456	0.377	0.312	0.258	0.215	0.178	0.149	0.124	0.104	0.087	0.073	0.061	5.929
21	0.811	0.660	0.538	0.439	0.359	0.294	0.242	0.199	0.164	0.135	0.112	0.093	0.077	0.064	0.053	5.973
22	0.803	0.647	0.522	0.422	0.342	0.278	0.226	0.184	0.150	0.123	0.101	0.083	0.068	0.056	0.046	6.011
23	0.795	0.634	0.507	0.406	0.326	0.262	0.211	0.170	0.138	0.112	0.091	0.074	0.060	0.049	0.040	6.044
24	0.788	0.622	0.492	0.390	0.310	0.247	0.197	0.158	0.126	0.102	0.082	0.066	0.053	0.043	0.035	6.073
25	0.780	0.610	0.478	0.375	0.295	0.233	0.184	0.146	0.116	0.092	0.074	0.059	0.047	0.038	0.030	6.097
30	0.742	0.552	0.412	0.308	0.231	0.174	0.131	0.099	0.075	0.057	0.044	0.033	0.026	0.020	0.015	6.177
35	0.706	0.500	0.355	0.253	0.181	0.130	0.094	0.068	0.049	0.036	0.026	0.019	0.014	0.010	0.008	6.215
40	0.672	0.453	0.307	0.208	0.142	0.097	0.067	0.046	0.032	0.022	0.015	0.011	0.008	0.005	0.004	6.233
45	0.639	0.410	0.264	0.171	0.111	0.073	0.048	0.031	0.021	0.014	0.009	0.006	0.004	0.003	0.002	6.242
50	0.608	0.372	0.228	0.141	0.087	0.054	0.034	0.021	0.013	0.009	0.005	0.003	0.002	0.001	0.001	6.246

Table A4 (continued)

Period	17%	18%	19%	20%	21%	22%	23%	24%	25%	30%	35%	40%	45%	50%
1	0.855	0.847	0.840	0.833	0.826	0.820	0.813	0.806	0.800	0.769	0.741	0.714	0.690	0.667
2	1.585	1.566	1.547	1.528	1.509	1.492	1.474	1.457	1.440	1.361	1.289	1.224	1.165	1.111
3	2.210	2.174	2.140	2.106	2.074	2.042	2.011	1.981	1.952	1.816	1.696	1.589	1.493	1.407
4	2.743	2.690	2.639	2.589	2.540	2.494	2.448	2.404	2.362	2.166	1.997	1.849	1.720	1.605
5	3.199	3.127	3.058	2.991	2.926	2.864	2.803	2.745	2.689	2.436	2.220	2.035	1.876	1.737
6	3.589	3.498	3.410	3.326	3.245	3.167	3.092	3.020	2.951	2.643	2.385	2.168	1.983	1.824
7	3.922	3.812	3.706	3.605	3.508	3.416	3.327	3.242	3.161	2.802	2.508	2.263	2.057	1.883
8	4.207	4.078	3.954	3.837	3.726	3.619	3.518	3.421	3.329	2.925	2.598	2.331	2.109	1.922
9	4.451	4.303	4.163	4.031	3.905	3.786	3.673	3.566	3.463	3.019	2.665	2.379	2.144	1.948
10	4.659	4.494	4.339	4.192	4.054	3.923	3.799	3.682	3.571	3.092	2.715	2.414	2.168	1.965
11	4.836	4.656	4.486	4.327	4.177	4.035	3.902	3.776	3.656	3.147	2.752	2.438	2.185	1.977
12	4.988	4.793	4.611	4.439	4.278	4.127	3.985	3.851	3.725	3.190	2.779	2.456	2.196	1.985
13	5.118	4.910	4.715	4.533	4.362	4.203	4.053	3.912	3.780	3.223	2.799	2.469	2.204	1.990
14	5.229	5.008	4.802	4.611	4.432	4.265	4.108	3.962	3.824	3.249	2.814	2.478	2.210	1.993
15	5.324	5.092	4.876	4.675	4.489	4.315	4.153	4.001	3.859	3.268	2.825	2.484	2.214	1.995
16	5.405	5.162	4.938	4.730	4.536	4.357	4.189	4.033	3.887	3.283	2.834	2.489	2.216	1.997
17	5.475	5.222	4.990	4.775	4.576	4.391	4.219	4.059	3.910	3.295	2.840	2.492	2.218	1.998
18	5.534	5.273	5.033	4.812	4.608	4.419	4.243	4.080	3.928	3.304	2.844	2.494	2.219	1.999
19	5.584	5.316	5.070	4.843	4.635	4.442	4.263	4.097	3.942	3.311	2.848	2.496	2.220	1.999
20	5.628	5.353	5.101	4.870	4.657	4.460	4.279	4.110	3.954	3.316	2.850	2.497	2.221	1.999
21	5.665	5.384	5.127	4.891	4.675	4.476	4.292	4.121	3.963	3.320	2.852	2.498	2.221	2.000
22	5.696	5.410	5.149	4.909	4.690	4.488	4.302	4.130	3.970	3.323	2.853	2.498	2.222	2.000
23	5.723	5.432	5.167	4.925	4.703	4.499	4.311	4.137	3.976	3.325	2.854	2.499	2.222	2.000
24	5.746	5.451	5.182	4.937	4.713	4.507	4.318	4.143	3.981	3.327	2.855	2.499	2.222	2.000
25	5.766	5.467	5.195	4.948	4.721	4.514	4.323	4.147	3.985	3.329	2.856	2.499	2.222	2.000
30	5.829	5.517	5.235	4.979	4.746	4.534	4.339	4.160	3.995	3.332	2.857	2.500	2.222	2.000
35	5.858	5.539	5.251	4.992	4.756	4.541	4.345	4.164	3.998	3.333	2.857	2.500	2.222	2.000
40	5.871	5.548	5.258	4.997	4.760	4.544	4.347	4.166	3.999	3.333	2.857	2.500	2.222	2.000
45	5.877	5.552	5.261	4.999	4.761	4.545	4.347	4.166	4.000	3.333	2.857	2.500	2.222	2.000
50	5.880	5.554	5.262	4.999	4.762	4.545	4.348	4.167	4.000	3.333	2.857	2.500	2.222	2.000

Table A5
Future Value Factor for One Dollar Compounded Continuously at *r* Percent for *n* Periods

$$FVF_{r\%,n} = e^{rn}$$

Period	1%	2%	3%	4%	5%	6%	7%	8%	9%	10%	11%	12%	13%	14%	15%	16%
1	0.990	0.980	0.971	0.962	0.952	0.943	0.935	0.926	0.917	0.909	0.901	0.893	0.885	0.877	0.870	1.174
2	1.970	1.942	1.913	1.886	1.859	1.833	1.808	1.783	1.759	1.736	1.713	1.690	1.668	1.647	1.626	1.377
3	2.941	2.884	2.829	2.775	2.723	2.673	2.624	2.577	2.531	2.487	2.444	2.402	2.361	2.322	2.283	1.616
4	3.902	3.808	3.717	3.630	3.546	3.465	3.387	3.312	3.240	3.170	3.102	3.037	2.974	2.914	2.855	1.896
5	4.853	4.713	4.580	4.452	4.329	4.212	4.100	3.993	3.890	3.791	3.696	3.605	3.517	3.433	3.352	2.226
6	5.795	5.601	5.417	5.242	5.076	4.917	4.767	4.623	4.486	4.355	4.231	4.111	3.998	3.889	3.784	2.612
7	6.728	6.472	6.230	6.002	5.786	5.582	5.389	5.206	5.033	4.868	4.712	4.564	4.423	4.288	4.160	3.065
8	7.652	7.325	7.020	6.733	6.463	6.210	5.971	5.747	5.535	5.335	5.146	4.968	4.799	4.639	4.487	3.597
9	8.566	8.162	7.786	7.435	7.108	6.802	6.515	6.247	5.995	5.759	5.537	5.328	5.132	4.946	4.772	4.221
10	9.471	8.983	8.530	8.111	7.722	7.360	7.024	6.710	6.418	6.145	5.889	5.650	5.426	5.216	5.019	4.953
11	10.368	9.787	9.253	8.760	8.306	7.887	7.499	7.139	6.805	6.495	6.207	5.938	5.687	5.453	5.234	5.812
12	11.255	10.575	9.954	9.385	8.863	8.384	7.943	7.536	7.161	6.814	6.492	6.194	5.918	5.660	5.421	6.821
13	12.134	11.348	10.635	9.986	9.394	8.853	8.358	7.904	7.487	7.103	6.750	6.424	6.122	5.842	5.583	8.004
14	13.004	12.106	11.296	10.563	9.899	9.295	8.745	8.244	7.786	7.367	6.982	6.628	6.302	6.002	5.724	9.393
15	13.865	12.849	11.938	11.118	10.380	9.712	9.108	8.559	8.061	7.606	7.191	6.811	6.462	6.142	5.847	11.023
16	14.718	13.578	12.561	11.652	10.838	10.106	9.447	8.851	8.313	7.824	7.379	6.974	6.604	6.265	5.954	12.936
17	15.562	14.292	13.166	12.166	11.274	10.477	9.763	9.122	8.544	8.022	7.549	7.120	6.729	6.373	6.047	15.180
18	16.398	14.992	13.754	12.659	11.690	10.828	10.059	9.372	8.756	8.201	7.702	7.250	6.840	6.467	6.128	17.814
19	17.226	15.678	14.324	13.134	12.085	11.158	10.336	9.604	8.950	8.365	7.839	7.366	6.938	6.550	6.198	20.905
20	18.046	16.351	14.877	13.590	12.462	11.470	10.594	9.818	9.129	8.514	7.963	7.469	7.025	6.623	6.259	24.533
21	18.857	17.011	15.415	14.029	12.821	11.764	10.836	10.017	9.292	8.649	8.075	7.562	7.102	6.687	6.312	28.789
22	19.660	17.658	15.937	14.451	13.163	12.042	11.061	10.201	9.442	8.772	8.176	7.645	7.170	6.743	6.359	33.784
23	20.456	18.292	16.444	14.857	13.489	12.303	11.272	10.371	9.580	8.883	8.266	7.718	7.230	6.792	6.399	39.646
24	21.243	18.914	16.936	15.247	13.799	12.550	11.469	10.529	9.707	8.985	8.348	7.784	7.283	6.835	6.434	46.525
25	22.023	19.523	17.413	15.622	14.094	12.783	11.654	10.675	9.823	9.077	8.422	7.843	7.330	6.873	6.464	54.598
30	25.808	22.396	19.600	17.292	15.372	13.765	12.409	11.258	10.274	9.427	8.694	8.055	7.496	7.003	6.566	121.510
35	29.409	24.999	21.487	18.665	16.374	14.498	12.948	11.655	10.567	9.644	8.855	8.176	7.586	7.070	6.617	270.426
40	32.835	27.355	23.115	19.793	17.159	15.046	13.332	11.925	10.757	9.779	8.951	8.244	7.634	7.105	6.642	601.845
45	36.095	29.490	24.519	20.720	17.774	15.456	13.606	12.108	10.881	9.863	9.008	8.283	7.661	7.123	6.654	1339.431
50	39.196	31.424	25.730	21.482	18.256	15.762	13.801	12.233	10.962	9.915	9.042	8.304	7.675	7.133	6.661	2980.958

Table A5 (*continued*)

Period	17%	18%	19%	20%	21%	22%	23%	24%	25%	30%	35%	40%	45%	50%
1	1.185	1.197	1.209	1.221	1.234	1.246	1.259	1.271	1.284	1.405	1.419	1.492	1.568	1.649
2	1.405	1.433	1.462	1.492	1.522	1.553	1.584	1.616	1.649	1.822	2.014	2.226	2.460	2.718
3	1.665	1.716	1.768	1.822	1.878	1.935	1.994	2.054	2.117	2.460	2.858	3.320	3.857	4.482
4	1.974	2.054	2.138	2.226	2.316	2.411	2.509	2.612	2.718	3.320	4.055	4.953	6.050	7.389
5	2.340	2.460	2.586	2.718	2.858	3.004	3.158	3.320	3.490	4.482	5.755	7.389	9.488	12.182
6	2.773	2.945	3.127	3.320	3.525	3.743	3.975	4.221	4.482	6.050	8.166	11.023	14.880	20.086
7	3.287	3.525	3.781	4.055	4.349	4.665	5.003	5.366	5.755	8.166	11.588	16.445	23.336	33.115
8	3.896	4.221	4.572	4.953	5.366	5.812	6.297	6.821	7.389	11.023	16.445	24.533	36.598	54.598
9	4.618	5.053	5.529	6.050	6.619	7.243	7.925	8.671	9.488	14.880	23.336	36.598	57.397	90.017
10	5.474	6.050	6.686	7.389	8.166	9.025	9.974	11.023	12.182	20.086	33.115	54.598	90.017	148.413
11	6.488	7.243	8.085	9.025	10.074	11.246	12.554	14.013	15.643	27.113	46.993	81.451	141.175	244.692
12	7.691	8.671	9.777	11.023	12.429	14.013	15.800	17.814	20.086	36.598	66.686	121.510	221.406	403.429
13	9.116	10.381	11.822	13.464	15.333	17.462	19.886	22.646	25.790	49.402	94.632	181.272	347.234	665.142
14	10.805	12.429	14.296	16.445	18.916	21.758	25.028	28.789	33.115	66.686	134.290	270.426	544.572	1096.633
15	12.807	14.880	17.288	20.086	23.336	27.113	31.500	36.598	42.521	90.017	190.566	403.429	854.059	1808.042
16	15.180	17.814	20.905	24.533	28.789	33.784	39.646	46.525	54.598	121.510	270.426	601.845	1339.431	2980.958
17	17.993	21.328	25.280	29.964	35.517	42.098	49.899	59.145	70.105	164.022	383.753	897.847	2100.646	4914.769
18	21.328	25.534	30.569	36.598	43.816	52.457	62.803	75.189	90.017	221.406	544.572	1339.431	3294.468	8103.084
19	25.280	30.569	36.966	44.701	54.055	65.366	79.044	95.583	115.584	298.867	772.784	1998.196	5166.754	13359.727
20	29.964	36.598	44.701	54.598	66.686	81.451	99.484	121.510	148.413	403.429	1096.633	2980.958	8103.084	22026.466
21	35.517	43.816	54.055	66.686	82.269	101.494	125.211	154.470	190.566	544.572	1556.197	4447.067	12708.165	36315.503
22	42.098	52.457	65.366	81.451	101.494	126.469	157.591	196.370	244.692	735.095	2208.348	6634.244	19930.370	59874.142
23	49.899	62.803	79.044	99.484	125.211	157.591	198.343	249.635	314.191	992.275	3133.795	9897.129	31257.043	98715.771
24	59.145	75.189	95.583	121.510	154.470	196.370	249.635	317.348	403.429	1339.431	4447.067	14764.782	49020.801	162754.791
35	70.105	90.017	115.584	148.413	190.566	244.692	314.191	403.429	518.013	1808.042	6310.688	22026.466	76879.920	268337.287
30	164.022	221.406	298.867	403.429	544.572	735.095	992.275	1339.431	1808.042	8103.084	36315.503	162754.791	729416.370	
35	383.753	544.572	772.784	1096.633	1556.197	2208.348	3133.795	4447.067	6310.688	36315.503	208981.289	*	*	
40	897.847	1339.431	1998.196	2980.958	4447.067	6634.244	9897.129	14764.782	22026.466	162754.791	*	*	*	
45	2100.646	3294.468	5166.754	8103.084	12708.165	19930.370	31257.043	49020.801	76879.920	729416.370	*	*	*	
50	4914.769	8103.084	13359.727	22026.466	36315.503	59874.142	98715.771	162754.791	268337.287	*	*	*	*	

* Not shown because of space limitations.

Table A6 (*continued*)
Present Value Factor for One Dollar Discounted Continuously at *r* Percent for *n* Periods

$$PVF_{r\%,n} = e^{-rn}$$

Period	1%	2%	3%	4%	5%	6%	7%	8%	9%	10%	11%	12%	13%	14%	15%	16%
1	0.990	0.980	0.970	0.961	0.951	0.942	0.932	0.923	0.914	0.905	0.896	0.887	0.878	0.869	0.861	0.852
2	0.980	0.961	0.942	0.923	0.905	0.887	0.869	0.852	0.835	0.819	0.803	0.787	0.771	0.756	0.741	0.726
3	0.970	0.942	0.914	0.887	0.861	0.835	0.811	0.787	0.763	0.741	0.719	0.698	0.677	0.657	0.638	0.726
4	0.961	0.923	0.887	0.852	0.819	0.787	0.756	0.726	0.698	0.670	0.644	0.619	0.595	0.571	0.549	0.619
5	0.951	0.905	0.861	0.819	0.779	0.741	0.705	0.670	0.638	0.607	0.577	0.549	0.522	0.497	0.472	0.449
6	0.942	0.887	0.835	0.787	0.741	0.698	0.657	0.619	0.583	0.549	0.517	0.487	0.458	0.432	0.407	0.383
7	0.932	0.869	0.811	0.756	0.705	0.657	0.613	0.571	0.533	0.497	0.463	0.432	0.403	0.375	0.350	0.326
8	0.923	0.852	0.787	0.726	0.670	0.619	0.571	0.527	0.487	0.449	0.415	0.383	0.353	0.326	0.301	0.278
9	0.914	0.835	0.763	0.698	0.638	0.583	0.533	0.487	0.445	0.407	0.372	0.340	0.310	0.284	0.259	0.237
10	0.905	0.819	0.741	0.670	0.607	0.549	0.497	0.449	0.407	0.368	0.333	0.301	0.273	0.247	0.223	0.202
11	0.896	0.803	0.719	0.644	0.577	0.517	0.463	0.415	0.372	0.333	0.298	0.267	0.239	0.214	0.192	0.172
12	0.887	0.787	0.698	0.619	0.549	0.487	0.432	0.383	0.340	0.301	0.267	0.237	0.210	0.186	0.165	0.147
13	0.878	0.771	0.677	0.595	0.522	0.458	0.403	0.353	0.310	0.273	0.239	0.210	0.185	0.162	0.142	0.125
14	0.869	0.756	0.657	0.571	0.497	0.432	0.375	0.326	0.284	0.247	0.214	0.186	0.162	0.141	0.122	0.106
15	0.861	0.741	0.638	0.549	0.472	0.407	0.350	0.301	0.259	0.223	0.192	0.165	0.142	0.122	0.105	0.091
16	0.852	0.726	0.619	0.527	0.449	0.383	0.326	0.278	0.237	0.202	0.172	0.147	0.125	0.106	0.091	0.077
17	0.844	0.712	0.600	0.507	0.427	0.361	0.304	0.257	0.217	0.183	0.154	0.130	0.110	0.093	0.078	0.066
18	0.835	0.698	0.583	0.487	0.407	0.340	0.284	0.237	0.198	0.165	0.138	0.115	0.096	0.080	0.067	0.056
19	0.827	0.684	0.566	0.468	0.387	0.320	0.264	0.219	0.181	0.150	0.124	0.102	0.085	0.070	0.058	0.048
20	0.819	0.670	0.549	0.449	0.368	0.301	0.247	0.202	0.165	0.135	0.111	0.091	0.074	0.061	0.050	0.041
21	0.811	0.657	0.533	0.432	0.350	0.284	0.230	0.186	0.151	0.122	0.099	0.080	0.065	0.053	0.043	0.035
22	0.803	0.644	0.517	0.415	0.333	0.267	0.214	0.172	0.138	0.111	0.089	0.071	0.057	0.046	0.037	0.030
23	0.795	0.631	0.502	0.399	0.317	0.252	0.200	0.159	0.126	0.100	0.080	0.063	0.050	0.040	0.032	0.025
24	0.787	0.619	0.487	0.383	0.301	0.237	0.186	0.147	0.115	0.091	0.071	0.056	0.044	0.035	0.027	0.021
25	0.779	0.607	0.472	0.368	0.287	0.223	0.174	0.135	0.105	0.082	0.064	0.050	0.039	0.030	0.024	0.018
30	0.741	0.549	0.407	0.301	0.223	0.165	0.122	0.091	0.067	0.050	0.037	0.027	0.020	0.015	0.011	0.008
35	0.705	0.497	0.350	0.247	0.174	0.122	0.086	0.061	0.043	0.030	0.021	0.015	0.011	0.007	0.005	0.004
40	0.670	0.449	0.301	0.202	0.135	0.091	0.061	0.041	0.027	0.018	0.012	0.008	0.006	0.004	0.002	0.002
45	0.638	0.407	0.259	0.165	0.105	0.067	0.043	0.027	0.017	0.011	0.007	0.005	0.003	0.002	0.001	0.001
50	0.607	0.368	0.223	0.135	0.082	0.050	0.030	0.018	0.011	0.007	0.004	0.002	0.002	0.001	0.001	*

* Discount factor is zero to three decimal places.

Period	17%	18%	19%	20%	21%	22%	23%	24%	25%	30%	35%	40%	45%	50%
1	0.844	0.835	0.827	0.819	0.811	0.803	0.795	0.787	0.779	0.741	0.705	0.670	0.638	0.607
2	0.712	0.698	0.684	0.670	0.657	0.644	0.631	0.619	0.607	0.549	0.497	0.449	0.407	0.368
3	0.600	0.583	0.566	0.549	0.533	0.517	0.502	0.487	0.472	0.407	0.350	0.301	0.259	0.223
4	0.507	0.487	0.468	0.449	0.432	0.415	0.399	0.383	0.368	0.301	0.247	0.202	0.165	0.135
5	0.427	0.407	0.387	0.368	0.350	0.333	0.317	0.301	0.287	0.223	0.174	0.135	0.105	0.082
6	0.361	0.340	0.320	0.301	0.284	0.267	0.252	0.237	0.223	0.165	0.122	0.091	0.067	0.050
7	0.304	0.284	0.264	0.247	0.230	0.214	0.200	0.186	0.174	0.122	0.086	0.061	0.043	0.030
8	0.257	0.237	0.219	0.202	0.186	0.172	0.159	0.147	0.135	0.091	0.061	0.041	0.027	0.018
9	0.217	0.198	0.181	0.165	0.151	0.138	0.126	0.115	0.105	0.067	0.043	0.027	0.017	0.011
10	0.183	0.165	0.150	0.135	0.122	0.111	0.100	0.091	0.082	0.050	0.030	0.018	0.011	0.007
11	0.154	0.138	0.124	0.111	0.099	0.089	0.080	0.071	0.064	0.037	0.021	0.012	0.007	0.004
12	0.130	0.115	0.102	0.091	0.080	0.071	0.063	0.056	0.050	0.027	0.015	0.008	0.005	0.002
13	0.110	0.096	0.085	0.074	0.065	0.057	0.050	0.044	0.039	0.020	0.011	0.006	0.003	0.002
14	0.093	0.080	0.070	0.061	0.053	0.046	0.040	0.035	0.030	0.015	0.007	0.004	0.002	0.001
15	0.078	0.067	0.058	0.050	0.043	0.037	0.032	0.027	0.024	0.011	0.005	0.002	0.001	0.001
16	0.066	0.056	0.048	0.041	0.035	0.030	0.025	0.021	0.018	0.008	0.004	0.002	0.001	*
17	0.056	0.047	0.040	0.033	0.028	0.024	0.020	0.017	0.014	0.006	0.003	0.001	*	*
18	0.047	0.039	0.033	0.027	0.023	0.019	0.016	0.013	0.011	0.005	0.002	0.001	*	*
19	0.040	0.033	0.027	0.022	0.018	0.015	0.013	0.010	0.009	0.003	0.001	0.001	*	*
20	0.033	0.027	0.022	0.018	0.015	0.012	0.010	0.008	0.007	0.002	0.001	*	*	*
21	0.028	0.023	0.018	0.015	0.012	0.010	0.008	0.006	0.005	0.002	0.001	*	*	*
22	0.024	0.019	0.015	0.012	0.010	0.008	0.006	0.005	0.004	0.001	*	*	*	*
23	0.020	0.016	0.013	0.010	0.008	0.006	0.005	0.004	0.003	0.001	*	*	*	*
24	0.017	0.013	0.010	0.008	0.006	0.005	0.004	0.003	0.002	0.001	*	*	*	*
25	0.014	0.011	0.009	0.007	0.005	0.004	0.003	0.002	0.002	0.001	*	*	*	*
30	0.006	0.005	0.003	0.002	0.002	0.001	0.001	0.001	0.001	*	*	*	*	*
35	0.003	0.002	0.001	0.001	0.001	*	*	*	*	*	*	*	*	*
40	0.001	0.001	0.001	*	*	*	*	*	*	*	*	*	*	*
45	*	*	*	*	*	*	*	*	*	*	*	*	*	*
50	*	*	*	*	*	*	*	*	*	*	*	*	*	*

* Discount factor is zero to three decimal places.

Appendix B: Cumulative Probabilities from the Standard Normal Distribution

Appendix B

Cumulative Probability, *N*(*d*), of Drawing a Value Less than or Equal to *d* from the Standard Normal Distribution

d	0	0.01	0.02	0.03	0.04	0.05	0.06	0.07	0.08	0.09
0	0.5000	0.5040	0.5080	0.5120	0.5160	0.5199	0.5239	0.5279	0.5319	0.5359
0.1	0.5398	0.5438	0.5478	0.5517	0.5557	0.5596	0.5636	0.5675	0.5714	0.5753
0.2	0.5793	0.5832	0.5871	0.5910	0.5948	0.5987	0.6026	0.6064	0.6103	0.6141
0.3	0.6179	0.6217	0.6255	0.6293	0.6331	0.6368	0.6406	0.6443	0.6480	0.6517
0.4	0.6554	0.6591	0.6628	0.6664	0.6700	0.6736	0.6772	0.6808	0.6844	0.6879
0.5	0.6915	0.6950	0.6985	0.7019	0.7054	0.7088	0.7123	0.7157	0.7190	0.7224
0.6	0.7257	0.7291	0.7324	0.7357	0.7389	0.7422	0.7454	0.7486	0.7517	0.7549
0.7	0.7580	0.7611	0.7642	0.7673	0.7704	0.7734	0.7764	0.7794	0.7823	0.7852
0.8	0.7881	0.7910	0.7939	0.7967	0.7995	0.8023	0.8051	0.8078	0.8106	0.8133
0.9	0.8159	0.8186	0.8212	0.8238	0.8264	0.8289	0.8315	0.8340	0.8365	0.8389
1	0.8413	0.8438	0.8461	0.8485	0.8508	0.8531	0.8554	0.8577	0.8599	0.8621
1.1	0.8643	0.8665	0.8686	0.8708	0.8729	0.8749	0.8770	0.8790	0.8810	0.8830
1.2	0.8849	0.8869	0.8888	0.8907	0.8925	0.8944	0.8962	0.8980	0.8997	0.9015
1.3	0.9032	0.9049	0.9066	0.9082	0.9099	0.9115	0.9131	0.9147	0.9162	0.9177
1.4	0.9192	0.9207	0.9222	0.9236	0.9251	0.9265	0.9279	0.9292	0.9306	0.9319
1.5	0.9332	0.9345	0.9357	0.9370	0.9382	0.9394	0.9406	0.9418	0.9429	0.9441
1.6	0.9452	0.9463	0.9474	0.9484	0.9495	0.9505	0.9515	0.9525	0.9535	0.9545
1.7	0.9554	0.9564	0.9573	0.9582	0.9591	0.9599	0.9608	0.9616	0.9625	0.9633
1.8	0.9641	0.9649	0.9656	0.9664	0.9671	0.9678	0.9686	0.9693	0.9699	0.9706
1.9	0.9713	0.9719	0.9726	0.9732	0.9738	0.9744	0.9750	0.9756	0.9761	0.9767
2	0.9772	0.9778	0.9783	0.9788	0.9793	0.9798	0.9803	0.9808	0.9812	0.9817
2.1	0.9821	0.9826	0.9830	0.9834	0.9838	0.9842	0.9846	0.9850	0.9854	0.9857
2.2	0.9861	0.9864	0.9868	0.9871	0.9875	0.9878	0.9881	0.9884	0.9887	0.9890
2.3	0.9893	0.9896	0.9898	0.9901	0.9904	0.9906	0.9909	0.9911	0.9913	0.9916
2.4	0.9918	0.9920	0.9922	0.9925	0.9927	0.9929	0.9931	0.9932	0.9934	0.9936
2.5	0.9938	0.9940	0.9941	0.9943	0.9945	0.9946	0.9948	0.9949	0.9951	0.9952

Example: Let $d = 1.15$. There is an 87.49% chance of drawing a value less than or equal to d from the standard normal distribution.

Appendix C: Key Formulas

Free Cash Flow

A firm's free cash flow (*FCF*) is derived from operating cash flow (*OCF*) and changes in asset and liability accounts as:

$$FCF = OCF - \Delta FA - (\Delta CA - \Delta A/P - \Delta accruals) \quad \text{(Eq. 2.2)}$$

Present Value of an Ordinary Annuity

The present value of an *n*-year ordinary annuity of $1 per year is:

$$PV = \frac{PMT}{r} \times \left[1 - \frac{1}{(1+r)^n}\right] \quad \text{(Eq. 3.7)}$$

Present Value of a Perpetuity

The present value of a perpetual stream of $1 annual payments is:

$$PV = PMT \times \frac{1}{r} = \frac{PMT}{r} \quad \text{(Eq. 3.10)}$$

Present Value of a Growing Perpetuity

The present value of a perpetual stream of payments, which grows at an annual rate *g*, is:

$$PV = \frac{CF_1}{r-g} \qquad r > g \quad \text{(Eq. 3.11)}$$

Effective Annual Interest Rate

The effective annual interest rate (*EAR*) can be derived from the stated rate *r* (given *m* compounding periods) as:

$$EAR = \left(1 + \frac{r}{m}\right)^m - 1 \quad \text{(Eq. 3.14)}$$

Measures of Risk

Variance of Returns

The variance of returns can be derived from a historical return series on N periods as:

$$\text{Variance} = \sigma^2 = \frac{\sum_{t=1}^{N}(R_t - \bar{R})^2}{N-1} \quad \textbf{(Eq. 6.3)}$$

Expected Return on a Portfolio

If the expected returns for individual assets in a portfolio are known, the expected return of an n-asset portfolio (with individual asset weights w_i) can be found as:

$$E(R_P) = w_1 E(R_1) + w_2 E(R_2) + \ldots + w_N E(R_N) \quad \textbf{(Eq. 7.1)}$$

The Capital Asset Pricing Model

The CAPM yields a unique expected return for an asset or portfolio as a linear function of that asset's beta (b_i) and the risk-free rate R_f:

$$E(R_i) = R_f + \beta_i \left(E(R_m) - R_f\right) \quad \textbf{(Eq. 7.2)}$$

Net Present Value

Finance's basic valuation model computes the NPV of a project or an asset, usually by subtracting the sum of a series of discounted cash inflows $\frac{CF_i}{(1 + r)^i}$ from a single cash outflow (CF_0):

$$NPV = CF_0 + \frac{CF_1}{(1+r)^1} + \frac{CF_2}{(1+r)^2} + \frac{CF_3}{(1+r)^3} + \ldots + \frac{CF_N}{(1+r)^N} \quad \textbf{(Eq. 8.1)}$$

Weighted Average Cost of Capital [without taxes]

The $WACC$ is a weighted average of the cost of debt and equity financing for a firm, in which the weights are the fractions of debt and equity in the firm's capital structure:

$$WACC = \left(\frac{D}{D+E}\right) r_d + \left(\frac{E}{D+E}\right) r_e \quad \textbf{(Eq. 10.3)}$$

The Weighted Average Cost of Capital [with taxes]

Incorporating corporate taxes allows calculation of a firm's $WACC$ when it must pay taxes at rate T_c on its income:

$$WACC = \left(\frac{D}{D+E}\right)(1-T_c) r_d + \left(\frac{E}{D+E}\right) r_e \quad \textbf{(Eq. 10.4)}$$

M&M Proposition I

Modigliani and Miller's famous Proposition I says that a firm's value (V) is given by capitalizing its expected net operating income (EBIT) at the rate r, and is independent of capital structure:

$$V = (E + D) = \frac{EBIT}{r} \quad \textbf{(Eq. 12.1)}$$

M&M Proposition II

Proposition II determines the rate at which the expected return on a levered firm's equity (r_l) must increase as debt is substituted for equity in its capital structure:

$$r_l = r + (r - r_d)\frac{D}{E} \qquad \textbf{(Eq. 12.2)}$$

Value of a Levered Firm [including only corporate taxes]

In the presence of corporate income taxes, the value of a levered firm is equal to the value of an otherwise equivalent unlevered firm plus the value of the interest tax shields on its debt:

$$V_L = V_U + PV \text{ tax shield} = V_U + T_C D \qquad \textbf{(Eq. 12.5)}$$

Gain From Leverage

In the presence of both corporate and personal taxes, the gain from leverage for a firm is a function of the effective tax rates on corporate profits (T_c), equity income received by investors (T_{ps}) and interest income received by investors (T_{pd}):

$$G_L = \left[1 - \frac{(1 - T_c)(1 - T_{ps})}{(1 - T_{pd})}\right] \times D \qquad \textbf{(Eq. 12.6)}$$

Put-Call Parity

The put-call parity formula shows the relationship that must hold between the values of the stock price (S), the put (P), the call (C), and the current price of the risk-free, zero-coupon bond (B).

$$S + P = B + C \qquad \textbf{(Eq. 15.1)}$$

The Black-Scholes Option Pricing Model

The value of a call option, C, is given as:

$$C = SN(d_1) - Xe^{-rt}N(d_2) \qquad \textbf{(Eq. 15.2)}$$

where:

$$d_1 = \frac{\ln\left(\frac{S}{X}\right) + \left(r + \frac{\sigma^2}{2}\right)t}{\sigma\sqrt{t}} \qquad \textbf{(Eq. 15.3)}$$

$$d_2 = d_1 - \sigma\sqrt{t}$$

S = current market price of underlying stock
X = strike price of option
t = amount of time before option expires (in years)
r = annual risk-free interest rate
s = annual standard deviation of underlying stock's returns
e = 2.718 (approximately)
N(X) = the probability of drawing a value less than or equal to "X" from the standard normal distribution

The Forward Premium or Discount [exchange rates]

The annualized forward discount or premium of a currency is:

$$\frac{F-S}{S}\times\frac{360}{N} \quad \textbf{(Eq. 16.1)}$$

The Parity Conditions of International Finance

Forward–Spot Parity

In equilibrium, the forward rate (F) observed for a currency should be equal to the expected future spot exchange rate, $E(S)$, for that currency:

$$E(S)=F \quad \textbf{(Eq. 16.2)}$$

Purchasing Power Parity

PPP expresses a currency's expected future spot exchange rate $[E(S^{\text{for/dom}})]$, relative to today's spot rate $(S^{\text{for/dom}})$, as a function of the relative expected inflation rates in the foreign, $E(i_{\text{for}})$, and domestic, $E(i_{\text{dom}})$, markets:

$$\frac{E(S^{\text{for/dom}})}{(S^{\text{for/dom}})}=\frac{[1+E(i_{\text{for}})]}{[1+E(i_{\text{dom}})]} \quad \textbf{(Eq. 16.4)}$$

Interest Rate Parity

IRP expresses a currency's forward exchange rate $(F^{\text{for/dom}})$, relative to today's spot rate $(S^{\text{for/dom}})$, as a function of the relative interest rates in the foreign (R_{for}) and domestic (R_{dom}) markets:

$$\frac{F^{\text{for/dom}}}{S^{\text{for/dom}}}=\frac{(1+R_{\text{for}})}{(1+R_{\text{dom}})} \quad \textbf{(Eq. 16.5)}$$

Real Interest Parity

The real interest parity relationship expresses interest rate parity in real rather than nominal terms:

$$\frac{1+R_{\text{for}}}{1+R_{\text{dom}}}=\frac{1+E(i_{\text{for}})}{1+E(i_{\text{dom}})} \quad \textbf{(Eq. 16.6)}$$

Forward Price of an Asset

Given a risk-free rate of interest R_f, the forward price (F) of an asset or commodity to be delivered n periods in the future can be derived from the current spot price (S_0) as:

$$F=S_0(1+R_f)^n \quad \textbf{(Eq. 17.1)}$$

Answers to Self-Test Problems

Chapter 2 Financial Statement and Cash Flow Analysis

ST2-1. Use the financial statements below to answer the questions concerning S&M Manufacturing's financial position at the end of the calendar year 2006.

a. How much cash and near cash does S&M have at year-end 2006?
b. What was the original cost of all of the firm's real property that is currently owned?
c. How much in total liabilities did the firms have at year-end 2006?
d. How much did S&M owe for credit purchases at year-end 2006?
e. How much did the firm sell during 2006?
f. How much equity did the common stockholders have in the firm at year-end 2006?
g. What is the cumulative total of earnings reinvested in the firm from its inception through the end of 2006?
h. How much *operating profit* did the firm earn during 2006?
i. What is the total amount if dividends paid out by the firm during the year 2006?
j. How many shares of common stock did S&M have outstanding at year-end 2006?

S&M Manufacturing, Inc.

Balance Sheet at December 31, 2006 ($000)

Assets		**Liabilities and Equity**	
Current assets		Current liabilities	
Cash	$ 140,000	Accounts payable	$ 480,000
Marketable securities	260,000	Notes payable	500,000
Accounts receivable	650,000	Accruals	80,000
Inventories	800,000	Total current liabilities	$1,060,000
Total current assets	$1,850,000	Long-term debt	
Fixed assets		Bonds outstanding	$1,300,000
Gross fixed assets	$3,780,000	Bank debt (long-term)	260,000
Less: Accumulated depreciation	1,220,000	Total long-term debt	$1,560,000
Net fixed assets	$2,560,000	Stockholders' equity	
Total assets	$4,410,000	Preferred stock	$ 180,000
		Common stock (at par)	200,000
		Paid-in capital in excess of par	810,000
		Retained earnings	600,000
		Total stockholders' equity	$1,790,000
		Total liabilities and equity	$4,410,000

S&M Manufacturing, Inc.

Income Statement for Year Ended December 31, 2006 ($000)

Sales revenue		$6,900,000
Less: Cost of goods sold		4,200,000
Gross profits		$2,700,000
Less: Operating expenses		
Sales expense	$ 750,000	
General and administrative expense	1,150,000	
Leasing expense	210,000	
Depreciation expense	235,000	
Total operation expenses		2,345,000
Earnings before interest and taxes		$ 355,000
Less: Interest expense		85,000
Net profit before taxes		$ 270,000
Less: Taxes		81,000
Net profits after taxes		$ 189,000
Less: Preferred stock dividends + retained earnings)		10,800
Earnings available for common stockholders		$ 178,200
Less: Dividends		75,000
To retained earnings		$ 103,200
Per share data		
Earnings per share (EPS)	$ 1.43	
Dividends per share (DPS)	$ 0.60	
Price per share	$15.85	

A:

a. $400,000 (only cash and marketable securities should be included $140,000 + $260,000)
b. $3,780,000 (net asset position + depreciation)
c. $2,620,000 (current liabilities + long-term debt)
d. $480,000 (accounts payable)
e. $6,900,000 (sales)
f. $1,010,000 (common stock at par + paid-in capital + retained earnings)
g. $600,000 (retained earnings)
h. $355,000 (EBIT)
i. $85,800 (preferred + common stock dividends)
j. 124,615 shares outstanding (178,200/1.43)

ST2-2. The partially complete 2006 balance sheet and income statement for Challenge Industries are given below, followed by selected ratio values for the firm based on its completed 2006 financial statements. Use the ratios along with the partial statements to complete the financial statements. *Hint:* Use the ratios in the order listed to calculate the missing statement values that need to be installed in the partial statements.

Challenge Industries, Inc.
Balance Sheet at December 31, 2006 (in $ thousands)

Assets		Liabilities and Equity	
Current assets		Current liabilities	
Cash	$ 52,000	Accounts payable	$150,000
Marketable securities	60,000	Notes payable	?
Accounts receivable	200,000	Accruals	80,000
Inventories	?	Total current liabilities	?
Total current assets	?	Long-term debt	$425,000
Fixed assets (gross)	?	Total liabilities	?
Less: Accumulated depreciation	240,000	Stockholders' equity	
		Preferred stock	?
Net fixed assets	?	Common stock (at par)	150,000
Total assets	?	Paid-in capital in excess of par	?
		Retained earnings	390,000
		Total shareholders' equity	?
		Total liabilities and shareholders' equity	?

Challenge Industries, Inc.
Income Statement for the Year Ended December 31, 2006
(in $ thousands)

Sales revenue		$4,800,000
Less: Cost of goods sold		?
Gross profits		?
Less: Operating expenses		
Sales expense	$690,000	
General and administrative expense	750,000	
Depreciation expense	120,000	
Total operating expenses		1,560,000
Earnings before interest and taxes		?
Less: Interest expense		35,000
Earnings before taxes		?
Less: Taxes		?
Net income (Net profits after taxes)		?
Less: Preferred dividends		15,000
Earnings available for common stockholders		?
Less: Dividends		60,000
To retained earnings		?

Challenge Industries, Inc.
Ratios for the Year Ended December 31, 2006

Ratio	Value
Total asset turnover	2.00
Gross profit margin	40%
Inventory turnover	10
Current ratio	1.60
Net profit margin	3.75%
Return on common equity	12.5%

A:

Challenge Industries, Inc.
Balance Sheet at December 31, 2006 (in $ thousands)

Assets		Liabilities and Equity	
Current assets		Current liabilities	
Cash	$ 52,000	Accounts payable	$ 150,000
Marketable securities	60,000	Notes payable	145,000
Accounts receivable	200,000	Accruals	80,000
Inventory	288,000	Total current liabilities	$ 375,000
Total current assets	600,000	Long-term debt	425,000
Fixed assets (gross)	2,040,000	Total liabilities	$ 800,000
Less: Accumulated depreciation	240,000	Stockholders' equity	$ 160,000
		Preferred stock	?
Net fixed assets	1,800,000	Common stock (at par)	150,000
Total assets	2,400,000	Paid-in capital in excess of par	900,000
		Retained earnings	390,000
		Total shareholders' equity	$1,600,000
		Total liabilities and shareholders' equity	2,400,000

Challenge Industries, Inc.
Income Statement for the Year Ended December 31, 2006
(in $ thousands)

Sales revenue		$4,800,000
Less: Cost of goods sold		2,880,000
Gross profits		1,920,000
Less: Operating expenses		
Selling expense	$690,000	
General and administrative expense	150,000	
Depreciation	120,000	
Total operating expenses		1,560,000
Earnings before interest and taxes		$ 360,000
Less: Interest expense		35,000
Earnings before taxes		$ 325,000
Less: Taxes		130,000
Net income (Net profits after taxes)		$ 195,000
Less: Preferred dividends		15,000
Earnings available for common stockholders		$ 180,000
Less: Dividends		60,000
To retained earnings		$ 120,000

ST2-3. Use the corporate income tax rate schedule in Table 2.6 of the chapter to calculate the tax liability for each of the following firms with the amounts of 2006 pretax income noted.

Firm	2006 Pretax Income	Tax Liability
A	$12,500,000	
B	200,000	
C	80,000	

a. What tax rate – average or marginal – is relevant to financial decisions for these firms?
b. Calculate, compare, and discuss the *average tax rates* for each of the firms during 2006.
c. Find the *marginal tax rates* for each of the firms at the end of 2006.
d. What relationship exists between the average and marginal tax rates for each firm?

A: **a.** The *marginal tax rate* is relevant to financial decisions for these firms, because it reflects the rate at which the next dollar of the firm's income will be taxed.

b.

Firm	2006 Pretax Income	Tax Liability	Average tax rate
A	$12,500,000	50,000 × 0.15=7,500	=4,275,000/12,500,000
		(75,000–50,000) × 0.25=6,250	=34.2%
		(100,000–75,000) × 0.34=8,500	
		(335,000–100,000) × 0.39=91,650	
		(10,000,000–335,000) × 0.34=3,286,100	
		(12,500,000–10,000,000) × 0.35=875,000	
		Total: 4,275,000	
B	200,000	50,000 × .15=7,500	=61,250/200,000
		(75,000–50,000) × 0.25=6,250	=30.63%
		(100,000–75,000) × 0.34=8,500	
		(200,000–100,000) × 0.39=39,000	
		Total: 61,250	
C	80,000	50,000 × 0.15=7,500	=15,450/80,000
		(75,000–50,000) × 0.25=6,250	=19.31%
		(80,000–75,000) × 0.34=1,700	
		Total: 15,450	

Companies A, B and C pay on average 34.2, 30.63 and 19.31 cents respectively on each dollar of pretax income earned.

c. Marginal tax rate: The tax companies will have to pay if they earn one more dollar–A: 35%; B: 39%; C: 34%

d. The observable pattern is that the higher the average tax rate the less the marginal tax rate in-creases and vice versa.

Chapter 3 Present Value

ST3-1. Starratt Alexander is currently considering investing specified amounts in each of four investment opportunities described below. For each opportunity, determine the amount of money Starratt will have at the end of the given investment horizon.

Investment A: Invest a lump sum of $2,750 today in an account that pays 6% annual interest and leave the funds on deposit for exactly 15 years.

Investment B: Invest the following amounts at the beginning of each of the next five years in a venture that will earn 9% annually and measure the accumulated value at the end of exactly 5 years:

Beginning of Year	Amount
1	$ 900
2	1,000
3	1,200
4	1,500
5	1,800

Investment C: Invest $1,200 at the end of each year for the next 10 years in an account that pays 10% annual interest, and determine the account balance at the end of year 10.

Investment D: Make the same investment as in investment C but place the $1,200 in the account at the *beginning* of each year.

A: Investment A: Future value is $6,590 = ($2,750 × FV(15,6%) = 2.3966)

Investment B: Future value = $900 × $(1.09)^5$ + $1,000 × $(1.09)^4$ + $1,200 × $(1.09)^3$ + $1,500 × $(1.09)^2$ + $1,800 × (1.09) = $8,094.53

Investment C: Future value is $19,116 ($1,200 × FVAF(10, 10%) = 15.93)

Investment D: $19,116 × 1.09=$20,836

ST3-2. Gregg Snead has been offered four investment opportunities, all equally priced at $45,000. Because the opportunities differ in risk, Gregg's required returns (i.e., applicable discount rates) are not the same for each opportunity. The cash flows and required returns for each opportunity are summarized below.

Opportunity	Cash Flows		Required Return
A	$7,500 at the end of 5 years		12%
B	Year	Amount	15%
	1	$10,000	
	2	12,000	
	3	18,000	
	4	10,000	
	5	13,000	
	6	9,000	
C	$5,000 at the *end of each year* for the next 30 years.		10%
D	$7,000 at the *beginning of each year* for the next 20 years.		18%

a. Find the present value of each of the four investment opportunities.
b. Which, if any, opportunities are acceptable?
c. Which opportunity should Gregg take?

A: **a.** PV of A: $7,500 × PV(5, 12%)=.5674 = $4,255.50
PV of B: $10,000/(1.15) + $12,000/$(1.15)^2$ + $18,000/$(1.15)^3$ + $10,000/$(1.15)^4$ + $13,000/$(1.15)^5$ $9,000/$(1.15)^6$ = $45,676.44
PV of C: $5,000 × PVAF(30, 10%)=9.4269 = $47,134
PV of D: $7,000 × PVAF(20, 18%)=5.3527 = $37,468 × 1.18 = $44,213
b. Opportunities B and C are acceptable because the present value of their cash flows is in excess of their current cost of $45,000. Opportunities A and D are not acceptable because their present values ore below their $45,000 cost.
c. None

ST3-3. Assume you wish to establish a college scholarship of $2,000 per year for a deserving student at the high school you attended. You would like to make a lump-sum gift to the high school to fund the scholarship into perpetuity. The school's treasurer assures you that they will earn 7.5% annually forever.

a. How much must you give the high school today to fund the proposed scholarship program?
b. If you wanted to allow the amount of the scholarship to increase annually after the first award (end of year 1) by 3% per year, how much must you give the school today to fund the scholarship program?
c. Compare, contrast, and discuss the difference in your response to parts a and b.

A: **a.** The present value of the proposed perpetuity is $2,000/.075 = $26,667
b. The present value of the growing perpetuity is $2,060/(.075–.03) = $2,060/.045 = $45,778
a. The amount that I need to give the high school if I want the scholarship to grow at 3% per year indefinitely, assuming they will be able to earn the proposed interest rate, is almost double the amount needed if the scholarship does not grow. This effect is due to the fact that we discount the annual cash flow by a smaller number in order to account for the annual growth in the scholarship.

ST3-4. Assume that you deposit $10,000 today into an account paying 6% annual interest and leave it on deposit for exactly 8 years.

a. How much will be in the account at the end of 8 years in interest is compounded:
  1. annually?
  2. semiannually?
  3. monthly?
  4. continuously?

b. Calculate the effective annual rate (EAR) for a (1) through a (4) above.

c. Based on your findings in parts a and b, what is the general relationship between the frequency of compounding and EAR?

A: **a.** 1. FV = $10,000 × FV (8, 6%)=1.5938 = $15,938
2. FV = $10,000 × FV (16, 3%)=1.6047 = $16,047
3. FV = $10,000 × FV (96, 0.5%)=1.6141 = $16,141
4. FV = $10,000 × $e^{(8 \times .06)}$ = $10,000 × $2.7182^{.48}$ = $10,000 × 1,6161 = $16,160

b. 1. EAR = $(1+0.06/1)^1 - 1$ = 6%
2. EAR = $(1+0.06/2)^2 - 1$ = 6.09%
3. EAR = $(1+0.06/12)^{12} - 1$ = 6.17%
4. EAR = $e^{0.06} - 1$ = 6.18%

c. The observable pattern shows that the more frequent the compounding, the higher the effective annual rate. Consequently, the higher annual rate is obtained when the compounding is continuous.

ST3-5. Imagine that you are a professional personal financial planner and one of your clients has asked you the following two questions. Use the value of money techniques to develop appropriate responses to each question.

a. I borrowed $75,000 and am required to repay it in 6 equal (annual) end-of-year installments of $3,344 and want to know what interest am I paying?

b. I need to save $37,000 over the next 15 years to fund my 3-year-old daughter's college education. If I made equal annual end-of-year deposits into an account that earns 7% annual interest, how large must this deposit be?

A: **a.** 9% (calculated with a financial calculator)

b. The amount of the annual, end-of-year deposits should be:
$37,000/FVAF (15, 7%)=25.129 = $1,472

Chapter 4 Bond Valuation

ST4-1. A 5-year bond pays interest annually. The par value is $1,000 and the coupon rate equals 7 percent. If the market's required return on the bond is 8 percent, what is the bond's market price?

A:
$$P = \frac{\$70}{1.08^1} + \frac{\$70}{1.08^2} + \frac{\$70}{1.08^3} + \frac{\$70}{1.08^4} + \frac{\$1,070}{1.08^5} = \$960.07$$

You could also obtain this answer by valuing the annuity of coupon payments and the lump sum principal amount separately as follows.

$$P_0 = \$70\left[\frac{1 - \frac{1}{(1+0.08)^5}}{0.08}\right] + \frac{\$1,000}{(1+0.08)^5}$$

$$= \$279.49 + \$680.58 = \$960.07$$

ST4-2. A bond that matures in 2 years makes semiannual interest payments. The par value is \$1,000, the coupon rate equals 4 percent, and the bond's market price is \$1,019.27. What is the bond's yield to maturity?

A: The YTM is the value of r that solves this equation.

$$\$1{,}019.27 = \frac{\$20}{\left(1+\frac{r}{2}\right)^1} + \frac{\$20}{\left(1+\frac{r}{2}\right)^2} + \frac{\$20}{\left(1+\frac{r}{2}\right)^3} + \frac{\$1{,}020}{\left(1+\frac{r}{2}\right)^4}$$

Because the bond sells at a premium, the YTM must be less than the coupon rate. We can try to find the YTM by trial and error. Inserting r = 0.035 into the equation produces a price of \$1,009.58. This price is too low, so we have chosen a YTM that is too high. Next try r = 0.03. At that interest rate, the market price is \$1,019.27, so the YTM = 3%.

An alternative approach to this problem uses the Excel function, =IRR. This function requires that you input the price of the bond as a negative value, followed by the positive cash flows that the bond promises.

	A
1	−1,019.27
2	20
3	20
4	20
5	20

Now in an empty cell type the function, =IRR(A1:A5), and Excel will return the value 1.5%. This is the YTM stated on a semiannual basis (equivalent to r/2 in the equation above), so multiply it times 2 to get the annual YTM of 3%. Note, you need to be sure that the cell in which you type the IRR formula is formatted in a way that allows you to see several decimal places. Otherwise, Excel may round off the YTM and you will not know it.

ST4-3. Two bonds offer a five percent coupon rate, paid annually, and sell at par (\$1,000). One bond matures in two years and the other matures in ten years. What are the YTMs on each bond? If the YTM changes to four percent, what happens to the price of each bond? What happens if the YTM changes to six percent?

Because the bonds currently sell at par, the coupon rate and the YTM must be equal at five percent. If the YTM drops to four percent, both bonds will sell at a premium, but the price of the ten-year bond will increase more than the price of the two-year bond.

$$P_{2-yr} = \$50\left[\frac{1-\frac{1}{(1+0.04)^2}}{0.04}\right] + \frac{\$1{,}000}{(1+0.04)^2}$$

$$= \$94.30 + \$924.56 = \$1{,}018.86$$

$$P_{10-yr} = \$50\left[\frac{1-\frac{1}{(1+0.04)^{10}}}{0.04}\right] + \frac{\$1{,}000}{(1+0.04)^{10}}$$

$$= \$405.55 + \$675.56 = \$1{,}081.11$$

Repeating the calculations above at r = 0.06 we find that the two-year bond's price falls to \$981.67 and the ten-year bond's price falls to \$926.40. This illustrates that long-term bond prices are more sensitive to changes in interest rates than are short-term bond prices.

Chapter 5 Stock Valuation

ST5-1. Omega Healthcare Investors (ticker symbol, OHI) pays a dividend on its Series B preferred stock of \$0.539 per quarter. If the price of Series B preferred stock is \$25 per share, what quarterly rate of return does the market require on this stock, and what is the effective annual required return?

A: The preferred stock valuation formula says that the price equals the dividend divided by the re-quired rate of return. Therefore, using the quarterly dividend and the quarterly required rate, we have

$\$25 = \$0.539/r$

$r = 0.02156$

This means that the effective annual required rate on the stock equals $(1.02156)^4 - 1 = 0.089$ or 8.9%.

ST5-2. The restaurant chain Applebee's International Inc. (ticker symbol, APPB) announced an increase of their quarterly dividend from \$0.06 to \$0.07 per share in December 2003. This continued a long string of dividend increases. Applebee's was one of few companies that had managed to increase its dividend at a double-digit clip for more than a decade. Suppose you want to use the dividend growth model to value Applebee's stock. You believe that dividends will keep growing at 10 percent per year indefinitely, and you think the market's required return on this stock is 11 percent. Let's simplify by assuming that Applebee's pays dividends annually and that the next dividend is expected to be \$0.31 per share. The dividend will arrive in exactly one year. What would you pay for Applebee's stock right now? Suppose you buy the stock today, hold it just long enough to receive the next dividend, and then sell it. What rate of return will you earn on that investment?

A: To calculate the price of the stock now, we simply divided next year's expected dividend, \$0.31, by the difference between the required rate of return and the dividend growth rate. This yields a price of \$0.31÷(0.11–0.10) = \$31.00.. Next, we have to calculate the expected price a year from now after the \$0.31 dividend has been paid. To do that, we need an estimate of the dividend two years in the future. If next year's dividend is \$0.31, then the following year's dividend should be 10 percent more or \$0.341 per share. This means that the price of Applebee's stock, just after the \$0.31 dividend is paid should be \$0.341÷(0.11–0.10) = \$34.10. Now calculate your rate of return. You purchase the stock for \$31. One year later you receive a dividend of \$0.31 and you immediately sell the stock for \$34.10, generating a capital gain of \$3.10. Your total return is therefore (\$34.10 + \$0.31 – \$31.00)÷\$31.00 = 0.11 or 11%. That shouldn't be a surprise because this is exactly the market's required return on the stock.

Chapter 6 The Trade-Off Between Risk and Return

ST6-1. Using Table 6.3, calculate the standard deviation of stock returns from 1999–2003. Over the last five years, were stocks more or less volatile than they were over the last ten years?

A: The table below illustrates the calculations need to solve this problem. First, calculate the average return. Next, subtract that average from each year's actual return, then square that difference. Add up the squared differences and divide by four to get the variance, and take the square root of the variance to get the standard deviation. Returns were more volatile over the past five years com-pared to the past ten years.

Year	Return (%)	Return – Average	Squared Difference
1999	23.6	21.1	445.2
2000	−10.9	−13.4	179.6
2001	−11.0	−13.5	182.2
2002	−20.9	−23.4	547.6
2003	31.6	29.1	847.8
Sum	12.4		2201.4
Average Return (%)	2.5		
Variance			550.3
Standard Dev. (%)			23.4

ST6-2. Table 6.3 shows that the average return on stocks from 1994-2003 was 12.5 percent. Not shown in the table are the average returns on bonds and bills over the same period. The average return on bonds was 8.7 percent, and for bills the average return was 4.2 percent. From these figures, recal-culate the risk premiums shown in Table 6.2 and compare recent history to the long-run numbers.

A: Table 6.2 (Revised) – A Comparison of Risk Premiums

	Risk Premium	
Comparison	1900–2003 (from Table 6.2)	1994–2003
Stocks – Bills	7.6%	8.3% (12.5% – 4.2%)
Stocks – Bonds	6.5%	3.8% (12.5% – 8.7%)
Bonds – Bills	1.1%	4.5% (8.7% – 4.2%)

ST6-3. Suppose that Treasury bill returns follow a normal distribution with a mean of 4.1 percent and a standard deviation of 2.8 percent. This implies that 68 percent of the time, Tbill returns should fall within what range?

A: For any normal distribution, 68 percent of the observations should fall within plus or minus one standard deviation of the mean. This means 68 percent of annual Tbill returns should fall within 1.3% and 6.9%.

Chapter 7 Risk, Return, and CAPM

ST7-1. Calculate the mean, variance, and standard deviations for a stock with the probability distribution outlined in the accompanying table:

A: The expected return is 0.10(–0.40) + 0.60(0.20) + 0.30(0.50) = 0.23. The variance equals 0.10 $(-0.4-0.23)^2 + 0.60(0.2-0.23)^2 + 0.30(0.50-0.23)^2 = 621\%^2$. The standard deviation is the square root of the variance, or 0.2492.

ST7-2. You invest $25,000 in T-bills and $50,000 in the market portfolio. If the risk-free rate equals two percent and the expected market risk premium is six percent, what is the expected return on your portfolio?

A: The portfolio is invested one-third in T-bills ($25K/$75K) and two-thirds in stocks ($50K/$75K). The risk-free rate is 2%. If the *market risk premium* is 6%, then the market's expected return is 8%. Therefore, the portfolio's expected return is 0.33(2%) + 0.67(8%) = 6%.

ST7-3. The risk-free rate equals four percent and the expected return on the market is ten percent. If a stock's expected return is 13 percent, what is the stock's beta?

A: Plug the known values into equation 7.2. 13% = 4% + B(10% – 4%) which implies that the beta equals 1.5.

Chapter 8 Capital Budgeting Process and Techniques

ST8-1. Nader International is considering investing in two assets – A and B. The initial outlay, annual cash flows, and annual depreciation for each asset is shown in the table below for assets' assumed five-year lives. As can be seen, Nader will use straight-line depreciation over each asset's five-year life. The firm requires a 12% return on each of those equally risky assets. Nader's maximum payback period is 2.5 years; its maximum discounted payback period is 3.25 years' and its minimum accounting rate of return is 30%.

	Asset A		Asset B	
Initial Outlay (CF_0)	$200,000		$180,000	
Year (t)	Cash Flow (CF_t)	Depreciation	Cash Flow (CF_t)	Depreciation
1	$ 70,000	$40,000	$80,000	$36,000
2	80,000	40,000	90,000	36,000
3	90,000	40,000	30,000	36,000
4	90,000	40,000	40,000	36,000
5	100,000	40,000	40,000	36,000

a. Calculate the accounting rate of return from each asset, assess its acceptability, and indicate which asset is best using the accounting rate of return.

b. Calculate the payback period for each asset, assess its acceptability, and indicate which asset is best using the payback period.

c. Calculate the discounted payback for each asset, assess its acceptability, and indicate which asset is best using the discounted payback.

d. Compute and contrast your findings in parts a, b, and c. Which asset would you recommend to Nader, assuming that they are mutually exclusive? Why?

A:

		Asset A			Asset B	
Invest		$200,000			$180,000	
Year	CF	12% PV	Depr.	CF	12% PV	Depr.
1	$ 70,000	62,500	$40,000	$80,000	71,429	$36,000
2	80,000	63,776	40,000	90,000	71,747	36,000
3	90,000	64,060	40,000	30,000	21,353	36,000
4	90,000	57,196	40,000	40,000	25,420	36,000
5	100,000		40,000	40,000		36,000

a. Accounting Rate of Return

	Asset A	Asset B
Year	NPAT	NPAT
1	$70,000 – $40,000 = $30,000	$80,000 – $36,000 = $44,000
2	$80,000 – $40,000 = $40,000	$90,000 – $36,000 = $54,000
3	$90,000 – $40,000 = $50,000	$30,000 – $36,000 = -$6,000
4	$90,000 – $40,000 = $50,000	$40,000 – $36,000 = $4,000
5	$100,000 – $40,000 = $60,000	$40,000 – $36,000 = $4,000
	Average = $46,000	Average = $20,000

$\frac{\$46,000}{\$100,000} = 46\%$ Acceptable $\qquad \frac{\$20,000}{\$90,000} = 22.22\%$ Not acceptable

Max		Asset A	Asset B
2.50	b. Payback	2.56 years / Not acceptable	2.33 years / Acceptable
3.25	c. Discounted payback at 12%	3.17 years/ Acceptable	3.62 years / Not Acceptable

d. They should take asset A because its accounting rate of return is acceptable as is its discounted payback.

ST8-2. JK Products, Inc. is considering investing in either of two competing projects that will allow the firm to eliminate a production bottleneck and meet the growing demand for its products. The firm's engineering department narrowed the alternatives down to tow – Status Quo (SQ) and High Tech (HT). Working with the accounting and finance personnel, the firm's CFO developed the following estimates of the cash flows for SQ and HT over the relevant 6-year time horizon. The firm has an 11 percent required return and views these projects as equally risky.

	Project SQ	Project HT
Initial Outflow (CF_0)	$670,000	$940,000
Year (t)	Cash Inflows (CF_t)	
1	$250,000	$170,000
2	200,000	180,000
3	170,000	200,000
4	150,000	250,000
5	130,000	300,000
6	130,000	550,000

a. Calculate the net present value (NPV) of each project, assess its acceptability, and indicate which project is best using NPV.
b. Calculate the internal rate of return (IRR) of each project, assess its acceptability, and indicate which project is best using IRR.
c. Calculate the profitability index (PI) of each project, assess its acceptability, and indicate which project is best using PI.
d. Draw the NPV profile for project SQ and HT on the same set of axes and use this diagram to explain why the NPV and IRR show different preferences for these two mutually exclusive projects. Discuss this difference in terms of both the "scale problem" and the "timing problem".
e. Which of the two mutually exclusive projects would you recommend JK Products undertake? Why?

A:

	Project SQ	Project HT
a. NPV	$87,313.87	$142,254.07*
b. IRR	16.07%*	15.17%
c. PI	1.13	1.15*

All measures indicate project acceptability
NPV > 0
IRR >11%
PI > 1.00
*Indicates the preferred project using each measure.

d.

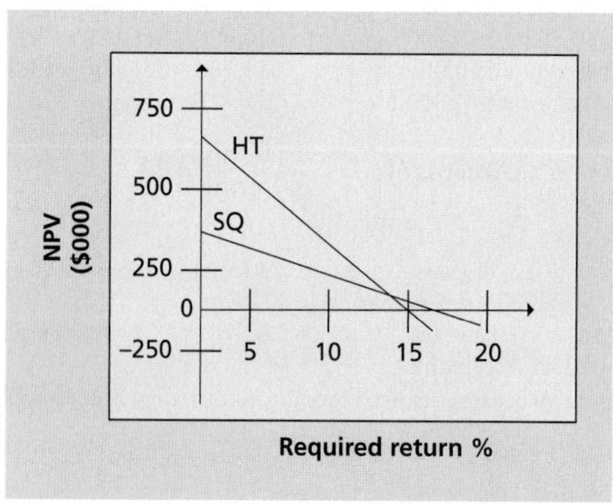

	Project	
Rate	SQ	HT
0%	$ 360,000	$ 710,000
11%	$87,313.87	$142,254.07
15.17%	-	0
16.07%	0	-

At 11% HT is preferred over SQ, but because the profiles cross somewhere beyond 11% and before the functions cross the required return axis the IRR of SQ exceeds the IRR of HT. This behavior can be explained by the fact that HT's larger scale causes its NPV to exceed that of SQ. The smaller project and the timing of SQ's cash flows – more in the early years – causes its IRR to exceed that of HT, which has more of its cash flows in later years.

e. Project HT is recommended because it has the higher NPV, the better technique. In addition its PI is higher than that of Project SQ.

Chapter 9 Cash Flow and Capital Budgeting

ST9-1. Claross, Inc. wishes to determine the relevant operating cash flows associated with the proposed purchase of a new piece of equipment having an installed cost of $10 million and falling into the 5-year MACRS asset class. The firm's financial analyst estimated that the relevant time horizon for analysis is 6 years. She expects the revenues attributable to the equipment to be $15.8 million in the first year and to increase at 5% per year through year 6. Similarly, she estimates all expenses other than depreciation attributable to the equipment to total $12.2 million in the first year and to increase by 4% per year through year 6. She plans to ignore any cash flows after year 6. The firm has a marginal tax rate of 40% and its required return on the equipment investment is 13%. (*Note:* Round all cash flow calculations to the nearest $0.01 million.)

a. Find the *relevant incremental cash flows* for years zero through 6.

b. Using the cash flows found in part a, determine the NPV and IRR for the proposed equipment purchase.

c. Based on your findings in part b, would you recommend that Claross, Inc. purchase the equipment? Why?

A: **a.**

				($million)			
Year	0	1	2	3	4	5	6
Initial Investment	–10						
Revenue (+5%/yr)		15.80	16.59	17.42	18.29	19.21	20.17
Expenses (+4%/yr		12.20	12.69	13.20	13.72	14.27	14.84
EBDT		3.60	3.90	4.22	4.57	4.94	5.33
–Depreciation*		2.00	3.20	1.92	1.15	1.15	0.58
EBT		1.60	0.70	2.30	3.42	3.79	4.75
–Taxes (40%)		0.64	0.28	0.92	1.37	1.52	1.90
EAT		0.96	0.42	1.38	2.05	2.27	2.85
+Depreciation*		2.00	3.20	1.92	1.15	1.15	0.58
Total Cash Flow	–10	2.96	3.62	3.30	3.20	3.42	3.43

* Depreciation:

Year	(1) Rate(from Table 9.1)	(2) Cost	(3) [(1) x (2)] Depreciation
1	0.2000	10.0	2.00
2	0.3200	10.0	3.20
3	0.1920	10.0	1.92
4	0.1152	10.0	1.15
5	0.1152	10.0	1.15
6	0.0576	10.0	0.58
Total			10.00

b. NPV at 13% = 3.21
IRR = 24%

c. Accept the project because the NPV is greater than zero and the IRR is greater than 13%.

ST9-2. Atech Industries wants to determine whether it would be advisable for it to replace an existing, fully depreciated machine with a new one. The new machine will have and after-tax installed cost of $300,000 and will be depreciated under a 3-year MACRS schedule. The old machine can be sold today for $80,000 after taxes. The firm is in the 40 percent tax bracket and requires a minimum return on the replacement decision of 15%. The firm's estimates of its revenues and expenses (excluding the depreciation) for both the new and the old machine (in $thousands) over the next four years are given below.

	New Machine		Old Machine	
Year	Revenue	Expenses (excl. depr)	Revenue	Expenses (excl. depr.)
1	$ 925	$740	$625	$580
2	990	780	645	595
3	1,000	825	670	610
4	1,100	875	695	630

Atech also estimated the values of various current accounts that would be impacted by the proposed replacement. They are shown below for both the new and old machine over the next four years. Currently (at time 0) the firm's net investment in these current accounts is assumed to be $110,000 with the new machine and $75,000 with the old machine.

New Machine

Year:	1	2	3	4
Cash	$20,000	$25,000	$ 30,000	$ 36,000
Accounts Rec.	90,000	95,000	110,000	120,000
Inventory	80,000	90,000	100,000	105,000
Accounts Pay	60,000	65,000	70,000	72,000

Old Machine

Year:	1	2	3	4
Cash	$15,000	$15,000	$15,000	$15,000
Accounts Rec.	60,000	64,000	68,000	70,000
Inventory	45,000	48,000	52,000	55,000
Accounts pay.	33,000	35,000	38,000	40,000

Atech estimates that after 4 years of detailed cash flow development, it will assume in analyzing this replacement decision that the year 4 incremental cash flows of the new machine over the old machine will grow at a compound annual rate of 2% from the end of year 4 to infinity..

a. Find the incremental *operating cash flows* (including any working capital investment) for years 1 to 4 for Atech's proposed machine replacement decision.

b. Calculate the *terminal value* of Atech's proposed machine replacement at the end of year 4.

c. Show the relevant cash flows (initial outlay, operating cash flows, and terminal cash flow) for years 1 to 4 for Atech's proposed machine replacement.

d. Using the relevant cash flows from part c, find the *NPV* and *IRR* for Atech's proposed machine replacement.

e. Based on your findings in part d, what recommendation would you make to Atech regarding its proposed machine replacement?

A: a.

Year:	0	1	2	3	4
NEW MACHINE					
Investment		−300,000			
Revenue		925,000	990,000	1,000,000	1,100,000
−Expenses(excl. depr.)		740,000	780,000	825,000	875,000
−Depreciation*		99,990	133,350	44,430	22,230
EBT		85,010	76,650	130,570	202,770
EAT [(1-0.40) 3 EBT]		51,006	45,990	78,342	121,662
−W/C Investment**		20,000	15,000	25,000	19,000
(1)Operating CF		31,006	30,990	53,342	102,662
OLD MACHINE					
A/T Sale Proceeds		+80,000			
Revenue		625,000	645,000	670,000	695,000
−Expenses(excl. depr.)		580,000	595,000	610,000	630,000
−Depreciation		0	0	0	0
EBT		45,000	50,000	60,000	65,000
EAT [(1−0.40) × EBT]		27,000	30,000	36,000	39,000
−W/C Investment***		12,000	5,000	5,000	3,000
(2)Operating CF		15,000	25,000	31,000	36,000
INCR. CF[(1)−(2)]	−220,000	16,006	5,990	22,342	66,662

* New Asset Depreciation

Year	Rate	Cost	Depreciation
1	.3333	$300,000	$ 99,990
2	.4445	300,000	133,350
3	.1481	300,000	44,430
4	.0741	300,000	22,230

** New Machine Working Capital Investment

NWC= Cash + Accounts Receivable + Inventory – Accounts Payable
ΔNWC= NWC–[Prior year's NWC]
Year 1 Δ NWC = $20,000+$90,000+$80,000–$60,000–[$110,000] = $20,000
Year 2 Δ NWC = $25,000+$95,000+$90,000–$65,000–[$130,000] = $15,000
Year 3 Δ NWC = $30,000+$110,000+$100,000–$70,000–[$145,000] = $25,000
Year 4 Δ NWC = $36,000+$120,000+$105,000–$72,000–[$170,000] = $19,000

*** Old Machine Working Capital Investment

NWC= Cash + Accounts Receivable + Inventory – Accounts Payable
ΔNWC= NWC-[Prior year's NWC]

Year 1 Δ NWC = $15,000+$60,000+$45,000–$33,000–[$75,000] = $12,000
Year 2 Δ NWC = $15,000+$64,000+$48,000–$35,000–[$87,000] = $5,000
Year 3 Δ NWC = $15,000+$68,000+$52,000–$38,000–[$92,000] = $5,000
Year 4 Δ NWC = $15,000+$70,000+$55,000–$40,000–[$97,000] = $3,000

b. Year 5 Operating CF = $66,662 × $(1+.02)^1$ = $67,995

$$\text{Terminal Value at end of Year 4} = \frac{\$67{,}995}{0.15 - 0.02} = \$523{,}038$$

c. Relevant Cash Flows
Total Year 4 CF = $66,662 + $523,038 = $589,700

Year	Cash Flow
0	-$220,000
1	16,006
2	5,990
3	22,342
4	589,700

d. NPV @ 15% = $150,301
IRR = 31.92%

e. Atech should undertake the proposed machine replacement because the *NPV* of $150,301 is greater than $0 and the *IRR* of 31.92% is above the firm's 15% required return.

ST9-3. Performance, Inc. is faced with choosing between two mutually exclusive projects with differing lives. It requires a return of 12% on these projects. Project A requires an initial outlay at time 0 of $5,000,000 and is expected to require annual maintenance cash outflows of $3,100,000 per year over its 2-year life. Project B requires an initial outlay at time 0 of $6,000,000 and is expected to require annual maintenance cash outflows of $2,600,000 per year over its 3-year life. Both projects are acceptable investments and provide equal quality service. The firm assumes that the replacement and maintenance costs for both projects will remain unchanged over time.

a. Find the *NPV* of each project over its life.
b. Which project would you recommend based on your finding in part a? What is wrong with choosing the best project based on its *NPV*?
c. Use the *equivalent annual cost (EAC)* method to compare the two projects.
d. Which project would you recommend based on your finding in part c? Compare and contrast this recommendation with the one you gave in part b.

A: **a.** Project A *NPV* = -$10,239,158
Project B *NPV* = -$12,244,761

b. Project A would be recommended because it has the lower cost *NPV*. The problem with this comparison is that Project A provides service for only 2 years versus Project B's 3-year service life.

c. *EAC* for Project A = $6,058,490
EAC for Project B = $5,098,094

d. B is preferred based on its lower *EAC*, which means that when costs are viewed on an annual basis it is less expensive than Project A. This recommendation is superior to the one made in part b because by looking at annual cost it resolves the issue of differing service lives when the replacement and maintenance costs are assumed unchanged over time.

Chapter 10 Risk and Capital Budgeting

ST10-1. A financial analyst for Quality Investments, a diversified investment fund, has gathered the following information for the years 2005 and 2006 on two firms—A and B—that it is considering adding to its portfolio. Of particular concern are the operating and financial risks of each firm.

	2005		2006	
	Firm A	Firm B	Firm A	Firm B
Sales ($ million)	10.7	13.9	11.6	14.6
EBIT ($ million)	5.7	7.4	6.2	8.1
Assets ($ million)			10.7	15.6
Debt ($ million)			5.8	9.3
Interest ($ million)			0.6	1.0
Equity ($ million)			4.9	6.3

a. Use the data provided to assess the *operating leverage* of each firm (using 2005 as the point of reference). Which firm has more operating leverage?

b. Use the data provided to assess the firms ROE (Cash to equity/Equity) assuming the firm's Return on Assets is 10% and 20% in each case. Which firm has more *financial leverage*?

c. Use your findings in parts *a* and *b* to compare, contrast the operating and financial risks of Firms A and B. Which firm is more risky? Explain.

A: **a.**

$$\text{Operating leverage} = \frac{\Delta\text{EBIT}}{\text{EBIT}} \div \frac{\Delta\text{sales}}{\text{sales}}$$

Firm A: [(6.2 – 5.7) ÷ 5.7] ÷ [(11.6 – 10.7) ÷ 10.7] = 0.0877 ÷ 0.0841 = 1.0428

Firm B: [(8.1 – 7.4) ÷ 7.4] ÷ [(14.6 – 13.9) ÷ 13.9] = 0.0946 ÷ 0.0504 = 1.8770

Firm B has more operating leverage than Firm A given its considerably higher ratio noted above. Based on 2005 sales, Firm B would experience a 1.8770% change in its EBIT for every 1% change in sales, whereas Firm A would only experience a 1.0428% change in EBIT for a 1% change in sales.

b.

	Firm A	Firm B
When Return on Assets Equals 10%		
EBIT($million)	0.10 × 10.7 = 1.07	0.10 × 15.6 = 1.56
Less: Interest($million)	0.60	1.00
Cash to Equity($million)	0.47	0.56
ROE	0.47 ÷ 4.9 = 9.59%	0.56 ÷ 6.3 = 8.89%
When Return on Assets Equals 20%		
EBIT($million)	0 .20 3 10.7 = 2.14	0.20 3 15.6 = 3.12
Less: Interest($million)	0.60	1.00
Cash to Equity($million)	1.54	2.12
ROE	1.54 ÷ 4.9 = 31.43%	2.12 ÷ 6.3 = 33.65%

Firm B has more financial leverage as demonstrated by the broader range of *ROEs* it expe-riences when the return on assets moves from 10% to 20%. Note that Firm B's *ROE* is lower than Firm A's at the 10% return on assets and its higher than Firm B's *ROE* at the 20% return on assets. Firm B's *ROE* has greater variability—is more responsive to changes in return on assets—than Firm A's *ROE*. Simply stated, Firm B has more financial risk than Firm A.

c. Based on the findings in parts **a** and **b**, its clear that Firm B is riskier than Firm A given that both its operating leverage (risk) and financial leverage (risk) are greater than that of Firm A.

ST10-2. Sierra Vista Industries (SVI) wishes to estimate its cost of capital for use in analyzing projects that are similar to those that already exist. The firm's current capital structure in terms of market value includes 40 percent debt, 10 percent preferred stock, and 50 percent common stock. The firm's debt has an average yield to maturity of 8.3 percent. Its preferred stock has a $70 par value, an 8 percent dividend, and is currently selling for $76 per share. SVI's beta is 1.05, the risk-free rate is 4 percent, and the return on the S&P 500 (the market proxy) is 11.4 percent. CVI is in the 40 percent marginal tax bracket.

a. What are SVI's pretax costs of debt, preferred stock, and common stock?

b. Calculate SVI's weighted average cost of capital (*WACC*) on both a pretax and after-tax basis. Which *WACC* should SVI use when making investment decisions?

c. SVI is contemplating a major investment that is expected to increase both its operating and financial leverage. Its new capital structure will contain 50 percent debt, 10 percent preferred stock, and 40 percent common stock. As a result of the proposed investment, the firm's average yield to maturity on debt is expected to increase to 9 percent, the market value of preferred stock is expected to fall to its $70 par value, and its beta is expected to rise to 1.15. What effect will this investment have on SVI's *WACC*? Explain your finding.

A: **a.** Cost of debt = 8.30%

Cost of preferred stock = (0.08 × \$70) ÷ \$76 = \$5.60 ÷ \$76 = 7.37%

Cost of common stock (using CAPM) = 4.00% + [1.05 × (11.40% – 4.00%)]
= 4.00% + 7.77%
= 11.77%

b. *WACC* (pretax) = (0.40 × 8.30%) + (0.10 × 7.37%) + (0.50 × 11.77%)
= 3.32% + 0.74% + 5.89%
= 9.95%

WACC (after-tax) = [(1.00 – 0.40) × (0.40 × 8.30%)] + (0.10 × 7.37%)
+ (0.50 × 11.77%)
= 1.99% + 0.74% + 5.89%
= 8.62%

c. Cost of debt = 9.00%

Cost of preferred stock = (0.08 × \$70) ÷ \$70 = \$5.60 ÷ \$70 = 8.00%

Cost of common stock (using CAPM) = 4.00% + [1.15 × (11.40% – 4.00%)]
= 4.00% + 8.51%
= 12.51%

WACC (after-tax) = [(1.00 – 0.40) × (0.50 × 9.00%)] + (0.10 × 8.00%)
+ (0.40 × 12.51%)
= 2.70% + 0.80 % + 5.00%
= 8.50%

As a result of the proposed risk-increasing investment SVI's after-tax *WACC* drops slightly from 8.62% to 8.50%. This result may seem a bit inconsistent with expectations, but can be explained by the fact that the increased financial leverage resulted in a higher proportion of debt in the firm's capital structure. In spite of the increased pretax costs of each source of financing, the tax-deductibility of the increased proportion of debt more than compensated for them, thereby lowering SVI's *WACC*.

Chapter 11 An Overview of Long-term Financing

ST11-1. Last year Guaraldi Instruments Inc. conducted an IPO, issuing 2 million common shares with a par value of \$0.25 to investors at a price of \$15 per share. During its first year of operation, Guaraldi earned net income of \$0.07 per share and paid a dividend of \$0.005 per share. At the end of the year, the company's stock was selling for \$20 per share. Construct the equity account for Guaraldi at the end of its first year in business, and calculate the firm's market capitalization.

A. Immediately after the IPO, during which Guaraldi Instruments sold 2 million shares with a par value of \$0.25 each at a price of \$15 each, the company's equity account would have the following entries:

Common stock, at par value (\$0.25 × 2 million)	\$ 500,000
Paid-in capital surplus ((\$15.00 – \$0.25) × 2 million)	29,500,000
Retained earnings	0
Total stockholders' equity	\$30,000,000

After the first year's net income (after dividend payments) are credited to Guaraldi's balance sheet, the equity accounts will have the following entries:

Common stock, at par value (\$0.25 × 2 million)	\$ 500,000
Paid-in capital surplus ((\$15.00 – \$0.25) × 2 million)	29,500,000
Retained earnings ((\$0.07 – \$0.005) × 2 million)	130,000
Total stockholders' equity	\$30,130,000

Guaraldi's market capitalization at the end of the first year would be \$40 million (\$20/share × 2 million shares).

ST11-2. The Bloomington Company needs to raise $20 million of new equity capital. Its common stock is currently selling for $42 per share. The investment bankers require an underwriting spread of 7 percent of the offering price, and the company's legal, accounting, and printing expenses as-sociated with the seasoned offering are estimated to be $450,000. How many new shares must the company sell to net $20 million?

The Bloomington Company needs to raise $20,000,000 + $450,000 = $20,450,000

7% × 42 = $2.94

The shares will net $39.06 a share ($42.00 – $2.94)

20,450,000/39.06 = 523,554 shares

ST11-3. Assume that Zurich Semiconductor Company (ZSC) wishes to create a sponsored ADR program worth $75 million to trade its shares on the NASDAQ stock market. Assume that ZSC is currently selling on the SWX Swiss Exchange for SF25.00 per share, and the current dol-lar/Swiss franc exchange rate is $0.8000/SF. American Bank and Trust (ABT) is handling the ADR issue for ZSC and has advised the company that the ideal trading price for high-technology shares on the NASDAQ is about $60 per share (or per ADR).

a. Describe the precise steps ABT must take to create an ADR issue meeting ZSC's preferences.

b. Assume that ZSC's stock price declines from SF25.00 to SF22.50 per share. If the exchange rate does not also change, what will happen to ZSC's ADR price?

c. If the Swiss franc depreciates from $0.8000/SF to $0.7500/SF, but the price of ZSC's shares remains unchanged in Swiss francs, how will ZSC's ADR price change?

A:

a. ZSC wants to start an ADR program equivalent to about $75 million.
Current ZSC stock price = SF25.00
Exchange rate: $0.8000/SF
Current ZSC stock price in dollars = SF25.00 × $0.8000 = $20.00/share.
Since the preferred ADR price is about $60/share, bundle three ZSC shares into each ADR
ADR price in dollars = 3 × $20/share = $60
To raise roughly $75 million, PSC must sell about 1,250,000 ADRs at $60 each.
To begin ADR creation process, ABT would purchase 3,750,000 shares of ZSC (1.25 ADR × shs/ADR).

Step 1: Purchase 3,750,000 ZSC shares = 3,750,000 × SF25.00/share = SF93,750,000

Step 2: Package stock into 1,250,000 ADRS and sell to US buyers for $60/ADR, raising 1,250,000 ADRs × $60/ADR = $75,000,000.

Step 3: Convert dollar proceeds from selling ADRs into Swiss francs to cover cost of purchasing stock $75,000,000 ÷ $0.8000/ SF = SF93,750,000; this covers ABT's costs.

b. New ADR price in dollars: SF22.50/share × 3 shares/ADR × $0.8000/SF = $54/ADR.

c. New ADR price in dollars: SF25.00/share × 3 shares/ADR × $0.7500/SF = $56.25/ADR.

Chapter 12 Capital Structure: Theory and Taxes

ST12-1. As Chief Financial Officer of the Uptown Service Corporation (USC), you are considering a recapitalization plan that would convert USC from its current all-equity capital structure to one including substantial financial leverage. USC now has 150,000 shares of common stock out-standing, which are selling for $80.00 each. The recapitalization proposal is to issue $6,000,000 worth of long-term debt at an interest rate of 7.0 percent and use the proceeds to repurchase 75,000 shares of common stock worth $6,000,000. USC's earnings in the next year will depend on the state of the economy. If there is normal growth, EBIT will be $1,200,000. EBIT will be $600,000 if there is a recession, and EBIT will be $1,800,000 if there is an economic boom. You believe that each economic outcome is equally likely. Assume there are no market frictions such as corporate or personal income taxes.

a. If the proposed recapitalization is adopted, calculate the number of shares outstanding, the per-share price and the debt-to-equity ratio for USC if the proposed recapitalization is adopted.

b. Calculate the earnings per share (EPS) and return on equity for USC shareholders under all three economic outcomes (recession, normal growth and boom), for both the current all-equity capitalization and the proposed mixed debt/equity capital structure.

c. Calculate the break-even level of EBIT, where earnings per share for USC stockholders are the same, under the current and proposed capital structures.

d. At what level of EBIT will USC shareholders earn zero EPS, under the current and the pro-posed capital structures?

A: **a.** If USC issues $6,000,000 worth of debt and repurchases 75,000 shares of stock worth $6,000,000, this implies that the shares will be repurchased at a price of $80 each ($6,000,000 ÷ 75,000 shares). After this transaction, 75,000 shares will remain outstanding, each worth $80, for a total equity value of $6,000,000. The debt-to-equity ratio will therefore be 1.0 ($6,000,000 debt ÷ $6,000,000 equity).

b.

Expected Operating Profits
Cash Flows to Stockholders and Bondholders Under Current and Proposed Capital Structure for USC
For Three Equally Likely Economic Outcomes

	Recession		Normal Growth		Boom	
EBIT	$600,000		$1,200,000		$1,800,000	
	All Equity Financing	50% Debt: 50% Equity	All Equity Financing	50% Debt: 50% Equity	All Equity Financing	50% Debt: 50% Equity
Interest (7.0%)	$ 0	$ 420,000	$ 0	$ 420,000	$ 0	$ 420,000
Net Income	$ 600,000	$ 180,000	$1,200,000	$ 780,000	$1,800,000	$1,380,000
Shares outstanding	150,000	75,000	150,000	75,000	150,000	75,000
Earnings per share	$ 4.00	$ 2.40	$ 8.00	$ 10.40	$ 12.00	$ 18.40
% Return on shares (P_0 = $80.00/share)	5.0%	3.0%	10.0%	13.00%	15.0%	23.0%

c. The break-even point is EBIT equal to twice the interest payment, or $840,000 (2 ×420,000 interest). At that level of EBIT, earnings per share will be $5.60 per share under both the current all-equity capitalization ($840,000 EBIT ÷ 150,000 shares O/S) and under the 50% debt, 50% equity capital structure [($840,000 EBIT – $420,000 Interest) ÷ 75,000 shares O/S].

d. Under the current all-equity capitalization, shareholders will earn positive EPS for any EBIT above zero, so EBIT = $0 is where EPS = $0. Under the proposed capital structure, EPS = $0 where EBIT = Interest payments = $420,000.

ST12-2. An unlevered company operates in perfect markets and has net operating income (EBIT) of $2,000,000. Assume that the required return on assets for firms in this industry is 8 percent. The firm issues $10 million worth of debt with a required return of 6.5 percent, and uses the proceeds to repurchase outstanding stock. There are no corporate or personal taxes.

a. What is the market value and required return of this firm's stock before the repurchase transaction, according to M&M Proposition I?

b. What is the market value and required return of this firm's remaining stock after the repurchase transaction according to M&M Proposition II?

A: **a.** Before the stock repurchase, the value of the firm under M&M Proposition I is EBIT/r = \$2,000,000/0.08 = \$25,000,000. The required return on the stock (all-equity financing) is 8.0%.

b. After the repurchase, the firm has \$10,000,000 debt and \$15,000,000 equity, so the debt-to-equity ratio is 0.6667 and the new required return on equity according to M&M Proposition II is:

$r_l = r + (r - r_d)D/E = 0.08 + (0.08 - 0.065) \times 0.6667 = 0.08 + 0.01 = 0.09$ or 9%.

ST12-3. Westside Manufacturing has EBIT of \$10 million; the firm has \$60 million of debt outstanding, with a required rate of return of 6.5 percent. The required rate of return on the industry is 10 percent. The corporate tax rate is 30 percent. Assume corporate taxes but no personal taxes.

a. Determine the present value of the interest tax shield of Westside Manufacturing, as well as the total value of the firm.

b. Determine the gain from leverage, if personal taxes of 10 percent on stock income and 35 percent on debt income exist.

A:

	Levered	Unlevered
EBIT	\$10,000,000	\$10,000,000
– Interest paid (0.065 × \$60,000,000)	(3,900,000)	0
= Taxable income	6,100,000	10,000,000
– Taxes (T_C = 0.30)	(1,830,000)	(3,000,000)
= Net income	4,270,000	7,000,000
+ Interest paid	3,900,000	0
= Total income available to investors	\$ 8,170,000	\$ 7,000,000

a. Present value of tax shield = Debt × T_C = \$60,000,000 × 0.30 = \$18,000,000

Value unlevered firm = Net income ÷ Capitalization rate
= \$7,000,000 ÷ 0.10
= \$70,000,000

Value of levered firm = Value unlevered firm + PV tax shields
= \$70,000,000 + \$18,000,000
= \$78,000,000.

b.

$$G_L = \left[1 - \frac{(1-T_c)(1-T_{ps})}{(1-T_{pd})}\right] \times D = \{1 - [(1-0.3)(1-0.1)] \div (1-0.35)\} \times \$60{,}000{,}000$$

$$= \{1 - [(0.7)(0.0)] \div 0.65\} \times \$60{,}000{,}000$$

$$= 0.0308 \times \$60{,}000{,}000$$

$$= \$1{,}846{,}153.85$$

ST12-4. You are the manager of a financially distressed corporation, with \$10 million in debt outstanding. This debt will mature in one month. Your firm currently has \$7 million cash on hand. Assume that you are offered the opportunity to invest in either of the two projects described below.

Project 1: The opportunity to invest \$7 million in risk-free Treasury bills, with a 4 percent annual interest rate (or a 0.333% per month interest rate)

Project 2: A high-risk gamble, which will pay off \$12 million in one month, if successful (probability = 0.25), but will only pay \$4,000,000, if unsuccessful (probability = 0.75)

a. Compute the expected payoff for each project, and state which one you would adopt if you were operating the firm in the shareholders' best interests? Why?
b. Which project would you accept if the firm was unlevered? Why?
c. Which project would you accept if the company was organized as a partnership rather than a corporation? Why??

A: **a.** Payoff for Project 1: $7,000,000 × 1.00333 = $7,023,333
Payoff for Project 2: 0.25 × $12,000,000 + 0.75 × $4,000,000 = $6,000,000

If you were operating in the shareholders' interests, project 2 would be accepted. It gives a higher potential payoff to shareholders if the project does well. Project 1 has a sure, but lower return, but its payoff will accrue to bondholders, rather than shareholders. This is in spite of the fact that project 2 clearly has a negative NPV – it pays off only $6,000,000 and requires a $7 million investment. Note that these are future payoffs – they need to be dis-counted at the appropriate cost of capital to determine NPV.

b. If the firm were unlevered, the firm would prefer project 1. The payoff for project is 1 is higher than the payoff for project 2. If the firm is unlevered, all of the return will accrue to shareholders, since there are no bondholders. An unlevered firm would reject project 2.

c. If the company were organized as a partnership rather than a corporation, then it would accept Project 1. In partnerships, the owners do not have the option to default on the firm's debt (i.e., they don't have limited liability), leaving the firm's assets in the hands of creditors. Therefore, without the option to default, partners have no incentive to under-invest. They will accept Project 1 because doing so reduces their expected losses when the firm goes bankrupt.

ST12-5 Run-and-Hide Detective Company currently has no debt and expects to earn $5 million in EBIT each year for the foreseeable future. The required return on assets for detective companies of this type is 10.0 percent, and the corporate tax rate is 35 percent. No taxes accrue on dividends or interest at the personal level. Run-and-Hide calculates a 5 percent chance that the firm will fall into bankruptcy in any given year. If bankruptcy does occur, it will impose direct and indirect costs totaling $8 million. If necessary, they will use the industry required return for discounting bankruptcy costs.

a. Compute the present value of bankruptcy costs for Run-and-Hide.
b. Compute the overall value of the firm.
c. Re-calculate the value of the company, assuming that the firm's shareholders face a 15 percent personal tax rate on equity income.

A: **a.** For any given year, the expected value of bankruptcy costs will be equal to the probability of bankruptcy (p = 0.05) times the cost to the firm if bankruptcy occurs ($8,000,000), or $400,000 per year. Since direct bankruptcy (B/R) costs are usually only incurred by unprofitable firms—that are not currently paying corporate income taxes—and since indirect B/R costs are things such as opportunity costs such as lost sales, loss of reputational capital and loss of key personnel, we will assume that all B/R costs are after-tax costs. The present value of bankruptcy costs, PV_{BR} , will then be equal to the sum of the stream of discounted expected annual bankruptcy costs, where the discount rate will be the industry required return (r = .10). Since this stream is a perpetuity, PV_{BR} will simply be the expected annual B/R costs divided by the discount rate:

$$PV_{BR} = \left[\frac{\$400,000}{0.10}\right] = \$4,000,000$$

b. The overall value of the firm is computed using equation 12.7, where V_U is the value of an unlevered firm (computed using equation 12.3), V_L is the value of a levered firm, and PVTS equals the present value of debt tax shields. Since there are, at present, no debt tax shields, we will simply compute firm value, *V*:

$$V_L = V = V_U + PV_{TS} - PV_{BR} \qquad \text{(Eq 12.7)}$$

$$V_U = \left[\frac{EBIT(1-T_c)}{r}\right] = \frac{\$5{,}000{,}000(0.65)}{0.10} = \frac{\$3{,}250{,}000}{0.10} = \$32{,}500{,}000$$

$$V = V_U - PV_{BR} = \$32{,}500{,}000 - \$4{,}000{,}000 = \$28{,}500{,}000$$

c. Incorporating a personal tax rate on equity income into the valuation model of an unlevered firm presented in equation 12.3 yields:

$$V_U = \left[\frac{EBIT(1-T_c)(1-T_{PS})}{r}\right] = \frac{\$5{,}000{,}000(0.65)(0.85)}{0.10} = \frac{\$2{,}762{,}500}{0.10} = \$27{,}625{,}000$$

And the new value of the firm, V, taking account of bankruptcy costs as well, becomes:

$$V = V_U - PV_{BR} = \$27{,}625{,}000 - \$4{,}000{,}000 = \$26{,}400{,}000$$

Chapter 13 Dividend Policy

ST13-1. What do record date, ex-dividend date, and payment date mean with regard to dividends? Why would you expect the price of a stock to drop by the amount of the dividend on the ex-dividend date? What rationale has been offered for why this does not actually occur?

A: When corporations announce dividend payments, they state that the dividend will be paid to shareholders of record on a certain date, with payment to be made several days later. This means the check will be made out to shareholders on the corporation's registry as of, say July 5, with payment actually being made on July 15. About three days before the record date, the company's stock will trade ex dividend, meaning that someone who purchases the stock before this ex dividend date will be recorded on the company's books before the record date and will receive the dividend payment. Someone who purchases the stock on or after the ex dividend date will not receive the dividend payment (it will go to the previous owner), as there will be insufficient time to record the new owner on the shareholders' registry before payment is made. The stock price should therefore drop by about the amount of the dividend payment on the ex-dividend date, because the new purchaser must be compensated for the fact that the upcoming cash payment will be made to the previous owner. Historically, the average price drop on the ex-dividend day for U.S. companies has been 50–65% of the amount of the dividend paid, and this has been interpreted as a personal income tax effect. Since personal tax rates on dividend income have traditionally been taxed at a higher rate than on realized capital gains, most individual investors eager to sell shares would prefer to sell before the ex-dividend date—receiving their return as capital gains—rather than wait to receive the highly taxed cash dividend. For some expected ex-dividend day price drop investors will be indifferent between receiving $1 worth of capital gains rather than $0.50–$0.65 worth of cash dividends.

ST13-2. What has happened to the total volume of share repurchases announced by U.S. public companies since 1982? Why did that year mark such an important milestone in the history of share repurchase programs in the United States?

A: The total value of share repurchases in the United States increased dramatically after 1982. During that year, the U.S. Securities and Exchange Commission (SEC) spelled out the legal rules covering share repurchases, and this "safe harbor" ruling clarified when corporate managers could execute repurchases without fear of being charged with insider trading by the SEC.

ST13-3. What has happened to the average cash dividend payout ratio of U.S. corporations over time? What explains this trend? How would your answer change if share repurchases were included in calculating U.S. dividend payout ratios?

Not only has the fraction of U.S. firms that pay dividends been declining steadily for the past 50 years, those companies that do pay regular cash dividends tend to pay out lower fractions of their earnings today than in the past. A relative handful of 200 or so NYSE listed firms account for over half of the value of dividend payments in the United States, though these companies are truly enormous and also account for the bulk of corporate profits each year. Several factors seem to account for this decline in the "propensity to pay" among dividend-paying firms, including the rise of institutional investors in U.S. markets (who presumably have less need for a regular cash payment than individual investors) and the increasing importance of technology and entrepreneurship in American business. These factors suggest both that corporate managers would have greater need to retain earnings for investment and that investors would have less desire to receive dividends. On the other hand, if share repurchases are included with regular cash dividends, than the picture of declining dividend payments reverses itself. By this measure, the aggregate "payout ratio" of large US businesses has been steadily (if slightly) increasing over time, though it is still the same relative handful of companies that pay dividend and execute share repurchase programs.

ST13-4. What does it mean to say that corporate managers "smooth" cash dividend payments? Why do managers do this?

A: Most firms will maintain a constant nominal dividend payment until the company's managers are convinced that corporate earnings have permanently changed. If the firm's "permanent earnings" increase, then managers will increase the nominal dividend payment a little each quarter or year until a new equilibrium level of dividend payments close to the target payout ratio is reached. The company will then maintain the quarterly or annual dividend at this nominal level until the firm's permanent earnings change again. This pattern of stable nominal dividend payments, followed by slow and steady increases as the firm's managers adjust to new levels of permanent earnings, gives the observed dividend series a smooth pattern, so managers are said to smooth dividends if they follow a constant nominal dividend payment policy with a partial adjustment strategy—as most do.

ST13-5. What are the key assumptions and predictions of the Signaling Model of Dividends? Are these predictions supported by empirical research findings?

A: The signaling model of dividends predicts that managers will begin paying dividends in order to differentiate their "strong" firms from weaker firms (with lower cash flows) in a market characterized by information asymmetries between managers and shareholders. In such an environment, investors cannot distinguish strong from weak companies, so managers of strong firms will incur all the costs (taxes, foregone investment, transactions costs of issuing new securities) of paying high dividends because their firms can afford to bear these costs while weaker firms cannot. Signaling with dividends is comparable to burning $100 bills in public; only the wealthiest individuals can afford to commit such a wasteful act, so the signal is credible to all who witness it. The signaling model predicts that the most profitable and most promising firms will pay the highest dividends. The prediction that more profitable firms will pay the highest dividends is partially supported by empirical research, but the most promising firms (high-tech and entrepreneurial companies) have low payouts, which contradicts the signaling model's predictions.

ST-6. What is the expected relationship between dividend payout levels and the growth rate and availability of positive-*NPV* projects under the agency cost model of dividends? What about the expected relationship between dividend payout and the diffusion of firm shareholders? Free cash flow? Consider a firm such as Microsoft awash in free cash flow, positive-*NPV* projects available, and a relatively diffuse shareholder base in an industry with increasing competition. Does either the agency model or signaling model adequately predict the dividend policy of Microsoft? Which does the better job?

A: The agency cost model predicts that firms with many positive-NPV investment projects will have less need to pay out cash as dividends in order to overcome agency costs than will firms with few positive-NPV projects. Thus high-growth firms will have low dividend payouts. As noted in 13-20 and 13-26 above, firms with a tight ownership structure have few agency problems between managers and shareholders, so have less need to make large dividend payments. Most economists agree that Microsoft should pay out more of its cash holdings (horde?) as dividends, and the firm recently has raised its payout level—though the current payments will not seriously reduce Microsoft's cash mountain in the foreseeable future.

Chapter 14 Entrepreneurial Finance and Venture Capital

ST14-1. You are seeking \$1.5 million from a venture capitalist to finance the launch of your online financial search engine. You and the VC agree that your venture is currently worth \$3 million, and when the company goes public in an IPO in five years, it is expected to have a market capitalization of \$20 million. Given the company's stage of development, the VC requires a 50 percent return on investment. What fraction of the firm will the VC receive in exchange for its \$1.5 million investment in your company?

A: Expected market value in 5 years = \$20 million
Required return on investment = 50%

Value of VC investment in 5 years = $\$1{,}500{,}000 \times 1.50^5 = \$1{,}500{,}000 \times 7.594 = \$11{,}390{,}625$

Fraction equity received = \$11,390,625 ÷ \$20,000,000 = **56.95%.**

ST14-2. An entrepreneur seeks \$12 million from a VC fund. The entrepreneur and fund managers agree that the entrepreneur's venture is currently worth \$30 million and that the company is likely to be ready to go public in four years. At that time, the company is expected to have net income of \$6 million, and comparable firms are expected to be selling at a price/earnings ratio of 25. Given the company's stage of development, the venture capital fund managers require a 40 percent compound annual return on their investment. What fraction of the firm will the fund receive in exchange for its \$12 million investment

A: Value of firm = Net income × P/E multiple = \$9 million × 25 = \$225 million

40% return is required on the investment
$12{,}000{,}000 \times (1.40)^4 = \$12{,}000{,}000 \times 3.842 = \$46{,}099{,}200$

\$46,099,200 ÷ \$225,000,000 = 20.49% of the firm.

ST14-3. Suppose that 6 out of 10 investments made by a VC fund are a total loss, meaning that the return on each of them is –100 percent. Of the remaining investments, three break even, earning a 0 percent return, while one investment pays off spectacularly and earns a 650 percent return. What is the realized return on the VC fund's overall portfolio?

A: This solution assumes that each of the 10 investments are for equal dollar amounts. Therefore, each investment gets a portfolio weight of 10%.

6 of 10 earn –100%, so expressed as a fraction of total portfolio (p/f) return:
$(0.6 \times -1.00) = -0.60$

3 of 10 earn 0% return, so expressed as a fraction of total p/f return: $(0.2 \times 0) = 0$

One investment earns 650% (0.1×6.50)

Portfolio return (R) is thus calculated as:
$R = (0.6 \times -1.00) + (0.3 \times 0) + (0.1 \times 6.50) = -0.60 + 0 + 0.65 = 0.05$

The portfolio's realized return will be 5.0 percent

Chapter 15 Options

ST15-1. Several call options on Cuban Cigars Inc. are available for trading. The expiration date, strike price, and current premium for each of these options appears below.

Strike	Expiration	Premium
$40	July	$6
$45	July	$3.50
$50	July	$1.75

An investor decides to purchase one call with a $40 strike and one with a $50 strike. At the same time, the investor sells two of the calls with a $45 strike price. Draw a payoff diagram for this portfolio of options. Your diagram should have two lines, one showing the portfolio's payoff on a gross basis and one showing the payoff net of the cost of forming the portfolio.

A: As the accompanying diagram shows, this portfolio has a zero payoff if the stock price is between $0 and $40 or if it is above $50. Between $40 and $45 the portfolio payoff rises with the stock price, but between $45 and $50 the payoff falls as the stock rises. To construct this portfolio, the investor pays $7.75 to buy two call options, and the investor receives $7 from selling two calls. Therefore, the net cost is $0.75, and the net payoff line is $0.75 below the gross payoff line.

Self-Test Problem 1

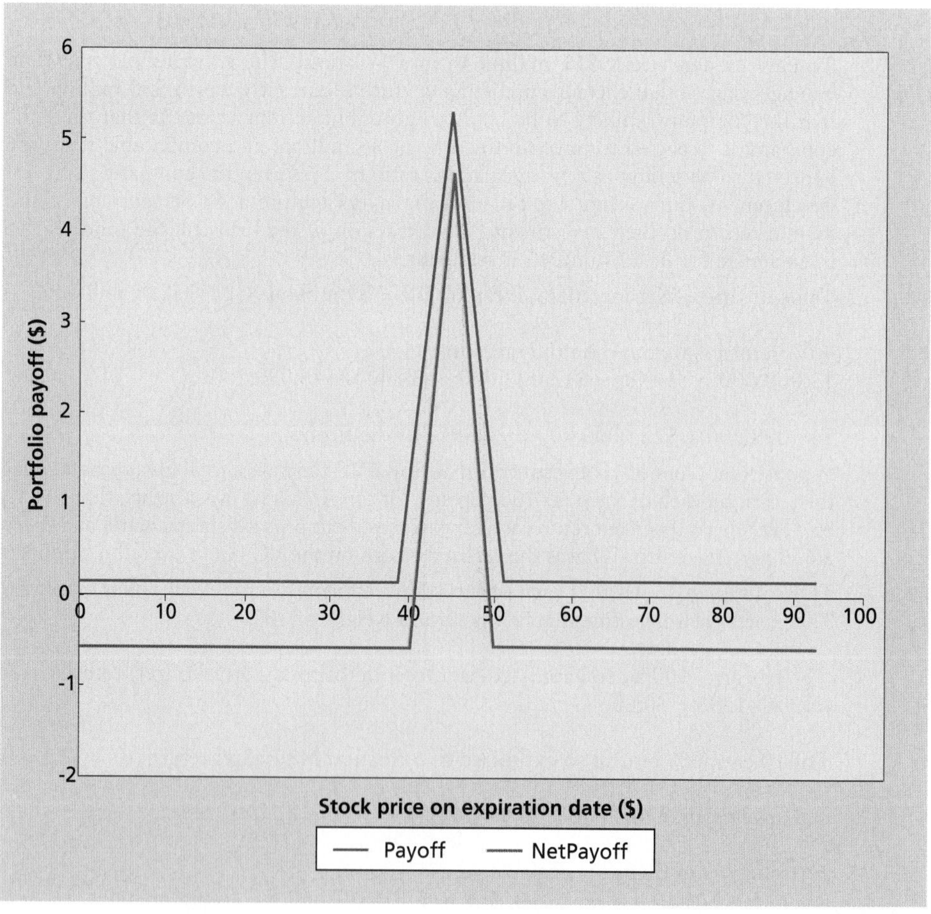

ST15-2. A stock currently sells for \$36. In the next six months, the stock will either go up to \$42 or it will fall to \$31. If the risk-free rate is 4% per year, calculate the current market price of a call option on this stock with an expiration date in six months and a strike price of \$35.

A: First draw the tree illustrating how the stock price will move and list the payoff of the option at each terminal node of the tree.

Stock values	Option pays
42	\$7
36	\$0

Next, calculate the hedge ratio. To do this, you imagine that you purchase one share of stock and "h" call options. If the stock price goes up, the payoff will be 42 + 7h, and if the stock price goes down the payoff on the portfolio will be 31 + 0h. Set these expressions equal to each other to find h:

$$42 + 7h = 31 + 0h$$

$$h = -11/7$$

This means that a perfectly hedged portfolio can be formed by purchasing 1 share of stock and selling 11/7 call options. If you plug h = -11/7 back into the equation from which it was derived you obtain

$$42 + 7(-11/7) = 31 + 0(-11/7)$$

$$31 = 31$$

This indicates that the perfectly hedged portfolio will pay \$31 with certainty in six months. This implies that the portfolio is identical to a Treasury bond that pays \$31 in six months. The price of such a Treasury bond would be 31 ÷ 1.02 = 30.39 (note: the discount factor is 1.02 because we are discounting at four percent for six months). But 30.39 must also be the net cost of buying 1 share of stock and selling 11/7 call options. Therefore we can write:

$$30.39 = 36 - (11/7)C$$

$$C = 3.57$$

Chapter 16 International Financial Management

ST16-1. Use Figure 16.1 to determine whether the British pound trades at a forward discount or a forward premium relative to the Japanese yen. Use the 6-month forward rate in your calculations.

A: To calculate the spot and forward exchange rates between pounds and yen, we must take the ratio of the exchange rate of each currency relative to the dollar.

$$\text{Spot Rate} = \frac{\$1.7733/£}{\$0.009138/¥} = ¥194.0578/£$$

$$\text{Fwd Rate} = \frac{\$1.7453/£}{\$0.009199/¥} = ¥189.7271/£$$

This calculation shows that one pound buys fewer yen on the forward market than on the spot market, so the pound trades at a forward discount and the yen trades at a forward premium.

ST16-2. Suppose the spot exchange rate equals ¥100/\$ and the six-month forward rate equals ¥101/\$. An investor can purchase a T-bill in the U.S. that matures in six months and earns an annual rate of return of 3%. What would be the annual return on a similar Japanese investment?

A: In order for the Interest Rate Parity to hold, we get:

101/100 = (1+x)/1.015
x = 0.0252

Therefore, the annualized return on Japanese investment will be 2 × 0.0252 = 5.03%

Chapter 17 Risk Management and Financial Engineering

ST17-1. A certain commodity sells for $150 today. The present value of the cost of storing this com-modity for one year is $10. The risk-free rate is 4 percent. What is a fair price for a one-year forward contract on this asset?

A: Use equation 17.2 to solve this problem. F = (150 + 10)(1.04) = 166.40

ST17-2. The spot exchange rate is $1.6666/£. The risk-free rate is 4 percent in the U.S. and 6 percent in the U.K. What is the forward exchange rate (assume a 1-year contract)?

A: Use equation 17.3 here, but remember that we need to express the exchange rates in terms of foreign currency per unit of domestic currency. If we treat the $ as the domestic currency, then the spot rate is 1/($1.6666/£) or £0.6000/$. So we have

F = 0.6000(1.06)/1.04 = 0.6115.

Chapter 18 Financial Planning

ST18-1. Some key financial data from the most recent annual report of Rancho, Inc. is listed below.

Sales	$12.7 million
Net income	$ 1.3 million
Total assets	$ 7.6 million
Total equity	$ 5.2 million
Dividends	$ 0.3 million

The firm's CFO wishes to use this data to estimate the firm's sustainable growth rate.

a. Use the data provided to calculate Rancho's net profit margin, assets-to-equity ratio, asset turnover ratio, and its dividend payout ratio.
b. Use your findings in part a to find Rancho's *sustainable growth rate*.
c. Interpret the sustainable growth rate calculated in part b. Does this rate of growth assure shareholder wealth maximization? Explain.
d. If the firm's Board feels that it is best for its shareholders to grow the firm more slowly, what alterations in each of the baseline assumptions would be necessary to achieve this objective?

A: **a.** m = net profit margin = $1.3 million ÷ $12.7 million = 0.1024
A/E = assets-to-equity ratio = $7.6 million ÷ $5.2 million = 1.46
S/A = asset turnover ratio = $12.7 million ÷ $7.6 million = 1.67
Note: $A/S = 1.0 \div S/A = 1.0 \div 1.67 = 0.599$
d = dividend payout ratio = $0.3 million ÷ $1.3 million = 0.231

b. Substituting the relevant values from part a into Equation 18.1, we get

$$g^* = [0.1024 \times (1.0 - 0.231) \times 1.46] \div [0.599-(0.1024 \times (1.0-0.231) \times 1.46)]$$
$$= 0.1150 \div 0.4840$$
$$= 0.2376 = 23.76\%$$

c. The 23.76 percent sustainable growth rate calculated in part b indicates that the firm can increase sales by this percentage in the coming year and maintain its balance sheet identity, i.e., its outflows (increases in assets) and inflows (increases in liabilities and equity) will be in balance. This growth rate *does not* assure wealth maximization of the wealth of Rancho's shareholders. It merely serves as a planning device that the firm can use to prepare for the consequences of its growth plans, which will be driven by the growth rate believed consistent with shareholder wealth maximization.

d. A lower profit margin (clearly not a good idea), a decrease in asset turnover (clearly not a good idea), a decrease in leverage, or an increase in the dividend payout ratio would lower Rancho's sustainable growth rate. Clearly the best strategy for lowering the firm's sustainable growth rate would be to either reduce leverage or pay out a larger percentage of net income as dividends.

ST18-2. Planet Inc. wishes to construct a pro forma income statement and a pro forma balance sheet for the coming year using the following data.

1. Sales are forecast to grow by 5% from \$809.5 million last year to \$850 million in the coming year.
2. Cost of goods sold is expected to represent 72% of forecast sales.
3. Operating expenses are expected to represent 11% of forecast sales.
4. Depreciation expense on the firm's existing net fixed assets, which currently total \$275 million, is expected to remain at \$55 million per year for at least four more years.
5. Planet's marginal tax rate is expected to remain at 40%.
6. Planet is expected to continue its policy of paying out 10% of net income as dividends.
7. Planet's net profit margin last year was 5.2%.
8. Planet wishes to maintain a minimum cash balance of \$8 million in the coming year.
9. The firm's accounts receivable are expected to equal about 15% of sales.
10. The firm's inventory has historically averaged about 12% of cost of goods sold.
11. Planet is planning to invest an additional \$35 million in fixed assets that will be depreciated on a straight-line basis over a 7-year life.
12. The firm's accounts payable, which totaled \$63.5 million at the end of last year, are expected to equal about 11% of cost of goods sold in the coming year.
13. Planet plans to maintain its notes payable of \$42 million requiring annual interest of 5%, which totals \$2.1 million.
14. The firm has \$80 million of long-term debt that matures as a lump-sum due and payable in full in 5 years. Annual interest of \$4.8 million must be paid on this debt.
15. Planet has no preferred stock outstanding and its retained earnings and common stock cur-rently total \$250 million.
16. Planet's total assets at the end of last year were \$435 million.
    - **a.** Use the preceding data to prepare Planet's pro forma income statement for the coming year.
    - **b.** Use the data provided and your findings in part a to prepare Planet's pro forma balance sheet for the coming year. Use notes payable as the balancing figure and ignore any change in annual interest expense caused by the change in notes payable.
    - **c.** Explain the balancing figure used to make notes payable the balancing figure in part b. Indicate the resulting amount of the *plug figure* needed to create the balancing figure. Will Planet be able to fund its planned growth internally? Explain.
    - **d.** Use Equation 18.2 along with Planet's relevant data to determine its *external funds required* (*EFR*). Compare this value to the *plug figure* you found in part c and explain in general terms why differences between these two values might result.

A: **a.**

Sales: $850	
Less: COGS (72% × 850)	612.0
Less: Operating expense (0.11 × $850)	93.5
Less: Depreciation expense [$55 + ($35 ÷ 7)]	60.0
Operating profit	$ 84.5
Less: Interest expense ($2.1 + $4.8)	6.9
Pretax income	$ 77.6
Less: Taxes (0.40 × $77.6)	31.0
Net income	$ 46.6
Less: Dividends (0.10 × $46.6)	4.7
To retained earnings	$ 41.9

b.

Planet Inc.
Balance Sheet
for the end of the Coming Year
($ in millions)

Cash	$ 8.0	Accounts payable (0.11 × $612)	$ 67.3
Accts rec. (0.15 3 $850)	127.5	Notes payable [$42.0	
Inventory (0.12 3 $612)	73.4	– ($481.2 – $458.9)]	19.7
Current assets	$208.9	Current liabilities	$ 87.0
Net fixed assets ($275 + $35		Long-term debt	80.0
– [$55 + ($35 ÷ 7)])	250.0	Retained earn. and common	
Total assets	$458.9	stock ($250 + $41.9)	291.9
		Total liabilities and equity	$458.9

c. The balancing figure of $19.7 of notes payable resulted from the fact that the initial notes payable of $42.0 were more than was necessary to allow Planet's total liabilities and equity to equal its forecast $458.9 of total assets. With the initial $42.0 of notes payable, Planet's total liabilities and equity would have totaled $481.2; in other words Planet had more financing than it needed to support its assets in the coming year. Therefore, using the notes payable as the balancing figure, the firm can pay down its notes by $22.3 million ($481.2 – $458.9) reducing them to $19.7 million ($42.0 – $22.3) as noted on the pro forma balance sheet. The $22.3 million reduction in notes payable is the *plug figure*. During the coming year Planet's internally generated financing is in excess of its need and it therefore it can pay down its notes payable as shown.

d. Using the data provided, the values of the key variables needed to apply Equation 18.2 to find the external funds required (*EFR*) are:

A/S = $435 million ÷ $809.5 million = 0.5374
ΔS = $850 million – $809.5 million = $40.5 million
AP/S = $63.5 million ÷ $809.5 million = .0784
m = net profit margin = .052
g = growth rate of sales = .050
d = dividend payout ratio = 0.10

Substituting these values into Equation 18.2 we get Planet's external funds required (*EFR*):

EFR = (0.5374 × $40.5 million) – (.0784 × $40.5 million)
– [.052 × $809.5 million × (1.00 + 0.05) × (1.00 – 0.10)]
= $21s.8 million – $3.18 million – $39.8 million
= –$21.19 million

The *EFR* of –$21.19 is very close to the –$22.3 million plug figure, which represented the reduction in notes payable discussed in part c. The difference in these two estimates is at-tributable to the fact that some of the assumptions in Equation 18.2 do not hold in the more detailed pro forma analysis. For example, in the *EFR* equation we assumed that the assets-to-sales ratio (*A/S*) was 0.5374, but in the pro forma calculations it becomes 0.5399 (\$458.9 million ÷ \$850 million). Other similar differences further contribute to the difference between the *EFR* and the *plug figure*.

ST18-3. The financial analyst for Sportif, Inc. has compiled sales and total cash disbursement estimates for the coming months of January through May. Historically, 60 percent of sales are for cash with the remaining 40 percent collected in the following month. The ending cash balance in January is \$1,000. The firm's minimum cash balance is \$1,000. The analyst plans to use this data to prepare a cash budget for the months of February through May.

Month	Sales	Total Cash Disbursements
January	\$ 5,000	\$6,000
February	6,000	8,000
March	10,000	8,000
April	10,000	6,000
May	10,000	5,000

a. Use the data provided to prepare Sportif's cash budget for the four months February through May.

b. How much total financing will Sportif need to meet its financial requirements for the period February to May?

c. If a pro forma balance sheet dated at the end of May were prepared from the information presented, how much would Sportif have in accounts receivable?

A: **a.**

	Jan.	Feb.	Mar.	Apr.	May
Sales (\$000)	\$5.0	\$6.0	\$10.0	\$10.0	\$10.0
Cash sales(0.60)	\$3.0	\$3.6	\$ 6.0	\$ 6.0	\$ 6.0
Collections(0.40_{t-1})		2.0	–2.4	4.0	4.0
Total Receipts		\$5.6	\$ 8.4	\$10.0	\$10.0
Less: Total disbursements		8.0	8.0	6.0	5.0
Net cash flow		–\$2.4	\$ 0.4	\$ 4.0	\$ 5.0
Add: Beginning cash		1.0	–1.4	–1.0	3.0
Ending cash balance		–\$1.4	\$–1.0	\$ 3.0	\$ 8.0
Less: Minimum cash balance		1.0	1.0	1.0	1.0
Required total financing (N/P)		\$2.4	\$ 2.0		
Excess cash balance (M/S)				\$ 2.0	\$ 7.0

b. Based on the cash budget prepared in part a, Spo rtif will need to be able to borrow up to \$2.4 thousand to cover its shortages in the months of February and March.

c. Sportif would have accounts receivable of \$4.0 thousand at the end of May. The receivables would represent the 40% of May's sales of \$10.0 thousand that would be uncollected at that time.

Chapter 19 Cash Conversion, Inventory, and Receivables Management

ST19-1. Aztec Products wishes to evaluate its cash conversion cycle (CCC). Research by one of the firm's financial analysts indicates that on average the firm holds items in inventory for 65 days, pays its suppliers 35 days after purchase, and collects its receivables after 55 days. The firm's annual sales (all on credit) are about \$2.1 billion, its cost of goods sold represent about 67 percent of sales, and purchases represent about 40 percent of cost of goods sold. Assume a 365-day year.

a. What is Aztec Products' *operating cycle (OC)* and *cash conversion (CCC)*?

b. How many dollars of resources does Aztec have invested in (1) inventory, (2) accounts re-ceivable, (3) accounts payable, and (4) the total CCC?

c. If Aztec could shorten its cash conversion cycle by reducing its inventory holding period by 5 days, what effect would it have on its total resource investment found in part b(4)?

d. If Aztec could shorten its CCC by 5 days, would it be best to reduce the inventory holding period, reduce the receivable collection period, or extend the accounts payable period? Why?

A: **a.** Operating cycle = Average age of inventory + Average collection period

OC = AAI + ACP
= 65 days + 55 days
= 120 days

Cash conversion cycle = Operating cycle – Average payment period

CCC = OC – APP
= 120 days – 35 days
= 85 days

b. (1) Inventory = ($2.1 billion × 67%) × (65/365) = $250.6 million
(2) Accounts receivable = ($2.1 billion) × (55/365) = $316.4 million
(3) Accounts payable = ($2.1 billion × 67% × 40%) × (35/365) = $54 million
(4) Total resources invested = $250.6 million + $316.4 million – $54 million
= $513.0 million

c. New inventory investment = ($2.1 billion × 67%) × [(65 – 5)/365]
= $231.3 million

Change in resource investment = Change in inventory investment
= $231.3 million – $250.6 million
= –$19.3 million

The total resource investment would be reduced by $19.3 million.

d. It would be best to reduce the receivable collection period because the receivables account for the largest annual dollar investment—$2.1 billion— whereas the annual inventory investment equals 67 percent of that amount, and annual purchases equal 40 percent of the inventory investment.

ST19-2. Vargas enterprises wishes to determine the economic order quantity (EOQ) for a critical and expensive inventory item that is used in large amounts at a relatively constant rate throughout the year. The firm uses 450,000 units of the item annually, has order costs of $375 per order, and its carrying costs associated with this item are $28 per unit per year. The firm plans to hold safety stock of the item equal to 5 days of usage, and it estimates that it takes 12 days to receive an order of the item once placed. Assume a 365-day year.

a. Calculate the firm's *EOQ* for the item of inventory described above.
b. What is the firm's *total cost* based upon the *EOQ* calculated in part a?
c. How many units of *safety stock* should Vargas hold?
d. What is the firm's *reorder point* for the item of inventory being evaluated? (*Hint:* Be sure to include the safety stock.)

A: **a.** S = 450,000 units; O = $375/order; C = $28/unit/year

$$\text{EOQ} = \sqrt{\frac{2SO}{C}} = \sqrt{\frac{2 \times 450{,}000 \times \$375}{\$28}} = \sqrt{12{,}053{,}571} = 3{,}472 \text{ units}$$

b. Total cost = (O × S/Q) + (C × Q/2)
= ($375 × 450,000/3,472) + ($28 × 3,472/2)
= $48,603 + $48,608
= $97,211

c. Daily usage = 450,000 ÷ 365 = 1,233 units
Safety stock = 5 days × 1,233 units/day = 6,165 units

d. Reorder point =(lead time in days × daily usage) + safety stock
= (12 days × 1,233 units/day) + 6,165 units
= 20,961 units

ST19-3. Belton Company is considering relaxing its credit standards to boost its currently sagging sales. It expects its proposed relaxation will increase sales by 20 percent from the current annual level of $10 million. The firm's average collection period is expected to increase from 35 days to 50 days and bad debts are expected to increase from 2 percent of sales to 7 percent of sales as a result of relaxing the firm's credit standards as proposed. The firm's variable costs equal 60 percent of sales and their fixed costs total $2.5 million per year. Belton's opportunity cost is 16 percent. Assume a 365-day year.

a. What is Belton's *contribution margin*?
b. Calculate Belton's *marginal profit from increased sales.*
c. What is Belton's *cost of the marginal investment in accounts receivable*?
d. What is Belton's *cost of marginal bad debts*?
e. Use your findings in parts b, c, and d to determine the net profit (cost) of Belton's proposed relaxation of credit standards. Should they relax credit standards?

A:
a. Contribution margin = 1.00 – variable cost percentage = 1.00 – 0.60 = 0.40 = 40%
b. Marginal profit from increased sales = Δsales × contribution margin
= ($10 million × 20%) × 40%
= $800,000
c. Cost of marginal investment in accounts receivable:
Investment in accounts receivable = Total variable cost/A/R turnover
After relaxation: ($12 million × 60%) / (365/50) = $986,301
Before relaxation: ($10 million × 60%) / (365/35) = $575,342
Marginal investment in A/R = $986,301 – $575,342 = $410,959
Cost of marginal investment in A/R = $410,959 × 16% = $65,753
d. Cost of marginal bad debts:
Cost of bad debts = annual sales × bad debt expense rate
After relaxation: $12 million × 7% = $840,000
Before relaxation: $10 million × 2% = $200,000
Cost of marginal bad debts = $840,000 – $200,000 = $640,000
e. Summary:

Marginal profit from increased sales =	$800,000
Less: Cost of marginal investment in A/R =	65,753
Less: Cost of marginal bad debts =	640,000
Net profit from proposed relaxation	$ 94,247

Recommendation: Belton Company should relax its credit standards as proposed because it will result in an annual increase in profits of $94,247.

Chapter 20 Cash, Payables, and Liquidity Management

ST20-1. Gale Supply estimates that its customers' payments are in the mail for 3 days, and once received they are processed in 2 days. After the payments are deposited in the firm's bank, the funds are made available to the firm by the bank in 2.5 days. The firm estimates its total annual collections, received at a constant rate, from credit customers to be $87 million. Its annual opportunity cost of funds is 9.5 percent. Assume a 365-day year.

a. How many days of collection float does Gale Supply have?
b. What is the current annual dollar cost of Gale Supply's collection float?
c. If the installation of an *electronic invoice presentment and payment (EIPP) system* would result in a 4 day reduction in Gale's collection float, how much could the firm earn annually on this float reduction?

d. Based on your findings in part c, should Gale install the *EIPP system* if its annual cost is $85,000? Explain your recommendation.

A: **a.** Collection float = Mail float + Processing float + Availability float
= 3.0 days + 2.0 days + 2.5 days
= 7.5 days

b. Average daily receipts = Annual receipts ÷ 365 days
= $87 million ÷ 365 days
= $238,356

Collection float ($) = Collection float (days) × Average daily receipts
= 7.5 days × $238,356
= $1,787,670

Annual dollar cost = Collection float ($) × Opportunity cost
= $1,787,670 × 9.5%
= $169,829

c. Annual earnings = Float reduction (days) × Average daily receipts × Opportunity cost
= 4.0 days × $238,356 × 9.5%
= $90,575

d. Gale should install the proposed EIPP system. The annual earnings of $90,575 exceed the annual cost of $85,000, thereby resulting in an annual profit contribution of $5,575 ($90,575 – $85,000).

ST20-2. Derson Manufacturing wishes to evaluate the credit terms offered by its four biggest suppliers of raw materials. The prime rate is currently 7.0 percent and Derson can borrow short-term funds at a spread 2.5 percent above the prime rate. Assume a 365-day year and that the firm always pays its suppliers on the last day allowed by their stated credit terms. The terms offered by each supplier are listed below:

Supplier 1: 2/10 net 40
Supplier 2: 1/15 net 60
Supplier 3: 3/10 net 70
Supplier 4: 1/10 net 50

a. Calculate the interest rate associated with not taking the discount from each supplier.

b. Assuming the firm needs short-term financing and considering each supplier separately, indicate whether the firm should take or not take the discount from each supplier.

c. If the firm did not need any short-term financing, when should it pay each of the suppliers?

d. If the firm could not obtain a loan from banks and other financial institutions and needed short-term financing, when should it pay each of the suppliers?

e. What impact, if any, would the fact that Derson could stretch its accounts payable (net period only) from Supplier 1 to day 90 without damaging its credit rating have on your recommendation with regard to Supplier 1 in part b? Explain you answer.

A: **a.** Rate = [%Discount ÷ (1.00 – %Discount)] × [365 ÷ (Credit per. – Cash disc. per.)]

Supplier	Calculation	Rate
1	[.02 ÷ (1.00 – .02)] × [365 ÷ (40 –10)] = .0204 × 12.17 =	24.83%
2	[.01 ÷ (1.00 – .01)] × [365 ÷ (60 –15)] = .0101 × 8.11 =	8.19%
3	[.03 ÷ (1.00 – .03)] × [365 ÷ (70 –10)] = .0309 × 6.08 =	18.79%
4	[.01 ÷ (1.00 – .01)] × [365 ÷ (50 –10)] = .0101 × 9.13 =	9.22%

b. Bank loan rate = Prime rate + Spread = 7.0% + 2.5% = 9.5%

Supplier 1: Take the discount: Interest rate of 24.83% > 9.5% Bank loan rate.
Supplier 2: Don't take discount: Interest rate of 8.19% < 9.5% Bank loan rate.

Supplier 3: Take the discount: Interest rate of 18.79% > 9.5% Bank loan rate.
Supplier 4: Don't take discount: Interest rate of 9.22% < 9.5% Bank loan rate.

c. If the firm needs no short-term financing, it should pay each supplier at the end of its cash discount period—days 10, 15, 10, and 10 for Suppliers 1, 2, 3, and 4, respectively. Clearly, the firm in this case should take the discounts rather than not take them and borrow unneeded funds from their suppliers.

d. If the firm needs short-term financing and cannot obtain a loan from banks and other financial institutions, it should not take the discounts offered by its suppliers and pay them at the end of the credit period—days 40, 60, 70, and 50 for Suppliers 1, 2, 3, and 4, respectively. This strategy results in borrowing from suppliers, given the need for funds and the lack of alternative lenders.

e. If Derson can stretch the net period for Supplier 1 to day 90 without damaging its credit rating, the firm would effectively be getting 2/10 net 90 terms from Supplier 1. The interest rate associated with not taking the discount under these terms would be:

$$\text{Rate} = [.02 \div (1.00 - .02)] \times [365 \div (90 - 10)] = .0204 \times 4.56 = 9.30\%$$

This result would change the recommendation for Supplier 1 given in part b to Take the discount because the interest rate of 9.30% < 9.5% bank loan rate.

ST20-3. Rosa Inc. has arranged a 1-year $2 million credit line with its lead bank. The bank set the interest rate at the prime rate plus a spread of 1.50 percent. The prime rate is expected to remain stable at 5.25 percent during the coming year. In addition, the bank requires Rosa to pay a 0.50 percent commitment fee on the *average unused portion* of the line. Assume a 365-day year.

a. Calculate the *effective borrowing rate (EBR)* on Rosa's line of credit during the coming year assuming an average loan balance outstanding during the year is $1.8 million.

b. Calculate Rosa's *EBR* on the line of credit during the coming year assuming the average loan balance outstanding during the year is $0.8million.

c. Compare and contrast the *EBRs* calculated for Rosa Inc. in parts **a** and **b**. Explain the causes of the differences in *EBRs*.

A:

a. Int. rate = Prime rate + Spread = 5.25% + 1.50% = 6.75%

EBR = [{(Intereset rate × Average. loan) + [Commitment fee × (Total credit line – Average loan)]}÷ Average loan] × (365 ÷ Days loan outstanding)
= [{(.0675 × $1.8 mil.) + [.0050 × ($2.0 mil. – $1.8 mil.)]} ÷ $1.8 mil.] × (365 ÷ 365)
= [($121,500 + $1,000) ÷ $1,800,000] × 1.00
= 6.81%

b. EBR = [{(Interest rate × Average loan) + [Commitment fee × (Total credit line – Average loan)]} ÷ Avg. loan] × (365 ÷ Days loan outstanding)
= [{(.0675 × $0.8 mil.) + [.0050 × ($2.0 mil. – $0.8 mil.)]} ÷ $0.8 mil.] × (365 ÷ 365)
= [($54,000 + $6,000) ÷ $800,000] × 1.00 = 7.50%

c. Note that the *EBR* of 6.81% in part a, where the average loan balance outstanding is $1.8 million and the average unused portion is $200,000 ($2.0 million - $1.8 million), is nearly 0.7% lower than the *EBR* of 7.50% in part b, where the average loan balance outstanding is $0.8 million and the average unused portion is $1.2 million ($2.0 million – $0.8 million). The higher cost in part b is primarily attributable to the fact that the commitment fee on the average unused portion in part b is $6,000 (0.0050 × $1,2 million) versus a commitment fee of only $1,000 (0.0050 × $200,000) in part a. When the higher commitment fees in part b are expressed as a percentage of its lower average loan ($0.8 million), its *EBR* is driven above the EBR in part a where the commitment fee is lower and the average loan ($1.8 million) is higher.

Chapter 21 Long-Term Debt Financing

ST21-1. The initial proceeds per bond, the size of the issue, the initial maturity of the bond, and the years remaining to maturity are shown in the following table for a number of bonds. In each case, the firm is in the 35 percent tax bracket, and the bond has a $1,000 par value.

Bond	Proceeds per Bond	Size of Issue	Initial Maturity of Bond	Years Remaining to Maturity
A	$ 975	50,000 bonds	10 years	5 years
B	1,020	25,000 bonds	20 years	15 years
C	1,000	100,000 bonds	25 years	12 years

a. Indicate whether each bond was sold at a discount, at a premium, or at its par value.
b. Determine the total discount or premium for each issue.
c. Determine the annual amount of discount or premium amortized for each bond.
d. Calculate the unamortized discount or premium for each bond.
e. Determine the after-tax cash flow associated with the retirement now of each of these bonds, using the values developed in part d.

A: Premium/discount per bond = Proceeds per bond – Par value per bond
Total Premium/discount = Premium/discount per bond × Size of issue (# of bonds)
Annual premium/discount amortized per bond = Prem/disc per bond ÷ Initial maturity (in years)
[Premiums added to earnings each year, so increase taxable income and taxes paid; Discounts deducted from earnings each year, so reduce taxable income and taxes paid]
Unamortized premium/discount per bond = Annual prem/disc per bond × Number years remaining
After-tax cash flow = [– (Unamortized pre/disc per bond × Size of issue × Corporate tax rate)]
[Retiring premium bonds: remaining prem realized as income, increasing taxes payable;
Retiring discount bonds: remaining disc deducted from income, reducing taxes payable]

Bond	Premium (+) or Discount (–) per Bond	Total Premium or Discount per Bond	Annual Premium or Discount per Bond	Unamortized Premium or Discount per Bond	After-Tax Cash Flows from Retiring Issue
A	–$25.00	–$1,250,000	–$2.50	–$12.50	+$218,750
B	+20.00	+500,000	+1.00	+15.00	–131,250
C	0	0	0	0	0

ST21-2. The principal, coupon interest rate, and interest overlap period are shown in the following table for a number of bonds.

Bond	Principal	Coupon Interest Rate	Interest Overlap Period
A	$ 15,000,000	6.5%	2 months
B	20,000,000	7.0%	3 months
C	15,000,000	6.0%	4 months
D	100,000,000	8.0%	6 months

a. Calculate the dollar amount of interest that must be paid for each bond during the interest overlap period.
b. Calculate the after-tax cost of overlapping interest for each bond if the firm is in the 40 percent tax bracket.

A: Interest payable during overlap = Coupon rate × Principal × [Months overlap ÷12]
After-tax cost of overlapping interest = Interest during overlap period × (1 – Tax rate)

Bond	Calculation of interest payable during overlap period	Interest payable during overlap period	After-tax cost of overlapping interest
A	$ 15,000,000 × 0.065 × [2 ÷ 12]	$ 162,500	$ 97,500
B	20,000,000 × 0.07 × [3 ÷ 12]	350,000	210,000
C	15,000,000 × 0.06 × [4 ÷ 12]	300,000	180,000
D	100,000,000 × 0.08 × [6 ÷ 12]	4,000,000	2,400,000

ST21-3. Well-Sprung Corporation is considering offering a new $100 million bond issue to replace an outstanding $100 million bond issue. The firm wishes to do this to take advantage of the decline in interest rates that has occurred since the original issue. The two bond issues are described in what follows. The firm is in the 30 percent tax bracket.

Old bonds. The outstanding bonds have a $1,000 par value and an 8.5 percent coupon interest rate. They were issued five years ago with a 20-year maturity. They were initially sold at a $30 per bond discount, and a $750,000 flotation cost was incurred. They are callable at $1,085.

New bonds. The new bonds would have a 15-year maturity, a par value of $1,000, and a 7.0 percent coupon interest rate. It is expected that these bonds can be sold at par for a floatation cost of $600,000. The firm expects a 3-month period of overlapping interest while it retires the old bonds.

a. Calculate the initial investment that is required to call the old bonds and issue the new bonds.

b. Calculate the annual cash flow savings, if any, expected from the proposed bond-refunding decision.

c. If the firm uses its after-tax cost of debt of 4.9 percent to evaluate low-risk decisions, find the net present value (*NPV*) of the bond-refunding decision. Would you recommend the proposed refunding? Explain your answer.

A: Steps in bond refunding decision: (1) Calculate the initial investment required to call the old bond issue and float the new one; (2) Find the annual cash flow savings from the new versus old bond issue, and; (3) Find the net present value of the refunding decision. Answers to parts a-f of this problem will be determined with this procedure.

(1) Finding the Initial Investment for the Bond Refunding Decision

(a) Call premium	
Before tax [($1,085 – $1,000) × 100,000 bonds]	$8,500,000
Less: Taxes (0.30 × $8,500,000)	(2,550,000)
After-tax cost of call premium	$5,950,000
(b) Floatation cost of new bond	650,000
(c) Overlapping interest on old bond	
0.085 × $100,000,000 × 3/12 × (1 – 0.3)	1,487,500
(d) Tax savings from unamortized discount on old bond	
–$30÷20 × 15 × 100,000 × 0.30	(675,000)
(e) Tax savings from unamortized flotation of old bond	
(15÷20 × $750,000 × 0.30)	(168,750)
Initial investment	$7,243,750

(2) Finding the Annual Cash Flow Savings for Bond Refunding Decision

Old bond	
(a) Interest cost	
Before tax (0.085 × $100,000,000)	$8,500,000
Less: Taxes (0.30 × $8,500,000)	(2,550,000)
After-tax interest cost	$5,950,000
(b) Tax savings from amortization of discount	
–$30÷20 × 100,000 × 0.30	(45,000)

(c) Tax savings from amortization of floatation cost	
[(\$750,000 ÷20) × 0.30]	(11,250)
(1) Annual after-tax debt payment	\$5,893,750
New bond	
(d) Interest cost	
Before tax (0.070 × \$100,000,000)	\$7,000,000
Less: Taxes (0.30 × \$7,000,000)	(2,100,000)
After-tax interest cost	\$4,900,000
(e) Tax savings from amortization of floatation cost	
[(\$600,000 ÷15) × 0.30]	(12,000)
(2) Annual after-tax debt payment	\$4,888,000
Annual cash flow savings [(1) – (2)]	\$1,005,750

(3) Finding the Net Present Value of the Bond Refunding Decision

(a) Present value of annual cash flow [from part (2)]	
\$1,005,750 × $PVA_{4.9\%,15\ years}$ = \$1,005,750 × 10.450	\$10,510,264
(b) Less: Initial investment (from (1)]	(7,243,750)
(c) Net present value (NPV) of refunding	\$3,266,514

Decision: The proposed refunding is recommended because the NPV of refunding of \$3,266,514 is greater than \$0.

ST21-4. Strident Corporation is attempting to determine whether to lease or purchase a new telephone system. The firm is in the 40 percent tax bracket, and its after-tax cost of debt is currently 4.5 percent. The terms of the lease and the purchase are as follows:

Lease. Annual beginning-of-year lease payments of \$22,000 are required over the 5-year life of the lease. The lessor will pay all maintenance costs; the lessee will pay insurance and other costs. The lessee will exercise its option to purchase the asset for \$30,000 paid along with the final lease payment.

Purchase. The \$100,000 cost of the telephone system can be financed entirely with a 7.5 percent loan requiring annual end-of-year payments of \$24,716 for five years. The firm in this case will depreciate the equipment under MACRS using a 5-year recovery period. (See Table 9.1 for applicable MACRS percentages.) The firm will pay \$3,500 per year for a service contract that covers all maintenance costs; the firm will pay insurance and other costs. The firm plans to keep the equipment and use it beyond its 5-year recovery period.

a. Calculate the after-tax cash outflows associated with each alternative.

b. Calculate the present value of each cash outflow stream using the after-tax cost of debt.

c. Which alternative, lease or purchase, would you recommend? Why?

A: Leasing the research equipment

Beginning of period lease payment: \$22,000
After-tax lease payment = 22,000 × (1 – 0.4) = \$13,200
N = 5 years
After-tax cost of debt: 4.5%

Present value of lease cash flows, beginning of years 1–5 (end of years 0–4):
$-\$13{,}200 - 13{,}200/1.045 - 13{,}200/(1.045)^2 - 13{,}200/(1.045)^3 - 43{,}200/(1.045)^4$
= –\$85,712

Purchasing the equipment
\$100,000 equipment cost

Depreciation, based on MACRS table:
Year 1: 20% × 100,000 = \$20,000
Year 2: 32% × 100,000 = \$32,000
Year 3: 19.2% × 100,000 = \$19,200
Year 4: 11.52% × 100,000 = \$11,520

Year 5: 11.52% × 100,000 = $11,520
Year 6: 5.76% × 100,000 = $ 5,760

Loan interest and principal:

Year	Principal balance	Payment	Interest	Principal	Ending Principal
1	$100,000	$24,716	$7,500	$17,216	$82,784
2	82,784	$24,716	6,209	18,508	64,276
3	64,276	$24,716	4,821	19,896	44,380
4	44,380	$24,716	3,329	21,388	22,992
5	22,992	$24,716	1,724	22,992	0

Loan cash flows:
Note that there are no inflows (revenues) given for the project. The cash inflows are the tax shields from depreciation and interest, the amount paid times the tax rate of 40%.

Maintenance costs: $3,500

After-tax cost of maintenance: $3,500 × (1 – 0.4) = $2,100

After-tax cash outflows associated with purchasing the telephone system:

End of Year	Loan Payments (1)	Maint. Costs (2)	Deprec (3)	Interest (4)	Total Deductions 2+3+4=(5)	Tax Shields 0.40×5=(6)	After-Tax Cash Outflows 1+2-6=(7)
1	$24,716	$3,500	20,000	$7,500	$31,000	$12,400	$15,816
2	$24,716	$3,500	32,000	6,209	41,709	16,684	11,532
3	$24,716	$3,500	19,200	4,821	27,521	11,008	17,208
4	$24,716	$3,500	11,520	3,329	18,349	7,340	20,876
5	$24,716	$3,500	11,520	1,724	16,744	6,698	21,518

Discounting the after-tax cash outflows at 4.5%: –$75,547

Since the present value of the after-tax cash outflows for the purchase alternative, –$75,547, is less than for the lease alternative, –85,712, it is less costly to purchase than to lease the equipment. This ignores the depreciation deduction for the purchase option for year 6, as well as year-6 maintenance payments made under the lease option after the asset is purchased in year 5.

Chapter 22 Mergers, Acquisitions and Corporate Control

ST22-1. Mega Service Corporation (MSC) is offering to exchange 2.5 shares of its own stock for each share of target firm Norman Corporation stock as consideration for a proposed merger. There are 10 million Norman Corp shares outstanding, and its stock price was $60 before the merger offer. MSC's preoffer stock price was $30. What is the control premium percentage offered? Now suppose that when the merger is consummated eight months later, MSC's stock price drops to $25. At that point, what is the control premium percentage and total transaction value?

A: The pre-offer value of Norman Corporation is $600 million (10 million shares × $60/share) and Mega Service Corporation offered 2.5 shares of its own stock (worth $30/share) as payment, or $75 per share of Norman Corp stock. The initial control premium offered is thus $15/share ($75 offer price – $60 market price) of Norman Corp stock a control premium percentage of 25% ($15 premium ÷ $60 initial market price).

When the merger is completed, and MSC's stock price has fallen to $25/share, the value actually received by Norman Corp shareholders is only $62.50/share

(\$25/share MSC stock × 2.5 shares MSC for each Norman Corp share). Norman shareholders will thus actually receive a control premium of \$2.50/share or 4.17% (\$2.50 premium ÷ \$60 initial market price). At that point the total transaction value is \$625 million (10 million shares × \$62.50/share).

ST22-2. You are the director of capital acquisitions for Morningside Hotel Company. One of the projects you are considering is the acquisition of Monroe Hospitality, a company that owns and operates of a chain of bed-and-breakfast inns. Susan Sharp, the owner of Monroe, is willing to consider selling her company to Morningside, but only if she is offered and all-cash purchase price of \$5 million. Your project analysis team estimates that the purchase of Monroe Hospitality will generate the following marginal after-tax cash flow:

Year	Cash Flow
1	\$1,000,000
2	1,500,000
3	2,000,000
4	2,500,000
5	3,000,000

If you decide to go ahead with this acquisition, it will be funded with Morningside's standard mix of debt and equity, at the firm's weighted average (after-tax) cost of capital of 9 percent. Morningside's tax rate is 30 percent. Should you recommend acquiring Monroe Hospitality to your CEO?

A: We use the 9% WACC to find the present value of the forecast marginal cash flow.

$$\begin{aligned}\text{Present Value} &= \frac{\$1{,}000{,}000}{(1.09)^1}+\frac{\$1{,}500{,}000}{(1.09)^2}+\frac{\$2{,}000{,}000}{(1.09)^3}+\frac{\$2{,}500{,}000}{(1.09)^4}+\frac{\$3{,}000{,}000}{(1.09)^5}\\ &= \$917{,}431+\$1{,}262{,}520+\$1{,}544{,}367+\$1{,}771{,}063+\$1{,}949{,}794\\ &= \$7{,}445{,}175\end{aligned}$$

Because the present value of the marginal cash flow from the purchase of Monroe Hospitality of \$7,445,175 is more than its \$5,000,000 all-cash purchase price, the CEO should purchase Monroe.

Chapter 23 Bankruptcy and Financial Distress

ST23-1. For a firm with outstanding debt of \$50 million, classify each of the following voluntary settlements as an extension, a composition, or a combination of the two.

a. Paying a group of creditors in full in six periodic installments and paying the remaining creditors 75 cents on the dollar immediately

b. Paying a group of creditors 50 cents on the dollar immediately and paying the remaining creditors 70 cents on the dollar in five periodic installments

c. Paying all creditors 30 cents on the dollar

A:

a. Paying a group in full in six installments (extension) and paying the remainder 75 cents on the dollar immediately (composition).

b. Paying a group 50 cents on the dollar immediately (composition) and paying the remainder 70 cents in five installments (composition and extension)

c. Paying all creditors 30 cents on the dollar (composition)

ST23-2. A firm has \$8 million in funds to distribute to its unsecured creditors. Three possible sets of unsecured creditor claims are presented. Calculate the settlement, if any, to be received by each creditor in each case shown in the following table.

Unsecured Creditors' Claims	Case I	Case II	Case III
Unpaid balance of second mortgage	$ 2,000,000	$ 2,500,000	$ 5,000,000
Accounts payable	2,500,000	3,000,000	4,000,000
Notes payable – bank	3,500,000	3,500,000	1,500,000
Unsecured bonds	4,000,000	5,000,000	5,500,000
Total	$12,000,000	$14,000,000	$16,000,000

A: In Case I, assuming each unsecured creditor has equal priority, each creditor will receive $8,000,000/$12,000,000 = $0.6667 on the dollar.

In Case II, each creditor will receive $8,000,000/$14,000,000 = $0.5714 on the dollar.

In Case III, each creditor will receive $8,000,000/$16,000,000 = $0.5000 on the dollar.

The actual amounts received are as follows:

Unsecured Creditor	Case I	Case II	Case III
Second mortgage	$1,333,333	$1,428,571	$2,500,000
Accounts payable	1,666,667	1,714,286	2,000,000
Notes payable	2,333,333	2,000,000	750,000
Unsecured bonds	2,666,667	2,857,143	2,750,000
Total	$8,000,000	$8,000,000	$8,000,000

ST23-3. Oxygen Filtration Systems recently failed and will be liquidated by a court-appointed trustee who will charge $500,000 for his services. The pre-liquidation balance sheet follows. Assume that the trustee liquidates the assets for $10.2 million, with $5.8 million coming from the sale of current assets and $4.4 million coming from fixed assets. Also assume that the unsecured bonds are subordinate to the notes payable. Prepare a table indicating the amount to be distributed to each claimant. Do the firm's owners receive any funds?

Oxygen Filtration Systems
Balance Sheet
As of December 31, 2006

Assets		Liabilities and Stockholder's Equity	
Cash	$ 600,000	Accounts payable	$ 2,500,000
Marketable securities	750,000	Notes payable – bank	4,000,000
Accounts receivable	1,750,000	Accrued wages[a]	750,000
Inventories	2,250,000	Unpaid employee benefits[b]	500,000
Prepaid expenses	900,000	Unsecured customer deposits[c]	500,000
Total current assets	$ 6,250,000	Taxes payable	1,000,000
		Total current liabilities	$ 9,250,000
Land	$ 3,000,000	First mortgage[d]	$ 3,000,000
Net plant	5,000,000	Second mortgage[d]	2,000,000
Net equipment	6,250,000	Unsecured bonds	3,500,000
Total fixed assets	$14,250,000	Total long-term debt	$ 8,500,000
Total assets	$20,500,000	Preferred stock (10,000 shares)	$ 500,000
		Common stock (20,000 shares)	2,000,000
		Retained earnings	250,000
		Total stockholders' equity	$ 2,750,000
		Total liabilities and stockholders equity	$20,500,000

[a] Represents wages of $2,000 or less per employee earned within 90 days of filing bankruptcy for 400 of the firm's employees.
[b] Unpaid employee benefits that were due in the 180-day period preceding the firm's bankruptcy filing, which occurred simultaneously with the termination of its business.
[c] Unsecured customer deposits not exceeding $900 each.
[d] First and second mortgages on the firm's total fixed assets.

A: Amount available for distribution: $10,200,000.

Distributions to Claimants		Cumulative Total
Trustee expenses	$ 500,000	$ 500,000
Employee wages	750,000	1,250,000
Employee benefits	500,000	1,750,000
Customer deposits	500,000	2,250,000
Taxes due	1,000,000	3,250,000
First mortgage	3,000,000	6,250,000
Second mortgage	1,400,000*	7,650,000
Unsecured Creditors		
Accounts payable	$2,500,000	
Notes payable	4,000,000	
Second mortgage**	600,000	
Unsecured bonds	3,500,000	
Total	$10,600,00	

Creditors through the first mortgage-holder will be paid in full, and the second mortgage-holder will receive $1,400,000 from the sale of secured assets, for a total initial payment of $7,650,000. This left $10,200,000 – $7,6500,000 = $2,550,000. The unsecured creditors' claims total $10,600,000. Assuming the unsecured creditors have equal priority, they will receive $2,550,000 ÷ $10,600,000 = $0.2406 on the dollar. This will be paid as follows:

	Shares of Proceeds	Actual Payouts
Accounts Payable	$ 601,415	$ 601,415
Notes payable	962,264	1,804,245***
Second mortgage	144,340	144,340
Unsecured bonds	841,981	0
Totals	$2,550,000	$2,550,000

Note that because the unsecured creditors' claims are not fully repaid, no funds are available for distribution to the firm's owners—both the preferred and common stockholders.

ST23-4. Express Trailers has a working capital/total assets ratio of 0.3, a retained earnings/total assets ratio of 0.15, an earnings before interest and taxes/ total asset ratio of 0.20, a market value of equity/book value of equity ratio of 0.5, and a sales/total assets ratio of 0.75. Calculate and in-terpret the company's Z score.

Altman's $Z = 1.2 \times X_1 + 1.4 \times X_2 + 3.3 \times X_3 + 0.6 \times X_4 + 1.0 \times X_5$

Where

X_1 = working capital /total assets = 0.45

X_2 = retained earnings/total assets = 0.25

X_3 = EBIT/total assets = 0.35

X_4 = Market value of equity/book value of debt = 0.60

X_5 = sales/total assets = 0.85

Altman's Z = 1.2 × 0.45 + 1.4 × 0.25 + 3.3 × 0.35 + 0.6 × 0.60 + 1.030.85 = 3.255

With a Z score of 3.255, the firm has a low probability of failure.

* $4,400,000 fixed asset sale proceeds – $3,000,000 first mortgage repayment

** $2,000,000 second mortgage – $1,400,000 paid from final asset sale proceeds

*** Because the unsecured bonds are subordinated to the notes payable, their claim of $841,981 passes to the notes payable, thereby increasing the notes payable proceeds to $1,804,245 (of $4.0 million due) and decreasing the amount recovered by the unsecured bonds to $0.

Glossary

A

ABC system An inventory control system that segregates inventory into three groups—A, B, and C. The A items require the largest dollar investment and the most intensive control, the B items require the next largest investment and less intensive control, and the C items require the smallest investment and the least intensive control.

absolute priority rules (APR) Rules contained in Chapter 7 of the Bankruptcy Reform Act of 1978 that specify the procedure by which secured creditors are paid first, then unsecured creditors, then preferred shareholders, and finally common stockholders.

accounting rate of return Calculation of a hurdle rate by dividing net income by the book value of assets, either on a year-by-year basis or by taking an average over the project's life.

accounts payable management A short-term financing activity that involves managing the time that elapses between the purchase of raw materials and mailing the payment to the supplier.

accredited investors Individuals or institutions that meet certain income and wealth requirements.

accrual-based approach Revenues are recorded at the point of sale and costs when they are incurred, not necessarily when a firm receives or pays out cash.

acquisition The purchase of additional resources by a business enterprise.

actively managed An approach to running a mutual fund in which the fund manager does research to identify under valued and over valued stocks.

activity ratios A measure of the speed with which a firm converts various accounts into sales or cash.

additional paid-in capital The difference between the price the company received when it sold stock in the primary market and the par value of the stock, multiplied by the number of shares sold. This represents the amount of money the firm received from selling stock, above and beyond the stock's par value.

adjustable rate preferred stock A corporate obligation used for short-term investments. These stocks take advantage of the dividend exclusion (of 70 percent or more) for stock in one corporation held by another corporation. In order to make this investment suitable for short-term holdings, the dividend rate paid on the stock is adjusted according to some rate index. This will stabilize the price, even if interest rates change during the forty-five-day holding period required to qualify for the dividend exclusion.

agency bonds Bonds issued by federal government agencies. Agency bonds are not explicitly backed by the full faith and credit of the U.S. government. Agencies issue bonds to promote the formation of credit in certain sectors of the economy such as real estate, education, and farming.

agency cost/contracting model of dividends A theoretical model that explains empirical regularities in dividend payment and share repurchase patterns, based on agency problems between managers and shareholders.

agency cost/tax shield trade-off model of corporate leverage This model expresses the value of a levered firm as the value of an unlevered firm, plus the present values of tax shields and the agency costs of outside equity, minus the present value of bankruptcy costs and the agency costs of debt.

agency costs Costs that arise due to conflicts of interest between shareholders and managers.

agency costs of (outside) equity In an efficient market, informed investors only pay a price per share that fully reflects the perks an entrepreneur is expected to consume after the equity sale, so the entrepreneur bears the full costs of her or his actions.

agency costs of debt Costs that must be weighed against the benefits of leverage in reducing the agency costs of outside equity.

agency problems The conflict between the goals of a firm's owners and its managers.

aggressive strategy When a company relies heavily on short-term borrowing, not only to meet the seasonal peaks each year but also to finance a portion of the long-term growth in sales and assets.

aging of accounts receivable A schedule that indicates the portions of the total accounts receivable balance that have been outstanding for specified periods of time.

all-in rate The base rate and the spread.

American call option An option that grants the right to buy an underlying asset, on or before the expiration date.

American Depositary Receipts (ADRs) Dollar-denominated claims, issued by U.S. banks, that represent ownership of shares of a foreign company's stock held on deposit by the U.S. bank in the issuing firm's home country.

American Stock Exchange A major stock exchange in the United States though not as large as the NYSE in terms of daily trading volume or the market capitalization of listed companies.

angel capitalists Wealthy individuals who make private equity investments on an ad hoc basis.

announcement date The day a firm releases the dividend record and payment dates to the public.

annual percentage rate (*APR*) The stated annual rate calculated by multiplying the periodic rate by the number of periods in one year.

annual percentage yield (*APY*) The annual rate of interest actually earned reflecting the impact of compounding frequency. The same as the *effective annual rate.*

annuity A stream of equal periodic cash flows.

annuity due An annuity for which the payments occur *at the beginning of each period.*

antitakeover amendments Adding defensive measures to corporate charters to avoid a hostile takeover.

antitrust Legislation intended to prevent mergers that are deemed to have anticompetitive effects on the business environment.

appreciate A currency appreciates when it buys more of another currency than it did previously.

arbitrage The process of buying something in one market at a low price and simultaneously selling it in another market at a higher price to generate an immediate, risk-free profit.

ask The price that an investor pays to a dealer to purchase a security. Also, the price at which a dealer stands ready to sell securities to investors.

asset substitution An investment that will increase firm value but does not earn a return high enough to fully redeem the maturing bonds.

assets-to-equity (A/E) ratio A measure of the proportion of total assets financed by a firm's equity. Also called the *equity multiplier.*

assignment An agreement of the creditors by which they pass the power to liquidate the firm's assets to an adjustment bureau, a trade association, or a third party.

at the money An option is at the money when the stock price equals the strike price.

automated clearinghouse (ACH) debit transfer A preauthorized electronic withdrawal from the payer's account.

availability float The time between deposit of a check and availability of the funds to a firm.

average age of inventory A measure of inventory turnover, calculated by dividing the turnover figure into 365, the number of days in a year.

average collection period (*ACP*) The average amount of time that elapses from a sale on credit until the payment becomes usable funds for a firm. Calculated by dividing accounts receivable by average sales per day. Also called the *average age of accounts receivable* or *days' sales outstanding* (*DSO*).

average investment in accounts receivable (*AIAR*) An estimate of the actual amount of cash tied up in accounts receivable at any time during the year.

average payment period (*APP*) The average length of time it takes a firm to pay its suppliers. Calculated by dividing the firm's accounts payable balance by its average daily purchases.

average tax rate A firm's tax liability divided by its pretax income.

B

backward integration A merger in which the acquired company provides an earlier step in the production process.

balloon payment A term loan agreement that requires periodic interest payments over the life of the loan followed by a large lump-sum payment at maturity.

bank account analysis statement A regular report (usually monthly) provided to a bank's commercial customers that specifies all services provided, including items processed and any charges assessed.

bankruptcy Occurs only when a company enters bankruptcy court and effectively surrenders control of the firm to a bankruptcy judge.

bankruptcy costs The direct and indirect costs of the bankruptcy process.

Bankruptcy Reform Act of 1978 The governing bankruptcy legislation in the United States today.

basis risk The possibility of unanticipated changes in the difference between the futures price and the spot price.

bear hug The potential acquirer approaches the target with both a merger offer and the threat of a proxy fight and/or hostile tender offer to gain the remaining shares needed to obtain voting control of the target if the merger offer is refused.

bearer bonds Bonds that both shelter investment income from taxation and provide protection against exchange rate risk.

best efforts The investment bank promises to give its best effort to sell the firm's securities at the agreed-upon price; but if there is insufficient demand for the issue, then the firm withdraws the issue from the market.

beta A standardized measure of the risk of an individual asset, one that captures only the systematic component of its volatility.

bid The price that an investor receives when they sell a security to a dealer. Also, the price at which a dealer stands ready to buy securities from investors.

bid-ask spread The difference between the price at which a dealer is willing to buy and the price at which the dealer will sell. By selling at the ask, which is higher than the bid, the dealer makes a profit on each trade.

boards of directors Elected by shareholders to be responsible for hiring and firing managers and setting overall corporate policies.

bond equivalent yield (*BEY*) The percentage return on zero-coupon bonds calculated as the difference between the par value and the purchase price.

bond ratings Grades assigned to bonds by specialized agencies that evaluate the capacity of bond issuers to repay their debts. Lower grades signify higher default risk.

book building A process in which underwriters ask prospective investors to reveal information about their demand for the offering. Through conversations with investors, the underwriter tries to measure the demand curve for a given issue, and the investment bank sets the offer price after gathering all the information it can from investors.

book value The value of a firm's equity as recorded on the firm's balance sheet.

bottom-up sales forecast A sales forecast that relies on the assessment by sales personnel of demand in the coming year on a customer-by-customer basis.

breakeven analysis The study of what is required for a project's profits and losses to balance out.

breakeven point (BEP) The level of sales or production that a firm must achieve in order to avoid losses by fully covering all costs. Calculated by dividing total fixed costs (FC) by the *contribution margin.*

brokers Agents who facilitate secondary-market trading by bringing buyers and sellers together.

bulge bracket Consists of firms that generally occupy the lead or co-lead manager's position in large, new security offerings, meaning that they take primary responsibility for the new offering (even though other banks participate as part of a syndicate), and as a result they earn higher fees.

business failure The unfortunate circumstance of a firm's inability to stay in business.

business risk Refers to the variability of a firm's cash flows, as measured by the variability of *EBIT*.

bust-up The takeover of a company that is subsequently split up.

C

call option An option that grants the right to buy an underlying asset at a fixed price.

call premium The amount by which the call price exceeds the par value of a bond. Paid by corporations to call bonds after a protection period ends.

call price The price at which a bond issuer may call or repurchase an outstanding bond from investors.

callable Bonds that the issuer can repurchase from investors at a predetermined price known as the *call price.*

cancellation option Option held by the venture capitalist to deny or delay additional funding for a portfolio company.

cannibalization Loss of sales of an existing product when a new product is introduced.

Capital Asset Pricing Model (CAPM) States that the expected return on a specific asset equals the risk-free rate plus a premium that depends on the asset's beta and the expected risk premium on the market portfolio.

capital budgeting The process of identifying which long-lived investment projects a firm should undertake.

capital budgeting function Selecting the best projects in which to invest the resources of the firm, based on each project's perceived risk and expected return.

capital gain The difference between the sale price and the original purchase price resulting from the sale of a capital asset, such as equipment or stock held as an investment.

capital investment Investments in long-lived assets such as plant, equipment, and advertising.

capital loss The loss resulting from the sale of a capital asset, such as equipment or stock held as an investment, at a price below its book, or accounting, value.

capital rationing The situation where a firm has more positive *NPV* projects than its available budget can fund. It must choose a combination of those projects that maximizes shareholder wealth.

capital spending Investments in long-lived assets such as plant, equipment, and advertising.

carrying cost The *variable cost per unit* of holding an item in inventory for a specified period of time. Used in calculating the EOQ.

cash application The process through which a customer's payment is posted to its account and the outstanding invoices are cleared as paid.

cash budget A statement of a firm's planned inflows and outflows of cash.

cash concentration The process of bringing the lockbox and other deposits together into one bank, often called the *concentration bank*.

cash conversion cycle (CCC) The elapsed time between the points at which a firm pays for raw materials and at which it receives payment for finished goods.

cash disbursements All outlays of cash by a firm in a given period.

cash discount A method of lowering investment in accounts receivable by giving customers a cash incentive to pay sooner.

cash flow approach Used by financial professionals to focus attention on current and prospective inflows and outflows of cash.

cash flow from operations Cash inflows and outflows directly related to the production and sale of a firm's products or services. Calculated as net income plus depreciation and other noncash charges.

cash position management The collection, concentration, and disbursement of funds for the company.

cash receipts All of a firm's cash inflows in a given period.

cash settlement An agreement between two parties, in which one party pays the other party the cash value of its option position, rather than forcing it to exercise the option by buying or selling the underlying asset.

cash-out statutes Antitrust "all-or-none" rules that disallow a partial tender offer/acquisition of a company and the ability to control that company with less than 100 percent ownership.

certification Assurance that the issuing company is in fact disclosing all material information.

Chapter 11 Section of the Bankruptcy Reform Act of 1978 that outlines the procedures for reorganizing a failed or failing firm, whether its petition is filed voluntarily or involuntarily.

Chapter 7 Section of the Bankruptcy Reform Act of 1978 that details the procedures to be followed when liquidating a failed firm.

clearing float The time between deposit of the check and presentation of the check back to the bank on which it is drawn.

closing futures price The price used to settle all contracts at the end of each day's trading.

coinsurance of debt The debt of each combining firm in a merger is insured with cash flows from two businesses.

collateral The specific assets pledged to secure a loan.

collateral trust bonds A bond secured by financial assets held by a trustee.

collection policy The procedures used by a company to collect overdue or delinquent accounts receivable. The approach used is often a function of the industry and the competitive environment.

collective action problem When individual stockholders expend time and resources monitoring managers, bearing the costs of monitoring management while the benefit of their activities accrues to all shareholders.

commercial paper The primary corporate obligation in the short-term market. Typically structured as an unsecured promissory note with a maturity of less than 270 days and sold to other corporations and individual investors. Most issues are also backed by credit guarantees from a financial institution and are sold on a discount basis.

common stock The most basic form of corporate ownership.

common-size income statement An income statement in which all entries are expressed as a percentage of sales.

competitively bid offer The firm announces the terms of its intended equity sale, and investment banks bid for the business.

composition A pro rata cash settlement of creditor claims.

compound interest Interest earned both on the principal amount and on the interest earned in previous periods.

conservative strategy When a company makes sure that it has enough long-term financing to cover its permanent investments in fixed and current assets as well as the additional seasonal investments in current assets that it makes during the various quarters each year.

consolidation A merger in which both the acquirer and target disappear as separate corporations, combining to form an entirely new corporation with new common stock.

constant nominal payment policy Based on the payment of a fixed-dollar dividend in each period.

constant payout ratio dividend policy Used by a firm to establish that a certain percentage of earnings is paid to owners in each dividend period.

continuous compounding Interest compounds at literally every moment as time passes.

contribution margin The sale price per unit (SP) minus variable cost per unit (VC).

contribution margin The sale price per unit minus variable cost per unit.

controlled disbursement A bank service that provides early notification of checks that will be presented against a company's account on a given day.

conversion premium The percentage increase in the underlying stock that must occur before it is profitable to exercise the option to convert a bond into shares.

conversion price The market price of a convertible bond, divided by the number of shares of stock that bondholders receive if they convert.

conversion ratio The number of shares bondholders receive if they convert their bonds into shares.

conversion value The market price of the stock, multiplied by the number of shares of stock that bondholders receive if they convert.

convertible bonds Securities that allow bondholders to change each bond into a stated number of shares of common stock.

corporate bonds Bonds issued by corporations.

corporate charter The legal document created at the corporation's inception to govern its operations.

corporate control The monitoring, supervision, and direction of a corporation or other business organization.

corporate finance The activities involved in managing money in a business environment.

corporate focus A focused firm concentrates its efforts on its core (primary) business; the opposite end of the spectrum from a diversified firm.

corporate governance function Developing ownership and corporate governance structures for companies that ensure that managers behave ethically and make decisions that benefit shareholders.

corporate venture capital funds Subsidiaries or standalone firms established by nonfinancial corporations eager to gain access to emerging technologies by making early-stage investments in high-tech firms.

corporation In U.S. law, a separate legal entity with many of the same economic rights and responsibilities as those enjoyed by individuals.

cost of marginal investment in accounts receivable The marginal investment in accounts receivable required to support a proposed change in credit policy multiplied by the required return on investment.

counterparty risk The risk that the counterparty in an over-the-counter options transaction will default on its obligation.

coupon A fixed amount of interest that a bond promises to pay investors.

coupon rate The rate derived by dividing the bond's annual coupon payment by its par value.

coupon yield The amount obtained by dividing the bond's coupon by its current market price (which does not always equal its par value).

coverage ratio A debt ratio that focuses more on income statement measures of a firm's ability to generate sufficient cash flow to make scheduled interest and principal payments.

covered interest arbitrage A trading strategy designed to exploit deviations from interest rate parity to earn an arbitrage profit.

cramdown procedure Used when a reorganization plan fails to meet the standard for approval by all classes, but at least one class of creditors has voted for a reorganization plan; or when the firm is clearly insolvent and the existing equity has no value.

credit monitoring The ongoing review of a firm's accounts receivable to determine if customers are paying according to the stated credit terms.

credit scoring Applies statistically derived weights for key financial and credit characteristics to predict whether or not a credit applicant with specific scores for each characteristic will pay the requested credit in a timely fashion.

credit terms The terms of sale for customers.

creditor control The creditor committee takes control of the firm and operates it until all claims have been settled.

cross exchange rate An exchange rate between two currencies calculated by taking the ratio of the exchange rate of each currency, expressed in terms of a third currency.

cross-default covenant In which the borrower is often considered to be in default on all debts if it is in default on any debt.

cross-hedging The underlying securities in a futures contract and the assets being hedged have different characteristics.

currency board arrangement An exchange rate system in which each unit of the domestic currency is backed by a unit of some foreign currency.

currency forward contract Exchange of one currency for another at a fixed date in the future.

currency swap A swap contract in which two parties exchange payment obligations denominated in different currencies.

current ratio A measure of a firm's ability to meet its short-term obligations, defined as current assets divided by current liabilities.

D

date of record The date on which the names of all persons who own shares in a company are recorded as stockholders and thus eligible to receive a dividend.

dealers Also called market makers, dealers faciliate secondary-market trading by standing ready to buy and sell securities with other investors.

debentures Unsecured bonds backed only by the general faith and credit of the borrowing company.

debt capital Borrowed money.

debt ratio A measure of the proportion of total assets financed by a firm's creditors.

debt-to-equity ratio A measure of the firm's financial leverage, calculated by divided long-term debt by stockholders' equity.

debtor in possession (DIP) The firm filing a reorganization petition.

decision tree A visual representation of the sequential choices that managers face over time with regard to a particular investment.

default risk The risk that the corporation issuing a bond may not make all scheduled payments.

deferred taxes Reflect the discrepancy between the taxes that firms actually pay and the tax liabilities they report on their public financial statements.

demand registration rights Agreements giving the venture capitalists the right to demand that a portfolio company's managers arrange for a public offering of shares in the company, to be paid for by the company itself.

depository transfer check (DTC) A method for transferring cash from the depository banks to the concentration bank. An unsigned check is drawn on one of the firm's bank accounts and deposited in another of the firm's bank accounts.

depreciate A currency depreciates when it buys less of another currency than it did previously.

derivative securities Securities such as options, futures, forwards, and swaps that derive their value from some underlying asset.

direct costs of bankruptcy Out-of-pocket cash expenses directly related to bankruptcy filing and administration.

direct lease A lessor acquires the assets that are leased to a given lessee.

direct quote An exchange rate quoted in terms of units of domestic currency per unit of foreign currency.

discount A bond sells at a discount when its market price is less than its par value.

discount investment An investment vehicle for which the investor pays less than face value at the time of purchase, and then receives the face value of the investment at its maturity date.

discounted payback The amount of time it takes for a project's discounted cash flows to recover the initial investment.

discounting Describes the process of calculating present values.

diversification The act of investing in many different assets rather than just a few.

divestiture Assets and/or resources of a subsidiary or division are sold to another organization.

dividend A periodic cash payment that firms make to investors who hold the firms' preferred or common stock.

dividend payout ratio The percentage of current earnings available for common stockholders paid out as dividends. Calculated by dividing the firm's cash dividend per share by its earnings per share.

dividend per share (*DPS*) The portion of the earnings per share paid to stockholders.

dividend yield Annual dividend per share divided by stock price.

double taxation problem Taxation of corporate income at both the company and the personal levels—the single greatest disadvantage of the corporate form.

dual-class recapitalization Organizational restructuring in which the parties wishing to concentrate control (usually management) buy all the shares of a newly issued Class B stock, which carries "super" voting rights (100 votes per share, for example).

due diligence Examination of potential security issuers in which investment banks are legally required to search out and disclose all relevant information about an issuer before selling securities to the public.

DuPont system An analysis that uses both income and balance sheet information to break the ROA and ROE ratios into component pieces.

E

earnings available for common stockholders Net income net of preferred stock dividends.

earnings per share (*EPS*) Earnings available for common stockholders divided by the number of shares of common stock outstanding.

economic exposure The risk that a change in prices will negatively impact the value of all cash flows of a firm.

economic failure A firm fails to earn a return that is greater than its cost of capital.

economic order quantity (EOQ) model A common tool used to estimate the optimal order quantity for big-ticket items of inventory. It considers operating and financial costs and determines the order quantity that minimizes overall inventory costs.

economies of scale Relative operating costs are reduced for merged companies because of an increase in size that allows for the reduction or elimination of overlapping resources.

economies of scope Value-creating benefits of increased size for merged companies.

effective Status of an offering before any shares can actually be sold to public investors.

effective annual rate (*EAR*) The annual rate of interest actually paid or earned, reflecting the impact of compounding frequency. Also called the *true annual return.*

effective borrowing rate (*EBR*) Generally determined as the total amount of interest and fees paid, divided by the average usable loan amount.

efficient markets hypothesis (EMH) Asserts that financial asset prices fully reflect all available information (as formally presented by Eugene Fama in 1970).

electronic bill presentment and payment (EBPP) A system in the business-to-consumer market under which consumers are sent bills in an electronic format and can then pay them via electronic means.

electronic depository transfer (EDT) The term used in the cash management trade for an *automated clearinghouse (ACH) debit transfer.*

electronic invoice presentment and payment (EIPP) A system in business-to-business transactions under which business customers are sent bills in an electronic format and then can pay them via electronic means.

employee stock ownership plan (ESOP) The transformation of a public corporation into a private company by the employees of the corporation itself.

entrepreneurial finance Study of the special challenges and problems involved with investment in and financing of entrepreneurial growth companies.

entrepreneurial growth companies (EGCs) Rapidly growing private companies that are usually technology-based and which offer both high returns and high risk to equity investors. These are the companies typically funded by venture capitalists.

equipment trust certificates A type of secured bond used to finance transportation equipment.

equity capital An ownership interest usually in the form of common or preferred stock.

equity carve-out Occurs when a parent company sells shares of a subsidiary corporation to the public through an initial public offering. The parent company may sell some of the subsidiary shares that it already owns, or the subsidiary may issue new shares.

equity claimants Owners of a corporation's equity securities.

equity kickers Warrants attached to another security offering (usually a bond offering) that give investors more upside potential.

equity multiplier A measure of the proportion of total assets financed by a firm's equity. Also called the *assets-to-equity (A/E) ratio.*

equivalent annual cost (EAC) method Represents the annual expenditure over the life of each asset that has a present value equal to the present value of the asset's annual cash flows over its lifetime.

euro The currency used throughout the countries that make up the European Union.

Eurobond A bond issued by an international borrower and sold to investors in countries with currencies other than that in which the bond is denominated.

Eurocurrency loan market A large number of international banks that stand ready to make floating-rate, hard-currency loans to international corporate and government borrowers.

European call option An option that grants the right to buy the underlying asset only on the expiration date.

ex-dividend A purchaser of a stock does not receive the current dividend.

excess earnings accumulation tax A tax levied by the IRS on a firm that has accumulated sufficient excess earnings to allow owners to delay paying ordinary income taxes.

exchange rate The price of one currency in terms of another currency.

exchangeable bonds Bonds issued by corporations which may be converted into shares of a company other than the company that issued the bonds.

exercise price The price at which an option holder can buy or sell the underlying asset.

exercise the option Pay (receive) the strike price and buy (sell) the underlying asset.

expectations theory In equilibrium, investors should expect to earn the same return whether they invest in long-term Treasury bonds or a series of short-term Treasury bonds.

expected return A forecast of the return that an asset will earn over some period of time.

expiration date The date on which the right to buy or to sell the underlying asset expires.

extension An arrangement wherein a firm's creditors are promised payment in full, although not immediately.

external financing function Raising capital to support companies' operations and investment programs.

external funds required The expected shortage or surplus of financial resources, given the firm's growth objectives.

extra dividend / special dividend The additional dividend that a firm pays if earnings are higher than normal in a given period.

F

factoring The outright sale of receivables to a third-party *factor* at a discount.

fair price provisions Antitrust rules that ensure that all target shareholders receive the same offer price in any tender offers initiated by the same acquirer, limiting the ability of acquirers to buy minority shares cheaply with a two-tiered offer.

fallen angels Bonds that received investment-grade ratings when first issued but later fell to junk status.

federal funds rate The interest rate that U.S. banks charge each other for overnight loans.

fiduciary Someone who invests and manages money on someone else's behalf.

field-banking system System characterized by many collection points, each of which may have a depository account at a local bank.

financial (or capital) lease A noncancelable contractual arrangement whereby the lessee agrees to make periodic payments to the lessor, typically for more than five years, to obtain an asset's services. Same as a capital lease.

financial deficit More financial capital for investment and investor payments than is retained in profits by a corporation.

financial engineering The process of using the principles of financial economics to design and price financial instruments.

financial intermediary (FI) An institution that raises capital by issuing liabilities against itself, and then lends that capital to corporate and individual borrowers.

financial leverage Using fixed-cost sources of financing, such as debt and preferred stock, to magnify both the risk and expected return on a firm's investments. Often refers to the presence of debt when firms finance their operations with debt and equity, leading to a higher stock beta.

financial management function Managing firms' internal cash flows and its mix of debt and equity financing, both to maximize the value of the debt and equity claims on firms and to ensure that companies can pay off their obligations when they come due.

financial risk Refers to how a firm chooses to distribute the business risk affecting a firm's cash lows between stockholders and bondholders.

financial synergies A merger results in less-volatile cash flows, lower default risk, and a lower cost of capital.

financial venture capital funds Subsidiaries of financial institutions, particularly commercial banks.

financing flows Result from debt and equity financing transactions.

firm-commitment An offering in which the investment bank underwrites the firm's securities and thereby guarantees that the firm will successfully complete its sale of securities.

five C's of credit A framework for performing in-depth credit analysis without providing a specific accept or reject decision.

fixed asset turnover A measure of the efficiency with which a firm uses its fixed assets, calculated by dividing sales by the number of dollars of net fixed asset investment.

fixed exchange rate An exchange rate system in which the price of one currency is fixed relative to all other currencies by government authorities.

fixed-for-floating currency swap A combination of a currency swap and an interest rate swap.

fixed-for-floating interest rate swap Typically one party will make fixed-rate payments to another party in exchange for floating-rate payments.

fixed-price offer An offer in which the underwriters set the final offer price for a new issue weeks in advance.

fixed-rate offerings Issues that have a coupon interest rate that remains constant throughout the issue's life.

flip To buy shares at the offer price and sell them on the first trading day.

float Funds that have been sent by the payer but are not yet usable funds to the payee.

floating exchange rate An exchange rate system in which a currency's value is allowed to fluctuate in response to market forces.

floating-rate bonds Bonds that make coupon payments that vary through time. The coupon payments are usually tied to a benchmark market interest rate. Also called variable-rate bonds.

floating-rate issues Debt issues with an interest (coupon) rate that periodically changes.

foreign bond A bond issued in a host country's financial market, in the host country's currency, by a nonresident corporation.

forward discount When one currency buys less of another on the forward market than it buys on the spot market.

forward exchange rate The exchange rate quoted for a transaction that will occur on a future date.

forward integration A merger in which the acquired company provides a later step in the production process.

forward premium When one currency buys more of another on the forward market than it buys on the spot market.

forward price The price to which parties in a forward contract agree. The price dictates what the buyer will pay to the seller on a future date.

forward rate In a currency forward contract, the forward price.

forward rate agreement (FRA) A forward contract in which the underlying asset is not an asset at all but an interest rate.

forward-spot parity An equilibrium relationship that predicts that the current forward rate will be an unbiased predictor of the spot rate on a future date.

free cash flow (*FCF*) The net amount of cash flow remaining after the firm has met all operating needs and paid for investments, both long-term (fixed) and short-term (current). Represents the cash amount that a firm could distribute to investors after meeting all its other obligations.

free cash flow theory of mergers Michael Jensen (1986) hypothesizes that managers will use free cash flow to invest in mergers that have negative net present values in order to build corporate empires from which the managers will derive personal benefits, including greater compensation.

full disclosure Requires issuers to reveal all relevant information concerning the company selling the securities and the securities themselves to potential investors.

fundamental principle of financial leverage States that substituting long-term debt for equity in a company's capital structure increases both the level of expected returns to shareholders—measured by earnings per share or *ROE*—and the risk (dispersion) of those expected returns.

fungibility The ability to close out a position by taking an offsetting position.

future value The value of an investment made today measured at a specific future date using *compound interest*.

futures contract Involves two parties agreeing today on a price at which the purchaser will buy a given amount of a commodity or financial instrument from the seller at a fixed date sometime in the future.

G

General Agreement on Tariffs and Trade (GATT) A trade treaty that extends free trade principles to broad areas of economic activity in many countries.

general cash offerings Most equity sales in the United States fall under this category.

general creditors Creditors who have no specific assets pledged as collateral, or the proceeds from the sale of whose pledged assets are inadequate to cover the debt.

Glass-Steagall Act Congressional act of 1933 mandating the separation of investment and commercial banking.

going-private transactions The transformation of a public corporation into a private company through issuance of large amounts of debt used to buy all (or at least a voting majority) of the outstanding shares of the corporation.

goodwill An intangible asset created if the restated values of the target in a merger lead to a situation in which its assets are less than its liabilities and equity.

Gordon growth model The valuation model, named after Myron Gordon, that views cash flows as a *growing perpetuity*.

Gramm-Leach-Bliley Act Act that allowed commercial banks, securities firms, and insurance companies to join together.

Green Shoe option An option to sell more shares than originally planned.

greenfield entry Internal expansion into a new market.

greenmail Targeted repurchase of shares, at an above-market price, by a company from a potential acquirer, paid to make the "raider" drop the threat of acquiring the company.

gross profit margin A measure of profitability that represents the percentage of each sales dollar remaining after a firm has paid for its goods.

growing perpetuity An annuity promising to pay a growing amount at the end of each year forever.

H

hedge ratio A combination of stock and options that results in a risk-free payoff.

hedging Procedures used by firms to offset many of the more threatening market risks.

Herfindahl Index (HI) A measure popularized by Comment and Jarrell (1995) to demonstrate the relationship between corporate focus and shareholder wealth.

high-yield bonds Bonds rated below investment grade (also known as junk bonds).

horizontal merger A combination of competitors within the same geographic market.

hostile takeover The acquisition of one firm by another through an open-market bid for a majority of the target's shares if the target firm's senior managers do not support (or, more likely, actively resist) the acquisition.

hubris hypothesis of corporate takeovers Richard Roll (1986) contends that some managers overestimate their own managerial capabilities and pursue takeovers with the belief that they can better manage their takeover target than the target's current management team can.

I

imaging services Disbursement services offered by banks and other vendors to allow both sides of the check, as well as remittance information, to be converted into digital images. The images can then be transmitted via the Internet or easily stored for future reference. Imaging services are especially useful when incoporated with *positive pay* services.

in the money A call (put) option is in the money when the stock price is greater (less) than the strike price.

income bonds An unsecured type of bond that pays interest only when the debtor company has positive earnings.

incremental cash flows Cash flows that directly result from a proposed investment. They effectively represent the *marginal costs* (*MC*) and *marginal benefits* (*MB*) expected to result from undertaking a proposed investment.

indenture A legal document stating the conditions under which a bond has been issued.

index fund A passively managed fund that tries to mimic the performance of a market index such as the S&P 500.

indirect bankruptcy costs Expenses or economic losses that result from bankruptcy but are not cash outflows spent on the process itself.

indirect quote An exchange rate quoted in terms of foreign currency per unit of domestic currency.

industry shock theory of takeovers Explains much of the activity in the wave of mergers as a reaction to some external shock to the industry, such as a change in regulation or the introduction of a fundamentally new technology.

initial margin The minimum dollar amount required of an investor when taking a position in a futures contract.

initial public offering (IPO) A corporation offers its shares for sale to the public for the first time; the first public sale of company stock to outside investors.

initial return The gain when an allocation of shares from an investment banker is sold at the first opportunity because the offer price is consistently lower that what the market is willing to bear.

insolvency bankruptcy A firm's liabilities exceed the fair market value of its assets.

insolvent A firm is insolvent when
(a) it is not paying its debts as they come due;
(b) within the immediately preceding 120 days a custodian (a third party) was appointed or took possession of the debtor's property; or (c) the fair market value of its assets is less than the stated value of its liabilities.

institutional venture capital funds Formal business entities with full-time professionals dedicated to seeking out and funding promising ventures.

integrated accounts payable Provides a company with outsourcing of its accounts payable or disbursement operations. The outsourcing may be as minor as contracting with a bank to issue checks and perform reconciliations or as major as outsourcing the entire payables function.

interest differential In an interest rate swap, only the differential is exchanged.

interest rate cap A call option on interest rates.

interest rate collar A strategy involving the purchase of an interest rate cap and the simultaneous sale of an interest rate floor, using the proceeds from selling the floor to purchase the cap.

interest rate floor A put option on interest rates.

interest rate parity An equilibrium relationship that predicts that differences in risk-free interest rates in two countries must be tied to differences in currency values on the spot and forward markets.

interest rate risk The risk that changes in market interest rates will cause fluctuations in a bond's price. Also, the risk of suffering losses as a result of unanticipated changes in market interest rates.

interest rate swap A swap contract in which two parties exchange payment obligations involving different interest payment schedules.

internal capital markets Created when the high-cash-flow businesses of a conglomerate generate enough cash to fund the riskier business ventures internally.

internal rate of return (*IRR*) The compound annual rate of return on a project, given its up-front costs and subsequent cash flows.

international common stock Equity issues sold in more than one country by nonresident corporations.

intrinsic value For a call, intrinsic value equals $S - X$ or zero, whichever is greater. For a put, it equals $X - S$ or zero, whichever is greater.

inventory turnover A measure of how quickly a firm sells its goods.

investment banks Financial institutions that assist firms in the process of issuing securities to investors. Investment banks also advise firms engaged in mergers and acquisitions, and they are active in the business of selling and trading securities in secondary markets.

investment flows Cash flows associated with the purchase or sale of both fixed assets and business equity.

investment-grade bonds Bonds rated Baa or higher by Moody's (BBB by S&P).

involuntary reorganization A reorganization initiated by an outside party, usually a creditor.

IPO underpricing Occurs when the offer price in the prospectus is consistently lower than what the market is willing to bear.

J

Jobs and Growth Tax Relief Reconciliation Act of 2003 Act of Congress that reduced the rate of personal taxation of dividend income, reducing the double taxation problem.

joint and several liability A legal concept that makes each partner in a partnership legally liable for all the debts of the partnership.

junk bonds Bonds rated below investment grade (also known as high yield bonds).

just-in-time (JIT) system An inventory management technique used to make sure that materials arrive exactly when they are needed for production, rather than being stored on-site. To work effectively it requires close teamwork among vendors and purchasing and production personnel.

L

law of one price A theory that says that the identical good trading in different markets must sell at the same price.

lead underwriter The investment bank that takes the primary role in assisting a firm in a public offering of securities.

league table Ranks investment banks, based on the total value of securities they underwrote globally during a given year.

lease-versus-purchase decision The alternatives available are to (1) lease the assets, (2) borrow funds to purchase the assets, or (3) purchase the assets using available liquid resources. Even if the firm has the liquid resources with which to purchase the assets, the use of these funds is viewed as equivalent to borrowing.

leasing Acquiring use of an asset by renting rather than by purchasing the asset.

lessee The user of the underlying asset who makes regular payments to the lessor.

lessor The owner of the asset who receives regular payments for its use by the lessee.

leveraged leases The lessor acts as an equity participant, supplying only about 20 percent of the cost of the asset, and a lender supplies the balance.

LIBOR The London Interbank Offered Rate. The rate that the most creditworthy international banks that deal in Eurodollars charge on interbank loans.

lien A legal contract specifying under what conditions a lender can take title to an asset if a loan is not repaid, and prohibiting the borrowing firm from selling or disposing of the asset without the lender's consent.

lifetime high prices The highest settlement prices recorded for a contract since its inception.

lifetime low prices The lowest settlement prices recorded for a contract since its inception.

limited partners One or more totally passive participants in a limited partnership, who do not take any active role in the operation of the business and who do not face personal liability for the debts of the business.

liquidation Winding up a firm's operations, selling off its assets, and distributing the proceeds to creditors.

liquidity crisis A firm is unable to pay its liabilities as they come due because assets cannot be converted into cash within a reasonable period of time.

liquidity preference theory States that the slope of the yield curve is influenced not only by expected interest rate changes, but also by the liquidity premium that investors require on long-term bonds.

liquidity ratios Measure a firm's ability to satisfy its short-term obligations as they come due.

listed securities Securities that trade on major stock exchanges.

loan amortization schedule Used to determine loan amortization payments and the allocation of each payment to interest and principal.

loan amortization A borrower makes equal periodic payments over time to fully repay a loan.

loans Private debt agreements arranged between corporate borrowers and financial institutions, especially commercial banks.

lockbox system A technique for speeding up collections that is popular because it affects all three components of float. Instead of mailing payments to the company, customers mail payments to a post office box, which is emptied regularly by the firm's bank.

London Interbank Offered Rate (LIBOR) The interest rate that banks in London charge each other for overnight loans. Widely used as a benchmark interest rate for short-term floating-rate debt.

long position To own an option or another security.

long-term debt Debt that matures more than one year in the future.

low-regular-and-extra policy Policy of a firm paying a low regular dividend supplemented by an additional cash dividend when earnings warrant it.

M

mail float The time delay between when payment is placed in the mail and when payment is received.

mail-based collection system Processing centers receive the mail payments, open the envelopes, separate the check from the remittance information, prepare the check for deposit, and send the remittance information to the accounts receivable department for application of payment.

maintenance clauses Specifying who is to maintain the assets and make insurance and tax payments.

maintenance margin Margin level required to maintain an open position.

majority voting system System that allows each shareholder to cast one vote per share for each open position on the board of directors.

managed floating rate system A hybrid currency system in which a government loosely fixes the value of the national currency.

management buyout (MBO) The transformation of a public corporation into a private company by the current managers of the corporation.

managerial entrenchment theory of mergers Shleifer and Vishny (1989) propose that unmonitored managers will try to build corporate empires through the pursuit of negative-NPV mergers, with the motive of making the management team indispensable to the firm because of its greater size and the team's supposed expertise in managing a large company.

managerial risk reduction theory Implies that acquiring firms' manager acquire other firms primarily to reduce the volatility of the combined firm's earnings, thus reducing the risk that they will be fired due to an unexpected decline in earnings.

managerial synergies Efficiency gains from combining the management teams of merged companies.

managerialism theory of mergers Poorly monitored managers will pursue mergers to maximize their corporation's asset size because managerial compensation is usually based on firm size, regardless of whether or not these mergers create value for stockholders.

manufacturing resource planning II (MRPII) Expands on MRP by using a complex computerized system to integrate data from many departments and generate a production plan for the firm along with management reports, forecasts, and financial statements.

margin account The account into which the investor must deposit the initial margin.

marginal tax rate The tax rate applicable to a firm's next dollar of earnings.

market capitalization The value of the shares of a company's stock that are owned by the stockholders: the total number of shares issued multiplied by the current price per share.

market extension merger A combination of firms that produce the same product in different geographic markets.

market portfolio A portfolio that contains some of every asset in the economy.

market power A benefit that might arise from a horizontal merger when competition is too weak (or nonexistent) to prevent the merged company from raising prices in a market at will.

market risk premium The additional return earned (or expected) on the market portfolio over and above the risk-free rate.

market/book (M/B) ratio A measure used to assess a firm's future performance by relating its market value per share to its book value per share.

marking-to-market Daily cash settlement of all futures contracts.

matching strategy When a company finances permanent assets (fixed assets plus the permanent component of current assets) with long-term funding sources and finances its temporary or seasonal asset requirements with short-term debt.

material requirements planning (MRP) A computerized system used to control the flow of resources, particularly inventory, within the production-sale process. Uses a master schedule to ensure that the materials, labor, and equipment needed for production are at the right places in the right amounts at the right times.

maturity date The date when a bond's life ends and the borrower must make the final interest payment and repay the principal.

McFadden Act Congressional act of 1927 that prohibited interstate banking.

merchant bank A bank capable of providing a full range of financial services.

merger A transaction in which two or more business organizations combine into a single entity.

mixed offerings Offerings in which some of the shares come from existing shareholders and some are new. Also, mergers financed with a combination of cash and securities.

mixed stream A series of unequal cash flows reflecting no particular pattern.

modified accelerated cost recovery system (MACRS) Set forth in the Tax Reform Act of 1986 to define the allowable annual depreciation deductions for various classes of assets.

monetary union An agreement between many European countries to integrate their monetary systems including using a single currency.

money market mutual funds Professionally managed short-term investment portfolios used by many small companies and some large companies.

money market yield (*MMY*) The yield for short-term discount instruments such as T-bills and commercial paper is typically calculated using algebraic approximations rather than more precise present value methods.

Monte Carlo simulation A sophisticated risk assessment technique that provides for calculating the decision variable, such as net present value, using a range or probability distribution of potential outcomes for each of a model's assumptions.

mortgage bonds A bond secured by real estate or buildings.

mortgage-backed securities (MBS) Debt securities that pass through to investors the principal and interest payments that homeowners make on their mortgages.

multinational corporations (MNCs) Businesses that operate in many countries around the world.

municipal bonds Issued by U.S. state and local governments. Interest received on these bonds is exempt from federal income tax.

mutually exclusive projects The situation that occurs when the *IRR*s of several projects exceed the hurdle rate (or the *NPV*s exceed $0), but only a subset of those projects can be undertaken at the given time.

N

naked option position To buy or to sell an option, without a simultaneous position in the underlying asset.

National Association of Securities Dealers Automated Quotation (Nasdaq) System An electronic system that facilitates trading in OTC stocks.

negative covenants Restrictions a borrower must accept in order to secure a loan. What a company must not do.

negotiated offer The issuing firm negotiates the terms of the offer directly with one investment bank.

net payoff The difference between the payoff received when the option expires and the premium paid to acquire the option.

net present value (*NPV*) The sum of the present value of all of a given project's cash flows, both inflows and outflows, discounted at a rate consistent with the project's risk. Also, a method for valuing capital investments.

net present value (*NPV*) profile A plot of a project's *NPV* (on the y axis) against various discount rates (on the x axis). It is used to illustrate the relationship between the *NPV* and the *IRR* for the typical project.

net profit margin A measure of profitability that represents the percentage of each sales dollar remaining after all costs and expenses, *including* interest, taxes, and preferred stock dividends, have been deducted.

net working capital A measure of a firm's liquidity calculated by *subtracting* current liabilities from current assets.

New York Stock Exchange The largest and most prestigious stock exchange in the world.

nominal return The stated return offered by an investment unadjusted for the effects of inflation.

noncash charges Expenses, such as depreciation, amortization, and depletion allowances, that appear on the income statement but do not involve an actual outlay of cash.

noncash expenses Tax-deductible expenses for which there is no corresponding cash outflow. They include depreciation, amortization, and depletion.

O

open interest The number of contracts that are currently outstanding.

opening futures price Price on the first trade of the day.

operating assets Cash, marketable securities, accounts receivable, and inventories that are necessary to support the day-to-day operations of a firm.

operating cash flow (*OCF*) The amount of cash flow generated by a firm from its operations. Mathematically, earnings before interest and taxes (*EBIT*) minus taxes plus depreciation.

operating cycle (*OC*) Measurement of the time that elapses from the firm's receipt of raw materials to begin production to its collection of cash from the sale of the finished product.

operating flows Cash inflows and outflows directly related to the production and sale of a firm's products or services.

operating lease A contractual arrangement whereby the lessee agrees to make periodic payments to the lessor, often for five years or less, to obtain an asset's services. The lessee generally receives an option to cancel, and the asset has a useful life longer than the lease.

operating leverage Measures the tendency of the volatility of operating cash flows to increase with fixed operating costs.

operating profit margin A measure of profitability that represents the percentage of each sales dollar remaining after deducting all costs and expenses other than interest and taxes.

operational synergy Economies of scale, economies of scope, and resource complementarities.

opportunity costs Lost cash flows on an alternative investment that the firm or individual decides not to make.

option premium The market price of the option.

order cost The *fixed dollar amount per order* that covers the costs of placing and receiving an order, which includes the cost of preparing, processing, and transmitting a purchase order, and the cost of receiving an order and checking it against the invoice. Used in calculating the EOQ.

ordinary annuity An annuity for which the payments occur *at the end of each period.*

ordinary corporate income Income resulting from the sale of the firm's goods and services.

out of the money A call (put) option is out of the money when the stock price is less (greater) than the strike price.

oversubscribe When the investment banker builds a book of orders for stock that is greater than the amount of stock the firm intends to sell.

ownership right agreements Agreements between venture capital investors and portfolio-company managers allocating ownership stakes and voting rights to venture capitalists, and usually mandating that the VCs will vote together on all contested issues.

P

paid-in capital The number of shares of common stock outstanding times the original selling price of the shares, net of the par value.

par value (bonds) The face value of a bond, which the borrower repays at maturity.

par value (common stock) An arbitrary value assigned to common stock on a firm's balance sheet.

par value (stock) An arbitrary value assigned to common stock on a firm's balance sheet.

participation rights Agreements giving the venture capitalists the right to participate, on equal terms, in any sale of portfolio-company stock to third parties that the company's managers might arrange for themselves.

passively managed An approach to running a mutual fund in which the fund manager makes no attempt to identify over valued or under valued stocks, but instead holds a diversified portfolio and attempts to minimize the costs of operating the fund.

payback period The amount of time it takes for a given project's cumulative net cash inflows to recoup the initial investment.

payment date The actual date on which a firm mails the dividend payment to the holders of record.

payment pattern The normal timing in which a firm's customers pay their accounts, expressed as the percentage of monthly sales collected in each month following the sale.

payoff The value received from exercising an option on the expiration date (or zero), ignoring the initial premium required to purchase the option.

payoff diagrams A diagram that shows how the expiration date payoff from an option or a portfolio varies, as the underlying asset price changes.

percentage-of-sales method Constructing pro forma statements by assuming that all items grow in proportion to sales.

perpetuity A level or growing cash flow stream that continues forever.

plug figure A line item on the pro forma balance sheet that represents an account that can be adjusted after all other projections are made, so that the balance sheet balances.

poison pills Defensive measures taken to avoid a hostile takeover.

political risk The risk that a government will take an action that negatively affects the values of firms operating in that country.

portfolio weights The percentage invested in each of several securities in a portfolio. Portfolio weights must sum to 1.0 (or 100%).

positive covenants Requirements a borrower must meet to secure a loan. What a company must do.

positive pay A bank service used to combat the most common types of check fraud. A company transmits a check-issued file, designating the check number and amount of each item, to the bank when the checks are issued. The bank matches the presented checks against this file and rejects any items that do not match.

preemptive rights These hold that shareholders have first claim on anything of value distributed by a corporation.

preferred habitat theory A theory that recognizes that the shape of the yield curve may be influenced by investors who prefer to purchase bonds having a particular maturity regardless of the returns those bonds offer compared to returns available at other maturities.

preferred stock A form of ownership that has preference over common stock with regard to income and assets.

premium A bond that sells for more than its par value.

prepackaged bankruptcy Companies prepare a reorganization plan that is negotiated and voted on by creditors and stockholders before the company actually files for Chapter 11 bankruptcy.

present value The value today of a cash flow to be received at a specific date in the future, assuming an opportunity to earn interest at a specified rate.

president or chief executive officer (CEO) The top company manager with overall responsibility and authority for managing daily company affairs and carrying out policies established by the board.

price stabilization Purchase of shares by an investment bank when a new issue begins to falter in the market, keeping the market price at or slightly above the offer price.

price/earnings (P/E) ratio A measure of a firm's long-term growth prospects that represents the amount investors are willing to pay for each dollar of a firm's earnings.

primary offering An offering in which the shares offered for sale are newly issued shares, which increases the number of outstanding shares and raises new capital for the firm.

primary security issues Security offerings that raise capital for firms.

primary-market transactions Sales of securities to investors by a corporation to raise capital for the firm.

prime lending rate The interest rate charged by banks on their most creditworthy borrowers.

prime rate The rate of interest charged by the largest U.S. banks on short-term loans to the best business borrowers, i.e., those with excellent credit records.

principal The amount of money on which interest is paid.

private placements Unregistered security offerings sold directly to accredited investors.

pro forma financial statements A forecast of what a firm expects its income statement and balance sheet to look like a year or two ahead.

processing float The time that elapses between the receipt of a payment by a firm and its deposit into the firm's account.

product extension mergers Diversification mergers that combine companies with similar but not identical lines of business.

profitability index (PI) A capital budgeting tool, defined as the present value of a project's cash inflows divided by its initial cash outflow.

project finance (PF) loans Loans usually arranged for infrastructure projects such as toll roads, bridges, and power plants.

Proposition I The famous "irrelevance proposition," which imagines that a company is operating in a world of frictionless capital markets, and in a world where there is uncertainty about corporate revenues and earnings.

Proposition II Asserts that the expected return on a levered firm's equity is a linear function of that firm's debt-to-equity ratio.

prospectus A document that describes the securities being offered for sale and the company offering them.

Protective covenants Provisions of the bond indenture that stipulate actions that the borrower must do (positive covenants) or actions that the borrower must not do (negative covenants).

protective put A portfolio containing a share of stock and a put option on that stock.

proxy fight A ploy used by outsiders to attempt to gain control of a firm by soliciting a sufficient number of votes to unseat existing directors.

proxy statements A document mailed to shareholders that describes the matters to be decided by a shareholder vote in an upcoming annual meeting. Shareholders can sign their proxy statements and grant their voting rights to other parties.

public company A corporation, the shares of which can be freely traded among investors without obtaining the permission of other investors and whose shares are listed for trading in a public security market.

purchase options The lessee may have the option to purchase the leased asset when the lease expires.

purchasing card programs Implemented by companies as a means of reducing the cost of low-dollar indirect purchases. Also called *procurement card programs*.

purchasing power parity An equilibrium relationship that predicts that currency movements are tied to differences in inflation rates across countries.

pure conglomerate mergers Unrelated diversification mergers that occur between companies in completely different lines of business.

pure discount bonds Bonds that pay no interest and sell below par value. Also called *zero-coupon bonds*.

pure stock exchange merger A merger in which stock is the only mode of payment.

put option An option that grants the right to sell an underlying asset at a fixed price.

put-call parity A relationship that links the market prices of stock, risk-free bonds, call options, and put options.

putable bonds Bonds that investors can sell back to the issuer at a predetermined price under certain conditions.

Q

qualified institutional buyers Institutions with assets exceeding $100 million.

quarterly compounding Interest compounds four times per year.

quick (acid-test) ratio A measure of a firm's liquidity that is similar to the current ratio except that it excludes inventory, which is usually the least-liquid current asset.

R

random walk A description of the movement of the price of a financial asset over time. When prices follow a random walk, future and past prices are statistically unrelated, and the best forecast of the future price is simply the current price.

ratchet provisions Contract terms that adjust downward the par value of the stock venture capitalists have purchased in a company in case the firm must sell new stock at a lower price than the VC originally paid. This preserves the venture capitalists' ownership stake in portfolio companies, at the expense of the company's managers.

ratio analysis Calculating and interpreting financial ratios to assess a firm's performance and status.

real interest rate parity An equilibrium relationship that predicts that the real interest rate will be the same in every country.

real option The right, but not the obligation, to take a future action that changes an investment's value.

real return Approximately, the difference between an investment's stated or nominal return and the inflation rate.

recapitalization Alteration of a company's capital structure to change the relative mix of debt and equity financing, leaving total capitalization unchanged.

redemption option Option for venture capitalists to sell a company back to its entrepreneur or founders.

refund To refinance a debt with new bonds at a lower interest rate.

registration statement The principal disclosure document for all public security offerings.

relevant cash flows All of the incremental, after-tax cash flows (initial outlay, operating cash flow, and terminal value) associated with a proposed investment.

renewal options In an operating lease, the lessee often has the option to renew a lease at its expiration.

reorganization The process in bankruptcy designed to allow businesses that are in temporary financial distress but are worth saving to continue operating while the claims of creditors are settled using a collective procedure.

repurchase rights Give the venture capitalists the right to force the company to buy back (repurchase) the shares held by the VC.

required rate of return The rate of return that investors require from an investment given the risk of the investment.

residual claimants Investors who have the right to receive cash flows only after all other claimants have been satisfied. Common stockholders are typically the residual claimants of corporations.

residual theory of dividends States that observed dividend payments will simply be a residual, the cash left over after corporations have funded all their positive-*NPV* investments.

resource complementarities A firm with a particular operating expertise merges with a firm with another operating strength to create a company that has expertise in multiple areas.

retained earnings The cumulative total of the earnings that a firm has reinvested since its inception.

return on common equity (*ROE*) A measure that captures the return earned on the common stockholders' (owners') investment in a firm.

return on total assets (*ROA*) A measure of the overall effectiveness of management in generating returns to common stockholders with its available assets.

reverse LBO (or second IPO) A formerly public company that has previously gone private through a leveraged buyout and then goes public again. Also called a second IPO.

reverse merger A merger in which the acquirer has a lesser market value than the target.

reverse stock split Occurs when a firm replaces a certain number of outstanding shares with just one new share. This is done to increase the stock price.

rights offerings A special type of seasoned equity offering that allows the firm's existing owners to buy new shares at a bargain price or to sell that right to other investors.

risk management The process of identifying firm-specific risk exposures and managing those exposures by means of insurance products. Also includes identifying, measuring, and managing all types of risk exposures.

risk premium The additional return that an investment must offer, relative to some alternative, because it is more risky than the alternative.

risk-management function Managing firms' exposures to all types of risk, both insurable and uninsurable, in order to maintain optimum risk-return trade-offs and thereby maximize shareholder value.

road show A tour of major cities taken by a firm and its bankers several weeks before a scheduled offering.

Rule 144A offering A special type of offer, first approved in April 1990, that allows issuing companies to waive some disclosure requirements by selling stock only to sophisticated institutional investors, who may then trade the shares among themselves.

S

S corporation An ordinary corporation in which the stockholders have elected to allow shareholders to be taxed as partners while still retaining their limited-liability status as corporate stockholders.

sale-leaseback arrangement One firm sells an asset to another for cash, then leases the asset from its new owner.

Samurai bonds Yen-denominated bonds issued by non-Japanese corporations.

Sarbanes-Oxley Act of 2002 (SOX) Act of Congress that established new corporate governance standards for U.S. public companies, and that established the Public Company Accounting Oversight Board (PCAOB).

scenario analysis A more complex form of *sensitivity analysis* that provides for calculating the decision variable, such as net present value, when a whole set of assumptions changes in a particular way.

seasoned equity offering (SEO) An equity issue by a firm that already has common stock outstanding.

secondary offering An offering whose purpose is to allow an existing shareholder to sell a large block of stock to new investors. This kind of offering raises no new capital for the firm.

secondary-market transactions Trades between investors that generate no new cash flow for the firm.

secured creditors Creditors who have specific assets pledged as collateral and who receive the proceeds from the sale of those assets.

Securities Act of 1933 The most important federal law governing the sale of new securities.

Securities and Exchange Commission Act of 1934 This act, and its amendments, established the U.S. Securities and Exchange Commission (SEC) and laid out specific procedures for both the public sale of securities and the governance of public companies.

securitization The repackaging of loans and other traditional bank-based credit products into securities that can be sold to public investors.

selling group Consists of investment banks that may assist in selling shares but are not formal members of the underwriting syndicate.

selling short Borrowing a security and selling it for cash at the current market price. An investor who sells short must eventually return the security to the lender by purchasing it at the then-current market price. Therefore, a short seller hopes that either (1) the price of the security sold short will fall, or (2) the return on the security sold short will be lower than the return on the asset in which the proceeds from the short sale were invested.

semiannual compounding Interest compounds twice a year.

sensitivity analysis A tool that allows exploration of the impact of individual assumptions on a decision variable, such as a project's net present value, by determining the effect of changing one variable while holding all others fixed.

serial bonds Bonds of which a certain proportion mature each year.

settlement date The future date on which the buyer pays the seller and the seller delivers the asset to the buyer.

settlement price The average price at which a contract sells at the end of a trading day.

share issue privatization (SIP) A government executing one of these will sell all or part of its ownership in a state-owned enterprise to private investors via a public share offering.

share repurchase program A company announcing this kind of program states that it will buy some of its own shares over a period of time.

shareholders Owners of common and preferred stock of a corporation.

shares authorized The shares of a company's stock that shareholders and the board authorize the firm to sell to the public.

shares issued The shares of a company's stock that have been issued or sold to the public.

shark repellents Antitakeover measures added to corporate charters.

shelf registration (Rule 415) A procedure that allows a qualifying company to file a "master registration statement," a single document summarizing planned financing over a two-year period.

short position To sell an option or another security.

short-term financing Accounts payable, commercial paper, and various types of short-term loans that are used by a firm to finance seasonal fluctuations in current asset investments and provide adequate liquidity to achieve its growth objectives and meet its obligations in a timely manner.

signaling model of dividends Assumes that managers use dividends to convey positive information to poorly informed shareholders.

simple interest Interest paid only on the initial principal of an investment, not on the interest that accrues in earlier periods.

sinking fund A provision in a bond indenture that requires the borrower to make regular payments to a third-party trustee for use in retiring the bond.

small business investment companies (SBICs) Federally chartered corporations established as a result of the Small Business Administration Act of 1958.

spin-off A parent company creates a new company with its own shares to form a division or subsidiary, and existing shareholders receive a pro rata distribution of shares in the new company.

split-off A parent company creates a new, independent company with its own shares, and ownership of the company is transferred to certain existing shareholders only, in exchange for their shares in the parent.

split-up The division and sale of all of a company's subsidiaries, so that it ceases to exist (except possibly as a holding company with no assets).

sponsored ADR An ADR for which the issuing (foreign) company absorbs the legal and financial costs of creating and trading the security.

spot exchange rate The exchange rate that applies to immediate currency transactions.

spot price The price that the buyer pays the seller in a current, cash market transaction.

spread The difference between the rate that a lender charges for a loan and the underlying benchmark interest rate. Lenders charge higher spreads to less creditworthy borrowers.

staged financing Method of investing venture capital in a portfolio company in stages, over time, with additional funding being provided each stage only if the company is achieving satisfactory results. Used by venture capitalists to minimize their risk exposure.

stand-alone companies Companies created for the sole purpose of constructing and operating a single project.

standard deviation A measure of volatility equal to the square root of variance.

stated annual rate The contractual annual rate of interest charged by a lender or promised by a borrower.

statutory merger A target integration in which the acquirer can absorb the target's resources directly with no remaining trace of the target as a separate entity.

stock dividend The payment to existing owners of a dividend in the form of stock.

stock option plans Plans set up to provide stock options to newly-hired managers of portfolio companies in order to give them incentives to manage the company to create value.

stock purchase warrants Instruments that give their holder the right to purchase a certain number of shares of a firm's common stock at a specified price over a certain period.

stock split Involves a company splitting the par value of its stock and issuing new shares to existing investors. For example, in a 2-for-1 split, the firm doubles the number of shares outstanding.

strategic merger Seeks to create a more efficient merged company than the two premerger companies operating independently.

strategic plan A multiyear action plan for the major investments and competitive initiatives that a firm's senior managers believe will drive the future success of the enterprise.

strike price The price at which an option holder can buy or sell the underlying asset.

subordinated debentures An unsecured bond that has a legal claim inferior to other outstanding bonds.

subordination Agreement by all subsequent or more-junior creditors to wait until all claims of the senior debt are satisfied in full before having their own claims satisfied.

subsidiary merger A merger in which the acquirer maintains the identity of the target as a separate subsidiary or division.

sunk costs Costs that have already been paid and are therefore not recoverable.

sustainable growth model Derives an expression that determines how rapidly a firm can grow while maintaining a balance between its outflows (increases in assets) and inflows (increases in liabilities and equity) of cash.

swap contract Agreement between two parties to exchange payment obligations on two underlying financial liabilities that are equal in principal amount but differ in payment patterns.

syndicated loan A large loan that is financed by several banks joining together in a syndicate, where each bank provides a small part of the total loan.

synergy An efficiency-enhancing effect resulting from a strategic merger.

systematic risk Risk that cannot be eliminated through diversification.

T

tailing the hedge Purchasing enough futures contracts to hedge risk exposure, but not so many as to cause overhedging.

takeover Any transaction in which the control of one entity is taken over by another.

target cash balance A cash total that is set for checking accounts to avoid engaging in *cash position management*.

target dividend payout ratio Under this policy, the firm attempts to pay out a certain percentage of earnings, but rather than let dividends fluctuate, it pays a stated dollar dividend and adjusts it toward the target payout slowly as proven earnings increases occur.

tax-loss carryforwards Negative income (net losses) can be used to offset taxes due on future income.

technical insolvency A firm is unable to pay its liabilities as they come due, although its assets are still greater than its liabilities.

tender offer The structured purchase of a target's shares in which the acquirer announces a public offer to buy a minimum number of shares at a specific price.

tender-merger A merger that occurs after an acquirer secures enough voting control of the target's shares through a tender offer to effect a merger.

term loan A loan made by a financial institution to a business, with an initial maturity of more than 1 year, generally 5 to 12 years.

term structure of interest rates The relationship between yield to maturity and time to maturity among bonds having similar risk.

terminal value The value of a project at a given future date.

time line A graphical presentation of cash flows over a given period of time.

time value The difference between an option's market price and its intrinsic value.

time value of money The financial concept that recognizes the fact that a dollar received today is more valuable than a dollar received in the future.

times interest earned ratio A measure of the firm's ability to make contractual interest payments, calculated by dividing earnings before interest and taxes by interest expense.

top-down sales forecast A sales forecast that relies heavily on macroeconomic and industry forecasts.

total asset turnover A measure of the efficiency with which a firm uses all its assets to generate sales; calculated by dividing the dollars of sales a firm generates by the dollars of asset investment.

total cost The sum of the *order costs* and the *carrying costs* that is minimized at the *economic order quantity (EOQ) model.*

total return A measure of the performance of an investment that captures both the income it paid and its capital gain or loss over a stated period of time.

total variable cost of annual sales (*TVC*) Calculated by multiplying the annual sales in units by the variable cost per unit and used to estimate the average investment in accounts receivable under a stated policy.

tracking stocks Equity claims based on (and designed to mirror, or track) the earnings of wholly owned subsidiaries of diversified firms.

transactions exposure The risk that movements in exchange rates will adversely affect the value of a particular transaction.

translation exposure or accounting exposure The risk that exchange rate movements will adversely impact reported financial results on a firm's financial statements.

Treasury bills Debt instruments issued by the federal government that mature in less than one year.

Treasury bonds Debt instruments issued by the federal government with maturities longer than 10 years.

Treasury Inflation-Protected Securities (TIPS) Notes and bonds issued by the federal government that make coupon payments that vary with the inflation rate.

Treasury notes Debt instruments issued by the federal government with maturities ranging from 1 to 10 years.

treasury stock Common shares that were issued and later reacquired by the firm through share repurchase programs and are therefore being held in reserve by the firm.

Treasury STRIP A zero-coupon bond representing one coupon payment or the final principal payment made by an existing Treasury note or bond.

triangular arbitrage A trading strategy in which traders buy a currency in a country where the value of that currency is too low and immediately sell the currency in another country where the currency value is too high.

trustee In bankruptcy, someone appointed by a judge to replace a firm's current management team and to oversee liquidation or reorganization.

turnover of accounts receivable (*TOAR*) Three-hundred-sixty-five divided by the *average collection period* (*ACP*). Used to calculate the *average investment in accounts receivable* (*AIAR*) when evaluating accounts receivable policies.

U

unanimous consent procedure (UCP) A reorganization plan instituted by consent of all creditors and equity classes.

underinvestment A situation of financial distress in which default is likely, yet a very profitable but short-lived investment opportunity exists.

underlying asset The asset from which an option or other derivative security derives its value.

underwrite The investment banker purchases shares from a firm and resells them to investors.

underwriting spread The difference between the net price and the offer price.

underwriting syndicate Consists of many investment banks that collectively purchase the firm's shares and market them, thereby spreading the risk exposure across the syndicate.

unseasoned equity offering An initial offering of shares by a company that does not currently have a public listing for trading its stock.

unsecured creditors Creditors who have no specific assets pledged as collateral, or the proceeds from the sale of whose pledged assets are inadequate to cover the debt.

unsponsored ADR An ADR in which the issuing firm is not involved with the issue at all and may even oppose it.

unsystematic risk Risk that can be eliminated through diversification.

V

variable growth model Assumes that the growth rate dividend will vary during different periods of time, when calculating the value of a firm's stock.

variance A measure of volatility equal to the sum of squared deviations from the mean divided by one less than the number of observations in the sample.

venture capital A professionally managed pool of money raised for the sole purpose of making actively managed direct equity investments in rapidly growing private companies.

venture capital limited partnerships Funds established by professional venture capital firms, and organized as limited partnerships.

venture capitalists Professional investors who specialize in high-risk/high-return investments in rapidly growing entrepreneurial businesses.

vertical merger Companies with current or potential buyer-seller relationships combine to create a more integrated company.

voluntary reorganization A strategy that sustains a firm so that the creditor can continue to receive business from it.

voluntary settlement A firm that becomes technically insolvent or bankrupt may make an arrangement with its creditors that enables it to bypass many of the costs involved in legal bankruptcy proceedings.

W

warrants Securities that grant rights similar to a call option, except that when a warrant is exercised, the firm must issue a new share, and it receives the strike price as a cash inflow.

wealth tax A tax levied on stock appreciation every period, regardless of whether the shares are sold or not.

weighted average cost of capital (*WACC*) The after-tax weighted-average required return on all types of securities issued by a firm, in which the weights equal the percentage of each type of financing in a firm's overall financial structure.

white knights "Friendly" acquirers who will top the price of an unwelcome bidder to avoid a hostile takeover.

wire transfer In the United States, the primary wire transfer system, known as *Fedwire*, is run by the Federal Reserve System and is available to all depository institutions.

working capital Refers to what is more correctly known as *net working* capital.

workout A firm that becomes technically insolvent or bankrupt may make an arrangement with its creditors that enables it to bypass many of the costs involved in legal bankruptcy proceedings.

World Trade Organization (WTO) An organization established by GATT to police world trading practices and to settle disputes between GATT member countries.

Yankee bonds Bonds sold by foreign corporations to U.S. investors.

Yankee common stock Stock issued by foreign firms in the U.S. market.

yield curve A graph that plots the relationship between yield to maturity and maturity for a group of similar bonds.

yield spread The difference in yield to maturity between two bonds or two classes of bonds with similar maturities.

yield to maturity The discount rate that equates the present value of the bond's cash flows to its market price.

Z

Z score The product of a quantitative model for forecasting bankruptcy that uses a blend of traditional financial ratios and a statistical technique known as multiple discriminant analysis. The Z score has been found to be about 90 percent accurate in forecasting it two years in the future.

zero growth model The simplest approach to stock valuation that assumes a constant dividend stream.

zero-balance accounts (ZBAs) Disbursement accounts that always have an end-of-day balance of zero. The purpose is to eliminate nonearning cash balances in corporate checking accounts.

Name Index

M

N

O

P

R

S

T

U

Company Index

Note: Fictitious company names are *italicized.*

C

D

E

M

N

O

Subject Index

Note: Bold page references indicate basic definitions.

A

D

E

F

G

H

M

S

T

U

V

W

Y

Z